ROLEX

Presents

The World of
Professional Golf

Founded by
Mark H. McCormack

2013

IMG

Editor: Bev Norwood
Contributors: Andy Farrell, Doug Ferguson, Donald (Doc) Giffin, Marino Parascenzo

All rights reserved
First published 2013
© IMG Operations, Inc. 2013

Designed and produced by Davis Design

ISBN-13: 978-1-878843-68-5
ISBN-10: 1-878843-68-0

Printed and bound in the United States.

Contents

APPENDIXES

Introduction

Rolex has done so many things over the years that were and are good for golf. Sponsorship of this publication is a prime example. My friends at Rolex, recognizing the historic and research value *The World of Professional Golf* has provided to the game continuously since the middle 1960s, stepped up in 2005 with the support necessary to continue its existence and the service it extends to the world of golf.

I well remember my conversations with my close friend and business manager, the late Mark McCormack, when he outlined his concept of filling a written gap in the game's history with an annual book carrying detailed stories and statistics covering every organized national and international tournament during that particular calendar year. The idea made complete sense to me and I encouraged him to proceed. He did, recruiting a group of talented golf journalists to work with him in producing the first edition that covered the 1966 season worldwide. Its publication has continued and grown in size and scope ever since, keeping pace with the tremendous growth of the game throughout the world.

Mark McCormack passed away in 2003, but his contribution to the historical record of golf did not die. Credit for this goes to IMG executives and others within the organization who considered the book an important continuing tribute to Mark and to the executives at Rolex, whose support has kept the literary chain intact.

Arnold Palmer
Orlando, Florida

Foreword
(Written in 1968)

It has long been my feeling that a sport as compelling as professional golf is deserving of a history, and by history I do not mean an account culled years later from the adjectives and enthusiasms of on-the-spot reports that have then sat in newspaper morgues for decades waiting for some patient drudge to paste them together and call them lore. Such works can be excellent when insight and perspective are added to the research, but this rarely happens. What I am talking about is a running history, a chronology written at the time, which would serve both as a record of the sport and as a commentary upon the sport in any given year — an annual, if you will....

When I embarked on this project two years ago (the first of these annuals was published in Great Britain in 1967), I was repeatedly told that such a compendium of world golf was impossible, that it would be years out of date before it could be assembled and published, that it would be hopelessly expensive to produce and that only the golf fanatic would want a copy anyway. In the last analysis, it was that final stipulation that spurred me on. There must be a lot of golf fanatics, I decided. I can't be the only one. And then one winter day I was sitting in Arnold Palmer's den in Latrobe, Pennsylvania, going through the usual motions of spreading papers around so that Arnold and I could discuss some business project, when Arnold happened to mention that he wanted to collect a copy of each new golf book that was published from now on, in order to build a golf library of his own. "It's really too bad that there isn't a book every year on the pro tour," he said. "Ah," I thought. "Another golf fanatic. That makes two of us." So I decided to do the book. And I have. And I hope you like it. If so, you can join Arnold and me as golf fanatics.

Mark H. McCormack
Cleveland, Ohio
January 1968

Mark H. McCormack
1930 – 2003

In 1960, Mark Hume McCormack shook hands with a young golfer named Arnold Palmer. That historic handshake established a business that would evolve into today's IMG, the world's premier sports and lifestyle marketing and management company —representing hundreds of sports figures, entertainers, models, celebrities, broadcasters, television properties, and prestigious organizations and events around the world. With just a handshake Mark McCormack had invented a global industry.

Sean McManus, President of CBS News and Sports, reflects, "I don't think it's an overstatement to say that like Henry Ford and Bill Gates, Mark McCormack literally created, fostered and led an entirely new worldwide industry. There was no sports marketing before Mark McCormack. Every athlete who's ever appeared in a commercial, or every right holder who sold their rights to anyone, owes a huge debt of gratitude to Mark McCormack."

Mark McCormack's philosophy was simple. "Be the best," he said. "Learn the business and expand by applying what you already know." This philosophy served him well, not only as an entrepreneur and CEO of IMG, but also as an author, a consultant and a confidant to a host of global leaders in the world of business, politics, finance, science, sports and entertainment.

He was among the most-honored entrepreneurs of his time. *Sports Illustrated* recognized him as "The Most Powerful Man in Sports." In 1999, ESPN's Sports Century listed him as one of the century's 10 "Most Influential People in the Business of Sport."

Golf Magazine called McCormack "the most powerful man in golf" and honored him along with Arnold Palmer, Gerald Ford, Dwight D. Eisenhower, Bob Hope and Ben Hogan as one of the 100 all-time "American Heroes of Golf." *Tennis* magazine and *Racquet* magazine named him "the most powerful man in tennis." Tennis legend Billie Jean King believes, "Mark McCormack was the king of sports marketing. He shaped the way all sports are marketed around the world. He was the first in the marketplace, and his influence on the world of sports, particularly his ability to combine athlete representation, property development and television broadcasting, will forever be the standard of the industry."

The London *Sunday Times* listed him as one of the 1000 people who influenced the 20th century. Alastair Cooke on the BBC said simply that "McCormack was the Oracle; the creator of the talent industry, the maker of people famous in their profession famous to the rest of the world and making for them a fortune in the process ... He took on as clients people already famous in their profession as golfer, opera singer, author, footballer, racing car driver, violinist—and from time to time if they needed special help, a prime minister, or even the Pope."

McCormack was honored posthumously by the Golf Writers Association of America with the 2004 William D. Richardson Award, the organization's highest honor, "Given to recognize an individual who has consistently made an outstanding contribution to golf."

Among McCormack's other honors were the 2001 PGA Distinguished Service Award, given to those who have helped perpetuate the values and ideals of the PGA of America. He was also named a Commander of the Royal Order of the Polar Star by the King of Sweden (the highest honor for a person living outside of Sweden) for his contribution to the Nobel Foundation.

Journalist Frank Deford states, "There have been what we love to call dynasties in every sport. IMG has been different. What this one brilliant man, Mark McCormack, created is the only dynasty ever over all sport."

Through IMG, Mark McCormack demonstrated the value of sports and lifestyle activities as effective corporate marketing tools, but more importantly, his lifelong dedication to his vocation—begun with just a simple handshake—brought enjoyment to millions of people worldwide who watch and cheer their heroes and heroines. That is his legacy.

Rolex is delighted to present *The World of Professional Golf 2013*, a retrospective of the highlights and results of the 2012 golf championships and tours worldwide. This comprehensive compilation is an invaluable resource for those who love golf.

At the beginning of 2012 Rolex was proud to welcome legendary golfer Tiger Woods to its family of Testimonees. Woods took home three PGA Tour victories over the course of the year, capturing his 74th title and moving past Jack Nicklaus into second place on the PGA Tour's All-Time Winners list.

Rolex was also pleased to congratulate Rolex Testimonee Luke Donald on defending his title at the BMW PGA Championship and winning the Transitions Championship on the PGA Tour, as well on finishing the season at World Number Two.

A major highlight of the year was the European team's historic comeback at the 2012 Ryder Cup, which took place in September at the Medinah Country Club in the United States. Rolex is a partner of the European Ryder Cup team, captained by Rolex Testimonee José Maria Olazabàl and accompanied by fellow Testimonees Luke Donald, Martin Kaymer and Nicolas Colsaerts.

Also of note was the announcement of the change in status of the Evian Masters from 2013. Rolex is thrilled to accompany the tournament as it grows in stature to become a Major in women's golf and looks forward to its continued partnership with the Evian Championship.

Rolex is committed to golf because we believe in the game — not only its development and promotion but also the etiquette and values that define it. The same excellence, performance and prestige reflected in the sport can also be found at the heart of every Rolex timepiece. And it is from this core that the company's involvement has flourished.

We hope that you will enjoy reliving the excitement of the 2012 season through *The World of Professional Golf 2013*.

Gian Riccardo Marini
Rolex SA
Chief Executive Officer

Rolex and Golf

Rolex is proud to be a major force at play behind the finest events, players and organizations in golf. The company's involvement began with Arnold Palmer in 1967. He, along with fellow Rolex Testimonees Jack Nicklaus and Gary Player — otherwise known as The Big Three — contributed to modernizing golf and giving it a worldwide dimension. Since 1967, the relationship between Rolex and golf has continuously grown and prospered. At present, Rolex is golf's leading supporter and is associated with the most important and prestigious entities governing the sport worldwide, as well as with golf's principal professional tours, competitions and athletes.

Tiger Woods

Luke Donald

Martin Kaymer

Phil Mickelson

Adam Scott

The Open Championship

Nicolas Colsaerts

Matteo Manassero

U.S. Open Championship

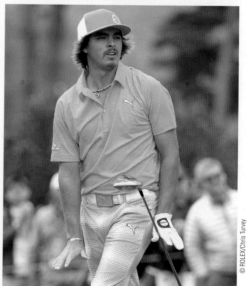

Rickie Fowler

Yani Tseng

Evian Masters

Bernhard Langer

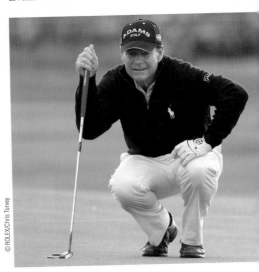

Tom Watson

Fred Couples

Asia Pacific Amateur Championship

The Rolex Rankings Top 10

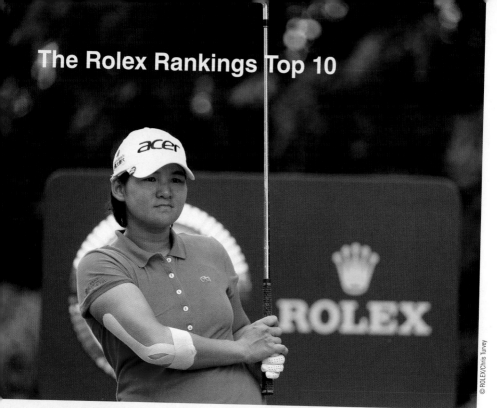

© ROLEX/Chris Turvey

1. Yani Tseng (Taiwan) 10.79 points

Andy Lions/Getty Images

2. Na Yeon Choi (Korea) 9.20 points

Scott Halleran/Getty Images

3. Stacy Lewis (USA) 8.52 points

4. Inbee Park (Korea) 8.12 points

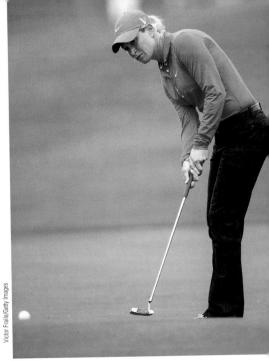

6. Suzann Pettersen (Norway) 7.13 points

5. Shanshan Feng (China) 7.37 points

7. So Yeon Ryu (Korea) 6.85 points

9. Ai Miyazato (Japan) 6.64 points

8. Jiyai Shin (Korea) 6.74 points

10. Mika Miyazato (Japan) 5.89 points

Rolex Rankings

The No. 1 player on the Rolex Rankings at the end of 2012 remained Yani Tseng, who had three wins before April (for a total of 15 victories in 15 months), but did not win again for the rest of the year. She lamented at the Wegmans LPGA Championship, "I just couldn't hit a shot, couldn't hit it on the green, couldn't hit on the fairway." A prolonged slump was not anticipated for the 23-year-old from Taiwan, who was Rolex Player of the Year for 2011 with two major championships, bringing her career total to five majors, the youngest player, male or female, to win that many.

Tseng had a 10.79 points average on the Rolex Rankings while No. 2 Na Yeon Choi, from Korea, had a 9.20 average. Choi won the U.S. Women's Open and the season-ending CME Group Titleholders event. The Rolex Rankings reflected the Korean dominance in women's golf for the year. Four of the top 10 and 37 of the top 100 players were from Korea, as were three of the four 2012 major championship winners.

Third on the Rolex Rankings with an 8.52 average was Stacy Lewis, who won the Rolex Player of the Year Award and was the first American winner since Beth Daniel in 1994. She had four victories on the LPGA Tour.

Inbee Park of Korea led the LPGA Tour money list and was fourth with an 8.12 average. Shanshan Feng, fifth with a 7.37 average, made history as the first Chinese player to win a major, at the Wegmans LPGA Championship, and was the worldwide leader with six victories. Feng won once on the LPGA Tour, twice on the Ladies European Tour, and three times on the Japan LPGA Tour.

The Ricoh Women's British Open was won by Jiyai Shin of Korea, ranked eighth in the world behind No. 6 Suzann Pettersen of Norway and No. 7 So Yeon Ryu of Korea. The Kraft Nabisco Championship was won by another Korean, Sun Young Yoo, ranked No. 23.

The Rolex Rankings — which was developed at the May 2004 World Congress of Women's Golf — is sanctioned by the five major women's professional golf tours: the Ladies Professional Golf Association (LPGA), Ladies European Tour (LET), Ladies Professional Golfers' Association of Japan (JLPGA), Korea Ladies Professional Golf Association (KLPGA), Australian Ladies Professional Golf (ALPG), and the Ladies' Golf Union (LGU).

The five major golf tours and the LGU developed the rankings and the protocol that governs the ranking while R2IT, an independent software development company, was retained to develop the software and to maintain the rankings on a weekly basis. The official events from all of the tours are taken into account and points are awarded according to the strength of the field, with the exception of the four major championships on the LPGA Tour schedule and the Futures Tour events, which have a fixed points distribution. The players' points averages are determined by taking the number of points awarded over a two-year rolling period and dividing that by the number of tournaments played, with a minimum divisor of 35.

The Rolex Rankings are updated and released following the completion of the previous week's tournaments around the world.

Rolex Rankings
(As of December 31, 2012)

Rank	Player	Country	No. of Events	Average Points	Total Points
1	Yani Tseng	Taiwan	50	10.79	539.64
2	Na Yeon Choi	Korea	55	9.20	505.83
3	Stacy Lewis	USA	53	8.52	451.30
4	Inbee Park	Korea	65	8.12	527.99
5	Shanshan Feng	China	60	7.37	442.06
6	Suzann Pettersen	Norway	47	7.13	335.34
7	So Yeon Ryu	Korea	50	6.85	342.57
8	Jiyai Shin	Korea	52	6.74	350.34
9	Ai Miyazato	Japan	49	6.64	325.51
10	Mika Miyazato	Japan	50	5.89	294.32
11	Cristie Kerr	USA	46	5.65	259.97
12	Paula Creamer	USA	47	5.36	251.69
13	Sun Ju Ahn	Korea	49	5.24	256.99
14	Catriona Matthew	Scotland	43	5.17	222.36
15	Amy Yang	Korea	46	5.10	234.41
16	Azahara Munoz	Spain	52	5.05	262.41
17	Karrie Webb	Australia	42	4.96	208.39
18	Brittany Lincicome	USA	46	4.68	215.38
19	Angela Stanford	USA	48	4.62	221.69
20	Chie Arimura	Japan	53	4.61	244.24
21	Mi-Jeong Jeon	Korea	59	4.39	259.30
22	I.K. Kim	Korea	43	4.36	187.47
23	Sun Young Yoo	Korea	47	4.15	195.05
24	Lexi Thompson	USA	39	4.10	159.88
25	Ji-Hee Lee	Korea	55	3.86	212.36
26	Se Ri Pak	Korea	35	3.76	131.55
27	Ha Neul Kim	Korea	43	3.59	154.16
28	Anna Nordqvist	Sweden	49	3.56	174.68
29	Brittany Lang	USA	47	3.56	167.49
30	Bo-Mee Lee	Korea	56	3.15	176.61
31	Hee Kyung Seo	Korea	52	3.14	163.25
32	Karine Icher	France	34	3.09	108.23
33	Sandra Gal	Germany	53	3.08	163.22
34	Sakura Yokomine	Japan	63	2.91	183.06
35	Miki Saiki	Japan	62	2.87	178.13
36	Chella Choi	Korea	48	2.84	136.15
37	Hee Young Park	Korea	54	2.66	143.88
38	Morgan Pressel	USA	48	2.59	124.46
39	Yuri Fudoh	Japan	46	2.54	116.65
40	Caroline Hedwall	Sweden	48	2.51	120.47
41	Rikako Morita	Japan	65	2.47	160.47
42	Soo-Jin Yang	Korea	40	2.44	97.73
43	Lydia Ko	New Zealand	12	2.43	85.13
44	Hyo-Joo Kim	Korea	16	2.41	84.46
45	Mayu Hattori	Japan	65	2.32	150.56
46	Jenny Shin	Korea	41	2.30	94.50
47	Haeji Kang	Korea	44	2.26	99.31
48	Caroline Masson	Germany	36	2.20	79.34
49	Ritsuko Ryu	Japan	65	2.18	141.92
50	Carlota Ciganda	Spain	26	2.15	75.27

Rank	Player	Country	No. of Events	Average Points	Total Points
51	Char Young Kim	Korea	38	2.10	79.79
52	Yoon-Kyung Heo	Korea	34	2.09	73.15
53	Je-yoon Yang	Korea	30	2.07	72.31
54	Candie Kung	Taiwan	49	2.01	98.29
55	Yukari Baba	Japan	65	2.01	130.35
56	Eun-Hee Ji	Korea	49	1.99	97.67
57	Meena Lee	Korea	52	1.92	99.83
58	Diana Luna	Italy	36	1.92	68.96
59	Beatriz Recari	Spain	52	1.91	99.49
60	Hiromi Mogi	Japan	62	1.91	118.49
61	Julieta Granada	Paraguay	51	1.91	97.30
62	Michelle Wie	USA	46	1.90	87.62
63	Shiho Oyama	Japan	38	1.89	71.74
64	Mi-Rim Lee	Korea	36	1.86	67.14
65	Hye-Youn Kim	Korea	41	1.84	75.63
66	Bo Bae Song	Korea	42	1.83	77.02
67	Katherine Hull	Australia	50	1.77	88.40
68	Melissa Reid	England	39	1.77	68.95
69	Ayako Uehara	Japan	63	1.75	110.17
70	Pornanong Phatlum	Thailand	47	1.71	80.54
71	Min-young Lee	Korea	34	1.71	59.91
72	Karin Sjodin	Sweden	36	1.71	61.62
73	Maria Hjorth	Sweden	43	1.71	73.59
74	Momoko Ueda	Japan	60	1.69	101.20
75	Giulia Sergas	Italy	52	1.66	86.47
76	Vicky Hurst	USA	51	1.64	83.76
77	Jung-Min Lee	Korea	27	1.64	57.28
78	Jessica Korda	USA	39	1.63	63.72
79	Katie Futcher	USA	49	1.61	78.98
80	Mina Harigae	USA	45	1.60	72.07
81	Lindsey Wright	Australia	45	1.59	71.72
82	Christel Boeljon	Netherlands	50	1.58	79.14
83	Sophie Gustafson	Sweden	51	1.55	79.03
84	Yumiko Yoshida	Japan	61	1.54	93.70
85	Ilhee Lee	Korea	41	1.53	62.84
86	Hee-Won Han	Korea	49	1.53	75.02
87	Soo-Yun Kang	Korea	53	1.51	79.92
88	Asako Fujimoto	Japan	63	1.51	94.98
89	Lizette Salas	USA	25	1.49	52.01
90	Na Ri Kim	Korea	59	1.48	87.05
91	Esther Lee	Korea	63	1.47	92.55
92	Jennifer Johnson	USA	39	1.46	56.90
93	Ha-na Jang	Korea	27	1.45	50.82
94	Lee-Anne Pace	South Africa	49	1.44	70.76
95	Gerina Piller	USA	39	1.43	55.83
96	Natalie Gulbis	USA	44	1.43	62.86
97	Junko Omote	Japan	65	1.40	91.11
98	Rui Kitada	Japan	67	1.40	93.87
99	Seul-A Yoon	Korea	39	1.40	54.62
100	Yeon-ju Jung	Korea	38	1.39	52.86

Rank	Player	Country	No. of Events	Average Points	Total Points
101	Yeong-Ran Cho	Korea	34	1.38	48.14
102	So-Hee Kim	Korea	57	1.37	78.22
103	Teresa Lu	Taiwan	58	1.37	79.50
104	Bo Kyung Kim	Korea	36	1.36	49.13
105	Ran Hong	Korea	40	1.35	53.91
106	Danielle Kang	USA	26	1.34	47.04
107	Saiki Fujita	Japan	53	1.34	70.80
108	Alison Walshe	Ireland	49	1.28	62.96
109	Mihoko Iseri	Japan	61	1.27	77.33
110	Karen Stupples	England	46	1.26	57.98
111	Kumiko Kaneda	Japan	62	1.25	77.43
112	Akane Iijima	Japan	62	1.24	77.17
113	Misuzu Narita	Japan	35	1.24	43.48
114	Young Kim	Korea	51	1.24	63.34
115	Jeong-Eun Lee	Korea	32	1.23	43.20
116	Cindy LaCrosse	USA	44	1.23	54.07
117	Hee-Won Jung	Korea	36	1.22	44.06
118	Na-Ri Lee	Korea	62	1.22	75.63
119	Dewi Claire Schreefel	Netherlands	49	1.21	59.05
120	Stacey Keating	Australia	49	1.18	57.64
121	Ji-Hyun Kim	Korea	27	1.17	40.84
122	Hyun-Ju Shin	Korea	56	1.15	64.41
123	Pernilla Lindberg	Sweden	54	1.14	61.61
124	Hye-Jin Jung	Korea	32	1.14	39.89
125	Sydnee Michaels	USA	36	1.13	40.67
126	Rye-Jung Lee	Korea	34	1.11	38.87
127	Chae-Young Yoon	Korea	37	1.10	40.63
128	Maiko Wakabayashi	Japan	63	1.08	68.31
129	Eun-Bi Jang	Korea	49	1.08	53.10
130	Mariajo Uribe	Colombia	37	1.08	40.05
131	You-Na Park	Korea	39	1.07	41.88
132	Nicole Castrale	USA	26	1.07	37.49
133	Hyun-Hwa Sim	Korea	35	1.07	37.47
134	Mi Jung Hur	Korea	37	1.04	38.56
135	Hyun-Hee Moon	Korea	32	1.03	36.14
136	Haru Nomura	Japan	53	1.02	54.05
137	Jodi Ewart	England	38	1.01	38.40
138	Megumi Kido	Japan	63	1.01	63.52
139	Liying Ye	China	56	1.01	56.40
140	Carly Booth	Scotland	35	1.01	35.20
141	Hye-Yong Choi	Korea	36	1.00	35.90
142	Juli Inkster	USA	26	0.98	34.18
143	Kyeong Bae	Korea	48	0.97	46.55
144	Kaori Ohe	Japan	63	0.96	60.50
145	Jimin Kang	Korea	43	0.96	41.15
146	Yuki Ichinose	Japan	58	0.94	54.70
147	Mindy Kim	Korea	42	0.93	39.26
148	Seung-Hyun Lee	Korea	36	0.93	33.59
149	Yuko Mitsuka	Japan	32	0.93	32.63
150	Becky Morgan	Wales	55	0.93	51.16

Rank	Player	Country	No. of Events	Average Points	Total Points
151	Song-Hee Kim	Korea	34	0.92	32.33
152	Shinobu Moromizato	Japan	60	0.91	54.78
153	Nikki Campbell	Australia	53	0.91	48.28
154	Trish Johnson	England	38	0.91	34.49
155	Akiko Fukushima	Japan	36	0.90	32.34
156	Miki Sakai	Japan	60	0.86	51.88
157	Ah-Reum Hwang	Korea	57	0.86	48.93
158	Florentyna Parker	England	42	0.85	35.87
159	Tiffany Joh	USA	45	0.85	38.36
160	Natsu Nagai	Japan	61	0.85	51.76
161	Ji-Na Yim	Korea	39	0.84	32.70
162	Mo Martin	USA	40	0.83	33.13
163	Nontaya Srisawang	Thailand	28	0.83	28.96
164	Anne-Lise Caudal	France	44	0.82	36.17
165	Belen Mozo	Spain	45	0.82	36.90
166	Laura Davies	England	63	0.82	51.38
167	Ji-Woo Lee	Korea	58	0.81	46.84
168	Yeo-Jin Kang	Korea	56	0.80	44.94
169	Sarah Jane Smith	Australia	42	0.79	33.21
170	Shin-Ae Ahn	Korea	33	0.79	27.49
171	Ashleigh Simon	South Africa	40	0.76	30.52
172	Line Vedel Hansen	Denmark	34	0.76	26.71
173	Paige MacKenzie	USA	37	0.76	28.08
174	Eun-A Lim	Korea	44	0.75	33.16
175	Joanna Klatten	France	39	0.75	29.31
176	Erina Hara	Japan	62	0.75	46.48
177	Jennifer Song	USA	41	0.74	30.30
178	Hyun-Ji Kim	Korea	34	0.74	25.80
179	Erika Kikuchi	Japan	56	0.73	41.03
180	Lydia Hall	Wales	28	0.73	25.61
181	Kaori Aoyama	Japan	59	0.73	42.89
182	Jin Eui Hong	Korea	33	0.73	25.42
183	Jeong Jang	Korea	14	0.72	25.30
184	Airi Saitoh	Japan	38	0.72	27.34
185	Veronica Zorzi	Italy	36	0.72	25.81
186	Kim Dana	New Zealand	26	0.72	25.05
187	Wendy Ward	USA	39	0.72	27.90
188	Beth Allen	USA	46	0.71	32.72
189	Becky Brewerton	Wales	46	0.71	32.51
190	Sei-Young Kim	Korea	30	0.70	24.66
191	Karen Lunn	Australia	50	0.70	34.76
192	Gwladys Nocera	France	52	0.69	36.13
193	Carin Koch	Sweden	26	0.69	24.24
194	Shiho Toyonaga	Japan	38	0.69	26.30
195	Amy Hung	Taiwan	45	0.69	31.09
196	Mamiko Higa	Japan	19	0.69	24.11
197	Young-Ae Ham	Korea	29	0.69	24.07
198	Ryann O'Toole	USA	44	0.67	29.63
199	Felicity Johnson	England	48	0.67	32.11
200	Ursula Wikstrom	Finland	32	0.67	23.31

Official World Golf Ranking
(As of December 31, 2012)

Ranking		Player	Country	Points Average	Total Points	No. of Events	2012 Points Lost	2012 Points Gained
1	(3)	Rory McIlroy	NIre	13.22	621.31	47	-364.26	596.98
2	(1)	Luke Donald	Eng	8.62	439.74	51	-447.49	345.77
3	(23)	Tiger Woods	USA	8.53	341.31	40	-172.24	369.87
4	(18)	Justin Rose	Eng	6.42	333.72	52	-210.39	337.65
5	(5)	Adam Scott	Aus	6.21	260.70	42	-212.62	215.02
6	(40)	Louis Oosthuizen	SAf	6.14	319.26	52	-179.83	334.84
7	(2)	Lee Westwood	Eng	6.03	313.71	52	-320.61	271.50
8	(21)	Bubba Watson	USA	5.30	259.43	49	-213.57	288.71
9	(33)	Jason Dufner	USA	5.29	269.84	51	-158.74	267.95
10	(38)	Brandt Snedeker	USA	5.23	271.70	52	-162.95	267.89
11	(10)	Webb Simpson	USA	5.13	256.37	50	-217.60	202.01
12	(16)	Ian Poulter	Eng	5.00	254.89	51	-171.41	232.11
13	(31)	Keegan Bradley	USA	5.00	259.85	52	-157.09	241.47
14	(9)	Charl Schwartzel	SAf	4.90	254.70	52	-222.23	205.40
15	(13)	Graeme McDowell	NIre	4.810	250.10	52	-245.16	252.30
16	(17)	Sergio Garcia	Esp	4.74	231.99	49	-148.07	194.26
17	(14)	Phil Mickelson	USA	4.69	229.87	49	-213.24	232.79
18	(6)	Steve Stricker	USA	4.65	190.60	41	-204.56	176.68
19	(42)	Peter Hanson	Swe	4.59	238.88	52	-148.72	234.54
20	(12)	Nick Watney	USA	4.54	235.98	52	-203.13	200.83
21	(11)	Matt Kuchar	USA	4.44	226.34	51	-246.09	218.04
22	(29)	Bo Van Pelt	USA	4.41	229.28	52	-159.96	206.93
23	(7)	Dustin Johnson	USA	4.36	209.21	48	-230.22	170.53
24	(56)	Ernie Els	SAf	4.34	225.54	52	-155.39	252.87
25	(37)	Zach Johnson	USA	4.25	212.34	50	-159.93	217.60
26	(19)	Hunter Mahan	USA	3.85	200.38	52	-212.04	209.85
27	(50)	Jim Furyk	USA	3.83	198.94	52	-146.65	209.36
28	(4)	Martin Kaymer	Ger	3.67	190.65	52	-274.42	131.00
29	(83)	Paul Lawrie	Sco	3.53	176.42	50	-97.43	187.31
30	(41)	Francesco Molinari	Ity	3.42	177.62	52	-167.98	181.16
31	(32)	Rickie Fowler	USA	3.37	171.84	51	-161.55	157.73
32	(110)	Carl Pettersson	Swe	3.34	173.51	52	-103.64	197.08
33	(49)	Gonzalo Fdez-Castano	Esp	3.31	132.51	40	-82.56	97.75
34	(271)	Branden Grace	SAf	3.17	164.57	52	-65.54	197.40
35	(27)	Bill Haas	USA	3.12	162.23	52	-172.44	149.30
36	(72)	Nicolas Colsaerts	Bel	3.10	161.29	52	-99.57	169.51
37	(8)	Jason Day	Aus	2.89	127.07	44	-195.34	79.00
38	(43)	John Senden	Aus	2.85	148.10	52	-128.54	118.23
39	(105)	Robert Garrigus	USA	2.84	147.56	52	-89.39	161.44
40	(57)	Ryan Moore	USA	2.76	132.58	48	-106.82	123.71
41	(175)	Scott Piercy	USA	2.71	141.12	52	-56.69	141.22
42	(26)	David Toms	USA	2.68	118.09	44	-144.12	87.20
43	(68)	Hiroyuki Fujita	Jpn	2.64	137.44	52	-102.30	122.28
44	(58)	Matteo Manassero	Ity	2.59	134.77	52	-106.99	132.29
45	(35)	Thomas Bjorn	Den	2.52	118.55	47	-134.83	92.00
46	(91)	David Lynn	Eng	2.42	116.26	48	-71.96	103.03
47	(86)	Jamie Donaldson	Wal	2.39	112.40	47	-77.85	103.53
48	(15)	K.J. Choi	Kor	2.30	119.51	52	-182.65	69.15
49	(82)	George Coetzee	SAf	2.27	117.84	52	-80.30	104.59
50	(163)	Thorbjorn Olesen	Den	2.20	114.26	52	-61.80	117.77

( ) Ranking in brackets indicates position as of December 31, 2011.

Ranking		Player	Country	Points Average	Total Points	No. of Events	2012 Points Lost	2012 Points Gained
51	(36)	Geoff Ogilvy	Aus	2.18	104.69	48	-128.46	80.02
52	(119)	Shane Lowry	Ire	2.15	107.70	50	-52.70	86.32
53	(207)	Henrik Stenson	Swe	2.14	111.07	52	-48.08	117.43
54	(44)	Miguel A. Jimenez	Esp	2.14	111.01	52	-138.17	91.56
55	(97)	Marcus Fraser	Aus	2.13	110.88	52	-66.46	91.19
56	(66)	Alexander Noren	Swe	2.13	110.78	52	-87.82	85.96
57	(103)	Richie Ramsay	Sco	2.13	110.75	52	-68.46	92.68
58	(118)	Rafa Cabrera Bello	Esp	2.12	110.19	52	-86.31	122.29
59	(85)	Padraig Harrington	Ire	2.09	108.42	52	-96.16	110.56
60	(253)	Marcel Siem	Ger	2.08	108.03	52	-51.09	120.55
61	(34)	Anders Hansen	Den	2.06	101.01	49	-131.97	71.06
62	(39)	Fredrik Jacobson	Swe	2.05	92.11	45	-114.36	49.39
63	(28)	Simon Dyson	Eng	2.02	105.11	52	-132.20	54.96
64	(60)	Greg Chalmers	Aus	2.02	104.93	52	-83.57	69.89
65	(162)	Bernd Wiesberger	Aut	2.02	104.77	52	-54.44	100.28
66	(543)	John Huh	USA	2.01	82.53	41	-32.95	104.14
67	(249)	Bud Cauley	USA	2.00	80.04	40	-33.55	84.67
68	(70)	Kevin Na	USA	1.99	103.53	52	-108.31	104.30
69	(186)	Thaworn Wiratchant	Tha	1.99	103.34	52	-47.38	100.42
70	(30)	Sang-Moon Bae	Kor	1.99	103.28	52	-107.87	72.46
71	(47)	Martin Laird	Sco	1.97	100.59	51	-152.04	103.34
72	(25)	K.T. Kim	Kor	1.95	101.48	52	-149.96	66.08
73	(80)	Brendan Jones	Aus	1.91	86.13	45	-68.88	80.39
74	(226)	Jonas Blixt	Swe	1.89	88.74	47	-33.22	83.29
75	(51)	Ryo Ishikawa	Jpn	1.88	97.81	52	-128.16	93.46
76	(148)	Kyle Stanley	USA	1.86	96.86	52	-79.40	112.58
77	(61)	Toru Taniguchi	Jpn	1.82	89.12	49	-78.70	61.78
78	(46)	Aaron Baddeley	Aus	1.80	88.39	49	-125.57	66.04
79	(1401)	Kristoffer Broberg	Swe	1.80	71.88	40	-3.75	75.64
80	(151)	Thongchai Jaidee	Tha	1.76	91.32	52	-63.22	92.67
81	(54)	Ben Crane	USA	1.74	85.32	49	-118.89	80.89
82	(63)	Vijay Singh	Fiji	1.74	90.20	52	-96.73	77.60
83	(144)	Brendon de Jonge	Zim	1.73	90.13	52	-70.28	93.52
84	(310)	Ben Curtis	USA	1.71	81.82	48	-45.78	99.94
85	(77)	Pablo Larrazabal	Esp	1.70	88.14	52	-79.02	68.69
86	(131)	Michael Thompson	USA	1.67	86.73	52	-48.55	81.58
87	(171)	Marc Leishman	Aus	1.67	86.64	52	-63.00	91.65
88	(101)	Fredrik Andersson Hed	Swe	1.66	84.79	51	-66.48	66.39
89	(392)	Gaganjeet Bhullar	India	1.65	67.80	41	-21.37	72.00
90	(22)	Alvaro Quiros	Esp	1.63	76.72	47	-142.56	31.84
91	(94)	Tim Clark	SAf	1.63	64.98	40	-74.02	71.65
92	(55)	Jonathan Byrd	USA	1.62	79.11	49	-122.67	73.48
93	(190)	Danny Willett	Eng	1.61	83.93	52	-54.38	88.22
94	(100)	Ross Fisher	Eng	1.60	75.14	47	-80.58	69.19
95	(107)	Seung-Yul Noh	Kor	1.60	83.06	52	-77.00	79.45
96	(187)	Jeev Milkha Singh	India	1.59	82.83	52	-51.11	80.58
97	(62)	Mark Wilson	USA	1.58	82.16	52	-129.35	94.36
98	(142)	Stephen Gallacher	Sco	1.57	80.21	51	-71.93	83.73
99	(74)	Jeff Overton	USA	1.55	80.55	52	-94.50	73.45
100	(81)	Koumei Oda	Jpn	1.54	80.05	52	-63.09	50.46

( ) Ranking in brackets indicates position as of December 31, 2011.

Ranking		Player	Country	Points Average	Total Points	No. of Events	2012 Points Lost	2012 Points Gained
101	(214)	Scott Jamieson	Sco	1.53	79.71	52	-40.83	79.22
102	(75)	Yuta Ikeda	Jpn	1.53	79.69	52	-91.60	68.63
103	(113)	Toshinori Muto	Jpn	1.53	79.39	52	-46.21	55.73
104	(123)	Robert Rock	Eng	1.51	78.48	52	-86.20	90.12
105	(45)	Y.E. Yang	Kor	1.51	78.26	52	-120.84	45.61
106	(154)	Charlie Wi	Kor	1.49	77.44	52	-65.60	81.78
107	(53)	Retief Goosen	SAf	1.48	69.43	47	-137.04	69.71
108	(64)	Joost Luiten	Hol	1.47	76.43	52	-82.02	46.30
109	(220)	Johnson Wagner	USA	1.43	74.28	52	-71.14	104.58
110	(591)	Casey Wittenberg	USA	1.43	58.48	41	-17.28	64.89
111	(157)	Juvic Pagunsan	Phi	1.41	56.57	40	-28.93	40.28
112	(174)	Ted Potter, Jr.	USA	1.40	61.72	44	-35.90	55.55
113	(87)	Thomas Aiken	SAf	1.40	72.54	52	-78.79	58.25
114	(1401)	Luke Guthrie	USA	1.39	55.50	40	-4.09	59.59
115	(98)	Chris Kirk	USA	1.39	72.09	52	-72.40	61.40
116	(316)	Kim Hyung-sung	Kor	1.38	67.61	49	-25.29	65.13
117	(76)	Charles Howell	USA	1.38	71.65	52	-89.05	60.20
118	(73)	Ryan Palmer	USA	1.37	70.07	51	-99.07	63.09
119	(106)	Raphael Jacquelin	Fra	1.37	71.43	52	-75.17	62.63
120	(165)	Jimmy Walker	USA	1.37	71.11	52	-59.83	75.60
121	(24)	Robert Karlsson	Swe	1.36	70.87	52	-149.20	35.73
122	(20)	Paul Casey	Eng	1.36	65.29	48	-149.68	28.69
123	(145)	Scott Stallings	USA	1.33	68.90	52	-53.06	55.36
124	(770)	Yoshinori Fujimoto	Jpn	1.32	52.73	40	-11.62	58.60
125	(300)	Matthew Every	USA	1.31	65.46	50	-32.69	72.22
126	(330)	Kevin Stadler	USA	1.30	67.80	52	-37.37	75.99
127	(201)	*Hideki Matsuyama	Jpn	1.29	51.67	40	-23.13	38.27
128	(108)	J.B. Holmes	USA	1.29	53.96	42	-70.02	56.62
129	(96)	Tommy Gainey	USA	1.28	66.48	52	-74.22	59.74
130	(146)	Kenichi Kuboya	Jpn	1.28	66.32	52	-45.30	44.12
131	(428)	Russell Henley	USA	1.27	50.97	40	-12.94	48.33
132	(259)	Victor Dubuisson	Fra	1.24	49.55	40	-28.25	50.91
133	(93)	Spencer Levin	USA	1.24	64.28	52	-90.11	62.51
134	(71)	Rory Sabbatini	SAf	1.23	64.13	52	-99.67	56.95
135	(125)	Andres Romero	Arg	1.23	60.32	49	-52.40	51.76
136	(117)	Brian Davis	Eng	1.23	63.74	52	-80.76	63.01
137	(79)	Sean O'Hair	USA	1.23	60.00	49	-83.93	52.44
138	(102)	Michael Hoey	NIre	1.22	63.49	52	-65.77	42.61
139	(212)	Chris Wood	Eng	1.20	60.18	50	-47.71	65.20
140	(274)	Harris English	USA	1.19	47.38	40	-25.98	48.10
141	(128)	Brad Kennedy	Aus	1.18	52.05	44	-32.97	31.05
142	(185)	Pat Perez	USA	1.18	57.89	49	-50.60	57.67
143	(209)	Blake Adams	USA	1.18	61.33	52	-42.31	57.65
144	(225)	Tom Gillis	USA	1.18	51.88	44	-44.78	59.47
145	(48)	Darren Clarke	NIre	1.18	55.20	47	-105.02	17.61
146	(104)	Jaco Van Zyl	SAf	1.17	61.06	52	-52.18	50.30
147	(175)	John Rollins	USA	1.17	61.00	52	-59.39	64.71
148	(120)	D.A. Points	USA	1.17	60.59	52	-79.42	69.14
149	(115)	Bryce Molder	USA	1.16	60.36	52	-66.04	50.14
150	(430)	Darren Fichardt	SAf	1.15	48.46	42	-17.67	50.60

( ) Ranking in brackets indicates position as of December 31, 2011.

Ranking		Player	Country	Points Average	Total Points	No. of Events	2012 Points Lost	2012 Points Gained
151	(129)	Davis Love	USA	1.14	48.04	42	-54.01	40.21
152	(52)	Gary Woodland	USA	1.14	56.96	50	-104.57	26.15
153	(265)	Ken Duke	USA	1.13	58.77	52	-34.18	59.24
154	(1031)	Richard Sterne	SAf	1.12	44.69	40	-11.60	53.94
155	(153)	Peter Lawrie	Ire	1.11	57.94	52	-54.11	50.46
156	(237)	Hwang Jung-gon	Kor	1.11	56.80	51	-19.97	46.28
157	(508)	Ryu Hyun-woo	Kor	1.11	45.38	41	-10.43	43.30
158	(195)	Soren Kjeldsen	Den	1.11	57.53	52	-54.61	61.57
159	(112)	Shingo Katayama	Jpn	1.10	51.83	47	-50.80	34.15
160	(1401)	Brian Harman	USA	1.10	43.65	40	-8.16	51.82
161	(166)	George McNeill	USA	1.09	50.19	46	-49.99	47.54
162	(378)	Prom Meesawat	Tha	1.09	45.77	42	-18.56	46.06
163	(124)	Gregory Bourdy	Fra	1.09	56.50	52	-59.90	43.19
164	(84)	Charley Hoffman	USA	1.08	56.28	52	-89.64	52.70
165	(320)	Bob Estes	USA	1.08	43.25	40	-24.37	45.25
166	(1401)	Charlie Beljan	USA	1.08	43.18	40	-2.69	45.87
167	(168)	Garth Mulroy	SAf	1.08	56.09	52	-39.04	43.56
168	(242)	Romain Wattel	Fra	1.06	53.86	51	-31.70	56.17
169	(197)	Cameron Tringale	USA	1.06	54.90	52	-48.62	53.65
170	(931)	Wu Ashun	Chn	1.05	42.12	40	-3.80	42.67
171	(138)	Kurt Barnes	Aus	1.05	42.09	40	-36.04	25.69
172	(767)	Lee Kyoung-hoon	Kor	1.04	41.51	40	-10.34	45.99
173	(143)	Mark Foster	Eng	1.02	50.98	50	-53.37	36.38
174	(216)	John Mallinger	USA	1.02	49.91	49	-42.62	48.45
175	(305)	Peter Senior	Aus	1.02	40.58	40	-18.48	35.80
176	(180)	Lee Slattery	Eng	1.01	52.65	52	-40.73	39.65
177	(612)	Graham DeLaet	Can	1.01	40.28	40	-18.31	49.01
178	(67)	Chez Reavie	USA	1.00	52.15	52	-61.51	23.48
179	(233)	J.J. Henry	USA	0.99	51.58	52	-43.16	54.00
180	(353)	Magnus A. Carlsson	Swe	0.99	45.56	46	-23.20	43.38
181	(116)	Hennie Otto	SAf	0.99	51.47	52	-53.88	28.22
182	(367)	Marc Warren	Sco	0.99	51.39	52	-24.35	50.20
183	(266)	Troy Matteson	USA	0.99	51.20	52	-35.45	54.10
184	(332)	Han Lee	USA	0.98	45.87	47	-22.08	43.73
185	(595)	Eduardo De La Riva	Esp	0.97	38.84	40	-11.16	40.21
186	(389)	Hideto Tanihara	Jpn	0.97	49.51	51	-25.05	50.56
187	(114)	Tomohiro Kondo	Jpn	0.96	47.23	49	-49.70	27.82
188	(326)	Julien Quesne	Fra	0.96	46.25	48	-28.86	46.75
189	(155)	Jbe' Kruger	SAf	0.94	48.97	52	-58.84	51.47
190	(251)	Liang Wen-chong	Chn	0.94	45.93	49	-32.14	45.71
191	(571)	Espen Kofstad	Nor	0.93	45.76	49	-9.66	44.77
192	(173)	Chad Campbell	USA	0.92	48.06	52	-48.43	39.36
193	(177)	Kiradech Aphibarnrat	Tha	0.92	47.90	52	-50.48	42.86
194	(408)	I.J. Jang	Kor	0.91	42.84	47	-19.95	43.70
195	(557)	John Daly	USA	0.90	46.79	52	-19.61	51.46
196	(444)	William McGirt	USA	0.90	46.77	52	-24.29	51.05
197	(59)	Robert Allenby	Aus	0.89	46.19	52	-103.72	31.65
198	(633)	Dicky Pride	USA	0.89	37.29	42	-20.67	46.63
199	(1401)	Shawn Stefani	USA	0.88	35.37	40	-3.43	38.81
200	(130)	Trevor Immelman	SAf	0.88	44.21	50	-49.71	33.43

( ) Ranking in brackets indicates position as of December 31, 2011.

Age Groups of Current Top 100 World Ranked Players

Under 25	25-28	29-32	33-36	37-40	Over 40
		Rose			
		Scott			
		Oosthuizen			
		Snedeker			
		Garcia	Donald		
		Watney	B. Watson		Mickelson
		Mahan	Dufner		Stricker
		F. Molinari	Poulter		Els
		Fdez-Castano	McDowell		Furyk
McIlroy	W. Simpson	B. Haas	P. Hanson		Paul Lawrie
Fowler	K. Bradley	Colsaerts	Kuchar		Senden
Grace	Schwartzel	Moore	Z. Johnson	Woods	Toms
Day	D. Johnson	Noren	Pettersson	Westwood	Fujita
Manassero	Kaymer	Ramsay	Garrigus	Van Pelt	Bjorn
Olesen	G. Coetzee	Siem	Piercy	Lynn	K.J. Choi
Lowry	Cabrera-Bello	Laird	Ogilvy	Donaldson	Jimenez
Huh	Wiesberger	Baddeley	Stenson	Jacobson	Harrington
Cauley	Na	de Jonge	Fraser	Chalmers	A. Hansen
Ishikawa	S.M. Bae	Larrazabal	Dyson	B. Jones	Wiratchant
Stanley	K.T. Kim	Leishman	Crane	Anderson-Hed	Taniguchi
Bhullar	Blixt	Quiros	Curtis	T. Clark	Jaidee
Willett	Broberg	R. Fisher	Byrd	M. Wilson	V. Singh
Noh	M. Thompson	Overton	K. Oda	Gallacher	Jeev M. Singh

2012 World Ranking Review

Major Movements

Upward				Downward			
Name	Net Points Gained	Position 2011	2012	Name	Net Points Lost	Position 2011	2012
Rory McIlroy	233	3	1	Martin Kaymer	143	4	28
Tiger Woods	198	23	3	Paul Casey	121	20	122
Louis Oosthuizen	155	40	6	Jason Day	116	8	37
Branden Grace	132	271	34	K.J. Choi	114	15	48
Justin Rose	127	18	4	Robert Karlsson	113	24	121
Jason Dufner	109	33	9	Alvaro Quiros	111	22	90
Brandt Snedeker	105	38	10	Luke Donald	102	1	2
Ernie Els	97	56	24	Darren Clarke	87	48	145
Carl Pettersson	93	110	32	K.T. Kim	84	25	72
Paul Lawrie	90	83	29	Eduardo Molinari	80	65	235
Peter Hanson	86	42	19	Gary Woodland	78	52	152
Scott Piercy	85	175	41	Simon Dyson	77	28	63
Keegan Bradley	84	31	13	Y.E. Yang	75	45	105
Bubba Watson	75	21	8	Robert Allenby	72	59	197
Robert Garrigus	72	105	39	Lucas Glover	70	69	259
Kristoffer Broberg	72	1401	79				
John Huh	71	543	66				
Nicolas Colsaerts	70	72	36				
Marcel Siem	69	253	60				
Henrik Stenson	69	207	53				

Highest-Rated Events of 2012

Event	No. of World Ranked Players Participating					World Rating Points
	Top 5	Top 15	Top 30	Top 50	Top 100	
1 PGA Championship	5	15	30	50	99	848
2 The Open Championship	4	14	28	47	81	759
3 U.S. Open Championship	5	15	28	48	74	756
4 Masters Tournament	5	14	29	49	69	730
5 The Players Championship	4	13	27	44	69	707
6 WGC-Cadillac Championship	5	15	30	50	68	741
7 WGC-Bridgestone Invitational	4	14	29	49	69	717
8 WGC-Accenture Match Play	5	14	28	48	64	710
9 The Barclays	5	14	27	38	62	673
10 Deutsche Bank Champ.	5	14	26	36	61	657
11 BMW Championship	5	15	27	32	52	602
12 Memorial Tournament	3	11	20	32	51	544
13 WGC-HSBC Champions	3	10	18	32	51	484
14 BMW PGA Championship	3	5	9	18	39	372
15 Northern Trust Open	1	8	15	27	52	460
16 The Tour Championship	5	15	24	27	30	469
17 Abu Dhabi HSBC Champ.	4	8	13	19	36	384
18 Wells Fargo Championship	3	6	13	23	43	409
19 Transitions Championship	1	6	15	23	44	397
20 DP World Tour Championship	3	6	12	21	37	381
21 BMW Masters	4	5	10	18	38	347
22 Arnold Palmer Invitational	0	5	15	22	45	366
23 Zurich Classic	2	5	11	18	29	308
24 Crowne Plaza Invitational	1	4	10	19	40	313
25 RBC Heritage	1	3	8	18	36	299
26 Waste Mgmt. Phoenix Open	0	4	9	15	38	294
27 Honda Classic	2	4	10	17	35	318
28 Shell Houston Open	2	6	10	17	35	304
29 Commercialbank Qatar Masters	2	5	8	16	26	263
30 Omega Dubai Classic	3	3	6	11	25	243
31 Barclays Singapore Open	1	4	5	8	26	218
32 AT&T National	1	3	7	11	37	259
33 AAM Scottish Open	1	2	5	15	28	247
34 Farmers Insurance Open	0	3	8	15	31	255
35 Greenbrier Classic	2	4	8	14	32	249
36 Alstom Open de France	1	4	6	12	29	237
37 Travelers Championship	1	4	8	13	30	256
38 Alfred Dunhill Links	0	2	6	13	29	223
39 Humana Challenge	0	3	5	12	30	227
40 World Challenge	1	8	17	18	18	250

World Golf Rankings 1968-2012

Year	No. 1	No. 2	No. 3	No. 4	No. 5
1968	Nicklaus	Palmer	Casper	Player	Charles
1969	Nicklaus	Player	Casper	Palmer	Charles
1970	Nicklaus	Player	Casper	Trevino	Charles
1971	Nicklaus	Trevino	Player	Palmer	Casper
1972	Nicklaus	Player	Trevino	Crampton	Palmer
1973	Nicklaus	Weiskopf	Trevino	Player	Crampton
1974	Nicklaus	Miller	Player	Weiskopf	Trevino
1975	Nicklaus	Miller	Weiskopf	Irwin	Player
1976	Nicklaus	Irwin	Miller	Player	Green
1977	Nicklaus	Watson	Green	Irwin	Crenshaw
1978	Watson	Nicklaus	Irwin	Green	Player
1979	Watson	Nicklaus	Irwin	Trevino	Player
1980	Watson	Trevino	Aoki	Crenshaw	Nicklaus
1981	Watson	Rogers	Aoki	Pate	Trevino
1982	Watson	Floyd	Ballesteros	Kite	Stadler
1983	Ballesteros	Watson	Floyd	Norman	Kite
1984	Ballesteros	Watson	Norman	Wadkins	Langer
1985	Ballesteros	Langer	Norman	Watson	Nakajima
1986	Norman	Langer	Ballesteros	Nakajima	Bean
1987	Norman	Ballesteros	Langer	Lyle	Strange
1988	Ballesteros	Norman	Lyle	Faldo	Strange
1989	Norman	Faldo	Ballesteros	Strange	Stewart
1990	Norman	Faldo	Olazabal	Woosnam	Stewart
1991	Woosnam	Faldo	Olazabal	Ballesteros	Norman
1992	Faldo	Couples	Woosnam	Olazabal	Norman
1993	Faldo	Norman	Langer	Price	Couples
1994	Price	Norman	Faldo	Langer	Olazabal
1995	Norman	Price	Langer	Els	Montgomerie
1996	Norman	Lehman	Montgomerie	Els	Couples
1997	Norman	Woods	Price	Els	Love
1998	Woods	O'Meara	Duval	Love	Els
1999	Woods	Duval	Montgomerie	Love	Els
2000	Woods	Els	Duval	Mickelson	Westwood
2001	Woods	Mickelson	Duval	Els	Love
2002	Woods	Mickelson	Els	Garcia	Goosen
2003	Woods	Singh	Els	Love	Furyk
2004	Singh	Woods	Els	Goosen	Mickelson
2005	Woods	Singh	Mickelson	Goosen	Els
2006	Woods	Furyk	Mickelson	Scott	Els
2007	Woods	Mickelson	Furyk	Els	Stricker
2008	Woods	Garcia	Mickelson	Harrington	Singh
2009	Woods	Mickelson	Stricker	Westwood	Harrington
2010	Westwood	Woods	Kaymer	Mickelson	Furyk
2011	Donald	Westwood	McIlroy	Kaymer	Scott
2012	McIlroy	Donald	Woods	Rose	Scott

(The World of Professional Golf 1968-1985; World Ranking 1986-2012)

Year	No. 6	No. 7	No. 8	No. 9	No. 10
1968	Boros	Coles	Thomson	Beard	Nagle
1969	Beard	Archer	Trevino	Barber	Sikes
1970	Devlin	Coles	Jacklin	Beard	Huggett
1971	Barber	Crampton	Charles	Devlin	Weiskopf
1972	Jacklin	Weiskopf	Oosterhuis	Heard	Devlin
1973	Miller	Oosterhuis	Wadkins	Heard	Brewer
1974	M. Ozaki	Crampton	Irwin	Green	Heard
1975	Green	Trevino	Casper	Crampton	Watson
1976	Watson	Weiskopf	Marsh	Crenshaw	Geiberger
1977	Marsh	Player	Weiskopf	Floyd	Ballesteros
1978	Crenshaw	Marsh	Ballesteros	Trevino	Aoki
1979	Aoki	Green	Crenshaw	Ballesteros	Wadkins
1980	Pate	Ballesteros	Bean	Irwin	Player
1981	Ballesteros	Graham	Crenshaw	Floyd	Lietzke
1982	Pate	Nicklaus	Rogers	Aoki	Strange
1983	Nicklaus	Nakajima	Stadler	Aoki	Wadkins
1984	Faldo	Nakajima	Stadler	Kite	Peete
1985	Wadkins	O'Meara	Strange	Pavin	Sutton
1986	Tway	Sutton	Strange	Stewart	O'Meara
1987	Woosnam	Stewart	Wadkins	McNulty	Crenshaw
1988	Crenshaw	Woosnam	Frost	Azinger	Calcavecchia
1989	Kite	Olazabal	Calcavecchia	Woosnam	Azinger
1990	Azinger	Ballesteros	Kite	McNulty	Calcavecchia
1991	Couples	Langer	Stewart	Azinger	Davis
1992	Langer	Cook	Price	Azinger	Love
1993	Azinger	Woosnam	Kite	Love	Pavin
1994	Els	Couples	Montgomerie	M. Ozaki	Pavin
1995	Pavin	Faldo	Couples	M. Ozaki	Elkington
1996	Faldo	Mickelson	M. Ozaki	Love	O'Meara
1997	Mickelson	Montgomerie	M. Ozaki	Lehman	O'Meara
1998	Price	Montgomerie	Westwood	Singh	Mickelson
1999	Westwood	Singh	Price	Mickelson	O'Meara
2000	Montgomerie	Love	Sutton	Singh	Lehman
2001	Garcia	Toms	Singh	Clarke	Goosen
2002	Toms	Harrington	Singh	Love	Montgomerie
2003	Weir	Goosen	Harrington	Toms	Perry
2004	Harrington	Garcia	Weir	Love	Cink
2005	Garcia	Furyk	Montgomerie	Scott	DiMarco
2006	Goosen	Singh	Harrington	Donald	Ogilvy
2007	Rose	Scott	Harrington	Choi	Singh
2008	Karlsson	Villegas	Stenson	Els	Westwood
2009	Furyk	Casey	Stenson	McIlroy	Perry
2010	McDowell	Stricker	Casey	Donald	McIlroy
2011	Stricker	D. Johnson	Day	Schwartzel	W. Simpson
2012	Oosthuizen	Westwood	B. Watson	Dufner	Snedeker

World's Winners of 2012

U.S. PGA TOUR

Hyundai Tournament of Champions	Steve Stricker
Sony Open	Johnson Wagner
Humana Challenge	Mark Wilson
Farmers Insurance Open	Brandt Snedeker
Waste Management Phoenix Open	Kyle Stanley
AT&T Pebble Beach National Pro-Am	Phil Mickelson
Northern Trust Open	Bill Haas
WGC - Accenture Match Play Championship	Hunter Mahan
Mayakoba Golf Classic	John Huh
Honda Classic	Rory McIlroy
WGC - Cadillac Championship	Justin Rose
Puerto Rico Open	George McNeill
Transitions Championship	Luke Donald
Arnold Palmer Invitational	Tiger Woods
Shell Houston Open	Hunter Mahan (2)
Masters Tournament	Bubba Watson
RBC Heritage	Carl Pettersson
Valero Texas Open	Ben Curtis
Zurich Classic of New Orleans	Jason Dufner
Wells Fargo Championship	Rickie Fowler
The Players Championship	Matt Kuchar
HP Byron Nelson Championship	Jason Dufner (2)
Crowne Plaza Invitational	Zach Johnson
Memorial Tournament	Tiger Woods (2)
FedEx St. Jude Classic	Dustin Johnson
U.S. Open Championship	Webb Simpson
Travelers Championship	Marc Leishman
AT&T National	Tiger Woods (3)
Greenbrier Classic	Ted Potter, Jr.
John Deere Classic	Zach Johnson (2)
True South Classic	Scott Stallings
RBC Canadian Open	Scott Piercy
WGC - Bridgestone Invitational	Keegan Bradley
Reno-Tahoe Open	J.J. Henry
PGA Championship	Rory McIlroy (2)
Wyndham Championship	Sergio Garcia

PGA TOUR PLAYOFFS FOR THE FEDEXCUP

The Barclays	Nick Watney
Deutsche Bank Championship	Rory McIlroy (3)
BMW Championship	Rory McIlroy (4)
Tour Championship	Brandt Snedeker (2)
The Ryder Cup	Europe

PGA TOUR FALL SERIES

Justin Timberlake Shriners Hospitals for Children Open	Ryan Moore
Frys.com Open	Jonas Blixt
McGladrey Classic	Tommy Gainey
Children's Miracle Network Hospitals Classic	Charlie Beljan

SPECIAL EVENTS

Tavistock Cup	Lake Nona
CVS Caremark Charity Classic	Morgan Pressel/Jay Haas (2)
PGA Grand Slam of Golf	Padraig Harrington
Callaway Golf Pebble Beach Invitational	Tommy Gainey (2)
World Challenge	Graeme McDowell
Franklin Templeton Shootout	Sean O'Hair/Kenny Perry (2)
PNC Father-Son Challenge	Davis Love/Dru Love

WEB.COM TOUR

Pacific Rubiales Colombia Championship	Skip Kendall
Panama Claro Championship	Edward Loar
Chile Classic	Paul Haley
Chitimacha Louisiana Open	Casey Wittenberg
Soboba Golf Classic	Andres Gonzales
TPC Stonebrae Championship	Alex Aragon
South Georgia Classic	Luke List
Stadion Classic	Hudson Swafford
BMW Charity Pro-Am	Nick Flanagan
Rex Hospital Open	James Hahn
Mexico Open	Lee Williams
Preferred Health Systems Wichita Open	Casey Wittenberg (2)
United Leasing Championship	Peter Tomasulo
Utah Championship	Doug LaBelle
Nationwide Children's Hospital Invitational	Ben Kohles
Cox Classic	Ben Kohles (2)
Price Cutter Charity Championship	Chris Wilson
Midwest Classic	Shawn Stefani
News Sentinel Open	Darron Stiles
Mylan Classic	Robert Streb
Albertsons Boise Open	Luke Guthrie
WNB Golf Classic	Luke Guthrie (2)
Chiquita Classic	Russell Henley
Neediest Kids Championship	David Lingmerth
Miccosukee Championship	Shawn Stefani (2)
Winn-Dixie Jacksonville Open	Russell Henley (2)
Web.com Tour Championship	Justin Bolli

CANADIAN TOUR

Times Colonist Island Savings Open	Andrew Roque
ATB Financial Classic	Michael Gligic
Syncrude Boreal Open	Cory Renfrew
Dakota Dunes Casino Open	Matt Hill
Canadian Tour Players Cup	Chris Killmer
Jamieson WFCU Windsor Roseland Charity Classic	Alan McLean
Canadian Tour Championship	Eugene Wong
Great Waterway Classic	Eugene Wong (2)

TOUR DE LAS AMERICAS

Abierto de Golf Los Lirios	Julian Etulain
International Open La Vitalicia	Rafael Romero
Challenge Latinoamericano Copa La Vitalicia	Venezuela
Abierto del Centro	Cesar Agustin Costilla
Abierto del Nordeste	Luciano Dodda
Televisa TLA Players Championship	Marco Ruiz
Taca Airlines Open	Marco Ruiz (2)

PGA TOUR LATINOAMERICA

Mundo Maya Open	Tommy Cocha
TransAmerican Power Products Open	Ariel Canete
65 Arturo Calle Colombian Open	Matias O'Curry
Brazil Open	Clodomiro Carranza
Roberto de Vicenzo Invitational Copa NEC	Alan Wagner
Lexus Peru Open	Sebastian Salem
Dominican Republic Open	Oscar Fraustro
Puerto Rico Classic	Sebastian Vazquez
Arturo Calle Colombian Coffee Classic	Sebastian Fernandez
Olivos Golf Classic - Copa Personal	Ariel Canete (2)
Visa Open de Argentina	Angel Cabrera

EUROPEAN TOUR

Abu Dhabi HSBC Golf Championship	Robert Rock
Commercialbank Qatar Masters	Paul Lawrie
Omega Dubai Desert Classic	Rafa Cabrera-Bello
Open de Andalucia Costa del Sol	Julien Quesne
Trophee Hassan II	Michael Hoey
Sicilian Open	Thorbjorn Olesen
Reale Seguros Open de Espana	Francesco Molinari
Madeira Islands Open	Ricardo Santos
Volvo World Match Play Championship	Nicolas Colsaerts
BMW PGA Championship	Luke Donald (2)
ISPS Handa Wales Open	Thongchai Jaidee
Nordea Masters	Lee Westwood (2)
Saint-Omer Open	Darren Fichardt
BMW International Open	Danny Willett
Irish Open	Jamie Donaldson
Alstom Open de France	Marcel Siem
Aberdeen Asset Management Scottish Open	Jeev Milkha Singh
The Open Championship	Ernie Els
Lyoness Open	Bernd Wiesberger (2)
Johnnie Walker Championship	Paul Lawrie (2)
Omega European Masters	Richie Ramsay
KLM Open	Peter Hanson
BMW Italian Open	Gonzalo Fernandez-Castano
Alfred Dunhill Links Championship	Branden Grace (5)
Turkish Airways World Golf Final	Justin Rose (2)
Portugal Masters	Shane Lowry
BMW Masters	Peter Hanson (2)
DP World Tour Championship	Rory McIlroy (5)

CHALLENGE TOUR

Gujarat Kensville Challenge	Maximilian Kieffer
Pacific Rubiales Colombia Classic	Phillip Archer
Barclays Kenya Open	Seve Benson
Allianz Open Cotes d'Armor - Bretagne	Eddie Pepperell
Telenet Trophy	Marco Crespi
Fred Olsen Challenge de Espana	Eduardo De La Riva
Karnten Golf Open	Gary Stal
Scottish Hydro Challenge	Sam Walker
Challenge Provincia di Varese	Raymond Russell
Credit Suisse Challenge	Gary Stal (2)
Double Tree by Hilton Acaya Open	Espen Kofstad
English Challenge	Chris Paisley
Finnish Challenge	Kristoffer Broberg
Norwegian Challenge	Kristoffer Broberg (2)
ECCO Tour Championship	Alessandro Tadini

Rolex Trophy — Kristoffer Broberg (3)
M2M Russian Challenge Cup — Alexandre Kaleka
Kazakhstan Open — Scott Henry
Allianz Golf Open Toulouse Metropole — *Julien Brun
Challenge de Catalunya — Brooks Koepka
Allianz Open de Lyon — Chris Doak
D+D Real Czech Challenge Open — Andreas Harto
Crowne Plaza Copenhagen Challenge — Kristoffer Broberg (4)
Apulia San Domenico Grand Final — Espen Kofstad (2)

ASIAN TOUR

Zaykabar Myanmar Open — Kieran Pratt
ICTSI Philippine Open — Mardan Mamat
Avantha Masters — Jbe' Kruger
SAIL-SBI Open — Anirban Lahiri
Handa Faldo Cambodian Classic — David Lipsky
Panasonic Open India — Digvijay Singh
ISPS Handa Singapore Classic — Scott Hend
Maybank Malaysian Open — Louis Oosthuizen (2)
CIMB Niaga Indonesian Masters — Lee Westwood
Ballantine's Championship — Bernd Wiesberger
Queen's Cup — Thaworn Wiratchant
Volvik Hildesheim Open J Golf Series — Lee In-woo
Worldwide Holdings Selangor Masters — Thaworn Wiratchant (2)
Yeangder Tournament Players Championship — Gaganjeet Bhullar
Mercuries Taiwan Masters — Tsai Chi-huang
CJ Invitational — K.J. Choi
Venetian Macau Open — Gaganjeet Bhullar (2)
Hero Indian Open — Thaworn Wiratchant (3)
CIMB Classic — Nick Watney (2)
WGC - HSBC Champions — Ian Poulter
Barclays Singapore Open — Matteo Manassero
UBS Hong Kong Open — Miguel Angel Jimenez
King's Cup — Arnond Vongvanij
Thailand Golf Championship — Charl Schwartzel
Iskandar Johor Open — Sergio Garcia (2)

ONEASIA TOUR

Enjoy Jakarta Indonesia Open — Nick Cullen
Volvo China Open — Branden Grace (3)
GS Caltex Maekyung Open — Bio Kim
SK Telecom Open — Bio Kim (2)
Thailand Open — Chris Wood
Charity High1 Resort Open — Matthew Griffin
Nanshan China Masters — Liang Wen-chong
Kolon Korea Open — Kim Dae-sub
Dongfend Nissan Cup — Asia-Pacific

JAPAN TOUR

Token Homemate Cup — Brendan Jones
Tsuruya Open — Hiroyuki Fujita
The Crowns — I.J. Jang
Japan PGA Championship — Toru Taniguchi
Totoumi Hamamatsu Open — Jay Choi
Diamond Cup — Hiroyuki Fujita (2)
Japan Tour Championship — Yoshinori Fujimoto
Gateway to the Open Mizuno Open — Brad Kennedy
Nagashima Shigeo Invitational — Lee Kyoung-hoon
Sun Chlorella Classic — Brendan Jones (2)

Kansai Open	Toshinori Muto
Vana H Cup KBC Augusta	Kim Hyung-sung
Fujisankei Classic	K.T. Kim
Toshin Golf Tournament	Wu Ashun
ANA Open	Hiroyuki Fujita (3)
Asia-Pacific Panasonic Open	Masanori Kobayashi
Coca-Cola Tokai Classic	Ryu Hyun-woo
Canon Open	Yuta Ikeda
Japan Open	Kenichi Kuboya
Bridgestone Open	Toru Taniguchi (2)
Mynavi ABC Championship	Han Lee
Mitsui Sumitomo Visa Taiheiyo Masters	Ryo Ishikawa
Dunlop Phoenix	Luke Donald (3)
Casio World Open	Hwang Jung-gon
Golf Nippon Series JT Cup	Hiroyuki Fujita (4)

AUSTRALASIAN TOUR

Victorian Open	Scott Arnold
Adroit Insurance Group Victorian PGA	Gareth Paddison
Coca-Cola Queensland PGA Championship	Andrew Tschudin
New Zealand PGA Pro-Am Championship	Michael Hendry
South Pacific Golf Open Championship	Brad Shilton
WA Goldfields PGA Championship	Peter Wilson
ISPS Handa Perth International	Bo Van Pelt
John Hughes Geely/Nexus Risk Services	
Western Australian Open	*Oliver Goss
Talisker Masters	Adam Scott
BMW New Zealand Open	*Jake Higginbottom
NSW PGA Championship	Matthew Stieger
Emirates Australian Open	Peter Senior
Australian PGA Championship	Daniel Popovic

AFRICAN TOURS

Africa Open	Louis Oosthuizen
Joburg Open	Branden Grace
Volvo Golf Champions	Branden Grace (2)
Dimension Data Pro-Am	Oliver Bekker
Telkom PGA Championship	Keith Horne
Platinum Classic	Jake Roos
Golden Pilsener Zimbabwe Open	Chris Swanepoel
Investec Royal Swazi Sun Open	Christiaan Basson
Vodacom Origins of Golf - Simola	Ryan Cairns
Sun City Challenge	Bryce Easton
Lombard Insurance Classic	Jake Roos (2)
Vodacom Origins of Golf - Zebula	Bryce Easton (2)
Indo Zambia Bank Zambia Open	Justin Harding
Vodacom Origins of Golf - De Zalze	Allan Versfeld
Vodacom Origins of Golf - Selborne	Adilson Da Silva
Wild Waves Golf Challenge	Trevor Fisher, Jr.
Vodacom Origins of Golf - Sishen	Trevor Fisher, Jr. (2)
Vodacom Origins of Golf Final	Branden Grace (4)
BMG Classic	Teboho Sefatsa
Suncoast Classic	Ruan de Smidt
ISPS Handa Matchplay Championship	Doug McGuigan
Nedbank Affinity Cup	Trevor Fisher, Jr. (3)
South African Open Championship	Henrik Stenson
Lion of Africa Cape Town Open	Jake Roos (3)
Nedbank Golf Challenge	Martin Kaymer
Nelson Mandela Championship	Scott Jamieson
Alfred Dunhill Championship	Charl Schwartzel (2)

U.S. LPGA TOUR

Honda LPGA Thailand	Yani Tseng
HSBC Women's Champions	Angela Stanford
RR Donnelley LPGA Founders Cup	Yani Tseng (2)
Kia Classic	Yani Tseng (3)
Kraft Nabisco Championship	Sun Young Yoo
LPGA LOTTE Championship	Ai Miyazato
Mobile Bay LPGA Classic	Stacy Lewis
HSBC LPGA Brasil Cup	Pornanong Phatlum
Sybase Match Play Championship	Azahara Munoz
ShopRite LPGA Classic	Stacy Lewis (2)
Wegmans LPGA Championship	Shanshan Feng (3)
Manulife Financial LPGA Classic	Brittany Lang
Walmart NW Arkansas Championship	Ai Miyazato (2)
U.S. Women's Open	Na Yeon Choi
Jamie Farr Toledo Classic	So Yeon Ryu
Safeway Classic	Mika Miyazato
CN Canadian Women's Open	*Lydia Ko (2)
Kingsmill Championship	Jiyai Shin
Navistar LPGA Classic	Stacy Lewis (3)
Sime Darby LPGA Malaysia	Inbee Park (3)
LPGA KEB-HanaBank Championship	Suzann Pettersen
Sunrise LPGA Taiwan Championship	Suzann Pettersen (2)
Lorena Ochoa Invitational	Cristie Kerr
CME Group Titleholders	Na Yeon Choi (2)

LADIES EUROPEAN TOUR

World Ladies Championship	Shanshan Feng
Lalla Meryem Cup	Karen Lunn (2)
Aberdeen Asset Management Scottish Open	Carly Booth
Turkish Airlines Ladies Open	Christel Boeljon (2)
UniCredit Ladies German Open	Anne-Lise Caudal
Deloitte Ladies Open	Carlota Ciganda
Allianz Ladies Slovak Open	Line Vedel
Deutsche Bank Ladies Swiss Open	Carly Booth (2)
Raiffeisenbank Prague Golf Masters	Melissa Reid
South African Women's Open	Caroline Masson
Evian Masters	Inbee Park (2)
Ladies Irish Open	Catriona Matthew
ISPS Handa Ladies British Masters	Lydia Hall
UNIQA Ladies Golf Open	Caroline Hedwall
Ricoh Women's British Ope	Jiyai Shin (2)
Tenerife Open de Espana Femenino	Stacey Keating
Lacoste Ladies Open de France	Stacey Keating (2)
China Suzhou Taihu Open	Carlota Ciganda (2)
Sanya Ladies Open	Cassandra Kirkland
Hero Women's Indian Open	Pornanong Phatlum (2)
Omega Dubai Ladies Masters	Shanshan Feng (6)

JAPAN LPGA TOUR

Daikin Orchid Ladies	Airi Saitoh
Yokohama Tire PRGR Ladies Cup	Bo-Mee Lee
T-Point Ladies	Ji-Hee Lee
Yamaha Ladies Open	Ritsuko Ryu
Studio Alice Ladies Open	Miki Saiki
Nishijin Ladies Classic	Maiko Wakabayashi
Fujisankei Ladies Classic	Kaori Ohe
Cyber Agent Ladies	Chie Arimura
World Ladies Championship Salonpas Cup	Sun-Ju Ahn

Fundokin Ladies	Inbee Park
Chukyo TV Bridgestone Ladies Open	Ji-Hee Lee (2)
Yonex Ladies	Shanshan Feng (2)
Resort Trust Ladies	Mi-Jeong Jeon
Suntory Ladies Open	*Hyo-Joo Kim
Nichirei Ladies	Hyun-Ju Shin
Earth Mondahmin Cup	Mayu Hattori
Nichi-Iko Ladies Open	Mi-Jeong Jeon (2)
Stanley Ladies	Chie Arimura (2)
Samantha Thavasa Girls Collection Ladies	Megumi Kido
Meiji Cup	Shanshan Feng (4)
NEC Karuzawa 72	Yumiko Yoshida
CAT Ladies	Mi-Jeong Jeon (3)
Nitori Ladies	Sun-Ju Ahn (2)
Golf 5 Ladies	Sun-Ju Ahn (3)
Japan LPGA Championship	Chie Arimura (3)
Munsingwear Ladies Tokai Classic	Natsu Nagai
Miyagi TV Cup Dunlop Ladies Open	Rikako Morita
Japan Women's Open	Shanshan Feng (5)
Fujitsu Ladies	Misuzu Narita
Masters Golf Club Ladies	So-Hee Kim
Hisako Higuch Morinaga Weider Ladies	Mi-Jeong Jeon (4)
Mizuno Classic	Stacy Lewis (4)
Itoen Ladies	Bo-Mee Lee (2)
Daio Paper Elleair Ladies Open	Miki Saiki (2)
Japan LPGA Tour Championship Ricoh Cup	Bo-Mee Lee (3)

AUSTRALIAN LADIES TOUR

Women's Victorian Open	Joanna Klatten
Moss Vale Golf Club ALPG Pro-Am	Cathryn Bristow
ActewAGL Royal Canberra Ladies Classic	Karen Lunn
Bing Lee Samsung NSW Open	*Lydia Ko
Gold Coast RACV Australian Ladies Masters	Christel Boeljon
ISPS Handa Women's Australian Open	Jessica Korda
ISPS Handa New Zealand Women's Open	Lindsey Wright

CHAMPIONS TOUR

Mitsubishi Electric Championship	Dan Forsman
Allianz Championship	Corey Pavin
ACE Group Classic	Kenny Perry
Toshiba Classic	Loren Roberts
Mississippi Gulf Resort Classic	Fred Couples
Encompass Insurance Pro-Am	Michael Allen
Liberty Mutual Insurance Legends of Golf	Michael Allen (2)/David Frost
Insperity Championship	Fred Funk
Senior PGA Championship	Roger Chapman
Principal Charity Classic	Jay Haas
Regions Tradition	Tom Lehman
Montreal Championship	Mark Calcavecchia
Constellation Senior Players Championship	Joe Daley
Nature Valley First Tee Open	Kirk Triplett
U.S. Senior Open Championship	Roger Chapman (2)
3M Championship	Bernhard Langer
Dick's Sporting Goods Open	Willie Wood
Boeing Classic	Jay Don Blake
Pacific Links Hawai'i Championship	Willie Wood (2)
SAS Championship	Bernhard Langer (2)
Greater Hickory Classic	Fred Funk (2)
AT&T Championship	David Frost (2)
Charles Schwab Cup Championship	Tom Lehman (2)

EUROPEAN SENIOR TOUR

Mallorca Senior Open	Gary Wolstenholme
Benahavis Senior Masters	Gary Wolstenholme (2)
ISPS Handa PGA Seniors Championship	Paul Wesselingh
Van Lanschot Senior Open	Massy Kuramoto
Berenberg Bank Masters	Tim Thelen
Bad Ragaz PGA Seniors Open	Tim Thelen (2)
The Senior Open Championship presented by Rolex	Fred Couples (2)
SSE Scottish Senior Open	Anders Forsbrand
Speedy Services Wales Senior Open	Barry Lane
Travis Perkins plc Senior Masters	Des Smyth
Pon Senior Open	Terry Price
French Riviera Masters	David J. Russell
Fubon Senior Open	Tim Thelen (3)
Nedbank Champions Challenge	Bernhard Langer (3)
ISPS Handa Australian Senior Open	Peter Fowler
MCB Tour Championship	David Frost (3)

JAPAN PGA SENIOR TOUR

Starts Senior	Naomichi Ozaki
ISPS Handa Cup Shakunetsu-no Masters	Takashi Miyoshi
Fancl Classic	Kazuhiro Takami
Komatsu Open	Naomichi Ozaki (2)
ISPS Handa Cup Akibare-no Masters	Gohei Sato
Japan PGA Senior Championship	Kiyoshi Murota
Japan Senior Open Championship	Frankie Minoza
Fuji Film Senior Championship	Kouki Idoki

Multiple Winners of 2012

PLAYER	WINS	PLAYER	WINS
Shanshan Feng	6	Russell Henley	2
Branden Grace	5	Zach Johnson	2
Rory McIlroy	5	Brendan Jones	2
Kristoffer Broberg	4	Stacey Keating	2
Hiroyuki Fujita	4	Bio Kim	2
Mi-Jeong Jeon	4	*Lydia Ko	2
Stacy Lewis	4	Espen Kofstad	2
Sun-Ju Ahn	3	Ben Kohles	2
Chie Arimura	3	Paul Lawrie	2
Luke Donald	3	Ji-Hee Lee	2
Trevor Fisher, Jr.	3	Tom Lehman	2
David Frost	3	Karen Lunn	2
Bernhard Langer	3	Hunter Mahan	2
Bo-Mee Lee	3	Ai Miyazato	2
Inbee Park	3	Louis Oosthuizen	2
Jake Roos	3	Naomichi Ozaki	2
Tim Thelen	3	Inbee Park	2
Yani Tseng	3	Kenny Perry	2
Thaworn Wiratchant	3	Suzann Pettersen	2
Tiger Woods	3	Pornanong Phatlum	2
Michael Allen	2	Justin Rose	2
Gaganjeet Bhullar	2	Marco Ruiz	2
Christel Boeljon	2	Miki Saiki	2
Carly Booth	2	Charl Schwartzel	2
Ariel Canete	2	Jiyai Shin	2
Roger Chapman	2	Brandt Snedeker	2
Na Yeon Choi	2	Gary Stal	2
Carlota Ciganda	2	Shawn Stefani	2
Fred Couples	2	Toru Taniguchi	2
Jason Dufner	2	Nick Watney	2
Bryce Easton	2	Lee Westwood	2
Fred Funk	2	Bernd Wiesberger	2
Tommy Gainey	2	Casey Wittenberg	2
Sergio Garcia	2	Gary Wolstenholme	2
Luke Guthrie	2	Eugene Wong	2
Jay Haas	2	Willie Wood	2
Peter Hanson	2		

World Money List

This list of the 350 leading money winners in the world of professional golf in 2012 was compiled from the results of men's (excluding seniors) tournaments carried in the Appendixes of this edition. This list includes tournaments with a minimum of 36 holes and four contestants and does not include such competitions as pro-ams and skins or skills contests. It does not include annual performance bonuses such as for the FedExCup (U.S.) and the Race to Dubai (Europe).

In the 47 years during which World Money Lists have been compiled, the earnings of the player in the 200th position have risen from a total of $3,326 in 1966 to $671,356 in 2012. The top 200 players in 1966 earned a total of $4,680,287. In 2012, the comparable total was $372,979,826.

The World Money List includes the official money lists of the U.S. PGA Tour, PGA European Tour, PGA Tour of Japan, Asian Tour, OneAsia Tour, Sunshine Tour, PGA Tour of Australasia, Tour de las Americas (to become PGA Tour Latinoamerica) and Canadian Tour (to become PGA Tour Canada), along with winnings in established unofficial tournaments when reliable figures could be obtained. The conversion rates used for 2012 were: Euro = US$1.29; Japanese yen = US$0.01; South African rand = US$0.12; Australian dollar = US$1.04; Canadian dollar = US$1.00.

POS.	PLAYER, COUNTRY	TOTAL MONEY
1	Rory McIlroy, N. Ireland	$11,301,228
2	Justin Rose, England	7,951,550
3	Tiger Woods, USA	7,388,061
4	Luke Donald, England	6,010,759
5	Louis Oosthuizen, South Africa	5,935,810
6	Jason Dufner, USA	5,839,495
7	Lee Westwood, England	5,459,415
8	Brandt Snedeker, USA	5,428,602
9	Bubba Watson, USA	5,231,247
10	Keegan Bradley, USA	4,783,908
11	Phil Mickelson, USA	4,758,850
12	Zach Johnson, USA	4,624,244
13	Nick Watney, USA	4,557,224
14	Matt Kuchar, USA	4,545,565
15	Hunter Mahan, USA	4,472,043
16	Graeme McDowell, N. Ireland	4,470,647
17	Ernie Els, South Africa	4,413,207
18	Webb Simpson, USA	4,346,758
19	Bo Van Pelt, USA	4,225,294
20	Carl Pettersson, Sweden	4,211,656
21	Ian Poulter, England	4,123,769
22	Peter Hanson, Sweden	4,116,162
23	Charl Schwartzel, South Africa	3,851,715
24	Jim Furyk, USA	3,825,472
25	Robert Garrigus, USA	3,729,530
26	Steve Stricker, USA	3,667,521
27	Dustin Johnson, USA	3,667,510
28	Adam Scott, Australia	3,601,181
29	Sergio Garcia, Spain	3,420,883

POS.	PLAYER, COUNTRY	TOTAL MONEY
30	Rickie Fowler, USA	3,345,460
31	Scott Piercy, USA	3,219,205
32	Nicolas Colsaerts, Belgium	3,073,957
33	Branden Grace, South Africa	3,055,050
34	Bill Haas, USA	3,003,951
35	Francesco Molinari, Italy	2,966,569
36	Ryan Moore, USA	2,858,944
37	John Huh, USA	2,752,713
38	Paul Lawrie, Scotland	2,697,189
39	Martin Kaymer, Germany	2,690,440
40	Ben Curtis, USA	2,673,815
41	Padraig Harrington, Ireland	2,598,767
42	Kyle Stanley, USA	2,429,357
43	Jonas Blixt, Sweden	2,320,545
44	Johnson Wagner, USA	2,305,007
45	Hiroyuki Fujita, Japan	2,298,990
46	Brendon de Jonge, Zimbabwe	2,280,252
47	Martin Laird, Scotland	2,279,123
48	Mark Wilson, USA	2,184,780
49	John Senden, Australia	2,159,551
50	Kevin Na, USA	2,132,443
51	Marc Leishman, Australia	2,088,654
52	Matteo Manassero, Italy	2,049,695
53	Matt Every, USA	1,972,166
54	Charlie Wi, Korea	1,942,314
55	Bud Cauley, USA	1,851,979
56	Ben Crane, USA	1,788,365
57	Vijay Singh, Fiji	1,783,305
58	Seung-Yul Noh, Korea	1,768,410
59	Marcel Siem, Germany	1,758,966
60	Henrik Stenson, Sweden	1,753,209
61	Ryo Ishikawa, Japan	1,727,168
62	Jimmy Walker, USA	1,691,794
63	Thorbjorn Olesen, Denmark	1,689,813
64	Sean O'Hair, USA	1,665,981
65	David Toms, USA	1,658,428
66	Jeff Overton, USA	1,642,670
67	Kevin Stadler, USA	1,618,386
68	Jonathan Byrd, USA	1,616,789
69	Tommy Gainey, USA	1,600,749
70	Charles Howell, USA	1,599,578
71	Rafa Cabrera-Bello, Spain	1,588,302
72	David Lynn, England	1,553,093
73	Ryan Palmer, USA	1,551,215
74	Thongchai Jaidee, Thailand	1,543,587
75	D.A. Points, USA	1,538,261
76	Ken Duke, USA	1,511,628
77	Tim Clark, South Africa	1,497,212
78	Jamie Donaldson, USA	1,491,094
79	John Rollins, USA	1,489,155
80	Gonzalo Fernandez-Castano, Spain	1,477,464
81	Jason Day, Australia	1,477,357
82	Marcus Fraser, Australia	1,472,312
83	Chris Kirk, USA	1,462,562

POS.	PLAYER, COUNTRY	TOTAL MONEY
84	Thomas Bjorn, Denmark	1,447,951
85	Richie Ramsay, Scotland	1,432,725
86	George Coetzee, South Africa	1,419,311
87	Michael Thompson, USA	1,408,374
88	Ted Potter, Jr., USA	1,385,040
89	Charlie Beljan, USA	1,380,808
90	Danny Willett, England	1,380,464
91	Rory Sabbatini South Africa	1,363,820
92	Geoff Ogilvy, Australia	1,362,721
93	Bernd Wiesberger, Austria	1,361,703
94	Brendan Jones, Australia	1,350,314
95	Greg Chalmers, Australia	1,349,329
96	Alexander Noren, Sweden	1,343,068
97	Brian Davis, England	1,318,032
98	Tom Gillis, USA	1,298,658
99	J.J. Henry, USA	1,297,802
100	William McGirt, USA	1,296,747
101	Scott Stallings, USA	1,296,197
102	Davis Love, USA	1,287,253
103	Spencer Levin, USA	1,283,616
104	Toru Taniguchi, Japan	1,283,587
105	Miguel Angel Jimenez, Spain	1,282,092
106	Cameron Tringale, USA	1,281,237
107	Shane Lowry, Ireland	1,280,554
108	Jeev Milkha Singh, India	1,278,795
109	Charley Hoffman, USA	1,276,663
110	Retief Goosen, South Africa	1,268,535
111	Dicky Pride, USA	1,266,003
112	Troy Matteson, USA	1,252,453
113	J.B. Holmes, USA	1,250,505
114	Brian Harman, USA	1,248,948
115	Blake Adams, USA	1,236,405
116	Pat Perez, USA	1,224,285
117	Aaron Baddeley, Australia	1,215,753
118	Ross Fisher, England	1,199,683
119	Harris English, USA	1,186,003
120	Bryce Molder, USA	1,171,015
121	Robert Rock, England	1,156,213
122	Greg Owen, England	1,151,622
123	Yuta Ikeda, Japan	1,150,351
124	John Mallinger, USA	1,149,877
125	George McNeill, USA	1,119,535
126	Daniel Summerhays, USA	1,116,422
127	K.J. Choi, Korea	1,110,748
128	Yoshinori Fujimoto, Japan	1,108,239
129	Stephen Gallacher, Scotland	1,085,623
130	John Merrick, USA	1,084,628
131	Fredrik Jacobson, Sweden	1,075,323
132	Hwang Jung-gon, Korea	1,071,754
133	Graham DeLaet, Canada	1,066,704
134	Jbe' Kruger, South Africa	1,065,345
135	Bob Estes, USA	1,063,269
136	Fredrik Andersson Hed, Sweden	1,038,448
137	Martin Flores, USA	1,037,769

POS.	PLAYER, COUNTRY	TOTAL MONEY
138	Brendan Steele, USA	1,033,528
139	Pablo Larrazabal, Spain	1,029,367
140	Garth Mulroy, South Africa	1,024,817
141	Josh Teater, USA	1,013,888
142	David Hearn, Canada	1,012,575
143	Anders Hansen, Denmark	1,010,638
144	Robert Allenby, Australia	1,009,705
145	Kim Hyung-sung, Korea	1,000,628
146	K.T. Kim, Korea	995,698
147	Raphael Jacquelin, France	985,414
148	Soren Kjeldsen, Denmark	980,773
149	Andres Romero, Argentina	978,161
150	Scott Jamieson, Scotland	972,214
151	Brian Gay, USA	960,658
152	Lee Kyoung-hoon, Korea	927,771
153	Chris Stroud, USA	906,028
154	Koumei Oda, Japan	904,256
155	Sang-Moon Bae, Korea	902,177
156	Thaworn Wiratchant, Thailand	897,366
157	Chad Campbell, USA	895,199
158	Kevin Streelman, USA	893,736
159	Toshinori Muto, Japan	887,508
160	Joost Luiten, Netherlands	883,048
161	Ricky Barnes, USA	876,408
162	Chris Wood, England	866,254
163	Han Lee, USA	865,222
164	Kenichi Kuboya, Japan	855,260
165	Boo Weekley, USA	848,347
166	Colt Knost, USA	848,197
167	Hideto Tanihara, Japan	837,756
168	I.J. Jang, Korea	833,671
169	Richard Sterne, South Africa	825,271
170	Peter Lawrie, Ireland	821,602
171	Jhonattan Vegas, Venezuela	801,803
172	Jason Bohn, USA	800,449
173	Thomas Aiken, South Africa	798,239
174	Simon Dyson, England	792,247
175	Alejandro Canizares, Spain	791,912
176	Masamichi Uehira, Japan	788,763
177	Troy Kelly, USA	788,523
178	John Daly, USA	783,553
179	Y.E. Yang, Korea	782,417
180	Will Claxton, USA	780,969
181	Rod Pampling, Australia	758,693
182	Jason Kokrak, USA	757,960
183	Ryu Hyun-woo, Korea	756,723
184	Roberto Castro, USA	755,095
185	Romain Wattel, France	753,608
186	Jerry Kelly, USA	743,201
187	David Mathis, USA	740,598
188	Liang Wen-chong, China	739,808
189	Victor Dubuisson, France	736,625
190	Marc Warren, Scotland	735,646
191	Masanori Kobayashi, Japan	735,188

POS.	PLAYER, COUNTRY	TOTAL MONEY
192	Harrison Frazar, USA	730,203
193	Trevor Immelman, South Africa	725,626
194	Luke Guthrie, USA	713,570
195	Gary Woodland, USA	702,879
196	Michael Hoey, N. Ireland	699,041
197	James Driscoll, USA	687,338
198	Jeff Maggert, USA	682,742
199	Shingo Katayama, Japan	674,023
200	Kim Do-hoon, Korea	671,356
201	Richard Lee, USA	664,377
202	Kunihiro Kamii, Japan	661,171
203	Tim Herron, USA	660,279
204	Robert Karlsson, Sweden	658,397
205	David Drysdale, Scotland	656,728
206	Brad Kennedy, Australia	649,326
207	Kevin Chappell, USA	647,510
208	David Howell, England	638,675
209	Richard Finch, England	635,321
210	Lee Slattery, England	635,301
211	Wu Ashun, China	633,477
212	Gaganjeet Bhullar, India	627,056
213	Alexandre Rocha, Brazil	625,563
214	Billy Mayfair, USA	619,961
215	Gary Christian, England	618,457
216	Justin Leonard, USA	615,155
217	D.J. Trahan, USA	611,142
218	Alvaro Quiros, Spain	606,753
219	Jaco Van Zyl, South Africa	599,546
220	Brett Rumford, Australia	598,952
221	Casey Wittenberg, USA	597,047
222	Bill Lunde, USA	593,598
223	Camilo Villegas, Colombia	581,679
224	Chez Reavie, USA	580,617
225	Kazuhiro Yamashita, Japan	577,440
226	Stewart Cink, USA	574,673
227	Tim Petrovic, USA	567,937
228	Julien Quesne, France	559,276
229	Juvic Pagunsan, Philppines	559,246
230	Billy Horschel, USA	557,952
231	Russell Knox, Scotland	553,834
232	Kiradech Aphibarnrat, Thailand	553,113
233	Gregory Bourdy, France	550,566
234	Tomohiro Kondo, Japan	550,117
235	Vaughn Taylor, USA	547,129
236	Anthony Wall, England	536,223
237	Prom Meesawat, Thailand	533,910
238	Bobby Gates, USA	530,193
239	Joel Sjoholm, Sweden	529,903
240	Nick O'Hern, Australia	519,691
241	Ryuichi Oda, Japan	519,654
242	Heath Slocum, USA	518,198
243	Jay Choi, USA	496,928
244	Richard Green, Australia	496,111
245	Shiv Kapur, India	484,257

POS.	PLAYER, COUNTRY	TOTAL MONEY
246	Yusaku Miyazato, Japan	483,951
247	Paul Casey, England	483,480
248	Tetsuji Hiratsuka, Japan	482,473
249	Fabrizio Zanotti, Paraguay	482,381
250	Lee Dong-hwan, Korea	480,909
251	Mark Foster, England	479,936
252	Matthew Baldwin, England	479,030
253	Scott Brown, USA	478,763
254	Billy Hurley, USA	476,631
255	Brendon Todd, USA	474,295
256	Joe Durant, USA	472,130
257	Prayad Marksaeng, Thailand	470,058
258	Chris DiMarco, USA	468,298
259	Keith Horne, South Africa	461,809
260	Darren Fichardt, South Africa	459,716
261	Bio Kim, Korea	454,812
262	Damien McGrane, Ireland	452,583
263	Kenny Perry, USA	451,544
264	Kyle Reifers, USA	448,960
265	Paul McGinley, Ireland	446,687
266	Mark Anderson, USA	445,185
267	Steve Webster, England	438,617
268	James Morrison, England	438,507
269	Kristoffer Broberg, Sweden	430,232
270	Stuart Appleby, Australia	430,219
271	Michael Campbell, New Zealand	428,930
272	Masahiro Kawamura, Japan	427,762
273	J.J. Killeen, USA	427,065
274	Felipe Aguilar, Chile	426,241
275	Danny Lee, New Zealand	425,780
276	Taichi Teshima, Japan	420,824
277	Daniel Chopra, Sweden	418,698
278	Nathan Green, Australia	417,859
279	Jorge Campillo, Spain	410,362
280	Magnus A. Carlsson, Sweden	408,138
281	Russell Henley, USA	402,574
282	Ricardo Gonzalez, Argentina	400,961
283	Anirban Lahiri, India	399,869
284	Hunter Haas, USA	399,364
285	Roland Thatcher, USA	396,801
286	Lee Janzen, USA	394,004
287	Katsumasa Miyamoto, Japan	392,428
288	Kris Blanks, USA	390,059
289	S.K. Ho, Korea	381,822
290	Kurt Barnes, Australia	381,785
291	Chapchai Nirat, Thailand	378,190
292	David Smail, New Zealand	377,494
293	S.S.P. Chowrasia, India	377,486
294	Scott Hend, Australia	372,667
295	Kevin Kisner, USA	371,926
296	Jonathan Moore, USA	370,927
297	Jose Maria Olazabal, Spain	366,168
298	Jarrod Lyle, Australia	363,685

POS.	PLAYER, COUNTRY	TOTAL MONEY
299	Luke List, USA	363,206
300	Erik Compton, USA	363,010
301	Takashi Kanemoto, Japan	361,694
302	Edoardo Molinari, Italy	361,054
303	Hennie Otto, South Africa	360,165
304	David Lipsky, USA	357,922
305	Graeme Storm, England	357,806
306	Emiliano Grillo, Argentina	352,667
307	Arjun Atwal, India	348,770
308	James Hahn, USA	346,405
309	Shunsuke Sonoda, Japan	344,835
310	Brandt Jobe, USA	344,332
311	Ricardo Santos, Portugal	339,464
312	Chris Couch, USA	335,848
313	Matt Bettencourt, USA	335,076
314	Tom Lewis, England	335,011
315	Mikko Ilonen, Finland	333,041
316	John Peterson, USA	327,091
317	Keiichiro Fukabori, Japan	325,740
318	Oliver Fisher, England	325,642
319	Thomas Levet France	325,158
320	Darren Clarke, N. Ireland	322,979
321	Yui Ueda, Japan	320,430
322	Andres Gonzales, USA	314,285
323	Robert Streb, USA	312,466
324	Alex Cejka, Germany	311,038
325	Shawn Stefani, USA	309,371
326	Mathew Goggin, Australia	309,236
327	Michio Matsumura, Japan	309,193
328	Siddikur, Bangladesh	306,342
329	Angel Cabrera, Argentina	305,885
330	Justin Hicks, USA	305,355
331	Ben Kohles, USA	303,977
332	Patrick Reed, USA	302,977
333	Lorenzo Gagli, Italy	301,069
334	Justin Bolli, USA	300,924
335	Kaname Yokoo, Japan	300,411
336	Matt Jones, USA	300,254
337	Gregory Havret, France	300,199
338	Robert Coles, England	299,734
339	Sushi Ishigaki, Japan	299,323
340	Kiyoshi Miyazato, Japan	296,761
341	Nick Cullen, Australia	295,195
342	Yasuharu Imano, Japan	293,411
343	Michael Hendry, New Zealand	293,226
344	Jean-Baptiste Gonnet, France	292,520
345	Rich Beem, USA	290,219
346	Miguel Angel Carballo, Argentina	289,513
347	Jim Herman, USA	289,001
348	Phillip Price, Wales	288,322
349	Cameron Beckman, USA	287,506
350	David Lingmerth, Sweden	287,148

World Money List Leaders

YEAR	PLAYER, COUNTRY	TOTAL MONEY
1966	Jack Nicklaus, USA	$168,088
1967	Jack Nicklaus, USA	276,166
1968	Billy Casper, USA	222,436
1969	Frank Beard, USA	186,993
1970	Jack Nicklaus, USA	222,583
1971	Jack Nicklaus, USA	285,897
1972	Jack Nicklaus, USA	341,792
1973	Tom Weiskopf, USA	349,645
1974	Johnny Miller, USA	400,255
1975	Jack Nicklaus, USA	332,610
1976	Jack Nicklaus, USA	316,086
1977	Tom Watson, USA	358,034
1978	Tom Watson, USA	384,388
1979	Tom Watson, USA	506,912
1980	Tom Watson, USA	651,921
1981	Johnny Miller, USA	704,204
1982	Raymond Floyd, USA	738,699
1983	Seve Ballesteros, Spain	686,088
1984	Seve Ballesteros, Spain	688,047
1985	Bernhard Langer, Germany	860,262
1986	Greg Norman, Australia	1,146,584
1987	Ian Woosnam, Wales	1,793,268
1988	Seve Ballesteros, Spain	1,261,275
1989	David Frost, South Africa	1,650,230
1990	Jose Maria Olazabal, Spain	1,633,640
1991	Bernhard Langer, Germany	2,186,700
1992	Nick Faldo, England	2,748,248
1993	Nick Faldo, England	2,825,280
1994	Ernie Els, South Africa	2,862,854
1995	Corey Pavin, USA	2,746,340
1996	Colin Montgomerie, Scotland	3,071,442
1997	Colin Montgomerie, Scotland	3,366,900
1998	Tiger Woods, USA	2,927,946
1999	Tiger Woods, USA	7,681,625
2000	Tiger Woods, USA	11,034,530
2001	Tiger Woods, USA	7,771,562
2002	Tiger Woods, USA	8,292,188
2003	Vijay Singh, Fiji	8,499,611
2004	Vijay Singh, Fiji	11,638,699
2005	Tiger Woods, USA	12,280,404
2006	Tiger Woods, USA	13,325,949
2007	Tiger Woods, USA	12,902,706
2008	Vijay Singh, Fiji	8,025,128
2009	Tiger Woods, USA	10,998,054
2010	Graeme McDowell, N. Ireland	7,371,586
2011	Luke Donald, England	9,730,870
2012	Rory McIlroy, N. Ireland	11,301,228

Career World Money List

Here is a list of the 50 leading money winners for their careers through the 2012 season. It includes players active on both the regular and senior tours of the world. The World Money List from this and the 46 previous editions of the annual and a table prepared for a companion book, *The Wonderful World of Professional Golf* (Atheneum, 1973) form the basis for this compilation. Additional figures were taken from official records of major golf associations. Conversion of foreign currency figures to U.S. dollars is based on average values during the particular years involved.

POS.	PLAYER, COUNTRY	TOTAL MONEY
1	Tiger Woods, USA	$123,603.903
2	Ernie Els, South Africa	83,039,652
3	Vijay Singh, Fiji	81,045,330
4	Phil Mickelson, USA	74,287,102
5	Jim Furyk, USA	64,145,767
6	Davis Love, USA	51,883,305
7	Retief Goosen, South Africa	49,496,523
8	Lee Westwood, England	49,246,608
9	Padraig Harrington, Ireland	49,167,995
10	Sergio Garcia, Spain	48,620,490
11	Luke Donald, England	45,128,008
12	David Toms, USA	41,725,611
13	Colin Montgomerie, Scotland	41,571,621
14	Bernhard Langer, Germany	41,340,979
15	Adam Scott, Australia	39,457,940
16	Steve Stricker, USA	38,857,934
17	Kenny Perry, USA	38,405,734
18	Nick Price, Zimbabwe	37,523,968
19	Fred Couples, USA	37,488,054
20	Hale Irwin, USA	37,065,855
21	Robert Allenby, Australia	35,695,275
22	Justin Leonard, USA	35,302,414
23	Justin Rose, England	35,014,706
24	Stewart Cink, USA	34,615,645
25	Mark Calcavecchia, USA	34,179,205
26	Tom Lehman, USA	33,055,191
27	Darren Clarke, N. Ireland	32,863,144
28	K.J. Choi, South Korea	32,674,526
29	Ian Poulter, England	32,541,610
30	Fred Funk, USA	31,747,333
31	Jay Haas, USA	31,060,442
32	Stuart Appleby, Australia	30,998,361
33	Tom Kite, USA	30,532,907
34	Geoff Ogilvy, Australia	30,196,620
35	Zach Johnson, USA	30,022,562
36	Mike Weir, Canada	29,667,294
37	Miguel Angel Jimenez, Spain	29,291,364
38	Rory McIlroy, N. Ireland	29,031,491
39	Rory Sabbatini, South Africa	28,718,995
40	Scott Verplank, USA	28,575,547

POS.	PLAYER, COUNTRY	TOTAL MONEY
41	Jeff Sluman, USA	28,091,058
42	Graeme McDowell, N. Ireland	28,086,635
43	Loren Roberts, USA	28,047,815
44	Paul Casey, England	28,041,693
45	Tom Watson, USA	27,918,703
46	Scott Hoch, USA	27,255,421
47	Chris DiMarco, USA	27,137,044
48	Gil Morgan, USA	27,120,452
49	Jose Maria Olazabal, Spain	27,117,366
50	Mark O'Meara, USA	26,662,724

These 50 players have won $1,984,365,922 in their careers.

Women's World Money List

This list includes official earnings on the U.S. LPGA Tour, Ladies European Tour, Japan LPGA Tour and Australian Ladies Tour, along with other winnings in established unofficial events when reliable figures could be obtained.

POS.	PLAYER, COUNTRY	TOTAL MONEY
1	Inbee Park, Korea	$3,185,020
2	Shanshan Feng, China	2,283,340
3	Na Yeon Choi, Korea	2,005,581
4	Stacy Lewis, USA	1,878,035
5	Mi-Jeong Jeon, Korea	1,654,761
6	Yani Tseng, Taiwan	1,490,992
7	Jiyai Shin, Korea	1,467,231
8	Ai Miyazato, Japan	1,378,642
9	Bo-Mee Lee, Korea	1,374,686
10	Suzann Pettersen, Norway	1,337,771
11	So Yeon Ryu, Korea	1,319,903
12	Chie Arimura, Japan	1,273,620
13	Sun-Ju Ahn, Korea	1,265,080
14	Azahara Munoz, Spain	1,230,751
15	Mika Miyazato, Japan	1,222,249
16	Miki Saiki, Japan	1,159,944
17	Ji-Hee Lee, Korea	978,167
18	Rikako Morita, Japan	954,437
19	Paula Creamer, USA	923,418
20	Mayu Hattori, Japan	896,022
21	Cristie Kerr, USA	892,314
22	Karrie Webb, Australia	884,973
23	Sakura Yokomine, Japan	867,366
24	Amy Yang, Korea	844,305
25	Ritsuko Ryu, Japan	838,302
26	Angela Stanford, USA	794,294

POS.	PLAYER, COUNTRY	TOTAL MONEY
27	Catriona Matthew, Scoland	785,236
28	Sun Young Yoo, Korea	781,587
29	Lexi Thompson, USA	721,011
30	Anna Nordqvist, Sweden	705,464
31	Yumiko Yoshida, Japan	697,994
32	Chella Choi, Korea	688,653
33	Hiromi Mogi, Japan	666,617
34	Brittany Lincicome, USA	656,631
35	Brittany Lang, USA	602,900
36	Hee Kyung Seo, Korea	600,403
37	So-Hee Kim, Korea	590,855
38	Sandra Gal, Germany	584,035
39	Karine Icher, France	576,628
40	Yuri Fudoh, Japan	566,049
41	I.K. Kim, Korea	561,302
42	Soo-Yun Kang, Korea	557,214
43	Esther Lee, Korea	541,772
44	Mihoko Iseri, Japan	530,042
45	Candie Kung, Taiwan	521,072
46	Morgan Pressel, USA	519,986
47	Haeji Kang, Korea	485,373
48	Julieta Granada, Paraguay	474,216
49	Beatriz Recari, Spain	461,381
50	Maiko Wakabayashi, Japan	448,387
51	Jenny Shin, Korea	447,731
52	Yukari Baba, Japan	434,573
53	Se Ri Pak, Korea	430,338
54	Hee Young Park, Korea	427,717
55	Kaori Ohe, Japan	420,264
56	Pornanong Phatlum, Thailand	419,084
57	Na-Ri Lee, Korea	415,225
58	Giulia Sergas, Italy	409,867
59	Junko Omote, Japan	408,269
60	Rui Kitada, Japan	407,833
61	Ayako Uehara, Japan	402,657
62	Vicky Hurst, USA	401,457
63	Misuzu Narita, Japan	397,144
64	Na-Ri Kim, Korea	387,984
65	Katherine Hull, Australia	382,822
66	Eun-Hee Ji, Korea	382,597
67	Megumi Kido, Japan	380,944
68	Yuki Ichinose, Japan	376,158
69	Meena Lee, Korea	374,312
70	Natsu Nagai, Japan	368,990
71	Akane Iijima, Japan	363,795
72	Ilhee Lee, Korea	355,780
73	Kumiko Kaneda, Japan	352,290
74	Hyun-Ju Shin, Korea	349,336
75	Young Kim, Korea	343,599
76	Jessica Korda, USA	339,320
77	Carlota Ciganda, Spain	338,397
78	Lindsey Wright, Australia	337,865
79	Miki Sakai, Japan	331,791

POS.	PLAYER, COUNTRY	TOTAL MONEY
80	Natalie Gulbis, USA	321,472
81	Caroline Masson, Germany	317,948
82	Karin Sjodin, Sweden	310,599
83	Shinobu Moromizato, Japan	306,745
84	Mina Harigae, USA	304,057
85	Caroline Hedwall, Sweden	302,927
86	Erina Hara, Japan	295,876
87	Katie Futcher, USA	290,213
88	Teresa Lu, Taiwan	281,959
89	Momoko Ueda, Japan	280,053
90	Gerina Piller, USA	276,462
91	Yeo-Jin Kang, Korea	271,595
92	Hee-Won Han, Korea	269,771
93	Asako Fujimoto, Japan	266,422
94	Yuko Fukuda, Japan	265,445
95	Erika Kikuchi, Japan	261,873
96	Airi Saitoh, Japan	260,493
97	Cindy LaCrosse, USA	258,034
98	Dewi Claire Schreefel, Netherlands	252,578
99	Jennifer Johnson, USA	245,999
100	Alison Walshe, USA	244,105
101	Pernilla Lindberg, Sweden	242,846
102	Lala Anai, Japan	242,778
103	Lizette Salas, USA	242,035
104	Eun-Bi Jang, Korea	239,664
105	Danielle Kang, USA	239,184
106	Diana Luna, Italy	232,770
107	Jodi Ewart, England	226,988
108	Nicole Castrale, USA	226,600
109	Christel Boeljon, Netherlands	224,593
110	Ah-Reum Hwang, Korea	224,303
111	Harukyo Nomura, Japan	223,325
112	Nikki Campbell, Australia	220,086
113	Bo-Bae Song, Korea	214,957
114	Stacey Keating, Australia	214,869
115	Saiki Fujita, Japan	214,687
116	Carly Booth, Scoland	210,766
117	Mariajo Uribe, Colombia	205,465
118	Lee-Anne Pace, South Africa	205,107
119	Mi Jung Hur, Korea	202,428
120	Laura Davies, England	202,211
121	Sydnee Michaels, USA	192,544
122	Da-Ye Na, Korea	188,170
123	Shiho Toyonaga, Japan	185,750
124	Sophie Gustafson, Sweden	182,264
125	Li-Ying Ye, China	173,618
126	Hiromi Takesue, Japan	172,900
127	Mo Martin, USA	171,345
128	Nobuko Kizawa, Japan	169,305
129	Becky Morgan, Wales	167,068
130	Michelle Wie, USA	166,642
131	Ha-Neul Kim, Korea	163,906
132	Trish Johnson, England	159,903

POS.	PLAYER, COUNTRY	TOTAL MONEY
133	Sarah Jane Smith, Australia	153,140
134	Jeong Jang, Korea	152,996
135	Hsuan-Yu Yao, Taiwan	151,904
136	Anne-Lise Caudal, France	150,862
137	Onnarin Sattayabanp, Thailand	150,032
138	Yui Kawahara, Japan	147,843
139	Belen Mozo, Spain	147,293
140	Amy Hung, Taiwan	142,351
141	Amanda Blumenherst, USA	133,305
142	Jimin Kang, Korea	133,130
143	Kaori Aoyama, Japan	132,018
144	Joanna Klatten, France	130,774
145	Florentyna Parker, England	130,090
146	Kotono Kozuma, Japan	129,760
147	Lydia Hall, Wales	129,112
148	Jennifer Song, USA	128,280
149	Gwladys Nocera, France	128,171
150	Karen Stupples, England	127,869
151	Jennie Lee, USA	126,455
152	Shiho Oyama, Japan	126,208
153	Mayumi Shimomura, Japan	124,356
154	Melissa Reid, England	122,476
155	Felicity Johnson, England	119,843
156	Veronica Felibert, Venezuela	119,388
157	Karen Lunn, Australia	118,804
158	Line Vedel, Denmark	118,031
159	Kaori Nakamura, Japan	115,551
160	Nachiyo Ohtani, Japan	115,222
161	Yun-Jye Wei, Taiwan	114,931
162	Mindy Kim, USA	112,891
163	Beth Allen, USA	112,152
164	Hiroko Fukushima, Japan	110,825
165	Nontaya Srisawang, Thailand	110,791
166	Kaori Yamamoto, Japan	108,250
167	Rebecca Hudson, England	106,583
168	Paige Mackenzie, USA	103,886
169	Maria Hjorth, Sweden	103,869
170	Juli Inkster, USA	103,315
171	Lorie Kane, Canada	103,126
172	Tao-Li Yang, China	102,038
173	Carin Koch, Sweden	101,380
174	Mikaela Parmlid, Sweden	100,027
175	Ji-Woo Lee, Korea	99,613

Senior World Money List

This list includes official earnings from the U.S. Champions Tour, European Senior Tour and Japan Senior Tour, along with other winnings in established official and unofficial tournaments when reliable figures could be obtained.

POS.	PLAYER, COUNTRY	TOTAL MONEY
1	Bernhard Langer, Germany	$2,474,468
2	Tom Lehman, USA	2,040,507
3	Michael Allen, USA	1,808,383
4	Mark Calcavecchia, USA	1,691,243
5	Fred Funk, USA	1,686,619
6	Jay Haas, USA	1,514,571
7	Kenny Perry, USA	1,489,617
8	Fred Couples, USA	1,435,995
9	Jay Don Blake, USA	1,378,180
10	Peter Senior, Australia	1,360,651
11	David Frost, South Africa	1,270,456
12	John Cook, USA	1,243,883
13	Corey Pavin, USA	1,173,198
14	Roger Chapman, England	1,099,706
15	Willie Wood, USA	1,054,869
16	Jeff Sluman, USA	1,020,307
17	Bill Glasson, USA	905,365
18	Kirk Triplett, USA	891,558
19	Brad Bryant, USA	876,249
20	Gary Hallberg, USA	798,163
21	Olin Browne, USA	777,629
22	Loren Roberts, USA	721,267
23	Mark Wiebe, USA	711,992
24	Russ Cochran, USA	695,860
25	Dan Forsman, USA	662,281
26	Chien Soon Lu, Taiwan	642,455
27	Joe Daley, USA	630,081
28	Mike Goodes, USA	614,521
29	Larry Mize, USA	599,069
30	Mark McNulty, Ireland	543,169
31	Duffy Waldorf, USA	540,872
32	Tom Kite, USA	512,338
33	Mark O'Meara, USA	498,980
34	Naomichi Ozaki, Japan	485,764
35	Steve Pate, USA	482,053
36	Tom Pernice, Jr., USA	479,776
37	Kiyoshi Murota, Japan	472,579
38	Joey Sindelar, USA	462,433
39	David Eger, USA	460,776
40	Barry Lane, England	447,696
41	John Huston, USA	441,892
42	Hale Irwin, USA	436,657
43	Brad Faxon, USA	406,042
44	Dick Mast, USA	394,456
45	Peter Fowler, Australia	372,795
46	Bobby Clampett, USA	366,307

POS.	PLAYER, COUNTRY	TOTAL MONEY
47	Kouki Idoki, Japan	363,200
48	Sandy Lyle, Scotland	360,258
49	Joel Edwards, USA	357,718
50	Tommy Armour, USA	352,954
51	Frankie Minoza, Philippines	334,850
52	Tim Thelen, USA	319,750
53	Rod Spittle, Canada	317,724
54	Bob Tway, USA	299,292
55	Andrew Magee, USA	287,387
56	Jeff Hart, USA	278,013
57	Tsuneyuki Nakajima, Japan	277,132
58	Kazuhiro Takami, Japan	273,262
59	Larry Nelson, USA	271,719
60	Jim Rutledge, Canada	270,434
61	Tom Watson, USA	267,807
62	Tom Jenkins, USA	263,427
63	Steve Lowery, USA	258,123
64	David Peoples, USA	254,284
65	Mark Brooks, USA	253,563
66	Boonchu Ruangkit, Thailand	252,413
67	Mark Mouland, Wales	247,515
68	Paul Wesselingh, England	243,412
69	Chip Beck, USA	227,017
70	Jim Thorpe, USA	226,597
71	Bob Gilder, USA	225,921
72	Craig Stadler, USA	223,253
73	Tom Purtzer, USA	220,008
74	Gil Morgan, USA	212,912
75	Ian Woosnam, Wales	207,313
76	Chris Williams, South Africa	204,131
77	Gary Wolstenholme, England	203,532
78	Peter Jacobsen, USA	198,840
79	Anders Forsbrand Sweden	197,287
80	Massy Kuramoto, Japan	196,573
81	Jeff Freeman, USA	196,387
82	Des Smyth, Ireland	191,135
83	Seiki Okuda, Japan	190,250
84	Tom Byrum, USA	186,480
85	Bruce Vaughan, USA	186,055
86	Morris Hatalsky, USA	172,502
87	Eduardo Romero, Argentina	171,910
88	Steve Jones, USA	164,934
89	Mike Reid, USA	164,672
90	David J. Russell, England	164,230
91	Philip Golding, England	163,131
92	Marc Farry, France	157,667
93	Mark James, England	155,318
94	P.H. Horgan, USA	153,800
95	Carl Mason, England	152,531
96	Gene Sauers, USA	148,072
97	Nick Price, Zimbabwe	145,328
98	Andy Bean, USA	143,990
99	D.A. Weibring, USA	136,858
100	Wayne Levi, USA	134,660

1. The Year in Retrospect

Sometimes it's hard to tell if Tiger Woods is being sincere or simply bluffing. Ever since he blazed through his sport by winning all four major championships in a span of 294 days, the golfing world has been desperate to find someone who would come along and present a serious challenge, or even show signs of — gasp — being better.

Sergio Garcia looked to be the heir apparent, and a few months before they clashed on the final nine at Medinah in the 1999 PGA Championship, Woods said, "I know I wasn't as talented as him. I wasn't as good as he is at 19." Garcia turned out to be a world-class player, though 13 years later, he still hasn't won a major. Aaron Baddeley won the Australian Open as an amateur, and he defended the title as a professional. Woods played a practice round with the 19-year-old Australian at Bay Hill one year and proclaimed there was "no way I ever hit it that good at 19. I was spraying it all over the lot, just trying to get up and down. I think Aaron has a very bright future ahead of him." It was another six years before Baddeley won his first PGA Tour event.

So there was a small dose of skepticism in 2009 when another 19-year-old, Rory McIlroy of Northern Ireland, made his professional debut in America at the Accenture Match Play Championship and defeated Louis Oosthuizen, Hunter Mahan and Tim Clark before losing in the quarter-finals to Geoff Ogilvy, the eventual champion. A few weeks later, Woods again was asked to look into the crystal ball. "He has all of the components to be the best player in the world, there's no doubt. It's just a matter of time and experience, and then basically gaining that experience in big events. Just give him some time, and I'm sure he'll be there," Woods said.

McIlroy made him look like a prophet in 2012. Rarely could anything be mentioned about McIlroy without the phrase "since Woods." He became the first player since Woods to win consecutive majors by at least eight shots when he captured the PGA Championship at Kiawah Island. He became the first player since Woods to win back-to-back FedExCup Playoff events. And at age 23, he became the youngest player since Woods to reach No. 1 in the world. And as the season ended, the questions going into the next year were of the variety that for so many years belonged exclusively to Woods. There was a growing gap between No. 1 and No. 2 in the world, so how much more could the kid separate himself from the rest of golf? It's not whether McIlroy will win a major, but how many? There was little doubt who would be the favorite at the Masters. McIlroy wound up winning the Mark H. McCormack Award for being at No. 1 in the World Ranking for more weeks than any other player after trading spots for much of the summer with Luke Donald. But even Donald could see what the future held when he said of McIlroy, "I think he'll be around for a long time."

If nothing else, McIlroy ended the argument about who was the best in golf. Even since Woods abandoned his roost atop the World Ranking in November 2010, that became a topic of discussion because not everyone was comfortable with who No. 1 was or even how they got there. Not since 1997-98, a period marked by Woods going through his first extensive swing overhaul under Butch Harmon, had the No. 1 looked like a game of musical chairs. At least in that era, when Woods, Greg Norman, Tom Lehman (for one week) and Ernie Els traded spots at the top, all of them had won major championships. This latest crop featured Lee Westwood, Martin Kaymer, Luke Donald and McIlroy. Westwood and Donald, both of whom earned the position with a combination of consistency and winning tournaments, never won a major. Kaymer won the 2010 PGA Championship, but he went to No. 1 by losing in the final of the 2011 Accenture Match Play Championship.

McIlroy first went to No. 1 by winning the Honda Classic against a strong field at PGA National and surviving a thrilling finish when Woods nearly caught him by closing birdie-eagle for a 62. McIlroy lasted only two weeks at No. 1. He returned a short time later and stayed there for another two weeks. Then came a three-week stay at No. 1. Finally, he seized control by winning his second major title at the PGA Championship, and he started to move away with consecutive FedExCup wins in the Deutsche Bank Championship and BMW Championship, where he was a combined 40 under par. And it was McIlroy at the PGA Championship who ended the streak of 16 players having won the previous 16 majors.

As a player, McIlroy's skill is undeniable, and it's clear now that Woods wasn't bluffing when he heaped praise on the kid a few years ago. He can swing as hard as he wants without ever losing his balance. He has cleaned up his ability to make short putts under pressure, one area that made some skeptical about him when he first turned pro. Despite all the attention and fame, he remained well-grounded. And as Woods said on more than one occasion when a friendship began to blossom in late summer, "He's such a nice kid." McIlroy was the whole package. He had youth, game, style and two majors.

Even so, there was no clarity to the year in golf until McIlroy began his run late in the summer. Going into the weekend of the final major, Woods led the PGA Tour with three wins. It was Woods who appeared to be closing in on a major, as the 36-hole leader in the U.S. Open at The Olympic Club, playing in the penultimate group in the Open Championship at Royal Lytham & St. Annes, and sharing the 36-hole lead going into the weekend at Kiawah Island.

A few months later, that seemed like old news. McIlroy was voted Player of the Year on the European Tour, the PGA Tour, by the British-based Association of Golf Writers and the Golf Writers Association of America, and the points-based award by the PGA of America. He won the Vardon Trophy (PGA of America) and Byron Nelson Award (PGA Tour) for the lowest scoring average, the honor which Woods once said was the best measure of great golf. He won the PGA Tour money title by nearly $2 million over Woods, and he matched Donald's feat of the previous year by capturing the money title on both sides of the Atlantic Ocean, easily winning the Race to Dubai for the European Tour honors.

While Woods predicted greatness for McIlroy long before he got there, the surprises in 2013 came from so many other corners. Stacy Lewis won the LPGA Tour's Rolex Player of the Year award, notable because an

American had not been the star of that tour since 1993. There were a pair of first-time major champions from unlikely sources. Bubba Watson made a remarkable escape from the trees right of the 10th fairway in a playoff to win the Masters and introduce the world to the unique brand of what he calls "Bubba Golf." Webb Simpson won the U.S. Open on the strength of others' mistakes. Ernie Els failed to qualify for the Masters for the first time in 20 years, and right when it looked as though he was headed to the twilight of his career, he was on the receiving end of a stunning collapse by Adam Scott at Royal Lytham & St. Annes to capture his fourth major victory. One of the indelible images from 2012 was Els sitting quietly in the locker room, gazing at the claret jug as if it were a newborn baby. Els became the third player in the last five majors to use a belly putter, and Royal & Ancient Chief Executive Peter Dawson dropped strong suggestions the day after Els won the Open that change was coming. It arrived in the final month when the R&A and the United States Golf Association agreed that anchored clubs — an edict directed at belly putters and broom-handle putters — would be banned starting in 2016.

Scott wasn't the only player to cough up a late lead. This was the year of the comeback, or the collapse, depending on the view. Kyle Stanley went from horror to heaven in one week, making a triple bogey on the last hole and losing in a playoff at Torrey Pines, only to make up an eight-shot deficit on the final day in Phoenix the following week. And the biggest comeback of all? That would be Europe, which appeared left for dead at Medinah on Saturday afternoon when it looked like the Americans would take an 11-5 lead into Sunday singles. Ian Poulter then made five straight birdies to pick up a late point, and Europe rode that momentum the next day to match the greatest rally in Ryder Cup history.

Lost in that amazing day was that McIlroy became confused by the time zone while watching television in his hotel room. He didn't realize that most times listed in America are Eastern. Chicago is in the Central time zone, and McIlroy might have missed his tee time if not for getting a ride in a police car to the golf course. Perhaps that was only fitting. No matter the circumstances, golf seemed to evolve around McIlroy this year.

McIlroy and Woods started the year by playing a practice round in the Abu Dhabi HSBC Golf Championship, and then they were in the same group for three of the four rounds. The edge would have seemed to have belonged to Woods when he went into the final round tied with Robert Rock of England, known more for his hair than anything he had done on the golf course. Rock went on to win, McIlroy was the runner-up, and thus began a roller coaster of a year. That ride began with an awesome climb that actually began late in the previous season when it appeared the kid was in trouble. Remember, he tried to hit a seven iron through a large root, and the tree won at the 2011 PGA Championship, with McIlroy injuring his left arm. The seriousness was laid to rest quickly, however, when he tied for third in Europe three weeks later. That began a stretch that carried into 2012 in which McIlroy finished no worse than fifth in 12 out of 13 tournaments. So when he arrived at the Accenture Match Play Championship, he was on the cusp of reaching No. 1 in the world for the first time in his career.

First came a showdown with Lee Westwood, a semi-final match that the British press filled with subplots over the testy exchange of tweets between the two players the previous summer, McIlroy leaving International Sports Management led by Chubby Chandler (Westwood's longtime agent). McIlroy overcame an early deficit with seven birdies in 10 holes to easily advance to the championship match. All he had to do was beat Hunter Mahan to rise to No. 1. Mahan delayed the inevitable with a 2-and-1 win. Much like Woods had said three years earlier, Mahan knew that McIlroy would be the top player. He just didn't want to be part of the coronation. Fittingly, that fell to Woods.

The stars moved across the country for the Florida swing at the Honda Classic, and McIlroy dazzled. One shot in particular showed his panache. From a mangled lie in the rough, he sized up his shot, pulled a seven iron and cleared the water by a yard, followed by a 50-foot birdie putt across the green. He had a two-shot lead going into the final round and looked like he had this one in the bag until hearing one explosive cheer after another ahead of him. That was Woods, making a 25-foot birdie on the tough par-three 17th, followed by a five iron to a tight pin that settled eight feet away for eagle. That gave Woods a 62, the lowest final round of his career. And yes, McIlroy heard. He responded with a birdie on the 13th, two clutch par saves from the bunker and held on for a two-shot win. At 22, he was the youngest to become No. 1 in the world since Woods first got there in 1997 at age 21. Westwood, meanwhile, closed with a 63 to tie for fourth. And it was Graeme McDowell who summed it up best when he said, "This golf season just got a lot more spicy." Rarely had there been so much anticipation heading to the first major of the year. By the end of the Florida swing, McIlroy, Donald, Woods, Phil Mickelson, Mahan and Justin Rose all had won on the PGA Tour. The stars were aligned. Without warning, McIlroy was more like a shooting star. Blazing one minute, gone the next.

It started at the Masters, where McIlroy was among the favorites as the reigning U.S. Open champion, but he'd had an unseemly collapse a year earlier when he blew a four-shot lead in the final round with an 80. He opened this Masters with a double bogey, but he was only one shot behind going into the weekend. Some thought the tournament was over, and that it was. He closed with a 77-76 weekend and tied for 40th. A year after he lost the Masters on the final nine Sunday, he lost this one on the first nine Saturday. That was only a blip, though, for he came roaring back at the Wells Fargo Championship at Quail Hollow and looked like he would win — and again go back to No. 1 in his see-saw battle with Donald — when he got into a three-way playoff with Rickie Fowler and unheralded D.A. Points. Fowler won on the first extra hole, though McIlroy was right there with a chance. It was starting to look like the glory days of Woods, who once seemed to always threaten to win even if someone else left with the trophy.

All that began to change at The Players Championship. McIlroy is not a big fan of the Stadium Course at the TPC Sawgrass, and it showed. He ruined a decent start by missing the island green at No. 17 to make double bogey, and then shot 76 the next day to miss the cut for the first time in more than a year. He shrugged. He thought he hit the ball as well as he did the previous week in a playoff loss at Quail Hollow. Move on. But two weeks later, he missed the cut at the BMW PGA Championship at Wentworth, and frustrations began to show when he tossed a club in disgust. He blamed that weekend off on not being properly prepared. A week later, he began the Memorial by taking a quadruple-bogey seven on the third hole of the tournament, and while he recovered for a 71, he was not so fortunate the next day with two double bogeys en route to a 79, and yet another missed cut. He added the St. Jude Classic to his schedule and tied for seventh, but in his title defense at the U.S. Open, he bogeyed three of the last four holes for a 77 and wound up missing yet another cut. The best player in golf? He sure didn't look like one. It had been nearly four years since McIlroy missed three successive cuts. At the U.S. Open, he was 19 shots worse after 36 holes than he was the previous year at Congressional. He played decently at Royal Portrush in the Irish Open, and then tied for 60th in the Open Championship and was going nowhere headed for the last major of the year.

That's when it all changed. McIlroy found something in his game at the Bridgestone Invitational, where he tied for fifth, and then just like that, everything was back to normal at the PGA Championship. He not only won a major, it was his second straight eight-shot win in a major. And to think only a month ago all anyone wanted to talk about was his slump. McIlroy said some people simply pushed the panic button too early, or were quick to attribute his poor play to his romance with tennis star Caroline Wozniacki, or even that he wasn't working as hard as he once did. That second major changed everything. Not since Seve Ballesteros in the 1980 Masters had a player so young already have two majors in the bag. The question was where he would go from there. A year ago after his U.S. Open title, McIlroy didn't handle the trappings of stardom very well, and it showed. He went some six months before his next official win. Would he learn this time around? "I think I heard Tiger say, 'You can have a good season, but to make a good season a great season, you need a major championship.' Now I've had two great seasons in a row no matter what happens from here in now. Hopefully, I can play some great golf from now until the end of the year and get myself ready for another great season next year, too," McIlroy said.

The answer was emphatic. McIlroy returned to No. 1, and this time he stayed there. Locked in a compelling Labor Day battle with Louis Oosthuizen at the Deutsche Bank Championship, McIlroy closed with a 67 to beat the former Open champion by one shot. A week later at Crooked Stick, against one of the best leaderboards of the season, McIlroy outlasted Mickelson, Westwood, Woods, Dustin Johnson, Adam Scott, Vijay Singh and Jim Furyk with a 67 on the final day to win the BMW Championship. That made him the No. 1 seed in the FedExCup going into the finale at the Tour Championship. He was only three shots behind going into the last day at East Lake, but he closed with a 74 and watched Brandt Snedeker win the tournament and claim the $10 million bonus. At this point, there was no disputing the best in golf, even without his name on the FedExCup trophy. McIlroy finished the year in style in Europe, finishing second and third, and responding to yet another missed cut by winning the DP World Tour Championship in Dubai. Not only did he win for the fifth time in the year, he won the Race to Dubai in convincing fashion.

"I had a few goals starting off this year," McIlroy said at the end of his season. "Obviously, I wanted to win a major. I think I wanted to win four times around the world — five. The Race to Dubai — I won. I guess getting to world No. 1, which I achieved earlier in the year. But I guess every goal that I set for myself at the start of 2012, I've achieved this year. So it doesn't really get much better than that."

Next up? More majors. He went into the 2013 season trying to join Woods, Mickelson, Tom Watson, Jack Nicklaus and Arnold Palmer as the only players to win a major in three successive years. McIlroy still had much to prove to be the next Tiger Woods, starting with those weekends off. McIlroy missed five cuts this year. Woods went seven years without ever missing cuts. "It's tough to say that Rory is a Tiger Woods–type player," said Graeme McDowell, McIlroy's closest friend on tour. "Tiger Woods is a once-in-a-lifetime player, and Rory is at least a once-in-a-decade type player. He's that good."

Woods used to say it couldn't be a great year without winning a major. He was willing to make a moderate exception for 2012. A great year? Maybe not. But it was nothing to complain about compared with the last two years.

He had gone two years without winning any tournament until he captured his Chevron World Challenge at the end of 2011. Sure, it was against only an 18-man field. But if anything, it was a harbinger that perhaps his game had finally turned the corner, that the swing changes with Sean Foley were becoming habit, and that he was ready to start his return to the top of golf. Instead, the early part of the season brought back the wrong kind of comparisons. "That never used to happen with the old Tiger." For only the ninth time in his career, he failed to win when he had at least a share of the 54-hole lead, this time Rock beating him in Abu Dhabi. Perhaps even more unsettling was his next event, the AT&T Pebble Beach National Pro-Am, when he was paired with Phil Mickelson on the final day. The tournament was wide open after 54-hole leader Charlie Wi four-putted for double bogey on the opening hole, but Woods could only watch hopelessly as Mickelson shot 64 to win going away. And in the second round of the Accenture Match Play Championship, Woods needed to birdie the 18th hole to extend the match against Nick Watney when he stuffed it into five feet. The birdie putt never even touched the hole. It raised questions whether Woods, who it seemed never missed, still had the magic to make putts that mattered. And just as fans began to wonder about his mental state, attention quickly shifted to his physical well-being when he quit after 11 holes in the final round of the Cadillac Championship at Doral because of soreness in his left Achilles tendon, the same injury that caused him to miss two majors and three months in 2011.

Would he ever be the same? And as silly as it sounded, would he ever win again? Considering his health issues, it was worth asking. But not for long. In the next tournament he played after withdrawing with injury, Woods built an early lead against McDowell and won the Arnold Palmer

Invitational at Bay Hill. It was his first PGA Tour win in 923 days, dating to the 2009 BMW Championship at Cog Hill and ending — by far — the longest drought of his career. He looked like the Woods of old, especially on a Bay Hill course that was fiery and firm and exposed even the slightest miss. Woods refused to acknowledge the drought, pointing to his win three months earlier at the Chevron World Challenge. But the way he slapped hands with caddie Joe LaCava after his final approach found the green, and the manner in which they hugged when it was over showed otherwise. It was a surreal moment. One week, Woods had a helicopter follow him out of Doral as the golf world wondered how badly he was hurt. Two weeks later, he was driving down the highway to his home in south Florida with his 72nd career PGA Tour victory and plenty of chatter that he was back. Next up? Augusta National. And just like that, Woods was considered one of the favorites to win his first major since the 2008 U.S. Open at Torrey Pines and his first green jacket since 2005. If only it were that easy.

Almost in sync with McIlroy, Woods went into a swoon. He went seven straight rounds without breaking 70. The Masters was particularly ugly, not so much because he tied for 40th for his worst finish ever at Augusta, but the way he kicked a club after missing a tee shot on the 16th hole in the second round. He followed that up by missing the cut at the Wells Fargo Championship, despite bizarre circumstances. Late in the second round, he pulled his approach to the par-five fifth hole into the pine trees, and a small crowd immediately swarmed the area. The ball was never found. After a raucous discussion that resembled a town hall meeting run amok, tour officials determined that a fan ran off with the ball and Woods was afforded a free drop. No matter. He still missed the cut, making it the first time he had missed a cut on the same golf course in his career. It also was the third straight year Woods failed to make a cut, including his withdrawal from The Players Championship a year earlier. The next stop was the TPC Sawgrass, not one of his favorite venues, and he tied for 40th. For the first time in his career, Woods play played three straight tournaments without finishing better than 40th. Was he back? If anything, he was back to where he started. And then, another rebirth.

It's one thing to win the Memorial, which he did for a record fifth time. What made this draw so much attention was that the U.S. Open was right around the corner, and Woods won at Muirfield Village with a shot that will be replayed for years. He birdied three of his last four holes in the final round, but it was the 16th hole that made tournament host Jack Nicklaus just about come out of his seat in the broadcast booth. Woods went long and faced what appeared to be an impossible chip to a pin some 50 feet away along a ridge. Woods took a full swing for a flop shot, hopeful of a reasonable shot at par. Too soft and it would turn away down the ridge. Too strong and it could run through the green and into the water. He holed it for a birdie-two. "I don't think under the circumstances I've seen a better shot," Nicklaus gushed. It was the 73rd win of his PGA Tour career, tying Woods with Nicklaus for second on the all-time list, just nine away from Sam Snead.

After he failed to win the U.S. Open despite having the 36-hole lead, a question surfaced at the AT&T National. Should not Snead's record of 82 tour wins be just as significant as the 18 majors won by Nicklaus that gets so much attention? Woods always emphasized the majors, and said while he was aware of the Snead mark, everyone talked about Nicklaus when he was growing up. Even so, he found Snead's consistency and longevity to be "truly amazing," and then he took another step toward that during a wild week at Congressional. No one could have imagined Woods being in the hunt on the weekend at a golf tournament outside the nation's capital with so few people watching. But a microburst of straight-line winds that hit the fabled Blue Course on Saturday morning toppled dozens of trees, some of them 50 feet tall, that cracked across the fairways. The tournament chose to keep fans off the course for the third round, and it was a minor miracle they got the course ready. With a full house back on Sunday, Woods won for the third time of the season when Bo Van Pelt failed to hold him off.

It was another sign that Woods was on his way back, but also another tease. He won his tournament before the Masters and had his worst score ever at Augusta. He won his last tournament before the U.S. Open and finished out of the top 20 despite the 36-hole lead. At least this time, he would play one more PGA Tour event, the Greenbrier Classic. Woods missed the cut, the first time since 2005 that he had missed two cuts in one year.

That turned out to be the last win of his season, which was somewhat surprising. There was talk in the summer that Woods might be voted Player of the Year *and* comeback player of the year on the PGA Tour. He got neither. The tour decided against a comeback award except for significant, career-threatening injury. And while Woods had the best season going into August, McIlroy took it from there. It was not without another tease, though, as Woods was tied for the lead going into the weekend at the PGA Championship before he fell back. There was little to doubt about his game. The mystery was what was going on in his head, and Woods conceded to some frailty after the majors were over. Some thought he struggled at the U.S. Open, and to a lesser extent the Open Championship, because he was trying too hard. Woods decided at the PGA Championship to not take himself so seriously, to relax and have some fun. He shot 74 in the third round to take himself out of the tournament. "I came out with probably the wrong attitude. And I was too relaxed and tried to enjoy it, and that's not how I play," he said. "I play intense and full systems go. That cost me."

He ended his PGA Tour season with three wins, second on the money list and second in the competition for the lowest adjusted scoring average, which in happier times would have constituted a down year. Woods called it a good one because of his health. Throw out the minor setback at Doral, and he had his busiest season in five years. He played the Honda Classic and the Greenbrier Classic for the first time as a pro, returned to the AT&T Pebble Beach National Pro-Am for the first time in 10 years and even added a few unofficial events to his schedule, the CIMB Classic in Malaysia and a medal-match exhibition in Turkey. He played 24 tournaments, practiced when he wanted and showed that he was on his way back to full health. As for his standing in golf? He still had a ways to go.

Donald, meanwhile, made a stubborn exit from the spotlight. The Englishman finished the year at No. 2 in the world. He was more disappointed than ever not to have won a major. And when he had put away his clubs for the year, there was a sense that he already had become a forgotten figure. To put that in a broader context, however, it was another example of how Donald elevated his game. He won three times, on three continents. He finished no worse than third in seven tournaments. And he was in the top 10 in half of the 24 tournaments he played around the world. That would have been a breakthrough season only two years ago. This was considered a minor letdown.

If this was the end of Donald's reign at No. 1, it should be noted for the type of game that brought him to the top and the fight he showed to stay there. Even before he left Northwestern University with an NCAA title, golf had entered the power era. The seven players before him who had ascended to No. 1 were Lee Westwood, Martin Kaymer, Tiger Woods, Vijay Singh, David Duval, Ernie Els and Greg Norman. There was a time, when Woods was at the peak of his powers, that another player could only dream of being No. 1 in the world, and those dreams belonged only to those who smash their drivers more than 300 yards. Donald gave hope to everyone with his work ethic, determination and a superb short game, which will always go a long way in golf. By year's end, Donald had been No. 1 a total of 56 weeks. Of the 16 players who have been No. 1 since the Official World Golf Ranking began in 1986, only four players have stayed there longer — Woods, Greg Norman, Nick Faldo and Seve Ballesteros.

Much like Lee Westwood the year before, the world No. 1 at the start of the season began slowly. Donald tied for 48th and tied for 56th in his opening two tournaments in the Middle East. And as the defending champion and top seed at the Accenture Match Play Championship, he had to play Els in the opening round. Donald lost in 14 holes. So when McIlroy went from reaching the championship match in Arizona to beating a strong field at the Honda Classic a week later to replace him at No. 1, that seemed to spell the end of Donald. Not so fast. Two weeks later, playing like someone who felt slighted, he closed with a 66 on the strong Copperhead course at Innisbrook to get into a four-man playoff at the Transitions Championship. On the first extra hole, Donald hit a seven iron out of the rough on the 18th hole to six feet and holed the birdie putt to win. Just like that, he was back on top. And he made it clear that while McIlroy was an immense talent, Donald wasn't about to give up the ranking without a battle. "I think people thought that my last year was maybe ... not a fluke, but I don't think many people thought I could do that all over again this year. Hopefully," Donald said, "I can prove them wrong."

And so began what looked to be a game of musical chairs between Donald and McIlroy, which carried on for the next five months. McIlroy went back to No. 1 a few weeks later without playing, Donald regained it with a third-place finish in New Orleans, back to McIlroy after his playoff loss at Quail Hollow, and then Donald reclaimed No. 1 by winning the BMW PGA Championship at Wentworth for his second win of the year. Donald stayed there the rest of the summer until the PGA Championship, and that's when McIlroy found another gear and left everyone in his wake. Donald went into 2012 with a lead of nearly two points in the World Ranking. He was 4.6 points behind at the end. But he at least made one point. "There's always going to be people who look at my game and say, 'He's No. 1?' That's just the way is. Whether they do or not, I don't really focus on that. I focus on what I can control, and that's just working hard. But I think I'm forcing people to respect me now."

He failed to earn their respect in the majors, though. Despite a solid year — Donald also won the prestigious Dunlop Phoenix on the Japan Golf Tour — his performance renewed attention on the best to have never won a major. Except for those who either don't understand or choose not to understand what the ranking is all about, there is little question that Donald earned his way to the top, much like Westwood before him. A major championship would serve as validation, for those two are the only players to be No. 1 without ever winning a major. Duval won his major two years after getting to No. 1, while Couples and Woosnam reached the top in the weeks leading up to their Masters wins.

Donald wound up playing seven majors as No. 1 in the world, and the pressure was mounting. That's one area his season was a disappointment. He opened with a 75 in the Masters and didn't break par until the final round, finishing in a tie for 32nd. He didn't make a single birdie in the opening round at Olympic Club and missed the cut in the U.S. Open. He was 10 shots behind at the Open Championship going into the final round and only a terrific Sunday gave him a tie for fifth. And he closed out the year at Kiawah Island by not breaking par until Sunday, never in the picture. "I knew it was always going to be tough to follow what I did last year, but still it's been a very successful year, won three times on three different tours and three different continents. There's a lot of my accomplishments I'm very proud of. Slightly disappointing it would be again, with the majors. That wasn't what I was looking for."

Westwood slipped even further. He ended the 2011 season at No. 2 in the world and didn't look like he was going away after a runner-up finish in Dubai, reaching the semi-finals of the Accenture Match Play Championship before losing to McIlroy, and closing with a 63 at the Honda Classic to finish fourth. He also won the Masters, just not the one he would have wanted. Two weeks after he tied for third at Augusta National, Westwood captured the CIMB Niaga Indonesian Masters and then won the Nordea Masters the week before the U.S. Open. Not only was he still within range of getting back to No. 1 in the world, he was in form to finally get that first major. One hole changed everything. Westwood was three shots out of the lead going into the final round of the U.S. Open when his ball clipped a towering cypress on the fifth hole and never came down. He had to go back to the tee, made double bogey and tied for 10th. That was followed by an indifferent performance at the Open Championship and a missed cut at the PGA Championship.

Westwood was at No. 7 when the year ended, facing a year of big changes. He decided to part ways with injured caddie Billy Foster. He moved his family to Florida as he takes up PGA Tour membership again for 2013 and he turns 40 in April. Only six players have captured their first major after turning 40 in the 160 years of championship golf. "I know my game is good enough to win when I play well enough. So that's what I try to do," Westwood said about the majors. "After that, it's out of your hands."

Two players are worthy of mention for taking steps forward, starting with Justin Rose. Even after what arguably had been his best year in golf, when he won twice on the PGA Tour in 2010, those wins came in a span of just over a month. What stood out this year was the consistency, along with winning against top-rated fields. Rose finished in the top 10 in half of the 28 tournaments he played around the world, and he was in the top five at nine tournaments, including the PGA Championship. He finished the year at No. 4 in the World Ranking, the highest of his career. And after all that, it was his 45-foot birdie putt from the back of the 17th green at Medinah that became the signature moment of Europe's stunning comeback to win the Ryder Cup. For Rose, perhaps the most significant trophy came in Miami. He had been left out of the last Ryder Cup team and was determined to get this year off on the right foot. Knowing his form was close, he dedicated himself to playing all four tournaments on the Florida swing of the PGA Tour and treat them as a body of work to see where he was. He was a winner in the WGC - Cadillac Championship, the biggest win of his career.

Rose's other win was unofficial, though it didn't hurt his status as being among the elite in golf. He won the Turkish Airways World Golf Final, an eight-man exhibition of medal matches that featured the world's best, a lineup that included McIlroy, Woods and Westwood. Rose mowed them down, beating Westwood on the final day for the $1.5 million prize. Along with the World Golf Championship title at Doral, that helped to elevate Rose to No. 2 on the World Money List with just under $8 million, second only to McIlroy. Rose, who once missed 21 successive cuts right after he turned pro at age 19, found a different version of consistency that he hopes will take him even further. "My golf is just so consistent at the moment, and the main thing is that I just don't have any skeletons in the closet, and I don't have that loose shot that is plaguing me all the time," he said in Turkey.

The other worth mentioning was Brandt Snedeker, who had only two wins in his previous five years on the PGA Tour and was known best for his roller-coaster final round in the 2008 Masters that left him so emotional he could barely speak through tears after tying for third. And it could be argued that his first win of the year was only because of an unimaginable failure. He closed with a 67 on the South Course at Torrey Pines and figured that might be good enough for second place in the Farmers Insurance Open, with Kyle Stanley appearing to be unflappable down the stretch. But on the par-five 18th, Stanley spun a wedge back into the water, went to the back of the green with his fifth shot and then took three putts for a triple bogey that sent him into a playoff. Snedeker won with a par on the second extra hole and made no apologies. He beat Stanley again a few weeks later in the Accenture Match Play Championship, but then injured a rib and wound up missing a full month in the summer, including the U.S. Open.

Snedeker returned in style at Royal Lytham & St. Annes by tying the Open Championship record for 36 holes at 130 with a course record-tying 64. He went 40 holes without a bogey, faltering ever so slightly on the weekend and tying for third. By then, however, he was quickly building a reputation as one of the best putters in golf, and he charmed the British galleries with his fast play and fast talk. He came up short of qualifying for the Ryder Cup, and when U.S. captain Davis Love made him a captain's pick, Snedeker made the captain look smart. He was runner-up at The Barclays, sixth at the Deutsche Bank Championship and finished off a wild FedExCup Playoffs by winning the Tour Championship to collect the $10 million bonus.

"I think it solidifies what I already know," he said. "I think when I play my best golf, my best golf is some of the best in the world. I've never had more confidence in myself than I have the last five weeks, and I made sure that I kept telling myself that all day," Snedeker said after his win at East Lake. "I am one of the best players in the world. This is supposed to happen." He moved into the top 10 in the world for the first time in his career and was starting to walk — quickly, as usual — with a swagger.

Snedeker's first win turned out to be a sign of things to come on the PGA Tour, and it wasn't a pretty picture for players who went into the final round with a big lead, particularly if that player was going after his first win. Stanley had a three-shot lead playing the 18th hole at Torrey Pines, which is why it was so memorable and evoked a few comparisons to Jean Van de Velde at Carnoustie in 1999. But when Snedeker rallied from a seven-shot deficit on the final day to win, it was the first of many. A week later, Spencer Levin had a six-shot lead over his closest competitor in the Waste Management Phoenix Open and stumbled badly on the final nine, allowing Stanley to make a remarkable turnaround. He rallied from eight shots behind on the final day to win. A week later in the AT&T Pebble Beach National Pro-Am, Mickelson came from six shots behind on the final day to win. Charlie Wi was the 54-hole leader by three shots over Ken Duke and four-putted for double bogey on the opening hole. And to cap off a wild West Coast swing, tour rookie John Huh started the final round of the Mayakoba Golf Classic in Mexico seven shots behind Daniel Summerhays and wound up the winner in a playoff over Robert Allenby. In all four cases, the 54-hole leader was going for his first PGA Tour victory. Of course, that wasn't the only explanation.

The most notorious case in the Year of the Comeback was Ernie Els, who started the last round at the Open Championship six shots behind Adam Scott. Els never looked like the winner until the Australian limped to the finish line with four straight bogeys. And the year ended with Jim Furyk and Davis Love tied for the lead going into Sunday at the McGladrey Classic. Neither of those veterans, with a combined 36 tour wins, held on. Instead, Tommy Gainey picked up his first PGA Tour win with a 60 to come from seven shots back. The PGA Tour slogan long has been, "These guys are good." Perhaps a new slogan should be, "No lead is safe." Not counting the events held opposite a major or World Golf Championship, there were 11 straight tournaments — from Jason Dufner at the HP Byron Nelson Championship to McIlroy at the PGA Championship — where the 54-hole leader failed to hang on.

There were other comebacks in a broader sense. Sergio Garcia had gone more than two full years without winning until he began to show some form toward the end of 2011 with two wins in Spain. And while there was nothing particularly glowing about his start to the season, it wasn't awful. But when he arrived at the Masters, the Spaniard made it sound as though it were the end of the world. He went into the weekend just one shot out of the lead, shot a 75 in the third round and then unloaded on Spanish reporters by saying he wasn't good enough to win a major that had eluded him throughout his career. "That's the reality," he told the Spanish press. "I'm not good enough and today I know it. I've been trying for 13 years and I don't feel capable of winning. I don't know what happened to me. Maybe it's something psychological. After 13 years, my chances are over. I'm not good enough for the majors. That's it."

Those were shocking words in any language, particularly for a player of Garcia's immense talent, one who first challenged Tiger Woods as a 19-year-old in the PGA Championship at Medinah, and who had played in the final group in three majors, losing one in a playoff. The low point came at the PGA Championship, where he missed the cut in his second straight major. He sulked, and playing partner Adam Scott had seen enough. They were born the same year (1980), are good friends, and until McIlroy came along, they had shown to be the best two players younger than Woods. "I said, 'Hey, listen, you've got to stop doing this. There's nothing wrong with your game. Don't embarrass yourself and carry on like that.' As much as I didn't want to watch that, as much as I don't want to play with a guy who's like that, I've known the guy a long time," Scott told *Golfweek* magazine. "'You're too good,' I told him. 'Just try and make it fun. Don't beat yourself up.'"

Among many talents, Garcia showed to be a good listener. One week later, he ended four years without winning on the PGA Tour when he captured the Wyndham Championship in Greensboro, North Carolina, and then he had a two-shot lead at Bethpage Black in The Barclays until he was overtaken by Nick Watney on the last day. No matter. Garcia made it to the Tour Championship for the first time since 2008, and he returned to Ryder Cup competition for the first time in four years. He and Luke Donald beat Woods and Steve Stricker, and Garcia won a crucial match against Furyk in singles. The year ended with three straight top-10s, including a win at the Iskandar Johor Open that returned Garcia closer to the elite at No. 16 in the world.

Louis Oosthuizen also showed signs of life. His 2011 season was so bad that he failed to qualify for the 125-man FedExCup Playoffs and even had to play twice in the Fall Series just to reach his minimum 15 tournaments. He might be the modern-day version of Byron Nelson, including the graceful swing, for the South African is equally content on his farm near Mossel Bay as he is on the golf course. He started the year by winning the Africa Open for the second straight time, only that was only the appetizer to his season. Oosthuizen hit his stride at the Masters with an albatross on the par-five second hole in the final round — the first ever on that hole — and was poised to win a green jacket until Bubba Watson's shot out of the trees on the first extra hole. A week earlier, Oosthuizen lost a two-shot lead in the final round of the Shell Houston Open and was the runner-up. A week after the Masters, he won the Maybank Malaysian Open. Much like McIlroy, he went into a summer swoon by missing four out of five cuts, including the U.S. Open. He didn't quite have the finish of McIlroy, though they played in the final group at the Deutsche Bank Championship, where McIlroy overcame a three-shot deficit and won by one shot. Oosthuizen had a stretch of six straight tournaments late in the year when he finished no worse than sixth. He can count two trophies from 2012, but perhaps the better measure is the World Ranking. He went into the season at No. 40 and finished the year at No. 6.

The most prolific winner among South Africans was Branden Grace, who, like Oosthuizen, came from humble roots and was a product of the Ernie Els and Fancourt Foundation. Grace earned his European Tour card through the qualifying tournament and wasted no time showing off his skills. He won the Joburg Open for his first win, and then a week later he withstood the Sunday pressure in the Volvo Golf Champions on The Links at Fancourt and got into a playoff with Els and Retief Goosen, the best of the Springboks from this generation who now have six majors among them. Grace won with a birdie on the first extra hole. It still wasn't enough to get him into Augusta National, though Grace wasn't through. He won the Volvo China Open two weeks after the Masters. He was never much a factor in the three majors or three World Golf Championships he played. But the 24-year-old South African with a big game ended his season with two more wins, the Vodacom Origins of Golf Final on the Sunshine Tour and the Alfred Dunhill Links Championship, giving him five wins — as many as McIlroy, though McIlroy's were against some of the best fields. Grace finished at No. 6 in the Race to Dubai standings, and No. 34 in the World Ranking. A pretty good start.

On the American side, the rookie who made the biggest splash was John Huh, born in New York of South Korean heritage. He tried to go to college in California but couldn't secure a scholarship and turned pro. He made it through every stage of the qualifying tournament, started strong with a tie for sixth at Torrey Pines, and then won the Mayakoba Golf Classic in Mexico by coming from seven shots behind on the last day and beating Robert Allenby in a playoff. The rest of his season was steady, but solid. That much was reflected in the fact that he received only half of the FedExCup points (Mexico was played opposite the Accenture Match Play Championship) and still made it all the way to the Tour Championship, securing a spot in at least the first three majors for 2013.

His year is significant in one other regard. There will never be another story like John Huh, someone who can put down $5,000 for his entry fee at Q-School and earn a spot on the PGA Tour, even if he has to go through every stage. In one of the biggest developments on the PGA Tour, officials decided to do away with the version of qualifying that had been around for a half-century. Starting in 2013, making it through Q-School will only earn a card to the PGA Tour's secondary tour. And typical of most new programs involving the PGA Tour, it's a bit complicated.

At the heart of this change were the "Fall Series" events that followed the FedExCup competition. The purses were smaller. The fields were weaker. The winner did not receive FedExCup points and did not receive an invitation to the Masters. For the PGA Tour to keep those sponsors, and an estimated $25 million in prize money, it had to make them official. The tour also was looking for a new umbrella sponsor for the smaller circuit to replace Nationwide. To make those events official, the PGA Tour decided to go to a wraparound season that starts in October and concludes with the Tour Championship in September. And once that was decided, it felt it was not prudent to offer PGA Tour cards through Q-School in December when the season would already have begun.

So how to distribute tour cards? In one of the more original ideas, Q-School effectively is being replaced by four tournaments called "The Finals." The field will be comprised of the top 75 players from the Web.com Tour (formerly known as the Nationwide Tour) and the next 75 players on the PGA Tour who failed to finish in the top 125 and qualify for the FedExCup Playoffs. Those approximately 150 players will start from scratch and play four $1 million events, with the top 25 on that special money list earning PGA Tour cards. The top 25 on the Web.com Tour season money list will be guaranteed cards, but still compete in "The Finals" to determine their priority ranking for the 2013-14 season. Instead of a player having to find his form for six days in the finals of Q-School, he now has four tournaments to find his game and earn his card.

If nothing else, it might be enough for John Daly to give it a try. "You get four chances to get a card. I think it's a great idea," said Daly, who has refused to go to Q-School since losing his card after the 2006 season. "And they're all $1 million purses, right? I'd have to give that a shot."

That wasn't the only big change that took place outside the ropes. Keegan Bradley won the PGA Championship in 2011 using a belly putter — a mid-length shaft that he anchored into his stomach — making him the first major champion with a long putter. Bradley told stories that afternoon about more players in the minor tours using belly putters, though not many paid close attention. He was a PGA Tour rookie, still relatively unknown. Phil Mickelson tried the belly putter briefly a few months later. There wasn't a wholesale shift, though it no longer was odd to see unconventional putters. And then Webb Simpson won the U.S. Open using a belly putter, making it two of the last three major champions. At Royal Lytham & St. Annes, it was Adam Scott bringing attention to anchoring. He had switched to a broom-handle version that he anchored against his chest, and he nearly won the Masters. He looked better than ever at the Open Championship and was on the verge of winning until four bogeys on his last four holes. That made a winner out of Ernie Els, who holed a 15-foot birdie putt with ... a belly putter. That made it three of the last five major champions, and it suddenly became an issue. Royal & Ancient Chief Executive Peter Dawson said as much in a press conference the day after Els won the claret jug, saying such putters were "firmly back on the radar."

"We appreciate that there is much speculation about this and that we need to clarify the position as soon as possible. And I think you're going to see us saying something about it one way or the other in a few months, rather than years," Dawson said. It took only four months. Instead of a decision on the putter itself, the R&A and USGA proposed a new rule that banned anchoring the club — any club — against the body. The new rule still had to go through a 90-day comment period, believed to be a formality, and it would not go into effect until the next Rules of Golf edition was issued in 2016. The anchored stroke had been around some 40 years, and it was Paul Azinger who first won with the belly putter in 2001.

The decision was controversial, even though several top players supported it. The major champions — Bradley, Simpson and Els — became the faces of this decision. The concern was that banning the stroke used for long putters would force recreational players from the game, at a time when the golf industry was concerned about fewer players in the game. Dawson and USGA Executive Director Mike Davis felt it was the right thing to do for golf. "Our conclusion is that anchored strokes threaten to supplant traditional strokes, which with all their frailties are integral to the longstanding character of our sport," Dawson said.

Guan Tianlang, a 14-year-old from China in the eighth grade, used a belly putter to win the Asia Pacific Amateur Championship and qualify for the Masters, making him the youngest player at Augusta National. He had only been using the belly putter for about six months, though he was an example of the governing bodies' concern — that kids would start using an anchored stroke at an early age. No longer might it be an act of desperation for players who struggled with putting, rather an advantage by those who saw it as a better way to putt.

It was a bigger issue on the men's tour than the LPGA Tour. Not many women use long putters, and besides, the LPGA Tour might have been too busy getting over the shock that an American — yes, an American — was the leading player for the first time since Beth Daniel in 1994. That player was Stacy Lewis, remarkable in her own right. She wore a back brace for seven years as a teenager to deal with scoliosis, and then required surgery. Her doctor was going to insert two rods into her back until he won a lottery at a charity event that earned him a golf lesson. Only then did he realize that Lewis was quite the golfer, and he opted instead for a single rod with five screws that would allow her more movement. Lewis took it from there, and she broke through by winning four times on the LPGA Tour to win the Rolex Player of the Year award.

The No. 1 player remained Yani Tseng, who looked like she might dwarf her competition with three wins before April, only to go into a mysterious slump. The South Koreans remained a force when Na Yeon Choi won the U.S. Women's Open, Inbee Park won the money list and Jiyai Shin won the Ricoh Women's British Open. Shanshan Feng made history as the first Chinese player to win a major at the Wegmans LPGA Championship, and she led the world of golf with six wins — one on the LPGA Tour, two on the Ladies European Tour and three times on the Japan LPGA Tour. It truly was a global performance, fitting in another year that showed how much the world of golf has become just that.

There was one other major development off the golf course involving a green jacket at Augusta National, just not one belonging to any of the players. The home of the Masters announced in August that it had invited two women to be members, ending the all-male membership that existed since the club was founded in 1932. Masters chairman Billy Payne called it a "joyous occasion." The club selected former Secretary of State Condoleezza Rice, who also is involved with the USGA, and Darla Moore, a South Carolina financier and a business protege of Hootie Johnson, who was the Augusta National chairman when this issue first mushroomed a decade ago. Johnson had said in July 2002, when the golfing world first heard of Martha Burk and her protest of the membership, that the club might one day invite a woman to join, "but that timetable will be ours and not at the point of a bayonet." True enough, no one saw this coming. It was announced the Monday of the FedExCup Playoffs on the PGA Tour, and it dominated news coverage for the next three days. The gender issue had returned in April during the Masters because IBM, one of the main corporate sponsors, appointed its first female CEO in the 100-year history of Big Blue, and the company's previous four CEOs were members. Virginia Rometty was at the Masters during the final round, though she wore a pink jacket. And perhaps as a sign that Augusta does things its own way, she was not announced as a member.

2. Masters Tournament

It took winning the 2012 Masters Tournament to expose the truth about Bubba Watson's name. Not that there was any great secret. It's just that until then, few thought to ask.

It turns out that on November 5, 1978, in Bagdad, Florida, Gerry Lester Watson named his newborn son Gerry Lester Watson Jr. And then noting that his son weighed 9½ pounds and had chubby cheeks, decided he looked like a football player and so he nicknamed him "Bubba," after a famous professional player of the time, Bubba Smith.

The easy-going Watson, 33, was noted as a left-hander of great power and possibly an underachiever, what with just three wins since joining the PGA Tour in 2006. And maybe as something of an odd duck by contemporary standards. He was self-taught and had no entourage — no swing coach, no short-game coach, no putting coach, no mind consultant. He was a distant 40-1 choice for this Masters. The coolness of the bookmakers was understandable. In Watson's three previous Masters, his best finish was a tie for 20th place. There was little to recommend him on Augusta National Golf Club's emerald expanses.

Tiger Woods, on the other hand, owner of four green jackets, gave the oddsmakers all they needed to make him the 6-1 favorite when he won the Arnold Palmer Invitational two weeks earlier. It was his first victory since 2009, after 30 months of personal problems, injuries and a swing change. The byword was — Tiger was back.

Next question — what about Rory McIlroy? Now ranked No. 2 in the world, McIlroy was ruined by the 10th hole in the final round in 2011, where a wild drive cost him a triple bogey and very possibly the Masters itself. There were those who wondered whether that would destroy his spirit. Well, a month later he ran off with the U.S. Open, his first major championship, then the Shanghai Masters, and then, just a month before this Masters, the Honda Classic. But now would he get back on the horse that threw him?

Others did not lack for pre-tournament attention. Phil Mickelson, a three-time winner, is always in the running, and the pundits wondered whether England's Lee Westwood, No. 3 in the world, might finally bring in that first major victory. Oddly enough, Luke Donald, No. 1 in the world, figured very lightly in pre-tournament chatter, which was a surprise because his disciplined game seemed to fit at Augusta National. Would Sergio Garcia finally put the pieces together? And if South Africa's Charl Schwartzel could figure out Augusta National in only his second visit in 2011, what would he do with another year under his belt? As for Australia's Jason Day, a kid who tied for second in his debut last year, can a win be far behind? Well, Bubba Watson was to answer all those questions.

And what is a Masters without a flap over Augusta National's all-male membership policy? An acrimonious dispute in 2006 with Hootie Johnson, then the chairman, surfaced again. The occasion this time: Long-time sponsor IBM got a new chief executive, who happened to be a woman,

Virginia Rometty. Since the IBM chief has long been a member of Augusta National, some thought the club should invite Mrs. Rometty to join. Masters Chairman Billy Payne repeated the club policy: Augusta National does not discuss membership issues publicly.

That said, it was on to the 2012 Masters.

First Round

Come Thursday morning, the 76th Masters Tournament opened on a note of nostalgia. The Big Three of the 1960s were reunited when Gary Player joined Arnold Palmer and Jack Nicklaus as honorary starters. Palmer, age 82, owned four Masters; Player, 76, three, and Nicklaus, 72, a record six. All three hit the fairway.

"I don't think any of us can see that far," Nicklaus said. "We can hear them land, though."

Behind them, the field of 95 ran the risk of hitting muddy balls from fairways softened by recent rain and also from intermittent showers in the first round.

Bubba Watson, the man who would be champion, had more than golf on his mind when he teed it up. "It's not fun because my baby's at home and I have to play," Watson was to say. Bubba and Angie had just welcomed their month-old adopted son, Caleb, and then Bubba had to leave for the Masters only a few days later.

Watson, teeing off in the next-to-last group with Rory McIlroy and Angel Cabrera, shot a solid three-under 69, his best start in his four Masters, despite a wind that stiffened late in the day. "Just trying to make pars and get out of here," said Watson. He did his scoring on the first nine — birdies at Nos. 3, 6 and 8. Coming in, he offset two bogeys with two birdies and was pleased to be just two off Lee Westwood's lead. "I shot three under," Watson said. "If you're not happy with that, then you have got problems."

England's Lee Westwood was 0-for-55 in the majors when he opened this Masters with a one-stroke lead on a 67, tying his all-time low in his 13th Masters. "Majors are my primary focus," Westwood said, reciting the golfer's anthem, and stubbornly, they always seemed to just slip from his grasp. He was runner-up to Mickelson in the 2010 Masters. He staked his claim this time with a burst of four straight birdies from No. 5, on putts of four, 10 and six feet, and two putts at the par-five eighth.

Westwood led by one over Sweden's Peter Hanson and South Africa's Louis Oosthuizen, winner of the 2010 Open Championship. Hanson, who missed the cut in 2011, his only other Masters, preferred the bolder approach. "My mindset was to be really aggressive off the tee and be pretty aggressive into the greens," he said, and with that strategy built his 68 on four birdies in six holes from No. 7, on some hot putting — a pair of 20-footers and a 30-footer. Oosthuizen's 68 came out of a wild second nine, with two bogeys and five birdies, four of them over the last five holes. "This golf course, you've got to be very patient," he said.

The anticipated Tiger Woods-Phil Mickelson duel never got off the ground. Woods bogeyed the last two holes for a 72. He'd hit just six of the 14 driving fairways, but found a bright side to the day. "My commitment to each and every shot ... my alignment, my setup," he said. "That's something I'm excited about." As for Mickelson, a lost-ball triple bogey at the par-four 10th cost him a 74, but that didn't dim his outlook. "So as poorly as I played...," he said, "I'm right there."

The question hovering over Rory McIlroy was natural: How would he do at the par-four 10th, where last year's Masters was yanked out of his grasp when he triple-bogeyed out of the left trees. This time, he crashed to a double bogey at No. 1. "Still 71 holes left in the tournament," he said, with that grin. He shot 71.

Charl Schwartzel, the man who took over when McIlroy self-destructed in 2011, birdied the last four holes to win. This time he had to make some great saves to survive. He missed the 11th green wide to the right but chipped stiff for his par. At the 12th, he blasted out of a bunker poorly, to 15 feet, then holed the par putt. And at the par-five 15th, he missed the green long, chipped back across and into the water, and still scraped out a bogey and shot 72. "It could easily have been a two- or three-under-par day," Schwartzel insisted.

Just when it seemed an inquiry on Luke Donald's card suggested he was in danger of being disqualified, came the official report — the birdie at No. 5 wasn't his error, it was due to "administrative error." Donald had declared the bogey that he made and shot 75. It was his worst start in eight Masters. "But the tournament's not over yet," Donald insisted.

Westwood would have had a co-leader at 67 if Augusta National hadn't proved to be a hole too long for Sweden's Henrik Stenson (71). Stenson eagled both par-fives on the first nine with 15-foot putts and was five under par and leading by two coming to the par-four 18th. But he drove into the trees on the right, punched out, was short with a four iron, long with a wedge, short with a chip and long with a putt, and it all added up to an eight that was great golf humor to everyone but the victim. "You make a little mistake...," said Stenson.

Some surprising names popped up on the leaderboard, and none more so than Scotland's Paul Lawrie, the Open Championship winner of 1999. He joined the group at 69 that included Spain's free-spirited Miguel Angel Jimenez and half of Italy's brother entry, Francesco Molinari, age 29. His big brother, Edoardo, 31, was well back at 75.

Apart from Westwood taking the lead, this Masters was definitely not proceeding as expected.

First-Round Leaders: Lee Westwood 67, Louis Oosthuizen 68, Peter Hanson 68, Paul Lawrie 69, Miguel Angel Jimenez 69, Francisco Molinari 69, Ben Crane 69, Jason Dufner 69, Bubba Watson 69.

Second Round

Like the azaleas and the dogwoods, Fred Couples blossoms every April at Augusta National. Here he was again — now age 52, his back still so sore he could barely warm up, now a star of the over-50 set on the Champions Tour, and he was tied for the halfway lead in this Masters, his 28th.

Could he actually work the magic that produced his Masters victory in 1992, at age 32? Maybe it's some kind of shared appetite for nostalgia, but it seemed to fans he was forever contending at Augusta National. He tied for 15th in 2011, finished sixth in 2010, tied third in 2006, and tied for sixth in 2004.

"For me to be tied at this moment ... it was incredible," said Couples. He did it with a day's-best 67 for a five-under-par 139 total, matching Jason Dufner, age 35, he of the solemn visage, apparently none the worse for wear after his stunning fold and loss to Keegan Bradley in the PGA Championship the previous August. Dufner shook off a double bogey at No. 4, shot 70, and wasn't excited. "I don't really think about it, to be honest with you," he said. "I'm just playing a round of golf."

Couples felt differently. "Very shocking, and it was a great day," Couples said, and then was reminded, to his surprise, that he started 71-68–139 last year and was in the hunt until a closing 73 tied him for 15th.

Couples surprised himself and the entire world of golf this time. How did he do it? Well, putts of three and four feet got birdies at the third and fourth. He birdied three straight from No. 7, from 20 feet, three feet and 35 feet. He birdied the par-five 15th on two putts from 25 feet and the par-three 16th on one putt from 20 feet.

Someone offered that 52-year-olds are not meant to win major championships. "Does that ever occur to you, or do you just figure, what the hell?" the questioner said.

"I stand out there and say 'What the hell' a lot," Couples said. "What do I have to lose here?"

Couples didn't get all the attention. Tiger Woods got a lot. Not that he wanted it. Television was proving to be the bane of his agonizing rebuilding program. After two early birdies, he started to slide, and television caught him in several instances showing his frustration. He shot 75, made the 36-hole cut and noted, "I've been around the block for a number of years, and I understand how to be patient."

Louis Oosthuizen, meanwhile, was one happy golfer. "I'm usually packing and picking kids up now," he said, noting that he had missed the cut in all three of his previous Masters appearances. He started the windy Friday morning double bogey-birdie-bogey-bogey from No. 2. "At three over after five," he said, dryly, "you get the feeling it's not going to be a good day." But he birdied three of the last five holes for a 72 to tie for third, a stroke off the lead.

Lee Westwood, like Henrik Stenson in the first round, found the course a hole too long. He was cruising along with the lead, then oops — he double-bogeyed the 18th, shot 73, and slipped down to a share of third. He consoled himself. "I'm not going to be too far off the lead," he said.

Luke Donald spared himself the embarrassment of world No. 1 missing the cut by scratching out a 73, but he was nine strokes off the lead. "I thought I was as prepared as I've been," he said. Charl Schwartzel (75) would need a miracle to repeat as champion. He was eight behind. And Rickie Fowler, a key figure in the youth movement, needed a miracle just to make the cut, and he got it at the 18th. His approach bounced off a fan's head, then off the grandstand, and he escaped with a par and made the cut at 74–148.

Boyish Sergio Garcia, now age 32, jumped into contention with a 68–140, one off the lead. "I'm pretty happy the way it came out," Garcia said, "but it's Friday, so I don't want to get ahead of myself." Rory McIlroy joined him at 140 with a five-birdie 69. Said McIlroy, equally cautious: "I wouldn't say I'm in a position to win yet." Meanwhile, speaking of whiz kids, whatever happened to Japan's Ryo Ishikawa? He missed the cut badly with his 76-77–153 total. He had one runner-up finish in seven PGA Tour stops, and nothing else was close.

The halfway cut came in at five-over 149, leaving 62 players in the field and taking out, among others, Paul Casey, Darren Clarke and K.J. Choi.

Bubba Watson, meanwhile, joined the tie for third place with a 71 salvaged from an unpromising start. He shook off bogeys at the fifth and the ninth and birdied Nos. 13 (after a near eagle), 15 and 16. "Anytime you shoot under par in a major, especially at the Masters, it's a good day," he said. He would be playing on the weekend, as they say, but this time it would be a matter of divided attention, a state familiar to new fathers. "Our new son's at home," he said, "so that's more important to me than trying to make a putt and win a golf tournament."

Second-Round Leaders: Fred Couples 67–139, Jason Dufner 70–139, Louis Oosthuizen 72–140, Lee Westwood 73–140, Sergio Garcia 68–140, Rory McIlroy 69–140, Bubba Watson 71–140, Paul Lawrie 72–141, Matt Kuchar 70–141, Miguel Angel-Jimenez 72–141

Third Round

While Bubba Watson crept closer to the lead, practically unnoticed, the third round of the Masters on Saturday was given over to the decline — but not fall — of Fred Couples, of Phil Mickelson and the wondrous flop shot, Peter Hanson's rocket ride to the top, and among other things, the doom of Tiger Woods, the amazing day of Ian Poulter, and the gallows humor of Sergio Garcia and Rory McIlroy.

Garcia and McIlroy, the once and current prodigies, respectively, opened the round a stroke off the lead and playing together — Garcia still seeking that first major championship, McIlroy seeking revenge on the course. So Garcia bogeyed No. 1, McIlroy double-bogeyed, and they staggered the rest of the way. They got their first birdie at the 12th, fell into each other's arms and exited laughing. "It would have been better," Garcia was to say, "if that were my girlfriend." Garcia shot 75, McIlroy 77. Said Garcia, now 0-for-54 in majors and not laughing: "I'm not good enough ... I don't have the thing I need to have."

The third round, first a scramble, turned into the Hanson-and-Mickelson show.

Hanson, in only his second Masters and never closer to the lead than seven strokes in his 17 previous majors, shot to the top with a remarkable 65. It was a stretch battle. Hanson, in the pairing ahead, heard the thunder when Mickelson holed a 20-foot putt to eagle the 13th hole. He responded by lofting a wedge to two feet at the 14th. The par-five 15th became a museum piece. Hanson birdied it from 15 feet, then Mickelson came along and hit a miraculous, scary flop shot off a tight lie from behind the green that could have gone across the green and into the pond in front. This was a heart-in-throat shot. Hanson put it best.

"When I ended up in that same spot on 15, I just sought the bump-and-run," Hanson said. "He just hits a full swing and goes straight up in the air."

"It wasn't the safest shot," Mickelson conceded. But he dropped it four feet from the flag and birdied. Then at the 18th, he hooked a seven iron to 12 feet for an inward 30 and a 66. Hanson birdied the 17th from 30 feet and the 18th off a six iron to three for his 65 and a nine-under 207, a stroke up on Mickelson. Was he prepared to sleep on the lead?

"I don't know," Hanson said, laughing. "It's a new situation to me."

Surely no one really expected Fred Couples to roll along and win this Masters, but he certainly was the sentimental favorite. That was plenty clear from the rolling cheers of the fans. "They yell for everybody," Couples said. A 75 knocked him seven strokes off the lead. "I'm not overly disappointed," he said, "but I am disappointed."

The same might be said of Tiger Woods. He started the round eight strokes off the lead and ended it 12 behind with a pedestrian 72. "It was so close to being a good round," said Woods. Ian Poulter's outing was anything but pedestrian. He parred No. 1, then held on for the ride — two birdies, two bogeys, two more birdies, two more bogeys on the front, shot 70 and finished seven behind.

The chase started to heat up. Louis Oosthuizen made his way like an old hand at Augusta, hitting 12 of 14 fairways and 15 greens, and birdieing three straight from No. 6 for a 69. He tasted the lead briefly and finished two off the lead. Matt Kuchar also held the lead briefly, then shot 70 and felt barely noticed. "It's nice to be under the radar," he said. Padraig Harrington (68) pushed his way into the picture with four straight birdies from the 13th, getting to five behind, and figured his two Open Championships and one PGA Championship took the pressure off him. "I'm going to win more majors," he said, curiously, "so I don't have to do it tomorrow." Hunter Mahan birdied three of the par-fives in a 68 and also was five off the lead.

If Oosthuizen was under the radar, Bubba Watson was incognito. Despite his five birdies, all the roars he heard were for Kuchar and Mickelson, playing ahead of him. "You're hearing all these different roars from different sections, so it's not the same guys all the time," Watson said. "You're wondering who it is, what's happening, but at the same time, it's doable out there." Watson dropped two shots over the first five holes, then birdied Nos. 6 and 8 to make the turn in par, and was one over with a bogey at the 11th. Then he felt the urgency.

"I didn't look at where I was until the last couple holes, and I heard some big roars and saw some numbers went up, at nine under," Watson said. "I knew I needed to make a couple of birdies to have a better chance." He got them — three on the last six holes, at 13, 15 and 18, the last on a six-foot putt for a 70 and a six-under 210 total, three shots off the lead. He was alone in fourth, his best position ever after three rounds in four Masters.

Third-Round Leaders: Peter Hanson 65–207, Phil Mickelson 66–208, Louis Oosthuizen 69–209, Bubba Watson 70–210, Matt Kuchar 70–211, Hunter Mahan 68–212, Padraig Harrington 68–212, Henrik Stenson 70–212, Lee Westwood 72–212, Paul Lawrie 72–213

Fourth Round

There are any number of ways to learn to play golf. Chi Chi Rodriguez hit a mashed tin can with a guava limb. Young Seve Ballesteros used a three iron, slashing at stones on a Spanish seacoast. Phil Mickelson, a right-hander, mirrored his dad on the tee and so learned to play left-handed. Bubba Watson, self-taught, hit wiffle balls as a kid, making them curve this way and that, at will. One day, this would let him shape shots to fit any occasion, as a disbelieving world discovered when he magically escaped from deep in the trees at Augusta National and won the 2012 Masters. But it was not the golfer's standard "dream come true."

Said Watson: "I never had a dream go this far."

Even dreaming of a playoff might have been too much, but that's where he ended up, charging to catch South Africa's Louis Oosthuizen, then beating him on the second extra hole after that incredible escape.

Other dreams died along the way. Peter Hanson, the third-round leader, shot 73 and tied for third, two out of the playoff. Matt Kuchar (69) bogeyed the 16th again and also tied for third, as did the always hopeful Lee Westwood (68), who birdied four of the last six holes but again fell short.

Phil Mickelson suffered the biggest crash when his tee shot at the par-three fourth glanced off the grandstand and left him in vegetation so thick he couldn't even take a penalty drop. He hacked with an upside-down club — once, twice — made a triple bogey-six and couldn't catch up, and shot 72. What will you take from this day? someone asked.

"Third place," Mickelson said.

Fate had a sense of theater. Watson and Oosthuizen were playing partners for the final round, with Oosthuizen leading by one. Watson three-putted the first for a bogey and birdied the second, and that's where the drama began.

Until Watson's playoff miracle, the shot of this Masters was Oosthuizen's four iron from 210 yards at the downhill, par-five No. 2. The ball landed short, rolled up between the front bunkers, curled to the right and slowly rolled toward the pin, then dropped, triggering an explosion for the first double eagle ever at No. 2, the fourth albatross-two in the Masters since Gene Sarazen's in 1935. It vaulted Oosthuizen into the lead. The man once considered a one-trick pony for winning the 2010 Open Championship and nothing else of prominence was suddenly closing in on the spring classic.

Oosthuizen bogeyed Nos. 4 and 10, birdied the 13th with two putts and the 15th from seven feet, and made five clutch par putts along the way.

Watson bogeyed the 12th, then raced to four straight birdies — two putts at the 13th, a wedge to six feet at the 14th, two putts at the 15th and an eight iron to eight feet at the 16th, tying Oosthuizen for the lead. They parred in. Watson shot 68, Oosthuizen 69, tying at 10-under 278, two ahead of the field.

At the first playoff hole, the 18th, they both narrowly missed birdie putts, Oosthuizen from 16 feet, Watson from eight. They went to the downhill, par-four 10th. Watson drove deep into the trees on the right and looked dead. But Oosthuizen brightened his outlook with a weak drive into the right rough. Augusta's rough isn't punishing, but it does affect play. Possibly that's why Oosthuizen's three-wood approach, from 231 yards, dropped short of the green.

Watson was back in the trees, beyond the gallery. "If I got a swing, I got a shot," he would say. "I attack. I always attack. I want to hit the incredible shot." His chance was coming up.

"I knew as soon as I was walking — before I even got to my ball. I was already looking at the gap. I saw everybody was standing."

Crucial point of technology: The modern ball is very hard to "work" — make curve — and then it only curves a little.

"I saw it was a perfect draw, a perfect hook," Watson said. "I hit my 52-degree, my gap wedge, hooked it about 40 yards, hit about 15 feet off the ground until it got under the tree and then it started rising. Pretty easy."

Watson's ball ended up 15 feet from the flag. Oosthuizen followed his weak approach with a too-long chip. "Didn't get the check on it that I thought I would," he said. He two-putted for a bogey. That left Watson the luxury of two-putting for a par and the win. His first putt stopped about three inches above the hole. The crowd started to roar for the new champion-to-be. Watson lifted his hand gently: Whoa, he was saying. Let's don't be too sure. Then he tapped in.

"I got in these trees and hit a crazy shot that I saw in my head," Watson said. This was a different kind of golfer. This was a Ballesteros kind of golfer.

"An unbelievable shot," Oosthuizen. It would stamp Watson for all time.

"I'm not ready for fame," Watson said. "I don't want to be famous. I just want to be me and play golf."

And raise his new son.

The Final Leaders: Bubba Watson 68–278 (won playoff), Louis Oosthuizen 69–278, Peter Hanson 73–280, Matt Kuchar 68–280, Phil Mickelson 72–280, Lee Westwood 68–280, Ian Poulter 69–283, Padraig Harrington 72–284, Justin Rose 68–284, Adam Scott 66–284

3. U.S. Open Championship

It was an unconventional way to prepare for a major championship. Webb Simpson warmed up by playing four days of casual golf with friends in the North Carolina sandhills.

"I honestly didn't do a whole lot of practicing once the Pinehurst trip came around," Simpson said. "It was needed for me, coming into a major, to just get my mind off things and just go and play golf.

"It might be an annual pre-U.S. Open trip now."

Simpson grew up not far from Pinehurst, in Raleigh, and was a scoring standard bearer for the 1999 U.S. Open there, when he was 13 years old. One of the players whose name he carried that week was Tom Watson, who offered him some advice: Every tournament is a level playing field, so keep working hard.

Adhering to Watson's advice to keep working, Simpson constructed a stunning weekend rally in the 112th U.S. Open Championship at The Olympic Club in San Francisco and registered a one-stroke victory to maintain Olympic's reputation as a welcoming place for unlikely champions. Thanks to a pair of 68s, Simpson rallied past two seasoned golfers and former U.S. Open winners, Jim Furyk and Graeme McDowell, to win in just his second U.S. Open and fifth start in a major championship.

Simpson completed 72 holes in one-over-par 281 and was one stroke ahead of McDowell and Michael Thompson.

Simpson, who now lives in Charlotte, had a breakout 2011 season in which he won twice on the PGA Tour and finished second to Luke Donald on the money list. He has come far since he turned professional in 2008 after an amateur career in which he was a member of the victorious American team in the 2007 Walker Cup. His college play at Wake Forest culminated in Simpson being the Atlantic Coast Conference Player of the Year in 2008. He reached the PGA Tour via the qualifying tournament, earned $1.2 million his first full season in 2009 and has never looked back.

A man of strong religious faith and devotion to his family, Simpson decided to skip the 2012 Open Championship in England because it was too close to the birth of his second child with his wife Dowd. Despite being 34 weeks pregnant, Dowd walked all 72 holes with her husband at The Olympic Club. To ease the tension as they watched the final groups come down the stretch trying to catch Simpson, the couple looked at pictures of their son, James, on Dowd's cellular phone.

With his victory Simpson became the first recipient of the Jack Nicklaus Medal. The traditional gold medal given to the winner was named in honor of Nicklaus, starting this year, because of his long association and success at the U.S. Open. One side of the new medal features an engraving of the Nicklaus swing.

Simpson also connected in the end with another past U.S. Open champion and Hall of Famer, Arnold Palmer. Simpson attended Wake Forest on a scholarship funded by Palmer, and in the days before the U.S. Open, he read of Palmer's seven-stroke collapse and loss in a playoff at The Olympic Club to Billy Casper in the 1966 U.S. Open.

"He's meant the world to me," Simpson said. "I played four years at Wake under his scholarship, which was a huge help. I've always been such a big fan of the King and what he represents. I had the opportunity to play in his tournament twice as an amateur, which kind of opened my eyes to the PGA Tour and how good these players are. He's meant the world to Wake Forest and couldn't have been a nicer guy to me through the years.

"Just the other day, I read the story (from 1966) and thought about it. Hopefully I can get a little back for him and make him smile."

Two days after his victory, Simpson was interviewed by telephone on Golf Channel's "Morning Drive" program. While he was on the line, Palmer called in to congratulate him. "I have a smile all the way across my face," the 82-year-old icon said proudly.

First Round

Just six players managed to better par in the opening round as The Olympic Club — its tilted fairways and small greens running firm, fast and provoking fury — won the day against the best golfers in the world.

A surprise leader often emerges on such days at the U.S. Open, and this championship proved to be no exception as a little-heralded 27-year-old from Alabama not only seized the lead, but actually put some space between himself and the field. Michael Thompson birdied six of his last 12 holes, needed 22 putts during his round and posted a four-under-par 66. That performance yielded a three-stroke lead.

It turned out that Thompson was not someone little-known to the United States Golf Association or to The Olympic Club membership. Five years earlier, in the 2007 U.S. Amateur, Thompson had lost in the final to Colt Knost, 2 and 1. Thompson said that after multiple times on the Lake Course that year, he grew fond of the place.

"I love this golf course," said Thompson, who put on his scoring run in the presence of Knost, playing in the same group of three. "It's the U.S. Open and I told my caddie a couple of times, I said, 'Man, this is so awesome being here.' I've been looking forward to hopefully playing in this event for over two years, since the U.S. Amateur. I just can't be more thrilled."

Tiger Woods was among those tied for second place after posting 69s. Others were 2010 U.S. Open champion Graeme McDowell, David Toms, Justin Rose and Nick Watney.

The day's best shot was played by Watney, who made the third albatross in U.S. Open history at the par-five 17th hole. He used a five iron from 190 yards. The ball landed on the front of the green then rolled to the back and into the hole. The two previous albatrosses, also known in America as double eagles, were by T.C. Chen (1987) and Shaun Micheel (2010). Watney's was the second in a major championship in 2012. Louis Oosthuizen had the other on the par-five second hole in the final round of the Masters.

The first-round scoring average for the 156 participants was a hefty 74.923, almost five strokes over par. Thirteen players shot in the 80s. The top three players in the World Ranking, playing together in the afternoon (a tradition the USGA started in 2008), were a combined 17 over par. No. 1 Luke Donald failed to make a birdie and returned a 79; No. 2 Rory McIlroy, the defending champion, struggled to a 77; and No. 3 Lee Westwood scraped out a 73 after standing four over par after six holes.

"There weren't a lot of opportunities out there," Donald lamented. Woods backed him up, saying, "This golf course, it's so demanding. This is one of those Opens where it's really hard to make birdie."

Yes, but Thompson had seven birdies, one by holing out from a bunker at the par-three third hole. "I just went out there and enjoyed the experience," Thompson said. "I didn't really care what happened today. I know what I'm working on right now is going to benefit me further on into the future."

Winless in the majors since his playoff victory over Rocco Mediate in the 2008 U.S. Open, Woods was playing in a marquee group with longtime rival Phil Mickelson and reigning Masters champion Bubba Watson. Mickelson posted a 76 and Watson struggled even more, finishing with a 78. Because of the course configuration, the group began on the ninth tee — believed to be the first time a major championship had started on a hole other than Nos. 1 and 10.

"I shot eight over, so not very good," Watson said of his bombs-away strategy. Players such as Toms and McDowell were much better playing more conservatively. A group at 70 included Jim Furyk and Matt Kuchar, two other control players. Also at 70 was 17-year-old Beau Hossler, who qualified at two nearby courses, Harding Park and Lake Merced. Hossler, a high school senior from Rancho Santa Margarita, California, already was playing in his second consecutive U.S. Open.

McIlroy, who a year ago chewed up a softened Congressional course on the way to a record 16-under 268 total and becoming the youngest U.S. Open champion since Bobby Jones, struggled all over the course. "Just anything a little off and it really punishes you," said McIlroy, age 23. "You have to be precise with your tee shots and your iron shots and leave it on the right side of the pins, and today I didn't really do any of that."

Meanwhile McDowell, his fellow countryman from Northern Ireland, was again proving his mettle. He had followed up his win at Pebble Beach in 2010 with a tie for 14th at Congressional. He and Toms posted their round in the more trying afternoon wave, when the sun baked out the fairways and greens.

First-Round Leaders: Michael Thompson 66, Tiger Woods 69, David Toms 69, Nick Watney 69, Justin Rose 69, Graeme McDowell 69, Jim Furyk 70, Matt Kuchar 70, Alistair Presnell 70, Robert Karlsson 70, Beau Hossler 70, Ian Poulter 70, J.B. Park 70, Jason Bohn 70

Second Round

There was a high level of excitement about the changes on the leaderboard on Friday at the U.S. Open. First, a 17-year-old amateur briefly found his way to the top. Later, a 17-year veteran ended the day with a share of the lead.

The latter man was Tiger Woods, the three-time U.S. Open champion, whose return to the top of the leaderboard was just about all anyone could talk about by the end of the second round. With a smartly played, hard-luck, even-par 70, Woods looked even more comfortable than the day before, and his one-under 139 total shared the halfway lead with two other major championship winners, David Toms and Jim Furyk. Toms also had a 70, while Furyk posted a 69 and was one of seven players who broke par.

That trio was two strokes ahead of four players including Graeme McDowell, who dropped three shots on the last four holes for a 72 and 141 total. Also at that figure were Belgium's Nicolas Colsaerts, winner of this year's Volvo World Match Play on the European Tour, who shot a 69; 2011 NCAA Division I golf champion John Peterson, who shot a 70, and first-round leader Michael Thompson, who needed a birdie at the tough par-three eighth, his last hole of the day, just to shoot 75.

Blake Adams, in his first U.S. Open, was alone in eighth place with 142, following a 70, while a large group at 143 included two-time winners on the 2012 PGA Tour, Hunter Mahan and Jason Dufner, The Players champion Matt Kuchar, and 2011 Masters winner Charl Schwartzel.

Woods wasn't feeling much discomfort, and he had much good karma to draw upon going forward. In only three other appearances in the U.S. Open had he led one of the first three rounds. In each he went on to win. He had never posted a score worse than par in the third round as the 36-hole leader in a major, and in his 14 major wins, Woods had never shot over par in the third round.

And Woods didn't look inclined to start now, not when he was leading the field in fairways hit and was third in greens in regulation, a ball-striking performance that augured well for him.

"I know it takes a bit out of us, but so be it," Woods said of the tiring round that nevertheless put him one step closer to his 15th major victory. "But I would much rather be out there than missing cuts or just making the cut. So it's a wonderful place to be with a chance to win your nation's Open."

The only disappointment for Woods was not holding on to the outright lead at two under par after sinking a five-foot putt at the par-three third hole. He followed up by suffering three consecutive bogeys, the third at the easy seventh when he three-putted from eight feet. He scratched back into a share of the lead with Furyk with a four-footer for birdie at No. 13.

While all this was going on, 17-year-old amateur Beau Hossler was making believers out of the gallery. He toured the second nine in one under par and then rolled in a six-foot birdie putt at the tough first hole, his 11th of the afternoon, that elevated him into the outright lead at two under par. He finished at 143 after a 73.

"I was pretty excited about it. I felt like I was getting a little bit into a zone," Hossler said. "Unfortunately, I kind of lost it coming in."

As for losing it. Hunter Mahan and Rickie Fowler each made a triple bogey in his round. Nick Watney wiped out his double eagle (albatross) from Thursday with a double bogey. Matt Kuchar made a double bogey, too. In all, there were 11 scores of triple bogey or more on the day and 89 double bogeys — and the course overall played slightly easier in yielding a 74.051 scoring average to the field.

Therefore, Hossler could be forgiven for his troubles. At 17 years and three months, Hossler became the youngest competitor to make the 36-hole cut in U.S. Open history. And he was still very much in the championship, tied for ninth place, something that could not be said for many top players who got dismissed. The cut of low 60 scores and ties came at eight-over 148 with 69 professionals and three amateurs advancing to the weekend.

Among the notable players eliminated at 149 were current Masters champion Bubba Watson and 2010 Open Championship winner Louis Oosthuizen. Notable players beyond that score included the world Nos. 1 and 2, respectively, Luke Donald and Rory McIlroy, the defending champion who made more bogeys in two rounds than he had in all of the 2011 U.S. Open at Congressional.

Other casualties included 14-year-old Chinese amateur Andy Zhang (157), the youngest player in U.S. Open history, who came through as an alternate in the sectional qualifying.

World No. 3 Lee Westwood shot 71–145 to be the highest remaining player in the World Ranking. But perhaps the most noteworthy survivor was Phil Mickelson. Capping his round with a nine-foot birdie putt on the home hole, Mickelson shot an even-par 70 to come in at 147. He trailed the leaders by eight strokes, a consideration he wasn't prepared yet to address. "I haven't really looked at the leaderboard. I've been more on the cut line," Mickelson said. "It depends on how Saturday goes."

But Woods wasn't the only one playing solid golf. He had worthy company in Furyk and Toms. Furyk, who had near-misses in the U.S. Open in 2006 and 2007, was steady tee to green, leading the field in greens hit in regulation, which helped him to a 69. A 40-foot birdie putt from off the third green was his highlight.

Toms, meanwhile, refused to give in, even with 30 putts on his day. "What I've done well this week is concentrate," said Toms after posting his 70, "...I've just really managed my game."

Second-Round Leaders: Jim Furyk 69–139, Tiger Woods 70–139, David Toms 70–139, John Peterson 70–141, Nicholas Colsaerts 69–141, Graeme McDowell 72–141, Michael Thompson 75–141, Blake Adams 70–142, Jason Dufner 71–143, K.J. Choi 70–143, Aaron Watkins 71–143, Fredrik Jacobson 71–143, Raphael Jacquelin 71–143, Matt Kuchar 73–143, Beau Hossler 73–143, Charl Schwartzel 70–143, Hunter Mahan 71–143

Third Round

Two former U.S. Open champions found their way to the top after 54 holes at The Olympic Club. The surprise was that one of them wasn't Tiger Woods. Instead, they were Jim Furyk and Graeme McDowell.

The Olympic Club was slightly more accommodating on a sun-drenched Saturday. But that didn't mean it was easy, playing to an average of just over 72. Just after 3 p.m. there was not one player under par, although later Furyk returned to that level and McDowell was able to join him.

The magnificent tree-lined layout clearly wasn't easy for Woods, who through two rounds had played largely impeccable golf. But while 13 players broke par, Woods had a flurry of bogeys that all but buried his chances of winning a fourth U.S. Open title and 15th major championship. He posted a 75 that left him five strokes behind at four-over 214.

Playing in the final pairing with Woods, Furyk handled the huge galleries and the course as well as anyone could expect, starting slowly, just like Woods, but holding it together with clutch putting to shoot 70 and complete three rounds at one-under 209.

"It is a little bit of a struggle at times," Furyk said. "I think you have to bide your time and get through certain holes each day trying to make pars. And there will be a couple of opportunities you get. There are some — if you can drive the ball in the fairway, there are some places you can get short irons in your hand and there are some pins that you can attack. You just have to be patient and wait for those moments instead of trying to force them."

Joining Furyk at 209 was McDowell, who shot a 68 and had a share of the third-round lead on the PGA Tour for only the second time in his career. "Probably for the first time this week, I actually enjoyed the round of golf," McDowell said, joking slightly, after he capped off his day with a four-foot putt for birdie at the 18th. "It was quite nice out there."

Fredrik Jacobson shot a 68 and was in third place alone at one-over 211. Lee Westwood, who earlier in the year at the Masters posted his seventh top-three finish in a major championship, a record for a player yet to win, shared the low round of the day with Casey Wittenberg, a 67. The English veteran was among four players who were three strokes behind, joined by Blake Adams, Nicolas Colsaerts and two-time U.S. Open champion Ernie Els, who chipped in for eagle at the par-five 16th, his second eagle of the week, for a 68.

An eclectic group at 213 included amateur Beau Hossler, who shot his second 70, Jason Dufner (70) and John Peterson (72), plus Webb Simpson, John Senden and Kevin Chappell, all of whom snuck into the picture with 68s. Chappell tied for third the previous year at Congressional.

Thirteen players were within four strokes of the lead. The year before no one was within six of Rory McIlroy.

Woods quickly fell out of the lead with two bogeys in the first three holes. He botched the par-fives when birdies could have salvaged the day. To top things off, he missed the green at the 18th with a wedge, then chucked his chip shot to lead to one last bogey. Only eight players had a score higher than his 75.

"I struggled on the greens today, quite a bit," said Woods, who needed 34 putts after 30 each of the first two days.

In recent years Woods has shown more of a penchant for weekend flame-outs. Two months earlier at the Masters, he backed up with a 74, and the year prior on Saturday at Augusta he posted an identical number. At Pebble Beach in 2010, he closed with a 75. But this was a shocking setback after he had appeared in command.

"Tomorrow, I'm just going to have to shoot a good round, and post early and see what happens," Woods said.

Woods wasn't the only big name to stumble. David Toms, who began the day tied atop the leaderboard with Woods and Furyk, never got on track with a 76. Another 40-something player also saw his hopes dim. On his 42nd birthday, Phil Mickelson, after a second consecutive 71, stood at eight-over 218 and knew he would need a monster rally for a shot at the title.

Third-Round Leaders: Graeme McDowell 68–209, Jim Furyk 70–209, Fredrik Jacobson 68–211, Lee Westwood 67–212, Ernie Els 68–212, Blake Adams 70–212, Nicolas Colsaerts 71–212, Webb Simpson 68–213, Kevin Chappell 68–213, John Senden 68–213, Beau Hossler 70–213, Jason Dufner 70–213, John Peterson 72–213

Fourth Round

Fog drifted onto The Olympic Club late on Sunday morning. For a final round that lacked clarity until the end, it seemed appropriate that the champion should emerge seemingly from out of nowhere, shrouded from attention for much of the day — and as it turned out, for much of the week as well. Nevertheless Webb Simpson proved a worthy winner of the U.S. Open.

A second consecutive two-under-par 68, built with a mid-round burst of birdies and saved at the end with a par save from a gnarly greenside lie at the 18th hole, enabled the 26-year-old to claim his first major championship victory.

Simpson made his way to the clubhouse with a one-over 281 total and then watched on television, seated with his wife Dowd in the basement locker room level, to see if anyone could catch him. No one did, including third-round co-leaders Jim Furyk and Graeme McDowell, who each needed a birdie at the home hole to tie and send the championship to an 18-hole Monday playoff.

Twenty-six players began the final round within six shots of the lead. One of them was Tiger Woods, who had never trailed after 54 holes in any of his 14 major victories. But Woods quickly blew himself out of the championship with a meltdown even more shocking than his disheveled display of golf the previous afternoon.

Beginning the day five strokes in arrears, Woods picked up where he left off — or make that dropped off. He went to six over par after six holes before leveling out, and only a few meaningless birdies at the end salvaged a 73 and a tie for 21st place at seven-over 287.

With Phil Mickelson dropping to a tie for 65th with a listless 78–296 effort, this marked the first U.S. Open since 2003 that neither Woods nor Mickelson finished among the top 10. Lee Westwood did finish in the top 10, coming home in 73–285 to tie for 10th, small consolation for a man still seeking his first major title. There was no luck for Ernie Els either. He got within two strokes of the lead after his third eagle of the championship at the seventh hole, but bogeyed the next two holes and never got closer. He shot a 72 for ninth place alone at 284. "I just made some soft errors," Els lamented.

So did Beau Hossler, the teenager who began the final day just four strokes behind the leaders and three ahead of his nearest challenger for low amateur, Jordan Spieth, who had just completed his freshman year at the University of Texas. Spieth ended up with the coveted low amateur prize, with a 69-70 weekend for a 287 total, tying Woods and others for

21st place. Hossler, who intends to become a Texas teammate of Spieth, shot a 76 to fall to 289 and a tie for 29th place.

Michael Thompson, the first-round leader, reached the clubhouse just after 5 p.m. with a score to beat, shooting a 67 to complete 72 holes in two-over 282. With a wedge to 10 feet, Thompson birdied the 16th and looked like he was going to match his first-round 66 — the low round of the championship — when another wedge set up a five-footer for birdie at the 17th. But he hit the putt through the break and had to settle for par.

"His speed had been good all day. Probably just a bit of nerves, but he played great," said David Toms, who with a 68 tied for fourth at 283.

"Coming up short leaves a really bitter taste in your mouth," Thompson said, "but at the same time, being in contention and having a chance to win is what were are out here playing for. And that's why we love the game is we love to compete and we love to be in that spotlight and have a chance."

With Thompson in, only three men looked capable of stepping up to beat him: Simpson and the two former U.S. Open champions, Furyk and McDowell.

Four birdies in a five-hole stretch gave Simpson a scent of the lead he hadn't been near all week. The run started with a seven iron to five feet at the tough par-four sixth, then he followed with two more birdies to cut a six-shot deficit in half.

Then Simpson knocked a wedge to three feet at the 10th hole and converted his sixth straight one-putt green that got him within one stroke of Furyk. With the pressure mounting, the birdies dried up. Simpson missed from five feet at the 15th and then couldn't convert at either of the back-to-back par-fives.

That turn of events looked ominous when Simpson's approach from the rough at the 18th drifted right of the green and disappeared into a circle of dirt that may have been the remnants of an old sprinkler head. There was a clump of grass behind the ball, but Simpson somehow scraped it out to three feet and buried the putt for a par.

"That was an impossible shot," said Nicolas Colsaerts, who played alongside Simpson. "With that lie he had, he was dead. That was kind of a miracle."

Both Furyk and McDowell had their chances at the 18th. McDowell, who hit only three fairways all afternoon, bogeyed four holes on the first nine. But when he banged home a 20-foot birdie at the 17th, he was somehow still alive. That was thanks to Furyk, who failed to birdie a single hole all day. Still, at the 16th hole, Furyk had the championship in his hands. He stood two over par for the day, one over for the championship.

An indecisive moment at the par-five 16th led to disaster for Furyk. Trying to draw a three wood around the trees, Furyk instead launched a duck hook into the trees. He couldn't recover and made bogey to fall one behind. A disappointing par at the 17th left him having to go for broke on the 18th to try to force a playoff.

When Furyk and McDowell arrived at the short but stout home hole, there had been only six birdies converted there all day, many with long downhill putts. With the greens remaining firm, players found it nearly impossible to get the ball close to the front-left hole location.

From a scruffy lie in the left rough, McDowell at least had an angle to work with and came through with a clutch shot from 115 yards out that settled 25 feet from the hole. It was Furyk's turn, and another hook proved devastating as his wedge approach sailed into a poor lie in the left greenside bunker. Instead of a birdie, Furyk suffered a bogey for a closing 74 and 283 total that dropped him into a tie for fourth place with Toms, Jason Dufner, John Peterson and Padraig Harrington.

"I was tied for the lead, sitting on the 16th tee," Furyk said. "I've got wedges in my hand, or reachable par-fives, on the way in, and one birdie wins the golf tournament. I'm definitely frustrated. I don't know how to put that one into words, but I had my opportunities and my chances and it was right there. It was, on the back nine, it was my tournament to win."

That left only McDowell, but after a long look at the left-breaking putt, he failed to get the ball on line from the start. It rolled harmlessly past the hole, leaving McDowell with a 73 and 282 total, tied for second with Thompson.

"Oh, wow," Simpson said, looking at his beaming wife, when McDowell's putt went asking.

Wow indeed. Of the last 18 players to tee off in the final round, Simpson was the only one to break par. "It hasn't set in yet," Simpson said. "Greensboro, my first win ... I was the overnight leader, and I won by three. And I just kind of dreamt it up in my head that I was going to win there. This feels much different. It hasn't sunk in at all. When Graeme missed on 18, and I realized I had won, I just kind of shook my head in disbelief. I couldn't believe it actually happened."

The Final Leaders: Webb Simpson 68–281, Michael Thompson 67–282, Graeme McDowell 73–282, David Toms 68–283, Padraig Harrington 68–283, John Peterson 70–283, Jason Dufner 70–283, Jim Furyk 74–283, Ernie Els 72–284, Casey Wittenberg 70–285, Retief Goosen 71–285, John Senden 72–285, Kevin Chappell 72–285, Lee Westwood 73–285

4. The Open Championship

Ernie Els had known disappointments in golf, not the least of which came in the 1996 Open Championship. He bogeyed two of the last three holes and Tom Lehman came away as the winner at Royal Lytham & St. Annes, the venue of this year's championship. It was one of his six runner-up finishes in the majors to go along with his U.S. Open victories in 1994 and 1997 and the Open Championship at Muirfield in 2002.

This year it was Adam Scott's time to have that disappointment while the 42-year-old South African experienced a rekindling of his highest ambitions.

Els had not won since claiming the South African Open, in December 2010. His slide began in July 2005 when he injured his left knee in a boating accident. In the next four years he won only once on the PGA Tour in America and three times in Europe.

In this time Els and Liezl, his wife, learned that Ben, their second child and first son, was autistic. At first they kept this to themselves, only revealing it to the public in 2008, when the Els family moved to Florida for more advanced autism treatment than could be found in Britain, where they had been living.

At the start of 2012 Els had fallen so far down the World Ranking that he was chasing a victory to get an invitation to the Masters. It never came. At the Transitions Championship in March, he lost after missing a series of short putts towards the end. "In March I looked like an absolute fool," Els said. "People were laughing at me and making jokes about me and really hitting me low, saying I was done and I should hang it up."

That could have been only a minority view, given the respect in which Els is held throughout the game. A ninth-place finish at the U.S. Open was a boost to his morale and showed the work he had undertaken on his long game, his fitness and his hand-eye coordination was paying off.

He arrived at Royal Lytham feeling good about his game. "It's an amazing game. You have to have a positive feel," Els said. "If you give yourself positive vibes, sometimes positive things happen. ... It's hard to explain. For some reason I felt something good was going to come out of this. Even if I didn't win, I was going to feel good about it because of the work I've put in. My game is back to where I feel I can compete."

Only Sir Henry Cotton, with 11 years between his second Open victory in 1937 and his third in 1948, had gone longer before reclaiming that famous prize of the Open, the Claret Jug. The trophy all but had Scott's name engraved on it for 2012 before Els came from six strokes behind with nine holes to play. He returned a 68 for a total of 273, seven under par, coming home in 32 strokes with a birdie on the final hole. Scott came back in 39 to finish on six under with a 75 that resulted from bogeys on his last four holes. Els never led while he was on the golf course. He signed his scorecard and waited on the putting green in hopes of a playoff while Scott completed the final two holes.

Both Els and Scott were shocked by the outcome. "Thankfully, he's young enough," Els said of his Australian friend. "He's 32 years old. He's got the next 10 years that he can win more than I've won. I've won four times now (in major championships); and I think he can win more than that."

First Round

The first round was played under surprisingly gentle conditions after there had been wind and rain on the practice days. There was an occasional shower but no wind, the course was soft and the greens were holding. All 156 competitors broke 80 for the first time in 14 years and 36 of them were under the par score of 70.

Adam Scott posted a 64, six under par, and was one stroke ahead of Paul Lawrie, Zach Johnson and Nicolas Colsaerts, and two strokes ahead of Brandt Snedeker. In addition to Lawrie and Johnson, five more former major champions were within three of the lead. Tiger Woods, Ernie Els, Rory McIlroy, Graeme McDowell and Bubba Watson all shot 67s along with Steve Stricker, Peter Hanson and Toshinori Muto.

"It was just like a nice walk in the park," Scott said. "It was not what we experienced in the practice rounds, I'm sure there are going to be some weather elements thrown at us the next three days so we'll have to knuckle down and handle that. But it was very pleasing to go out and play some solid golf and take advantage of the calm conditions."

Plenty of players still struggled. Luke Donald and Padraig Harrington both had 70s; Ian Poulter, Tom Watson, Keegan Bradley and Rickie Fowler 71s; Sergio Garcia, Louis Oosthuizen and Paul Casey 72s; Phil Mickelson and Lee Westwood 73s; Justin Rose 74; Darren Clarke 76, and Martin Kaymer 77.

Scott had a course record and lowest round ever in a major championship in his sights until he bogeyed the final hole. After a bogey at the third hole, Scott collected eight birdies in the next 13 holes to be seven under par with two holes to play. Two pars would better Tom Lehman's course record of 64. If Scott could make one more birdie, he would become the first player to score a 62 in the Open or any major championship.

"I know there has never been a 62," said Scott, who found himself thinking of that going to the 17th tee. " ...I also probably realized then I wasn't going to be the guy to shoot 62. It's one of those things you don't want going through your mind, thinking of your final score and stuff like that. So I got rid of that quickly and got on to playing the 17th. Unfortunately I dropped one up the last."

Scott pulled a two-iron shot off the tee into thick rough on the 18th and did not put his third close enough to save par. But Scott had played some superb golf. His game was resurrected by the use of a long putter, and the friendly Australian now seemed to have become a harder-edged competitor after hiring Steve Williams, formerly with Woods, as his caddie. He had opened with a 62 and romped to a victory in the 2011 WGC - Bridgestone Invitational.

In 2012, Scott's first rounds in the major championships had been poor. "I've been playing well in the majors this year but shooting myself in the foot in the first round," Scott said. "That's where a guy with experience like Steve can help. He wanted me to go to the first tee today like it was the 72nd and you have three to win. Really switch yourself on. That was a good trigger to have."

No one would know then that Scott would come to the 72nd hole needing a three to win the Open, but that morning, at the only venue on the Open rota to begin with a par-three hole, it was the ideal settler for Scott.

"These greens are always kept at a speed where if there's no wind we all feel comfortable that we can hole at lot of putts," Scott said. "The greens are very flat and there are very subtle breaks, but if you get your eye in, they roll pure, so you can hole a lot of putts."

Lawrie, with his 65, chipped in at the third and fifth holes while scoring three birdies in a row, then holed a long putt at the sixth hole for a par. "It was probably the strangest start of my career," said Lawrie, the 1999 Open champion. "I didn't really hit many good shots, but I was three under. Obviously we get enough bad luck, it is nice when it goes our way now and again. After that I played some solid golf and hit the ball in all the right places."

For his 65, Colsaerts was helped by holing his eight-iron shot from 200 yards for an eagle-two at the second hole. The other returning a 65, Johnson, had won the previous week at the John Deere Classic and that form had traveled with him across the Atlantic. The former Masters champion got to six under par for the day with four birdies on the second nine before his second bogey of the day at the 17th hole.

Partly, Johnson was inspired by playing in the group with the defending champion, Clarke, and the 2002 champion, Els. "They are fun to play with," Johnson said. "They've got great rhythm and great tempo. It's easy to be with them."

That was truer of Els, with his 67, than of Clarke. "I don't think you could publish my thoughts right now," Clarke said after his 76.

First-Round Leaders: Adam Scott 64, Paul Lawrie 65, Zach Johnson 65, Nicolas Colsaerts 65, Brandt Snedeker 66, Ernie Els 67, Bubba Watson 67, Graeme McDowell 67, Tiger Woods 67, Toshinori Muto 67, Rory McIlroy 67, Steve Stricker 67, Peter Hanson 67

Second Round

With an afternoon tee time, Adam Scott was not surprised to find he was no longer leading when his round started, but it was not expected that Brandt Snedeker was the one at the top of the leaderboard. Snedeker matched the 64 by Scott the previous day and his total of 130, 10 under par, tied the Open record for the first 36 holes set by Sir Nick Faldo with the same 66-64 scores at Muirfield in 1992.

Scott followed with a 67 that left him one stroke behind Snedeker, and both were well ahead of the rest until Tiger Woods picked up two strokes on the last three holes, finishing with a dramatic hole-out from a greenside bunker on the 18th, to finish in third place with a 67 and a 134 total. A short time later, Denmark's Thorbjorn Olesen birdied the last two holes for a 66 to be next at 135.

There was a sizable presence at four under par, 136, with Paul Lawrie, Graeme McDowell, Matt Kuchar, Thomas Aiken and Jason Dufner, who matched Olesen's 66. Ernie Els, at 137 after his 70, rounded out the top 10 leaders.

It took heroic effort just for the second round to get underway. A heavy rain overnight had fallen on the saturated ground. Despite pumping out water from the bunkers, the water table was so high that a few contained water for the rest of the day, in some cases the rest of the week. The organizers had a bigger headache preparing the site for spectators, but they managed an on-time start to play at 6:30 a.m.

Snedeker admitted to being surprised by his score, saying in his press conference, "I am sure everybody in this room is in about as much shock as I am right now."

Remarkably, Snedeker had yet to record a bogey in his card. He was the first since Woods at St. Andrews in 2000 to complete the first 36 holes of a major championship without a bogey. Known as a streaky putter, the 31-year-old from Nashville, Tennessee, was on a roll here. "I'm making every 25-footer I look at, so that makes it a lot easier," Snedeker said. "I'm getting some good breaks and playing some pretty good golf."

Snedeker had not been in any of Royal Lytham's 206 bunkers in the first two days. "To hit it in no bunkers around here, you have to get lucky," Snedeker admitted. "I've gotten very fortunate when I was hitting bad shots and haven't gone into bunkers or particularly heavy rough. I don't expect that stat to hold over the weekend. I'm fully prepared to hit it in a few bunkers."

Teeing off after Snedeker had taken the lead, Scott said, "That doesn't matter, that's usual in these tournaments. I saw that he was 10 under after a few holes and I just had to stay patient and wait for my opportunities. They are hard to come by until you get to the seventh."

Scott dropped a shot at the third hole but reached the green at the seventh in two strokes and two-putted for his first birdie of the day. He holed a 45-foot putt for a birdie at the 10th, then made another two-putt birdie at the 11th. "It was a bit of a slow start, but I built my momentum from the seventh onwards," Scott said. "I didn't take any unnecessary risks, so it was kind of stress-free.

A large crowd had gathered at the 18th to see the late starters and Scott did not disappoint them. He hit a nine-iron shot to three feet and capped off the round with a fourth birdie. "It was the first time this week coming up the 18th with the grandstands almost full," he said. "The best 18th hole in golf is always at the Open Championship. It was great. A warm reception and a few Aussie flags, so it was good to see them supporting."

It was Woods who stole the show at the 18th, despite having hit his approach shot into the middle bunker on the right of the green. "It wasn't as hard as it may have looked," Woods said. "I was on an upslope, so I could take out that steepness coming off the bunker and land the ball on the flat. So I just threw it up there and played it about a cup outside the left. It landed on my spot and rolled to the right." And into the hole.

There were plenty of casualties falling down the leaderboard. Nicolas Colsaerts suffered a precipitous drop to 142 after a 77 that included a triple-bogey eight at the seventh, where the Belgian drove into a bunker. Rory McIlroy had a 75 and also fell to two over par.

Among those who just made the cut at three over were Bubba Watson, Lee Westwood, Keegan Bradley, John Daly and Rickie Fowler. A total of 83 players qualified for the weekend, but not among them were Justin Rose and Sergio Garcia (144), Tom Lehman and David Duval (145), Martin Kaymer and Sandy Lyle (146), Darren Clarke (147), and Paul Casey and Phil Mickelson (151). Mickelson had a 78 with three double bogeys.

Second-Round Leaders: Brandt Snedeker 64–130, Adam Scott 67–131, Tiger Woods 67–134, Thorbjorn Olesen 66–135, Paul Lawrie 71–136, Matt Kuchar 67–136, Graeme McDowell 69–136, Jason Dufner 66–136, Thomas Aiken 68–136, Ernie Els 70–137

Third Round

"It's a great leaderboard," said Adam Scott, looking back after his score of 68 saw him move from one stroke behind Brandt Snedeker at the halfway stage to four strokes ahead of everyone with one round to play. "And a four-shot lead doesn't seem to be very much this year on any golf tournament that I've watched. It doesn't mean that much."

Scott finished with a total of 11-under-par 199. A superb last nine from Graeme McDowell for a 67 and a late rally from Snedeker for a 73 put his nearest challengers at 203, seven under. Tiger Woods started poorly, recovered well but couldn't quite finish off the round, and was at 70 and 204. Zach Johnson, whose 66 was the best score of the day, and Ernie Els, with his 68, were tied for fifth place at 205.

While taking nothing for granted, after many come-from-behind victories on various tours this year, Scott played a round that was worthy of his advantage while paired in the final group with Snedeker. At the fifth hole Snedeker missed a short putt and recorded his first bogey of the week. At the next he found his first bunker of the championship. Both Scott and Snedeker birdied the par-five seventh, but then Snedeker had bogeys on the next two holes, plus the 11th and 14th holes. Scott birdied the eighth from 30 feet to go out in 32.

Scott had the chance at the 11th for an eagle from 30 feet to go 13 under but took two putts for his third birdie of the day. He dropped a stroke at the 13th but played steadily with pars the rest of the way. "It was a solid round," Scott said. "I think a 68 accurately reflects the way I played. I certainly made a couple of nice putts. I may have left a few chances out there, but considering the circumstances and how much trouble there is on this course, it was all solid stuff."

It was yet another calm day, but with many difficult hole locations there was no repeat of the record-equaling scores of the first two days. "They have put the pins in tough spots for the last two days," Scott said. That made it tough for anyone to make an upward run on the leaderboard. Lee Westwood had a 71 to be at 214, and Rory McIlroy dropped to 215 after a 73. Luke Donald was at 209 after a 71, with 10 strokes still between him and the leader.

Mark Calcavecchia, the 52-year-old former champion, was at 208 with what he called an "adventuresome" round of 69 with six birdies, three bogeys and a double bogey. These three players — Dustin Johnson, Louis Oosthuizen and Bill Haas — all shot 68s in both the second and third rounds to be, respectfully, at 209, 208 and 207.

Zach Johnson made a prominent move after starting at one under par and getting to five-under 205. The key to his round of six birdies and two bogeys was not getting into trouble. He missed only one fairway and his two dropped shots were both from three-putting. "I don't think I could play more aggressively than I did today," Johnson said. "I knew if I was going to get back into the tournament I had to make a move of some sort. For me that was making sure I got it on the fairways and the greens."

Els joined Johnson at 205 with a round of 68, striking the ball superbly and playing some fine golf. He birdied the most difficult hole of the day, the sixth, and then seventh to be out in 32. His only dropped shot came at the 14th, but he took that back with a birdie at the 17th. "I did a lot of good things today," Els said. "I struck it nicely and gave myself a lot of opportunities."

Playing with Els was another South African, Thomas Aiken, who had a 71 to be at 207. "I've played with Ernie quite a few times," Aiken said. "I get along well with him and we played a practice round together on Tuesday. But it gets a bit despondent when the crowd is going 'Ernie, Ernie' all the time. There were a few cheers for me, but he is such a great guy, really down to earth."

Els admitted to using his relationship with the gallery to his advantage. "You can feed off this crowd," he said. "This crowd really knows the game well and knows the golf course well. They know when you've hit a good shot or a poor one. The Open is very special in that way."

Birdies on the 16th and 18th holes limited the damage of Snedeker's round to a 73. "Those two late birdies salvaged what could have been a horrific round into a pretty awful one, so I've still got a chance," Snedeker said. "It was one of these things when you find out if you have some guts or not. I could have packed up and gone home today but I didn't. It was just one of those days when you shake your head and wonder what you're doing out there. The short miss at the fifth was the first poor putt I've hit all week, and then I found out how tough these bunkers are. I found a few of them today and they are not much fun."

McDowell had to be patient as he played the first seven holes in one over par, but he was four under for the last 11 holes, completing his 67. A nine-iron shot to 12 feet set up a birdie at the eighth, and then he birdied three of the fearsome last par-fours. A 15-footer went in at the 13th, a 40-footer at the next, and a 12-footer at the 17th. On the wrong side of a ridge on the 18th, he was happy to two-putt.

"I felt the tournament was slipping away and really needed to dig deep for some patience," McDowell said. "The birdie on the eighth settled me down, and from the 14th tee onwards, it's probably as good as I've swung the club all week. I hit some nice shots and made some nice putts."

By posting his total of 203 ahead of Snedeker, McDowell ensured that he would go out in the final pairing with Scott. McDowell said, "For sure, since I was a young boy I dreamed of coming down that last fairway on a Sunday afternoon in the last group of the Open Championship."

Third-Round Leaders: Adam Scott 68–199, Graeme McDowell 67–203, Brandt Snedeker 73–203, Tiger Woods 70–204, Zach Johnson 66–205, Ernie Els 68–205, Thorbjorn Olesen 71–206, Bill Haas 68–207, Thomas Aiken 71–207, Bubba Watson 68–208, Louis Oosthuizen 68–208, Mark Calcavecchia 69–208, Matt Kuchar 72–208

Fourth Round

Late into the Sunday afternoon the championship looked to be Adam Scott's. In the same pairing, Graeme McDowell said, "I honestly thought when he striped it down the middle of 15, this guy is going to win and win it well. I felt Adam's name was on the trophy, I really did. Little did I know."

Then Scott bogeyed the last four holes and Ernie Els produced one of the great finishes in championship history. Six strokes behind with nine holes to play, Els came home in 32 to post a 68 and a total of 273, seven under par. After holing his birdie putt on the 18th green, Els went off to wait on the putting green.

When Scott bogeyed the last hole, not even a playoff was required. Scott finished with a 75 and a total of 274. While Scott stood wondering what had just happened, Els was stunned. "Amazing, I'm still numb," Els said an hour later. "It's just crazy, crazy, crazy."

"I really do feel for my buddy, Scottie," Els said at the prize-giving and in his post-round interview. "I've been there before. I've blown majors before and I just hope he doesn't take it as hard as I did." Els said as much to Scott personally after the trophy presentation.

Starting the day tied for fifth place, six strokes behind Scott, Els dropped a shot further back with a bogey at the second hole and was still seven strokes back with 14 holes to play. He holed a putt from six feet for par at the sixth. He two-putted from 20 feet for his par-five on the seventh and missed a good birdie chance from six feet at the eighth and missed another from eight feet at the ninth.

"I was really angry with myself at the ninth," Els said. "But that got me into a different mindset. It really got me aggressive. I hit a lot of drivers on the back nine and I was trying to make birdies. I felt good. For once I wasn't thinking ahead, I wasn't thinking back, I was right in the moment. I was really just hitting the shot in the moment. When you've been around as long as I have, you've seen a lot of things happen. I felt the course is such that if you have any doubt, it was going to bite you. There are too many bunkers, too much trouble, and there was a lot of breeze. I felt I was going to hit the shots I needed and that I still had a chance."

For the first time during the championship there was a decent breeze, helping to make the course slightly firmer than on previous days. While others struggled to adapt, Els went on to produce a mighty performance on the inward nine. He hit a driver and then a sand wedge to the green at the 10th, and finally he holed a significant putt, from 18 feet, and he was headed in the right direction.

At the short 12th Els hit a six iron to seven feet and made another birdie. A huge drive at the 14th left just a sand-wedge approach and he made a 12-footer to get to six under par. Playing two holes ahead of Scott, Els still found himself three behind, but there was no stopping him now. Another pounding drive at the 18th left him in perfect position. He hit a wedge to 15 feet and received a huge ovation from the standing gallery in the grandstands.

"They were behind me all week," Els said. "The last four holes we had a magnificent crowd. They were really rooting for me and it really inspired me."

When Els rolled in the putt on the final green the crowd rose to him again. His 68 put Els on a total of 273 and meant he now had 39 rounds in the 60s in the Open, two ahead of the previous record-holder, Sir Nick Faldo.

The roar from the 18th green rolled back over the links and hit Scott and McDowell in the 17th fairway. Scott was about to make a crucial mistake, but McDowell had already played his way out of the championship. He closed with a 75 to share fifth place at 278 with Luke Donald, who finished strongly with a 69. One stroke further ahead, tied for third place, were Tiger Woods and Brandt Snedeker, after rounds of 73 and 74 respectively. A triple bogey on the sixth hole and three bogeys in a row from the 13th ended Woods's hopes.

Scott had a nervous start, going bogey-birdie-bogey, then dropped another shot at the sixth. But after that he kept finding fairways and greens, the sort of solid play that would bring him the championship. He holed from 15 feet at the 14th for a birdie to get back to one over par for the day and 10 under for the week. He led by four strokes over Els, who had just completed the 16th.

"I was surprisingly calm the whole round," Scott said. "A little nervous on the first tee but less so than yesterday ... but once I was out there I felt completely in control. And even in the last few holes, I didn't feel it was a case of nerves or anything like that."

Scott missed the green at the 15th with a four iron and found a bunker. He came out to 10 feet but missed the putt. One stroke was gone but he had three still in hand. His approach to the 16th flew over the flag and ran to the back of the green. He took three putts for another bogey. Scott pulled his six-iron approach to the 17th and missed the green to the left, in some thick rough. His chip came out heavy and he missed a long putt for his par. The third successive bogey meant he was now tied with Els.

On the 18th tee, Scott took a three wood and found the second of three bunkers on the left. The ball was up against the face of the bunker and he could only chip out sideways. He now needed to get up and down from around 150 yards out. His approach was on line but pulled up eight feet short of the hole. He missed the putt on the left to come home in 39 strokes for the closing 75 and total of six under par.

Scott had little time to compose himself before speaking to the media, but he acquitted himself well. "It was a sloppy finish," he said. "I wasn't out of position all week until I managed to get myself into trouble on the last few holes. Obviously, I'm disappointed. I let a great chance slip through my fingers. But I don't think I've ever played so well in a major championship, so that's a good thing moving forward. Today is just one of those days, that's why they call it golf."

The Final Leaders: Ernie Els 68–273, Adam Scott 75–274, Tiger Woods 73–277, Brandt Snedeker 74–277, Luke Donald 69–278, Graeme McDowell 75–278, Nicolas Colsaerts 65–279, Thomas Aiken 72–279, Geoff Ogilvy 67–280, Miguel Jimenez 67–280, Ian Poulter 67–208, Alexander Noren 69–280, Vijay Singh 70–280, Dustin Johnson 71–280, Matt Kuchar 72–280, Mark Calcavecchia 72–280, Thorbjorn Olesen 74–280, Zach Johnson 75–280

5. PGA Championship

In the Emerald Isle, where the wee people go tripping through the heather, wonderful mysteries abound. From the distant, misty past, there are the stones of Newgrange. Of more recent history, just over a century ago, there is the theft of the Crown Jewels of Ireland. And of more immediate vintage, there was the disappearance of Rory McIlroy, and this was of particular interest coming into the 94th PGA Championship.

Nothing is known of Newgrange or the crown jewels, but with respect to McIlroy, the question was — who was that playing slipshod golf under his name? Consider, first, that the glowing predictions of McIlroy's future got even brighter when he ran away with the 2011 U.S. Open Championship by a record eight strokes. Then early in the PGA Tour's 2012 season, he added to his considerable portfolio with a two-stroke victory in the Honda Classic over Tom Gillis and Tiger Woods.

But suddenly, in four starts from mid-May, McIlroy missed the cut three times, in The Players Championship, the Memorial Tournament and the U.S. Open, followed by a tie for 60th in the Open Championship. It was a slump — but at age 23? How to explain it? One possibility, some offered, was that he'd been afflicted with romance in the person of Danish tennis player Caroline Wozniacki. Whatever the reason, McIlroy was clearly off his game. But then came a flicker of encouragement.

The week before the PGA, McIlroy tied for fifth place in the WGC - Bridgestone Invitational. He said he hadn't felt that good since back in May. How did he get straightened out? "It's just stuff like working it out," he said, "and finding a way to get back to where you were." It seems he found his way. He went out and won the PGA Championship, the fourth and final major of the year, by a ridiculous eight strokes over a wind-whipped Ocean Course near Charleston, on Kiawah Island, a barrier island on the coast of South Carolina.

Even a fabulist would be hard-pressed to sell the kind of story McIlroy came up against. He won against a bunch of challengers that included the famous, the faded, the unknown, the little-known, insiders, outsiders, resurrected and who-knows-what. The famous included, of course, Tiger Woods. The unknown and little-known? There was England's David Lynn, who finished second, and Holland's Joost Luiten, perhaps the most obscure of the obscure. Then there was John Daly, the hero of Crooked Stick, 1991, who brought wild hair and the wild swing to golf. And Vijay Singh, 49, a two-time PGA champion. And so it went, for four grinding days across a course that, truth be known, would have been no problem without the winds off the Atlantic.

In such a field, through turbulent weather across a 7,606-yard course, McIlroy came from behind against Woods, defending champion Keegan Bradley, Ian Poulter and a surprisingly strong Carl Pettersson, among others. McIlroy showed superb control in winds that blew for the last three rounds and were brutally strong in the second. With his long, high shots, he took advantage of a course that was softened by rains. And in his march to the championship, he posted these remarkable statistics: He went the first 22 holes and the last 23 without a bogey, and made just seven overall.

"To sit up here and see this trophy and call myself a multiple major champion," McIlroy told the media, "...not many people have done it, and yeah, I'm very privileged to join such an elite list of names."

First Round

It's not often that something other than the event takes over the story, but this time, traffic did, what with thousands daily clogging the two-lane road serving the Ocean Course on Kiawah Island. Three comments could sum up the week:

Said Tiger Woods on Monday: "I don't know how the spectators are going to get around this place. First of all, I don't know how they're going to get to it."

Said Charleston's newspaper, *The Post and Courier*, on Friday: "Anyone driving to the PGA Championship today may just want to pull over and watch golf at the Charleston Municipal Golf Course instead."

Said World Golf Hall of Fame writer Dan Jenkins on Twitter on Saturday: "Good leaderboard, but the real heroes this week are the fans. What it takes to get here, be here and leave here is legendary."

PGA officials did avoid one problem, however. They declared all the sandy reaches of the Ocean Course to be "through the green," meaning there were no bunkers. Players could ground their clubs in the sand and even take practice swings. So there would be no repeat of Dustin Johnson's debacle in 2010 at Whistling Straits.

It took a little getting used to. "I thought, just have a practice swing, just to see what it feels like," said Adam Scott. "I think that's the most odd thing I've ever experienced."

Then there was another element. Sorry to dredge up that old Scottish adage, but it did fit nicely for the first round of this PGA Championship. Goes the saying: "If it's nae wind and nae rain, it's nae golf." It paraphrases comfortably for the PGA: "If it's nae wind, the Ocean Course is nae dragon." And the Ocean Course was said to be a real dragon. The one Colin Montgomerie played in 22 under par to win the 1997 World Cup individual championship.

When the PGA opened on an sultry August Thursday, the healthcare people could measure the heat and humidity by the number of people who had to be treated for heat problems. There were 180 the first day. On the other hand, golf people could measure the wind by the scores. There was little or nae of it. So of the 156 starters, 65 shot par or better, and of those, 45 broke par, and of those, 24 were in the 60s. This was no way for a proper dragon to behave.

Leading this unceremonious assault was the improbable Willibrordus Adrianus Maria Luiten, 26, of Holland, who answers more readily to "Joost" (pronounced "Yoast"), owner of one victory on the European Tour. While everyone was fixed on the marquee names, Luiten was happily demolishing the Ocean Course with six birdies, an eagle and no bogeys that put him at eight under with four holes to play and flirting with a 63, the record for the majors. Then, alas, he realized where he was. Said Luiten: "You can't deny that you get nervous when you start playing so well in a major and take a big lead." He bogeyed the last four holes for a 68.

That cleared the way for beefy Carl Pettersson, a native Swede and now a naturalized American citizen. He went bogey-free and made six birdies on putts of five, six, 25, 25 (two putts), one and seven feet. "I think we've seen it about as easy as it can get," said Pettersson, whose best finish in seven PGAs was a tie for 24th.

Tiger Woods, now 36 and in the throes of trying to reinvent himself — he had won three times already in 2012 — shot a 69 and came away feeling he'd missed a great opportunity. He made six birdies, but also took three bogeys. No matter. "Anything in the 60s is going to be a good start in a major championship," Woods said, "and I'm right there."

A stroke off the lead, in a group at 67, was the interesting combination of Gary Woodland, who had done so little, and Rory McIlroy, who has done so much. Said Woodland, the power hitter who had fallen quiet: "When I drive it like that, I'm playing a game that most guys can't play out here."

Truth is, despite McIlroy's performance, observers were wondering where he would go from here. He'd won the 2011 U.S. Open by a record eight strokes and won the Honda Classic in March, then missed three cuts in four starts, fizzled in the Open Championship, and finally pulled out of the spin and tied for fifth in the Bridgestone Invitational the week before the PGA. McIlroy had played the Ocean Course a number of times, but stepped out on Thursday with what looked like a suicidal amount of practice. "I played nine holes on Monday, nine holes on Tuesday, and that was it," he said. "I'm pretty comfortable with the golf course." And he proved it. He shot 67, one off the lead, and one of only five bogey-free rounds, joining Pettersson, the leader at 66, Geoff Ogilvy (68), Aaron Baddeley (68) and Ben Curtis (69).

McIlroy birdied his first hole, the 10th, off a wedge to 12 feet. The gem of his five birdies, on a bogey-free day, came at the brutish 14th (his fifth), playing at 249 yards. He fired a towering three iron to 12 feet, plunking the shot down safely away from the severe slopes off the corners. He saved par at the par-three 17th after bouncing his tee shot off a woman and into a bunker. He splashed out to four feet and saved par.

Also at 67 were Spain's Gonzalo Fernandez-Castano and Sweden's Alex Noren.

Keegan Bradley, surprise winner of the 2011 PGA — after he'd apparently choked it away — opened his bid for a repeat with a 68 built on five birdies and an eagle at the par-five 11th, and told of the joys of winning. "Any time I get announced as the PGA Champion," he said, "it gives me chills."

John Daly knew those chills, after his stunning victory in the 1991 PGA. The much troubled Daly, 46 now and given to wearing loud pants, shot 68 with a game its best in years. "It's up and down, but so is my life," Daly said. "Everybody's life is up and down. It's how we battle to get through it."

The PGA wasn't starting out as a rousing final major for the year's major winners. Masters champion Bubba Watson, trying to learn to be a new father, shot a two-birdie 73. U.S. Open champion Webb Simpson, also a new father, shot three-birdie 79 under balmy conditions. And Open Championship winner Ernie Els had a three-birdie, three-bogey par 72.

It also was not a promising start for two other prominent golfers who are still seeking that first major. World No. 1 Luke Donald double-bogeyed the 17th and shot 74, and No. 4 Lee Westwood had a two-birdie 75.

First-Round Leaders: Carl Pettersson 66, Gary Woodland 67, Rory McIlroy 67, Gonzalo Fernandez-Castano 67, Alex Noren 67, John Daly 68, Geoff Ogilvy 68, Keegan Bradley 68, Joost Luiten 68, Aaron Baddeley 68, Adam Scott 68, Scott Piercy 68, Graeme McDowell 68

Second Round

Winds came up strong off the Atlantic, steady all day and gusting to 38 mph, snapping flags across the Ocean Course, and somewhere, Pete Dye, the architect, had to be smiling. Just the way he planned it. The wind brought his devilish design to life. The Ocean Course may look like a classic British links course, but with elevated and bunkered greens, golfers would have to fly the ball in. The low "wind-cheater" shots wouldn't work. Golf became an exercise in aerodynamics: What is the effect of a 30 mph wind on a golf ball measuring 1.68 inches in diameter and traveling at X speed?

The horror stories were rampant. Of a four-iron shot going only 150 yards into the wind. Of having to play 30, 40 yards wide of the target, hoping the crosswind would bring it back. Gentlemen, start your guesswork.

This is why Rory McIlroy's caddie, J.P. Fitzgerald, was to say: "The biggest moment of the week was the birdie at the 14th on Friday, when he held a four iron into the wind and put it on the green."

"Playing it along the ground is not an option here," said Phil Mickelson, after his 71. "You've got to tackle these crosswinds."

At day's end, the par-72 Ocean Course, soft touch in the first round, now in the wind played at an average of 78.1 — the highest since the PGA Championship was changed from match play to stroke play in 1958. Only five players broke par. There were 39 scores in the 80s and two in the 90s. The players weren't amused about it all.

Two-time PGA champion Vijay Singh, with a three-under 69, was the only one to break 70. "If you had a golf course like this and asked me to play in windy conditions, I'd say no," Singh said.

The course was shortened by 147 yards, to 7,521, but that was it for concessions to the wind.

"The PGA didn't get too shy about their set-up," said Northern Ireland's Graeme McDowell, four off the lead after a 76. "I guess they want us all back to level par as soon as possible."

The cut came in at six-over 150, leaving 73 players for the last two rounds.

The surreal day produced some surreal results. Matt Kuchar went from 72 to 82, Rickie Fowler 74-80, Hunter Mahan 72-80 and Jose Maria Olazabal 74-86. Also missing the cut, surprisingly, were Lee Westwood (77), Sergio Garcia (75), Webb Simpson (72), Brandt Snedeker (78) and Jason Day (80).

Three players were able to stay the course. Tiger Woods, Carl Pettersson and Vijay Singh tied at four-under 140 to share a one-stroke lead on Ian Poulter.

Woods's putter, which gave him 23 one-putt greens through the first two rounds, cost him a three-putt bogey from 30 feet and the solo lead at his last hole. His three-birdie, two-bogey 71 dropped him into the tie.

"Holy cow, we're starting the ball so far off line to have it come back in," Woods said. "There's so much drift to this wind, and it doesn't matter whether you hook it or slice it. It's still gonna drift."

Pettersson, starting from No. 10, bogeyed two of his first three holes, and closed with three straight bogeys for a 74. "I thought shooting two over today was like shooting two under yesterday," Pettersson said. "I hit some squirrelly shots, which is typical when it's blowing 30 miles an hour."

Singh, 49 and just six months from Champions Tour eligibility (he's suggested he's not interested), was playing perhaps his best of the season and was happy just to get the day in. "After a while, you don't really think about your score," he said. The par-threes were stubborn. He parred three of them but bogeyed the 14th and wondered, "I don't know what Dye was thinking when he made 14."

The jury was still out on Rory McIlroy after he struggled to a 75, even though he was still just two off the lead. Actually, it was a good 75. He was heading for worse in the wind, what with bogeys at Nos. 5, 7, 10 and 13. He stopped the bleeding at the par-three 14th, with the remarkable wind-beating tee shot to 12 feet.

"It could have been a couple shots better, of course," McIlroy said. "You can't get aggressive with this weather. You don't even care where the pin is. You just try to hit it on the green somewhere."

Ian Poulter came in just a shot off the lead after a bogey at the 18th gave him a 71, and it was a weary Ian Poulter. "You're fighting the wind," he said. "Six-hour rounds ... is going to wear you out." Defending champion Keegan Bradley, after an opening 68, made six bogeys over an 11-hole stretch from No. 4, shooting 77 for a 145, and wasn't discouraged. "I'm only five back," Bradley said. "If it's like this, any round under par, you'll be okay, no matter what."

World No. 1 Luke Donald barely made it through the turn. From the seventh, he went bogey-bogey-bogey-double bogey and shot 76 and just made the cut at 150. "I actually played decently and got nothing out of it," he said.

When the day closed, the wind was still the story. Spain's Gonzalo Fernandez-Castano (78) was asked what was the toughest part of the course in the wind. "Well," he said, "it's everything." France's Marcel Siem (73) on whether it was a satisfying day: "No." And Blake Adams (72), on being informed he was the only player to go through the first 15 holes without a bogey: "Oh, yeah?"

Then there was tomorrow. "I don't know what the forecast is," Woods said, "but if it's anything like this, it's going to be tough."

Second-Round Leaders: Carl Pettersson 74–140, Vijay Singh 69–140, Tiger Woods 71–140, Ian Poulter 71–141, Jamie Donaldson 73–142, Rory McIlroy 75–142, Aaron Baddeley 75–143, Adam Scott 75–143, Blake Adams 72–143, Trevor Immelman 72–143

Third Round

When a golfer saves par out of a tree, it's time to take him seriously. This was Rory McIlroy, at No. 3 in the third round. Until then, it was the Tiger Woods-Vijay Singh-Carl Pettersson show, give or take. But McIlroy birdied the first two holes — No. 1 from 15 feet and No. 2 from long range on two putts — and took the bait and tried to drive the green at the risk-reward No. 3, shortened to 317 yards. And his ball disappeared. The television blimp came to the rescue. It showed the ball lodged in the limb of that stunted, dead-looking cypress near the green, about seven feet off the ground. McIlroy reached up, pulled it out from under the bark — saving himself a lost ball stroke-and-distance penalty — took a penalty drop, pitched on and holed a six-foot putt to save his par. Things like that say this is a guy's time.

"I'm just glad I didn't try to play that ball from the tree," McIlroy quipped, recalling hurting his hand hitting a tree root in the 2011 Masters.

McIlroy went on to birdie three more holes and bogeyed No. 9, and a Saturday that had started with sunshine and somewhat gentler winds got hit by a huge storm in the afternoon. Play had to be called for the day, leaving 27 players to finish the round Sunday morning.

Bo Van Pelt was the leader in the clubhouse with a no-bogey 67 for a three-under 213, but it was an iffy spot, with so many others in better shape and still to finish.

With play halted, McIlroy was six under for the championship through No. 9, tied with Vijay Singh, 49, who hadn't been in contention in a major in six years. Singh birdied the first from 15 feet and the seventh from 25 before play was stopped. Tiger Woods ran off the tracks under kinder conditions Saturday. He bogeyed the fourth after hitting a spectator with his tee shot, bogeyed the par-three fifth after hitting his tee shot into some mounds, and then bogeyed the par-five seventh with two poor shots and a wedge over the green. "I got off to a rough start today and couldn't get anything going," Woods said, through a spokesman. Adam Scott birdied four times and was at five under after nine, and Pettersson, with a birdie and a bogey, was four under through No. 8. McIlroy had caught fire, logging five birdies and a bogey through No. 9.

"To be four under through nine is a great position to be in," McIlroy said. "And you know, the conditions today were a lot better than they were yesterday."

Jimmy Walker, a three-time winner on the Web.com Tour, who missed the cut in his only other PGA start, moved into contention with a 31 on the second nine and a 67. Denmark's Thomas Bjorn rushed into the picture with birdies on his first four holes, then bogeyed seven of the last 14 for a 74.

David Lynn, the little-known Englishman, made peace with the crosswinds and edged into contention. "Tried to slow things down today in a left-to-right wind," he said. His reward: a no-bogey 32 on the front and a 68 to get to one under.

And that's where everything stood at the end of a stormy Saturday. Came Sunday morning, Van Pelt woke to find that he had slid down the leaderboard without swinging a club. McIlroy picked up where he'd left off Saturday. After a bogey at the 13th, he birdied the 15th and 16th (to take the lead, as it turned out, for good). He made a tough save out of a bunker at the 17th, shot a 67, a seven-under 209 total and a three-stroke lead to take into the final round.

"I think I hit every fairway, only missed a couple greens," McIlroy said. "Just one more round like that, and I'll be happy."

Going into the final round, he led by three over Carl Pettersson, who finished with a par 72, and was four up on Bo Van Pelt (67), Trevor Immelman (70) and Adam Scott (70).

Tiger Woods couldn't recover from his first-nine 40 and shot 74, tying with Vijay Singh, who double-bogeyed the 15th and also shot 74. They trailed McIlroy by five going into the final round.

McIlroy went back to his room on the island for a short nap and a change of clothes. He had earlier decided on a red shirt for the final round, but only if he weren't paired with Woods, whose red shirt and black slacks were his Sunday trademark. They weren't paired for Sunday. He wore the red.

"Might have to do it from now on," he was to say later. "No wonder he wins so much."

Third-Round Leaders: Rory McIlroy 67–209, Carl Pettersson 72–212, Bo Van Pelt 67–213, Trevor Immelman 70–213, Adam Scott 70–213, Steve Stricker 67–214, Peter Hanson 70–214, Vijay Singh 74–214, Tiger Woods 74–214

Fourth Round

As Rory McIlroy would recount: On arriving at the Ocean Course Monday of the PGA Championship, he went to his locker and looked out the window, at the beach and ocean. "I was thinking to myself, 'I just have a good feeling about this week. Something about this just feels right,'" he said. "I felt it from the start of the week, that it could be special."

Thus equipped, McIlroy proceeded to play only nine holes of practice one day, nine holes another, and that was it.

"I'm pretty comfortable with the course," McIlroy had said.

Take a spectacular game and a booming confidence, add a dash of ESP, and that will add up to special every time. But even the bubbly McIlroy couldn't have dreamed how special this one would be. McIlroy, who won the 2011 U.S. Open by a record eight strokes, left landmarks all over this PGA. These included an eight-stroke victory that broke Jack Nicklaus's record of seven in the PGA, and at age 23 years, three months and eight days, becoming the youngest to win two majors since Seve Ballesteros, with the 1979 Open Championship and the 1980 Masters, eclipsing Tiger Woods's own mark.

The only marquee names within reach of McIlroy never got close in the final round. Tiger Woods and Vijay Singh both started five strokes behind. Woods bogeyed twice coming home, shot 72 and finished tied for 11th. "I came out with probably the wrong attitude yesterday," Woods said. "And I was too relaxed, and that's not how I play." Singh ran into a bad patch, posting only two birdies but five bogeys and a double at the 17th for a 77 and a tie for 36th.

With McIlroy rolling along, there was a little competition, thanks to Ian Poulter, playing four groups ahead. Poulter started the final round six behind, ran off six birdies through No. 7, and twice got within two strokes. But three straight bogeys from the 13th held him to a 69 and a tie for third.

"I knew I had a chance to be fairly close, and I was fairly close," Poulter said. "I just couldn't get any closer. Rory has played some immense golf out there today, and when he plays like he's playing this week, everyone should take note. The guy's pretty good."

England's David Lynn, playing in the United States for the first time, made only one bogey and closed fast with birdies at the 16th and 17th for a 68 and a 283 total to become the answer to: "Who finished second to McIlroy in the 2012 PGA?"

Piled up behind him in a tie for third at 284 were Poulter, defending champion Keegan Bradley (68), Justin Rose (66) and Carl Pettersson (72), who missed finishing second by a two-stroke penalty for touching a leaf on his backswing in a hazard. "It's one of those stupid rules," said Pettersson, a contender from the start.

McIlroy wasted no time pulling away. He birdied the second from six feet after a pitch from dirt under a tree, then the third from 12. He had a breathtaking birdie at the par-five No. 7. He two-putted from 60 feet, but the second was a tap-in. He escaped a bogey at No. 9, holing his par from 10 feet. The momentum, and the fever of the crowd, built from there. He birdied the 12th from 15 feet, the 16th from six, and saved the most dramatic moment for the last.

He came to the 18th tee leading by seven, and still relishing his eight-shot win in the U.S. Open, he audaciously told his caddie, J.P. Fitzgerald, "I'm going to win this one by eight, as well."

He put his approach on the edge of the green, about 20 feet from the cup, and rolled the putt in. He raised his putter and gave that huge smile. A 66, a 275 total, 13 under. So ended a run of 16 majors with 16 different winners.

Where most golfers never think of "a number," McIlroy had one fixed in his mind. "I said, look, if I get to 12 under par, no one is going to catch me," he said in the media interview, "and I was able to go one better than that. I was a little frustrated with how I was playing earlier in the year. I wanted to go out there and prove people wrong. That's what I did."

On a long, tough Ocean Course, that ran from capricious to brutal under Atlantic winds, he went bogey-free through his first 22 holes and his last 23, and made just seven bogeys all week. In the end, Rory McIlroy was asked which part of his game could have been better. That's like asking an artist which of his masterpieces was his favorite. He gave that big grin.

"It was all good," McIlroy said.

The Final Leaders: Rory McIlroy 66–275, David Lynn 68–283, Justin Rose 66–284, Keegan Bradley 68–284, Ian Poulter 69–284; Carl Pettersson 72–284, Blake Adams 67–285, Jamie Donaldson 70–285, Peter Hanson 71–285, Steve Stricker 71–285

6. The Ryder Cup

Over the years, certain Ryder Cups were tagged with a name for an issue or event that distinguished them from the others. There was, for example, "The Concession" in 1969, in which Jack Nicklaus conceded Tony Jacklin's three-foot putt on the final hole to allow him and his team a gracious tie rather than expose Jacklin to the risk of missing it.

"The Barnesie" was named for big, beefy, beer-drinking Brian Barnes — his presence begs for alliteration — beating Nicklaus twice in singles in the same day in 1975 at Laurel Valley, after Arnold Palmer, the United States captain, rigged the draw for the afternoon session.

The Ryder Cup in 1991 became "The War by the Shore," adding a touch of hostility to what was supposed to be a friendly competition. In the 1995 edition, Oak Hill became "Choke Hill" after the favored Americans fumbled away what looked to be a sure victory.

The 2012 Ryder Cup — held at Medinah Country Club outside of Chicago in late September — would take on three names, depending on how one looked at it. For Europeans, it was the Miracle at Medinah; for Americans, the Meltdown at Medinah, after they held a huge 10-6 advantage going into the singles on the last day, and lost.

But before the matches reached that point, they already had a name: "The First Ryder Cup without Seve."

This was the 39th playing of the Ryder Cup overall, but it was only the 17th since 1977, the year the Ryder Cup was saved. The United States had enjoyed such success that the original Great Britain and Ireland side had to get help. The Ryder Cup was nearly dying of disinterest until Nicklaus recommended the side be expanded to include Europe. Which, at the time, meant Severiano Ballesteros, the fiery and brilliant Spaniard. Before long, the Ryder Cup had evolved into the most compelling international golf competition, and the Europeans began to dominate.

This was the first Ryder Cup without Ballesteros. He died of a brain tumor on May 7, 2011, at 54 years of age. He ran up a 20-12-5 record, but more to the point, he had breathed life — actually, fire — into the European side. Ballesteros was their spiritual leader in life, and then in death. His memory was invoked everywhere. The European captain Jose Maria Olazabal, a fellow Spaniard, friend and former teammate, summoned Ballesteros's memory even in the Sunday team uniform. The Europeans dressed in Ballesteros's Sunday best — navy blue slacks and sweater and white shirt, but bearing his silhouette on the sleeve. They honored Ballesteros in another way. That escape and victory were pure Ballesteros.

By the time the last putt fell — or in this case, was conceded — this was the kind of Ryder Cup that had earned some kind of name. The signs were there. Tiger Woods would go without a point. The two trusted picks of U.S. captain Davis Love, Jim Furyk and Steve Stricker, would produce one point between them. And it was a player who didn't qualify on performance points and who had to be a captain's pick, and who was outranked by seven teammates in the World Ranking, who would lead Europe. It was almost as though the many-colored Ian Poulter assured his teammates as Ballesteros did a frightened Olazabal in his first Ryder Cup: "You play your game, I'll take care of the rest."

First Day

A day when two rookies hit the Ryder Cup like a seismic disturbance was marked first by deafening silence, where it should have been, and then thunderous noise, where it shouldn't.

And then there was the demonstrative Ian Poulter, often recognized for his colorful clothing and exotic cars, and emerging as the European knight errant. Ballesteros had his fiery temperament, Colin Montgomerie his imperious reserve, and now came England's Poulter, with clenched fists, gaping mouth and bulging eyes.

On Friday morning, the thousands of fans jammed at the first tee were already roaring when, at 7:20 a.m., Northern Ireland's Graeme McDowell stepped up to hit the first shot of the 2012 Ryder Cup. The fans fell quiet.

"The silence was deafening," McDowell said, "and it made my mind go blank."

Then that afternoon, big-hitting American Bubba Watson took to the same first tee. He waved his arms, whipping the crowd into a roar, and told them to keep it up *while* he was hitting. Then he blasted a drive down the middle. At this point, you knew this wasn't going to be your daddy's Ryder Cup.

The Europeans were leading early in all four morning matches, but the United States came back to take two of the first four points and came out ahead on the first day with a 5-to-3 margin.

Paul Azinger once labeled Seve Ballesteros "The King of Gamesmanship." In the Spirit of Seve, then, let the gamesmanship begin. In the opening match, Rory McIlroy's tee shot at the par-three No. 2 ended up near a sprinkler head in the collar of the green. Graeme McDowell wanted a free drop, but Jim Furyk argued that the sprinkler head wouldn't interfere with his swing. Rules officials agreed. That meant McDowell would have to chip from the rough rather than putt from the fringe, where the drop would have left him. Furyk's move paid off. McDowell chipped badly, setting up a bogey, and the Americans, Furyk and Brandt Snedeker, won with a par. But it only delayed things. The European pair of McIlroy and McDowell won, 1 up, in the first morning foursomes match.

Watson and Webb Simpson led all the way in the most decisive win of the day, winning 5 and 4 over Paul Lawrie and Peter Hanson in the opening afternoon fourballs match.

But two rookies were stealing the show — American Keegan Bradley and Europe's big-hitting Nicolas Colsaerts, like Poulter, a captain's pick and the first Belgian ever to play in the Ryder Cup.

U.S. captain Davis Love paired Bradley with Phil Mickelson in two matches on the first day. "Oh, baby," Bradley was to say. "I wish we could go 36 holes more." Said Mickelson: "I love, love playing with this man. He plays with such excitement, and man, can he roll the rock."

The excitable Bradley, age 26, and the low-key Mickelson, 42, a perfect fit, breezed through both of their matches. They whipped Luke Donald and

Sergio Garcia in the morning foursomes, 4 and 3, winning four straight holes from the 12th. Bradley's 25-foot birdie was the knockout punch. Then against McIlroy and McDowell in the afternoon fourballs, they birdied the first three holes — Bradley the first from 10 feet, Mickelson from eight, then Bradley from eight — and were 4 up on Bradley's birdie at No. 8, on their way to a 2-and-1 win. "We were trying to claw our way back, but Keegan and Phil were just too strong," McIlroy said.

Colsaerts, making his debut in the afternoon fourballs, left teammate Lee Westwood shaking his head in wonder. Colsaerts poured in putts from everywhere for eight birdies and an eagle, and shot a 10-under-par 62 on his own ball — the best round ever by a rookie — as he and Westwood beat Tiger Woods and Steve Stricker, 1 up, blocking an American sweep for the afternoon.

"I dreamt about it, yes," Colsaerts said. "It's difficult to imagine you're going to do so well."

"It was unbelievable to watch," said Westwood, who had no birdies. "He'll look back on that and smile."

Colsaerts's eight birdies ranged in length from four feet to 22 feet. He eagled the par-five 10th with a second shot from the rough to within six feet of the hole, and at the par-three 17th he put his tee shot 20 feet from the hole while Woods fired his to three feet. Then Colsaerts holed his for a birdie.

So Woods's match-play problems dragged on. It was the fourth time in his seven Ryder Cups that he lost both opening-day matches.

Poulter teamed with Justin Rose for a 2-and-1 win over Woods and Stricker in the morning, then sat out the afternoon.

"There's momentum for the U.S. team right now," Rose said. "But that could all swing back in our favor tomorrow."

First Morning Foursomes: Rory McIlroy and Graeme McDowell (Europe) won 1 up over Jim Furyk and Brandt Snedeker; Phil Mickelson and Keegan Bradley (USA) won 4 and 3 over Luke Donald and Sergio Garcia; Jason Dufner and Zach Johnson (USA) won 3 and 2 over Lee Westwood and Francesco Molinari; Ian Poulter and Justin Rose (Europe) won 2 and 1 over Steve Stricker and Tiger Woods.

First Afternoon Fourballs: Bubba Watson and Webb Simpson (USA) won 5 and 4 over Paul Lawrie and Peter Hanson; Phil Mickelson and Keegan Bradley (USA) won 2 and 1 over Rory McIlroy and Graeme McDowell; Dustin Johnson and Matt Kuchar (USA) won 3 and 2 over Justin Rose and Martin Kaymer; Lee Westwood and Nicolas Colsaerts (Europe) won 1 up over Tiger Woods and Steve Stricker.

Second Day

The Americans enjoyed a robust outing on Saturday, which could best be described in the prevailing sentiment in the media center: "It ain't over till it's over — but *this* one is over."

This was the general idea after the United States went 5-3 in the second and last day of team matches, thus leaving the Europeans hanging on the ropes of a 10-6 deficit. It would be all but insurmountable in the 12 singles matches on Sunday. And the situation was loaded with irony. In the 1999 Ryder Cup, the Americans faced precisely the same huge deficit, and inspired by captain Ben Crenshaw's faith, they scored the greatest comeback in Ryder Cup history.

The Americans were off and running Saturday, taking a 3-1 lead in the morning foursomes, then rolling to two wins in the fourballs, a performance spiked by the emotional Poulter, who won Europe a stay of execution. First off in the morning, Poulter and Justin Rose took the lead with a par at the 10th and scored a 1-up win over Bubba Watson and Webb Simpson. In the afternoon, partner Rory McIlroy had little to do while Poulter made an electrifying five birdies over the last five holes to beat Zach Johnson and Jason Dufner, 1 up. Poulter's spree included a bunker blast to tap-in range at the 15th, a 30-foot curling putt at the 16th and a downhill 12-footer at the 18th.

"It was incredible to watch," McIlroy said. "He made everything."

Said Poulter, lifting his overall record to 11-3-0: "It's pretty fun, this Ryder Cup."

Poulter's spree came right after Luke Donald and Sergio Garcia held off Tiger Woods and Steve Stricker, 1 up. Woods got nothing for a dazzling five birdies on the second nine. "I've played well the last two afternoons and I didn't get a point," said Woods, winless for the first time going into the Sunday singles. The stunner came at the par-three 17th, where Woods fired his tee shot to five feet only to see Donald stick his to two feet. They halved in birdies, and the Europeans won on a half at the 18th when Stricker missed a 10-foot birdie try.

Observers noted that the U.S. lead might have been one point larger — that is, a near-lock on the cup — if Love hadn't sat out his hottest pairing in the afternoon. Phil Mickelson and Keegan Bradley, who had yet to play the 18th hole, ran off Luke Donald and Lee Westwood by a whopping 7-and-6 margin in the morning. They took the first hole off Mickelson's wedge to one foot for a birdie, then won the second when Westwood hit his tee shot into the water.

Nothing went right for the Europeans. They three-putted the 12th for a bogey against the U.S. close-out birdie after Mickelson hit a wedge to one foot. Then U.S. captain Davis Love sat them out. The sharp question was, "Why?" Love had earlier said that no one would play five matches, that he wanted the players rested. Even Woods sat out in the morning, for the first time in his seven Ryder Cups. "It was nice to get a little bit of rest," Woods said.

Even so, it seemed Love was about to be roasted by the media when Mickelson took the microphone in the post-match interview and explained that he and Bradley had asked to be sat out.

After the Mickelson-Bradley frolic, Dufner and Zach Johnson needed nothing more than eight pars from the 10th for a 2-and-1 decision against the erratic play of Nicolas Colsaerts and Sergio Garcia. Jim Furyk and Brian Snedeker led all the way for a 1-up victory over Rory McIlroy and Graeme McDowell to wrap up a 3-1 morning.

The U.S. lead was up 5-1 for the day with the two early fourballs wins in the afternoon. Dustin Johnson birdied the 17th to give him and Matt Kuchar a 1-up win over Colsaerts and Paul Lawrie. Then Bubba Watson and Webb Simpson ran away from Justin Rose and Francesco Molinari, 5 and 4. "On our own ball, we got in our rhythm," Watson said. "I did the par-fives and he did the rest." Watson won the seventh and the close-out 14th, and Simpson won a mix of three.

The two sides were left to consider their positions heading into the singles — one having to guard against overconfidence, the other to search for hope.

"We're excited," Love said. "But we know it's not over yet."

"I believe momentum will come our way," Olazabal said. "Why not tomorrow?"

There was the echo of Ben Crenshaw's words from 1999: "I'm a big believer in fate. I have a good feeling about this."

Second Morning Foursomes: Justin Rose and Ian Poulter (Europe) won 1 up over Bubba Watson and Webb Simpson; Keegan Bradley and Phil Mickelson (USA) won 7 and 6 over Lee Westwood and Luke Donald; Jason Dufner and Zach Johnson (USA) won 2 and 1 over Nicolas Colsaerts and Sergio Garcia; Jim Furyk and Brandt Snedeker (USA) won 1 up over Rory McIlroy and Graeme McDowell.

Second Afternoon Fourballs: Dustin Johnson and Matt Kuchar (USA) won 1 up over Nicolas Colsaerts and Paul Lawrie; Bubba Watson and Webb Simpson (USA) won 5 and 4 over Justin Rose and Francesco Molinari; Sergio Garcia and Luke Donald (Europe) won 1 up over Tiger Woods and Steve Stricker; Rory McIlroy and Ian Poulter (Europe) won 1 up over Jason Dufner and Zach Johnson.

Third Day

European captain Jose Maria Olazabal had a four-point deficit hanging around his neck like an albatross, and he was desperate, plotting his course for the 12-match singles. He badly needed early points. His best bets were his big guns, so he had Luke Donald leading off, followed by Ian Poulter, then Rory McIlroy.

"Obviously, we couldn't hide anything," Olazabal said. "We knew that they would know that."

United States captain Davis Love, needing only 4½ points, scattered his strength. He had Bubba Watson leading off, Phil Mickelson fourth and Dustin Johnson sixth. For insurance, he had Steve Stricker 11th and Tiger Woods last.

It didn't matter. In a lightning strike, the Europeans swept the first four matches and rolled to one of the greatest comeback victories in Ryder Cup history, 14½ points to 13½. Those first four matches were the key.

Big-hitting Bubba Watson and the super-steady Luke Donald led off the singles. Watson got the crowd roaring again on the first tee, but it was his last hurrah. He fell behind with a bogey at No. 2, and Donald led the rest of the way. Donald's 2-and-1 win cut the U.S. lead to 10-7.

Paul Lawrie, the long-quiet 1999 Open champion, came in with Europe's second point in a brisk 5-and-3 win over Brandt Snedeker. Lawrie birdied the fourth hole, eagled the sixth, and led from there, reducing the U.S. lead to 10-8. Was this Brookline in reverse?

"We don't want to get ahead of ourselves," Lawrie said, "but right now, it's looking pretty good."

Match No. 3, the third to finish, was the marquee match, and it almost didn't happen. Rory McIlroy misunderstood his schedule, then needed police transportation to rush him to his tee time. He managed a few practice putts and was off against American rookie sensation Keegan Bradley. McIlroy never trailed, and went ahead for good with a birdie at the 14th, and won, 2 and 1. The U.S. lead was down to 10-9.

Ian Poulter, Europe's histrionic hero, saved his best for last in Match No. 2 (the fourth to finish). He took the lead over Webb Simpson with a par at the par-three 17th. At the 18th, with a Ballesteros flourish, he hit a spectacular approach from behind the trees to within 12 feet of the pin, setting up a 2-up victory that gave Europe a sweep of the first four matches to tie the U.S. at 10-10.

With the two closing wins Saturday, that was six straight for the Europeans. The 2012 Ryder Cup was starting over.

Dustin Johnson stopped the European rampage with a 3-and-2 win over Nicolas Colsaerts in the No. 6 match and got a shock. "I looked up at the board, and they've gotten four points already...," Johnson said. A ragged back nine started with Colsaerts four-putting for a bogey at the par-five 10th and ended with Johnson birdieing the 14th and 15th. The U.S. was back on top, 11-10.

From there, it was nip-and-tuck.

Justin Rose put on a putting circus, holing a 35-footer for a winning birdie to squelch Phil Mickelson's terrific flop shot at the 17th, then holing a 12-footer for another at the 18th. Rose won, 1 up, and it was 11-11.

Zach Johnson led all the way in his 2-and-1 win over Graeme McDowell, putting the U.S. ahead again, 12-11. But it was 12-12 after Europe's Lee Westwood sailed past Matt Kuchar, 3 and 2.

The unfortunate Jim Furyk, as he had several times this season, faltered in the stretch. He bogeyed the last two holes, leaving Sergio Garcia a 1-up winner and letting Europe taste the lead for the first time, 13-12. But enter gritty rookie Jason Dufner. Posting four birdies and two eagles (one conceded), he beat Peter Hanson 2 up, giving the U.S. new life, at 13-13.

Europe's clincher came in Match 11, and it fell, almost cruelly, to Germany's Martin Kaymer, slumping since winning the 2010 PGA Championship and benched for both sessions Saturday. Still, he was 1 up on Steve Stricker going into the 18th. The tension was excruciating.

Kaymer, hitting first, drove into a fairway bunker, then put his second to the back-left of the green. Stricker split the fairway, then hit his approach 40 feet past the pin. He badly misread his birdie try and knocked it eight feet wide. Kaymer rolled his six feet past. Then it got tighter. Stricker holed the return putt for his par.

Now Kaymer faced the putt of his young career. He and almost everyone there — the teams, the spectators and the media — instantly recalled the similar putt that another German, Bernhard Langer, by now a friend and mentor to Kaymer, had missed in his match against Hale Irwin to hand the trophy to America in the 1991 Ryder Cup, known then and ever since as The War by the Shore.

Kaymer also remembered Olazabal's words back at the 16th: "We need your point. And I don't really care how you do it. Just deliver."

Kaymer did — holing the six-footer for a 1-up victory and a 14-13 edge to complete the Miracle at Medinah for Europe.

"Now I know how it really feels to win the Ryder Cup," Kaymer said.

Said a dejected Stricker: "I'm disappointed that I let 11 other players down..."

In the final match, Woods bogeyed the 18th, then conceded Francesco Molinari's three-foot par putt, allowing him to win the hole and halve the last match. "The cup (had been) retained by Europe," Woods said. "So it was already over."

So Europe had the victory, its fifth in the last six playings and a 9-7-1 record since 1979.

Let the post-mortems begin:

Did Davis Love play into Olazabal's hands with his lineup?

Said Love: "We could have laid them out there in about any order ... It wouldn't have really mattered. ... the (other) team plays like that, you're going to get beaten."

Ian Poulter: "Whether it was Seve up there looking down on us or Seve on the shirt — it was enough, it was enough for us."

Jose Maria Olazabal: "Seve will always be present. Seve will always be present with this team."

Third Day Singles: Luke Donald (Europe) won 2 and 1 over Bubba Watson; Ian Poulter (Europe) won 2 up over Webb Simpson; Rory McIlroy (Europe) won 2 and 1 over Keegan Bradley; Justin Rose (Europe) won 2 up over Phil Mickelson; Paul Lawrie (Europe) won 5 and 3 over Brandt Snedeker; Dustin Johnson (USA) won 3 and 2 over Nicolas Colsaerts; Zach Johnson (USA) won 2 and 1 over Graeme McDowell; Sergio Garcia (Europe) won 2 up over Jim Furyk; Jason Dufner (US) won 2 up over Peter Hanson; Lee Westwood (Europe) won 3 and 2 over Matt Kuchar; Martin Kaymer (Europe) won 1 up over Steve Stricker; Francesco Molinari (Europe) halved with Tiger Woods.

7. Women's Major Championships

Kraft Nabisco Championship

The word "unheralded" gets bandied about a lot in sports. It's generally applied to someone who's relatively unknown, or of whom little is expected. But it's only trotted out when an unheralded does something to come to everyone's attention. Such as to win.

Yes to all of the above for South Korea's Sun Young Yoo. First, she certainly was unheralded in the 2010 Sybase Match Play Championship, previously her one shining moment. As a 23-year-old unknown, she swept through five players perched in the top 12 of the Rolex Rankings to score her only win. Coming into that Sybase event, she had missed the cut in three of the six LPGA starts. Among her victims were Cristie Kerr, No. 5 at the time; Yani Tseng, then No. 4, and Jiyai Shin, merely No. 1 in the world. And then came Yoo's disarming disclaimer. "Everybody's good this week," she said, "so I think the ranking number's just a number."

Yoo got a nickname at the Sybase event: "Giant-killer."

Even so, she was pretty much forgotten by the time she arrived at the 2012 Kraft Nabisco Championship, the first major championship on the LPGA schedule.

To Yoo's credit, she stuck close to the leaders all the way at Mission Hills' tough par-72 Dinah Shore course. She was three strokes off the lead in the first round, two in the second round, and three in the third round, and was pretty much ignored. Being ignored is the fate of the unheralded. They are also expected to politely go away at some point. Yoo was not about to oblige.

And she won it the hard way. After shooting 69-69-72-69, she had the clubhouse lead with a nine-under-par 279 total. Fellow South Korean I.K. Kim was about to beat her on the final hole. There, Kim left her birdie putt a foot short. So just a tap-in par, and she would be the champion. But amazingly, she missed it. The ball horseshoed around the hole and stayed out. She tapped in for bogey and a tie and, shattered, off she went into the playoff with Yoo. It was mercifully short. Yoo holed an 18-foot birdie putt on the first extra hole for her second LPGA win and her first major. From unheralded to champion. How did that sound?

"I don't think any words can describe how I feel right now," Yoo said. "I'm still nervous. I wasn't nervous on the course, but now I'm really nervous."

Yani Tseng, No. 1 on the Rolex Rankings, and winner of the 2010 Kraft Nabisco Championship, prudently practiced everything before coming to Mission Hills — drives, fairway woods, short game, putting, and even her ceremonial championship jump into Poppie's Pond.

"I thought I jumped pretty cool two years ago, but my friends say it wasn't a good jump," Tseng said. "So after that I go in my swimming pool and try to jump in a different pose to see what's the best. This year

I think maybe if I had a lead on the last hole and I can be thinking what's the best pose for me to jump. I don't know. I will think about it after I'm winning."

Tseng was, of course, the odds-on favorite at the Kraft Nabisco Championship. She arrived having won three of the LPGA's first five events of the season, and the last two in a row, including the Kia Classic the week before. But Tseng, who either led or shared the lead in her previous eight rounds, found herself in a strange place in the first round — third, behind South Korea's Amy Yang, who shot 66, and Australia's Lindsey Wright, 67, both seeking their first LPGA wins. Tseng made six birdies and shot a four-under 68 and wasn't pleased. "I didn't hit many good shots," she said. "But you can still see my name on the first page of the leaderboard, so I'm happy it's only the first day of the tournament."

At the other end of the emotion spectrum was Wright, who had been taking medication in her battle against clinical depression. "I could have shot 80 today and I'd still feel really great," said Wright, who birdied five of her last nine holes. "I don't feel like I'm swimming with weights and dragging around 10 pounds of excess baggage."

Yang, with eight birdies and two bogeys in her 66, faced the prospect of Tseng in pursuit. "She's very tough to beat right now," Yang said. "She's hitting the ball so good."

Paula Creamer, co-low American at 69, and owner of the 2010 U.S. Women's Open, looked forward to playing with Tseng. "She's the best player in the world," Creamer said, "and it's good to play with people that are going to push you."

Yoo, three back at 69, was among those unmentioned.

Tseng didn't wait long to get back to the top. In the second round, she birdied the last hole for another 68 that gave her a one-shot lead at 136 over South Korea's Haeji Kang (68). "I felt more energy coming out today," said Tseng, who then headed out to play some basketball, a sport she loved but that required, she felt, something more than her 5-foot-6 size for her to be competitive. Kang, 22, South Korean via New Zealand and Australia, had one win on the developmental Futures Tour but none in her four years on the LPGA Tour. She was edgy about playing in the final pairing in the third round. "I've never been in the championship group, so I'm really looking forward to it," she said. "But I'm a little nervous because I'm going out with Yani. I'll just do my best and see what happens."

If Tseng practiced her jump into the pond, Na Yeon Choi didn't even want to think about it. Choi tied the day's-low 67 and was three back at 139, and winning the Kraft was at least a possibility. "Every day I look at the pond, but I don't know how to swim and I'm very scared of water because I had a very bad experience when I was young," Choi said. "I told my caddie last year, if I win this tournament I can't jump in the water. So even this year, I talked to my caddie. But you know — if I win this tournament, I think I can do it."

Sun Young Yoo came to people's attention with another 69 that left her just two off the lead, at 138. Her reaction suggested a gift of precognition. Yoo said she'd been hitting the ball well since the Donnelley Founders Cup two weeks earlier, and, of course, was hoping to make a few putts.

And then she added: "I have two days to go. I have a great feeling and I'm looking forward to it."

Karin Sjodin, a big-hitting Swede and former collegiate star at Oklahoma State University, was the next to take a run at Yani Tseng. Sjodin, 28, looking for her first win, had never made the cut in the Kraft Nabisco Championship but shot 68 in the blustery winds in the third round to tie Tseng at nine-under 207. The LPGA Tour has been a learning process for Sjodin. "I never realized what my weaknesses were, because I could just bomb it up there," she said. "Coming out here, all of a sudden, there are a lot of people who hit it farther. It took awhile to work on those things. Now I know what I want to do and how to work at it."

Tseng hit a snag. After making only three bogeys over the first three rounds, she bogeyed three holes on the back nine and shot her worst score so far, a one-under 71. She saved more damage with a birdie at the par-three 17th, on a six iron to two feet. "I hung in there," Tseng said. "On the back nine, I got my emotions in it ... maybe it was the wind. But I'm happy I hung in there."

Whiz Kid Lexi Thompson, 17, got to the fringe of contention with a sizzling start and a 68 that left her within five shots of the lead. She birdied four of the first five holes and had to calm herself down. "I was thinking I was definitely shooting a low score, but I was trying not to get ahead of myself," she said. She nursed her round home against 40 mph gusts for the last several holes, hitting knock-downs and three-quarter shots, and escaped with a bogey after hitting over the green at the 18th. "I was happy to get away with just a bogey," she said.

The stage for the finale was set quietly. with Yoo fighting the winds for a 72 and I.K. Kim shooting her third straight 70 to tie for fourth at 210, three shots off the lead.

The final round was not a nice, tense shootout. It was part-mad dash, part-scramble before it ended up in the playoff. Down the frantic stretch, five players held the lead. Tseng and Sjodin started off tied with a one-shot lead. Tseng lost her share in the first two holes, with Sjodin taking over. She took a three-stroke lead with an eagle at the second, then bogeyed twice through the turn, handing the lead to Hee Kyung Seo, who proceeded to bogey the 15th and 16th, causing a four-way tie for the lead. Tseng might have joined the final playoff, but pushed her birdie try at the 18th and missed by an inch, shooting 73 and finishing a solo third by a stroke.

When it came to contenders, Yoo, who never finished better than seventh in a major, wasn't in a promising position. She started three shots off the lead and suffered two early bogeys. Then she surged down the stretch with three birdies in five holes, and parred the last three. A 69 gave her the clubhouse lead at 279, but with the late developments, only thoughts of a good payday.

Kim, playing behind her, rolled along bogey-free, then birdied the 16th on a 15-foot putt, then the 17th on a 20-footer to break a three-way tie for the lead. At the 18th, she just missed on a long birdie try and sat a foot from the hole with her par putt for the win.

"I thought I had no chance," Yoo said. "I thought I.K. was going to make the putt."

So did everyone else, especially Kim herself. But when her tap-in rimmed around the hole and stayed out, she lifted her left hand to her mouth and turned away while the gallery groaned. She had just joined that forlorn few in history of those who somehow missed the unmissable. Most notably, Doug Sanders in the 1970 Open Championship and Scott Hoch in the 1989 Masters.

"I played it straight," she was to say, "and it actually broke to the right, even that short putt," Kim said.

She gathered herself and tapped in the bogey, but she was done for. In the playoff, at the 18th, Kim barely cleared the water with her drive and was short with a birdie try from the fringe. "It was just hard to focus on what's going on," she said. "Because I was still a little bit bummed..."

Yoo hit the green routinely, then rolled in her 18-foot putt for the birdie and the win.

There was sadness all around for Kim, except, it seemed, from Yoo. Came the question in the interview room: "Do you feel a little sad for her?"

Said Yoo: "I mean, it happens. It's golf. It's a crazy game. It happened to me before, too. I mean, everybody's playing to win out here, but I don't think I can..." And she stopped, then added, "she did great today."

As for herself, Yoo said: "I didn't think about winning today. I didn't want to let myself down, but I think I did better than what I was expecting."

Wegmans LPGA Championship

Shanshan Feng started the final round three shots off the lead, pleased to be in the hunt but not thinking much more about it, minding her own business and not looking at leaderboards. Then about the time she approached the 16th, she noticed a couple members of the media had shown up in her thin gallery. She had been around long enough that, though she'd never won, she knew what it meant. Then a few more showed up, and then others, and the gallery was picking up. The pulse of the tournament was quickening around her. She hadn't led at all since the start of the championship, but she couldn't very well dismiss these signs.

"Then I thought, well, maybe I have a chance," she said.

"I have two goals," Feng said, on leaving the final green with the club-house lead, to begin the nervous wait on the players still on the course. "I want to win a tournament on the LPGA Tour and I want to finish in the top 10 in a major."

This was the Wegmans LPGA Championship at Locust Hill Golf Club, outside Rochester, New York, and in a little while, the young lady from China was about to accomplish both goals at the same time.

Feng, 22, was the only player from China to win on the LPGA Tour, so she would have to be, therefore, the first Chinese to win on the tour and the first to win a major championship, but there was a nice, historic ring to introducing her that way.

Feng was introduced to golf by her father, a Chinese golf official. She liked it, practiced hard, and moved to the United States in 2007, worked under an instructor, and won her LPGA playing card that same year. Her record did not command much attention at Locust Hill. She had won three times on the Japan Tour (once in 2012) and once on the Ladies European Tour. Her play in the majors was unexciting. Overall, her best finish was a tie for 22nd in the Kraft Nabisco just six weeks earlier. Otherwise, her finishes ranged from a tie for 30th to a tie for 73rd. In four previous LPGAs, she missed one cut and finished in the 50s three times. She did manage some excitement to start the 2012 season, tying for fifth, second and third in her first three events. Then came four ties ranging from 22nd to 62nd.

And nothing much was happening at Locust Hill. Then she began noticing the media people following her about the time they began to notice her — with just a few holes to play.

Feng played the par-72 Locust Hill course in 72-73-70-67–282 and won by two strokes over Mika Miyazato (69), Stacy Lewis (70), Suzann Pettersen (70) and Eun-Hee Ji (72). Feng's closing 67 was the tournament-best over the course toughened by heavier rough in response to the beatings it had been taking. Where the previous two champions, Cristie Kerr and Yani Tseng, each finished at 19 under, Feng won at six under.

Where Feng went unnoticed most of the way, Tseng, No. 1 in the Rolex Rankings, was center stage from the start. Tseng, who owned five majors already at age 23, won the 2011 LPGA here by 10 shots on her 19-under performance. And she opened the 2012 season on a rampage, winning three of the first five events. And then, mysteriously, she began playing more like the back-of-the-pack players. She opened the LPGA with her worst score of the year, a four-over 76, at which she was easily in danger of missing the cut. "I just couldn't hit a shot, couldn't hit on the green, couldn't hit on the fairway," Tseng said. "It was really tough for me out there. I know it's my mental problem. I'm hitting so well on the driving range, and when I get on the first tee, there's something wrong."

Tseng's 76 consisted of two birdies and six bogeys, and even so, left her just seven shots off the lead. It was a sunny day and the breeze was light, but only 16 players broke par on the toughened Locust Hill. For all of the prominent names in the field, the first round was led by a trio of little known players — Spain's Beatriz Recari, a one-time winner, and Italy's Giulia Sergas and America's Ryann O'Toole, both seeking their first win, tied at three-under 69. Recari bogeyed her second hole, saved par on the next two, then made three straight birdies and turned at two under. "I would sum up the round as very confident off the tee, and I had a great feeling on the greens," she said. Kerr, who won by a record 12 strokes in 2010, marveled at the rough after her two-under 70. "It's just gobbling up golf balls," she said. As to her own round: "I ended up being patient, and I'm happy with that."

The course was littered with great tries. Jeong Jang, for one, got to five under, then bogeyed four of her last five holes for a 70, tying with an all-star cast: Kerr, Mika and Ai Miyazato (not related), Na Yeon Choi, Paula Creamer and Se Ri Pak, who started the Korean invasion with her victories in 1998. She had been slumping recently and had an injured shoulder. "I feel great to be back," Pak said. "Low expectations help a lot. Even though I feel 100 percent, you never know."

Feng was quietly in a large group at 72 that included Stacy Lewis, Inbee Park and Sun Young Yoo.

Se Ri Pak celebrated her good feelings with a 71 in the stiff breezes of the second round that carried her into a one-stroke lead at 141. "I'm happy to be back in this seat," she said in the media interview room, where she had spent so many happy days. "Before I teed off, I knew it was tougher because of the wind. It was very difficult." She struggled on the front nine, even saving par on four straight holes, despite what seemed to be a problem with her left arm. "I'm slowly better every day," Pak said. "Out of an injury, you don't have high expectations."

The number of par-shooters shrank. Where 16 broke par in the first round, only 12 did in the windy second, and only three players broke 70 — Eun-Hee Ji, with the day's-low 68, in a six-way tie at 143; Mi Jung Hur and Karin Sjodin, each with a 69 and among the 24 players within four strokes of Pak. This group include Shanshan Feng, at 73–145.

Stacy Lewis made four birdies and four bogeys for another 72. "Today, the wind was brutal," she said. "Once we hit nine, from then on it was blowing pretty hard. In the middle of the back nine, I was counting the number of holes we had left."

Yani Tseng added a plump 75 to her opening 76, but was spared by the generosity of the cut, which she made on the number at a most forgiving seven-over 151 total, five higher than in 2011. "I did my best," she said. "I hung in there." The laboring Michelle Wie did not hang in there. She shot 82–156. Also gone were Angela Stanford (76–152) and Natalie Gulbis (77–153).

Feng improved to a two-under 70 in the third round, but gained only a stroke on the leader, Eun-Hee Ji (69–212). "I'm a little bit nervous," Ji said, but it didn't show in her game. She hit 11 of the 14 driving fairways, and all told had hit 39 greens in regulation in the 54 holes. Karrie Webb leaped to within a stroke by birdieing three of her last five holes — including dropping a 15-foot putt at the 17th hole — for a 68–213 total. "I think my patience level has been quite good — for me," said Webb, who has seven majors in her 38 career wins but whose best finish in 10 starts this season was a tie for fourth. Stacy Lewis, a two-time winner this season, and fresh from winning the ShopRite Classic the week before, birdied the 17th and pulled within two of the lead with a 70. "It's a lot easier coming from behind," Lewis said. "I almost like being at the back and coming up and surprising someone." Paula Creamer hit 10 fairways and 16 greens but her putter held her to a 73 and a one-under 215, three off the lead. Se Ri Pak, the second-round leader, faded out with a 76 in the third round.

And so the race tightened. Where 24 players were within four shots of the lead after 36 holes, now there were 13 after 54 holes.

The fourth round was marked first by Yani Tseng completing her alien appearance. She closed the way she opened, with a 76, and would tie for 59th, 13 over par. In the four rounds she hit only 22 fairways and 41 greens in regulation. "The way I played this week," Tseng said, "if I went to a par-three course I would be four over."

The path for Feng would open up as obstacles cleared themselves away. Paul Creamer, for one, began the day tied with Feng and started to move with a birdie at No. 4, but stalled out with a bogey at No. 9. Karrie Webb, second starting the last round, could manage only a par 72. Pettersen was tied with Feng through the 12th, then fell behind with bogeys at the 13th and 14th, finishing with a 70 and tying for second at 284. Eun-Hee Ji, who started with a one-stroke lead, ran into trouble and had to rally for birdies at 13, 15 and 16 to get back to the tie for second place. Mika Miyazato shot 69 and Stacy Lewis 70 and joined the tie for second, two behind Feng, who had finished at 282.

Playing in front of the leaders, Feng methodically made her way through the field to a bogey-free 67, the lowest round of the championship, on these five birdies:

• No. 2, she set up her first birdie with a pitching wedge to 15 feet.
• No. 6, she punched a five iron from 171 yards into the wind to 10 feet.
• No. 8, a par-five, she hit a hybrid second from 205 yards to 12 feet below the hole and two-putted.
• No. 12, she lofted a wedge to 15 feet.
• No. 17, after bunkering her drive, she hit a seven iron up the fairway, then hit a wedge to 12 feet.

And at the 18th, she missed the green but chipped out of heavy rough to inside two feet for the par and the 67. But there wasn't a sense of urgency when she set out.

"For me, I never thought 'I must win,'" Feng said. "I knew I was three behind, so I knew I had a chance. I wasn't nervous at all because I didn't know I was leading."

The sense of urgency finally came as she waited to see whether the leaders would catch her. But one by one, they fell short, and then history was hers. It was time to celebrate. But Feng, with her first victory and her first major, couldn't.

"I don't know how to celebrate," she said. "It happened too soon."

Next, the outlook for golf in China. Given the inspiration of Se Ri Pak on women's golf in Korea, would Feng expect something similar in China?

"I would say yes," Feng said. "You know, all of the Asians are good. That's what my parents told me — all of the Asians are good at controlling small things. I don't know if it's true or not. But I will say, if the Koreans can, the Chinese can."

U.S. Women's Open

Na Yeon Choi, then 10 years of age, was staying up past her bedtime. The family understood. In fact, all of her country understood. Halfway around the world, a young South Korean named Se Ri Pak was in the process of winning one of the most prestigious women's golf events in the world. It would prove to be a landmark event. Choi and girls all over the country were inspired by Pak's historic accomplishment in 1998 — the first South Korean woman to win the U.S. Women's Open. In fact, she was the first South Korean to make a mark in professional golf, and in doing so, launched the Korean domination of the LPGA Tour, and she would go on to a Hall of Fame career.

The U.S. Women's Open returned to Blackwolf Run in 2012, 14 years later, and when Choi, now 24, holed her final putt, for a four-stroke victory, Pak was there to congratulate her with a hug and a smile. Choi was also the latest installment of Korean domination of the U.S. Women's Open, which Pak had started. Choi made it four of the past five U.S. Women's Opens won by Koreans. It was American Paula Creamer, in 2010, who interrupted the string.

"Se Ri really inspired me to become an LPGA player — she inspired all the Korean players," Choi said. "My dream when I was 10 was just to be out here on the LPGA Tour. And 14 years later, I'm here right now, and I made it."

Although there is no conclusion to be drawn from their performances, it is interesting to note that Pak won the 1998 Open in a 20-hole playoff against amateur Jenny Chuasiriporn. They tied in regulation at six-over-par 290, then tied at 73 in the 18-hole playoff, and had to go to sudden death, with Pak winning by holing an 18-foot birdie putt on the second hole. Choi shot Blackwolf Run in 71-72-65-73–281, seven under.

The key was the tournament-low 65 in the third round, not only the fifth-lowest score in the history of the Women's Open, but a remarkable score on a course that was set up tougher and also buffeted by 25 mph winds. There was only one other score in the 60s — Amy Lang's 69 — and 19 in the 80s. Choi had been chasing the leaders, and suddenly she had a six-shot lead.

The 53rd U.S. Women's Open got under way, on a fiercely hot July day in America's dairyland, Wisconsin, with a rather ringing statement.

"The U.S. Open is where it's at," Cristie Kerr was saying. "This is the stage I want to perform on." It's fair to say she was speaking for the 154 other starters. Kerr, 34, knew the stage well. She won the 2007 Women's Open. But she was impatient. She hadn't won since the 2010 LPGA Championship. She dealt herself in on this championship with a three-under-par 69 for a share of the first-round lead with Brittany Lincicome and Lizette Salas.

"That proved to myself that I was there," Kerr said. This was a moment of triumph. She had just escaped a bogey at the opening hole — from a watered tee shot to a curling 18-foot par putt.

The heat was the No. 1 topic, however. The temperature hit 98 degrees and the heat index 105. "It was a bad combination," said Lincicome. "The U.S. Open is one of those weeks where you're mentally drained after each round, so you have to focus really hard on every shot."

The weather and the course were a bad combination, too. The field was packed tight. Japan's Ai Miyazato, Spain's Beatriz Recari, Jennie Lee and 17-year-old Lexi Thompson were at 70, one off the lead, and in a crush right behind, at 71, was Na Yeon Choi. World No. 1 Yani Tseng shot 74, and World No. 2, Stacy Lewis, shot 77 and also gave her golf bag a few smacks. Blackwolf Run played at an average of 4.16 over par, giving up 14 rounds under par but also exacting 38 rounds in the 80s.

For Se Ri Pak, it was replay and reunion. "Actually, very exciting to be back again," she said. "Of course, it was 14 years ago, but the funny things I remember was at the playoff, the last couple holes. I have great memories about '98, so no matter what, I feel really great to be out."

There was no mistaking the stir that went through Blackwolf Run in the second round. Michelle Wie, her game still afflicted with whatever was afflicting it. She had missed six cuts in eight starts this season. She shot 74 in the first round, but now she toured the course in a sparkling 66, getting to within a stroke of Suzann Pettersen, leading at 68–139. Suddenly, the young Michelle — a strange thought, since she was only 22 and had recently graduated from Stanford University — was back. Or at least the one it seems the golf world thought she was. It was quite confusing.

Wie was famous young — only 12 when she qualified for an LPGA Tour event in 2002, and her parents also had her playing, as a teenager, in a number of events against the best in the world, the men on the PGA Tour. Then the magic disappeared. "I don't know if anyone gave up on me or not," she said. "But I never gave up on myself, and today was a good reminder to myself what I can do and I still have it." Cautiously, a confidence-booster is the most she would call that 66. "It's nice to know that I made the cut, for sure," she said.

By then Wie had hurled herself into contention, tied with Kerr (71), who wasn't sure her 2007 victory would be of any real use. "I always draw on that experience," Kerr said. "But it's hard to predict what's an advantage and what's not an advantage. You just don't know." They were tied for second, a stroke behind Suzann Pettersen. Pettersen was more assertive. "My game is very solid," she said. "My ball striking is good. My short game is good. And my putting has been really good so far." And this after she overslept and had to hurry to make her tee time.

Lizette Salas, co-leader in the first round, drifted with a 73, and the other, Lincicome, stumbled badly to an 80 and made the cut right on the number, 149, and was the reverse of the upbeat Pettersen. "I did nothing right today," Lincicome said. "I couldn't drive the ball. I couldn't do anything right. I couldn't putt."

World Nos. 1, 2 and 3, respectively, changed positions. Tseng improved to a 72 and Lewis to a 69 to tie at two-over 146. And Ai Miyazato slipped to a 74 and was at even-par 144. Defending champion So Yeon Ryu shot 71–145.

The weather had cooled just a bit, but was to turn a bit cooler on the weekend. "Which I'm all for," Pettersen said. "It's been two really hot days."

The weather did cool for the third round, and the brisk winds came up, lifting scores like so many kites. Choi, it seemed, was playing by herself in the calm. As Cristie Kerr would put it, after a 77 of her own, "Na Yeon beat the field by about 12 shots today."

Choi, in fact, shot the tournament low, a seven-under 65, with eight birdies and one bogey, and took a six-stroke lead over Amy Yang, whose 69 was the only other score in the 60s. Only three others broke the par of 72, and 19 shot 80 or better. The course played to an average of 76.89.

"This is a very special golf course, and I am honored," Choi said. She also seemed safe. Nobody had ever come from more than five strokes behind in the final round to win the Women's Open.

The tributes were many and varied. Among them: "It was pretty crazy, that 65," said Michelle Wie, who started the day one off the lead and ended up 10 behind after shooting 78.

Choi produced the 65 from a magical day with her short irons, an obedient putter and faith in her caddie.

"I tried to put the ball exactly where I want," she said, "and when my caddie gave me number (yardage), I just trust that number and swing at it."

Choi's historic round is in the books like this: She birdied Nos. 1, 2, 7 and 8 going out, and 10, 11, 12 and 17 coming in. She hit wedges for four of the birdies to two, three, four and 15 feet; eight iron for three, to four, 15 and 20 feet, and a seven iron to 15 feet. The only flaw in her masterpiece was a three-putt bogey from 50 feet at the 13th.

Choi was on the verge of shedding golf's weariest tag: "The best never to have won a major." She had won five times on the LPGA Tour and seven times on the Korean Ladies' tour. Before she could add a major, there was the matter of her discomfort with the lead. She didn't play well with the lead. She admitted to that.

"I'm pretty sure I'll be nervous tomorrow," she said. "It will be a lot of pressure, but I know what I have to do and I know what I can control."

A six-stroke lead going into the final round of any tournament is just about what the oddsmakers like to call a mortal lock. It might be even more so in the U.S. Women's Open, given the difficulty of the course, the tough field, and the sheer pressure of the event itself. Still, she was confident.

Even so, the cracks appeared on the home stretch. At the par-four 10th, she pulled her tee shot into a lateral water hazard on the left and opted to return to the tee and take a penalty stroke and hit again. But she caught the rough, finally reached the green and two-putted from 12 feet for a triple-bogey eight. Her six-stroke lead was down to two over Yang, who parred the hole.

The old problem had cropped up. She had to deal with it. "That moment, I thought I might screw up today," Choi said. "But I thought I needed to fix that. I can do it. So I tried to think what I have to do. So my decide is I have to talk with my caddie. So I started to talk with my caddie, about just like what airplane tomorrow, or about the car or about the vacation."

The chat steadied her, and she rebounded with a birdie at the 11th, on a five-foot putt, and salvaged a par at the 12th after chopping out of deep rough.

The fates all but proclaimed her the champion at the par-three 13th. Her tee ball was heading for the Sheboygan River, but bounced twice off rocks and ended up 15 feet behind the green.

"Even after the first bounce, I didn't know if it would end up in the water," the relieved Choi said. "But after the second bounce, it kicked to the left. I looked at my caddie, and all the winners who have won the tournament, they had a little bit of luck. So I thought maybe today I had luck from that tee shot, and then that's why I can win today."

Choi got up and down for par, went ahead by four on Yang's bogey at the 14th, then five with a birdie at the 16th. She came home with a cautious bogey for a one-over 73 and her four-stroke win.

Se Ri Pak, who tied for ninth, 11 strokes behind, was there at the 18th green to congratulate Choi and welcome her with the champagne shower. Choi recalled watching Se Ri and dreaming late into the night.

"And 14 years later, I'm here right now," she said. "I made it."

Ricoh Women's British Open

After missing the previous two major championships, Jiyai Shin made a triumphant return to her best form by winning the Ricoh Women's British Open by nine strokes at Royal Liverpool Golf Club, in Hoylake, England. Shin, the former Rolex world No. 1 who had struggled with injuries in recent times, took a brave decision to miss two months of the season after undergoing an operation to remove a small bone in her left wrist. During her recuperation, Shin kept positive that she could resume competition at the highest level by watching recordings of her previous victories, including this championship in 2008 at Sunningdale. Shin said that win "changed my life," taking her from Korea to a new home in Atlanta and fulfilling her dream to become one of the best players in the game. "This tournament is special for me," she said.

Her nine-stroke victory over Inbee Park after finishing as the only player under par for the championship on 279, nine under par, was a master class in playing a tough course in tough conditions with patience and determination. And no little skill, including a new course record in the second round. The margin of victory was a record for the event since it became a major championship in 2001, although Ayako Okamoto had won by 11 strokes in 1984 at Woburn. It also meant Asian players had won all four major championships in a season for the first time and seven in a row. Another quality Shin showed was endurance after she won the Kingsmill Championship in America after a nine-hole playoff that only finished on the Monday morning of the Open week.

This was the second year in a row that the Ricoh Women's British Open was played at a new venue from the traditional rota of the men's Open Championship. In 2011 it was Carnoustie, and in benign conditions the modest length of the course for the women was considered not quite the full experience compared to the layout's "Carnastie" reputation.

But at 6,660 yards, Hoylake was not just in superb condition but also a fearsome test throughout the week. The date of the championship was pushed from its usual late July slot to September due to a clash of dates with the Olympics and Britain's bountiful summer of sport. For those visitors asking why the event was not being staged in summer, warm, balmy September days are plentiful, just not on this occasion. Even the practice days produced some gruesome weather, so there was no hiding the challenge that was to come.

After only arriving in Britain on Tuesday, Shin rested up and headed out for her only practice round on Wednesday. But as the weather deteriorated, Shin decided only nine holes was advisable, so it meant she saw the second nine for the first time in Thursday's first round. A one-under 71 was a fine return, sparked off by a chip-in birdie at the third hole, and put Shin just one off the lead of So Yeon Ryu and Haeji Kang. Conditions were improved from the previous two practice days, but there was a still a tricky breeze and the odd shower. Kang was the first to post her 70, with Ryu, the 2011 U.S. Women's Open champion, becoming the co-leader later in the day.

While Kang was still awaiting a victory on the LPGA circuit, Ryu, officially a rookie in 2012, won the Jamie Farr Toledo Classic in August to feel she had backed up her major win from the previous year. This was her first experience of links golf. "This is my first time playing in England, so this type of golf, I never played this type of golf course," Ryu said. "It's really tough but fun. Always the first experience, really fun and a little tough, but I want to enjoy this type of golf course."

Among those alongside Shin at one under were both Miyazatos, Ai and Mika, plus Karrie Webb, a three-time champion. "I think it counts for a little bit," Webb said of her experience in the event. "But you've still got to go out there and hit the shot, and you've got to commit to the lines that you want to hit your shots on, and do it, because there's really no — I think that there's a lot of links courses that there's a side to miss on, and I don't think this course, especially off the tee, there's a side to miss on. You've just got to get up there and hit a good shot."

At the other end of the scale, also on 71, was 16-year-old Charley Hull, an English amateur who was aiming to go to the qualifying tournament for the Ladies European Tour at the end of the year. Hull made the cut at the Kraft Nabisco Championship before going on to the Curtis Cup, where she was a member of the winning Great Britain and Ireland team. Hull matched the same score she recorded in the opening round of the Kraft but not her feat there of birdieing the first hole.

She said she was not as nervous has she had been in California. "I just pretend I'm out there playing with my mates," she said. "I know it's a major but that's how I think of it." Hull heralds from the same club that Ian Poulter represents, Woburn, and the pair have been in Twitter contact. Her home course, a former venue for the Ricoh Women's British Open, helped prepare Hull despite being an inland course rather than a links. Asked about the Hoylake course, Hull said: "Oh, yeah, I like them long. I like them narrow, as well. I come from Woburn and that's quite tight."

An even younger player, 15-year-old Lydia Ko, was in a group of players at even par that included Cristie Kerr and Yani Tseng, the champion for the previous two years. Ko arrived in Britain after winning the U.S. Women's Amateur and then becoming the youngest-ever winner on the LPGA circuit at the Canadian Open. The Korean-born New Zealander appears to have a maturity beyond her years. Asked after the expectations upon her tender shoulders, Ko said: "Yeah, they are probably expecting a big thing from me, and yeah, but I'm not going to take that much interest. Just got to play my own game. It's not like I'm going to play any better by thinking that they want me to play really good."

On Friday no one was playing golf. Or rather, a third of the field got out on the course but play was only possible for 78 minutes before it was suspended due to winds that were gusting up to 60 mph. Suzann Pettersen tweeted: "The sport we played this morning had nothing to do with golf." Of the 18 players who teed off on the front nine, only Angela Stanford made a par at the first hole and Felicity Johnson had a quintuple-bogey nine (followed by a mere double bogey two holes later). Caroline Masson started with three consecutive double-bogey sixes. But it was at the exposed 12th hole where play ground to a halt. Players had tap-in putts roll 10 feet away due to the gusts, and Cristie Kerr needed four goes to get her ball to stay on the tee. "It's a day to be short," said Michelle Wie, "because I felt like a beanpole out there."

With the winds maintaining their strength into the afternoon, it was not possible to resume play and officials decided to scrub out the morning scores. Susan Simpson, the tournament director, said the wind was gusting to 25 mph when play started but conditions quickly deteriorated. "Competitors began their rounds in extremely adverse weather and conditions worsened despite our belief that they would remain stable," she said. "It would have been unfair to those competitors not to declare play null and void and cancel all scores for the round in question." If players were relieved with that news, there was a little controversy about the decision to cut to only 50 players so that 36 holes could be played on Sunday.

But the interruption worked perfectly for Shin. She got to sleep in on Friday and ended up resting all day. Then she teed off for her second round just before midday on Saturday in the best conditions of the week. In the middle of the day it was warm and sunny and the wind coming off the Irish Sea dropped to the gentlest of breezes. The Welsh Hills across Dee Estuary were once more a scenic backdrop rather than a potential hazard to a gale-propelled wayward shot.

Shin took full advantage of the kinder conditions. She chipped in for an eagle at the 10th, her first hole, and then birdied the next three holes. Another birdie came at the par-five 16th as she played the second nine in 31, and despite cooler and windier conditions later in the round, she played the front nine in 33 with two more birdies. She hit all 18 greens in regulation, missed only one fairway and did not find a bunker. Her eight-under-par 64 was a new women's course record at Hoylake by three strokes. Four men have shot 65 in majors at Royal Liverpool: Tiger Woods, Sergio Garcia, Ernie Els and Chris DiMarco — all in the Open Championship in 2006.

"It is probably my best round in a major," Shin said. "I can't believe I had a 64 on such a tough course. The wind was blowing strong again towards the end, but I kept my timing and my tempo." It helped with the latter that she was playing with compatriot Inbee Park — they ended up playing all four rounds together. Shin explained: "Normally I don't watch other players, but Inbee has a great tempo and that is good for me to see." Park had the next-best score of the day, a 68 that was four worse than Shin and put her in second place on the leaderboard, five adrift. Six shots behind were Mika Miyazato and Webb, who both had 70s. Juli Inkster, 52, had a 69 to just make the cut, but Pettersen, Sophie Gustafsson and youngster Hull missed the cut, while Laura Davies had to withdraw with an Achilles injury.

A long Sunday began with Shin returning a 71 in which her lead was briefly cut to one by Webb. But Shin responded with three birdies in a row from the 11th, and after the briefest of lunch breaks took a three-shot lead over the Australian, who had a 68. Park had a 72 and was six behind.

The weather had turned cold and wet and windy again and the conditions told as the day wore on. Webb dropped four shots in the first three holes, which took the pressure off the leader when Shin had a triple bogey at the first hole in the fourth round. But any suggestion that the Korean would be upset by the setback was soon dismissed. She had birdies at the sixth and seventh holes before a bogey at the eighth, but her nearest challengers were struggling. Webb slumped to an 82 with three double-bogey sixes, while Park had a 76 in which her only birdies came at the 16th and 18th holes. The latter meant she held on to second place by one shot over Paula Creamer, who had consistent rounds of 73, 72, 72 and 72 but finished in a sprint with an eagle and two birdies on the back nine. Mika Miyazato was fourth on two over, while Webb shared fifth place with Ryu on three over. Ko took the amateur honors after finishing in a tie for 17th place despite rounds of 76 and 78 on the final day.

Shin dropped a shot at the 11th but then had birdies at the 13th, 15th and 16th holes to briefly lead by 11 strokes before a bogey at the 17th. A huge setting sun finally emerged to spotlight Shin's progress up the 18th hole and her second victory in the championship. "The weather was really tough but I just kept focused on each single shot. After I made the winner's putt it felt like, oh my God, I was so excited," Shin said.

"I think this course is made for me. After last week I had great confidence here and I have great memories of this tournament. Always when I come to the British Open I really enjoy myself. I was thinking that my game was not good for a links course, but finally I had a great tempo with my swing and got to know it works on a links course too. When I won at Sunningdale it was a totally different type of course, so Sunningdale was my favorite golf course, but also here, Royal Liverpool is my favorite golf course too."

8. American Tours

If Rory McIlroy, the Northern Ireland whiz kid, hadn't come of age with his eight-stroke win in the 2011 U.S. Open, he certainly did in the 2012 PGA Championship, and at the final tee in the final round. There, at the 18th, preparing to hit his drive, he turned to his caddie and said, "I'm going to win this one by eight, as well."

And with that and a few other smash performances, McIlroy, a mere 23 years of age, made 2012 his year.

Back at the 18th tee at the PGA: McIlroy had come through a tough field at the difficult Ocean Course at Kiawah Island, South Carolina, that turned harsh in the Atlantic winds, then heaped more pressure on himself with the brash statement that he would win by eight. He'd have to birdie the final hole to do that. Well, it was simple enough — hit a good drive, put the approach 25 feet from the pin, then hole the putt for a 66 and the record eight-stroke win, breaking Jack Nicklaus's long-standing margin.

"I think I heard Tiger say, 'You can have a good season, but to make a good season a great season, you need a major championship," McIlroy said. "Now I've had two great seasons in a row." His season was this great: He won the Honda Classic, PGA Championship, Deutsche Bank Championship and BMW Championship. He topped the U.S. money list with $8,047,952 (and also won the European Tour money title and led the World Money List with $11,301,228), and was elected Player of the Year by his colleagues and the American golf writers.

In the other major championships:

Masters Tournament — Left-handed Bubba Watson made a shot for the ages, getting a wedge to hook about 40 yards on a 135-yard shot from the pine needles back in the trees at No. 10, the second playoff hole against Louis Oosthuizen. The ball ended up 10 feet from the cup. Watson two-putted for the winning par.

U.S. Open Championship — Webb Simpson, in his second U.S. Open, finished with a 68 and won his first major title while behind him Jim Furyk bogeyed two of his last three holes and Graeme McDowell missed a 25-foot birdie try on the 18th.

The Open Championship — Ernie Els won his fourth major title by a stroke when Australia's Adam Scott blew a four-stroke lead with four straight closing bogeys.

Tiger Woods was "back," even if he wasn't all the way back to his former dominating self. His year started with a scare. He withdrew in the fourth round of the WGC - Cadillac Championship in March with a sore left Achilles tendon, the injury that bothered him in 2011. Two weeks later, he won the Arnold Palmer Invitational, his first win in two and a half years. He added the Memorial Tournament and the AT&T National, and though he fell short in the majors, his favorites, it still was an outstanding season. He started the year at 23rd in the Official World Golf Ranking, and rose to third, and was second in U.S. money winnings to McIlroy at $6.1 million (and third on the World Money List with $7.4 million, behind Justin Rose with $7.9 million).

The biggest news of 2012 occurred off the course when the PGA Tour revised the methods for golfers to qualify. First came an abrupt change to the developmental Nationwide Tour, which in June had a new sponsor and became the Web.com Tour, the latest version of the circuit that began as the Ben Hogan Tour in 1990. The Web.com Tour, in turn, will be come the route to the PGA Tour. Beginning in 2013, the qualifying tournament — the famed "Q-School" — will award cards to the Web.com Tour. This would also entail changes to the schedule.

The PGA Tour in 2013 also will begin operating two struggling neighbor tours — the Canadian Tour and the Tour de Las Americas. They will be known as the PGA Tour Canada and PGA Tour Latinoamerica.

In addition:

• John Huh, who won the Mayakoba Golf Classic and had three other top-10 finishes, was named Rookie of the Year. Huh is the first player of Korean descent to win the honor.

• There were six multiple winners on the PGA Tour in 2012: McIlroy (four), Woods (three), and Jason Dufner, Zach Johnson, Hunter Mahan and Brandt Snedeker (two each).

• Charlie Beljan, 28, a rookie trying to gain his card for 2013, won it with the season's most dramatic performance. It came in the final event, the aptly named (in this case) Children's Miracle Network Hospitals Classic. Beljan needed both a miracle and a hospital in the second round when he shot 64 in the grip of a severe panic attack that had him gasping for breath and his heart hammering. He spent the night in a hospital and went on to win the tournament and gain his card. "I thought I literally had a chance to die," Beljan said.

• From the statistics department: Bubba Watson was the longest hitter, averaging 315.5 yards per drive; Jerry Kelly the most accurate, hitting 73 percent of the fairways; Rory McIlroy led in scoring (68.87 strokes per round); Justin Rose in hitting greens in regulation (70.34 percent), and Keegan Bradley was first in the all-around category.

• Wildest win in years: Australia's Mark Leishman started the final round of the Travelers Championship six strokes off the lead, shot 62, then sat and watched for over two hours as a host of pursuers, including Bubba Watson and Charley Hoffman, fell short, leaving him with his first victory. Said Leishman: "Golf is a funny game, a really funny game."

U.S. PGA Tour

Hyundai Tournament of Champions
Maui, Hawaii
Winner: Steve Stricker

How comfortable is a comfortable lead? Alas, that's not a subject that Steve Stricker can really address. He doesn't seem comfortable with any lead, as he demonstrated again in the PGA Tour's 2012 season-opening Hyundai Tournament of Champions. There always seems to be that patch of heavy seas no matter how smooth the sailing. This time, it was a five-shot lead he took into the final round, and in only six holes it was down to one. But, once again, he pulled his nerves and his game back together and won by three.

"I've been there before," Stricker was to say. "It's not a great feeling, either."

Actually, this was the fourth time in the last two years that Stricker, nearing age 45, lost a healthy lead. It was also the fourth time that he recovered in time to win. It was his career 12th win and ninth since turning 40.

Stricker shot the par-73 Plantation course in 68-63-69-69, trailing by one stroke in the first round, leading by five through the middle two rounds, then pulling back from the brink in the final round to beat Martin Laird by three shots. It looked easy — a 23-under-par total of 269. But it wasn't.

The 10-under 63 in the second round is what sent Stricker on his way. He played the last five holes in five under, including an eagle at the par-five 15th, off a three wood to 12 feet from the hole, that gave him a five-stroke lead on Webb Simpson. He then birdied the 17th on a 15-footer and the 18th with two putts. Said Stricker, who played the par-fives in nine under through the first two rounds: "I felt like I was going to make every putt I looked at for a while." Kevin Na had the hottest finish, eagle-eagle. He holed a 221-yard five iron at the par-four 17th, then hit a three wood to 10 feet at the 18th for a 64 and a 137 total, six strokes off the lead.

Stricker's first stumble came in the third round. His five-shot lead was slipping away, but he came to life and birdied the last four holes for a 69. So he led by five going into the final round. He'd been there before: In 2010, his six-shot lead shrank to two in only six holes, but he hung on to win. In 2011 at the Memorial Tournament, he led by three strokes with five holes to play, and won by one. And at the John Deere Classic, he went from a five-shot lead to a two-shot deficit on the final nine, but rallied to win by one.

This time, the scene was Stricker standing dejected, behind the sixth green. His five-shot lead was down to one. Then he holed a 25-footer for birdie at the eighth, tapped in for another at the ninth, dropped a two-footer at the 16th, then birdied the 18th for the three-stroke win.

Said Stricker: "It's always tough trying to win, and it's even more tough when you have a lead like I did."

Sony Open
Honolulu, Hawaii
Winner: Johnson Wagner

As far as can be determined, there is no measurable relationship between the growing of a mustache and success in golf. It is probably best to put it down as coincidence that Johnson Wagner, 31, 20 pounds lighter and a thick mustache heavier, came from behind in the final round to win the Sony Open in Hawaii, the second tournament of 2012. And it seems he had a hunch it was coming. "I was definitely telling people to expect something early this year," Wagner said. Usually my confidence is low. I'm kind of shy, in a little shell. And for some reason, I just had way more energy and confidence going into this year."

It was quite a chase they had at Waialae Country Club. Take, for example, Duffy Waldorf, he of the flowery shirts, in the third round. He happened to notice the scoreboard at No. 9 and saw that he was tied for 40th — and only five shots out of the lead. "Well," he told himself, "if I go make some birdies, I might get back in it." (He did, and he was, briefly.)

After opening with 68-66, Wagner drew within two of the lead with another 66 in third round, behind Matt Every (68) and surprising Jeff Maggert (64), at 47 making a comeback from shoulder surgery.

The chase turned into a scramble in the final round. Harrison Frazar took the lead with a birdie at the 10th but could make only pars the rest of the way and shot 67 to tie for second. Charles Howell birdied the 18th for a 69 to join the tie. Sean O'Hair (67) joined the group when his 30-foot putt for eagle at the 18th just missed. And Carl Pettersson had perhaps the most significant finish in the group. Pettersson shook off a double bogey at No. 2 and birdied four of the last six holes for a 67 and a share of second. Pettersson, a native Swede who played his college golf at North Carolina State University, became an American citizen during the off-season.

After two birdies and two bogeys through the seventh, Wagner birdied Nos. 9 and 10, then pretty well locked it up with a birdie at the 15th, where he put a nine-iron approach into the fringe, hole-high and just 15 feet from the cup. He readily parred in for a 67 and a 13-under 267 total to win by two. Coming into the year, he'd had two victories and only five other top-10 finishes in 139 starts on the PGA Tour.

Then it was time to explain the mustache. "Kind of made a deal with myself in December," Wagner said, "that if I was to get into the Masters, then I was going to keep the mustache, for at least this year." And for those who doubted the power of the mustache, he had a warning. "Look," he added, "this is not a one-month mustache. This is potentially a 10-year mustache."

Humana Challenge
La Quinta, California
Winner: Mark Wilson

It was the kind of week in Southern California where if you wanted to check the scoreboard in the Humana Challenge — the old Bob Hope Desert Classic — you had to go look in the lake. Smart thinking held that it would take a heavy hitter to power his way through those violent January winds that battered the tournament's three courses. But it was slight Mark Wilson, age 37, 5-feet-8 and 145 pounds, a routine hitter at best, averaging drives of 280 yards, who tamed the tough conditions for his fifth PGA Tour victory. It was his time: All five of his victories came before mid-March.

"The only thing I can think of is the break in November and December," Wilson said, trying to explain that timing. "I clear my mind of golf. I've really had a clear mind, focused on what I'm doing."

The Bob Hope tournament had run for 46 years under various names. The Humana Challenge kept the pro-am format but was reduced from five to four rounds and was played over three agreeable Palm Springs-area courses — La Quinta Country Club, PGA West Palmer and PGA West Nicklaus. Wilson shot them in 66-62-67-69–264, 24 under par, to win by two over John Mallinger, Robert Garrigus and Jonathan Wagner, who won the Sony Open in Hawaii the previous week.

It was the second-round 62 that lifted Wilson into the chase, tying him for the lead with Ben Crane (63) and David Toms (65). It wasn't even low for the day. Ryan Moore, after bogeying Nos. 2 and 3, eagled No. 4 and birdied 11 of 12 holes for a 61 on the Nicklaus course. What with everyone beating up on the courses, the 61 only got Moore to within five of the lead.

The winds hit during the third round, knocking a scoreboard into a lake, felling trees and delaying play. The net effect for Wilson was that he had to get up before sunrise on Sunday to complete his third round (67), then went back to get his kids ready for day care at his in-laws' home, then came back for the free-for-all in the final round.

Wilson led by three to start the last nine, but had to hold off a host of challengers. Eight players were within two shots of the lead when the final group neared the final turn. It came down to the 18th. Wagner holed a seven-foot putt for a 65 to finish at 22 under. Mallinger tied when he missed his birdie try from 15 feet and shot 66. Garrigus missed an eagle try from 35 feet and tied with a 68. Then Wilson, in the dimming light, holed a 10-footer for a birdie and the two-stroke victory.

And maybe the calendar wasn't the only key to Wilson's success. There were his "rituals."

"I start every round with two long tees, one short tee, and a quarter and a penny and a divot fixer in my pocket," said Wilson, adding that he is not superstitious.

Farmers Insurance Open
La Jolla, California
Winner: Brandt Snedeker

Brandt Snedeker stumbled home with a 74 in the third round and figured, he was so far out of it, that was the last he would see of Kyle Stanley, who was streaking off into the distance. But an amazed Snedeker did see him again — in a playoff after Stanley's stunning collapse. Stanley would leave in tears, and Snedeker, after coming from seven shots behind in the final round, would leave with the Farmers Insurance Open trophy.

"It's just crazy," said Snedeker. "I told him I was sorry. There's nothing else you can say."

Stanley, 24, in his second year on the PGA Tour, was one hole from getting his first victory. Then, like Jean van de Velde in the Open Championship, he folded on the final hole, suffering a triple bogey-eight. Then he three-putted the second playoff hole for a bogey, and Snedeker had his third PGA Tour victory. This was getting to be a habit for Snedeker. In his previous two wins, he came from five back at the 2007 Wyndham Championship and from six in the 2011 Heritage Classic.

At Torrey Pines, the field alternated between the North and South courses in the first two rounds, playing three rounds on the tougher South course.

Stanley shared the lead in the first round with a 62 at the North course, was the solo leader in the next two rounds (68-68), and came into the final round five ahead of John Huh and John Rollins and seven up on Snedeker (67-64-74-67). Stanley lost no time padding his lead. Four birdies and a bogey on the front nine put him seven ahead through the turn. Even after bogeys on the 11th and 12th, he was leading by four when he came to the par-five 18th, which he'd already played in eagle-birdie-par. He hit his drive 300 yards with ease and laid up about 80 yards short rather than challenge the pond in front of the green. Then he crashed.

Stanley pitched on, but incredibly, his ball bit and spun back down the green and into the water. After a penalty drop, he took no chances, wedging 45 feet past the cup. Then he three-putted for a triple bogey-eight and a 74. Stanley could barely find the words. "I'm kind of in shock," he said.

They tied at 16-under 272, and the playoff ended at the second extra hole, the par-three 16th, on a bit of good luck for Snedeker. His tee shot bounced over the green and was headed for a canyon, but caromed off a TV tower and stopped. He chipped to five feet and got his par. Stanley was on, again about 45 feet away, and again he three-putted, this time for a losing bogey.

The loss brought Stanley to tears. "I know I'll be back," he said. "It's just tough to swallow now."

Said Snedeker: "He's an unbelievably talented player. I wouldn't be surprised if he's contending again really soon."

Waste Management Phoenix Open
Scottsdale, Arizona
Winner: Kyle Stanley

It figured to be the defining moment of Kyle Stanley's young career. There he was, age 24, in his second year on the PGA Tour and just one hole from his first victory, and then his dreams were crushed. This was in the Farmers Insurance Open, where he blew a four-stroke lead with one hole to play. It left him in tears. He vowed he would be back some day. But in a week?

Stanley didn't merely bounce back and get that first win in the Waste Management Phoenix Open the following week, he came from eight shots behind in the final round to do it.

"I'm not sure I expected to recover this quickly," Stanley admitted. "I think the biggest challenge was seeing if I could put last week behind me. I think I did."

Of course, if one player can come from so far behind, it usually means someone else had to fold, and that unfortunate was Spencer Levin. He took a three-shot lead through the second round, and going into the fourth he was leading the field by six strokes, and Stanley by eight. Levin's first victory was at his fingertips.

"He's playing so good, you don't expect him to come back to the field," Bubba Watson offered. "You're going to have to go chase him down."

Levin had had only two bogeys over the first three rounds, and shot 63 in the second, with six birdies and an eagle. But the rest is an old and painful tale in golf. Stanley made up four of his eight-shot deficit on the front nine when he birdied the second, third and eighth while Levin had a birdie and two bogeys.

The pieces fell into place from there. Stanley birdied the 11th, 13th and 14th holes, and the unfortunate Levin bogeyed the 11th and 12th, birdied the 14th, then went through a nightmare at the par-five 15th. His tee shot bounced off a cart path and ended up against cactus in the desert area. He had to hack the ball with his putter from an awkward stance, and after his caddie plucked pieces of cactus from his pants and shirt, he hit his next into water near the green. That was the final blow — a double bogey.

"It just wasn't my day," Levin said. "You have a six-shot lead and lose, you gave it away. What are you going to do? I tried my best."

Stanley, a big hitter despite standing only 5-foot-11 and weighing 165 pounds, tied Levin with a birdie at the par-five 13th off a 376-yard drive. He took the lead with a 12-foot birdie at the 14th. Levin closed with a 75 and finished third. Stanley got his first win on a total of 69-66-69-65–269, 15 under par, beating Ben Crane by one stroke, but he didn't get it without a thought for Levin.

Said Stanley: "He's way too good of a player not to bounce back." Talk about a guy knowing whereof he speaks.

AT&T Pebble Beach National Pro-Am
Pebble Beach, California
Winner: Phil Mickelson

It's a bit awkward in the telling, but the singular thing that happened at the AT&T Pebble Beach National Pro-Am was that Phil Mickelson pulled a Tiger Woods — on Tiger Woods.

It's legendary, the way golfers wilted with Woods coming up behind them. This time, it was Mickelson who came from behind and Woods played the other role.

Actually, the scene was a bit distorted by the fact that Mickelson and Woods, playing together, weren't in a classic shootout. They were chasing winless Charlie Wi. Mickelson made a brilliant charge to the win, and Woods faded. This definitely wasn't the old script.

This was the old Crosby Clambake, the February Frolic with professionals and amateurs of celebrity and CEO status playing Pebble Beach, Spyglass and the Monterey Peninsula Country Club. Wi ended up the unfortunate main victim.

Opening with a 61 at Monterey Peninsula, Wi held or shared the lead through the first three rounds, much encouraged at the thought of nabbing that first PGA Tour victory. There was a catch. "I'm sure I'll be fighting my demons all day," Wi said, and sure enough, they popped up immediately. He three-putted No. 1 for a double bogey, never really recovered, and closed with three straight birdies for his fifth runner-up finish. And he was now 0-for-163 on the tour.

But who noticed? It was the heavyweight bout just ahead of him that took center stage. Woods began the final round four off Wi's lead, and Mickelson was two behind him. Mickelson opened the battle at the par-five No. 2. He burned the hole with a long eagle putt and tapped in for a birdie, then went on a birdie-birdie-eagle tear from No. 4, on putts of 15, one and 20 feet and made the turn in five-under 31.

Woods birdied the sixth and seemed ready to turn up the heat. But he stumbled to three straight bogeys from No. 7 and turned in 38. He seemed set for a two-shot leap when he holed a bunker shot for birdie at No. 12 with Mickelson needing a 30-footer for par. But Mickelson holed it. Then three more birdies gave him a 64. Woods made two more bogeys and shot 75.

Mickelson, shooting 70-65-70-64–269, 17 under par, beat Wi by two strokes and topped Woods by nine.

"All I had to do was get off to a good, solid start," a puzzled Woods said. "And I didn't do that."

It was Mickelson's fourth win at Pebble Beach and his 40th on the PGA Tour, and significantly, also the fifth straight time he scored better than Woods when they played together in the final round. How to explain this amazing reversal?

"I am inspired playing with him," Mickelson said. "I think most people are, but he seems to bring out the best in me, and the last four or five years, I've played some of my best golf playing with him and I really enjoy it."

Northern Trust Open
Pacific Palisades, California
Winner: Bill Haas

It seemed to most that Bill Haas didn't have much to worry about. He had the clubhouse lead by a shot in the Northern Trust Open, and only two guys could catch him, and to do that, both needed birdies at Riviera Country Club's tough 18th hole, which had yielded only six birdies all day. Phil Mickelson, fresh from winning the AT&T Pebble Beach National Pro-Am, had played it in even par and Keegan Bradley in one over. Haas had just parred it for a 69 and a seven-under-par 277 total. Still, Haas kept warming up on the practice range.

Then came a thunderous roar from the 18th green. It was Mickelson, holing a 25-footer.

Playoff.

Mickelson turned to Bradley. "Join me," he said.

Bradley did, from 12 feet, both scoring 71s. There would be a three-way playoff.

It figured to be a beauty. All three were noted for heroic finishes. Just last September, Haas escaped from a watery lie to set up an $11.4 million payday at The Tour Championship. Bradley overcame an impossible deficit to win the PGA Championship last August. As for Mickelson — any number of feats.

They parred the first playoff hole, the 18th, then went to the 10th, a risk-reward par-four of only 312 yards — an enticing hole for anyone willing to risk reaching it. All three could reach it, therefore all three had to try. Nobody could afford to be left behind. They hadn't dominated it. Haas had played it 4-3-3-4, Mickelson 3-5-4-3 and Bradley 5-4-4-3. Mickelson was short, and his flop shot second ended up in the back bunker. Bradley was in a greenside bunker and blasted out 15 feet long, just off the green. Haas hit long, into the thick back rough, and played wide right to avoid the bunker and ended up 40 feet from the cup. He putted, trying for a two-putt par, and darned if the thing didn't drop.

"I never expected to make a 40-footer, especially in that situation," said Haas, now sporting his fourth PGA Tour title. "I guess it was meant to be."

Haas, shooting 72-68-68-69, trailed until late in the final round and stepped into an opportunity when Mickelson authored some loose play, leaving himself a 50-footer at the 14th and a 70-footer at the 15th. He bogeyed both, this after leading from the start with some free-wheeling golf. In the first round, he reached the 587-yard 11th with a dangerous "driver off the deck" into the wind — using his driver off the fairway. In the second, he had a hole-out eagle and a chip-in birdie, and in the third, he clipped a tree limb, hit behind a bottle brush, and threaded a nine iron through five trees, then found a spectator down flat on the other side.

"I thought for sure I took him out," Mickelson said. It turned out the guy was lying still so as not to disturb Mickelson's ball, there in the hem of his shorts. Haas's 40-footer was just the final straw.

WGC - Accenture Match Play Championship
Marana, Arizona
Winner: Hunter Mahan

To Hunter Mahan, between the acclaim from television people including Johnny Miller and Nick Faldo and the chanting of the fans, it sounded more like the Rory McIlroy Admiration Society than a golf tournament. "Deep down," Mahan said, "you wanted to postpone that crowning of the No. 1 player in the world."

Thus inspired, Mahan — after making his way through five other guys — came head-to-head with McIlroy in the final of the WGC - Accenture Match Play Championship. Mahan cooled the cheering section by winning three straight holes on the front nine, then held McIlroy off for a 2-and-1 victory, his fourth PGA Tour victory and his second WGC win.

But first, some interesting golf got played along the way at Dove Mountain, in the cactus and rocks of Arizona's high Sonoran Desert. For example:

• Luke Donald, No. 1 in the world and No. 1 seed, got knocked out in the first round, 5 and 4, by the lowest seed, No. 64 Ernie Els. He even shanked a shot and hit two balls into the water. "I don't know where to start to explain," Donald said, "other than I didn't have control of my golf ball." Donald, who never trailed in his 2011 victory, became the fourth straight champion to lose in the first round the following year.

• Jason Day (7), a member of the youth movement, rallied from three down with three to play to beat Spain's Rafael Cabrera-Bello (58) in 19 holes. Then he got crushed by John Senden (39), 6 and 5.

• Tiger Woods (19) got up and down from a bunker, holing a 10-foot putt on the 18th for a 1-up win over Spain's Gonzalo Fernandez-Castano (46). Then he was ousted when his five-foot birdie putt at the last never touched the hole, giving Nick Watney (14) a 1-up win. It was the third straight time Woods, a three-time winner, didn't get out of the second round.

Mahan, the No. 21 seed, beat Zach Johnson (44), Y.E. Yang (53), Steve Stricker (5), Matt Kuchar (13) and Mark Wilson (40). McIlroy (2) beat George Coetzee (63), Anders Hansen (34), Miguel Angel Jimenez (50), Sang-Moon Bae (42) and Lee Westwood (3).

McIlroy never led in the final and lost a great chance when he missed a four-foot par putt at No. 1. Mahan took the lead at the par-three No. 6, off a nine iron to two feet. McIlroy lost the seventh on a double bogey, then the eighth on a bogey. This wasn't the McIlroy who racked up seven birdies in a 10-hole stretch against Westwood in their morning semi-final. McIlroy finally won a hole at the 11th, with a chip-in eagle, and birdied the 14th to cut Mahan's lead to 2 up, but couldn't get any closer. "It feels good because you're going against the game's best," Mahan said. "I needed everything to win."

Mayakoba Golf Classic
Riviera Maya, Mexico
Winner: John Huh

The Mayakoba Golf Classic came down to a battle between two rookies — one real, the other moaning that he played like one.

Introducing John Huh, 21, an American of Korean parentage, graduate of the 2011 qualifying tournament playing in his fifth PGA Tour start. He scored his first win in a grinding eight-hole playoff against Australian veteran Robert Allenby, 40, who took a two-stroke lead into the final hole, double-bogeyed, and blew the chance for his first tour win since 2001.

"I mean, I had this tournament in the bag — a two-shot lead with one hole to play — and just played it like a rookie," Allenby lamented.

"It's amazing," said Huh, who had ties for sixth and 12th. "It's my rookie year, and playing in my fifth event. I just couldn't put it in words ... it's really hard to explain. It's major. I mean, it was my dream."

The key to Huh's breakthrough win was Allenby's amazing crash. Allenby was playing brilliantly, ripping off five straight birdies from No. 2 and adding three more through the 14th. Then came the fatal error at the 18th. "Disappointed that I didn't hit three wood off 18 in regulation," Allenby said. He had opted for the driver instead, and ended up in the trees on the right. It cost him a double bogey and a 65. Huh himself was blistering the par-71 El Camaleon course. He birdied Nos. 1 and 3, eagled No. 5 and birdied No. 8, the came home with birdies at Nos. 13, 14 and 17 for a no-bogey, tournament-low 63, tying Allenby at 13-under 271.

The playoff alternated between the par-four 18th and the par-three 10th. They matched pars for seven holes, then at the eighth (No. 10), Huh chipped from the right rough to two feet and got his par. Allenby put his tee shot into a hazard on the right, chipped to 15 feet, but missed the tying par putt. It was the fifth eight-hole playoff in tour history and the first since 1983, but three holes short of the record, when Cary Middlecoff and Lloyd Mangrum were declared co-winners after an 11-hole marathon in the 1949 Motor City Open.

Allenby and Huh chased the leaders through the first three rounds before moving ahead in the last, Allenby shooting 69-67-70-65 and Huh 67-70-71-63. They got some needed help from golfers getting out of their way. Matt Every had five birdies through the 13th, then bogeyed the 16th. Colt Knost made six birdies, but cooled off with a bogey at the 12th. Alejandro Canizares birdied six times through the 11th, but bogeyed the 12th and 14th. Daniel Summerhays, who made only eight cuts in 29 starts as a rookie in 2011, had the toughest victim story. He led by two going into the final round, his first 54-hole lead on the tour, then suffered five bogeys on the front nine and shot 73. He had the consolation of scoring his best finish, a tie for fifth.

Honda Classic
Palm Beach Gardens, Florida
Winner: Rory McIlroy

Ah, the resilience of youth.

One week, Rory McIlroy was frustrated and getting beaten in the Accenture World Match Play. The next, he was standing up to a super-hot Tiger Woods and winning the Honda Classic.

The reward, in addition to a rousing payday, was the No. 1 spot in the Official World Golf Ranking.

"It was always a dream of mine to become the world No. 1," said McIlroy, 22, from Northern Ireland. "But I didn't know that I would be able to get here this quickly."

McIlroy had to withstand the famous Woods pressure down the final stretch to do it.

McIlroy was at the 13th green, trying to protect his lead, when he was hit by a thunderous roar from up ahead. "It definitely wasn't a birdie roar," McIlroy said. It sure wasn't. It was Woods making an eagle at the par-five 18th — his second of the day — wrapping up a bogey-free 62, eight under par at PGA National's Champion course. "It could have really been something special if a few putts would have gone in," he said. He held the clubhouse lead at 10-under 270, and McIlroy still had a long way to go.

The Honda Classic had something for everyone. For example, PGA Tour rookie Brian Harman, 25, who carries peanut butter-and-jelly sandwiches in his bag, broke the course record by three shots with a nine-under 61 in the second round. He would go on to his best finish, a tie for 12th. At the other end was journeyman Tom Gillis, age 43, tasting the lead and finally tying Woods for second. He found the secret. "I wasn't going to try too hard," he said.

McIlroy shot the first three rounds in 66-67-66, taking the lead in the third, and his big test would come in the final round, where he led Gillis and Harris English by two, but was a whopping nine ahead of Woods.

Woods plunged into the battle with an eagle at the par-five third, ground away with four birdies, including a tense 25-foot putt at the 17th, then fired a five iron to eight feet at the 18th and eagled again for his 62 and went for a bite to eat.

McIlroy, meanwhile, was holding his own, effectively if unimpressively. He birdied the eighth, bogeyed the 12th, and was at the 13th lining up his putt when the thunder from Woods's eagle at the 18th rolled over him. McIlroy responded by dropping the eight-footer for a birdie and a two-stroke lead. He was in trouble at the 14th, his tee shot in deep rough. He hacked out a par.

"I knew if I could just play the last five holes at even par, it was going to be good enough," McIlroy said. He did and had his fifth career win, the third on the PGA Tour, and the No. 1 spot in the world, climbing over Luke Donald.

"Congrats!" Donald messaged him: "Enjoy the view!"

WGC - Cadillac Championship
Miami, Florida
Winner: Justin Rose

Justin Rose and Bubba Watson were having such a dandy time of it that hardly anybody noticed Tiger Woods improving by five shots, shooting a 67 — and losing ground.

This was in the second round of the WGC - Cadillac Championship at the Doral Blue Monster that was more blue than monster when these guys were done with it. In the final round, Rose fit neatly between a sagging Watson and a charging Rory McIlroy to take his fourth PGA Tour win and his first in the World Golf Championships. And he didn't even know he'd done it when he did.

After sticking close through the first three rounds — 69-64-69 — he closed with a 70 and a 16-under 272 total, and went to the practice range to stay warm in case there was a playoff. He knew Watson had to birdie the last to tie him. It finally dawned on him — no birdie, no roar, no tie. He'd won.

"Definitely a fantastic feeling," Rose said. "It sets up a very exciting year."

But a questionable one for Tiger Woods. He'd shot 72-67-68 and was eight shots off the lead going into the final round, then pulled up with an injured left Achilles tendon. "After hitting my tee shot at 12, I decided it was necessary to withdraw," Woods said. This was the Achilles tendon he'd hurt in the 2011 Masters, and it cost him three months of the season.

Rose and the big-hitting Watson took center stage in the second round when they had 17 birdies between them — eight by Rose (64), while Watson had nine birdies, an eagle and a bogey for a 62. This included an improbable birdie at the par-four No. 6, where he sliced a nine iron around a tree into a left-to-right wind to six feet.

Watson shot 67 in the third round and held a three-stroke lead over Rose and Keegan Bradley (66) going into the final round, which had a touch of carnival to it. Take Sergio Garcia. He watered four shots at the par-four third and made a 12, and Paul Casey aced the 13th. Watson's game got away from him early. After a birdie at No. 1, he stumbled through four bogeys on the front. Rose started three behind Watson, then found himself two behind Bradley at the turn. Bradley then shot 41 on the back. McIlroy (67), eight behind to start, charged with five birdies and an eagle, but fell short by two bogeys and finished third.

Rose was the steadiest of the bunch. He took a two-stroke lead at the 14th, sticking a wedge shot to five feet, setting up a birdie. He'd had three birdies and a bogey to that point, then bogeyed the 18th from a bunker for a 70 that he didn't know was good enough until he heard the silence.

"It was all about controlling what I could control," Rose said.

Puerto Rico Open
Rio Grande, Puerto Rico
Winner: George McNeill

Some say golf teaches life lessons. If so, then George McNeill figures he learned a thing or two the hard way. About winning, for example.

"Winning is tough at anything," he said. "Doesn't matter — playing golf, playing tennis, trying to be the best person, smartest person in the class." This was McNeill after winning the Puerto Rico Open at Trump International, his second win on the PGA Tour but first since the Frys.com Open in 2007. He was a rookie then. Winning seemed to come pretty easy.

"I think I was a little dumb, for lack of a better word," said McNeill. "I really didn't know any better. I've been out here awhile now. It's my sixth year, and I've had six second-place finishes and two playoff losses, and seems like — wow — it's getting harder and harder and harder to win."

So now, in his 145th start, it was a wiser and cagier McNeill who came from behind down the closing stretch to pluck the Puerto Rico Open right off the fingertips of young Japanese whiz Ryo Ishikawa. That's when the tournament had got the toughest. McNeill tied Matt Jones for the lead at 66 in a wind-whipped first round. "Just had to judge it right," said Jones, after five birdies and a bogey. "I had unbelievable ball-striking. I think I was pin-high every hole except 17."

McNeill likened it to his days as a college golfer at Florida State University. "It's just like Florida," he said. "So it felt comfortable, and I hit it pretty well and putted pretty well." McNeill shot 70 in the second round and fell three behind Jones, but regained the lead in the third with a wild 67. He eagled the par-five fifth, tripped at Nos. 7 and 8 on three-putt bogeys, then birdied five of the 10 holes coming in to lead by a stroke at 13-under 203, up by one on Henrik Stenson (65) and Kevin Stadler (66), who birdied four of the first five holes.

McNeill would outrun them, but now the problem was up ahead — Ishikawa, who closed with a 68 and held a one-shot clubhouse lead at 273. "I made three birdies in the last four holes, and it was a great experience for me to be very close to the winning experience," said Ishikawa, 20, a nine-time winner on the Japan Tour, who failed to qualify for the WGC - Cadillac Championship being played at Doral the same week.

It looked as though McNeill was going to be turned away again. But he pulled himself together and raced home with three straight birdies for a 69 and won by two with a 16-under 272.

"I was really nervous, but I knew what I had to do," McNeill said. "Basically, I just had to bear down and get it done. If not, then somebody else was going to win. I was trying to have control of myself, and that's all I was looking for."

Transitions Championship
Palm Harbor, Florida
Winner: Luke Donald

The tournament couldn't have been better named — the Transitions Championship. Rory McIlroy's Twitter message said it all: "Well I enjoyed it while it lasted! Congrats Luke Donald! Impressive performance!"

McIlroy, who wasn't in the field, had spent all of two weeks as No. 1 in the World Ranking, and now was transitioning right back out when Donald retook the spot in a four-man playoff, ending one of the tour's wilder tournaments.

It opened with Padraig Harrington emerging from a long spell in the shadows with a 10-under-par 61 in the first round on Innisbrook's Copperhead Course. He faded and was replaced by Jason Dufner, last seen self-destructing at the PGA Championship the previous August. Dufner took the lead on two remarkable bogey-free 66s. And next, two other big names resurfaced after long absences — Retief Goosen, who would falter under his chronically bad back, and Jim Furyk, who would stick around for the final act.

Donald kept pace as well as he could, but his first three rounds of 67-68-70 got him no closer than three strokes. The final round turned into a chase. At one point, eight players either led or shared the lead. Then in the last hour, there was a six-way tie, until two players fell out — Ken Duke, missing a five-foot par putt at the 17th, and Ernie Els, with two closing bogeys.

It would boil down on that steamy March Sunday into a four-man dead heat, a tie at 13-under 271. Robert Garrigus birdied the last two holes for a 64 and the clubhouse lead. Sang-Moon Bae dropped a six-foot par putt at the 18th for a 68. Donald started the final round three shots off the lead, then birdied four times in a seven-hole stretch around the turn, well on his way to the 66 that clinched his spot in the first playoff in the Transitions' 12 years.

It lasted one hole. All four were putting for birdie. Furyk was dead when his eight iron from the rough ended up 40 feet from the flag. Bae's 18-footer fell away. Garrigus pulled his seven-footer. That left the steady Donald facing an uphill 157-yard shot from the rough to a pin nestled over the bunker. He opted for his seven iron.

"You never quite know, out of the rough," Donald said. "Sometimes it comes out soft and sometimes it comes out a little hot. That one — just when it was in the air, looked good to me."

It ended up about six feet beneath the cup. He rolled it in. The birdie gave him his fifth win in his last 31 starts around the globe and also returned him to the top of the rankings, a message for those who thought 2011 was a fluke.

"I don't think many people thought I could do that all over again this year," Donald said. "Hopefully I can prove them wrong."

Well, he was off to a great start.

Arnold Palmer Invitational
Orlando, Florida
Winner: Tiger Woods

This week in Orlando, Florida, observers figured there was a real sign that Tiger Woods was playing his old game. It came in the second round of the Arnold Palmer Invitational. He was putting for birdie on every hole. Woods did birdie seven holes, adding to four birdies in the first round. His bogey at the par-three 17th was his only bogey over the first 36 holes.

Two rounds later, Woods had the same observers shuffling through the records book.

This was Woods's first victory since the domestic incident late in 2009 that led to his fall from grace. He had gone 27 PGA Tour events and 923 days without winning. This was his record seventh victory at Palmer's event at the Bay Hill Club and his 72nd tour victory, one short of Jack Nicklaus for second place on the career list.

"It's not like winning a major championship or anything," Woods said. "But it certainly feels really good."

Woods trailed Charlie Wi and Jason Dufner (66s) in the first round, tied Wi for the lead in the second round, and led from there, playing Bay Hill in 69-65-71-70–275, 13 under par, beating Northern Ireland's Graeme McDowell by five strokes.

Said McDowell: "I said to myself, if I could get within a couple coming into 16, maybe I could have a shot. Every time I got close to him, I made a mistake." He went from a 63 in the second round to a fragmented 74 in the final round, when after a double bogey, he made a 45-foot birdie putt and a 50-footer for eagle, then bogeyed three of the last seven holes.

Woods's performance would have to rank as a surprise. It was only two weeks ago, in the WGC - Cadillac Championship, that he was taken off the course with tightness in his left Achilles tendon, the injury that forced him to miss three months of the 2011 season. The injury was in the back of his mind from the start of the week.

"I got to the range, started warming up, starting getting tight," Woods said. "I'm going to have to monitor it."

Woods cruised untroubled and took a one-stroke lead over McDowell in the third round, despite a weird occurrence at the 15th hole. Just as he was hitting his tee shot, a teenager fainted and a woman screamed when she saw it. Woods hooked the tee shot out of bounds and double-bogeyed. Then McDowell tied him with a birdie at the 17th. Woods retook the lead at the par-five 16th with a birdie out of a fairway bunker.

In the fourth round, while McDowell was lurching to a 74, Woods shook off a bogey at No. 2 and made four birdies on the front nine. The last, at No. 8, was vintage Woods — an eight iron from 182 yards, just clearing the bank and rolling to four feet. A bogey at the 14th cut his lead as McDowell struggled.

"I am excited, no doubt," Woods said. "I'm looking forward to the momentum I've built here."

Shell Houston Open
Humble, Texas
Winner: Hunter Mahan

For Hunter Mahan at the Shell Houston Open, it was a case of winning through psychology.

"That's a pretty surreal thing to think about," said Mahan, after coming from behind in the final round to take a one-stroke victory at Redstone Golf Club, becoming the first two-time winner of the season. "It shows me what I can do, shows me what I'm capable of."

Not that winning is simple, of course, but a good frame of mind and a dollop of self-belief can go a long way, Mahan said, summarizing some recent work with a sports psychologist who encouraged him to quit beating himself up for misfires and such.

"I feel I showed myself I don't have to be perfect to win," Mahan said.

It came after the field went through frustrating storm delays and settled into a good dogfight in the third round. That's when South Africa's Louis Oosthuizen completed his second-round 66 Saturday morning and began his third round with bogeys on the first two holes. An 11-foot birdie putt at No. 6 was a relief. "After that, I felt real comfortable," he said. He played the last 11 holes in seven under for another 66, a 17-under 199 total and a two-stroke lead on Mahan, who was riding an amazing putter. At Nos. 5, 6, 10 and 14 he birdied from 23, 34, 28 and 28 feet for a 65. "That," Mahan allowed, "was a nice stretch there."

The final round was more grind than race. Said Phil Mickelson, the defending champion: "I think there's a really hot round out there." But he shot a pedestrian 71 and tied for fourth. Oosthuizen's round was anything but pedestrian. After an early bogey-birdie exchange, he double-bogeyed

Nos. 5 and 8 and bogeyed 9 and 10, and finished third on a 75. "I'm not going to be bothered about the way I played the front nine," he said. Carl Pettersson, first-round co-leader, parred the last eight holes for a 71 and fell short by a stroke.

Mahan wasn't perfect, but he was steady, getting birdies at Nos. 9 and 10, and then came to a crystallizing moment at the last hole. He split the fairway, then hit a 203-yard approach to 21 feet and two-putted for the par.

"Feels great to come to 18 knowing you got to have a par to win, and hit two good shots and make an easy par," he said. That wrapped up a card of 69-67-65-71 for a 16-under 272 and the one-stroke win.

Ernie Els left in a fit of pique. He'd had to win to get an automatic berth in the Masters the next week, but finished six back. So he would miss the Masters for the first time since 1993. Of course, Masters officials might issue him a special invitation, as they did for Greg Norman in 2002. But Els slammed that door shut.

"To go through all of this, and then get an invite — I wouldn't take it," he said. "They can keep it."

Masters Tournament.
Augusta, Georgia
Winner: Bubba Watson

See Chapter 2.

RBC Heritage
Hilton Head Island, South Carolina
Winner: Carl Pettersson

The RBC Heritage had overtones of a soap opera, which asked the question, can a fat man find happiness and fulfillment in golf?

Carl Pettersson, his robust old self, gave a blunt answer: 70-65-66-69 adds up to a "You bet."

"Just because you don't look like an athlete doesn't mean you're not an athlete," said Pettersson. "We're not running a marathon out here. We're walking 18 holes."

The Heritage became a weighty issue — pun intended — when Pettersson, 34, and Carl Knost, 26, were paired. Pettersson had dropped 30 pounds in the belief that he would play better, then put it back on when the opposite occurred. Knost was still Knost, at 5-foot-11 and 215 pounds.

Said Pettersson, after they whipped through the third round: "Two fat guys played in three hours, 48 minutes."

And said Pettersson, after he'd posted a five-stroke victory: "It's great to be fit and everything, but I feel like I'm fit enough to get around 18 holes."

Knost, who had one top-20 finish, a tie for third in the Mayakoba Classic in February, birdied three of his last five holes to join a tie for the first-round lead at four-under 67. He took the solo lead in the second with a 66–133. It was a glimmer of hope for the man who turned pro with such promise, after winning both the U.S. Amateur and the U.S. Public Links Championship in 2007. "I felt I was ready for this level," said Knost. "And apparently I wasn't."

Pettersson and Knost were paired as the fat men in the third round, wisecracking their way around the Harbour Town Links. Pettersson erased a two-shot deficit with five straight birdies on the front nine and birdied the 18th for a 66 and a one-stroke lead over Knost, who helped with a case of nerves. Knost bogeyed No. 1 after a 190-yard drive, then eagled No. 2, and had some shaky moments after that, "I could have got rattled pretty easy after that start," he said. "But I'm really proud of the way I hung in." Pettersson remained realistic on his own chances. "I'm not Phil (Mickelson) or Tiger (Woods) or anybody," he said.

Knost started the final round bogey-birdie-double bogey, and that pretty well ended his bid for that first win. And Pettersson birdied three of the first five — on a 24-foot putt at No. 1, a 16-footer at No. 4, and on two putts from 40 at No. 5. He was on his way to a one-bogey 69, a 14-under 270 total and the five-shot win. Zach Johnson emerged as his real threat with three quick birdies going out, but he was choppy from there and shot 70, finishing five behind. Knost, with 74, finished third, six back.

With the victory topping Pettersson's upbeat season so far, the question was how did he put the weight back on? "Well," Pettersson said, "you drink 10 beers and eat a tub of ice cream before bed..."

Valero Texas Open
San Antonio, Texas
Winner: Ben Curtis

You could tell how they did by the way they carried on at the finish. Matt Every was frustrated. Scott Piercy snapped his putter over his knee. You didn't need a translator for that. Ben Curtis had tears in his eyes and his voice was quivery.

That was a happy man, and a relieved one. For Curtis, taking the Valero Texas Open, at the testing TPC San Antonio, was as much about redemption as winning. Remember, Curtis was a no-name when he came out of nowhere to win the 2003 Open Championship. And then came a long dry spell, which he broke with two victories in 2006, in the Booz Allen Classic and the 84 Lumber Classic, both now ex-tournaments. Then came a long slide down the money list until in 2012 he needed invitations to get into tournaments. He was splitting his time between the PGA Tour and the European Tour, trying to find a home. The Texas Open, in mid-April, was just his fourth PGA Tour stop of the year.

"It's been a tough couple years just fighting through it," Curtis said.

The Texas win didn't come easy. Curtis opened with a bogey-free 67, four behind Matt Every, then shot another in the second round before a storm delay to take the lead at 10-under 134, two ahead of David Mathis (67) and Every, who completed a 73 Saturday morning.

The leaders didn't lose ground in the third, but no one came away unscathed. Curtis himself seemed on the edge of collapse, stumbling to two double bogeys, including an awkward one at the par-five No. 8, where he hit twice from an adjoining fairway. He pulled out a one-over 73 and kept the lead by three over Every, who scrambled to two birdies for his own 73 and stayed in second place, tied with John Huh, three behind. "Overall, not bad," Every said. "I have a chance to win." Huh nearly withdrew after the first round, when he went five over on his first three holes and shot 77. But 68-67 middle rounds kept him in the hunt. It was a three-man battle down the final nine.

Huh made a great try but that opening 77 left him too much to do. He closed with a 69, tying Every at 281. Said Huh: "I didn't really expect too much, final round." Every missed four birdie tries of nine feet or less and shot 71. "A little bummed out," he said. "I mean, they got to go in sometime. Saving for something bigger, I guess."

Curtis locked up the win with a 12-foot birdie putt at the 18th for a 72, winning by two with his nine-under 279. "I think deep down," Curtis said, "you realize all the hard work you put in finally paid off."

As to why Piercy wanted to teach his putter a lesson: He was four under for the day and flirting with a high finish and then made nine at the par-five 18th.

Zurich Classic of New Orleans
Avondale, Louisiana
Winner: Jason Dufner

Those who expected Bubba Watson to set the world on fire after winning the Masters spectacularly two weeks previously would have to wait a little longer. (He could only manage a tie for 18th this time.) Conversely, those whoever thought Jason Dufner was buried under the collapse of his world at the 2011 PGA Championship also miscalculated.

Dufner had said after the PGA — and some thought it was just brave talk — that he would be back. And here he was, at age 35, plucking the Zurich Classic out of Ernie Els's hands in a playoff for his first victory in 164 PGA Tour starts.

"To get the monkey off my back — it's a great feeling," Dufner said. And just in time. He would be getting married the next week.

There was good reason to believe his fold in the PGA had done him in. Five times in his career — twice in 2012 — he led through two rounds, only to wilt.

"There's been a good bit of pressure," Dufner said. "People talking about, 'Why can't you close the deal?' Friends, family, media, even people in my inner circle. But when you're leading going into weekends and you're finishing 24th, then there's going to be some questions."

Dufner quieted them all by holding off a hard-charging Els, then beating him with a birdie on the second playoff hole. Dufner shot the TPC Louisiana in 67-65-67-70, and Els closed with a flawless 67 that included an eagle at the par-five seventh. They tied at a course-record 19-under 269.

When Dufner holed a 30-footer for eagle at the 18th in the second round, he found himself in uncomfortable territory — the halfway lead. He didn't need to be reminded about his earlier performances. He'd had at least a share of the 36-hole lead in two of his last four tournaments. "I've been trying to think what I can do better, emotionally," he said. "There's a lot of different things that go into winning besides hitting the golf ball well."

Putting was part of it, and he was a putting fiend this time. In the third round, he birdied three of the first five holes, dropping a 50-footer at No. 4 and a 25-footer at No. 5, setting up a 67 that gave him a two-stroke lead going into the final round. In the fourth, he saved par with a 44-footer at the 16th. It was a new twist. Tour statistics had him 98th in scoring in the third round and 108th for the fourth.

Pressure is what Dufner wasn't handling, but he handled it this time. He and Els tied with pars on the first extra hole. On the second, also at the par-five 18th, Els missed his birdie from 19 feet. Dufner's eagle try from 60 feet missed, leaving him two feet from a birdie. He tapped it in for his first win.

"It helps pay for the wedding," Dufner said, managing a grin. "They're more expensive than I thought."

Wells Fargo Championship
Charlotte, North Carolina
Winner: Rickie Fowler

Tiger Woods may well have made a fashion statement with his red ensemble for Sundays, but it's hard to say whether Rickie Fowler's all-orange motif would ever catch on. But at least now he had a victory to go with it, with his first PGA Tour win in the Wells Fargo Championship.

It seemed that Fowler had been at it for a very long time — the orange did attract attention — but he was only age 23 and in his third season and 67th start on the tour when he beat Rory McIlroy, also 23, and D.A. Points, 35, with a brilliant wedge approach at the first playoff hole at Quail Hollow. It was the par-four 18th, and it had yielded only four birdies in the final round.

"I didn't want to play it safe," said Fowler, facing a 133-yard shot to a tricky pin. "I had a good number, and I was aiming right of the hole, with the wind coming from the right, and if I hit the perfect shot, it comes down right on the stick ... I hit the perfect shot at the right time, and I was going for it."

It did come down on the stick — to four feet. And when both McIlroy and Points could only par, Fowler dropped the putt for a birdie and his breakthrough win.

It was good timing. The golf world was wondering whether Fowler's promise was real. Fowler had come close a number of times but couldn't break through, except for a win in Korea. He'd shown so much talent that it seems people forgot he was so young.

Fowler drew praise from his competitors. McIlroy, winner of the 2010 Wells Fargo Championship, said, "You couldn't call the 18th today a birdie hole, not with that pin. ... For Rickie to go out and play that hole the way he did, he deserved to win." Said Points: "The shot he hit was spectacular."

Fowler trailed Webb Simpson by one in the first round and Nick Watney by six in the second. Simpson led going into the final round, with Points one behind, McIlroy two, and Fowler three, part of a 10-player jam within four strokes.

Points, a one-time winner, had the Wells Fargo in hand until the final hole. He hadn't bogeyed in 40 holes, since the 13th in the second round, and came to the 18th leading by a shot. And he bogeyed. The 71 dropped him into the tie. McIlroy's chance to win in regulation evaporated when he missed a 15-foot birdie putt at the 18th and shot 70. Fowler was leading until he went from bunker to bunker and bogeyed No. 16 and posted a six-birdie, three-bogey 69. The win left Fowler reaching for words to express himself.

"Definitely some relief, satisfaction," he said. "I'm definitely happy. It's not a bad thing, winning. It's kind of fun."

The Players Championship
Ponte Vedra Beach, Florida
Winner: Matt Kuchar

They were beginning to call him "Mr. Top 10." That was apt. Coming into The Players Championship in May, Matt Kuchar had last won in August 2010, in the Barclays. Starting with the 2011 season, he'd had 13 top-10 finishes. So one of the game's brightest smiles got about 100 megawatts brighter when that final putt dropped in The Players Championship. Kuchar beamed.

"Such an amazing feeling," he said. "It really is magical." Kuchar seems to have a way with words. As when, in the third round, he hit a poor tee shot at the 14th and said, "Oh, stinker!"

But Kuchar prevailed, shooting the TPC Sawgrass in 68-68-69-70, for a 13-under 275 total and a two-stroke win for his fourth PGA Tour victory. The Pete Dye course, ordinarily a vexing test, was agreeable enough in the first round, giving up 65s to Ian Poulter and Martin Laird. Both birdied the island 17th, and Poulter had the only bogey between them.

Kuchar worked his way to the top in the second round with another 68, tying Zack Johnson (66) and Kevin Na (69) at 136. Na, the maddening fidgeter, took the third-round lead with a 68 despite being "on the clock" — timed for slow play. He pleaded for patience from his colleagues. "Honestly, I'm trying," Na said. "Just bear with me." Kuchar trailed him by one going into the final round and would need help. He got it from Na himself — a 76 in the final round. It turned into a tight race.

"It's fun to be back in position with a chance to win," said Kuchar. Zach Johnson eagled the second and got within two with a birdie at the 11th, but cooled down the stretch and shot 68. Rickie Fowler birdied Nos. 11, 12, 16 and 17 but negated them with a double bogey and two singles for a 70. Ben Curtis started four off the lead and made a sizzling run with six birdies over the last 10 holes, but a double bogey at the eighth helped hold him to a 68.

Kuchar bogeyed the first, then settled in for two birdies going out and added birdies at the 12th and 16th, the latter on a 15-foot putt that opened his lead to three. Laird, starting from six back, sprinted to six birdies through the 13th. Bogeys at the 14th and 18th stopped him. Kuchar's three-putt bogey at the island 17th only cut into his winning margin.

This Players had its other interesting points. Among them: Luke Donald, World No. 2, rocketed to solo sixth with a closing 66, including a 30 on the last nine. Rory McIlroy missed the cut for the third time in his three Players and vowed to make it if it took 20 years. And Tiger Woods, who had a rare missed cut the week before at the Wells Fargo Championship, played all four rounds, finished 12 back and noted, "Just need to be a little bit more consistent."

HP Byron Nelson Championship
Irving, Texas
Winner: Jason Dufner

They ought to give an award for having a great time, then give it to Jason Dufner and retire it.

You score your career-first win late in April, get married the next week, and take your second win in May — all in the span of 22 days.

"You probably couldn't dream it any better than what's been going on here," Dufner said, on wrapping up the HP Byron Nelson Championship at the TPC Four Seasons. If his collapse at the 2011 PGA Championship with four holes to play hadn't been erased by his win in the Zurich Classic, then this one should have done the job. Shooting 67-66-69-67–269, 11 under par, Dufner clung to a tenuous one-stroke lead from the second round, and he won by that.

Dufner made his move in the second round, birdieing four of the last five holes to take the lead. It was the fourth time in the 2012 season that he'd had the 36-hole lead — remarkable for a player, now 35, who had been practically faceless since turning professional in 2000.

Nine players either led or shared the lead at one point in the heavy winds in the third round. Dufner broke free with a two-birdie, one-bogey 69, setting up his spirited finish. But he had to survive some real threats in the fourth.

J.J. Henry had the victory in his sights. After an ace at the par-three No. 5 and two late birdies, he was looking good. But he overshot the par-three 17th and double-bogeyed, tumbling out of the solo lead. "It's disappointing, but that's golf," said Henry, who tied for third.

Dicky Pride, whose only win came in 1994, birdied three straight from the 15th for a 67 and the clubhouse lead at 10 under. That was the target number for Dufner, in the final group, playing the 18th.

"I knew if I made birdie that I would win," Dufner said. "Par would be a playoff, but the playoffs aren't much fun. My experiences in them aren't too great." Yes, he beat Ernie Els to take the Zurich a few weeks earlier, but he lost twice in 2011, including to Keegan Bradley in that agonizing episode in the PGA Championship.

Dufner had bogeyed the second and third holes, then birdied four of the next seven. A bogey at the 11th cooled him, but he birdied the 16th out of a bunker to get to 10 under, where Pride already sat, then needed the birdie at the 18th for the win, and he went after it. He drove confidently into the middle of the fairway, then lofted a wedge to 25 feet and coolly dropped the putt for the win, joining Hunter Mahan as the only two two-time winners this season. So much for Dufner's incredible 22 days.

Said Dufner: "Amanda and I are lucky to be in the position we're in and to have each other and enjoy what's going on around us right now."

Crowne Plaza Invitational
Fort Worth, Texas
Winner: Zach Johnson

Jason Dufner, the hottest man on the PGA Tour with two victories in the previous three weeks — now ranked 14th in the world — was leading the Crowne Plaza Invitational by two strokes with 10 holes to play. The man grinding so hard to catch him was former Masters champion Zach Johnson, who hadn't won for two years. How would the oddsmakers dope this one out?

Right. Dufner, hands-down. But the oddsmakers don't know golf. In what turned into a bizarre match-play situation down the stretch, Johnson would win going away — almost. There was the incident on the final green, when Johnson moved his ball out of Dufner's way, then failed to return his ball marker to its original spot. That's a two-stroke penalty. It gave him a two-over 72 and cut his winning margin to one, on a 268 total, 12 under par at Colonial Country Club.

"There's a number of adjectives I'm calling myself right now, and 'lucky' would be the biggest one," said Johnson, shooting 64-67-65-72 for his eighth tour victory.

Dufner had more than just two victories to show for his recent weeks. He got married as well.

"I'm not going to use that as an excuse," Dufner was quick to offer. "I didn't have it today. I couldn't get the ball in the fairway."

The tournament came down to a series of two-shot swings down the final stretch, with Johnson and Dufner kicking the lead back and forth like a soccer ball. It started early:

• At the par-four second, Dufner, leading by one, bunkered his drive, then three-putted from 28 feet for a bogey. Johnson holed a 28-footer for a birdie and was ahead by one.

• At the par-five 11th, Johnson's tee shot ricocheted off a tree and into the fairway. He finished the hole with an 18-foot birdie putt, getting to 15 under. Dufner also hit into the trees, but his ball stayed there. He had to punch out, finished with a two-putt bogey from 23 feet, and fell two behind.

• At the par-four 12th, Dufner holed an eight-footer for birdie. Johnson bunkered his tee shot and bogeyed, and they were tied.

• Johnson edged ahead with a birdie at the 14th, then had it all but in his pocket when Dufner chopped up the par-four 15th for a triple bogey that knocked him four behind. Johnson's bogey at the 16th and the penalty double bogey at the 18th cut his margin to one.

Johnson's penalty episode could have been disastrous had a rules official not asked his caddie whether he had replaced his marker. The warning came in time for Johnson to add the penalty before he'd signed his scorecard. Johnson was asked about the close call with disqualification. "Let's just count it as a hypothetical and move on," a relieved Johnson said.

Said Dufner: "It would be extremely unfortunate for him, and extremely lucky for me."

Memorial Tournament
Dublin, Ohio
Winner: Tiger Woods

As one writer put it, borrowing from William Blake, "This was Tiger, Tiger, burning brightest..."

The current Tiger Woods, staying in the hunt for three rounds and 14 holes. And then the original Tiger Woods materialized over the last four, wrenching out three birdies — one of them miraculously — coming from behind for his second victory of the year, his record fifth Memorial Tournament win, and the 73rd PGA Tour win of his career, matching Jack Nicklaus, tournament host and designer of Muirfield Village Golf Club.

"To be able to tie Jack," said Woods, age 36, careful to remind everyone, "at such a young age ... to do it with Jack here, it just makes it that much more special."

After rounds of 70-69-73, Woods went into the final round trailing winless Spencer Levin by four shots and restless Rory Sabbatini by three. Then, still trailing by two, he exploded down the final four holes. He birdied the par-five 15th after just missing a 30-foot eagle putt, and at the 18th, he put his approach to about nine feet and locked things up with another birdie for a five-under 67, a nine-under 279 and a two-stroke win.

It was the birdie at the 220-yard, par-three 16th that set him up. Woods hit his eight-iron tee shot into heavy grass behind the green, some 50 feet from a flag that sat dangerously close to the fronting pond. He opted for a full-swing flop shot, hoping to save his par. Too weak and the ball would die short, too strong and it could be in the water beyond. Woods just wanted to get close. He took a big swipe and lifted the ball out. It landed gently and trickled down toward the hole.

"I didn't think it was going to get there at one point," Woods said. "It was one of the hardest shots I've ever pulled off."

The finish was painful for Spencer Levin, who let another slip away. He led by two going into the final nine, then came undone and shot 75. "I've got to find a way to get tougher on the back nine," he said. The finish was devastating for Rickie Fowler. Three off the lead entering the last round, he shot 84. "One of those days," he said. "And this isn't going to be the last bad one."

And it was tantalizing for Sabbatini. He seemed on the verge of winning until Woods's hot finish, and he ended up needing a hole-out eagle from 118 yards at the 18th to tie. But his wedge shot from well below his feet off a grassy slope flew right over the pin. He had to settle for a two-putt par for a 72 and a tie for second with Andres Romero (67), leaving Woods to sum up his day.

"It was good stuff," Woods said. "I hit the ball great today. Better than I have in years."

FedEx St. Jude Classic
Memphis, Tennessee
Winner: Dustin Johnson

Maybe golf is a bit like riding a bicycle — you don't really forget how. Dustin Johnson made something of a case for that notion when, in his second start after being off injured for nearly three months, he came from behind to win the FedEx St. Jude Classic early in June, in the process blunting Rory McIlroy's recovery from a mini-slump and thwarting John Merrick and Nick O'Hern in the bid for that first win.

Johnson had pulled a back muscle lifting a jet ski in March and didn't return until the Memorial Tournament late in May, tying for 19th. And now, a week later, he was scoring his sixth PGA Tour victory. He surged in the final round, ending a leapfrog chase with two late birdies to beat Merrick by a stroke at TPC Southwind.

"Well, it feels really good," the laconic Johnson said. "Especially having so much time off."

In something of a class reunion, Jeff Maggert and Davis Love, both age 48, were both in the hunt. But Maggert showered five bogeys through each of the last two rounds, shot 73-72 and tied for 27th. Love, himself out for about six weeks with a rib injury, tied for third. Someone had asked what a win would mean for him. Said Love, the American Ryder Cup captain: "A lot of Ryder Cup points."

After sticking close with a 70-68 start, Johnson made his move in the third round with a 67 sparked by an eagle at the par-five third. He was just a stroke out of the lead behind Love (68), O'Hern (67) and Merrick (69). "Today is probably the first day where I actually hit it nicely all day long," Johnson said.

The chase in the fourth round was this hot: Johnson birdied No. 1 and created a seven-way tie for the lead.

The most prominent dropout was McIlroy, who led by two with four birdies through the 11th, then stumbled home with two bogeys and a double bogey at the 18th and sank to a tie for seventh.

Johnson gave the boys something to shoot at. After three birdies and a bogey going out, he came down the stretch and birdied the 16th from 11 feet and the 17th from nine, finishing with a 66 and a nine-under 271 total for the clubhouse lead. Then only Merrick and O'Hern had a chance to catch him. But O'Hern watered his drive and Merrick put his near a cart path. Merrick parred and finished second, and O'Hern bogeyed and tied for third. The pursuit had gotten hot, but Johnson ignored the leaderboard. "I was just trying to play my game," he said. "And you know — I did that."

It was a troubled McIlroy who came to the St. Jude after missing three straight cuts, but a reassured one heading for the U.S. Open the next week. "I'm happy I came," he said. "I feel like I'm well prepared. ... Looking forward to getting to San Francisco."

U.S. Open Championship
San Francisco, California
Winner: Webb Simpson

See Chapter 3.

Travelers Championship
Cromwell, Connecticut
Winner: Marc Leishman

Little Alice woke up on the riverbank to discover she hadn't been down the rabbit hole after all. Marc Leishman, on the other hand, hadn't even fallen asleep, but he woke up in Wonderland anyway.

Leishman started the final round six strokes off the lead and had finished well ahead of the frontrunners in the Travelers Championship. He retired to the clubhouse, convinced that after his 68-66-70 in the first three rounds, the closing 62 wouldn't win for him.

"I didn't think it was going to be enough," Leishman said. "Golf," he added, "is a funny game, a really funny game."

That being the case, Leishman, a 28-year-old Australian, had the last laugh. He finished at 14-under-par 266 at the TPC River Highlands and then decided to hang around, just in case. There were 13 twosomes still behind him. He'd have to wait nearly two and a half hours. And then the just-in-case happened. All the players he had outrun stalled out down the stretch, leaving him with his first victory, a one-stroke win over Bubba Watson (65) and Charley Hoffman (66).

"Waking up this morning, I definitely didn't think I was going to be in this situation," said Leishman, the PGA Tour's Rookie of the Year in 2009. "But I'll gladly take it."

Not that he didn't earn it. He birdied holes two, four, six, seven and eight going out, and 13, 14 and 17 coming home for a bogey-free 62. But he would need a lot of help, and he got it.

• Bubba Watson spiked his own guns. He started the final round four behind and had five birdies through the 13th. But at the short par-four 15th, he watered his tee shot, parred home from there and tied for second.

• Brian Davis, the third-round co-leader at 12 under, bogeyed the 13th out of a hazard, shot 70 and tied for fourth.

• James Driscoll, two behind through the turn, drove out of bounds at the 10th and double-bogeyed, then also drove out of bounds at the 14th and quadruple-bogeyed. A 72 dropped him to a tie for 18th.

• Tim Clark was 13 under when he blew a great opportunity at the par-five 13th. He hit the green in two, but knocked his eagle putt off the green and could only par. Then he missed a 30-inch par putt at the 17th. "I pretty much knew I was going to miss (it)," he said. He shot 67 and tied for fourth.

• Charley Hoffman came from three behind to lead by two through the 13th, but double-bogeyed the 17th off a watered drive, then bogeyed the 18th from a bunker, shot 66 and tied Watson for second.

• Roland Thatcher, after overcoming three early bogeys, needed a birdie at the 18th to tie Leishman, but bunkered his approach and bogeyed for a 70 and a tie for fourth.

Leishman acknowledged the gifts. "But," he added, "I'm not going to give this back or anything."

AT&T National
Bethesda, Maryland
Winner: Tiger Woods

A violent storm came howling in from the west late Friday night, hitting the Washington, D.C., area with 70 mph winds, uprooting trees, knocking down power lines and stopping the third round of the AT&T National in its tracks. Officials barred spectators and volunteers from the course for Saturday's third round and delayed the start until Congressional Country Club could be cleared of fallen trees and debris. It took a big story to upstage that one.

Enter Tiger Woods.

Woods, shooting 72-68-67-69, worked his way up the leaderboard to an eight-under 276 total and a two-stroke victory over Bo Van Pelt after a slugfest down the stretch. It was the rejuvenated Woods's third victory of the season and his career 74th, carrying him past Jack Nicklaus into second place on the PGA Tour's all-time win list, eight behind Sam Snead. Woods, coming back from a variety of problems, took a certain vengeful pleasure from the victory.

"I remember there was a time when people were saying I could never win again," Woods said. "That was, I think — what? — six months ago. Here we are. Four months ago? Four months ago, OK."

Apart from brief moves by Hunter Mahan and Zimbabwe's Brendon de Jonge, the AT&T was essentially a Tiger Woods–Bo Van Pelt battle as they kept pace with each other. Van Pelt led the first round by one, and Woods was five behind him. They tied in the second, five behind Hunter Mahan, and they were tied again going into the final round, one behind the bulky de Jonge, who left the chase abruptly in a flurry of bogeys, shooting 77. Adam Scott shot 31 on the front nine and tied for the lead, then hurt himself with two late bogeys. By then, the fun had already begun.

Woods took the lead three times, but Van Pelt wouldn't let him get away, catching him with a birdie of his own each time. It came down to the last three holes. Van Pelt had the edge at the par-five 16th, smashing a 345-yard tee shot, leaving himself only a six iron to the green. Woods hit a spectator with his stray tee shot, laid up, then hit his approach over the green and down the slope. But Van Pelt's approach was short, and he didn't get his next on, turning the birdie opportunity into a bogey, matching Woods. Then Van Pelt self-destructed with bogeys at the 17th and 18th, and Woods parred both for the two-stroke win.

"I'll be disappointed for a while," Van Pelt said. "Probably about my flight home tonight and about two hours tomorrow."

For Woods, it was another moment in history, passing Nicklaus in victories. "I've had a pretty good career," he said. "To do it at 36 — I feel like I have a lot of years ahead of me. I've had a number of good years in my career, and I feel like I've got a lot more ahead of me."

Greenbrier Classic
White Sulphur Springs, West Virginia
Winner: Ted Potter, Jr.

For Ted Potter, Jr., the immediate future wasn't especially bright.

Potter, 28, finally on the PGA Tour after years of frustration, had arrived at the Greenbrier Classic in July having missed the cut in his five previous starts, ranked 218th in the world, and trailing by four strokes with four holes to play. Things did not look promising.

But seven holes later — that's four holes of regulation plus three playoff holes — Potter had his first victory, up in the forested mountains of West Virginia. "It was just a big relief," said Potter, the sixth first-time winner this season. "All the struggles the last few weeks, knowing that now I've got a couple years to improve on my game and win some more tournaments."

First, though, came the improbable finish, chasing Troy Kelly, who had all but a lock on the victory. Potter made up his four-shot deficit with a long putt for a birdie at the 15th, another for eagle at the 17th and a five-footer for another birdie at the 18th, catching Kelly, who missed birdie putts on the last two holes. Potter shot 69-67-64-64 and Kelly in 69-67-62-66, tying at 16-under 264 on the agreeable par-70 Old White TPC, where 63 players finished under par.

They tied in pars on the first two playoff holes. On the third, the par-three 18th, Kelly didn't get his tee shot over the ridge in the middle of the green and left himself a 45-footer for birdie. Potter put his tee shot just four feet from the cup. Kelly missed on his long try, and Potter dropped his short putt for the win.

Neither player was making an impression earlier in the going. Vijay Singh and Jeff Maggert, both approaching senior status, were in the mix. Singh led the first round with some of his brightest golf in years, shooting a seven-under 63, topping a day in which 62 players broke par on the friendly course. Maggert was in a group at 64. (Both would fade from view with one-birdie 74s, Singh in the second round, Maggert in the third.) Webb Simpson, the recently crowned U.S. Open champion, took over with a 66 in the rain-delayed second round, then led the third round by two with a 65. That's when Kelly (62) and Potter (64) jumped in.

They could thank Simpson for being in the running. He was leading by a stroke on the final nine, but after going 50 consecutive holes without a bogey, he made three in the row from the 12th and was gone. Said Simpson: "I'm probably going to learn something from it."

The tournament had a bigger surprise earlier. Tiger Woods and Phil Mickelson both missed the cut. "I didn't have the feel for the distances," said Woods, missing for only the ninth time on the tour. Said Mickelson: "I certainly struggled on these greens, but nothing that should have led to these scores."

John Deere Classic
Silvis, Illinois
Winner: Zach Johnson

It was the second hole of the playoff in the John Deere Classic, and Zach Johnson's prospects definitely were not promising. His tee shot lay in a fairway bunker, 193 yards from a tough pin position at the 18th. He opted for his six iron and fired away.

"I saw it hit the green, bounce a little left, and after that I couldn't see it," Johnson said. No matter. The frantic gallery told him all he needed to know. "I liked that crescendo from the crowd," he said. The ball had stopped just inches from the hole. When Troy Matteson's desperate birdie try from 43 feet missed, Johnson tapped in for his second win of the season, his career ninth (including the Masters) and a 3-0 record in playoffs. And also ending the Steve Stricker Invitational — Stricker having been after his fourth straight victory here.

It would seem the loss would have crushed Matteson, who had led all the way after his opening 10-under-par 61. Not quite. Said Matteson, who missed 11 cuts in 21 starts: "You lose to a shot like that — it's an unbelievable shot. And for how I played this year, this has been a really good finish for me. I'm not disappointed at all, really."

Matteson, playing the TPC Deere Run course in 61-68-66-69, had led from the start until the final nine, when a double bogey at the 15th knocked him to 18 under and a stroke behind Johnson, who was surging up ahead. Johnson was on the 18th green, completing a bogey-free round and a card of 68-65-66-65 when he heard a huge outburst behind him. "I didn't know what the roar was for," Johnson said. That was Matteson, catching him with a 60-foot putt for an eagle back at the par-five 17th. They tied at 20-under 264, ending another full-field assault on what can be charitably described as a user-friendly course. Only two of 76 finishers didn't break par for four rounds.

Johnson and Matteson tied, awkwardly enough, with double bogeys on the first playoff hole — the 18th — after both hit into the water, Johnson from the same bunker. The second time set the stage for Johnson's six iron beauty.

"It's one of the best results of my career," said Johnson. It's up there. It's probably way up there."

Until then, Stricker was the big story of the week — whether he would join Tom Morris, Jr., Walter Hagen, Gene Sarazen and Tiger Woods as the winner of a tournament four straight times. Could he do it? "I don't feel the pressure that I have to go out and win this week," Stricker had said, "but I'm going to try like mad to do it again." He stayed in the hunt all week, but a three-bogey stumble down the final stretch shut him out. His closing 70 tied him for fifth, four shots back.

The Open Championship
Lytham St Annes, Lancashire, England
Winner: Ernie Els

See Chapter 4.

True South Classic
Madison, Mississippi
Winner: Scott Stallings

The question was, how could a guy score his first victory and win nearly $2 million as a rookie one year, then come back out the next and miss 13 cuts in his first 18 starts? Answer: A couple of herniated disks and some torn rib cartilage ought to do the trick.

"I hurt my confidence and hurt everything that came along with it," said Scott Stallings, age 27. "I learned a lot of lessons through that."

One lesson — once he got everything fixed — was how to make birdies in bunches, which he showed in the True South Classic, played opposite of the Open Championship. He came through the steamy July heat and storms of Mississippi with a 24-under-par 264 total, playing Annandale Golf Club in 68-64-64-68, for a two-stroke victory over Jason Bohn. Billy Horschel, four-time All-American at the University of Florida, had his best finish to date, a solo third, four strokes back.

The rain-softened course dictated play. Said Bohn, after a first-round 64: "There is very little roll (in the fairways), but that makes the fairways wider. You can play more aggressively off the tee — use drivers where you might use a three wood." That, coupled with the lift-clean-place provision part of the way, helped keep scores low.

The weather became a real factor. Players struggled in the dense heat and humidity. A number of caddies couldn't make it through the second round, and two players withdrew. Even Horschel, a Florida native told of drinking a bottle of water at every hole. "That's the most I've ever sweat," he said. Not that it mattered. He shot 63–131 for a one-stroke lead on Stallings after 36 holes. "The way I'm playing, I don't want to go home," he said. But after a 66 in the third round, he couldn't get much going and finished with a two-birdie, one-bogey 71 for third place.

Stallings interrupted a neat, workman-like round Sunday at the 14th with a stray drive that led to a bogey — his first after 54 holes without one. His last bogey, and one of only three in the tournament, came at the 13th in the first round. He soon made up for that bit of lost ground. At the 16th, he stuck his approach to three feet and birdied, and followed that with a 12-footer for another at the 17th. He was leading by three.

"It made that tee shot on 18 a lot easier," Stallings said.

Bohn cut into his lead with a closing birdie, but Stallings was nothing but comfortable. He came up the 18th fairway with a smile and a wave for the gallery. After those two middle 64s, his Sunday 68 may have looked almost drab, but it was the work of a guy avoiding trouble. The victory was something of a bonus.

"I'm just happy to be playing," Stallings had said. "I'm just happy to get up in the morning and do what I love."

RBC Canadian Open
Ancaster, Ontario, Canada
Winner: Scott Piercy

"This course takes the juices out of it for me," Scott Piercy was saying. That was Piercy after yawning his way to an eight-under-par 62 in the first round of the RBC Canadian Open at Hamilton Golf & Country Club. Later, in a less eloquent variation on the theme, he was to note: "This golf is boring golf for me."

The problem was, Piercy likes to have a bash at a course, and Hamilton, reachable at some 7,000 yards but heavy on the rough, requires patience more than power. But he managed to stay awake and alert. The thought of winning will do that for a player. So with his nervous energy on a tight leash, he added three more rounds of 67 for a 17-under 263 and his second PGA Tour victory, a one-stroke win over Robert Garrigus, a one-time winner, and William McGirt, enjoying his career-best finish.

Piercy, age 33, in his fourth year on the tour, burst into the tournament with that 62 on a soggy lift-clean-place day that included eagles at both par-fives, No. 17 (his eighth hole) and No. 4 (his 13th), then birdies on three of his last five holes.

Hamilton was not agreeable to everybody. While Jim Furyk and Ernie Els were missing the cut, Piercy's 67 gave him a share of the 36-hole lead with McGirt (66) at 11-under 129. Piercy was headed just once, by Garrigus, who took the third-round lead with a 64–194, 16 under, that broke a 57-year-old record that had stood since it was set in the 1955 Canadian Open at Weston Golf & Country Club — by Arnold Palmer, in his first career win. Said Garrigus: "Oops — sorry, Arnie."

Garrigus's chances died in the final round when he went missing putts by the handfuls — six inside eight feet, even four-footers for birdies at the third and the par-three 13th. "I should have won this tournament by seven shots," Garrigus said. "If I could have just made a putt today."

Piercy started the fourth round two behind and did what he had to do — fight the temptation to bomb away. And so he raced past Garrigus with four straight birdies from No. 2. Then things got dicey. At the 14th, after a stray tee shot, he had to play out of the trees and then hole a six-footer to save his bogey. He chipped in for birdie at the 15th, then parred in for his 67, and got the win when Garrigus and McGirt, playing behind him, failed to catch him.

Next question: Was it still boring golf? Piercy realized he had offended some people with his comments and backtracked diplomatically in a hurry.

"I like to hit driver a lot," he said, "and this course, I felt, took the driver out of my hands. ... I did say, however, that at the end of the week, if the score is good, it's exciting. So I'm pretty excited."

WGC - Bridgestone Invitational
Akron, Ohio
Winner: Keegan Bradley

You should not be able to come from six shots behind in the final round, shouldn't be able to dig your ball out of a plugged lie at the final hole, shouldn't get it within 15 feet of the cup, and shouldn't be able to hole that pressure putt, and shouldn't be able to win. But Keegan Bradley did all those things in the WGC - Bridgestone Invitational that hot August week at Firestone Country Club — except for the winning part.

The unfortunate Jim Furyk pretty much did that part for him. Furyk, who had folded in some recent tournaments, this time played beautifully for 71 holes, led all the way, then crashed with a double bogey at the 72nd. Bradley was there to pick up the victory. He knew the feeling, in a way. Bradley blew a chance to win the 2011 Bridgestone Invitational, but down the final nine he did what Furyk did on the final hole — folded. The last thing Bradley expected was to win.

"My hope, standing on the 18th tee," Bradley said, "was to make birdie and maybe force a playoff. But you just never know..."

Furyk played the Firestone South course in 63-66-70 in the first three rounds, no easy task for an average hitter on the par-70, 7,400-yard brute. Everyone was helped by a course running hard and fast in the hot weather. Consider that in the second round, his tee shot at the 464-yard 18th went 371 yards, leaving him a wedge to the green. In the third round, at the 648-yard 16th, Louis Oosthuizen had a six-iron second to the green, and Bubba Watson a wedge. Furyk cranked production out of his approach game and putting to lead by two in the first round, and going into the last, he was one ahead of Oosthuizen, four ahead of Bradley. Furyk opened the final round with three straight birdies, leaving Oosthuizen two behind and Bradley all but dead, six back.

It evolved into a Furyk-Bradley battle. Furyk bogeyed the sixth, parred nine straight, then birdied the 16th. Bradley charged to within one with birdies at Nos. 3, 7, 10, 11, 14 and 16. Furyk, with that precious one-shot lead, got a great break at the 18th. His tee shot went wide left but bounced off a tree and back into the fairway. He then hit a seven iron long, into the heavy collar behind a bunker. From an awkward stance, he barely got over the bunker to the greenside rough. Then he chipped weakly, five feet short, and two-putted for an agonizing double-bogey six. Bradley blasted from a plugged lie to 15 feet from the cup.

"I didn't think for a second I was going to miss it," said Bradley, and he didn't, getting his par and wrapping up a card of 67-69-67-64, 13-under 267, and a one-stroke win.

Furyk was crushed. "I led the golf tournament the entire way and lost it on the last hole," he said. "I have no one to blame but myself."

Reno-Tahoe Open
Reno, Nevada
Winner: J.J. Henry

The scoring wasn't in eagles and birdies at the Reno-Tahoe Open, it was in points, but that didn't matter to J.J. Henry. It all added up to winning.

"It's been a long time coming," said Henry, puzzled by his long dry spell. "I've been out here 12 straight years, so I've done something right. But it's been six years since I've won."

Henry, who had three top-10 finishes this season, scored a one-point victory over Brazil's Alexandre Rocha, 43 points to 42. The Reno-Tahoe Open, held opposite the WGC - Bridgestone Invitational in August, was played under the modified-Stableford system, last used on the PGA Tour in the old International in 2006. The system awards two points for a birdie, five for an eagle and eight for a double eagle. Pars get zero, and one point is docked for a bogey, three for double bogeys or worse.

"At times," Henry said, after taking the lead in the third round, "you feel like you're more of a mathematician than a golfer."

Even so, the golfer still had to get the ball into the hole, and Henry rang up points in a bunches — 15 of his 43 — with his three eagles. He got the first in the first round, holing out a 167-yard approach at the par-four 12th. The next, in the second round, was conventional, on a 25-foot putt after he hit the green in two at the 636-yard eighth. In the third, he just missed the green with his tee shot at the 308-yard, par-four 14th, and chipped in from 35 feet.

Argentina's Andres Romero birdied four of his first six holes en route to the first-round lead on 14 points. "I had a good feeling on the greens," he said. Rocha, describing himself as a chronic slow-starter, was anything but in the second round. He streaked to a birdie-birdie-birdie-eagle start and took the lead with 24 points. Henry's second eagle led him to within two.

The Stableford calls for a different strategy. "If you're playing a medal play and you had maybe a couple-shot lead, maybe you'd play a little differently," Henry said. "I don't know. But I'm really not even going to look at who's behind me." With that approach, he piled up 14 points in the third round, taking a three-point lead on Rocha. Henry ran out of eagles in the final round, but three birdies in a four-hole stretch on the front nine had him in good shape. Rocha needed an eagle at the par-five 18th to become the first Brazilian to win on the PGA Tour, but he did well to scratch out a birdie after hitting his approach into the gallery. Henry locked up the win with a two-putt par from 12 feet.

It turned out the scoring system did matter to Henry. If the tournament had been played at stroke play, he and Rocha would have tied at 271.

PGA Championship
Kiawah Island, South Carolina
Winner: Rory McIlroy

See Chapter 5.

Wyndham Championship
Greensboro, North Carolina
Winner: Sergio Garcia

Sergio Garcia didn't exactly have warm and fuzzy memories of Sedgefield Country Club, so in the Wyndham Championship he was either getting even with Donald Ross, the late and legendary designer, or else Ross had owed him one. It just depended on one's point of view.

As for Garcia, age 32, he took full responsibility for blowing the 2009 Wyndham Championship, letting a three-stroke lead slip away midway through the final round. "That year," Garcia said, "I was pretty much in control and I lost it myself. The course," he added, curiously giving Sedgefield a life of its own, "didn't do anything wrong to me."

This time, Garcia did just about everything right, ringing up his eighth PGA Tour victory and his first since 2008. The win meant more than that, however, and more than the $936,000 first prize. To him, it meant he just might have locked up a spot on the European Ryder Cup team after falling out of the top 10 on the points list when he missed the cut at the PGA Championship the week before the Wyndham.

"Everybody knows how much the Ryder Cup means to me," Garcia had said earlier in the week. "So I was very disappointed last week. I have a chance this week. I'm going to give it my best shot."

Garcia shot 67-63-66-66–262, 18 under par, and made just four bogeys for the week in his two-stroke win over Tim Clark. The difference, he said, was in the putting.

"I did hit the ball nicely last week," Garcia said. "I putted like a dog."

After trailing by five in the first round, Garcia rocketed into the chase in the second with a seven-under 63, fueled by five birdies over eight holes from No. 8, trailing Jimmy Walker (62–128) by two. Then Garcia moved to the top in the third, birdies at the 12th and 13th spurring him to a one-stroke lead.

The final round got dicey, especially when rain stalled play and forced Garcia and 37 others to finish on Monday. Garcia fell back into a tie with a bogey at the 12th, then came the spurt that set up his win — four birdies over five holes. He had a chip and a tap-in at the 13th, a bunker shot to five feet at the 15th, a tee shot to two feet at the par-three 16th, and then tacked on another birdie at the 17th that gave him the luxury of bogeying the 18th and still winning by two.

Some furious golf had come and gone. Carl Pettersson, for example — a member at Sedgefield — took the first-round lead with a 62 and was only one up on Tim Clark and David Mathis. Clark stayed steady with three 67s and finished second by two.

Now, for Garcia, what did the Wyndham win really mean?

"Hopefully," Garcia said, "this will secure my spot on the Ryder Cup team."

PGA Tour Playoffs for the FedExCup

The Barclays
Farmingdale, New York
Winner: Nick Watney

All Nick Watney had to do to brighten his year was to make two adjustments — one to his putting, the other to his attitude.

They came together at just the right time, late in August, in The Barclays, the first of the four FedExCup Playoffs, this at Bethpage Black, New York's U.S. Open-caliber municipal course. He got into the chase from the start and, unlike his earlier underachieving play, he stayed in it and topped the 123-man field for a three-stroke victory, his first win of 2012, and first since the AT&T National over a year earlier.

It was a rich yield at $1.44 million, but it also was the first step toward the $10 million FedExCup bonus, and it made him part of the Ryder Cup chatter.

"It's been not quite the year I wanted," Watney said. "But this makes it all forgotten."

First came the attitude adjustment. He tended to get discouraged when things went wrong. Then came the putting change from a club pro from near Bethpage. He'd been getting back too far on his heels. "It's the best I've putted all year, by far," Watney said.

Bethpage Black, a par 71, got tougher as the week wore on, and Watney stuck with it and played it in 65-69-71-69–274, 10 under, for a three-stroke win over Brandt Snedeker, who posted a 70 while other challengers slipped behind. Watney worked his way through the leaderboard with no apparent trouble. He tied for second, one behind Padraig Harrington (64) in the first round, and shared the halfway lead with Sergio Garcia (68), and then entered the final round two behind Garcia (69). He fell three behind with a bogey at No. 5, three-putting from 40 feet. Then he caught fire for three birdies over four holes — a two-putt at the par-five seventh, a 30-footer at the par-three eighth, and at the 10th, a four-footer against Garcia's three-putt bogey. Watney creaked coming in from the 11th, with three bogeys and two birdies, the last at the 18th for his three-shot cushion. Garcia, who broke a four-year drought in the Wyndham, closed with a shaky 75 and tied for third with Dustin Johnson (68).

It wasn't a good week for marquee players. Bubba Watson and Luke Donald tied for 10th, Rory McIlroy for 24th, and Tiger Woods and Phil Mickelson, both closing with 76s, tied for 38th.

So Watney stood atop the standings for the second of the four playoffs, and he had to be — the speculators held — right up there with Steve Stricker and Jim Furyk as pick candidates with Ryder Cup captain Davis Love. Would he ask?

"I don't want to be lobbying," Watney said. "It's his decision. The best way to enter the conversation is to play your way into the conversation."

Which is what Watney had just done.

Deutsche Bank Championship
Norton, Massachusetts
Winner: Rory McIlroy

As Louis Oosthuizen was to put it, "He's not No. 1 in the world for nothing." This was Oosthuizen after falling just short of catching Rory McIlroy, who demonstrated in the Deutsche Bank Championship that he can win in whatever way he has to. This wasn't the Rory McIlroy who ran away from everyone, as he did in taking a U.S. Open and a PGA Championship, each by eight shots. And it wasn't the McIlroy who came rocketing from nowhere with a final-round 62, as he did in the Quail Hollow Championship. This Rory McIlroy had to scratch his way from behind, then hang on, but with a game that was almost vintage weekender, in order to take his third win of the season and the fifth in 52 PGA Tour starts. And the pressure couldn't have been greater, coming from Oosthuizen, Tiger Woods, Dustin Johnson and Phil Mickelson.

"I had a couple of wobbles coming in," McIlroy said, "but I did enough, and I'm very excited to get a victory."

McIlroy's play was patchy, but his numbers were very good — 65-65-67-67–264, 20 under par and a one-stroke win over Oosthuizen at TPC Boston. He trailed by three in the first round, in which Tiger Woods shot his lowest opening round in three years, a 64, and found himself two off the lead, tied for third behind South Korea's Seung-Yul Noh (62). A second 65 lifted McIlroy into a one-stroke lead over Oosthuizen (65) in the second round. "Now that I'm in the tournament," McIlroy said, "I just want to play as well as I can."

It didn't seem that would be enough, not from the show Oosthuizen put on in the third round. He birdied the second, paused to catch his breath, then ran off seven straight birdies from the third. "You get those days," he was to say, "where you just look at a putt and you hole it." A bogey at the 17th marred the card, but he got the stroke back with a birdie at the 18th, shot 63 and led McIlroy by three going into the final round. (Lost in the fireworks was the extraordinary crash of former Masters champion Charl Schwartzel. Having already suffered three double bogeys, Schwartzel got the fourth at the 18th by four-putting from three feet for a 79.)

All doubts aside, McIlroy erased the three-shot deficit with birdies over the first four holes, but that was no preview of his finish. Instead, he would turn ragged. One tee shot went 170 yards and had the distinction of being the only one to find the fairway on the last five holes. Then there was the bunker shot that left him a six-footer to save par (he did), and then pitching across the green and needing a five-footer for bogey (he made it). He beat Oosthuizen (71) by one. It was one of the scruffiest 67s McIlroy ever shot, but it worked.

BMW Championship
Carmel, Indiana
Winner: Rory McIlroy

Anyone wanting to know how it feels to be Rory McIlroy — first, you have to be holding a trophy. A new one about every week or so.

"The more you win, the more you pick up trophies, it becomes normal," McIlroy was saying.

McIlroy, still a whiz but not so much a kid anymore, at age 23, forgot to add "habit-forming" to the act of winning, of which he was doing more than his share (statistically speaking) as 2012 rolled along. The occasion for his observation was the BMW Championship early in September, in the FedExCup Playoffs, which he took rather handily with a performance of 64-68-69-67–268, 20 under par at rain-softened Crooked Stick, and two strokes better than Phil Mickelson and Lee Westwood.

McIlroy had to take this one pretty much on his own. There were no great gaffes, no gifts, no favors. As Mickelson put it: "A lot of people stayed in neutral and Rory geared ahead."

In the final round, McIlroy faced the cream of golf. Mickelson, who had raced to a 64 in the third round to share the lead with Vijay Singh, turned his fourth round into one of his up-and-down performances — five birdies and three bogeys for a 70. Two killer shots kept the short-game master from tying McIlroy, simple wedges that missed the green and cost him bogeys at Nos. 7 and 12. Singh broke down with bogeys at 14, 16 and 17 and shot 73. Westwood started the final round tied with McIlroy, a shot behind Mickelson and Singh, but just couldn't get enough done and shot 69. Tiger Woods started three off the lead and stayed there with a 68. Bubba Watson posted a day's-best 65, but that merely jumped him up the leaderboard by 25 spots to a tie for 12th.

"Rory's putting on a show out there," Woods said, "and we've got one more tournament (to go)."

There was a way to measure the pressure McIlroy felt from this cast: He missed only one fairway in the final round.

McIlroy broke out of a four-way tie with birdies at the ninth and 10th. Westwood tied him with a birdie at the 13th, but poor chip shots cost him a bogey at the 14th and a par at the 15th. McIlroy added two more birdies — at the 15th, a two-putt from 15 feet after a four iron from 226 yards, then birdied the 16th from 15 feet for a three-stroke lead. That took the sting out of his only bogey, that at the 18th.

"By that time, I had sort of done enough," he said. And so he had won again — the Honda Classic in March, and then in four straight starts from mid-August, he won the PGA Championship, two weeks later tied for 24th in the Barclays, then won the Deutsche Bank and the BMW, back-to-back.

"It feels," McIlroy said, "like this is what you're supposed to do."

Tour Championship
Atlanta, Georgia
Winner: Brandt Snedeker

That old golf expression, "Putt for dough," took on a new meaning at the Tour Championship — meaning $11.44 million, in fact.

Brandt Snedeker putted the East Lake course silly to take the PGA Tour Playoffs' crowning tournament and all that went with it — the $1.44 million first prize and the $10 million annuity from the FedExCup bonus pool.

"I putted great all week," Snedeker said. "You needed to do that in this wind and on this golf course." True, Snedeker's putter did take over, but first he had to get to the greens, and that meant taming the winds in the blustery third round. He shot a remarkable bogey-free 64 to tie Justin Rose (68), also bogey-free. "It was so tough today," Snedeker said. "The wind made it so hard to hit the fairways because it seemed it would move the ball five yards one way or the other, and these fairways might be 15 yards wide. Just every iron shot has to be hit so crisply to control your distances, and I did a great job of that today."

Snedeker shot 68-70-64-68–270, 10 under, three ahead of Rose for his fourth tour title. Lee Westwood, closing with 76-74, brought up the rear in the exclusive 30-man field, 25 strokes behind.

The tournament started as the Marquee Open — Rory McIlroy vs. Tiger Woods, or vice versa, depending on one's outlook. They were playing together for the fifth time in the FedExCup Playoffs, and the first round went to Woods in this one. He shot 66 and tied Rose for the lead, and McIlroy shot 69. "I enjoy playing with Rory," Woods said. "He's a great kid." Said McIlroy: "Wish I could have shot a couple shots better. But I'm in a good position going into tomorrow." Neither would be a real threat the rest of the way. Woods tied for eighth, eight strokes back, and McIlroy tied for 10th, nine back.

Snedeker's putter stayed hot in the final round. He made birdie putts of 10, 18 and 40 feet, and a par putt of 11, and chipped in for birdie from 28 feet at the 17th, and his closing 68 gave him the three-shot win over Rose (71). Snedeker took the outright lead with a birdie at No. 3, but he had one really scary moment. He watered his tee shot at No. 6 and double-bogeyed. He still had the lead, then underlined his intentions by sinking the 40-footer for birdie at No. 8. For the week, Snedeker made 12 putts of 10 feet or longer, and he didn't miss a putt inside eight feet.

Then Snedeker was off to Chicago for his debut in the Ryder Cup, comforted by a singular thought. Said Snedeker: "This win solidified to me what I already knew — when I play my best, I am one of the best players in the world."

The Ryder Cup
Medinah, Illinois
Winner: Europe

See Chapter 6.

PGA Tour Fall Series

Justin Timberlake Shriners Hospitals for Children Open
Las Vegas, Nevada
Winner: Ryan Moore

"Just one of those nice days," Ryan Moore said, in the glow of a 10-under-par 61 in the first round of the Justin Timberlake Shriners Hospitals for Children Open. Three days later, he might have been saying, "Just one of those nice weeks." Except that it wasn't exactly a cakewalk winning the early October opener of the PGA Tour's four-event Fall Series.

It was a survival race at the TPC Summerlin, what with golfers hurling all kinds of low numbers. For all of the fireworks, it wasn't until Moore birdied the 16th in the final round that he finally took the lead over portly Zimbabwean Brendon de Jonge, then made it to the finish line for a one-stroke victory. It looked like a lark on the card — 61-68-65-66 and the whopping 24-under 260 total. But it was a battle all the way. His opening 61, for example, was just good for a one-stroke lead over de Jonge.

"The last couple days were tough," said Moore, who lives in Las Vegas and was accompanied by family.

Moore shot 68 in the second round and was puzzled by good putts that burned the holes and lipped out, "All in all," he said, "I like my position going into the weekend." And that position was a stroke behind de Jonge (66) and Sweden's Jonas Blixt, who shot his second straight 64. "I've been working on my ball-striking," Blixt said. "It's not really there yet, but I got a hot putter and it's been helping me out a lot the last two days." He could have shot much better, except for the water at the 17th. He doubled-bogeyed. "I don't know why they always put water on 17, on the par-threes," he said.

Blixt wasn't kidding about the hot putter. He shot 66 in the third round and noted, "I just had a good time. I got hot in the end and made some putts." That is, he birdied six of the last seven holes. He shot 66 to tie Moore (65) and de Jonge (66). Moore shot a disarming and bogey-free 65. "I didn't do anything amazing," he said. "I just did what I've been doing — put it in play, gave myself a bunch of wedges, nine irons into greens." And they were tied at 19-under 194 going into the final round.

There, Blixt left the party with a 70 and finished third. Moore birdied the second and third holes to edge ahead, then went two ahead with a birdie at the seventh. De Jonge caught him with birdies at the eighth, the ninth, and they were tied through the 15th. At the par-five 16th, de Jonge missed the fairway and Moore inched ahead with a birdie, then parred the last two for the one-stroke win.

Next, the question was the champion's dinner, what with his side of the family and his wife's side of the family turning out. "Yeah," Moore said, "I think I will be buying."

Frys.com Open
San Martin, California
Winner: Jonas Blixt

Hockey players often make good golfers. It's something about the similarity between the slap shot and the golf swing. Sweden's Jonas Blixt, a frustrated hockey player, carried the notion to the highest level when he broke through in the Frys.com Open in October. He was the third rookie to win on the PGA Tour in 2012.

Oddly enough, Blixt, 28, wasn't feeling all that good about his game at CordeValle Golf Club that week in early October. And so, unable to figure out what was wrong, he resorted to the most basic of approaches to the game. "Just give it a good hit and see what happens," he said. "Just focus. You can't do anything better than your best. That's what I did on every shot."

Having thus made his peace with the game, Blixt stayed in the hunt, shooting the first three rounds in 66-68-66. The third round was where he really warmed up. After a bogey at No. 3, he played the last 10 holes in six under for the 66 that left him two off the lead. He birdied the first two holes of the final round — that was eight birdies in 12 holes — and was finally cooled down by bogeys at Nos. 3 and 4. From there, he birdied Nos. 6, 15 and 17 and parred all the others for a 68 and a 16-under 268 to win by one over Tim Petrovic (64) and Jason Kokrak (68), tied at 269.

CordeValle was a shooting gallery. Nick O'Hern, for example, who had five wins in Australia but was still looking for that first on the PGA Tour, bolted into the first-round lead on a nine-under 62. Then just a sprinkling of bogeys cost him a run of pars, 71-71-71, and dropped him to a tie for 22nd. John Mallinger shot 62 in the second round to open a four-stroke lead, and when someone mentioned he had gone two rounds without a bogey, Mallinger shushed him. "Let's not talk about that," he said, not wanting to break the spell. But maybe that broke the spell. He ran his string to 38 bogey-free holes, then bogeyed twice early in the second round, and broke down with five bogeys on the front nine of the final round, and shot 72 and tied for fourth.

Blixt turned in the kind of performance that is a joy to fans of statistics. After hitting 71 percent of the fairways in the first round, he hit only 50, 57 and 50 percent, respectively. The key was on the greens. For the tournament, he hit 67 percent of the greens in regulation, and needed just 25, 28, 27 and 25 putts, respectively.

How does a boy in hockey-happy Sweden end up in golf? First off, through a golf-happy dad. And second: "I never really got big enough or good enough to play ice hockey."

And then he added: "The tough guys play hockey. You know — the guys with no teeth."

McGladrey Classic
St. Simons Island, Georgia
Winner: Tommy Gainey

The McGladrey Classic was the Tale of Two Big Ones for part-golfer, part-folk hero Tommy "Two Gloves" Gainey. One got away, the other did not.

The one that got away was the magic number, 59, the almost unreachable figure golfers dream about. Gainey had come from seven strokes back in the final round and needed a birdie at the final hole for that 59, to become just the sixth player in PGA Tour history to reach that number. But he just missed the 20-foot putt.

He got the other big one, though. Gainey, 37, small-town boy and self-made golfer from Camden, South Carolina, tapped in for a par and a 60, thus going in seven years from wrapping insulation around water tanks to playing forgettable mini-tours, to becoming a folk hero on the Golf Channel's "Big Break" reality show, to his first win on the PGA Tour.

"Oh, man," said Gainey, who got his nickname from wearing two golf gloves, "I tell you, you're out here on the PGA Tour. Ninety-nine percent of these guys have already won ... majors, big tournaments. I'm very proud to be in this tournament, and very proud to win. And wow — it's been a whirlwind day."

Of all those seven years, the last two hours were the longest. Gainey was never closer than six shots to the lead and was seven behind going into the final round. The tap-in at the last wrapped up his card of 69-67-68-60–264, 16 under at Sea Island. Davis Love and Jim Furyk, so recently Ryder Cup captain and his pick, respectively, could still wipe out Gainey's two-stroke lead, and they had 10 holes left in which to do it.

"Got a long way to go," a nervous Gainey said, meaning himself, not them.

The leaderboard had changed fast — Bud Cauley and Marco Dawson leading the first round, Arjun Atwal the second, and Love and Furyk the third. Gainey then picked Sea Island to pieces in the fourth, going out in 31, with birdies at Nos. 1, 3, 5 and 9, then racing home in 29, on birdies at 11, 13, 14 and 16 and an eagle at the 15th. In a string of seven threes from the 11th, Gainey tied for the lead on a 20-foot birdie putt at the 14th, then holed out a 40-foot bunker shot at the par-five 15th, and a 20-foot birdie putt at the 16th. It was then that the 59 was gettable.

"I wasn't thinking about 59," Gainey said. "See, all I did all day was just try to make birdies ... when you're seven shots back, your chances of winning — with the leaders Davis Love and Jim Furyk — it don't bide in your favor, man." Gainey paused then.

"I'm just waiting," Two Gloves said, "for somebody to slap me up side the head or pinch me or something, to wake me up."

Children's Miracle Network Hospitals Classic
Lake Buena Vista, Florida
Winner: Charlie Beljan

Think of Ben Hogan dragging his injured body through the 1950 U.S. Open. Think of Ken Venturi, staggering through extreme heat in the 1964 U.S. Open. Then consider Charlie Beljan slumping to the turf, gasping for breath, his heart racing, his blood pressure spiking at the Children's Miracle Network Hospitals Classic. He was playing like a guy saying, "I'm going to win this thing or die trying," which he believed he very nearly did. Ironically, Beljan, 28, needed both a hospital and a miracle to win the season finale and at last gain his PGA Tour playing card. For Beljan, former University of New Mexico and mini-tour player, who came through the qualifying school for 2012 and who then made only eight cuts in 21 starts coming into this last chance, it was quite a leap of faith.

Beljan's scoring looked like a good, solid, first-timer's card — 68-64-71-69–272, 16 under par across the Magnolia and Palm courses at Walt Disney World, both par-72s. The numbers hid an extraordinary tale.

"I thought I literally had a chance to die," Beljan said.

His opening 68 left him four behind Charlie Wi. Then came the miracle. He shot an eight-under 64 while in the grip of a full-blown panic attack — 18 holes of gasping for breath, stooped over or on the ground, a hammering heart, numbness in his arms, a spiked blood pressure, and worst of all, a sense of impending death. Paramedics followed, but could do little. "He kept saying he thought he was going to die," said his caddie, Rich Adcox. And somehow, Beljan was playing remarkable golf. He made two eagles, for example, played the par-fives in six under, and made only two bogeys. "It was awesome to watch," said Ed Loar, his playing partner

Adcox tried to get Beljan to quit. "It's only a golf tournament," he said. "You've got many more."

But Beljan had already set the course. "The position I'm in," he said before he started, "it's kind of hard not to show up." He was 139th on the money list and had to finish about 10th to crack the all-exempt top 125 to earn his card for 2013. Finally, the long, frightening day was over. Beljan signed for his miracle 64 and was wheeled out on a stretcher and taken to a hospital. After about 90 minutes' sleep overnight, he ignored the doctors' cautions and came out for the third round, saying, "It's nice to be able to walk around and smile." He shot 71 and led by two. In the final round, he ran off five birdies in six holes from No. 7, holing 30-footers for two of them, for a five-stroke lead. Then he double-bogeyed, birdied, and shot 69 for a 16-under 272 to win by two over Matt Every and Robert Garrigus and lock up that playing card.

The 2012 season needed a great finishing chapter, and Charlie Beljan had just written it.

Special Events

Tavistock Cup
Orlando, Florida
Winner: Lake Nona

"Bragging rights," is what Graeme McDowell called it, and he didn't leave much wiggle room for all comers after host Lake Nona Country Club took the 2012 Tavistock Cup by two strokes. "I think it's definite bragging rights," said the Northern Irishman, a former U.S. Open champion. "I mean, four in a row speaks for itself." And five of the last six maybe speaks a little louder.

All six Lake Nona players broke par on the second and last day, led by Retief Goosen and Ross Fisher's five-under 67s. Ben Curtis, Peter Hanson and Gary Woodland rounded out the Lake Nona team. The event was a Lake Nona-Isleworth showdown of Florida clubs when it began in 2004, and became a four-club event in 2011. Host Lake Nona won this one with a 41-under-par total, followed by Isleworth, at 39; Queenwood, of England, 31; and Albany, of Nassau, Bahamas, 26, despite the presence of Tiger Woods.

Woods was the focus, playing his first golf since withdrawing from the Cadillac Championship less than two weeks earlier with an injured Achilles tendon. With the Masters two weeks away, he pronounced himself fit and showed it with birdies on four of his first seven holes, paired with Justin Rose on the Albany team in the first-round better-ball. He shot a par 72 in the second. Had he come back too soon?

"There are times when I played through some things that I probably shouldn't have," Woods said. "That cost me a little bit. I've been on the sideline for months at a time because of it. For the first time, I did the right thing, and hence I'm back in a week versus I could have been out for a lot longer."

CVS Caremark Charity Classic
Barrington, Rhode Island
Winners: Morgan Pressel and Jay Haas

They opened with a nine-under-par 62 in better-ball to tie for the first-round lead. Then the LPGA's Morgan Pressel and Champions Tour star Jay Haas struck a bit of lightning around old Rhode Island Country Club in the second-round scramble — a birdie-par start followed by nine straight birdies from the third and capped off with an eagle at the 12th. They parred in for a 12-under 59 and a 21-under 121 total and a two-stroke win in the CVS Caremark Charity Classic over Lexi Thompson and Corey Pavin, Suzann Petterson and Fred Funk.

"In this format, you expect to make a lot of birdies, but not quite like we did," said Haas, who capped the birdie streak with a hole-out eagle from 74 yards at the par-four 12th after Pressel stuck her approach to 10 feet. "When you hole out from like 80 yards, you luck out," Pressel said. And said Haas: "Morgan freed me up. She had a great shot and allowed me to go for it."

Tournament founders and native New Englanders Billy Andrade and Brad Faxon enjoyed a whiff of success when they tied for the first-round lead at 62. Said Andrade: "I haven't had this feeling of being tied for the lead in a really long time. We had a great day." But true to the fate of busy hosts trying to compete, they couldn't sustain the effort and finished in a tie for fifth in the 10-team field. This was the 14th playing of their charity event. They have yet to win it.

PGA Grand Slam of Golf
Southhampton Parish, Bermuda
Winner: Padraig Harrington

Padraig Harrington, a three-time major winner who hadn't won anything for two years, felt he talked his way into the title in the PGA Grand Slam of Golf in Bermuda.

"Every day I play, I always try to enjoy the day, talk to my playing partners," Harrington said, after taking a two-shot lead in the first round. "Today it was better than ever. Everybody was up for a chat. I play better when the whole group enjoys it. If the guys had any sense," he added, with that grin, "they shouldn't talk to me tomorrow."

But who could resist that Irish gift? And so Harrington, substituting for Open champion Ernie Els in this October exhibition for the winners of the four majors, played Port Royal in 66-67–133 for a one-stroke win over U.S. Open champion Webb Simpson (69-65–134). Masters champion Bubba Watson (68-71) and Keegan Bradley (72-67), substituting for PGA champion Rory McIlroy, tied at 139.

Simpson was closing fast in the second round until they got to what he figured was the turning point, a three-hole stretch from the 11th. "I had some good looks and played them even," Simpson said, "and he played them three under." Harrington birdied all three and was on his way.

When you haven't won anything for a couple years, even a made-for-television frolic in Bermuda feels like a million bucks. Well, the actual figure was $600,000, but it was the thought that counted. "They don't come around anywhere near as often as you believe," he said, "and when you win, make sure you enjoy it."

Callaway Golf Pebble Beach Invitational
Pebble Beach, California
Winner: Tommy Gainey

Unlike a lot of golfers, Tommy "Two Gloves" Gainey wasn't shy about checking the leaderboard, so at the final hole of the Callaway Golf Pebble Beach Invitational, he knew where he stood, and it was a precarious position.

"I knew I needed the putt to win," said Gainey, suddenly facing a three-footer that under the pressure of the moment had become so much longer. So Two Gloves, so nicknamed for wearing two golf gloves, bore down and rolled it in for a three-under-par 69 and an 11-under 277 total for a one-shot win over Kirk Triplett (68) and William McGirt (69) in the tournament for players from the PGA, Champions, LPGA and Web.com tours. Both missed birdie tries at the 18th. Gainey, who gained fame from a TV reality golf show, had scored his first PGA Tour victory at the McGladrey Classic in October with a final-round 60.

Gainey coolly manufactured this win. He started the final round two behind third-round leader Robert Streb and birdied three straight from the fifth. He got to 12 under at the par-five 14th, then bogeyed the next two. He swallowed hard at the 18th. "When I saw my ball headed towards that bunker, I was just hoping it'd get in and stay there," Gainey said. It did, and he splashed out to three feet.

"Winning here is awesome," Gainey said. "You can't ask for more than winning at Pebble Beach."

Hall-of-Famer Annika Sorenstam, making a rare appearance in her retirement, played in a foursome that included Juli Inkster, and closed with a 69 and finished at one over.

World Challenge
Thousand Oaks, California
Winner: Graeme McDowell

Graeme McDowell, a native of Northern Ireland and a resident of Orlando, Florida, seems to have found a home at Sherwood Country Club. In the World Challenge, McDowell shot 69-66-68-68–271, 17 under par, to win by three strokes. There's something about Sherwood that suits him. It was the 10th time in 12 rounds that he shot in the 60s. His affinity for the course shows in his record: He finished second in 2009 and won in 2010. In fact, this was McDowell's first victory since he beat host Tiger Woods in the same tournament in 2010, the year of his U.S. Open victory.

"This really caps off my season," said McDowell, who won over Keegan Bradley to pick up the $1 million first prize in the 18-player field early in December. "We try not to put winning on a pedestal," he added, "but this one feels very sweet because it's been a grind all year." McDowell played in the final group in both the U.S. Open and the Open Championship but ran out of steam.

Woods, who finished eight shots behind, tied for fourth, founded the tournament to raise money for the learning centers and youth activities of his Tiger Woods Foundation. When a title sponsor could not be found for 2012, Northwestern Mutual signed on as a "presenting sponsor," a less expensive role, and Woods himself "bridged the gap," he said, by contributing a "good number." The Associated Press reported Woods's contribution to be $4 million, for a total of $18.4 million donated since 1999, representing Woods's earnings in the three tournaments that support his Foundation — World Challenge, AT&T National and Deutsche Bank Championship.

Franklin Templeton Shootout
Naples, Florida
Winners: Sean O'Hair and Kenny Perry

It was like a couple of kids having fun, Sean O'Hair was saying. That was he and Kenny Perry teaming for a 31-under-par 185 total and a one-stroke victory in the Franklin Templeton Shootout at Tiburon Golf Club early in December. They jumped into the lead in the second round and held it through the third and final round to edge Charles Howell and Rory Sabbatini. Jason Dufner and Vijay Singh were third in the 10-team field at 28 under.

It was Perry's third victory in the event. The other two came with John Huston, in 2005, and Scott Hoch in 2008.

"That was the best thing," O'Hair said. "We just had a ton of fun, just like being a kid, enjoying what you do." With a 64 in the opening modified alternate-shot format, they were two shots behind Davis Love and Brandt Snedeker. Then they took the lead in the second round, birdieing the last six holes for a 61 in the better-ball format. "We got pretty hot," O'Hair said. "Kenny did a great job when I wasn't in the hole, then I did a pretty good job when Kenny wasn't in the hole."

Then they birdied five of the last six holes in the final-round scramble to lock up the one-stroke win, becoming the seventh second-round leaders to go on to win, finding it a bit like a game of tag. "I knew they were going to probably catch up to us at some point, but I knew we had holes to catch back up to them," Perry said.

PNC Father-Son Challenge
Orlando, Florida
Winner: Davis Love and Dru Love

It was something of a case of father-knows-best. "Neither one of us hit good shots into the 18th," Davis Love was saying, "and I was more nervous over the chip, but it was great to leave the last putt for Dru."

Love chipped to eight feet and his son Dru, a freshman at the University of Alabama, rolled in the curling putt for an 11-under-par 61 and a one-stroke victory in the revived PNC Father-Son Challenge at the Ritz-Carlton Golf Club. The Loves, runners-up the last time the event was played in 2008, shot the two-golfer scramble in 60-61, 23-under 121, for a one-stroke win over Larry and Josh Nelson, the 2004 and 2008 champions, who shot 62-60–122. Vijay and Qass Singh carded a 61 and finished third in this event for fathers who have won major championships or The Players.

The Nelsons had a chance to tie at the final hole, but Larry's 12-foot putt hit the back of the cup and rimmed out. "That is one of the toughest (lip-outs) of my career," said Nelson.

Two fathers played with their daughters. Fuzzy and Gretchen Zoeller shot 65-60–125, and Bernhard and Christian Langer 62-65–127.

Two of the standbys returned. Jack and Gary Nicklaus tied for sixth at 62-63–125, and Arnold Palmer and grandson Will Wears finished 18th and last at 80-76–156.

Web.com Tour

Casey Wittenberg was finally rewarded for all those years of struggle — he won twice — and four others matched him, adding spark to a brisk season on what started out 2012 as the Nationwide Tour, the "developmental" circuit as the PGA Tour calls it. But it was all upstaged by a shift in golf.

One minute they were watching the Nationwide Tour, the next the Web.com Tour. On June 27, 2012, the PGA Tour announced that the circuit would have a new umbrella sponsor. Web.com, a web services provider, would replace Nationwide Insurance, effective immediately. Chief among other changes was that the Web.com Tour would now be the path to the PGA Tour, replacing the qualifying tournament, which would now be the port of entry to the Web.com Tour.

This was the last year in which the top 25 on the money list go right to the PGA Tour. Beginning in 2013, the top 75 on the money list will join with Nos. 126-200 on the PGA Tour money list to play the Web.com Tour Final, a four-event series that will give 50 players their PGA Tour card for the following season.

Thus history turned a page on the developmental tour. It started as the Ben Hogan Tour in 1990 and ran for three years, followed by the Nike Tour for seven, the Buy.com Tour for three, and the Nationwide for nine and a half years.

Wittenberg scored both of his wins on the Nationwide Tour before the change. He took the Chitimacha Louisiana Open with a splash — two eagles, 22 birdies and just two bogeys, and won by a tournament-record eight shots. He added the Preferred Health Systems Wichita Open, birdieing four of the last nine holes. "I wanted to go win the tournament and not let it come to me," he said. With six other top-10 finishes, Wittenberg amassed $433,453 and won the Player of the Year Award, but most important, headed the coveted top 25 on the money list who got their PGA Tour playing cards.

The season was a festival for rookies. They accounted for 11 victories, and four had two apiece — Ben Kohles, Luke Guthrie, Shawn Stefani and Russell Henley. Better yet, Kohles and Guthrie won theirs back-to-back. At 22, they also were the youngest of the "Class" of 2012, as top-25s came to be known.

Kohles was unquestionably the new star of the year. He arrived at the Nationwide Children's Hospital Invitational as an amateur, checked "professional" on his registration form, then proceeded to win his first start as a pro. He was the first player in tour history to win in his pro debut, and he did it with a flair. He birdied two of his last three regulation holes, then ironically won in a playoff over Guthrie, who himself would win twice about a month later. "What more can you ask for in your first pro event than to win?" Kohles said.

What more could you ask for than to win your next start? Kohles did it, coming from behind with a nine-under 62 in the final round to finish at 24 under and win by three in the Cox Classic. That made him the first player in tour history to win his first two starts in two weeks as a pro. "I'm pretty shocked myself," he said. "What are you supposed to do better than this?"

His strategy might be a hint to how he might play on the PGA Tour. "Attack, attack, attack," said Kohles. "Anything can happen behind us. We were just pedal-to-the-metal down to the end."

Guthrie used a similar approach in taking his first victory, the Albertsons Boise Open in September. "Pick a conservative target but make sure you play aggressively to it," he said. "Attack the easy holes and hunker down and make pars." He started the final round par-birdie-eagle, shot 65 and a tournament-record 22-under total and won by four.

At the WNB Golf Classic the next week, Guthrie rallied from five shots behind with a closing 66, holing a 12-foot par putt at the final hole to win by one for his second win to go with four other top-10 finishes. "You go through these runs where the hole gets bigger, your mind slows down and it seems easy," he said. "The trick is to have more days like this than the bad ones."

Guthrie, incidentally, was balancing golf with academics, finishing his studies in the fall to get his degree at the University of Illinois.

The other two double-winners were Shawn Stefani (Midwest Classic and Miccosukee Championship) and Russell Henley (Chiquita Classic and Winn-Dixie Jacksonville Open).

For Alex Aragon, the TPS Stonebrae Championship in April wasn't the tournament of the year, it was the tournament of a lifetime. The first good sign: He started by locking his keys in the trunk of his car on Thursday, but he made his tee time, thanks to a two-hour fog delay. He played all 18 holes on Thursday, but because of more fog, he hit only his first tee shot on Friday, the day his wallet was stolen at a nearby gas station. Then he played 33 holes on Saturday and 21 on Sunday. It was worth it. Aragon got his first career win. Said Aragon: "I kept saying to myself all day, I was going to win the tournament."

Rookie Robert Streb, 25, bashed his way to his first victory and a spot in the coveted top 25 at the Mylan Classic early in September. In the final round, he hit 13 of the 14 driving fairways, 13 greens, and had just one bogey in 36 holes and only three for the tournament, and shot a course-record 18-under-par 266 to win by four. Said Streb, the sixth rookie and 13th first-timer in 20 events to win on the tour: "I guess I've reached my goals for now. It's nice, because I can figure out what I'm doing the rest of the year."

Canadian Tour

This was a real debut: You're not only a rookie, but you're making your first start, and it's in the tour's opening tournament. Comes the final round, and you birdie the last seven holes, shoot 61 and win the thing by three. That was Andrew Roque, age 23, of Monterey Park, California, winning the Canadian Tour's Times Colonist Island Savings Open at Uplands Golf Club, Victoria, British Columbia, in June.

And talk about getting into the zone: "I knew where I stood," said Roque, "but I didn't realize that I made seven birdies in a row." Which left him with a tough question: What does he do for an encore?

Thus began the 26th and final season of the Canadian PGA Tour as a stand-alone circuit. It would emerge in 2013 as PGA Tour Canada. The various financial and organizational concerns would now be in the hands of the PGA Tour, which earlier had absorbed the Tour de Las Americas, and which became the PGA Tour Latinoamerica, for Central and South America and the Caribbean. "This," said PGA Tour Commissioner Tim Finchem, "gives us geographic integration throughout the Americas..." Or pole-to-pole golf in the Western Hemisphere.

So, in the season opener, Roque left his mark with his breakthrough win, overrunning local favorite Cory Renfrew, also making his first start, and triggering a run of six first-time winners over the eight events on the schedule (excluding the Canadian Open, co-sanctioned with the PGA Tour and won by Scott Piercy). The group was led by North Vancouver's Eugene Wong, 2010 Jack Nicklaus Award winner, who scored not only his first victory but the second as well, back-to-back.

Ontario's Michael Gligic won at the second stop, the ATB Financial Classic at Windermere Golf Club in Edmonton. Gligic closed with a 67 to tie Matt Marshall, of Scottsdale, Arizona, who had birdied the first four holes of the final round and led by as many as four strokes. Then he bogeyed four straight coming in and had to sink an eight-foot birdie putt to tie Gligic in regulation. Gligic just missed a winning three-foot putt on the first extra hole, then won on the second with a par. "You can never really practice those three-footers to win a tournament," Gligic said.

Renfrew, denied his first win by Roque's birdie binge in the season opener, got it in the Syncrude Boreal Open at Ft. McMurray, Alberta. Renfrew closed with a course-record 63 and tied Ontario's Matt Hill, then beat him on the fourth extra hole.

It was Hill's turn next, and at the Dakota Dunes Casino Open at Saskatoon. Ironically, it was in another four-hole playoff, this against former PGA Tour player Will Strickler. Hill, the 2009 NCAA Individual Champion and Jack Nicklaus Award winner, shot four rounds of 68 or better to become the third straight Canadian to win a tournament, which hadn't been done since 2009. The victory carried Hill to the top of the money-winning list, where he stayed the rest of the season.

Chris Killmer, of Bellingham, Washington, became the fifth straight first-timer, taking the Canadian Tour Players Cup with a par on the fourth playoff hole against Philadelphia's Vince Covello. They entered the final round as co-leaders, four ahead of the field, and put on a show. Killmer eagled the 12th and Covello birdied four of the last seven holes, both shooting two-under 69s to tie at 15-under-par 269. Both missed chances to win on the first three playoff holes, and then at the fourth, Covello was wide right with his five-foot par putt, and Killmer took the opportunity and holed his par putt for the win. "I'm on top of the world right now," Killmer said.

Alan McLean, 41, a Scot raised in South Africa, was or wasn't technically a first-time winner, depending, when he took the Jamieson WFCU Windsor Roseland Charity Classic. He had won before, but this was his first since joining the Canadian Tour, his first in 132 starts. McLean made five birdies on the final nine, four of them in succession from the 11th, and added another on an eight-foot putt at the 17th. He shot 66 and a 10-under 270 to edge Hugo Leon by two. As for winning, no matter where: "You never get tired of that feeling," McLean said.

Wong, 21, won the Canadian Tour Championship with a miracle shot on the final hole, then closed out by winning the season finale, the Great Waterway Classic.

"My caddie and I were walking up the fairway," said Wong, "and he said, 'It would be nice to hole it right now, wouldn't it?' And I said 'Yeah, it would.'" Whereupon Wong's approach from 133 yards took two hops and went into the hole to edge Joe Panzeri by a stroke. The win put Wong in the clouds. "My confidence is really high now," he said. "I know I can compete with the pros, and I'm happy to get my first win. So there's one milestone down."

Two weeks later, Wong scored his second win with a final-round six-under 65 to nip Daniel Im in the Great Waterway. "It's been a pretty unbelievable stretch for me," Wong said.

The victory lifted Wong up the money list. Matt Hill topped it with $48,273, followed by Gligic at $42,950 and Wong at $33,936. James Love had the lowest stroke average, 68.75, and Wong was second at 68.88.

With the tournaments ending in early September, it was on to the fall qualifying tournament for the hopefuls. Under the operational guidelines of the new PGA Tour Canada, the debut season in 2013 would consist of at least eight tournaments, each with a purse of at least $150,000. As with the PGA Tour Latinoamerica, the top five finishers at the end of the season would have a berth on the Web.com Tour, the last step up to the PGA Tour — the "big" tour.

PGA Tour Latinoamerica

Let the record show that the new PGA Tour Latinoamerica was officially born at 7:30 a.m., September 5, 2012, when Jesus Rivas, of Colombia, hit the first tee shot of the Mundo Maya Open. He went on to shoot a one-under-par 71 and tie for 34th at two-under 286, 18 shots behind the winner. Rivas won $1,020. It may not have been much for him or the new tour, but it was a start.

There was a rather nice, storybook ring to it, a touch of Hollywood.

The PGA Tour Latinoamerica, a brand-new tour for Latin America under the umbrella of the PGA Tour, was making its debut into the world of professional golf with the Mundo Maya Open, and Argentina's Tommy Cocha, age 21 and just 21 months a professional, was making his own debut, in a sense. He won it — his first victory as a pro. There was a kind of harmony there.

The Latinoamerica tour was the reincarnation of the Tour de Las Americas, which ran for 12 seasons, and of earlier tours that plied golf in the region but just couldn't quite make it work. But the new tour had the money and the muscle of the PGA Tour with it. The Latinoamerica was an immediate upgrade. Players would qualify for points under the Official World Golf Ranking, and the new tour would provide access to the developmental Web.com Tour. The top five players on the money-winning list would have a berth on the Web.com Tour, the next step to the big tour itself. Thus the new tour would provide a channel for future talents of the caliber of Camilo Villegas, Andres Romero and Angel Cabrera. Much the same thing happened far to the north, where the struggling Canadian PGA Tour became PGA Tour Canada. The addition of the two feeder tours essentially made the entire Western Hemisphere the golf ground of the PGA Tour, not only stabilizing the professional game throughout both regions but also effectively pre-empting any thoughts of expansion by any other tours.

But back to the action:

What started out as a tour for all of Latin America quickly turned into a playground for Argentines: They won eight of the 11 events.

Cocha, who stands just 5-feet-5 and weighs 128 pounds, won the Mundo Maya Open by five strokes, shooting Yucatan Country Club at Merida, Mexico, in 20-under 268. Cocha started the final round leading by four, and despite some pressure from Mexico's Oscar Fraustro, he was never in real trouble. He birdied Nos. 4, 5, 8, 14 and 16, going up by as many as six and never falling below four. "I felt it could be a great week," Cocha said, "but I never thought I'd get to 22 under par because of the difficulty of the course." He made 27 birdies and only five bogeys for the week.

Argentina's Ariel Canete won twice to top the money list with $91,395. He had to play 34 holes on the final day to take the rain-plagued TransAmerican Open at LaHerradura Golf Club in Monterrey, Mexico. Seven different players topped the leaderboard in the long grind, but Canete didn't notice. "When you are scoring and playing that well, you don't get that tired," said Canete, after a closing 68 gave him a two-stroke win. He posted his second win early in August, winning the Olivos Golf Classic at home in Buenos Aires. "It's like a major championship for us (Argentines)," Canete said, after shooting a pair of 67s in the 36-hole wrap-up to win by two again. The victory gave him six top-five finishes in the 10 starts.

Argentina's Matias O'Curry put his law degree on hold and saw the bold move pay off in a win at the Colombian Open — by eight strokes, the most decisive in the Latinoamerica's first season. He led by seven going into the final round, but didn't grow complacent or defensive at Club El Rincon in Bogota. "This is really awesome," said O'Curry. "I was lucky to stay out of trouble most of the time."

Also chiming in for Argentina: Clodomiro Carranza, in the Brazil Open, made up six strokes in the final round and won the first playoff in the new tour, beating Mexico's Jose de Jesus Rodriguez. Alan Wagner was about to miss his fourth straight cut, but rallied and birdied the last two holes to take the Roberto de Vicenzo Invitational. And Sebastian Fernandez dropped a 15-foot birdie putt on the first playoff hole to beat Colombia's Jose Manuel Garrido in the Colombian Coffee Classic.

Interrupting the All-Argentine party were Peru's Sebastian Salem, winning the Lexus Peru Open by a stroke; Mexico's Fraustro, cruising by four in the Dominican Republic Open, and Mexico's Sebastian Vazquez, 22, taking the Puerto Rico Classic by two in his second start.

The finale in December, the Argentina Open, was left to a familiar figure, that of Angel Cabrera, native son and winner of the 2007 U.S. Open and the 2009 Masters. Cabrera entered the final round a stroke behind Fraustro, then posted nine birdies against a single bogey for a 64 and an 18-under 270 for a four-stroke win, his first win since the 2009 Masters.

The Tour de Las Americas, which ran for 12 seasons, closed its books with these final six entries, spanning March to June:

Paraguay's Marco Ruiz led the transition to the new tour by winning the last two tournaments, the TLA Players Championship in Mexico, then the Taca Airlines Open in Peru. He topped the money list with $26,884.

The final season began with Argentina's Julian Etulain taking the Los Lirios Open in Chile. Venezuela's Rafael Romero then won the La Vitalicia International Open in Venezuela, followed by two more Argentines — Cesar Costilla, in the Centro Open, and Luciano Dodda in the Nordeste Open, both played in Argentina. With Ruiz's two wins, the TLA books were closed, and the Latinoamerica's books were about to open.

9. European Tours

Rory McIlroy was so good in 2012 that the discussion inevitably turned to how many Europeans could be considered to have had a better season in the modern era. Many made the case that only the double major-winning seasons of Nick Faldo in 1990 and Padraig Harrington in 2008 could emphatically be placed ahead of the Northern Ireland star's efforts.

At the age of 23 McIlroy matched Luke Donald's feat from 2011 of winning the money lists on both the PGA Tour and the European Tour, as well as finishing the year as the undisputed world No. 1. But McIlroy also won a major championship. His second came in a similar style to the first at the 2011 U.S. Open. McIlroy won the U.S. PGA Championship by eights shots in another runaway performance at Kiawah Island that left his rivals breathless.

McIlroy first became the world No. 1 at the Honda Classic in America in March, but a lackluster early summer caused him to miss cuts at The Players Championship, the BMW PGA Championship at Wentworth and the Memorial Tournament. After a seventh-place finish at the St. Jude Classic, McIlroy then missed the cut in defense of his U.S. Open crown. At Wentworth McIlroy admitted to "taking his eye off the ball" in his practice regime, and some observers suggested his relationship with superstar tennis player Caroline Wozniacki was to blame for his loss of form.

However, a longer-term view would be that since dating Wozniacki shortly after winning the 2011 U.S. Open had done wonders for McIlroy's fitness and work ethic while he had matured both as a golfer and a person. Hard work with his coach Michael Bannon duly paid off. After finishing fifth at the WGC - Bridgestone Invitational, he was flying again, winning at Kiawah the next week. Two imperious victories followed in the PGA Tour's FedExCup Playoffs at the Deutsche Bank Championship and the BMW Championship, and although he slipped to 10th at the Tour Championship, he could be forgiven for wondering how the mathematics prevented him from winning the FedExCup itself.

Winning his second major at the U.S. PGA Championship seemed to unleash his best golf, just as it did for Tiger Woods in 1999. But no longer was McIlroy winning tournaments when at his best and blowing the rest away — as he has done for both his major wins. He also won when not at his best or by doing whatever it takes to get the job done. Witness his control down the stretch at the Honda Classic, parring in from the 14th when under pressure from the course, the wind and a late-charging Woods. And also his five birdies after falling two behind to Justin Rose at the DP World Tour Championship in Dubai. "I just wanted to finish the season the way I thought it deserved to be finished," McIlroy said. "I've played so well throughout the year, and I didn't want to just let it tail off sort of timidly. I wanted to come here and finish in style."

Donald, who retained the BMW PGA Championship but lost his world No. 1 crown during the year, marveled: "Rory has been the best player all year and that was some finish by him. A lot of grit and determination, and he's proved that once again he's the best player in the world. It's capped off an amazing year for him. I think he'll be around for a long time, but it's good, he'll push me to work harder."

Not that McIlroy will be working any less hard. His goals for 2013? "I guess the same. To be focused on the majors, try to win more of those. I've won one in '11, one in '12, it would be nice to keep that run going next year. As I've said, just try to keep improving as a player. I can feel like I can improve in different areas of the game still. That's the challenge and the fun of practice, trying to get better all the time."

Of McIlroy's five wins during the season only two counted on the European Tour, at the U.S. PGA and the season-ending World Tour Championship in Dubai. But such was his consistency — 10 top-10 finishes in 15 events with runner-up spots at the Abu Dhabi HSBC Championship, the WGC - Accenture Match Play and the BMW Masters — that he had sealed the Race to Dubai money title with a third-place finish in the Barclays Singapore Open, or rather once Louis Oosthuizen lost in a playoff for that title against Matteo Manassero.

Oosthuizen won twice on the European Tour in 2012, alongside McIlroy, Paul Lawrie, whose resurgence in form aged 43 was sparked by playing with his teenage sons, Peter Hanson and Bernd Wiesberger. Oosthuizen was pipped for second place on the Race to Dubai by Rose, who won his first WGC title at the Cadillac Championship. Once again the leading spots on the money list were dominated by those players who also played in America and got to enter all the majors and WGC events.

But the newcomer on the European Tour was undoubtedly Branden Grace, who lived the dream after winning his card at the qualifying tournament. The 24-year-old South African had a disappointing rookie season on the European Tour in 2009, but this time he immediately made his mark by winning the Joburg Open in the second week of the season. The following week he returned home to George and beat his heroes Ernie Els and Retief Goosen in a playoff at the Volvo Champions at Fancourt. He then won the Volvo China Open and in October, the week after winning on the Sunshine Tour, he claimed the biggest of his four European Tour wins, and five in all, at the Alfred Dunhill Links Championship.

It was a wire-to-wire win after opening with a 60 at Kingsbarns and he was inspired by staying for the week with the 2010 Open champion Oosthuizen. "Getting my card at Tour School and that first win just did me the world's best," Grace said. "I think the confidence that I got after that just lifted me up sky high and everything has just been going my way. But I think any golfer out there would dream of winning at St. Andrews. When you dream of turning professional, you are dreaming and striving to win a tournament of this caliber, and to win it on this place, the Home of Golf, was amazing. It was more than just a couple of dreams coming true when I lifted the trophy on that bridge."

The 2012 season will also be remembered for another Ryder Cup victory for Europe. It was Europe's fifth win in six attempts but was hardly just another victory. Mid-afternoon on the Saturday America led 10-4 and anything but a home win at Medinah seemed absurd. Although led by Ian Poulter's five birdies to close out a second fourball victory, the visitors still were left hanging on by the fingernails at 10-6. But the momentum was heading their way. A thrilling final-day comeback was completed when Martin Kaymer ensured Europe would retain the Cup, and Woods's concession to Francesco Molinari at the last left the scoreline 14½-13½. For Europe's captain, Jose Maria Olazabal, it was a deserved victory that lifted him alongside his great amigo Seve Ballesteros, whose inspiration was often quoted in those dramatic moments.

But Ryder Cup success is not everything these days and most of the team either were, or would shortly become, not just members of the PGA Tour but based in America. Even Lee Westwood, whose reluctance to leave his hometown of Worksop is well known, decided to move to Florida in the hope of winning that elusive major championship. The European Tour's response to what might be seen as a brain drain has been to schedule some of their biggest events early and late in the season, but players have to travel to the Middle East and Asia to do that, while South Africa has also been fertile ground for adding tournaments. But with players based in America from March to September, tournaments in Europe itself have suffered from not seeing the star players often enough — McIlroy, for example, has won 10 times in his career but never in Europe.

A double whammy has been the economic austerity in Europe that has seen countries like Spain drastically reduce their commitment to the tour. "We are of course slightly disappointed that we have lost events in the Eurozone countries and we are working on that for next year," said George O'Grady, chief executive of the European Tour. "The depth of that crisis is very, very strong. And I think we know if accountants are put in charge of the issue, the big thing is to cut costs wherever you can; whereas the strength of the European Tour is you market your way out of problems with tremendous value for money we feel."

O'Grady acknowledged that more work needed to be done for tournaments and players in the middle and bottom tiers of the tour. However, a new "Final Series" was announced for 2013 with four concluding events offering over $30 million in prize money. It starts with the BMW Masters, continues with the HSBC Champions and Turkish Open and culminates at the Dubai finale. Play in two of the first three and players will qualify for the bonus pool; play all three and points earned from those events will be increased by 20 percent. It is a modest attempt to keep the No. 1 spot alive until the final week but without the complexity of the FedExCup.

"We can't guarantee that and we actually don't want to," said Keith Waters, chief operating officer of the European Tour, "because we feel it's there on an individual if he actually plays incredibly well and much better than everybody else, he has the right to win the Race earlier in the season. That's what sport is about, and we don't want to contrive the points to such a degree that it all comes down to the last nine holes."

Often, it will anyway. O'Grady added: "We did examine a FedEx Series proposal and whether we imitated the PGA Tour, but I think our system is cleaner. In each of the first four years the current world No. 1 player has won the Race to Dubai, and surely that's the way it should be." In 2012, it certainly was for Rory McIlroy.

Africa Open
East London, Eastern Cape, South Africa
Winner: Louis Oosthuizen

See Africa Tours chapter.

Joburg Open
Johannesburg, South Africa
Winner: Branden Grace

See Africa Tours chapter.

Volvo Golf Champions
George, South Africa
Winner: Branden Grace

See Africa Tours chapter.

Abu Dhabi HSBC Golf Championship
Abu Dhabi, United Arab Emirates
Winner: Robert Rock

When Robert Rock birdied the last two holes of his third round of the Abu Dhabi HSBC Golf Championship, it was almost a dream to be paired with Tiger Woods in the final round. This was an apparently resurgent Woods, in his first appearance in the tournament and for the new season, who had just returned a 66 to claim top spot on the leaderboard before Rock joined him. Rock, ranked 117th in the world at the start of the week, then delivered a popular upset by outscoring the former world No. 1 with a 70 to a 72. Rock finished on 275, 13 under, and beat Rory McIlroy by one, with Woods sharing third place with Thomas Bjorn and Graeme McDowell.

Woods started the last day well with birdies at Abu Dhabi's second and third holes, but Rock matched him each time. Then Woods bogeyed the next two holes and the theme for the day was set. Rock went three clear with a birdie at the sixth, although when he bogeyed the eighth and Woods birdied the ninth, the gap was back to one. But Woods bogeyed the 10th and then parred his way to the clubhouse. He hit only two fairways and six greens in regulation during the round. "I was just a little off," Woods said, but in truth he rarely looked like making a birdie on the back nine.

Instead, Rock recovered from a bogey at the 13th by holing from 10 feet for a birdie at the 14th and from six feet for another at the 16th. When he pushed his drive on a sandy and rocky patch next to a water hazard, he dropped back down the fairway and made sure of taking no worse than a bogey-six. It was his second victory after winning in Italy in 2011, and the former assistant at Swinger Golf Centre in Lichfield was serenaded with the theme from the Rocky movies by spectators, some of whom had attended the Pakistan-England Test cricket match in the same city which had ended the previous day.

"It's pretty hard to believe I managed to win today," Rock said. "It doesn't get an awful lot harder than playing with Tiger Woods, so I guess, barring a major, I know I can handle that again and that's nice to know. I was just determined to try and play the way I had been playing, and hopefully without being too nervous, I could continue to hit some decent shots. But he's such a good player that if he decides to play his very, very best, you're probably not going to beat him."

McIlroy was left ruing an incident on the fringe of the ninth green in the second round when he brushed sand from a bunker away from his line of play. Luke Donald, his playing partner, immediately pointed out the infringement to McIlroy who equally quickly admitted to a "brain freeze." The two-shot penalty was the difference between first and second place on Sunday.

Commercialbank Qatar Masters
Doha, Qatar
Winner: Paul Lawrie

When Paul Lawrie won the Commercialbank Qatar Masters in 1999, he went on to win the Open Championship the same year. Holding the giant pearl-in-oyster trophy after winning again in 2012, the 43-year-old was asked if another claret jug might be on its way. "Now wouldn't that be nice to get that again?" he replied.

When Lawrie wins, conditions are rarely easy, and Doha was once more exposed to some fierce winds. Lawrie scored a 69 in the first round, three behind leader Gonzalo Fernandez-Castano, in the strong breezes of Thursday, but early on Friday play in the second round had to be suspended as gales battered the course. The tournament resumed on Saturday and was cut to 54 holes. Lawrie returned a 67 to take a one-stroke lead over Nicolas Colsaerts and then on Sunday simply ran away with the title. He scored a 65, chipping in for an eagle at the ninth and again for a birdie at the 17th, to finish at 15 under par on a total of 201. He won by four shots over Jason Day, the Australian who also closed with a 65, and Sweden's Peter Hanson. John Daly finished in fourth place, his best result since a runner-up spot at the Italian Open in 2009.

Day had four birdies in a row to start his final round and also to start the back nine, but Lawrie was always in command. Sergio Garcia briefly tied the Scot at the top of the leaderboard before slipping back to fifth place, but Lawrie immediately regained the outright lead by his eagle at the ninth. He then birdied the 11th, 14th and 16th holes before the second chip-in at the 17th. It was not just a spectacular display of short game skills but a fine exhibition of ball-striking with his irons.

Lawrie said he had been playing and practicing more at home, having been inspired by his promising teenage sons, Craig and Michael. Including the Dubai World Championship at the end of 2011, this was Lawrie's fourth top-10 finish in a row. He had never had three successive top-10s before. "I don't think I can play much better than that," he said. "I've been playing well for a long, long time, but it's just nice to come out one ahead and shoot seven under."

Omega Dubai Desert Classic
Dubai, United Arab Emirates
Winner: Rafa Cabrera-Bello

Rafa Cabrera-Bello won the Austrian Open in 2009 with a final round of 60. The 27-year-old Spaniard opened the Omega Dubai Desert Classic with a 63 but only regained the lead late in the fourth round to claim his second title on the European Tour. In between, some of the game's biggest names seemed well placed to take the huge teapot trophy. Former winners Rory McIlroy and Thomas Bjorn shared the halfway lead on 13 under after both had rounds of 66 and 65. Yet both faltered on the back nine on Saturday and the third-round lead was claimed by Lee Westwood after a 67. When the Worksop man holed a long putt from off the front of the second green for an eagle to go two ahead of the field, it seemed another flawless display of front-running would ensue. It did not. Westwood hardly holed another putt all day. Although his only bogey came at the fifth, his only birdie was at the par-five 13th where he missed a good chance of an eagle. All down the inward nine, chances went astray.

Cabrera-Bello, only a stroke off the lead at the end of the second and third holes, had been patiently waiting his turn. He birdied the second, but it was on the back nine that he made his move. He birdied the short 11th and then the 12th. Westwood and Stephen Gallacher, with an eagle at the 13th, made it a three-way tie at the top, but at the 17th Cabrera-Bello made the decisive break. His second shot finished five feet away and he holed for a three. His rounds of 63, 69, 70 and 68 left him on 270, 18 under par. Both Westwood and Gallacher had a chance to tie with a birdie at the last, but neither could get up and down for a four.

"It's an unbelievable feeling and it's been a really spectacular week for me," said Cabrera-Bello, who started it with nine birdies in 11 holes. "With so many big, big names I felt really proud of myself. I wanted to fight, I stayed calm, I did everything that I've read we should do in these type of situations." He was the third successive Spaniard to win the title after Miguel Angel Jimenez and Alvaro Quiros, and the fifth in all including Seve Ballesteros and Jose Maria Olazabal. "It's a really amazing feeling for me to be a little bit a part of the same history they are."

McIlroy tied for fifth place and Bjorn tied for ninth, but it was Westwood who felt he should have won and he departed without talking to the media. The following day he took to Twitter to announce his "16-hour sulk" was over. He added: "Well, tossed that one away nicely! Carnage on the greens! Managed not to break or smash anything post round! Waved the putter at it 33 times. Not even good enough for the monthly medal with form like that."

Avantha Masters
Gurgaon, India
Winner: Jbe' Kruger

See Asia/Japan Tours chapter.

Open de Andalucia Costa del Sol
Andalucia, Spain
Winner: Julien Quesne

Although a new name to many, Julien Quesne became the 400th different winner on the European Tour in some style. The 31-year-old Frenchman not only scored the lowest round of his career but equaled the Aloha course record set in the opening round by Matteo Manassero, the eventual runner-up. Quesne birdied four of the last five holes and at the final hole hit a four iron to five feet to claim a two-stroke win over Manassero and a three-shot advantage over Eduardo De La Riva, who had led after the second and third rounds.

Quesne, who only took up golf at the age of 17, had won twice on the Challenge Tour, where he had returned in 2011 after losing his card in his rookie European Tour campaign the previous year. He had rounds of 68, 72 and 67 to lie three strokes off the lead going into the final round. Manassero was hoping for a win to get him into the world's top 50 in time for an invitation to the Masters, while De La Riva had qualified off the Spanish order of merit and only a win would secure his status on the European Tour. The Spaniard closed with a 70 to equal his best finish of third at the 2011 Madrid Masters, while Manassero, who had twin scores of 68 over the weekend, was left to rue a second-round 73 that was nine strokes worse than his opening effort.

Quesne matched that 64 on the final day by going to the turn in 32 and then starting a winning bid from the 14th. He holed from 12 feet there, from 15 feet at the next, and laid a lag putt from 60 feet and from down on the lower tier stone dead for a two-putt birdie at the 16th. Then came the stunning climax that gave him all the insurance he needed with his rivals still out on the course.

Antonio Garrido was the first official European Tour winner at the 1972 Spanish Open, so it was appropriate for the 400th winner to come in the 40th anniversary season. It was also appropriate that Quesne, who had never before finished in the top 10, won an event promoted by one of his heroes, Miguel Angel Jimenez. The new champion knew a gift he could give the host that would be appreciated. "I've been dreaming about this moment since I was 10," he said. "It wasn't easy with Matteo, Miguel and Eduardo (De La Riva) all playing well. My four iron on 18 was the best shot I've ever hit. I'm very proud that I won shooting a 64, finishing with a birdie on 18, the toughest hole on the course. I will remember this day for the rest of my life. I'm particularly happy that I won the tournament organized by my favorite player, Miguel. I'll send him a case of Bordeaux wine, because I know he likes it so much."

Trophee Hassan II
Agadir, Morocco
Winner: Michael Hoey

A third victory in 25 starts was the reward for Michael Hoey after a brilliant weekend of golf at the Trophee Hassan II. Hoey was presented with a bejeweled golf dagger for winning at the Golf du Palais Royal, the course inside the royal residence in Agadir. But after an opening 74, the 33-year-old from Northern Ireland was more concerned about missing the cut. With high winds and thunder delaying play until the afternoon of the second day, Hoey did not complete a reviving 67 until Saturday morning, at which point he was still eight strokes behind halfway leader Damien McGrane. But twin scores of 65 for the last two rounds gave him a three-stroke winning margin over McGrane, who closed with rounds of 71 and 70. Although McGrane birdied the first two holes of the final round to go three clear of the field, he found himself trailing once Hoey, who had also birdied the second, had claimed four more in a row from the fifth to be out in 31.

Despite a bogey at the 10th, Hoey birdied the 14th, 15th and 17th holes to give himself a cushion at the last. With his win at the Alfred Dunhill Links Championship the previous autumn also counting for Ryder Cup points, Hoey went back to second place on the qualifying table, offering the possibility of a third of the European team being from Northern Ireland if he were to join Rory McIlroy, Graeme McDowell and Darren Clarke at Medinah.

"It's all a bit surreal at the moment, but it always feels like that for me," he said. "I was really trying to stay in the present all day and go through the routines of one shot at a time. I actually hit all the right shots at the right times over the closing holes, which was really satisfying. I was thinking that I might struggle to make the cut after shooting two over in the first round, but I started swinging the club really well and the confidence was there, so it was great to back that up with the scores too. The second round was a good 67 and then to shoot two 65s over the weekend was pretty special."

Jamie Donaldson set a course record of 61 in the final round after playing the second nine — but his first half after starting at the 10th — in 28. A ball in the water for a bogey at the par-five fifth halted thoughts of a 59, but at the ninth he clocked up his third eagle of the day to share third place with Robert Coles and Phillip Price. Matteo Manassero scored a 65 in the third round to tie McGrane for the 54-hole lead but faded with a closing 72 when he needed to win to return to the world's top 50 and earn an invitation to the Masters.

Sicilian Open
Sicily, Italy
Winner: Thorbjorn Olesen

It was an impressive maiden victory on the European Tour for Thorbjorn Olesen at the Sicilian Open. At 22, Olesen became the youngest Dane to win on the circuit in only his second year on tour. He had won on the Challenge Tour in 2010 as he earned promotion to the European Tour and finished as a runner-up three times in 2011. But here he took the top spot on the podium after a stirring duel with Chris Wood, a young Englishman also looking for his maiden victory.

Olesen took the 54-hole lead at Verdura after a 67 in very difficult, windy conditions on the seaside course. The Dane led by three, but Wood was six behind before he put in a great final-round charge. His closing 64 equaled the course record set by first-round leader Peter Lawrie on the opening day. Wood went out in 30, including an eagle at the fourth from only five feet. Olesen started with a nervous chip at the first which cost a bogey, but birdied the second to set up an outward 33.

Wood, who holed from 40 feet at the 12th, edged in front for the second time as he birdied the 14th, his seventh and last birdie of the day, combined with Olesen later bogeying the 13th. But as Wood bogeyed the tricky 17th, Olesen hit a brilliant pitch from the rough at the par-five 14th to set up a birdie that put him back in front. Pars at the last four holes meant Olesen had a closing 69 for a 273 total of 15 under par and a one-stroke victory over Wood. Compatriot Soren Kjeldsen, one of seven previous Danish winners on the European Tour, tied for third place with Nicolas Colsaerts, while Jose Manuel Lara was fifth.

"It feels amazing," Olesen said. "I had three seconds last year, so to finally get my first win is great. I've been playing some great golf this year, without all parts of my game coming together. But this week my long and short game both came together, and it feels fantastic to finally get over the line. I saw he (Wood) was doing well when I arrived at the ninth, so I knew I had to go for it and make birdies, so it kind of made up my mind for me that I had to play attacking golf. I was definitely a bit nervous. I was just trying to focus on one shot at a time, but that's very difficult to do because your mind keeps thinking of other things. The chip on the 14th was the most crucial shot of the week and I'm really happy to finish with a par on 18, because it's a really tough golf hole. So when I found the green with my second shot, I was very happy."

Maybank Malaysian Open
Kuala Lumpur, Malaysia
Winner: Louis Oosthuizen

See Asia/Japan Tours chapter.

Volvo China Open
Tianjin, China
Winner: Branden Grace

See Asia/Japan Tours chapter.

Ballantine's Championship
Seoul, South Korea
Winner: Bernd Wiesberger

See Asia/Japan Tours chapter.

Reale Seguros Open de Espana
Seville, Spain
Winner: Francesco Molinari

After battling through three stormy, wet and windy days at the Real Club in Seville, Francesco Molinari got his reward when the sun came out with a stirring final round which took him from four behind to a three-stroke victory in the Reale Seguros Open de Espana. Molinari was the only player from his half of the draw for the first two days who got into contention over the weekend. After rounds of 70, 71 and 74, the 29-year-old Italian showed exactly why he is reckoned to have one of the best swings in the game. His closing 65 included seven birdies in the first 14 holes and then he parred in for an eight-under-par total of 280. It was a target that no one else could match. Spaniards Alejandro Canizares and Pablo Larrazabal shared runner-up honors with Soren Kjeldsen, a former winner of the Open de Andulacia on the same course, on five under. Simon Dyson, who led by one over Larrazabal and Kjeldsen, fell back with a 76 to tie for 12th place.

Dyson made the perfect start with birdies at the first and second holes, holing out from a bunker at the latter, but then the Englishman's form deserted him. Up ahead Molinari had birdied the first, third and fifth holes and then had four more in six holes from the ninth. He took the lead with his birdie at the 10th and noticed the fact when he saw a leaderboard at the 12th. "The others still had a few birdie chances, so I knew I needed a couple more myself," Molinari said. They duly arrived at the 13th and 14th holes and, despite the best conditions of the week in Seville, no one else challenged for the title down the stretch.

It was Molinari's third victory on the European Tour and 18 months after his last at the 2010 HSBC Champions. Having already won his home championship, Molinari was thrilled to win the centenary version of the Spanish Open and on the anniversary weekend of Seve Ballesteros's death. "For those reasons, this makes it very special to win here," he said. "I knew I was playing well. I just needed some putts to drop. I was also hoping the other guys would not go too far under par and everything worked out perfectly."

Having made his debut for Europe in the Ryder Cup in 2010, the victory put Molinari in position to make a run at another appearance. "Everybody is desperate to make the team, but unfortunately for us there are only 12 spots. It's going to be hard. There are a lot of great players in Europe at the moment."

Madeira Islands Open
Madeira, Portugal
Winner: Ricardo Santos

Ricardo Santos created history for his nation by becoming the first Portuguese golfer to win on home soil on the European Tour at the Madeira Islands Open. Santos was cheered home to a four-stroke victory at Santo da Serra after a stunning closing round of 63. The 29-year-old from Faro had nine birdies in a bogey-free effort that left him at 266, 22 under par, a record total for the tournament. "This is huge for my career," said the rookie. "It is very emotional and I haven't got the words to describe how I feel. To win my first European Tour event in my own country is very special."

Another 63 the previous day had left Carlos Del Moral three shots clear with a round to play, but the Spaniard had a triple-bogey seven at the ninth hole and slipped away to finish tied for fourth after a 73. Denmark's Andreas Harto briefly took the lead after an outward 30 but had three bogeys in four holes from the 12th, so the 23-year-old had to settle for third place, one behind Magnus Carlsson, who matched Harto's 67 to finish at 18 under.

But in the end it was a comfortable victory for the home man, who started the day four adrift. He birdied the third, fifth, seventh and eighth holes to be out in 32 and then birdied the 12th and 13th holes to move to the top of the leaderboard. The fairy tale had the perfect ending when he added birdies at each of the last three holes, landing a putt from long range at the 17th to send the gallery into ecstasy. "The putt on the 17th was unbelievable, and I knew then that victory was mine," he said.

"It was a sensational round, definitely the best of my career. It was amazing to have the crowds here supporting me. It would be difficult to imagine a better win than this. I didn't have many bad moments in the round, but the supporters were always there to pick me up and keep me going. This is a huge moment in my career. I just played very solidly all the way round. I kept hitting fairways and greens and trying to hole putts, and luckily my putting was incredible today."

Santos graduated from the Challenge Tour in 2011, having won The Princess event in Denmark and also finishing tied for 10th at this tournament, which is co-sanctioned by both circuits. Victory, however, upgraded Santos's status to qualify for some of the main tour's biggest events, such as the BMW PGA Championship.

Volvo World Match Play Championship
Casares, Andalucia, Spain
Winner: Nicolas Colsaerts

Nicolas Colsaerts advanced to the semi-finals of the Volvo World Match Play Championship in 2011 and beat Graeme McDowell along the way. A year later the 29-year-old Belgian got to the final and again defeated the Northern Irishman at Finca Cortesin in Spain. "It means everything," Colsaerts said after claiming the biggest title of his career. "Where do I start? I felt that I had a pretty good shot at it last year in the same format, and I was a little disappointed not to get to the final.

"Two days ago I was in my room taking a nap thinking I was going to fly home. It means so much to be here, it's fantastic." Under the group format of the early stages, Colsaerts halved his opening match against Charl Schwartzel and then lost to Retief Goosen by one hole on Friday morning. Thinking that would be the end of his participation, he booked a tee time for nearby Valderrama for Saturday morning and retired to his room. But at the end of the afternoon, after Goosen had beaten Schwartzel 4 and 3,

Colsaerts was required for a sudden-death playoff and could not be found, Eventually his caddie knocked on the door of his on-site hotel room and Colsaerts just got to the tee on time. By winning the playoff against the former Masters champion, Colsaerts had to forget about Valderrama and on Saturday beat Justin Rose 4 and 3 and then Brandt Snedeker by the same score in the quarter-finals.

But early on Sunday morning Colsaerts lost the first four holes against Paul Lawrie, only to claw his way back into the match, and after a brief delay due to a thunderstorm he eventually beat the 1999 Open champion at the 20th hole. McDowell beat Robert Karlsson and Jbe' Kruger in the group stages, then overcame Richard Finch before Sergio Garcia three-putted from short distance at the 19th hole to send McDowell into the semi-finals. There he saw off Rafa Cabrera-Bello by two holes.

It was a cold and windy day and 30 mph gusts caused problems for both players in the final. The winner carded five bogeys and a double but also showed his immense power by eagling the third hole. Three times McDowell drew even on the front nine after Colsaerts had gone ahead, but on the back nine the 2010 U.S. Open champion went two down before winning the 15th and losing the 16th. Colsaerts missed a short putt at the par-three 17th to extend the match but then sealed it at the last.

Colsaerts won his first title at the Volvo China Open in 2011, was third at this tournament the same year, and in 2012 had been fourth at the Volvo Champions event and second at the Volvo China Open. Clearly he likes the company.

"I played well in tough conditions. Wind like this, you know it's going to be very difficult. Graeme McDowell, he's won the U.S. Open, so he's used to playing in tough conditions. I knew that it was going to be a tough game in conditions like these."

BMW PGA Championship
Virginia Water, Surrey, England
Winner: Luke Donald

Luke Donald first became the world No. 1 by winning the 2011 BMW PGA Championship at Wentworth in a playoff against Lee Westwood, the then world leader. When he defended the title a year later, his first successful defense, he again became the world No. 1 but in somewhat more relaxed circumstances. Firstly, the then world's best, Rory McIlroy, missed the cut, as he had in his previous outing at The Players Championship. McIlroy admitted he had "taken his eye off the ball" and, after spending the Saturday morning on the practice range, he departed on Eurostar to Paris to visit his tennis player girlfriend, Caroline Wozniacki, at the French Open.

Donald just needed to finish in the top eight to overtake McIlroy, and after taking a two-shot lead over Justin Rose into the final round, the 34-year-old from High Wycombe claimed a four-stroke victory over Rose and Paul Lawrie. In stunning sunshine and in front of record crowds, Donald was able to enjoy a triumphant march up the final hole with a handsome lead. "I played nicely this whole week," said Donald.

"Today was the most difficult in terms of pressure and having never defended a title before. I knew I had to be mistake-free and fortunately I got it done. But to play the back nine like that against players like Justin Rose and Paul Lawrie was pleasing, and I certainly enjoyed the walk down 18 more than last year with a four-shot lead. This is our biggest event on the European Tour and the number of people who came here this week to support me and the tournament speaks volumes. To come here and defend and get back to No. 1 is very sweet indeed."

Donald made a slow start on Sunday, with a bogey at the par-five fourth meaning he was now tied for the lead with his playing partner Rose. But from that moment, Donald took charge with birdies at the sixth and seventh holes before a 25-footer for a birdie at the short 10th put him three ahead. Further birdies at the 12th and 16th, and otherwise pars, meant Donald finished on 15 under par with a total of 273 after rounds of 68, 68, 69 and 68. He joined Sir Nick Faldo and Colin Montgomerie as the only players to win the title two years in a row.

"After the fourth I didn't give him (Rose) another hole where he was teeing off first other than the 18th. I got the job done," Donald said. "I was just trying to keep my head down and plug away. I was swinging well and I've putted well all week."

Rose suffered dizzy spells on Thursday morning and was not certain of teeing off until after spending an hour with a doctor. He opened with a 67 but closed with a 70, while Lawrie had a best-of-the-day 66 to grab a share of second place.

ISPS Handa Wales Open
City of Newport, Wales
Winner: Thongchai Jaidee

A wet and windy Celtic Manor must have felt a long way away from his home of Thailand, but Thongchai Jaidee battled through the conditions to win his first European Tour title outside of Asia. All four of his previous titles had come on his home continent, but the 42-year-old claimed the ISPS Handa Wales Open by one stroke. A group of four players shared second place: Gonzalo Fernandez-Castano, Thomas Bjorn, Richard Sterne and Joost Luiten, with Ross Fisher and Paul McGinley a stroke further back.

It was Luiten and Fisher, both one stroke behind Thongchai going into the final round, who provided the stiff challenge to the champion and both shared the lead on the final day. Thongchai was out in three over par but then responded with a brilliant run of four birdies in six holes from the 10th. An 18-footer for birdie at the 15th put him two clear of Luiten. Both men bogeyed the 16th, which meant a six at the last from Thongchai still meant he clung on to the win.

"I want to say thank you to all my family, all the supporters and the sponsors here," he said. "Conditions were quite tough for me. I tried to hit everything on the fairway — that's the main thing — then hit the ball on the green. It was very, very tough for me, not like Thailand!"

There was a controversial element to the final day when Fisher, still only one behind at the time, was penalized one stroke at the 14th for slow play. It was the second time in four holes that he had exceeded the time limit of 40 seconds for a shot. Fisher was informed by chief referee John Paramor and he admitted the news left him rattled. Fisher was enjoying a return to the scene of his Ryder Cup appearance in 2010 and took the halfway lead with a second round of 66 but closed with a 73, while Luiten and Thongchai had 72s. Thongchai finished on 278, six under par, with Fernandez-Castano closing with a 67 and Bjorn and Sterne rounds of 68. McGinley, the 45-year-old former Ryder Cup player, signed off with a 65.

Nordea Masters
Stockholm, Sweden
Winner: Lee Westwood

Lee Westwood warmed up for the following week's U.S. Open with a brilliant performance to win the Nordea Masters at Bro Hof Slott in Stockholm. Westwood opened with a 68 before a 64 on the second day put him in front by three strokes. He maintained that lead with a 68 in the third round and closed with a 69 to win by five strokes over Ross Fisher. Westwood finished on 19 under par with a total of 269.

It was the third time Westwood had won the title. He claimed it as his maiden victory in 1996 and during his Order of Merit–winning season of 2000. It was the 22nd win on the European Tour for the 39-year-old but a first for three years since the Portugal Masters in 2009.

"It feels really special winning here another time," Westwood said. "I've won it in three decades now, which just shows how old we're getting! I played really well this week. You don't win tournaments by five shots without playing well. I missed a few short putts on the front nine, had a lot of chances the first 10 holes and could have really put some breathing space between me and the field.

"Having said that, when I needed to on the back nine — when they got a bit closer and put me under a bit of pressure — I managed to make a great eagle at 12, good birdie at 15 and pull away. I hit some really solid shots. It didn't look like I was hitting it close on the last three holes, but I can tell you those last three holes I hit it exactly where I wanted to every time."

Fisher, after being penalized for slow play on the back nine during the final round of the Wales Open the week before, was putting pressure on Westwood before finding water at the 13th for a double bogey. He also dropped a shot at the 14th before finishing with a burst of three birdies in a row from the 15th hole. He closed with a 71 to finish one ahead of home favorite Peter Hanson, Finland's Mikko Ilonen and Sergio Garcia, who finished with a fine 67.

Saint-Omer Open
Lumbres, France
Winner: Darren Fichardt

With high winds battering Aa Saint Omer Golf Club over the weekend, only three players ended under par at the Saint-Omer Open. It was the experienced Darren Fichardt who showed how to cope best as the 37-year-old won the tournament for both regular European Tour players and Challenge Tour campaigners. It was a third victory on the European Tour for the South African but his first since the Qatar Masters in 2003. In the meantime Fichardt had struggled with injuries and only won his card back though the qualifying tournament at the end of 2011.

But with all his experience of winning down in South Africa — this was Fichardt's 17th career victory — he knew how to keep a steady head. After opening with rounds of 68 and 69, Fichardt surged into the lead on Saturday with another 69 that put him five clear of Simon Wakefield. The Englishman briefly narrowed the deficit to two strokes after three holes in the final round, but a double bogey at the fifth hole stalled his advance. Compatriot Gary Lockerbie, who said the event felt like a "major" to the Challenge Tour players, made a charge with a closing 69 and birdies at the 16th and 17th put him at two under par.

Wakefield finished one behind in third place after a 72, but Fichardt was clear at the head of the field. His only birdie on the final day came at the eighth, but bogeys coming home were of no consequence. He closed with a 73 for a five-under-par total of 279 and won by three strokes over Lockerbie. "It was messy today," Fichardt said. "It definitely wasn't pretty. I was absolutely terrified and I was happy we didn't have to play any more holes.

"To win is awesome. The last four years I've had injuries and missed out at the qualifying school a couple of times, and you wonder if you'll ever make it back. So it was amazing to get my card back last year, and to win on my ninth start this season is a dream come true. The exemption for next season is very welcome."

BMW International Open
Cologne, Germany
Winner: Danny Willett

After 19 top-10 finishes in 105 tournaments on the European Tour, Danny Willett finally won his maiden title in the 106th at the BMW International Open. But it took him four extra holes to eventually beat Marcus Fraser at Gut Larchenhof in Cologne. Willett, the son of a vicar from Sheffield, is a former English Amateur champion and Walker Cup player, but despite a runner-up finish to Martin Kaymer in the 2010 Alfred Dunhill Links Championship, his consistency as a professional had not yet brought the ultimate reward.

Until a wet and windy day in Cologne. Willett had opened with a 65 to be one off the lead, shared by Fraser. Rounds of 70 and 69 put Willett ahead after three rounds but only by a stroke over Chris Wood and Joel Sjoholm, while Fraser was among those two behind. Marcel Siem provided some excitement for the home fans earlier on the last day, but it came down to a duel between Willett and Fraser. Bogeys at the 11th and 15th holes from Willett left him one behind after Fraser birdied the 16th, but then the Australian dropped a shot at the last for a 71 and an 11-under total of 277. Willett parred in for a 73 to tie Fraser but only after slicing his drive into trees at the last and having to play a big, booming hook onto the green with a long iron for his approach.

Four times the pair played the 18th again in the playoff. On the second occasion, Willett had a chance to end proceedings but his four-footer for victory lipped out. On the fourth extra hole, Willett was able to get up and down, but Fraser three-putted. "Danny is such a great guy and he's an awesome player," said Fraser. "It's the first of many tournaments for him, that's for sure. He's going to be a future star on the European Tour. It was nice to have a chance, but unfortunately I couldn't do it."

"This is my fourth year on tour now," said Willett. "I've had a lot of good finishes, been in contention a couple of times. To polish it off, it feels good. Ideally I would have won earlier, but I'm probably a little bit more mature now than I was when I first came on tour. It would have been good to win a few years ago, but a win is a win. The guys out here are brilliant. They play week in, week out, and it's competitive. I've had some ups and downs in the last 18 months as everyone knows, but I'm injury-free now and back to playing well and I'd like to thank everyone back home for supporting me. I'll keep working hard and hopefully we can do it again."

Irish Open
Portrush, County Antrim, Northern Ireland
Winner: Jamie Donaldson

For the first time in the history of the European Tour an event was sold out for all four days. The excitement surrounding the playing of the Irish Open at Royal Portrush had built for months beforehand with Northern Ireland's three recent major champions, Rory McIlroy, Graeme McDowell and Darren Clarke, heading the field. With speculation over whether the Open Championship might return to the links that gave Max Faulkner the claret jug in 1951, a successful week was ensured with 112,280 spectators attending and local charities benefiting to the tune of £100,000. Given the weather was often wet, windy and cold, the vast galleries never flagged as local man Michael Hoey acknowledged: "All of the players are saying this is by far the best tournament they have been to crowd-wise."

But none of the home favorites could get into contention, and it was Jamie Donaldson who claimed his maiden title on the European Tour. The 36-year-old Welshman, now based in Macclesfield, had won three times on the Challenge Tour, but this was his 255th event on the main circuit over 12 seasons.

But when he made his first hole-in-one on the European Tour at the sixth hole on Thursday, Donaldson got the feeling that it might be his week. An opening 68 left him three off the lead, but rounds of 67 and 69 put him one ahead of Anthony Wall going into the final round. While Wall was taking a triple-bogey eight at the second hole, Mikael Lundberg made an early charge with a closing 65 to finish at 13 under par. But although Donaldson avoided looking at the leaderboards, he kept collecting birdies, including a stunning finish of five in the last seven holes, for a 66 that left him four clear of Wall, Rafa Cabrera-Bello and Fabrizio Zanotti on 18 under par.

Wall said of the winner: "I've never doubted him. He's a class act and a super, super player, and he deserves everything he gets because he does work hard and he's got loads of talent."

"To have a hole in one the first time in a tournament, and to win it, as well, is very special," Donaldson said. "I didn't really look at any leaderboards on the way around. I didn't really know what was going on." Ironically, his success came just days after breaking from his caddie of five years, Jamie Baker. "He's a great mate and he did great for me for four or five years. He's a good mate of mine and I think he'll just be happy obviously to see me win, really."

Alstom Open de France
Paris, France
Winner: Marcel Siem

Just a fortnight after losing out at the BMW International on home soil, Marcel Siem returned to the winner's circle for the first time in eight years at the Alstom Open de France. In Cologne, Siem found water on the seventh hole when leading and missed out, but at Golf National in Paris he survived hitting into the lake on the first hole as well as a brilliant charge from Francesco Molinari. Siem was two behind going into the last round, but the men ahead of him, leaders David Howell and Anders Hansen, and George Coetzee all faded. Going in the opposite direction was Molinari, who put a double bogey at the first hole behind him to rack up nine birdies. Six of those birdies came on the inward half as the Italian closed with a 64 to set the target at seven under par.

Siem managed to save par despite finding the water at the first, and with five birdies, including importantly at the 14th and 15th holes, he arrived at the 18th in front by two. A bogey there did not matter as he returned rounds of 68, 68, 73 and 67 for an eight-under total of 276. He beat Molinari by one stroke with local hero Raphael Jacquelin one further back. Howell shared fourth place with David Lynn and Ian Poulter, although without the two bogeys at the 17th and 18th holes Poulter would have shared second place. Lee Westwood finished down the field after a 76 in the third round during which he sprained an ankle, but a closing 70 proved there were no lasting effects with the Open Championship fast approaching.

Siem's victory earned him a place at Royal Lytham and St. Annes, as well as giving him a first title since his maiden victory at the Dunhill Championship in South Africa in 2004. "I'm so happy. This means a lot to me," he said. "First, after eight years it doesn't matter what kind of tournament you win; it's huge, because you've got the confidence again. Every time I've played consistent golf this year, and there were so many times up there, I couldn't make it. Stupid things happened the whole time.

"It means so much to me to win after that long stretch. It's all about winning in the end, and it puts so much pressure every time you don't win and people start talking, you will never win again and stuff like that, so it's very important for me. I love this golf course. I always loved it and I love it even more or even better now. I'm super happy."

Aberdeen Asset Management Scottish Open
Inverness, Scotland
Winner: Jeev Milkha Singh

Jeev Milkha Singh got more than he expected as he relaxed with a cup of tea and a slice of cake after signing off with a 67 in the Aberdeen Asset Management Scottish Open. Singh was three behind the leader Marc Warren when the Indian retired to the clubhouse. But his day got better still as Singh ended up in a playoff and holed a 15-footer for birdie on the 18th to beat Francesco Molinari at the first extra hole. It was a fourth European Tour win for the 40-year-old and his first for four years. He had earlier returned rounds of 66, 70 and 68 for a total of 271, 17 under par.

Molinari was the leader for the first three rounds. He opened with a course-record 62 that included 10 birdies and was a continuation of his fine form from the French Open the previous week. Molinari was 10 under for 15 holes at Castle Stuart but could not carry on to break the 60 barrier. However, with a 29 for his last nine holes in Paris and a score of 30 for his first nine here, it added up to an 18-hole stretch in 59 shots.

Molinari still headed the field going into the final day, but Singh, who was five behind and in 16th place, started with four birdies in the first six holes and added another at the 10th before parring in. But it was Warren, a former winner of the Johnnie Walker Championship at Gleneagles, who delighted the home crowd with five birdies of his own in the first 12 holes. Victory beckoned, but he had a nightmare finish. He three-putted at the 15th for a double bogey, found a bush at the 16th for a bogey and also dropped a shot at the last. He finished tied for third with Alex Noren, one shot outside the playoff. As well as missing out on a second win in Scotland, Warren also failed to claim a debut appearance in the Open Championship. Instead, the final place on offer at Royal Lytham went to Singh.

With Warren falling back and Noren bogeying the 18th and Molinari bogeying the 15th, it meant a playoff with the Italian, who failed to match his brother Edoardo, the 2010 Scottish Open champion, and ended up as a runner-up for the second week running. Singh said: "I was just enjoying a cup of tea and some chocolate cake and watching it on television, and suddenly got excited. I think God has been kind, and I think the field came back and put me in a position to go in for a playoff. I'm very fortunate."

The Open Championship
Lytham St. Annes, Lancashire, England
Winner: Ernie Els

See Chapter 4.

Lyoness Open
Atzenbrugg, Austria
Winner: Bernd Wiesberger

An hour away from his home town of Vienna, at the Diamond Country Club in Atzenbrugg, Bernd Wiesberger could not have been happier when he rolled in a 30-footer for a birdie on the final hole to win the Lyoness Open. It gave the 26-year-old Austrian a three-stroke victory over Thomas Levet and Shane Lowry and his second European Tour title, three months after winning the Ballantine's Championship.

Wiesberger started the final round four strokes behind Thorbjorn Olesen and was even par for the day through the first eight holes. But then he exploded into life with seven birdies in the last 10 holes. Four came in five holes from the ninth and then he added further birdies at the 15th and 16th holes before the grandstand finish at the last. He closed with a 65, after rounds of 71, 66 and 67, for a 19-under-par total of 269.

Wiesberger became the second Austrian to win the title after Markus Brier. "It's the best day of my life so far," Wiesberger said. "It seems like it went my way, especially the last two holes. I had such a great country and such great fans backing me. I'm very proud to be following in such big footsteps (as Brier). I'm sure I'm not going to be the last home winner. When Jose Manuel Lara holed a similar putt to win the tournament two years ago, I always imagined I'd have a putt like that to win here. I actually said that to my caddie walking up the 18th hole, and when it went in, I just couldn't believe it."

Levet had five birdies in nine holes en route to a 68, while Lowry closed with a 66 as the pair finished on 16 under. Rikard Karlberg was fourth and Olesen took fifth place on 14 under. Still on a high after finishing tied for ninth at the Open Championship the previous week, Olesen opened with a 64 and led for the first three rounds before slipping back with a closing 74. Little went the Dane's way and bogeys at the last two holes meant he did not even hang on to a share of second place.

Johnnie Walker Championship
Auchterarder, Perthshire, Scotland
Winner: Paul Lawrie

Paul Lawrie won the Johnnie Walker Championship with such relative ease that the question loomed large of who would be the two wild cards picked by Jose Maria Olazabal for the European Ryder Cup team. Lawrie's place in the team for Medinah was secured before he arrived at Gleneagles, and free from any such worries he cruised to a four-stroke victory over Brett Rumford.

Only one place remained up for grabs, and although Martin Kaymer was not present in Scotland, the German was confirmed as the 10th automatic qualifier when Niclas Colsaerts failed to finish in the top two here. The Belgian started well, lying just two shots off the lead after the first day, but faded to a tie for 19th place, 10 strokes adrift of the winner. Kaymer joined Rory McIlroy, Graeme McDowell, Luke Donald, Sergio Garcia, Lee Westwood, Francesco Molinari, Justin Rose, Peter Hanson and Lawrie.

However, Colsaerts only had to be patient for one more day before Olazabal selected him alongside Ian Poulter as his wild cards. While there was no surprise at all at Poulter being picked, Colsaerts had not been so certain, with experienced players like Padraig Harrington also to be considered. But Olazabal was adamant that the big-hitting Belgian was the right man and would be the sole rookie on the European team. Colsaerts said: "I've gone from being nervous about making the team to being nervous about wanting to get there."

Lawrie said that knowing the pressure to make the team was off had helped him play his best golf. He returned scores of 68, 69, 67 and 68 for a 16-under-par total of 272 on the revamped PGA Centenary Course that would host the 2014 Ryder Cup. One ahead going into the final day, Lawrie went further ahead when his playing partner, Romain Wattel, bogeyed the first hole, and five birdies kept him clear of the field. He became the first Scot in the modern era to win three times in his home country, having also won the Open at Carnoustie in 1999 and the Dunhill Links at St. Andrews in 2001.

"I feel calmer in Scotland for some reason and I play some of my best golf too," Lawrie said. "It was probably one of the best ball-striking weeks in my career. There's no question I'm hitting the ball extremely well this week. The course is obviously very good and the course played quite long, and I've hit the ball a bit longer this week. I've been working on rhythm, and when you hit it a bit longer, it helps a bit. It's been a fantastic week."

Omega European Masters
Crans Montana, Switzerland
Winner: Richie Ramsay

Paul Lawrie was close to pulling off a second consecutive victory, but at least there were successive wins from Scots as Richie Ramsay claimed the Omega European Masters high in the Alps at Crans-sur-Sierre. Ramsay matched Lawrie's winning margin of the previous week, four strokes, with a superb display over the weekend. After opening with rounds of 69 and 68, Ramsay eased into top gear with a 64 in the third round with six birdies and no bogeys. Due to conditions under foot, the sixth hole had been reduced from a par-four to a par-three, so the overall par for the third round was 70 rather than 71.

Ramsay led by one stroke over Lawrie and Danny Willett and needed a birdie at the first hole of the final round to retain a share of the lead when Lawrie made an eagle. But the former Open champion suffered four bogeys on the first nine to drop out of contention, while Ramsay went out in five-under 31. He dropped shots at the 13th and 17th holes, but they were cancelled out by his eagle at the 14th. A closing 66 gave him a total of 267, 16 under par. Willett hung on to second place alongside Marcus Fraser, Romain Wattel and Fredrik Andersson-Hed, while Lawrie finished a further shot back tied for sixth place with Bernd Wiesberger and Felipe Aguilar.

A former U.S. Amateur champion, Ramsay won the South African Open in 2009. But in the intervening period, Ramsay had further matured as a golfer. "Between then and now I've made a lot of big decisions about my career. Today was vindication of that," said the 29-year-old. "It's an incredible place to play golf, so to win here is very special. You can get caught up looking at the scenery, but I knew I had a job to do here today. I had a clear goal in mind and all the way round I was imagining I was playing a round with my best mates from back home. I performed unbelievably well against two of the most in-form players around; Paul (Lawrie) is playing the golf of his life and Danny is one of the best young players around. So it was always going to be difficult, but I managed to pull it off."

KLM Open
Hilversum, Netherlands
Winner: Peter Hanson

A monster putt for eagle on the final green gave Peter Hanson not only victory at the KLM Open but peace of mind after a traumatic weekend off the course at Hilversumsche. Hanson's one-year-old son Tim was hospitalized with a respiratory virus. For a while Hanson was not sure if he would continue playing, but he was persuaded to stay in the Netherlands by his wife and it turned out for the best both on the course and at home.

Hanson had rounds of 66, 66, 67 and 67 for a total of 266, 14 under par, and won by two strokes over Pablo Larrazabal and Richie Ramsay, the winner the previous week. Hanson started the final round one behind a quartet of players that included Larrazabal, Graeme Storm, Scott Jamieson and Gonzalo Fernandez-Castano. But it turned into a duel between Hanson and Larrazabal, and when Hanson followed successive bogeys with a birdie at the 15th hole and Larrazabal bogeyed the 16th, the pair were tied. At the 18th it was Hanson who got his blow in first by holing from across the green for an eagle, something the Spaniard could not match.

For the 34-year-old Swede it was a fifth European Tour victory, his first for two years and a perfect way to warm up for the Ryder Cup. But all he was really thinking about was matters at home. "It's always a nice feeling to win, but especially this week with how things have been with my son being a little bit ill," said Hanson. "He has managed to get over that and he's getting better and better, which is the most important thing.

"When he was put into hospital on Friday, I was panicking. He was not good for 12 to 14 hours there and as a parent that makes you feel very vulnerable. I just wanted to go back home and look after the family, but my wife convinced me to stay. They were in good hands; there was nothing I could do and she was telling me that, but when your kids get sick you don't think straight."

On how he was able to keep his mind on his golf, Hanson said: "When we get a chance to lift these trophies, something just clicks in your head. I was just trying to stay focused. This was needed. It's been a bit of a slow summer for me, so this came at a perfect time to get confidence back and feel ready for the Ryder Cup."

BMW Italian Open
Turin, Italy
Winner: Gonzalo Fernandez-Castano

Freed from the distraction of just failing to make the Ryder Cup team and having stayed at home until his children had returned to school, a relaxed Gonzalo Fernandez-Castano claimed the BMW Italian Open after a terrific duel with Garth Mulroy. Fernandez-Castano won by two strokes in the end, but it all came down to the last two holes, which Mulroy played in five-five (bogey-par) to the Spaniard's four-four (par-birdie). The 31-year-old won the Italian Open for the second time and a sixth time in all on the European Tour, having won the Singapore Open late in 2011 to kick-start his campaign to earn a spot in compatriot Jose Maria Olazabal's team.

"Not making the Ryder Cup was disappointing," he said. "I had a victory, two second-place finishes and one third, and it hasn't been good enough. It's tough. You have to play well in the big events, and that's what I didn't do this year unfortunately. I have talked to Ollie about the Ryder Cup many, many times. I can laugh about it now, but it hasn't been easy.

"I just needed to believe in myself and put the Ryder Cup out of my head, which I've done this week. I changed my schedule a little. I normally travel on a Tuesday but I arrived here on Wednesday, mainly because I wanted to see the kids start school. It was a completely different frame of mind for the week. I didn't know the course, so everything was new to me. I just followed my caddie's instructions and it worked. The main thing was my attitude. I didn't get too frustrated out there or try too hard. I just let it happen."

After rounds of 68, 65 and 67, Fernandez-Castano went into the last round one behind Mulroy but claimed a share of the lead with a birdie at the first. The lead change hands regularly, but they were tied heading into the back nine. The Spaniard had five birdies coming home for a 64 and a 24-under-par total of 264, while Mulroy had four birdies but then, crucially, dropped a shot at the 17th hole. Gregory Bourdy and Matteo Manassero shared third place, two behind Mulroy.

The Ryder Cup
Medinah, Illinois
Winner: Europe

See Chapter 6.

Alfred Dunhill Links Championship
St. Andrews & Fife, Scotland
Winner: Branden Grace

A week after returning to South Africa to record his fourth win of the season, Branden Grace struck gold again when he claimed the Alfred Dunhill Links Championship. It was a fifth win of the year and a fourth on the European Tour, for which he qualified from the qualifying tournament the previous December. The 24-year-old South Africa led from start to finish but had to survive a late charge from Thorbjorn Olesen, who finished as the runner-up. Grace finished on 22 under par to win by two strokes over the Dane and claim the biggest title of his career.

It was a stunning opening for Grace when he set a new course record at Kingsbarns with a 12-under-par 60. He became the 14th player to score a 60 on the European Tour after an eagle and 11 birdies, including five in a row to finish the round. Needing an eagle at his final hole, the par-five ninth, to shoot a 59, he missed the green but chipped up to a foot. He led by two over Victor Dubuisson, who equaled the course record on the Old Course at St. Andrews. The Frenchman had 11 birdies in 15 holes before bogeying the seventh hole (his 16th) for a 62 to match Curtis Strange's record score from the 1987 Dunhill Nations Cup. Grace went to St. Andrews the next day and returned a 67 to take a five-stroke lead and then had a 69 at Carnoustie to stay four ahead of Olesen.

But in the final round, back at the Old Course, Olesen made three birdies going out, and when Grace bogeyed the 11th they were tied. But then Grace pulled away again with birdies at the next three holes from 10, 12 and 14 feet. He bogeyed the Road Hole but birdied the last, and although Olesen birdied two of the last three holes, Grace had the victory. Alexander Noren, who was part of the winning pro-am team, took third place, four behind the winner, while former champion Stephen Gallacher had to settle for a fifth-place tie after playing the ball of his playing partner's amateur at the 16th and ending up with a quadruple-bogey eight.

"I've really dreamt of this moment my whole life," said Grace, who was inspired by Louis Oosthuizen's Open win at St. Andrews two years earlier. "I had goosebumps thinking this morning about Louis and the possibility of holding a trophy here myself. It was a tough day, but the putter started working and that's all I needed to do."

Turkish Airlines World Golf Final
Belek, Antalya, Turkey
Winner: Justin Rose

Justin Rose continued a fine run of form and drew on his Ryder Cup heroics from Medinah to win the Turkish Airlines World Golf Final. The unofficial eight-man event at Antalya featured medal match play and finished on a Friday morning to prevent coverage of the tournament clashing with the Portugal Masters on the weekend. The event was a precursor to a Turkish Open appearing as an official event on the European Tour in 2013.

EUROPEAN TOURS / 185

Rose beat his Ryder Cup teammate Lee Westwood 66-67 in the final to win $1.5 million. Rose also beat Westwood in the group stages (67-70) as he finished with three wins out of three, though Westwood also qualified for the semi-finals from a group that also included Americans Webb Simpson and Hunter Mahan. In the other group a big showdown was eagerly awaited between Tiger Woods and Rory McIlroy, but the Irishman was already out of contention after losing his first two matches. Woods had lost to Charl Schwartzel 69-70 before beating Matt Kuchar 68-73 and still needed a win over McIlroy to make sure of qualifying and duly won 64-70.

But it was Schwartzel who topped the group after winning all three of his group matches, but Westwood produced a superb round in the semi-finals to beat the South African 61-67, while Rose defeated Woods 69-70. Rose had finished runner-up at the Tour Championship and then birdied the last two holes to beat Phil Mickelson in the singles at the Ryder Cup. Rose led from the start in the final against Westwood after birdieing the first, but was only one ahead when he holed a long putt for a two at the 17th, bringing back memories of the 17th at Medinah.

Rose said: "He hit a great shot into 17 and I really felt like I needed to make that putt, and the 17th against Phil came to mind, just drawing on positive experiences. I think the Tour Championship sparked the good play for sure. I had not had a good FedExCup Playoff run until then, it was nice to get in contention. I played in the last group every day in the Tour Championship and that's something I really enjoyed. That prepared me well for the Ryder Cup and I came off that with great feelings, the most amazing pressure putts of my life, and the 17th green has been really good to me again this week."

Portugal Masters
Algarve, Portugal
Winner: Shane Lowry

By winning the Portugal Masters, Shane Lowry became only the second player in the history of the European Tour, after Pablo Martin, to win on the circuit both as an amateur and a professional. Lowry won the Irish Open in 2009 as an amateur and immediately turned professional but had to wait three years to add to his tally of titles. When he did, it was in handsome style as he beat Ross Fisher by one stroke at Oceanico Victoria at Vilamoura. A superb run on the back nine took Lowry to the title including a birdie at the 10th and then a holed seven iron at the 11th for an eagle. He also birdied the 15th and 17th holes and a bogey at the last did not matter.

Lowry closed with a 66 after rounds of 67, 70 and 67 as he finished on a total of 270, 14 under par. He had started the final round four adrift of Bernd Wiesberger, but the Austrian slipped back with a 73. He finished in fourth place, one behind a resurgent Michael Campbell, who was one behind Fisher. Campbell, the 2005 U.S. Open champion, fell out of the world top-1,300 but here recorded his best finish for four years and had four rounds in the 60s for the first time in nine years.

Lowry, the 25-year-old Irishman, won his first European Tour event and his 99th. He was still three behind at the turn, but the 11th changed everything. "I thought then this could be my day and thankfully it is," he said. "We had a long wait on the 12th tee, which was good, I had time to compose myself."

Spurred on by plenty of support from his countrymen on the Algarve, Lowry added: "I cannot believe this. I can't explain how I feel really. It's a dream come true. I'm over the moon. Everyone was referring to me as the fella who won the Irish Open as an amateur, but now I've won such a prestigious event I don't know what to say."

ISPS Handa Perth International
Perth, Western Australia
Winner: Bo Van Pelt

See Australasian Tour chapter.

BMW Masters
Shanghai, China
Winner: Peter Hanson

Peter Hanson capped a wonderful few weeks by claiming the biggest win of his career at the BMW Masters. In September the 35-year-old Swede won for the first time in two years at the KLM Open in the Netherlands before playing a part in Europe's Ryder Cup victory at Medinah. Hanson was not happy with his captain, Jose Maria Olazabal, for not playing him in either session on the second day, but here defeated many of his teammates with a handsome performance at Lake Malaren in Shanghai. Hanson won by one stroke over Rory McIlroy, who won the inaugural unofficial event at Lake Malaren a year earlier, with Luke Donald three strokes further back in third place and Ian Poulter finishing in fourth place.

After an opening 66, Hanson scored a 64 in the second round to lead by two over McIlroy, although that advantage was cut to one shot after a third-round 70. Hanson matched McIlroy's 67 in the final round to finish on a 21-under score of 267, but what appeared to be a comfortable victory suddenly became more problematic. Hanson was four ahead after five holes and three birdies in a row from the 11th hole, but McIlroy suddenly ignited on the back nine with an inward 31. An eagle at the 15th and a birdie at the next cut the deficit to two shots, and then Hanson, who had been in a bunker, had to hole from 15 feet for a par at the short 17th. At the 18th, Hanson's approach finished in a tricky spot on the bank of a bunker. After being informed there was no relief available, he got down in a chip and two putts for a closing bogey.

"It was a little bit tense," said Hanson. "Rory made a tremendous effort with his eagle on 15 and birdie on 16, so it put quite a bit of pressure on me. I was trying to play it a little bit safe, but against the world No. 1 you still have to hit the shots. This is by far my biggest win in my career.

I think all of the work I have put in to try to be ready for the Ryder Cup — that's really what paid off both in Holland and even now a couple of weeks later.

"I was working really hard all the way from the U.S. PGA when I knew that I had a good chance to make the team, with my mindset of being as prepared as I ever could be for the Ryder Cup. I've been hitting it nice and especially the putter has been feeling great. That's the main reason I'm standing here with this beautiful trophy."

Barclays Singapore Open
Singapore
Winner: Matteo Manassero

See Asia/Japan Tours chapter.

UBS Hong Kong Open
Hong Kong
Winner: Miguel Angel Jimenez

See Asia/Japan Tours chapter.

South African Open Championship
Ekurhuleni, South Africa
Winner: Henrik Stenson

See African Tours chapter.

DP World Tour Championship
Dubai, United Arab Emirates
Winner: Rory McIlroy

Rory McIlroy was assured of winning the Race to Dubai money title after Louis Oosthuizen failed to win a playoff at the Barclays Singapore Open. But the 23-year-old from Northern Ireland was keen to finish the season on a high and he did just that by making five birdies over the last five holes to win the DP World Tour Championship at Jumeirah Golf Estates in Dubai. McIlroy duly lifted both the trophy for the tournament and that for being the European No. 1 at the conclusion of the 2012 season. It was his fifth win of the year but only the second that counted on the European Tour, the other being his second major triumph at the U.S. PGA Championship. In the process McIlroy matched Luke Donald from 2011 in winning the money lists on both the PGA and the European tours, as well as ending the year as the world No. 1. McIlroy had rounds of 66, 67, 66 and 66 for a 23-under total of 265. He beat Rose by two shots with Donald and Charl Schwartzel tying for third place three shots further back.

It was Donald, the leader or co-leader from the moment he posted a first round of 65, who started the last day as McIlroy's chief opponent. The world No. 1 and No. 2 were tied for the lead and in the last pairing, a fitting finale and hardly the anti-climax that some had predicted with the money title wrapped up. On Saturday evening at the 18th Donald had chalked up 100 holes without a dropped shot on the Earth course, dating back to the eighth hole of the second round in 2011. But his streak lasted only two more holes before a bogey at the third.

McIlroy had bogeyed the first but birdied the ninth to take a one shot lead, only it was no longer a private duel. Justin Rose suddenly entered the picture as he set a new course record of 62. Out in 32, Rose birdied the 10th and 13th holes, eagled the 14th and birdied the 15th. McIlroy birdied the 11th but dropped a shot at the 13th to find himself two behind. And Rose still had the par-five 18th to play. On the back of the green in two, Rose hit the most amazing putt from over 90 feet, dying the ball on top of a ridge and then seeing it pick up pace again and finish just an inch from the hole. "I knew it was hero or zero there," said the Englishman. "I was one roll away from looking like an idiot. I actually got goosebumps. I thought it was going to go in for a second."

Rose had posted the target at 21 under par, but by then McIlroy had moved up several gears. After the bogey at 13, he got his four at the par-five 14th, drove just short of the 15th and got up and down for a three, holed from 20 feet at the 16th, and hit a fine tee shot to six feet at the short 17th, before laying up at the 18th and pitching and putting for his closing four. It was a stunning performance.

"I knew I needed to do something special over the closing few holes," said McIlroy. "I really couldn't have wished for a better ending. I saw Justin make a charge. I heard the cheers, but to finish like that was great. I said I wanted to win both trophies this week and that is exactly what I've managed to do, even though I didn't get off to the best of starts with a bogey on the first."

Nelson Mandela Championship
Durban, South Africa
Winner: Scott Jamieson

See Africa Tours chapter.

Alfred Dunhill Championship
Mpumalanga, South Africa
Winner: Charl Schwartzel

See Africa Tours chapter.

Challenge Tour

Kristoffer Broberg made the most dramatic entrance ever onto the Challenge Tour. While a friend from Stockholm reckons no one practices harder than the 26-year-old Swede, Broberg was still plying his trade on the Nordic League, a Scandinavian mini-tour, early in 2012. But two victories on that circuit, prompted by an upturn in his putting fortunes, gave him a chance on the Challenge Tour. He made his debut in Brittany in May, but it was not until August that his season went ballistic. He won his second ever Challenge Tour event at the Finnish Challenge by six strokes. The next week he won the Norwegian Challenge by holing a 60-foot birdie putt on the second playoff hole to beat Alvaro Velasco. The following week he was third at the ECCO Tour Championship and the week after that he won again at the Rolex Trophy, holing a 40-footer on the final green to win by one stroke at 27 under par.

Broberg was the fifth player to win an instant promotion to the European Tour with three wins in a season, but none of the others had done it in only five tournaments. Broberg said: "It's so amazing, I'm just so happy. I couldn't believe it when that putt on the last hole dropped in. I always go for putts, so I never considered just rolling it up to the hole, I've always been positive with my putts. I didn't putt very well today, but it's great to know I can make big putts when I need to. I can't describe how it feels — it hasn't really hit me yet, but I'm sure it will. At the moment I want to keep playing as much as I can, because I'm playing the best golf of my life."

A month and a half later Broberg returned to the Challenge Tour and extended his winning streak to four out of five when he won the Crowne Plaza Copenhagen Challenge by three strokes. He was the third player to win at least four times in a season on the Challenge Tour. It put him on top of the rankings, but a seventh-place finish in the Apulia San Domenico Grand Final meant he slipped behind Espen Kofstad, who won the closing tournament to become the first Norwegian to be the Challenge Tour No. 1.

In contrast to Broberg's dramatics, Kofstad won just twice but both times in Puglia, having earlier won the Doubletree by Hilton Acaya Open. The 25-year-old went into the last event 11th on the rankings, but rounds of 66, 66, 67 and 67 for 19 under par gave him a four-stroke victory over Joachim B. Hansen and James Busby. "I might have to move here. I don't know what it is about this place. I love the food and the climate is really nice. I seem to cope very well with the greens here. I find them very easy to read and I holed some great putts this week," said Kofstad, who did not drop a shot over the weekend at San Domenico. "At the start of the season my coach and I decided the target would be three wins and a place in the top 10. I've only won twice, but I'll take it."

Busby, a 26-year-old Englishman, had turned professional eight years earlier but a month later suffered a car crash and was out of the game for two years. He entered the Grand Final in 45th place on the rankings — he was the last man in — but rose to 16th to grab a European Tour card for 2013. Busby holed a six-foot putt on the last green to get his card. "That putt at the last just summed up how I was feeling for the entire second nine — absolutely petrified," he said. "It's the stuff of dreams really. Up until today I was thinking about preparing for the qualifying tournament, so I can't really put into words how delighted I am right now."

Seve Benson, who had played previously on the European Tour for three years and won the Barclays Kenya Open earlier in the season, also had a good last week to jump into the top 21 who received their cards for the main circuit. The others were: Hansen, Andreas Harto, Gary Lockerbie, Magnus A. Carlsson, Simon Wakefield, Alessandro Tadini, Chris Doak, Scott Henry, Chris Paisley, Eddie Pepperell, Maximilian Kieffer, Justin Walters, Gary Stal, Mark Tullo, Morten Orum Madsen and Daniel Brooks.

10. Asia/Japan Tours

When they start describing a golfer as "age-defying" instead of "veteran" or some such designation of advancing years, then he's had a mind-boggling year. That was the case of Thailand's Thaworn Wiratchant, who at 46 turned a wealth of experience, a sharp short game and a will to win into the Asian Tour's 2012 Player of the Year Award.

Thaworn won three tournaments — the Queen's Cup in June, where he birdied the 16th and eagled the 18th to win by three, his first victory in nearly two years; the Selangor Masters in September by four, and the Hero Indian Open in October, where after a wild day off the tee, he won in a playoff. The three wins gave him a record 15 on the Asian Tour. He also topped the year's money-winning list with $738,046.

"The first time I joined the Asian Tour, I couldn't make the cut," Thaworn said. "I never thought I would come this far."

Success for the 40-somethings in the 27 tournaments was not limited to Thaworn.

Singapore's Mardan Mamat, 44, ended a six-year drought, taking the ICTSI Philippine Open by five shots. "There was a time," said Mamat, "when I said it was time for me to be a golf coach." He mentioned that to his wife. "But she said, 'In your dreams.'" (Lost in the bustle was the story of Filipino whiz Miguel Nabuena, only 17, who trailed Mamat by just a stroke entering the final nine. Then he triple-bogeyed the 10th and was on his way to a tie for 11th. As Thaworn had noted earlier, there are new players coming in. Nabuena would bear watching.)

Digvijay Singh, 40, took the Panasonic Open India, his first win since joining the tour in 2000. Two other 40-somethings won outside the Asian Tour. Thongchai Jaidee, 43, scored his first win in Europe in the ISPS Wales Open, and Jeev Milkha Singh, 41, got his third, the Scottish Open.

But youth were served as well in 2012. India's Gaganjeet Bhullar, 24, won twice, the Yeangder Tournament Players Championship and the Venetian Macau Open, and had six other top-10s to finish fifth on the money list.

Anirban Lahiri, 25, also from India, scored his second tour victory in the SAIL-SBI Open, and tied for 31st in the Open Championship in Britain. And Thailand's Arnond Vongvanij, 24, enjoyed a distinction that few his age could boast of. He beat both Thaworn and Mamat in the King's Cup in November. "I never thought I would win," he said. His secret: "I putted well and had some luck."

Two stars from the world stage also found success in Asia. Spain's Sergio Garcia shot 61 in the final round to win the rain-shortened Iskandar Johor Open in mid-December, the week after South African Charl Schwartzel, scoring his first victory since the 2010 Masters, ran away with the Thailand Golf Championship by 11 shots. "Winning," he said, "is not as easy as everyone thinks it is." (Aside to momentum-watchers: The week following this frolic, Schwartzel won the European Tour's Alfred Dunhill Championship by 12 shots.)

On the OneAsia Tour, in its fourth season, South Korea's Bio Kim, 21, was the only multiple winner on the 11-tournament schedule. He took the lead in the third round in the Caltex Maekung Open and turned it into a five-stroke victory. "People who win here," Bio observed, "tend to go on to greater things." Then the next week, he held or shared the lead all the way for a three-stroke win in the SK Telecom Open. He ended up topping the money list with $380,745.

In October, former teen whiz Kim Dae-sub seemed stuck in a pretty nice rut. Dae-sub, freshly returned from his mandatory 20-month Korean military stint showing no trace of nearly two years without tournament golf, came from behind to win the Kolon Korea Open — his third. The other two were as an amateur, the first in 1998 when he was 16. "I always dream I would win the Korea Open as a professional, but I didn't think it would happen this year," he said.

China's Liang Wen-chong plucked himself a nifty feather in the Nanshan China Masters, beating two former major winners, South Africa's Louis Oosthuizen (British Open) and South Korea's Y.E. Yang (U.S. PGA).

Did South Africa's Branden Grace, 23, throw his name into the Youth Derby? He opened the season with back-to-back wins in South Africa, then added the OneAsia's Volvo China Open in April. "To have won three now, before May, is unbelievable," Grace said. "Now I want to win every week."

On the Japan Tour, though younger players had their moments, two of Japan's most talented veterans — Hiroyuki Fujita and Toru Taniguchi — were the frontrunners of the 2012 season.

The 43-year-old Fujita moved into the No. 1 spot on the money list in the season's second month and never relinquished it, although 44-year-old Taniguchi had a remote shot at his third money title until Fujita walked away with his fourth victory of the year in the season-ending Nippon Series. The two, who stand fifth (Taniguchi) and sixth (Fujita) on the all-time tour money list, have 34 wins between them. In 2012, Taniguchi took the major PGA Championship and the Bridgestone Open, Fujita the Tsuruya Open, Diamond Cup and ANA Open prior to his third straight Nippon Series triumph that upped his final earnings to ¥173,154,307.

Australian Brendan Jones, 37, with two, was the only other multiple winner, and 40-year-old Kenichi Kuboya landed the Japan Open Championship.

Among the seven first-time winners — eight if you count Luke Donald's victory in the rich Dunlop Phoenix — were youngsters Lee Kyoung-hoon, 20, and Yoshinori Fujimoto, 22, who won the Tour Championship, along with, among others, the circuit's first victor from China — Wu Ashun — and two Korean-Americans — Han Lee and Jay Choi.

Ryo Ishikawa, the dashing young gallery favorite, avoided a second consecutive shutout year when he won the late-season Taiheiyo Masters, but Shingo Katayama, his stardom predecessor, went winless for a fourth year in a row.

Major Champions

Ten years between victories, Ernie Els held the Claret Jug for the second time after winning the Open Championship in a stunning finish.

Rory McIlroy, PGA Championship

Webb Simpson, U.S. Open Championship

Bubba Watson, Masters Tournamentn

Bubba Watson came in with a 68 for a 278 total and won in a playoff with Louis Oosthuizen.

Streeter Lecka/Getty Images

Streeter Lecka/Getty Images

Louis Oosthuizen lost despite an albatross.

Phil Mickelson started with 74 but tied for third.

Jamie Squire/Getty Images

Streeter Lecka/Getty Images

Matt Kuchar's closing 69 left him two shots back.

Lee Westwood's 67 led the first round.

U.S. Open

With 68s on the weekend at the U.S. Open, Webb Simpson won a major on just his fifth try.

Graeme McDowell dropped four shots in the final round but steadied himself to tie for second.

David Toms closed with a 68 to share fourth.

Jim Furyk bogeyed two of the last three.　　Michael Thompson had 66 to start, 67 to finish.

The Open Championship

David Cannon/The R&A

Ernie Els came home in 32 with a birdie at the last, but to win Els needed Adam Scott to finish with four consecutive bogeys.

Adam Scott was stunned by his late collapse.

Graeme McDowell was in the last group.

Brandt Snedeker led after two rounds.

Tiger Woods shared third despite his 73.

PGA Championship

Rory McIlroy became the first since Tiger Woods to win consecutive majors by at least eight strokes when he won the PGA Championship.

Out of the blue David Lynn posted two 68s on the weekend to take second place.

Justin Rose's 66 lifted him into a tie for third.

Keegan Bradley shot 68s on the first and last days.

Ian Poulter earned a share of third place.

Ryder Cup

Ross Kinnaird/Getty Images

Martin Kaymer secured the Ryder Cup for Europe, holing the clinching putt in the same situation as Bernhard Langer had when he missed in 1991.

Andy Lions/Getty Images

Ian Poulter kept Europe's hopes alive on Saturday.

David Cannon/Getty Images

Dustin Johnson had a 3-0 record.

Andrew Redington/Getty Images

Jose Maria Olazabal was sitting pretty with the Ryder Cup.

David Cannon/Getty Images

Phil Mickelson teamed well on the first two days.

David Cannon/Getty Images

Justin Rose (3-2) and Poulter (4-0) led the European Team.

Ross Kinnaird/Getty Images

At age 23 Rory McIlroy became the youngest since Tiger Woods to reach No. 1 in the world and won money titles in the U.S. and Europe.

Andy Lions/Getty Images

Andrew Redington/Getty Images

Tiger Woods passed Jack Nicklaus in wins.   Luke Donald won three, including the BMW PGA.

Peter Hanson was fourth in money in Europe.

Brandt Snedeker won the FedExCup bonus.

Lee Westwood won a Masters in Indonesia.

Ian Poulter topped the HSBC Champions.

Hunter Mahan took the Accenture title.

Zach Johnson had a two-victory season.

Jason Dufner won twice.

Dustin Johnson claimed the FedEx St. Jude title.

Nicolas Colsaerts's rise to prominence included winning the Volvo World Match Play Championship.

Matt Kuchar became The Players champion.

Carl Pettersson wore the Heritage's plaid jacket.

Nick Watney won The Barclays.

Matteo Manassero was the Singapore winner.

Steve Stricker started with a win in Hawaii.

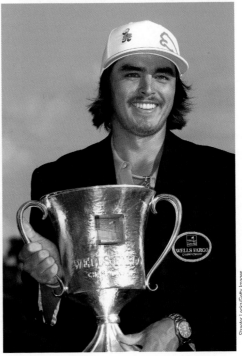

Hiroyuki Fujita won four times in Japan.

Rickie Fowler claimed the Wells Fargo prize.

Asian Tour

Zaykabar Myanmar Open
Yangon, Myanmar
Winner: Kieran Pratt

Truth be told, even Kieran Pratt's family had to be writing him off in the Zaykabar Myanmar Open, opening the Asian Tour's 2012 season. Could anyone that far out for so long have a chance? He trailed by six shots in the first round, by eight through the second and by five in the third. In other words, Pratt, age 23, an Australian in his second season on the tour, would still be looking for that first win when this was over. Well, now Pratt will be looking for that second one.

"Walking up 14, 15 and 16," said Pratt, who was feeling a long way off the lead in the final round, "I kind of felt the leaders were going nowhere. I told myself if I could get a couple of birdies, I could force a playoff." Then an eagle at the par-five 18th, on a 15-foot putt, did the trick, giving him a card of 70-69-66-68–273 at Royal Mingalardon, tying at 15 under with fellow Aussie Adam Blyth and Thailand's Kiradech Aphibarnrat.

They played off at the 18th. Kiradech was eliminated by a par on the first trip. On the second, Pratt won with a birdie while Blyth was scratching out a great par after hitting his tee shot so far that it bounced off a cart path and into the water.

The Myanmar Open actually was pretty much in the hands of Aussie Scott Hend from the start. He was leading by two going to the ninth in the final round, then watered two shots and took a quadruple bogey. That opened the door to everyone, especially Pratt.

"It was pretty cool and unexpected to sneak into the playoff," he said. Nobody disagreed

ICTSI Philippine Open
Manila, Philippines
Winner: Mardan Mamat

For Singapore's Mardan Mamat, now age 44, with two Asian Tour wins in his bag, it was back to the basics of golf in the ICTSI Philippine Open.

Case in point: Mamat's two-under-par 70 that kept him in the lead in the third round. "Yesterday, I hit the ball well but didn't putt it well," Mamat said. "Today, I didn't hit it well but putted well."

The lesson was clear in how Mamat handled the tough Wack Wack course, patiently shooting 69-70-70-71 for an eight-under-par 280, breaking from a three-round struggle for a five-stroke victory over Korea's Mo Joong-kyung, whose challenge fizzled in a closing 74. Mo opened the final round two behind Mamat, then stumbled to five over par in the first seven holes. "I just hit two bad shots," Mo said. "The way Mardan was playing ... I was just focused on finishing second."

Another great story fizzled out in the final round. Filipino whiz Miguel Tabuena, age 17, was only a stroke behind Mamat entering the last round and fell hard. He was three over on the first nine, then triple-bogeyed No. 10 off a wild drive, shot 81 and tied for 11th.

Mamat, who hadn't won since the 2006 Singapore Masters, took a three-stroke lead in the last round with a birdie at the fourth hole while Mo and Tabuena had shaky starts. He made the turn in 35 and was leading by six shots. "After the eighth hole, I was quite relieved," Mamat said. "You can pick up a big number there and I managed to get a par. It may have looked easy, but it wasn't easy."

Mamat credited his wife's encouragement for his win. "There was a time when I said it was time for me to be a golf coach," Mamat said. "But she said, not in your dreams."

Avantha Masters
Gurgaon, India
Winner: Jbe' Kruger

First, a word about Jbe' Kruger's first name. It's actually a nickname for his given names — James Barry — and would be "J.B." anywhere else. But a nickname by any other name ... At all events, in the Avantha Masters, Kruger was amazed at how easy that first win came in the final round. Well, he'd had plenty of experience in not getting there.

"It's a big relief now that I've won," said Kruger, who took it by two with a 14-under 274 total, "but I think I needed all those second-place finishes to appreciate this. There was no pressure, even when I made my only bogey of the day at the 17th."

It helped when his closest pursuers — Spain's Jorge Campillo (67) and Germany's Marcel Siem (70) — made timely bogeys at the 14th and tied for second in the Asian-European Tour co-sanctioned event. If "Jbe'" is a tough nickname, "Bridesmaid" would have been tougher. Kruger had come close a number of times, most notably in his second season, 2010, when he was runner-up three times.

One of his biggest threats was erased when Scotland's Peter Whiteford was disqualified for signing an incorrect scorecard in the third round. (He didn't realize the ball had moved. TV viewers said it did.)

Kruger, shooting the par-72 DLF Golf Club in 70-69-66-69, edged into a one-stroke lead in the third round. It was tantalizing. "If it's meant to be my week, it'll be mine," Kruger said, "so I don't want to think too far yet."

Still, he was tempted after birdies at the fourth, sixth and eighth put him out in three-under 33. He added the 11th and was on his way.

SAIL-SBI Open
New Delhi, India
Winner: Anirban Lahiri

The SAIL-SBI Open came down to two clubs — the belly putter and the disobedient driver. In different sets of hands, of course.

The belly putter belonged to India's Anirban Lahiri, thanks to his father. It was the key to his second Asian Tour victory. The driver belonged to Thai veteran Prom Meesawat. It disobeyed him just once, and there went the tournament.

Lahiri, playing Delhi Golf Club in 65-69-67-73, led through the first three rounds, then got caught by Prom (72-64-68-70) at 14-under 274. The playoff went one hole. Lahiri drove into the fairway and put his third within three feet of a birdie. Prom drove into the bushes on the right, took an unplayable lie penalty drop, and finally needed a 40-footer for par. He said the heck with it and picked up his ball. "I managed to hit all the fairways during regulation play," Prom said, "but unfortunately I had to miss my only one in the playoff."

Lahiri, 23, switched to the belly putter in 2011, when his regular putter got cranky and his dad, he said, began carping on him to try the long one. "I just gave in to him," he said.

Lahiri made his big move going out in the third round. After an early birdie-bogey exchange, he birdied Nos. 3, 4 and 9, then birdied three more over the first five holes coming home. He bogeyed twice, then birdied the 18th for a 67 and took a three-stroke lead into the fourth.

Lahiri closed with a 73 and wasn't pleased. "I've hit it much better the past three days," he said. "I found two bushes today, and I also dropped five shots." Even so, as a good son, he was happy that he listened to his dad.

Handa Faldo Cambodian Classic
Siem Reap, Cambodia
Winner: David Lipsky

If there was one thing David Lipsky learned when he graduated at the top of his class in the Asian Tour qualifying tournament, it was that he had the right stuff. Just two months later, a cross-country putt and a chip-in birdie, and the 23-year-old American rookie had his first victory, taking the inaugural Handa Faldo (yes, that Faldo) Cambodian Classic in a playoff over the Philippines' Elmer Salvador.

"I won in qualifying and I knew I had the game in me," Lipsky said. "I'm happy it showed up here."

And it showed up just in time. Lipsky opened with a one-over-par 73 at the Angkor Golf Resort, seven behind Korea's Baek Seuk-hyun. A 68 in the second round left him eight behind Korea's Kim Hyung-sung and Thailand's Chinnarat Phadungsil. And a 67 in the third round still left him seven behind Kim going into the final. Lipsky's prospects were looking a bit thin.

The fourth round turned into a scramble when Kim slid out of the lead. Six players were tied for the lead at one point. Then Lipsky and Salvador — he started from four back — began to pull away. Lipsky struck with a huge birdie putt. "On 15, I saw that everyone was bunched at 13 under, and I had a 50-foot putt," he said, "and I jarred it and thought I could have a chance to win." Salvador, 42, missed on two birdie chances — a three-footer at the 14th and a 10-footer at the 18th. "My putting," said Salvador, tying with a 68, "was sometimes good, sometimes bad." It was on to the playoff. Lipsky ended it fast, chipping in on the first hole.

"I really can't believe I'm here right now," said Lipsky, just five tournaments into his first season.

Panasonic Open India
New Delhi, India
Winner: Divijay Singh

India's Digvijay Singh was getting on — he was 40 years of age now — and beginning to feel left out. He'd been banging his head against the wall for 12 years but couldn't break through. "It was frustrating," Singh said. "Everybody had won but me."

He was at the Panasonic Open India and on the fringe of contending, but still the fates toyed with him. He trailed all the way and was three behind starting the fourth round. The picture wasn't all that promising, not until the final nine. And then he raced home, wrapping up a card of 70-73-68-66–277, 11 under par at Delhi Golf Club.

"The 13th was the turning point that got me going," Singh said. "I made my second birdie of the day on No. 7 and couldn't convert anything until the birdie on 13. From then on, the birdies started flowing in."

He left a bunch of former tour winners behind. Bangladesh's Siddikur shot a two-bogey 68 and India's Gaganjeet Bhullar a one-bogey 70 and tied for second, two strokes back. Thailand's Boonchu Ruangkit, now 55, shot a bogey-free 67 to finish a solo fourth. Boonchu scared the leaders, getting four birdies coming in on the course he first played as an amateur in 1985. "I like this course because you have to plan your shots," he said. "It's not about blasting off the tees."

Singh caught a spark from that birdie at the 13th, then birdied the 14th, 16th and 18th.

When he dropped that final putt, he was greeted by Asian star Jyoti Randhawa, his brother-in-law and the man who introduced him to golf. Randhawa tied for 19th.

"I wasn't disheartened when I lost my Asian Tour card last year," Singh said. "I told myself this is where I am and I should make the most of it."

ISPS Handa Singapore Classic
Singapore
Winner: Scott Hend

It took the lively imagination of Scott Hend to carry golf into one of the unexplored corners of wedded bliss best left unexplored. Said Hend, describing the agonizing wait to learn whether he had won the ISPS Handa Singapore Classic: "It's sort of like you're going out and have to wait for your wife to do her hair or something. You're just sitting around and pacing around, and that's what I was feeling then."

Hend had played the first two rounds at the par-70 Orchid Country Club in 67-68, and trailed by six strokes in the first round and four through the second. Then came his vexing predicament. The tournament was cut to three rounds because of stormy weather. The big-hitting Australian shot six-under 64 in the third round and held the clubhouse lead at 199. But a number of players still had a shot at him. And he had to wait almost an hour.

"I just wanted for it to be over and know whether I've won or not," Hend said. "Luckily for me, I won."

They fell short, one by one. Sri Lanka's Mithun Perera shot 65, Taiwan's Lu Wei-chih 66, Spain's Javi Colomo 67, and finally, America's David Lipsky missed a birdie putt on the 18th and shot 66. They all tied for second at 200.

For Hend, who had three domestic wins in Australia and one Asian win in 2008, this was extra sweet because he had taken time off to sort out some things in his game. "It's amazing," he said. "Especially to have four weeks off and come back and win. It's great to see the hard work pay off."

Maybank Malaysian Open
Kuala Lumpur, Malaysia
Winner: Louis Oosthuizen

If the playoff loss to Bubba Watson in the Masters left any scars on Louis Oosthuizen, they weren't visible the following week at the Maybank Malaysian Open. Shaking off his Masters pain, jet lag from a 30-hour trip, severe heat and a strong field, Oosthuizen took command in the second round and made off with the title by a comforting three strokes in the co-sanctioned Asian-European Tour event at Kuala Lumpur Golf Club.

"Coming here and winning after what happened last week showed me that I can pull it off," said Oosthuizen, the former Open Championship winner. "I'm a little bit surprised because I thought I would be tired."

Charl Schwartzel needed only 24 putts in his opening eight-under 64, but the magic faded. Oosthuizen, after trailing by two, took over in the second round and went on to post a card of 66-68-69-68–271, 17 under, three better than Scotland's Stephen Gallacher. It was his first win on the Asian Tour, his fifth on the European.

Oosthuizen had to complete his third-round 69 on Sunday after a weather delay and took a one-stroke lead into the fourth round. He all but locked up the win with a birdie at the 13th. "I had a seven iron in my hand and the wind changed a little bit, so I went to an eight iron," Oosthuizen said. "I hit a beautiful shot and made that putt." He also birdied the 16th for a cushy margin in what might have been a difficult time. It turned out that the Masters loss didn't hurt his sense of humor, either.

When officials handed Oosthuizen the trophy and the champion's navy blue jacket, he gave a little smile. "It would have been better," he said, "if I had the green jacket."

CIMB Niaga Indonesian Masters
Jakarta, Indonesia
Winner: Lee Westwood

If a player has an eight-shot lead heading into the final round, what more could he ask of the fates? Well, in the case of Lee Westwood in the CIMB Niaga Indonesian Masters, he could ask them to get him to the house before he ran out of gas. That eight-shot lead wasn't as cushy as it seemed. Thanks to lightning delays, Westwood had to play a 32-hole marathon on the final day. Under the heavy April heat and humidity of Indonesia, Westwood was wilting fast as he was grinding out a two-stroke victory over Thai veteran Thaworn Wiratchant. Westwood, No. 3 in the world, shot 65-68-65-74, a 16-under-par 272 total at Royal Jakarta Golf Club for his first win of 2012 and career 38th.

"You never know how to play with such a big lead — you don't know if you should attack or defend," said Westwood, the 10th on the Asian Tour to successfully defend his title. And there was the punishing heat. "Today was hard," he said. "It was draining out there, and I was really feeling it on the back nine."

Two weeks earlier, Westwood fell short again in his bid for that first major, in the Masters, this time finishing third, and took a week off. "It was good to recharge my batteries because the Masters always takes a lot out of you," he said. So, refreshed, he opened at Jakarta with three straight birdies and took a two-stroke lead. Fighting the elements, he built his lead to five at the halfway point, then to eight after three rounds, during the Sunday marathon. Then came the wilt. The conditions were tough even for Southeast Asians. "I felt tired at the 12th but I held on," said Thaworn, a 12-time winner.

"I lost concentration out there," Westwood said. "That has been the story for me since last year."

Ballantine's Championship
Seoul, South Korea
Winner: Bernd Wiesberger

Austria's Bernd Wiesberger, a second-year player and unknown, found his way into what the golfers call "The Zone" and came racing from back in the pack to the lead in the second round of the Ballantine's Championship.

It was strange territory for him. "I couldn't really do anything wrong," he said. "I felt like everything was going in the right direction."

After opening with a 72, Wiesberger touched Seoul's Blackstone Resort course for a flawless seven-under-par 65 and a one-stroke lead. He bumped that up to five and rode it home for his breakthrough win. He took the co-sanctioned Asian-European Tour tournament by five on a card of 72-65-65-68–270, 18 under. That last leg was a bit scary.

"I can't say I wasn't nervous on the first tee," he offered, "but when I got the first shot out there on the fairway, it was a bit of a relief." He made things easy on himself from there. He birdied the par-five fifth and made the turn in one-under 35, parred to the 14th, birdied the 15th and 16th, and came home for a five-shot win over Richie Ramsay (65).

France's Victor Dubuisson, 22, was the only other player to lead, shooting a 68 in the wind-blown first round, four strokes and a host of players ahead of Wiesberger. He double-bogeyed the fourth when the wind took his ball into the water, but he shook it off like a vet. "I wasn't really upset because I didn't hit a bad shot," he said. He tied for third. It was Wiesberger's time.

"To play the way I did this week is very special," Wiesberger said. "I just wanted to get my hands on the trophy, and I did that pretty well."

Queen's Cup
Koh Samui, Thailand
Winner: Thaworn Wiratchant

One look at his ball, and Thaworn Wiratchant knew he was in a classic case of choose your own poison. In the final round of the Queen's Cup, he was at Santiburi Samui's No. 4 hole, his tee shot sitting on a cart path. He was entitled to a free drop, but his nearest point of relief was stony ground. Which to play from — cart path or stony ground?

Thaworn, a veteran of the Asian Tour, quickly opted for the stony ground. He hit a great approach to 12 feet, then sank the putt for his first birdie of the day. He was on the way to a three-stroke win, his first victory in nearly two years, tying countryman Thongchai Jaidee with a tour-record 13th.

"There was pressure from the first tee," Thaworn said. "My experience helps with the mental game. It helps me calm down."

Calm nerves were needed at the wind-battered Santiburi, which he shot in 70-67-72-68–277, seven under par. His didn't get his three-stroke margin until the last few holes in a stretch battle with Bangladesh's Siddikur, who lost the lead when he missed a two-foot par putt at the 15th hole. "I was done after that," Siddikur said.

Thaworn then birdied the 16th from five feet and eagled the 18th from 12 to lock up the win. "The second shot on the 18th," Thaworn said. "It was the first time I could smile today."

The tour got another look at the future in the person of the Philippines' Miguel Tabuena, a mere 17 years of age, who tied for the lead in the first three rounds, then sagged to a 76 and tied for 10th place.

"I played really well the whole week," Tabuena said. "It's just a different ball game going into the last day. I haven't reached that yet."

Volvik Hildesheim Open J Golf Series
Jecheon, South Korea
Winner: Lee In-woo

Thailand's Thaworn Wiratchant, who won his 13th Asian Tour title in the Queen's Cup a week earlier, had a strategy for getting that 14th, but he classified it "top secret ... in case they copy and make me lose," he said with a chuckle.

No matter. It didn't work. Native son Lee In-woo kept his poise under the pressure from the veteran star and took his first tour victory in the inaugural Volvik Hildesheim Open J Golf Series. Lee closed with a four-under-par 68 at Hildesheim Country Club, squeaking out a one-stroke win over Thaworn and Korea's Lee Sang-hee.

"When I took a share of the third-round lead yesterday, I told myself that this was my chance of winning again, and I cannot waste it," said Lee, 40, whose only other victory came in 2005 on the Korean Golf Tour. Thaworn closed with a 69, and Lee Sang-hee a 67 to tie for second.

Ma Soo-kil and Lee Sang-hee had the distinction of sharing the first-round lead with six-under-par 66s in the new tournament, co-sponsored by the Asian and Korean tours. They already had made their marks — Ma topped the Korean qualifying tournament in 2011, and Sang-hee, 20, was the youngest winner on the Korean Golf Tour.

But neither was around when the third round ended in a traffic jam, with six tied for the lead. It unraveled quickly.

"The turning point was at the 17th," said Thaworn, after bogeying the par-three hole. Then he missed on a 20-foot birdie try at the 18th. "That's golf," he said.

"What made this victory even sweeter," In-woo said, was that I managed to win against a strong field that included players from the Asian Tour."

Worldwide Holdings Selangor Masters
Shah Alam, Malaysia
Winner: Thaworn Wiratchant

Thaworn Wiratchant, age 45, the venerable and durable Thai star, rang up a record 14th Asian Tour victory in the Worldwide Holdings Selangor Masters, but he had to share the spotlight with Michael Tran, a mere 22. It underlined the spread of professional golf in Asia that Tran is from Vietnam — the only one from that country on the tour.

Tran stayed close to Thaworn much of the way and shared the halfway lead with him at nine under before tailing off with two double bogeys going out in the final round. "When I made the turn, I saw I had no chance to win," Tran said. "I just said to myself, 'Enjoy the last nine holes.' I stopped trying to force things to happen." For the history books, he shot the Kota Permai Club in 67-68-73-68–276, 12 under, tied for third, four behind Thaworn. It was his first top-10 finish in his three seasons.

Thaworn (66-69-68-69–272) launched his run at the win in the first round with a sparkling eagle at the par-five 12th, hitting the pin with his three-wood approach. "I've never hit that green in two," he said, "so I got lucky there." Thaworn's veteran nerves pulled him through a shaky stretch in the third round. He dropped three shots at Nos. 8 and 9 — "I said, 'I'm dead' — then righted himself spectacularly, holing a 60-foot putt for a birdie at the 10th.

"The first time I joined the Asian Tour, I couldn't make the cut," said Thaworn, cradling the record. "I never thought I would come this far. I don't have a complete or perfect swing, but I practiced hard to ensure I could maintain the same swing. I believe in my swing."

Yeangder Tournament Players Championship
Taipei, Taiwan
Winner: Gaganjeet Bhullar

Not that golf is quite this simple, but India's Gaganjeet Bhullar decided it was time for him to win again, and so he did, taking the weather-shortened Yeangder Tournament Players Championship by a comfortable four shots.

Said Bhullar, "I told myself that I've got to win this tournament, no matter what." It was a little more involved than that, of course, but he shot 66-69-69–204, 12 under par at the par-72 Linkou International course, only briefly pressured by American Jason Knutzon, a two-time winner (his first-round 66 included a hole-in-one at the par-three No. 5), and Thailand's Thaworn Wiratchant, a 14-time winner.

Bhullar took the lead in the second round, starting with a birdie at the first hole and an eagle at the fourth, then rebounding from a bogey at the seventh and double bogey at the 14th on his way to a 69. He led by a stroke going into the third and last round, and ran up four birdies against a bogey through the 10th. Bogeys at the 11th and 13th cut his lead to one. "I told myself that I had to make another birdie," Bhullar said. And he got two, at the 16th and 18th.

Knutzon closed with a 71 and offered, "I wish we were able to keep playing." Thaworn (72) missed finishing a solo second by the margin of a slow-play penalty stroke.

Whether a golfer can talk himself into winning is one thing. But as the Philippines' Angelo Que demonstrated, it seems he can talk his way out of it. Que took the first-round lead with a 65 and then noted, "I'm really surprised to be ahead. When I start this good, I feel that I may find ways to mess it up." Then he shot 75 in the second round.

Asia-Pacific Panasonic Open
Hyogo
Winner: Masanori Kobayashi

See Japan Tour section.

Mercuries Taiwan Masters
Taipei, Taiwan
Winner: Tsai Chi-huang

One of golf's scariest phenomena, "sleeping on the lead" — in which the leader twitches at the thought of coming failure — was put to a severe test in the Mercuries Taiwan Masters. Taiwan's Tsai Chi-huang took a whopping six-shot lead into the final round — and nearly flunked. But he held himself together, shot 76, and such was the generosity of his pursuers that he still won by four shots.

"Honestly, I couldn't sleep last night," the frazzled Tsai said. "I was wondering if I could make it to the end. I felt like I was still sleeping when I was on the first tee box."

So the tale ended with Tsai posting scores of 74-69-65-76, a four-under 284 total at the Taiwan Golf and Country Club. His third-round 65 was a gift that kept on giving. He shot it on his 44th birthday, getting the six-stroke lead going into the final round, and most of it held up, delivering his second Taiwan Masters victory the next day.

In the windy weather of the fourth round, nobody could mount a serious threat to the sleepwalking Tsai. The Philippines' Antonio Lascuna, who started seven shots back, managed a 73 to finish second at even-par 288. "I saw the scores and I knew I had a chance to win," said Lascuna, winless in his six seasons. "But I was playing par golf for most of the second nine and couldn't score."

Tsai did get a brief scare. Chan Yih-shin, a two-time winner, cut his luxurious lead to two at one point, but bogeyed the 16th and double-bogeyed the 18th, and slipped to a tie for third.

Said Tsai, of what was looking like a nightmare for a while: "It was only when I finished that I knew my dream had come true."

CJ Invitational
Yeoju, South Korea
Winner: K.J. Choi

They're not likely to be found in any golf instruction book, much less heard on the practice tee, but it turns out that three secrets are the heart of K.J. Choi's game.

"I was starting to warm up when I came back in the morning to complete my third round," Choi was saying at the CJ Invitational hosted by Choi, his own charity tournament, in October. "But once I got through those nine holes, three key elements came back into my game — see, feel and trust."

And so Choi again played the less-than-accommodating host and won his own tournament. It was up for grabs while he was shooting 69-65-68 in the first three rounds, but rejuvenated, he closed with a 67 for a 269 total, 15 under par at Haesley Nine Bridges, and a two-stroke win over Jang Dong-kyu and Bae Sang-moon. Choi donated his $118,875 first prize to his K.J. Choi Foundation.

Thanks to fog delays, Choi had to finish his third round on Sunday morning, making a birdie and a bogey coming in for his 68. After a brief break, he started the final round with two birdies over the first four holes. A bogey at the ninth slowed him, then he ran off three consecutive birdies from the 11th and parred in for a 67 and his sixth win on the Asian Tour.

Australia's Scott Hend charged back into the hunt with an eagle at the par-four 12th and a birdie at the 13th. But bogeys at the 15th and 16th spilled him to a tie for fifth. "You're cruising along ... and suddenly you get smashed," Hend said.

Said Choi, of his three golf senses: "I could see, feel and trust every aspect of my ball-striking ... I was really confident that I would go on and win."

Venetian Macau Open
Macau
Winner: Gaganjeet Bhullar

India's Gaganjeet Bhullar, a mere 24 years of age, had reduced golf to its simplest logical terms.

Said Bhullar: "When you know mentally that you're striking the ball well, it'll be a matter of putting, and if you putt well, you will score."

Say yes to all of the above and you've wrapped up Bhullar in the Venetian Macau Open, a wire-to-wire cruise to a two-stroke victory. Bhullar's exercise in logic came after the eight-under 63 in the first round gave him the two-stroke lead he would carry the rest of the way. He added 68-69-68 for a 16-under 268 at Macau Golf and Country Club. He even spotted the field a bogey at the first hole. He bounced back with an eagle at No. 2, on a 35-foot putt, and had seven birdies, two of them from 40 feet.

It was his second victory of the year, following the Yeangder Tournament Players Championship a month earlier, and it was also his fourth Asian Tour win.

"I canned that putt (on No. 2), and it changed the whole game plan," Bhullar said. And after his second-round 68: "Not as good as yesterday, but ... it's not a bad score. I'm just going to stick to my routine and see what happens."

In the third round, Bhullar missed a three-foot par putt at the 17th and a three-footer for birdie at the 18th, and shot 69 to keep his two-stroke lead. "That's not the finish I was thinking of," Bhullar said. "I'm feeling positive and I'm feeling good." In the final round, he birdied four of the first seven holes, and after a few bumps, he birdied the 18th for the two-stroke win.

"I had to believe in myself," Bhullar said. "I did it, and it was really special."

Hero Indian Open
Bengaluru, India
Winner: Thaworn Wiratchant

Thailand's Thaworn Wiratchant, veteran star of the Asian Tour, took what is commonly and charitably referred to as the "scenic route" for much of the Hero Indian Open. Meaning that he saw parts of the Karnataka course rarely seen, which led him to observe, after the fact: "To be honest, I didn't expect to win with the way I was driving the ball this week."

Fortunately for Thaworn, the rest of his game pulled him through for a playoff victory over Scotland's Richie Ramsay, who was about to convert a sponsor's invitation into a wire-to-wire win. All Ramsay needed was a par at the 18th. Instead, he three-putted for a bogey and fell into a tie with Thaworn, who had already finished with a birdie at the last, sticking his seven-iron approach to a foot. Thaworn shot 69-68-67-66 and Ramsay 66-66-70-68 to tie at 14-under-par 270.

It was a bitter finish for Ramsay. He had led or shared the lead all the way. Both stumbled through the playoff, but Ramsay worse than Thaworn. Ramsay put his tee shot into the creek, then after a penalty drop put his third at the back of the green, chipped 10 feet past the hole and two-putted for a double bogey. Thaworn put his approach into a greenside bunker, blasted out, then two-putted for a winning bogey. It was his third win of the year and his tour-record 15th. Irony hung in the air afterward.

Earlier, Ramsay had noted: "As long as you're hitting fairways, there are a lot of chances out there. The minute you're off the fairways, then you are going to struggle."

CIMB Classic
Kuala Lumpur, Malaysia
Winner: Nick Watney

The way the guys were battering the Mines Resort course, Nick Watney wasn't even thinking of winning until, oh, at the 13th on the last day. That's when, after trailing all the way, and sometimes badly, he found himself tied for the lead.

It was the co-sanctioned CIMB Classic in October, the PGA Tour's first venture into the Asian Tour and a kind of dress rehearsal for when the tournament will become a full PGA Tour event in 2013. And it was a scoring carnival that left Watney doubting from the start. Out of the no-cut field of 48, only two players failed to break par for the tournament — Malaysia's Shaaba Hussin, at one over, and Australia's Scott Hend, dead last at three over.

Watney zipped up the leaderboard, shooting 71-65-65-61, but he was hardly confident. "After the first round, I thought I was out of it," Watney said. He was eight behind Troy Matteson (63), then he was still eight behind Robert Garrigus (64) in the second. Through the third, he was four behind Garrigus (69) and Bo Van Pelt (62).

Watney, who won the Barclays two months earlier, started the fourth round with two birdies and soon had caught fire and was making a run at a 59. He had it in sight with six birdies over seven holes from the 11th. Then he drove into the rough at the 18th. "So the 59 went out the window right there," he said. "I was more concerned with just winning the tournament." He bogeyed the 18th for a 22-under 262 total, winning by one over Garrigus (66) and Van Pelt (66).

"I was just trying to keep my head down," Watney said. "And it worked out for me"

WGC - HSBC Champions
Guangdong, China
Winner: Ian Poulter

The thrill of the Ryder Cup had all but faded, and the 2012 season was winding down, and now Ian Poulter wanted something for himself.

"I've only been one season without a victory, and I certainly didn't want to go another one," Poulter was to say. "As well as I've played ... it would have been a disappointment to have gone this year without winning."

That was a reasonable hope, but he needed some help before he could reach it in the WGC - HSBC Champions in Guangdong, China. For one, Louis Oosthuizen was perking right along. He tied for the first-round lead with Adam Scott at 65 on the par-72 Mission Hills Olazabal course, then shot 63 in the second for a WGC record 16-under-par 128 total for 36 holes. Oosthuizen added a 70 in the third round and was tied by Lee Westwood's sizzling 61 at 18 under. Poulter (65) was four strokes behind going into the final round.

There were still obstacles. But Westwood and Oosthuizen were deserted by their putting. Phil Mickelson missed a five-foot par putt at the 12th hole. Ernie Els missed a three-foot par putt at the 14th, then just missed a birdie at the 18th. Defending champion Martin Kaymer made five birdies in six holes coming in, but triple-bogeyed the 17th.

Poulter, after starting the final round four strokes off the lead, then scored eight birdies in groups of twos — holes Nos. 2-3, 7-8, 10-11, and then holed a five-footer at the 14th and a 20-footer at the 15th for a three-stroke lead. He bogeyed the 17th hole, then sealed his two-stroke win with a 10-footer for par at the 18th, playing the course in 69-68-65-65–267, 21 under.

Poulter won $1.2 million, but said, in his love of cars, he had already spent it. "Yes, it was a vehicle, and yes," he said, "it was very expensive."

Barclays Singapore Open
Singapore
Winner: Matteo Manassero

For all of his youth, Italy's Matteo Manassero, age 19, had about run out of steam in the weather-whipped Barclays Singapore Open. Storms had forced one round into another until, by Sunday, Manassero had to finish 15 holes of the third round, and then after a 27-minute rest, play the 18 holes of the fourth. "On 13, I was not feeling that great, I was really flat," he said. "No more energy left. But the adrenaline throughout the day kept me going." South Africa's Louis Oosthuizen, the 2010 Open champion, age 30, had to finish 13 holes on Sunday, then play the final round. Manassero shot 70-68-64-69 and Oosthuizen 70-69-65-67, and they tied at 13-under 271, three ahead of Rory McIlroy (65–274).

Manassero then holed a 12-foot putt for eagle on the third playoff hole to win the co-sanctioned Asian-European Tour tournament, his third European Tour title.

They were practically locked in a playoff even during the round. Oosthuizen, down three, charged into a tie with three birdies from No. 9, but then bogeyed the next two. Manassero parred 10 straight holes, then bogeyed the 15th off a short approach. Oosthuizen took his only lead of the day with a birdie at the 18th on a two-foot putt. Manassero then caught up with a two-putt birdie from 60 feet, forcing the playoff.

For Oosthuizen, it was a case of the stubborn ball. "I was putting beautifully today but the ball just didn't go in," he said. "It's been a story for the last four weeks."

For Manassero, it was a relief to win since tailing off after being the youngest to win on the European Tour at 17. "I didn't have great results for something like a year," he said. "It was frustrating."

UBS Hong Kong Open
Fanling, Hong Kong
Winner: Miguel Angel Jimenez

For Spain's pony-tailed Miguel Angel Jimenez, there's nothing like a good cigar and a bottle of wine to deal with the advancing years. That might stop the doctors in their tracks, but it works for him.

Not that the formula would be recommended for youth, but Rory McIlroy, the defending champion, could have used some kind of help. He couldn't get moving and missed the cut by three strokes on his 73-72 start.

And so Jimenez was sipping a celebratory glass shortly after winning the Asian-European Tour co-sanctioned UBS Hong Kong Open in November, having become at age 48 years and 318 days the oldest player ever to win on the European Tour.

"There is maybe olive oil in my joints, and drinking the nice Rioja wine and those things keep me fit and flexible," Jimenez said. "Well, the most important thing, I do what I like to do in my life, and golf has given me all this pleasure."

It was Jimenez's third Hong Kong Open victory — the others coming in 2004 and 2007 — and it gave him six wins on the Asian Tour and 19 on the European Tour. Jimenez played the Hong Kong Golf Club's par-70 Fanling course in 65-67-68-65–265, 15 under par, to win by one over Sweden's Fredrik Andersson Hed. Jimenez charged to four straight birdies from No. 7 and rolled on to his third straight bogey-free round.

"Becoming the oldest winner on the tour at 48 — my goodness," said Jimenez. "Twenty-four years I've been on the tour. I've been around a long time. But I still love it, and that is fantastic, to love what you're doing, and enjoy yourself, keep fit, keep working myself and stretching a lot. That's the main thing to do, keep the body to compete with the new guns."

King's Cup
Khon Kaen, Thailand
Winner: Arnond Vongvanij

Thailand's Supakorn Utaipat surged into the second-round lead of the King's Cup and was not in the most confident frame of mind. This was only his second start on the Asian Tour. "And honestly, I'm feeling nervous," he said. "I've never been in this position before."

Consider, then, the case of Thailand's Arnond Vongvanij, 23, a rookie on the tour, and finding himself in position to win in the final round.

Vongvanij entered the final round trailing Singapore's Mardan Mamat by three strokes and set about changing that. Going out, he birdied Nos. 2, 7, 8 and 9 to turn in 32. Coming in, he birdied Nos. 11, 14 and 16, then at the par-three 17th holed a 10-foot putt for his eighth and final birdie, taking the lead and then completing a bogey-free round by saving par from off the green at the 18th. He wrapped up a total of 65-70-67-64–266 for a two-stroke victory over Mamat and Thai star Thaworn Wiratchant.

"I just kept playing one shot at a time," Vongvanij said, "and it was really a close fight all the way, as Mardan was also making birdies. It was tough not to feel any pressure, and I tried to steady my nerves after every hole."

Vongvanij, it turns out, had some practice at steadying his nerves. He was born in Hawaii and grew up in Thailand, then moved to Florida at age 12 to play golf, and he played college golf for the University of Florida.

Vongvanij entered the tournament with four top-10 finishes for an already good rookie season. As to his breakthrough win: "I putted well," he said, "and had some luck.

Thailand Golf Championship
Bangkok, Thailand
Winner: Charl Schwartzel

Bubba Watson was speaking for himself, of course, but he said it for everyone at the Thailand Golf Championship. "Schwartzel played pretty (well)," Watson said, "and my best stuff probably wouldn't have been as good."

That was as good a way as any to describe Charl Schwartzel's wire-to-wire frolic to the title, an 11-shot victory over a field that didn't lack for muscle. Beyond Watson, tying for second place, there were Sergio Garcia, in fourth, and Lee Westwood and Nicolas Colsaerts far, far behind as Schwartzel tore up the Amata Spring Country Club course with rounds of 65-65-68-65–263, 25 under par, breaking Westwood's tournament record by three shots.

Schwartzel was more relieved than anything. Surprisingly for a golfer of his evident talents, this was his first win since the 2011 Masters. "I'm very happy the way my game has started getting back," he said, after his opening 65. That gave him just a one-stroke lead over Thailand's Thitiphun Chuayprakong, 20, who would go on to tie for second with Watson and be thankful that he had played with Schwartzel.

Schwartzel birdied the first two holes to start the tournament, and he was on his way. "I found many fairways," he said, adding, "You're not going to win the golf tournament after Round 1, but you sure can lose it."

Not this time. He just piled on birdie after birdie, and made only one bogey in the entire tournament. He entered the final round leading by five, birdied No. 1, and left the others fighting for second place.

"Winning," he would say, to smiles all around, "is not as easy as everyone thinks it is."

Iskandar Johor Open
Johor Bahru, Malaysia
Winner: Sergio Garcia

Despite his great experience, Sergio Garcia let the weather scramble get to him for a while at the Asian Tour's season-ending Iskandar Johor Open. "It's hard to keep up mentally," Garcia said, "and I sort of did that yesterday morning, where I finished poorly." He was speaking of the second round, when storms and delays reduced the tournament to three rounds.

Garcia proved his point, and then some, in the third and final round. He blistered Horizon Hills Golf and Country Club for a bogey-free, 11-under-par 61 and a three-stroke victory, his second win of the year, after the Wyndham Championship on the PGA Tour. He made history — the lowest final round by a winner ever on the Asian Tour.

"It has been a long week because of the weather, and I couldn't have asked for a better way to end the week," Garcia said. "It has been a great experience as this is my first time in Malaysia, and to be able to win is a treat."

Garcia birdied seven of the first nine holes and made the turn at 29, then birdied the 13th and 14th just before a long rain delay hit. Then he returned and birdied the 15th and 16th. He posted a card of 68-69-61–198, 18 under, holding off American Jonathan Moore, who also shot 61 but couldn't close the gap and was three back, at 201, for his second runner-up finish of the season.

"I had a clear focus today," Moore said. "I didn't have any fear over any shots."

Thailand's Thaworn Wiratchant closed with a 65 and tied for fifth place, locking up the tour's money-winning title at $738,046. He won it in 2005, but now he was nearly 46 years old. Said Thaworn: "I never thought I could win the Order of Merit at this age."

OneAsia Tour

Enjoy Jakarta Indonesia Open
Jakarta, Indonesia
Winner: Nick Cullen

"This means the world to me," Australia's Nick Cullen was saying, on winning the Enjoy Jakarta Indonesia Open. He was speaking figuratively, of course, but the observation had its literal side, too, for a struggling 27-year-old who had finally scored his first win as a professional. The OneAsia Tour's season-opener was also sanctioned by the Japan Tour, and so he now had exemptions on both circuits. That may not be the entire world, but it was a start.

As Cullen was playing the demanding Emeralda Golf Club in 72-66-67-74–279, nine under par, the win almost didn't happen. He was on-again, off-again, and he was leading by four shots with five holes to play and then stumbled badly at the par-four 14th hole. He drove into a mess and could only chip back to the fairway, and then hit his approach over the green and ended up with a triple bogey. More experienced golfers than Cullen have folded under such disappointment, but he pulled himself together and birdied the 17th, holing a 20-foot putt to edge into the lead over New Zealand's David Smail. Cullen faced one final test. He missed the green at the 18th and the best he could do with his chip was five feet. But he braced himself and dropped the putt for the save and a one-stroke win over Smail, a five-time winner on the Japan Tour.

"I haven't holed many putts all week, so the last two were very timely," Cullen understated. They were enough to thwart Smail, who led through the first two rounds, then double-bogeyed twice and fell six behind with a 74 in the third.

"I haven't had a win now for seven years," Smail lamented. "To finally stumble home would be nice."

Volvo China Open
Tianjin, China
Winner: Branden Grace

Add South Africa's Branden Grace, age 23, to the rising tide of youth in world golf. Actually, you don't have to add him. He did it himself with a three-stroke victory in the co-sanctioned OneAsia-European Tour Volvo China Open to underline a hot start to the young season.

"To have won three now, before May, is unbelievable," he said. "Now I want to win every week."

He opened the season with back-to-back wins in South Africa — the Joburg Open, co-sanctioned by the Sunshine and European tours, and the Volvo

Golf Champions. His success carried him to China's Binhai Lake Golf Club in mid-April, where he opened without fanfare with a five-under-par 67, two behind England's Matthew Baldwin. And he was one off the halfway lead with a 67 that sparkled with an eagle after he drove the green at the tempting par-four No. 7. "I hit straight at it, got a nice bounce forward to five feet, and rolled the putt in," Grace said. But poor Paul Casey. The once-promising Englishman couldn't say anything like that. His day: A 10 at the par-five 12th and two double bogey-sevens in a 79.

Grace followed with a 64 for the third-round lead by three over Belgium's Nicolas Colsaerts, the defending champion. Grace gave nothing away in the final round. He finished with a one-bogey 69 for a 21-under 267 to win by three over Colsaerts. "I thought I could have got a little meaner on Branden today," said Colsaerts (69). "I left him a bit too much breathing space."

Ambition blossomed for Grace. "I've played one of the majors, but a few more are the aim," he said. "I will also head to the States to try to get a bit more experience there."

GS Caltex Maekyung Open
Seoul, South Korea
Winner: Bio Kim

South Korea's Bio Kim was a bit star-struck on his first crack at the PGA Tour. Now older and wiser, at 21, Kim was becoming a star himself. In the OneAsia Tour's GS Caltex Maekyung Open, he jumped into the lead in the third round and barreled home from there for a five-shot victory, the second win of his young career, and in the tournament he wanted most of all.

"People who win here," Kim said, "tend to go on to greater things."

Kim got his runaway win off a 69-69-67-68–273, 15-under-par performance at Nam Seoul Country Club. But he had to fend off a lot of comers along the way. His opening 69, for example, left him a stroke behind an eight-way tie for the lead. He still was a shot back at the halfway point when Park Sang-hyun turned a carom off a tree branch into a birdie at the 16th and a 69–137. Kim, on the other hand, double-bogeyed out of the rough. But he got the shot back when his downhill, 30-foot putt at the 18th hit the stick and dropped for a birdie.

Kim's big chance came at the 14th in the third round. Park bogeyed out of the trees and Kim birdied for a two-stroke swing and the lead. He looked nervous only once, and that was in the final round, with a bogey at No. 1. A birdie at the next calmed him, and four more for the 68 wrapped things up and had him thinking of returning to the PGA Tour, where he was just 19 when he first won his card.

"I was playing with all the best players in the world and I was trying too hard to keep up," he said. "Next time around, I will be better prepared."

SK Telecom Open
Jeju Island, South Korea
Winner: Bio Kim

There was more noise than Bio Kim cared to hear in the SK Telecom Open. In the third round, the news from up ahead wasn't very sweet to his ears. Hur In-hoi, who started six shots off the lead, made up all six in a hurry, starting with four birdies and an eagle on his way to a Pinx Golf Club course-record nine-under-par 63. Next, it was Park Sang-hyun in the fourth round. Said Kim: "I could hear a few roars up front, but I'm glad I had no idea what was going on. I would probably have tried to be a bit more aggressive — and that could have been dangerous."

But Kim, who led or shared the lead all the way, ignored the noise and posted his second straight OneAsia Tour victory, a three-stroke decision over Park on a card of 68-68-67-67–270, eight under. After missing the cut in his first outing, the Nanshan China Open, he was now two-for-three for 2012, winning both the GS Caltex Maekyung Open and the SK Telecom, and he shot all eight rounds in the 60s. But this one looked iffy for a while.

What Kim heard going on up ahead was Park tearing up the course with three birdies and an eagle in his first four holes. Park made the turn in 30, then eagled the 10th for a two-stroke lead, but bunkered his tee shot and bogeyed the par-three 17th. Behind him, Kim birdied the 14th, then salvaged an amazing birdie at the par-five 16th, hitting his third from a thick clump of grass to four feet. Park followed by bogeying the 18th, and Kim came along and parred and heard one final roar. It was for him.

Thailand Open
Nalornpathom, Thailand
Winner: Chris Wood

Chris Wood, the lanky, 6-foot-5 Englishman, had been waiting a long time for that first win, and just as he was about to take it, he had to wait again. A rainstorm swept in and halted play in the Thailand Open just as he was marching up the 17th. It was one of the longest hours of his life. But he got through it and picked up that breakthrough win by two strokes over Korea's Jang Dong-kyu.

"It's brilliant — I am really, really pleased," said Wood, playing in his first OneAsia Tour event. Wood, one of five European Tour regulars in the tournament, played Suwan Golf and Country Club in 67-64-67-67–265, 23 under par.

Wood, 24, first came to attention when he finished fifth as an amateur in the 2008 Open Championship. Then as a pro in the 2009 Open Championship, he came within a stroke of joining Tom Watson and Stewart Cink in the playoff. The closest he came to winning this season was a pair of top-three finishes on the European Tour. He escaped trouble at the final hole in the third round when his ball stopped short of the water. He saved his par to take the solo lead heading into the final round. "I will just try to play the same game again tomorrow," he said. But would he?

In fact, he did. He was four under through the sixth, then bogeyed the eighth. But he got the stroke back at the 11th with a birdie on a 30-foot putt, then got another on a 35-footer at the 15th.

"It's hard winning," Wood said. "I always felt that once I got one win, it would give me the confidence to go on and win more."

Charity High1 Resort Open
Gohan, South Korea
Winner: Matthew Griffin

Just four years earlier, Matthew Griffin was Australia's top amateur and ranked No. 3 in the world. He knew golf too well to expect pro rewards to come easy. Even so, it was a great relief when he scored his first big victory, taking the Charity High1 Resort Open.

"This is what I've worked for all my life, so it is absolutely thrilling to finally get there," said Griffin, 29, holding off all comers with his 67-70-69-72—278 performance, nine under par.

First came the early encouragement, a bogey-free 67 in the first round that left him one behind the leader, Jason Kang. "The game has been coming along very nicely," he said. "Hopefully I'll get a win soon." The second round perked him up even more. His 70 included his only bogey in 36 holes, and tied him at 137 with Korea's Lee Jun-seok. Lee, a professional for just three years, was encouraged by making the cut. "Making the field was a result — playing the weekend is a bonus," Lee said.

Griffin proved his golf maturity in the third round, coming through rain and buffeting winds to shoot a 69 and take a two-shot lead. "It was a tough day for scoring," Griffin said. "I had to hit a few different clubs off the tees because of the wind."

He had to prove himself one more time. There was the pressure of the final round complicated by the pressure of favorite native sons. He held up. His par 72 was good for a one-stroke win over Kang Kyung-nam (68) and Park Sang-hyun (71).

"It gives me a lot of security," said Griffin, "and it also repays the faith that my supporters and sponsors have shown over the years."

Nanshan China Masters
Nanshan, China
Winner: Liang Wen-chong

The Nanshan China Masters meant different things to different golfers.

To Liang Wen-chong, the winner, it was quite exciting, though he could have done with a tad less excitement than a five-hole playoff. "I have never been involved in something like this," Liang said. "Thanks to Y.E. for making it so exciting."

It was anything but exciting to Y.E. Yang. He was the one who lost. "I'm a bit disappointed," Yang said. And needing a rest. "It was very tiring to have to play five extra holes," he said.

For South Africa's Louis Oosthuizen, the 2010 Open Championship winner and playoff runner-up in the Masters back in April, it was a wasted chance. "It's a bit frustrating when I think of the missed opportunities," he said. He was speaking of his 71-72 start on the par-71 Nanshan International. He finished stronger, 69-67, but only enough to tie for fourth.

Liang himself nearly wasted a big opportunity. He led or shared the lead through the first three rounds on 68-67-68, but in the final round an opening bogey and a double bogey out of a hazard at No. 7 cost him a 73. Yang birdied twice on the first nine and shot 69 to tie Liang at 276. Australia's Aaron Townsend shared the lead with them through the turn and took the lead with a birdie at the 11th, but bogeyed two of the last five holes, shot 72 and missed the playoff by a stroke.

That sent Liang and Yang to the 18th for a playoff. They played it five times. On the fifth trip, Liang holed a 12-foot birdie putt for the win. The key was falling behind at the 10th. "I actually felt more relaxed," Liang said. "I played the back nine better."

Kolon Korea Open
Cheonan, South Korea
Winner: Kim Dae-sub

All golfers need to get away from the game for a while, but a two-year hitch in the military might not quite be everyone's idea of getting away. That, however, was it for former South Korean teenage whiz Kim Dae-sub. He had to do a mandatory 20 months in the South Korean military, and although he practiced during that span, he had to go without tournament golf. And just two months after his discharge, he found enough game to win the Kolon Korea Open on the OneAsia Tour in October.

It was, by the way, his third Korea Open. He won the first two as an amateur — at age 16 in 1998, and again in 2001, after which he turned professional. He didn't live up to his promise as a pro, except to win six times on the domestic Korean Tour, which made this win so satisfying.

"I always dreamed I would win the Korea Open as a professional, but I didn't think it would happen this year," he said. "This is the happiest day of my life."

Kim Dae-sub was dogged in his move up the leaderboard. Shooting Woo Jeong Hills Country Club in 72-68-70-69, he trailed Kang Kyung-nam by four in the first round, then by three, and when Kang blew to a 77 in the third round, he tied Kim Dae-hyun (66) at 210.

Dae-sub broke the tie with an 18-foot birdie putt at No. 2 against Dae-hyun's three-putt bogey, and took control from there to win by two at five-under 279.

"I am just trying to play steady and not expect too much," said Dae-sub, and for a guy who had just come back from a two-year break, he did all right.

Dongfeng Nissan Cup
Shenzhen, China
Winner: Asia-Pacific

Next up from the Wide World of Whiz Kids — Chinese amateur Guan Tianlang, all of 14 and making his debut on the global stage amidst the professionals in the second Dongfeng Nissan Cup at the CTS Tycoon Club.

Playing for Team China against Asia-Pacific in the Ryder Cup-style competition would be one more big entry for his resume when he played in the 2013 Masters as the youngest ever. Guan earned the berth in November by winning the Asia-Pacific Amateur, co-sponsored by Augusta National Golf Club and the R&A.

"He plays so well that it's easy to forget how young he is," said New Zealand's Mark Brown, after beating the kid, 2 and 1, as Asia-Pacific came storming from behind in singles to beat China, 14½-9½.

China led in better-ball, 4-2. Guan was teamed with China's No. 1, Liang Wen-chong, in a 2-and-1 loss to Australia's Andre Stolz and Scott Laycock. Guan (1-2) got his point in the alternate-shot format, when he and Liang beat Japan's Yosuke Tsukada and Soushi Tajima, 2 and 1 The teams tied, 3-3, leaving China with a 7-5 lead going into the singles.

There, Asia-Pacific rolled, 9½-2½, to retain the trophy they won in the inaugural in 2011.

The Chinese team would pretty much be the one to represent the country when golf returns to the Olympic Games at Rio de Janeiro in 2016. They'll probably be led by Guan Tianlang. By then, he would be all of 18 or so.

Emirates Australian Open
Sydney, New South Wales
Winner: Peter Senior

See Australasian Tour.

Australian PGA Championship
Coolum, Queensland
Winner: Daniel Popovic

See Australasian Tour.

Japan Tour

Token Homemate Cup
Kuwana, Mie
Winner: Brendan Jones

Brendan Jones called it "a dream start," which made it a bit of a nightmare for the other contenders for the season-opening Token Homemate Cup on the 2012 Japan Tour. By far Australia's most successful campaigner in Japan in recent years, Jones thundered from behind in Sunday's final round with a nine-under-par 62 that gave him a two-stroke victory. He was 15 under par at 269 in posting his 11th victory in his decade on the Japan Tour.

The turn of events on the last day was particularly shocking for Shingo Katayama, the tour's spotlight player for many years before the emergence of Ryo Ishikawa. Winless since the 2008 season, Katayama carried a one-stroke lead into the final round at Token Tado Country Club at Nagoya. His third-round 65 for 204 put him a shot in front of Mamo Osanai, three ahead of Jones and others. Forgotten then was Tatsunori Nukaga, the leader the first two days with rounds of 64 and 69 before plunging from contention with a 77 Saturday.

Grouped with Ishikawa and Satoshi Tomiyama, the 37-year-old Jones made three front-nine birdies Sunday, then really caught fire on the back side, reeling off six more birdies, four in a row starting at the 14th hole, where he went in front to stay. "I feel unbelievable," said the Aussie, who had played in just one previous tournament since the first of the year.

Ryuichi Oda, with 65–271, took second, a stroke ahead of Osanai (67) and two in front of Katayama (69), Tomiyama (67) and Hideto Tanihara (65). Ishikawa, without a title since 2010, dropped into a tie for 10th with 71–277.

Tsuruya Open
Kawanishi, Hyogo
Winner: Hiroyuki Fujita

Age doesn't seem to be slowing Hiroyuki Fujita down. Now 42 years old, Fujita had been a top-10 finisher in five of his previous seven starts when he teed it up in the Tsuruya Open, which two years earlier had been one of his previous 11 victories on the Japan Tour. He made it an even dozen on April 22 when he rolled to a four-stroke triumph, 15 under par at 269.

Though a contender all week at Yamanohara Golf Club near Osaka, Fujita didn't take the lead and command of the competition until the final round. He opened with a three-under-par 68, tied for eighth place, as long-time Japanese star Shingo Katayama came up with his best round in recent seasons — 62 — in quest of his first win on the tour since 2008.

It was downhill after that for Katayama as Ryuichi Oda took first place with 66-67–133, a shot ahead of Fujita and Hwang Jung-gon (68-66s).

The third round belonged to American Han Lee, who tacked a 63 onto his 67-69 start to head Fujita (68) by three and five others by four, but his lead disappeared early on Sunday. The two-time Canadian Amateur champion lost four strokes on the first five holes, eventually shooting 78, and Fujita zipped past him en route to 67 and the four-shot win over 20-year-old South Korean rookie Lee Kyoung-hoon, playing in just his second tournament in Japan.

The Crowns
Togo, Aichi
Winner: I.J. Jang

When I.J. Jang arrived for his first shot at the Japan Tour in 2006, he came with high promise as the leading money winner on the 2005 Korean Tour. He quickly lived up to expectations when he won the Mitsubishi Diamond Cup tournament by three strokes early that season. Who would have thought then that it would be seven years before Jang won again in the Land of the Rising Sun?

The 39-year-old South Korean parlayed a hot weekend display of shot-making into a two-stroke victory in the venerable Crowns tournament, the third stop on the tour. Jang produced a pair of 66s Saturday and Sunday on the Wago course of Nagoya Golf Club for an eight-under total of 272, two in front of Australia's Steven Conran and Yoshikazu Haku, the third-round co-leaders.

Those two were in it from the opening bell. They started with 66s, a shot behind leader Kenichi Kuboya, the veteran winner who shot 65. Conran, a frequent contender over the years whose only victory in Japan came in 2004, matched that 65 Friday to jump four strokes in front as Kuboya put up a 70 and Haku a 71. Jang had opening rounds of 71-69 to remain in the picture. He moved within two with the first 66 when Conran could only manage a 73 Saturday but remained in a first-place tie with Haku, who shot 67.

Jang ran off five birdies and took a single bogey Sunday in nailing down the victory, commenting afterward: "Even though I've had chances to win every year, I'd forgotten what it feels like to actually do it."

Japan PGA Championship
Tochigi
Winner: Toru Taniguchi

Perhaps at times overlooked when Japan's greatest players are discussed, Toru Taniguchi continues, at age 44, to add to his fine reputation and record. Taniguchi enhanced both in early May when he went wire to wire and landed his fourth major title on the Japan Tour, scoring a one-stroke victory in the Japan PGA Championship. It was his second PGA title (2010) and 18th win on the circuit.

The Japanese veteran, who stands fifth on the all-time Japan Tour money list, faltered only once on his way to the win. He launched the title run with a seven-under-par 65 in the opening round at Karasuyama Country Club, a shot ahead of unknown Juvic Pagusan, who eventually finished third from last in the field.

Taniguchi followed with 70 the next day that gave him a three-shot lead over Keiichiro Fukabori (72-66) but still left him dissatisfied because of "so many silly errors" — four bogeys to go with six birdies, including four on the par-fives. Scoring soared so high on a windswept Saturday that, despite a 76, Taniguchi retained a two-stroke lead. Koumei Oda shot 70, the day's low round, and moved into a tie for second with I.J. Jang, the winner of the previous week's Crowns (71). Fukabori matched Taniguchi's 76 and stayed three back with Hideto Tanihara.

Taniguchi nursed his lead Sunday to the final hole, where, needing a par for the victory, he two-putted the double-decker green from 50 feet for 73–284 to edge Fukabori, who shot 71 for 285. He was the only other player to break par over the distance.

Totoumi Hamamatsu Open
Hamamatsu, Shizuoka
Winner: Jay Choi

American Jay Choi spoiled Yoshinori Fujimoto's first real bid to pick off a victory in his rookie season. Fujimoto, the most recent high-caliber product from golf-reputed Tohoku Fukushi University, led the field in the Totoumi Hamamatsu Open for three days, but fell a stroke short of victory when Choi closed with a seven-under-par 65 and edged him by a lone shot.

Choi, the first American to win on the Japan circuit since Tiger Woods's victory in the 2005 Dunlop Phoenix, moved steadily up the standings after his opening 68 only placed him in a tie for 28th place. The co-leaders that first day at 64 went different directions the rest of the week. Fujimoto took sole possession of the lead with 70–134 Friday as overall scoring completely turned around. Jang Dong-kyu, the other 64-shooter Thursday, collapsed Friday and missed the cut with an 82. Choi's 71–139 jumped him into a tie for eighth, as Aussie Brendan Jones (65-71), the Token Homemate winner, and Hiroshi Iwata (66-70) settled into second place.

Fujimoto retained his two-stroke margin with 68–202 Saturday with veteran winner Hideto Tanihara taking over the runner-up position with 66–204. The American reached a third-place tie with South Korean S.K. Ho (67) with his 68, but they trailed by five shots at 207.

As Choi applied the pressure with his seven-birdie finish, Fujimoto succumbed to the pressure in the stretch. He bogeyed two of the last four holes, shot 71 and fell that one stroke short as Choi become the tour's initial first-time winner of 2012.

Diamond Cup
Noda, Chiba
Winner: Hiroyuki Fujita

Perhaps it was appropriate that Hiroyuki Fujita became the first double winner in 2012 when he nailed down a three-stroke victory in the Diamond Cup tournament in Chiba. Although he seems to have hovered just under the radar picking up the circuit's top stars, Fujita clearly has been the most consistent among all of Japan's leading players for more than a decade.

Fujita was 31 before he won his first tour event in 2001. He won 12 times after that, has never finished lower than 17th on the money list, was ninth or better every season since 2007, and finished second to K.T. Kim in 2010. He entered the 2012 campaign sixth on the all-time money list with earnings of more than a billion yen.

At the Diamond Cup, Fujita charged into the lead on the second day and never relinquished first place, even with a rather erratic final round. He started the week in a second-place tie with Kim at 66, two behind Jay Choi, who was still riding the momentum of his victory the previous Sunday in the Totoumi Hamamatsu Open, then jumped three strokes in front of the American when he followed with 65–131 to Choi's 70–134. Fujita took the three-shot margin into the final round with 70–201, then over Takashi Kanemoto.

On the adventurous Sunday, Fujita managed only a 73 for the winning, 14-under-par 274, absorbing two double bogeys and a pair of bogeys to go with five birdies. But he had no serious challengers, and Thailand's little-known Kiradech Aphibarnrat slipped into second place with 72–277.

Japan Tour Championship
Kasama, Ibaraki
Winner: Yoshinori Fujimoto

Yoshinori Fujimoto chose a fancier stage to land his first victory on the Japan Tour. Disappointed by a poor finish two weeks earlier in the Totoumi Hamamatsu tournament that cost him that initial title, the 22-year-old rookie made the major Japan Tour Championship win No. 1 and scooped up the Citibank Cup in the process. With two other top-10s among his five starts, Fujimoto zoomed into second place on the money list.

Unlike his performance in the Totoumi Hamamatsu when he rode the lead all the way until two bogeys derailed him in the stretch, Fujimoto made two early birdies in the final round and steadily rolled to a three-under-par 68 and the two-stroke victory. He joined Jay Choi, who beat him in the Totoumi Hamamatsu, as the year's initial two first-time winners. He was the first rookie in Japan Tour history to make a major his first victory.

The number was 64 the first two days. Masanori Kobayashi shot it Thursday to lead by two over Masahiro Kawamura and Brendan Jones, the Token Homemate winner in April. Then, on Friday, K.T. Kim, the 2010 leading money winner, matched that score for 134 and a share of the lead with Kim Do-hoon (67-67) as Kobayashi came unglued with a 79. Fujimoto moved into a tie for fourth with a pair of 68s, then seized the lead for good with 67–203 in the third round.

Masamichi Uehira, who shared second place Saturday with Kawamura, birdied two of the last three holes to snare second place with 69–273.

Gateway to the Open Mizuno Open
Kasaoka, Okayama
Winner: Brad Kennedy

Perhaps as a 37-year-old rookie on the 2011 Japan Tour, Brad Kennedy was tuning up for things to come when he made an impressive fifth-place finish in the Gateway to the Open Mizuno Open. In any event, when he returned to Kasaoka in 2012, he went four positions better and walked off with an impressive three-stroke victory, his first in Japan and a companion piece on his record for his win in the New Zealand Open in 2011. Again, because the Mizuno Open is the Japan qualifier for the Open Championship in Britain, he again earned a spot at Royal Lytham in July, along with other high finishers Toshinori Muto, Koumei Oda and Hiroyuki Fujita.

Victory seemed highly unlikely for Kennedy when, coming off two straight missed-cuts, he started the week in 40th place with a par 72. But when he followed with rounds of 68 and 65, Kennedy climbed into a first-place tie with Yui Ueda, both at 205, 11 under par after 54 holes. They had a shot on Kim Hyung-sung, two on four others, including Yoshinori Fujimoto, the previous week's winner.

Ueda, whose only victory came in the 2007 Token Homemate Cup, had led or shared the lead from the start with 67-68-70 rounds. But he fell behind early Sunday as Kennedy came out hot with birdies at the first two holes and never let up. Kennedy turned in 32, birdied the next two holes, bogeyed the par-three 12th, and parred in around a final birdie at the 15th for 66–271, three in front of Muto and Toru Taniguchi, who was already qualified for the Open Championship. Ueda's 72 dropped him into a 10-way tie for fifth.

Nagashima Shigeo Invitational
Chitose, Hokkaido
Winner: Lee Kyoung-hoon

It seemed as if it was just a matter of time before Lee Kyoung-hoon, South Korea's latest male rookie standout, would notch his first victory on the Japan Tour. It turned out to be just a few months as the rookie capped his strong start on the circuit with a two-stroke victory in early July in the Nagashima Shigeo Invitational Sega Sammy Cup in Hokkaido.

Lee had finished in a second-place group in the Tsuruya Open, the season's second event, and followed with three other top-10s in his next six starts before his wire-to-wire victory at the North Country Golf Club, which jumped him in second place on the money list, close behind leader Hiroyuki Fujita.

The 20-year-old jumped off with 65 Thursday, a shot in front of fellow Korean Cho Min-gyu, then shared the 36-hole lead when Yasuharu Imano matched the 65 for 134, 10 under par. Despite missing five short birdie putts, Lee remained on top after 54 holes, tied then with another Korean, Kim Hyung-sung at 204, Lee putting up a four-birdie, two-bogey 70 as Kim shot 68 for his 204.

The winner was on top of his game Sunday, polishing off the triumph with birdies on the last two holes for 65–269 and the two-shot win over playing partner Kim. Ryo Ishikawa, still looking for his first 2012 victory, finished with 66, in a quartet of players four strokes behind Lee.

Sun Chlorella Classic
Otaru, Hokkaido
Winner: Brendan Jones

Experienced winning trumped decades of frustration at the Sun Chlorella Classic. For longer than he cared to remember, 42-year-old Yoshinobu Tsukada had been searching without success for a victory on the Japan Tour. He was on the verge of it at Otaru Country Club, taking a one-stroke lead into the final round, but Australian Brendan Jones, with 11 Japan Tour victories under his belt, snuffed out his hopes with a steady two-under-par 70 that gave him a two-stroke victory over Tsukada (73), South Korean Lee Seong-ho and 20-year-old amateur Hideki Matsuyama.

Jones, who won the season-opening Token Homemate Cup, was just the second multiple winner of 2012, the other being Hiroyuki Fujita, whom he supplanted atop the money list with his second Sun Chlorella victory, nine seasons after the first one.

Tsukada was never out of the lead the first three days, putting together rounds of 67-68-67. He shared first place on Thursday with Chinese newcomer Wu Ashun and Friday with Jones (69-66) and Lee Kyoung-hoon (70-65), before holding the top spot alone Saturday with the 202, one in front of Jones and Thailand's Kiradech Aphibarnrat.

The lead changed hands twice Sunday before Jones moved in front to stay on the back nine.

Kansai Open
Sakai, Osaka
Winner: Toshinori Muto

Although it had the smallest purse of the season (¥60,000,000), the Kansai Open, long an overlooked tournament during the season, drew a respectable field in mid-August as it came after a three-week break on the somewhat-depleted schedule. Toshinori Muto made the most of the opportunity when he rolled to a wire-to-wire victory at Izumigaoka Country Club at Osaka.

The 34-year-old Muto, whose fourth career victory came in the high-profile Dunlop Phoenix the previous November, lashed together four consecutive rounds in the 60s, starting with a first-round 64 that set him a stroke in front of Norio Shinozaki and Shunsuke Sonoda. He widened his margin to two Friday with 65–129, as Sonoda shot 66–131 and Shinozaki 68–133. South Korea's Kim Hyung-sung, Muto's eventual major threat, was three back at 132.

Muto's third-round 68–197 maintained his two-shot edge, then over Shinozaki (66) and Yuta Ikeda, who came up with a 62, the week's lowest round. The victory didn't come without considerable travail Sunday. Muto's lead slipped away when he bogeyed the 13th, 14th and 15th holes to drop into a tie with Kim, playing in the group ahead of him. Muto rallied, though, with a game par at the 16th and he birdied the 18th for 266, 18 under par, nipping Kim (67) by a stroke.

Vana H Cup KBC Augusta
Shima, Fukuoka
Winner: Kim Hyung-sung

Kim Hyung-sung followed suit at the Vana H Cup KBC Augusta tournament. Fellow South Korean Bae Sang-moon, whose win in the KBC Augusta was his first in Japan and spurted him toward the tour's money title, was playing The Barclays in the United States and couldn't defend, so Kim duplicated Bae's feat, picking up his initial win on the Japan Tour at Keya Golf Club at Shima, eking out a one-stroke victory over Akio Sadakata.

The triumph wiped out a long period of frustration for Kim — three winless seasons in Japan following three victories on the Korean Tour and second-place finishes in two of the previous three events.

The week started uneventfully at Keya for Kim, whose opening 69 left him in a 24th-place tie, six strokes behind leader Yoshinori Fujimoto, the Tour Championship winner, who shot a nine-under-par 63. When the 32-year-old Kim came back with 64–133 and Fujimoto shot 70 in the second round, the South Korean found himself in a third-place tie with him, two behind new leader Kurt Barnes of Australia.

Kim's 68 Saturday for 201 jumped him into the lead, a stroke ahead of Sadakata, as Barnes slipped to 73–204 and a third-place tie with Kazuhiro Yamashita. An ebb-and-flow of birdies left Kim and Sadakata even through 14 holes Sunday before the Japanese pro slipped with a bogey at the 15th. They then matched pars to the finish.

Fujisankei Classic
Fujikawaguchiko, Yamanashi
Winner: K.T. Kim

Things had not gone particularly well in 2012 for South Korean star K.T. Kim after his No. 1 finish on the Japan Tour two years earlier and his strong performances in international events, including the 2011 Presidents Cup. Kim had a glimmer of hope going into the Fujisankei Classic, though, off his fifth-place finish in the Kansai Open following a pair of bottom-of-the-standings finishes and two missed cuts in the previous four events.

Kim moved steadily up the ladder at Fujizakura Country Club, birdied three of the last five holes, including the 18th, for 68–276 to edge Yuta Ikeda, already finished with 67–277. It was Kim's fifth victory in Japan and first since winning the Shigeo Nagashima Invitational in mid-2011. It came on his 26th birthday, a present to himself.

His advance up the standings went like this: 70 and tie for 15th, five behind first-round leader Katsumasa Miyamoto; 70–140 and tie for sixth, three behind co-leaders Prayad Marksaeng (68-69) and Kim Hyung-sung (71-66); 68–208 and tie for fourth, three behind Prayad (68) going into Sunday.

The Thailand pro, a three-time winner on the tour in 2008, slipped to 73 Sunday and dropped into a third-place tie at 278 with Hiroyuki Fujita, who stood second on the money list.

Toshin Golf Tournament
Inabe, Mie
Winner: Wu Ashun

It was a first in more ways than one. When China's Wu Ashun won a four-hole playoff in the weather-plagued Toshin Golf Tournament, it was his and his country's first victory on the Japan Tour. And it ended in a one-of-a-kind way in virtual darkness at the Ryosen Golf Club. Officials kept shortening the par-five 18th hole as light faded over the playoff until Wu sank a six-foot birdie putt the fourth time around to defeat high-ranking Yuta Ikeda, who finished second the week before in the Fujisankei Classic.

The two players had teed off in the final round in a four-way tie for second place, two shots behind Masamichi Uehira, a former star on the developmental Japan Challenge Tour, who posted rounds of 66-63–129 on the heels of I.J. Jang's opening 63. Wu and Ikeda had identical rounds of 65-66–131 to deadlock K.T. Kim (66-65) and Ryu Hyun-woo (64-67).

When play resumed after horrid weather forced cancellation of the Saturday round and held up action for more than two hours Sunday, Wu and Ikeda matched birdies and bypassed Uehira. Then Ikeda blinked with a double bogey on the 14th hole, but he birdied the 18th for a matching 67–198 with the 27-year-old Chinese pro to force the playoff.

Said Wu: "I've been in playoffs (in China) when it was dark, but never where they changed the distance like today."

ANA Open
Kitahiroshima, Hokkaido
Winner: Hiroyuki Fujita

What was further triumph for one player was continued frustration for another when the ANA Open ended as the Japan Tour entered its stretch run. Hiroyuki Fujita raced from an 18th-place position at the halfway point to a one-stroke victory that enhanced his position as the money leader, while Yuta Ikeda was finishing in second place for a third time in a row, the first time that had happened on the tour since 1997.

It was a remarkable finish on the Wattsu course of Sapporo Golf Club. Fujita started the final round two shots behind South Korea's Kim Hyung-sung, the KBC Augusta winner, then shot a 68 for a 16-under-par 272 and expected to be in a playoff. Instead, Ikeda, Kim and Australian Kurt Barnes all bogeyed the last hole, China's charging Liang Wen-chong failed to birdie the 18th after posting birdies on the two previous holes, and Fujita had his third win of the season and 14th of his career in Japan. He supplanted the idle Brendan Jones atop the money list in his bid for his first season title.

For Ikeda, the four-way finish with Liang, Barnes and Kim at 273 was particularly galling after his playoff loss the previous week in the Toshin Tournament and one-shot loss in the Fujisankei. The early-round leaders — Tetsuji Hirasuka (65) and Kim Do-hoon (70-64–134) — were out of the picture over the weekend.

Asia-Pacific Panasonic Open
Miki, Hyogo
Winner: Masanori Kobayashi

How would one gauge the chances of Masanori Kobayashi winning the strong-field Asia-Pacific Panasonic Open? He teed it up at Higashi Hirono Golf Club on the heels of four consecutive missed cuts, seven in all in 2012 in Japan, and no finish higher than 12th since early May. Or, after he started with a 74, tied for 110th place 12 strokes behind leader Yuta Ikeda in the joint Japan and Asian Tours event?

Kobayashi, a 36-year-old veteran who scored the only victory of his long career in 2011 at the Hamamatsu Open, overcame those negatives in steps up the standings but was still six strokes and in 15th place behind leader Masamichi Uehira (66-68-65–199) going to the final 18 holes. Teeing off nearly an hour before the leaders, Kobayashi burned up the front nine with an eagle and five birdies for an outgoing 28, tacked three more birdies onto a lone bogey coming home and went to the clubhouse with his nine-under-par 62–267 to await the outcome.

Koumei Oda, a five-time winner on the tour, had the best shot at him among the contenders, but he bogeyed the 17th hole and failed to birdie the 18th to finish lone second with 67–268. Uehira shot 71–270 to take third. Hiroyuki Fujita, seeking his second straight and fourth 2012 win, led after two rounds with 64-68–132, but dropped to 13th place at the end.

Coca-Cola Tokai Classic
Miyoshi, Aichi
Winner: Ryu Hyun-woo

The wait continued for Shingo Katayama after the Coca-Cola Tokai Classic, compliments of a 31-year-old rookie from South Korea named Ryu Hyun-woo. Katayama, the toast of the Japan Tour for years, seemingly hit a wall with his game after capturing his fifth money title and scoring his 24th, 25th and 26th circuit victories in 2008.

Only occasionally a contender in the ensuing seasons, the colorful 39-year-old appeared to have No. 27 finally in hand when he raced from five strokes back into the clubhouse lead with a closing 66–282 at Miyoshi Country Club and leader Ryu tripled-bogeyed his 70th hole. But the South Korean, winless in Japan, parred in for 71 and a matching 282, then won the playoff when Katayama bogeyed to his par on the first extra hole.

The lead changed hands in each of the first three rounds in the late September tournament in Aichi Prefecture. Tadahiro Takayama had it first with 68, then Masahiro Kawamura (70-70) and Park Eun-shin (72-68) took over in the second round. Ryu, four strokes behind at the midpoint, jumped in front Saturday with 67–211, as Katayama drifted into a 12th-place tie with a 73 and 216 before leap-frogging in front with the 66 and the wait and the subsequent fruitless playoff.

Canon Open
Yokohama, Kanagawa
Winner: Yuta Ikeda

Yuta Ikeda's decisive victory in the Canon Open the first week of October was a landmark win in more ways than one for him. It brought him his 10th title less than a month after he had to settle for a third straight second-place finish and, with it, an epic achievement. At 26 years, nine months, Ikeda became the youngest player in recorded tour history to reach that win total, surpassing the great Masashi (Jumbo) Ozaki, who had nine wins by the time he turned 27 on his way to the 94 he put on his remarkable record.

Ikeda never trailed at Yokohama's Totsuka Country Club as he won the Canon Open for the second time in four seasons and moved up to No. 2 on the money list behind Hiroyuki Fujita. Ikeda's 17-under-par 271 was three strokes better than Taichi Teshima and South Korean Hwang Jung-gon.

Ikeda started with a six-under-par 66, tied for the lead with little-known Yuki Sato, then outdistanced the field the rest of the way. His second-round 68–134 moved him three strokes in front of Hwang, Aussie Brad Kennedy and veteran Shigeki Maruyama, all with 68-69 cards, and Masamichi Uehira (69-68), as Sato faded with 76. Another 68 the third day gave Ikeda a two-stroke cushion over Hwang (67), Teshima (65) and Ryo Ishikawa (66) which he finessed to victory Sunday with a 69, producing an eagle, three birdies and two bogeys as Hwang and Teshima finished with 70s.

Japan Open
Naha, Okinawa
Winner: Kenichi Kuboya

Kenichi Kuboya's victory in the battle for survival that was the 2012 Japan Open came unexpectedly in more ways than one. For one thing, the 40-year-old arrived in Okinawa in a terrible slump, having made just one cut in his previous 10 starts and having won money in just six 2012 tournaments.

For another, when he checked in with a one-under-par 70, the lowest score anybody shot Sunday, and posted an eight-*over*-par 292, the best score in the house, he started packing for departure. After all, Juvic Pagunsan was two strokes better than that through 16 holes. But the 34-year-old Filipino ex-caddie fell victim to a double bogey at the 17th and a bogey at the 18th for 75, and his 293 total cost him a playoff shot.

The surprise victory was Kuboya's career sixth and a second major title to go with his 2002 Japan PGA Championship. In a way, the Naha Golf Club course and the blustery weather were the real winners that mid-October weekend. A lone 69 by Okinawan Yusaku Miyazato was the lowest score all week. It was tough going from the beginning as five players led with one-over 72s Thursday. Veteran Tetsuji Hiratsuka, also 40, a six-time winner in Japan with several other victories elsewhere in Asia, moved into a three-stroke lead the second day with 73-70—143 and remained two ahead of Pagunsan (76-72-70) and Koumei Oda (73-73-72) after 54 holes with his 73—218.

When Hiratsuka faltered Sunday, Pagunsan, trying to become the first Filipino winner of the championship since the revered Ben Arda landed the title in 1973, slipped in front and had the victory beckoning before the fatal final holes. The win was a switch for Kuboya, who lost the 2011 Open in a playoff to Sang-Moon Bae.

Bridgestone Open
Chiba
Winner: Toru Taniguchi

Talk about contrasts!

Back in May, Toru Taniguchi dominated the Japan PGA Championship, leading from wire to wire to score his 18th career victory. Five months later when he was defending a title that he won by five shots in 2011, Taniguchi picked up No. 19 the hard way, chipping in on the final hole for an eagle that gave him a one-stroke victory in the Bridgestone Open.

His third Bridgestone win (2004, too) wasn't assured, though, until Hiroyuki Fujita, the leading money winner and third-round co-leader, failed to birdie the 18th minutes later. The 44-year-old Taniguchi shot 66 for a 12-under-par 272 and the ¥30-million purse moved him into second place on the money list behind Fujita. The two stand fourth and fifth among the circuit's career money winners.

For three rounds, Fujita seemed headed for his fourth win of the season, particularly after he fired a 64 to take a two-stroke lead over Taniguchi the first day. Even though he slipped to 72 Friday, he remained in a three-way tie for the lead with Yusaku Miyazato (70-66) and Sushi Ishigaki (68-68), a shot ahead of Taniguchi (71). Things were still tight after 54 holes with Fujita (69) and Lee Dong-hwan (67) in front at 205, just a stroke in front of Taniguchi (69), Ishigaki (70) and Ryuichi Oda, whose 65 was the best of the day.

Taniguchi spurted two in front with four birdies on the front nine Sunday, faltered with bogeys at the 13th and 14th, but birdied the 16th before the deciding eagle on the final hole.

Mynavi ABC Championship
Kato, Hyogo
Winner: Han Lee

Han Lee made better use of his second 63 of the 2012 Japan Tour season. The first one came in the third round of year's second tournament, but he threw away a three-shot lead in the Tsuruya Open the next day with a closing 78. The 35-year-old American did little over the next six months, a tie for sixth in the Kansai Open his only top-10, before he came up with another 63 in the Mynavi ABC Championship. This time it happened in the final round and turned a five-stroke deficit into a one-stroke victory, his first in five years in Japan.

Lee, whose most impressive prior golf achievements were successive victories in the Canadian Amateur that preceded seasons on the U.S. Nationwide and Asian Tours, finished a shot ahead of Katsumasa Miyamoto with his 17-under-par 271 and two in front of K.T. Kim, 2010's leading money winner and the third-round leader. Kim, who already had the 2012 Fujisankei title under his belt, had seized a three-stroke lead from Kazuhiro Yamashita (65) the second day with 67-65–132 and retained it Saturday, a stroke ahead of Miyamoto, when he followed with 71–203.

With rounds of 67-71-70, Lee trailed him by five when he teed off a half hour before the leaders Sunday. His round was flawless. Four times he paired birdies and he finished off the nine-under-par round with his fourth birdie in a row on the par-five 18th, then awaited the outcome. Miyamoto closed with 68 to edge Kim (70) and Kaname Yokoo (68) by a stroke for second place. Yokoo was five under par on his final four holes. Lee was the seventh first-time winner of the season.

Mitsui Sumitomo Visa Taiheiyo Masters
Gotemba, Shizuoka
Winner: Ryo Ishikawa

Things had not gone well by his standards for Ryo Ishikawa on the Japan Tour in 2012. The young Japanese golfing superstar had done nothing in international major events since the Presidents Cup in 2011 and had missed three cuts and had only five top-10 finishes in his 15 starts in Japan when he signed in at the Mitsui Sumitomo Visa Taiheiyo Masters in November.

Now 21 but already five years beyond his astonishing victory in the 2007 Munsingwear Open as a 15-year-old high schooler, Ishikawa drew confidence from an improving game and being back on the Taiheiyo Club's Gotemba course, where he had scored his ninth and most recent victory in 2010. He slipped into the lead for the first time all season in the third round and took home his 10th title, closing with 68 for a 15-under-par 273 and a one-stroke victory over Michio Matsumura, the first-round leader (65).

Han Lee, the Korean-born American, gunned for two straight victories in the early rounds. The 35-year-old, who won the Mynavi ABC Championship two weeks earlier, replaced Matsumura in first place Friday, his 69-65 rounds producing a two-stroke lead over Ishikawa, Matsumura and New Zealand's David Smail.

The darling of the galleries took over Saturday. Ishikawa shot his second straight 69 and inched a shot in front of Matsumura and Lee, then tucked away the win Sunday with the 68, but not without a scare in the rain at the end. After sailing through the first 12 holes, he absorbed bogeys at the 13th, 16th and 17th holes, enabling Matsumura to catch him with birdies at the last two holes before Ishikawa birdied the par-five 18th for the win. Hideki Matsuyama, the 20-year-old amateur sensation who won the Taiheiyo Masters in 2011, finished in a tie for fourth with Lee.

Another record fell to Ishikawa. He became the youngest player with 10 wins on his record in Japan Tour history.

Dunlop Phoenix
Miyazaki
Winner: Luke Donald

A trend was revived in 2012 when Luke Donald ran away with the Dunlop Phoenix. Visitors from overseas had carted away the tournament title 30 times in its 40-year history, but two of the victories by Japan Tour regulars had come the previous two seasons.

Englishman Donald, the No. 1-ranked international player of 2011, made sure it didn't happen three years in a row with a crushing, wire-to-wire victory, his third of the season on a third different tour. The five-stroke win, along with victories in America (PGA Tour's Transition) and his homeland (BMW PGA Championship), elevated him to No. 2 in the World Ranking.

The dominant performance in the week preceding his near-miss showing in the European Tour's Race to Dubai finale went this way:

First round: A six-under-par 65 despite two bogeys, tied for the lead with Australian Brendan Jones, a two-time winner during the Japan Tour season, and veteran Hideto Tanihara.

Second round: A flawless 64–129, four strokes in front of Japan's Shunsuke Sonoda and six ahead of Hiroyuki Fujita, the circuit's leading money winner.

Third round: A par 71–200, retaining the four-shot margin, then over Jones (67) and Sonoda (71).

Final round: A somewhat-erratic 68 for 268 and the five-stroke victory that included an eagle, three birdies and a pair of bogeys. Hideki Matsuyama, the brilliant young Japanese amateur, shot 67 to nail second place, a shot ahead of Koumei Oda, who shot 64, and two in front of Fujita and Jones.

Casio World Open
Geisei, Kochi
Winner: Hwang Jung-gon

For the second consecutive week, a tournament's first-round leader was the last man standing at the end of the week. Hwang Jung-gon emulated the wire-to-wire feat of Luke Donald in the Dunlop Phoenix and marched to victory in the Casio World Open, the second win on the Japan Tour for the 20-year-old, second-year player from South Korea.

Hwang did it with a finishing flash. Just a stroke ahead of non-winner Kunihiro Kamii playing the final hole, Hwang rolled in a short eagle putt for a three-under-par 69 and 19-under 269, a final three-shot margin at Kochi Kuroshio Country Club.

For two days. Hwang shared the lead. He and S.K. Ho opened with 65s, two in front of Kenichi Kuboya, Masamichi Uehira and Kamii. Yusaku Miyazato, 32, brother of international star Ai Miyazato, shot 67 Friday and joined Hwang (70) at the top at 135. They led K.T. Kim (69-67), 2010's leading money winner, and Kamii (69) by a stroke. Hwang finally had first place to himself after a bogey-free 68 in the third round, taking a one-stroke lead over Kamii and Kim, who also had 68s. Kamii, seeking his first tour win, challenged Hwang all day Sunday. They were tied after 15 holes before Hwang birdied the 16th and chalked up the eagle on the final green. Money leader Hiroyuki Fujita tied for ninth place, the ¥4,315,000 check leaving him just short of clinching his first No. 1 title.

Golf Nippon Series JT Cup
Tokyo
Winner: Hiroyuki Fujita

Hiroyuki Fujita left no doubt about who was the best player in Japan in 2012. Having already all but clinched his first money-winning title when he teed off in the season-ending Golf Nippon Series JT Cup, a tournament he had won the two previous Decembers, Fujita quickly left the field in his dust with a runaway, five-stroke victory at Tokyo's Yomiuri Country Club.

The 43-year-old Japan Tour veteran, the oldest No. 1 since Naomichi (Joe) Ozaki topped the list in 1999, blistered the course the first day with a nine-under-par 61 for a three-shot lead. No player got any closer than five shots the rest of the way as Fujita registered his fourth win of the season — nobody else won more than twice — and the 15th of his 16-year career. He was 10th or better in 13 of his 25 starts during his impressive season, missing the cut just twice all year, as he finished with winnings of ¥173,154,307, ¥72 million ahead of runner-up Toru Taniguchi, the money leader in 2002 and 2007.

Fujita followed the opening 61 with a 66–127, five ahead of Han Lee, the ABC winner, who shot 62. A 68–195 the third day widened Fujita's gap to six over a foursome of runners-up — Lee, Taniguchi, K.T. Kim and Ryo Ishikawa — and he breezed home with 67 for 262 to complete the tour's third straight wire-to-wire victory performance. Toshinori Muto shot his second 64 of the week Sunday and shared second place with Lee (66) in the limited-field tournament consisting of the year's winners and the top 25 on the money list.

11. Australasian Tour

As much as he might like to, Adam Scott will probably never forget the northern summer of 2012. But it will not be until later in his career that the lasting impact of the 141st Open Championship can be gauged. Either Royal Lytham & St. Annes will represent a vital stepping stone to winning his first major championship or the one he should never have let slip away. For the second year running Scott finished runner-up in a major and for the second time he was pipped by a South African. At Augusta National in 2011, Charl Schwartzel finished with four birdies in a row to beat Scott and compatriot Jason Day. At Lytham, Scott finished with four bogeys in a row to hand victory to Ernie Els.

Scott played golf of such sustained quality for the first 68 holes that he was four ahead with four to play. He led after an opening 64 and resumed his place at the top of the leaderboard with a round to go. When he dropped a shot from a bunker at the 15th and lipped out for a par at the 16th, it was no time to panic. But as the Australian walked down the 17th fairway, Els rolled in a birdie putt on the final green and suddenly the alarm bells were ringing. Scott missed the 17th green in the worst place possible and dropped another shot. On the last tee he was now only tied for the lead and drilled a three wood into a fairway bunker. By the time he got to the green, his putt to force a playoff seemed unlikely to fall. It did not.

Such a crushing defeat might have sent a lesser man into despair. But in his moment of torment, Scott had two things going for him. Firstly, his immediate reaction was as mature as it was classy. "It was a very sloppy finish," he admitted. "I wasn't out of position all week until I managed to get myself into trouble on the last few holes. Obviously, I'm disappointed. I let a great chance slip through my fingers. But I don't think I've ever played so well in a major championship, so that's a good thing moving forward. Today is just one of those days, that's why they call it golf."

Secondly, his tormentor, a long-time friend, reacted with both compassion and class. "I really feel for my buddy, Scottie," Els said. "I really do. I've been there before. I've blown majors before and I just hope he doesn't take it as hard as I did. Thankfully, he's young enough. He's 32 years old. He's got the next 10 years that he can win more than I've won. I've won four now; I think he can win more than that."

Such a public show of faith was exactly what Scott needed to hear, but it remains to be seen about Els's prediction. As well as overcoming any lingering demons, over the next few years Scott will also have to address his putting once more. It was turning to the broom-handle putter that ignited Scott's current run of form that saw him end 2012 as the fifth-best ranked player in the world. But the R&A and the USGA have indicated that anchoring extended putters will be outlawed in 2016, so the likes of Scott will have to adapt once more.

Before doing so, Scott got to return home and claim one of the titles that first inspired him to become a professional golfer. Scott won the Talisker Masters at Kingston Heath after a superb duel with defending champion Ian

Poulter over the weekend. "This has been a long time coming," he said. "I had some close calls about 10 years ago, so this is pretty sweet to be in the gold jacket and hold this trophy that I've been admiring since I was a little kid. Winning the Australian Open was like getting the monkey off my back a couple of years ago, but this is certainly something I've wanted to achieve for a long time. Maybe I can set the theme of winning jackets and turn it green next year before I come back to defend."

Scott added: "It's the only week of the year, maybe one other, where I've put four really solid rounds together and the result shows. I'm really, really happy with what I was able to do this week, and especially today. It was great to be a part of it. The way Ian and I played the last two days was the highest standard of golf there is. You could have brought anyone down here and they would have had to be on their game to play that way."

At the Emirates Australian Open there was a shock win when Peter Senior claimed the Stonehaven Cup for the second time, 23 years after his first victory. In strong winds at The Lakes, Senior used all his experience to hold his game together and at the age of 53 become the oldest ever winner of the title. After three seasons on the Champions Tour in America, Senior felt he was back to playing some of his best golf after taking a sabbatical for much of his 40s.

Apart from wins for Australia's best player and one of its wily veterans, the spring run of tournaments on the PGA Tour of Australasia were dominated by a new wave of talented young players. Not one but two amateurs claimed victories, Oliver Goss at the Western Australian Open and Jake Higginbottom at the BMW New Zealand Open. While Goss followed his playoff win in Perth with third place in the Asian Amateur Championship and was planning to go to college in America in 2013, Higginbottom immediately turned professional. Other promising young professionals to win were Matthew Stieger at the NSW PGA Championship and Daniel Popovic at the Australian PGA Championship.

With another fine finish at the PGA, Senior took the Order of Merit title, while Bio Kim clinched the OneAsia Order of Merit. On the latter circuit, there were victories for Nick Cullen and Matt Griffin, while Kieran Pratt won the Myanmar Open on the Asian Tour and Brad Kennedy the Mizuno Open in Japan, where there was also a win for Japanese Tour regular Brendan Jones. But the biggest overseas win for an Australian came at the Travelers Championship on the PGA Tour where Marc Leishman came from six shots back and tied for 20th after three rounds to win with a closing round of 62. Leishman finished more than two hours before the leaders and only realized he might have a chance of a playoff when Charley Hoffman had a double bogey at the 17th hole. When Hoffman bogeyed the last as well, Leishman had his maiden win in the States.

Victorian Open
Melbourne, Victoria
Winner: Scott Arnold

Scott Arnold claimed his first professional title when he won the Victorian Open at Spring Valley in Melbourne. The 26-year-old from New South Wales turned professional in 2010 after becoming the Australian Amateur champion the previous year and briefly being ranked the world's No. 1 amateur player. Arnold beat Kurt Barnes by one stroke in a tight finish after New Zealand's Michael Hendry slipped to third place.

Hendry, after rounds of 65 and 66, led by six shots going into the weekend but closed with twin 73s. Arnold drew level after three rounds with scores of 71, 66 and 67 before a 68 left him on a 12-under-par total of 272. Barnes had an adventurous closing round of 66 which included two eagles and a double bogey. Barnes made three birdies before his first eagle at the seventh but then suffered a double at the 11th. Two birdies and two bogeys followed in the next four holes, but he was still two behind when Arnold, who had three birdies going out but bogeyed the ninth and 11th holes, birdied the 16th. Barnes then eagled the 17th, but Arnold made a birdie to stay one ahead as both parred the last.

"It's great, especially the way I did it as well, I just sort of hung in there all day," said Arnold, the son of a professional. "Barnesey was really putting the heat on. I didn't play fantastic golf but was still playing within myself and getting done what I needed to do."

Adroit Insurance Group Victorian PGA Championship
Creswick, Victoria
Winner: Gareth Paddison

Gareth Paddison survived an ugly finish to the Adroit Insurance Group Victorian PGA Championship. It all started with a triple-bogey six on the 13th hole at Forest Resort and continued with bogeys at the 15th, 16th and 18th holes. At the same time, his nearest challenger, James McLean, also dropped six shots over the closing stretch with bogeys at the 12th, 15th and 16th holes and then his own triple bogey at the last. McLean, the second-round leader, eventually dropped to four under and a tie for seventh place, while Paddison, with rounds of 67, 69, 67 and 74, finished on a total of 277, seven under par. He crept home one in front of Leighton Lyle, an Australian who had finished sometime earlier on six under after a 69. Peter O'Malley and David McKenzie, both after 66s, plus Marcus Cain and Andre Stolz all shared third place.

It was a fourth Australasian Tour victory for the 31-year-old New Zealander, while the left-hander also has a victory on the Challenge Tour in Europe. He said: "Relief would be the only word to describe how I was feeling at the last, just because of how many shots I had dropped and because it really wasn't a true reflection on how I felt I played, so it was just nice to cross the line. At the end of the day a win is a win, you only need to get there by one shot and so it was very satisfying."

Coca-Cola Queensland PGA Championship
Toowoomba, Queensland
Winner: Andrew Tschudin

Originally from Melbourne, Andrew Tschudin claimed his first title in Australia in his new adopted home of Toowoomba. Tschudin won the Coca-Cola Queensland PGA Championship at City Golf Club by one stroke after the tournament was reduced to 54 holes. Heavy rain on Saturday meant the third round had to be suspended with the leaders about to tee off and play could not resume until Sunday afternoon.

Tschudin had been three behind Andrew Martin going into what turned out to be the final round, but he added a six-under 64 to early scores of 67 and 68 for an 11-under-par total of 199. The 39-year-old Tschudin birdied the last three holes to set the clubhouse total and then watched as 24-year-old Brody Ninyette, playing only his fourth Australasian Tour event, took a double bogey at the last and then Martin, who came out short at the 18th, miss the chip shot he needed to hole to force a playoff. Martin, after a 68, and Ninyette, with a 67, finished on 200, with Rohan Blizard one of those tying for fourth after a closing 63.

Tschudin, who had won twice in Korea and three times on the Hooters Tour in America, moved to Toowoomba a year ago. "To win in Australia is something I've always wanted to do," he said. "And to do it in what is now my hometown, with Amanda and friends around, makes it more special."

New Zealand PGA Pro-Am Championship
Queenstown, New Zealand
Winner: Michael Hendry

Michael Hendry birdied the first five holes, almost gave that advantage away on one hole when he took a quadruple-bogey seven on the 16th, but still hung on to claim the New Zealand PGA Pro-Am Championship. Hendry fell behind Australian Andrew Martin but rebounded to birdie the par-five 17th, while Martin took a six at the same hole and then bogeyed the last. Martin, a 27-year-old Australian, had led by five strokes at The Hills in Queenstown after rounds of 67 and 64 but finished with scores of 71 and 72 over the weekend. He still led by two over Hendry going into the final round, but four bogeys in a row to end the front nine allowed the local man to set the pace on the inward half.

The 32-year-old Hendry had rounds of 69, 68, 67 and 68 for a 16-under-par total of 272. He won by two over Martin and Mark Brown, with Ryan Fox fourth and Jin Jeong in fifth. Hendry had won the Indonesia Open in 2010 on the OneAsia Tour, but this was a proud moment for the Kiwi.

"Winning in Indonesia was satisfying because it was my first win, but being able to win at home in front of friends and family and putting my name on that cup, which has been one of my goals ever since I turned professional, is just awesome," said Hendry. "I felt the love out there. I had a lot of people as I was walking off greens saying, 'come on Mike you can do it, keep it going, you're playing great.' You don't often get that overseas."

South Pacific Golf Open Championship
Noumea, New Caledonia
Winner: Brad Shilton

After seven years on the PGA Tour of Australasia, Brad Shilton won for the first time at the South Pacific Golf Open Championship. Shilton was the only player to participate in all five editions of the tournament and secured a one-stroke victory over Matthew Griffin, who won the event in 2011. The 33-year-old from New Zealand returned scores of 67, 68, 65 and 71 for a 13-under-par total of 271. Griffin, the halfway leader after a second round of 64 as he attempted to defend his title, came from five strokes back with a round to play with a closing 67. But while Shilton saw Griffin hole a good putt at the 16th and thought it was for a birdie, it turned out it was for a bogey, and when Shilton birdied the 17th he was two ahead. A three-putt on the 18th green ultimately did not matter.

"I'm stoked, it's been a pretty long time coming, so to finally get it done is awesome," said Shilton. "I still felt like I was playing OK, I tried to stay controlled and the whole day just really kept my head on. To finish pretty strong at the end, making a few birdies coming in, was awesome. I got a wee bit nervy I suppose, but that's going to happen. Considering I haven't been in that position for ages, especially in one of these events, I am pretty proud of that."

Adam Bland closed with a 64 to share third place on 11 under with Henry Epstein, who set a new course record at Tina Golf Course in Noumea, New Caledonia, with an opening 63 and was Shilton's nearest challenger trailing by three shots after three rounds.

Western Australia Goldfields PGA Championship
Kalgoorlie, Western Australia
Winner: Peter Wilson

Peter Wilson claimed his first title at the Western Australia Goldfields PGA Championship by beating Glenn Joyner by two strokes. With fierce winds battering the Kalgoorlie Golf Course all week, Wilson posted scores of 74, 70, 70 and 69 for a five-under total of 283. Joyner, who led Wilson by one with a round to play, closed with a 72 for three under, while a third Victorian, Andrew Kelly, at one under, was the only other player to finish in red figures for the tournament.

Joyner, who at 48 was also looking for his first title, could not keep pace with 34-year-old Wilson's six-under-par run over the first 11 holes. Wilson was five ahead at one point and then cruised in for victory. "It's just so good to win one finally," he said. "I just had a hot start. I started to think about it for a while there, but I got it done in the end."

Joyner praised the Kalgoorlie course, saying: "I can promise you if the guys that are voting on it come here and play, it won't be voted number 73 in Australia for long. It's in the top 20, I think."

ISPS Handa Perth International
Perth, Western Australia
Winner: Bo Van Pelt

At a new tournament co-sanctioned by the European Tour and the PGA Tour of Australasia it was two invited Americans who stole the show. Bo Van Pelt won his private duel with Ryder Cup star Jason Dufner to claim the inaugural ISPS Handa Perth International at Lake Karrinyup, near Perth. After rounds of 70, 67 and 68, Van Pelt out-scored Dufner 68-69 on the final day to secure a two-stroke victory. Van Pelt finished on 16 under par with a total of 272, while Dufner ended up three clear of third-place Alejandro Canizares. Michael Hendry was fourth, and Paul Casey, finally showing some form after an injury-hit season, was among those tied for fifth place.

Van Pelt made six birdies in each of the third and four rounds, but maybe the most dramatic was the 60-footer he made on the 18th green on Saturday evening to claim a one-stroke lead. It meant Dufner was always playing catch-up on Sunday, and he never quite managed to put enough pressure on Van Pelt. "Bo played really good today, put a lot of pressure on me to make something happen, and I couldn't quite do it," said Dufner. "It is hard chance winning when someone plays as well as Bo did."

It was the second year running that Van Pelt, who only has one official PGA Tour victory, had won overseas as he won the CIMB Classic on the Asian Tour in 2011 and he left Perth to defend that title the following week.

"It's a great feeling to come out on top, I have a lot of respect for Jason and his game, he's a world-class player and I knew it was going to be tough today," said Van Pelt. "Any time you get a win, it's special; to come this far and to play against a great field, a co-sanctioned event, it's something that I'll cherish forever. I've won a tournament in the States and I've won a tournament in Malaysia, and now to win one in Australia, as much as golf means over here, it means a lot to me to come to a country that treasures golf and to win a title. You know, the weather was fantastic, the people were great, and I really enjoyed the golf course. I'll be spreading the word of what a great event this is and guys need to come and check it out."

John Hughes Geely/Nexus Risk Services WA Open
Perth, Western Australia
Winner: Oliver Goss

It took five extra holes to settle which amateur would win the John Hughes Geely/Nexus Risk Services Western Australia Open at Royal Perth. Finally 18-year-old Oliver Goss, who won the Western Australia state amateur title in March, defeated Brady Watt, who had held a two-shot lead going into the final round. Goss had rounds of 72, 66, 68 and 66 to finish on 272, 16 under par, as did Watt after his own 66 in the third round and a closing 68. The 66s by Goss and Watt were the new course record after the Royal Perth course was revamped until experienced winner Brett Rumford closed with a 65 to take third place on 14 under par.

Goss had a chance at an eagle on the 18th in regulation, but both he and Watt birdied to head for the playoff, where both again birdied the 18th on both the first two playoff holes. They then moved to the short par-four eighth hole, where Goss finally triumphed after three more holes. He became the first amateur to win the Western Australia Open since Stephen Leaney in 1991.

"It was definitely hot out there; I was glad when it was over after 18 holes and five extra playoff holes; I am pretty knackered to be honest," said Goss. "I guess things were just flowing and I definitely putted better today than I have any other day, I think that's what made the difference. It feels pretty surreal, it hasn't really sunk in at the moment, but I bet it will tomorrow morning. I like to think it's quite a good achievement and I am really happy."

Talisker Masters
Melbourne, Victoria
Winner: Adam Scott

Adam Scott, the highest ranked player in the field, and Ian Poulter, the defending champion, delivered a thrilling weekend duel before Scott won the Talisker Masters by four strokes at Kingston Heath. Playing together in the third round, the pair produced 17 birdies, with Poulter's 64, one outside the course record, putting him one ahead of Scott. But the Australian had his revenge the following day, only dropping one shot and collecting six birdies. Three of those birdies came in a row from the sixth and Poulter had to match those birdies at the seventh and eighth to stay just one back.

But Poulter found bunker problems at the 12th to make a bogey-six and then dropped a shot at the 14th to fall three behind. He got one back at the 16th but gave it back at the next, while Scott, who had parred in relentlessly, closed with a birdie at the last to finish on 17 under par. He had rounds of 67, 70, 67 and 67 for a total of 271, while Poulter closed with a 72 and handed the gold jacket to the Australian. New Zealanders Mark Brown and Gareth Paddison tied for third place four strokes behind Poulter.

This was Scott's 19th career win, but only his second in his homeland after he claimed the 2009 Australian Open. "This has been a long time coming. I had some close calls about 10 years ago, so this is pretty sweet to be in the gold jacket and hold this trophy that I've been admiring since I was a little kid," said Scott. "Winning the Australian Open was like getting the monkey off my back a couple of years ago, but this is certainly something I've wanted to achieve for a long time. Maybe I can set the theme of winning jackets and turn it green next year before I come back to defend.

"It's the only week of the year, maybe one other, where I've put four really solid rounds together and the result shows. I'm really, really happy with what I was able to do this week, and especially today. It was great to be a part of it with Poults. The way Ian and I played the last two days was the highest standard of golf there is. You could have brought anyone down here and they would have had to be on their game to play that way."

BMW New Zealand Open
Christchurch, New Zealand
Winner: Jake Higginbottom

For the second time in a month an amateur won on the PGA Australasian Tour. Jake Higginbottom followed Oliver Goss at the Western Australian Open by claiming the BMW New Zealand Open at Clearwater Resort in Christchurch. The 19-year-old Australian came from three behind Kiwi Mark Brown to win by one over fellow Australians Peter Wilson and Jason Norris, who split the first and second prizes. Higginbottom, who was also the leading amateur in the event in 2011, didn't collect a penny. Not since Harry Berwick in 1956 had an amateur won the New Zealand Open.

Higginbottom opened the final round with one of three bogeys but also had eight birdies, five of them coming in a seven-hole stretch on the back nine, but he was not assured of victory until tapping in at the final hole. He had rounds of 72, 70, 72 and 67 for a seven-under total of 281. Norris closed with a 66 and Wilson a 68, but Brown slipped down to fourth place with a 73.

"I was a bit shaky to start with, but it's actually good to be a couple behind after the front nine. I knew I had to go out there and make a few birdies and that's what I did," Higginbottom said. "I think I was the most nervous I've ever been on the short putt on the last. I don't think it's sunk in yet, but it's a good feeling, it means a lot to me. It's good to come over here and play against all the professionals and see that you're just as good."

NSW PGA Championship
New South Wales
Winner: Matthew Stieger

After winning the BMW New Zealand Open, Jake Higginbottom turned professional in time to tee-up in the NSW PGA Championship and celebrated with a course-record 65 in the first round at Mt. Broughton. Higginbottom was tied for 18th at the end of the tournament, but Callan O'Reilly set up the chance of a second successive victory by an amateur when he got the 54-hole lead after a third round of 66. But it was yet another of Australia's promising young players who secured the title as Matthew Stieger beat fellow tour rookie Daniel Nisbet by three strokes.

The 21-year-old only turned professional two months earlier and this was his sixth tournament. He had rounds of 67, 67, 71 and 68 for a 15-under-par total of 273. Stieger came from one behind O'Reilly with two birdies, an eagle at the 11th (where O'Reilly had a double bogey for a four-shot swing) and no bogeys. Nisbet closed with a 69 while O'Reilly had a 75 to slump to a share of sixth place. With a two-year exemption, Stieger was immediately into the field for the Australian Open and the following week's Australian PGA.

"I don't have to pre-qualify in the morning, which is a massive bonus!" said Stieger. "I was a bit worried about getting into next week and then the PGA. Everything was still up in the air for the next year and I didn't know where I was heading, so to come out with a win just solves a lot of problems."

Emirates Australian Open
Sydney, New South Wales
Winner: Peter Senior

Experience came to the fore on a difficult final day of the Emirates Australian Open with gales so strong at one point that play was suspended for three hours in the middle of the day. Typically, 63-year-old Tom Watson, possibly playing for the last time in Australia, had the best round of the day with a 69, one of only six scores under par. But it was another senior golfer who took victory, with the 53-year-old Peter Senior becoming the oldest ever winner of the Stonehaven Cup. Senior's closing 72 at The Lakes gave him a four-under-par total of 284.

Senior started the final round three strokes behind John Senden, who was the third-round leader for the second successive year. This time he had a double bogey at the first hole and slumped to an 82. His playing partner, the world No. 4 Justin Rose, also struggled, returning a 76 to share fourth place with Kim Felton and Kieran Pratt. Brendan Jones scored a 71 to finish one behind Senior, while Cameron Percy was third a further stroke back.

While Jones eagled the 17th hole to be four under for the last seven holes and set the clubhouse target, Senior recovered from two bogeys on the front nine with birdies at the 10th and 12th holes. But it was his steadiness under the pressure of the situation and conditions that was the key to his success. "It was one of the toughest days I have seen on a golf course," said Senior. "When the conditions are that tough, I feel that half the guys are out of the competition because they think it is going to be too difficult."

Senior won his first Stonehaven Cup in 1989, but after scaling down his tournament play in his 40s, he rededicated himself to the game after joining the U.S. Champions Tour. "My son Mitch has caddied for me for the last two years and we've lost three playoffs, so it feels unbelievable finally to win with him on the bag," Senior said. "Mitch's one percent is looking pretty good!"

Australian PGA Championship
Coolum, Queensland
Winner: Daniel Popovic

Daniel Popovic won the qualifying tournament for the PGA Tour of Australasia but hardly got to play in 2012 after his father was diagnosed with terminal cancer. But his decision to play in the Australian PGA Championship paid dividends from the moment he opened with an eight-under 64 at the Palmer Coolum Resort. The 26-year-old went on to lead or share the lead each day before claiming a four-stroke victory over Rod Pampling and Anthony Brown. Geoff Ogilvy and Brad Kennedy were a further shot behind, tied for fourth place.

Popovic became the sentimental favorite after revealing after the first round how he was playing with his father in mind. Two ahead with a round to play, Popovic had to withstand a superb charge from Pampling, who took the lead by birdieing the first six holes. He added another at the 12th, but his finish was a disaster with bogeys at the 16th and 17th holes and a double bogey at the last. Out in two under, Popovic kept his composure to birdie the 12th and 17th holes and claim a comfortable maiden victory. The win catapulted the victor from 1,251st place on the World Ranking to 363rd.

"Unbelievable, just unbelievable, there are no words to explain how good it sounds," said Popovic, whose name joined a host of legends on the Joe Kirkwood Cup. "I knew if I had that same mentality of what I had every single day leading into every round this week I was going to be fine, which I did, and I turned up today and I was more confident than any of the other days.

"That is the difference because of my father, that is the difference as to why I am so confident and do back myself and do push myself so hard on the golf course now. For him it's going to be a relief and he said he is so proud of me and so is my mum, they have all their friends over there, he is going to be over the moon and I cannot wait to give him a big bear hug. We are going to have a pretty big party I think when we get back."

12. African Tours

Pride of place in South African golf in 2012 was shared by two players — one of its greatest ever, Ernie Els, and one who might make that claim at some point in his career, Branden Grace. That the latter was once at the former's foundation only made their achievements more poignant.

It was no surprise that a fourth South African in five years won a major championship. But after Trevor Immelman, Louis Oosthuizen and Charl Schwartzel showed how much talent the country possesses, it was Els who showed their was life in the old man yet — well, 42-year-old — as he won a second Open Championship 10 years after the first. It took a decade for Els to add a fourth major title, but that did not look a likely happening earlier in the year when he failed to qualify for the Masters.

Not since his debut in 1994 had Els missed a trip to Augusta, and though he had chances to clock up a win on the PGA Tour to qualify, his erratic putting always seemed to intervene at the crucial moment. But after spending most of the year working with a vision expert, Dr. Sherylle Calder, the belief and confidence were slowly returning. At Royal Lytham & St. Annes, where twice he had let the claret jug slip through his hands, Els took advantage of a dramatic collapse by Adam Scott. The Australian bogeyed the last four holes when he appeared to have the championship wrapped up, but on the inward half, which he played in 32, Els was sublime and, when it really mattered, he holed magnificently from 15 feet for the winning birdie.

"In March I looked like an absolute fool," Els admitted. "People were laughing at me and making jokes about me and really hitting me low, saying I was done and I should hang it up. But it's an amazing game. You have to have a positive feel. If you give yourself positive vibes, sometimes positive things happen. I've been in such a negative mode for a while, and now that I've started to feel more positive, obviously things happen, especially on the back nine where I haven't got the job done. At the U.S. Open I had an outside chance but didn't quite capitalize. But I feel comfortable here at Lytham and when you are comfortable on a course, you can hit the shots. On the back nine I didn't miss a shot. I hit really good shots, and to make the pressure putts, that was the whole goal."

Els received a rapturous reception from the galleries as his charge to the line intensified. He remains a much-loved figure in the game, and not least for his gracious victory speech and compassion for "my good buddy" Scott. And then there is what he has given back to the game, including his foundation at Fancourt, which has benefited the likes of Oosthuizen and Grace.

Grace started the year at 271st in the World Ranking but finished it in 34th place. In fact, the 24-year-old had ended 2011 on an upward curve after regaining his European Tour card at the qualifying tournament. It was at home that he started the year with a bang by winning the Joburg Open and then, the following week, the Volvo Golf Champions at Fancourt, where he defeated two of his great compatriots, Els and Retief Goosen, in a playoff. "Although I was disappointed to miss out on winning, it was nice to see Branden make his mark as one of the world's best players in front of his home crowd," Els said. "Not so long ago he was a member of our Foundation and we're all so proud of what he has gone on to achieve. He's an inspiration to our current crop of members."

Grace was not finished yet. He won the Volvo China Open and then the Vodacom Origins of Golf Final. His biggest win of all came in the Alfred Dunhill Links Championship at St. Andrews, Carnoustie and Kingsbarns, where he led from start to finish. He went on to finish sixth on the Race to Dubai money list on the European Tour, where four of his five wins came. No one else managed to win more than two. Two of his wins counted on the Sunshine Tour and a 12th-place finish at the Alfred Dunhill Championship at Leopard Creek meant he topped his home circuit's Order of Merit ahead of George Coetzee and Jaco Van Zyl.

"The Order of Merit is very important," Grace said. "Every guy that plays golf out here on the Sunshine Tour wants his name on the trophy at the end of the season," said Grace. "I'm very chuffed. Winning the Order of Merit is all I wanted to do this year. It's been a great finish to an awesome season. Reflection will come now. I've sat back a little bit and thought about what I've done, but not everything has sunk in yet. I think that when I have this break now I can really sit back, tick it off and realize that it's been a great year. Hopefully, 2013 can be remotely as good as this was."

Oosthuizen had a highly consistent season, winning the Africa Open and the Malaysian Open. And his albatross at the second hole of the final round at Augusta National looked for a while to have secured him a second major title. It was not to be as he was beaten by Bubba Watson's wonder shot from the trees at the 10th hole in the playoff, but the 2010 Open champion continued to impress throughout the year. He finished third on the European Tour's Race to Dubai behind Rory McIlroy and Justin Rose and rose from 40th to sixth on the World Ranking.

For Schwartzel, it was a year that only came to life at the very end, but when it did, he was right back to his best. In his last five events of the year, he finished fifth, third, second and then won the last two — by 11 strokes at the Thailand Championship and by 12 strokes at the Alfred Dunhill Championship. "Last week I got that win by a big margin, and normally when you come back the next week it's hard to put up the same show," Schwartzel said at Leopard Creek. "To me that's the most satisfying — to continue the form that I had up in Bangkok after the flight and the jetlag and come here and play the same sort of golf."

Coetzee secured a spot as the fifth South African in the year-end World Ranking in 49th place and so joined Grace in qualifying for the 2013 Masters from the top 50. He did not win in 2012, but his consistency suggested that wins, both at home and on the European Tour, will come in the future. Two players clocked up three victories on the Sunshine Tour, Trevor Fisher, Jr. and Jake Roos, the latter winning all three in playoffs.

Perhaps the buoyancy of South Africa can be measured from the fact that as some European countries, including Spain, were withdrawing events from the European Tour, South Africa was due to host six on the 2013 schedule. It is becoming a rich proving ground.

Africa Open
East London, Eastern Cape, South Africa
Winner: Louis Oosthuizen

Louis Oosthuizen successfully defended the title at the Africa Open with a two-stroke victory over Tjaart van der Walt at East London. It was not until the par-three 17th that the result was decided. Oosthuizen holed from 35 feet for a birdie-two, while van der Walt three-putted for a bogey. It had been a terrific struggle between the two all day, with double U.S. Open champion Retief Goosen taking third place but falling out of contention after taking three to get down from the edge of the 10th green.

Oosthuizen won the Africa Open in 2011 as his first win after claiming the 2010 Open Championship. This was his next win and the 29-year-old took the lead after two rounds following scores of 69 and a 62 that was one outside Richard Sterne's course record. He was joined at 21 under after three rounds by the 37-year-old van der Walt, who had a 65 but could not repeat the drama of his second-round 64 which contained a hole-in-one at the second, courtesy of a six iron, followed by an eagle from 20 feet at the third.

It was van der Walt who started better on the final day with three birdies in a row. Oosthuizen was two behind after starting with a birdie and a bogey and still trailed despite an eagle at the third. In fact, Oosthuizen only parred two holes on the first nine. It was after his second bogey of the day at the fifth that he got going. He drove the green at the 310-yard par-four sixth for the first of four birdies in six holes. That included a rare three at the ninth and a two-putt four at the 11th to take the lead. Van der Walt responded at the 13th to tie, but the 17th was crucial. Oosthuizen closed with a 67 for a 27-under-par total of 265, while van der Walt finished off with a 69.

"It was a real dogfight for most of the day," said Oosthuizen. "Tjaart's one of those who won't go away. What happened on 17, it was going to be one of us who faltered. If I two-putted, he would probably have made that short putt. One of us needed to make some big putt to put a lot of pressure on the other guy, and it was just fortunate for me that it went my way."

Joburg Open
Johannesburg, South Africa
Winner: Branden Grace

Branden Grace is attached to the George Golf Club and came through the Ernie Els Foundation at nearby Fancourt. But the 23-year-old South African was not due to play in the Volvo Golf Champions at Fancourt until he became the last player to qualify by winning the Joburg Open. Grace earned his first European Tour victory and his second on the Sunshine Tour, after his Coco-Cola Championship win in 2010, by one stroke over Jamie Elson at Royal Johannesburg. Grace closed with a level-par 72 and parred the entire back nine to pip Elson, who was the only player to make a run at Grace. Elson, who only gained his tour card at the qualifying tournament by holing a 40-footer on the last hole, scored his second 63 of the week and birdied six of the first eight holes and holed from 30 feet at the last for an eagle. His clubhouse target of 16 under par was what Grace had to beat, and the South African still had nine holes to play. A bogey at the second and a birdie at the ninth were his only deviations from par as Grace finished on 270, 17 under par. He had earlier rounds of 67, 66 and 65. It was his charge at the end of the third round that set up the victory for Grace. He birdied his last three holes on Saturday as yet another thunderstorm interrupted play, and on the resumption of the third round on Sunday morning finished with two birdies in three holes to lead by three over Richard Finch and George Coetzee, both of whom faded in the final round.

"It's a dream come true," said Grace. "It was pretty tough out there today. I played really nicely, I hit the ball superb, I think, and the putter was just cold — I couldn't get the speed of the greens going today. Fortunately at the end of the day it was enough. I had goose bumps when the applause started as we walked up to the 18th. I will never forget that moment — walking up to the 18th green and knowing that it was my week." Grace said he was helped throughout by his caddie Zack Rasego, the bagman for Louis Oosthuizen's 2010 Open Championship victory. As for getting to tee up at the following week's Volvo Champions, Grace added: "Everyone has been asking me whether I'm playing the Volvo tournament next week, and the answer was always no, but now it's all yes."

Volvo Golf Champions
George, South Africa
Winner: Branden Grace

Could it get better for Branden Grace than being a last-minute invitee to the Volvo Golf Champions at The Links at Fancourt, just nearby George Golf Club where the 23-year-old is attached? Yes, it could. Grace ended up winning for the second successive week and did so by beating two of South Africa's most illustrious major champions in a playoff. A birdie-four at the 18th hole for Grace saw him collecting the trophy ahead of Ernie Els and Retief Goosen. The trio tied at 12 under par on a total of 280, and although Grace missed a short birdie putt for the victory in regulation, he promptly managed it at the second time of asking despite giving two decades' worth of age and experience to his opponents.

After Nicolas Colsaerts broke the course record with an opening nine-under 64 — followed by scores of 76, 69 and 72 to finish one outside the playoff after a bogey at the last — Grace led by four strokes at halfway after rounds of 68 and 66. But after two days of fine conditions, the wind got up on day three and a 75 from Grace meant he only shared the 54-hole lead with Colsaerts. Grace's bid to back-to-back titles then stalled with a double bogey at the third and a bogey at the fourth on the final day. He recovered with two birdies to turn in 37 and then birdied the 12th, 13th and 16th holes. "When I missed the putt in regulation, I didn't really think I had a bad putt," he said. "I might have slightly misread the line a little bit, but I think it's one of those things where you don't want to overdo it."

Grace closed with a 71, while Goosen had a 70 and Els a 67. Els, who was out in 34, birdied the 11th and holed from 18 feet for an eagle at the 13th and only just missed his eagle try at the last. Goosen's challenge appeared to be over after a double bogey at the ninth, but he eagled the 13th and birdied three of the last four holes.

Grace hit the best drive in the playoff. Els hooked his drive into the left rough and had to lay up. Goosen was just short of the green in two but chipped poorly and missed his long birdie try, while Els had a 25-footer for a four which slipped by. Both Els and Goosen were using belly-putters, but Grace utilized a standard-length putter to putt from the front of the green to within tap-in range. He made no mistake with the winning putt.

"I'm really ecstatic. It's a dream come true to win such a big event, pretty much the best tournament I've played in so far," said Grace, who became the first player to win his first two European Tour events back-to-back since Fred Couples in 1995. Having gained his European Tour card at the qualifying tournament the month before, Grace had moved from 271st on the World Ranking at the start of the year to 92nd. "Just standing on the tee with Ernie and Retief was unbelievable on the playoff," he said. "There was a calm about me, the whole playoff hole actually. I think I was more nervous and more pumped up going down the last hole when I walked up the fairway. But now I've beaten Ernie and Retief in a playoff and I know that I can do it again."

Jose Maria Olazabal, the European Ryder Cup captain, took fifth place, two strokes behind Charl Schwartzel.

Dimension Data Pro-Am
George, South Africa
Winner: Oliver Bekker

For his second victory on the Sunshine Tour Oliver Bekker reckoned he had claimed one of the biggest titles on the circuit. The Dimension Data Pro-Am is played under a similar format to that of the AT&T Pebble Beach National Pro-Am and the Alfred Dunhill Links Championship. Each player is partnered by an amateur in a fourball better-ball competition while the professionals compete in a stroke-play event across three courses — The Links, Montagu and Outeniqua courses at Fancourt in George. Bekker opened with a 65 at Montagu, then had a 70 at Outeniqua and a 71 at The Links, recovering from a double bogey and a bogey in the first three holes, before returning to Montagu for the final round. Holding the lead throughout the final day, he closed with a 70 for a total of 276, 13 under par. He won by two strokes over Tyrone Ferreira, who eagled the 18th, and Thomas Aiken. Birdies at the ninth, 10th and 11th holes put Bekker firmly in control, but then he bogeyed the 13th and 15th. Although now only leading by one, he remained calm and holed from 10 feet at the last for a celebratory birdie.

"It's an awesome feeling to win the Di Data. It's one of the premier events on our tour — it's what you dream about on the Sunshine Tour," said the 27-year-old from Stellenbosch. "Every time I finish with a win everybody looks so excited, but I am just relieved that I managed to stay in front. It's like a weight has lifted off your shoulders."

The team event was won for the second successive year by Jean Hugo and Sunshine Tour executive director Selwyn Nathan on 31 under par.

Telkom PGA Championship
Johannesburg, South Africa
Winner: Keith Horne

Apart from a brief trial during the Dubai Desert Classic, the first time Keith Horne planned to use the belly putter he started with a four-putt but went on to win the tournament. Horne had been practicing with the implement at home for a month, but after that hiccup on the opening hole, it worked perfectly. A double bogey to start at the Country Club Johannesburg led to an opening 70, but a 63 in the second round put Horne in the lead. He birdied the last four holes of his third-round 67 to lead by two going into the final round, and three birdies in the first six holes kept him in front despite a charge from Alex Haindl, who eagled the sixth to get within one but dropped back with a double bogey at the ninth. Horne calmly strung together a run of pars before finishing with a bogey and a birdie for a 69. With a total of 269, 19 under par, Horne won by three strokes over Haindl, Jaco Ahlers and Darren Fichardt.

It was the fifth win of Horne's Sunshine Tour career, which dates back to 1996, and the biggest as it came at South Africa's second oldest tournament. "It has been a long time coming," said the 40-year-old. "I'm over the moon that I can tick this off. I would've been disappointed to have played in South Africa for so long and never won a big tournament. And this is a big one. It's been going for many years with so many big names on the trophy. I really feel like I'm a big player in South Africa now."

Platinum Classic
Rustenburg, South Africa
Winner: Jake Roos

It took five extra holes but Jake Roos finally holed from three feet to win the Platinum Classic at Mooinooi. Roos was the first to benefit with events on the winter series of the Sunshine Tour attracting world ranking points for the first four places for the first time. Roos had tied on 202, 14 under par, alongside Anthony Michael, who tied the course record with a 63, and Chris Swanepoel, who closed with a 65.

Roos had collected two opening rounds of 66 and only birdies at the last two holes brought him the score of 70 that joined the leaders in the clubhouse. Warren Abery, however, went in the opposite direction by bogeying the last two holes to finish two adrift and behind Ulrich van den Berg and Dean Burmester, who tied for fourth place. Roos's winning birdie in the playoff came at the 16th, where a cobra slithering across the fairway could not detract from the exciting finish. For the 31-year-old Roos, it was a third victory on the Sunshine Tour and the third to come in extra time, while this was the last week his wife Rhone was due to caddie for him before taking up a new job.

"It was grueling but I felt good in the playoff," said Roos. "I felt relaxed, so I knew as long as I was in there, I had a good chance."

Golden Pilsener Zimbabwe Open
Harare, Zimbabwe
Winner: Chris Swanepoel

Chris Swanepoel claimed his third victory on the Sunshine Tour but only after a huge comeback on the final day and then beating Trevor Fisher, Jr. in a playoff at the Golden Pilsener Zimbabwe Open. Swanepoel had rounds of 71, 69 and 69 to lie five strokes off the lead before a closing 64 at Royal Harare to set the clubhouse target at 273, 15 under par. It was a stunning round with only four pars. The 27-year-old from Pretoria opened with four birdies in a row and added six more plus an eagle at the 12th but also suffered not one but two double bogeys, at the ninth and 15th holes. But he recovered each time, and birdies at the 16th and 18th holes set a challenge that Fisher could not beat, having dropped shots at the 15th and the last, where he missed from four feet for his par. Fisher closed with a 69, while rookie Ruan de Smidt, who shared the 54-hole lead, finished with a 71 to take third place, with Colin Nel four strokes further back in fourth place.

Swanepoel and Fisher returned to the 18th and parred it on the first extra hole. But the next time Fisher pulled his drive into the trees, and while Swanepoel was on the green in regulation and two-putted for a par, Fisher missed his 15-footer to keep the playoff alive.

"This is a nice win," said Swanepoel. "Against Fisher — he's a really good player and a good guy. I feel sorry for him, but unfortunately there can only be one winner, we can't split it. I love playing out here on this fantastic course, it has a lovely layout. It's my first playoff win in three tries, and it's an incredible feeling,"

Investec Royal Swazi Sun Open
Mbabane, Swaziland
Winner: Christiaan Basson

Five days after his 30th birthday, and five weeks before his wedding, Christiaan Basson showed why he was made an Investec ambassador following the 2011 tournament by winning the latest version of the Investec Royal Swazi Sun Open. Basson held his nerve to eagle the 12th and then finish with six pars to win the modified-Stableford event by just one point. His 50 points just held off Desvonde Botes, the leader after the second and third rounds, and rookie Danie van Tonder, while Dean Burmester finished in fourth place on 45 points.

While von Tonder fought his way into contention with a bumper haul of 21 points in the third round, Basson was highly consistent at the Royal Swazi Sun course. He had a 68 for 10 points on day one, then added a 64 which netted 17 points in the second round, followed by a 67 for 11 points and a closing 67 for 12 points on the final day.

This was a second Sunshine Tour win for the King David Golf Club professional from Cape Town. "I'm ecstatic to have won in Swaziland," he said. "I signed with Investec after this tournament last year, so winning here is first prize, and first prize! I can't tell you how much it means to me. I was so relieved when I sunk that last putt. My wedding is in just over a month, and I'm really looking forward to it. This does a fair amount for my stress levels. On the course, my immediate plan is to play the remainder of the Sunshine Tour season and then head to European Tour qualifying at the end of the year."

Vodacom Origins of Golf - Simola
Eastern Cape, South Africa
Winner: Ryan Cairns

On a day when everything went right for Ryan Cairns, his decision not to give in to his fears over a delicate chip at the playoff hole was instrumental in claiming his first victory at the Vodacom Origins of Golf event at Simola. Cairns first equaled the course record with a 62, coming home in 30 strokes with six birdies in the last seven holes, and then defeated Vaughn Groenewald in sudden-death by chipping in for an eagle.

The pair finished on 15 under par with a total of 201, three clear of Louis de Jager and Jake Redman, who was the second-round leader. Groenewald closed with a 66 in which he dropped only one shot at the 14th. He was also looking good in the playoff until a stroke of genius from Cairns.

"With Vaughn in close on the playoff hole, I knew I had to hit that shot properly," said the 29-year-old Zimbabwean. "It was actually a tight lie and I was going to putt it because I didn't want to duff it in front of all of those people." But he changed his mind and secured the victory that proves his career is headed in the right direction. "It's a work in progress," he said. "You never stop working. And now that I know what my routine is every day that has worked, I'm just going to stick to doing the same thing."

Sun City Challenge
Sun City, South Africa
Winner: Bryce Easton

Bryce Easton needed not one but two eagles at the 18th hole to win the Sun City Challenge. Easton came to the last hole on the Lost City course two adrift and hit his approach at the par-five to 10 feet. He holed the putt to make it a four-way playoff with Allan Versfield, Brandon Pieters and Andrew Georgiou. Then, the 24-year-old from Durban did it all again at the 18th — approach to 10 feet and holed the putt. Pieters had an eagle chance from 20 feet but lipped out, while Georgiou and Versfield missed birdie chances. It was Easton's maiden win on the Sunshine Tour, a year after he won the first event on the Big Easy development circuit in 2011.

"Once I got to 18, I was a bit surprised to see the lead was nine under," said Easton. "Once I saw I had a chance, it became a little easier knowing exactly what I had to do. The hole kind of sets up for me, so I could fade the ball into the pin, even though it was close to the water."

The quartet tied at 207, nine under par, with Easton compiling rounds of 66, 69 and 72. Versfield birdied the last two holes to make the playoff, but Pieters bogeyed the last and Georgiou parred it after dropping a shot at the 17th. James Kamte had a chance to win with an eagle at the last, or join the playoff with a birdie, but found the water and shared fifth place with Justin Waters and Theunis Spangenberg.

Lombard Insurance Classic
Mbabane, Swaziland
Winner: Jake Roos

Jake Roos played the 19 holes of his life to win the Lombard Insurance Classic. After rounds of 66 and 70, Roos produced a closing 63 at Royal Swazi Sun Country Club to tie defending champion Justin Harding at 17 under par on a total of 199. Harding had six birdies and three bogeys before an eagle at the 17th gave him a closing 67. But Roos only dropped one shot, at the third, and rolled out the birdies, with seven in the first 13 holes. Then he eagled the 17th and had a birdie-two at the 18th. Back at the 18th in the playoff, Harding missed the green, and while Roos lipped out from 20 feet for another two, the par was good enough for his second win of the season and his fourth Sunshine Tour win in all, all four having come in extra holes.

"The playoffs have been good to me, so I'm grateful. It's really a fairytale story," said Roos. "I didn't have any expectations at the start of the round, I just tried to move as far up as possible. Then I climaxed at the end with an eagle-birdie finish. You get those days where you're in the zone. You just plod along, even though everything is going your way, and don't think about it too much. You don't get those days often, so when they come around you just flow with it."

Andrew Georgiou finished in third place, three strokes out of the playoff, but it was the 31-year-old Roos who was celebrating. "My wife was here this week with me. It was her birthday, and then we found out a couple of weeks ago that she is pregnant. We're excited about starting a family together and the timing couldn't have been better. We have some money now to buy nappies."

Vodacom Origins of Golf - Zebula
Limpopo, South Africa
Winner: Bryce Easton

Bryce Easton won for the second time in three tournaments at the Vodacom Origins of Golf event at Zebula and in an unusual prize-giving was handed the trophy by an elephant. Easton had rounds of 68, 64 and 68 for a 16-under-par total of 200 to win by three strokes over Doug McGuigan. The pair were tied at the start of the final round, but in windy conditions McGuigan slipped four behind after a double bogey at the fifth hole and a bogey at the seventh. Easton closed with birdies at two of the last three holes, so McGuigan's eagle at the last did not concern him, it just secured second place, one ahead of Dean Burmester and with Colin Nel in fourth.

"I'm over the moon. The goal was just to get that first win, and I was ecstatic when I got that one out of the way. This week I put myself in a good position and here we are again," Easton said. "I love being in the thick of things. As a junior I always enjoyed it because it made me concentrate. That's why I play — to execute great shots and produce under pressure. It's an awesome feeling when you do that under pressure." But equally as impressive was the composure he showed on a tricky day in the wind. "Even before I won at Sun City I started to feel very comfortable on tour. I've been playing well and I feel like I'm coming to events now looking to win and not just make the cut or make the pre-qualifier like last year. To get two wins in three weeks is great."

Indo Zambia Bank Zambia Open
Lusaka, Zambia
Winner: Justin Harding

Justin Harding led from the front as he sealed victory at the Indo Zambia Bank Zambia Open. Leading by a stroke going into the final round at Lusaka Golf Club, Harding eventually won by two over Divan van den Heever. Three ahead going to the par-five last hole, a regulation finish meant Harding did not have to match the closing birdie of his nearest rival. It was a third victory on the Sunshine Tour by the 26-year-old from Cape Town, who collected four birdies in a row despite the windy conditions. Harding had rounds of 71, 72, 69 and 68 for a 12-under-par total of 280. Van den Heever had opened with a 75 but closed with scores of 70, 68 and 69. Des Terblanche, who returned a 67 in the final round, and J.G. Claassen shared third place a stroke behind the runner-up.

"I've been hitting the ball pretty well for the past three days. If you just put it in play around this golf course, then it is playable. I played the par-fives relatively well. The greens are good and I made my fair share of putts today, which hasn't happened in a while," Harding said. "I managed to keep it together. At the beginning of the day I knew that if I could shoot a round under par I would have a chance. It was awesome walking up there (the 18th green) and seeing the crowds."

Vodacom Origins of Golf - De Zalze
Stellenbosch, South Africa
Winner: Allan Versfeld

Allan Versfeld converted his Rookie of the Year title from 2011 into a maiden Sunshine Tour victory at the Vodacom Origins of Golf tournament at De Zalze. The 21-year-old South African came from three behind compatriot Ockie Strydom to win by three after adding a 67 to earlier rounds of 65 and 66. Versfeld finished on 198, 18 under par, while Strydom, whose advantage had been built on twin rounds of 64, slipped to a 73 to finish on 15 under. Keith Horne took third place on 11 under, one ahead of a large group who tied for fourth place.

Strydom was caught as early as the fifth hole in a final round in which he suffered two double bogeys while Versfeld had two eagles, at the eighth and 14th holes. There was a bogey at the par-five sixth which put Strydom back in the lead only briefly, but Versfeld was four ahead going to the last and could afford a second bogey. Just back from a stint in Europe, Versfeld, who was taught the game at age 10 by his father, took his opportunity impressively.

"It's awesome. I'm so happy to get the first win out of the way," Versfeld said. "I think it was my best round under the pressure. I played well the previous two days, but it all came together on the final day."

Vodacom Origins of Golf - Selborne
KwaZulu-Natal, South Africa
Winner: Adilson Da Silva

Adilson Da Silva thought his putting problems had returned in the final round of the Vodacom Origins of Golf tournament at Selborne Park. But then five birdies in six holes spurted the Brazilian into the lead and he hung on for a one-shot victory over Danie van Tonder and Doug McGuigan. It was a 10th victory on the Sunshine Tour for the 40-year-old Da Silva, who left his homeland at age 16 when a benefactor encouraged him to take his chance in Africa.

Da Silva started the final round one behind McGuigan and began by three-putting the first and fourth holes and missing short birdie chances at the second and third. But his fortunes turned with birdies at the sixth and seventh, then he chipped in at the ninth and holed 25-footers at the 10th and 11th. A closing 69, following rounds of 69 and 66, gave Da Silva a 12-under-par total of 204. McGuigan closed with a 71 and van Tonder a 67 as the pair finished two ahead of Desvonde Botes.

"I was very lucky to come to Africa," said Da Silva. "My parents would never have had the means to afford it. Now, with this win, it feels like I can build up to something good again. It was such a bad start, though, and I was really worried. My putting has been a nightmare. I've been hitting the ball so well, but just couldn't hole putts."

Wild Waves Golf Challenge
KwaZulu-Natal, South Africa
Winner: Trevor Fisher, Jr.

Trevor Fisher, Jr. won for the first time in three years at the Wild Waves Golf Challenge and in so doing pushed his season earnings past the one million rand mark, his best ever season on the Sunshine Tour. Victory at the Wild Coast Sun Country Club left the 33-year-old Fisher in fifth place on the Order of Merit, but he was the leading player to base himself in South Africa rather than playing mainly in Europe or America.

Fisher scored a bogey-free 66 in the final round to beat Ross Wellington by two strokes. The pair had been tied after two rounds as both returned scores of 64 and 67 (or 67 and 64 in Wellington's case). They were still tied when they got to the 15th, but a two-shot swing ensued when Fisher claimed his fourth birdie of the day and Wellington three-putted. "I could breathe a little easier after that, but it is never easy closing out a tournament," Fisher said.

Wellington birdied the 17th to get back within one, but then bogeyed the last for a 68, while Fisher finished on a 13-under-par total of 197. Oliver Bekker finished in third place, one behind Wellington, while Danie van Tonder was fourth.

Vodacom Origins of Golf - Sishen
Kathu, South Africa
Winner: Trevor Fisher, Jr.

Back-to-back birdies at the 18th hole gave Trevor Fisher, Jr. back-to-back victories at the Vodacom Origins of Golf tournament at Sishen. After winning at Wild Coast the previous week, Fisher looked second best here as Christiaan Basson led by two strokes playing the final hole. But Fisher was four under for the last four holes, and after an eagle at the 15th and a birdie at the 16th, the 33-year-old hit his approach to 15 feet at the last. While Basson three-putted for a bogey, hitting his first putt from the back of the green 10 feet past the hole, Fisher holed his birdie attempt to set up extra holes. At the same hole for the playoff, Basson missed the green while Fisher holed from a similar position for a winning birdie.

Fisher had rounds of 67, 69 and 66 for a 14-under total of 202. Basson finished on the same mark after a closing 65. Doug McGuigan finished two strokes outside the playoff in third place, and Danie van Tonder continued his fine form with another fourth place.

"So I'm very chuffed. But I didn't think I was going to win coming down the last five holes," said Fisher. "I bleed for Christiaan, because I've been in his situation a few times where you've got a lead and somebody snatches it away from you. The eagle on 15 was a big swing for me, even though Christiaan made birdie there. Then the first putt on 18 was perfect. You don't sink them all the time, so it's nice when they go in. Christiaan was putting so well that I was surprised when he missed his putt to get me into the playoff."

Vodacom Origins of Golf Final
George, South Africa
Winner: Branden Grace

Returning to his hometown of George, Branden Grace claimed his second victory of the year at The Links at Fancourt. It was here that the 23-year-old made his name by following his victory at the Joburg Open with an upset, playoff win against his illustrious compatriots Ernie Els and Retief Goosen at the Volvo Golf Champions. He also went on to win the Volvo China Open, so victory at the Vodacom Origins of Golf Final was his fourth of a breakthrough year.

Grace did it in style on a windy final day at Fancourt. His closing 68 included a four-under inward half of 33 and was the best score of the day by three shots. After earlier rounds of 69 and 72, Grace finished on 209, 10 under par. He beat Allan Versfeld, the second-round leader who closed with a 75, by three shots and was eight ahead of Divan van den Heever, who had a final round of 77, in third place.

"This was one of the toughest days I have played on The Links," Grace said. "The wind was brutal, and when the rain came, it became extra tough. But being a member here just helped a little bit when it really counted."

BMG Classic
Johannesburg, South Africa
Winner: Teboho Sefatsa

A month after securing the 2012 Big Easy Tour Order of Merit crown, Teboho Sefatsa claimed his first victory on the Sunshine Tour at the BMG Classic. The 29-year-old Sefatsa, a professional attached to host venue Glendower, used his local knowledge to return rounds of 70, 68 and 68 for a 10-under-par total of 206. He beat Merrick Bremner by a stroke and was two ahead of Matthew Carvell, the 36-hole leader, and Desvonde Botes.

An intense hailstorm on Saturday, which caused damage to the greens and left many broken car windshields, meant the second round was suspended overnight. But play could resume the next morning, and when the third round began it was Sefatsa who made the best start with a birdie at the first and an eagle at the second. Two ahead going to the 18th, Sefatsa could afford a closing bogey while Bremner finished with a 69 and Carvell a 71.

"I wasn't feeling the pressure until the final hole," he said. "I knew I had one hand on the trophy and I just needed to put the other one on it. I was ecstatic after I made that last putt," he said. "I've finally broken through and it feels fantastic. It hasn't totally hit me yet, but I'm sure when I get home it will sink in. My career really takes off from here — this is where the hard work begins."

Suncoast Classic
Durban, South Africa
Winner: Ruan de Smidt

Ruan de Smidt celebrated his 23rd birthday by sharing the lead on the opening day of the Suncoast Classic. Two days later he was able to celebrate his maiden victory. A 69 made him the co-leader on day one, while a 68 the next day put him three ahead. De Smidt closed with a 71 for a total of 208, eight under par, and a four-stroke win over Vaughn Groenewald. Jacques Blaauw was third on three under par.

De Smidt, who stuck to his two iron rather than driver in the seaside winds and on the rolling fairways of the Durban Country Club, won the Sunshine Tour qualifying tournament in 2011 but as a rookie was required to pre-qualify for most tournaments. Now his victory would mean automatic entry to events, perfect timing with the summer swing about to start. He bogeyed his first hole in the final round, but three birdies put him well clear before a nervy bogey-bogey-birdie finish.

"I didn't feel nervous until the last tee shot. I had a three-stroke lead and I just wanted to hit it into the fairway. I'm very happy and excited for the end of the year now that I've got my first win," he said. "I've definitely got a lot more confidence now. Last week I missed the cut — I played terribly. This week's win really turns that around and I'm looking forward to my next year of golf," he said.

ISPS Handa Matchplay Championship
Pretoria, South Africa
Winner: Doug McGuigan

Doug McGuigan won the biggest title of the year when he claimed the ISPS Handa South African Match Play Championship at Zwartkop. The 42-year-old beat top-seed Darren Fichardt in the quarter-finals and then defeated Merrick Bremner 5 and 3 in the semi-finals. While Jaco Ahlers also won his semi-final 5 and 3 over P.H. McIntyre, he could not find a way past McGuigan in the final, who won by one hole. McGuigan trailed for much of the early action until he drew level at the 12th and then went ahead at the 16th. Ahlers almost holed a remarkable flop shot over a bunker at the last, but McGuigan two-putted from the fringe to seal his victory.

"It was probably the longest 35- or 40-footer I've had to hit," he said. "I've won five times in my career, but to beat these guys one-on-one like this is a very satisfying personal achievement. And to win at this age — although there have been guys who have won at this age — well, I'm hoping I'm one of those guys who peak after 40."

Daniel Slabbert won the ISPS Handa Disabled Matchplay Championship by beating Conrad Stolz 2 and 1. Slabbert, 21, who has an artificial left leg, hopes to turn professional after completing his studies.

Nedbank Affinity Cup
Sun City, South Africa
Winner: Trevor Fisher, Jr.

Trevor Fisher, Jr. was so disenchanted with his play the week before the Nedbank Affinity Cup that he withdrew from the event. When he later thought better of his decision and changed his mind, entries had closed, so he phoned the sponsors and received a last-minute invitation. It was a wise decision because Fisher claimed his third win of the season at the Lost City course at Sun City.

Fisher had rounds of 69, 67 and 71 for a nine-under total of 207 and a one-stroke victory over Desvonde Botes, who closed with a 67, and Bradford Vaughan, who had a 68 in the final round. But it was a rollercoaster final day for the 23-year-old Fisher. He shared the lead with Dean Burmester at the start of the round and went three clear at the turn. But after a birdie at the 11th, he had a triple bogey at the 12th and then found water at the short 13th and did well to make a bogey.

Fisher was still one behind with two holes to play but holed from six feet for a birdie at the 17th and then birdied the par-five 18th to seal the victory. "It was a tough day out there and it became a real fight, so I'm glad to have come out on top," he said.

South African Open Championship
Ekurhuleni, South Africa
Winner: Henrik Stenson

Such was Henrik Stenson's loss of form since winning the 2009 Players Championship that he did not qualify for the DP World Tour Championship in 2011 and he started 2012 outside the world's top 200. The 36-year-old Swede arrived at the South African Open standing 113th in the world and 59th on the Race to Dubai. To get back to the season-ending event in Dubai the following week Stenson had to stay in the top 60 on the money list and he did that in style with a three-stroke victory at Serengeti Golf and Wildlife Estates. It was his first victory anywhere since winning at Sawgrass and his first win on the European Tour since he claimed the Dubai Classic and WGC - Accenture Match Play early in 2007. It was also his second win in South Africa as he won the Nedbank Challenge in 2008.

"I've had to fight hard the last few years on the golf course and I'm very pleased to pick up this win," Stenson said.

Building on recent better form, Stenson opened with rounds of 66 and 65 to take a three-stroke lead at halfway and kept that advantage despite George Coetzee scoring a 63 in the third round to lie second alongside Magnus Carlsson. Hennie Otto set a course record of 62 early on Sunday morning, but the leaders found scoring more difficult. Stenson had a double bogey at the ninth to be out in 38 but had three birdies coming home at the 10th, 16th and 17th, and with Coetzee dropping a shot at the 15th there was a three-shot swing over three holes. Both players closed with 71s as Stenson finished on 271, 17 under par. Thomas Aiken and Martin Kaymer shared third place, one behind Coetzee, with Charl Schwartzel fifth and young Englishman Tommy Fleetwood in sixth to retain his card at the end of his rookie season. The winner of the Challenge Tour in 2011 started the week 124th on the money list and needed to climb at least five places, which he did and more.

Lion of Africa Cape Town Open
Western Cape, South Africa
Winner: Jake Roos

Jake Roos never makes it easy on himself and the Lion of Africa Cape Town Open followed the same pattern as his previous four victories on the Sunshine Tour. In each case, including the Platinum Classic and Lombard Classic in 2012, Roos went to a playoff before taking the trophy. At Royal Cape Golf Club, Roos needed to beat three other players in extra time and it took a 15-foot birdie putt at the second additional hole for Roos to prevail. "There's nothing to lose when you get into playoffs," he said, "so you can just relax and let yourself go. Other than that, I don't know how to explain how I've won so many. But as I walked up to the green on that second playoff hole, I had a good feeling about the putt. I saw the line immediately, and I told myself that I could hole it."

Roos had rounds of 71, 67, 73 and 68 to finish on nine under par with a total of 279. He tied with Jaco Van Zyl, who closed with a 66, Tyrone van Aswegen, after a 67, and Mark Williams, who closed with a 71 after taking the lead into the final round. Roos had birdied the 18th in regulation to get into the playoff, while Williams arrived at the 18th with a one-shot lead, but a poor drive led to a closing bogey.

Nedbank Golf Challenge
Sun City, South Africa
Winner: Martin Kaymer

Martin Kaymer made it a German double at the Nedbank Golf Challenge after Bernhard Langer had won the 54-hole Champions Challenge portion of the event the previous day. Buoyed by the win for his mentor and hero, Kaymer was also enjoying the confidence-boosting benefit of holing the putt at Medinah that guaranteed Europe would retain the Ryder Cup. In only his second appearance in the tournament at Sun City, Kaymer returned scores of 72, 69, 70 and 69 for an eight-under-par total of 280 and a two-stroke victory over Charl Schwartzel. American Bill Haas was third, Louis Oosthuizen fourth and defending champion Lee Westwood fifth in the 12-man event.

Kaymer took the lead in the third round and set out one ahead of Oosthuizen on the final day. He started brilliantly with an eagle at the second hole but immediately suffered a double bogey at the next. Straying offline is never recommended at the Gary Player Country Club, especially with the fairways narrowed this year after the low scoring of 2011. But the jungle can be treacherous, and after Kaymer made three birdies in a row from the ninth, he hooked his drive at the par-five 14th deep into the undergrowth. However, in a moment of good fortune that suggested it was his day, Kaymer's ball came to rest in a small clearing and he was able to chip back to the fairway and eventually collect a birdie-four. He dropped a shot at the next but then parred in, while Schwartzel's challenge ended at the 17th when he came up short of the green and failed to get up and down.

Kaymer, who had dropped to 32nd on the World Ranking after being the number one two years earlier, had not won all season and he was keen not to miss out after winning every season since 2008. "I'm very happy to finally win this year, that was the most important thing for me, because I was practicing very hard, I played very well the last few weeks and months, but it just did not happen for me on the golf course. I said to Craig, my caddie, we have to win one tournament every year and this is our last chance, fortunately we could bring it home," he said. "There was a little bit more pressure today, everybody was talking about the German double. I am very fortunate that everything worked out the way I was hoping it would and obviously very nice from Bernhard that he congratulated me straight away. Bernhard has been a very, very big help for me."

Langer had a two-stroke victory over Jay Haas with a total of 209, seven under par. Langer jumped in front of the elite, eight-man field with an opening 68 and stretched the lead for four strokes the second day, an adequate margin to allow for a 74 in the final round. Haas finished on 211 and Ian Woosnam was in third place on 214.

Nelson Mandela Championship
Durban, South Africa
Winner: Scott Jamieson

Scott Jamieson became the first player in the history of the European Tour to win an event with a closing round of 57. While the circumstances meant Jamieson's feat will be no more than a footnote in the record books, his maiden victory in the Nelson Mandela Championship will remain a career highlight. For two days rain washed out any chance of play at Royal Durban. Over the weekend 36 holes were possible for the field of 156, but four par-fours had to be reduced to par-threes, reducing the par of the course from an already modest 69 to a positively minute 65. Jamieson tied with Eduardo De La Riva and Steve Webster on seven under par, and then the 29-year-old Scot won the playoff at the second extra hole.

All three players who made the playoff played in the morning on the final day and had a long wait while the afternoon wave went out. Webster set the target at 123 after a 60 and then De La Riva, who had just got his card back in the European Tour qualifying tournament, joined him after a 61 that included a bogey at the final hole. Jamieson started on the 10th and went to the turn in 26 with five birdies. He added three more on the front nine and matched the 57 of Jaco Van Zyl. Although they are the lowest scores ever recorded on the European Tour, they do not count officially as the first sub-60 rounds on the circuit.

Jamieson had finished on the ninth, where he drove the green but missed from 12 feet for an eagle. Tim Clark was the leading contender among the afternoon players, but a double bogey at the 17th meant he missed out on the playoff by one shot. De La Riva went out at the first extra hole at the 18th, where Webster's 30-footer for birdie came up just short. Second time around on the same hole, Webster found rough off the tee and then had to get a free drop off the practice putting green after pulling his approach. He failed to get up and down, which meant a par from Jamieson gave the Scot the opening event on the 2013 European Tour.

"To get your name on any European trophy is a fantastic achievement," said Jamieson, "but it's a little more special when it's for someone like Nelson Mandela."

Alfred Dunhill Championship
Mpumalanga, South Africa
Winner: Charl Schwartzel

Until the previous week, Charl Schwartzel had not won since claiming his Masters green jacket in 2011. There had been a few chances, but during 2012 there were also some niggling injuries. However, as the year drew to a close he was right back on top form as he won the Thailand Championship by 11 strokes. Just a few days later he returned to one of his favorite venues at Leopard Creek and won the Alfred Dunhill Championship by 12 strokes. It was a domineering performance that was founded on back-to-back rounds of 64 on the second and third days. He had opened with a 67 and closed with a 69 for a 24-under-par total of 264. Gregory Bourdy was his closest pursuer, 10 shots back overnight, but had a double bogey on the seventh hole and fell into a tie for third place with Garth Mulroy, Andy Sullivan and Nelson Mandela champion Scott Jamieson. But it was Swede Kristoffer Broberg who took second place after coming from nowhere to win four times on the Challenge Tour in 2012.

But Schwartzel was in a league of his own. In his last five events of the year, dating back to the South African Open, he was 84 under par with a sequence of fifth, third, second, win, win. This was his eighth European Tour title and a second win in the Alfred Dunhill Championship at Leopard Creek, having also won at the event's new home in 2004. Since then he has also finished runner-up four times here.

"It's always been a special place for me," he said. "This is where I can almost say my career started and it's always stayed close to my heart. It's nice to have continued my form from last week. I was saying a month and a half ago it's been a pretty disappointing year. Slowly and surely I started to swing the club a lot better. ... It started at the SA Open and from there got better and better. It's been a pretty good year now!"

Keith Horne twice holed in one on the 12th hole with an eight iron in the second and third rounds, but the BMW car parked beside the tee was only available for an ace on Sunday. However, the sponsors awarded the South African an alternative car for his feat, while Magnus A. Carlsson claimed the initial prize when he holed in one at the 12th on the final day.

13. Women's Tours

Funny how things come full circle.

A year earlier, at the end of the 2011 season, Yani Tseng was saying how she wished the year would never end. She might have been saying the same thing at the end of the 2012 season, but for a completely different reason.

Tseng started the year like a conqueror, winning three of the first five events (that made it 15 victories in 15 months). It turned out, those were her only wins of the year. Three wins is a great year by any measure, but in another chapter of one of golf's great mysteries, Tseng's game went into a sudden dive. She didn't break par for 12 straight rounds, and missed two cuts, back-to-back. As she said, after a 76 in the first round of the Wegmans LPGA Championship: "I just couldn't hit a shot, couldn't hit on the green, couldn't hit on the fairway."

But Tseng's cooling-off, while it may have cleared the way for others, did not knock her off the top of the Rolex Rankings. She finished the year with 97 weeks as No. 1. Behind her were: 2. Na Yeon Choi; 3. Stacy Lewis; 4. Inbee Park; 5. Shanshan Feng; 6. Suzann Pettersen; 7. So Yeon Ryu; 8. Jiyai Shin; 9. Ai Miyazato, and 10. Mika Miyazato (they're both Japanese, from Okinawa, but not related).

The rankings reflected the South Korean dominance. Four of the top 10 are South Koreans, 37 of the top 100, and 142 of the top 500.

The year was marked by a number of surprises, the two biggest being the emergence of China and the emergence of more youth.

One victory does not a global power make, of course, but one episode in June made a point in history. Shanshan Feng, 22, said she had two goals: "I want to win a tournament on the LPGA Tour, and I want to finish in the top 10 in a major." She did both by winning the Wegmans LPGA Championship, becoming the first Chinese to win on the tour. Will the Chinese one day become a global force? she was asked. "If the Koreans can," she said, "the Chinese can."

Lexi Thompson held the title of youngest ever to win on the LPGA Tour, at 16, less than a year, when along came Lydia Ko, 15, winning the CN Canadian Women's Open in August. And an amateur, at that, fresh from winning the U.S. Women's Amateur. "Just playing against the big names — it's nerve-racking," said the Korean-born New Zealander. Said Suzann Pettersen: "It feels like you're being beaten by a kid." Exactly.

Feng's win in the Wegmans LPGA Championship prevented a sweep of the majors by the South Koreans.

• Sun Young Yoo got a major gift in the Kraft Nabisco Championship — I.K. Kim blowing a winning one-foot putt for par on the final hole. Yoo beat the shaken Kim in the playoff, then uttered one of the quotes of the year. Asked if she felt sorry for Kim, she replied: " ...it happens. It's golf."

• Na Yeon Choi, who made no secret that she's uncomfortable playing with the lead, threatened to squander a six-shot edge in the final round, but pulled herself together to win the U.S. Women's Open. She built the lead with an amazing 65 in the third round, in blustery winds that blew many scores into the 80s. She did it with her short irons, an obedient putter and faith in her caddie. Choi would also add the season-ending CME Group Titleholders title.

• Jiyai Shin took command with a 64 in the second round, then came though heavy weather in a 36-hole wrap-up the final day to take her second Ricoh Women's British Open. "My goal was one under par every day, so my goal was four under," Shin said. She beat that by five — and won by nine. This was the week after she ended a two-year drought by winning the Kingsmill Championship.

Elsewhere on the LPGA in 2012:

Stacy Lewis, who led the LPGA in victories with four, was the first American since Beth Daniel in 1994 to win the Rolex Player of the Year Award.

Inbee Park, a two-time winner, topped the money list with $2.2 million, followed by Na Yeon Choi, $1.9 million, and Lewis, $1.8 million.

On a schedule that listed 28 tournaments — 15 of them in the United States — Japan's Ai Miyazato and Norway's Suzann Pettersen also won two each.

And the tribulations of Michelle Wie, long the poster girl for the LPGA, marched on. She graduated from Stanford University in the spring, but golf proved to be a little tougher. In 23 starts, she missed 10 cuts and finished just once in the top 10.

The Oddity of the Year Award went to the Sybase Match Play Championship. Morgan Pressel was three up with six holes to play in a semi-final against Spain's Azahara Munoz when she was hit with a slow-play penalty. "Pace of play is an issue," Pressel conceded, "but in that situation, I'm not sure it should have been called." Munoz went on to score her first tour win.

The Oddity of the Year Award II went to Lexi Thompson. The Whiz Kid, now 17, was still a kid. She passed up the Sybase to go to her high school prom. That was no ordinary prom date she had. She had more than 100 military applicants on her Facebook page, and she chose a U.S. Marine, Lance Cpl. Mark Scott.

U.S. LPGA Tour

ISPS Handa Women's Australian Open
Victoria, Australia
Winner: Jessica Korda

See Australian Ladies Tour section.

Honda LPGA Thailand
Chonburi, Thailand
Winner: Yani Tseng

If Japan's Ai Miyazato had learned one thing about playing against Taiwan's Yani Tseng, it was not to count her birdies until they hatched. And so at the final hole of the Honda LPGA Thailand, after she stuck her approach stiff, she folded her arms and waited.

Tseng, age 23, wasn't rated No. 1 in the world for nothing. "I saw that Ai hit it so close...," she was to say, "so I tell myself, 'I need to get this close.'"

Tseng had 104 yards to the pin. "I just tried to keep it low and not spin too much," she said. Close? Make that tap-in range.

Dutifully, Miyazato birdied for a 67, and Tseng tapped in for a 66 and a one-stroke victory at 19-under-par 269 at Siam Country Club for her first win of the year, her LPGA 13th and career 33rd.

It didn't take long for the mid-February event to become a two-woman chase. Miyazato opened with the lead on a no-bogey 67, and the veteran Karrie Webb jumped out front with a 65–133 in the lightning-interrupted second round, with Miyazato at 70–137 and Tseng at 75–138. Miyazato and Tseng, playing together, matched 65s to come through the third round 1-2 on the leaderboard.

Then the chase was on in the fourth. Miyazato birdied the par-five No. 1, but Tseng eagled it, and they were tied at 15 under. Tseng added three birdies and led Jiyai Shin by three and Miyazato by four at the turn. Tseng kept it interesting with two bogeys and a birdie through the 13th while Miyazato had two birdies, and they were 1-2 coming to the 17th and stayed that way with birdies. It came down to the final hole. Miyazato hit it stiff, Tseng stiffer.

Said the frustrated Miyazato: "I knew it wouldn't be easy today. I expected her to play that way."

Said Tseng, who played the last three rounds in 20 under par: "I had some luck out there."

Countered Miyazato: "I really enjoyed playing with Yani, but the next time, I want to win."

HSBC Women's Champions
Singapore
Winner: Angela Stanford

If it wasn't a sign that this was Angela Stanford's week, then there's no such thing as a sign.

She suffered a pro golfer's worst nightmare on her last hole of the first round, the par-five No. 9. She absolutely topped a fairway wood. But she swallowed her embarrassment and smacked her next to within 30 feet and rolled in the putt. Said Stanford: "I've never topped a shot and made birdie on the same hole."

The escape helped her to a tournament-low 66, six under par. She then shot 70-71-71, tying through the next three rounds and finishing at 10-under 278, then winning in a playoff at the HSBC Women's Champions at Tanah Merah Country Club.

Stanford was tied with Katie Futcher and Jenny Shin through the second and third rounds, then needed and got a big boost from Shin, who led through most of the final round. Shin led by a stroke through the 17th when play was suspended because of lightning. Shin, age 19, who turned professional in 2010 and was in her 18th LPGA event, conceded that her lack of experience might have led to her jitters when play resumed. At the final hole, she knocked her tee shot out of bounds and two-putted for a double bogey and a 71. Stanford bogeyed and fell into tie with Shin, China's Shanshan Feng (69) and Korea's Na Yeon Choi (68).

The playoff stayed at the par-four 18th. Feng bowed out with a bogey the first time, Choi with a bogey the second. On the third try, Shin missed her par from four feet, and Stanford got hers from three for her fifth tour win but not really the one she wanted.

"I haven't won a major yet," Stanford said, "but they call this Asia's major, so it's the closest thing to me."

If it was Stanford's week, it sure wasn't Michelle Wie's. She put down some astonishing numbers — 79-81-75-75, a 22-over 310 and one spot ahead of dead-last Singapore amateur Sock Hwee Koh. Where was the cut when a body needed it?

RR Donnelley LPGA Founders Cup
Phoenix, Arizona
Winner: Yani Tseng

Taiwan's Yani Tseng, No. 1 on the Rolex Rankings, is pretty much accustomed to having her own way in tournaments. She's either brushing away competition like so many pesky mosquitoes or else she's coming from behind and overrunning everyone in her way. Neither was the case in the RR Donnelley LPGA Founders Cup in mid-March, the tour's first tournament of the season in the United States.

Tseng led or shared the lead from the start, challenged every step of the way before notching her second win of the year and 14th tour victory. She shot the par-72 Wildfire Golf Club in 65-70-67-68, an 18-under-par 270 total, nipping Korea's Na Yeon Choi (68) and Japan's Ai Miyazato (69) by a stroke.

"It was little drama out there," Tseng said. "I didn't play very well on the front nine. It was like hail on the first hole and it was like hail three holes. I just was really patient."

Patience was the byword for everybody in the final round. The warm Arizona weather abruptly turned varied, with a vengeance — 40 degrees, rain, wind, hail and lightning, with three delays, all of which translated into an eight-hour round that had the leaders finishing in failing light. Miyazato said it for everybody: "Thank God we finished."

Tseng started the final round tied with Miyazato, but stumbled on the front nine and trailed her by three at the turn. Said Tseng: "I told myself, 'We have nine more holes. You still have a good chance on the back nine. Just play like on the first day.'" That was a seven-hole stretch on the back in seven under, with an eagle and five birdies. Does one just summon up something like that? Tseng did, getting five birdies coming in. The run started at the 10th, where she came out after a delay facing a 25-foot birdie putt. She dropped it. She then added birdies at Nos. 11, 13, 14 and 15 to lock up the win.

"I'm just very proud because ... I just hung in there," Tseng said.

Kia Classic
Carlsbad, California
Winner: Yani Tseng

It was like a warm-up lap in a race. Taiwan's Yani Tseng, No. 1 on the Rolex Rankings, loosened up in the first round with a 67. That tied her for the lead. Then with the blood up and the senses sharpened, she just ran away, adding 68-69-70, leading, respectively, by two, three and finally six strokes for her second straight LPGA Tour victory and her third of the season. And it was only mid-March.

Tseng's biggest threats were the greens at the La Costa Legends course. Jennifer Johnson, a member, readily agreed after her 68 in the first round. "The greens are a little bumpy," she said, "and I think that's where I have an advantage, just knowing sometimes they don't break."

By the third round, Tseng was frustrated when her short birdie putt at the 17th went wobbling off to the right. "You can see very clear, the ball is jumping to the right," she said. "It's not like I misread it or something." All told, she missed four putts from six feet and closer.

Among other noteworthy episodes in Tseng's stroll:

• In the first round, she hit only eight of the 14 driving fairways, and 12 greens, and still shot 67.

• Nothing helps a putting average like hole-outs. In the second round, Tseng holed out from a bunker for a birdie at the par-four 10th and chipped in for another at the par-four 13th.

• A miraculous break saved her at the 18th in the third round. Her tee shot strayed to the right, but uncannily rolled down a cart path and across a narrow bridge, a drive of 370 yards. "That," Tseng conceded, "was a pretty lucky shot." She ended up two-putting for par from 45 feet, but it was more like a save. Her second putt was from eight feet.

Tseng's six-shot win was very nearly seven. She three-putted the last hole from 30 feet. It was her only three-putt of the week.

The next stop would be the Kraft Nabisco Championship, the first major, the following week. Said Tseng: "I can't wait to start."

Kraft Nabisco Championship
Rancho Mirage, California
Winner: Sun Young Yoo

See Chapter 7.

LPGA LOTTE Championship
Kapolei, Oahu, Hawaii
Winner: Ai Miyazato

One day, Ai Miyazato's dad took her aside and said, "Let me give you some fatherly advice," or words to that effect. Whereupon Miyazato minded her dad — the advice being a putting tip — and put it to good and proper use and took the wind-whipped LPGA LOTTE Championship for the eighth win of her career.

It was a four-stroke win in the books, but it wasn't as decisive as it looked, what with Meena Lee ending the suspense and the duel with a double bogey at the final hole.

Miyazato methodically worked her way up the leaderboard, shooting the par-72 Ko Olina in 71-65-70-70–276, 12 under par, while needing — thanks to dad — just over 27 putts per round. She trailed by three in the first round, tied Spain's Azahara Munoz in the second and moved three strokes clear of Munoz and Cristie Kerr in the third. Then came a tough final round.

Miyazato was four ahead of Lee starting the final round, but saw her encouraging edge slip away until she finally fell behind at the par-three 12th, on a bogey off a bunkered tee shot. Lee then slipped back on a bogey, a three-putt at the 14th. Miyazato took the gift and ran with it. She birdied the 15th, saved par on a tough 10-foot putt at the 16th, then rolled in a 25-footer for a birdie at the 17th. In the exchange, Lee, playing up ahead, trailed by just one. Then she crashed at the 18th, bunkering her approach and three-putting from 30 feet for a double bogey, and Miyazato won by four.

The win had a certain liberating effect, as well. With it, Miyazato stepped out of the shadow of Yani Tseng, World No. 1. This was her fifth top-10 finish in six events, and in two of them she finished second to Tseng.

"It was," Miyazato said, "very nice."

Tseng, who had already won three times, tied for 10th. "Just not my day out there," she said.

Mobile Bay LPGA Classic
Mobile, Alabama
Winner: Stacy Lewis

Stacy Lewis's finish was so iffy, it took a second glance for one to realize that she'd had an all-star kind of outing in the Mobile Bay LPGA Classic. That three-under-par 69 she shot in the final round was her worst round of the week.

The iffy part was real enough, too. Lewis led from the second round and was ahead by a comfortable five strokes early in the final round, then tailed off. But she perked up in time to pull out a one-stroke win over Lexi Thompson, age 17, the fast-rising rookie. It was Lewis's second LPGA win, after the 2011 Kraft Nabisco Championship.

"I'm getting more comfortable in this situation," said Lewis. "It's definitely been coming."

Lewis played Magnolia Grove's Crossings course in 68-67-67-69, a 17-under 271 total, but she nearly wasted the effort by stagnating down the final stretch just as Thompson was getting up steam.

"I wasn't trying to birdie or do any of that," Lewis said. "Just hit some good shots and made a couple putts, and then from there things just (seemed) to level off."

Thompson finished with a bogey-free 65 and was signing autographs as Lewis two-putted for a winning par at the 18th and raised her arms in relief.

Lewis had opened the last round with birdies on the first two holes, going five ahead, then went calm until the two holes that wrapped up the drama. At the 15th, she hooked her approach into the water.

"Double (bogey) was going to put me out of the tournament," she said, "so I needed to get up and down there." She did, limiting the damage to a bogey, but it cost her the outright lead. She got it right back at the par-five 16th on what she considered her shot of the week. She missed the green but set up a birdie with a brilliant chip. "You could probably put 10 balls there and maybe get four or five of them up and down," she said. "To hit the shot I did under the pressure was huge."

HSBC LPGA Brasil Cup
Rio de Janeiro, Brazil
Winner: Pornanong Phatlum

It was a new year, a new — and fourth — HSBC LPGA Brasil Cup, and a new country heard from in this kind of officially unofficial event dabbling in an Olympic Games kind of spirit in golf. It's something of a warm-up for golf in the Olympics at Rio de Janeiro in 2016.

This time it was Thailand heard from, in the person of Pornanong Phatlum, a four-year member of the tour. Phatlum tied France's Karine Icher with a 66 in the first round, then opened the second and final round with five birdies on the front nine to run away with the tournament. Her 67 gave her a four-stroke win over Taiwan's Amy Hung at the par-73 Itanhanga Golf

Club. Paula Creamer (69) and Chelia Choi (67) tied for third, five shots back.

"I'm so excited today," Phatlum said. "I played really well today, and I played my own game."

The event, with a field of 30 playing two rounds, was officially an exhibition. The victory was recorded as Phatlum's first LPGA victory, but her winnings, $108,000, were not official. Phatlum gives the event four winners from four different countries — Scotland's Catriona Matthew in 2009, followed by America's Meaghan Francella and Colombia's Mariajo Uribe.

Sybase Match Play Championship
Gladstone, New Jersey
Winner: Azahara Munoz

The record will show that Spain's Azahara Munoz defeated Candie Kung to win the Sybase Match Play Championship — her first LPGA Tour victory — but for all of its finality and riches, it was merely the anticlimax to the tournament. The big show at Hamilton Farm Golf Club was the slow play penalty on Morgan Pressel in the semi-finals that helped get Munoz to the finals.

The episode led to hurt feelings, anger, tears and, apparently, making up.

Pressel and Munoz were both slow and both were warned after nine holes. Then they were being timed ("put on the clock") after the 11th. Pressel won the 12th with a par to go 3 up — seemingly. Then came the bad news. When they got to the 13th tee, a rules official informed her that she had been penalized for slow play. That meant she lost the previous hole, and in the rules scramble, Pressel ended up being not 3 up but 1 up with six holes to play. Next, Pressel accused Munoz of touching her putting line with her putter at the 15th. There was no evidence that Munoz did, and no penalty. She responded by winning the hole, and when Pressel bogeyed the next two, Munoz was a 2-and-1 winner.

Later, Pressel complained that she got penalized even though Munoz was slower. "I know I was slow, and I apologized," Munoz said. "I didn't do anything wrong. She was slow, I wasn't, not when the clock was on. When the clock is on, the clock is on."

In the championship match that afternoon, Munoz went 2 up when Kung stumbled at the 11th and 12th. Kung got a hole back at the 14th, but Munoz took the 16th with a bogey and won, 2 and 1, and celebrated her first victory. Along the way, she beat Lindsey Wright, Karrie Webb, Jodi Ewart and Stacy Lewis before reaching the big flap.

Munoz, age 24, former NCAA champion out of Arizona State University in her third year on the LPGA Tour, had five top-25 finishes this season, including top-fours in the last two events.

ShopRite LPGA Classic
Galloway, New Jersey
Winner: Stacy Lewis

The lesson was fresh, and it was a tough one for Stacy Lewis. Just three stops ago, in the final round of the Mobile Bay Classic, she checked the leaderboard and saw she had a five-stroke lead. Then: "I made the mistake of playing safe," she said. Before she knew it she was having to scramble to escape with a one-stroke win. She wasn't about to make that error again.

In her 65-65-71–201 performance at Stockton Seaview in the ShopRite LPGA Classic, it was that second-round 65 that won it for her. "I took so much from Mobile," she was to say. She birdied three of the first five holes, and after a double bogey at No. 6, a quick check of the leaderboard told her she had a two-stroke lead by the turn. "Let's see how big we can get this," she told herself. Keeping her head down, she birdied five of her last 10 holes and was 12 under par and six strokes up on Anna Nordqvist going into the final round. Before long, she was getting out of sight en route to her third LPGA win.

"I wasn't really playing aggressively," Lewis said. "I was just playing smart." Nobody raised a serious challenge. Katherine Hull shot a 68 to finish second, four behind. Japan's Mika Miyazato, who tied Lewis for the first-round lead at 65, closed with a 68 and tied for third with Spain's Azahara Munoz (69). Lewis birdied Nos. 4, 7 and 8 and led by a staggering nine shots. Then the wobblies set in. Her chipping went sour and she bogeyed the ninth, double-bogeyed the par-three 11th and bogeyed the 12th as well.

"I think I just started taking a few chip shots for granted," Lewis said. "When I made the double and the bogey on 11 and 12, I was actually pretty nervous."

Later, she made one final check. "I had a six-shot lead at that point," she said. "That was when I said, 'All right, it's center of the green, two-putt, and move on.'"

Wegmans LPGA Championship
Pittsford, New York
Winner: Shanshan Feng

See Chapter 7.

Manulife Financial LPGA Classic
Waterloo, Ontario, Canada
Winner: Brittany Lang

It was like that old school lesson for Brittany Lang. She had to keep doing it over until she got it right for her first victory on the LPGA Tour, on the tour's first visit to Waterloo, Ontario. It all started when she missed a short birdie putt at the final hole. After a 69-65-67 start, Lang finished with a 67 and fell into a tie at 16-under 268 with Chella Choi (63), Hee

Kyung Seo (67) and Inbee Park (69). It was back to Grey Silo's par-five 18th for the playoff.

Choi bowed out on the first trip, Park on the second. On the third, Lang blasted out of a bunker to six feet, then turned to Luke, her brother and caddie. Said Lang: "He said to me, 'Just because you're nervous doesn't mean you're going to miss the putt.'"

Oh. Then armed with that truth, Lang holed the putt. Ironically, after that miss in regulation, she had just birdied the 18th three straight times. She'd had only two bogeys all week.

"It feels amazing," said Lang, a runner-up five times. "I can't believe it took me seven years to win a tournament out here. I hadn't been that good under pressure, and I'm getting better. I'm so thankful that it happened this week, and I'll only get stronger from here."

Rolex world No. 2 Stacy Lewis, the tour's hottest at the moment with two victories and two top-five finishes in her last four events, opened with a one-over 72 that put her down in the pack. But she fought back with rounds of 64-69-64, including a chip-in eagle at the last to tie for fifth, missing the playoff by a shot. "I'm just proud of the way I came back," she said. Rookie Sandra Changkija shot an eight-under 63, tying the tour's season-low for the first-round lead. She went on to tie for 10th.

Then there was the forlorn Michelle Wie, now 22. She had improved, but barely. After missing six straight cuts, this time she closed with a 74 and tied for 68th.

Walmart NW Arkansas Championship
Rogers, Arkansas
Winner: Ai Miyazato

After an disappointing start to her LPGA career, Venezuela's Veronica Felibert knew a rookie's thrill of almost winning, then the sobering reality of faltering and getting overrun by a seasoned professional. Felibert led through the first two rounds, and then Japan's Ai Miyazato came from five strokes behind to win the Walmart NW Arkansas Championship at Pinnacle Country Club. If Felibert needed any consolation, she could note that Miyazato overran a crowded leaderboard, and also that Rolex world No. 1 Yani Tseng, a three-time winner this season, missed the cut for the first time in over a year. Her 73-74 start made it six straight rounds that she was over par.

Felibert started with 65-66, and Miyazato (68-68) trailed her by five going into the last. "I didn't have any expectation and I didn't have any pressure on the front nine," Miyazato said. "So that's why I could focus on my game and have four birdies on the front."

She got to 12 under par with her sixth birdie of the day at the par-three 15th. She bogeyed the 17th, but regained the shot at the par-five 18th — a three-wood second to the front fringe, a chip to five feet and a left-to-right downhill put for a birdie, a 65 and the 12-under 201 for a one-stroke win over Mika Miyazato (no relation) and Azahara Munoz. Felibert closed with a 72 and tied for fourth.

It was Miyazato's second win of the season, her ninth overall. Experience helped her shake off a bogey at the 17th, she said. "Afterwards, I just like in three seconds I was able to (be) back in myself," she said.

Felibert, a former University of Southern California player who spent two years on the developmental Symetra Tour, was nearly a story of the year. In her four LPGA starts, she missed the cut in three, tied for 70th and came to the NW Arkansas ranked 723rd in the world. Of her closing 72, she said: "I didn't feel nervous, but my swing wasn't there. I just played with what I got and it wasn't enough."

U.S. Women's Open
Kohler, Wisconsin
Winner: Na Yeon Choi

See Chapter 7.

Evian Masters
Evians-les-Bains, France
Winner: Inbee Park

See Ladies European Tour section.

Jamie Farr Toledo Classic
Sylvania, Ohio
Winner: So Yeon Ryu

Sometimes second place doesn't look so bad.

Angela Stanford came to that conclusion on the final nine of the Jamie Farr Toledo Classic, when the leaderboard showed that So Yeon Ryu was on a tear. "When you see somebody's running away with it, you continue to chase them, but if I can't catch her," she reasoned, "I'd like to be second." She got her wish.

Second, that is, by seven shots.

Ryu was deep in the hunt through the first three rounds, shooting 67-68-67, and was tied for the lead going into the last round. Then it was all over. A burst of birdies carried her well out of reach on a nine-under-par 62 at Highlands Meadows and a 20-under 264 total. Stanford did give chase, closing with a 66 to finish at 13 under.

Ryu thought of her dry spell after winning the 2011 U.S. Women's Open before she was a member of the LPGA Tour. "Everyone had really high expectations," she said. "I had no wins after that, so some were disappointed for me. So I really wanted to win as soon as possible, and today I made it."

Ryu inched her way out of the tie in the fourth round. She birdied the third hole with an approach out of light rough to eight feet to take the lead. She went up by two at the fifth with a birdie from 12 feet. Then after her lead was cut to one, she birdied the ninth from 30 feet. Next came an unreal spell — five birdies from six feet or less. Then she capped her day with a two-footer at the 18th. But it wasn't the end. "This," she said, "is just my turning point. I want to win again."

A tournament that ended with fireworks started with them — the putting rampage by Sweden's Pernilla Lindberg in a first-round 64. Lindberg, who went on to tie for 18th, holed a 50-footer, a 40-footer and three from 25 feet, all for birdies. "It felt," she said, "like every putt had a chance to go in."

Safeway Classic
North Plains, Oregon
Winner: Mika Miyazato

There was the curious tale of two golfers named Miyazato — Ai and Mika. Both Japanese, both from Okinawa, and not related. It was said the way to tell them apart was that Mika was the one who couldn't win. Then along came the Safeway Classic.

Where the old Mika would have fallen short, the new one went wire-to-wire, shooting 65-68-70–203, 13 under par at Pumpkin Ridge, to grab her first victory and by two strokes.

"It was my dream to win and play on the LPGA Tour," said Miyazato, the sixth first-time winner of the year. Miyazato, age 22, in her fourth season on the tour, had five top-10 finishes in her past six events, including two ties for second.

Miyazato stamped the Safeway as hers in the first round, racing to four straight birdies at one point, then birdieing the 18th, the toughest hole on the course, to tie rookie Sydnee Michaels at 65.

"To begin the season, I was not so very good," Miyazato said. "I'm gaining more confidence."

In the second round, Miyazato birdied two of her last four holes for a 68 and a two-stroke lead, and then came the final round and the big test. She upped her lead to three, then made her first bogey in 40 holes at the 10th. "I'm so angry with myself," she said. Then she narrowly escaped at the par-three 11th. Her tee shot was headed for the creek, but bounced off a rock and landed near the green. "Maybe lucky for me," she was to say. She saved par with a 25-foot putt.

Lincicome birdied the last two holes for a 67, and Park bagged five birdies in eight holes and shot 70, to take the clubhouse lead at 11 under. Miyazato held her ground, birdied the 17th on a five-footer, and came in with a 70, two shots better.

Then there were two Miyazatos on the 18th green. Ai, who tied for 16th, came rushing out to hug Mika. Said Ai, a nine-time winner: "I knew her time was going to come soon."

CN Canadian Women's Open
Coquitlam, British Columbia, Canada
Winner: Lydia Ko

Just 15 years old and she's in the World Golf Hall of Fame already.

Well, in a manner of speaking.

Lydia Ko, New Zealand's entry in golf's youth movement — who likes school and going to movies with her friends — won the U.S. Women's Amateur early in August. But why come all that way for just one title? So she entered the CN Canadian Women's Open a few weeks later and became the youngest ever to win on the LPGA Tour, and the first amateur to win the Canadian Women's Open and fifth to win on the LPGA Tour.

"It's nerve-racking, playing with the pros and actually playing against the pros," the kid said. The feeling was mutual. Said Suzann Pettersen: "It feels like you're being beaten by a kid." Well?

This was no come-from-behind surge down the stretch. Playing the par-72 Vancouver Golf Club course in 68-68-72-67–275, 13 under, Ko tied for the lead in the second round and led the rest of the way. She won by three over Inbee Park, who as low pro got the $300,000 first prize. And this wasn't a teenage field. World No. 1 Yani Tseng, for example, led the first round with a 66, with Ne Yeon Choi at 67, and Ko tied with Park at 68. Ko showed great poise in the second round. She parred the first 11 holes, birdied three straight from the 12th, then added another at the 17th in a no-bogey 68 to share the lead, and took the solo lead in the third.

The pros were dumbfounded. "This is our job," an admiring Stacy Lewis said. "It isn't supposed to be her job, and yet she's beating us."

Ko was especially impressive in the final round. She not only shook off the greatest pressure, she shot her best round, a 67, to win by three. The Hall of Fame was on the phone in an instant. Ko was happy to provide her golf glove, and surely had dreams of joining it someday.

Kingsmill Championship
Williamsburg, Virginia
Winner: Jiyai Shin

The Kingsmill Championship came down to Jiyai Shin trying to end a victory drought of nearly two years and Paula Creamer trying to end one of just over two, and needing an 81-hole tournament in which to do it — 72 holes of regulation and a grinding nine-hole playoff that Sunday darkness forced into Monday morning. It was the LPGA Tour's longest ever between two players.

Daylight found Creamer three-putting for a bogey at the ninth extra hole, and Shin winning with a two-putt par. It was seeing Creamer miss her short par putt that scared Shin about her own. "I was really nervous with it," Shin said. "But after, I was really happy."

The three-putt shocked Creamer, too. "I thought I hit a great putt, that first one," she said. "I felt good over the next one."

Except for a brief interlude by hot-putting Danielle Kang, 19 (she would tie for third), it was a Shin-Creamer duel, both coming back from injuries. Shin shot a stunning nine-under 62 in the first round, then added 68-69-69, leading the first and second rounds. Creamer (65-67-65-71) led the third, and they tied at 268, 16 under at the par-71 Kingsmill River course. Creamer led Shin by two going into the final round, then made a double bogey and two singles in the fourth, the last when she missed a five-footer for a winning par at the final hole.

They battled away in pars for eight extra holes at the par-four 18th Sunday evening, then came out Monday morning to the par-four 16th. It was over in 20 minutes. Creamer knocked her 30-foot birdie try five feet past, missed the par return and bogeyed. Shin two-putted from 15 feet for her winning par. Then both were headed to the Women's British Open.

Creamer refused to be discouraged. "I played great this whole tournament," she said. "I'm going to go and try and win a major."

Shin said: "I can't believe, because I did a hand operation in June. I'm really happy it's coming quick."

Ricoh Women's British Open
Hoylake, England
Winner: Jiyai Shin

See Chapter 7.

Navistar LPGA Classic
Prattville, Alabama
Winner: Stacy Lewis

It was getting to be pretty late in the Navistar LPGA Classic when Stacy Lewis finally looked up, and much to her surprise, there was quite a golf tournament going on around her. With her as the target, that is.

"Lexi was within one when we got to the 16th green," Lewis said, "and that's the only time all day I actually knew what was going on."

It was then Lewis discovered that Lexi Thompson, who led through the first two rounds and who had been chasing her ever since, had just about caught up. "Making birdie there on 16 was huge," Lewis said. It gave her a two-stroke edge to see her home for her third victory of the season, one that carried another number of great importance: 56.

The win, in the final full-field event of the season in mid-September, gave Lewis a 56-point lead over Jiyai Shin in the Rolex Player of the Year race with the season winding down. And Lewis wanted that POY award.

But first, she had to get through the Navistar, which turned into a battle between the young (Lewis, age 27, in her fourth year on the tour) and the much younger (Thompson, 17, in her second year, and defending the title she'd won at age 16). Thompson shot the par-72 Senator course in 63-69 and led by one at the halfway point, but was four up on Lewis. Then, after making only one bogey in 36 holes, she made two and a double bogey in the third round, shooting 74, and fell five behind Lewis, who took the lead with a 65. The fourth round was a duel, though Lewis was sticking to her tunnel vision.

Lewis bogeyed No. 2 and birdied Nos. 5 and 9. Thompson birdied three straight from No. 10 on putts of six, one and 10 feet. Thompson missed birdie putts on three of the last four holes and shot 66, while Lewis birdied the 16th, posted a 69 for an 18-under 270 to win by two.

"It's unbelievable," Lewis said. "Winning never gets easier."

Sime Darby LPGA Malaysia
Kuala Lumpur. Malaysia
Winner: Inbee Park

Korea's Na Yeon Choi shared the first-round lead and held the solo lead through the second and third, so going into the final round she was exactly where she didn't want to be. "Actually, I don't like leading a tournament — that feeling," Choi said. "I like chasing better."

Unfortunately, Choi, ranked No. 4 in the Rolex Rankings, got her wish in the final round, but she came up short. Fellow Korean Inbee Park, who opened with 69-68-65, rode a birdie spurt on the final nine to a 67 and beat Choi by two with a 269 total, 15 under par, in the Sime Darby LPGA Malaysia at Kuala Lumpur Golf and Country Club.

"I was nervous coming to the 17th and 18th, as I knew I was leading and it was tough from there," Park said. So tough, in fact, that she bogeyed both holes. It was Park's second win of the year, after the Evian Masters in July, and her career-third.

Choi, trying for her seventh LPGA Tour win, double-bogeyed the par-three 17th and closed with a 71 to finish second. "I played well on the front nine, but I had one bogey, on the ninth," Choi said. "I think I had back luck on the 17th as well."

Starting out, Choi knew the tension of the defending champion. "I think I put extra pressure on myself," she said. "A lot of people expect me to win again this year. That makes me a little nervous, a little more pressured."

She shot six-under 65, tying with Australia's Karrie Webb, who was seeking her first victory of the season. "The thing I was most proud of was that I just settled in," Webb said. "I didn't want to try to force anything." Webb closed with a 68 and finished third.

Park, who trailed by as much as five shots through the first three rounds, caught fire down the final nine, birdieing the 10th, 11th, 13th and 14th to take the lead. "Playing aggressively helped me and got me the birdies," Park said. "My golf has improved a lot — hitting, chipping and putting."

LPGA KEB-HanaBank Championship
Incheon, South Korea
Winner: Suzann Pettersen

Playing to protect a big lead — sometimes it's a trap, sometimes not. As with any trap, the golfer doesn't really know till she's in it. Norway's Suzann Pettersen found this out the hard way in the LPGA KEB-HanaBank Championship. She was able to escape with her first win of the season, her ninth on the tour, but it took her a three-hole playoff against Scotland's Catriona Matthew to do it.

Pettersen played Sky 72 Golf Club beautifully in the first two rounds, with a course-record 63, nine under par, followed by a 68 for a 13-under 131 total and a five-stroke lead over South Korea's So Yeon Ryu going into the third and final round. Choicer yet, she was up by seven over Matthew. And it all disappeared.

"I might have gone out trying to be a little bit protective," Pettersen admitted, "which obviously does not fit my game at all." She double-bogeyed the par-three third hole, then bogeyed the eighth, and then another double bogey at the par-three 12th dropped her two strokes behind the charging Matthew. Time for a chat with the caddie. She told him if she was going to make bogeys, she might as well fire at the pins. He agreed. "Why don't you just play as aggressively as you have all week," he told her. She responded with a birdie at the 14th, and when Matthew bogeyed the 16th, they were tied at 11 under. Pettersen won it with a birdie on their third playoff visit to the par-five 18th.

"I felt I played pretty well," Pettersen offered, "but it was just not a scoring day."

Taiwan's Yani Tseng, defending champion and ranked No. 1 in the world, finished third. Michelle Wie, playing on a sponsor's exemption, tied for 30th.

Sunrise LPGA Taiwan Championship
Yang Mei, Taiwan
Winner: Suzann Pettersen

Sunday of the Sunrise LPGA Taiwan Championship came up windy and drizzling and not at all conducive to good golf. Ah, said Norway's Suzann Pettersen — just the way I like it.

Said Pettersen, winner of the HanaBank event the week before: "Coming from behind, being a little bit of an underdog, knowing that they predicted tougher conditions, that was just up my alley."

This underdog had her days. Pettersen trailed South Korea's Inbee Park by four strokes in the first round, and then they hooked up in one of the tour's grittiest scraps. Pettersen had to rally in the final round for the win, her second of the season and 10th on the tour. Park led or shared the lead with 65-69-64 through the first three rounds. Pettersen shot 69-65-66 and trailed by two going into the final round and the disagreeable weather.

"I like a challenge," Pettersen said. "I'm looking forward to tomorrow."

So was World No. 1 Yani Tseng, native daughter and huge favorite at the Sunrise Golf Club. But she couldn't crack the Pettersen-Park battle and finished third.

Park, seeking her third win of the year, drew some strength from Pettersen. "She's playing great, and that really helps me with my game," she said. And so they shot it out over the last three rounds, Park taking a two-shot lead into the last.

Pettersen wasted no time, getting within one with a birdie at the first, and they were tied when Park bogeyed the fifth. They matched birdies and bogeys through the next two holes. Pettersen bogeyed the 11th, then rebounded with a birdie at the 12th and they were tied again. Pettersen broke into the lead for good on Park's bogey at the 14th, went up by two with a birdie at the 15th, and finally birdied the 18th for a 69 to Park's 74 for her three-stroke win with a 19-under 269 total. And the weather helped.

"It was tough enough to where I managed to keep my focus," Pettersen said. "Really playing with my heart, playing with my instinct."

Mizuno Classic
Shima, Mie
Winner: Stacy Lewis

See Japan LPGA Tour section.

Lorena Ochoa Invitational
Guadalajara, Mexico
Winner: Cristie Kerr

Not that it's likely to find its way into the supply of good golf omens, but getting locked in the bathroom was worth at least a chuckle or some kind of inspiration for Cristie Kerr in the Lorena Ochoa Invitational.

"I didn't even lock the door," said Kerr. She was getting alarmed. She was due on the tee. "And I'm kicking and kicking, trying to open the door," she said. Well, this scene out of *Caddyshack* took place in the third round, when Kerr was still trying to catch the leaders. She got within two of Inbee Park, the 54-hole leader. From there, it was a Mexican holiday at Guadalajara Country Club for Kerr and Stacy Lewis. Kerr was on her way to her 15th career victory but her first since 2010. And Lewis locked up the Rolex Player of the Year Award, the first American to win it in 18 years, since Beth Daniel in 1994.

Kerr hung close to the leaders through the first three rounds, then fought off a case of nerves and parred the last three holes, outrunning Park to win the 36-player invitational. Kerr shot 67-69-67-69–272, 16 under par, for a one-shot win over Park, who could only manage a four-birdie, four-bogey 72. "Coming in those last couple holes, it didn't feel like I had won before," Kerr said. "I kind of just squeaked in. I won by a shot. That's all it takes. I've lost plenty of tournaments by a shot, but winning by a shot feels a lot better."

It was definitely feel-good time for Stacy Lewis, too. She tied for fourth and clinched the Player of the Year Award. It was almost a formality. She came into the tournament leading Park by 58 points. Park would have had to win the Ochoa and the season-ending Titleholders and have Lewis finish outside the top 10 to beat her. It was almost a formality, but that didn't dampen the thrill.

"It's just crazy to think that there have been so many great American players," Lewis said, "and I am the one after Beth."

CME Group Titleholders
Naples, Florida
Winner: Na Yeon Choi

South Korea's Na Yeon Choi was making quite a name for herself: "The Golfer Who Hates the Lead."

Choi was at it again in the LPGA's season-ending CME Group Titleholders in November, chafing at the thought of being out front, then playing better down the stretch to add the title to her U.S. Women's Open to make it a great 2012. She won by two shots over countrywoman So Yeon Ryu, herself signing off with the Rolex Rookie of the Year Award.

"I was very nervous last night," Choi would admit later, of a disturbed Saturday night's sleep. "I told people that leading the tournament, there's always extra pressure. Even on the front nine, when I had the double bogey and the tie for first place, I felt more comfortable than leading. Maybe that sounds a little weird. I like chasing somebody, and then I can play more aggressive."

It worked this time. But it didn't in the Sime Darby event in October. She fell behind Inbee Park and couldn't catch up. But there's something of a pattern emerging. Choi had to recover from a triple bogey in the final round of the Women's Open. This time it was a double bogey, when she missed the green badly at No. 3 and slipped into a four-way tie for the lead. But she quickly regained the lead at the par-five No. 4, hitting a three wood from 240 yards that bounced short of the green and rolled up inside 10 feet. She dropped the putt for an eagle and led the rest of the way. She played the par-72 TwinEagles Club in 67-68-69-70—274, 14 under.

Choi was comfortably one shot behind in each of the first two rounds. The third-round 69 forced her out front. It had a special meaning to her. Said Choi: "I'm just happy I have to play just 18 more holes and finish this year." As for goals: "I want to make good result this week," said Choi, who lives in Orlando, Florida, "to buy a new house."

Ladies European Tour

Gold Coast RACV Ladies Masters
Ashmore, Queensland, Australia
Winner: Christel Boeljon

See Australian Ladies Tour section.

ISPS Handa Women's Australian Open
Melbourne, Victoria, Australia
Winner: Jessica Korda

See Australian Ladies Tour section.

ISPS Handa New Zealand Women's Open
Christchurch, New Zealand
Winner: Lindsey Wright

See Australian Ladies Tour section.

World Ladies Championship
Haikou, Hainan, China
Winner: Shanshan Feng

Shanshan Feng made history as the first player from mainland China to win on the Ladies European Tour. Feng, who came into the tournament as No. 12 on the Rolex Rankings, won the inaugural World Ladies Championship at Mission Hills Haikou on Hainan Island. Rounds of 66, 69 and 71 put Feng at 206, 10 under par, and one ahead of Thailand's Pornanong Phatlum, with Sweden's Pernilla Lindberg a shot further behind in third. The 54-hole tournament was a three-in-one event, with a professional team event and an amateur individual event running alongside the main competition. China, thanks to Feng and Li-Ying Ye, who finished tied for fourth, took the team title with a total of 415, 17 under par, two clear of Thailand, with Sweden third and Italy in fourth place.

Italian Diana Luna led the individual tournament after 13 holes of the final round but fell back into a tie with Feng after a bogey at the 16th and then took a triple bogey at the final hole. Her second went over the green onto rocks that were in a hazard. After a penalty drop, she took four more shots to hole out.

Feng said: "I wasn't really shooting a low score today. I think at one time I was three behind, but I wasn't worried at all because I knew I would have more chances on the back nine and I would catch up and finally I got it. I was really focusing on the team score and I saw the Thailand team was really strong. Me and my partner, we were talking about it and we said, 'no, we can't let them catch us.'"

The amateur event was won by 16-year-old Jing Yan, a Chinese national team member who was born and raised in Singapore, with a total of 216 by two strokes over world No. 1 amateur Lydia Ko.

Lalla Meryem Cup
Agadir, Morocco
Winner: Karen Lunn

Karen Lunn made a strong charge on the homeward half to win the Lalla Meryem Cup at the Ocean course in Agadir. The 46-year-old Australian claimed her 10th title on the Ladies European Tour by coming home in 31 with five birdies to win by three strokes over Marianne Skarpnord and Tandi Cunningham. Lunn returned rounds of 72, 66, 68 and 66 for a 16-under-par total of 272.

After a poor start to the week, the former British Open champion worked her way up to a stroke behind Jade Schaeffer with a round to play. But with the Frenchwoman stuttering, her challenge fading with a double bogey at the 12th, it was the veteran Australian, who had won the Royal Canberra Classic on the ALPG circuit two months earlier, who took advantage. She had three birdies in a row to start the back nine, with a 50-footer at the 12th putting her in front, and although Skarpnord briefly tied her for the lead, the Norwegian dropped a shot at the 15th, where Lunn birdied. Another birdie at the 16th sealed the victory. Skarpnord, who was watched on the weekend by her boyfriend Richard Green, who had missed the cut in the concurrent Hassan II Trophy, closed with a 69, while South Africa's Cunningham finished strongly with a 67.

"We got to the turn and I think there were seven or eight players within two shots of the lead, so it was game on for anyone," said Lunn. "I just managed to play the back nine really well and made some putts and that's what you have to do. No matter how many times you win, every one is very difficult. I never actually got nervous today until I got in front after 15. I was like, it's up to me now."

Aberdeen Asset Management Ladies Scottish Open
East Lothian, Scotland
Winner: Carly Booth

After a home victory for Catriona Matthew at the Aberdeen Asset Management Ladies Scottish Open in 2011, there was another home triumph for another ambassador for the sponsors in the form of the exciting 19-year-old Carly Booth. A young prodigy of high talent — and not just in golf as a former Scottish title winner at gymnastics — Booth became the youngest club champion in Britain when she took the title at Dunblane New at the age of just 11. Once ranked the top junior in Europe, Booth became the youngest player to represent Great Britain and Ireland in the Curtis Cup in 2008 before turning professional at age 17. Both she and her elder brother benefited from playing on the 15-hole course built by their father

Wally in their back garden at home in Comrie, Perthshire. Taking time to settle into the professional ranks, Booth just missed a spot in the top 30 of the LET qualifying at the end of 2011 and started the season on the LET Access Series, winning the Dinard Open just a fortnight before getting a sponsor's invitation to play in her national championship. Her maiden victory on the main circuit means she is exempt until the end of the 2014 season.

The fiendish bunkers built by her father helped prepare Booth for the Archerfield course and her bunker play was crucial, not least at the last as she came out of the sand safely for her third shot at the par-five, then putted up to two feet before tapping in for a one-stroke victory over Florentyna Parker and Frances Bondad. It was the third vital par save in a row for the Scot, who took the lead for good once Parker three-putted at the 16th for a bogey while Booth got up and down from 30 yards. Booth closed with a 71 after rounds of 70 and 71, for a four-under total of 212, while Parker, who shared the lead with a round to play, had a 72 and Bondad a 67. Trish Johnson shared fourth place with Stacey Keating and Mel Reid after a closing 68 in which she had seven birdies in the first 11 holes.

Booth said: "I'm still 19 and I've just won my first Ladies European Tour event, so I'm just happy. The last putt was only about two feet and I only just got it in the hole. I must have just felt the nerves there. I was fine all the way up until that putt, put it that way. I just didn't feel anything until I holed that putt because I realized, 'This is it!' It was the longest two-foot putt I've ever had to hole."

Turkish Airlines Ladies Open
Belek, Antalya, Turkey
Winner: Christel Boeljon

On a course that requires disciplined golf over four days, Christel Boeljon successfully retained her title at the Turkish Airlines Ladies Open at the National Golf Club in Belek, Antalya. It was a year ago that Boeljon claimed her first individual title, having won a team event for Holland as her first official LET event in 2009. And since then the 24-year-old Dutchwoman has not looked back, taking part in Europe's Solheim Cup victory in Ireland, then winning the opening event of the 2012 season at the Australian Ladies Masters. On a tight, tree-lined course, Boeljon shared or held the lead outright throughout the tournament. An opening three-under 70 put her among five co-leaders; a 73 in the second round meant she shared the halfway lead with Ursula Wikstrom, while a 69 on day three put her two clear. Another 73 to close gave Boeljon a three-stroke victory over Wikstrom, who had a 74, and by five over Carin Koch and Carlota Ciganda.

Ciganda, who started three behind, took advantage of Boeljon's bogey at the first with two birdies in the first three holes to tie for the lead. But then the young Spaniard dropped six shots in the next eight holes, while Boeljon had three birdies in a row from the fifth. Wikstrom got within one thanks to a birdie at the 11th but then went bogey, birdie, bogey, double bogey. Boeljon, who bogeyed the 10th and then birdied the 13th, was still four clear despite a bogey at the 15th, where Wikstrom's challenge fizzled. A ball in the water at the last ultimately did not matter.

"To be able to defend is quite an honor and quite special, so I'm very pleased," said Boeljon. "It's a tough course because you need to put the ball in the right place and you need to putt well. Your short game needs to be good, so it's all around a good golf course."

UniCredit Ladies German Open
Munich, Germany
Winner: Anne-Lise Caudal

Laura Davies felt the pain of a playoff defeat even more at the UniCredit Ladies German Open because of the bonus prize offered by the presenting sponsor. As well as a first prize of €52,500, Anne-Lise Caudal also claimed an Audi A5 cabriolet car. Caudal won the playoff at the second extra hole with a birdie at the 18th. Both parred the 18th for the first extra hole, but next time Davies missed from 12 feet for a birdie to leave Caudal with a 10-footer for victory. The 27-year-old from France duly converted the chance for her second tour victory. It came four years after her first, at the Portuguese Open in 2008.

"I can't believe it yet. It was an amazing week this week after a tough first round, plus two: a lot of emotion right now," said Caudal. "I was pretty confident with my wedge at the second extra hole. I had a wedge in my hand to hit to the pin, and I just breathed a lot and tried to calm down because my heart was pretty fast. I just breathed and believed in what I'm doing."

Caudal opened with a 74 but then reeled off three 67s in a row for a 13-under total of 275. She and Davies started the final round two shots behind a trio of leaders, Pernilla Lindberg, Rebecca Hudson and Bree Arthur. Hudson closed with a 71 to finish in third place, two shots behind the playoff. Davies's 67 included birdies at the 14th and 15th holes, only for her to three-putt at the 16th to fall out of the lead. She made a birdie from eight feet at the last to tie but could not match it in the playoff.

Davies said: "It's a cruel playoff to lose really, because not only do you lose the money, you lose the sub prize of a car, which is very unusual on the European Tour, so for whoever wins this tournament, it's a really special win. It's like a double hit, but Anne-Lise deserves it."

Deloitte Ladies Open
Rotterdam, Netherlands
Winner: Carlota Ciganda

Two days after her 22nd birthday and a year after turning professional, Carlota Ciganda won her first LET title at the Deloitte Ladies Open at Broekpolder, near Rotterdam. Ciganda, from Pamplona, was a highly talented amateur who first played on the LET at the age of 14 and finished third in the Tenerife Open in 2008. She also created history at Arizona State University by winning back-to-back Pac-10 Championships in 2009-2010.

After turning professional Ciganda won an LET Access Series event in Murcia and in 2012 won the Spanish professional title.

Rounds of 71 and 67 in Holland put Ciganda one ahead of Ursula Wikstrom going into the final round. After a lengthy delay due to heavy overnight rain, both players went out in 33, with Ciganda holing long putts at the first and ninth holes. Wikstrom had briefly tied for the lead and did so again when Ciganda three-putted at the 11th, but the Finn dropped shots at the 12th and 16th holes to fall two behind. Both players birdied the last as the rain returned, but the young Spaniard had held her nerve to finish on 207, nine under par, after a 69. Wikstrom finished two back, with Lee-Anne Pace three further back in third place.

"I am very happy. It's a very good feeling and I am very happy because I played very good golf. I was feeling calm and I was fine," Ciganda said.

Allianz Ladies Slovak Open
Brezno, Tale, Slovakia
Winner: Line Vedel

Denmark's Line Vedel claimed her maiden victory when she defeated Caroline Masson by two strokes at the Allianz Ladies Slovak Open. The 23-year-old from Aabenraa was helped by a suspension of an hour and 20 minutes on the final day. After starting the day tied with Finland's Jenni Kuosa, Vedel bogeyed two of the first three holes, but upon the resumption she birdied five holes out of nine from the sixth, where she holed from 60 feet. Vedel, in her second season on tour, had rounds of 71, 69 and 69 to finish on 209, seven under par. Masson also closed with a 69 to be two ahead of Nontaya Srisawang and Veronica Zorzi, who tied for third place. Carly Booth and Trish Johnson were among those tied for seventh, but Kuosa closed with an 82 to be 47th.

"I'm thrilled and excited. It's just a big relief, I'd say, because I knew I can play against the best, but also doing it, that's another factor. I knew it was a tough day today and with my start I kind of felt the pressure a bit, but I just tried to keep patient. I've been hitting the ball well all week and putted alright as well, so I hung in there. I felt the nerves on the last couple of holes, but I managed to hang in there, so it feels great."

Vedel had her mother Susanne caddieing for her. "Normally it's my dad and when my boyfriend/coach is available, he's on the bag, so they've got some competition now."

Deutsche Bank Ladies Swiss Open
Ticino, Switzerland
Winner: Carly Booth

Carly Booth won for the second time in little over a month by eagling the fourth hole of a playoff against the German pair of Anja Monke and Caroline Masson. Booth leapt high into the air when the winning putt fell, and then jumped into the arms of her caddie, European Tour player Tano Goya. Her boyfriend, Goya, claimed he would retire from the post of caddie with a 100 percent record. It was an early 20th birthday present for Booth, who also had her first hole-in-one at the 13th hole of the first round.

Booth won a tournament on the Access Series before winning the Scottish Open on an invitation. "I said to myself after the Scottish, I'm going to try to get two wins before my 20th and I just did it," she revealed. Booth had rounds of 70, 71, 67 and 68 for a total of 276, 12 under par, as she tied with Monke, who closed with 66, and Masson, who finished with 68. Masson ended up a runner-up for the second week running after the first attempts at the par-five 18th ended with all three players making birdies. Then Booth hit a five iron to 10 feet and made the winning putt.

"I'm overwhelmed, speechless, so happy," Booth said. "It was tough. We birdied three out of three and I was thinking someone's going to have to eagle to win this. I was just trying to hit a positive putt. I wasn't trying to think about it, and I think with having the experience of winning previously in the Scottish I had grasped the feeling of trying to stay calm and positive."

Raiffeisenbank Prague Golf Masters
Prague, Czech Republic
Winner: Melissa Reid

Melissa Reid claimed one of the most emotional victories ever on the Ladies European Tour at the Raiffeisenbank Prague Masters at Albatross Golf Resort. It was Reid's first tournament since the death of her mother, Joy, four weeks earlier at the German Open. Reid's parents had attended the players' party at the start of the week and were driving back to their hotel when they were involved in a car crash. Joy Reid died the following day from internal injuries.

Reid immediately withdrew from the tournament and only returned to the circuit in Prague, scoring rounds of 68 and 67 to take the lead going into the final round. With a congested leaderboard in difficult conditions, Reid returned a 72 for a total of 207, nine under par, to finish one ahead of Diana Luna, with Rachel Bailey and Rebecca Hudson in third place. Reid birdied the 17th to go one ahead of Luna but then needed to hole from six feet at the last for a par and the victory. It was only after the ball had dropped that the tears started to flow as Reid was embraced by many friends and competitors.

"To be honest I wasn't that nervous," Reid said. "I think with something like what's happened to my family and me the last four weeks nothing really seems that difficult anymore. I spoke to my coach when I went back a couple of weeks after and he said to me, 'I don't know when it's going to be, but this will make you a stronger person,' and my best friends have said that as well and I honestly think it will. It will make me fight and nothing will seem as bad as what I've been through, so yeah, I actually felt very calm and I knew I was going to hole the putt on 18."

South African Women's Open
KwaZulu-Natal, South Africa
Winner: Caroline Masson

It was windy all week at Selborne Park during the South African Women's Open, but such were the gales on the final day that play was suspended for an hour in the morning. In overcoming the treacherous conditions, Caroline Masson also claimed her first LET title. Masson finished as the only player under par as the 23-year-old German beat home favorite Lee-Anne Pace and England's Danielle Montgomery by one stroke.

Scores in the 60s were few and far between during the week, and Masson took the lead with an opening three-under 69. A 75 the next day left her still in a tie for the lead with three other players, but it was her 71 in the final round which really stood out. She had a birdie at the third hole, but the most impressive thing was that she did not drop a shot, finishing on a total of 215. Pace made up ground with a 70 as Montgomery returned a 72, while the lowest round of the week was the 68 of South Africa's Melissa Eaton-Jackson, who jumped to ninth place.

"It was such a tough day with the wind," said Masson. "Not having a bogey was pretty good. I hung in there and made my pars. I got lucky a few times, and I had a few birdie chances but didn't make those putts. But all in all I'm really happy with the way I played."

Evian Masters
Evians-les-Bains, France
Winner: Inbee Park

Inbee Park became the last winner of the Evian Masters. With the course at the Evian Royal Resort being closed for a year for redevelopments, the tournament is due to return in 2013 as The Evian, moved from July to September and recognized as a major championship on the LPGA Tour as well as on the Ladies European Tour. Having just got the pace of the greens to perfection in securing a two-stroke victory, Park may not want any changes to the course, but with a skydiver delivering a Korean flag to her at the prize-giving, the 24-year-old was too busy enjoying her victory in similar fashion to athletes at the just-started London Olympic Games.

Park birdied the last three holes to seal the victory over Stacy Lewis and Karrie Webb, as putts from 10, three and 25 feet fell to her delight. She had started the day tied for the lead with Lewis and on the back nine was joined in the lead by Webb, who chipped in at the 13th, and Natalie Gulbis. But once Park had birdied the 13th she kept her nose in front despite the late charges of Webb, who birdied the last two holes, and Lewis, who birdied the 16th and eagled the 18th.

Lewis started the week in superb form by equaling Helen Alfredsson's course record of nine-under 63. Park trailed by eight after a 71, but a 64 on Friday put her within three of the American, who had followed up with a 69. After a 73 on Saturday, Lewis lost sole possession of the lead with Park joining her after a 70.

Scoring was again low on the final day, with Shanshan Feng holing a bunker shot at the last hole to set the clubhouse target at 14 under par. She ended tied for fourth place with Gulbis and 17-year-old Korean amateur Hyo Joo Kim. Webb, the 2006 winner, and Lewis, who struggled with her putting and a cracked driver, finished one shot better with rounds of 67 and 68 respectively. Park's closing 66 left her on a 17-under total of 271 as she collected a second LPGA title following her 2008 U.S. Women's Open triumph.

Park said: "In the Olympics when I was watching all the athletes have their flags on when they had a medal, I wanted to do that also. I did it today, so I'm very happy. I really had a tough time the last five years putting here and didn't play good here. I was not really confident with the greens. This year I came and the greens were a lot quicker than the last five years. I like the fast greens, so I think that really suited me as well."

Ladies Irish Open
Co. Meath, Ireland
Winner: Catriona Matthew

A trio of players from the European team which won the 2011 Solheim Cup at Killeen Castle returned to County Meath to top the leaderboard at the Ladies Irish Open. Catriona Matthew led from start to finish to claim her fifth LET title but was pushed all the way by defending champion Suzann Pettersen and former winner Laura Davies. Matthew had seven birdies in her last eight holes in an opening round of 67 and added a 71 in the second round to lead by two strokes over Carly Booth and Pernilla Lindberg.

But it was the experienced Pettersen and Davies who made a last-day charge. Davies was hampered by an Achilles tendon injury first suffered three months earlier and aggravated during a charity football match at the Evian Masters. However, the Englishwoman closed with a 68 for three under par, but it was Pettersen's 69 that put the pressure on Matthew. The Norwegian got within one with a birdie at the 12th and tied for the lead after a 20-foot birdie at the 15th. Matthew, playing in the group behind, also birdied the hole, but then Pettersen birdied the 16th before dropping a shot at the 17th. Matthew birdied the 17th to lead by two, so a bogey at the last meant a 71 for a seven-under total of 209 and a one-stroke win.

"I'm absolutely delighted," said Matthew, 42. "It's always difficult going out in the lead. I was just kind of trotting along there at seven under and saw Suzann making some birdies. I think she thought she was in the Solheim Cup again."

ISPS Handa Ladies British Masters
Denham, Buckinghamshire, England
Winner: Lydia Hall

Having suffered a mini-crisis earlier in her round, Lydia Hall kept her composure at the exciting 17th hole at the Buckinghamshire Golf Club, where the Ladies European Tour has its headquarters, to win the ISPS Handa Ladies British Masters. While Ashleigh Simon had a double bogey and, in front of the final pairing, American Beth Allen had a triple bogey, Hall hit her drive over the lake, a carry of 244 yards, and onto the green at the short par-four. She three-putted for a four, as had Allen, who was leading by one at the time but had laid up on the fairway and put her second in a bunker, where the ball was imbedded, and she elected to take a penalty drop.

Hall had duffed a chip in the rough at the short 12th for a double bogey and had a bogey at the 13th but rallied with a birdie at the 14th and produced a composed finish before a bogey at the last. A co-leader on the first day after a 66, Hall had further rounds of 71 and 72 for a seven-under total of 209 and a one-shot win over Allen. A group of six players tied for third place two behind: Simon, who led with a round to play but closed with a 76, Trish Johnson, Stacy Lee Bregman, Rebecca Artis, Henrietta Zuel and Mikaela Parmlid.

Hall, a 24-year-old from Bridgend, won her maiden title alongside a new caddie, veteran bagman Lee Griffiths, who is from the same Welsh town. "It was good to have Lee on the bag, who is experienced, as he kept me calm and focused throughout the round," Hall said. "I've been waiting to win a tournament for the last five years since I came on tour."

England's Charley Hull finished tied for 18th as a 16-year-old amateur.

UNIQA Ladies Golf Open
Wiener Neustadt, Austria
Winner: Caroline Hedwall

In her first tournament in two months due to a hip injury, Caroline Hedwall surprised even herself by defending her title at the UNIQA Ladies Golf Open at Fohrenwaldh in Austria. Hedwall won four times on tour in 2011 as she took both rookie and player of the year honors, but her second season as a professional was interrupted by an injury at the U.S. Women's Open. The 23-year-old Swede was only allowed to hit full shots three weeks before arriving in Wiener Neustadt. But she opened with a 67 to share the lead with Australian Alison Whitaker and went two ahead after a second round of 66.

Hedwall closed with a 70 for a 13-under-par total of 203. She won by four strokes over Laura Davies, a three-time former winner who got within one shot at the turn before her challenge stalled, and Mikaela Parmlid. Whitaker, who holed her third shot for an eagle at the last, finished a further shot back alongside Linda Wessburg and Anne-Lise Caudal.

"I'm very happy and especially coming back from injury," Hedwall said.

"This is more than I could have hoped for. I definitely wasn't expecting to win and I just wanted to make the cut when I came here, but I found my game and played really well."

Ricoh Women's British Open
Hoylake, England
Winner: Jiyai Shin

See Chapter 7.

Tenerife Open de Espana Femenino
Tenerife, Spain
Winner: Stacey Keating

A week after being disqualified from the Ricoh Women's British Open after signing for an incorrect score, Stacey Keating was smiling again after claiming her first victory at the Tenerife Open de Espana Femenino at Golf Las Americas.

But it took a playoff for the 26-year-old Australian to see off the challenge of third-round leader Caroline Masson. The German was aiming for a second win of the season, but on a hot and breezy final day in the Canary Islands, their close duel went to a 73rd hole. Playing the par-five 18th again, Masson put her second shot in the water and Keating holed from five feet for a winning birdie.

Keating had returned scores of 70, 69, 70 and 70 for a nine-under total of 279, which was matched by Masson's closing 71. Trish Johnson was third a shot behind, and Nikki Garrett, who led for the first two rounds after an opening 64, was fourth.

"I've probably had the worst week of my life and the best week of my life in two weeks," said Keating, who was comforted by compatriots Karrie Webb and Karen Lunn between tournaments. "It was very disappointing last week, but this makes up for it, I can tell you."

Masson said: "If you hit the worst shot of the week in a playoff it's a bit unlucky, but you don't deserve to win and Stacey played well."

Lacoste Ladies Open de France
Saint-Jean-de-Luz, Aquitaine, France
Winner: Stacey Keating

The turnaround in Stacey Keating's fortunes continued in a positive direction when she won for the second tournament in a row at the Lacoste Ladies Open de France just a fortnight after collecting her maiden title in Tenerife. Clearly on a confidence high, the Australian opened with an eight-under 62 at Chantaco Golf Club, where former U.S. Open champion Catherine Lacoste was president for 35 years, and after rounds of 71 and 69 she closed with a 64 to finish on a 14-under total of 266. A bogey at the last might have cost her the victory, but Diana Luna also dropped a shot at the 18th, missing the par putt after her chip for birdie had lipped out. Luna had a 64 in the second round and led after days two and three but came up one short.

It was a superb final-round tussle with both players having four birdies in a row on the front nine, but Luna was denied for the third year running at the French Open, having lost playoffs to Trish Johnson and Felicity Johnson the previous two years.

Having been disqualified at the Women's British Open, Keating said the turnaround was due to knowing nothing that bad could ever happen again. "Nothing on the golf course can hurt me like that now," she said.

Keating was presented with the trophy by Sophie Lacoste, alongside Lorena Ochoa, who finished tied for 22nd in a rare appearance since retiring as the world No. 1 two years earlier, and Europe's winning Ryder Cup captain Jose Maria Olazabal.

"Ten years ago my dream was to meet Lorena Ochoa, so standing here is unbelievable, so thank you to Lorena for playing in this event," said Keating. "I think Europe's win in the Ryder Cup also deserves a round of applause!"

China Suzhou Taihu Open
Suzhou, China
Winner: Carlota Ciganda

Carlota Ciganda extended her lead at the top of the Order of Merit as the 22-year-old Spanish rookie cruised to a seven-stroke victory in the China Suzhou Taihu Open at the Suzhou Taihu International Golf Club. The runner-up was her closest challenger for the money title, Caroline Masson, who finished four clear of Florentyna Parker and Julie Greciet who tied for third place.

Ciganda, who won her first title in the Netherlands earlier in the season, did not drop a shot in an opening 65, added a 70 on day two, and closed with a course-record 65, again not dropping a shot to par. Her 17-under total for 54 holes of 199 was one better than Yani Tseng's tournament record from 2011.

"I was just thinking about playing my game, having fun, and I liked the course from the beginning," Ciganda said. "I was playing good, I was confident and I think it's one of those weeks that everything goes right and I was lucky. I was making putts, hitting to the fairway, hitting lots of greens."

Sanya Ladies Open
Sanya, China
Winner: Cassandra Kirkland

Going into the Sanya Ladies Open in 90th place on the Order of Merit, Cassandra Kirkland needed a good result to secure her card for the following season. A maiden victory, when she had never finished better than fifth before in six seasons on tour, sorted all that out for the 28-year-old from Paris. Coming from a shot behind going into the last round, Kirkland won by two shots over compatriot Jade Schaeffer and England's Holly Aitchison. Recovering from an opening 73, Kirkland posted scores of 69 and 70 for a total of 210, six under par at the breezy Yalong Bay course in Sanya. Nine players shared fourth place, three behind the winner, including Order of Merit leader Carlota Ciganda, Numa Gulyanamitta, the 36-hole leader, and 16-year-old Chinese professional Xi Yu Lin.

Kirkland had to overcome the absence of her six iron, lost by her caddie the previous week and a club she would have used at least five times in the second round alone. But it was a holed sand wedge from 65 yards for an eagle at the 14th hole in the final round that virtually clinch the victory.

"This win is totally unexpected because I've struggled so much this year and I didn't have my six iron, so I guess I didn't have any expectations this week and I didn't put any pressure on myself. I didn't feel stressed out there, so it was really good," Kirkland said.

Hero Women's Indian Open
New Delhi, India
Winner: Pornanong Phatlum

Two days before her 23rd birthday, Thailand's Pornanong Phatlum won the Hero Women's Indian Open for the third time. Phatlum also won at the DLF Country Club outside New Delhi in 2008 and 2009, before the event was co-sanctioned by the Ladies European Tour. This was her first LET title but her fifth on the Ladies Asian Golf Tour. After an opening 72, Phatlum had rounds of 65 and 66 over the weekend for a 13-under-par total of 203. She won by four strokes over defending champion Caroline Hedwall and by six over compatriot Nontaya Srisawang. "It's like a big tournament; I won and in two days it will be my birthday, so it's going to be a big present for me," said Phatlum. "I love winning at this golf course and I like to play here very much."

Hedwall set a course record of 62 in the second round to lie one behind Phatlum and Bree Arthur, but the Thai golfer went to the turn in 31 with three birdies and an eagle. Hedwall got back within one after a two-shot swing at the 15th, but while Phatlum birdied the last two holes, Hedwall found water with her second at the par-five 18th after her drive finished in a divot. Tied for eighth place was 14-year-old amateur Aditi Ashok, who had shared the first-round lead with a 69. Ashok was only 13 when she won a professional event on the Hero India circuit in 2010.

Omega Dubai Ladies Masters
Dubai, United Arab Emirates
Winner: Shanshan Feng

After becoming the first player from China to win a major title at the LPGA Championship, Shanshan Feng finished the season in grand style with victory at the Omega Dubai Ladies Masters. The 23-year-old won by five strokes at the Emirates Golf Club in a dominating display which left little doubt where the trophy would go. It was a second LET title for Feng after she started the season with victory at the World Ladies Championship, and the eighth win of her career.

Feng led from start to finish, sharing the lead on the opening day with a six-under 66. A 65 the next day put her four ahead, and a 67 in the third round meant she was five ahead going into the last day. Feng rolled in a 20-footer on the third hole for an eagle and never looked back, closing with a 69. She set a new record-winning total of 267, 21 under, three better than the previous record. "I'm very happy because I had the lead for three days in a row and I don't want to give it away on the last day," said Feng, who was making her debut in the event. "This looks like a major to me. I've always heard about it, that it's very nice. Finally I got a chance to play, and I like it, I like the golf course: of course, I shot 21 under."

Dewi-Claire Schreefel set a new course record of 63 in the third round to become Feng's nearest challenger on the final day and closed with a 69 to finish alone in second place, four shots ahead of Caroline Masson and Becky Brewerton.

Masson had a chance to overtake Spain's Carlota Ciganda at the top of the ISPS Handa Order of Merit when she was lying in second place, but then suffered a triple bogey at the 12th hole. Ciganda finished in a tie for 10th place to become the first player since Laura Davies in 1985 to win the Order of Merit and the Rookie of the Year title in the same year. The 22-year-old from Pamplona, who won twice and had nine other top-10 finishes, was also voted the Players' Player of the Year by LET members.

"It's an honor to win the ISPS Handa Order of Merit as a rookie and I'm very happy," said Ciganda. "It's a real privilege to follow Laura Davies in achieving this rare double. I played with her a lot this year and I think it was very good for me because I learned so many things. She's so talented and I think she's one of the best players of all time in golf."

Japan LPGA Tour

Daikin Orchid Ladies
Nanjo, Okinawa
Winner: Airi Saitoh

The opening event of the 2012 Japan LPGA Tour season produced one of the least likely winners. Though just 22 years old, Airi Saitoh had already made two unsuccessful ventures on the circuit, moved up for a third time from the developmental Step-Up Tour and, in just her 11th career start, won the Daikin Orchid Ladies in a playoff against two experienced winners in the early March season opener.

Gaining a two-stroke lead in Saturday's second round from Friday's six deadlocked front-runners with an eight-under-par 64, Saitoh pieced together an inconsistent par round Sunday. She gave up the lead when she double-bogeyed the first hole, regained it with four birdies over the next 15 holes, only to bogey the 17th and 18th and drop into a three-way tie at 206 with Ji-Hee Lee (67) and Yuko Mitsuka (66), who had 19 victories between them.

Lee went out on the first extra hole when she failed to match birdies on the par-five 18th with Saitoh and Mitsuka, then Saitoh was gifted the title when Mitsuka muffed a par putt from inside three feet on the next hole.

Yokohama Tire PRGR Ladies Cup
Kanan, Kochi
Winner: Bo-Mee Lee

Bo-Mee Lee joined the ever-growing list of South Korean winners on the Japan LPGA Tour when the Yokohama Tire PRGR Ladies Cup, the first tournament cancelled in wake of the devastating earthquake in 2011, returned to action. Although not a household name on the international scene, Lee's credentials as she entered her first full season in Japan included three victories and 12 other top-10s when she was the top player on the 2010 Korean LPGA Tour.

Again, it took two extra holes to decide the winner at Kanan. Both Lee and fellow Korean Sun-Ju Ahn, the tour's leading money winner the two previous years, brushed past Ayako Uehara, Mi-Jeong Jeon and Yuri Fudoh, the second-round co-leaders at just one-under-par 143, to finish at three-under 213 Sunday. Fudoh, holder of 50 titles on the tour and winner of more than a billion yen in her brilliant career, had opened in front with 68 but fell back with a pair of 75s on the weekend.

Lee shot 69 and Ahn 67 in the final round to set up the playoff, and Lee won it with a par to Ahn's bogey on the second extra hole, becoming the second first-time winner of the young season.

T-Point Ladies
Kamo, Kagoshima
Winner: Ji-Hee Lee

Ji-Hee Lee only waited two weeks before setting aside her playoff loss in the season-opening Daikin Orchid tournament and posting her 16th victory on the Japan LPGA Tour. Lee, whose success in Japan is third only to Mi-Jeong Jeon (17 wins) and Ok-Hee Ku (23 wins) among the many South Koreans who have played in Japan, mustered a solid finish to score a one-stroke victory in the T-Point Ladies over non-winner Soo-Yun Kang.

Three off the pace the first day as Ayako Uehara, Mayu Hattori and Kaori Ohe led with 68s, Lee moved a stroke closer Saturday as the leaderboard shuffled, Eun-Bi Jang jumping into the lead at 72-66–138, a shot ahead of Kang (72-67) and Ritsuko Ryu (70-69).

One stroke behind Kang after a bogey at the 11th hole Sunday at Kagoshima Takamaki Country Club, Lee birdied the next two holes to take the lead and added another at the 17th to solidify the one-shot margin of victory. Ryu (72) and Jang (73) finished third, two off the lead.

Yamaha Ladies Open
Fukuroi, Shizuoka
Winner: Ritsuko Ryu

Talk about repetition. When Ritsuko Ryu won her first tournament on the Japan LPGA Tour in the 2011 Nitori Ladies, she birdied three of the last four holes for the victory. In contention in the previous two events of 2012, Ryu duplicated the feat in the Yamaha Ladies Open to capture a two-stroke triumph at Katsuragi Golf Club in Shizuoka Prefecture.

Mayu Hattori had the upper hand after a first round in which her three-under 69 was the only sub-par round on a tough day. Her three-stroke lead looked even better when heavy rains washed out the Saturday round and forced the Yamaha to a 36-hole event.

Ryu was four shots off the lead at the start of Sunday's round, but her three birdies from the 15th hole in gave her a 68 and 141 total, two better than Hattori, who shot 74, Li-Ying Ye (67), Yuki Ichinose (68) and Hiromi Mogi (71). "It was very windy out there," Ritsuko noted, "but I managed to play my best golf today."

Studio Alice Ladies Open
Miki, Hyogo
Winner: Miki Saiki

In one way, Miki Saiki's victory in the Studio Alice Ladies Open was surprising, almost shocking, but otherwise it really wasn't.

What was totally unexpected was the last-minute collapse of Jiyai Shin, the world-class South Korean star and former leading money winner on the U.S. LPGA Tour, who blew a four-stroke lead on the final two holes at Hanayashiki Golf Club. On the other hand, the 27-year-old Saiki had the credentials to make the birdie-par-birdie finish that nailed the victory. It was her fourth win since she became the fastest victor ever on the Japan LPGA Tour when she took the 2007 Fujisankei Classic just 112 days after turning pro. "I was able to hit some big shots in clutch situations," she mentioned afterward. "That's going to be a nice confidence boost."

Shin (70-68) led Saiki (71-69) by two strokes after 36 holes, having taken the lead from two-time money leader Sun-Ju Ahn and reigning amateur champion Mamiko Higa, who had opened with three-under-par 69s Friday. Shin had built her lead to four and seemed to be coasting toward her first win anywhere in more than a year and sixth in Japan when the bottom fell out. She finished with 72–210, one behind Saiki's 69–209.

Nishijin Ladies Classic
Kikuyo, Kumamoto
Winner: Maiko Wakabayashi

It had been a long time since Maiko Wakabayashi won her first and only title on the Japan LPGA Tour and things hadn't looked very promising when she arrived for the Nishijin Ladies Classic after missing the cut badly (74-82) the previous week in the Studio Alice event.

Instead, Wakabayashi, whose only circuit victory came in the 2008 Sankyo Open, turned things completely around, put together three steady rounds at Kumamoto Airport Country Club and posted a two-stroke triumph over a threatening Hiromi Mogi. Leading by just a stroke, Wakabayashi birdied the final hole for a three-under-par 69 and the two-shot win with her 209 total.

She had entered the final round in a tie for the lead with Bo-Mee Lee, the first-round leader (69), after putting up a pair of 70s. The South Korean faded Sunday with a 74, leaving it up to Mogi, a five-time winner on tour, to challenge Wakabayashi. Mogi's 68 wasn't good enough.

Fujisankei Ladies Classic
Ito, Shizuoka
Winner: Kaori Ohe

A week earlier, Kaori Ohe blew a good chance for her first win on the Japan LPGA, but she found it to be a positive experience when the same situation developed at the Fujisankei Classic. "I was in the last group (one back) on the final day last week, so I wasn't that nervous today," Ohe pointed out after holding on for a one-stroke victory.

Even if she wasn't on edge, the 22-year-old had a shaky finish. Coasting home with a four-stroke lead, Ohe struggled with a double bogey at the par-four 18th for 70 and 207, just enough to offset the closing birdie of veteran winner Mi-Jeong Jeon, who also shot 70 Sunday on the Fuji course at the Kawana Hotel Golf Club.

Lost in the final shuffle was Akane Iijima, a six-time winner on tour.

She put up rounds of 68 and 67 to handle the lead through the first two rounds. After Saturday's second round, Iijima led Ohe by two strokes, Jeon by three, Ohe making the biggest move with a seven-under-par 65 and Jeon shooting 68. But Iijima plunged into a tie for sixth Sunday with a 76 as Ohe became the season's third first-time winner.

Cyber Agent Ladies
Ichihara, Chiba
Winner: Chie Arimura

Chie Arimura made up for lost time at the Cyber Agent Ladies tournament in late April. An injured left wrist had sidelined her through the off-season and the first three events of 2012. Two top-10 finishes upon her return to action set up Arimura for an impressive victory in the Cyber Agent, the 11th in the JLPGA career of the 24-year-old, who won three times and finished third on the 2011 money list.

After sharing the lead the first two days at Tsurumai Country Club, Arimura broke away with a bogey-free, seven-under-par 65 and 201 total to win by five strokes over Sakura Yokomine, who jumped into second place with a 66.

"There were some pretty tough times because of the injury to my wrist, but through it all I learned how to concentrate better on the golf itself," she observed.

Arimura started with 68, tied for the lead with formidable opponents Inbee Park and Mi-Jeong Jeon, then repeated that score Saturday. That kept her on top but deadlocked with Ji-Woo Lee, who followed a 70 with 66 for her 136. Park slipped two off the pace, joined at 138 by Jiyai Shin (72-66). Nobody had the firepower to compete with Arimura Sunday.

World Ladies Championship Salonpas Cup
Tsukubamirai, Ibaraki
Winner: Sun-Ju Ahn

Sun-Ju Ahn's march to her second straight No. 1 spot at the end of the season in 2011 began in early May when she scored a decisive victory in the World Ladies Championship, so it seemed appropriate when she accepted the Salonpas Cup again with her first victory of 2012. But it wasn't quite so easy this time.

Ahn wound up in a tie with talented American Morgan Pressel, the 2010 winner, and fellow South Korean Inbee Park at eight-under-par 208 on Ibaraki Golf Club's West course before snatching the title again with a six-foot birdie putt on the first hole of the ensuing playoff. The first major championship of the season was shortened to 54 holes by a Thursday rain-out.

Ahn, who had lost in another playoff in the Yokohama Tire tournament and had two other top-five finishes earlier in the season, trailed Pressel by three strokes going into the final round. Pressel had posted rounds of

65 and 68, sharing the first-round lead with Jiyai Shin before moving two shots ahead Saturday when Shin took a 70. Pressel's game deteriorated midway through the final round as she came back to the field with four bogeys. Ahn birdied the 18th hole for 72 to tie Park, who closed with 68, and Pressel, who struggled home with 75, before she birdied the 18th again in the playoff to notch her ninth win in Japan.

Fundokin Ladies
Asakura, Fukuoka
Winner: Inbee Park

Inbee Park's victory in the Fundokin Ladies tournament shouldn't have surprised anybody. Her record in the five events she played earlier in the season indicated a win was in the books, and the reputable South Korean validated that a week after failing to land another major title when she lost in the playoff in the Salonpas World Championship. Never finishing lower than 16th in her first five starts of the Japanese season, Park broke from a first-place tie after 36 holes to post a two-stroke victory, the fourth in Japan for the player who also competes on the U.S. LPGA Tour.

Park's main protagonist at Fukuoka Country Club was China's Shanshan Feng, who jumped off to a three-stroke lead over Park in the opening round with a bogey-free 67. Park, the 2008 U.S. Women's Open champion, moved to a tie for the lead with Feng in the second round, producing four early birdies and a 69 to overtake the Chinese star (72) at five-under-par 139.

Feng gained the upper hand on the front nine Sunday with a birdie-bogey swing against Park at the eighth hole, but the South Korean birdied the 11th and 12th holes to move a stroke in front. She then cozied a two-stroke lead to the finish when Feng bogeyed the 14th hole. Park shot 68 to Feng's 70 for a final, seven-under-par 209. Sun-Ju Ahn maintained her lead on the money list with a solid, fifth-place finish at 212.

Chukyo TV Bridgestone Ladies Open
Toyota, Aichi
Winner: Ji-Hee Lee

Ji-Hee Lee surely has nothing but good things to say about Chukyo Golf Club's Ishino course, considering that she has won three of her 17 Japan LPGA Tour titles there.

The third one came in mid-May of the 2012 season, a decisive, three-stroke victory as she never trailed and closed with a five-under-par 67 and 200 total. She became the year's first two-time winner and moved into third place on the money list behind fellow South Koreans Sun-Ju Ahn and Mi-Jeong Jeon. She won the T-Point Ladies in March.

Lee shared the first-round lead at 68 with Jeon, a shot in front of Rikako Morita and Hiromi Mogi, then took command of the tournament Saturday. She fired a crisp 65 and advanced three shots in front of Jeon (68), four ahead of Morita (68). The winner shook off an early bogey Sunday and birdied six of her last 10 holes to put the title away. Morita birdied seven of her final 13 holes for 66 to claim second place, a shot ahead of Jeon (68). Defending champion Harukyo Nomura's 64 on Sunday was the best round of the week.

Yonex Ladies
Nagaoka, Niigata
Winner: Shanshan Feng

Shanshan Feng's victory in the Yonex Ladies tournament in late May certainly had no unexpected element to it. The 22-year-old Chinese golfer merely embellished an already-gaudy 2012 record when she became the fourth straight player from overseas to capture an event. Earlier in the season she had a win on the Ladies European Tour, a playoff loss on the U.S. LPGA Tour and a runner-up finish two weeks earlier in the Fundokin Ladies in Japan.

The win didn't come easily. For two days, the front-runners were Yukari Baba, the 2011 Japan Women's Open champion, and rookie Serena Aoki, who both opened with 69s. The diminutive Baba inched a stroke in front of Aoki Saturday with a five-under-par 67 and at 136 had a three-shot advantage over Feng (70-69) as she sought her third Japan LPGA title entering the final round at Yonex Country Club at Nagaoka in Niigata Prefecture.

The Chinese star, the most successful of the emerging standouts from the mainland power, overtook Baba Sunday, posting a four-birdie, one-bogey 69 while Baba could muster only a par round with pairs of birdies and bogeys for her 72–208. Feng then birdied the second hole of the ensuing playoff, the fourth of the season, to record her third victory in Japan. Her win followed three consecutive victories by South Koreans Ji-Hee Lee, Inbee Park and Sun-Ju Ahn.

Resort Trust Ladies
Miyota, Nagano
Winner: Mi-Jeong Jeon

The strong South Korean presence on tour projected again when Mi-Jeong Jeon, one of the country's most successful players in overseas competition, locked down her 18th victory in Japan in the Resort Trust Ladies. It was the third win by a South Korean in the last four events and reshuffled the top of the money list, placing compatriots Jeon, Ji-Hee Lee and 2011 leader Sun-Ju Ahn in the top three spots.

Jeon, who had two runner-up finishes earlier in the season, led the Resort Trust from the start. She shared the first-round lead at 65 with Lee Friday at Grandee Karuizawa Golf Club, inched a stroke in front of Lee Saturday with 68–133, and showed her experience Sunday when she shook off potential calamity with a flurry on late birdies. She pulled away to a three-under-par 69 and a three-stroke victory over Lee, whose two earlier 2012 victories ran her total in Japan to 17. Jeon's winning score was 14-under-par 202.

For 13 holes in Sunday's final round, Jeon did not have the look of a winner. She absorbed her fourth bogey of the day there, but the 28-year-old turned things around completely down the stretch, ringing up birdies at the 14th, 15th and 17th holes to pull away from Lee and the rest of the field. Lee shot 71–205 to take second place, a stroke in front of Mihoko Iseri. Ahn, who finished 11th, had led the money list the previous week.

Suntory Ladies Open
Kobe, Hyogo
Winner: Hyo-Joo Kim

There seems to be something about tour golf in Japan that breeds phenomenal young winners. Five years after Ryo Ishikawa burst on the international scene at age 15 with a victory in the Japan Tour's Munsingwear Open, 16-year-old South Korean youngster Hyo-Joo Kim made a similar startling debut on the Japan LPGA Tour.

Like Ishikawa's feat on the men's circuit, Kim became the youngest winner ever on the JLPGA Tour, carving out a remarkable, 11-under-par 61 final round to win the Suntory Ladies Open by four strokes. Unlike Ishikawa, Kim was not the youngest female winner ever on any world tour. She was four months older than American Lexi Thompson, who was just seven months beyond her 16th birthday when she won the 2011 Navistar tournament on the U.S. LPGA Tour.

The Japanese high school sophomore didn't exactly come out of the blue. Earlier in the year, Kim won the season opener on the Korea Tour by nine strokes. She attracted little attention in the early rounds of her first start in Japan, though, posting a pair of 71s at Rokko Kokusai Golf Club, and was seven strokes behind leader Mayu Hattori (67-67-69–203) in a tie for sixth place at 210 after 54 holes.

Hattori slumped to a 74 Sunday and the rest of the field had no chance against the new South Korean whiz, who brutalized the front nine with a seven-birdie 29 and added four more birdies coming in for the flawless 61 and the four-stroke victory over Miki Saiki, the Studio Alice winner in April, who started the day even with Kim and shot a fine but futile 65.

Nichirei Ladies
Chiba
Winner: Hyun-Ju Shin

The South Korean parade continued at the Nichirei Ladies tournament in mid-June, this time in the person of Hyun-Ju Shin, who had encountered a dry spell after racking up five victories in the late 2000s. Shin became the sixth different player from her country to win in a seven-event stretch and the eighth South Korean victor of the 2012 season.

Shin, who hadn't won in two years, surged from three shots off the pace with a final-round, five-under-par 67 on Sodegaura Country Club's Shinsode course to pick off a one-stroke victory. With 205, she edged Ritsuko Ryu and Chie Arimura of Japan and Soo-Yun Kang, the South Korean leader after 36 holes.

Yuri Fudoh, Japan's greatest female player in the 2000s with her 50 career victories, showed signs of her past prowess with a bogey-free 66 in the opening round, but led four players, including Shin, by just a shot. The 35-year-old star slipped to 73 Saturday and yielded first place to 36-year-old Kang, who played and won in America in her earlier years but had never won in Japan. Kang posted 68-67–135 and led Kaori Ohe by a stroke.

Shin's final-round exploits began with birdies on the first three holes. She birdied six of the first 11 holes around a bogey at the eighth and parred in for the win. Ryu made a strong bid in the stretch, going eagle-bogey-birdie-birdie on the final holes for 68, good enough only to tie Arimura (68), the Cyber Agent winner, and Kang (71.)

Earth Mondahmin Cup
Sodegaura, Chiba
Winner: Mayu Hattori

Mayu Hattori's spectacular finish in the inaugural Earth Mondahmin Cup tournament restored a measure of prestige for Japanese women's golf. For the first time in eight tournaments, the title wound up in the hands of a player from the circuit's homeland as Hattori snatched an unlikely victory with a birdie-eagle finish to win by a stroke at Camellia Hills Country Club.

Before Hattori's closing heroics, the run of victories by overseas women — six South Koreans and a Chinese — seemed likely to be extended. South Korean Sun-Ju Ahn, the circuit's leading money winner the previous two seasons who launched the streak in early May with her win in the Salonpas Cup, was four under par through 10 holes in the final round. Hattori, who shared the second-round lead with Ahn and Sakura Yokomine at 133, dimmed her hopes with bogeys at the 10th and 13th.

Then came the abrupt turnaround. Ahn bogeyed the 15th, then the 17th, where Hattori picked up two shots with her birdie before sinking a long putt for the winning eagle on the 495-yard, par-five home hole. The 68 gave Hattori her fourth career win. Her 15-under-par 201 was one better than the 202s of Yokomine (69) and Chie Arimura (68). Ahn, who had opened the tournament with a leading 64, slipped to 70 Sunday and placed fourth at 202.

Nichi-Iko Ladies Open
Toyama
Winner: Mi-Jeong Jeon

As the South Korean domination continued with her victory in the Nichi-Iko Ladies Open, Mi-Jeong Jeon strengthened her position as the leader of the pack. With her second win of the season, Jeon widened her money-list lead to nearly ¥20 million over the 2011 champion Sun-Ju Ahn and remarked afterward: "If I keep finishing strong, the money title will be there for me."

Jeon rode first place all the way in the Nichi-Iko Open at Yatsuo Country Club in winning for the 19th time in Japan, one stroke ahead of Erina Hara with her eight-under-par 208. She opened with a 66, two in front of Mayu Hattori, the previous week's champion and only Japanese winner on the circuit in two months.

Miki Saiki, the Studio Alice victor, shot 67 Saturday and overtook Jeon as the South Korean managed just a one-under-par 71 for 137. Foul weather shrouded the course Sunday, and Jeon's second straight 71, the product of two birdies and a bogey, was just enough to edge Hara, who closed with a 69 for 209. Saiki plunged to 76 and finished fourth. Hattori took third place with 71–211.

Stanley Ladies
Susano, Shizuoka
Winner: Chie Arimura

Chie Arimura successfully defended her title in the Stanley Ladies tournament, but in a rather bizarre turn of events. Rain and fog plagued the golf at Shizuoka Prefecture's Tomei Country Club so intensely from the first day on that only 27 holes were played, but enough, the Japan LPGA decided, to make it an official victory. It was Arimura's second of the season and 12th of her career.

Heavy rains during Friday's opening round forced a carryover of play into Saturday and the decision to make the Stanley a 36-hole event. When those results were in, Rikako Morita had the lead with a six-under-par 66, a stroke in front of Erina Yamato and Arimura, who had a bogey-free 67.

Dense fog prevented a normal start of the Sunday round, forcing a nine-hole finish on Tomei's back nine. Arimura nudged ahead with an even-par 36 to Morita's 38 for a final, five-under-par 103, one stroke ahead of Morita, Bo-Bae Song of South Korea (33) and China's Tao-Li Yang (36).

Ironically, it was the tour's first 27-hole event since the same tournament in 2007 when a typhoon swept through the area.

Samantha Thavasa Girls Collection Ladies
Ibaraki
Winner: Megumi Kido

Faced with a classic situation that seemed certain to spell collapse, Megumi Kido staged a remarkable finish to polish off her first victory in the inaugural Samantha Thavasa Girls Collection Ladies.

After racing to a four-stroke lead after the first two rounds at Eagle Point Golf Club with a pair of six-under-par 66s, Kido entered the final 18 holes pitted against the likes of Mi-Jeong Jeon, the leading money winner; Yuri Fudoh, one of the tour's all-time greats with 50 wins on her record, and Jiyai Shin, South Korea's international star just back in action following hand surgery.

Kido had things in hand Sunday until she double-bogeyed the par-three ninth hole and dropped into a tie with Fudoh and Shin and was just a shot ahead of Jeon, a slip-up that would doom most winless 22-year-olds. But the young Japanese pro, who had two top-10 finishes in her previous three starts, bounced back. Matching their birdies with three birdies of her own on the next five holes, Kido pulled out to a two-stroke lead and rode it home, aided by a final birdie at the 17th, to a 70 for 202 and a two-stroke win over Jeon (68), three over Shin (68) and So-Hee Kim (66) and four over Fudoh (69). Kido was the season's fifth first-time winner.

Meiji Cup
Kitahiroshima, Hokkaido
Winner: Shanshan Feng

What a way to celebrate a birthday!

Chinese sensation Shanshan Feng picked the 23rd anniversary of her birth to become the most dominant player, not only on the Japan LPGA Tour, but in all of women's golf in 2012 with a playoff victory in the Meiji Cup in Hokkaido. It was her second win of the year in Japan to go with a victory on the Ladies European Tour and, most impressively, one in the U.S. in the major LPGA Championship.

Furthermore, her victim in the Meiji playoff was Sun-Ju Ahn, the circuit's leading money winner the previous two seasons, who carried a two-stroke lead into the final round at Sapporo International Country Club. Trailing by four after 36 holes, Feng ran off five birdies in the middle of the final round and posted 67–209, then waited as Ahn and Shinobu Moromizato, in the final pairing, futilely sought birdies on the back nine and shot 71 and 69, respectively, for matching 209s. Legendary Yuri Fudoh just missed the playoff, falling a stroke short with her 67–210.

Moromizato, who hadn't won since her great, six-victory season of 2009, went out of the playoff when she couldn't match the birdies of Feng and Ahn on the first extra hole. Three holes later, the young Chinese star dropped a 45-foot eagle putt for her fourth victory in Japan and a companion for her May win in the Yonex Ladies. She became the fourth double winner of 2012 and jumped to eighth on the money list, even though she had played for just the sixth time in Japan.

NEC Karuizawa 72
Karuizawa, Nagano
Winner: Yumiko Yoshida

Surprisingly, the dominance of the South Koreans in the victory column in the early months of 2012 was penetrated, not in most cases by the home country's most prominent players, but instead mostly by ladies who entered the season with records devoid of titles in their pro careers.

For the fourth time in 2012, a Japanese player came up with her first tour victory when Yumiko Yoshida hung tough through six extra holes to win the NEC Karuizawa 72 tournament, joining earlier first-time winners

Airi Saitoh (Daikin Orchid), Kaori Ohe (Fujisankei) and Megumi Kido (Samantha Thavasa.)

The 25-year-old, who had four top-10s and only three missed cuts earlier in the year, came from two off the pace in the final round with a bogey-free 67, her fifth birdie at the 18th putting her in the playoff against Eun-Bi Jang, who made her first bogey since midway through the opening round at that hole to drop into the tie with her 68 and 11-under-par 205. Six playoff holes later, Yoshida dropped a six-foot birdie putt for her maiden victory.

Jang, who was also seeking her first win, shared the first-day lead on 68 with Junko Omote and Tomoko Kusakabe, who repeated that score Saturday to edge a stroke in front of Jang (69) and long-time star Yuri Fudoh (69-68). Yoshida was two back with 71-67–138. Fudoh, who won her 50th tournament in early 2011, missed the playoff with 70–207 and finished third.

CAT Ladies
Hakone, Kanagawa
Winner: Mi-Jeong Jeon

There are come-from-behind victories and there are resounding come-from-behind victories. Mi-Jeong Jeon authored one that fit the latter description in the CAT Ladies tournament as she strengthened her hold on the top spot on the money list and locked up her third victory of the year and 20th in her eighth season in the country.

Though only two strokes off the pace entering the final round at Dai-hakone Country Club in Hakone, the talented South Korean trailed seven players. But while the five co-leaders and two runners-up were struggling with par, Jeon was tearing up the final nine with birdies on her way to a 65, the day's lowest score by four shots, and a four-stroke victory with her 13-under-par 206.

The stage was set Saturday when Mayu Hattori (72-67), Bo-Mee Lee (71-68) and Yumiko Yoshida (71-68), all 2012 winners, along with Rikako Morita (69-70) and Onnarin Sattayabanphot (73-66) log-jammed the lead and had the upper hand on Jeon, tied for eighth place with Junko Omote and Erika Kikuchi, all with 71-70 scores.

After nine holes Sunday Jeon had lost ground, running three behind Hattori and was two shy of Lee and one back of Morita. After that, as Jeon said later, "the putts were amazing." She birdied the 10th, 11th, 13th, 15th and 18th, the 11th from 35 feet and two others from 17 feet for an incoming 32 and the winning 65. Hattori, Morita and Lee all shot 71s to tie for second.

Nitori Ladies
Tomakomai, Hokkaido
Winner: Sun-Ju Ahn

Just when her South Korean compatriot Mi-Jeong Jeon was showing signs of pulling away in the race for the money title, Sun-Ju Ahn made it clear she wasn't going to let her bid for a third title in a row get away from her.

Ahn wasn't in the CAT Ladies field the previous week when Jeon scored her second 2012 win and fattened her lead to ¥30 million. She was on hand for the Nitori Ladies tournament, though. She overcame a slow start (72) at Katsura Golf Club at Tomakomai, Hokkaido, with a nine-under-par 63 middle round and scored her second win of the season and 10th of her career in Japan with a 68–202.

Jeon nearly kept pace, piecing together three rounds in the 60s for a 204 and her fourth second-place finish of the season, finishing two behind Ahn. Ahn took an early bogey in the final round, but followed with five birdies over a seven-hole stretch and parred home for the triumph. Little-known Lala Anai, who opened on top with 66 and trailed Ahn by two after 36 holes, finished fifth behind Rikako Morita (65) and Soo-Yun Kang (70) at 207.

Golf 5 Ladies
Mizunami, Gifu
Winner: Sun-Ju Ahn

Sun-Ju Ahn reinforced her return to top form when she followed up her victorious final-round performance in the previous week's Nitori Ladies tournament with another fine finish and her third win of the season in the Golf 5 Ladies.

Ahn clinched with a sparkling birdie on the 18th hole for 66 and a 15-under-par total of 201, avoiding a playoff with fellow South Korean Ji-Hee Lee, already finished with a birdie of her own at the 18th for 202. The back-to-back wins moved Ahn within range of money leader Mi-Jeong Jeon in her quest for a third straight No. 1 season finish and separated the two South Koreans from the rest of the pack in the standings.

Chie Arimura, who also was bidding for her third 2012 victory, had the upper hand entering the final round at Mizunami Country Club. Her consecutive 67s the first two days gave her a one-stroke lead over Ahn, Ah-Reum Hwang and Megumi Kido. She shot 69 Sunday, failing to make a birdie over the last six holes, and tied for third at 203 with Rikako Morita, whose 65 was the day's best round.

Japan LPGA Championship
Koka, Shiga
Winner: Chie Arimura

Chie Arimura made it a three-way race for top honors in the 2012 season with her first major victory and third win of the year when she hung on to a one-stroke lead and captured the Japan LPGA Championship Konika Minolta Cup.

The three wins matched the 2012 victory records of Mi-Jeong Jeon and Sun-Ju Ahn, the top two money list leaders, and gave additional credence to her plans to play on the U.S. LPGA Tour in 2013.

Arimura reversed her final-round fortunes from the preceding week, when she failed to hold the Golf 5 lead she took into the last 18 holes, but the victory did not come comfortably. Arimura took over the top spot the second day with 65–134, a shot ahead of first-time 2012 winner Yumiko Yoshida, and widened the margin to three over Yoshida and Na-Ri Kim (71s) with her Saturday 69–203.

Enter Inbee Park in the final round. The solid international player began the Sunday round eight strokes behind Arimura. By day's end, Park had put together a seven-under-par 65 that included eight birdies, five in a row at the end of the round, to post a 276. Arimura rallied from a bogey at the par-five 15th with pars on the final three holes for 72–275 and the one-stroke victory.

Munsingwear Ladies Tokai Classic
Mihama, Aichi
Winner: Natsu Nagai

It was a long time in coming. Natsu Nagai, who had labored with little success for 11 years on tour, finally broke through with a victory in mid-September in the Munsingwear Ladies Tokai Classic. The victory came unexpectedly when Mi-Jeong Jeon, the money list leader, double-bogeyed the final hole at Shin Minami Aichi Country Club when a birdie would have forced a playoff.

Nagai, who started the final round at 67-71–138, five strokes behind Jeon, who already had won three times in 2012, fired a brilliant, six-under-par 66 for 204 and headed for the practice range, anticipating a likely playoff that never happened. When Saturday's runners-up Bo-Mee Lee and Miki Saiki, with 70s, finished at 206, Nagai became the fifth first-time winner of the season.

Jeon seemed headed for her fourth victory of 2012 when she opened the tournament with a leading 64 and remained three shots in front when she shot 69 for 133. Lee and Saiki were next with 69-67s, but Nagai, who had never finished better than fifth in more than a decade on the tour, prevailed with her sparkling finish.

Miyagi TV Cup Dunlop Ladies Open
Rifu, Miyagi
Winner: Rikako Morita

Encouraged by three runner-up finishes earlier in the season, Rikako Morita broke through with a two-stroke victory in the Miyagi TV Cup Dunlop Ladies Open as the circuit moved into its fall stretch of strong tournaments.

Morita prevailed in a final-round joust with Hiromi Mogi and Esther Lee, shooting a five-under-par 67 to complete a 202 total at Rifu Golf Club in Miyagi Prefecture, picking up her second career victory, the earlier win coming in the Hisako Higuchi Ladies in 2010. The ¥12 million purse jumped her into fourth place on the money list.

Yuri Fudoh, who had been riding her brilliant, 50-win record since early 2011 with occasional spurts of contention, jumped off in front the first day with a 67 in one of the few long-standing tournaments she has never won. She fell back Saturday as Mogi, a four-time career winner, moved in front with 68-66–134, a shot ahead of Morita and Esther Lee, both with 71-64–135 cards.

The three remained close and the lead changed hands several times Sunday before Morita's sixth birdie of the round at the 16th hole, along with bogeys by the other two players, gave her the final two-stroke margin. Mogi and Lee both closed with 70s.

Japan Women's Open
Yokohama, Kanagawa
Winner: Shanshan Feng

China's impressive Shanshan Feng expanded on her already sparkling season when she won the Japan Women's Open, a Japan Tour major title to go with her victory earlier in the season in the LPGA Championship in America. It was her fifth win of the year.

With a typhoon closing in on Yokohama and play underway at seven on Sunday morning, Feng came out on top in a four-way battle down the stretch on the testing West course of Yokohama Country Club, shooting 71 for an even-par 288 and a one-stroke victory over Inbee Park. She became the fourth three-time winner of the season and inserted herself into the money race, even though it was just her eighth start in Japan.

The 23-year-old pride of China was never out of the lead. With 68, the only round below 70, Feng began with a two-stroke lead over Megumi Kido and Na-Ri Kim. Indicative of the bad weather effect and the tough layout of the course, Maiko Wakabayashi shot the second day's best round — par 72. That's why Feng's 75–143 was still good enough to keep her a shot ahead of Kido and two in front of Kim.

Even on a calm Saturday, the scores remained high. Kido shot 73 and Feng 74 to share first place at one-over-par 217, Feng failing to make a birdie. She made three on the front nine Sunday to get to one under par. An early triple bogey ended Kido's hopes, and Park, with her international win in the Evian Masters and Japanese victory in the Fundokin, couldn't catch Feng with her 70–289. Two-time winner Ji-Hee Lee, with 69–290, finished third.

Fujitsu Ladies
Chiba
Winner: Misuzu Narita

Another young woman emerged as a first-time winner on the Japan LPGA Tour when, just after turning 20, Misuzu Narita captured the Fujitsu Ladies tournament with a strong finish in front of an appreciative gallery at Tokyu Seven Hundred Club in her home prefecture of Chiba.

Six days after her birthday, Narita overcame a five-stroke deficit with a final-round 67 to score a two-shot victory over a disappointed Lala Anai, another player seeking her initial win on the tour. Narita's nine-under-par 207 made her the sixth maiden victor of 2012.

After 45 holes, it was Anai's tournament to win or lose. She led for two rounds after opening with a sparkling 65 and following with a 70 to establish a three-stroke lead over Megumi Kido. She shot a steady front nine the final day with a birdie at the eighth hole and eight pars, but she couldn't finish it off. While Narita was overtaking her with two outgoing birdies and another at the 11th, Anai stumbled with bogeys at the 10th, 14th and 18th. Narita polished off the victory with back-to-back birdies at the par-five 16th and par-three 17th.

Masters Golf Club Ladies
Miki, Hyogo
Winner: So-Hee Kim

Disappointment continued for Sakura Yokomine, one of the tour's most successful players, when she finished on the short end of a three-way playoff in the Masters Golf Club Ladies. On the other hand, the result ended five frustrating years for the victor, South Korea's So-Hee Kim, who coincidentally won her only previous title in Japan by beating two others in overtime.

The two players and Yumiko Yoshida, the NEC Kariuizawa 72 winner in August, tied for first with 11-under-par 205s. Yoshida went out on the first extra hole when she failed to match birdies by Kim and Yokomine, and Kim won when she sank a six-foot birdie putt after Yokomine missed for par from 10 feet.

It was another setback for Yokomine, an 18-tournament winner who was No. 1 with record earnings and six victories in 2009 but has won only three times since then, most recently in the 2011 Resort Trust Ladies. She was in bogeyless control the first two days at the Masters Golf Club in Hyogo Prefecture, opening with a 65, two ahead of Kim, and following with a 67–132, inching anther stroke in front of the South Korean (68).

Yokomine widened the gap to five early in the final round, but lost her touch coming home, shooting a one-over-par 73 to fall into the fatal tie with Kim (70) and Yoshida, who birdied three of the last five holes for 67 and her 205.

Hisako Higuchi Morinaga Weider Ladies
Ichihara, Chiba
Winner: Mi-Jeong Jeon

Mi-Jeong Jeon strengthened her hold on the No. 1 position on the money list with a solid performance and three-stroke victory in the Hisako Higuchi Morinaga Weider tournament. With her fourth win of the season, Jeon opened a gap of ¥23 million on Sun-Ju Ahn, her fellow South Korean who led the money list the last two years.

With 21 Japanese victories, the 29-year-old Jeon moved within two of Ok-Hee Ku, South Korea's all-time career winner in Japan. She never trailed at Ichihara's Morinaga Takataki Country Club in building the 12-under-par 204 winning score.

After sharing the first-round lead with Hiromi Takesue at 67, Jeon fashioned a two-stroke solo margin over Asako Fujimoto Saturday with 69–136. She polished off the victory with a workman-like performance Sunday, posting five birdies against a lone bogey on the first 13 holes to make things easy in the final stretch. She shot 68. Compatriot Young Kim had a 67 to claim the runner-up slot at 207, Fujimoto shot 70–208, and nobody else was within seven strokes of the winner.

Mizuno Classic
Shima, Mie
Winner: Stacy Lewis

Missing from the impressive roster of international winners of the Mizuno Classic since it became an official event on the U.S. and Japan LPGA Tours in 1999 was the name of an American player. Stacy Lewis took care of that omission in stylish fashion in 2012 with a stunning victory in the important event that had implications beyond the triumph itself.

As the 27-year-old Lewis blazed home with birdies on the last three holes to capture her fourth victory of the season, she virtually clinched the LPGA's coveted Rolex Player of the Year award, something no American had accomplished since Beth Daniel won it in 1994.

"I felt it coming yesterday. I just didn't make any putts," said Lewis after posting her eight-under-par 64 that turned a seven-stroke deficit into a one-shot victory at 11-under-par 205. "Putts just started falling today." She rang up 10 birdies on the Kintetsu Kashikojima Country Club course in Shima, concluding with three dazzlers from 25, 12 and 25 feet to edge Bo-Mee Lee, the second-round leader.

The South Korean, winner of the Yokohama Tire in March, had shot a 64 of her own the day before to open a four-stroke margin over Rikako Morita, the Miyagi TV Dunlop winner in September. Ayako Uehara and Jiyai Shin, the Mizuno winner in 2008 and 2010, led on a windy Friday with 68s.

Itoen Ladies
Chonan, Chiba
Winner: Bo-Mee Lee

Bo-Mee Lee, who started the run of South Korean winners on the Japan LPGA Tour in the Yokohama Tire, the season's second tournament, increased the total to 15 when she won again in the Itoen Ladies in early November with the season nearing its end.

Just as in March, Lee had to go extra holes to nail down the victory, her second in her second season in Japan, and again she had to beat a top-level player — first, Sun Ju Ahn in the Yokohama Tire, this time Chie Arimura, who was chasing Mi-Jeong Jeon for the money title. Second-place money of ¥7,920,000 left her some ¥22 million behind Jeon, who missed the cut in the Itoen.

Arimura, who already had three wins on her 2012 record, got away fast with a sparkling 64, leading Hiromi Mogi by two. Lee was back in a 14th-place tie at 69, but scooted up into a deadlock for third the second day with 67–136 as Mogi shot 68 to overtake Arimura (70) at 134, 10 under par at Chonan's Great Island Club in Chiba Prefecture.

Arimura's shot at first-place money took a hit when she bogeyed the 54th hole for 70–204, forcing her into a tie with Lee (68–204.) She lost the playoff when Lee birdied the first extra hole.

Daio Paper Elleair Ladies Open
Fukushima
Winner: Miki Saiki

Miki Saiki joined the ranks of the multiple winners in 2012 when she broke away from a tight battle with money leader Mi-Jeong Jeon and took a three-stroke victory in the Daio Paper Elleair Ladies Open. In scoring her second win of the year, Saiki became the seventh player to post at least two victories after 35 events of the 36-tournament season.

Despite settling for second place, Jeon clinched the No. 1 position on the money list, moving well out of reach of her closest pursuers. Saiki, in turn, climbed to fifth as she paired the Elleair with her April victory in the Studio Alice tournament.

It was virtually a duel between Saiki and Jeon all week at Fukushima's Itsuura Teien Country Club. They left the rest of the field behind the first day when Jeon, seeking her fifth win of the season, shot a six-under-par 66, Saiki a 67, and nobody else better than 69. They matched 70s in the second round, then Saiki pulled away with a closing, bogey-free 68 to Jeon's 72 for a 205 total and a three-stroke triumph, the fifth of her five-year pro career.

Japan LPGA Tour Championship Ricoh Cup
Miyazaki
Winner: Bo-Mee Lee

Bo-Mee Lee capped an outstanding first season in Japan with an impressive victory in the Japan LPGA Tour Championship Ricoh Cup, the year-ending major championship. Lee, who won in just her second start in Japan in the Yokohama Tire tournament in March and again in her last previous start, prevailed over the elite 30-player field at Miyazaki Country Club, closing with a three-under-par 69–275 for a two-stroke victory.

The year-end surge jumped Lee into second place on the money list behind South Korean compatriot Mi-Jeong Jeon, who finished in a 16th-place tie but had already wrapped up the title.

The tournament outcome was a disappointment for Japanese standout Sakura Yokomine. She started with 67, tied for the lead with Lee, and moved a stroke in front of her Friday with 69–136 in her bid for a 19th tour victory that would have kept alive her feat of winning at least once every year since her 2005 rookie season. Instead, Yokomine stumbled badly with 76 the third day and Lee regained the lead with 69–206.

Inbee Park, who won earlier in the season in Japan and twice as a regular on the U.S. LPGA Tour, then was Lee's only serious threat going into Sunday's final round, two back at 208 and four ahead of Yokomine in third place. Park could only match Lee's solid 69, though, and finished second by four shots over Miki Saiki, the previous week's winner, who shot 65, the low round of the week. Yuri Fudoh, the storied 50-tournament winner, tied for fifth, finishing the year without a win for just the second time since 1998.

Australian Ladies Tour

Women's Victorian Open
Melbourne, Victoria
Winner: Joanna Klatten

France's Joanna Klatten celebrated her first title as a professional in the Women's Victorian Open with a glass of beer before having to sober up and play two extra holes. South Korean Haeji Kang holed out with a wedge shot from just over 100 yards for an eagle-two at the 18th hole to tie Klatten and force the playoff. "They handed a beer to me and supposed it was over, but I did tell them it was not over, she could hole the shot," said Klatten, age 26. "But I still had it. So when she holed the shot, I don't drink, so one beer got me a little bit tipsy. I was a little bit worried. I went to hit some balls and I tried to chug as much water as I could to sober up." After Klatten holed a 15-footer for a par at the first extra hole, she finally claimed the victory with a par at the 18th after Kang missed from three feet.

The final two rounds were played at Spring Valley alongside the men's version of the Victorian Open with alternate pairings of men and women players. Klatten opened with a 74 at Woodlands, and then had rounds of 70 and 68 at Spring Valley to finish on 212, seven under par. Kang tied with a closing 72, while Rebecca Flood finished two shots behind after a closing 76, nine shots higher than her second-round effort. Klatten had an eight at the par-three 10th in the second round but was 11 under for the last 25 holes, including a run of eagle-birdie-birdie to finish.

ActewAGL Royal Canberra Ladies Classic
Yarralumla, Australian Capital Territory
Winner: Karen Lunn

Karen Lunn, with her sister Mardi acting as her caddie, won the ActewAGL
Royal Canberra Ladies Classic by four strokes after her 40-foot putt for
an eagle at the last dropped into the hole. It was a special way to finish
off the victory, but it was not always so comfortable. Lunn finished at 12
under par on a total of 207 after rounds of 71, 66 and 70. She led by three
strokes going into the final round, and three birdies in a row from the
fourth extended that lead to six. However, two bogeys early on the back
nine followed by an eagle by Vicky Thomas at the 16th meant the lead
was down to two. At the 17th Lunn hit her tee shot into a bunker in front
of the green, but she managed to get up and down to keep the two-shot
cushion going to the last hole.

"I'm absolutely thrilled to win this event," said Lunn, the 1993 Women's
British Open champion. "It makes it even more special that Mardi was on
the bag. My cousin was in the crowd and it was nice to see some familiar
faces from Cowra in the gallery. It has just made the day even more special."
The Lunn sisters spent part of their childhood in Cowra, not far away.

Thomas took second place, one ahead of Stacey Keating and England's
Kym Larratt.

Bing Lee Samsung NSW Open
Sydney, New South Wales
Winner: Lydia Ko

At the age of 14 and 280 days Lydia Ko became the youngest winner of
a professional tournament when she claimed the Bing Lee Samsung NSW
Open at Oatlands in Sydney. Ryo Ishikawa was 15 years and 245 days in
winning on the Japanese tour, while the previous youngest female winner
was Amy Yang, who was 16 years and 192 days when she won the Australian Masters in 2006. Ko, the New Zealander who won the inaugural
McCormack Medal as the leading women's amateur in 2011, almost won
the same event at the age of 13 but missed a short putt on the last green
to lose by one to Caroline Hedwall.

This time Ko was in charge from the moment she added an eight-under
64 to her opening 69. She led by four strokes going into the final round
and another 69 ensured victory by four strokes over Becky Morgan with
a 14-under total of 202. Australians Kristie Smith and Lindsey Wright finished a stroke further back in third place. Wright, Ko's nearest challenger
overnight, drew within two strokes of the leader but dropped a shot at the
11th, where Ko, having missed the green, holed from five feet for her par.

"I got more nervous as the day went on," Ko said. "When Lindsey got
within two shots, I started to think back to last year with Caroline. Obviously, I am very happy to win, it means a lot to me." She added: "To be
part of history is a miracle. It's not something you can have by clicking
your fingers."

Gold Coast RACV Australian Ladies Masters
Ashmore, Queensland
Winner: Christel Boeljon

Christel Boeljon patiently reeled in So Yeon Ryu to win the Gold Coast RACV Australian Ladies Masters. It was a second victory for the 24-year-old from the Netherlands after her win Turkey in 2011. But the Solheim Cup player had work to do to overhaul Ryu, the U.S. Women's Open champion, whose second round of 61 had put the Korean four shots clear at halfway. With preferred lies in operation, Ryu's score did not officially tie Karrie Webb's course record at Royal Pines, while her 36-hole total of 17-under 127 also did not count as a new tour record. But Boeljon, with a 65 after an opening 66, kept on Ryu's coattails, and twin weekend rounds of 68, as opposed to Ryu's 69 and 72, put Boeljon one clear. She finished on a total of 267, 21 under par.

Ryu was still three ahead going into the final round, but Boeljon made her move with birdies at the seventh, 10th and 13th. She bogeyed the next, but both she and Ryu birdied the 15th before the Korean bogeyed the 16th. Now tied heading to the par-five, Ryu was in a greenside bunker in two but came out long and two-putted for her par. Boeljon was hoping to two-putt for a birdie, but her approach effort came up five feet short. Retaining her composure, Boeljon holed for the victory. "My first putt, I was not really happy: it was a bit far away for my liking," she said. "I am really happy I finished with a birdie and it's unbelievable."

Ryu tied for second place with Diana Luna and Ha-Neul Kim, both of whom came home in 31 for closing 67s.

ISPS Handa Women's Australian Open
Melbourne, Victoria
Winner: Jessica Korda

Jessica Korda not only emerged with her first victory after a six-way playoff but completed an usual family double at the ISPS Handa Women's Australian Open. Korda's father, Petr, was a leading tennis player who won the Australian Open in Melbourne in 1998. Jessica even celebrated her victory at Royal Melbourne with her father's trademark scissor kick.

Korda missed the cut at the Australian Masters, but in the opening LPGA event of the year — the tournament was tri-sanctioned with the ALPG and the LET — rounds of 72, 70 and 73 put her one in front of the field with a round to play. Three birdies in the first eight holes on a rainy final day made the 18-year-old from Florida a clear favorite, but then she dropped three shots in the next two holes. A birdie at the 11th steadied her round before she suffered three birdies in a row from the 14th. Korda ran from the 16th green to the 17th tee as she claims it calms her down and then got a birdie-four followed by a closing par.

A 74 left Korda on a three-under total of 289, but she only got into the playoff because just ahead of her the Korean pair of So Yeon Ryu, the U.S. Open champion, and Hee Kyung Seo both bogeyed the 18th hole. Both closed with 73s, while Brittany Lincicome and Juliet Granada, after 71s, and Stacy Lewis, with a 70, also finished on three under, one stroke ahead of Jenny Shin, while world No. 1 Yani Tseng was a stroke further back.

Lincicome had the best chance at the first playoff hole, but her three-footer for victory horseshoed out of the hole back towards her. All six players, playing in two groups of three, parred the 18th on the first extra hole, but on the same hole at the second time of asking Korda rolled in a 25-footer for a birdie that no one else could match.

"I knew what the putt did because I'd had it before and it did not move. All I had to do was just hit it," she said. "It started breaking. I thought, 'Oh my goodness no, don't lip out, don't break too early.' I was overwhelmed by everything."

Korda, who said the Taylor Swift song "Enchanted" calmed her during the playoff, became the sixth youngest winner on the LPGA. "When we spoke on Monday, Dad said Melbourne had been good to him. As I was walking around here, there was a Melbourne sign on every green. It made me smile because it reminds me of the good times. It is a really special place for my family. For my first win, I honestly could not have thought of a better place," said Korda. On her father's reaction, she revealed: "That he was so proud of me and we'll talk about the three-putts later."

ISPS Handa New Zealand Women's Open
Christchurch, New Zealand
Winner: Lindsey Wright

Lydia Ko was one of six players tied for the lead going into the final round of the ISPS Handa Women's New Zealand Open, but the 14-year-old could not add to her winning sequence, including her national amateur and a professional title in Australia. Instead it was the 32-year-old Lindsey Wright who claimed the title at Pegasus in Christchurch. Wright could not overhaul the amateur 18 years her junior at the NSW Open, but here Wright finished with a 68, after earlier rounds of 70 and 68, while Ko slipped back down the leaderboard with a 74. But there were plenty of other players around to challenge Wright. Jessica Speechley, a 22-year-old Australian, had an eagle and five birdies in an outward half of 29, and her 65 set the clubhouse target at nine under par. She was joined there by American Alison Walshe, one of the overnight co-leaders, who closed with a 69. So Wright came to 18th needing a birdie to win by one and converted a putt from 12 feet to take the title. Stephanie Na and Lorie Kane shared fourth place on eight under par.

Wright, who finished second at the 2009 LPGA Championship, had taken time out of the game due to a lack of form and could not have been more delighted to claim the victory. "It's still sinking in. I putted really well all day and the last six holes I was really nervous," said Wright. "I haven't been in this position for a while and I thought to myself 'I can win this.' I looked at the leaderboard and saw Alison Walshe up there and Speechley at nine under and thought 'no, I can make this putt. Just keep your head down, just hit a great putt.' My caddie was more shocked than I was I think."

14. Senior Tours

England's Roger Chapman, obscure in European golf and unknown on the Champions Tour in the United States, stunned the golf world by winning both the Senior PGA Championship and the U.S. Senior Open — two of the tour's five majors — and was asked to explain the secret to his sudden success.

Said Chapman: "I can't put my finger on why."

And so in the 2012 season, Chapman took his place along side Tom Lehman, winner of the Tradition; Joe Daley, the Senior Players Championship, and Fred Couples, the Senior Open in Britain.

In 606 starts on the European Tour, Chapman had one victory, the 2000 Brazil Open. So it came as quite a surprise to all when, against one of the toughest fields of the year in the Senior PGA Championship, he led all the way and won by two shots.

"Having led wire-to-wire, that to me is the greatest thing I've ever done," said Chapman. Said John Cook, his frustrated playing companion in the final round: "I can't say it was fun to watch, but it was impressive to watch."

Chapman reversed things in the U.S. Senior Open. He trailed all the way until the final round, then closed with a 66 to win by two.

Chapman cooled off for the rest of the season, and there being no Surprise of the Year Award, he had to make do with his two majors and $1,021,985 in winnings, 13th on the money list.

Tom Lehman, one of six players to win two individual titles, finished second on the money list with $1.9 million, and won the Player of the Year Award on the strength of his titles — the Regions Tradition, a major, and the season-ending Charles Schwab Cup Championship. Given the $1 million annuity, the Schwab was worth $1.4 million to Lehman, moving him to note, "To chase a white ball and call it work is so much fun."

Bernhard Langer, who won two tournaments, topped the money list with $2.1 million, making a great comeback from the thumb injury that idled him much of the 2011 season. Langer was impressively consistent. In addition to the two wins, he was runner-up five times. Langer was dazzling in his second win, the SAS Championship. He hit 87 percent of the fairways and one-putted 11 times in his closing 63. He had two kinds of golf for the week. "Good," he said, "or really good."

Fred Couples, nursing that chronic bad back, played in only 11 tour events, but won twice — Mississippi Gulf Resort Classic and the Senior Open Championship — and had five other top-10 finishes. He was elected to the World Golf Hall of Fame, and he took the news calmly. "I mean it's surprising. But I don't think it's surprising like, 'Oh my God, I got in there,'" he said. "I have been on tour a long time. I think when people talk about people in the Hall of Fame they are all great players. I don't believe that I'm a great player, but I'm a darn good player.

"I'm a truist. I don't know what a great player is. I know there are a lot of them... But I believe that golf is a little bit different than a lot of sports when you start talking about the Hall of Fame because we get to play for so long. A lot of it comes from just being around forever. I think I was just in the right spot."

Joe Daley, long-aspiring journeyman, finally broke through and got his first win and first major at the same time, in the Constellation Senior Players Championship.

Fred Funk underlined his year with a tough win over Lehman in the Insperity Championship, then amazingly went bogey-free for all three rounds to win the Greater Hickory Classic. Willie Wood broke out of a 16-year drought in a big way, with two wins, in the Pacific Links Hawai'i Championship and the Dick's Sporting Goods Open.

Kirk Triplett turned 50 in late March, broke through in the senior ranks at the Nature Valley First Tee Open in July, his eighth start. It was his first win since 2006. He trailed through the first two rounds, then went six under through the first 11 holes in the third, shot 66 and won by two. The win and four other top-10 finishes won him the Rookie of the Year Award.

The year was characteristically good for pithy utterances. Among them:

• "I really wanted that putt," said Kenny Perry, on holing a 10-foot bogey putt on the final hole of the ACE Group Classic. Not that he needed it. He just wanted to shoot 20 under. He did, and won by five.

• "I wish I had a tournament next week," said Willie Wood after winning the Pacific Links Hawai'i Championship, for his second Champions Tour victory after the Dick's Sporting Goods Open three weeks earlier, his first win of any kind in about 16 years.

• "I never had a five-shot lead — Fuzzy told me to play like I was broke," said Michael Allen, on taking Fuzzy Zoeller's advice and winning the Encompass Insurance Pro-Am, ending an 0-for-40 stretch.

• "Big day tomorrow," said aching Mark Calcavecchia after winning the Montreal Championship, looking forward to a visit to the chiropractor, then getting his dog to the veterinarian.

On the Japan Senior Tour, Naomichi (Joe) Ozaki, who delayed his switch to senior golf until he was 56 years old, promptly won two of the six tournaments he played on the eight-event schedule in 2012 and led the Order of Merit standings. The tour's majors went to Filipino Frankie Minoza (Senior Open) and Kiyoshi Miyoshi, who won the Senior PGA for the third time and has eight victories on the Senior Tour.

Paul Wesselingh, 51, was named the European Senior Tour Rookie of the Year after winning once and notching six other top-10 finishes in 14 starts in 2012. He finished fifth on the Order of Merit.

Champions Tour

Mitsubishi Electric Championship
Ka'upulehu-Kona, Hawaii
Winner: Dan Forsman

This was the Mitsubishi Electric Championship, kicking off the 2012 Champions Tour and reviving Dan Forsman's career.

"That shot could've gone anywhere," Forsman was saying. "It could've been long, over, behind the green in a bunker, right or left." This was at the par-four 11th in the second round, a five iron from 185 yards out of "gnarly" rough that, instead of going wild, ended up just eight feet past the flag. Forsman got his birdie. "And it was a super boost," he said. "It got me thinking, 'I could turn a corner here. It could be a good day.'"

It was, in fact, a great day. Forsman was back in the pack through the first nine. Then he scorched the second nine for six birdies, starting with a tap-in at the 10th hole. Then came the inspiring 11th. He closed the run with an 11-footer at the 17th and a two-footer at the 18th for a seven-under-par 65 at the Hualalai Resort and a two-stroke lead to carry into the final round.

Forsman had opened with a 67, two behind co-leaders Tom Lehman, the tour's 2011 Player of the Year, and Bruce Vaughan. Then he led the rest of the way, shooting 65-69 — the final round in brisk winds — for a 15-under 201 total and a two-stroke win over Jay Don Blake (67–203), who ended the 2011 season with a victory in the Charles Schwab Championship.

Forsman held off the pack with three birdies over the first 11 holes of the final round. After a bogey, he finished with a birdie and five pars, twice getting up and down out of bunkers, making a birdie at the par-five 14th and saving par at the 16th. It was quite a rebirth for a guy who had won twice on the tour but struggled through 2011 with a sore hip.

"I sat home over the holidays and kept thinking, 'What will it take to get through the door,'" Forsman said. "I kept thinking, 'I've got to do the little things that all add up.'"

He did them, and they added up to a win.

Allianz Championship
Boca Raton, Florida
Winner: Corey Pavin

Corey Pavin had nothing but an eight iron left to the green — but what an eight iron. This wasn't your routine approach from a comfortable lie in the fairway. This was Pavin trying to chop the ball from against a gnarled tree root, but having to hold the club upside-down and swing left-handed. Just your basic impossible shot.

It came in the final round of the Allianz Championship, the second stop and first full field on the 2012 Champions Tour. Pavin, battling Mark Calcavecchia and Peter Senior, had missed the green at Broken Sound's par-three 14th and had that awful lie. He couldn't afford a penalty drop. But could he afford to risk a crazy shot?

"It's not like I practice turning eight irons over and hit them left-handed," said the gritty Pavin, grinning. Somehow, he popped the ball to the green, to within five feet of the hole, saved his par and his skin, and went on to beat Senior on the first hole of a playoff with a 12-foot birdie putt. It was Pavin's first win on the Champions Tour, in his 35th start, and his first win in more than five years, dating back to the 2006 U.S. Bank Championship.

Pavin led the first round by two with an eight-under-par 64 he tried to ignore. "When you start thinking about how many birdies you're making, you tend to mess up," Pavin said. He finished with 70-71 to tie Senior at 11-under 205.

Calcavecchia blew amazingly hot and cold. In the second round, he went three over in the first three holes, then made seven birdies the rest of the way for a 68. In the last round, he was leading Pavin by three, then bogeyed six of his last seven for a 73, dropping to a tie for seventh. Calc shrugged. Pavin's miracle shot and his own six bogeys in seven holes — both one in a million. "That's the way it goes," he said.

ACE Group Classic
Naples, Florida
Winner: Kenny Perry

The moment of crisis for Kenny Perry in the ACE Group Classic arrived when he was playing the final hole. He was leading, but he'd hit his tee shot far to the left and was in trouble. Scrambling from there, he was facing a 10-foot putt for bogey.

"I really wanted that putt," Perry said. Not that he was in any danger. He was leading by six strokes. "I really wanted to shoot 20 under," Perry said. "I didn't want to fall back to 19 like I did at Colonial one year. I had a seven-stroke lead coming in, and I doubled and I went from 21 to 19 (under). I said, 'I ain't doing that this week.'"

So Perry holed that 10-footer for a 70, a 20-under 196 and a five-stroke win over Bernhard Langer for his second Champions Tour victory. His 64-62 start set the tour's 36-hole record of 126.

"That's amazing," said Perry. "So many great players have played this tour, and to be able to now say I've had the lowest 36 of all time is pretty neat." Perry made 20 birdies in those 36 holes, including a streak of four in the first round, another of three in the second, leading an assault on the Talon course at TwinEagles, in which 49 of 77 in the field finished under par, and 11 of them in double figures.

Larry Mize kicked off the assault with a 62 in the first round. Perry took over in the second, leading off the way he had in the first, with five birdies on the front nine. He added six on the back, interrupted by one bogey for his 62.

Said Langer, six back with his 65–131: "It looks like we're all playing for second place." He had eagled the 17th for the third straight time, shot 70, and finished second. Perry had frustrated the field.

"It was tough to get any pressure on him," Tom Lehman said.

Said Langer: "I played well. It's just that Perry ran off with it."

Toshiba Classic
Newport Beach, California
Winner: Loren Roberts

Loren Roberts, whose range of emotion consists of a big smile when another birdie putt drops, admitted he'd been getting nervous.

"I was getting a little worried about it," Roberts said. He meant not having won in 34 tournaments, and he had become accustomed to winning.

"This was huge for me," he said. He was referring to the Toshiba Classic, and how he made it his 13th Champions Tour victory. And just when he was wondering whether, at age 57, he had what it took to win again. He did, coming from behind and surviving a late shake to post a card of 66-70-69–205, for a two-stroke win at Newport Beach Country Club. He beat a tough field — Tom Kite (69), Bernhard Langer (70) and Mark Calcavecchia (73), all tied for second.

The tournament started with fireworks, with Langer, Bobby Clampett and Olin Browne tying for the lead at six-under 65. Langer eagled the par-four sixth on an eight iron from 143 yards. Clampett birdied three of the last four holes, and Browne birdied the par-five 18th with the last of his 27 putts.

On Saturday, the second round was a time to be survived. Chilling winds and heavy rain hit Newport Beach, right on the Pacific. Calcavecchia bogeyed Nos. 4 and 6 at the height of the storm, and came back out after a suspension of play to birdie five of the last 11 holes for a 67 and a two-stroke lead on Fred Couples (69) and Roberts (70).

With Calcavecchia running into trouble fast in the final round — he dropped four shots over four holes from the fourth — Roberts was about to turn the tournament into a rout, but a crabby patch hauled him back. He had five birdies and a bogey through the 13th, then broke down into bogeys at 14, 16 and 17.

"I let everybody in the game," Roberts said. "I got out of rhythm."

He calmed himself and holed a five-foot birdie putt on the 18th to lock it up by two.

Said Roberts, with a grin: "We did make it interesting."

Mississippi Gulf Resort Classic
Biloxi, Mississippi
Winner: Fred Couples

It seems that a fellow who could come back from a storm delay the next day and complete a 63 on a course he hadn't seen before he teed it up the first day, and who led all the way, ought to have won in some degree of comfort.

But no. Fred Couples, making the Mississippi Golf Resort Classic his first start of the year, suffered two late hiccups at Fallen Oak, and bogey-proof Michael Allen kept the pressure on. So Couples needed to hole an eight-foot birdie putt on the last hole for the win. He got it, but not without drama.

The first act came in the storm-interrupted first round, when Couples came out the next morning and birdied his last six holes for a nine-under 63 and a one-stroke lead. He tied for the lead in the second with a 70, and then in the last, was cruising along with four birdies through the 14th. And then came the bumps.

"I had a two-shot lead, sitting on a par-five," said Couples, coming to the 15th. "I felt like I could have made birdie to put it out of reach, and make a six. So then your mind jumps. I hadn't won since last October and I hadn't played much. It's not like riding a bike. They say you just get back up and go. You get a little jumpy.

"And on 17, I was trying to cut it and the wind held it, and I got in that bunker and couldn't get a stance. I got it up and down for bogey."

At the par-four 18th, the toughest hole on the course, Couples split the fairway with his drive, then stuck his approach eight feet from the hole. He nailed it for a 69 and his seventh tour win.

Allen, falling short by a stroke, was far from brokenhearted. "I didn't think I'd have a chance to tie," he said. But a guy who plays his last 35 holes in 10 under and who has only one bogey in 54 holes almost always has a chance.

Encompass Insurance Pro-Am
Lutz, Florida
Winner: Michael Allen

When Michael Allen won for the first time, taking the 2009 Senior PGA Championship, he ended an 0-for-334 drought. "Seems like only yesterday," he said. This was after scoring his second victory in the Encompass Insurance Pro-Am in April, ending an 0-for-40 stretch.

"I knew it was going to come again soon," Allen said. The question was, how to do it? He got the answer from a good friend.

"I've never had a five-shot lead," Allen said. "Fuzzy told me to play like I was broke."

Fuzzy Zoeller's tip did the trick. After a 66-67 start, Allen simply outran a formidable chaser, Kenny Perry, and shot the par-71 TPC Tampa Bay in 68 for a 12-under 201 total, winning by three.

Said Allen: "You never quite know what you really have to do until it's over."

The first thing Allen had to do was get out of that first-round mess. After two opening birdies, he double-bogeyed the fourth and was falling behind. Then he birdied five of seven from No. 7, bogeyed the 15th, then birdied the 18th for a 66 and a tie for second behind Bruce Fleisher, who insisted his 65 shouldn't have been. "I keep telling friends and family that this is not for 63-year-olds," Fleisher said. He followed with a 78 and disappeared.

Allen enjoyed a brief flurry in the second round — birdied the 11th, eagled the 12th on a 40-foot putt, birdied the 18th — for a 67 and a five-shot lead. But what pleased him most were two par saves — after a watered shot at the 14th and on a 15-foot putt at the 17th. "Those were really nice," he said.

Despite the five-stroke lead, he started the last round shakily, bogeying the third and fourth. But he settled down, and playing "like he was broke," birdied Nos. 5, 7, 12, 14 and 17, holding off Perry, who was charging to a 65, three strokes short.

Said Allen: "It's been a long time since I beat these guys. It's very nice to get on 18 and go, 'Man, I got them all.'"

Liberty Mutual Insurance Legends of Golf
Savannah, Georgia
Winners: Michael Allen and David Frost

The way they were beating up on Savannah Harbor, Tom Purtzer was almost in awe over what might be the winning score at the Liberty Mutual Insurance Legends of Golf. "I bet it would take 30 under if the weather is like it was today," Purtzer said. The April weather turned from balmy to rainy. Even so, he missed by only a shot.

Michael Allen and David Frost were on a tear, combining for a 29-under 187 to win the 35-twosome event by a stroke. Frost touched on the key in better-ball play.

"Hopefully, we don't play the same holes badly," Frost said. "That's the only question out here." They answered the question by shooting Savannah Harbor in 62-63-62 without a bogey. Frost said he felt less pressure playing with Allen, who won the Encompass Insurance Pro-Am the previous week, his first win after going 40 consecutive tournaments without one. "It took so long to win the second one," Allen said. "Then I had the breakthrough last week. It was great having David on my side."

They started the Liberty with five straight birdies and tied for second in the first round at 10 under, two behind Purtzer and Brad Bryant. They took turns in the second round, Frost making four birdies in the first seven holes, then Allen five over the next six to tie Purtzer and Bryant at 19 under.

"For sure, Michael couldn't have done it without me," Frost cracked, when it was over. It was his eagle chip at the 14th that got them to 29 under. "I was a little nervous over that chip," Frost said. "The ball was lying downhill. But it came out just right." Later, when the rains hit, John Cook cut their margin to one with a 45-foot birdie at the 18th.

The second straight win — or half-win — strengthened Allen's perch atop the Champions Tour money list. There was another plus.

"Now I know my kids will jump all over me and tell me how great I am," Allen said.

Insperity Championship
The Woodlands, Texas
Winner: Fred Funk

It was something of a 20th anniversary for Fred Funk at The Woodlands. He scored the first of his eight PGA Tour victories there in 1992, and now, in 2012, his seventh Champions Tour win, a gritty one-shot decision over Tom Lehman.

They turned the tournament into a nose-to-nose battle practically all the way. Lehman, age 53, raced to the top in the first round with an eagle and five birdies over the first eight holes coming home for a seven-under-par 65 and a one-stroke lead over Funk and Tom Jenkins. It was a great performance considering he'd once hated the course because of his early struggles on it.

For Funk, age 55, health was his problem for the past three years — a staph infection, knee replacement and two thumb surgeries.

"I wasn't sure whether I was going to have a career," said Funk, who made just two bogeys in the entire tournament. He tied for the second-round lead with a four-birdie 69 when Lehman turned erratic coming in, three birdies and three bogeys, and shot 70. Never separated by more than a stroke, they were one ahead of Mike Goodes (67) and Brad Bryant (68).

The Insperity came down to the final nine, and for Lehman, it was a bogey and a par that did him in. He led by a stroke at the turn, bogeyed the 10th, then birdied three straight from the 12th for a two-stroke lead. But he overshot the green at the par-five 15th and only parred. "The whole tournament turned on 15," he was to say. Funk tied him with three straight birdies from the 14th.

The par-four 18th settled it. Funk hit a five iron from 174 yards to two feet. Lehman hit a seven iron from 157 to 12 feet. He grazed the hole and parred, and Funk rolled in his two-footer for the win.

"I haven't been this disappointed after a tournament in a long time," Lehman said.

Said Funk: "It was a storybook type of week."

Senior PGA Championship
Benton Harbor, Michigan
Winner: Roger Chapman

The instant Roger Chapman's name appeared on the leaderboard, there in the first round, the question popped up everywhere: "Who's he?"

This was the Senior PGA Championship in May, and they didn't come any more obscure than the 53-year-old Englishman. In 606 starts on the European Tour, he had one win, a playoff victory over Padraig Harrington in the 2000 Brazil Open. Beyond that, his career could be summed up as a small handful of missed chances, a lot of futility, and a few years as a rules official while waiting to turn 50 and heading for senior golf.

Chapman's name hit the leaderboard in the front nine of the first round, after three quick birdies from No. 7, and it stayed there the rest of the way. Heads nodded among the knowing observers: "Don't worry — he won't last." They quit nodding when his lead reached a ridiculous nine early in the final round. He could still be caught, but it would have taken a grotesque collapse — followed by thoughts of self-harm — to blow it by then. Chapman did slip when his mind strayed, but — shooting 68-67-64-72–271, 13 under par at Harbor Shores — he still had plenty of breath left to win by two.

"Having led wire-to-wire, that to me is the greatest thing I've ever done," said Chapman.

Said runner-up John Cook, weary from chasing him all the way: "I can't say it was fun to watch, but it was impressive to watch."

Chapman built his lead to an absurd nine shots in the final round with birdies at Nos. 4, 6 and 7, and then he began thinking of a good friend and coach, George Will, who died two years ago.

"Your mind starts to wander a bit," Chapman said. He bogeyed four of the last 10 holes, and these coupled with Cook's surge cut his winning margin to two. "It's difficult," Chapman said, "when you haven't been in that position before."

Chapman spoke of the "negative man" who sits on your shoulder, telling you all the things that could go wrong. This time, Chapman wasn't listening.

Principal Charity Classic
West Des Moines, Iowa
Winner: Jay Haas

Jay Haas was raised in Belleville, Illinois, went to Wake Forest University and lives in South Carolina, so why would he enjoy homecookin' at Glen Oaks Country Club at West Des Moines, Iowa? But there's some kind of affinity between the two. That's one way of explaining how, early in June, Haas became the first to win the Principal Charity Classic three times.

"I don't know what it is," said Haas, after shooting 66-65-66–197, 16 under par. "I just feel comfortable here."

And the folks at Glen Oaks are comfortable with him, nowhere more than at the par-three 14th. They love to see him come by. When anybody makes a birdie there, beer is half-price. But he was only good for one beer this time, the birdie in the final round, but it sparked the finish that carried him to a five-shot victory. Kirk Triplett, Champions Tour rookie, had to shoot a course-record 62 just to tie Larry Mize to get that close.

Haas, who won the tournament in 2007 and 2008, was in the hunt from the start in this one. His 66 had him two behind first-round leader Mike Goodes, who launched his 64 with four straight birdies, then restrained his imagination. "You don't want to start thinking about how good you are after four," Goodes said.

Haas was in a familiar position in the second round, when he leaped to a three-stroke lead on Mize. He led by three in the second round when he won in 2007.

"It wasn't comfortable then, it probably won't be comfortable now," Haas said. "But it beats being three behind." He set about getting comfortable from the start, birdieing the second and seventh holes, then the 11th, and the beer birdie at the 14th put him up by four with four to play. He stuck his tee shot to two feet at the par-three 16th for another birdie, then a bogey at the 17th, only his third of the week, left him with the five-shot win.

Regions Tradition
Shoal Creek, Alabama
Winner: Tom Lehman

The big question facing Tom Lehman, age 53, on winning his second consecutive Regions Tradition, was — why was he wearing his golf cap turned backward on the final hole? A fashion statement?

"I'm sure they thought it was stupid," Lehman said, meaning his two daughters, college students, who came to Shoal Creek for the second of the Champions Tour's five major championships. "They probably thought I was doing it to be cool or something. The fact of the matter is that when you putt and it's raining, the water drips off the bill onto the ball. It's very distracting. The putt I missed on 17 — two drops fell off my hat onto my ball when I was on my backstroke and it really distracted me."

The miss — the final round was played in a drizzle and occasional rain — cost him his fourth bogey of the tournament in a card of 69-69-68-68–274, 14 under, and cut his winning margin to two over Bernhard Langer (66) and Chien Soon Lu (66).

"My goal was to get off to a good start and put pressure on him," said Langer, who birdied four of the first seven holes. "He responded extremely well to it." Langer, recovering from thumb surgery and looking for his first win of the season, misfired at the eighth and ninth, and the four birdies coming home weren't enough. Lu eagled No. 6 and made four birdies on the back for his best tour finish.

Lehman trailed through the first two rounds, then took the lead for good in the third and locked it up in the rainy fourth. "I don't like playing in rain," Lehman said. "I just feel like I lose the rhythm of my swing."

Lehman made six birdies, including a 30-footer at the seventh that broke a brief tie with Langer, but the joy of his round was the clutch 12-foot par-saver at the 14th. "It really started pouring and that was a really difficult putt," Lehman said. "That might have been the biggest putt of the day."

Montreal Championship
Sainte-Julie, Quebec, Canada
Winner: Mark Calcavecchia

Mark Calcavecchia was cruising along in the final round of the Montreal Championship when, as he sometimes does, he started to get a little nervous. So he called for some expert help.

"I made some nice four-footers for pars," Calcavecchia said. "I get a little shaky on those, on occasion, and for some reason today, I just felt good on them, and then that 16th happened (a chip-in eagle), and I figured even if I bogeyed the last two holes, I'd be fine. At 17, I hit a bad iron into the green and then had a Tiger Woods thought." No matter the luxurious cushion, Calcavecchia figured that if he let one slide, goodness knows what might follow.

"I really wanted to keep the round clean," said Calcavecchia, who had only two bogeys for the week, both in the first round, and he went the last 40 holes bogey-free.

And so summoning the resolve of Tiger Woods, he kept the round clean, completing a card of 69-67-64–200, 16 under par at Richelieu Valley's Vercheres Course, for a four-stroke victory over Brad Bryant.

The tournament didn't look all that good for him at the outset. Russ Cochran, age 53, and a three-time Champions Tour winner, had run off seven birdies against just one bogey for a six-under 66 to lead the first round by two. Cochran birdied all four par-fives, no little feat considering the crosswinds and the bunkers. "So you've got to shape the ball right," the left-hander said.

Bob Tway, 53, still seeking that first Champions win, came to the top with a 65 in the second round and led Calcavecchia by one. Then Calc went on his romp in the final round. He tore through the front nine with five birdies, then added a birdie at the 11th and the eagle at the 16th, tying the course record with a 64 for the four-shot win. Then Calcavecchia's life was going to the dogs.

"Big day tomorrow," Calcavecchia said. It was on to the trusted chiropractor early on Monday, then get the dogs to the veterinarian in the afternoon.

Constellation Senior Players Championship
Pittsburgh, Pennsylvania
Winner: Joe Daley

For 12 years, Joe Daley's career had been defined by "the putt." In the 2000 PGA Tour qualifying tournament, his four-foot putt dropped into the hole and popped right back out, bouncing off a defective cup liner. He missed his playing card by a shot.

Now his career could be defined by another putt, a downhill 18-foot curler at the final hole that dropped in — and stayed in — for a birdie that locked up the 2012 Constellation Senior Players Championship. After some 20 years as a golf junkie, Daley finally was a real winner. The $405,000 first prize was just one taste of the dessert. The other: He was now exempt for a year. And he did it under severe heat at Fox Chapel Golf Club — 90-plus degrees and the cream of the Champions Tour — Tom Lehman, Mark Calcavecchia and Fred Couples.

"It was my competition — not them," Daley said. "I'm my own competition. Have been for years."

Daley was high in the mix all the way, playing Fox Chapel in 66-64-68-68 for a 14-under 266 total, and won by two over Lehman.

Daley was paired with Couples and Calcavecchia in the last round and took the lead as they faltered. Couples, who hurt his bad back in the third round, closed with a 71, tying for fourth with Calcavecchia, four back. Calcavecchia birdied the 13th and 15th, but bogeyed the 16th and 17th, and shot 72. His putter had betrayed him. He needed 34 putts.

Up ahead, Lehman gave Daley something to think about. He finished erratically, stalling out with three birdies and three bogeys over the last six holes, but he took the clubhouse lead with 69–268. "In a nutshell, it was too many mistakes," he said.

Daley started the final round tied with Calcavecchia at 12 under. He took the lead with birdies at the ninth and 10th, bogeyed the 17th out of a bunker, then holed the 18-footer at the 18th for the two-stroke win.

"All I was keying on was what I had next, and kept my emotions under control," Daley said. "So here I am."

Nature Valley First Tee Open
Monterey, California
Winner: Kirk Triplett

When it comes to distinctions, Kirk Triplett can claim one for the books. He went from the oldest winner on the Web.com Tour (then the Nationwide Tour) to one of the youngest on the Champions Tour in less than a year. Triplett won the Web.com's News Sentinel Open at age 49 in August 2011, then after turning 50 in March 2012, he won the Champions' Nature Valley First Tee Open at Pebble Beach the first week in July, in which the pros play with 81 juniors from the First Tee program.

"To win anywhere is special," said the affable Triplett, joining an exclusive group who have won on the PGA Tour, the Web.com Tour and the Champions Tour — Olin Browne, Ron Streck, Keith Fergus, Tom Lehman and Gary Hallberg. "But," Triplett added, "to win at Pebble Beach is extra special. To do it in my first Champions Tour try is great." Triplett won three times on the PGA Tour, the last the 2006 Chrysler Classic.

In his first seven Champions starts, Triplett had three top-10 finishes, the best a tie for second in the Principal Charity Classic. Now, in his eighth start, he was on the fringe of contention through the first two rounds, alternating over Pebble Beach and Del Monte, both par 72s. Triplett opened with a pair of 70s, trailing John Cook and Tom Kite by three in the first round, and trailing Kite and Brad Bryant by four in the second.

Triplett exploded in the final round with an eagle at Pebble Beach's par-five second, then raced off to three more birdies on the front at the third, seventh and ninth holes. He added a birdie at the 11th, took his only bogey at the par-three 12th, and chipped in for his fifth and final birdie at the par-four 16th, wrapping up scores of 70-70-66 for a 10-under 206 total and a two-stroke win over McNulty.

"I really hadn't been playing that well," Triplett said. "But I'm doing a lot better lately, and feeling more comfortable out there."

U.S. Senior Open Championship
Lake Orion, Michigan
Winner: Roger Chapman

Ruling out black magic, it would take some doing to explain England's Roger Chapman and his debut on the Champions Tour.

Chapman, 53, with only one victory to his credit in 25 years on the European Tour, surprised everyone by winning the Senior PGA Championship in May, then doubly stunned everyone by winning the U.S. Senior Open in July. Two wins — two majors.

Chapman's explanation: "I can't put my finger on why."

He led wire-to-wire in taking the Senior PGA. In the U.S. Senior Open, he came from behind in the final round. Chapman did allude to a certain confidence in his swing. It produced a total of 68-68-68-66–270, 10 under par, and a two-stroke victory at Indianwood. But he needed a big assist from Bernhard Langer. Langer squandered the four-shot lead he carried into the fourth round, shot 72, and tied for second with Fred Funk, Tom Lehman and Corey Pavin. Langer's decline started with a double bogey out of the trees at the par-four No. 2. "If I shoot under par from that point on, I'll still be in good shape," Langer said. "But I couldn't make a putt."

The door was open, and Chapman came confidently striding through. He started four behind Langer and picked up speed immediately. He birdied the second and eighth, then the 11th and 14th, and after bogeying the 16th out of a bunker, he came to a dramatic moment in his rebirth. At the 195-yard, par-three 17th, he fired a five iron to tap-in range for his final birdie, restoring his two-stroke lead. "I have to say that was my best shot ever played," Chapman said.

He had another moment at the 18th. He drove into the gallery on the left, but ended up in a good lie. He reached the green safely and two-putted for his par, locking up his two-stroke win and a sense of liberation.

"I wanted to prove to myself and to other people that Benton Harbor (Senior PGA) wasn't a one-off event," Chapman said. "That was in the back of my mind."

The Senior Open Championship presented by Rolex
Ayrshire, Scotland
Winner: Fred Couples

See European Senior Tour section.

3M Championship
Blaine, Minnesota
Winner: Bernhard Langer

At the 3M Championship at TPC Twin Cities, it was a week for shooting one's age, what with Gil Morgan matching his with a 65 and Hale Irwin bettering his by two years with a 65. Bernhard Langer was beginning to think he'd have to shoot his own to win — 54. But the gods of golf intervened and all Langer needed for his first win of the season was a 10-under-par 62.

"Winning is always special," said Langer, who rallied from six shots behind, "but this is pretty important because it's been awhile since I've won and especially after what I've been through the last few weeks..." Langer was referring to letting leads slip away in the final round recently in the Senior Open Championship and the U.S. Senior Open. "It was very important for my confidence to pull off a win here sooner than later," he said. He shot 67-69-62–198, 18 under, for his first win since February 2011, shortly before his thumb surgery.

It came at the expense of David Peoples, who was in a drought of his own — 0-for-50 on the Champions Tour. Peoples, who shot 62 in the second round, might have won this one except that after opening a five-shot lead early in the final round, he fell into a trap of his own making.

"I got into my own little world," said Peoples. "I felt, 'Just don't make any mistakes and you'll be all right.' I should have looked at the boards. I had no idea."

Langer went five under on the front nine, then added birdies at Nos. 11, 12, 14 and 15, and at the par-five 18th he put his approach to eight feet to set up his clinching birdie. Peoples, who had parred 10 straight holes, finished bogey-bogey-birdie. "I just didn't feel like I was aggressive enough on that back nine," said Peoples, runner-up by two.

Said Langer: "It's not easy to play with a big lead. You start to protect a little bit and you don't shoot at the flag..."

Dick's Sporting Goods Open
Endicott, New York
Winner: Willie Wood

It was a matter of two big breaks for Willie Wood in the Dick's Sporting Goods Open — one he made for himself, the other made for him by the unfortunate Michael Allen. They added up to Wood's first victory on the Champions Tour and his first since his only win on the PGA Tour, the 1996 Deposit Guarantee Classic.

"It was quite exciting, said Wood, who was making his eighth start, this one through the Monday qualifier. "I hung in there, hung in there, and things turned out great."

Though it was the reverse for Allen. He watered his tee shot on the first playoff hole, essentially ending it right there.

Wood shot 67-68-68 and Allen 66-71-66 to tie at 13-under 203 at En-Joie Golf Club, one ahead of Joey Sindelar (66), Kenny Perry (67), Tom Lehman (67) and Brad Faxon (71).

Wood manufactured his big break the dramatic way. He was facing a 35-foot putt at the last hole to tie Allen, the clubhouse leader. The ball slowed as it neared the hole, then broke right and toppled in. Allen had his dramatic moment earlier. At the par-five 12th, he hit a hybrid from 235 yards to 10 feet and dropped the putt for an eagle.

The playoff ended abruptly. Wood found the fairway with his tee shot, but Allen pulled his left into the water. Wood parred for the win, ending years of frustration. In addition to the victory on the PGA Tour, he'd had 22 other top-10 finishes, and also 12 top-10s on the Nationwide Tour, without a win.

"I knew when I turned 50 that I would have a new challenge ahead of me," Wood said.

Perry, Bernhard Langer and John Huston shared the first-round lead on 65s, and Huston was the solo leader in the second round but faded to a 77 in the final. Faxon had the round of the tournament in his second-round 66 — a double bogey out of the trees, eight birdies and 12 one-putt greens. "I've played a lot of good golf hitting the ball sideways," Faxon said.

Boeing Classic
Snoqualmie, Washington
Winner: Jay Don Blake

Jay Don Blake had got a reprieve on the first playoff hole that he hadn't expected.

"I've got my hand out of my pocket, ready to shake his hand," said Blake. "I didn't expect him to miss it."

Mark O'Meara didn't expect to miss the six-foot birdie putt, either. But it slid away, and they went back to the tee at TPC Snoqualmie's par-five 18th to try again. This time, Blake put his approach on the back fringe. O'Meara missed the green with his three iron, then pitched on to 15 feet. Blake chipped to tap-in range. O'Meara missed on his birdie try, and Blake tapped in for the birdie and his third Champions Tour win. This was late in August — Blake's time of the year. He won the Songdo IBD in September in 2011 (in a playoff that included O'Meara). Then he followed that with the Charles Schwab Cup Championship in November.

"I guess this time of year is when things happen for me," Blake said. "I worked hard at it. Now the hard work is finally paying off. What a joy."

O'Meara, of course, wasn't sharing in any joy. "It wasn't very much fun," he said. As for Blake: "He deserved to win. He hit a good pitch shot on the last hole."

The question at the end was whether it would be a three-way playoff. Blake shot 68-70-68 and O'Meara 74-64-68 to tie at 10-under 206. Willie Wood, who won the Dick's Sporting Goods Open the week before, needed an eagle at the 18th to tie them. But Wood birdied and finished second.

There was history in the making for a while. Tom Jenkins, age 64, taking the lead from Mark Calcavecchia in the second round, shot a 65 and was one round from becoming the oldest winner in tour history. The question was inevitable: How would he do in he final round? "I'm not going to talk much about how I'm going to do," Jenkins said. "But if I can get on that 18th tee with a five-shot lead, I'll guarantee I'll win." (Alas, he shot 78.)

Pacific Links Hawai'i Championship
Kapolei, Hawaii
Winner: Willie Wood

"I wish I had a tournament next week," Willie Wood was saying. It was an understandable sentiment. Wood, 51, was on a roll. Surging in the final round, Wood made the Pacific Links Hawai'i Championship not only his second Champions Tour victory but his second in three events. But he's got to take it easy on the nerves. In the Dick's Sporting Goods Open, he had to make a long birdie putt on the final hole to tie Michael Allen, then par the first playoff hole for his first win. This time he had to birdie the last two holes to edge a faltering Bill Glasson by a stroke.

Woods, who shot Kapolei Golf Club in 68-68-66–202, 14 under par, was tagging along through the first two rounds. Australia's Peter Senior, winless in his 65 tour starts over three years, got some encouragement with a seven-under-par 65 for a one-stroke lead in the first round. "It'd be nice to have a win," said Senior, a runner-up five times. Glasson would thwart Senior this time, rolling to a 65 in the second round for a four-stroke lead going into Sunday. Glasson birdied three of the last five holes and noted, "Finishing the way I did is going to help tomorrow." But golf is such a contrary game.

Glasson's four-stroke lead melted under three birdies and five bogeys on the final nine. "I got a little iffy between clubs," Glasson said. The stumble left him with 72 and second by a shot, his best finish in his 47 tour starts.

Wood, five behind to start, cruised along to six birdies, the last two off a chip to five feet at the par-five 17th, then a 20-footer at the 18th for his winning 66. "I had a great back nine," Wood said. "And I got a little bit lucky with the way Bill finished."

True, Wood needed help from the unfortunate Glasson, but he did his part by going all 54 holes without a bogey.

SAS Championship
Cary, North Carolina
Winner: Bernhard Langer

It would seem that Bernhard Langer likes nothing better than a nice, deep hole to climb out of.

At the 3M Championship in August, it was six shots going into the final round. He shot 62 to win his first of the year. This time, with the Champions Tour resuming early in October with the SAS Championship at Prestonwood, it was a mere four strokes. He shot a bogey-free 63 this time. Mark up No. 2, by two strokes on a 13-under 203 total.

"I knew I had to go deeper and lower to make up some ground," said Langer, who had trailed on 68-72. "And thank goodness it was nine under, because Jay Don came very close to tying me."

Jay Don Blake, who won the Boeing Classic late in August, was the victim this time. It wasn't a Langer-Blake duel until the final round. Russ Cochran (66) led the first round, and in the second, Fred Funk (67) and

Steve Pate (67) led Blake by one, Langer by four. As the others faded in the last round, Blake was shooting 68, but Langer was on a tear. He birdied three straight from No. 4, parred the seventh, and birdied the eighth and ninth. He added four more birdies on the back nine, including the 17th and 18th, to put the tournament almost out of reach. Blake needed a birdie at the 18th to tie. But he hit a tree with his drive and bogeyed.

"Probably the rhythm I was in wasn't very good because I was just making pars," Blake said. "You just feel like you have to be more aggressive. But sometimes being aggressive doesn't always work out. Trying to be too aggressive on 18 kind of hurt me." Actually, it killed his slim chances.

Langer won this one on accuracy and putting. He hit 87 percent of the fairways in each round, and in the final round he one-putted 11 times, including five of his last six holes. Apart from two bad shots, he had two kinds of golf for the week. "Good," he said, "or really good."

Greater Hickory Classic
Conover, North Carolina
Winner: Fred Funk

Golfers routinely go before the media to review their rounds — "go over your birdies and bogeys" is the expression. For Fred Funk, in the Greater Hickory Classic, he'd have to say, "What bogeys?"

Funk strung out three bogey-free rounds to take the Greater Hickory Classic, and in the process he stretched two other streaks — 60 holes without a bogey, since the No. 13 in the final round of the SAS Championship the previous week, and 84 holes at Rock Barn, dating to No. 7 in the second round of the 2011 Greater Hickory.

Funk, trailing only in the first round, shot the par-72 Rock Barn in 66-66-69–201, 15 under, grabbing a one-stroke win over Duffy Waldorf with a birdie at the final hole.

"I really wanted to win here really bad," said Funk, 56, notching his second Champions title of 2012 and his eighth on the tour. "I've been knocking at the door on this tournament a lot ... but I was feeling the heat. When you get in contention, you always want to finish it."

Funk trailed only in the first round, by a stroke, when Dan Forsman's back pain eased long enough to let him shoot 65.

Funk came through two crucial holes swimmingly. The first was in the second round, where he had a close brush with a bogey. "I jump-started my round with a save on No. 2," he said. "I drove it into the bunker and had to wedge it out for par." With that crisis past, he came to the next, that in the final round at the final hole, the par-five 18th. There, playing ahead of him, Waldorf came up just short on a 20-foot birdie try.

"I assumed Duffy was going to birdie No. 18," Funk said. "When I saw that I needed a birdie to win, I played real aggressive with my tee shot. I just smoked a three wood and hit a great chip. Still, I was pretty nervous about that putt."

Nervous about a two-footer? Only long enough to get it down.

AT&T Championship
San Antonio, Texas
Winner: David Frost

The way Mark Calcavecchia was making his way through the AT&T Championship, there didn't seem to be much room for anyone else. So it came as something as a surprise in the final round to Bernhard Langer and David Frost to find themselves in a playoff.

"I wasn't planning on this," Frost said. "Only when I hit it close on 13 (setting up a birdie) did I think that it was just Bernhard and I." But they were the ones left with a chance to win. Frost shot 71-71-66, overcoming a six-stroke deficit in the final round to tie with Langer (74-68-66) at eight-under 208. Both parred the last hole of regulation. Langer was short into a bunker with his approach, blasted six feet past and holed the putt. Frost missed a 25-footer for his birdie and tapped in for a par.

They tied on the first playoff hole, then Frost holed a 10-footer for birdie for the win, making the biggest comeback in the event's 26 years.

But it looked like Calcavecchia's tournament after the first two rounds. Playing with a surgically repaired right hand, Calcavecchia shot a five-under-par 67 in the first round, against a storm that brought rain, lightning, heavy winds and chilling temperatures in the 40s to TPC San Antonio. "It feels like he's shooting 59 out there," said Jay Haas, relieved that he got in with a par 72. The storm forced a delay of play and kicked the round over into a morning finish the next day. Kenny Perry completed a 70 to hold second, three strokes back.

Calcavecchia stretched his lead to four with a 69 in the second round, but he knew the feeling. "My back was a little bit spasmy," he said. "And when that happens, I hunch over a little bit to protect it. When I do that, I get both-way misses." He missed the fairway wide to the right at the 14th and 15th, then missed the 17th by 50 yards to the left. He birdied it, but the bad signs were there. He shot 74 and finished third, two back.

Charles Schwab Cup Championship
Scottsdale, Arizona
Winner: Tom Lehman

When a man can summon a final kick to birdie four of the last five holes and win $1.4 million, what more can he say? Tom Lehman found the words. "To chase a white ball and call it a job," he said, after winning the Champions Tour season-ending Charles Schwab Cup, "is so much fun."

Thus ended the 2012 tour early in November, with Lehman racing off with a six-stroke victory — his second win of the year — and taking the $440,000 first prize and the $1 million annuity from the year-long points chase.

"It was a great week from start to finish," said Lehman, who took the lead in the third round and kept it, shooting the Desert Mountain Cochise course in 68-63-62-65–258, 22 under par. Jay Haas, after a 60 in the second round, closed with a 69 to finish second.

Lehman played with his emotions running high. The Cochise course is where he first worked with noted golf instructor Jim Flick, who was dying of cancer. "I decided I can't play this round of golf with tears in my eyes," Lehman said. "I have to wait until business is finished."

He had opened with a 68, four off defending champion Jay Don Blake's lead, and his 63 in the second round was hugely upstaged by Haas's 60. "It was a magical day," said Haas, who credited magic or something for some of his birdies. Like the one at No. 10, where he missed the green and then chipped in, and at No. 11, where he mis-hit his seven-footer and watched it roll in anyway.

Lehman took the lead with a third-round 62, then broke free late in the fourth. He kicked off his birdie run with a scary escape from the rough to nail the 14th from 12 feet, holed 12-footers at the 15th and 16th, and tapped in at the par-five 18th after just missing an eagle.

Before the tournament, Lehman was asked about his prospects. "If I win, I win," he said. There were no "if's" about this one.

European Senior Tour

Mallorca Senior Open
Son Servera, Mallorca, Spain
Winner: Gary Wolstenholme

Gary Wolstenholme, England's most decorated amateur, continued to verify his decision to turn professional when the European Senior Tour beckoned as the circuit launched its 2012 season in early May with the Mallorca Senior Open in Spain. With his second Senior Tour victory at Mallorca, Wolstenholme registered his 12th top-10 finish among his 28 starts since making that move when he turned 50. He won by two at Pula Golf Club with his 69 finish and eight-under-par 205, breaking from a second-round tie with tour rookie Paul Wesselingh, a fellow Englishman.

Wesselingh, who tied for second at 208 with tour veterans Mike Harwood (70) and Chris Williams (67), got off to a flying start in his first senior appearance, sharing the first-round lead with American journeyman Dick Mast at 68. Mast led the January qualifier and Wesselingh was second.

Wolstenholme overtook Wesselingh the second day with a seven birdie-two bogey 66 as the long-time club pro put up another 68 and Mast fell back with a one-over 72. Aussie Harwood slipped a stroke behind the leaders with Paraguay's Angel Franco and Spain's Juan Quiros when he bogeyed the last two holes after taking the lead.

A 25-foot birdie putt on the first hole and a string of three straight birdies in the middle of Sunday's final round sparked Wolstenholme's winning run, while Wesselingh's hopes virtually died when he double-bogeyed the sixth hole.

Benahavis Senior Masters
Benahavis, Spain
Winner: Gary Wolstenholme

Freshman-of-the-year in 2011, Gary Wolstenholme staked an early claim on the mythical title of sophomore-of-the-year with his come-from-behind victory in the Benahavis Senior Masters two weeks after capturing the tour's opening Mallorca Open.

Just one stroke off the lead after 36 holes at La Quinta Golf and Country Club and four back of Mark James at one point early in the final round, Wolstenholme surged to a five-under-par 66 and posted a 200 total, one in front of Mark Mouland, the leader for two days, who shot 68, and James, who closed with 67. It was Wolstenholme's third win on the circuit.

Mouland, also a second-season player with a 2011 victory to his credit, jumped off fast Friday with a course-record-equaling 64. He birdied seven of his first 11 holes, then parred in, but led South African Chris Williams by just a stroke, Delroy Cambridge and Anders Forsbrand by two.

Mouland clung to that one-shot margin, facing the Sunday challenges of Wolstenholme, James, Australia's Mike Harwood and all-time victory leader Carl Mason. After a slow start, Wolstenholme produced five birdies in the middle of the round and established the winning margin with a 15-foot birdie putt at the 17th hole.

ISPS Handa PGA Seniors Championship
Hexham, England
Winner: Paul Wesselingh

A long period of intense preparation paid off quickly for Paul Wesselingh. The English club professional followed up a runner-up finish in Spain with a win in the weather-shortened ISPA Handa PGA Seniors Championship in just his fourth start on the European Senior Tour.

"I've spent the last four or five years working really hard to get ready for the Senior Tour, so this victory feels fantastic," said Wesselingh, who raced from a four-shot deficit at the start of the final round at De Vere Slaley Hall to a 67 and six-under-par 210 total, edging defending champion Andrew Oldcorn and Anders Forsbrand by a stroke. Interestingly, Wesselingh won the Senior PGA title two years after David J. Russell, whom he succeeded as head professional at Kedleston Park, Derby, in 2001.

Before heavy weather moved in Friday, Mark James put up his fourth straight 67 to take the first-round lead, a shot ahead of Bob Cameron, following his 67-67-67–201 runner-up finish in the Benahavis Masters. Flooding rains led to the decision to shorten the tournament to 54 holes as it took two days to complete a second round. When the field had muddled to a finish Saturday, James remained in front. His 72–139 gave him a two-stroke lead over Forsbrand (70-71) and Oldcorn (72-69).

Wesselingh was just one under par after 11 holes Sunday before launching a run of four straight birdies. Forsbrand tied him with a birdie at the 16th, but he bogeyed the 17th, and neither he nor Oldcorn could muster a necessary birdie at the last hole to catch Wesselingh, who had already finished. James slipped to 74 and dropped to fourth place.

Van Lanschot Senior Open
The Hague, Netherlands
Winner: Massy Kuramoto

Massy Kuramoto revived memories of the glory days he enjoyed in the 1980s and early 1990s on the Japan Tour with his victory in the Van Lanschot Senior Open, his second win on the European Senior Tour but his first ever outside of his native country. He won the Handa Cup Senior Masters when the circuit visited Japan in 2010. With 28 victories, the short-statured Kuramoto still stands seventh on the Japan Tour's career money list despite the inflation of prize money.

Kuramoto broke from an eight-man horde of challengers one stroke behind Gordon Brand, Jr. after 36 holes in the Dutch tournament to post a 69, the low score of the week, and a two-stroke victory at Royal Haagsche Golf and Country Club in The Hague.

His winning score was even-par 216 as windy conditions on the links-style course affected play all three days. Brand, who won his only senior title in 2010, handled it best the first two days. He opened with a 71, the only player to break Royal Haagsche's par of 72, and in front by two strokes. He went five over on his last four holes Saturday, but clung to the one-stroke lead with his 75–136 over the big group that included Kuramoto (75-72).

Brand faltered early Sunday, and Englishman John Harrison led the field much of the day but lost four strokes on three holes on the back nine. The 56-year-old Kuramoto recovered from an early bogey with four birdies, the last at the 15th hole giving him a cushion for the two-shot final margin over Scot Andrew Oldcorn (70), who had to settle for a runner-up position in a second straight tournament.

Berenberg Bank Masters
Munich, Germany
Winner: Tim Thelen

Tim Thelen is full of surprises. The Minnesota-born Texan had nothing more impressive than a pair of U.S. PGA Club Pro championships decking his playing record when he led the 2011 qualifier for the European Senior Tour and finished third in the Berenberg Bank Masters and second in Holland in his first two starts after turning 50 in June of that year.

Back at the Berenberg Bank tournament a year later thanks to those two high finishes, the American stirred up a zany final round at Worthsee Golf Club in Munich, Germany, and wound up accepting the winner's trophy from tournament ambassador Gary Player. Thelen shot a closing, five-under-par 67 for 201 and a three-stroke victory at the end of a wild and wooly afternoon.

Thelen started the third consecutive torridly hot day a stroke behind second-round leader Mark Mouland of Wales (66-67–133) after rounds of 66-68. He promptly roared in front when he jarred his six-iron second shot on the par-five opening hole for an albatross-deuce, double-bogeyed the second, birdied the third and bogeyed the fifth and sixth. It was all gravy after that, though, as the 51-year-old Yankee birdied the ninth and 10th with 20-foot birdie putts and closed with three more birdies on the final four holes.

Mouland (71) and Barry Lane and Peter Fowler (69s), the first-round co-leaders with 65s, tied for second at 204, a shot ahead of home country favorite Bernhard Langer (69–205.)

Bad Ragaz PGA Seniors Open
Bad Ragaz, Switzerland
Winner: Tim Thelen

Tim Thelen wasted no time proving that he is for real as a serious contender on the European Senior Tour, following his surprising victory in the Berenberg Bank Masters with another win a week later in the Bad Ragaz PGA Seniors Open in Switzerland.

Again, the unsung American, who never won on any national tour in his homeland, withstood the challenges of top European stars in racking up a two-stroke victory with his third consecutive round in the 60s, finishing with a three-under-par 67 for 198, two in front of Mark James, the ex-Ryder Cup captain and five-times winner as a senior, and three ahead of Ian Woosnam, the sterling Welsh pro. He joined Gary Wolstenholme as a double victor on the 2012 tour.

Although David J. Russell led the first day with 64 and James (65) and Thelen (66) were close behind, Thursday's big splash was made by Bob Charles, the game's first left-handed major winner. The knighted New Zealander, now 76 years old, beat his age by 10 strokes in a rare appearance on the European Senior Tour.

Not surprisingly, the soft-spoken Charles faded with subsequent 73-72 rounds as Thelen fired a 65 the second day and moved into a three-stroke lead at 131 over Woosnam, fellow American Mike Cunning and South Africa's Chris Williams. In control early in the final round, Thelen dropped two shots at the start of the back nine. Woosnam and James mounted challenges before Tim birdied the 15th and 17th holes to establish the eventual two-shot margin.

The Senior Open Championship presented by Rolex
Ayrshire, Scotland
Winner: Fred Couples

Decisive and abrupt turns of fortune seem to becoming commonplace in the final rounds of The Senior Open Championship presented by Rolex. In 2011, a four-putt green midway through Sunday's finish did in front-runner Mark Calcavecchia. In 2012, it was Bernhard Langer who encountered similar disaster. The German star, locked in a final-round battle for the coveted title with Fred Couples, was blown away by a three-stroke swing at the 12th hole, and the classy American went on to win his second senior major.

Couples stood off a late challenge by Gary Hallberg to post a 67 and take the victory with his nine-under-par 271. Hallberg, who had shot a brilliant 63 in blustery weather on the famous Ailsa course of Scotland's Turnberry resort two days earlier, trailed by only a stroke after he birdied the 71st hole before Couples birdied the final two holes for the two-shot victory.

The 54-year-old Langer was otherwise the dominant player at Turnberry. The 2010 Senior Open champion jumped off to a one-stroke lead Thursday with a flawless 64 as he sought redress for his near-miss two weeks earlier in the U.S. Senior Open. Then Hallberg entered the picture the second day with his 63 to leapfrog into the lead with 134, three shots ahead of Tom Lehman (66-71) and Langer, who suffered a triple bogey and 73 for his 137.

Back came Langer Saturday with 66–203, and enter Couples, whose 64 jumped him into second place at 205 as Hallberg slipped to 73–207. The Langer-Couples duel virtually ended at the 12th hole Sunday, where a bad drive and a pot-bunkered second shot led Langer to the double bogey as Couples was taking charge with his second consecutive birdie.

SSE Scottish Senior Open
Fife, Scotland
Winner: Anders Forsbrand

Sweden, which has had its share of successes on the regular male and female tours, made its first serious mark in senior golf when Anders Forsbrand snatched a one-stroke victory in the 20th SSE Scottish Senior Open at Fairmont St. Andrews in historic St. Andrews. Forsbrand, one of the first Swedes to gain prominence in international golf, became his country's first winner on the European Senior Tour with the victory in his second season.

Forsbrand, competitively stale when he came onto the circuit in 2011 after seven years coaching the game in Austria, became a factor in 2012. He was a runner-up in the early season PGA Seniors Championship before winning at Fairmont St. Andrews, his first professional victory since winning his sixth European Tour title in the 1995 German Masters.

The 51-year-old Swede carried a three-stroke lead into the final round and shot a solid, five-under-par 67, holding off the challenge of English newcomer Philip Golding with his 17-under-par 199. After opening with a 72, six back of leaders Forsbrand and Frenchman Marc Farry, Golding produced consecutive 64s to put heat on Forsbrand at the finish.

Forsbrand led by two playing the final hole, enough of a cushion when Golding, playing in just his second senior event, birdied before the winner tapped in for par and the victory.

Speedy Services Wales Senior Open
Caernarvonshire, Conwy, Wales
Winner: Barry Lane

Barry Lane, who challenged and finished second to Australian Peter Fowler on the 2011 Order of Merit, was back at it in the latter stages of the 2012 season, this time pursuing leader Roger Chapman.

Englishman Lane moved into second place in the standings when he landed the Speedy Services Wales Senior Open title, but he had to fend off compatriot Philip Golding, who came within a stroke of forcing a playoff for a second week in a row in just his third start on the circuit.

Golding, who finished with a pair of 64s in the Scottish Senior Open the previous weekend, opened the tournament at Conwy Golf Club with another one, took a two-shot lead over Welshman Mark Mouland and remained in front by a shot despite a two-over-par 74 amid strong winds the second day.

Lane took over the runner-up spot with 72-67–139 and battled Golding on even terms in the final round until Golding bogeyed the 11th hole to surrender the lead for the first time. They traded birdies before Lane gave himself what turned out to be a necessary cushion when he hit a four-iron approach six inches from the cup at the 17th for a tap-in birdie. When the surprising Golding left a 12-foot birdie putt short on the final hole, Lane's bogey for 70–209 gave him his fourth title in three seasons on the Senior Tour. Anders Forsbrand, the Scottish Open victor, and Fowler tied for third at 212.

Travis Perkins plc Senior Masters
Woburn, England
Winner: Des Smyth

Des Smyth, an Irishman, admires Woburn Golf Club in England so much that he's thinking about moving there. No wonder. Not only did he win the Travis Perkins plc Senior Masters there for the second time in three years in early September, but he raved about the course and its condition after posting a one-stroke victory.

Smyth, one of the few European Senior Tour players who also has victories on America's Champions Tour, broke from a deadlock with Spaniard Juan Quiros with a birdie-bogey swing at the 11th hole Sunday. He rode the two-shot lead to the final hole before finishing a stroke in front of Peter Fowler, the 2011 Order of Merit winner, who closed with 67–207 to the 68–206 registered by Smyth.

"This was a comfortable round," said the 59-year-old Drogheda native after winning his fifth EST title. "I felt in control all day. It (Woburn) is a really quality course. I might even come and live here. It's that nice."

Smyth trailed by three the first day after Denis Durnian shot the only round in the 60s (69) and led eight others by a shot. Quiros, one of those eight, shot 68–138 Saturday to forge the tie with Smyth (66).

Mark James, the Ryder Cup player and captain and winner of 29 overall titles who was accorded an honorary life European Tour membership earlier in the week, carved out a 65 Saturday and followed with 67 Sunday to finish third at 208.

Pon Senior Open
Vorbeck, Germany
Winner: Terry Price

Terry Price turned things upside down at the Pon Senior Open in Vorbeck, Germany. The Australian had never reached the top 20 in his six previous 2012 starts on the European Senior Tour and rested 63rd on the Order of Merit. So it was without warning that Price blew away the field in the most decisive finish of the season at Winston Golf.

After sharing the first-round lead with Scotsman Ross Drummond, he took command of the standings and rolled to a 16-under-par 200 and a six-stroke victory, the first senior victory for the 51-year-old pro from Down Under.

He and Drummond opened with 67s, but German national hero Bernhard Langer loomed just a stroke back. When Price followed with a 66–133, he left Drummond (72), Langer (73) and the rest of the players in his dust. He led Brits Bill Longmuir and Glenn Ralph by three.

On Sunday, Price was at the top of his game. He birdied two of the first three holes and ran off four in a row in the middle of the round on his way to a 67. Only Barry Lane, the second-place player on the Order of Merit, bettered that score among the contenders, his 66 putting him in a second-place tie with Frenchman Marc Farry (69) at 206. Price was the fourth first-time winner on the circuit in 2012.

French Riviera Masters
Tourrettes, Provence, France
Winner: David J. Russell

His own hot round and playoff prowess combined with miscues by his closest competitors led Englishman David J. Russell to his second victory on the European Senior Tour in the French Riviera Masters.

The 58-year-old Russell, whose lone previous win on the circuit came in 2010, produced a seven-under-par 65 in the final round on the Terre Blanche Resort and Golf Club course in Provence. It was enough to edge a stroke in front of Order of Merit leader Roger Chapman, but only enough to put him in a playoff with surprising American Tim Thelen, who shot his second straight 66 as he sought his third victory of the season. The two men finished at 208 and went back to the 18th tee three times before Thelen took his first bogey in 39 holes and lost to Russell's par.

Although missed short putts at the 52nd and 54th holes "cost me," his third-place finish clinched the No. 1 position on the Order of Merit for Chapman, whose outstanding season was highlighted by his triumphs in the U.S. Senior Open and Senior PGA Championships, official victories on the European circuit.

Chapman shot 71 after taking a one-stroke lead into the final round on rounds of 71-67–138. At that point, Thelen, the Berenberg and Bad Ragaz winner in July, was four back at 76-66–142 and Russell was another shot behind at 69-74–143. But none of the five other players ahead of them Saturday night could match the pace of Russell and Thelen Sunday, although Paul Wesselingh shot 69 and tied Chapman at 209.

Fubon Senior Open
Taipei, Taiwan
Winner: Tim Thelen

Tim Thelen put an exclamation point on his emergence from relative obscurity when the circuit made its mid-November stop in Taiwan. With two back-to-back victories already in the bag, Thelen virtually waltzed to a five-stroke victory in the Fubon Senior Open, becoming the year's only three-time winner in the process. Only one other American — John Grace in 2000 — achieved that much success in the tour's history.

"Words cannot describe how incredible this is for me," enthused the 51-year-old Texas resident after signing for a 69–202. "I had been a playing pro for 23 years and was delighted just to get on the Senior Tour (he led the 2011 qualifier), but to win three times this year is just unfathomable."

Thelan's major obstacle at Miramar Golf & Country Club was Kim Jong-duck, who staked out a three-stroke lead at the 36-hole mark with an exceptional, nine-under-par 63 for 130. Thelen, who had lost in a playoff in the last previous event in September, had that second-place position at 66-67–133 after sharing the first-day lead with Sweden's Peter Dahlberg.

Things turned around quickly Sunday. As Kim was faltering with four bogeys and a double bogey on the front nine on his way to an 81, Thelen followed six pars with a pair of birdies at the seventh and eighth holes to race five strokes in front. He coasted home with two more birdies and his lone bogey of the week. South African Chris Williams (70) and Filipino Frankie Minoza (71), who won the Japan Senior Open two weeks earlier, tied for second at 207.

ISPS Handa Australian Senior Open
Perth, Australia
Winner: Peter Fowler

Peter Fowler validated his past credentials when he scored a hands-down victory in the ISPS Handa Australian Senior Open at the end of November.

Twenty-nine years earlier, he captured the prized Australian Open Championship and a year ago capped an accomplished season by landing the Order of Merit title on the European Senior Tour.

So, it was not surprising when Fowler raced to a six-stroke victory at Royal Perth Golf Club with three solid, unspectacular rounds and a nine-under-par 207, unchallenged after sharing the first-round lead with Terry Price, a 2012 winner on the tour. They both shot 67s and led by two strokes.

Fowler jumped three strokes in front of Tim Elliot (69-71) the second day with 70–137 and was never threatened in Sunday's final round. Three early birdies led him to another 70 and the six-shot triumph over Mike Harwood (71) and David Merriman (72). With the pairing of Australian Open and Senior Open titles, Fowler joined the exclusive company of Wayne Grady, Peter Senior and Harwood.

MCB Tour Championship
Poste de Flacq, Mauritius
Winner: David Frost

Talk about that well-known golf expression — horses for courses. David Frost and the Constance Belle Mare Plage course on the Indian Ocean island nation of Mauritius fit that phrase to a "tee."

Since first playing in the tournament there in 2009, the 53-year-old Frost has won twice, finished second and fifth, and gone a cumulative 38 under par. The second victory, in early December, gave him the MCB Tour Championship for the second time in three years in the season-ending event.

The South African, a regular with two victories on the U.S. Champions Tour during 2012, never trailed this time in the MCB Tour Championship, but he had to recover from serious trouble amid the final round and birdie the last hole to hang up a one-stroke victory over Australia's Peter Fowler and Englishman Barry Lane. His 74 gave him an 11-under-par 205 to the 206s of Fowler (68) and Lane (70).

With earlier rounds of 64 and 67, Frost established a four-stroke lead over three-time winner Tim Thelen (68-67), the surprising American, and was five ahead of Lane (70-66). Frost's game melted Sunday when he triple-bogeyed the sixth hole, then, after birdieing the 10th, bogeyed the 11th and double-bogeyed the 12th before recovering with two birdies in the stretch run for the 74.

Roger Chapman tied for 15th in Mauritius, but the Englishman, winner of both the Senior Open and Senior PGA in America, official events on the European Senior Tour, easily succeeded Fowler as the Order of Merit money leader and John Jacobs Trophy winner with earnings of €356,751. Lane and Thelen finished second and third in the final standings.

Japan PGA Senior Tour

Starts Senior
Chiba
Winner: Naomichi Ozaki

Naomichi (Joe) Ozaki, the youngest of the famous golfing family triumvirate and the fourth-standing money winner all-time on the Japan Tour, made his initial mark as a senior with a narrow, one-stroke victory in the Starts Senior tournament, the June opener of the Japan Senior Tour.

Ozaki joined older brother Tateo (Jet) as a winner on the over-50 circuit, starting on that tour at 56 after continuing to campaign on the regular circuits well into his 50s. The older (by two years) Tateo Ozaki, 58, holds four titles on the Japan Senior Tour.

Naomichi Ozaki never trailed in the Starts Senior at Hirakawa Country Club. He began the week with a five-under-par 67, tied for the lead with Yutaka Hagawa, winner of 2011's Total Energy Philanthropy tournament, then went in front alone with 68–135, four strokes ahead of runner-up Seiki Okuda. Hagawa plummeted with 79–146.

Okuda took a run at Ozaki in the final round with a 70, but fell a shot short as Ozaki put up a 73 for the winning 208.

ISPS Handa Cup Shakunetsu-no Senior Masters
Fukuoka
Winner: Takashi Miyoshi

Takashi Miyoshi returned to the winner's circle on the Japan Senior Tour in the ISPS Handa Cup Shakunetsu-no Senior Masters four winless years after his seven-victory spurt over seven seasons in the opening decade of the 2000s.

A pair of one-under-par 71s was all that Miyoshi needed to post a one-stroke victory over four other players — Kiyoshi Murota and Takaaki Fukuawa with 72-71s and Hideki Kase and Yasuo Sone with 70-73s.

Miyoshi was tied with Tomoo Ozaki, trailing Kase, Sone and Tateo Ozaki by a shot after the opening round, as nobody in the field found the 60s in the final round on the Yahata course of the Kyusyu Golf Club.

Fancl Classic
Susono, Shizuoka
Winner: Kazuhiro Takami

Kazuhiro Takami has to fancy the Fancl Classic. He won his first senior tour event two years earlier in that tournament at Susono Country Club in Shizuoka Prefecture and nailed No. 2 in the same tournament in 2012.

Victory was much more difficult the second time around. The winner by five strokes in 2010, Takami needed two extra holes in a three-man playoff to pick off his second senior title. He and seasoned winners Tsuneyuki (Tommy) Nakajima and Filipino Frankie Minoza finished with nine-under-par 207s. Nakajima bowed out on the first hole with a par, then Takami birdied again when he and Minoza replayed the 18th hole.

Takami and Hawaiian David Ishii, a leading money winner earlier in his career on the Japan Tour, shared the stage the first two days, both shooting 66s in the opening round. Ishii edged a shot in front Saturday with a 68 to Takami's 69 but then slipped to a 74 Sunday. Minoza shot 67 and Nakajima, one of his country's all-time greats, 70 the last day to force the playoff when Takami posted a 72.

Komatsu Open
Komatsu, Ishikawa
Winner: Naomichi Ozaki

Naomichi (Joe) Ozaki became the first double winner of the season as the Komatsu Open went extra holes for a second year in a row and the circuit had its second consecutive playoff.

Suichi Sano, whose only senior victory came in the PGA Philanthropy tournament in 2004, had opened the Komatsu with a seven-under-par 65, but had the likes of Ozaki (68), Masahiro (Massy) Kuramoto (66) and Tsuneyuki (Tommy) Nakajima (67), among others, in hot pursuit.

In fact, Kuramoto and Hiroshi Ueda took over first place the second day at 136, Kuramoto with 70 and Ueda 68 as Sano struggled to a 75. Ozaki shot 69 and, with Masami Ito (66-71), trailed by one. Kuramoto slipped to 72 Sunday, but Ueda put up a 67 for 203 and Ozaki brought about the playoff with a 66.

The two matched pars, then birdies on the first two extra holes before Ozaki birdied again for the triumph.

ISPS Handa Cup Akibare-no Senior Masters
Hokkaido
Winner: Gohei Sato

It seemed to take Gohei Sato nearly as long to win the playoff as it did to play the tournament when he won his first senior title in the 36-hole ISPS Handa Cup Akibare-no Senior Masters at Noboribetsu Country Club in Hokkaido.

For seven holes, Sato and Satoshi Higashi matched pars, and in one case bogeys, after tying for first place with eight-under-par 136 totals. Sato finally made a birdie at the eighth extra hole to end the marathon.

Sato shared the first-round lead with Hawaii's David Ishii, a former Order of Merit winner on the regular Japan Tour. Both shot four-under-par 68s. Sato repeated the 68 in the final round, but was overtaken by Satoshi

Higashi, who added a 66 to his opening 70 for the matching 136. Yutaka Hagawa, who won the 2011 Total Energy Philanthropy tournament, also shot 66 the second day, but fell a stroke short of the playoff.

Japan PGA Senior Championship
Hyogo
Winner: Kiyoshi Murota

Kiyoshi Murota, who had already enjoyed considerable success on the Japan Senior Tour, put another feather in his cap when he won the Japan PGA Senior Championship in early October. It was his eighth circuit victory and, more impressively, his third PGA Championship and fourth senior major. Murota, who had only six wins on the regular tour, captured previous PGAs in 2005 and 2009 and the Japan Senior Open Championship in 2011.

This time the 57-year-old won by two strokes with his 11-under-par 277 at Hyogo Prefecture's Tojonomori Country Club, besting the reputable Hajime Meshiai in a duel over the final three rounds.

After Takaaki Fukuzawa and Hisao Inoue, the first-round leaders, quickly faded from contention, Murota stepped in front with 70-67–137, two ahead of Meshiai (71-68). Meshiai crept a stroke closer with his third-round 68–207 to Murota's 69–206 as Yutaka Hagawa kept his hopes alive at 209 with a 67, matching Murota's second-round score as the lowest scores of the week.

Murota came up with a 71 the final day for the victory over Meshiai and his 72–279.

Japan Senior Open Championship
Aichi
Winner: Frankie Minoza

Frankie Minoza emerged from a tightly packed group of strong contenders to capture the Japan Senior Open Championship, the tour's richest and most prestigious tournament. The 53-year-old Minoza, who has carried the Philippines flag in international competition for three decades, eked out a one-stroke victory with a closing 71 for a four-under-par 284 total at Aichi's Higashi Nagoya Golf Club.

He and three others teed off Sunday a stroke behind senior rookie Kouki Idoki, 50, and his steady 212. Idoki, whose second and most recent victory on the Japan Tour came in 1993, and Englishman Barry Lane had seized first place the second day with 70-70–140s after Minoza had begun the tournament a shot in front of six players with a 69.

Idoki took sole possession of the lead with his par 72 Saturday. One stroke back were two former Senior Open champions — Kiyoshi Murota (71), who had won the Japan Senior PGA, his eighth senior title, three weeks earlier, and Tsuneyuki (Tommy) Nakajima, one of Japan's all-time greats with 52 career victories who shot 68, the week's low round — along with Minoza (72) and Lane (73). With the 71 Sunday, the Filipino edged

Murota and Nakajima, who shot 72s, and Idoki, who took a 73. It was Minoza's second senior victory and ninth over the years in Japan.

Fuji Film Senior Championship
Chiba
Winner: Kouki Idoki

Kouki Idoki was not going to let another one get away. After leading for two rounds going into the final day and losing by a stroke the previous Sunday in the Japan Senior Open, Idoki bounced back in stunning fashion in the Fuji Film Senior Championship, the finale of the season.

Grabbing the first-round lead with a six-under-par 66, the 50-year-old circuit newcomer retained first place the second day with 66-70–136, then pulled away Sunday to a four-shot victory with his closing 68 for 204. He was the third first-time winner of the season.

The opening 66 at Chiba's Country Club of Japan gave Idoki a two-stroke lead over Kim Jong-duck, Satoshi Higashi and Boonchu Ruangkit, Thailand's leading senior who led the European Senior Tour's Order of Merit in 2010. Kim closed the gap to one with a 69 to Idoki's 70 on Saturday. Seiki Okuda and consistent challengers and winners Kiyoshi Murota and Tsuneyuki Nakajima (70-68s) threatened at 138, but nobody came close to Idoki Sunday as he ended a 19-year victory drought.

Naomichi Ozaki, the year's only two-time winner, jumped into a second-place tie with Okuda at 208 with a closing 69 and wrapped up the Order of Merit title.

APPENDIXES

American Tours

Hyundai Tournament of Champions

Kapalua Resort, Plantation Course, Maui, Hawaii
Par 36-37–73; 7,411 yards

January 6-9
purse, $5,600,000

	SCORES				TOTAL	MONEY
Steve Stricker	68	63	69	69	269	$1,120,000
Martin Laird	68	70	67	67	272	650,000
Jonathan Byrd	67	71	67	68	273	369,000
Webb Simpson	68	68	69	68	273	369,000
K.J. Choi	70	73	69	65	277	245,000
Harrison Frazar	74	69	66	68	277	245,000
Chris Kirk	75	66	70	67	278	190,000
Bryce Molder	71	70	67	70	278	190,000
Ben Crane	72	71	68	68	279	165,000
Rory Sabbatini	73	70	68	68	279	165,000
Johnson Wagner	72	72	68	67	279	165,000
Kevin Na	73	64	71	72	280	130,000
Scott Piercy	72	71	69	68	280	130,000
D.A. Points	71	69	71	69	280	130,000
Nick Watney	73	71	68	68	280	130,000
Keegan Bradley	69	72	75	65	281	105,000
Sean O'Hair	73	70	70	69	282	99,000
Bubba Watson	74	69	72	69	284	91,500
Mark Wilson	72	71	69	72	284	91,500
Bill Haas	73	73	70	69	285	84,000
Aaron Baddeley	75	68	74	69	286	80,000
Michael Bradley	68	75	75	69	287	74,500
Scott Stallings	74	69	74	70	287	74,500
Gary Woodland	73	71	73	72	289	70,000
Brendan Steele	76	76	72	71	295	68,000
David Toms	76	74	75	71	296	66,000
Jhonattan Vegas	75	73	76	74	298	64,000

Sony Open

Waialae Country Club, Honolulu, Hawaii
Par 35-35–70; 7,068 yards

January 12-15
purse, $5,500,000

	SCORES				TOTAL	MONEY
Johnson Wagner	68	66	66	67	267	$990,000
Harrison Frazar	67	68	67	67	269	363,000
Charles Howell	67	67	66	69	269	363,000
Sean O'Hair	67	67	68	67	269	363,000
Carl Pettersson	65	67	70	67	269	363,000
Matt Every	66	64	68	72	270	178,062.50
Brian Gay	69	69	65	67	270	178,062.50
D.A. Points	68	69	64	69	270	178,062.50
Michael Thompson	70	65	68	67	270	178,062.50
Brendon de Jonge	71	62	67	71	271	137,500
David Hearn	66	66	70	69	271	137,500
John Rollins	70	68	69	64	271	137,500
Keegan Bradley	67	67	68	70	272	97,166.67
Chris DiMarco	70	65	70	67	272	97,166.67

	SCORES				TOTAL	MONEY
Chris Stroud	68	68	67	69	272	97,166.67
Brendon Todd	68	68	68	68	272	97,166.67
Jeff Maggert	69	65	64	74	272	97,166.66
Ted Potter, Jr.	68	68	66	70	272	97,166.66
Tadd Fujikawa	69	66	71	67	273	69,025
William McGirt	67	67	70	69	273	69,025
George McNeill	69	70	66	68	273	69,025
Joe Ogilvie	71	68	66	68	273	69,025
Will Claxton	66	69	69	70	274	47,575
Colt Knost	66	71	69	68	274	47,575
Spencer Levin	67	67	68	72	274	47,575
Scott Piercy	69	68	65	72	274	47,575
John Senden	68	67	68	71	274	47,575
Kyle Stanley	66	68	70	70	274	47,575
Kris Blanks	68	66	69	72	275	32,755.56
Bud Cauley	66	68	70	71	275	32,755.56
Stewart Cink	70	66	71	68	275	32,755.56
Jerry Kelly	70	66	70	69	275	32,755.56
Rory Sabbatini	67	71	68	69	275	32,755.56
Sang-Moon Bae	68	68	66	73	275	32,755.55
Graham DeLaet	63	72	68	72	275	32,755.55
Billy Mayfair	68	67	68	72	275	32,755.55
Duffy Waldorf	69	66	66	74	275	32,755.55
K.J. Choi	65	73	67	71	276	22,000
Gavin Coles	69	66	71	70	276	22,000
J.J. Killeen	68	69	69	70	276	22,000
Chris Kirk	69	70	68	69	276	22,000
Corey Pavin	70	67	68	71	276	22,000
Webb Simpson	66	72	70	68	276	22,000
Steve Stricker	66	69	67	74	276	22,000
Josh Teater	69	67	70	70	276	22,000
Vijay Singh	71	67	71	68	277	14,708.58
Stephen Ames	67	68	67	75	277	14,708.57
Bobby Gates	68	68	70	71	277	14,708.57
Pat Perez	66	67	71	73	277	14,708.57
Tom Pernice, Jr.	69	70	67	71	277	14,708.57
Daniel Summerhays	69	69	67	72	277	14,708.57
Jhonattan Vegas	67	71	67	72	277	14,708.57
John Huh	72	65	70	71	278	12,980
Jonas Blixt	72	67	68	72	279	12,540
Tim Herron	68	71	70	70	279	12,540
Zach Johnson	72	65	72	70	279	12,540
Doug LaBelle	66	67	70	76	279	12,540
Jeff Overton	69	70	69	71	279	12,540
Tommy Biershenk	71	66	70	73	280	11,880
Roberto Castro	67	69	73	71	280	11,880
Kevin Chappell	72	67	67	74	280	11,880
Ken Duke	66	69	68	77	280	11,880
Brian Harman	72	66	69	73	280	11,880
Koumei Oda	72	65	70	73	280	11,880
Greg Owen	69	69	69	73	280	11,880
Seung-Yul Noh	66	72	71	72	281	11,440
Erik Compton	71	68	70	73	282	11,275
Harris English	67	70	70	75	282	11,275
Jarrod Lyle	69	70	70	74	283	11,110
Justin Leonard	71	68	69	76	284	11,000
Alex Aragon	69	70	71		210	10,725
Chad Campbell	70	69	71		210	10,725
Billy Hurley	68	71	71		210	10,725
Ryuji Imada	71	68	71		210	10,725
Jason Kokrak	69	70	72		211	10,340
Alexandre Rocha	70	69	72		211	10,340
Tadahiro Takayama	70	69	72		211	10,340

	SCORES			TOTAL	MONEY
Nathan Green	69	69	74	212	10,120
Tommy Gainey	73	66	75	214	9,955
Steve Wheatcroft	69	68	77	214	9,955

Humana Challenge

PGA West, Palmer Course: Par 36-36–72; 6,950 yards
PGA West, Nicklaus Course: Par 36-36–72; 7,060 yards
La Quinta CC: Par 36-36–72; 6,924 yards
La Quinta, California

January 19-22
purse, $5,600,000

	SCORES				TOTAL	MONEY
Mark Wilson	66	62	67	69	264	$1,008,000
Johnson Wagner	68	67	66	65	266	418,133.34
Robert Garrigus	73	64	61	68	266	418,133.33
John Mallinger	67	65	68	66	266	418,133.33
Jeff Maggert	69	65	69	64	267	224,000
John Senden	69	64	68	67	268	194,600
David Toms	63	65	72	68	268	194,600
Ben Crane	65	63	70	71	269	156,800
Bobby Gates	68	63	71	67	269	156,800
Zach Johnson	68	65	65	71	269	156,800
Brandt Snedeker	64	68	66	71	269	156,800
Brendon de Jonge	65	71	70	64	270	123,200
Jason Dufner	71	63	68	68	270	123,200
Sang-Moon Bae	64	69	72	66	271	95,200
Gary Christian	66	68	73	64	271	95,200
Martin Laird	66	69	67	69	271	95,200
Pat Perez	67	67	74	63	271	95,200
Rory Sabbatini	68	68	68	67	271	95,200
Harris English	69	62	73	68	272	72,800
Steve Marino	65	68	68	71	272	72,800
Camilo Villegas	63	68	72	69	272	72,800
Stephen Ames	66	67	70	70	273	56,000
Bob Estes	64	70	71	68	273	56,000
Matt Kuchar	71	67	70	65	273	56,000
Josh Teater	71	66	67	69	273	56,000
James Driscoll	69	70	68	67	274	42,280
Paul Goydos	70	69	69	66	274	42,280
Jarrod Lyle	68	67	67	72	274	42,280
Brendon Todd	66	67	69	72	274	42,280
Miguel Angel Carballo	69	66	70	70	275	31,857.78
Bud Cauley	66	67	71	71	275	31,857.78
Kevin Chappell	65	68	72	70	275	31,857.78
Chris DiMarco	68	64	72	71	275	31,857.78
William McGirt	67	71	68	69	275	31,857.78
Kevin Na	66	68	73	68	275	31,857.78
Brett Quigley	67	68	70	70	275	31,857.78
Jason Bohn	68	70	71	66	275	31,857.77
Cameron Tringale	68	64	71	72	275	31,857.77
Ken Duke	67	65	74	70	276	24,080
Lee Janzen	69	66	72	69	276	24,080
Chez Reavie	70	70	70	66	276	24,080
Roberto Castro	68	70	70	69	277	18,512
Erik Compton	67	69	72	69	277	18,512
Brian Gay	69	68	72	68	277	18,512
Chris Kirk	68	63	74	72	277	18,512
Ryan Moore	72	61	75	69	277	18,512
Carl Pettersson	71	70	67	69	277	18,512
Kyle Reifers	69	69	67	72	277	18,512

	SCORES				TOTAL	MONEY
Ricky Barnes	68	69	72	69	278	13,820.80
Joe Durant	68	71	70	69	278	13,820.80
Charles Howell	69	70	68	71	278	13,820.80
George McNeill	73	65	71	69	278	13,820.80
Phil Mickelson	74	69	66	69	278	13,820.80
Blake Adams	66	71	72	70	279	12,488
Brian Harman	69	69	69	72	279	12,488
Troy Kelly	71	70	67	71	279	12,488
Justin Leonard	69	68	70	72	279	12,488
Jeff Overton	67	70	73	69	279	12,488
Ted Potter, Jr.	64	73	73	69	279	12,488
Michael Thompson	71	67	69	72	279	12,488
Bo Van Pelt	67	71	69	72	279	12,488
Jimmy Walker	70	66	71	72	279	12,488
Charlie Wi	71	71	68	69	279	12,488
Bill Haas	71	69	70	70	280	11,816
Spencer Levin	68	67	72	73	280	11,816
Kevin Kisner	68	73	68	72	281	11,368
Danny Lee	69	69	69	74	281	11,368
Jamie Lovemark	68	68	73	72	281	11,368
Nick O'Hern	68	70	71	72	281	11,368
John Rollins	68	68	72	73	281	11,368
Brendan Steele	70	69	70	72	281	11,368
Tommy Biershenk	68	64	72	78	282	10,976
Marco Dawson	72	70	68	73	283	10,808
Kevin Sutherland	69	68	73	73	283	10,808
Charlie Beljan	71	69	69	75	284	10,640

Farmers Insurance Open

Torrey Pines, La Jolla, California
South Course: Par 36-36—72; 7,569 yards
North Course: Par 36-36—72; 6,874 yards

January 26-29
purse, $6,000,000

	SCORES				TOTAL	MONEY
Brandt Snedeker	67	64	74	67	272	$1,080,000
Kyle Stanley	62	68	68	74	272	648,000
(Snedeker defeated Stanley on second playoff hole.)						
John Rollins	70	65	68	71	274	408,000
Bill Haas	63	71	70	72	276	264,000
Cameron Tringale	67	72	66	71	276	264,000
John Huh	64	71	68	74	277	208,500
Hunter Mahan	69	65	74	69	277	208,500
Martin Flores	65	67	75	71	278	162,000
Justin Leonard	65	70	71	72	278	162,000
Rod Pampling	64	75	68	71	278	162,000
D.A. Points	70	70	67	71	278	162,000
Jimmy Walker	73	65	70	70	278	162,000
Bud Cauley	69	70	73	67	279	96,666.67
Stewart Cink	69	68	72	70	279	96,666.67
Rickie Fowler	68	70	71	70	279	96,666.67
Bill Lunde	74	68	68	69	279	96,666.67
Bryce Molder	71	70	68	70	279	96,666.67
Vijay Singh	64	75	71	69	279	96,666.67
Ryo Ishikawa	69	69	69	72	279	96,666.66
Scott Piercy	70	68	68	73	279	96,666.66
Bubba Watson	69	71	68	71	279	96,666.66
Robert Allenby	68	67	73	72	280	57,600
Jonas Blixt	70	70	65	75	280	57,600
Keegan Bradley	69	68	73	70	280	57,600

	SCORES				TOTAL	MONEY
Pat Perez	66	70	71	73	280	57,600
Camilo Villegas	65	72	70	73	280	57,600
Aaron Baddeley	70	72	69	70	281	41,700
Brendon de Jonge	70	70	69	72	281	41,700
James Driscoll	68	69	70	74	281	41,700
Tim Herron	68	70	69	74	281	41,700
Seung-Yul Noh	69	72	71	69	281	41,700
Nick O'Hern	69	70	74	68	281	41,700
Sang-Moon Bae	65	67	72	78	282	29,100
Cameron Beckman	68	72	74	68	282	29,100
Michael Bradley	69	71	70	72	282	29,100
Roberto Castro	70	72	71	69	282	29,100
Greg Chalmers	65	72	72	73	282	29,100
Trevor Immelman	71	70	71	70	282	29,100
John Merrick	74	66	70	72	282	29,100
Chris Riley	67	70	72	73	282	29,100
Justin Rose	71	68	70	73	282	29,100
Marc Turnesa	66	72	74	70	282	29,100
Blake Adams	75	67	70	71	283	18,720
Ricky Barnes	69	70	73	71	283	18,720
Harris English	67	72	72	72	283	18,720
Charles Howell	72	69	69	73	283	18,720
Dustin Johnson	66	72	70	75	283	18,720
Spencer Levin	62	76	73	72	283	18,720
Tom Pernice, Jr.	69	72	69	73	283	18,720
Paul Goydos	68	72	69	75	284	14,940
Geoff Ogilvy	72	70	67	75	284	14,940
Kevin Chappell	73	69	69	74	285	13,785
Marco Dawson	67	73	72	73	285	13,785
Chris DiMarco	68	70	72	75	285	13,785
Ernie Els	71	70	72	72	285	13,785
Charley Hoffman	71	68	74	72	285	13,785
J.J. Killeen	72	69	67	77	285	13,785
Marc Leishman	72	69	70	74	285	13,785
Andres Romero	68	73	72	72	285	13,785
Bobby Gates	76	64	70	76	286	13,020
Richard H. Lee	72	69	73	72	286	13,020
Jhonattan Vegas	69	68	73	76	286	13,020
Nick Watney	69	68	75	74	286	13,020
Mark D. Anderson	73	68	73	74	288	12,660
Chez Reavie	72	67	75	74	288	12,660
Tommy Biershenk	70	71	72	76	289	12,240
Gary Christian	72	70	71	76	289	12,240
Steve Marino	69	71	74	75	289	12,240
Josh Teater	64	77	72	76	289	12,240
Duffy Waldorf	70	69	75	75	289	12,240
Chris Kirk	70	72	72	76	290	11,880
Greg Owen	75	67	71	78	291	11,760
Colt Knost	66	74	74	79	293	11,640
Miguel Angel Carballo	70	72	73		215	11,460
Jarrod Lyle	73	69	73		215	11,460
Brendon Todd	70	71	75		216	11,160
Boo Weekley	71	67	78		216	11,160
Gary Woodland	70	72	74		216	11,160
Troy Kelly	68	72	78		218	10,920

Waste Management Phoenix Open

TPC Scottsdale, Scottsdale, Arizona
Par 35-36–71; 7,216 yards

February 2-5
purse, $6,100,000

	SCORES				TOTAL	MONEY
Kyle Stanley	69	66	69	65	269	$1,098,000
Ben Crane	69	67	68	66	270	658,800
Spencer Levin	65	63	68	75	271	414,800
D.J. Trahan	72	70	64	66	272	292,800
Kevin Na	66	73	69	65	273	222,650
Brendan Steele	71	69	69	64	273	222,650
Bubba Watson	66	70	67	70	273	222,650
Jason Dufner	64	72	68	70	274	170,800
John Rollins	70	70	65	69	274	170,800
Webb Simpson	65	69	68	72	274	170,800
Bo Van Pelt	65	71	71	67	274	170,800
John Huh	68	66	69	72	275	128,100
Trevor Immelman	67	70	69	69	275	128,100
Chris Stroud	68	70	66	71	275	128,100
Keegan Bradley	68	70	71	67	276	100,650
Harris English	70	69	68	69	276	100,650
Bryce Molder	70	69	71	66	276	100,650
Rod Pampling	67	71	71	67	276	100,650
Chris Couch	70	68	72	67	277	68,842.86
Martin Flores	71	68	68	70	277	68,842.86
Bill Haas	69	68	69	71	277	68,842.86
Pat Perez	69	73	66	69	277	68,842.86
Mark Wilson	70	69	74	64	277	68,842.86
Greg Chalmers	68	69	67	73	277	68,842.85
Marc Leishman	70	68	68	71	277	68,842.85
Rickie Fowler	69	69	71	69	278	43,310
Harrison Frazar	66	67	73	72	278	43,310
Derek Lamely	66	70	72	70	278	43,310
Jeff Maggert	70	68	68	72	278	43,310
Phil Mickelson	68	70	67	73	278	43,310
Jeff Quinney	69	71	70	68	278	43,310
Gary Woodland	71	71	70	66	278	43,310
Robert Allenby	71	69	70	69	279	31,545.72
Matt Kuchar	69	68	72	70	279	31,545.72
Carl Pettersson	70	69	70	70	279	31,545.72
Charles Howell	69	68	71	71	279	31,545.71
George McNeill	71	70	70	68	279	31,545.71
Seung-Yul Noh	67	72	68	72	279	31,545.71
Heath Slocum	73	69	69	68	279	31,545.71
Ricky Barnes	71	70	71	68	280	23,790
Matt Jones	67	72	67	74	280	23,790
Sung Kang	67	73	69	71	280	23,790
Jarrod Lyle	66	72	70	72	280	23,790
Josh Teater	68	69	71	72	280	23,790
J.B. Holmes	71	70	72	68	281	17,860.80
Sean O'Hair	74	68	70	69	281	17,860.80
D.A. Points	69	73	70	69	281	17,860.80
Ian Poulter	72	69	70	70	281	17,860.80
Chez Reavie	66	76	72	67	281	17,860.80
Bud Cauley	72	67	72	71	282	14,713.20
Ken Duke	69	72	71	70	282	14,713.20
Bill Lunde	67	73	69	73	282	14,713.20
Scott Piercy	68	70	70	74	282	14,713.20
Brandt Snedeker	71	70	73	68	282	14,713.20
Graham DeLaet	71	69	72	71	283	13,725
J.J. Killeen	70	70	72	71	283	13,725
Kevin Kisner	69	71	74	69	283	13,725

	SCORES				TOTAL	MONEY
Billy Mayfair	68	73	70	72	283	13,725
Ryan Palmer	64	72	76	71	283	13,725
Johnson Wagner	68	69	73	73	283	13,725
James Driscoll	67	70	71	76	284	13,115
Dustin Johnson	68	70	74	72	284	13,115
Martin Laird	72	70	73	69	284	13,115
John Merrick	69	73	72	70	284	13,115
Blake Adams	69	70	74	72	285	12,566
Aaron Baddeley	72	67	74	72	285	12,566
Cameron Beckman	69	69	73	74	285	12,566
David Hearn	69	69	73	74	285	12,566
Kenny Perry	70	72	72	71	285	12,566
Ted Potter, Jr.	71	69	73	75	288	12,078
Kevin Stadler	70	71	76	71	288	12,078
Kevin Sutherland	71	70	72	75	288	12,078
Kevin Streelman	68	74	78	69	289	11,773
Camilo Villegas	71	67	75	76	289	11,773
Bobby Gates	73	67	75	75	290	11,590
Charley Hoffman	71	71	77	72	291	11,468
Stephen Gangluff	69	73	74	79	295	11,346
Ryan Moore	72	70	77	78	297	11,224

AT&T Pebble Beach National Pro-Am

Pebble Beach GL: Par 36-36–72; 6,816 yards
Monterey Peninsula CC: Par 36-36–72; 6,836 yards
Spyglass Hill GC: Par 36-36–72; 6,858 yards
Pebble Beach, California

February 9-12
purse, $6,400,000

	SCORES				TOTAL	MONEY
Phil Mickelson	70	65	70	64	269	$1,152,000
Charlie Wi	61	69	69	72	271	691,200
Ricky Barnes	70	66	70	67	273	435,200
Aaron Baddeley	66	72	69	67	274	307,200
Dustin Johnson	63	72	70	70	275	243,200
Kevin Na	66	69	70	70	275	243,200
Ken Duke	64	73	65	74	276	206,400
Padraig Harrington	68	66	72	70	276	206,400
Jason Kokrak	68	67	72	70	277	153,600
Spencer Levin	69	69	71	68	277	153,600
Greg Owen	68	67	72	70	277	153,600
Kevin Streelman	70	69	68	70	277	153,600
Brendon Todd	67	69	69	72	277	153,600
Jimmy Walker	69	68	71	69	277	153,600
Steven Bowditch	71	67	72	68	278	102,400
Bob Estes	67	70	69	72	278	102,400
Richard H. Lee	65	71	73	69	278	102,400
Hunter Mahan	65	70	70	73	278	102,400
Tiger Woods	68	68	67	75	278	102,400
Robert Garrigus	68	69	71	71	279	71,936
Brian Gay	69	65	74	71	279	71,936
Brian Harman	64	73	71	71	279	71,936
Davis Love	70	70	70	69	279	71,936
Ryan Moore	72	64	71	72	279	71,936
Danny Lee	63	73	74	70	280	51,040
Geoff Ogilvy	70	69	68	73	280	51,040
Vijay Singh	68	68	71	73	280	51,040
Kevin Stadler	69	70	73	68	280	51,040
Miguel Angel Carballo	69	71	69	72	281	40,693.34
Sean O'Hair	68	74	69	70	281	40,693.34
Brian Davis	70	74	68	69	281	40,693.33

	SCORES				TOTAL	MONEY
Zach Johnson	67	72	72	70	281	40,693.33
Rocco Mediate	71	66	76	68	281	40,693.33
Ryan Palmer	72	71	64	74	281	40,693.33
Mark D. Anderson	69	71	71	71	282	31,552
Mathew Goggin	69	71	69	73	282	31,552
Charley Hoffman	67	73	73	69	282	31,552
John Huh	71	71	71	69	282	31,552
Josh Teater	64	71	77	70	282	31,552
Jonas Blixt	70	69	69	75	283	21,849.60
Joseph Bramlett	66	69	73	75	283	21,849.60
Harris English	75	68	70	70	283	21,849.60
Jim Furyk	69	69	74	71	283	21,849.60
Tom Gillis	74	72	66	71	283	21,849.60
Nathan Green	66	76	71	70	283	21,849.60
Heath Slocum	74	71	68	70	283	21,849.60
Daniel Summerhays	65	73	73	72	283	21,849.60
D.J. Trahan	70	69	71	73	283	21,849.60
Nick Watney	66	73	69	75	283	21,849.60
Roberto Castro	70	68	73	73	284	15,584
Bobby Gates	72	70	69	73	284	15,584
Joe Ogilvie	68	73	70	73	284	15,584
Ian Poulter	69	72	72	71	284	15,584
Gary Christian	72	70	70	73	285	14,656
Hunter Haas	72	69	72	72	285	14,656
Tom Pernice, Jr.	72	70	70	73	285	14,656
Roland Thatcher	71	68	70	76	285	14,656
Matt Bettencourt	73	69	70	74	286	14,208
John Mallinger	70	71	72	73	286	14,208
Pat Perez	67	72	74	73	286	14,208
Sang-Moon Bae	68	73	72	74	287	13,760
Shane Bertsch	68	75	65	79	287	13,760
Tim Petrovic	70	70	72	75	287	13,760
Cameron Tringale	71	71	70	75	287	13,760
Lee Janzen	72	71	70	75	288	13,376
Kyle Reifers	69	72	72	75	288	13,376
Stuart Appleby	72	71	70	76	289	13,120
D.A. Points	72	65	74	78	289	13,120
Kris Blanks	70	72	72		214	12,224
Kevin Chappell	71	70	73		214	12,224
Graham DeLaet	66	77	71		214	12,224
Martin Flores	73	73	68		214	12,224
Billy Horschel	70	72	72		214	12,224
Ryuji Imada	67	74	73		214	12,224
Kent Jones	71	74	69		214	12,224
Martin Laird	70	71	73		214	12,224
Derek Lamely	74	68	72		214	12,224
Bryce Molder	67	74	73		214	12,224
John Peterson	70	75	69		214	12,224
Sam Saunders	72	68	74		214	12,224

Northern Trust Open

Riviera Country Club, Pacific Palisades, California
Par 35-36–71; 7,298 yards

February 16-19
purse, $6,600,000

	SCORES				TOTAL	MONEY
Bill Haas	72	68	68	69	277	$1,188,000
Keegan Bradley	71	69	66	71	277	580,800
Phil Mickelson	66	70	70	71	277	580,800
(Haas defeated Bradley and Mickelson on second playoff hole.)						
Sergio Garcia	69	76	70	64	279	259,875

	SCORES				TOTAL	MONEY
Dustin Johnson	71	70	67	71	279	259,875
Jarrod Lyle	73	65	71	70	279	259,875
Jimmy Walker	72	66	72	69	279	259,875
Jonathan Byrd	68	70	69	73	280	191,400
J.B. Holmes	67	73	70	70	280	191,400
Bo Van Pelt	74	68	68	70	280	191,400
Aaron Baddeley	73	69	66	73	281	158,400
Jim Furyk	72	70	69	70	281	158,400
Fredrik Jacobson	72	72	71	67	282	123,750
Pat Perez	72	65	70	75	282	123,750
Justin Rose	70	70	71	71	282	123,750
Bubba Watson	70	69	72	71	282	123,750
Adam Scott	73	71	69	70	283	86,365.72
Brandt Snedeker	75	70	68	70	283	86,365.72
Michael Thompson	72	72	71	68	283	86,365.72
Zach Johnson	71	69	71	72	283	86,365.71
Marc Leishman	70	69	71	73	283	86,365.71
Bryce Molder	74	67	66	76	283	86,365.71
Ryan Moore	72	69	68	74	283	86,365.71
Kevin Chappell	73	67	73	71	284	49,940
K.J. Choi	69	71	74	70	284	49,940
Matt Kuchar	69	69	75	71	284	49,940
Hunter Mahan	67	75	70	72	284	49,940
Ryan Palmer	76	69	68	71	284	49,940
Kevin Stadler	71	71	72	70	284	49,940
Kyle Stanley	74	68	70	72	284	49,940
Cameron Tringale	70	74	69	71	284	49,940
Johnson Wagner	73	71	68	72	284	49,940
Vijay Singh	74	70	71	70	285	38,940
Briny Baird	71	70	72	73	286	31,927.50
Retief Goosen	73	67	72	74	286	31,927.50
J.J. Killeen	71	69	71	75	286	31,927.50
Jason Kokrak	76	67	70	73	286	31,927.50
Carl Pettersson	68	70	76	72	286	31,927.50
Nick Watney	73	70	69	74	286	31,927.50
Charlie Wi	75	69	70	72	286	31,927.50
Y.E. Yang	72	72	69	73	286	31,927.50
Erik Compton	73	72	69	73	287	25,080
Brendon de Jonge	73	69	71	74	287	25,080
Graham DeLaet	73	68	73	74	288	20,512.80
Padraig Harrington	74	70	74	70	288	20,512.80
David Hearn	70	73	74	71	288	20,512.80
Jeff Overton	73	72	71	72	288	20,512.80
John Senden	73	70	72	73	288	20,512.80
Harrison Frazar	71	74	74	70	289	16,676
Bobby Gates	73	72	69	75	289	16,676
George McNeill	76	67	73	73	289	16,676
Bud Cauley	74	70	71	75	290	15,477
Jason Dufner	72	72	73	73	290	15,477
Tommy Gainey	70	73	70	77	290	15,477
Spencer Levin	73	66	73	78	290	15,477
Luke Donald	70	72	71	78	291	14,916
John Mallinger	71	71	75	74	291	14,916
Kevin Streelman	74	70	71	76	291	14,916
Ken Duke	69	72	78	73	292	14,520
Ernie Els	73	68	73	78	292	14,520
Vaughn Taylor	72	71	73	76	292	14,520
Ricky Barnes	71	71	77	74	293	13,992
Jason Day	73	71	75	74	293	13,992
Rickie Fowler	75	69	70	79	293	13,992
Billy Mayfair	72	73	72	76	293	13,992
Joe Ogilvie	71	71	72	79	293	13,992
Cameron Beckman	70	75	71	78	294	13,530

	SCORES			TOTAL	MONEY
Stewart Cink	69	71	74	80	294	13,530
Troy Matteson	68	75	77	75	295	13,200
Brendan Steele	69	74	74	78	295	13,200
Gary Woodland	73	71	74	77	295	13,200
Matt Bettencourt	73	70	77	76	296	12,804
Ryo Ishikawa	73	70	76	77	296	12,804
Sung Kang	72	71	73	80	296	12,804
Bill Lunde	73	72	74	78	297	12,540
Kevin Na	74	71	78	77	300	12,408

WGC - Accenture Match Play Championship

Ritz-Carlton Golf Club, Dove Mountain, Marana, Arizona

Par 36-36–72; 7,849 yards

February 22-26

purse, $8,500,000

FIRST ROUND

Ernie Els defeated Luke Donald, 5 and 4.
Peter Hanson defeated Jason Dufner, 2 and 1.
Kyle Stanley defeated K.J. Choi, 2 and 1.
Brandt Snedeker defeated Retief Goosen, 21 holes.
Robert Rock defeated Adam Scott, 1 up.
Mark Wilson defeated Bo Van Pelt, 3 and 2.
Dustin Johnson defeated Jim Furyk, 20 holes.
Francesco Molinari defeated Thomas Bjorn, 20 holes.
Martin Kaymer defeated Greg Chalmers, 4 and 2.
David Toms defeated Rickie Fowler, 1 up.
Matt Kuchar defeated Jonathan Byrd, 1 up.
Bubba Watson defeated Ben Crane, 3 and 2.
Steve Stricker defeated Kevin Na, 2 and 1.
Louis Oosthuizen defeated Aaron Baddeley, 2 and 1.
Y.E. Yang defeated Graeme McDowell, 2 and 1.
Hunter Mahan defeated Zach Johnson, 19 holes.
Rory McIlroy defeated George Coetzee, 2 up.
Anders Hansen defeated K.T. Kim, 5 and 3.
Miguel Angel Jimenez defeated Sergio Garcia, 2 and 1.
Keegan Bradley defeated Geoff Ogilvy, 4 and 3.
Jason Day defeated Rafa Cabrera-Bello, 19 holes.
John Senden defeated Simon Dyson, 4 and 3.
Charl Schwartzel defeated Gary Woodland, 4 and 2.
Sang-Moon Bae defeated Ian Poulter, 4 and 3.
Lee Westwood defeated Nicholas Colsaerts, 3 and 1.
Robert Karlsson defeated Fredrik Jacobson, 6 and 5.
Nick Watney defeated Darren Clarke, 5 and 4.
Tiger Woods defeated Gonzalo Fernandez-Castano 1 up.
Matteo Manassero defeated Webb Simpson, 3 and 2.
Martin Laird defeated Alvaro Quiros, 1 up.
Ryo Ishikawa defeated Bill Haas, 1 up.
Paul Lawrie defeated Justin Rose, 1 up.

(Each losing player received $45,000.)

SECOND ROUND

Hanson defeated Els, 5 and 4.
Snedeker defeated Stanley, 2 and 1.
Wilson defeated Rock, 3 and 2.
Johnson defeated Francesco Molinari, 7 and 5.
Kaymer defeated Toms, 2 up.
Kuchar defeated Watson, 3 and 2.
Stricker defeated Oosthuizen, 1 up.

Mahan defeated Yang, 5 and 3.
McIlroy defeated Hansen, 3 and 2.
Jimenez defeated Bradley, 2 and 1.
Senden defeated Day, 6 and 5.
Bae defeated Schwartzel, 1 up.
Westwood defeated Karlsson, 3 and 2.
Watney defeated Woods, 1 up.
Laird defeated Manassero, 2 and 1.
Lawrie defeated Ishikawa, 1 up.

(Each losing player received $95,000.)

THIRD ROUND

Hanson defeated Snedeker, 5 and 3.
Wilson defeated Johnson, 4 and 3.
Kuchar defeated Kaymer, 4 and 3.
Mahan defeated Stricker, 4 and 3.
McIlroy defeated Jimenez, 3 and 1.
Bae defeated Senden, 1 up.
Westwood defeated Watney, 3 and 2.
Laird defeated Lawrie, 3 and 1.

(Each losing player received $140,000.)

QUARTER-FINALS

Wilson defeated Hanson, 4 and 3.
Mahan defeated Kuchar, 6 and 5.
McIlroy defeated Bae, 3 and 2.
Westwood defeated Laird, 4 and 2.

(Each losing player received $270,000.)

SEMI-FINALS

Mahan defeated Wilson, 2 and 1.
McIlroy defeated Westwood, 3 and 1.

PLAYOFF FOR THIRD-FOURTH PLACE

Wilson defeated Westwood, 1 up.

(Wilson earned $600,000; Westwood earned $490,000.)

FINAL

Mahan defeated McIlroy, 2 and 1.

(Mahan earned $1,400,000; McIlroy earned $850,000.)

Mayakoba Golf Classic

El Camaleon Golf Club, Riviera Maya, Mexico,
Par 36-35–71; 6,987 yards

February 23-26
purse, $3,700,000

	SCORES				TOTAL	MONEY
John Huh	67	70	71	63	271	$666,000
Robert Allenby	69	67	70	65	271	399,600
(Huh defeated Allenby on eighth playoff hole.)						
Matt Every	67	71	69	66	273	214,600
Colt Knost	69	71	67	66	273	214,600

	SCORES				TOTAL	MONEY
Alejandro Canizares	67	72	69	66	274	129,962.50
Dicky Pride	68	72	68	66	274	129,962.50
Chris Stroud	69	66	68	71	274	129,962.50
Daniel Summerhays	69	65	67	73	274	129,962.50
Michael Allen	68	71	66	71	276	99,900
Will Claxton	66	68	71	71	276	99,900
J.J. Henry	72	69	68	67	276	99,900
Briny Baird	71	69	67	70	277	74,925
Rich Beem	70	71	69	67	277	74,925
Richard S. Johnson	70	66	72	69	277	74,925
Billy Mayfair	70	68	70	69	277	74,925
Stephen Ames	69	70	70	69	278	46,990
Mark D. Anderson	67	72	73	66	278	46,990
Charles Howell	67	71	69	71	278	46,990
Tom Lehman	70	72	70	66	278	46,990
Seung-Yul Noh	68	70	73	67	278	46,990
Greg Owen	67	67	73	71	278	46,990
Tim Petrovic	72	72	66	68	278	46,990
Kevin Stadler	68	68	72	70	278	46,990
Vaughn Taylor	71	69	72	66	278	46,990
Marc Turnesa	67	72	67	72	278	46,990
Matt Bettencourt	69	72	72	66	279	27,935
Chad Campbell	70	71	71	67	279	27,935
Brian Harman	71	71	65	72	279	27,935
William McGirt	69	72	73	65	279	27,935
Billy Horschel	69	72	70	69	280	23,495
Sung Kang	68	76	69	67	280	23,495
Russell Knox	74	67	68	71	280	23,495
Johnson Wagner	73	70	71	66	280	23,495
Spencer Levin	73	71	69	68	281	19,980
Patrick Sheehan	70	73	71	67	281	19,980
Esteban Toledo	72	69	71	69	281	19,980
Craig Barlow	71	68	71	72	282	15,170
Nathan Green	73	69	68	72	282	15,170
Hunter Haas	68	75	71	68	282	15,170
Troy Kelly	72	73	68	69	282	15,170
Jarrod Lyle	73	69	71	69	282	15,170
John Merrick	71	67	74	70	282	15,170
Heath Slocum	73	71	69	69	282	15,170
Steve Wheatcroft	75	70	70	67	282	15,170
Garrett Willis	70	72	69	71	282	15,170
Martin Flores	77	67	73	66	283	10,779.34
Billy Hurley	73	71	69	70	283	10,779.33
Michael Thompson	72	72	71	68	283	10,779.33
Gary Christian	73	70	73	68	284	9,040.34
David Hearn	68	73	77	66	284	9,040.34
Fred Funk	73	71	72	68	284	9,040.33
Skip Kendall	71	72	70	71	284	9,040.33
Will MacKenzie	72	73	69	70	284	9,040.33
Chris Riley	73	72	70	69	284	9,040.33
Erik Compton	71	69	76	69	285	8,362
Brian Gay	72	68	74	71	285	8,362
Tim Herron	70	74	70	71	285	8,362
John Peterson	73	72	72	68	285	8,362
Jose de Jesus Rodriguez	71	73	70	71	285	8,362
Brandt Jobe	74	70	72	70	286	8,066
Jerry Kelly	73	71	72	70	286	8,066
Josh Teater	68	75	71	72	286	8,066
Cameron Beckman	72	71	71	74	288	7,733
Gavin Coles	71	71	76	70	288	7,733
Robert Damron	73	72	71	72	288	7,733
Edward Loar	69	74	68	77	288	7,733
Jose Maria Olazabal	72	72	74	70	288	7,733

	SCORES				TOTAL	MONEY
Brett Wetterich	71	72	73	72	288	7,733
Charley Hoffman	75	70	72	72	289	7,437
Paul Stankowski	72	70	74	73	289	7,437
Charlie Beljan	73	67	79	71	290	7,289
Boo Weekley	75	69	76	70	290	7,289
Stephen Gangluff	70	75	71	76	292	7,141
Kirk Triplett	73	71	69	79	292	7,141
Garth Mulroy	71	74	76	72	293	7,030

Honda Classic

PGA National, Champion Course, Palm Beach Gardens, Florida   March 1-4
Par 35-35–70; 7,158 yards   purse, $5,700,000

	SCORES				TOTAL	MONEY
Rory McIlroy	66	67	66	69	268	$1,026,000
Tom Gillis	68	64	69	69	270	501,600
Tiger Woods	71	68	69	62	270	501,600
Lee Westwood	70	69	70	63	272	273,600
Justin Rose	66	66	71	70	273	216,600
Charl Schwartzel	71	66	67	69	273	216,600
Rickie Fowler	69	72	67	66	274	183,825
Dicky Pride	66	67	71	70	274	183,825
Graeme McDowell	73	64	69	69	275	153,900
Kevin Stadler	66	71	69	69	275	153,900
Chris Stroud	70	69	67	69	275	153,900
Keegan Bradley	67	68	68	73	276	115,425
Greg Chalmers	68	69	68	71	276	115,425
Brian Harman	73	61	69	73	276	115,425
D.A. Points	71	70	68	67	276	115,425
Fredrik Jacobson	70	71	67	69	277	94,050
Brandt Jobe	70	69	69	69	277	94,050
Harris English	66	69	66	77	278	79,800
Jeff Overton	71	65	70	72	278	79,800
Vaughn Taylor	68	66	74	70	278	79,800
Stuart Appleby	69	71	71	68	279	59,280
Ernie Els	70	68	70	71	279	59,280
Spencer Levin	72	69	67	71	279	59,280
Davis Love	64	72	71	72	279	59,280
Henrik Stenson	70	69	70	70	279	59,280
Erik Compton	67	71	71	71	280	43,035
Charles Howell	68	67	72	73	280	43,035
Troy Matteson	70	69	75	66	280	43,035
Ryan Palmer	66	71	72	71	280	43,035
Gary Christian	73	67	67	74	281	34,627.50
Ben Crane	67	69	75	70	281	34,627.50
Robert Garrigus	71	69	70	71	281	34,627.50
Ted Potter, Jr.	72	64	72	73	281	34,627.50
Mark Wilson	70	70	68	73	281	34,627.50
Y.E. Yang	70	70	70	71	281	34,627.50
Robert Allenby	72	68	73	69	282	26,267.50
Stewart Cink	70	67	75	70	282	26,267.50
Martin Flores	66	72	74	70	282	26,267.50
John Huh	68	69	75	70	282	26,267.50
Rocco Mediate	69	67	73	73	282	26,267.50
Carl Pettersson	67	70	74	71	282	26,267.50
Anthony Kim	70	69	75	69	283	21,660
Jason Kokrak	71	68	71	73	283	21,660
Sean O'Hair	70	69	72	73	284	18,810
Heath Slocum	70	71	70	73	284	18,810

	SCORES				TOTAL	MONEY
Charlie Wi	71	68	75	70	284	18,810
John Mallinger	74	67	69	75	285	14,313.34
Kenny Perry	70	71	70	74	285	14,313.34
Cameron Tringale	72	69	70	74	285	14,313.34
Sang-Moon Bae	70	71	71	73	285	14,313.33
Michael Bradley	70	70	73	72	285	14,313.33
Brian Davis	68	70	74	73	285	14,313.33
Tim Herron	71	69	71	74	285	14,313.33
Scott Langley	70	69	73	73	285	14,313.33
Michael Thompson	74	66	72	73	285	14,313.33
Kris Blanks	69	72	72	73	286	12,711
Brendon de Jonge	68	72	74	72	286	12,711
J.B. Holmes	70	70	71	75	286	12,711
Robert Karlsson	72	69	75	70	286	12,711
Chris Kirk	71	70	72	73	286	12,711
Seung-Yul Noh	66	74	75	71	286	12,711
Jason Bohn	70	70	72	75	287	12,084
Ken Duke	67	69	74	77	287	12,084
Bob Estes	67	69	73	78	287	12,084
William McGirt	69	71	72	75	287	12,084
Rory Sabbatini	69	72	69	77	287	12,084
Colt Knost	71	70	79	68	288	11,571
Nick O'Hern	69	71	71	77	288	11,571
Jhonattan Vegas	71	69	73	75	288	11,571
Jimmy Walker	67	67	73	81	288	11,571
Padraig Harrington	70	68	72	79	289	11,286
Rod Pampling	69	71	71	79	290	11,172
Ricky Barnes	72	69	75	75	291	11,058
Jose Maria Olazabal	73	67	74	78	292	10,944
Brendan Steele	68	73	75	77	293	10,830
Ryan Moore	70	71	71	82	294	10,716

WGC - Cadillac Championship

TPC Blue Monster at Doral, Miami, Florida
Par 36-36–72; 7,334 yards

March 8-11
purse, $8,500,000

	SCORES				TOTAL	MONEY
Justin Rose	69	64	69	70	272	$1,400,000
Bubba Watson	70	62	67	74	273	845,000
Rory McIlroy	73	69	65	67	274	516,000
Peter Hanson	70	65	69	71	275	362,500
Charl Schwartzel	68	69	70	68	275	362,500
Luke Donald	70	68	69	69	276	260,000
John Senden	76	67	68	65	276	260,000
Keegan Bradley	69	67	66	75	277	165,000
Matt Kuchar	72	67	66	72	277	165,000
Steve Stricker	69	70	69	69	277	165,000
Bo Van Pelt	73	65	70	69	277	165,000
Aaron Baddeley	69	74	68	67	278	120,000
Graeme McDowell	75	67	67	70	279	101,000
Francesco Molinari	75	68	71	65	279	101,000
Adam Scott	66	68	74	71	279	101,000
Johnson Wagner	70	69	67	73	279	101,000
Charles Howell	70	67	71	72	280	92,000
Zach Johnson	70	68	67	75	280	92,000
Nick Watney	71	73	69	67	280	92,000
Greg Chalmers	71	70	68	72	281	85,000
Jason Day	73	67	70	71	281	85,000
Robert Karlsson	75	68	70	68	281	85,000

	SCORES				TOTAL	MONEY
Martin Kaymer	73	64	70	74	281	85,000
Thomas Bjorn	68	68	75	71	282	76,000
Marcus Fraser	76	68	69	69	282	76,000
Martin Laird	72	73	66	71	282	76,000
Hunter Mahan	71	72	66	73	282	76,000
Robert Rock	75	70	68	69	282	76,000
Jason Dufner	66	72	73	72	283	67,500
Bill Haas	74	70	70	69	283	67,500
Anders Hansen	70	72	69	72	283	67,500
Garth Mulroy	73	71	69	70	283	67,500
Lee Westwood	76	67	68	72	283	67,500
Gary Woodland	71	70	70	72	283	67,500
Jonathan Byrd	72	70	70	72	284	60,500
K.J. Choi	74	67	70	73	284	60,500
Nicolas Colsaerts	73	70	70	71	284	60,500
Branden Grace	78	72	64	70	284	60,500
Dustin Johnson	75	68	73	68	284	60,500
Juvic Pagunsan	69	71	72	72	284	60,500
Chez Reavie	78	68	67	71	284	60,500
Webb Simpson	75	66	66	77	284	60,500
Darren Clarke	74	74	68	69	285	55,500
Phil Mickelson	72	71	71	71	285	55,500
Rickie Fowler	74	70	72	70	286	52,000
Retief Goosen	74	71	71	70	286	52,000
Miguel Angel Jimenez	69	71	73	73	286	52,000
Brandt Snedeker	75	69	70	72	286	52,000
Mark Wilson	72	70	72	72	286	52,000
Hennie Otto	73	66	71	77	287	49,000
Paul Casey	76	71	68	73	288	46,875
Ben Crane	73	71	73	71	288	46,875
K.T. Kim	74	72	70	72	288	46,875
Kyle Stanley	69	69	76	74	288	46,875
Gonzalo Fernandez-Castano	74	70	73	72	289	45,250
Geoff Ogilvy	73	73	70	73	289	45,250
Jbe' Kruger	72	71	73	74	290	44,250
Alvaro Quiros	69	74	71	76	290	44,250
Y.E. Yang	72	67	76	76	291	43,500
Sergio Garcia	75	74	68	76	293	42,000
Paul Lawrie	70	74	72	77	293	42,000
Louis Oosthuizen	77	70	74	72	293	42,000
Ian Poulter	76	77	71	69	293	42,000
Tadahiro Takayama	74	73	75	71	293	42,000
Rafa Cabrera-Bello	75	70	75	74	294	40,500
Pablo Larrazabal	76	73	71	75	295	39,750
Vijay Singh	75	73	72	75	295	39,750
Fredrik Jacobson	72	76	71	77	296	39,000
Alexander Noren	74	75	72	76	297	38,500
Tetsuji Hiratsuka	78	73	70	77	298	38,000
Sang-Moon Bae	79	76	73	71	299	37,750
Simon Dyson	74	72	73	81	300	37,500
Tiger Woods	72	67	68		WD	
David Toms	72	70			WD	

Puerto Rico Open

Trump International Golf Club, Rio Grande, Puerto Rico
Par 36-36–72; 7,569 yards

March 8-11
purse, $3,500,000

	SCORES				TOTAL	MONEY
George McNeill	66	70	67	69	272	$630,000
Ryo Ishikawa	70	67	69	68	274	378,000
Henrik Stenson	70	69	65	71	275	203,000
Boo Weekley	70	68	71	66	275	203,000
Scott Brown	69	72	65	70	276	133,000
Matt Jones	66	67	72	71	276	133,000
Kevin Stadler	69	69	66	73	277	112,875
Daniel Summerhays	68	70	68	71	277	112,875
Blake Adams	74	68	68	68	278	94,500
Graham DeLaet	69	70	68	71	278	94,500
Brandt Jobe	76	69	67	66	278	94,500
Todd Hamilton	68	69	73	69	279	77,000
Roland Thatcher	69	71	68	71	279	77,000
Roberto Castro	69	69	70	72	280	57,750
Ben Curtis	67	73	68	72	280	57,750
J.J. Killeen	70	69	69	72	280	57,750
William McGirt	71	69	68	72	280	57,750
Jeff Overton	68	73	69	70	280	57,750
Brendon Todd	70	73	66	71	280	57,750
Will Claxton	69	72	70	70	281	40,775
Jamie Lovemark	70	72	68	71	281	40,775
Dicky Pride	71	72	67	71	281	40,775
Andres Romero	71	67	70	73	281	40,775
Angel Cabrera	69	75	69	69	282	33,600
Miguel Angel Carballo	71	72	72	68	283	26,150
Jerry Kelly	71	70	70	72	283	26,150
Kevin Kisner	68	70	71	74	283	26,150
Edward Loar	75	70	70	68	283	26,150
David Mathis	70	75	71	67	283	26,150
Seung-Yul Noh	71	74	69	69	283	26,150
Rod Pampling	71	74	69	69	283	26,150
James Driscoll	70	73	70	71	284	17,780
Joe Durant	71	73	71	69	284	17,780
Lee Janzen	69	71	74	70	284	17,780
Richard S. Johnson	71	69	73	71	284	17,780
Kent Jones	71	72	68	73	284	17,780
Will MacKenzie	74	71	67	72	284	17,780
Troy Matteson	71	72	72	69	284	17,780
Shaun Micheel	69	72	70	73	284	17,780
Patrick Sheehan	74	71	66	73	284	17,780
Derek Tolan	73	72	70	69	284	17,780
Michael Bradley	72	71	72	70	285	11,900
Erik Compton	71	71	71	72	285	11,900
Nathan Green	71	71	72	71	285	11,900
Emiliano Grillo	72	73	73	67	285	11,900
Vaughn Taylor	70	70	70	75	285	11,900
Garrett Willis	72	72	68	73	285	11,900
Briny Baird	71	74	69	72	286	8,484
Charlie Beljan	71	73	68	74	286	8,484
Matt Bettencourt	72	72	75	67	286	8,484
Gavin Coles	69	71	72	74	286	8,484
Brendon de Jonge	69	70	69	78	286	8,484
Matt Every	71	73	70	72	286	8,484
Danny Lee	70	70	71	75	286	8,484
Ted Potter, Jr.	72	71	72	71	286	8,484
Kyle Reifers	75	70	69	72	286	8,484
Duffy Waldorf	73	69	74	70	286	8,484

	SCORES				TOTAL	MONEY
Mark D. Anderson	70	75	74	68	287	7,700
Robert Gamez	73	72	73	69	287	7,700
J.J. Henry	73	72	74	68	287	7,700
Heath Slocum	75	70	71	71	287	7,700
Marc Turnesa	73	71	71	72	287	7,700
Brian Davis	69	70	72	77	288	7,385
Billy Horschel	72	73	69	74	288	7,385
Bill Lunde	73	71	70	74	288	7,385
Rocco Mediate	74	68	76	70	288	7,385
Peter Lonard	72	70	71	76	289	7,210
Marco Dawson	72	73	72	73	290	7,105
J.B. Holmes	73	72	73	72	290	7,105
Ken Duke	73	70	73	75	291	7,000
Jeff Curl	72	73	77	71	293	6,895
Stephen Gangluff	74	67	75	77	293	6,895
Tommy Biershenk	77	68	72	77	294	6,790

Transitions Championship

Innisbrook Resort, Copperhead Course, Palm Harbor, Florida   March 15-18
Par 36-35–71; 7,340 yards   purse, $5,500,000

	SCORES				TOTAL	MONEY
Luke Donald	67	68	70	66	271	$990,000
Sang-Moon Bae	69	66	68	68	271	410,666.67
Jim Furyk	66	70	66	69	271	410,666.67
Robert Garrigus	67	72	68	64	271	410,666.66
(Donald won on first playoff hole.)						
Ken Duke	68	67	69	68	272	193,187.50
Ernie Els	70	67	68	67	272	193,187.50
Jeff Overton	68	69	69	66	272	193,187.50
Scott Piercy	69	68	73	62	272	193,187.50
Bo Van Pelt	70	68	69	66	273	159,500
Jason Dufner	66	66	71	71	274	132,000
Matt Kuchar	73	67	69	65	274	132,000
Webb Simpson	68	69	69	68	274	132,000
Kevin Streelman	68	69	69	68	274	132,000
Chris DiMarco	70	67	69	69	275	101,750
Charley Hoffman	69	71	67	68	275	101,750
Bud Cauley	68	71	69	68	276	85,250
Sergio Garcia	68	68	70	70	276	85,250
Geoff Ogilvy	72	68	70	66	276	85,250
Michael Thompson	68	70	71	67	276	85,250
Jason Day	69	72	67	69	277	53,838.89
Padraig Harrington	61	73	72	71	277	53,838.89
Jerry Kelly	69	68	71	69	277	53,838.89
John Mallinger	72	66	66	73	277	53,838.89
Bryce Molder	67	71	73	66	277	53,838.89
Louis Oosthuizen	73	68	68	68	277	53,838.89
Chez Reavie	68	70	67	72	277	53,838.89
David Toms	67	72	67	71	277	53,838.89
Retief Goosen	69	68	65	75	277	53,838.88
Kris Blanks	73	68	70	67	278	32,755.56
Greg Chalmers	70	70	68	70	278	32,755.56
Justin Leonard	69	70	72	67	278	32,755.56
Kenny Perry	66	70	72	70	278	32,755.56
Justin Rose	67	70	75	66	278	32,755.56
Will Claxton	64	74	68	72	278	32,755.55
William McGirt	66	68	73	71	278	32,755.55
Brandt Snedeker	69	72	67	70	278	32,755.55

	SCORES				TOTAL	MONEY
Gary Woodland	68	71	68	71	278	32,755.55
Brian Davis	69	71	69	70	279	23,100
Bill Lunde	68	73	68	70	279	23,100
Shaun Micheel	71	69	66	73	279	23,100
Kevin Na	71	68	69	71	279	23,100
Kyle Reifers	70	68	70	71	279	23,100
John Senden	66	70	70	73	279	23,100
Jason Bohn	66	71	70	73	280	18,700
Jamie Lovemark	70	67	69	74	280	18,700
Robert Allenby	69	72	69	71	281	15,246
K.J. Choi	71	70	73	67	281	15,246
Zach Johnson	71	68	72	70	281	15,246
George McNeill	67	68	72	74	281	15,246
Cameron Tringale	66	71	70	74	281	15,246
Arjun Atwal	71	70	67	74	282	13,117.50
John Daly	69	72	70	71	282	13,117.50
Jimmy Walker	70	69	71	72	282	13,117.50
Nick Watney	69	72	70	71	282	13,117.50
Brian Gay	70	70	72	71	283	12,265
Peter Hanson	70	70	75	68	283	12,265
Sung Kang	68	73	71	71	283	12,265
Joe Ogilvie	67	73	71	72	283	12,265
Greg Owen	70	70	69	74	283	12,265
Pat Perez	71	70	70	72	283	12,265
Andres Romero	70	68	75	70	283	12,265
Mark Wilson	71	70	70	72	283	12,265
James Driscoll	70	70	73	71	284	11,660
D.A. Points	69	72	73	70	284	11,660
Vijay Singh	71	70	72	71	284	11,660
Chris Couch	67	68	73	77	285	11,275
Tom Gillis	72	69	71	73	285	11,275
J.J. Henry	70	71	73	71	285	11,275
Marc Leishman	71	70	71	73	285	11,275
Kevin Chappell	69	69	75	73	286	10,890
Stewart Cink	67	74	72	73	286	10,890
Troy Matteson	70	69	71	76	286	10,890
Jonathan Byrd	72	69	76	71	288	10,670
Rory Sabbatini	68	72	72	77	289	10,560
Michael Bradley	71	70	74	75	290	10,450
Jesper Parnevik	69	72	75	75	291	10,340
Charlie Wi	70	71	73	78	292	10,230

Arnold Palmer Invitational

Bay Hill Club & Lodge, Orlando, Florida
Par 36-36–72; 7,381 yards

March 22-25
purse, $6,000,000

	SCORES				TOTAL	MONEY
Tiger Woods	69	65	71	70	275	$1,080,000
Graeme McDowell	72	63	71	74	280	648,000
Ian Poulter	71	69	68	74	282	408,000
Bud Cauley	70	73	68	72	283	209,571.43
Brian Davis	70	73	70	70	283	209,571.43
Ryan Moore	71	71	71	70	283	209,571.43
Kevin Na	73	68	69	73	283	209,571.43
Johnson Wagner	71	69	69	74	283	209,571.43
Bubba Watson	69	70	72	72	283	209,571.43
Ernie Els	71	70	67	75	283	209,571.42
Jim Furyk	72	72	70	70	284	132,000
Tim Herron	74	71	68	71	284	132,000

	SCORES				TOTAL	MONEY
Trevor Immelman	73	69	71	71	284	132,000
Zach Johnson	71	68	72	73	284	132,000
Jason Dufner	66	69	77	73	285	96,000
Brian Harman	77	69	71	68	285	96,000
Justin Rose	69	69	74	73	285	96,000
Henrik Stenson	72	74	69	70	285	96,000
Chris Stroud	70	69	72	74	285	96,000
Charles Howell	73	68	68	77	286	69,900
Seung-Yul Noh	73	73	67	73	286	69,900
Greg Owen	73	74	67	72	286	69,900
John Rollins	71	72	71	72	286	69,900
Kevin Chappell	73	69	73	72	287	49,800
Matt Every	73	72	72	70	287	49,800
Phil Mickelson	73	71	71	72	287	49,800
Vijay Singh	71	68	75	73	287	49,800
Jimmy Walker	69	72	76	70	287	49,800
Bill Haas	73	72	72	71	288	39,900
J.B. Holmes	71	75	74	68	288	39,900
Sean O'Hair	69	72	70	77	288	39,900
Charlie Wi	66	68	76	78	288	39,900
Sergio Garcia	72	67	75	75	289	33,900
George McNeill	73	72	73	71	289	33,900
Daniel Summerhays	72	70	73	74	289	33,900
Kris Blanks	71	72	73	74	290	27,650
K.J. Choi	69	72	72	77	290	27,650
Martin Laird	72	68	74	76	290	27,650
Rod Pampling	75	70	73	72	290	27,650
Webb Simpson	73	66	73	78	290	27,650
Michael Thompson	74	72	72	72	290	27,650
Chad Campbell	71	76	69	75	291	20,400
Brian Gay	72	73	71	75	291	20,400
Hunter Mahan	72	73	71	75	291	20,400
Andres Romero	73	74	73	71	291	20,400
Josh Teater	74	73	67	77	291	20,400
Camilo Villegas	73	69	74	75	291	20,400
Robert Allenby	72	75	72	73	292	15,264
Marc Leishman	70	71	72	79	292	15,264
Dicky Pride	74	73	72	73	292	15,264
Scott Stallings	74	72	75	71	292	15,264
Gary Woodland	75	68	70	79	292	15,264
Ryo Ishikawa	73	74	71	75	293	13,760
Fredrik Jacobson	77	70	73	73	293	13,760
Lee Janzen	74	72	71	76	293	13,760
Skip Kendall	71	73	75	74	293	13,760
D.J. Trahan	76	70	70	77	293	13,760
Boo Weekley	74	72	72	75	293	13,760
Charley Hoffman	76	71	72	75	294	13,140
Justin Leonard	75	70	73	76	294	13,140
Nick Watney	68	73	79	74	294	13,140
Mark Wilson	77	70	71	76	294	13,140
Bobby Gates	74	72	75	74	295	12,720
William McGirt	73	74	77	71	295	12,720
Brandt Snedeker	73	73	77	72	295	12,720
Martin Flores	74	72	73	79	298	12,300
Billy Hurley	75	72	75	76	298	12,300
Anthony Kim	69	74	72	83	298	12,300
Colt Knost	76	71	76	75	298	12,300
Jeff Overton	76	70	69	84	299	11,940
Chez Reavie	73	74	77	75	299	11,940
Jhonattan Vegas	76	70	79	75	300	11,760
Tom Gillis	79	66	79	78	302	11,580
John Huh	77	70	74	81	302	11,580

Shell Houston Open

Redstone Golf Club, Tournament Course, Humble, Texas
Par 36-36–72; 7,457 yards

March 29-April 1
purse, $6,000,000

	SCORES				TOTAL	MONEY
Hunter Mahan	69	67	65	71	272	$1,080,000
Carl Pettersson	65	70	67	71	273	648,000
Louis Oosthuizen	67	66	66	75	274	408,000
Keegan Bradley	67	69	69	71	276	236,250
Brian Davis	68	65	69	74	276	236,250
Phil Mickelson	65	70	70	71	276	236,250
Jeff Overton	69	70	69	68	276	236,250
Bud Cauley	67	69	73	68	277	168,000
James Driscoll	67	66	71	73	277	168,000
J.B. Holmes	68	67	71	71	277	168,000
Cameron Tringale	69	70	70	68	277	168,000
Ernie Els	70	69	69	70	278	132,000
Pat Perez	68	69	71	70	278	132,000
Jim Herman	68	70	73	68	279	105,000
John Huh	66	70	70	73	279	105,000
Greg Owen	66	69	76	68	279	105,000
Boo Weekley	69	67	70	73	279	105,000
Harris English	69	68	73	70	280	84,000
Bryce Molder	70	70	69	71	280	84,000
John Senden	72	65	69	74	280	84,000
Angel Cabrera	65	70	76	70	281	56,325
Marc Leishman	70	70	69	72	281	56,325
Ryan Palmer	71	68	66	76	281	56,325
Scott Piercy	70	70	70	71	281	56,325
Kyle Reifers	68	69	74	70	281	56,325
Henrik Stenson	69	68	72	72	281	56,325
Vaughn Taylor	69	67	72	73	281	56,325
Lee Westwood	68	70	70	73	281	56,325
Rod Pampling	73	69	70	70	282	37,328.58
Mark Anderson	71	70	70	71	282	37,328.57
Jonas Blixt	70	66	74	72	282	37,328.57
Ben Crane	69	70	73	70	282	37,328.57
Jeff Maggert	66	66	76	74	282	37,328.57
Johnson Wagner	68	71	70	73	282	37,328.57
Y.E. Yang	69	71	69	73	282	37,328.57
Roberto Castro	71	69	73	70	283	27,650
Mathew Goggin	70	72	70	71	283	27,650
Brandt Jobe	68	69	71	75	283	27,650
Danny Lee	69	68	72	74	283	27,650
Shawn Stefani	71	71	71	70	283	27,650
Steve Stricker	68	70	75	70	283	27,650
Blake Adams	67	71	73	73	284	21,000
Erik Compton	71	67	73	73	284	21,000
Brendon de Jonge	70	70	72	72	284	21,000
Tommy Gainey	68	67	71	78	284	21,000
Sean O'Hair	70	71	69	74	284	21,000
Chad Campbell	69	67	75	74	285	16,140
Fred Couples	67	73	71	74	285	16,140
Troy Kelly	71	71	72	71	285	16,140
Jhonattan Vegas	72	70	72	71	285	16,140
Tommy Biershenk	72	67	72	75	286	14,208
Thomas Bjorn	69	69	70	78	286	14,208
Will Claxton	70	72	70	74	286	14,208
Jamie Lovemark	70	70	74	72	286	14,208
John Merrick	70	72	72	72	286	14,208
Cameron Beckman	74	67	73	73	287	13,380
Jason Bohn	69	72	73	73	287	13,380

	SCORES				TOTAL	MONEY
Nathan Green	70	70	70	77	287	13,380
Tim Herron	74	68	68	77	287	13,380
John Mallinger	70	70	70	77	287	13,380
Troy Matteson	73	69	72	73	287	13,380
Shaun Micheel	70	72	71	75	288	12,960
Rickie Fowler	68	70	74	77	289	12,660
Graeme McDowell	70	69	73	77	289	12,660
Joe Ogilvie	71	69	74	75	289	12,660
Steve Wheatcroft	68	72	73	76	289	12,660
Ricky Barnes	66	74	74	76	290	12,300
Billy Mayfair	70	71	71	78	290	12,300
Miguel Angel Carballo	74	68	73	76	291	12,060
Ted Potter, Jr.	74	68	72	77	291	12,060
Padraig Harrington	69	73	74		216	11,700
Bill Lunde	69	71	76		216	11,700
Omar Uresti	71	69	76		216	11,700
Jimmy Walker	72	70	74		216	11,700
Kris Blanks	69	72	76		217	11,160
Hunter Haas	73	65	79		217	11,160
Brian Harman	69	73	75		217	11,160
Charley Hoffman	74	68	75		217	11,160
Kyle Stanley	73	69	75		217	11,160
Robert Allenby	72	68	78		218	10,740
Chris Stroud	69	73	76		218	10,740
Lucas Glover	73	66	80		219	10,380
William McGirt	70	72	77		219	10,380
Kevin Stadler	73	69	77		219	10,380
Duffy Waldorf	71	71	77		219	10,380
Chris DiMarco	73	69	78		220	10,080
Daniel Summerhays	72	69	80		221	9,960
Ryan Moore	71	66	85		222	9,840
Colt Knost	69	73	81		223	9,720
Justin Leonard	69	72	83		224	9,600

Masters Tournament

Augusta National Golf Club, Augusta, Georgia   April 5-8
Par 36-36–72; 7,435 yards   purse, $8,000,000

	SCORES				TOTAL	MONEY
Bubba Watson	69	71	70	68	278	$1,440,000
Louis Oosthuizen	68	72	69	69	278	864,000
(Watson defeated Oosthuizen on second playoff hole.)						
Peter Hanson	68	74	65	73	280	384,000
Matt Kuchar	71	70	70	69	280	384,000
Phil Mickelson	74	68	66	72	280	384,000
Lee Westwood	67	73	72	68	280	384,000
Ian Poulter	72	72	70	69	283	268,000
Padraig Harrington	71	73	68	72	284	232,000
Justin Rose	72	72	72	68	284	232,000
Adam Scott	75	70	73	66	284	232,000
Jim Furyk	70	73	72	70	285	200,000
Fred Couples	72	67	75	72	286	156,800
Sergio Garcia	72	68	75	71	286	156,800
Hunter Mahan	72	72	68	74	286	156,800
Graeme McDowell	75	72	71	68	286	156,800
Kevin Na	71	75	72	68	286	156,800
Ben Crane	69	73	72	73	287	124,000
Bo Van Pelt	73	75	75	64	287	124,000
Charles Howell	72	70	74	72	288	96,960
Fredrik Jacobson	76	68	70	74	288	96,960

	SCORES				TOTAL	MONEY
Francesco Molinari	69	75	70	74	288	96,960
Geoff Ogilvy	74	72	71	71	288	96,960
Brandt Snedeker	72	75	68	73	288	96,960
Jason Dufner	69	70	75	75	289	70,400
Anders Hansen	76	72	73	68	289	70,400
Paul Lawrie	69	72	72	76	289	70,400
Keegan Bradley	71	77	73	69	290	56,800
Jonathan Byrd	72	71	72	75	290	56,800
Rickie Fowler	74	74	72	70	290	56,800
Vijay Singh	70	72	76	72	290	56,800
Scott Stallings	70	77	70	73	290	56,800
Angel Cabrera	71	78	71	71	291	45,280
Luke Donald	75	73	75	68	291	45,280
Zach Johnson	70	74	75	72	291	45,280
Sean O'Hair	73	70	71	77	291	45,280
Nick Watney	71	71	72	77	291	45,280
Sang-Moon Bae	75	71	69	77	292	37,600
Thomas Bjorn	73	76	74	69	292	37,600
Bill Haas	72	74	76	70	292	37,600
Aaron Baddeley	71	71	77	74	293	32,000
Rory McIlroy	71	69	77	76	293	32,000
Henrik Stenson	71	71	70	81	293	32,000
Tiger Woods	72	75	72	74	293	32,000
Kevin Chappell	71	76	71	76	294	26,400
Martin Kaymer	72	75	75	72	294	26,400
Webb Simpson	72	74	70	78	294	26,400
Ross Fisher	71	77	73	74	295	22,560
Steve Stricker	71	77	72	75	295	22,560
*Patrick Cantlay	71	78	74	72	295	
Stewart Cink	71	75	81	69	296	19,960
Robert Karlsson	74	74	77	71	296	19,960
Charl Schwartzel	72	75	75	74	296	19,960
David Toms	73	73	75	75	296	19,960
Scott Verplank	73	75	75	74	297	18,880
*Hideki Matsuyama	71	74	72	80	297	
Miguel Angel Jimenez	69	72	76	81	298	18,560
Martin Laird	76	72	74	77	299	18,240
Edoardo Molinari	75	74	76	74	299	18,240
Y.E. Yang	73	70	75	81	299	18,240
Trevor Immelman	78	71	76	76	301	17,920
Gonzalo Fernandez-Castano	74	75	76	77	302	17,760
*Kelly Kraft	74	75	77	80	306	

Out of Final 36 Holes

K.T. Kim	74	76	150	Johnson Wagner	79	74	153
John Senden	74	76	150	Tim Clark	73	81	154
Paul Casey	76	75	151	Darren Clarke	73	81	154
Harrison Frazar	73	78	151	Lucas Glover	75	79	154
Larry Mize	76	75	151	Mark Wilson	76	78	154
Jose Maria Olazabal	75	76	151	Ian Woosnam	77	77	154
Kyle Stanley	75	76	151	Simon Dyson	78	77	155
Tom Watson	77	74	151	*Corbin Mills	74	81	155
Mike Weir	72	79	151	Alvaro Quiros	78	77	155
Robert Garrigus	77	75	152	Brendan Steele	76	80	156
Bernhard Langer	72	80	152	Ben Crenshaw	76	83	159
Ryan Palmer	75	77	152	*Randal Lewis	81	78	159
Rory Sabbatini	72	80	152	Craig Stadler	81	82	163
K.J. Choi	77	76	153	Sandy Lyle	86	78	164
Ryo Ishikawa	76	77	153	Gary Woodland			WD
Bryden MacPherson	77	76	153	Jason Day			WD
Chez Reavie	79	74	153				

(Professionals who did not complete 72 holes received $5,000.)

RBC Heritage

Harbour Town Golf Links, Hilton Head Island, South Carolina
Par 36-35–71; 7,101 yards

April 12-15
purse, $5,700,000

	SCORES				TOTAL	MONEY
Carl Pettersson	70	65	66	69	270	$1,026,000
Zach Johnson	71	68	66	70	275	615,600
Colt Knost	67	66	69	74	276	387,600
Billy Mayfair	72	70	67	69	278	250,800
Kevin Stadler	72	71	67	68	278	250,800
Matt Bettencourt	73	69	68	69	279	198,075
Boo Weekley	70	66	70	73	279	198,075
Harris English	68	68	73	71	280	153,900
Matt Every	68	72	73	67	280	153,900
Jim Furyk	68	75	67	70	280	153,900
Charley Hoffman	74	65	71	70	280	153,900
Kevin Na	70	68	69	73	280	153,900
Mark Anderson	73	71	69	68	281	106,875
Brian Davis	72	68	68	73	281	106,875
Robert Garrigus	71	66	70	74	281	106,875
Vaughn Taylor	67	73	70	71	281	106,875
Rory Sabbatini	70	72	68	72	282	85,500
Brandt Snedeker	71	67	69	75	282	85,500
Kevin Streelman	74	68	70	70	282	85,500
Greg Chalmers	71	69	73	70	283	66,405
D.A. Points	74	68	71	70	283	66,405
John Rollins	70	72	70	71	283	66,405
Michael Thompson	71	70	70	72	283	66,405
Cameron Beckman	73	71	66	74	284	47,310
Chad Campbell	67	70	72	75	284	47,310
Jason Dufner	78	66	67	73	284	47,310
Bob Estes	71	67	75	71	284	47,310
Mark Wilson	73	72	68	71	284	47,310
Stephen Ames	71	74	66	74	285	34,698.75
Kevin Chappell	70	72	73	70	285	34,698.75
Brendon de Jonge	72	70	71	72	285	34,698.75
Charles Howell	72	68	77	68	285	34,698.75
Trevor Immelman	71	71	71	72	285	34,698.75
Lee Janzen	71	70	73	71	285	34,698.75
Jerry Kelly	72	69	72	72	285	34,698.75
Geoff Ogilvy	74	67	74	70	285	34,698.75
Bud Cauley	71	68	74	73	286	24,510
Tim Clark	73	67	72	74	286	24,510
Luke Donald	75	69	71	71	286	24,510
J.J. Henry	72	70	72	72	286	24,510
Spencer Levin	73	72	71	70	286	24,510
John Mallinger	69	72	73	72	286	24,510
Heath Slocum	71	71	70	74	286	24,510
Jason Bohn	70	71	69	77	287	16,473
Michael Bradley	74	64	71	78	287	16,473
Gary Christian	71	68	76	72	287	16,473
Graham DeLaet	74	68	73	72	287	16,473
Tom Gillis	70	71	74	72	287	16,473
Matt Kuchar	72	69	69	77	287	16,473
Marc Leishman	71	71	70	75	287	16,473
Jeff Maggert	74	71	69	73	287	16,473
John Daly	70	74	68	76	288	13,366.50
Tommy Gainey	70	70	68	80	288	13,366.50
Webb Simpson	71	74	70	73	288	13,366.50
Charlie Wi	68	73	73	74	288	13,366.50
Stuart Appleby	73	69	71	76	289	12,825
James Driscoll	72	72	75	70	289	12,825

	SCORES				TOTAL	MONEY
Hunter Haas	71	74	67	77	289	12,825
Chez Reavie	69	71	70	79	289	12,825
Will Claxton	70	72	73	75	290	12,369
Ken Duke	72	72	73	73	290	12,369
Shaun Micheel	72	73	76	69	290	12,369
Kyle Stanley	71	72	75	72	290	12,369
Joe Durant	70	71	77	73	291	12,027
Nick O'Hern	74	69	78	70	291	12,027
Briny Baird	74	69	71	78	292	11,856
Fredrik Jacobson	71	67	74	81	293	11,742
Sean O'Hair	73	69	79	73	294	11,628
Lucas Glover	72	72	74	78	296	11,514
Brian Harman	71	70	74	82	297	11,343
Rocco Mediate	73	71	74	79	297	11,343

Valero Texas Open

TPC San Antonio, San Antonio, Texas
Par 36-36–72; 7,522 yards

April 19-22
purse, $6,200,000

	SCORES				TOTAL	MONEY
Ben Curtis	67	67	73	72	279	$1,116,000
Matt Every	63	74	73	71	281	545,600
John Huh	77	68	67	69	281	545,600
Bob Estes	72	72	70	69	283	244,125
Brian Gay	73	69	71	70	283	244,125
Brendan Steele	73	74	69	67	283	244,125
Charlie Wi	72	69	71	71	283	244,125
Hunter Haas	66	74	77	67	284	179,800
Ryan Moore	72	72	71	69	284	179,800
Cameron Tringale	72	65	76	71	284	179,800
Kris Blanks	74	73	68	70	285	148,800
David Hearn	74	74	71	66	285	148,800
Charley Hoffman	72	74	71	69	286	112,840
Matt Kuchar	70	76	67	73	286	112,840
Frank Lickliter	71	70	74	71	286	112,840
Seung-Yul Noh	73	71	68	74	286	112,840
Kevin Streelman	71	70	74	71	286	112,840
Bud Cauley	70	72	77	68	287	78,120
Brian Harman	72	73	71	71	287	78,120
Fredrik Jacobson	68	76	71	72	287	78,120
Jerry Kelly	72	74	75	66	287	78,120
David Mathis	69	67	77	74	287	78,120
Scott Piercy	76	65	74	72	287	78,120
Miguel Angel Carballo	70	73	76	69	288	51,460
Martin Flores	71	73	70	74	288	51,460
Nathan Green	73	71	72	72	288	51,460
Tim Herron	74	69	74	71	288	51,460
Chris Stroud	72	73	69	74	288	51,460
Blake Adams	71	69	79	70	289	42,160
Bill Lunde	73	70	76	70	289	42,160
Daniel Summerhays	74	68	74	73	289	42,160
Matt Jones	77	71	70	72	290	36,683.34
Billy Hurley	71	77	68	74	290	36,683.33
Ryan Palmer	71	69	74	76	290	36,683.33
Greg Chalmers	72	72	69	78	291	29,915
Tom Gillis	72	72	73	74	291	29,915
Derek Lamely	68	75	78	70	291	29,915
Justin Leonard	74	70	73	74	291	29,915
Spencer Levin	71	75	73	72	291	29,915

	SCORES				TOTAL	MONEY
Patrick Reed	71	74	74	72	291	29,915
Robert Damron	76	72	73	71	292	22,940
J.J. Henry	74	74	73	71	292	22,940
Skip Kendall	71	73	73	75	292	22,940
Russell Knox	72	71	74	75	292	22,940
Will MacKenzie	72	76	70	74	292	22,940
*Jordan Spieth	75	70	72	75	292	
J.J. Killeen	73	71	73	76	293	18,062.67
Paul Stankowski	73	74	73	73	293	18,062.67
Kevin Kisner	73	70	73	77	293	18,062.66
Tommy Biershenk	70	74	74	76	294	15,148.67
Chad Campbell	73	71	75	75	294	15,148.67
Scott Langley	72	76	73	73	294	15,148.67
Kyle Reifers	70	75	74	75	294	15,148.67
Ricky Barnes	74	74	74	72	294	15,148.66
Garrett Willis	75	72	78	69	294	15,148.66
Graham DeLaet	73	74	75	73	295	14,074
Bobby Gates	77	71	75	72	295	14,074
Billy Mayfair	70	73	73	79	295	14,074
Garth Mulroy	71	71	76	77	295	14,074
Marco Dawson	71	73	78	74	296	13,640
David Duval	75	73	77	71	296	13,640
Harrison Frazar	72	74	72	78	296	13,640
Stephen Ames	74	74	73	76	297	13,206
Cameron Beckman	68	76	75	78	297	13,206
Will Claxton	75	71	74	77	297	13,206
Danny Lee	75	71	76	75	297	13,206
Briny Baird	73	73	78	74	298	12,710
Harris English	70	73	80	75	298	12,710
Hank Kuehne	72	74	74	78	298	12,710
Shaun Micheel	77	71	77	73	298	12,710
Joe Ogilvie	72	73	80	75	300	12,338
Patrick Sheehan	72	71	82	75	300	12,338
Scott Dunlap	72	76	77	76	301	12,090
Ted Purdy	76	72	76	77	301	12,090
Billy Horschel	74	74	77	77	302	11,904
Nick O'Hern	73	74	76	81	304	11,780
Rich Beem	69	78	79		226	11,594
Brendon de Jonge	72	75	79		226	11,594
Mark Anderson	71	77	79		227	11,408
Diego Velasquez	73	75	80		228	11,284
Zack Miller	72	76	84		232	11,160

Zurich Classic of New Orleans

TPC Louisiana, Avondale, Louisiana
Par 36-36–72; 7,341 yards

April 26-29
purse, $6,400,000

	SCORES				TOTAL	MONEY
Jason Dufner	67	65	67	70	269	$1,152,000
Ernie Els	66	68	68	67	269	691,200
(Dufner defeated Els on second playoff hole.)						
Luke Donald	73	65	66	67	271	435,200
Graham DeLaet	68	67	66	71	272	281,600
Ryan Palmer	72	67	64	69	272	281,600
Steve Stricker	66	68	69	70	273	230,400
Ken Duke	65	68	71	70	274	199,466.67
Cameron Tringale	65	70	68	71	274	199,466.67
John Rollins	67	66	69	72	274	199,466.66
Rickie Fowler	71	65	69	70	275	160,000

	SCORES				TOTAL	MONEY
David Mathis	72	69	69	65	275	160,000
Justin Rose	72	67	68	68	275	160,000
Jonas Blixt	68	70	71	67	276	116,480
Ben Curtis	67	70	68	71	276	116,480
J.B. Holmes	71	67	68	70	276	116,480
Scott Piercy	72	66	69	69	276	116,480
Webb Simpson	68	72	67	69	276	116,480
Alex Cejka	70	69	67	71	277	80,640
Brendon de Jonge	73	69	69	66	277	80,640
Jeff Overton	72	67	73	65	277	80,640
Camilo Villegas	69	66	74	68	277	80,640
Jimmy Walker	70	71	68	68	277	80,640
Bubba Watson	71	71	65	70	277	80,640
Bobby Gates	71	65	74	68	278	51,840
David Hearn	68	73	68	69	278	51,840
Colt Knost	70	70	72	66	278	51,840
George McNeill	70	70	67	71	278	51,840
Patrick Reed	71	70	70	67	278	51,840
Chris Stroud	66	71	72	69	278	51,840
Mark Anderson	69	70	72	68	279	36,408.89
Kris Blanks	69	68	72	70	279	36,408.89
Greg Chalmers	70	64	72	73	279	36,408.89
Erik Compton	69	68	72	70	279	36,408.89
Fred Funk	72	67	72	68	279	36,408.89
Russell Knox	69	64	74	72	279	36,408.89
William McGirt	70	69	70	70	279	36,408.89
Greg Owen	70	69	71	69	279	36,408.89
Daniel Summerhays	68	70	68	73	279	36,408.88
Miguel Angel Carballo	69	70	73	68	280	25,600
K.J. Choi	71	68	73	68	280	25,600
Brian Davis	71	67	72	70	280	25,600
Tim Herron	69	68	71	72	280	25,600
Charles Howell	71	66	72	71	280	25,600
John Senden	72	70	69	69	280	25,600
Daniel Chopra	66	70	72	73	281	17,938.29
Matt Jones	72	70	68	71	281	17,938.29
Geoff Ogilvy	76	66	71	68	281	17,938.29
David Toms	72	68	70	71	281	17,938.29
Stuart Appleby	69	69	70	73	281	17,938.28
James Driscoll	73	65	70	73	281	17,938.28
Kyle Reifers	69	68	70	74	281	17,938.28
Will Claxton	72	69	70	71	282	14,924.80
Peter Hanson	74	68	70	70	282	14,924.80
J.J. Henry	69	72	70	71	282	14,924.80
Danny Lee	72	68	74	68	282	14,924.80
John Merrick	72	70	69	71	282	14,924.80
Briny Baird	69	71	74	69	283	14,208
Jason Kokrak	70	70	69	74	283	14,208
Graeme McDowell	69	73	69	72	283	14,208
Rocco Mediate	71	65	73	74	283	14,208
Vaughn Taylor	69	71	73	70	283	14,208
Tommy Biershenk	74	67	71	72	284	13,632
Chris DiMarco	71	70	70	73	284	13,632
Troy Kelly	69	72	73	70	284	13,632
Hank Kuehne	71	70	70	73	284	13,632
David Duval	72	69	70	74	285	13,056
Brian Gay	70	70	74	71	285	13,056
Lucas Glover	70	72	71	72	285	13,056
Garth Mulroy	70	72	72	71	285	13,056
Seung-Yul Noh	70	69	71	75	285	13,056
Kevin Streelman	69	73	72	74	288	12,672
Michael Bradley	72	68	75		215	12,288
Tommy Gainey	73	69	73		215	12,288

	SCORES			TOTAL	MONEY
Mathew Goggin	70	72	73	215	12,288
Charley Hoffman	69	73	73	215	12,288
Scott Verplank	69	73	73	215	12,288
Chris Couch	72	69	75	216	11,904
Gavin Coles	72	70	75	217	11,776
Alexandre Rocha	72	70	77	219	11,648

Wells Fargo Championship

Quail Hollow Club, Charlotte, North Carolina
Par 36-36–72; 7,442 yards

May 3-6
purse, $6,500,000

	SCORES				TOTAL	MONEY
Rickie Fowler	66	72	67	69	274	$1,170,000
Rory McIlroy	70	68	66	70	274	572,000
D.A. Points	66	68	69	71	274	572,000
(Fowler defeated McIlroy and Points on first playoff hole.)						
Webb Simpson	65	68	69	73	275	312,000
Ben Curtis	69	70	71	67	277	237,250
Ryan Moore	65	70	68	74	277	237,250
Lee Westwood	71	72	68	66	277	237,250
Nick Watney	68	64	72	74	278	201,500
Jonas Blixt	68	73	67	71	279	156,000
Jonathan Byrd	69	69	72	69	279	156,000
Brian Davis	66	74	69	70	279	156,000
Jason Day	70	70	69	70	279	156,000
James Driscoll	71	70	69	69	279	156,000
Seung-Yul Noh	68	70	70	71	279	156,000
Stewart Cink	65	69	71	75	280	100,750
Robert Garrigus	69	72	68	71	280	100,750
George McNeill	70	68	68	74	280	100,750
Sean O'Hair	72	69	69	70	280	100,750
John Senden	66	68	72	74	280	100,750
David Toms	74	65	70	71	280	100,750
Arjun Atwal	68	69	75	69	281	67,600
Ben Crane	70	64	73	74	281	67,600
Martin Flores	68	70	71	72	281	67,600
Hunter Haas	68	68	75	70	281	67,600
Geoff Ogilvy	71	70	65	75	281	67,600
Will Claxton	71	72	70	69	282	47,125
Jim Furyk	71	71	71	69	282	47,125
Sung Kang	71	70	70	71	282	47,125
Martin Laird	72	70	69	71	282	47,125
Phil Mickelson	71	72	68	71	282	47,125
Kevin Stadler	68	74	70	70	282	47,125
Roberto Castro	68	72	72	71	283	34,450
Ken Duke	72	71	72	68	283	34,450
Spencer Levin	72	68	70	73	283	34,450
Billy Mayfair	67	71	73	72	283	34,450
Patrick Reed	66	74	69	74	283	34,450
Heath Slocum	69	67	75	72	283	34,450
Josh Teater	69	73	71	70	283	34,450
Camilo Villegas	71	70	69	73	283	34,450
Chad Campbell	72	71	72	69	284	24,700
Brendon de Jonge	67	73	72	72	284	24,700
Tommy Gainey	68	72	69	75	284	24,700
Richard H. Lee	70	69	69	76	284	24,700
Rocco Mediate	68	69	75	72	284	24,700
John Merrick	70	68	74	72	284	24,700
Troy Matteson	74	69	70	72	285	19,500

	SCORES				TOTAL	MONEY
Carl Pettersson	69	72	70	74	285	19,500
Robert Karlsson	71	67	73	75	286	16,536
Jeff Overton	68	71	70	77	286	16,536
Dicky Pride	69	72	73	72	286	16,536
Brendan Steele	71	72	71	72	286	16,536
Jimmy Walker	69	73	73	71	286	16,536
Kevin Chappell	72	71	71	73	287	15,047.50
Tom Gillis	73	68	69	77	287	15,047.50
Ryuji Imada	69	72	72	74	287	15,047.50
Hunter Mahan	73	68	75	71	287	15,047.50
Sang-Moon Bae	69	69	77	73	288	14,235
Gary Christian	73	70	74	71	288	14,235
Brian Harman	67	74	72	75	288	14,235
J.J. Henry	73	69	71	75	288	14,235
J.B. Holmes	71	71	69	77	288	14,235
Chris Kirk	75	67	73	73	288	14,235
Andres Romero	70	71	73	74	288	14,235
Cameron Tringale	69	74	70	75	288	14,235
Aaron Baddeley	69	73	75	72	289	13,455
David Hearn	70	72	76	71	289	13,455
Marc Leishman	75	67	74	73	289	13,455
Johnson Wagner	71	66	74	78	289	13,455
Brandt Jobe	72	70	73	75	290	13,000
Zach Johnson	70	71	77	72	290	13,000
Kyle Reifers	70	72	69	79	290	13,000
Gavin Coles	72	71	75	74	292	12,740
Alexandre Rocha	68	75	73	77	293	12,610
Harris English	70	72	77	75	294	12,480

The Players Championship

TPC Sawgrass, Ponte Vedra Beach, Florida
Par 36-36–72; 7,215 yards

May 10-13
purse, $9,500,000

	SCORES				TOTAL	MONEY
Matt Kuchar	68	68	69	70	275	$1,710,000
Ben Curtis	68	71	70	68	277	627,000
Rickie Fowler	72	69	66	70	277	627,000
Zach Johnson	70	66	73	68	277	627,000
Martin Laird	65	73	72	67	277	627,000
Luke Donald	72	69	72	66	279	342,000
Bo Van Pelt	71	70	70	69	280	296,083.34
Kevin Na	67	69	68	76	280	296,083.33
Jhonattan Vegas	68	74	68	70	280	296,083.33
Carl Pettersson	71	72	69	69	281	247,000
David Toms	69	74	73	65	281	247,000
Blake Adams	66	73	72	71	282	199,500
Jonathan Byrd	68	70	72	72	282	199,500
Geoff Ogilvy	70	73	70	69	282	199,500
Brendon de Jonge	69	71	72	71	283	137,987.50
Bob Estes	73	69	76	65	283	137,987.50
Peter Hanson	73	71	71	68	283	137,987.50
Martin Kaymer	73	69	70	71	283	137,987.50
Spencer Levin	74	68	72	69	283	137,987.50
David Mathis	72	71	69	71	283	137,987.50
Adam Scott	68	70	74	71	283	137,987.50
Henrik Stenson	71	71	71	70	283	137,987.50
Chris Couch	72	71	71	70	284	95,000
John Huh	75	66	72	71	284	95,000
Tim Clark	71	70	71	73	285	66,547.50

	SCORES				TOTAL	MONEY
Brian Davis	68	70	72	75	285	66,547.50
Jim Furyk	72	70	72	71	285	66,547.50
Bill Haas	68	71	74	72	285	66,547.50
Phil Mickelson	71	71	70	73	285	66,547.50
Pat Perez	69	75	70	71	285	66,547.50
Ian Poulter	65	76	71	73	285	66,547.50
John Rollins	72	72	69	72	285	66,547.50
Kevin Stadler	68	71	73	73	285	66,547.50
Charlie Wi	71	67	73	74	285	66,547.50
Keegan Bradley	72	70	74	70	286	46,835
Tom Gillis	70	71	73	72	286	46,835
Jeff Maggert	70	71	71	74	286	46,835
Johnson Wagner	69	73	69	75	286	46,835
Jimmy Walker	71	70	71	74	286	46,835
Kris Blanks	69	74	72	72	287	37,050
J.J. Henry	71	73	74	69	287	37,050
Bryce Molder	72	72	70	73	287	37,050
Alvaro Quiros	72	72	72	71	287	37,050
Tiger Woods	74	68	72	73	287	37,050
Marc Leishman	73	70	73	72	288	31,350
Ricky Barnes	74	69	72	74	289	26,334
Harrison Frazar	68	76	69	76	289	26,334
Brian Gay	71	72	71	75	289	26,334
Ryan Moore	69	72	75	73	289	26,334
Josh Teater	71	71	76	71	289	26,334
Brian Harman	73	68	76	73	290	22,496
Chris Kirk	71	73	72	74	290	22,496
Justin Rose	76	68	75	71	290	22,496
Kevin Streelman	72	68	72	78	290	22,496
Michael Thompson	68	71	75	76	290	22,496
Sergio Garcia	73	71	68	79	291	21,280
Trevor Immelman	72	72	72	75	291	21,280
Robert Karlsson	70	74	76	71	291	21,280
Rod Pampling	71	72	78	70	291	21,280
Nick Watney	71	70	76	74	291	21,280
Robert Allenby	72	72	75	73	292	20,520
Sung Kang	75	68	72	77	292	20,520
Lee Westwood	71	70	74	77	292	20,520
Stewart Cink	71	72	78	72	293	19,855
Harris English	70	67	79	77	293	19,855
George McNeill	70	73	82	68	293	19,855
Heath Slocum	73	70	78	72	293	19,855
Jason Dufner	73	71	76	75	295	19,285
David Hearn	69	75	77	74	295	19,285
Graham DeLaet	71	73	76	76	296	18,905
Justin Leonard	75	68	74	79	296	18,905
Cameron Tringale	73	71	77	76	297	18,620

HP Byron Nelson Championship

TPC Four Seasons Resort, Irving, Texas
Par 35-35–70; 7,166 yards

May 17-20
purse, $6,500,000

	SCORES				TOTAL	MONEY
Jason Dufner	67	66	69	67	269	$1,170,000
Dicky Pride	66	68	69	67	270	702,000
Jonas Blixt	68	70	67	66	271	312,000
Joe Durant	70	71	65	65	271	312,000
J.J. Henry	68	68	67	68	271	312,000
Marc Leishman	65	69	71	66	271	312,000

	SCORES			TOTAL	MONEY
Ken Duke	69	67	72	66	274	209,625
Phil Mickelson	70	69	69	66	274	209,625
Jason Bohn	70	70	67	68	275	156,000
Jason Day	68	68	67	72	275	156,000
Robert Garrigus	71	70	68	66	275	156,000
Ryan Palmer	64	70	72	69	275	156,000
Pat Perez	67	67	72	69	275	156,000
Vijay Singh	68	70	66	71	275	156,000
Padraig Harrington	68	69	70	69	276	107,250
Matt Kuchar	66	68	72	70	276	107,250
David Mathis	68	71	70	67	276	107,250
Scott Piercy	66	70	70	70	276	107,250
Rich Beem	68	70	68	71	277	78,780
James Driscoll	67	71	70	69	277	78,780
Andres Gonzales	66	72	69	70	277	78,780
Danny Lee	71	71	68	67	277	78,780
D.A. Points	68	69	72	68	277	78,780
Keegan Bradley	67	68	71	72	278	53,950
Chad Campbell	68	66	73	71	278	53,950
John Mallinger	70	70	69	69	278	53,950
John Rollins	71	67	71	69	278	53,950
Gary Woodland	68	70	74	66	278	53,950
Roberto Castro	74	67	68	70	279	40,439.29
Alex Cejka	65	73	76	65	279	40,439.29
Todd Hamilton	70	70	71	68	279	40,439.29
Derek Lamely	69	70	71	69	279	40,439.29
Greg Owen	67	71	70	71	279	40,439.28
Andres Romero	72	67	70	70	279	40,439.28
Jimmy Walker	70	68	69	72	279	40,439.28
Erik Compton	70	71	71	68	280	30,615
Tim Herron	70	72	67	71	280	30,615
Kevin Kisner	67	74	71	68	280	30,615
Billy Mayfair	69	68	71	72	280	30,615
John Merrick	71	70	69	70	280	30,615
Graham DeLaet	71	68	69	73	281	22,132.50
Ernie Els	70	69	70	72	281	22,132.50
Bob Estes	73	68	65	75	281	22,132.50
Charley Hoffman	66	69	74	72	281	22,132.50
Charles Howell	68	73	68	72	281	22,132.50
Richard H. Lee	68	72	74	67	281	22,132.50
Chris Riley	67	74	73	67	281	22,132.50
Duffy Waldorf	72	70	69	70	281	22,132.50
Mathew Goggin	69	71	73	69	282	15,748.58
Ricky Barnes	67	71	74	70	282	15,748.57
Scott Brown	70	69	73	70	282	15,748.57
Chris Couch	68	70	75	69	282	15,748.57
Nathan Green	68	71	70	73	282	15,748.57
Brandt Jobe	70	69	71	72	282	15,748.57
Bill Lunde	66	75	69	72	282	15,748.57
Blake Adams	66	71	75	71	283	14,430
Arjun Atwal	72	69	73	69	283	14,430
Greg Chalmers	70	71	70	72	283	14,430
Brian Davis	73	65	73	72	283	14,430
Brian Gay	71	71	71	70	283	14,430
Hunter Haas	69	73	69	72	283	14,430
Kyle Reifers	70	72	71	70	283	14,430
Shane Bertsch	70	70	68	76	284	13,715
J.J. Killeen	70	72	72	70	284	13,715
D.J. Trahan	72	68	71	73	284	13,715
Boo Weekley	69	68	73	74	284	13,715
Ryuji Imada	67	68	79	71	285	13,390
Nick O'Hern	70	71	71	74	286	13,260
Gavin Coles	71	69	71	76	287	13,000

	SCORES				TOTAL	MONEY
Seung-Yul Noh	73	69	70	75	287	13,000
Jhonattan Vegas	67	74	73	73	287	13,000
Harrison Frazar	68	70	77		215	12,675
Robert Gamez	74	68	73		215	12,675
Bobby Gates	71	70	75		216	12,415
Alexandre Rocha	69	72	75		216	12,415
Rocco Mediate	70	71	76		217	12,155
Tim Petrovic	67	74	76		217	12,155
Jerry Kelly	68	71	79		218	11,960
Stephen Gangluff	71	71	78		220	11,830

Crowne Plaza Invitational

Colonial Country Club, Fort Worth, Texas
Par 35-35–70; 7,204 yards

May 24-27
purse, $6,400,000

	SCORES				TOTAL	MONEY
Zach Johnson	64	67	65	72	268	$1,152,000
Jason Dufner	65	64	66	74	269	691,200
Tommy Gainey	66	67	73	67	273	435,200
Jim Furyk	69	69	68	68	274	307,200
Harris English	65	70	73	67	275	216,960
Rickie Fowler	68	68	70	69	275	216,960
John Huh	70	66	69	70	275	216,960
Chris Kirk	71	69	70	65	275	216,960
Ryan Palmer	68	67	70	70	275	216,960
Jonas Blixt	73	67	66	71	277	160,000
Jonathan Byrd	72	68	67	70	277	160,000
Ben Crane	70	71	68	68	277	160,000
Sergio Garcia	66	73	71	68	278	113,066.67
Kevin Na	70	71	71	66	278	113,066.67
Kyle Reifers	65	72	72	69	278	113,066.67
Chris Stroud	69	73	67	69	278	113,066.67
David Hearn	71	72	65	70	278	113,066.66
Charley Hoffman	69	70	69	70	278	113,066.66
Tim Clark	70	69	71	69	279	72,228.58
Roberto Castro	67	74	68	70	279	72,228.57
Tom Gillis	65	69	69	76	279	72,228.57
Trevor Immelman	70	71	69	69	279	72,228.57
Geoff Ogilvy	70	70	70	69	279	72,228.57
Louis Oosthuizen	71	67	68	73	279	72,228.57
Bo Van Pelt	69	64	71	75	279	72,228.57
Ken Duke	68	75	66	71	280	47,360
Martin Flores	68	73	70	69	280	47,360
Matt Kuchar	72	69	67	72	280	47,360
Ryan Moore	67	69	70	74	280	47,360
Carl Pettersson	70	69	71	70	280	47,360
Bryce Molder	72	64	75	70	281	37,120
Seung-Yul Noh	70	69	72	70	281	37,120
Greg Owen	69	68	71	73	281	37,120
Corey Pavin	71	70	67	73	281	37,120
Boo Weekley	72	71	68	70	281	37,120
Y.E. Yang	73	69	66	73	281	37,120
Sung Kang	70	69	69	74	282	29,440
J.J. Killeen	72	70	69	71	282	29,440
Hunter Mahan	69	71	68	74	282	29,440
John Senden	69	71	72	70	282	29,440
Chad Campbell	71	71	69	72	283	23,040
Kevin Chappell	70	67	70	76	283	23,040
John Daly	70	69	70	74	283	23,040

	SCORES				TOTAL	MONEY
Brendon de Jonge	67	74	68	74	283	23,040
Brandt Jobe	67	75	70	71	283	23,040
Charlie Wi	68	69	75	71	283	23,040
Blake Adams	69	72	70	73	284	16,240
Greg Chalmers	70	69	72	73	284	16,240
Will Claxton	72	69	71	72	284	16,240
Chris DiMarco	66	74	73	71	284	16,240
John Mallinger	71	72	70	71	284	16,240
Rory Sabbatini	71	71	71	71	284	16,240
Vijay Singh	70	69	70	75	284	16,240
Michael Thompson	69	71	71	73	284	16,240
Bill Haas	72	71	70	72	285	14,656
David Mathis	71	67	71	76	285	14,656
Kris Blanks	73	69	73	71	286	14,144
Jason Bohn	70	70	71	75	286	14,144
Jerry Kelly	72	70	69	75	286	14,144
Kelly Kraft	71	71	64	80	286	14,144
Marc Leishman	72	68	74	72	286	14,144
Josh Teater	70	71	72	73	286	14,144
Aaron Baddeley	71	70	73	73	287	13,568
William McGirt	70	71	73	73	287	13,568
Pat Perez	69	74	70	74	287	13,568
Miguel Angel Carballo	75	68	70	75	288	13,120
Bobby Gates	71	67	72	78	288	13,120
Andrés Romero	66	71	78	73	288	13,120
Mark Wilson	71	71	72	74	288	13,120
Gary Christian	70	73	72	74	289	12,736
George McNeill	72	69	72	76	289	12,736
Nick Watney	71	71	72	76	290	12,544
Hunter Haas	71	72	73		216	12,224
Edward Loar	72	71	73		216	12,224
Brendon Todd	70	71	75		216	12,224
Gary Woodland	70	70	76		216	12,224
Sang-Moon Bae	70	70	77		217	11,904
Heath Slocum	70	73	75		218	11,776
Justin Leonard	69	73	77		219	11,648

Memorial Tournament

Muirfield Village Golf Club, Dublin, Ohio
Par 36-36–72; 7,265 yards

May 31-June 3
purse, $6,200,000

	SCORES				TOTAL	MONEY
Tiger Woods	70	69	73	67	279	$1,116,000
Andres Romero	69	73	72	67	281	545,600
Rory Sabbatini	69	69	71	72	281	545,600
Spencer Levin	67	72	69	75	283	272,800
Daniel Summerhays	69	71	74	69	283	272,800
Jonathan Byrd	71	70	72	71	284	215,450
Matt Every	69	75	71	69	284	215,450
Justin Rose	73	72	71	69	285	192,200
Aaron Baddeley	69	72	73	72	286	167,400
Ryo Ishikawa	72	70	71	73	286	167,400
Greg Owen	72	71	76	67	286	167,400
Luke Donald	71	73	75	68	287	142,600
J.B. Holmes	72	75	74	67	288	119,866.67
Bo Van Pelt	73	69	75	71	288	119,866.67
Jim Furyk	72	68	75	73	288	119,866.66
Davis Love	74	72	71	72	289	99,200
Vijay Singh	72	73	69	75	289	99,200

	SCORES				TOTAL	MONEY
Kevin Stadler	72	73	71	73	289	99,200
Blake Adams	69	77	71	73	290	72,540
K.J. Choi	74	71	77	68	290	72,540
John Huh	71	74	76	69	290	72,540
Dustin Johnson	71	71	73	75	290	72,540
Hunter Mahan	72	73	77	68	290	72,540
Charl Schwartzel	73	72	73	72	290	72,540
Ricky Barnes	72	72	76	71	291	40,776.93
Brian Davis	73	72	74	72	291	40,776.93
Branden Grace	74	72	75	70	291	40,776.93
Chris Kirk	75	70	75	71	291	40,776.93
Stewart Cink	71	73	73	74	291	40,776.92
Nicolas Colsaerts	72	74	73	72	291	40,776.92
David Hearn	70	75	70	76	291	40,776.92
Trevor Immelman	71	70	75	75	291	40,776.92
David Mathis	71	71	74	75	291	40,776.92
Pat Perez	74	73	72	72	291	40,776.92
Kyle Reifers	71	70	73	77	291	40,776.92
Scott Stallings	66	73	75	77	291	40,776.92
Cameron Tringale	72	74	73	72	291	40,776.92
Greg Chalmers	71	71	77	73	292	24,800
Erik Compton	67	75	75	75	292	24,800
Brendon de Jonge	73	71	74	74	292	24,800
Troy Matteson	72	69	76	75	292	24,800
Ryan Moore	70	73	71	78	292	24,800
Nick O'Hern	74	73	74	71	292	24,800
Jeff Overton	72	72	78	70	292	24,800
Johnson Wagner	72	72	73	75	292	24,800
Lucas Glover	74	68	75	76	293	17,577
Rod Pampling	72	74	73	74	293	17,577
Adam Scott	70	72	77	74	293	17,577
Henrik Stenson	74	68	71	80	293	17,577
Fred Couples	74	73	76	71	294	15,438
Steve Stricker	73	70	75	76	294	15,438
Bud Cauley	70	76	77	72	295	14,539
Rickie Fowler	71	71	69	84	295	14,539
Seung-Yul Noh	72	73	75	75	295	14,539
Charlie Wi	71	75	75	74	295	14,539
Robert Allenby	73	74	77	72	296	14,074
Jhonattan Vegas	74	73	75	74	296	14,074
Chris DiMarco	73	72	73	79	297	13,702
Ernie Els	70	75	74	78	297	13,702
Marc Leishman	72	75	75	75	297	13,702
Geoff Ogilvy	71	74	79	73	297	13,702
Harris English	71	75	80	72	298	13,206
Ryuji Imada	75	72	71	80	298	13,206
Brendan Steele	72	75	74	77	298	13,206
Jimmy Walker	72	73	78	75	298	13,206
Brandt Jobe	73	74	79	73	299	12,834
Mark Wilson	70	76	78	75	299	12,834
Scott Piercy	70	75	80	75	300	12,648
Ben Crane	72	75	74	80	301	12,524
Robert Garrigus	71	76	79	77	303	12,338
Camilo Villegas	73	74	82	74	303	12,338

FedEx St. Jude Classic

TPC Southwind, Memphis, Tennessee
Par 35-35–70; 7,244 yards

June 7-10
purse, \$5,600,000

	SCORES				TOTAL	MONEY
Dustin Johnson	70	68	67	66	271	\$1,008,000
John Merrick	66	69	69	68	272	604,800
Chad Campbell	68	67	70	68	273	268,800
Davis Love	68	68	68	69	273	268,800
Nick O'Hern	70	67	67	69	273	268,800
Ryan Palmer	74	66	67	66	273	268,800
Robert Allenby	68	70	67	69	274	168,700
Ken Duke	68	68	73	65	274	168,700
Rory McIlroy	68	65	72	69	274	168,700
Seung-Yul Noh	67	69	72	66	274	168,700
Greg Owen	72	67	71	65	275	134,400
Kevin Stadler	69	65	71	70	275	134,400
Martin Flores	72	70	69	65	276	98,933.34
William McGirt	71	69	68	68	276	98,933.34
Padraig Harrington	68	68	71	69	276	98,933.33
Kevin Kisner	69	66	70	71	276	98,933.33
Jeff Overton	67	72	68	69	276	98,933.33
Henrik Stenson	72	66	70	68	276	98,933.33
Arjun Atwal	67	74	70	66	277	67,872
Woody Austin	72	68	67	70	277	67,872
John Daly	68	69	76	64	277	67,872
Luke Guthrie	69	71	67	70	277	67,872
J.B. Holmes	70	64	72	71	277	67,872
Martin Laird	72	70	67	69	278	49,280
Bryce Molder	69	71	69	69	278	49,280
Duffy Waldorf	71	69	69	69	278	49,280
Roberto Castro	73	68	66	72	279	38,080
Daniel Chopra	72	65	71	71	279	38,080
Charles Howell	69	71	71	68	279	38,080
Fredrik Jacobson	69	72	66	72	279	38,080
J.J. Killeen	68	69	74	68	279	38,080
Jeff Maggert	66	68	73	72	279	38,080
Boo Weekley	70	67	73	69	279	38,080
Brendon de Jonge	71	68	71	70	280	29,540
Bob Estes	72	68	71	69	280	29,540
Bill Lunde	71	68	71	70	280	29,540
Patrick Sheehan	71	70	71	68	280	29,540
Ryo Ishikawa	72	67	73	69	281	24,640
Kent Jones	72	68	73	68	281	24,640
George McNeill	72	68	72	69	281	24,640
Shaun Micheel	71	70	68	72	281	24,640
Tim Clark	69	71	69	73	282	18,512
Gavin Coles	70	72	71	69	282	18,512
Robert Garrigus	74	65	73	70	282	18,512
David Hearn	72	69	70	71	282	18,512
Dustin Morris	71	69	67	75	282	18,512
Sean O'Hair	70	69	71	72	282	18,512
Chris Riley	70	71	74	67	282	18,512
Stuart Appleby	72	68	73	70	283	13,294.40
Shane Bertsch	71	68	73	71	283	13,294.40
Bart Bryant	72	70	70	71	283	13,294.40
Gary Christian	70	71	71	71	283	13,294.40
Tommy Gainey	72	70	71	70	283	13,294.40
Lee Janzen	68	71	73	71	283	13,294.40
Troy Kelly	68	71	74	70	283	13,294.40
Danny Lee	69	70	71	73	283	13,294.40
Troy Matteson	70	72	72	69	283	13,294.40

	SCORES				TOTAL	MONEY
Kyle Stanley	71	70	73	69	283	13,294.40
J.J. Henry	67	74	72	71	284	12,376
Paul Stankowski	69	69	74	72	284	12,376
Cameron Beckman	72	70	68	75	285	11,984
Will Claxton	72	70	74	69	285	11,984
Chris Couch	70	70	69	76	285	11,984
John Peterson	72	65	73	75	285	11,984
Brett Wetterich	71	71	71	72	285	11,984
Zack Miller	70	70	77	69	286	11,592
Y.E. Yang	68	71	73	74	286	11,592
Craig Barlow	72	68	72	75	287	11,368
Steven Bowditch	74	66	73	74	287	11,368
Neal Lancaster	72	70	74	72	288	11,144
Omar Uresti	70	72	73	73	288	11,144
Billy Horschel	72	69	70	78	289	10,920
Matt McQuillan	71	69	76	73	289	10,920
Robert Gamez	72	69	74	77	292	10,696
Mathew Goggin	70	71	73	78	292	10,696
Jonathan Fly	78	64	75	76	293	10,528

U.S. Open Championship

The Olympic Club, San Francisco, California
Par 34-36–70; 7,170 yards

June 14-17
purse, $8,000,000

	SCORES				TOTAL	MONEY
Webb Simpson	72	73	68	68	281	$1,440,000
Michael Thompson	66	75	74	67	282	695,916
Graeme McDowell	69	72	68	73	282	695,916
David Toms	69	70	76	68	283	276,841
Padraig Harrington	74	70	71	68	283	276,841
John Peterson	71	70	72	70	283	276,841
Jason Dufner	72	71	70	70	283	276,841
Jim Furyk	70	69	70	74	283	276,841
Ernie Els	75	69	68	72	284	200,280
Casey Wittenberg	71	77	67	70	285	163,594
Retief Goosen	75	70	69	71	285	163,594
John Senden	72	73	68	72	285	163,594
Kevin Chappell	74	71	68	72	285	163,594
Lee Westwood	73	72	67	73	285	163,594
K.J. Choi	73	70	74	69	286	118,969
Steve Stricker	76	68	73	69	286	118,969
Adam Scott	76	70	70	70	286	118,969
Aaron Watkins	72	71	72	71	286	118,969
Martin Kaymer	74	71	69	72	286	118,969
Fredrik Jacobson	72	71	68	75	286	118,969
Nick Watney	69	75	73	70	287	86,348
*Jordan Spieth	74	74	69	70	287	
Raphael Jacquelin	72	71	73	71	287	86,348
Justin Rose	69	75	71	72	287	86,348
Tiger Woods	69	70	75	73	287	86,348
Blake Adams	72	70	70	75	287	86,348
Matt Kuchar	70	73	71	74	288	68,943
Nicolas Colsaerts	72	69	71	76	288	68,943
Davis Love	73	74	73	69	289	53,168
Alistair Presnell	70	74	75	70	289	53,168
Morgan Hoffmann	72	74	73	70	289	53,168
Francesco Molinari	71	76	72	70	289	53,168
Robert Karlsson	70	75	72	72	289	53,168
Kevin Na	74	71	71	73	289	53,168

	SCORES				TOTAL	MONEY
Scott Langley	76	70	70	73	289	53,168
Charlie Wi	74	70	71	74	289	53,168
*Beau Hossler	70	73	70	76	289	
Charl Schwartzel	73	70	74	73	290	44,144
Hunter Mahan	72	71	73	74	290	44,144
Sergio Garcia	73	71	71	75	290	44,144
Zach Johnson	77	70	73	71	291	38,816
Rickie Fowler	72	76	71	72	291	38,816
*Patrick Cantlay	76	72	71	72	291	
Ian Poulter	70	75	73	73	291	38,816
Alex Cejka	78	69	70	74	291	38,816
Matteo Manassero	76	69	73	74	292	31,979
Bob Estes	74	73	71	74	292	31,979
Angel Cabrera	72	76	69	75	292	31,979
Steve LeBrun	73	75	69	75	292	31,979
Hunter Hamrick	77	67	71	77	292	31,979
Simon Dyson	74	74	74	71	293	24,912
Jesse Mueller	75	73	74	71	293	24,912
Nicholas Thompson	74	74	72	73	293	24,912
Hiroyuki Fujita	75	71	73	74	293	24,912
Branden Grace	71	74	73	75	293	24,912
Michael Allen	71	73	77	73	294	21,995
Jeff Curl	73	75	71	75	294	21,995
Jonathan Byrd	71	75	71	77	294	21,995
Bo Van Pelt	78	70	76	71	295	19,955
Jason Day	75	71	76	73	295	19,955
J.B. Park	70	74	77	74	295	19,955
Matthew Baldwin	74	74	73	74	295	19,955
Kevin Streelman	76	72	72	75	295	19,955
Darron Stiles	75	71	73	76	295	19,955
Marc Warren	73	72	74	77	296	18,593
Phil Mickelson	76	71	71	78	296	18,593
K.T. Kim	74	72	74	77	297	18,113
Stephen Ames	74	73	79	72	298	17,633
Keegan Bradley	73	73	75	77	298	17,633
Rod Pampling	74	73	74	78	299	17,153
Jason Bohn	70	75	78	78	301	16,833
Joe Ogilvie	73	75	76	79	303	16,512

Out of Final 36 Holes

Thomas Bjorn	78	71	149	Spencer Levin	74	77	151
Gregory Bourdy	74	75	149	Toru Taniguchi	78	73	151
Roberto Castro	75	74	149	Gary Woodland	74	77	151
Joe Durant	78	71	149	Stewart Cink	77	75	152
Robert Garrigus	72	77	149	Paul Claxton	75	77	152
Lucas Glover	76	73	149	Samuel Osborne	76	76	152
Bill Haas	76	73	149	D.A. Points	72	80	152
Brian Harman	77	72	149	Anthony Summers	76	76	152
Justin Hicks	75	74	149	Shane Bertsch	78	75	153
Charles Howell	72	77	149	Matt Bettencourt	76	77	153
Mikko Ilonen	75	74	149	Tommy Biershenk	74	79	153
Ryo Ishikawa	71	78	149	Michael Campbell	79	74	153
Dustin Johnson	75	74	149	George Coetzee	78	75	153
Martin Laird	77	72	149	James Hahn	73	80	153
Casey Martin	74	75	149	Peter Hanson	78	75	153
Louis Oosthuizen	77	72	149	Colt Knost	75	78	153
Carl Pettersson	75	74	149	Bill Lunde	81	72	153
*Alberto Sanchez	72	77	149	David Mathis	78	75	153
Lee Slattery	79	70	149	Robert Rock	75	78	153
Bubba Watson	78	71	149	Vijay Singh	75	78	153
Mark Wilson	76	73	149	Tadahiro Takayama	77	76	153
Y.E. Yang	74	75	149	Aaron Baddeley	75	79	154

Sang-Moon Bae	77	73	150	*Brooks Koepka	77	77	154
Rafa Cabrera-Bello	74	76	150	Kyle Thompson	82	72	154
Ben Crane	77	73	150	*Cameron Wilson	77	77	154
Martin Flores	71	79	150	Brian Gaffney	77	78	155
Jim Herman	78	72	150	Brice Garnett	78	77	155
Edward Loar	76	74	150	Hunter Haas	81	74	155
Rory McIlroy	77	73	150	Trevor Immelman	80	75	155
Alexander Noren	75	75	150	G. Fernandez-Castano	80	76	156
Geoff Ogilvy	76	74	150	Lee Dong-hwan	77	79	156
Scott Piercy	75	75	150	*Andy Zhang	79	77	156
Alvaro Quiros	75	75	150	Tim Weinhart	78	79	157
Chez Reavie	80	70	150	Miguel A. Jimenez	81	77	158
Kyle Stanley	73	77	150	*Nick Sherwood	78	80	158
Olin Browne	77	74	151	Mark McCormick	82	77	159
Tim Clark	77	74	151	Scott Smith	78	81	159
Luke Donald	79	72	151	Soren Kjeldsen	85	75	160
Anders Hansen	72	79	151	Steve Marino	84	78	162
Tim Herron	74	77	151	Dennis Miller	80	82	162
Brendan Jones	76	75	151	Cole Howard	80	84	164
Peter Lawrie	74	77	151	Brian Rowell	86	82	168

(Professionals who did not complete 72 holes received $2,000.)

Travelers Championship

TPC River Highlands, Cromwell, Connecticut
Par 35-35–70; 6,844 yards

June 21-24
purse, $6,000,000

	SCORES				TOTAL	MONEY
Marc Leishman	68	66	70	62	266	$1,080,000
Charley Hoffman	67	67	67	66	267	528,000
Bubba Watson	66	71	65	65	267	528,000
Tim Clark	66	69	66	67	268	236,250
Brian Davis	67	67	64	70	268	236,250
John Rollins	68	67	65	68	268	236,250
Roland Thatcher	66	67	65	70	268	236,250
Brendon de Jonge	72	65	66	66	269	174,000
Fredrik Jacobson	65	66	70	68	269	174,000
Matt Kuchar	67	68	66	68	269	174,000
Padraig Harrington	69	67	65	69	270	132,000
Hunter Mahan	70	69	70	61	270	132,000
Chez Reavie	66	71	65	68	270	132,000
Vaughn Taylor	70	70	65	65	270	132,000
Will Claxton	65	67	69	70	271	102,000
Heath Slocum	70	66	69	66	271	102,000
Cameron Tringale	69	70	68	64	271	102,000
Stuart Appleby	68	65	67	72	272	75,600
Gary Christian	66	68	72	66	272	75,600
James Driscoll	68	66	66	72	272	75,600
Tommy Gainey	66	68	70	68	272	75,600
Seung-Yul Noh	68	68	68	68	272	75,600
Rory Sabbatini	71	66	68	67	272	75,600
Nathan Green	65	69	70	69	273	49,800
Brian Harman	70	65	69	69	273	49,800
Billy Horschel	71	67	67	68	273	49,800
Bo Van Pelt	70	67	67	69	273	49,800
Charlie Wi	70	65	70	68	273	49,800
Blake Adams	69	64	70	71	274	36,525
Charlie Beljan	73	67	68	66	274	36,525
Keegan Bradley	68	68	70	68	274	36,525
Robert Karlsson	68	68	66	72	274	36,525
Billy Mayfair	68	66	71	69	274	36,525

	SCORES				TOTAL	MONEY
Garth Mulroy	68	69	69	68	274	36,525
Webb Simpson	66	69	68	71	274	36,525
Camilo Villegas	68	64	70	72	274	36,525
Aaron Baddeley	67	68	69	71	275	24,000
Greg Chalmers	67	69	69	70	275	24,000
Chris Couch	72	67	66	70	275	24,000
Tim Herron	72	68	67	68	275	24,000
J.B. Holmes	70	62	75	68	275	24,000
Brandt Jobe	67	72	64	72	275	24,000
Jerry Kelly	66	72	68	69	275	24,000
Derek Lamely	68	71	68	68	275	24,000
Vijay Singh	71	69	67	68	275	24,000
Chris Stroud	71	68	69	67	275	24,000
Roberto Castro	67	70	71	68	276	14,584.62
Chris DiMarco	67	70	71	68	276	14,584.62
Ken Duke	67	69	73	67	276	14,584.62
Billy Hurley	69	67	72	68	276	14,584.62
Ryan Moore	72	67	69	68	276	14,584.62
Louis Oosthuizen	69	69	70	68	276	14,584.62
Johnson Wagner	69	70	69	68	276	14,584.62
Lucas Glover	70	66	71	69	276	14,584.61
J.J. Henry	73	67	65	71	276	14,584.61
Jeff Maggert	69	66	72	69	276	14,584.61
Rocco Mediate	66	70	69	71	276	14,584.61
Patrick Reed	73	66	68	69	276	14,584.61
Kevin Streelman	68	69	67	72	276	14,584.61
Gavin Coles	73	65	70	69	277	13,140
Kyle Stanley	70	67	70	70	277	13,140
Richard H. Lee	72	67	69	70	278	12,900
Ian Poulter	68	71	68	71	278	12,900
Harris English	69	71	67	72	279	12,600
Zach Johnson	72	65	70	72	279	12,600
Bryce Molder	71	67	67	74	279	12,600
Sean O'Hair	70	68	69	73	280	12,360
Graham DeLaet	68	68	70	75	281	12,240
Arjun Atwal	71	68	70	74	283	12,060
Jamie Lovemark	70	70	68	75	283	12,060
Miguel Angel Carballo	71	69	70		210	11,640
George McNeill	73	66	71		210	11,640
John Merrick	72	65	73		210	11,640
Nick O'Hern	68	69	73		210	11,640
Tim Petrovic	71	69	70		210	11,640
Stephen Gangluff	67	71	73		211	11,040
Neal Lancaster	72	68	71		211	11,040
David Mathis	64	73	74		211	11,040
Patrick Sheehan	68	72	71		211	11,040
D.J. Trahan	73	67	71		211	11,040
Brian Gay	68	72	72		212	10,560
Jason Kokrak	74	66	72		212	10,560
Danny Lee	69	70	73		212	10,560
Angel Cabrera	74	66	73		213	10,140
Scott Dunlap	75	65	73		213	10,140
Tom Pernice, Jr.	74	66	73		213	10,140
John Peterson	70	70	73		213	10,140
Bart Bryant	71	69	74		214	9,840

AT&T National

Congressional Country Club, Bethesda, Maryland
Par 36-35–71; 7,529 yards

June 28-July 1
purse, $6,500,000

	SCORES				TOTAL	MONEY
Tiger Woods	72	68	67	69	276	$1,170,000
Bo Van Pelt	67	73	67	71	278	702,000
Adam Scott	75	67	70	67	279	442,000
Robert Garrigus	70	67	73	70	280	255,937.50
Billy Hurley	69	73	66	72	280	255,937.50
Seung-Yul Noh	70	68	69	73	280	255,937.50
Jhonattan Vegas	71	70	68	71	280	255,937.50
Jason Day	69	72	70	70	281	195,000
Hunter Mahan	70	65	73	73	281	195,000
Nick Watney	70	72	69	71	282	175,500
Brendon de Jonge	68	69	69	77	283	143,000
Brian Harman	72	73	71	67	283	143,000
Martin Laird	72	69	73	69	283	143,000
John Mallinger	70	72	68	73	283	143,000
Ryan Palmer	74	67	69	74	284	113,750
Chez Reavie	72	72	67	73	284	113,750
Sang-Moon Bae	75	68	68	74	285	91,000
Greg Chalmers	72	71	72	70	285	91,000
John Huh	72	73	67	73	285	91,000
Greg Owen	70	75	67	73	285	91,000
Daniel Summerhays	70	73	69	73	285	91,000
Stewart Cink	70	68	74	74	286	58,592.86
Ben Crane	77	70	71	68	286	58,592.86
Jeff Overton	79	69	68	70	286	58,592.86
Rod Pampling	71	67	75	73	286	58,592.86
Kyle Stanley	72	75	68	71	286	58,592.86
Charley Hoffman	72	68	71	75	286	58,592.85
Sean O'Hair	73	72	67	74	286	58,592.85
Roberto Castro	74	73	70	70	287	44,200
Troy Matteson	73	70	69	75	287	44,200
Pat Perez	69	69	72	77	287	44,200
Marc Leishman	70	70	71	77	288	39,325
Jimmy Walker	68	69	75	76	288	39,325
Bud Cauley	73	71	71	74	289	31,443.75
Ben Curtis	74	74	73	68	289	31,443.75
Martin Flores	75	71	72	71	289	31,443.75
Jim Furyk	73	73	74	69	289	31,443.75
Hunter Haas	74	72	73	70	289	31,443.75
Brandt Jobe	70	72	70	77	289	31,443.75
Andres Romero	73	71	74	71	289	31,443.75
Heath Slocum	76	70	70	73	289	31,443.75
Bobby Gates	74	68	75	73	290	24,700
Bryce Molder	78	69	72	71	290	24,700
Will Claxton	73	75	71	72	291	20,202
Dustin Johnson	70	76	71	74	291	20,202
K.T. Kim	72	74	72	73	291	20,202
D.J. Trahan	75	72	71	73	291	20,202
Cameron Tringale	74	65	76	76	291	20,202
Blake Adams	72	75	72	73	292	15,527.78
Ricky Barnes	74	72	72	74	292	15,527.78
Brian Davis	74	69	72	77	292	15,527.78
Graham DeLaet	74	74	71	73	292	15,527.78
George McNeill	73	72	73	74	292	15,527.78
Vijay Singh	68	70	73	81	292	15,527.78
Charlie Wi	70	75	74	73	292	15,527.78
Chris DiMarco	76	71	74	71	292	15,527.77
William McGirt	72	76	73	71	292	15,527.77

		SCORES			TOTAL	MONEY
Kevin Chappell	72	73	72	76	293	14,430
Harris English	71	74	73	75	293	14,430
Ryan Moore	73	75	73	72	293	14,430
James Driscoll	70	76	73	76	295	13,910
Ryuji Imada	72	74	73	76	295	13,910
Trevor Immelman	74	68	77	76	295	13,910
Rory Sabbatini	74	73	73	75	295	13,910
Y.E. Yang	76	72	72	75	295	13,910
Patrick Cantlay	72	71	71	82	296	13,455
Bob Estes	74	74	73	75	296	13,455
Erik Compton	73	73	72	79	297	13,130
Charles Howell	70	73	74	80	297	13,130
Brendan Steele	71	76	74	76	297	13,130
J.J. Killeen	72	75	73	79	299	12,870
Brendon Todd	72	76	73	79	300	12,740
Gary Woodland	72	74	75	80	301	12,610
Arjun Atwal	76	72	74		222	12,350
*Beau Hossler	71	74	77		222	
Justin Leonard	75	71	76		222	12,350
Davis Love	70	76	76		222	12,350
J.B. Holmes	72	70	81		223	12,025
Vaughn Taylor	71	76	76		223	12,025
J.J. Henry	77	71	76		224	11,830

Greenbrier Classic

The Old White TPC, White Sulphur Springs, West Virginia
Par 34-36–70; 7,234 yards

July 5-8
purse, $6,100,000

		SCORES			TOTAL	MONEY
Ted Potter, Jr.	69	67	64	64	264	$1,098,000
Troy Kelly	69	67	62	66	264	658,800
(Potter defeated Kelly on third playoff hole.)						
Charlie Beljan	70	62	67	67	266	353,800
Charlie Wi	67	66	68	65	266	353,800
Daniel Summerhays	68	67	68	64	267	244,000
Martin Flores	64	68	69	67	268	219,600
Roberto Castro	71	64	71	63	269	177,510
Ken Duke	66	68	65	70	269	177,510
Kevin Na	69	67	68	65	269	177,510
Sean O'Hair	66	68	69	66	269	177,510
Webb Simpson	65	66	65	73	269	177,510
John Daly	68	67	70	65	270	119,560
Graham DeLaet	67	70	64	69	270	119,560
David Hearn	69	68	67	66	270	119,560
Jerry Kelly	66	66	70	68	270	119,560
Scott Piercy	66	68	68	68	270	119,560
Blake Adams	67	70	64	70	271	85,400
Kevin Chappell	69	66	69	67	271	85,400
Davis Love	69	66	68	68	271	85,400
Jeff Overton	70	65	67	69	271	85,400
Carl Pettersson	71	65	66	69	271	85,400
Jonathan Byrd	64	68	70	70	272	58,560
Will Claxton	73	65	69	65	272	58,560
Garth Mulroy	65	74	67	66	272	58,560
Steve Stricker	69	67	68	68	272	58,560
Steve Wheatcroft	70	68	64	70	272	58,560
Gavin Coles	68	68	69	68	273	42,395
J.B. Holmes	65	68	66	74	273	42,395
Jeff Maggert	64	68	74	67	273	42,395

	SCORES				TOTAL	MONEY
Seung-Yul Noh	68	67	67	71	273	42,395
Rod Pampling	69	67	70	67	273	42,395
Pat Perez	71	66	69	67	273	42,395
Bill Haas	68	69	65	72	274	32,940
Billy Horschel	66	70	67	71	274	32,940
Dustin Johnson	71	67	68	68	274	32,940
Billy Mayfair	69	65	68	72	274	32,940
Vijay Singh	63	74	68	69	274	32,940
Ricky Barnes	69	67	69	70	275	24,400
Kris Blanks	72	66	71	66	275	24,400
Patrick Cantlay	67	70	67	71	275	24,400
Bob Estes	69	65	68	73	275	24,400
Ryuji Imada	71	68	67	69	275	24,400
Richard H. Lee	67	70	69	69	275	24,400
Tim Petrovic	69	68	69	69	275	24,400
Brandt Snedeker	71	68	69	67	275	24,400
Keegan Bradley	68	68	66	74	276	16,909.20
John Huh	71	68	68	69	276	16,909.20
Kenny Perry	70	66	71	69	276	16,909.20
D.A. Points	69	69	70	68	276	16,909.20
Brendon Todd	70	69	68	69	276	16,909.20
*Justin Thomas	67	71	66	72	276	
Sang-Moon Bae	69	70	71	67	277	14,548.50
Chris Couch	68	68	72	69	277	14,548.50
Brendon de Jonge	74	64	68	71	277	14,548.50
Edward Loar	73	64	69	71	277	14,548.50
Ben Curtis	70	68	69	71	278	13,664
Troy Matteson	70	67	71	70	278	13,664
Kyle Reifers	68	70	71	69	278	13,664
Scott Stallings	67	70	70	71	278	13,664
Kevin Streelman	67	68	74	69	278	13,664
D.J. Trahan	69	69	71	69	278	13,664
Cameron Tringale	71	67	70	70	278	13,664
Spencer Levin	73	64	72	70	279	13,176
John Merrick	69	70	68	73	280	12,932
Fran Quinn	68	67	74	71	280	12,932
Johnson Wagner	68	69	67	76	280	12,932
Hunter Haas	69	67	72	73	281	12,627
Charley Hoffman	66	72	73	70	281	12,627
K.J. Choi	66	73	73	70	282	12,322
Brian Harman	69	68	69	76	282	12,322
Russell Knox	69	68	74	71	282	12,322
Tommy Gainey	73	66	74	70	283	12,078
Marc Leishman	70	69	73	72	284	11,834
Roland Thatcher	71	68	72	73	284	11,834
Tom Watson	70	68	71	75	284	11,834
Arjun Atwal	70	69	72	75	286	11,590

John Deere Classic

TPC Deere Run, Silvis, Illinois
Par 35-36–71; 7,257 yards

July 12-15
purse, $4,600,000

	SCORES				TOTAL	MONEY
Zach Johnson	68	65	66	65	264	$828,000
Troy Matteson	61	68	66	69	264	496,800
(Johnson defeated Matteson on second playoff hole.)						
Scott Piercy	65	69	67	65	266	312,800
John Senden	69	64	67	67	267	220,800
Luke Guthrie	65	68	71	64	268	174,800

	SCORES				TOTAL	MONEY
Steve Stricker	65	67	66	70	268	174,800
Scott Brown	70	66	66	67	269	154,100
Chris DiMarco	66	67	68	69	270	124,200
Billy Hurley	68	68	64	70	270	124,200
Lee Janzen	67	65	71	67	270	124,200
Ryan Moore	67	69	66	68	270	124,200
Kevin Streelman	68	69	68	65	270	124,200
K.J. Choi	65	72	67	67	271	81,266.67
Ben Crane	66	67	73	65	271	81,266.67
Tommy Gainey	69	66	69	67	271	81,266.67
Nick Watney	68	68	69	66	271	81,266.67
Erik Compton	68	69	66	68	271	81,266.66
J.J. Henry	67	64	69	71	271	81,266.66
Gary Christian	65	66	70	71	272	53,820
Brendon de Jonge	68	68	67	69	272	53,820
Brian Harman	65	65	69	73	272	53,820
Seung-Yul Noh	68	69	66	69	272	53,820
Rory Sabbatini	67	68	72	65	272	53,820
Kyle Stanley	68	69	69	66	272	53,820
Blake Adams	71	67	68	67	273	35,880
Stuart Appleby	66	69	67	71	273	35,880
Alex Cejka	67	68	71	67	273	35,880
Robert Garrigus	65	66	71	71	273	35,880
Dicky Pride	67	68	73	65	273	35,880
Chris Couch	67	67	70	70	274	27,945
Bobby Gates	66	68	67	73	274	27,945
Chris Kirk	68	68	68	70	274	27,945
Danny Lee	70	68	70	66	274	27,945
Jeff Overton	69	68	69	68	274	27,945
Jimmy Walker	66	71	68	69	274	27,945
Jerry Kelly	69	69	69	68	275	19,805.56
Bill Lunde	66	72	70	67	275	19,805.56
Carl Pettersson	68	69	71	67	275	19,805.56
Josh Teater	69	69	69	68	275	19,805.56
Roland Thatcher	69	68	72	66	275	19,805.56
Chad Campbell	68	70	66	71	275	19,805.55
Tim Clark	67	68	68	72	275	19,805.55
Tom Gillis	66	69	69	71	275	19,805.55
Spencer Levin	66	71	69	69	275	19,805.55
Ricky Barnes	64	67	71	74	276	12,460.89
Kevin Chappell	70	68	73	65	276	12,460.89
Randall Hutchison	68	68	71	69	276	12,460.89
Jeff Maggert	68	62	72	74	276	12,460.89
Vaughn Taylor	72	66	70	68	276	12,460.89
Duffy Waldorf	66	69	69	72	276	12,460.89
Mark Wilson	69	68	69	70	276	12,460.89
Y.E. Yang	68	65	70	73	276	12,460.89
Jamie Lovemark	71	66	64	75	276	12,460.88
Tommy Biershenk	66	66	71	74	277	10,534
Jonathan Byrd	72	66	66	73	277	10,534
Billy Horschel	70	68	65	74	277	10,534
John Merrick	67	67	70	73	277	10,534
Marco Dawson	70	68	74	66	278	10,028
Matt Every	71	65	68	74	278	10,028
Martin Flores	67	67	72	72	278	10,028
Hunter Haas	67	69	74	68	278	10,028
Chris Riley	68	70	71	69	278	10,028
Camilo Villegas	71	66	69	72	278	10,028
Steve Wheatcroft	67	70	69	72	278	10,028
*Jordan Spieth	70	67	72	69	278	
Matt Bettencourt	68	70	69	72	279	9,614
Ted Potter, Jr.	67	66	74	72	279	9,614
Chez Reavie	67	70	70	73	280	9,430

	SCORES				TOTAL	MONEY
Chris Stroud	68	70	70	72	280	9,430
Mathias Gronberg	69	69	69	74	281	9,246
J.J. Killeen	68	68	72	73	281	9,246
Bud Cauley	69	69	75	69	282	9,108
Scott Dunlap	70	68	68	77	283	9,016
Nathan Green	67	69	72	76	284	8,924
Alexandre Rocha	70	68	73	75	286	8,832
Mark Anderson	69	67	73	80	289	8,740

The Open Championship

See European Tours chapter.

True South Classic

Annandale Golf Club, Madison, Mississippi
Par 36-36–72; 7,199 yards

July 19-22
purse, $3,000,000

	SCORES				TOTAL	MONEY
Scott Stallings	68	64	64	68	264	$540,000
Jason Bohn	64	67	68	67	266	324,000
Billy Horschel	68	63	66	71	268	204,000
Bud Cauley	67	66	70	66	269	144,000
Scott Brown	72	66	67	65	270	109,500
Will Claxton	67	67	68	68	270	109,500
William McGirt	70	69	64	67	270	109,500
J.J. Killeen	66	68	69	68	271	93,000
Josh Teater	73	64	71	64	272	87,000
Hunter Hamrick	68	68	69	68	273	75,000
Ryuji Imada	66	71	67	69	273	75,000
Chris Kirk	67	68	69	69	273	75,000
Woody Austin	71	67	66	70	274	54,600
Gary Christian	67	68	69	70	274	54,600
Chris Couch	69	69	67	69	274	54,600
Jerry Kelly	69	69	68	68	274	54,600
Heath Slocum	69	67	67	71	274	54,600
Roberto Castro	67	69	69	70	275	42,000
Luke Guthrie	65	68	72	70	275	42,000
Willie Wood	66	73	67	69	275	42,000
Jason Gore	66	68	66	76	276	26,700
David Hearn	71	67	70	68	276	26,700
J.J. Henry	70	67	71	68	276	26,700
Russell Knox	67	71	71	67	276	26,700
Jonathan Randolph	67	69	68	72	276	26,700
Patrick Reed	73	65	66	72	276	26,700
Chris Riley	70	70	69	67	276	26,700
Duffy Waldorf	68	69	68	71	276	26,700
Boo Weekley	67	73	66	70	276	26,700
Garrett Willis	66	71	71	68	276	26,700
Stuart Appleby	69	71	69	68	277	16,650
Shane Bertsch	68	71	69	69	277	16,650
Glen Day	70	71	70	66	277	16,650
Brendon de Jonge	70	66	68	73	277	16,650
Ken Duke	68	67	70	72	277	16,650
Tommy Gainey	70	68	66	73	277	16,650
Skip Kendall	68	71	69	69	277	16,650
Len Mattiace	69	70	70	68	277	16,650
Steven Bowditch	66	67	71	74	278	12,900
Mathew Goggin	66	71	72	69	278	12,900

	SCORES				TOTAL	MONEY
Gene Sauers	73	67	68	70	278	12,900
Tim Petrovic	70	67	71	71	279	9,917.15
Paul Stankowski	66	70	72	71	279	9,917.15
Cameron Beckman	69	71	65	74	279	9,917.14
Michael Bradley	68	72	66	73	279	9,917.14
Gavin Coles	68	68	72	71	279	9,917.14
Brian Gay	71	70	70	68	279	9,917.14
Rocco Mediate	67	69	71	72	279	9,917.14
Eric Axley	73	67	69	71	280	7,215
Matt Bettencourt	66	66	76	72	280	7,215
Guy Boros	70	69	66	75	280	7,215
Mark Brooks	71	68	72	69	280	7,215
Jason Kokrak	69	66	74	71	280	7,215
Steve Lowery	66	75	70	69	280	7,215
Alexandre Rocha	67	73	70	70	280	7,215
Vaughn Taylor	72	67	69	72	280	7,215
Marco Dawson	67	71	72	71	281	6,660
Kevin Kisner	68	71	72	70	281	6,660
Dicky Pride	75	66	71	69	281	6,660
Chris Stroud	69	66	76	70	281	6,660
Kyle Thompson	69	72	67	73	281	6,660
Alex Cejka	70	69	73	70	282	6,450
Ted Purdy	69	72	71	70	282	6,450
Mark Anderson	68	73	73	69	283	6,300
Scott Dunlap	71	69	76	67	283	6,300
Patrick Sheehan	69	69	71	74	283	6,300
Arjun Atwal	70	71	70	73	284	6,150
Robert Gamez	68	71	71	74	284	6,150
Bill Lunde	70	71	74	70	285	6,000
Roland Thatcher	71	69	76	69	285	6,000
Omar Uresti	68	72	74	71	285	6,000
Matt Jones	69	70	75	72	286	5,850
Brendon Todd	72	67	72	75	286	5,850
Kyle Reifers	69	70	72	76	287	5,760

RBC Canadian Open

Hamilton Golf & Country Club, Ancaster, Ontario, Canada
Par 35-35–70; 6,966 yards

July 26-29
purse, $5,200,000

	SCORES				TOTAL	MONEY
Scott Piercy	62	67	67	67	263	$936,000
Robert Garrigus	64	66	64	70	264	457,600
William McGirt	63	66	66	69	264	457,600
Josh Teater	67	65	68	66	266	214,933.34
Bud Cauley	70	63	67	66	266	214,933.33
Chris Kirk	69	66	63	68	266	214,933.33
Vijay Singh	65	67	69	67	268	162,066.67
Bo Van Pelt	65	66	67	70	268	162,066.67
Scott Stallings	69	66	63	70	268	162,066.66
Gary Christian	71	68	65	66	270	119,600
Retief Goosen	68	70	63	69	270	119,600
Nathan Green	70	67	65	68	270	119,600
Kevin Kisner	69	65	67	69	270	119,600
Troy Matteson	65	68	69	68	270	119,600
Tim Clark	70	62	72	67	271	85,800
Brian Davis	69	68	65	69	271	85,800
J.B. Holmes	68	68	64	71	271	85,800
Seung-Yul Noh	72	66	68	65	271	85,800
Will Claxton	70	66	68	68	272	54,715.56

	SCORES				TOTAL	MONEY
Gavin Coles	65	69	70	68	272	54,715.56
Martin Flores	69	67	68	68	272	54,715.56
Tom Gillis	70	65	73	64	272	54,715.56
Brian Harman	74	63	71	64	272	54,715.56
Ken Duke	70	65	67	70	272	54,715.55
Ryan Palmer	69	67	64	72	272	54,715.55
Brendon Todd	69	66	66	71	272	54,715.55
Cameron Tringale	67	69	67	69	272	54,715.55
Thomas Aiken	69	66	69	69	273	34,580
Stuart Appleby	65	69	69	70	273	34,580
Arjun Atwal	69	67	67	70	273	34,580
Brian Gay	70	67	70	66	273	34,580
Jhonattan Vegas	65	74	67	67	273	34,580
Jimmy Walker	68	68	69	68	273	34,580
Scott Dunlap	69	69	66	70	274	28,080
Matt Kuchar	67	69	68	70	274	28,080
Brandt Snedeker	70	67	71	66	274	28,080
J.J. Henry	67	70	68	70	275	23,400
Bill Lunde	66	70	67	72	275	23,400
Tom Pernice, Jr.	68	70	67	70	275	23,400
Chez Reavie	68	70	72	65	275	23,400
Patrick Sheehan	68	66	69	72	275	23,400
Miguel Angel Carballo	68	71	72	65	276	17,680
Billy Horschel	71	68	73	64	276	17,680
Ryo Ishikawa	67	69	73	67	276	17,680
Garth Mulroy	73	63	69	71	276	17,680
Charl Schwartzel	65	74	69	68	276	17,680
Daniel Summerhays	67	68	69	72	276	17,680
Ricky Barnes	71	67	68	71	277	12,805
Michael Bradley	69	68	70	70	277	12,805
John Daly	69	69	73	66	277	12,805
Tommy Gainey	69	65	69	74	277	12,805
Colt Knost	71	67	71	68	277	12,805
Richard H. Lee	70	67	70	70	277	12,805
Hunter Mahan	70	69	72	66	277	12,805
Heath Slocum	67	70	70	70	277	12,805
Graham DeLaet	69	69	70	70	278	11,648
John Huh	67	70	70	71	278	11,648
Russell Knox	68	66	73	71	278	11,648
Greg Owen	63	72	73	70	278	11,648
Ted Potter, Jr.	69	66	72	71	278	11,648
Patrick Cantlay	69	70	74	66	279	10,868
Daniel Chopra	72	65	68	74	279	10,868
Matt Every	70	69	71	69	279	10,868
Trevor Immelman	70	67	74	68	279	10,868
Jerry Kelly	70	68	72	69	279	10,868
Jeff Overton	71	68	71	69	279	10,868
Kyle Stanley	71	68	71	69	279	10,868
Chris Stroud	72	67	74	66	279	10,868
Michael Thompson	68	70	73	68	279	10,868
Camilo Villegas	69	64	73	73	279	10,868
David Hearn	68	68	72	72	280	10,244
Jason Kokrak	69	67	72	72	280	10,244
Kevin Streelman	68	71	72	70	281	10,088
*Albin Choi	69	68	72	72	281	
Matt Hill	70	69	71	73	283	9,932
Matt McQuillan	70	67	77	69	283	9,932
Tim Herron	70	68	73	73	284	9,724
Spencer Levin	68	71	70	75	284	9,724
Harrison Frazar	69	69	77	71	286	9,568

WGC - Bridgestone Invitational

Firestone Country Club, South Course, Akron, Ohio
Par 35-35–70; 7,400 yards

August 2-5
purse, $8,500,000

	SCORES				TOTAL	MONEY
Keegan Bradley	67	69	67	64	267	$1,400,000
Jim Furyk	63	66	70	69	268	665,000
Steve Stricker	68	68	68	64	268	665,000
Louis Oosthuizen	67	65	68	69	269	365,000
Rory McIlroy	70	67	67	68	272	276,500
Justin Rose	70	69	66	67	272	276,500
Jason Dufner	67	66	73	68	274	210,000
Aaron Baddeley	73	66	71	66	276	128,750
K.J. Choi	71	72	67	66	276	128,750
Luke Donald	66	69	71	70	276	128,750
Matt Kuchar	70	70	70	66	276	128,750
Lee Slattery	65	71	72	68	276	128,750
David Toms	68	67	73	68	276	128,750
Bo Van Pelt	70	69	66	71	276	128,750
Tiger Woods	70	72	68	66	276	128,750
Simon Dyson	66	71	70	70	277	90,000
John Senden	66	70	69	72	277	90,000
Kyle Stanley	69	73	68	67	277	90,000
Bill Haas	67	71	70	70	278	82,000
Dustin Johnson	69	68	73	68	278	82,000
Scott Piercy	69	70	70	69	278	82,000
Nick Watney	69	70	72	67	278	82,000
Bubba Watson	66	73	72	67	278	82,000
K.T. Kim	67	67	74	71	279	74,500
Graeme McDowell	70	67	70	72	279	74,500
Geoff Ogilvy	67	70	72	70	279	74,500
Charl Schwartzel	69	75	72	63	279	74,500
Carl Pettersson	67	70	71	72	280	72,000
Rafa Cabrera-Bello	66	65	77	73	281	68,000
Jason Day	75	70	70	66	281	68,000
Sergio Garcia	67	72	71	71	281	68,000
Retief Goosen	67	72	73	69	281	68,000
Martin Kaymer	68	72	72	69	281	68,000
Martin Laird	68	72	68	73	281	68,000
Ian Poulter	74	69	69	69	281	68,000
Jamie Donaldson	68	73	75	66	282	62,500
Branden Grace	72	70	66	74	282	62,500
Johnson Wagner	71	74	68	69	282	62,500
Y.E. Yang	69	71	74	68	282	62,500
Thomas Bjorn	71	70	74	68	283	59,000
Zach Johnson	68	73	68	74	283	59,000
Francesco Molinari	74	70	69	70	283	59,000
Phil Mickelson	71	69	73	71	284	56,500
Alvaro Quiros	70	71	72	71	284	56,500
Nicolas Colsaerts	73	68	74	70	285	53,000
Ernie Els	73	73	68	71	285	53,000
Marc Leishman	70	72	70	73	285	53,000
Adam Scott	71	70	71	73	285	53,000
Mark Wilson	72	71	73	69	285	53,000
Ryo Ishikawa	71	72	70	73	286	49,000
Fredrik Jacobson	71	73	73	69	286	49,000
Paul Lawrie	72	68	74	72	286	49,000
Brandt Snedeker	71	70	70	75	286	49,000
Danny Willett	72	74	73	67	286	49,000
Jonathan Byrd	73	73	69	72	287	46,500
Greg Chalmers	71	75	71	70	287	46,500
Gonzalo Fernandez-Castano	71	73	70	73	287	46,500

	SCORES				TOTAL	MONEY
Hunter Mahan	73	73	69	72	287	46,500
Bernd Wiesberger	70	71	74	72	287	46,500
Rickie Fowler	70	80	69	69	288	44,500
Yoshinori Fujimoto	73	74	71	70	288	44,500
Marcel Siem	76	71	70	71	288	44,500
Peter Hanson	73	71	71	74	289	43,500
Joost Luiten	72	71	77	69	289	43,500
Kevin Na	72	76	72	69	289	43,500
Sang-Moon Bae	72	66	76	76	290	43,000
Toshinori Muto	73	71	73	74	291	42,625
Jeev Milkha Singh	73	74	71	73	291	42,625
Robert Allenby	73	79	72	68	292	42,250
Lee Westwood	68	72	81	73	294	42,000
Michael Hoey	78	75	70	72	295	41,625
Robert Rock	76	72	74	73	295	41,625
Ted Potter, Jr.	72	72	75	80	299	41,250
Tom Lewis	78	76	74	73	301	41,000
Oliver Bekker	77	72	76	77	302	40,750
Ben Crane	66	75			WD	
Toru Taniguchi	72	78			WD	
Thongchai Jaidee	73				WD	

Reno-Tahoe Open

Montreux Golf & Country Club, Reno, Nevada
Par 36-36–72; 7,432 yards

August 2-5
purse, $3,000,000

	POINTS				TOTAL	MONEY
J.J. Henry	10	12	14	7	43	$540,000
Alexandre Rocha	8	16	9	9	42	324,000
Andres Romero	14	7	10	6	37	204,000
John Mallinger	11	11	10	2	34	144,000
John Daly	10	9	9	5	33	114,000
Justin Leonard	5	10	11	7	33	114,000
Josh Teater	11	-3	14	9	31	100,500
Todd Hamilton	9	6	8	7	30	87,000
Tom Pernice, Jr.	7	6	11	6	30	87,000
Brendan Steele	6	10	7	7	30	87,000
Kevin Stadler	5	8	11	5	29	75,000
J.B. Holmes	1	17	5	5	28	66,000
Richard H. Lee	4	5	8	11	28	66,000
Kevin Chappell	7	5	9	6	27	55,500
John Merrick	6	11	7	3	27	55,500
Stuart Appleby	8	1	10	7	26	49,500
Joe Durant	8	9	7	2	26	49,500
Bill Lunde	4	10	14	-3	25	45,000
Jason Bohn	4	6	8	6	24	40,500
Padraig Harrington	7	7	9	1	24	40,500
Ricky Barnes	11	5	7	0	23	31,200
Matt Bettencourt	8	12	0	3	23	31,200
Gary Christian	5	11	12	-5	23	31,200
Scott Dunlap	3	9	2	9	23	31,200
Brett Wetterich	4	11	4	4	23	31,200
Cameron Beckman	6	4	3	9	22	22,200
Glen Day	6	1	8	7	22	22,200
Billy Horschel	4	3	6	9	22	22,200
Chris Kirk	9	8	5	0	22	22,200
D.J. Trahan	-2	10	10	4	22	22,200
Hunter Haas	10	8	1	2	21	17,400
Hwang Jung-gon	2	11	0	8	21	17,400

	POINTS			TOTAL	MONEY
Lee Janzen	1	7	11	2	21	17,400
J.J. Killeen	4	6	8	3	21	17,400
Seung-Yul Noh	13	3	9	-4	21	17,400
Marc Turnesa	5	7	1	8	21	17,400
Guy Boros	7	4	6	3	20	13,800
Patrick Cantlay	10	5	4	1	20	13,800
Stewart Cink	3	5	7	5	20	13,800
Chris Riley	3	9	7	1	20	13,800
Billy Mayfair	9	1	5	4	19	12,000
Dicky Pride	1	8	3	7	19	12,000
Brian Gay	4	4	8	2	18	9,900
Russell Knox	5	3	4	6	18	9,900
John Rollins	8	1	5	4	18	9,900
Brendon Todd	8	4	6	0	18	9,900
Steve Wheatcroft	-1	13	4	2	18	9,900
Charlie Beljan	5	4	7	1	17	7,540
Shane Bertsch	7	1	7	2	17	7,540
Troy Kelly	3	8	6	0	17	7,540
Jason Kokrak	3	4	6	4	17	7,540
John Peterson	6	7	-2	6	17	7,540
Heath Slocum	7	7	1	2	17	7,540
Miguel Angel Carballo	6	2	5	3	16	6,810
Richard S. Johnson	4	3	3	6	16	6,810
Danny Lee	10	6	5	-5	16	6,810
Rod Pampling	0	9	5	2	16	6,810
John Riegger	7	5	7	-3	16	6,810
Boo Weekley	1	6	0	9	16	6,810
Erik Compton	2	9	4	0	15	6,570
Nick O'Hern	7	8	-3	3	15	6,570
Brandon Brown	-1	14	-3	3	13	6,480
Arjun Atwal	7	14	-1	-8	12	6,360
Kevin Kisner	1	6	2	3	12	6,360
Ted Purdy	4	3	7	-2	12	6,360
David Duval	6	8	-2	-1	11	6,240
Jake Sarnoff	6	3	4	-4	9	6,180
Nathan Green	-1	9	-6	6	8	6,120
Bryce Molder	9	0	-1	-1	7	6,060
Scott Smith	0	9	-1	-2	6	6,000

PGA Championship

Kiawah Island Resort, Ocean Course,
Kiawah Island, South Carolina
Par 36-36–72; 7,676 yards

August 9-12
purse, $8,000,000

	SCORES				TOTAL	MONEY
Rory McIlroy	67	75	67	66	275	$1,445,000
David Lynn	73	74	68	68	283	865,000
Justin Rose	69	79	70	66	284	384,500
Keegan Bradley	68	77	71	68	284	384,500
Ian Poulter	70	71	74	69	284	384,500
Carl Pettersson	66	74	72	72	284	384,500
Blake Adams	71	72	75	67	285	226,000
Jamie Donaldson	69	73	73	70	285	226,000
Peter Hanson	69	75	70	71	285	226,000
Steve Stricker	74	73	67	71	285	226,000
Ben Curtis	69	77	73	67	286	143,285.71
Bubba Watson	73	75	70	68	286	143,285.71
Tim Clark	71	73	73	69	286	143,285.71
Geoff Ogilvy	68	78	70	70	286	143,285.71

		SCORES			TOTAL	MONEY
Graeme McDowell	68	76	71	71	286	143,285.71
Tiger Woods	69	71	74	72	286	143,285.71
Adam Scott	68	75	70	73	286	143,285.71
John Daly	68	77	73	69	287	99,666.66
Padraig Harrington	70	76	69	72	287	99,666.66
Bo Van Pelt	73	73	67	74	287	99,666.66
Louis Oosthuizen	70	79	70	69	288	72,666.66
Joost Luiten	68	76	75	69	288	72,666.66
Robert Garrigus	74	73	74	67	288	72,666.66
Pat Perez	69	76	71	72	288	72,666.66
Seung-Yul Noh	74	75	74	65	288	72,666.66
Jimmy Walker	73	75	67	73	288	72,666.66
Thorbjorn Olesen	75	74	71	69	289	51,900
Miguel Angel Jimenez	69	77	72	71	289	51,900
Jason Dufner	74	76	68	71	289	51,900
Marc Leishman	74	72	71	72	289	51,900
Trevor Immelman	71	72	70	76	289	51,900
John Senden	73	74	72	71	290	42,625
Greg Chalmers	70	76	72	72	290	42,625
Bill Haas	75	73	69	73	290	42,625
Luke Donald	74	76	74	66	290	42,625
Fredrik Jacobson	71	75	73	72	291	34,750
Rich Beem	72	76	72	71	291	34,750
Y.E. Yang	73	74	74	70	291	34,750
Phil Mickelson	73	71	73	74	291	34,750
Marcel Siem	72	73	71	75	291	34,750
Vijay Singh	71	69	74	77	291	34,750
J.J. Henry	72	77	70	73	292	25,750
Jim Furyk	72	77	70	73	292	25,750
Aaron Baddeley	68	75	74	75	292	25,750
Gary Woodland	67	79	75	71	292	25,750
David Toms	72	78	72	70	292	25,750
Martin Laird	71	74	79	68	292	25,750
Paul Lawrie	73	75	71	74	293	18,625
Ernie Els	72	75	73	73	293	18,625
Dustin Johnson	71	79	72	71	293	18,625
Thomas Bjorn	70	79	74	70	293	18,625
Retief Goosen	73	75	75	70	293	18,625
Scott Piercy	68	78	78	69	293	18,625
Francesco Molinari	70	75	74	75	294	16,810
Sang-Moon Bae	72	78	71	73	294	16,810
Darren Clarke	73	76	72	73	294	16,810
Brendon de Jonge	71	78	72	73	294	16,810
K.J. Choi	69	77	75	73	294	16,810
Charl Schwartzel	70	77	74	74	295	16,100
Ryo Ishikawa	69	77	79	70	295	16,100
K.T. Kim	69	77	77	73	296	15,900
Gonzalo Fernandez-Castano	67	78	75	77	297	15,650
Chez Reavie	74	76	73	74	297	15,650
Ken Duke	71	78	74	74	297	15,650
George McNeill	71	76	80	70	297	15,650
Alex Noren	67	80	73	78	298	15,350
Marcus Fraser	74	75	78	71	298	15,350
Toru Taniguchi	72	76	78	73	299	15,150
John Huh	72	78	79	70	299	15,150
Zach Johnson	72	73	76	79	300	15,000
Matt Every	72	76	74	82	304	14,900
Cameron Tringale	69	78	77	82	306	14,800

Out of Final 36 Holes

Thomas Aiken	72	79	151
Robert Allenby	75	76	151
George Coetzee	73	78	151
Nicolas Colsaerts	73	78	151
Hiroyuki Fujita	72	79	151
Sergio Garcia	76	75	151
Anders Hansen	72	79	151
Davis Love	72	79	151
Ted Potter, Jr.	74	77	151
Webb Simpson	79	72	151
Johnson Wagner	75	76	151
Bernd Wiesberger	72	79	151
Jonathan Byrd	73	79	152
Rafa Cabrera-Bello	71	81	152
Stewart Cink	74	78	152
Jason Day	72	80	152
Robert Karlsson	74	78	152
Hunter Mahan	72	80	152
William McGirt	73	79	152
Ryan Moore	73	79	152
Bob Sowards	75	77	152
Lee Westwood	75	77	152
Mark Wilson	76	76	152
Jeff Coston	74	79	153
Simon Dyson	73	80	153
Branden Grace	74	79	153
Charles Howell	76	77	153
Thongchai Jaidee	73	80	153
Matteo Manassero	71	82	153
Bryce Molder	75	78	153
Scott Stallings	74	79	153
Rickie Fowler	74	80	154
Brendan Jones	76	78	154
Matt Kuchar	72	82	154
John Rollins	72	82	154
Mike Small	76	78	154
Chris Stroud	73	81	154
Michael Thompson	73	81	154
Bud Cauley	80	75	155
Lucas Glover	77	78	155
Darrell Kestner	75	80	155
Shaun Micheel	72	83	155
Alan Morin	74	81	155
Jeff Overton	74	81	155
Rory Sabbatini	73	82	155
Brandt Snedeker	77	78	155
Nick Watney	73	82	155
Danny Balin	77	79	156
Angel Cabrera	76	80	156
Roger Chapman	78	78	156
Spencer Levin	78	78	156
Charley Hoffman	81	76	157
Pablo Larrazabal	77	80	157
Kelly Mitchum	76	81	157
Ryan Palmer	71	86	157
Rod Perry	75	82	157
Charlie Wi	79	78	157
Brian Cairns	75	83	158
Tommy Gainey	77	81	158
Martin Kaymer	79	79	158
Mitch Lowe	79	79	158
Kyle Stanley	80	78	158
Alvaro Quiros	76	83	159
Jeev Milkha Singh	76	83	159
Frank Bensel	84	76	160
Mark Brooks	78	82	160
Matt Dobyns	81	79	160
Jose Maria Olazabal	74	86	160
D.A. Points	73	87	160
Brian Gaffney	76	85	161
Brian Davis	75	87	162
Marty Jertson	80	82	162
Robert Rock	76	86	162
Paul Scaletta	75	87	162
Corey Prugh	78	85	163
Mark Brown	78	86	164
Paul Casey	79	85	164
Bill Murchison	82	86	168
Michael Frye	79	90	169
Doug Wade	83	93	176

Wyndham Championship

Sedgefield Country Club, Greensboro, North Carolina
Par 35-35–70; 7,130 yards
(Event completed on Monday—rain.)

August 16-20
purse, $5,200,000

	SCORES				TOTAL	MONEY
Sergio Garcia	67	63	66	66	262	$936,000
Tim Clark	63	67	67	67	264	561,600
Bud Cauley	66	65	66	68	265	353,600
Chad Campbell	71	64	65	66	266	214,933.34
Carl Pettersson	62	68	68	68	266	214,933.33
Jimmy Walker	66	62	71	67	266	214,933.33
Nicolas Colsaerts	67	65	69	66	267	162,066.67
Bill Haas	68	65	67	67	267	162,066.67
Jason Dufner	68	67	63	69	267	162,066.66
Harris English	66	64	68	70	268	124,800
Davis Love	67	66	66	69	268	124,800
Troy Matteson	64	68	68	68	268	124,800

	SCORES				TOTAL	MONEY
John Merrick	66	69	67	66	268	124,800
Brendon de Jonge	68	68	67	66	269	88,400
Matt Every	65	66	68	70	269	88,400
Richard H. Lee	66	69	65	69	269	88,400
Charl Schwartzel	67	68	66	68	269	88,400
Scott Stallings	64	70	67	68	269	88,400
Bobby Gates	69	67	65	69	270	67,600
John Huh	69	65	69	67	270	67,600
Justin Leonard	68	68	64	70	270	67,600
Angel Cabrera	67	71	66	67	271	48,273.34
Chris Kirk	66	69	69	67	271	48,273.34
Graham DeLaet	69	67	67	68	271	48,273.33
Trevor Immelman	67	68	68	68	271	48,273.33
Rocco Mediate	70	65	68	68	271	48,273.33
Webb Simpson	66	63	71	71	271	48,273.33
Tim Herron	76	61	67	68	272	36,920
Rod Pampling	68	66	70	68	272	36,920
Brandt Snedeker	67	67	68	70	272	36,920
Patrick Cantlay	70	68	66	69	273	30,160
Will Claxton	69	66	65	73	273	30,160
Charles Howell	67	69	71	66	273	30,160
Heath Slocum	68	67	67	71	273	30,160
Kyle Thompson	69	67	68	69	273	30,160
Nick Watney	66	69	70	68	273	30,160
Gary Christian	67	70	67	70	274	21,320
Russell Knox	68	68	69	69	274	21,320
Ryan Moore	71	68	68	67	274	21,320
Jeff Overton	69	69	67	69	274	21,320
D.A. Points	68	68	67	71	274	21,320
Kyle Reifers	67	72	66	69	274	21,320
Kevin Streelman	68	66	68	72	274	21,320
Josh Teater	67	71	69	67	274	21,320
Y.E. Yang	67	69	69	69	274	21,320
Billy Horschel	69	67	66	73	275	14,742
Kevin Kisner	68	71	70	66	275	14,742
Nick O'Hern	68	71	67	69	275	14,742
Kevin Stadler	73	65	68	69	275	14,742
Jamie Donaldson	68	66	71	71	276	12,542.40
Tommy Gainey	66	67	68	75	276	12,542.40
Jerry Kelly	72	67	69	68	276	12,542.40
Dicky Pride	69	68	67	72	276	12,542.40
Alexandre Rocha	68	68	69	71	276	12,542.40
Jonas Blixt	72	67	67	71	277	11,856
Derek Lamely	69	68	70	70	277	11,856
David Mathis	63	71	73	70	277	11,856
Blake Adams	67	71	67	73	278	11,440
Scott Dunlap	70	69	67	72	278	11,440
Ryuji Imada	67	70	70	71	278	11,440
Chez Reavie	67	69	71	71	278	11,440
Charlie Wi	72	67	70	69	278	11,440
Troy Kelly	71	68	69	71	279	11,128
Billy Mayfair	69	70	74	67	280	11,024
Jeff Maggert	68	71	74	68	281	10,920
Arjun Atwal	66	69	75	72	282	10,660
Cameron Beckman	73	66	69	74	282	10,660
Tom Pernice, Jr.	70	68	74	70	282	10,660
Brendan Steele	72	65	71	74	282	10,660
Stuart Appleby	67	71	69	76	283	10,296
Ben Kohles	72	67	70	74	283	10,296
Camilo Villegas	72	67	70	74	283	10,296
Jason Kokrak	66	69	77	73	285	10,036
Chris Stroud	68	70	72	75	285	10,036
Paul Casey	68	70	77	75	290	9,880

PGA Tour Playoffs for the FedExCup

The Barclays

Bethpage State Park, Farmingdale, New York
Par 36-35–71; 7,468 yards

August 23-26
purse, $8,000,000

	SCORES			TOTAL	MONEY
Nick Watney	65	69	71	69	274	$1,440,000
Brandt Snedeker	70	69	68	70	277	864,000
Sergio Garcia	66	68	69	75	278	464,000
Dustin Johnson	67	71	72	68	278	464,000
Graham DeLaet	75	67	72	65	279	281,000
Brian Harman	65	75	68	71	279	281,000
Louis Oosthuizen	70	71	68	70	279	281,000
Lee Westwood	69	72	68	70	279	281,000
Greg Chalmers	70	70	68	72	280	232,000
Bud Cauley	71	71	72	67	281	160,888.89
Tim Clark	70	72	67	72	281	160,888.89
Luke Donald	68	74	69	70	281	160,888.89
Bob Estes	69	66	72	74	281	160,888.89
Tom Gillis	69	72	68	72	281	160,888.89
David Hearn	70	73	67	71	281	160,888.89
William McGirt	68	74	67	72	281	160,888.89
Bubba Watson	70	70	70	71	281	160,888.89
Kevin Stadler	72	69	65	75	281	160,888.88
Padraig Harrington	64	75	75	68	282	96,960
J.B. Holmes	71	69	73	69	282	96,960
Geoff Ogilvy	70	72	69	71	282	96,960
John Senden	68	68	72	74	282	96,960
Josh Teater	72	71	69	70	282	96,960
Ricky Barnes	71	72	70	70	283	56,700
Roberto Castro	76	67	69	71	283	56,700
Jason Day	70	70	77	66	283	56,700
Harris English	70	69	71	73	283	56,700
Rickie Fowler	67	70	75	71	283	56,700
Rory McIlroy	69	73	69	72	283	56,700
Ryan Moore	69	69	70	75	283	56,700
Ryan Palmer	75	68	68	72	283	56,700
Carl Pettersson	73	66	73	71	283	56,700
Charl Schwartzel	71	69	69	74	283	56,700
Scott Stallings	72	70	71	70	283	56,700
Bo Van Pelt	70	69	74	70	283	56,700
John Huh	70	67	77	70	284	40,200
Ian Poulter	68	71	76	69	284	40,200
Tommy Gainey	70	70	73	72	285	32,000
Zach Johnson	68	75	72	70	285	32,000
Matt Kuchar	72	68	73	72	285	32,000
Phil Mickelson	68	74	67	76	285	32,000
Greg Owen	68	73	72	72	285	32,000
Pat Perez	66	70	77	72	285	32,000
Jimmy Walker	66	74	74	71	285	32,000
Tiger Woods	68	69	72	76	285	32,000
Jonas Blixt	67	73	73	73	286	21,080
Gary Christian	66	71	77	72	286	21,080
Chris Kirk	68	71	76	71	286	21,080
Billy Mayfair	71	72	71	72	286	21,080
Bryce Molder	70	73	71	72	286	21,080
Rod Pampling	70	73	74	69	286	21,080
Justin Rose	67	72	79	68	286	21,080

	SCORES				TOTAL	MONEY
Vijay Singh	68	67	76	75	286	21,080
Ernie Els	68	72	72	75	287	18,000
Brian Gay	71	72	72	72	287	18,000
Charles Howell	71	69	77	70	287	18,000
Troy Kelly	74	66	74	73	287	18,000
Sean O'Hair	71	72	73	71	287	18,000
John Rollins	72	69	74	72	287	18,000
Henrik Stenson	73	65	78	71	287	18,000
Steve Stricker	69	71	73	74	287	18,000
Adam Scott	70	69	74	75	288	17,280
Kevin Streelman	69	72	76	72	289	17,040
Michael Thompson	71	68	77	73	289	17,040
Blake Adams	71	69	78	72	290	16,720
Troy Matteson	68	73	76	73	290	16,720
Trevor Immelman	75	66	75	75	291	16,240
Fredrik Jacobson	71	68	79	73	291	16,240
George McNeill	67	76	71	77	291	16,240
Seung-Yul Noh	71	71	78	71	291	16,240
Robert Garrigus	73	68	77	74	292	15,760
Martin Laird	70	68	77	77	292	15,760
K.J. Choi	67	71	80	75	293	15,440
Jeff Maggert	69	74	74	76	293	15,440
James Driscoll	73	70	75	77	295	15,200

Deutsche Bank Championship

TPC Boston, Norton, Massachusetts
Par 36-35–71; 7,214 yards

August 31-September 3
purse, $8,000,000

	SCORES				TOTAL	MONEY
Rory McIlroy	65	65	67	67	264	$1,440,000
Louis Oosthuizen	66	65	63	71	265	864,000
Tiger Woods	64	68	68	66	266	544,000
Dustin Johnson	67	68	65	70	270	352,000
Phil Mickelson	68	68	68	66	270	352,000
Brandt Snedeker	69	70	65	67	271	288,000
Jeff Overton	64	71	69	68	272	258,000
Adam Scott	69	69	68	66	272	258,000
Bryce Molder	65	69	68	71	273	232,000
Ryan Moore	64	68	70	72	274	208,000
Kevin Stadler	68	71	69	66	274	208,000
John Senden	66	69	70	70	275	184,000
Keegan Bradley	71	73	63	69	276	145,600
Jim Furyk	69	72	65	70	276	145,600
Seung-Yul Noh	62	71	75	68	276	145,600
Steve Stricker	69	69	68	70	276	145,600
Lee Westwood	68	71	69	68	276	145,600
Jason Dufner	67	66	70	74	277	116,000
Webb Simpson	69	70	66	72	277	116,000
Jonas Blixt	67	72	71	68	278	86,666.67
Troy Matteson	72	67	70	69	278	86,666.67
John Merrick	68	72	68	70	278	86,666.67
Dicky Pride	69	72	69	68	278	86,666.67
D.A. Points	68	65	71	74	278	86,666.66
Nick Watney	72	69	66	71	278	86,666.66
William McGirt	69	72	69	69	279	54,444.45
Pat Perez	69	72	69	69	279	54,444.45
Vijay Singh	73	69	68	69	279	54,444.45
Bo Van Pelt	69	71	70	69	279	54,444.45
Luke Donald	67	72	70	70	279	54,444.44

	SCORES			TOTAL	MONEY
Ernie Els	69	69	71	70	279	54,444.44
Tom Gillis	69	69	71	70	279	54,444.44
David Hearn	67	69	68	75	279	54,444.44
Charley Hoffman	67	67	69	76	279	54,444.44
Matt Every	71	68	68	73	280	40,300
Bill Haas	71	72	68	69	280	40,300
Chris Kirk	63	70	75	72	280	40,300
Matt Kuchar	70	74	68	68	280	40,300
Greg Chalmers	69	68	73	71	281	34,400
J.B. Holmes	72	69	69	71	281	34,400
Hunter Mahan	68	72	70	71	281	34,400
Aaron Baddeley	68	74	70	70	282	28,000
Bob Estes	71	69	73	69	282	28,000
Robert Garrigus	71	67	73	71	282	28,000
Marc Leishman	72	71	70	69	282	28,000
Kyle Stanley	70	70	71	71	282	28,000
Zach Johnson	70	71	71	71	283	21,520
George McNeill	71	70	72	70	283	21,520
Ian Poulter	67	71	75	70	283	21,520
Charl Schwartzel	68	65	79	71	283	21,520
Roberto Castro	72	72	69	71	284	18,826.67
Jason Day	68	73	72	71	284	18,826.67
Geoff Ogilvy	72	69	73	70	284	18,826.67
Jimmy Walker	73	71	72	68	284	18,826.67
John Huh	71	73	69	71	284	18,826.66
Johnson Wagner	70	71	69	74	284	18,826.66
Bud Cauley	68	73	71	73	285	18,000
Carl Pettersson	71	70	75	69	285	18,000
Padraig Harrington	70	74	75	67	286	17,760
Blake Adams	69	73	74	71	287	17,360
Brendon de Jonge	70	73	73	71	287	17,360
J.J. Henry	69	73	72	73	287	17,360
Josh Teater	71	71	71	74	287	17,360
Sean O'Hair	70	74	69	75	288	16,880
Scott Piercy	72	70	73	73	288	16,880
Tommy Gainey	72	70	71	76	289	16,480
Scott Stallings	70	73	74	72	289	16,480
Mark Wilson	74	70	74	71	289	16,480
Harris English	70	73	73	74	290	15,840
Martin Flores	72	71	73	74	290	15,840
Kevin Na	69	75	73	73	290	15,840
Ted Potter, Jr.	69	68	72	81	290	15,840
Daniel Summerhays	71	70	72	77	290	15,840
Rickie Fowler	71	72	72	76	291	15,200
Brian Harman	71	73	72	75	291	15,200
Graeme McDowell	74	70	75	72	291	15,200
Jonathan Byrd	72	72	73	75	292	14,880
Sang-Moon Bae	69	72	77	78	296	14,720

BMW Championship

Crooked Stick Golf Club, Carmel, Indiana
Par 36-36–72; 7,516 yards

September 6-9
purse, $8,000,000

	SCORES			TOTAL	MONEY
Rory McIlroy	64	68	69	67	268	$1,440,000
Phil Mickelson	69	67	64	70	270	704,000
Lee Westwood	68	65	68	69	270	704,000
Robert Garrigus	67	69	66	69	271	352,000
Tiger Woods	65	67	71	68	271	352,000

	SCORES				TOTAL	MONEY
Dustin Johnson	68	67	67	70	272	278,000
Adam Scott	68	68	66	70	272	278,000
Vijay Singh	65	66	69	73	273	248,000
Jim Furyk	69	70	67	68	274	232,000
Ryan Moore	66	66	73	70	275	208,000
Bo Van Pelt	64	69	71	71	275	208,000
Zach Johnson	67	69	68	72	276	162,000
Chris Kirk	68	68	69	71	276	162,000
Ian Poulter	68	68	69	71	276	162,000
Bubba Watson	69	71	71	65	276	162,000
Greg Chalmers	74	70	68	66	278	108,600
Tom Gillis	69	67	73	69	278	108,600
Padraig Harrington	70	65	70	73	278	108,600
John Huh	70	66	73	69	278	108,600
Troy Matteson	70	66	71	71	278	108,600
Seung-Yul Noh	68	66	73	71	278	108,600
Louis Oosthuizen	68	69	68	73	278	108,600
Justin Rose	67	70	70	71	278	108,600
Ben Curtis	70	69	68	72	279	73,600
Sergio Garcia	69	69	71	70	279	73,600
Kevin Na	72	71	68	69	280	62,800
Steve Stricker	68	73	68	71	280	62,800
Brendon de Jonge	71	66	71	73	281	53,200
Luke Donald	66	72	72	71	281	53,200
Jason Dufner	72	67	73	69	281	53,200
Ernie Els	68	71	69	73	281	53,200
Geoff Ogilvy	68	71	74	68	281	53,200
Charl Schwartzel	69	68	72	72	281	53,200
J.B. Holmes	70	74	67	71	282	43,200
Graeme McDowell	68	67	69	78	282	43,200
Kyle Stanley	68	70	69	75	282	43,200
Graham DeLaet	64	70	74	75	283	36,800
Bob Estes	71	69	71	72	283	36,800
Scott Piercy	72	71	72	68	283	36,800
Brandt Snedeker	69	69	71	74	283	36,800
Ben Crane	67	71	74	72	284	30,400
Rickie Fowler	67	70	73	74	284	30,400
Brian Harman	73	69	70	72	284	30,400
Charlie Wi	70	72	72	70	284	30,400
Bill Haas	71	64	72	78	285	22,880
Ryan Palmer	66	73	73	73	285	22,880
Pat Perez	72	72	67	74	285	22,880
Kevin Stadler	69	73	73	70	285	22,880
Johnson Wagner	70	71	72	72	285	22,880
Nick Watney	70	69	72	74	285	22,880
Jeff Overton	74	72	67	73	286	19,253.34
Matt Every	68	71	71	76	286	19,253.33
Webb Simpson	64	75	73	74	286	19,253.33
Charley Hoffman	75	72	69	71	287	18,480
Matt Kuchar	69	73	72	73	287	18,480
Bud Cauley	69	72	74	73	288	18,080
D.A. Points	74	71	68	75	288	18,080
John Senden	70	69	76	73	288	18,080
Keegan Bradley	71	70	75	73	289	17,600
Tim Clark	71	71	73	74	289	17,600
Dicky Pride	76	71	71	71	289	17,600
Martin Laird	69	68	72	81	290	17,200
Mark Wilson	72	76	70	72	290	17,200
Jimmy Walker	67	76	72	76	291	16,960
David Hearn	69	70	77	76	292	16,720
Marc Leishman	75	73	71	73	292	16,720
Bryce Molder	77	72	70	75	294	16,480
William McGirt	77	72	72	74	295	16,320

	SCORES				TOTAL	MONEY
Carl Pettersson	75	72	70	79	296	16,160
Hunter Mahan	70	73	80	77	300	16,000

Tour Championship

East Lake Golf Club, Atlanta, Georgia
Par 35-35–70; 7,154 yards

September 20-23
purse, $8,000,000

	SCORES				TOTAL	MONEY
Brandt Snedeker	68	70	64	68	270	$1,440,000
Justin Rose	66	68	68	71	273	864,000
Luke Donald	71	69	67	67	274	468,000
Ryan Moore	69	70	65	70	274	468,000
Webb Simpson	71	68	70	66	275	304,000
Bubba Watson	69	66	70	70	275	304,000
Jim Furyk	69	64	72	72	277	272,000
Hunter Mahan	68	73	71	66	278	248,000
Tiger Woods	66	73	67	72	278	248,000
Robert Garrigus	68	69	69	73	279	205,760
Dustin Johnson	69	67	73	70	279	205,760
Matt Kuchar	67	69	70	73	279	205,760
Rory McIlroy	69	68	68	74	279	205,760
Bo Van Pelt	67	68	71	73	279	205,760
Sergio Garcia	69	73	71	68	281	167,200
Zach Johnson	68	69	70	74	281	167,200
Phil Mickelson	69	71	72	69	281	167,200
Scott Piercy	67	73	71	70	281	167,200
Adam Scott	68	73	70	72	283	156,800
Jason Dufner	70	70	71	73	284	152,000
Carl Pettersson	71	67	75	71	284	152,000
Steve Stricker	67	73	73	73	286	147,200
Keegan Bradley	70	73	70	74	287	140,800
Rickie Fowler	71	68	72	76	287	140,800
Louis Oosthuizen	70	71	69	77	287	140,800
John Senden	72	68	73	75	288	134,400
Ernie Els	72	75	71	71	289	132,800
Nick Watney	75	74	70	74	293	131,200
John Huh	74	70	73	77	294	129,600
Lee Westwood	72	73	76	74	295	128,000

Final Standings – PGA Tour Playoffs for the FedExCup

RANK	NAME	FEDEXCUP POINTS	BONUS MONEY
1	Brandt Snedeker	4,100	$10,000,000
2	Rory McIlroy	2,827	3,000,000
3	Tiger Woods	2,663	2,000,000
4	Nick Watney	2,215	1,500,000
5	Phil Mickelson	2,073	1,000,000
6	Justin Rose	1,770	800,000
7	Louis Oosthuizen	1,635	700,000
8	Dustin Johnson	1,527	600,000
9	Luke Donald	1,275	550,000
10	Lee Westwood	1,205	500,000
11	Ryan Moore	1,105	300,000
12	Zach Johnson	1,073	290,000
13	Bubba Watson	1,005	280,000
14	Jason Dufner	853	270,000
15	Jim Furyk	790	250,000

RANK	NAME	FEDEXCUP POINTS	BONUS MONEY
16	Webb Simpson	785	245,000
17	Sergio Garcia	733	240,000
18	Matt Kuchar	707	235,000
19	Hunter Mahan	693	230,000
20	Steve Stricker	685	225,000
21	Keegan Bradley	655	220,000
22	Bo Van Pelt	647	215,000
23	Robert Garrigus	637	210,000
24	Carl Pettersson	613	205,000
25	Adam Scott	560	200,000
26	Ernie Els	510	195,000
27	Scott Piercy	483	190,000
28	Rickie Fowler	475	185,000
29	John Huh	460	180,000
30	John Senden	445	175,000

The Ryder Cup

Medinah Country Club, Medinah, Illinois
Par 434 454 534–36, 544 354 434–36–72; 7,658 yards

September 28-30

FIRST DAY
Morning Foursomes

Rory McIlroy and Graham McDowell (Europe) defeated Jim Furyk and Brandt Snedeker, 1 up.

McIlroy/McDowell	4	4	4	3	4	3	4	4	3	4	4	4	4	4	5	5	3	4
Furyk/Snedeker	4	3	4	4	4	4	4	3	4	6	5	4	3	4	3	3	3	5

Phil Mickelson and Keegan Bradley (US) defeated Luke Donald and Sergio Garcia, 4 and 3.

Donald/Garcia	4	3	4	4	4	4	5	3	4	4	4	5	3	6	4
Mickelson/Bradley	4	2	4	4	5	5	5	3	3	4	4	4	2	5	3

Jason Dufner and Zach Johnson (US) defeated Lee Westwood and Francesco Molinari, 3 and 2.

Westwood/Molinari	4	3	4	4	4	5	4	3	4	5	4	4	3	5	5	5
Dufner/Johnson	5	2	4	5	4	4	5	3	3	4	4	4	3	5	3	4

Ian Poulter and Justin Rose (Europe) defeated Steve Stricker and Tiger Woods, 2 and 1.

Poulter/Rose	4	3	5	3	5	4	5	4	4	3	4	4	4	4	4	3
Stricker/Woods	4	5	4	4	5	5	4	4	4	4	5	5	3	5	3	4	3

POINTS: Europe 2, United States 2

Afternoon Fourballs

Bubba Watson and Webb Simpson (US) defeated Paul Lawrie and Peter Hanson, 5 and 4.

Lawrie				4		4	4	4	5	3	4		3	3	3	4
Hanson		4		3							4					
Watson				3			3	4	2					4		
Simpson	3	3		3	4					4	4	4	3	3		

Mickelson and Bradley (US) defeated McIlroy and McDowell, 2 and 1.

McIlroy	4	3	4	4		4	5	3		4	4	4	3	4	3	4	2
McDowell					4				3								
Mickelson		2		4		5	4		4		4	4	3	5		4	2
Bradley	3		3					2		4					3		

Dustin Johnson and Matt Kuchar (US) defeated Justin Rose and Martin Kaymer, 3 and 2.

```
Rose       3     4       3       4 5 4 3 3 4 4 4
Kaymer           3   4 5     5 3
Johnson          2               3 4     4   3 4 3
Kuchar     4     4 3 4 3 4        5     4           4
```

Lee Westwood and Nicolas Colsaerts (Europe) defeated Woods and Stricker, 1 up.

```
Westwood                         4           4 5   4
Colsaerts  4 2 4 3 4     4 3 3 3 4     2     3     2
Woods      3   4   4       3   4 3     3 4   3 2
Stricker       2   4     4 4     4       4       4       4
```

POINTS: Europe 3, United States 5

SECOND DAY
Morning Foursomes

Rose and Poulter (Europe) defeated Watson and Simpson, 1 up.

```
Rose/Poulter      3 4 4 4 5 4 5 4 3 5 3 4 4 4 4 6 3 4
Watson/Simpson    4 4 3 4 4 4 5 4 4 6 3 5 4 4 4 5 3 4
```

Bradley and Mickelson (US) defeated Westwood and Donald, 7 and 6.

```
Westwood/Donald      4 5 4 4 4 5 5 3 4 5 4 5
Bradley/Mickelson    3 2 4 4 4 4 4 3 3 4 4 4
```

Dufner and Zach Johnson (US) defeated Colsaerts and Garcia, 2 and 1.

```
Colsaerts/Garcia    4 3 4 5 5 4 5 3 3 5 3 6 4 5 4 3 4
Dufner/Johnson      4 2 4 4 5 5 5 3 3 5 4 4 3 5 4 4 3
```

Furyk and Snedeker (US) defeated McIlroy and McDowell, 1 up.

```
McIlroy/McDowell    4 3 4 4 5 4 5 3 4 5 4 4 3 4 4 3 3 4
Furyk/Snedeker      3 3 4 4 4 4 5 4 4 5 3 4 3 4 4 4 3 4
```

POINTS: Europe 4, United States 8

Afternoon Fourballs

Dustin Johnson and Kuchar (US) defeated Colsaerts and Lawrie, 1 up.

```
Colsaerts      3 4     4     4 3       4       4
Lawrie       4     4     4       4 5   4 3   3 4 3
Johnson      4   4         5       4   3 4   5 2
Kuchar           2   3 4 5   3 4 4   4       3       4
```

Watson and Simpson (US) defeated Rose and Molinari, 5 and 4.

```
Rose         4 3   4     4 5 2   5         3
Molinari         4     4       3   3 4   5
Watson           3           4             4
Simpson      4     3 4 4     2 3 4 3 4 2
```

Garcia and Donald (Europe) defeated Woods and Stricker, 1 up.

```
Garcia       3       3 4       4     3       4     4
Donald         3 4     4 5 2 3 5   4     4 3     2
Woods              4 5       4       2 4 4 3 2 4
Stricker     4 4 4 4 3     3 4     4 3
```

McIlroy and Poulter (Europe) defeated Dufner and Zach Johnson, 1 up.

```
McIlroy          4     4           4   2
Poulter      4 4     3     4 5 3 4 4   4   4 3 3 2 3
Dufner             4 4 4 4 4 3 4   4 4 3 4       3
Johnson      3 3                   4       4 4 2
```

POINTS: Europe 6, United States 10

THIRD DAY
Singles

Donald (Europe) defeated Watson, 2 and 1.
```
Donald    3 3 4 3 5 5 4 3 4 4 3 4 4 4 4 4 3
Watson    3 4 4 4 5 5 4 3 4 4 5 4 4 3 3 3
```

Poulter (Europe) defeated Simpson, 2 up.
```
Poulter   3 4 4 5 4 5 4 3 4 5 4 3 3 5 4 4 3 3
Simpson   3 3 4 3 5 4 6 4 4 4 4 4 3 5 4 4 4 4
```

McIlroy (Europe) defeated Bradley, 2 and 1.
```
McIlroy   4 3 4 3 4 3 5 3 3 5 4 5 3 4 3 4 3
Bradley   4 3 4 5 4 4 5 2 4 4 4 3 5 4 4 3
```

Rose (Europe) defeated Mickelson, 1 up.
```
Rose       3 2 4 5 5 4 3 3 3 5 4 4 3 5 4 4 2 3
Mickelson  4 4 4 4 4 4 5 2 4 5 3 4 3 4 4 4 3 4
```

Lawrie (Europe) defeated Snedeker, 5 and 3.
```
Lawrie    4 3 4 3 3 4 5 3 3 5 4 3 3 5 3
Snedeker  4 3 4 4 4 4 5 3 4 4 5 5 4 4
```

Dustin Johnson (US) defeated Colsaerts, 3 and 2.
```
Colsaerts 5 3 4 4 4 4 4 3 3 6 5 4 3 5 4 5
Johnson   3 3 4 6 4 3 4 3 4 5 4 5 4 4 3 4
```

Zach Johnson (US) defeated McDowell, 2 and 1.
```
McDowell  5 3 4 5 4 4 6 3 3 5 4 4 4 5 4 4 3
Johnson   4 3 3 4 5 4 5 3 4 5 4 4 4 5 4 4 3
```

Garcia (Europe) defeated Furyk, 1 up.
```
Garcia    4 2 5 4 4 4 5 4 4 3 4 3 5 4 4 3 4
Furyk     4 3 4 4 4 4 5 3 4 4 4 3 4 4 4 4 4 5
```

Dufner (US) defeated Hanson, 2 up.
```
Hanson    3 3 5 4 4 5 5 3 4 4 4 3 4 4 4 3 5
Dufner    3 3 4 4 3 5 3 2 4 5 5 5 2 5 3 4 4 4
```

Westwood (Europe) defeated Kuchar, 3 and 2.
```
Westwood  4 3 4 4 4 5 4 3 4 5 4 3 4 3 4
Kuchar    4 3 4 5 4 4 4 3 5 4 4 5 4 4 4 4
```

Kaymer (Europe) defeated Stricker, 1 up.
```
Kaymer    4 3 4 4 4 4 5 3 3 5 5 4 5 4 5 4 3 4
Stricker  4 2 4 4 4 5 5 3 4 4 5 5 3 5 4 4 4 4
```

Molinari (Europe) halved with Woods.
```
Molinari  4 3 3 5 5 5 4 3 4 4 5 4 4 4 4 4 4
Woods     4 4 4 4 5 4 3 3 4 5 4 3 5 4 4 3 5
```

TOTAL POINTS: Europe 14½, United States 13½

PGA Tour Fall Series

Justin Timberlake Shriners Hospitals for Children Open

TPC Summerlin, Las Vegas, Nevada
Par 35-36–71; 7,223 yards

October 4-7
purse, $4,500,000

	SCORES				TOTAL	MONEY
Ryan Moore	61	68	65	66	260	$810,000
Brendon de Jonge	62	66	66	67	261	486,000
Jonas Blixt	64	64	66	70	264	306,000
Jason Day	69	68	64	65	266	216,000
Bill Lunde	67	69	67	66	269	180,000
Richard H. Lee	66	68	71	65	270	156,375
Scott Piercy	67	66	73	64	270	156,375
Blake Adams	65	70	68	68	271	135,000
Jason Bohn	71	66	64	70	271	135,000
Tim Herron	63	68	68	73	272	112,500
Jimmy Walker	67	66	66	73	272	112,500
Nick Watney	66	66	71	69	272	112,500
Bobby Gates	70	67	66	70	273	72,500
Mathew Goggin	68	69	70	66	273	72,500
John Huh	63	69	72	69	273	72,500
Colt Knost	68	67	66	72	273	72,500
Russell Knox	66	67	68	72	273	72,500
Jeff Overton	70	66	68	69	273	72,500
Heath Slocum	67	67	74	65	273	72,500
Brendan Steele	69	67	70	67	273	72,500
Michael Thompson	70	66	68	69	273	72,500
Angel Cabrera	68	70	67	69	274	39,487.50
Bob Estes	69	68	68	69	274	39,487.50
Robert Garrigus	66	68	73	67	274	39,487.50
John Mallinger	70	65	72	67	274	39,487.50
Kevin Na	68	66	70	70	274	39,487.50
Patrick Reed	65	69	70	70	274	39,487.50
Kevin Streelman	68	67	68	71	274	39,487.50
Josh Teater	70	65	67	72	274	39,487.50
David Hearn	68	70	69	68	275	29,250
Kevin Stadler	66	68	72	69	275	29,250
Camilo Villegas	70	66	68	71	275	29,250
Ricky Barnes	68	69	70	69	276	25,425
Justin Leonard	64	69	71	72	276	25,425
Chris Riley	68	70	69	69	276	25,425
Stewart Cink	68	69	68	72	277	18,922.50
Ken Duke	66	68	68	75	277	18,922.50
Chris Kirk	64	68	71	74	277	18,922.50
Edward Loar	67	68	70	72	277	18,922.50
George McNeill	70	68	72	67	277	18,922.50
John Merrick	69	67	72	69	277	18,922.50
Andres Romero	68	66	72	71	277	18,922.50
Vijay Singh	66	66	71	74	277	18,922.50
Daniel Summerhays	68	63	72	74	277	18,922.50
Steve Wheatcroft	69	69	71	68	277	18,922.50
Tommy Biershenk	68	70	70	70	278	11,857.50
Scott Brown	69	67	72	70	278	11,857.50
Daniel Chopra	68	67	73	70	278	11,857.50
Nathan Green	68	68	74	68	278	11,857.50
David Mathis	68	68	72	70	278	11,857.50
Ryan Palmer	67	70	66	75	278	11,857.50
Marc Turnesa	70	68	70	70	278	11,857.50
Jhonattan Vegas	68	68	69	73	278	11,857.50

	SCORES				TOTAL	MONEY
Chad Campbell	73	65	74	67	279	10,305
Robert Karlsson	69	68	70	72	279	10,305
Billy Mayfair	70	66	72	71	279	10,305
Vaughn Taylor	65	72	70	72	279	10,305
J.J. Killeen	66	68	75	71	280	10,035
Sean O'Hair	67	70	71	72	280	10,035
Harris English	71	66	73	71	281	9,900
Will Claxton	70	68	71	73	282	9,720
Erik Compton	66	71	75	70	282	9,720
Troy Kelly	68	70	70	74	282	9,720
Matt Bettencourt	68	70	73	72	283	9,495
J.B. Holmes	70	67	73	73	283	9,495
Roberto Castro	69	66	71	78	284	9,315
Davis Love	68	67	73	76	284	9,315
Gary Christian	68	68	76	73	285	9,135
Rod Pampling	70	68	72	75	285	9,135
Hunter Hamrick	69	69	77	71	286	9,000
John Daly	69	63	86	77	295	8,910

Frys.com Open

CordeValle Golf Club, San Martin, California
Par 35-36–71; 7,368 yards

October 11-14
purse, $5,000,000

	SCORES				TOTAL	MONEY
Jonas Blixt	66	68	66	68	268	$900,000
Jason Kokrak	68	66	67	68	269	440,000
Tim Petrovic	70	68	67	64	269	440,000
John Mallinger	66	62	70	72	270	196,875
Alexandre Rocha	69	67	66	68	270	196,875
Vijay Singh	70	66	66	68	270	196,875
Jimmy Walker	73	68	67	62	270	196,875
Jeff Overton	68	69	68	66	271	155,000
Russell Knox	70	68	65	69	272	140,000
Gary Woodland	66	72	66	68	272	140,000
Martin Flores	71	67	68	67	273	106,000
Charles Howell	66	69	66	72	273	106,000
Zack Miller	70	69	66	68	273	106,000
Bryce Molder	71	67	66	69	273	106,000
Patrick Reed	73	67	70	63	273	106,000
Steven Bowditch	71	64	71	68	274	72,500
Scott Dunlap	70	63	70	71	274	72,500
Ernie Els	71	68	69	66	274	72,500
Danny Lee	69	67	67	71	274	72,500
Jeff Maggert	67	71	67	69	274	72,500
Chez Reavie	73	65	68	68	274	72,500
Ben Curtis	69	71	65	70	275	45,071.43
Mathew Goggin	69	70	69	67	275	45,071.43
David Mathis	68	70	67	70	275	45,071.43
Nick O'Hern	62	71	71	71	275	45,071.43
D.A. Points	68	67	69	71	275	45,071.43
Jhonattan Vegas	65	67	71	72	275	45,071.43
Greg Owen	66	69	68	72	275	45,071.42
Brian Gay	69	71	67	69	276	31,791.67
Billy Horschel	67	65	73	71	276	31,791.67
Garth Mulroy	73	67	67	69	276	31,791.67
Camilo Villegas	70	66	72	68	276	31,791.67
Brian Davis	72	69	69	66	276	31,791.66
Jerry Kelly	69	68	67	72	276	31,791.66
Nicolas Colsaerts	65	68	71	73	277	24,125

	SCORES				TOTAL	MONEY
Tim Herron	70	65	73	69	277	24,125
Matt Jones	70	66	70	71	277	24,125
Davis Love	69	67	72	69	277	24,125
Bill Lunde	69	67	69	72	277	24,125
John Rollins	71	69	64	73	277	24,125
Derek Ernst	65	72	72	69	278	20,000
Rocco Mediate	67	71	69	71	278	20,000
J.J. Killeen	67	72	70	70	279	17,000
Richard H. Lee	71	67	69	72	279	17,000
John Merrick	72	68	68	71	279	17,000
Rod Pampling	70	68	69	72	279	17,000
Mark Anderson	71	70	68	71	280	12,842.86
Patrick Cantlay	67	70	68	75	280	12,842.86
Frank Lickliter	71	64	72	73	280	12,842.86
Heath Slocum	70	70	69	71	280	12,842.86
D.J. Trahan	73	66	69	72	280	12,842.86
Scott Brown	73	68	69	70	280	12,842.85
Chris Riley	70	69	73	68	280	12,842.85
Robert Karlsson	70	68	72	71	281	11,600
Charlie Beljan	69	67	75	71	282	11,250
Bud Cauley	68	72	71	71	282	11,250
Will Claxton	67	69	71	75	282	11,250
Erik Compton	69	71	72	70	282	11,250
Nathan Green	72	66	68	76	282	11,250
Vaughn Taylor	67	74	70	71	282	11,250
Kelly Kraft	72	69	69	73	283	10,850
Billy Mayfair	72	69	72	70	283	10,850
Angel Cabrera	71	68	70	75	284	10,700
Stephen Ames	71	68	73	73	285	10,450
Cameron Beckman	71	70	72	72	285	10,450
Stephen Gangluff	70	67	74	74	285	10,450
Ryuji Imada	70	70	77	68	285	10,450
Miguel Angel Carballo	73	65	74	75	287	10,200
Kevin Streelman	72	69	72	75	288	10,050
Garrett Willis	67	70	78	73	288	10,050
Todd Hamilton	73	67	72	78	290	9,900
J.B. Holmes	71	70	79	72	292	9,800

McGladrey Classic

Sea Island Golf Club, Seaside Course, St. Simons Island, Georgia
Par 35-35–70; 7,055 yards

October 18-21
purse, $4,000,000

	SCORES				TOTAL	MONEY
Tommy Gainey	69	67	68	60	264	$720,000
David Toms	65	67	70	63	265	432,000
Jim Furyk	66	65	66	69	266	272,000
Brendon de Jonge	66	69	68	65	268	165,333.34
Davis Love	65	66	66	71	268	165,333.33
D.J. Trahan	66	67	66	69	268	165,333.33
Chad Campbell	66	67	69	67	269	124,666.67
Greg Owen	64	69	71	65	269	124,666.67
Charles Howell	66	68	67	68	269	124,666.66
Arjun Atwal	67	63	69	71	270	92,000
Charlie Beljan	66	71	68	65	270	92,000
David Mathis	69	69	65	67	270	92,000
Michael Thompson	65	68	69	68	270	92,000
Mark Wilson	68	69	66	67	270	92,000
Blake Adams	68	68	69	66	271	64,000
Daniel Chopra	68	69	66	68	271	64,000

	SCORES				TOTAL	MONEY
Harris English	71	66	66	68	271	64,000
Kyle Reifers	67	68	67	69	271	64,000
Scott Stallings	68	70	67	66	271	64,000
Scott Brown	67	70	70	65	272	41,714.29
Sean O'Hair	73	66	67	66	272	41,714.29
Brendan Steele	67	71	66	68	272	41,714.29
Camilo Villegas	65	71	68	68	272	41,714.29
Bud Cauley	62	70	68	72	272	41,714.28
Ken Duke	67	68	68	69	272	41,714.28
Bill Lunde	68	68	68	68	272	41,714.28
Stuart Appleby	69	68	67	69	273	22,550
Roberto Castro	69	66	68	70	273	22,550
Will Claxton	70	66	65	72	273	22,550
Ben Crane	68	71	62	72	273	22,550
Ben Curtis	68	69	66	70	273	22,550
James Driscoll	67	69	71	66	273	22,550
Joe Durant	65	71	67	70	273	22,550
Mathew Goggin	67	66	68	72	273	22,550
Brian Harman	67	72	65	69	273	22,550
Russell Knox	71	68	67	67	273	22,550
Jason Kokrak	68	70	66	69	273	22,550
Danny Lee	65	70	69	69	273	22,550
Rory Sabbatini	69	65	67	72	273	22,550
Vijay Singh	66	68	68	71	273	22,550
Henrik Stenson	67	68	69	69	273	22,550
Boo Weekley	64	71	69	69	273	22,550
Kevin Chappell	71	66	68	69	274	12,826.67
Billy Horschel	68	69	66	71	274	12,826.67
Rocco Mediate	70	68	67	69	274	12,826.67
Garth Mulroy	68	70	66	70	274	12,826.67
Brian Gay	65	68	69	72	274	12,826.66
Peter Tomasulo	67	67	68	72	274	12,826.66
Tim Herron	69	66	71	69	275	10,240
Zach Johnson	65	70	70	70	275	10,240
Mark Anderson	69	70	69	68	276	9,413.34
Jeff Overton	69	70	69	68	276	9,413.34
Gavin Coles	67	65	70	74	276	9,413.33
Nathan Green	72	67	68	69	276	9,413.33
David Hearn	66	71	71	68	276	9,413.33
Matt Jones	72	67	66	71	276	9,413.33
Jason Day	67	67	72	71	277	8,920
Matt Every	67	72	68	70	277	8,920
Martin Flores	65	69	72	71	277	8,920
Billy Hurley	66	71	70	70	277	8,920
Alexandre Rocha	68	68	70	72	278	8,640
Heath Slocum	69	68	71	70	278	8,640
Kyle Thompson	67	72	69	70	278	8,640
Stewart Cink	69	70	67	73	279	8,360
Chris Kirk	69	70	68	72	279	8,360
Zack Miller	68	71	68	72	279	8,360
Chase Wright	67	71	68	73	279	8,360
Marco Dawson	62	75	70	73	280	8,160
Justin Leonard	68	70	70	75	283	8,080
Rod Pampling	64	71	72	77	284	8,000
Cameron Beckman	66	73	68	80	287	7,920
Jason Bohn	69	67	73		209	7,600
Steven Bowditch	68	66	75		209	7,600
Angel Cabrera	68	71	70		209	7,600
Gary Christian	67	69	73		209	7,600
Ryuji Imada	70	69	70		209	7,600
Richard H. Lee	67	71	71		209	7,600
Billy Mayfair	72	66	71		209	7,600
Robert Allenby	69	70	71		210	7,120

	SCORES			TOTAL	MONEY
Brian Davis	74	65	71	210	7,120
Edward Loar	68	70	72	210	7,120
Carl Paulson	68	71	71	210	7,120
John Rollins	69	70	71	210	7,120
Jonas Blixt	72	67	72	211	6,840
Erik Compton	69	69	73	211	6,840
Alex Cejka	70	67	75	212	6,680
J.J. Killeen	66	71	75	212	6,680
Chris DiMarco	72	67	75	214	6,560

Children's Miracle Network Hospitals Classic

Walt Disney World Resort, Lake Buena Vista, Florida　　　　November 8-11
Magnolia Course: Par 36-36–72; 7,516 yards　　　　purse, $4,700,000
Palm Course: Par 36-36–72; 6,957 yards

	SCORES				TOTAL	MONEY
Charlie Beljan	68	64	71	69	272	$846,000
Matt Every	67	69	70	68	274	413,600
Robert Garrigus	68	68	70	68	274	413,600
Brian Gay	69	69	67	70	275	225,600
Scott Stallings	66	70	71	69	276	165,087.50
Josh Teater	71	67	67	71	276	165,087.50
Boo Weekley	70	67	72	67	276	165,087.50
Charlie Wi	64	71	70	71	276	165,087.50
Mark Anderson	68	67	74	68	277	112,800
Tom Gillis	72	66	70	69	277	112,800
Tim Herron	71	70	67	69	277	112,800
Jerry Kelly	71	68	72	66	277	112,800
Russell Knox	66	72	72	67	277	112,800
Joey Snyder	69	70	72	66	277	112,800
Cameron Beckman	70	68	69	71	278	77,550
Charles Howell	68	67	73	70	278	77,550
Ryan Palmer	70	70	67	71	278	77,550
Kevin Streelman	68	68	72	70	278	77,550
Jonas Blixt	70	71	68	70	279	49,454.45
Harris English	68	67	73	71	279	49,454.45
Matt Jones	71	64	73	71	279	49,454.45
Daniel Summerhays	71	71	68	69	279	49,454.45
Daniel Chopra	69	67	70	73	279	49,454.44
Brendon de Jonge	69	68	70	72	279	49,454.44
Scott Dunlap	72	68	68	71	279	49,454.44
Sean O'Hair	73	68	67	71	279	49,454.44
Henrik Stenson	68	67	71	73	279	49,454.44
Martin Flores	72	69	71	68	280	31,255
Ryuji Imada	69	66	73	72	280	31,255
Robert Karlsson	71	70	72	67	280	31,255
Vaughn Taylor	70	68	68	74	280	31,255
Roland Thatcher	69	73	67	71	280	31,255
Camilo Villegas	65	71	70	74	280	31,255
Roberto Castro	69	71	72	69	281	23,735
Kevin Chappell	67	69	72	73	281	23,735
Gavin Coles	71	71	70	69	281	23,735
Billy Horschel	71	70	71	69	281	23,735
Derek Lamely	73	68	69	71	281	23,735
D.J. Trahan	74	67	68	72	281	23,735
Stuart Appleby	74	68	69	71	282	16,045.80
Matt Bettencourt	67	74	71	70	282	16,045.80
Stewart Cink	69	69	75	69	282	16,045.80
Ken Duke	67	74	69	72	282	16,045.80

	SCORES				TOTAL	MONEY
Tommy Gainey	65	71	70	76	282	16,045.80
Colt Knost	67	71	71	73	282	16,045.80
Davis Love	73	68	70	71	282	16,045.80
Nick O'Hern	69	73	73	67	282	16,045.80
Brendan Steele	67	75	72	68	282	16,045.80
Garrett Willis	73	69	70	70	282	16,045.80
Miguel Angel Carballo	71	65	74	73	283	11,248.67
Will Claxton	72	67	71	73	283	11,248.67
Jeff Maggert	72	70	68	73	283	11,248.67
William McGirt	71	71	69	72	283	11,248.67
Justin Leonard	73	67	73	70	283	11,248.66
Edward Loar	69	74	72	68	283	11,248.66
Brian Harman	66	72	73	73	284	10,622
Tom Pernice, Jr.	74	68	73	69	284	10,622
Ted Potter, Jr.	75	68	69	72	284	10,622
Jason Kokrak	71	68	74	72	285	10,340
Chris Stroud	70	66	77	72	285	10,340
Cameron Tringale	75	67	72	71	285	10,340
Ben Curtis	69	70	75	72	286	10,058
Nathan Green	71	72	71	72	286	10,058
Kyle Reifers	69	74	70	73	286	10,058
Carl Paulson	71	70	74	72	287	9,823
John Rollins	70	70	75	72	287	9,823
Marco Dawson	68	72	74	74	288	9,541
J.J. Killeen	71	70	71	76	288	9,541
Alexandre Rocha	71	70	75	72	288	9,541
Gary Woodland	73	68	74	73	288	9,541
Alex Cejka	72	71	69	77	289	9,212
Chris DiMarco	72	71	71	75	289	9,212
Patrick Sheehan	69	73	72	75	289	9,212
Jason Bohn	73	70	70	77	290	8,977
Chris Kirk	73	70	72	75	290	8,977
Shane Bertsch	69	71	75	76	291	8,836
Chez Reavie	68	74	74	76	292	8,742
Mathew Goggin	69	74	72	79	294	8,648

Special Events

Tavistock Cup

Lake Nona Golf & Country Club, Orlando, Florida
Par 36-36–72; 7,215 yards

March 19-20
purse, $2,170,000

FIRST DAY
(Team fourball–better ball)

Group 1
Tiger Woods and Justin Rose (Albany) tied with Bubba Watson and Charles Howell (Isleworth), -9 to -9.

Group 2
Ben Curtis and Peter Hanson (Lake Nona) defeated Soren Kjeldsen and Paul McGinley (Queenwood), -9 to -7.

Group 3
Tim Clark and Ernie Els (Albany) defeated Adam Scott and Thomas Bjorn (Queenwood), -8 to -6.

Group 4
Bo Van Pelt and Sean O'Hair (Isleworth) defeated Ross Fisher and Retief Goosen (Lake Nona), -13 to -9.

Group 5
Daniel Chopra and Robert Allenby (Isleworth) tied with David Howell and Tom Lewis (Queenwood), -4 to -4.

Group 6
Ian Poulter and Trevor Immelman (Albany) tied with Graeme McDowell and Gary Woodland (Lake Nona), -6 to -6.

SECOND DAY
(Singles stroke play – cumulative team score)

Group 1
Tim Clark (Albany) E
Robert Allenby (Isleworth) -5
Ben Curtis (Lake Nona) -2
Paul McGinley (Queenwood) -2

Group 2
Ernie Els (Albany) -5
Charles Howell (Isleworth) -1
Retief Goosen (Lake Nona) -5
Soren Kjeldsen (Queenwood) -1

Group 3
Trevor Immelman (Albany) E
Daniel Chopra (Isleworth) -1
Ross Fisher (Lake Nona) -5
David Howell (Queenwood) -1

Group 4
Justin Rose (Albany) -2
Bo Van Pelt (Isleworth) E
Peter Hanson (Lake Nona) -1
Adam Scott (Queenwood) -2

Group 5

Ian Poulter (Albany) +4
Bubba Watson (Isleworth) -3
Gary Woodland (Lake Nona) -1
Tom Lewis (Queenwood) -3

Group 6

Tiger Woods (Albany) E
Sean O'Hair (Isleworth) -3
Graeme McDowell (Lake Nona) -3
Thomas Bjorn (Queenwood) -5

TWO-DAY TOTAL: Lake Nona -41, Isleworth -39, Queenwood -31, Albany -26

(Each member of the Lake Nona team received $110,000; each member of the Isleworth
team received $80,000; each member of the Queenwood team received $60,000; and each
member of the Albany team received $50,000. Els, Allenby, Goosen, Fisher and Bjorn
received $70,000 for the lowest scores on the second day.)

CVS Caremark Charity Classic

Rhode Island Country Club, Barrington, Rhode Island   June 18-19
Par 36-35–71; 6,688 yards   purse $1,300,000

	SCORES		TOTAL	MONEY (Team)
Morgan Pressel/Jay Haas	62	59	121	$300,000
Suzann Pettersen/Fred Funk	64	59	123	185,000
Lexi Thompson/Corey Pavin	63	60	123	185,000
Brittany Lincicome/Brett Quigley	65	60	125	150,000
Yani Tseng/Jeff Sluman	64	62	126	121,666.67
Lorena Ochoa/Mark Calcavecchia	64	62	126	121,666.67
Billy Andrade/Brad Faxon	62	64	126	121,666.66
Cristie Kerr/John Cook	64	63	127	110,000
Juli Inkster/Dana Quigley	62	66	128	105,000
Annika Sorenstam/Peter Jacobsen	73	64	137	100,000

PGA Grand Slam of Golf

Port Royal Golf Course, Southampton Parish, Bermuda   October 23-24
Par 36-35–71; 6,845 yards   purse, $1,350,000

	SCORES		TOTAL	MONEY
Padraig Harrington	66	67	133	$600,000
Webb Simpson	69	65	134	300,000
Keegan Bradley	72	67	139	225,000
Bubba Watson	68	71	139	225,000

Callaway Golf Pebble Beach Invitational

Pebble Beach GL: Par 36-36–72; 6,828 yards
Spyglass Hills GC: Par 36-36–72; 6,953 yards
Del Monte GC: Par 36-36–72; 6,365 yards
Pebble Beach, California

November 15-18
purse, $300,000

	SCORES				TOTAL	MONEY
Tommy Gainey	69	69	70	69	277	$60,000
William McGirt	66	71	72	69	278	24,300
Kirk Triplett	66	69	75	68	278	24,300
Billy Horschel	70	69	68	72	279	10,600
Tommy Armour	71	71	70	68	280	9,000
John Cook	70	72	69	71	282	6,875
James Hahn	76	66	66	74	282	6,875
Robert Streb	69	68	69	76	282	6,875
Jimmy Walker	72	74	69	67	282	6,875
Jason Bohn	70	73	69	71	283	4,900
Bobby Gates	69	72	77	65	283	4,900
Bryce Molder	71	67	77	68	283	4,900
D.A. Points	74	70	68	71	283	4,900
Daniel Summerhays	70	72	72	69	283	4,900
Olin Browne	69	70	77	69	285	3,733.33
Fred Funk	73	73	71	68	285	3,733.33
Mark Brooks	73	73	72	67	285	3,733.33
Gary Hallberg	74	71	71	70	286	3,025
Jason Kokrak	72	70	69	75	286	3,025
John Mallinger	67	69	76	74	286	3,025
Nicholas Thompson	72	71	76	67	286	3,025
Russ Cochran	70	65	74	78	287	2,458.33
Russell Henley	68	73	76	70	287	2,458.33
Scott Stallings	64	74	78	71	287	2,458.33
Josh Teater	73	73	74	67	287	2,458.33
Lee Williams	71	79	67	70	287	2,458.33
Chris Stroud	72	69	73	73	287	2,458.33
Martin Flores	72	72	74	70	288	2,200
Luke Guthrie	69	75	73	72	289	2,110
Justin Hicks	69	73	77	70	289	2,110
Annika Sorenstam	70	69	81	69	289	2,110
Blake Adams	71	76	72	71	290	2,060
Gary Christian	70	75	72	74	291	2,000
Juli Inkster	76	69	75	71	291	2,000
Joe Ogilvie	72	76	72	71	291	2,000
Shawn Stefani	73	71	75	72	291	2,000
Cameron Tringale	74	70	76	71	291	2,000
David Mathis	71	75	71	75	292	1,930
Cheyenne Woods	71	71	73	77	292	1,930
Paul Haley	68	72	79	75	294	1,900
Graham Cliff	74	73	73	76	296	1,880
Mark Brown	68	70	81	81	300	1,860
Trevor Immelman	73	73	72		WD	1,830
Charlie Wi	71	76	72		WD	1,830

World Challenge

Sherwood Country Club, Thousand Oaks, California
Par 36-36–72; 7,027 yards

November 29-December 2
purse, $4,000,000

	SCORES				TOTAL	MONEY
Graeme McDowell	69	66	68	68	271	$1,000,000
Keegan Bradley	69	69	67	69	274	500,000
Bo Van Pelt	70	68	70	70	278	300,000
Jim Furyk	69	69	71	70	279	201,667
Tiger Woods	70	69	69	71	279	201,667
Rickie Fowler	73	67	70	69	279	201,666
Webb Simpson	70	73	69	69	281	160,000
Steve Stricker	73	71	68	70	282	150,000
Hunter Mahan	71	73	71	68	283	142,500
Bubba Watson	71	74	67	71	283	142,500
Matt Kuchar	73	69	72	70	284	132,500
Nick Watney	67	73	71	73	284	132,500
Dustin Johnson	74	68	72	71	285	124,500
Brandt Snedeker	75	68	73	69	285	124,500
Jason Day	71	75	72	69	287	122,500
Jason Dufner	73	68	75	71	287	122,500
Ian Poulter	73	72	71	72	288	121,000
Zach Johnson	74	70	70	79	293	120,000

Franklin Templeton Shootout

Tiburon Golf Course, Naples, Florida
Par 36-36–72; 7,288 yards

December 7-9
purse, $3,000,000

	SCORES			TOTAL	MONEY (Each)
Sean O'Hair/Kenny Perry	64	61	60	185	$375,000
Charles Howell/Rory Sabbatini	66	63	57	186	235,000
Jason Dufner/Vijay Singh	66	63	59	188	140,000
Stewart Cink/Carl Pettersson	67	62	60	189	97,500
Jerry Kelly/Steve Stricker	68	63	58	189	97,500
Davis Love/Brandt Snedeker	62	65	62	189	97,500
Keegan Bradley/Brendan Steele	67	64	60	191	81,250
Dustin Johnson/Ian Poulter	67	65	59	191	81,250
Bud Cauley/Rickie Fowler	66	67	63	196	77,500
Justin Leonard/Scott Verplank	70	67	63	200	75,000
Fredrik Jacobson/Greg Norman	72	68	63	203	72,500
Mark Calcavecchia/Mike Weir	70	71	65	206	70,000

PNC Father-Son Challenge

Ritz-Carlton Golf Club, Orlando, Florida
Par 36-36–72; 7,120 yards

December 15-16
purse, $1,000,000

	SCORES		TOTAL	MONEY (Won by professional)
Davis Love/Dru Love	60	61	121	$200,000
Larry Nelson/Josh Nelson	62	60	122	80,000
Vijay Singh/Qass Singh	62	61	123	57,000
David Duval/Nick Karavites	63	61	124	49,500
Mark O'Meara/Shaun O'Meara	61	63	124	49,500
Fuzzy Zoeller/Gretchen Zoeller	65	60	125	47,000
Jack Nicklaus/Gary Nicklaus	62	63	125	47,000

	SCORES			TOTAL	MONEY (Won by professional)
Fred Funk/Taylor Funk	61	64		125	47,000
Hale Irwin/Steve Irwin	62	64		126	45,000
Bernhard Langer/Christina Langer	62	65		127	44,000
Lee Janzen/Connor Janzen	63	65		128	43,500
Steve Elkington/Sam Elkington	66	63		129	42,750
Raymond Floyd/Robert Floyd	64	65		129	42,750
Lanny Wadkins/Tucker Wadkins	66	65		131	41,750
Sandy Lyle/James Lyle	66	65		131	41,750
Nick Faldo/Matthew Faldo	63	69		132	41,000
Lee Trevino/Daniel Trevino	69	65		134	40,500
Arnold Palmer/Will Wears	80	76		156	40,000

Web.com Tour

Pacific Rubiales Colombia Championship

Country Club de Bogota, Bogota, Colombia
Par 35-36–71; 7,102 yards

February 16-19
purse, $600,000

	SCORES				TOTAL	MONEY
Skip Kendall	70	67	66	71	274	$108,000
Andres Gonzales	69	70	68	68	275	52,800
Andrew Svoboda	70	66	67	72	275	52,800
James Hahn	70	69	67	70	276	26,400
Kirk Triplett	72	68	64	72	276	26,400
Tom Hoge	71	66	72	68	277	19,425
Kevin Johnson	70	70	70	67	277	19,425
Bronson La'Cassie	70	72	68	67	277	19,425
Charles Warren	71	69	66	71	277	19,425
Michael Connell	68	72	69	69	278	16,200
Oscar Serna	72	70	67	70	279	14,400
Brian Smock	66	68	74	71	279	14,400
Jason Allred	73	68	69	70	280	10,285.72
Peter Lonard	66	70	74	70	280	10,285.72
Tyrone van Aswegen	68	71	72	69	280	10,285.72
Paul Claxton	68	70	71	71	280	10,285.71
Ryan Hietala	69	68	72	71	280	10,285.71
Billy Horschel	66	66	76	72	280	10,285.71
Michael Sim	70	65	74	71	280	10,285.71
Scott Gardiner	72	69	71	69	281	6,291.43
Fabian Gomez	70	69	74	68	281	6,291.43
Travis Hampshire	70	71	71	69	281	6,291.43
Steve LeBrun	74	69	67	71	281	6,291.43
Troy Merritt	72	70	69	70	281	6,291.43
Dicky Pride	70	68	73	70	281	6,291.43
Erik Flores	67	68	74	72	281	6,291.42

Panama Claro Championship

Panama Golf Club, Panama City, Panama
Par 35-35–70; 7,102 yards

March 1-4
purse, $550,000

	SCORES				TOTAL	MONEY
Edward Loar	66	68	68	74	276	$99,000
Ryan Armour	72	69	68	68	277	36,300
Luke List	71	71	67	68	277	36,300
Cameron Percy	75	69	66	67	277	36,300
Brian Smock	71	64	73	69	277	36,300
Justin Bolli	65	70	73	71	279	19,800
Brad Fritsch	70	70	71	69	280	17,737.50
Peter Lonard	69	69	73	69	280	17,737.50
Derek Fathauer	71	70	67	73	281	11,550
Aaron Goldberg	68	70	73	70	281	11,550
Justin Hicks	64	75	67	75	281	11,550
Mike Lavery	73	71	72	65	281	11,550
Steve LeBrun	71	72	68	70	281	11,550
David Lingmerth	69	70	70	72	281	11,550
B.J. Staten	70	71	70	70	281	11,550
Shawn Stefani	69	70	70	72	281	11,550
Darron Stiles	73	68	72	68	281	11,550
Tim Wilkinson	68	68	73	72	281	11,550
Brad Adamonis	71	71	68	72	282	6,435
Michael Connell	69	70	71	72	282	6,435
Glen Day	73	71	68	70	282	6,435
Jim Herman	68	73	71	70	282	6,435
Kevin Johnson	75	69	63	75	282	6,435
Casey Wittenberg	72	69	74	67	282	6,435
Ben Briscoe	76	68	68	71	283	4,111.25
Josh Broadaway	72	72	64	75	283	4,111.25
Daniel Chopra	72	69	68	74	283	4,111.25
Cesar Costilla	70	69	71	73	283	4,111.25
Skip Kendall	72	72	69	70	283	4,111.25
Troy Merritt	72	71	69	71	283	4,111.25
Philip Pettitt, Jr.	69	69	72	73	283	4,111.25
Chris Wilson	74	69	68	72	283	4,111.25

Chile Classic

Prince of Wales Country Club, Santiago, Chile
Par 36-36–72; 6,711

March 8-11
purse, $600,000

	SCORES				TOTAL	MONEY
Paul Haley	67	64	64	71	266	$108,000
Joseph Bramlett	71	68	66	64	269	64,800
Paul Claxton	70	66	66	68	270	40,800
Steven Alker	68	67	71	66	272	24,800
Alex Aragon	69	67	66	70	272	24,800
Rob Oppenheim	69	69	65	69	272	24,800
Brad Elder	68	67	66	72	273	19,350
Brian Stuard	68	68	67	70	273	19,350
Benjamin Alvarado	71	69	65	69	274	16,200
Camilo Benedetti	67	69	68	70	274	16,200
Brice Garnett	68	71	69	66	274	16,200
David Lingmerth	70	69	67	69	275	11,760
Alex Prugh	66	72	66	71	275	11,760
Mark Tullo	69	67	69	70	275	11,760
Will Wilcox	69	68	71	67	275	11,760

	SCORES				TOTAL	MONEY
Tim Wilkinson	74	67	66	68	275	11,760
Glen Day	71	69	68	68	276	8,120
Troy Merritt	69	68	70	69	276	8,120
Alistair Presnell	67	68	69	72	276	8,120
Shawn Stefani	70	70	67	69	276	8,120
Robert Streb	70	67	69	70	276	8,120
Lee Williams	74	66	69	67	276	8,120
Rahil Gangjee	72	68	65	72	277	5,424
Russell Henley	71	68	67	71	277	5,424
Bio Kim	69	71	68	69	277	5,424
Aron Price	70	71	69	67	277	5,424
Darron Stiles	72	66	66	73	277	5,424

Chitimacha Louisiana Open

Le Triomphe Country Club, Broussard, Louisiana
Par 36-35–71; 7,004 yards

March 22-25
purse, $500,000

	SCORES				TOTAL	MONEY
Casey Wittenberg	66	66	63	65	260	$90,000
Fabian Gomez	69	66	68	65	268	37,333.34
Paul Claxton	67	65	68	68	268	37,333.33
Chris Riley	65	70	66	67	268	37,333.33
Woody Austin	69	65	67	68	269	16,950
Camilo Benedetti	66	63	70	70	269	16,950
Brad Fritsch	70	68	69	62	269	16,950
Rob Oppenheim	65	67	68	69	269	16,950
Darron Stiles	69	65	65	70	269	16,950
Kent Jones	70	67	68	65	270	12,500
Andrew Svoboda	67	67	69	67	270	12,500
Omar Uresti	67	70	65	68	270	12,500
Jason Gore	70	66	66	69	271	9,375
Andrew Loupe	67	69	66	69	271	9,375
Patrick Sheehan	67	66	70	68	271	9,375
Shawn Stefani	70	65	68	68	271	9,375
Lee Williams	70	67	67	68	272	8,000
Andres Gonzales	69	68	66	70	273	6,300
Adam Hadwin	69	63	68	73	273	6,300
Justin Hicks	69	66	69	69	273	6,300
Tag Ridings	68	68	69	68	273	6,300
Brian Stuard	68	67	69	69	273	6,300
Steve Wheatcroft	69	68	68	68	273	6,300
Jonas Blixt	69	67	67	71	274	4,350
Justin Bolli	66	69	70	69	274	4,350
Jim Herman	67	68	71	68	274	4,350
Robert Streb	68	67	69	70	274	4,350

Soboba Golf Classic

Country Club at Soboba Springs, San Jacinto, California
Par 36-35–71; 7,101 yards

April 5-8
purse, $750,000

	SCORES				TOTAL	MONEY
Andres Gonzales	67	70	68	71	276	$135,000
Andrew Svoboda	71	70	66	71	278	81,000
Michael Letzig	72	70	67	70	279	43,500
Alistair Presnell	72	68	71	68	279	43,500

	SCORES				TOTAL	MONEY
Camilo Benedetti	75	67	68	70	280	27,375
Adam Hadwin	71	71	65	73	280	27,375
Justin Hicks	70	73	70	67	280	27,375
Nicholas Thompson	71	72	70	68	281	23,250
Luke List	73	70	70	69	282	20,250
Philip Pettitt, Jr.	71	74	72	65	282	20,250
Jim Renner	72	70	70	70	282	20,250
Paul Claxton	70	75	69	69	283	13,821.43
Joe Durant	72	67	74	70	283	13,821.43
Reid Edstrom	71	69	74	69	283	13,821.43
Jason Gore	71	73	68	71	283	13,821.43
Cameron Percy	74	71	68	70	283	13,821.43
Omar Uresti	71	71	73	68	283	13,821.43
Will Wilcox	72	72	68	71	283	13,821.42
Justin Bolli	69	72	72	71	284	9,090
Robert Damron	70	72	69	73	284	9,090
Jim Herman	71	71	72	70	284	9,090
Aron Price	72	70	71	71	284	9,090
Robert Streb	71	73	69	71	284	9,090
Jason Allred	70	71	72	72	285	6,525
Aaron Goldberg	71	68	72	74	285	6,525
Scott Parel	72	74	69	70	285	6,525
Andre Stolz	72	74	70	69	285	6,525

TPC Stonebrae Championship

TPC Stonebrae, Hayward, California
Par 35-35–70; 7,100 yards

April 12-15
purse, $600,000

	SCORES				TOTAL	MONEY
Alex Aragon	67	70	67	66	270	$108,000
Paul Haley	68	66	69	68	271	44,800
Matt Harmon	71	68	71	61	271	44,800
Duffy Waldorf	67	69	67	68	271	44,800
Bio Kim	75	68	66	63	272	22,800
Rob Oppenheim	69	68	67	68	272	22,800
Russell Knox	73	67	66	67	273	19,350
Tyrone van Aswegen	69	67	64	73	273	19,350
Josh Broadaway	66	70	67	71	274	16,800
Michael Putnam	66	68	69	71	274	16,800
Camilo Benedetti	67	72	68	68	275	12,720
Ben Briscoe	73	66	68	68	275	12,720
Bubba Dickerson	68	70	68	69	275	12,720
Jim Renner	71	67	66	71	275	12,720
Wes Roach	69	69	67	70	275	12,720
Ben Martin	65	75	69	67	276	8,417.15
Hudson Swafford	69	73	68	66	276	8,417.15
Steve Friesen	69	68	70	69	276	8,417.14
Rahil Gangjee	70	68	69	69	276	8,417.14
Travis Hampshire	70	68	69	69	276	8,417.14
Justin Searles	71	72	65	68	276	8,417.14
Brian Smock	70	68	69	69	276	8,417.14
Steve Allan	68	71	71	67	277	5,760
Richard Scott	69	71	68	69	277	5,760
Brian Stuard	66	69	68	74	277	5,760

South Georgia Classic

Kinderlou Forest Golf Club, Valdosta, Georgia
Par 36-36–72; 7,781 yards

April 26-29
purse, $625,000

	SCORES				TOTAL	MONEY
Luke List	67	68	69	68	272	$112,500
Brian Stuard	67	69	72	66	274	67,500
Woody Austin	74	66	64	73	277	42,500
Justin Hicks	71	67	73	67	278	25,833.34
Richard Scott	69	70	69	70	278	25,833.33
Robert Streb	66	73	69	70	278	25,833.33
Scott Gardiner	69	70	72	68	279	18,828.13
Fabian Gomez	71	71	70	67	279	18,828.13
Kevin Foley	70	72	69	68	279	18,828.12
Will MacKenzie	70	67	69	73	279	18,828.12
Andrew Buckle	71	70	69	70	280	14,375
Darron Stiles	70	68	71	71	280	14,375
Duffy Waldorf	71	73	69	67	280	14,375
Reid Edstrom	71	72	69	69	281	10,937.50
Peter Lonard	72	71	71	67	281	10,937.50
Rob Oppenheim	73	71	72	65	281	10,937.50
Alex Prugh	71	70	70	70	281	10,937.50
Aaron Goldberg	74	68	73	67	282	7,111.12
Ben Briscoe	72	68	66	76	282	7,111.11
Brice Garnett	71	67	72	72	282	7,111.11
Justin Peters	72	68	70	72	282	7,111.11
Sam Saunders	69	70	75	68	282	7,111.11
David Skinns	71	69	74	68	282	7,111.11
B.J. Staten	72	69	71	70	282	7,111.11
Hudson Swafford	71	71	71	69	282	7,111.11
Lee Williams	73	68	72	69	282	7,111.11

Stadion Classic

University of Georgia Golf Club, Athens, Georgia
Par 35-36–71; 7,240 yards

May 3-6
purse, $550,000

	SCORES				TOTAL	MONEY
Hudson Swafford	66	70	69	62	267	$99,000
Lee Janzen	65	72	66	65	268	48,400
Luke List	66	67	70	65	268	48,400
Billy Horschel	69	63	69	68	269	26,400
Tyrone van Aswegen	67	68	65	70	270	22,000
Jim Herman	66	66	70	69	271	19,800
Justin Bolli	70	69	66	67	272	15,445.84
Kevin Foley	68	69	68	67	272	15,445.84
Woody Austin	67	68	66	71	272	15,445.83
Paul Claxton	68	71	66	67	272	15,445.83
James Hahn	70	65	69	68	272	15,445.83
Bio Kim	70	67	64	71	272	15,445.83
Bubba Dickerson	70	69	67	67	273	10,633.34
Jason Gore	68	65	71	69	273	10,633.33
David May	70	66	68	69	273	10,633.33
Steven Alker	70	68	72	64	274	8,250
Cliff Kresge	68	66	68	72	274	8,250
Aron Price	67	66	71	70	274	8,250
Shawn Stefani	68	68	66	72	274	8,250
Andrew Svoboda	69	69	68	68	274	8,250
Jason Allred	69	68	69	69	275	6,160

	SCORES				TOTAL	MONEY
Martin Piller	67	69	71	68	275	6,160
Robert Streb	69	68	72	66	275	6,160
Nicholas Thompson	68	71	68	69	276	4,913.34
Brandon Brown	65	69	69	73	276	4,913.33
Justin Hicks	70	68	67	71	276	4,913.33

BMW Charity Pro-Am

Thornblade Club, Greer, South Carolina:
Par 35-36–71; 7,024 yards
Greenville Country Club, Greenville, South Carolina:
Par 36-36–72; 6,688 yards
Carolina Country Club, Spartanburg, South Carolina:
Par 36-36–72; 6,877 yards

May 17-20
purse, $600,000

	SCORES				TOTAL	MONEY
Nick Flanagan	67	70	67	67	271	$108,000
Cameron Percy	68	62	75	66	271	64,800
(Flanagan defeated Percy on third playoff hole.)						
Darron Stiles	64	68	74	66	272	34,800
Robert Streb	66	68	70	68	272	34,800
Brad Fritsch	67	68	68	70	273	21,900
Sam Saunders	66	71	69	67	273	21,900
Aaron Watkins	67	66	73	67	273	21,900
D.J. Brigman	65	74	69	66	274	16,800
Scott Gardiner	72	69	69	64	274	16,800
Alistair Presnell	67	72	69	66	274	16,800
Alex Prugh	68	70	66	70	274	16,800
Brent Delahoussaye	67	67	72	69	275	11,400
James Hahn	70	65	69	71	275	11,400
Jim Herman	65	73	68	69	275	11,400
Justin Hicks	71	66	71	67	275	11,400
Fernando Mechereffe	69	69	69	68	275	11,400
Casey Wittenberg	69	72	69	65	275	11,400
Camilo Benedetti	69	67	74	66	276	8,100
Joseph Bramlett	66	76	66	68	276	8,100
Reid Edstrom	67	66	74	69	276	8,100
James Sacheck	69	73	67	67	276	8,100
John Chin	69	72	68	68	277	5,485.72
Derek Fathauer	66	74	69	68	277	5,485.72
Paul Stankowski	68	70	68	71	277	5,485.72
Steve LeBrun	68	68	67	74	277	5,485.71
Scott Parel	68	69	69	71	277	5,485.71
Tag Ridings	71	66	70	70	277	5,485.71
Ron Whittaker	69	69	68	71	277	5,485.71

Rex Hospital Open

TPC Wakefield Plantation, Raleigh, North Carolina
Par 36-35–71; 7,257 yards

May 31-June 3
purse, $550,000

	SCORES				TOTAL	MONEY
James Hahn	67	68	69	67	271	$99,000
Scott Parel	67	69	67	68	271	59,400
(Hahn defeated Parel on second playoff hole.)						
Jin Park	69	71	65	67	272	28,600
Jim Renner	63	71	67	71	272	28,600

	SCORES				TOTAL	MONEY
B.J. Staten	66	68	66	72	272	28,600
Dustin Bray	67	71	69	66	273	18,425
Jeff Curl	65	69	70	69	273	18,425
Will Wilcox	67	72	68	66	273	18,425
Oscar Serna	67	66	72	69	274	15,950
Darron Stiles	70	68	69	68	275	12,191.67
Andrew Svoboda	68	68	70	69	275	12,191.67
Nicholas Thompson	67	69	70	69	275	12,191.67
Lee Williams	70	69	69	67	275	12,191.67
Shane Bertsch	65	69	70	71	275	12,191.66
Steven Bowditch	65	70	70	70	275	12,191.66
Brad Adamonis	72	68	66	70	276	7,466.25
Paul Claxton	70	69	70	67	276	7,466.25
Brent Delahoussaye	71	69	67	69	276	7,466.25
Reid Edstrom	65	70	68	73	276	7,466.25
Derek Fathauer	69	68	70	69	276	7,466.25
Jim Herman	67	71	67	71	276	7,466.25
Justin Hicks	66	66	71	73	276	7,466.25
Brian Stuard	71	67	68	70	276	7,466.25
Scott Gardiner	66	70	70	71	277	4,785
Scott Langley	70	69	69	69	277	4,785
Ryan Nelson	69	71	65	72	277	4,785
Alex Prugh	68	67	70	72	277	4,785

Mexico Open

El Bosque Golf Club, Leon, Mexico
Par 36-36–72; 6,810 yards

June 7-10
purse, $625,000

	SCORES				TOTAL	MONEY
Lee Williams	69	67	68	70	274	$112,500
Paul Haley	65	71	71	68	275	67,500
Scott Gutschewski	70	69	71	66	276	42,500
Philip Pettitt, Jr.	68	74	67	68	277	27,500
Tyrone van Aswegen	69	70	67	71	277	27,500
Julian Etulain	70	71	70	67	278	18,906.25
Aaron Goldberg	72	68	68	70	278	18,906.25
Matt Hendrix	68	70	67	73	278	18,906.25
Andy Pope	73	70	65	70	278	18,906.25
Brian Stuard	67	73	71	67	278	18,906.25
Casey Wittenberg	70	68	72	68	278	18,906.25
Tim Wilkinson	73	67	73	66	279	14,375
Alex Coe	68	72	69	71	280	11,718.75
Matt Harmon	76	69	66	69	280	11,718.75
Troy Merritt	69	73	68	70	280	11,718.75
Dawie Van der Walt	71	68	69	72	280	11,718.75
Andy Bare	71	70	71	69	281	9,062.50
Adam Hadwin	68	71	70	72	281	9,062.50
Doug LaBelle	70	70	65	76	281	9,062.50
Hudson Swafford	68	69	77	67	281	9,062.50
Jeff Gove	71	72	69	70	282	7,250
Ben Martin	72	67	76	67	282	7,250
Scott Gardiner	69	70	66	78	283	6,250
Adam Long	70	72	71	70	283	6,250
Brad Adamonis	69	73	72	70	284	5,125
Justin Bolli	67	71	71	75	284	5,125
John Chin	73	69	73	69	284	5,125
Aron Price	71	73	75	65	284	5,125

Preferred Health Systems Wichita Open

Crestview Country Club, Wichita, Kansas
Par 35-36–71; 6,913 yards

June 21-24
purse, $600,000

	SCORES				TOTAL	MONEY
Casey Wittenberg	63	70	67	66	266	$108,000
Jim Herman	66	64	68	70	268	52,800
Justin Hicks	66	70	65	67	268	52,800
Joseph Bramlett	68	64	71	68	271	23,625
Scott Gardiner	66	67	73	65	271	23,625
Brice Garnett	67	66	69	69	271	23,625
Hudson Swafford	67	66	70	68	271	23,625
Duffy Waldorf	68	69	68	67	272	18,600
Paul Haley	68	68	69	68	273	14,400
Matt Harmon	66	68	71	68	273	14,400
Steve LeBrun	66	70	68	69	273	14,400
Cameron Percy	67	71	70	65	273	14,400
Richard Scott	68	68	70	67	273	14,400
Charles Warren	66	69	72	66	273	14,400
Jason Allred	71	66	68	69	274	9,000
Jason Gore	65	68	68	73	274	9,000
Kevin Johnson	65	68	71	70	274	9,000
Bronson La'Cassie	67	68	72	67	274	9,000
David Lingmerth	69	69	70	66	274	9,000
Luke List	71	64	68	71	274	9,000
Tag Ridings	67	69	69	69	274	9,000
Jeff Corr	69	69	70	67	275	5,485.72
Michael Letzig	69	68	70	68	275	5,485.72
Ben Martin	68	66	73	68	275	5,485.72
Bryan DeCorso	68	68	70	69	275	5,485.71
Doug LaBelle	69	69	69	68	275	5,485.71
Aron Price	68	68	69	70	275	5,485.71
Darron Stiles	68	67	69	71	275	5,485.71

United Leasing Championship

Victoria National Golf Club, Newburgh, Indiana
Par 36-36–72; 7,239 yards

June 28-July 1
purse, $550,000

	SCORES				TOTAL	MONEY
Peter Tomasulo	70	72	65	70	277	$99,000
David Lingmerth	67	70	72	68	277	59,400
(Tomasulo defeated Lingmerth on fourth playoff hole.)						
Richard Scott	70	72	65	71	278	37,400
Derek Fathauer	70	68	70	71	279	20,735
Scott Gardiner	73	69	71	66	279	20,735
Morgan Hoffmann	71	68	69	71	279	20,735
Chris Riley	72	66	69	72	279	20,735
Aaron Watkins	74	69	67	69	279	20,735
Justin Hicks	71	69	70	70	280	15,400
Nicholas Thompson	70	72	65	73	280	15,400
Scott Parel	71	71	67	72	281	11,660
Cameron Percy	72	69	68	72	281	11,660
Tag Ridings	68	72	68	73	281	11,660
Brian Stuard	70	67	70	74	281	11,660
Roger Tambellini	71	68	71	71	281	11,660
Glen Day	71	71	68	72	282	8,250
Scott Gutschewski	72	70	67	73	282	8,250
Bio Kim	71	69	71	71	282	8,250

	SCORES				TOTAL	MONEY
Will MacKenzie	69	70	68	75	282	8,250
Aron Price	72	71	70	69	282	8,250
Aaron Goldberg	70	72	68	73	283	5,720
Jamie Lovemark	75	67	73	68	283	5,720
Martin Piller	67	71	69	76	283	5,720
Alistair Presnell	68	68	69	78	283	5,720
Charles Warren	69	72	75	67	283	5,720

Utah Championship

Willow Creek Country Club, Sandy, Utah   July 12-15
Par 35-36–71; 7,104 yards   purse, $550,000

	SCORES				TOTAL	MONEY
Doug LaBelle	64	68	69	68	269	$99,000
Scott Gutschewski	67	67	69	67	270	36,300
James Hahn	68	66	71	65	270	36,300
Michael Putnam	67	66	63	74	270	36,300
Sam Saunders	70	68	65	67	270	36,300
Craig Bowden	70	66	68	67	271	19,800
Andy Pope	68	69	68	67	272	17,737.50
Ron Whittaker	67	69	71	65	272	17,737.50
Brian Anderson	68	68	69	68	273	11,550
Camilo Benedetti	66	69	68	70	273	11,550
Andres Gonzales	66	66	69	72	273	11,550
Russell Henley	69	70	67	67	273	11,550
Morgan Hoffmann	64	67	72	70	273	11,550
James Love	66	68	69	70	273	11,550
Richard Scott	70	69	68	66	273	11,550
Brian Stuard	69	65	69	70	273	11,550
Nicholas Thompson	70	69	65	69	273	11,550
Lee Williams	68	66	71	68	273	11,550
Josh Broadaway	70	68	67	69	274	7,150
Jin Park	68	67	72	67	274	7,150
Aaron Watkins	67	68	69	70	274	7,150
Brad Fritsch	64	70	73	68	275	5,028.58
Matt Davidson	68	71	69	67	275	5,028.57
Trevor Murphy	71	62	70	72	275	5,028.57
Robert Streb	67	68	65	75	275	5,028.57
Peter Tomasulo	69	70	67	69	275	5,028.57
Tyrone van Aswegen	70	62	70	73	275	5,028.57
Matt Weibring	70	67	72	66	275	5,028.57

Nationwide Children's Hospital Invitational

The OSU Golf Club, Scarlet Course, Columbus, Ohio   July 26-29
Par 36-35–71; 7,141 yards   purse, $800,000

	SCORES				TOTAL	MONEY
Ben Kohles	66	69	67	70	272	$144,000
Luke Guthrie	72	65	69	66	272	86,400
(Kohles defeated Guthrie on first playoff hole.)						
Cliff Kresge	69	71	64	69	273	46,400
Casey Wittenberg	68	67	70	68	273	46,400
Kevin Foley	69	70	69	66	274	32,000
Aaron Watkins	72	67	65	71	275	28,800
Joseph Bramlett	69	66	70	71	276	23,280

	SCORES				TOTAL	MONEY
Trevor Murphy	63	68	73	72	276	23,280
James Sacheck	66	70	70	70	276	23,280
Nicholas Thompson	69	66	71	70	276	23,280
Lee Williams	71	69	66	70	276	23,280
Camilo Benedetti	68	68	69	72	277	17,600
Cameron Percy	69	70	70	68	277	17,600
Scott Gutschewski	72	68	69	69	278	13,200
Doug LaBelle	68	70	70	70	278	13,200
David Lingmerth	71	68	68	71	278	13,200
Fernando Mechereffe	68	68	73	69	278	13,200
Alex Prugh	68	69	71	70	278	13,200
David Skinns	70	71	67	70	278	13,200
Brice Garnett	72	67	71	69	279	10,000
John Kimbell	73	68	67	71	279	10,000
John Chin	70	69	71	70	280	6,933.34
Luke List	68	69	72	71	280	6,933.34
Robert Streb	66	72	71	71	280	6,933.34
Steve Allan	67	69	71	73	280	6,933.33
Paul Claxton	72	69	72	67	280	6,933.33
Andres Gonzales	71	68	72	69	280	6,933.33
Philip Pettitt, Jr.	70	68	71	71	280	6,933.33
Michael Sim	70	66	70	74	280	6,933.33
Shawn Stefani	69	71	71	69	280	6,933.33

Cox Classic

Champions Run, Omaha, Nebraska
Par 35-36–71; 7,145 yards

August 2-5
purse, $650,000

	SCORES				TOTAL	MONEY
Ben Kohles	65	66	67	62	260	$117,000
Dawie Van der Walt	68	66	69	60	263	70,200
Justin Bolli	67	67	66	64	264	31,200
Luke Guthrie	62	63	71	68	264	31,200
Adam Hadwin	68	67	63	66	264	31,200
Jim Herman	63	69	68	64	264	31,200
Russell Henley	64	68	64	69	265	20,962.50
Justin Hicks	67	69	64	65	265	20,962.50
Steve LeBrun	66	64	71	65	266	17,550
Luke List	67	67	66	66	266	17,550
Rob Oppenheim	69	61	69	67	266	17,550
Aaron Goldberg	62	70	66	69	267	14,950
Steve Allan	68	64	70	66	268	11,830
Josh Broadaway	67	65	68	68	268	11,830
Reid Edstrom	67	65	68	68	268	11,830
Brad Fritsch	66	64	70	68	268	11,830
Shawn Stefani	69	66	66	67	268	11,830
Fabian Gomez	64	70	68	67	269	8,775
Jeff Gove	70	66	70	63	269	8,775
Tag Ridings	65	63	71	70	269	8,775
Brian Stuard	66	63	70	70	269	8,775
Jeff Curl	68	66	68	68	270	5,785
Scott Gutschewski	67	68	67	68	270	5,785
David Lingmerth	67	65	68	70	270	5,785
Peter Lonard	66	64	72	68	270	5,785
Alex Prugh	66	67	68	69	270	5,785
Jim Renner	66	66	67	71	270	5,785
Wes Roach	66	67	68	69	270	5,785
B.J. Staten	69	64	68	69	270	5,785

Price Cutter Charity Championship

Highland Springs Country Club, Springfield, Missouri
Par 36-36–72; 7,060 yards

August 9-12
purse, $625,000

	SCORES				TOTAL	MONEY
Chris Wilson	68	67	65	67	267	$112,500
Scott Harrington	65	68	66	68	267	67,500
(Wilson defeated Harrington on first playoff hole.)						
Andy Winings	67	71	65	65	268	42,500
Camilo Benedetti	66	72	63	68	269	27,500
Matt Hendrix	63	72	68	66	269	27,500
Stuart Anderson	67	72	63	68	270	20,234.38
Robert Streb	69	68	68	65	270	20,234.38
Michael Letzig	65	69	67	69	270	20,234.37
David Lingmerth	67	67	65	71	270	20,234.37
Luke Guthrie	68	67	69	67	271	16,250
James Nitties	64	71	66	70	271	16,250
Alex Aragon	65	70	69	68	272	13,125
James Hahn	69	68	67	68	272	13,125
Aron Price	68	70	69	65	272	13,125
Jim Herman	65	70	71	67	273	10,312.50
Philip Pettitt, Jr.	71	64	69	69	273	10,312.50
Nicholas Thompson	70	64	66	73	273	10,312.50
Matt Weibring	69	69	69	66	273	10,312.50
Joseph Bramlett	67	72	70	65	274	6,828.13
Josh Broadaway	65	71	68	70	274	6,828.13
Rob Oppenheim	66	72	68	68	274	6,828.13
Michael Putnam	70	68	68	68	274	6,828.13
Doug Barron	64	71	68	71	274	6,828.12
Glen Day	70	67	66	71	274	6,828.12
Paul Haley	65	73	65	71	274	6,828.12
Richard Scott	69	69	66	70	274	6,828.12

Midwest Classic

Nicklaus Golf Club at LionsGate, Overland Park, Kansas
Par 36-35–71; 7,251 yards

August 16-19
purse, $550,000

	SCORES				TOTAL	MONEY
Shawn Stefani	68	68	67	64	267	$99,000
Russell Henley	68	66	67	68	269	48,400
Luke List	70	68	64	67	269	48,400
Tag Ridings	68	68	66	68	270	24,200
Matt Weibring	65	69	65	71	270	24,200
Luke Guthrie	69	67	70	65	271	19,112.50
Ben Martin	69	68	65	69	271	19,112.50
Jason Gore	65	70	68	69	272	15,950
Jason Schultz	68	67	68	69	272	15,950
Robert Streb	68	69	70	65	272	15,950
Guy Boros	71	69	65	68	273	11,275
Christopher DeForest	66	67	68	72	273	11,275
Scott Gardiner	70	68	65	70	273	11,275
Jamie Lovemark	72	66	63	72	273	11,275
James Nitties	68	66	66	73	273	11,275
Duffy Waldorf	70	65	69	69	273	11,275
Derek Fathauer	67	71	67	69	274	8,250
Brice Garnett	74	66	65	69	274	8,250
David Skinns	68	69	69	68	274	8,250
Lee Janzen	70	70	67	68	275	5,767.15

	SCORES				TOTAL	MONEY
Cliff Kresge	72	68	67	68	275	5,767.15
Justin Bolli	68	68	68	71	275	5,767.14
Michael Connell	66	70	66	73	275	5,767.14
Louis de Jager	70	68	66	71	275	5,767.14
Bryan DeCorso	69	63	69	74	275	5,767.14
Hudson Swafford	70	67	68	70	275	5,767.14

News Sentinel Open

Fox Den Country Club, Knoxville, Tennessee   August 23-26
Par 35-36–71; 7,110 yards   purse, $500,000

	SCORES				TOTAL	MONEY
Darron Stiles	67	66	66	67	266	$90,000
Scott Gardiner	67	70	68	62	267	37,333.34
D.J. Brigman	67	69	68	63	267	37,333.33
Nicholas Thompson	68	68	67	64	267	37,333.33
Erik Flores	66	65	69	68	268	20,000
John Daly	70	66	66	67	269	16,187.50
Scott Dunlap	66	69	67	67	269	16,187.50
Brice Garnett	67	68	70	64	269	16,187.50
Jeff Gove	68	67	69	65	269	16,187.50
Adam Hadwin	68	66	68	68	270	12,500
Matt Weibring	71	67	65	67	270	12,500
Casey Wittenberg	63	72	69	66	270	12,500
Patrick Sheehan	65	69	66	71	271	10,500
Josh Broadaway	66	72	67	67	272	8,250
Kevin Kisner	67	71	70	64	272	8,250
Cliff Kresge	70	68	69	65	272	8,250
James Sacheck	69	65	67	71	272	8,250
B.J. Staten	68	70	64	70	272	8,250
Dawie Van der Walt	69	69	67	67	272	8,250
Gavin Coles	68	70	67	68	273	5,825
Matt Davidson	69	70	66	68	273	5,825
Michael Putnam	68	69	68	68	273	5,825
Alexandre Rocha	67	69	70	67	273	5,825
Brian Stuard	69	66	73	66	274	4,028.58
Shane Bertsch	66	68	70	70	274	4,028.57
Justin Bolli	72	66	67	69	274	4,028.57
Jeff Corr	68	67	72	67	274	4,028.57
Nathan Green	68	71	68	67	274	4,028.57
Doug LaBelle	65	72	68	69	274	4,028.57
Jin Park	70	69	67	68	274	4,028.57

Mylan Classic

Southpointe Golf Club, Canonsburg, Pennsylvania   August 30-September 3
Par 35-36–71; 6,951 yards   purse, $600,000

	SCORES				TOTAL	MONEY
Robert Streb	64	69	69	64	266	$108,000
Brad Fritsch	66	64	72	68	270	44,800
Cliff Kresge	66	65	70	69	270	44,800
Matt Weibring	71	63	69	67	270	44,800
Ben Kohles	68	70	66	67	271	24,000
Nicholas Thompson	67	67	68	70	272	21,600
John Chin	66	69	70	68	273	17,460

	SCORES				TOTAL	MONEY
Justin Hicks	67	70	71	65	273	17,460
Kevin Kisner	66	71	66	70	273	17,460
Will MacKenzie	66	72	68	67	273	17,460
Dawie Van der Walt	69	70	66	68	273	17,460
Jason Allred	70	68	65	71	274	12,600
Steve Friesen	69	69	69	67	274	12,600
James Hahn	70	70	68	66	274	12,600
Scott Gardiner	70	68	68	69	275	9,900
Jim Herman	70	68	72	65	275	9,900
Edward Loar	64	69	74	68	275	9,900
Peter Lonard	69	65	74	67	275	9,900
Steven Alker	68	71	67	70	276	7,800
Nate Smith	67	73	66	70	276	7,800
Casey Wittenberg	65	67	72	72	276	7,800
Joseph Bramlett	70	66	72	69	277	6,000
Richard H. Lee	68	67	71	71	277	6,000
Jin Park	70	70	67	70	277	6,000
Shawn Stefani	68	72	71	66	277	6,000

Albertsons Boise Open

Hillcrest Country Club, Boise, Idaho
Par 36-35–71; 6,698 yards

September 13-16
purse, $725,000

	SCORES				TOTAL	MONEY
Luke Guthrie	64	71	62	65	262	$130,500
Scott Gardiner	67	66	64	69	266	47,850
Richard H. Lee	67	62	71	66	266	47,850
Michael Putnam	62	65	68	71	266	47,850
Steve Wheatcroft	66	68	63	69	266	47,850
Tyrone Van Aswegen	62	68	67	70	267	26,100
Shawn Stefani	68	68	69	63	268	22,595.84
Jeff Gove	63	68	67	70	268	22,595.83
Billy Horschel	68	65	67	68	268	22,595.83
Glen Day	63	69	70	67	269	18,125
Jim Renner	67	69	65	68	269	18,125
Casey Wittenberg	67	66	64	72	269	18,125
J.J. Killeen	71	66	68	65	270	12,808.34
Danny Lee	66	68	71	65	270	12,808.34
Joe Durant	67	69	66	68	270	12,808.33
Luke List	67	65	68	70	270	12,808.33
Scott Parel	67	70	67	66	270	12,808.33
Matt Weibring	65	67	69	69	270	12,808.33
Steven Bowditch	69	68	68	66	271	8,182.15
Dawie Van der Walt	65	65	73	68	271	8,182.15
Woody Austin	70	65	66	70	271	8,182.14
Russell Henley	68	68	67	68	271	8,182.14
Ben Kohles	66	66	70	69	271	8,182.14
Ben Martin	69	65	67	70	271	8,182.14
Tim Wilkinson	69	67	66	69	271	8,182.14

WNB Golf Classic

Midland Country Club, Midland, Texas
Par 36-36–72; 7,354 yards

September 20-23
purse, $550,000

	SCORES				TOTAL	MONEY
Luke Guthrie	72	66	67	66	271	$99,000
Danny Lee	72	63	65	72	272	48,400
Cameron Percy	68	68	66	70	272	48,400
Aaron Goldberg	66	73	66	68	273	24,200
Brett Wetterich	71	69	66	67	273	24,200
Morgan Hoffmann	68	64	70	74	276	19,800
Jamie Lovemark	66	69	69	73	277	17,737.50
Michael Putnam	68	72	69	68	277	17,737.50
Guy Boros	72	71	67	68	278	13,750
Brice Garnett	69	71	67	71	278	13,750
Justin Hicks	68	70	67	73	278	13,750
Adam Long	71	70	65	72	278	13,750
Tim Wilkinson	67	71	71	69	278	13,750
Jason Allred	71	69	67	72	279	9,075
Scott Dunlap	73	69	66	71	279	9,075
Luke List	67	71	72	69	279	9,075
Tim Petrovic	68	72	66	73	279	9,075
Alex Prugh	71	72	65	71	279	9,075
Nate Smith	69	70	70	70	279	9,075
Jeff Corr	72	71	70	67	280	6,636.67
Jeff Gove	73	70	69	68	280	6,636.67
Steve Allan	69	71	70	70	280	6,636.66
Adam Hadwin	73	70	69	69	281	4,592.50
Matt Hendrix	70	70	73	68	281	4,592.50
Bio Kim	72	71	71	67	281	4,592.50
Derek Lamely	70	71	69	71	281	4,592.50
Tag Ridings	69	70	73	69	281	4,592.50
Jason Schultz	73	68	72	68	281	4,592.50
Aaron Watkins	71	69	69	72	281	4,592.50
Lee Williams	74	66	70	71	281	4,592.50

Chiquita Classic

The Club at Longview, Weddington, North Carolina
Par 36-36–72; 7,065 yards

September 27-30
purse, $550,000

	SCORES				TOTAL	MONEY
Russell Henley	66	65	65	70	266	$99,000
Patrick Cantlay	69	67	65	65	266	48,400
Morgan Hoffmann	68	67	66	65	266	48,400
(Henley defeated Cantlay and Hoffman on first playoff hole.)						
Brad Fritsch	67	64	65	72	268	26,400
Scott Dunlap	66	71	66	68	271	20,900
Robert Streb	69	69	66	67	271	20,900
Russell Knox	68	65	70	70	273	17,737.50
Fernando Mechereffe	69	66	67	71	273	17,737.50
Justin Hicks	69	66	68	71	274	14,850
Lee Janzen	66	67	70	71	274	14,850
Kevin Johnson	71	68	66	69	274	14,850
Aaron Goldberg	69	67	69	70	275	12,100
Casey Wittenberg	70	66	71	68	275	12,100
Marco Dawson	71	64	72	69	276	9,075
Chris Epperson	70	66	68	72	276	9,075
Skip Kendall	66	69	70	71	276	9,075

	SCORES				TOTAL	MONEY
Jeff Klauk	68	70	66	72	276	9,075
Philip Pettitt, Jr.	69	69	69	69	276	9,075
Nicholas Thompson	68	69	70	69	276	9,075
Travis Hampshire	70	68	71	68	277	6,636.67
Aaron Watkins	68	68	70	71	277	6,636.67
Daniel Chopra	69	69	66	73	277	6,636.66
Derek Fathauer	70	66	72	70	278	4,714.29
Kevin Foley	68	71	69	70	278	4,714.29
Tom Hoge	67	70	72	69	278	4,714.29
Andrew Svoboda	72	67	69	70	278	4,714.29
Jeff Gove	70	68	68	72	278	4,714.28
Jason Kokrak	66	68	71	73	278	4,714.28
Dawie van der Walt	67	69	69	73	278	4,714.28

Neediest Kids Championship

TPC Potomac at Avenel Farm, Potomac, Maryland
Par 35-35–70; 7,139 yards

October 4-7
purse, $600,000

	SCORES				TOTAL	MONEY
David Lingmerth	66	66	74	66	272	$108,000
Casey Wittenberg	67	69	68	69	273	64,800
Philip Pettitt, Jr.	66	71	68	69	274	34,800
Alistair Presnell	65	70	70	69	274	34,800
Chris Wilson	70	68	67	70	275	24,000
Morgan Hoffmann	69	69	72	68	278	20,850
Bronson La'Cassie	67	67	75	69	278	20,850
Reid Edstrom	69	72	67	71	279	16,200
Tom Hoge	69	65	69	76	279	16,200
Josh Persons	65	68	69	77	279	16,200
Sam Saunders	66	73	71	69	279	16,200
Will Wilcox	65	71	69	74	279	16,200
Luke List	68	72	66	74	280	12,000
Brian Stuard	68	70	73	69	280	12,000
Rob Oppenheim	68	72	70	71	281	10,800
Stuart Anderson	69	73	71	69	282	7,880
Camilo Benedetti	69	68	74	71	282	7,880
D.J. Brigman	66	70	70	76	282	7,880
Glen Day	67	73	72	70	282	7,880
Joe Durant	73	69	72	68	282	7,880
Brad Fritsch	67	66	74	75	282	7,880
Cliff Kresge	70	69	73	70	282	7,880
Michael Putnam	71	69	70	72	282	7,880
Tag Ridings	72	70	70	70	282	7,880
Nick Flanagan	70	72	69	72	283	4,800
Jeff Gove	69	69	70	75	283	4,800
Adam Hadwin	69	72	72	70	283	4,800
Paul Haley	70	72	73	68	283	4,800
Robert Streb	68	72	73	70	283	4,800

Miccosukee Championship

Miccosukee Golf & Country Club, Miami, Florida   October 11-14
Par 35-36–71; 7,200 yards   purse, $600,000

	SCORES				TOTAL	MONEY
Shawn Stefani	68	71	62	68	269	$108,000
Alistair Presnell	71	67	69	67	274	64,800
Russell Henley	70	70	69	69	278	40,800
Steve LeBrun	68	67	73	71	279	28,800
Christopher DeForest	65	70	72	73	280	22,800
Kevin Tway	67	75	67	71	280	22,800
Jamie Lovemark	71	70	69	71	281	19,350
Jin Park	72	68	72	69	281	19,350
Travis Hampshire	69	71	69	73	282	15,600
Morgan Hoffmann	66	72	73	71	282	15,600
Cameron Percy	67	70	73	72	282	15,600
Aron Price	69	71	71	71	282	15,600
Steve Allan	68	74	68	73	283	9,975
Doug Barron	69	73	69	72	283	9,975
Craig Bowden	72	67	73	71	283	9,975
Scott Gardiner	69	69	72	73	283	9,975
David Lingmerth	71	70	70	72	283	9,975
Josh Persons	75	68	70	70	283	9,975
Wes Short, Jr.	74	66	72	71	283	9,975
Nicholas Thompson	69	72	68	74	283	9,975
Lee Janzen	68	72	76	68	284	6,240
Bronson La'Cassie	69	70	73	72	284	6,240
Scott Parel	70	70	72	72	284	6,240
Brian Stuard	69	73	69	73	284	6,240
Andrew Svoboda	69	73	67	75	284	6,240

Winn-Dixie Jacksonville Open

Dye's Valley Course, Ponte Vedra, Florida   October 18-21
Par 35-35–70; 6,864 yards   purse, $600,000

	SCORES				TOTAL	MONEY
Russell Henley	66	70	69	65	270	$108,000
B.J. Staten	68	66	68	68	270	64,800
(Henley defeated Staten on first playoff hole.)						
Ben Martin	67	69	68	68	272	40,800
Aaron Watkins	68	71	68	67	274	28,800
Patrick Cantlay	68	67	68	72	275	21,900
Kevin Foley	67	69	72	67	275	21,900
Wes Roach	70	69	67	69	275	21,900
Troy Merritt	67	71	69	71	278	18,000
Robert Streb	70	66	67	75	278	18,000
Camilo Benedetti	66	71	72	70	279	13,800
Brad Fritsch	68	70	70	71	279	13,800
Fabian Gomez	69	70	70	70	279	13,800
Matt Hendrix	68	73	69	69	279	13,800
Ron Whittaker	69	66	73	71	279	13,800
Blayne Barber	67	69	74	70	280	8,440
Joseph Bramlett	68	70	72	70	280	8,440
Josh Broadaway	70	69	70	71	280	8,440
Matt Harmon	70	68	70	72	280	8,440
Doug LaBelle	65	70	74	71	280	8,440
Michael Letzig	70	70	67	73	280	8,440
James Nitties	69	66	72	73	280	8,440

	SCORES				TOTAL	MONEY
Tag Ridings	73	67	69	71	280	8,440
Brett Wetterich	71	66	72	71	280	8,440
Woody Austin	67	73	68	73	281	4,960
Glen Day	69	66	73	73	281	4,960
Lee Janzen	68	69	69	75	281	4,960
Andy Pope	69	70	69	73	281	4,960
Chris Wilson	69	68	73	71	281	4,960
Andy Winings	67	69	74	71	281	4,960

Web.com Tour Championship

TPC Craig Ranch, McKinney, Texas
Par 36-35–71; 7,438

October 25-28
purse, $1,000,000

	SCORES				TOTAL	MONEY
Justin Bolli	65	71	67	65	268	$180,000
James Hahn	70	67	64	69	270	108,000
Adam Hadwin	69	69	68	65	271	58,000
Morgan Hoffmann	68	72	67	64	271	58,000
Justin Hicks	65	69	67	71	272	40,000
Russell Henley	70	67	68	68	273	34,750
Cliff Kresge	65	73	67	68	273	34,750
Edward Loar	67	73	66	69	275	31,000
Brad Fritsch	65	71	71	69	276	26,000
Luke Guthrie	66	72	67	71	276	26,000
David Lingmerth	68	71	69	68	276	26,000
Casey Wittenberg	68	71	67	70	276	26,000
Kevin Foley	68	73	71	65	277	17,666.67
Doug LaBelle	70	71	68	68	277	17,666.67
Luke List	74	68	67	68	277	17,666.67
Sam Saunders	71	69	68	69	277	17,666.67
Ben Martin	69	69	69	70	277	17,666.66
Michael Putnam	65	72	67	73	277	17,666.66
Camilo Benedetti	72	73	66	67	278	12,120
Brice Garnett	69	72	66	71	278	12,120
Cameron Percy	72	72	66	68	278	12,120
Tag Ridings	65	73	69	71	278	12,120
Darron Stiles	71	69	69	69	278	12,120
Peter Tomasulo	69	69	69	72	279	9,600
Scott Gardiner	67	70	73	70	280	8,400
Robert Streb	70	72	73	65	280	8,400
Matt Weibring	67	74	69	70	280	8,400

Canadian Tour

Times Colonist Island Savings Open

Uplands Golf Club, Victoria, British Columbia
Par 35-35–70; 6,420 yards

June 7-10
purse, C$150,000

	SCORES				TOTAL	MONEY
Andrew Roque	64	70	71	61	266	C$24,000
Lucas Lee	65	69	70	65	269	11,700
Cory Renfrew	68	67	66	68	269	11,700
Derek Gillespie	67	66	71	66	270	7,200
Scott Harrington	69	71	68	65	273	5,700
Matt Jager	72	69	65	67	273	5,700
Nick Taylor	67	70	69	68	274	4,800
Jeff Rangel	70	68	66	70	274	4,800
Tyler Aldridge	69	70	68	68	275	4,350
Roger Sloan	71	68	69	68	276	3,750
Mark Hubbard	73	68	67	68	276	3,750
Jaime Gomez	69	70	67	70	276	3,750
Matt Hoffman	70	72	70	65	277	2,900
Wes Heffernan	69	70	68	70	277	2,900
Matt Marshall	67	69	70	71	277	2,900
James Allenby	68	70	71	69	278	2,250
Adam Cornelson	73	67	69	69	278	2,250
Wil Collins	70	70	69	69	278	2,250
Gordy Scutt	67	68	73	70	278	2,250
Vince Covello	72	70	66	70	278	2,250
Kyle Kallan	73	66	73	67	279	1,687.50
Jae Woo Im	74	66	71	68	279	1,687.50
Ryan Williams	72	70	69	68	279	1,687.50
Kyle Stough	73	69	68	69	279	1,687.50
Nathan Leonhardt	69	69	70	71	279	1,687.50
Jeff Burton	67	71	68	73	279	1,687.50

ATB Financial Classic

Windermere Golf Club, Edmonton, Alberta
Par 35-36–71; 6,743 yards

June 21-24
purse, C$175,000

	SCORES				TOTAL	MONEY
Michael Gligic	65	70	68	67	270	C$28,000
Matt Marshall	69	71	62	68	270	16,800
(Gligic defeated Marshall on second playoff hole.)						
Nick Taylor	69	65	71	67	272	8,050
Ryan Williams	64	70	70	68	272	8,050
Joe Panzeri	67	62	72	71	272	8,050
Dodge Kemmer	67	68	67	70	272	8,050
Hugo Leon	65	72	69	67	273	5,775
Wilson Bateman	69	72	65	68	274	4,900
Scott Harrington	64	70	69	71	274	4,900
Matt Hill	68	71	65	70	274	4,900
Garrett Sapp	68	69	66	71	274	4,900
Dan Buchner	70	66	70	69	275	3,675

	SCORES				TOTAL	MONEY
Darren Wallace	66	69	69	71	275	3,675
James Love	68	68	67	72	275	3,675
Chris Killmer	68	67	73	68	276	2,712.50
Riley Wheeldon	67	72	70	67	276	2,712.50
Will Strickler	67	70	74	65	276	2,712.50
Derek Gillespie	71	68	69	68	276	2,712.50
Michael McCabe	68	69	69	70	276	2,712.50
Russell A. Surber	68	67	70	71	276	2,712.50
Creighton Honeck	67	70	69	71	277	2,100
Jason Scrivener	71	65	69	72	277	2,100
Steven Lecuyer	67	69	68	73	277	2,100
Garrett Frank	70	70	68	70	278	1,881.25
James Allenby	73	67	63	75	278	1,881.25

Syncrude Boreal Open

Fort McMurray Golf Club, Ft. McMurray, Alberta
Par 36-36–72; 6,886 yards

June 28-July 1
purse, C$150,000

	SCORES				TOTAL	MONEY
Cory Renfrew	71	64	73	63	271	C$24,000
Matt Hill	72	66	66	67	271	14,400
(Renfrew defeated Hill on fourth playoff hole.)						
Nate McCoy	67	65	71	71	274	9,000
Daniel Im	72	66	70	69	277	6,600
Roger Sloan	69	68	69	71	277	6,600
Andrew Roque	69	69	73	68	279	4,837.50
Kent Eger	69	70	69	71	279	4,837.50
Tyler Aldridge	71	69	67	72	279	4,837.50
Sebastian Saavedra	70	70	67	72	279	4,837.50
Michael McCabe	73	67	71	69	280	3,600
Mark Hubbard	69	71	69	71	280	3,600
Joe Panzeri	69	70	70	71	280	3,600
Matt Marshall	73	71	64	72	280	3,600
Craig Hocknull	73	70	72	66	281	2,700
Lucas Lee	70	69	70	72	281	2,700
Devin Carrey	71	72	65	73	281	2,700
Brock Mackenzie	74	71	67	70	282	2,115
Kevin Stinson	75	69	71	67	282	2,115
David Dragoo	73	66	71	72	282	2,115
Tarquin MacManus	71	72	74	65	282	2,115
Jae Woo Im	69	70	69	74	282	2,115
Boyd Summerhays	73	71	69	70	283	1,650
Tyler Harris	72	71	69	71	283	1,650
Brian Kontak	72	69	71	71	283	1,650
Joel Dahmen	70	71	68	74	283	1,650
Cody Slover	71	71	67	74	283	1,650

Dakota Dunes Casino Open

Dakota Dunes, Saskatoon, Saskatchewan
Par 36-36–72; 7,301 yards

July 5-8
purse, C$150,000

	SCORES				TOTAL	MONEY
Matt Hill	67	68	66	68	269	C$24,000
Will Strickler	69	70	64	66	269	14,400
(Hill defeated Strickler on fourth playoff hole.)						

	SCORES				TOTAL	MONEY
Joel Dahmen	71	66	65	68	270	7,400
James Allenby	69	67	65	69	270	7,400
Jose de Jesus Rodriguez	67	67	66	70	270	7,400
Michael Gligic	65	71	70	65	271	5,400
Derek Gillespie	67	72	62	72	273	4,950
Creighton Honeck	69	68	70	67	274	4,350
Tyler Harris	69	67	68	70	274	4,350
Wes Homan	71	65	67	71	274	4,350
Danny Sahl	74	66	68	67	275	3,750
Kent Eger	70	70	71	65	276	3,150
Hugo Leon	69	71	67	69	276	3,150
Nathan Stamey	67	70	66	73	276	3,150
Mark Hubbard	70	71	70	66	277	2,260.71
Adam Hadwin	72	67	71	67	277	2,260.71
Scott Harrington	70	67	70	70	277	2,260.71
Chan Song	74	68	66	69	277	2,260.71
Matt Marshall	73	67	65	72	277	2,260.71
Brad Tilley	70	66	68	73	277	2,260.71
Nick Taylor	70	66	68	73	277	2,260.71
Roger Sloan	72	65	75	66	278	1,725
Jason Scrivener	68	71	69	70	278	1,725
Jesse Smith	68	69	67	74	278	1,725
Kyle Stough	71	70	70	68	279	1,537.50
Brandon Harkins	69	66	69	75	279	1,537.50

Canadian Tour Players Cup

Pine Ridge Golf Club, Winnipeg, Manitoba   July 12-15
Par 36-35–71; 6,601 yards   purse, C$150,000

	SCORES				TOTAL	MONEY
Chris Killmer	66	64	70	69	269	C$24,000
Vince Covello	66	68	66	69	269	14,400
(Killmer defeated Covello on fourth playoff hole.)						
David Lang	68	68	70	68	274	9,000
Josh Habig	66	72	71	67	276	6,600
Matt Richardson	69	67	72	68	276	6,600
Mark Hubbard	68	67	75	67	277	5,175
Trey Denton	68	71	67	71	277	5,175
Jon McLean	67	68	75	68	278	4,050
David Dragoo	69	69	72	68	278	4,050
Ryan Williams	69	69	71	69	278	4,050
Jose de Jesus Rodriguez	67	70	71	70	278	4,050
Matt Hill	70	67	70	71	278	4,050
Lucas Lee	71	70	71	67	279	2,650
Michael McCabe	66	71	72	70	279	2,650
Steven Lecuyer	70	70	69	70	279	2,650
Michael Gligic	72	69	68	70	279	2,650
Wes Heffernan	69	70	69	71	279	2,650
Matt Makinson	69	68	69	73	279	2,650
Kyle Kallan	73	69	69	69	280	1,975
Tyler Harris	68	70	71	71	280	1,975
Darren Wallace	69	65	74	72	280	1,975
Sebastian Saavedra	70	69	73	69	281	1,650
Kevin Stinson	68	70	72	71	281	1,650
Adam Cornelson	73	68	73	67	281	1,650
Jaime Gomez	67	72	75	67	281	1,650
Garrett Sapp	67	70	70	74	281	1,650

RBC Canadian Open

See U.S. PGA Tour section.

Jamieson WFCU Windsor Roseland Charity Classic

Roseland Golf & Curling Club, Windsor, Ontario
Par 35-35–70; 6,943 yards

August 18-21
purse, C$100,000

	SCORES				TOTAL	MONEY
Alan McLean	70	69	65	66	270	C$16,000
Hugo Leon	69	67	70	66	272	9,600
Garrett Frank	65	69	71	69	274	5,400
Michael Gligic	70	66	67	71	274	5,400
Danny Sahl	70	68	71	66	275	4,000
Brandon Harkins	70	72	69	65	276	3,225
Wes Heffernan	70	66	69	71	276	3,225
James Allenby	65	69	70	72	276	3,225
Will Strickler	69	66	68	73	276	3,225
Roger Sloan	70	69	69	69	277	2,500
Kent Eger	69	71	69	68	277	2,500
Michael McCabe	72	67	69	69	277	2,500
Ryan Williams	72	68	70	68	278	1,933.33
Cory Renfrew	68	72	70	68	278	1,933.33
Joe Panzeri	65	73	69	71	278	1,933.33
Matt Marshall	70	68	73	68	279	1,600
George Bradford	71	69	70	69	279	1,600
Tyler Harris	71	69	70	69	279	1,600
Darren Wallace	71	70	71	69	281	1,207.14
Eugene Choe	67	73	70	71	281	1,207.14
David Byrne	65	76	69	71	281	1,207.14
Zachary Bixler	70	73	67	71	281	1,207.14
Jeff Rangel	71	68	69	73	281	1,207.14
Tyler Aldridge	72	69	67	73	281	1,207.14
Dodge Kemmer	67	72	69	73	281	1,207.14

Canadian Tour Championship

Scarboro Golf & Country Club, Toronto, Ontario
Par 35-36–71; 6,554 yards

August 23-26
purse, C$100,000

	SCORES				TOTAL	MONEY
Eugene Wong	68	67	68	67	270	C$16,000
Joe Panzeri	70	64	70	67	271	9,600
Cody Slover	68	71	67	68	274	6,000
Carlos Sainz, Jr.	71	64	72	68	275	3,925
Matt Daniel	66	69	72	68	275	3,925
Brian Unk	68	68	69	70	275	3,925
Trey Denton	70	66	67	72	275	3,925
Mark Hubbard	71	65	77	64	277	2,900
Nick Taylor	71	71	68	67	277	2,900
David Markle	68	71	68	70	277	2,900
Nathan Stamey	71	69	71	67	278	2,120
Sejun Yoon	72	71	68	67	278	2,120
Dodge Kemmer	66	70	74	68	278	2,120
David Dragoo	71	68	69	70	278	2,120
Matt Makinson	69	67	69	73	278	2,120
Joel Dahmen	76	66	74	63	279	1,600
James Allenby	72	69	68	70	279	1,600

	SCORES				TOTAL	MONEY
Derek Gillespie	72	69	67	71	279	1,600
*Mackenzie Hughes	72	67	72	69	280	
Tyler Aldridge	67	69	74	70	280	1,260
Will Strickler	68	72	69	71	280	1,260
Stuart Anderson	71	68	68	73	280	1,260
Hugo Leon	69	69	67	75	280	1,260
Stephen Bidne	68	67	69	76	280	1,260
Wes Homan	71	70	72	68	281	1,006
Jeff Rangel	72	70	70	69	281	1,006
Michael McCabe	77	66	68	70	281	1,006
Nate McCoy	72	68	69	72	281	1,006
Kyle Stough	68	70	68	75	281	1,006

Great Waterway Classic

Smuggler's Glen, Gananoque, Ontario
Par 35-36–71; 6,572 yards

September 6-9
purse, C$100,000

	SCORES				TOTAL	MONEY
Eugene Wong	67	66	68	65	266	C$16,000
Daniel Im	70	69	63	65	267	9,600
David Dragoo	64	65	71	70	270	6,000
Roger Sloan	68	68	70	65	271	4,400
Trey Denton	67	66	70	68	271	4,400
Danny Sahl	69	66	69	68	272	3,333.33
Tyler Harris	65	66	73	68	272	3,333.33
Jaime Gomez	63	68	72	69	272	3,333.33
Oliver Tubb	71	67	70	65	273	2,700
Carlos Sainz, Jr.	65	65	74	69	273	2,700
Will Strickler	68	65	69	71	273	2,700
Wes Heffernan	67	70	69	69	275	2,300
Nick Taylor	68	67	73	68	276	1,820
Garrett Frank	68	70	71	67	276	1,820
Wil Collins	70	68	70	68	276	1,820
Joe Panzeri	66	64	76	70	276	1,820
Mark Hoffman	65	69	71	71	276	1,820
Cory Renfrew	70	69	73	65	277	1,400
Steve Saunders	71	71	69	66	277	1,400
Kyle Stough	67	69	71	70	277	1,400
Matt Richardson	69	67	72	70	278	1,250
Steven Lecuyer	72	69	72	66	279	1,100
Darren Wallace	67	73	69	70	279	1,100
Kent Eger	69	67	71	72	279	1,100
Yohann Benson	72	64	70	73	279	1,100
Michael Gligic	69	63	73	74	279	1,100

Stacy Lewis was awarded the Rolex Player of the Year trophy after winning four times.

Inbee Park, the Evian Masters champion, was the leading money winner with over $3.1 million.

Matthew Lewis/Getty Images

Na Yeon Choi won the U.S. Women's Open.

Andy Lyons/Getty Images

Jiyai Shin won the Ricoh Women's British.

David Cannon/Getty Images

Shanshan Feng won the Wegmans LPGA.

Sun Young Yoo was Kraft Nabisco champion.

Ai Miyazato had two LPGA Tour victories.

Yani Tseng stayed No. 1 on Rolex Rankings.

Suzann Pettersen had two wins.

So Yeon Ryu was the Jamie Farr champion.

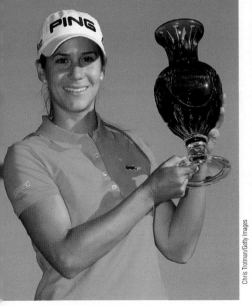

Azahara Munoz won the Sybase title.

Mika Miyazato was 10th on the Rolex Rankings.

Cristie Kerr won Lorena Ochoa's tournament.

Carlota Ciganda led the Ladies European Tour.

Amateur star Lydia Ko won the Canadian title.

Lexi Thompson was 29th in world earnings.

Pornanong Phatlum had a LET victory in India.

Bernhard Langer led the U.S. Champions money list, had two victories and 17 top-10 finishes.

Tom Lehman won twice, including the Charles Schwab Cup Championship.

Fred Couples won the Senior Open in Britain.
Englishman Roger Chapman won two majors.

Joe Daley won the Constellation title.

Fred Funk won at Insperity and Hickory.

Michael Allen won back-to-back in April.

Willie Wood posted two Champions victories.

David Frost was the AT&T champion.

Tour de las Americas

Abierto de Golf Los Lirios

Los Lirios Golf Club, Rancagua, Chile
Par 36-36–72

March 15-18
purse, US$40,000

	SCORES				TOTAL	MONEY
Julian Etulain	64	72	70	67	273	US$7,200
Julio Zapata	70	70	67	69	276	4,800
Sergio Acevedo	70	75	67	66	278	3,600
Emilio Dominguez	73	69	69	68	279	3,200
Tommy Cocha	67	72	70	71	280	2,600
Tomas Aravena	70	69	73	69	281	2,200
Cristobal Beltramin	66	71	74	71	282	2,000
Cristian Espinoza	72	72	72	67	283	1,350
Rafael Gomez	72	72	69	70	283	1,350
Cesar Agustin Costilla	74	70	69	70	283	1,350
Juan P. Luna	68	71	72	72	283	1,350
Julian Saltaleggio	70	72	75	68	285	940
Daniel Barbetti	69	71	67	78	285	940
Wolmer Murillo	74	70	71	71	286	814
Sebastian Fernandez	70	71	72	73	286	814
Matías O'Curry	71	72	70	73	286	814
Jesus Amaya	74	71	74	68	287	620
Nicolas Geyger	75	68	71	73	287	620
Luis Moreno	71	74	69	73	287	620
Christian Leon	72	73	69	73	287	620

International Open La Vitalicia

Barquisimeto Golf Club, Barquisimeto, Venezuela
Par 71

March 22-25
purse, US$120,000

	SCORES				TOTAL	MONEY
Rafael Romero	69	68	66	67	270	US$21,600
Rafael Campos	68	69	67	67	271	13,680
Jesus Amaya	66	67	66	73	272	9,600
Otto Solis	66	72	69	66	273	6,960
Daniel Barbetti	67	72	67	67	273	6,960
Ariel Canete	70	70	68	67	275	5,040
Nelson Ledesma	70	69	71	66	276	3,720
Julian Etulain	71	67	69	69	276	3,720
Sebastian Fernandez	70	68	71	68	277	2,880
Julio Zapata	69	72	66	70	277	2,880
Pablo Acuna	67	70	68	72	277	2,880
Alfredo Adrian	64	69	80	65	278	2,040
Emilio Dominguez	69	71	72	66	278	2,040
Manuel Merizalde	71	71	69	67	278	2,040
Paulo Pinto	68	71	72	67	278	2,040
Oscar Alvarez	68	67	73	70	278	2,040
Cristian Espinoza	69	69	70	70	278	2,040
Diego Vanegas	65	70	71	72	278	2,040
Raul Sanz	73	70	68	68	279	1,560

	SCORES				TOTAL	MONEY
Rafael Gomez	73	69	72	66	280	1,248
Luciano Giometti	70	65	76	69	280	1,248
Sebastian Saavedra	71	67	71	71	280	1,248
Juan Lizarralde	70	67	72	71	280	1,248
Patricio Salem	66	72	70	72	280	1,248

Challenge Latinoamericano Copa La Vitalicia

Lagunita Country Club, Caracas, Venezuela   March 27-30
Par 70; 6,909 yards   purse, US$64,000

FIRST DAY
(Alternate-shot Foursomes)

Alfredo Adrian and Otto Solís (Venezuela) defeated Hector Cespedes and Rafael Romero (South America), 2 and 1.
Diego Vanegas and Patricio Salem (SA) halved with Danielle Cabriles and Juan C. Berastegui.
Christian Espinoza and Juan Lizarralde (SA) defeated Diego Larrazabal and Cipriano Castro, 3 and 2.
Raul Sanz and Wolmer Murillo (VEN) defeated Joaquín Estevez and Jesus Amaya, 3 and 1.

POINTS: Venezuela 2½, South America 1½

SECOND DAY
(Fourball)

Cabriles and Berastegui (VEN) defeated Estevez and Cespedes, 2 and 1.
Vanegas and Salem (SA) defeated Adrian and Solís, 2 and 1.
Larrazabal and Castro (VEN) defeated Espinoza and Lizarralde, 2 up.
Sanz and Murillo (VEN) defeated Amaya and Romero, 1 up.

POINTS: Venezuela 5½, South America 2½

FINAL DAY
(Singles)

Adrian (VEN) defeated Jesus Amaya, 1 up.
Estevez (SA) defeated Berastegui, 1 up.
Sanz (VEN) defeated Cespedes after match conceded.
Romero (SA) defeated Murillo, 1 up.
Cabriles (VEN) defeated Salem, 2 up.
Solís (VEN) defeated Espinoza, 5 and 4.
Castro (VEN) defeated Lizarralde, 4 and 3.
Larrazabal (VEN) defeated Vanegas, 2 and 1.

TOTAL POINTS: Venezuela 11½, South America 4½.

(Each member of the Venezuela team received US$5,000; each member of the South America team received US$3,000.)

Abierto del Centro

Cordoba Golf Club, Villa Allende, Argentina
Par 35-36–71; 6,794 yards

April 12-15
purse, Arg$350,000

	SCORES				TOTAL	MONEY
Cesar Agustin Costilla	70	71	69	70	280	US$13,120
Cesar Monasterio	69	71	71	70	281	7,029
Nicolas Geyger	72	70	68	72	282	4,158
Emilio Dominguez	68	69	71	74	282	4,158
Mauricio Molina	73	68	74	68	283	2,928
Marco Ruiz	73	72	70	68	283	2,928
*Jorge Fernandez Valdes	73	69	69	73	284	
Franco Barrera	72	72	69	73	286	2,284
Ariel Canete	71	71	70	74	286	2,284
Julio Zapata	71	76	70	70	287	1,768
Rafael Echenique	68	75	72	72	287	1,768
Paulo Pinto	75	69	71	72	287	1,768
Gustavo Acosta	71	72	74	71	288	1,410
Clodomiro Carranza	73	72	72	71	288	1,410
Hernan Rey	73	71	71	73	288	1,410
Diego Vanegas	72	75	73	69	289	1,245
Rafael Campos	74	73	71	71	289	1,245
Luis Carbonetti	72	70	72	75	289	1,245
Matías O'Curry	70	70	76	74	290	1,148
Juan Lizarralde	74	71	73	73	291	1,125

Abierto del Nordeste

Chaco Golf Club, Resistencia, Chaco, Argentina
Par 36-36–72; 6,749 yards

May 16-19
purse, Pesos 280,000

	SCORES				TOTAL	MONEY
Luciano Dodda	67	69	67	70	273	US$9,029
Clodomiro Carranza	67	67	69	71	274	4,966
Miguel Fernandez	72	66	69	68	275	2,671
Roberto Coceres	71	70	66	68	275	2,671
Cesar Costilla	68	68	69	70	275	2,671
Daniel Barbetti	67	71	71	68	277	2,032
Nelson Ledesma	69	67	74	68	278	1,862
Tommy Cocha	69	69	68	72	278	1,862
Marco Ruiz	71	73	68	67	279	1,636
Eduardo Argiro	71	72	67	69	279	1,636
Ariel Canete	73	68	71	68	280	1,376
Lucas Juncos	70	72	67	71	280	1,376
Daniel Altamirano	70	69	69	72	280	1,376
Nicolas Geyger	70	69	69	72	280	1,376
Julian Etulain	71	65	71	73	280	1,376
David Ferreyra	72	72	69	68	281	1,193
Leandro Marelli	69	72	69	71	281	1,193
Julio Nunez	71	71	68	71	281	1,193
Rodolfo Gonzalez	72	70	72	68	282	1,063
Julio Zapata	73	70	71	68	282	1,063
Manuel Relancio	74	70	70	68	282	1,063
Sergio Acevedo	65	77	71	69	282	1,063
Rafael Gomez	71	69	70	72	282	1,063
Paulo Pinto	73	67	68	74	282	1,063

Televisa TLA Players Championship

Acapulco Princess, Acapulco, Mexico
Par 35-35–70; 6,355 yards

May 25-27
purse, US$70,000

	SCORES			TOTAL	MONEY
Marco Ruiz	65	64	64	193	US$12,600
Mauricio Azcue	65	65	64	194	7,980
Rafael Gomez	66	62	67	195	5,600
Manuel Inman	70	66	60	196	4,060
Diego Vanegas	65	69	62	196	4,060
Julian Etulain	64	70	63	197	2,940
Tommy Cocha	65	67	66	198	2,170
Nicolas Geyger	62	67	69	198	2,170
Andres Echavarria	66	67	66	199	1,610
Nelson Ledesma	66	66	67	199	1,610
Jose Trauwitz	65	66	68	199	1,610
Gerardo Loroima	66	64	69	199	1,610
Daniel Barbetti	68	66	66	200	1,330
Diego Larrazabal	66	69	66	201	1,260
Julio Zapata	69	68	65	202	1,125
Ary Rodriguez	71	63	68	202	1,125
Ariel Canete	68	66	68	202	1,125
Jose de Jesus Rodriguez	67	66	69	202	1,125
Jesus Osmar	66	69	68	203	933
Matias O'Curry	69	66	68	203	933
Esteban Toledo	66	67	70	203	933

Taca Airlines Open

Country Club La Planicie, Lima, Peru
Par 35-37–72

May 31-June 3
purse, US$50,000

	SCORES				TOTAL	MONEY
Marco Ruiz	66	67	69	70	272	US$9,000
Diego Vanegas	69	65	74	68	276	5,700
Maximiliano Godoy	72	69	69	67	277	4,000
Rafael Campos	73	67	71	68	279	2,663
Mauricio Azcue	75	65	69	70	279	2,663
Nelson Ledesma	71	68	69	71	279	2,663
Daniel Barbetti	72	72	68	69	281	1,610
Mario Hurtado	71	69	71	70	281	1,610
Ulises Mendez	74	71	72	65	282	1,270
Ariel Canete	71	71	73	67	282	1,270
Armando Zarlenga	73	70	68	71	282	1,270
Clodomiro Carranza	71	73	67	71	282	1,270
Juan Luna	72	71	72	68	283	1,045
Tommy Cocha	72	72	69	70	283	1,045
Manuel Relancio	74	72	70	68	284	895
Emilio Dominguez	71	71	69	73	284	895
Matias O'Curry	74	69	68	73	284	895
Mauricio Molina	75	69	67	73	284	895
Luis Graf	71	70	73	71	285	745
Sebastian Fernandez	73	68	73	71	285	745

PGA Tour Latinoamerica

Mundo Maya Open

Yucatan Country Club, Meridia, Mexico
Par 36-36–72; 7,282 yards

September 5-8
purse, US$150,000

	SCORES				TOTAL	MONEY
Tommy Cocha	68	64	66	68	266	US$27,000
Oscar Fraustro	68	70	68	65	271	16,200
Ariel Canete	73	67	65	67	272	10,200
Rafael Campos	70	66	70	67	273	6,600
*Sebastian Vazquez	69	71	64	69	273	
Andres Echavarria	67	65	70	71	273	6,600
Santiago Rivas	68	69	71	69	277	5,400
Christian Espinoza	71	72	69	66	278	4,675
Philippe Gasnier	70	68	72	68	278	4,675
Jose de Jesus Rodriguez	65	71	69	73	278	4,675
Armando Favela	67	67	71	74	279	4,050
Bronson Burgoon	72	71	68	69	280	3,450
Matias O'Curry	71	70	68	71	280	3,450
Clodomiro Carranza	72	69	67	72	280	3,450
Dustin Garza	66	68	77	70	281	2,700
Hugo Leon	73	68	70	70	281	2,700
Horacio Leon	69	68	72	72	281	2,700
Byron Smith	70	72	70	70	282	2,250
Vince Covello	68	75	68	71	282	2,250
Jose Octavio Gonzalez	72	67	68	75	282	2,250

TransAmerican Power Products Open

La Herradura Golf Club, Monterrey, Mexico
Par 36-36–72; 6,983 yards

September 13-16
purse, US$150,000

	SCORES				TOTAL	MONEY
Ariel Canete	68	67	67	68	270	US$27,000
Tommy Cocha	67	69	69	67	272	16,200
Nicolas Geyger	71	68	67	67	273	7,800
Cody Slover	72	67	65	69	273	7,800
Armando Favela	69	69	68	67	273	7,800
Benjamin Alvarado	70	69	68	67	274	5,400
Matias O'Curry	68	68	68	71	275	5,025
Christian Espinoza	70	66	69	71	276	4,650
Rafael Campos	68	71	71	67	277	3,900
Jose de Jesus Rodriguez	68	71	68	70	277	3,900
Mauricio Molina	69	72	66	70	277	3,900
Clodomiro Carranza	71	67	68	71	277	3,900
Oscar Fraustro	71	69	71	68	279	3,150
Santiago Russi	71	68	71	70	280	2,475
Fernando Figueroa	71	68	71	70	280	2,475
Julio Santos	68	70	75	67	280	2,475
Sebastian MacLean	66	71	72	71	280	2,475
Sebastian Saavedra	67	68	75	70	280	2,475
Horacio Leon	66	68	71	75	280	2,475
Brad Tilley	69	72	68	72	281	1,875
Pablo Del Grosso	70	68	73	70	281	1,875

65 Arturo Calle Colombian Open

El Rincon de Cajica Golf Club, Bogota, Colombia
Par 36-36–72

September 20-23
purse, US$125,000

	SCORES				TOTAL	MONEY
Matias O'Curry	71	69	68	71	279	US$22,500
Nelson Ledesma	72	74	71	70	287	11,000
Andres Echavarria	66	76	73	72	287	11,000
Sebastian MacLean	74	74	69	71	288	6,000
Sebastian Saavedra	72	74	72	72	290	4,750
Ariel Canete	68	75	73	74	290	4,750
Bruce McDonald	71	75	72	73	291	4,031
Benjamin Alvarado	69	75	73	74	291	4,031
*Marcelo Rozo	76	70	71	74	291	
Hugo Leon	72	76	73	71	292	3,250
Sebastian Fernandez	75	73	72	72	292	3,250
Luciano Dodda	75	70	73	74	292	3,250
Jose Manuel Garrido	73	72	73	74	292	3,250
Dan Olsen	73	75	72	73	293	2,275
Manuel Inman	71	73	75	74	293	2,275
Rafael Campos	72	74	73	74	293	2,275
David Vanegas	71	79	69	74	293	2,275
Ryan Thornberry	74	75	69	75	293	2,275
Manuel Merizalde	75	75	74	70	294	1,875
Mauricio Azcue	75	73	72	75	295	1,750

Brazil Open

Sao Fernando Golf Club, Sao Paulo, Brazil
Par 35-36–71

October 3-6
purse, US$130,000

	SCORES				TOTAL	MONEY
Clodomiro Carranza	68	66	70	65	269	US$23,400
Jose de Jesus Rodriguez	65	71	65	68	269	14,040
(Carranza defeated Rodriguez on first playoff hole.)						
Matias O'Curry	70	69	70	62	271	8,840
Andres Echavarria	68	67	72	67	274	5,119
Christian Espinoza	70	69	66	69	274	5,119
Jorge Monroy	72	65	66	71	274	5,119
Rafael Campos	64	68	66	76	274	5,119
Mauricio Molina	70	64	71	70	275	3,900
Marco Ruiz	71	66	68	70	275	3,900
Armando Favela	72	71	68	65	276	3,510
Byron Smith	68	71	70	68	277	3,250
Alvaro Jose Arizabaleta	68	69	72	69	278	2,633
Hernan Rey	70	70	69	69	278	2,633
Oscar David Alvarez	68	69	68	73	278	2,633
Armando Zarlenga	72	66	67	73	278	2,633
Drew Kittleson	68	71	72	68	279	2,145
Nicolas Geyger	70	66	73	70	279	2,145
Daniel Altamirano	71	66	74	69	280	1,702
Felipe Velazquez	68	72	71	69	280	1,702
Carlos Franco	73	68	68	71	280	1,702
Philippe Gasnier	68	68	71	73	280	1,702
Jesus Amaya	73	69	65	73	280	1,702

Roberto de Vicenzo Invitational Copa NEC

San Eliseo Golf Club, San Vicente, Buenos Aires, Argentina
Par 36-36–72

October 11-14
purse, US$125,000

	SCORES				TOTAL	MONEY
Alan Wagner	69	72	64	68	273	US$22,500
Oscar Fraustro	72	72	67	64	275	11,000
Ariel Canete	72	67	70	66	275	11,000
Daniel Stapff	70	70	71	65	276	5,167
Julio Zapata	72	68	68	68	276	5,167
Armando Favela	69	67	69	71	276	5,167
Oscar David Alvarez	66	74	71	66	277	4,188
Daniel Altamirano	70	70	72	66	278	3,625
Julian Etulain	68	71	68	71	278	3,625
Matias O'Curry	70	70	67	71	278	3,625
Ulises Mendez	71	69	68	71	279	3,125
Pablo Del Grosso	70	70	70	70	280	2,750
Sebastian Saavedra	65	69	69	77	280	2,750
Oreste Focaccia	73	71	70	67	281	2,375
Maximiliano Godoy	69	72	74	67	282	2,000
Pablo Acuna	72	70	73	67	282	2,000
Jose de Jesus Rodriguez	72	72	69	69	282	2,000
Francisco Bide	69	74	68	71	282	2,000
Ramon Bescansa	71	69	70	72	282	2,000
Jorge Fernandez-Valdes	72	69	72	70	283	1,563
Luciano Dodda	70	72	68	73	283	1,563

Lexus Peru Open

Los Inkas Golf Club, Lima, Peru
Par 36-36–72

November 1-4
purse, US$125,000

	SCORES				TOTAL	MONEY
Sebastian Salem	71	71	67	66	275	US$22,500
Andres Echavarria	73	69	71	63	276	8,250
Maximiliano Godoy	73	70	68	65	276	8,250
Carlos Franco	68	70	70	68	276	8,250
Clodomiro Carranza	69	67	71	69	276	8,250
Nelson Ledesma	69	69	70	69	277	4,188
Bronson Burgoon	66	73	68	70	277	4,188
Sebastian Fernandez	69	68	69	71	277	4,188
Jaime Clavijo	69	72	70	67	278	3,125
Rafael Claux	71	70	69	68	278	3,125
Byron Smith	68	68	71	71	278	3,125
Jose Manuel Garrido	70	67	70	71	278	3,125
Felipe Velazquez	72	68	66	72	278	3,125
Manuel Villegas	70	68	70	71	279	2,250
Pablo Acuna	70	66	71	72	279	2,250
Jesus Amaya	69	71	67	72	279	2,250
Marco Ruiz	70	73	69	68	280	1,750
Sebastian Vazquez	69	70	71	70	280	1,750
David Vanegas	69	70	71	70	280	1,750
Bruce McDonald	75	67	68	70	280	1,750
Paul Imondi	69	73	64	74	280	1,750

Dominican Republic Open

Cana Bay Golf Club, Punto Cana, Dominican Republic
Par 36-36–72

November 8-11
purse, US$125,000

	SCORES				TOTAL	MONEY
Oscar Fraustro	70	70	67	71	278	US$22,500
Marcelo Rozo	73	71	70	68	282	13,500
Ariel Canete	73	70	68	72	283	7,250
Paul Imondi	69	67	72	75	283	7,250
Dustin Garza	70	71	72	71	284	4,750
Emilio Dominguez	74	70	73	67	284	4,750
Julio Zapata	70	72	72	71	285	3,766
Sebastian Saavedra	74	68	73	70	285	3,766
Sebastian Fernandez	70	74	72	69	285	3,766
Luciano Giometti	69	70	77	69	285	3,766
Maximiliano Godoy	75	67	70	74	286	3,000
Luciano Dodda	70	74	71	71	286	3,000
Santiago Quirarte	70	71	73	73	287	2,417
Ronaldo Francisco	69	72	74	72	287	2,417
Mauricio Molina	75	70	74	68	287	2,417
Gibby Martens	70	73	76	69	288	1,875
Bruce McDonald	70	71	75	72	288	1,875
Carlos Velez	72	69	78	69	288	1,875
Jesus Osmar	71	69	73	75	288	1,875
Hernan Rey	68	71	76	73	288	1,875

Puerto Rico Classic

Dorado Beach Resort, East Course, San Juan, Puerto Rico
Par 36-36–72

November 15-18
purse, US$250,000

	SCORES				TOTAL	MONEY
Sebastian Vazquez	65	72	66	71	274	US$22,500
Jorge Fernandez-Valdes	67	69	69	71	276	13,500
Julio Zapata	67	71	68	71	277	8,500
Gustavo Acosta	74	70	66	69	279	6,000
Emilio Dominguez	71	70	70	69	280	5,000
Ryan Thornberry	73	69	69	70	281	4,500
Paul Imondi	70	70	73	69	282	3,896
Christian Espinoza	70	72	70	70	282	3,896
Ariel Canete	71	68	71	72	282	3,896
Ronaldo Francisco	74	69	67	73	283	3,375
Jorge Monroy	70	71	72	72	285	2,875
Clodomiro Carranza	73	69	70	73	285	2,875
Eduardo Argiro	70	72	69	74	285	2,875
Alex Ching	72	72	71	71	286	2,313
Felipe Velazquez	71	72	71	72	286	2,313
*Edward Figueroa	73	68	71	74	286	
Otto Solis	73	71	74	69	287	2,063
Gibby Martens	72	70	73	72	287	2,063
Omar Beltran	73	72	72	71	288	1,750
Mauricio Azcue	77	69	67	75	288	1,750
Jaime Clavijo	70	69	73	76	288	1,750

Arturo Calle Colombian Coffee Classic

Club Campestre de Cali, Calle, Colombia
Par 36-36–72

November 29-December 2
purse, US$125,000

	SCORES				TOTAL	MONEY
Sebastian Fernandez	68	69	68	70	275	US$22,500
Jose Manuel Garrido	68	67	71	69	275	13,500
(Fernandez defeated Garrido on first playoff hole,)						
Bruce McDonald	67	69	73	67	276	7,250
Matias O'Curry	72	68	65	71	276	7,250
Oscar Fraustro	72	65	71	69	277	4,563
Clodomiro Carranza	69	69	68	71	277	4,563
Michael Buttacavoli	69	65	69	74	277	4,563
Christian Espinoza	67	71	70	70	278	3,750
Jesus Amaya	67	71	68	72	278	3,750
Diego Velasquez	76	68	66	69	279	3,125
Marcelo Rozo	67	69	70	73	279	3,125
Diego Vanegas	66	70	70	73	279	3,125
Armando Favela	71	70	75	64	280	2,500
Pablo Acuna	67	73	69	71	280	2,500
Santiago Rivas	69	74	72	66	281	2,125
Julian Etulain	69	71	75	66	281	2,125
Ariel Canete	71	69	69	72	281	2,125
Tommy Cocha	70	73	71	68	282	1,688
Oscar David Alvarez	69	71	72	70	282	1,688
Alex Ching	70	71	70	71	282	1,688
Felipe Velazquez	66	74	70	72	282	1,688

Olivos Golf Classic - Copa Personal

Olivos Golf Club, Buenos Aires, Argentina
Par 36-35–71; 6,740 yards

December 6-9
purse, US$125,000

	SCORES				TOTAL	MONEY
Ariel Canete	71	70	67	67	275	US$22,500
Clodomiro Carranza	74	67	71	65	277	11,000
Jose Coceres	70	70	69	68	277	11,000
Fabian Gomez	69	69	70	70	278	6,000
Alex Ching	72	65	69	73	279	5,000
Bruce McDonald	72	68	71	69	280	4,344
Tommy Cocha	69	71	69	71	280	4,344
Carlos Franco	68	69	74	70	281	3,875
Emilio Dominguez	70	72	73	67	282	3,375
Benjamin Alvarado	74	68	68	72	282	3,375
Pablo Del Grosso	72	69	69	72	282	3,375
Paulo Pinto	72	72	67	72	283	2,625
Jorge Fernandez-Valdes	74	69	68	72	283	2,625
Andres Echavarria	72	74	66	71	283	2,625
Ryan Thornberry	74	70	70	70	284	2,000
Julio Nunez	73	71	68	72	284	2,000
Cesar Agustin Costilla	72	71	73	68	284	2,000
Vicente Fernandez	67	74	73	70	284	2,000
Julio Santos	68	73	71	72	284	2,000
Mauricio Molina	71	72	70	72	285	1,563
Matias O'Curry	73	73	69	70	285	1,563

Visa Open de Argentina

Nordelta Golf Club, Buenos Aires, Argentina   December 13-16
Par 36-36–72   purse, US$125,000

	SCORES				TOTAL	MONEY
Angel Cabrera	65	70	71	64	270	US$22,500
Miguel Carballo	69	68	69	68	274	11,000
Oscar Fraustro	68	67	70	69	274	11,000
Andres Echavarria	66	74	69	67	276	5,500
Julio Zapata	74	67	67	68	276	5,500
Sebastian MacLean	68	74	70	65	277	4,500
Daniel Vancsik	71	70	68	69	278	4,188
Alan Wagner	72	70	70	67	279	3,750
Hernan Rey	71	71	67	70	279	3,750
Clodomiro Carranza	69	70	74	68	281	3,375
*Alejandro Tosti	69	73	69	70	281	
Rafael Campos	67	73	73	70	283	3,125
Benjamin Alvarado	71	69	73	71	284	2,750
Scott Dunlap	71	72	66	75	284	2,750
Hector Cespedes	69	74	71	71	285	2,125
Leandro Marelli	74	71	69	71	285	2,125
Jorge Fernandez-Valdes	75	67	71	72	285	2,125
Horacio Leon	66	74	71	74	285	2,125
Daniel Altamirano	65	71	74	75	285	2,125
Sebastian Fernandez	72	71	71	72	286	1,535
Manuel Garcia	70	73	70	73	286	1,535
Ariel Canete	67	71	74	74	286	1,535
Nelson Ledesma	72	72	68	74	286	1,535
Mauricio Azcue	72	72	67	75	286	1,535

European Tours

Africa Open

See African Tours chapter.

Joburg Open

See African Tours chapter.

Volvo Golf Champions

See African Tours chapter.

Abu Dhabi HSBC Golf Championship

Abu Dhabi Golf Club, Abu Dhabi, United Arab Emirates
Par 36-36–72; 7,600 yards

January 26-29
purse, €2,078,350

	SCORES				TOTAL	MONEY
Robert Rock	69	70	66	70	275	€347,024
Rory McIlroy	67	72	68	69	276	231,349
Thomas Bjorn	73	71	65	68	277	107,577
Graeme McDowell	72	69	68	68	277	107,577
Tiger Woods	70	69	66	72	277	107,577
George Coetzee	71	72	65	70	278	67,670
Matteo Manassero	73	65	71	69	278	67,670
Keith Horne	71	71	68	69	279	44,662
Paul Lawrie	70	69	68	72	279	44,662
Francesco Molinari	74	67	66	72	279	44,662
Thorbjorn Olesen	70	67	71	71	279	44,662
Sergio Garcia	71	69	71	69	280	34,668
Jean-Baptiste Gonnet	68	71	69	72	280	34,668
Anders Hansen	71	70	72	68	281	30,608
Gareth Maybin	68	70	72	71	281	30,608
Romain Wattel	74	69	69	69	281	30,608
Simon Dyson	72	72	68	70	282	25,194
Gonzalo Fernandez-Castano	72	74	65	71	282	25,194
Mark Foster	75	67	69	71	282	25,194
James Kingston	72	69	67	74	282	25,194
David Lynn	74	70	67	71	282	25,194
Charl Schwartzel	70	70	72	70	282	25,194
Lee Westwood	72	72	68	70	282	25,194
Alejandro Canizares	71	71	70	71	283	20,717
Nicolas Colsaerts	69	75	71	68	283	20,717
Robert Karlsson	67	72	72	72	283	20,717
Liang Wen-chong	70	71	70	72	283	20,717
Jeev Milkha Singh	75	70	67	71	283	20,717
Jaco Van Zyl	75	70	68	70	283	20,717
Jamie Donaldson	74	68	67	75	284	17,282
Johan Edfors	70	71	70	73	284	17,282
Richard Finch	68	71	71	74	284	17,282
Richard S. Johnson	71	72	70	71	284	17,282
Graeme Storm	74	69	68	73	284	17,282
David Drysdale	70	72	71	72	285	14,367
Lorenzo Gagli	72	73	67	73	285	14,367
Stephen Gallacher	72	72	70	71	285	14,367

	SCORES				TOTAL	MONEY
Peter Hanson	74	69	64	78	285	14,367
Padraig Harrington	71	69	72	73	285	14,367
Marcel Siem	72	74	70	69	285	14,367
Anthony Wall	70	75	71	69	285	14,367
Markus Brier	72	71	74	69	286	11,660
Ross Fisher	73	72	68	73	286	11,660
Miguel Angel Jimenez	72	69	70	75	286	11,660
Jose Manuel Lara	70	70	74	72	286	11,660
Joost Luiten	71	71	73	71	286	11,660
Peter Whiteford	73	73	68	72	286	11,660
Thomas Aiken	72	70	72	73	287	8,745
Gary Boyd	73	73	68	73	287	8,745
Rafa Cabrera-Bello	76	70	71	70	287	8,745
K.J. Choi	71	75	68	73	287	8,745
Ben Curtis	72	71	70	74	287	8,745
Luke Donald	71	72	73	71	287	8,745
Michael Hoey	70	76	69	72	287	8,745
Richie Ramsay	69	71	77	70	287	8,745
S.S.P. Chowrasia	74	72	74	68	288	6,288
Rhys Davies	75	71	70	72	288	6,288
Bradley Dredge	73	71	72	72	288	6,288
Soren Hansen	72	73	69	74	288	6,288
Andrea Pavan	73	72	69	74	288	6,288
Alexander Noren	73	72	74	70	289	5,518
Joel Sjoholm	73	71	72	73	289	5,518
Oliver Fisher	71	71	75	73	290	4,685
Marcus Fraser	71	71	73	75	290	4,685
Ricardo Gonzalez	72	73	71	74	290	4,685
Richard Green	75	71	72	72	290	4,685
David Horsey	75	70	69	76	290	4,685
Raphael Jacquelin	71	74	69	76	290	4,685
Jose Maria Olazabal	72	74	78	71	295	3,956

Commercialbank Qatar Masters

Doha Golf Club, Doha, Qatar
Par 36-36–72; 7,412 yards
(Event shortened to 54 holes—wind.)

February 2-5
purse, €1,913,171

	SCORES			TOTAL	MONEY
Paul Lawrie	69	67	65	201	€316,020
Jason Day	68	72	65	205	164,688
Peter Hanson	69	69	67	205	164,688
John Daly	67	73	67	207	94,808
Sergio Garcia	72	68	68	208	62,763
Jean-Baptiste Gonnet	71	72	65	208	62,763
Ricardo Gonzalez	71	67	70	208	62,763
Soren Hansen	71	71	66	208	62,763
Nicolas Colsaerts	69	68	72	209	38,429
Victor Dubuisson	72	68	69	209	38,429
Martin Kaymer	71	70	68	209	38,429
Gonzalo Fernandez-Castano	66	75	69	210	27,542
Anders Hansen	70	73	67	210	27,542
Michael Hoey	71	71	68	210	27,542
Keith Horne	73	69	68	210	27,542
Scott Jamieson	73	69	68	210	27,542
Jose Maria Olazabal	71	70	69	210	27,542
Marcel Siem	71	69	70	210	27,542
Lee Westwood	71	70	69	210	27,542
Andrew Dodt	71	69	71	211	21,464

	SCORES			TOTAL	MONEY
Thongchai Jaidee	72	71	68	211	21,464
James Kingston	70	69	72	211	21,464
Brett Rumford	74	69	68	211	21,464
Chris Wood	72	72	67	211	21,464
Thomas Bjorn	79	65	68	212	17,160
Jorge Campillo	73	71	68	212	17,160
Alejandro Canizares	72	69	71	212	17,160
Richard Finch	69	74	69	212	17,160
Richard Green	70	73	69	212	17,160
Gregory Havret	71	72	69	212	17,160
Simon Khan	71	68	73	212	17,160
Pablo Larrazabal	71	70	71	212	17,160
Shaun Micheel	71	74	67	212	17,160
Anthony Wall	74	66	72	212	17,160
Rafa Cabrera-Bello	72	69	72	213	12,135
George Coetzee	70	73	70	213	12,135
Carlos Del Moral	71	70	72	213	12,135
Mark Foster	73	70	70	213	12,135
Peter Hedblom	72	71	70	213	12,135
Mikko Ilonen	73	71	69	213	12,135
Maarten Lafeber	72	68	73	213	12,135
Lee Slattery	72	71	70	213	12,135
Jaco Van Zyl	71	71	71	213	12,135
Marc Warren	72	68	73	213	12,135
Romain Wattel	73	71	69	213	12,135
Martin Wiegele	71	72	70	213	12,135
Felipe Aguilar	77	68	69	214	7,600
Alex Cejka	73	69	72	214	7,600
S.S.P. Chowrasia	73	71	70	214	7,600
Ben Curtis	71	70	73	214	7,600
Rhys Davies	74	71	69	214	7,600
David Drysdale	73	72	69	214	7,600
Oliver Fisher	70	74	70	214	7,600
Retief Goosen	73	71	70	214	7,600
Branden Grace	75	68	71	214	7,600
David Lynn	71	69	74	214	7,600
Christian Nilsson	74	71	69	214	7,600
Matthew Zions	73	72	69	214	7,600
Markus Brier	72	70	73	215	4,835
Marcus Fraser	73	70	72	215	4,835
Miguel Angel Jimenez	73	69	73	215	4,835
Richard S. Johnson	75	69	71	215	4,835
Peter Lawrie	71	73	71	215	4,835
Graeme McDowell	73	72	70	215	4,835
Thorbjorn Olesen	72	71	72	215	4,835
Alvaro Quiros	72	71	72	215	4,835
Soren Kjeldsen	73	71	72	216	3,887
Ricardo Santos	77	68	71	216	3,887
Thomas Aiken	73	72	72	217	3,188
Francesco Molinari	71	72	74	217	3,188
Jamie Moul	77	66	74	217	3,188
Oliver Wilson	72	72	73	217	3,188
Michael Jonzon	71	74	73	218	2,835
Shiv Kapur	75	70	73	218	2,835
Damien McGrane	78	67	73	218	2,835
Kenneth Ferrie	74	71	74	219	2,829

Omega Dubai Desert Classic

Emirates Golf Club, Dubai, United Arab Emirates
Par 35-37–72; 7,301 yards

February 9-12
purse, €1,924,297

	SCORES				TOTAL	MONEY
Rafa Cabrera-Bello	63	69	70	68	270	€315,532
Stephen Gallacher	69	65	68	69	271	164,434
Lee Westwood	69	65	67	70	271	164,434
Marcel Siem	65	69	68	71	273	94,661
George Coetzee	69	66	69	70	274	62,666
Scott Jamieson	65	68	70	71	274	62,666
Soren Kjeldsen	68	69	70	67	274	62,666
Rory McIlroy	66	65	72	71	274	62,666
Thomas Bjorn	66	65	73	71	275	38,369
Nicolas Colsaerts	66	72	67	70	275	38,369
Joel Sjoholm	71	66	66	72	275	38,369
Romain Wattel	66	71	70	69	276	32,563
Ben Curtis	70	67	67	73	277	29,093
Estanislao Goya	68	68	72	69	277	29,093
Martin Kaymer	66	67	70	74	277	29,093
Gregory Bourdy	66	67	73	72	278	25,038
Jamie Donaldson	74	67	69	68	278	25,038
Johan Edfors	69	71	68	70	278	25,038
Francesco Molinari	70	68	69	71	278	25,038
Brett Rumford	70	71	67	71	279	21,725
Henrik Stenson	72	64	70	73	279	21,725
Nicholas Thompson	68	71	72	68	279	21,725
Chris Wood	71	67	69	72	279	21,725
Gregory Havret	73	67	69	71	280	19,406
Edoardo Molinari	69	72	68	71	280	19,406
Seung-Yul Noh	69	70	69	72	280	19,406
Bernd Wiesberger	70	72	68	70	280	19,406
David Drysdale	70	70	71	70	281	16,850
Ignacio Garrido	72	71	70	68	281	16,850
Jbe' Kruger	69	73	70	69	281	16,850
Peter Lawrie	67	74	70	70	281	16,850
Gareth Maybin	71	70	70	70	281	16,850
Fred Couples	70	73	71	68	282	14,436
Simon Dyson	72	68	68	74	282	14,436
Joost Luiten	69	73	69	71	282	14,436
Danny Willett	71	71	70	70	282	14,436
John Daly	71	72	67	73	283	12,685
David Howell	69	74	69	71	283	12,685
Alvaro Quiros	70	70	71	72	283	12,685
Jeev Milkha Singh	67	73	70	73	283	12,685
Richard Sterne	66	71	74	72	283	12,685
Oscar Floren	67	71	71	75	284	10,034
Thongchai Jaidee	69	70	74	71	284	10,034
James Kingston	72	70	71	71	284	10,034
Pablo Larrazabal	70	73	72	69	284	10,034
Matteo Manassero	71	70	70	73	284	10,034
Damien McGrane	75	65	72	72	284	10,034
Thorbjorn Olesen	70	73	72	69	284	10,034
Ricardo Santos	70	73	71	70	284	10,034
Anthony Wall	71	72	67	74	284	10,034
Jorge Campillo	72	70	69	74	285	7,194
Branden Grace	71	71	71	72	285	7,194
Peter Hanson	71	70	71	73	285	7,194
Paul Lawrie	71	70	69	75	285	7,194
Richie Ramsay	69	71	73	72	285	7,194
Robert Rock	73	67	69	76	285	7,194
Tommy Fleetwood	72	70	72	72	286	5,585

	SCORES				TOTAL	MONEY
Peter Hedblom	70	71	68	77	286	5,585
David Lynn	69	72	73	72	286	5,585
Richard McEvoy	69	70	74	73	286	5,585
Floris De Vries	70	73	72	72	287	4,733
Marcus Fraser	74	69	71	73	287	4,733
Soren Hansen	72	69	73	73	287	4,733
Sean McNamara	72	71	71	73	287	4,733
Mark O'Meara	69	74	69	75	287	4,733
Alejandro Canizares	73	69	72	74	288	3,797
Robert Coles	76	67	71	74	288	3,797
Ross Fisher	67	74	72	75	288	3,797
Ricardo Gonzalez	71	72	72	73	288	3,797
Shane Lowry	68	70	73	77	288	3,797
Fabrizio Zanotti	71	72	73	74	290	2,840
Tom Lewis	70	70	75	76	291	2,837
Jose Manuel Lara	71	72	72	77	292	2,834
Todd Hamilton	71	71	75	76	293	2,825
Colin Montgomerie	71	69	77	76	293	2,825
Peter Richardson	70	71	71	81	293	2,825
Jake Shepherd	73	70	75	75	293	2,825
Martin Wiegele	72	69	73	79	293	2,825
Fredrik Andersson Hed	69	71	77	79	296	2,814
Miguel Angel Jimenez	70	73	76	77	296	2,814
Federico Colombo	74	69	79	77	299	2,810

Avantha Masters

See Asia/Japan Tours chapter.

Open de Andalucia Costa del Sol

Aloha Golf Club, Andalucia, Spain
Par 36-36—72; 6,881 yards

March 15-18
purse, €1,000,000

	SCORES				TOTAL	MONEY
Julien Quesne	68	72	67	64	271	€166,660
Matteo Manassero	64	73	68	68	273	111,110
Eduardo De La Riva	67	69	68	70	274	62,600
David Lynn	70	68	68	69	275	50,000
Raphael Jacquelin	70	68	69	69	276	38,700
Hennie Otto	67	71	68	70	276	38,700
Mark Foster	69	70	69	69	277	24,350
Miguel Angel Jimenez	69	68	69	71	277	24,350
Shane Lowry	71	72	67	67	277	24,350
Jaco Van Zyl	69	71	71	66	277	24,350
Gregory Bourdy	70	72	66	70	278	16,340
Borja Etchart	71	71	66	70	278	16,340
Simon Khan	70	69	66	73	278	16,340
Edoardo Molinari	73	65	71	69	278	16,340
Phillip Price	69	72	66	71	278	16,340
Graeme Storm	70	69	69	71	279	14,100
Alex Haindl	68	71	70	71	280	12,933
Robert Rock	69	69	70	72	280	12,933
Marcel Siem	69	71	67	73	280	12,933
Bradley Dredge	74	67	68	72	281	11,167
Darren Fichardt	69	71	67	74	281	11,167
Marcus Fraser	69	70	72	70	281	11,167
Soren Hansen	73	68	71	69	281	11,167
Pablo Larrazabal	68	69	71	73	281	11,167

	SCORES				TOTAL	MONEY
Damien McGrane	69	68	71	73	281	11,167
Andrew Dodt	70	74	70	68	282	9,200
Tommy Fleetwood	68	69	72	73	282	9,200
Ignacio Garrido	69	71	70	72	282	9,200
Jean-Baptiste Gonnet	69	72	68	73	282	9,200
Andrea Pavan	70	69	70	73	282	9,200
Anthony Wall	67	77	70	68	282	9,200
Oliver Wilson	71	67	74	70	282	9,200
Fredrik Andersson Hed	70	73	71	69	283	7,111
Matthew Baldwin	72	71	69	71	283	7,111
Niclas Fasth	67	73	72	71	283	7,111
Gregory Havret	71	69	71	72	283	7,111
Michael Hoey	69	69	74	71	283	7,111
Gareth Maybin	72	68	69	74	283	7,111
Richie Ramsay	72	71	71	69	283	7,111
Andy Sullivan	74	67	74	68	283	7,111
Simon Thornton	72	70	72	69	283	7,111
Oliver Fisher	71	69	68	76	284	5,700
Keith Horne	73	70	69	72	284	5,700
David Horsey	70	72	71	71	284	5,700
Joakim Lagergren	68	70	73	73	284	5,700
Joost Luiten	72	71	68	73	284	5,700
Rafa Cabrera-Bello	71	70	69	75	285	4,700
Alejandro Canizares	70	73	68	74	285	4,700
Alastair Forsyth	71	70	71	73	285	4,700
Lloyd Kennedy	67	73	71	74	285	4,700
Jeev Milkha Singh	72	69	71	73	285	4,700
Javi Colomo	70	73	73	70	286	3,438
Victor Dubuisson	72	72	69	73	286	3,438
Stephen Gallacher	75	69	71	71	286	3,438
Santiago Luna	70	74	70	72	286	3,438
George Murray	72	72	71	71	286	3,438
Gary Orr	71	73	70	72	286	3,438
Ricardo Santos	71	72	72	71	286	3,438
Mike Weir	68	73	72	73	286	3,438
David Drysdale	71	71	73	73	288	2,700
Estanislao Goya	72	69	69	78	288	2,700
Pedro Oriol	70	72	73	73	288	2,700
Wil Besseling	73	71	70	75	289	2,500
Gary Boyd	70	73	74	73	290	2,250
David Dixon	73	70	78	69	290	2,250
Michael Jonzon	73	71	74	72	290	2,250
Marc Warren	74	70	70	76	290	2,250
Adrien Bernadet	73	70	70	78	291	1,950
Lorenzo Gagli	73	69	69	80	291	1,950
Andrew Johnston	71	73	76	76	296	1,830

Trophee Hassan II

Golf du Palais Royal, Agadir, Morocco
Par 36-36-72; 6,844 yards

March 22-25
purse, €1,502,250

	SCORES				TOTAL	MONEY
Michael Hoey	74	67	65	65	271	€250,000
Damien McGrane	65	68	71	70	274	166,660
Robert Coles	73	70	65	67	275	77,500
Jamie Donaldson	72	68	74	61	275	77,500
Phillip Price	68	66	72	69	275	77,500
Keith Horne	69	70	70	67	276	45,000
Matteo Manassero	69	70	65	72	276	45,000
Edoardo Molinari	68	70	71	67	276	45,000

	SCORES				TOTAL	MONEY
Ignacio Garrido	69	71	69	68	277	28,230
James Kingston	70	67	70	70	277	28,230
Jose Manuel Lara	70	65	70	72	277	28,230
Pablo Larrazabal	74	68	67	68	277	28,230
Hennie Otto	69	69	70	69	277	28,230
Robert-Jan Derksen	68	69	70	72	279	22,050
David Horsey	72	70	71	66	279	22,050
Craig Lee	73	68	70	68	279	22,050
Matthew Baldwin	70	68	68	74	280	17,888
Bradley Dredge	74	68	66	72	280	17,888
Mikko Ilonen	72	69	66	73	280	17,888
Shane Lowry	73	68	71	68	280	17,888
Francesco Molinari	70	68	73	69	280	17,888
Richie Ramsay	68	70	73	69	280	17,888
Andy Sullivan	72	72	68	68	280	17,888
Anthony Wall	69	73	69	69	280	17,888
Daniel Denison	73	66	71	71	281	14,025
Branden Grace	74	67	67	73	281	14,025
Richard McEvoy	69	72	70	70	281	14,025
Gary Orr	72	67	71	71	281	14,025
Brett Rumford	71	66	75	69	281	14,025
Joel Sjoholm	70	66	70	75	281	14,025
Graeme Storm	68	72	69	72	281	14,025
Jaco Van Zyl	75	68	70	68	281	14,025
Jbe' Kruger	75	68	71	68	282	11,775
George Murray	72	72	71	67	282	11,775
Thorbjorn Olesen	72	67	72	72	283	11,250
Benjamin Hebert	73	70	73	68	284	10,950
Jorge Campillo	68	69	72	76	285	9,750
Carlos Del Moral	72	67	73	73	285	9,750
Tommy Fleetwood	74	70	72	69	285	9,750
Andrew Johnston	72	69	72	72	285	9,750
Jamie Moul	76	67	71	71	285	9,750
Timothy O'Neal	70	73	71	71	285	9,750
Julien Quesne	72	70	73	70	285	9,750
Felipe Aguilar	71	68	71	76	286	7,500
Richard Bland	72	72	70	72	286	7,500
David Drysdale	71	71	75	69	286	7,500
Kim Do-hoon	76	65	72	73	286	7,500
Joost Luiten	70	66	73	77	286	7,500
James Morrison	77	67	69	73	286	7,500
Chris Wood	74	70	69	73	286	7,500
Fabrizio Zanotti	72	69	74	71	286	7,500
Christian Cevaer	75	69	73	70	287	5,550
Scott Jamieson	72	70	74	71	287	5,550
Mark Murphy	72	68	71	76	287	5,550
Marcel Siem	73	71	72	71	287	5,550
Danny Willett	71	67	75	74	287	5,550
Steven O'Hara	71	69	76	72	288	4,650
Alejandro Canizares	67	72	78	72	289	4,275
Rhys Davies	75	69	72	73	289	4,275
Raphael Jacquelin	73	71	70	75	289	4,275
Steve Webster	72	72	74	71	289	4,275
Estanislao Goya	71	72	74	73	290	3,825
Pablo Martin	76	67	77	70	290	3,825
Markus Brier	77	66	73	75	291	3,450
Thongchai Jaidee	74	70	71	76	291	3,450
Garth Mulroy	73	65	77	76	291	3,450
Andrew Dodt	73	71	72	76	292	3,075
Kenneth Ferrie	68	75	74	75	292	3,075
Edouard Dubois	73	71	78	72	294	2,850
Jean-Baptiste Gonnet	71	72	72	80	295	2,740
Lorenzo Gagli	69	75	76	82	302	2,250

Sicilian Open

Verdura Golf & Spa Resort, Sicily, Italy
Par 36-36–72; 7,375 yards

March 29-April 1
purse, €989,970

	SCORES				TOTAL	MONEY
Thorbjorn Olesen	68	69	67	69	273	€166,660
Chris Wood	67	71	72	64	274	111,110
Nicolas Colsaerts	67	71	69	69	276	56,300
Soren Kjeldsen	65	72	71	68	276	56,300
Jose Manuel Lara	69	70	70	68	277	42,400
Shane Lowry	67	70	74	67	278	30,000
Andrew Parr	71	69	67	71	278	30,000
Anthony Wall	69	72	71	66	278	30,000
Estanislao Goya	65	73	72	69	279	21,200
Alvaro Velasco	67	74	70	68	279	21,200
Rich Beem	69	69	73	69	280	15,275
John Daly	71	67	72	70	280	15,275
Pelle Edberg	70	66	75	69	280	15,275
Richard Green	67	70	74	69	280	15,275
Tom Lewis	68	73	70	69	280	15,275
Gareth Maybin	68	73	70	69	280	15,275
Tim Sluiter	69	71	71	69	280	15,275
Graeme Storm	68	73	69	70	280	15,275
Alex Haindl	66	74	74	67	281	11,188
Scott Jamieson	68	73	74	66	281	11,188
Sihwan Kim	67	73	72	69	281	11,188
Peter Lawrie	64	72	72	73	281	11,188
Scott Pinckney	69	70	70	72	281	11,188
Richie Ramsay	71	69	76	65	281	11,188
Lloyd Saltman	71	68	69	73	281	11,188
Bernd Wiesberger	67	71	75	68	281	11,188
Christian Cevaer	69	71	74	68	282	9,350
Victor Dubuisson	71	67	75	69	282	9,350
Julien Guerrier	68	69	73	72	282	9,350
Maarten Lafeber	68	68	77	69	282	9,350
Lloyd Kennedy	70	71	75	67	283	7,900
Ben Mannix	72	68	73	70	283	7,900
Richard McEvoy	68	70	75	70	283	7,900
James Morrison	66	74	75	68	283	7,900
Phillip Price	70	70	71	72	283	7,900
Steve Webster	70	71	68	74	283	7,900
Matthew Baldwin	70	71	71	72	284	6,800
Shiv Kapur	71	68	76	69	284	6,800
David Lynn	67	69	79	69	284	6,800
Simon Wakefield	69	67	74	74	284	6,800
Wil Besseling	71	70	74	70	285	5,800
Alastair Forsyth	67	72	76	70	285	5,800
Michael Jonzon	69	69	77	70	285	5,800
Craig Lee	67	73	73	72	285	5,800
Garth Mulroy	70	67	74	74	285	5,800
Victor Riu	66	72	74	73	285	5,800
Magnus A. Carlsson	70	69	77	70	286	4,500
Carlos Del Moral	71	68	75	72	286	4,500
Sam Hutsby	67	70	78	71	286	4,500
Andrea Maestroni	69	71	75	71	286	4,500
Gary Orr	66	73	75	72	286	4,500
Scott Strange	70	69	77	70	286	4,500
Alessandro Tadini	71	67	77	71	286	4,500
Robert Coles	69	69	80	69	287	3,600
Kim Do-hoon	68	71	79	69	287	3,600
Richard Bland	69	72	75	72	288	3,075
Paul Broadhurst	69	70	77	72	288	3,075

	SCORES				TOTAL	MONEY
Jordi Garcia	68	72	75	73	288	3,075
Joakim Lagergren	66	73	76	73	288	3,075
Jose-Filipe Lima	73	68	75	73	289	2,700
Andrew Marshall	71	70	76	72	289	2,700
Taco Remkes	70	70	75	74	289	2,700
Jamie Donaldson	65	71	80	74	290	2,500
Mikael Lundberg	69	70	77	77	293	2,400
Tjaart van der Walt	69	70	81	74	294	2,300

Maybank Malaysian Open

See Asia/Japan Tours chapter.

Volvo China Open

See Asia/Japan Tours chapter.

Ballantine's Championship

See Asia/Japan Tours chapter.

Reale Seguros Open de Espana

Real Club de Golf de Seville, Seville, Spain
Par 36-36–72; 7,134 yards

May 3-6
purse, €1,988,550

	SCORES				TOTAL	MONEY
Francesco Molinari	70	71	74	65	280	€333,330
Alejandro Canizares	74	72	68	69	283	149,140
Soren Kjeldsen	71	70	71	71	283	149,140
Pablo Larrazabal	71	72	69	71	283	149,140
Jorge Campillo	68	72	73	72	285	77,400
Thorbjorn Olesen	73	72	70	70	285	77,400
Markus Brier	74	73	72	67	286	46,320
Nicolas Colsaerts	72	72	71	71	286	46,320
Matteo Manassero	70	70	76	70	286	46,320
Gareth Maybin	73	75	71	67	286	46,320
Graeme Storm	70	71	74	71	286	46,320
Simon Dyson	71	69	71	76	287	31,650
Richard Green	76	72	71	68	287	31,650
Gregory Havret	72	74	72	69	287	31,650
Marcel Siem	71	72	72	72	287	31,650
Anders Hansen	72	73	76	67	288	25,960
Peter Lawrie	71	73	71	73	288	25,960
Richie Ramsay	73	71	77	67	288	25,960
Robert Rock	68	72	76	72	288	25,960
Jarmo Sandelin	75	72	74	67	288	25,960
Gregory Bourdy	73	66	80	70	289	22,300
Carlos Del Moral	74	73	69	73	289	22,300
Thongchai Jaidee	73	69	74	73	289	22,300
Lee Slattery	74	71	74	70	289	22,300
Matthew Baldwin	69	73	75	73	290	20,500
Joel Sjoholm	75	72	70	73	290	20,500
Rafa Cabrera-Bello	70	73	75	73	291	18,400
Sam Hutsby	70	73	73	75	291	18,400
Gary Orr	70	72	77	72	291	18,400
Romain Wattel	73	74	72	72	291	18,400
Fabrizio Zanotti	72	73	75	71	291	18,400
Darren Fichardt	75	68	73	76	292	14,875

	SCORES				TOTAL	MONEY
Alex Haindl	72	75	74	71	292	14,875
Shaun Micheel	67	77	73	75	292	14,875
James Morrison	71	76	77	68	292	14,875
Jeev Milkha Singh	73	74	71	74	292	14,875
Simon Thornton	73	73	74	72	292	14,875
Marc Warren	72	74	74	72	292	14,875
Danny Willett	68	73	79	72	292	14,875
Fredrik Andersson Hed	74	73	76	70	293	12,400
Richard Bland	73	71	77	72	293	12,400
George Murray	74	74	73	72	293	12,400
Adrian Otaegui	73	73	77	70	293	12,400
Robert-Jan Derksen	72	75	75	72	294	11,200
Borja Etchart	73	74	72	75	294	11,200
Thomas Aiken	71	76	77	71	295	9,800
Emiliano Grillo	73	72	77	73	295	9,800
Craig Lee	71	76	76	72	295	9,800
Jose María Olazabal	75	72	75	73	295	9,800
Chris Wood	72	73	76	74	295	9,800
Kenneth Ferrie	72	74	81	69	296	8,400
Edoardo Molinari	74	74	78	70	296	8,400
Johan Edfors	74	74	78	71	297	7,000
Gonzalo Fernandez-Castano	76	72	78	71	297	7,000
*Jack Hiluta	72	73	81	71	297	
James Kingston	74	68	78	77	297	7,000
Jose Manuel Lara	74	74	74	75	297	7,000
Christian Nilsson	71	76	76	74	297	7,000
Joakim Lagergren	73	74	74	77	298	5,900
Andy Sullivan	73	75	76	74	298	5,900
Phillip Price	73	73	78	75	299	5,600
Bradley Dredge	72	75	80	73	300	5,300
Mark Haastrup	75	73	75	77	300	5,300
Manuel Quiros	76	72	80	73	301	5,000
Raphael Jacquelin	76	70	79	77	302	4,800
Raul Quiros	73	73	83	75	304	4,600
Felipe Aguilar	75	72	85	74	306	4,300
Michael Jonzon	73	74	77	82	306	4,300

Madeira Islands Open

Santo da Serra, Madeira, Portugal
Par 36-36–72; 6,825 yards

May 10-13
purse, €675,000

	SCORES				TOTAL	MONEY
Ricardo Santos	68	67	68	63	266	€112,500
Magnus A. Carlsson	66	66	71	67	270	75,000
Andreas Harto	67	71	66	67	271	42,255
Carlos Del Moral	69	67	63	73	272	24,624
Joakim Lagergren	66	66	70	70	272	24,624
Mikael Lundberg	69	70	64	69	272	24,624
John Parry	71	70	65	66	272	24,624
Oliver Wilson	66	65	72	69	272	24,624
David Dixon	68	68	70	67	273	14,310
Alastair Forsyth	69	68	70	66	273	14,310
H.P. Bacher	67	69	71	68	275	11,030
Julien Guerrier	70	69	68	68	275	11,030
Sihwan Kim	68	66	70	71	275	11,030
Morten Orum Madsen	66	69	74	66	275	11,030
Gary Orr	69	69	68	69	275	11,030
Richard Bland	68	67	69	72	276	8,606
Chris Doak	70	68	70	68	276	8,606

	SCORES				TOTAL	MONEY
Charlie Ford	67	68	70	71	276	8,606
Alex Haindl	69	68	71	68	276	8,606
Ben Parker	66	72	71	67	276	8,606
Andy Sullivan	68	64	76	68	276	8,606
Matthew Baldwin	67	70	69	71	277	7,324
Chris Paisley	69	69	69	70	277	7,324
Victor Riu	72	69	70	66	277	7,324
Alessandro Tadini	70	68	70	69	277	7,324
Knut Borsheim	68	69	68	73	278	6,716
Shiv Kapur	70	68	68	72	278	6,716
Daniel Denison	70	71	67	71	279	6,008
Tyrone Ferreira	74	66	70	69	279	6,008
Thomas Norret	69	68	70	72	279	6,008
Lloyd Saltman	68	73	72	66	279	6,008
Alvaro Velasco	64	72	72	71	279	6,008
Nick Dougherty	69	71	68	72	280	5,006
Niclas Fasth	73	68	71	68	280	5,006
Jordi Garcia	72	66	71	71	280	5,006
James Heath	69	69	71	71	280	5,006
Jarmo Sandelin	70	67	73	70	280	5,006
Johan Wahlqvist	70	70	70	70	280	5,006
Warren Abery	67	72	71	71	281	4,320
Stephen Dodd	73	68	70	70	281	4,320
Emiliano Grillo	73	68	69	71	281	4,320
Jamie McLeary	69	69	73	70	281	4,320
Adam Gee	68	71	69	74	282	3,780
Lloyd Kennedy	71	65	74	72	282	3,780
Andrew McArthur	70	68	74	70	282	3,780
Raymond Russell	71	70	69	72	282	3,780
Joachim B. Hansen	70	70	71	72	283	3,240
Lasse Jensen	71	69	71	72	283	3,240
Pedro Oriol	69	70	71	73	283	3,240
Florian Praegant	73	68	71	71	283	3,240
Bjorn Akesson	73	68	69	74	284	2,835
Tommy Fleetwood	66	70	72	76	284	2,835
Andre Bossert	69	72	72	72	285	2,256
Benjamin Hebert	70	69	73	73	285	2,256
Nuno Henriques	73	67	73	72	285	2,256
Chris Lloyd	74	67	71	73	285	2,256
Jean-Francois Lucquin	73	68	74	70	285	2,256
Charles-Edouard Russo	74	66	72	73	285	2,256
Sam Walker	69	72	74	70	285	2,256
Markus Brier	69	72	72	73	286	1,822
Roope Kakko	70	69	70	77	286	1,822
Antonio Rosado	72	69	72	73	286	1,822
Sion E. Bebb	69	69	74	75	287	1,654
Anthony Snobeck	70	71	75	71	287	1,654
Andrea Perrino	70	71	74	73	288	1,519
Tim Sluiter	69	71	80	68	288	1,519
Steven Tiley	71	69	72	77	289	1,418
Jamie Elson	70	70	77	73	290	1,316
Steven Jeppesen	73	68	74	75	290	1,316
Maarten Lafeber	71	70	77	74	292	1,230

Volvo World Match Play Championship

Finca Cortesin Golf Club, Casares, Andalucia, Spain
Par 37-35–72; 7,290 yards

May 17-20
purse, €2,750,000

FIRST ROUND

Ian Poulter defeated John Senden, 3 and 2.
Brandt Snedeker defeated Thomas Bjorn, 5 and 4.
Paul Lawrie defeated Peter Hanson, 2 and 1.
Sergio Garcia defeated Alvaro Quiros, 2 and 1.
Graeme McDowell defeated Robert Karlsson, 1 up.
Charl Schwartzel halved with Nicolas Colsaerts.
Justin Rose defeated Robert Rock, 7 and 6.
Rafa Cabrera-Bello defeated Martin Kaymer, 3 and 2.

SECOND ROUND

Tom Lewis defeated Senden, 1 up.
Bjorn defeated Branden Grace, 2 and 1.
Lawrie halved with Camilo Villegas.
Quiros defeated Tetsuji Hiratsuka, 5 and 4.
Karlsson halved with Jbe' Kruger.
Retief Goosen defeated Colsaerts, 1 up.
Rock defeated Darren Clarke, 2 up.
Cabrera-Bello defeated Richard Finch, 4 and 2.

THIRD ROUND

Poulter defeated Lewis, 4 and 3.
Grace defeated Snedeker, 4 and 3.
Villegas defeated Hanson, 6 and 4.
Garcia defeated Hiratsuka, 4 and 2.
McDowell defeated Kruger, 4 and 3.
Goosen defeated Schwartzel, 4 and 3.
Rose defeated Clarke, 6 and 4.
Finch defeated Kaymer, 1 up.

(Each eliminated player received €50,000)

ROUND OF TOP 16

Garcia defeated Lewis, 4 and 3.
McDowell defeated Finch, 3 and 2.
Lawrie defeated Bjorn, 5 and 4.
Goosen defeated Rock, 3 and 2.
Snedeker defeated Villegas, 3 and 2.
Colsaerts defeated Rose, 4 and 3.
Quiros defeated Poulter, 4 and 3.
Cabrera-Bello defeated Karlsson, 1 up.

(Each losing player received €70,000.)

QUARTER-FINALS

McDowell defeated Garcia, 19 holes.
Lawrie defeated Goosen, 6 and 5.
Colsaerts defeated Snedeker,4 and 3.
Cabrera-Bello defeated Quiros, 3 and 1

(Each losing player received €92,500.)

SEMI-FINALS

Colsaerts defeated Lawrie, 20 holes.
McDowell defeated Cabrera-Bello, 2 up

(Each losing player received €180,000.)

FINAL

Colsaerts defeated McDowell, 1 up.

(Colsaerts received €700,000; McDowell received €360,000.)

BMW PGA Championship

Wentworth Club, Virginia Water, Surrey, England
Par 35-37–72; 7,302 yards

May 24-27
purse, €4,513,497

	SCORES				TOTAL	MONEY
Luke Donald	68	68	69	68	273	€750,000
Paul Lawrie	69	71	71	66	277	390,850
Justin Rose	67	71	69	70	277	390,850
Peter Lawrie	66	71	72	71	280	225,000
Branden Grace	69	69	73	70	281	190,800
Richard Sterne	71	68	72	71	282	157,500
Ernie Els	68	73	70	72	283	116,100
Francesco Molinari	68	70	74	71	283	116,100
Marcel Siem	71	67	76	69	283	116,100
David Drysdale	66	70	78	70	284	78,300
David Higgins	70	70	74	70	284	78,300
James Morrison	68	64	81	71	284	78,300
Ian Poulter	71	73	69	71	284	78,300
Alvaro Quiros	67	70	77	70	284	78,300
Rafa Cabrera-Bello	68	70	74	73	285	63,450
S.S.P. Chowrasia	69	76	71	69	285	63,450
Martin Kaymer	71	69	76	69	285	63,450
Fredrik Andersson Hed	70	68	77	71	286	55,950
Peter Hedblom	68	70	74	74	286	55,950
Charl Schwartzel	69	71	79	67	286	55,950
George Coetzee	68	77	76	66	287	48,825
Victor Dubuisson	70	71	76	70	287	48,825
Alexander Noren	70	74	73	70	287	48,825
Julien Quesne	74	71	72	70	287	48,825
Robert Rock	68	76	74	69	287	48,825
Paul Streeter	71	74	74	68	287	48,825
Federico Colombo	69	74	71	74	288	40,725
Simon Khan	71	74	70	73	288	40,725
Garth Mulroy	71	70	76	71	288	40,725
Jose Maria Olazabal	70	72	76	70	288	40,725
Jeev Milkha Singh	70	74	70	74	288	40,725
Marc Warren	68	76	72	72	288	40,725
Niclas Fasth	67	73	78	71	289	33,375
Richard Finch	76	67	74	72	289	33,375
Ricardo Gonzalez	71	67	77	74	289	33,375
Jbe' Kruger	72	73	74	70	289	33,375
Paul McGinley	73	71	73	72	289	33,375
Lee Westwood	70	75	70	74	289	33,375
Andrew Dodt	69	73	76	72	290	28,800
Miguel Angel Jimenez	71	70	76	73	290	28,800
Gareth Maybin	70	70	76	74	290	28,800
Damien McGrane	71	72	75	72	290	28,800
Thomas Bjorn	74	70	78	69	291	24,300

	SCORES				TOTAL	MONEY
Kenneth Ferrie	68	74	77	72	291	24,300
Scott Jamieson	68	75	75	73	291	24,300
Richard S. Johnson	67	75	75	74	291	24,300
Matteo Manassero	74	69	77	71	291	24,300
Danny Willett	69	71	79	72	291	24,300
Alex Cejka	75	70	76	71	292	19,800
Tommy Fleetwood	72	73	72	75	292	19,800
Edoardo Molinari	69	70	76	77	292	19,800
Chris Wood	73	71	80	68	292	19,800
Jamie Donaldson	67	73	77	76	293	16,650
Pablo Martin	69	70	76	78	293	16,650
Bernd Wiesberger	68	73	83	69	293	16,650
Thongchai Jaidee	71	72	79	72	294	13,838
Jose Manuel Lara	72	71	78	73	294	13,838
Sam Little	72	73	76	73	294	13,838
Christian Nilsson	74	70	77	73	294	13,838
Bradley Dredge	71	72	78	74	295	12,600
Robert-Jan Derksen	71	71	81	73	296	11,475
Gregory Havret	75	67	83	71	296	11,475
Mikko Ilonen	74	70	79	73	296	11,475
Steve Webster	69	74	81	72	296	11,475
Oscar Floren	74	71	80	72	297	9,900
Richard Green	72	73	79	73	297	9,900
Pablo Larrazabal	70	75	77	75	297	9,900
Ben Curtis	70	75	81	72	298	8,775
Shane Lowry	71	74	79	74	298	8,775
James Kingston	71	74	85	71	301	7,475
Brett Rumford	70	74	79	78	301	7,475
Colin Montgomerie	69	74	78	81	302	6,747

ISPS Handa Wales Open

Celtic Manor Resort, City of Newport, Wales
Par 36-35–71; 7,378 yards

May 31-June 3
purse, €2,249,718

	SCORES				TOTAL	MONEY
Thongchai Jaidee	71	68	67	72	278	€372,720
Thomas Bjorn	71	72	68	68	279	148,777
Gonzalo Fernandez-Castano	69	74	69	67	279	148,777
Joost Luiten	74	69	64	72	279	148,777
Richard Sterne	73	69	69	68	279	148,777
Ross Fisher	70	66	71	73	280	72,680
Paul McGinley	72	73	70	65	280	72,680
Peter Lawrie	72	73	69	67	281	50,243
Joel Sjoholm	69	74	70	68	281	50,243
Romain Wattel	73	72	68	68	281	50,243
Carlos Del Moral	75	68	66	74	283	38,539
David Drysdale	72	71	71	69	283	38,539
David Lynn	73	71	67	72	283	38,539
Gregory Bourdy	74	69	68	73	284	32,203
George Coetzee	71	71	68	74	284	32,203
Paul Lawrie	74	69	71	70	284	32,203
Chris Wood	72	67	74	71	284	32,203
Magnus A. Carlsson	77	67	70	71	285	25,092
Robert Coles	73	69	72	71	285	25,092
Federico Colombo	79	68	67	71	285	25,092
Mark Foster	72	69	69	75	285	25,092
Raphael Jacquelin	76	65	72	72	285	25,092
Richard McEvoy	71	70	69	75	285	25,092
Thorbjorn Olesen	73	68	71	73	285	25,092

	SCORES				TOTAL	MONEY
Brett Rumford	74	70	70	71	285	25,092
Tim Sluiter	68	72	68	77	285	25,092
Jaco Van Zyl	72	69	71	73	285	25,092
Pablo Larrazabal	69	74	71	72	286	19,903
Matteo Manassero	76	68	68	74	286	19,903
Damien McGrane	71	71	69	75	286	19,903
Lee Slattery	67	71	76	72	286	19,903
Fabrizio Zanotti	70	69	75	72	286	19,903
Jean-Baptiste Gonnet	74	69	75	69	287	17,555
Marcel Siem	68	75	66	78	287	17,555
Emiliano Grillo	73	69	71	75	288	15,431
Keith Horne	79	66	68	75	288	15,431
Joakim Lagergren	72	72	74	70	288	15,431
Tom Lewis	74	71	72	71	288	15,431
George Murray	75	71	69	73	288	15,431
Simon Thornton	69	73	77	69	288	15,431
Matthew Zions	76	71	68	73	288	15,431
Knut Borsheim	74	71	76	68	289	12,971
Oscar Floren	78	69	67	75	289	12,971
Marcus Fraser	70	77	71	71	289	12,971
Stephen Gallacher	77	70	75	67	289	12,971
Oliver Fisher	76	71	73	70	290	11,629
Francesco Molinari	74	69	73	74	290	11,629
Rich Beem	77	68	73	73	291	9,169
David Horsey	71	73	74	73	291	9,169
David Howell	73	69	75	74	291	9,169
Andrew Johnston	75	72	71	73	291	9,169
Simon Khan	75	70	74	72	291	9,169
Maarten Lafeber	74	72	72	73	291	9,169
Steven O'Hara	70	72	73	76	291	9,169
Reinier Saxton	74	71	75	71	291	9,169
Oliver Wilson	73	73	74	71	291	9,169
Jamie Elson	71	75	73	73	292	6,485
Tommy Fleetwood	75	68	78	71	292	6,485
Lorenzo Gagli	77	70	66	79	292	6,485
Miguel Angel Jimenez	76	71	74	71	292	6,485
James Morrison	77	70	72	73	292	6,485
Ricardo Gonzalez	73	72	76	72	293	5,591
Andrew Marshall	72	74	75	72	293	5,591
Colin Montgomerie	74	72	72	75	293	5,591
Gregory Havret	75	72	71	76	294	5,144
Benjamin Hebert	73	72	75	75	295	4,920
Daniel Denison	78	67	75	76	296	4,584
Steen Tinning	73	73	73	77	296	4,584
Graeme Storm	80	67	80	70	297	4,249
Fredrik Andersson Hed	71	75	79	73	298	3,715
Niclas Fasth	74	73	70	81	298	3,715
Andrea Pavan	76	71	74	78	299	3,351
Jamie Moul	78	67	77	80	302	3,348
Scott Hend	80	66	70	87	303	3,345

Nordea Masters

Bro Hof Slott Golf Club, Stockholm, Sweden   June 6-9
Par 36-36–72; 7,607 yards   purse, €1,508,982

	SCORES				TOTAL	MONEY
Lee Westwood	68	64	68	69	269	€250,000
Ross Fisher	70	68	65	71	274	166,660
Sergio Garcia	69	69	70	67	275	77,500

	SCORES				TOTAL	MONEY
Peter Hanson	67	68	69	71	275	77,500
Mikko Ilonen	70	69	68	68	275	77,500
Joakim Lagergren	70	68	69	69	276	52,500
Felipe Aguilar	69	70	68	70	277	38,700
Jeev Milkha Singh	73	66	68	70	277	38,700
Richard Sterne	69	67	73	68	277	38,700
Pelle Edberg	69	69	70	70	278	26,888
Ignacio Garrido	67	69	73	69	278	26,888
Gregory Havret	70	69	68	71	278	26,888
Alexander Noren	74	66	66	72	278	26,888
Darren Fichardt	70	70	68	71	279	22,050
Marcus Fraser	72	70	65	72	279	22,050
Andy Sullivan	68	71	69	71	279	22,050
Roope Kakko	70	68	72	70	280	18,720
Andrew Marshall	73	70	66	71	280	18,720
Reinier Saxton	70	70	70	70	280	18,720
Anthony Wall	69	70	70	71	280	18,720
Bernd Wiesberger	69	71	67	73	280	18,720
Richard Bland	67	70	68	76	281	15,375
Jens Dantorp	76	67	66	72	281	15,375
Daniel Denison	68	70	70	73	281	15,375
Jamie Donaldson	72	69	68	72	281	15,375
Emiliano Grillo	68	68	76	69	281	15,375
Thorbjorn Olesen	71	68	69	73	281	15,375
Lloyd Saltman	71	64	75	71	281	15,375
Chris Wood	71	66	74	70	281	15,375
Kristoffer Broberg	71	68	71	72	282	11,888
Carlos Del Moral	68	67	72	75	282	11,888
Johan Edfors	72	69	69	72	282	11,888
Estanislao Goya	70	68	69	75	282	11,888
Edoardo Molinari	72	69	69	72	282	11,888
Scott Strange	71	69	72	70	282	11,888
Romain Wattel	72	71	70	69	282	11,888
Peter Whiteford	71	69	69	73	282	11,888
Magnus A. Carlsson	65	72	73	73	283	9,900
Richard Green	72	69	68	74	283	9,900
Michael Jonzon	68	68	70	77	283	9,900
Pablo Martin	75	66	70	72	283	9,900
Alejandro Canizares	68	71	72	73	284	8,850
Gary Orr	72	70	71	71	284	8,850
Tjaart van der Walt	72	68	70	74	284	8,850
Lucas Bjerregaard	73	68	74	70	285	8,100
Robin Wingardh	68	73	71	73	285	8,100
Matthew Baldwin	67	76	71	72	286	7,050
Rafa Cabrera-Bello	71	69	69	77	286	7,050
Pablo Larrazabal	71	70	68	77	286	7,050
Gareth Maybin	74	67	72	73	286	7,050
Matthew Nixon	71	71	70	74	286	7,050
Mark Foster	70	71	71	75	287	5,850
Thongchai Jaidee	73	70	72	72	287	5,850
Maarten Lafeber	71	65	77	74	287	5,850
Michael Hoey	70	68	77	73	288	4,740
David Howell	72	70	70	76	288	4,740
Jason Knutzon	72	71	68	77	288	4,740
David Lynn	70	73	72	73	288	4,740
Jaco Van Zyl	69	74	71	74	288	4,740
Daniel Gaunt	71	72	72	74	289	4,200
Knut Borsheim	76	67	72	75	290	3,825
Andrew Dodt	71	69	74	76	290	3,825
*Robert Karlsson	72	70	75	73	290	
Jesper Kennegard	73	70	72	75	290	3,825
Graeme Storm	73	70	72	75	290	3,825
Julien Guerrier	70	71	73	77	291	3,225

	SCORES				TOTAL	MONEY
Joakim Haeggman	72	70	73	76	291	3,225
Brett Rumford	69	71	74	77	291	3,225
Tim Sluiter	70	73	74	74	291	3,225
Niclas Fasth	69	74	74	75	292	2,850
Niklas Bruzelius	71	71	75	76	293	2,495
Edouard Dubois	75	66	74	78	293	2,495
Richard McEvoy	71	72	74	77	294	2,247
Jamie Elson	73	70	75	81	299	2,244
Mark Haastrup	73	69	74	91	307	2,241

Saint-Omer Open

Aa Saint-Omer Golf Club, Lumbres, France
Par 36-35–71; 6,846 yards

June 14-17
purse, €508,085

	SCORES				TOTAL	MONEY
Darren Fichardt	68	69	69	73	279	€83,330
Gary Lockerbie	69	75	69	69	282	55,550
Simon Wakefield	67	72	72	72	283	31,300
Wil Besseling	71	69	73	73	286	19,675
Pelle Edberg	70	72	72	72	286	19,675
Charlie Ford	74	69	73	70	286	19,675
Adam Gee	67	72	75	72	286	19,675
Bjorn Akesson	75	72	70	70	287	11,233
Magnus A. Carlsson	73	72	71	71	287	11,233
James Heath	71	70	74	72	287	11,233
Chris Paisley	71	76	72	69	288	8,375
Simon Thornton	71	69	75	73	288	8,375
Mark Tullo	78	68	67	75	288	8,375
Justin Walters	73	68	77	70	288	8,375
Carlos Aguilar	72	73	73	71	289	6,406
Christophe Brazillier	77	69	75	68	289	6,406
Daniel Brooks	76	69	71	73	289	6,406
Alastair Forsyth	69	72	74	74	289	6,406
Chris Gane	73	73	71	72	289	6,406
Alexandre Kaleka	71	75	73	70	289	6,406
Sihwan Kim	67	69	81	72	289	6,406
Michael Lorenzo-Vera	75	71	72	71	289	6,406
Julien Guerrier	71	72	74	73	290	5,200
Andreas Harto	72	74	70	74	290	5,200
David Howell	73	70	73	74	290	5,200
Raymond Russell	68	75	74	73	290	5,200
Reinier Saxton	71	72	74	73	290	5,200
Joachim B. Hansen	75	71	75	70	291	4,231
Berry Henson	69	74	77	71	291	4,231
Maarten Lafeber	74	72	76	69	291	4,231
Mikael Lundberg	73	74	68	76	291	4,231
Andrew Marshall	72	71	76	72	291	4,231
Thomas Norret	70	73	73	75	291	4,231
Taco Remkes	74	70	73	74	291	4,231
Steven Tiley	69	75	76	71	291	4,231
Federico Colombo	73	70	74	75	292	3,400
Edouard Dubois	70	75	75	72	292	3,400
Jamie Elson	70	73	75	74	292	3,400
Rikard Karlberg	75	71	73	73	292	3,400
Florian Praegant	71	74	76	71	292	3,400
Lloyd Saltman	70	74	77	71	292	3,400
Benn Barham	70	72	80	71	293	2,700
Rafa Echenique	74	72	72	75	293	2,700
Thomas Feyrsinger	75	72	76	70	293	2,700

	SCORES				TOTAL	MONEY
Benjamin Hebert	75	72	74	72	293	2,700
Shiv Kapur	73	74	75	71	293	2,700
Espen Kofstad	76	69	77	71	293	2,700
Ben Parker	76	71	73	73	293	2,700
Andrea Perrino	73	68	74	78	293	2,700
Roope Kakko	70	73	76	75	294	2,000
Jason Knutzon	73	71	79	71	294	2,000
Craig Lee	72	72	77	73	294	2,000
Raul Quiros	68	74	78	74	294	2,000
Gary Stal	72	74	73	75	294	2,000
Matthew Zions	73	72	72	77	294	2,000
Stuart Davis	74	72	73	76	295	1,483
Klas Eriksson	73	74	72	76	295	1,483
Jordi Garcia	74	73	70	78	295	1,483
Andrew Johnston	74	69	77	75	295	1,483
Nicolas Meitinger	75	70	75	75	295	1,483
Andy Sullivan	70	71	80	74	295	1,483
Chris Doak	75	72	74	75	296	1,125
Raphael Eyraud	71	76	75	74	296	1,125
Tyrrell Hatton	72	70	78	76	296	1,125
Fredrik Henge	77	69	73	77	296	1,125
Colm Moriarty	69	77	77	73	296	1,125
Dominique Nouailhac	74	73	76	73	296	1,125
Anthony Snobeck	69	73	79	75	296	1,125
Matthew Southgate	73	73	77	73	296	1,125
Guillaume Cambis	75	71	70	82	298	780
Daniel Denison	71	70	81	76	298	780
David Dixon	77	69	76	76	298	780
Agustin Domingo	74	71	82	71	298	780
Carl Suneson	72	75	80	71	298	780
Andrew Parr	74	73	81	71	299	736
Alvaro Velasco	75	72	75	77	299	736
Jean-Francois Lucquin	71	76	74	79	300	732
Floris De Vries	74	73	83	73	303	728
David McKenzie	76	70	78	79	303	728
Johan Wahlqvist	75	71	80	78	304	723
Sam Hutsby	71	75	76	84	306	720

BMW International Open

Golf Club Gut Larchenhof, Cologne, Germany
Par 36-36–72; 7,228 yards

June 21-24
purse, €2,000,000

	SCORES				TOTAL	MONEY
Danny Willett	65	70	69	73	277	€333,330
Marcus Fraser	64	74	68	71	277	222,220
(Willett defeated Fraser on fourth playoff hole.)						
Gonzalo Fernandez-Castano	71	69	69	69	278	103,333
Paul McGinley	65	70	77	66	278	103,333
Chris Wood	65	70	70	73	278	103,333
Marcel Siem	68	71	68	72	279	65,000
Henrik Stenson	70	68	71	70	279	65,000
Thomas Bjorn	69	70	70	71	280	42,900
Ross Fisher	70	70	70	70	280	42,900
Thongchai Jaidee	70	71	68	71	280	42,900
Joel Sjoholm	67	66	72	75	280	42,900
Simon Dyson	68	70	73	70	281	30,300
Keith Horne	66	73	67	75	281	30,300
David Lynn	69	70	74	68	281	30,300
Andrew Marshall	71	67	70	73	281	30,300

	SCORES				TOTAL	MONEY
Thomas Norret	67	69	73	72	281	30,300
Fabrizio Zanotti	64	71	72	74	281	30,300
Carlos Del Moral	68	75	70	69	282	24,080
Pelle Edberg	66	74	69	73	282	24,080
Mark Foster	69	74	70	69	282	24,080
Steve Webster	69	70	69	74	282	24,080
Oliver Wilson	69	73	67	73	282	24,080
Niclas Fasth	68	69	77	69	283	20,500
Shiv Kapur	66	70	75	72	283	20,500
Bernhard Langer	72	67	72	72	283	20,500
Paul Lawrie	72	70	72	69	283	20,500
Mikael Lundberg	68	74	68	73	283	20,500
Matthew Nixon	71	66	72	74	283	20,500
Robert-Jan Derksen	69	70	75	70	284	17,500
Sergio Garcia	71	67	79	67	284	17,500
David Howell	72	70	70	72	284	17,500
Pablo Larrazabal	69	71	72	72	284	17,500
Gary Boyd	71	69	72	73	285	15,040
Oscar Floren	67	70	73	75	285	15,040
Dylan Frittelli	69	68	74	74	285	15,040
Stephen Gallacher	67	73	72	73	285	15,040
Ricardo Gonzalez	70	72	76	67	285	15,040
Rhys Davies	69	69	77	71	286	12,800
Richard Green	67	73	73	73	286	12,800
Andrew Johnston	71	72	73	70	286	12,800
Joost Luiten	68	69	74	75	286	12,800
Christian Nilsson	68	71	76	71	286	12,800
Richard Sterne	69	69	69	79	286	12,800
David Drysdale	69	70	73	75	287	10,400
Soren Kjeldsen	67	73	76	71	287	10,400
Damien McGrane	76	66	73	72	287	10,400
Colin Montgomerie	69	74	72	72	287	10,400
Phillip Price	70	71	78	68	287	10,400
Marc Warren	73	70	70	74	287	10,400
Julien Guerrier	68	74	72	74	288	8,800
Gregory Havret	66	76	77	69	288	8,800
Miguel Angel Jimenez	68	74	75	72	289	8,000
Simon Khan	69	71	73	76	289	8,000
Thomas Aiken	72	71	76	71	290	6,500
Rich Beem	71	70	76	73	290	6,500
Alastair Forsyth	69	71	75	75	290	6,500
Michael Jonzon	68	74	73	75	290	6,500
Richard McEvoy	69	71	72	78	290	6,500
Simon Thornton	71	72	74	73	290	6,500
Wil Besseling	71	69	76	75	291	5,300
Michael Campbell	70	68	78	75	291	5,300
John Daly	68	73	77	73	291	5,300
Peter Whiteford	70	73	70	78	291	5,300
Federico Colombo	73	68	75	76	292	4,700
Steven O'Hara	69	72	71	80	292	4,700
Alex Cejka	68	75	74	76	293	4,200
Pablo Martin	70	73	76	74	293	4,200
Julien Quesne	75	68	77	73	293	4,200
Jordi Garcia	72	71	77	74	294	3,725
James Kingston	71	72	74	77	294	3,725

Irish Open

Royal Portrush Golf Club, Portrush,
County Antrim, Northern Ireland
Par 36-36–72; 7,143 yards

June 28-July 1
purse, €2,000,000

	SCORES				TOTAL	MONEY
Jamie Donaldson	68	67	69	66	270	€333,330
Rafa Cabrera-Bello	71	67	70	66	274	149,140
Anthony Wall	67	71	67	69	274	149,140
Fabrizio Zanotti	69	71	68	66	274	149,140
Mark Foster	66	67	73	69	275	77,400
Mikael Lundberg	69	66	75	65	275	77,400
David Drysdale	70	70	70	66	276	51,600
Padraig Harrington	67	67	72	70	276	51,600
Craig Lee	73	68	67	68	276	51,600
Simon Dyson	67	72	71	67	277	33,900
Ross Fisher	68	71	72	66	277	33,900
Mikko Ilonen	66	72	72	67	277	33,900
Rory McIlroy	70	69	71	67	277	33,900
Francesco Molinari	70	67	73	67	277	33,900
Paul Waring	69	65	73	70	277	33,900
Graeme McDowell	71	68	73	66	278	27,600
Richie Ramsay	69	70	72	67	278	27,600
Richard Bland	68	69	73	69	279	23,733
Edouard Dubois	66	73	71	69	279	23,733
Thongchai Jaidee	67	72	74	66	279	23,733
Thorbjorn Olesen	72	70	66	71	279	23,733
Gary Orr	68	68	74	69	279	23,733
Matthew Zions	66	71	73	69	279	23,733
John Daly	70	71	72	67	280	20,500
Bradley Dredge	68	71	73	68	280	20,500
Lorenzo Gagli	68	66	76	70	280	20,500
James Morrison	68	70	71	71	280	20,500
Michael Hoey	70	67	74	70	281	18,700
Romain Wattel	69	70	75	67	281	18,700
Jbe' Kruger	69	73	71	69	282	17,200
Andrew Marshall	66	71	73	72	282	17,200
Jeev Milkha Singh	65	71	75	71	282	17,200
Gregory Bourdy	65	67	80	71	283	14,833
Gary Boyd	71	71	72	69	283	14,833
Alex Haindl	68	70	76	69	283	14,833
David Howell	71	71	72	69	283	14,833
Paul Lawrie	69	72	76	66	283	14,833
Simon Thornton	70	70	75	68	283	14,833
Darren Clarke	71	69	73	71	284	12,600
Estanislao Goya	70	70	70	74	284	12,600
Christian Nilsson	69	71	73	71	284	12,600
Ricardo Santos	69	72	73	70	284	12,600
Marc Warren	71	68	74	71	284	12,600
Matthew Baldwin	70	69	74	72	285	10,200
Jorge Campillo	71	69	73	72	285	10,200
Alejandro Canizares	67	70	73	75	285	10,200
Oscar Floren	66	72	73	74	285	10,200
Stephen Gallacher	72	69	74	70	285	10,200
Emiliano Grillo	68	74	74	69	285	10,200
Richard Sterne	70	69	73	73	285	10,200
Robert-Jan Derksen	69	71	72	74	286	8,200
Shane Lowry	72	68	76	70	286	8,200
Peter Whiteford	67	70	76	73	286	8,200
Paul McGinley	69	70	76	72	287	7,000
Steven O'Hara	69	69	77	72	287	7,000
Lee Slattery	70	69	77	71	287	7,000

	SCORES				TOTAL	MONEY
Marcel Siem	69	71	77	71	288	6,200
Mark Murphy	69	73	73	74	289	5,900
Joel Sjoholm	70	72	75	72	289	5,900
Rich Beem	69	72	75	74	290	5,300
Sam Little	71	68	76	75	290	5,300
George Murray	72	68	77	73	290	5,300
Mark O'Sullivan	68	72	78	72	290	5,300
Damien McGrane	71	71	74	75	291	4,800
Robert Rock	71	71	74	76	292	4,600
Joost Luiten	72	69	78	74	293	4,400
Fredrik Andersson Hed	68	73	82	71	294	4,200
Phillip Price	71	70	75	79	295	4,000
Johan Edfors	72	68	77	80	297	3,725
Simon Khan	72	70	78	77	297	3,725

Alstom Open de France

Le Golf National, Paris, France
Par 36-35–71; 7,347 yards

July 5-8
purse, €3,150,000

	SCORES				TOTAL	MONEY
Marcel Siem	68	68	73	67	276	€525,000
Francesco Molinari	71	68	74	64	277	350,000
Raphael Jacquelin	68	71	70	69	278	197,190
David Howell	70	70	67	72	279	133,770
David Lynn	67	72	72	68	279	133,770
Ian Poulter	72	69	69	69	279	133,770
Brendan Steele	70	70	71	69	280	86,625
Henrik Stenson	68	73	69	70	280	86,625
Soren Kjeldsen	70	71	71	69	281	66,780
Justin Rose	71	73	68	69	281	66,780
Michael Campbell	71	74	70	67	282	52,762
Nicolas Colsaerts	70	72	69	71	282	52,762
David Drysdale	70	70	72	70	282	52,762
Anders Hansen	70	68	69	75	282	52,762
Thongchai Jaidee	66	75	70	72	283	45,360
Alexander Noren	70	67	74	72	283	45,360
George Coetzee	70	68	70	76	284	38,692
Branden Grace	72	69	72	71	284	38,692
Shane Lowry	70	70	74	70	284	38,692
Matteo Manassero	66	75	72	71	284	38,692
Graeme McDowell	72	69	71	72	284	38,692
Marc Warren	76	69	68	71	284	38,692
Johan Edfors	71	73	68	73	285	32,760
Philip Golding	71	70	72	72	285	32,760
Retief Goosen	77	68	67	73	285	32,760
Emiliano Grillo	73	71	68	73	285	32,760
Shiv Kapur	72	69	71	73	285	32,760
Mark Foster	71	72	72	71	286	28,980
Scott Jamieson	71	74	70	71	286	28,980
Jose María Olazabal	73	70	70	73	286	28,980
Robert Coles	71	72	69	75	287	24,885
Gonzalo Fernandez-Castano	67	76	72	72	287	24,885
Kenneth Ferrie	72	72	72	71	287	24,885
James Morrison	73	70	70	74	287	24,885
Christian Nilsson	65	75	76	71	287	24,885
Richard Sterne	73	70	72	72	287	24,885
Gary Boyd	66	75	74	73	288	21,735
Jaco Van Zyl	69	72	78	69	288	21,735
Steve Webster	68	74	75	71	288	21,735

	SCORES				TOTAL	MONEY
Robert-Jan Derksen	73	70	71	75	289	18,900
Lorenzo Gagli	69	75	71	74	289	18,900
Gregory Havret	70	73	74	72	289	18,900
Jean-Francois Lucquin	73	71	74	71	289	18,900
Lee Westwood	70	73	76	70	289	18,900
Fabrizio Zanotti	72	73	72	72	289	18,900
Jeev Milkha Singh	68	74	75	73	290	16,695
Niclas Fasth	72	71	73	75	291	14,490
Ignacio Garrido	73	72	70	76	291	14,490
Ricardo Gonzalez	72	73	72	74	291	14,490
Hu Mu	71	70	76	74	291	14,490
Joost Luiten	74	69	73	75	291	14,490
Bernd Wiesberger	72	72	71	76	291	14,490
Peter Lawrie	73	72	72	75	292	12,285
Thomas Aiken	70	74	73	76	293	11,025
Mikko Ilonen	71	73	76	73	293	11,025
Damien Perrier	70	72	79	72	293	11,025
Rafa Cabrera-Bello	70	74	77	73	294	9,450
Ricardo Santos	71	69	80	74	294	9,450
Tjaart van der Walt	68	75	74	77	294	9,450
Keith Horne	72	71	73	79	295	8,820
Federico Colombo	67	76	76	77	296	7,560
Carlos Del Moral	70	75	71	80	296	7,560
Julien Guerrier	69	74	79	74	296	7,560
Peter Hanson	72	73	76	75	296	7,560
Pablo Larrazabal	70	74	74	78	296	7,560
Craig Lee	73	71	74	78	296	7,560
Thomas Norret	69	76	79	72	296	7,560
Felipe Aguilar	74	69	76	79	298	6,142
Danny Willett	71	73	80	74	298	6,142
Martin Kaymer	73	72	78	77	300	5,740

Aberdeen Asset Management Scottish Open

Castle Stuart Golf Links, Inverness, Scotland
Par 36-36–72; 7,193 yards

July 12-15
purse, €3,136,252

	SCORES				TOTAL	MONEY
Jeev Milkha Singh	66	70	68	67	271	€518,046
Francesco Molinari	62	70	67	72	271	345,360
(Singh defeated Molinari on first playoff hole.)						
Alexander Noren	66	66	70	70	272	174,999
Marc Warren	68	69	64	71	272	174,999
Matthew Baldwin	67	68	71	67	273	111,278
Soren Kjeldsen	65	72	64	72	273	111,278
Thomas Levet	68	69	66	70	273	111,278
Phillip Price	68	69	68	69	274	69,834
Henrik Stenson	69	69	66	70	274	69,834
Peter Whiteford	71	65	66	72	274	69,834
Alejandro Canizares	64	71	68	72	275	50,790
S.S.P. Chowrasia	67	67	69	72	275	50,790
Ignacio Garrido	68	69	67	71	275	50,790
Anders Hansen	68	67	65	75	275	50,790
Shane Lowry	66	69	69	71	275	50,790
Luke Donald	67	68	68	73	276	38,388
Padraig Harrington	69	69	67	71	276	38,388
Fredrik Jacobson	66	72	67	71	276	38,388
Raphael Jacquelin	65	71	69	71	276	38,388
Martin Laird	68	70	64	74	276	38,388
Pablo Larrazabal	67	70	66	73	276	38,388

	SCORES				TOTAL	MONEY
Phil Mickelson	73	64	65	74	276	38,388
Andy Sullivan	69	69	69	69	276	38,388
Robert-Jan Derksen	71	68	66	72	277	31,394
Stephen Gallacher	68	72	65	72	277	31,394
Richard Green	68	69	67	73	277	31,394
Peter Lawrie	66	69	68	74	277	31,394
Louis Oosthuizen	69	70	66	72	277	31,394
Fredrik Andersson Hed	71	68	66	73	278	25,844
Simon Dyson	68	69	67	74	278	25,844
Alastair Forsyth	71	68	68	71	278	25,844
Thongchai Jaidee	68	70	67	73	278	25,844
Martin Kaymer	67	68	69	74	278	25,844
Andrew Marshall	66	72	68	72	278	25,844
Marcel Siem	71	69	69	69	278	25,844
Robert Coles	66	71	71	72	280	19,582
Nicolas Colsaerts	68	69	72	71	280	19,582
David Dixon	68	71	69	72	280	19,582
Niclas Fasth	70	70	67	73	280	19,582
David Horsey	68	72	67	73	280	19,582
Andrew Johnston	69	70	67	74	280	19,582
Jbe' Kruger	72	68	68	72	280	19,582
David Lynn	71	67	71	71	280	19,582
Matteo Manassero	69	64	73	74	280	19,582
Thorbjorn Olesen	70	65	73	72	280	19,582
Chris Wood	68	72	67	73	280	19,582
Felipe Aguilar	69	71	70	71	281	14,609
Rafa Cabrera-Bello	70	68	65	78	281	14,609
Oscar Floren	67	72	71	71	281	14,609
Marcus Fraser	69	71	69	72	281	14,609
Lee Slattery	71	67	73	70	281	14,609
Gregory Bourdy	73	67	70	72	282	11,190
George Coetzee	69	69	72	72	282	11,190
Ernie Els	70	70	68	74	282	11,190
Andrea Pavan	70	67	69	76	282	11,190
Tim Sluiter	73	66	72	71	282	11,190
Anthony Wall	67	68	72	75	282	11,190
Rhys Davies	72	68	68	75	283	9,014
Maarten Lafeber	68	72	72	71	283	9,014
Steve Webster	69	68	75	71	283	9,014
Thomas Aiken	68	67	76	73	284	7,460
Daniel Denison	70	70	71	73	284	7,460
Miguel Angel Jimenez	69	71	76	68	284	7,460
Mikael Lundberg	72	68	72	72	284	7,460
Steven O'Hara	69	71	69	75	284	7,460
Jose María Olazabal	69	70	72	73	284	7,460
Joel Sjoholm	70	68	71	75	284	7,460
Ross Fisher	68	70	69	78	285	5,617
Branden Grace	72	68	73	72	285	5,617
David Howell	70	67	77	71	285	5,617
Jose Manuel Lara	68	72	69	76	285	5,617
Alex Haindl	70	68	69	80	287	4,658
James Morrison	72	67	74	74	287	4,658
Ricardo Gonzalez	69	64	75	80	288	4,653
*Jack McDonald	70	70	68	80	288	
Richard Wallis	72	68	73	76	289	4,650
Tjaart van der Walt	70	70	73	77	290	4,647

The Open Championship

Royal Lytham & St. Annes Golf Club, Lytham St. Annes, Lancashire, England
Par 34-36–70; 7,086 yards

July 19-22
purse, €6,347,075

	SCORES				TOTAL	MONEY
Ernie Els	67	70	68	68	273	€1,136,880
Adam Scott	64	67	68	75	274	656,864
Brandt Snedeker	66	64	73	74	277	375,802
Tiger Woods	67	67	70	73	277	375,802
Luke Donald	70	68	71	69	278	246,324
Graeme McDowell	67	69	67	75	278	246,324
Thomas Aiken	68	68	71	72	279	180,006
Nicolas Colsaerts	65	77	72	65	279	180,006
Mark Calcavecchia	71	68	69	72	280	100,551
Miguel Angel Jimenez	71	69	73	67	280	100,551
Dustin Johnson	73	68	68	71	280	100,551
Zach Johnson	65	74	66	75	280	100,551
Matt Kuchar	69	67	72	72	280	100,551
Alexander Noren	71	71	69	69	280	100,551
Geoff Ogilvy	72	68	73	67	280	100,551
Thorbjorn Olesen	69	66	71	74	280	100,551
Ian Poulter	71	69	73	67	280	100,551
Vijay Singh	70	72	68	70	280	100,551
Steve Alker	69	69	72	71	281	64,107
Bill Haas	71	68	68	74	281	64,107
Hunter Mahan	70	71	70	70	281	64,107
Louis Oosthuizen	72	68	68	73	281	64,107
Matthew Baldwin	69	73	69	71	282	48,554
Simon Dyson	72	67	73	70	282	48,554
Peter Hanson	67	72	72	71	282	48,554
James Morrison	68	70	72	72	282	48,554
Carl Pettersson	71	68	73	70	282	48,554
Steve Stricker	67	71	73	71	282	48,554
Nick Watney	71	70	69	72	282	48,554
Bubba Watson	67	73	68	74	282	48,554
Jason Dufner	70	66	73	74	283	38,107
Rickie Fowler	71	72	70	70	283	38,107
Anirban Lahiri	68	72	70	73	283	38,107
Keegan Bradley	71	72	68	73	284	32,843
Jim Furyk	72	70	71	71	284	32,843
Paul Lawrie	65	71	76	72	284	32,843
John Senden	70	71	75	68	284	32,843
Gary Woodland	73	70	70	71	284	32,843
K.J. Choi	70	73	71	71	285	25,896
Padraig Harrington	70	72	70	73	285	25,896
Troy Matteson	70	72	71	72	285	25,896
Francesco Molinari	69	72	71	73	285	25,896
Kyle Stanley	70	69	70	76	285	25,896
Richard Sterne	69	73	73	70	285	25,896
Greg Chalmers	71	68	71	76	286	18,744
Rafa Echenique	73	69	71	73	286	18,744
Bob Estes	69	72	74	71	286	18,744
Ross Fisher	72	71	74	69	286	18,744
Justin Hicks	68	74	69	75	286	18,744
Simon Khan	70	69	71	76	286	18,744
Pablo Larrazabal	73	70	71	72	286	18,744
Joost Luiten	73	70	69	74	286	18,744
Lee Westwood	73	70	71	72	286	18,744
Thomas Bjorn	70	69	72	76	287	16,232
Harris English	71	71	70	75	287	16,232
Gonzalo Fernandez-Castano	71	71	72	73	287	16,232

	SCORES				TOTAL	MONEY
Yoshinori Fujimoto	71	70	73	73	287	16,232
Fredrik Jacobson	69	73	73	72	287	16,232
Greg Owen	71	71	71	74	287	16,232
Jamie Donaldson	68	72	72	76	288	15,601
Rory McIlroy	67	75	73	73	288	15,601
Ted Potter, Jr.	69	71	74	74	288	15,601
Dale Whitnell	71	69	72	76	288	15,601
Sang-Moon Bae	72	71	71	75	289	15,032
Retief Goosen	70	70	75	74	289	15,032
Charles Howell	72	71	74	72	289	15,032
Garth Mulroy	71	69	72	77	289	15,032
Lee Slattery	69	72	75	73	289	15,032
Aaron Baddeley	71	71	74	74	290	14,527
Adilson Da Silva	69	74	71	76	290	14,527
Jeev Milkha Singh	70	71	76	73	290	14,527
Chad Campbell	73	70	74	74	291	14,022
Brendan Jones	69	74	72	76	291	14,022
Martin Laird	70	69	82	70	291	14,022
Toshinori Muto	67	72	74	78	291	14,022
Juvic Pagunsan	71	72	73	75	291	14,022
Warren Bennett	71	70	75	76	292	13,453
Branden Grace	73	69	71	79	292	13,453
Thongchai Jaidee	69	71	74	78	292	13,453
Tom Watson	71	72	76	73	292	13,453
Rafa Cabrera-Bello	70	71	76	77	294	13,074
John Daly	72	71	77	74	294	13,074
Andres Romero	70	69	77	82	298	12,885

Out of Final 36 Holes

George Coetzee	74	70			144	4,421
Nick Cullen	73	71			144	4,421
Marcus Fraser	71	73			144	4,421
Sergio Garcia	72	72			144	4,421
Anders Hansen	68	76			144	4,421
Raphael Jacquelin	72	72			144	4,421
Jbe' Kruger	68	76			144	4,421
Marc Leishman	69	75			144	4,421
Koumei Oda	72	72			144	4,421
Richie Ramsay	71	73			144	4,421
Justin Rose	74	70			144	4,421
Charl Schwartzel	69	75			144	4,421
Marcel Siem	74	70			144	4,421
Steven Tiley	72	72			144	4,421
Aaron Townsend	70	74			144	4,421
Mark Wilson	72	72			144	4,421
Y.E. Yang	74	70			144	4,421
Stewart Cink	72	73			145	3,600
David Duval	74	71			145	3,600
Gregory Havret	73	72			145	3,600
K.T. Kim	75	70			145	3,600
Tom Lehman	73	72			145	3,600
Morten Orum Madsen	74	71			145	3,600
Scott Pinckney	68	77			145	3,600
Bo Van Pelt	71	74			145	3,600
Jonathan Byrd	74	72			146	3,600
Alejandro Canizares	74	72			146	3,600
*Alan Dunbar	75	71			146	
Ashley Hall	71	75			146	3,600
Todd Hamilton	72	74			146	3,600
Ryo Ishikawa	74	72			146	3,600
Martin Kaymer	77	69			146	3,600
Barry Lane	73	73			146	3,600

	SCORES			TOTAL	MONEY
Sandy Lyle	74	72		146	3,600
Steven O'Hara	74	72		146	3,600
Sam Walker	76	70		146	3,600
Robert Allenby	75	72		147	3,600
Stephen Ames	74	73		147	3,600
Daniel Chopra	73	74		147	3,600
Darren Clarke	76	71		147	3,600
Toru Taniguchi	72	75		147	3,600
Michael Thompson	74	73		147	3,600
Hiroyuki Fujita	76	72		148	3,284
Andrew Georgiou	74	74		148	3,284
Lucas Glover	72	76		148	3,284
John Huh	75	73		148	3,284
Troy Kelly	72	76		148	3,284
Brad Kennedy	75	73		148	3,284
Justin Leonard	75	73		148	3,284
Tadahiro Takayama	77	71		148	3,284
Ben Curtis	75	74		149	3,284
Trevor Immelman	74	75		149	3,284
Alvaro Quiros	74	75		149	3,284
Chez Reavie	74	75		149	3,284
Robert Rock	78	71		149	3,284
Johnson Wagner	73	76		149	3,284
Tim Clark	76	74		150	3,284
Kodai Ichihara	77	73		150	3,284
Davis Love	71	79		150	3,284
Prayad Marksaeng	75	75		150	3,284
Kevin Na	73	77		150	3,284
Paul Casey	72	79		151	3,284
Phil Mickelson	73	78		151	3,284
Elliot Saltman	76	75		151	3,284
Angel Cabrera	71	81		152	2,969
James Driscoll	76	76		152	2,969
Paul Broadhurst	75	78		153	2,969
Richard Finch	74	79		153	2,969
Michael Hoey	79	75		154	2,969
Grant Veenstra	77	79		156	2,969
*Manuel Trappel	74	83		157	
Ian Keenan	76	83		159	2,969
Mardan Mamat	77			DQ	

Lyoness Open

Diamond Country Club, Atzenbrugg, Austria
Par 36-36–72; 7,386 yards

July 25-28
purse, €994,270

	SCORES				TOTAL	MONEY
Bernd Wiesberger	71	66	67	65	269	€166,660
Thomas Levet	65	70	69	68	272	86,855
Shane Lowry	70	68	68	66	272	86,855
Rikard Karlberg	70	67	66	70	273	50,000
Thorbjorn Olesen	64	68	68	74	274	42,400
Chris Doak	73	66	68	68	275	32,500
Benjamin Hebert	72	66	64	71	275	32,500
Richard Bland	69	67	68	72	276	23,700
Scott Jamieson	71	67	70	68	276	23,700
Emiliano Grillo	70	68	69	70	277	19,200
Pablo Larrazabal	64	76	68	69	277	19,200
Robert-Jan Derksen	72	68	69	69	278	16,650
Chris Wood	71	69	70	68	278	16,650

	SCORES				TOTAL	MONEY
Niclas Fasth	69	70	72	68	279	15,300
David Drysdale	71	69	70	70	280	14,100
Alastair Forsyth	68	72	72	68	280	14,100
Oliver Wilson	68	70	68	74	280	14,100
Felipe Aguilar	67	71	75	68	281	11,538
Gregory Bourdy	70	69	68	74	281	11,538
Mathias Gronberg	70	75	67	69	281	11,538
Steven O'Hara	71	70	67	73	281	11,538
Taco Remkes	70	71	70	70	281	11,538
Tim Sluiter	76	68	73	64	281	11,538
Tjaart van der Walt	74	69	71	67	281	11,538
Romain Wattel	72	69	72	68	281	11,538
Damien McGrane	71	69	68	74	282	9,650
Thomas Norret	69	72	70	71	282	9,650
Victor Riu	69	74	72	67	282	9,650
Steve Webster	70	71	73	68	282	9,650
Magnus A. Carlsson	72	71	71	69	283	8,600
Mikael Lundberg	66	74	72	71	283	8,600
Brett Rumford	71	73	68	71	283	8,600
Daniel Denison	69	70	72	73	284	7,314
Rafa Echenique	73	71	67	73	284	7,314
Peter Hedblom	70	70	71	73	284	7,314
Sam Little	71	73	71	69	284	7,314
Christian Nilsson	74	69	73	68	284	7,314
Wade Ormsby	71	69	67	77	284	7,314
Ricardo Santos	78	66	70	70	284	7,314
Gary Boyd	73	72	71	69	285	5,700
Jorge Campillo	76	68	71	70	285	5,700
Eduardo De La Riva	73	72	72	68	285	5,700
Stephen Gallacher	72	72	71	70	285	5,700
Ignacio Garrido	73	71	70	71	285	5,700
Ross McGowan	73	66	75	71	285	5,700
David McKenzie	65	74	70	76	285	5,700
Roland Steiner	74	71	71	69	285	5,700
Alessandro Tadini	71	71	70	73	285	5,700
Agustin Domingo	69	71	74	72	286	4,500
Andrew Marshall	72	71	69	74	286	4,500
*Lukas Nemecz	75	70	72	69	286	
Julien Quesne	73	72	73	68	286	4,500
Wil Besseling	65	72	72	78	287	3,800
Kenneth Ferrie	70	73	70	74	287	3,800
David Higgins	67	71	74	75	287	3,800
Phillip Price	73	71	73	70	287	3,800
Carl Suneson	72	72	69	75	288	3,300
Tommy Fleetwood	73	72	70	74	289	3,050
Andrea Pavan	69	74	75	71	289	3,050
Joakim Haeggman	70	75	73	72	290	2,800
Miles Tunnicliff	72	70	73	75	290	2,800
Paul Waring	70	75	71	74	290	2,800
Oscar Floren	68	69	79	75	291	2,600
Jamie Moul	73	70	74	75	292	2,500
*Manuel Trappel	73	72	72	75	292	
James Byrne	72	71	73	78	294	2,350
Michael Jonzon	71	73	71	79	294	2,350
Peter Gustafsson	74	71	76	74	295	2,200
Christoph Pfau	71	73	75	78	297	2,100

Johnnie Walker Championship

Gleneagles Hotel, Auchterarder, Perthshire, Scotland
Par 36-36–72; 7,060 yards

August 23-26
purse, €1,766,562

	SCORES				TOTAL	MONEY
Paul Lawrie	68	69	67	68	272	€296,119
Brett Rumford	67	70	71	68	276	197,408
Fredrik Andersson	73	69	70	65	277	91,798
Maarten Lafeber	68	73	67	69	277	91,798
Romain Wattel	74	68	63	72	277	91,798
Stephen Gallacher	75	67	65	71	278	49,926
Francesco Molinari	68	72	71	67	278	49,926
Colin Montgomerie	72	68	69	69	278	49,926
Richie Ramsay	69	71	70	68	278	49,926
Thomas Bjorn	70	71	68	70	279	31,848
Rafa Cabrera-Bello	72	68	69	70	279	31,848
Paul Waring	71	67	72	69	279	31,848
Peter Whiteford	72	69	71	67	279	31,848
Craig Lee	70	73	70	67	280	27,184
Gregory Bourdy	72	66	71	72	281	24,519
Victor Dubuisson	69	72	71	69	281	24,519
Anders Hansen	72	72	71	66	281	24,519
Thorbjorn Olesen	68	72	69	72	281	24,519
Gary Boyd	74	70	64	74	282	20,153
Jorge Campillo	73	68	70	71	282	20,153
Nicolas Colsaerts	69	70	71	72	282	20,153
Edouard Dubois	71	70	71	70	282	20,153
Richard Finch	69	67	78	68	282	20,153
James Morrison	71	71	72	68	282	20,153
Marcel Siem	75	69	71	67	282	20,153
Chris Doak	76	66	69	72	283	16,613
Mark Foster	68	68	75	72	283	16,613
Ricardo Gonzalez	71	69	76	67	283	16,613
David Lynn	71	70	73	69	283	16,613
Alexander Noren	72	69	70	72	283	16,613
Chris Wood	70	70	75	68	283	16,613
Knut Borsheim	67	73	69	75	284	13,788
Rhys Davies	72	68	75	69	284	13,788
Ross Fisher	76	68	71	69	284	13,788
David Howell	70	69	71	74	284	13,788
Pablo Larrazabal	75	67	73	69	284	13,788
Scott Pinckney	72	70	69	74	285	12,260
Tjaart van der Walt	73	70	71	71	285	12,260
Fabrizio Zanotti	73	71	70	71	285	12,260
Matthew Nixon	71	69	72	74	286	11,193
Lloyd Saltman	77	67	71	71	286	11,193
Matthew Southgate	73	67	72	74	286	11,193
Robert Coles	72	71	71	73	287	9,594
Bradley Dredge	71	73	70	73	287	9,594
Tommy Fleetwood	71	70	73	73	287	9,594
Emiliano Grillo	71	71	77	68	287	9,594
Scott Jamieson	76	68	73	70	287	9,594
Simon Thornton	75	69	71	72	287	9,594
David Dixon	75	69	72	72	288	8,351
Andrew Marshall	71	73	74	71	289	7,995
Stephen Dodd	73	68	74	75	290	7,285
Peter Lawrie	72	72	76	70	290	7,285
Damien McGrane	73	71	73	73	290	7,285
Johan Edfors	71	72	73	75	291	5,774
Chris Gane	70	73	74	74	291	5,774
Daniel Gaunt	70	73	72	76	291	5,774
Gary Orr	74	67	73	77	291	5,774

	SCORES				TOTAL	MONEY
Victor Riu	74	70	73	74	291	5,774
Joel Sjoholm	72	71	74	74	291	5,774
Oliver Fisher	73	70	75	74	292	4,797
Shiv Kapur	72	72	74	74	292	4,797
Richard McEvoy	72	72	76	72	292	4,797
Benjamin Hebert	70	73	72	78	293	4,353
Jose Manuel Lara	72	71	79	71	293	4,353
Lloyd Kennedy	70	72	77	75	294	4,087
Alex Haindl	72	72	80	72	296	3,909
Markus Brier	73	71	81	78	303	3,731

Omega European Masters

Crans-sur-Sierre Golf Club, Crans Montana, Switzerland
Par 36-35–71; 6,891 yards

August 30-September 2
purse, €2,125,116

	SCORES				TOTAL	MONEY
Richie Ramsay	69	68	64	66	267	€350,000
Fredrik Andersson Hed	65	73	67	66	271	139,708
Marcus Fraser	68	68	69	66	271	139,708
Romain Wattel	67	70	68	66	271	139,708
Danny Willett	67	67	68	69	271	139,708
Felipe Aguilar	68	69	68	67	272	63,000
Paul Lawrie	69	66	67	70	272	63,000
Bernd Wiesberger	68	70	68	66	272	63,000
Jamie Donaldson	69	69	66	69	273	44,520
Anders Hansen	68	70	67	68	273	44,520
Miguel Angel Jimenez	77	65	66	66	274	36,190
David Lynn	73	68	65	68	274	36,190
Julien Quesne	68	65	70	71	274	36,190
Michael Campbell	70	71	67	67	275	29,610
Mathias Gronberg	70	69	65	71	275	29,610
Marcel Siem	68	72	68	67	275	29,610
Lee Slattery	68	74	69	64	275	29,610
Jaco Van Zyl	69	68	67	71	275	29,610
Darren Fichardt	70	72	67	67	276	24,832
Oliver Fisher	65	73	72	66	276	24,832
Tommy Fleetwood	70	66	73	67	276	24,832
Brett Rumford	71	68	67	70	276	24,832
Scott Barr	66	72	71	68	277	22,155
Robert Coles	66	70	73	68	277	22,155
Michael Jonzon	71	67	69	70	277	22,155
Sam Little	67	71	68	71	277	22,155
Simon Dyson	69	70	67	72	278	18,690
Johan Edfors	67	74	66	71	278	18,690
Estanislao Goya	74	66	71	67	278	18,690
David Howell	66	70	69	73	278	18,690
Thomas Levet	68	70	68	72	278	18,690
Joost Luiten	71	71	63	73	278	18,690
Alexander Noren	71	69	69	69	278	18,690
Gregory Bourdy	63	75	72	69	279	14,910
David Drysdale	68	74	67	70	279	14,910
Lorenzo Gagli	70	70	71	68	279	14,910
Stephen Gallacher	67	71	73	68	279	14,910
Gregory Havret	69	72	70	68	279	14,910
Matteo Manassero	71	70	70	68	279	14,910
Steve Webster	69	71	69	70	279	14,910
Alex Cejka	69	71	69	71	280	11,760
S.S.P. Chowrasia	71	71	67	71	280	11,760
Peter Hedblom	72	70	67	71	280	11,760

	SCORES				TOTAL	MONEY
Jason Knutzon	70	72	66	72	280	11,760
Jyoti Randhawa	68	73	71	68	280	11,760
Richard Sterne	72	69	69	70	280	11,760
Graeme Storm	68	70	67	75	280	11,760
Fabrizio Zanotti	69	72	68	71	280	11,760
Rhys Davies	66	75	71	69	281	8,820
Victor Dubuisson	68	71	69	73	281	8,820
Rikard Karlberg	72	67	66	76	281	8,820
Maarten Lafeber	69	73	71	68	281	8,820
Shane Lowry	69	71	68	73	281	8,820
Mardan Mamat	71	71	68	71	281	8,820
Scott Hend	71	70	74	67	282	6,930
Michael Hoey	70	68	72	72	282	6,930
*Adrien Saddier	70	72	71	69	282	
Marc Warren	76	66	68	72	282	6,930
Peter Hanson	69	69	76	69	283	6,195
David Lipsky	70	70	68	75	283	6,195
Richard Finch	70	68	73	73	284	5,670
Benjamin Hebert	72	69	71	72	284	5,670
Berry Henson	68	73	69	74	284	5,670
Ross Fisher	70	70	72	73	285	4,725
Mark Foster	72	70	72	71	285	4,725
Richard McEvoy	69	71	69	76	285	4,725
Colin Montgomerie	72	68	71	74	285	4,725
Hennie Otto	70	72	75	68	285	4,725
Tjaart van der Walt	70	70	69	76	285	4,725
Phillip Price	68	71	74	73	286	3,990
Marcus Both	72	70	72	73	287	3,282
Darren Clarke	72	70	74	71	287	3,282
Ignacio Garrido	72	70	72	73	287	3,282
Raphael Jacquelin	72	70	71	74	287	3,282
Angelo Que	71	71	72	73	287	3,282
Markus Brier	67	72	71	80	290	3,134
Gonzalo Fernandez-Castano	71	71	73	75	290	3,134
Branden Grace	70	72	68	80	290	3,134
Jose Manuel Lara	68	74	70	78	290	3,134
*Benjamin Rusch	75	67	72	76	290	

KLM Open

Hilversumsche Golf Club, Hilversum, Netherlands

September 6-9

Par 35-35–70; 6,906 yards

purse, €1,802,700

	SCORES				TOTAL	MONEY
Peter Hanson	66	66	67	67	266	€300,000
Pablo Larrazabal	69	65	64	70	268	156,340
Richie Ramsay	71	66	64	67	268	156,340
Scott Jamieson	68	64	66	71	269	90,000
Gonzalo Fernandez-Castano	67	65	66	73	271	64,440
Henrik Stenson	68	70	64	69	271	64,440
Graeme Storm	63	66	69	73	271	64,440
Gregory Bourdy	69	68	69	66	272	38,610
Nicolas Colsaerts	70	65	67	70	272	38,610
Anders Hansen	70	67	68	67	272	38,610
Richard Sterne	70	68	66	68	272	38,610
Bradley Dredge	69	66	70	68	273	27,864
Richard Finch	70	69	70	64	273	27,864
Marcus Fraser	69	68	66	70	273	27,864
Marc Warren	69	71	66	67	273	27,864
Bernd Wiesberger	68	71	65	69	273	27,864

	SCORES				TOTAL	MONEY
Richard Bland	67	72	67	68	274	22,860
Tommy Fleetwood	67	73	66	68	274	22,860
Lorenzo Gagli	69	67	67	71	274	22,860
Richard S. Johnson	70	67	69	68	274	22,860
Matthew Baldwin	71	68	69	67	275	19,800
Jamie Donaldson	70	67	70	68	275	19,800
Martin Kaymer	65	71	68	71	275	19,800
Richard Kind	67	69	71	68	275	19,800
Fabrizio Zanotti	65	74	71	65	275	19,800
Felipe Aguilar	66	74	66	70	276	16,830
Thomas Aiken	71	69	70	66	276	16,830
Darren Fichardt	70	67	68	71	276	16,830
Raphael Jacquelin	65	70	71	70	276	16,830
Damien McGrane	70	67	70	69	276	16,830
Danny Willett	66	69	66	75	276	16,830
Rich Beem	73	67	68	69	277	13,968
Darren Clarke	72	68	67	70	277	13,968
Oliver Fisher	67	71	69	70	277	13,968
Peter Lawrie	69	69	71	68	277	13,968
David Lynn	69	70	68	70	277	13,968
Alejandro Canizares	66	74	70	68	278	11,880
Shiv Kapur	67	67	70	74	278	11,880
Maarten Lafeber	70	69	72	67	278	11,880
Shaun Micheel	71	68	68	71	278	11,880
Garth Mulroy	71	65	69	73	278	11,880
Simon Thornton	71	64	68	75	278	11,880
Alex Cejka	71	68	69	71	279	10,260
David Drysdale	70	69	67	73	279	10,260
Chris Wood	69	69	70	71	279	10,260
Paul Casey	67	72	73	68	280	8,460
Federico Colombo	70	70	70	70	280	8,460
Simon Dyson	70	66	74	70	280	8,460
Richard Green	69	69	68	74	280	8,460
*Daan Huizing	72	68	68	72	280	
Craig Lee	66	70	71	73	280	8,460
Jaco Van Zyl	68	68	70	74	280	8,460
Sam Walker	69	68	73	70	280	8,460
Robert-Jan Derksen	70	69	68	74	281	6,480
Andrew Johnston	67	69	72	73	281	6,480
Phillip Price	69	71	71	70	281	6,480
Steve Webster	66	71	71	73	281	6,480
Knut Borsheim	71	69	70	72	282	5,220
Robert Coles	71	66	74	71	282	5,220
Victor Dubuisson	72	67	70	73	282	5,220
Jamie Elson	72	66	73	71	282	5,220
Matteo Manassero	71	69	68	74	282	5,220
Sam Little	71	69	70	73	283	4,680
Johan Edfors	69	71	74	70	284	4,320
Soren Kjeldsen	71	68	70	75	284	4,320
Brett Rumford	73	67	73	71	284	4,320
Gareth Maybin	69	71	74	72	286	3,870
Lee Slattery	69	70	76	71	286	3,870
Gary Orr	70	69	76	73	288	3,600
Steven O'Hara	69	71	76	73	289	3,420
Niclas Fasth	69	70	72	79	290	3,280
Paul Waring	67	69	81	77	294	2,700

BMW Italian Open

Royal Park I Roveri, Turin, Italy
Par 36-36–72; 7,282 yards

September 13-16
purse, €1,508,982

	SCORES				TOTAL	MONEY
Gonzalo Fernandez-Castano	68	65	67	64	264	€250,000
Garth Mulroy	66	67	66	67	266	166,660
Gregory Bourdy	69	64	70	65	268	84,450
Matteo Manassero	69	69	65	65	268	84,450
Gary Boyd	69	70	68	63	270	49,650
Nicolas Colsaerts	71	67	65	67	270	49,650
Martin Kaymer	70	66	67	67	270	49,650
Pablo Larrazabal	69	66	66	69	270	49,650
Rafa Cabrera-Bello	67	69	65	70	271	33,600
Anders Hansen	70	68	67	67	272	27,800
Jaco Van Zyl	71	69	68	64	272	27,800
Marc Warren	68	65	72	67	272	27,800
Victor Dubuisson	66	69	69	69	273	22,575
Keith Horne	66	71	68	68	273	22,575
Sam Little	67	68	69	69	273	22,575
Shane Lowry	70	67	67	69	273	22,575
Richard Bland	66	66	71	71	274	18,720
Bradley Dredge	67	69	70	68	274	18,720
David Howell	66	70	72	66	274	18,720
Mikael Lundberg	70	65	71	68	274	18,720
Sam Walker	70	69	68	67	274	18,720
Tommy Fleetwood	69	69	69	68	275	16,050
Emiliano Grillo	68	70	67	70	275	16,050
Michael Hoey	71	67	72	65	275	16,050
Hennie Otto	70	67	67	71	275	16,050
Joel Sjoholm	64	71	69	71	275	16,050
Kristoffer Broberg	72	68	69	67	276	13,125
Mark Foster	72	66	70	68	276	13,125
Lorenzo Gagli	69	68	68	71	276	13,125
Mikko Ilonen	69	70	70	67	276	13,125
Scott Jamieson	68	69	72	67	276	13,125
Robert Karlsson	70	70	68	68	276	13,125
Damien McGrane	73	65	72	66	276	13,125
Lee Slattery	65	71	69	71	276	13,125
Fredrik Andersson Hed	70	68	70	69	277	9,750
Alex Cejka	67	70	72	68	277	9,750
Robert Coles	70	66	71	70	277	9,750
Johan Edfors	67	72	69	69	277	9,750
Gregory Havret	70	69	69	69	277	9,750
Peter Hedblom	73	66	70	68	277	9,750
Andrew Johnston	71	67	69	70	277	9,750
Shiv Kapur	67	69	70	71	277	9,750
Gareth Maybin	66	71	71	69	277	9,750
Graeme Storm	69	68	69	71	277	9,750
Oliver Wilson	75	65	67	70	277	9,750
Dylan Frittelli	70	67	70	71	278	7,050
Raphael Jacquelin	67	70	75	66	278	7,050
Francesco Molinari	68	69	76	65	278	7,050
Phillip Price	68	69	66	75	278	7,050
Robert Rock	70	70	75	63	278	7,050
Richard Sterne	67	68	71	72	278	7,050
Fabrizio Zanotti	72	68	68	70	278	7,050
Thomas Aiken	70	67	69	73	279	5,400
Peter Lawrie	70	70	70	69	279	5,400
Richard McEvoy	66	68	73	72	279	5,400
Thorbjorn Olesen	71	67	73	68	279	5,400
Felipe Aguilar	73	67	72	68	280	4,275

	SCORES				TOTAL	MONEY
Edouard Dubois	67	72	69	72	280	4,275
Estanislao Goya	71	68	71	70	280	4,275
Soren Kjeldsen	70	69	71	70	280	4,275
Joakim Lagergren	70	65	72	73	280	4,275
Steve Webster	72	67	69	72	280	4,275
Thomas Norret	70	67	69	75	281	3,600
Jose María Olazabal	70	70	76	65	281	3,600
Bernd Wiesberger	70	69	69	73	281	3,600
Stephen Dodd	68	71	73	70	282	3,008
Darren Fichardt	69	67	75	71	282	3,008
Alastair Forsyth	68	71	72	71	282	3,008
Todd Hamilton	73	67	72	70	282	3,008
Paul Waring	71	69	68	74	282	3,008
Jorge Campillo	70	68	71	74	283	2,250
Ignacio Garrido	70	70	76	68	284	2,246
Shaun Micheel	71	68	71	74	284	2,246
Anthony Wall	71	69	74	72	286	2,241

The Ryder Cup

See American Tours chapter.

Alfred Dunhill Links Championship

St. Andrews Old Course: Par 36-36–72; 7,279 yards
Carnoustie Championship Course: Par 36-36–72; 7,412 yards
Kingsbarns Golf Links: Par 36-36–72; 7,150 yards
St. Andrews & Fife, Scotland

October 4-7
purse, €3,696,952

	SCORES				TOTAL	MONEY
Branden Grace	60	67	69	70	266	€617,284
Thorbjorn Olesen	63	69	68	68	268	411,520
Alexander Noren	64	72	65	69	270	231,852
Joel Sjoholm	65	67	70	70	272	185,185
Fredrik Andersson Hed	64	71	66	72	273	102,222
George Coetzee	71	72	68	62	273	102,222
Victor Dubuisson	62	73	70	68	273	102,222
Stephen Gallacher	67	70	65	71	273	102,222
Raphael Jacquelin	69	67	68	69	273	102,222
Lee Slattery	67	70	68	68	273	102,222
Danny Willett	66	69	68	70	273	102,222
Steve Webster	70	72	68	64	274	63,704
Magnus A. Carlsson	66	68	73	68	275	58,148
Ricardo Gonzalez	71	72	63	69	275	58,148
David Drysdale	66	72	70	68	276	48,254
Oliver Fisher	66	74	67	69	276	48,254
Mark Foster	72	69	66	69	276	48,254
Anton Haig	65	68	73	70	276	48,254
Thongchai Jaidee	65	71	67	73	276	48,254
Graeme Storm	68	66	72	70	276	48,254
Chris Wood	69	70	68	69	276	48,254
Thomas Aiken	72	68	67	70	277	38,519
Ross Fisher	70	69	69	69	277	38,519
Ashley Hall	64	73	69	71	277	38,519
Mikko Ilonen	72	71	66	68	277	38,519
Edoardo Molinari	71	68	70	68	277	38,519
James Morrison	70	69	71	67	277	38,519
Brett Rumford	71	70	69	67	277	38,519
Gonzalo Fernandez-Castano	70	69	70	69	278	31,852

	SCORES				TOTAL	MONEY
Darren Fichardt	71	66	72	69	278	31,852
Emiliano Grillo	70	69	67	72	278	31,852
Padraig Harrington	71	73	66	68	278	31,852
Paul Waring	69	66	70	73	278	31,852
Alejandro Canizares	66	70	71	72	279	24,074
Bradley Dredge	69	69	72	69	279	24,074
Ernie Els	73	70	65	71	279	24,074
Lorenzo Gagli	69	67	72	71	279	24,074
Mathias Gronberg	74	66	69	70	279	24,074
Peter Hanson	72	70	69	68	279	24,074
David Howell	71	72	67	69	279	24,074
Scott Jamieson	68	74	68	69	279	24,074
Martin Kaymer	70	71	69	69	279	24,074
Maarten Lafeber	71	71	65	72	279	24,074
Shane Lowry	69	69	71	70	279	24,074
Marc Warren	70	70	69	70	279	24,074
Oliver Wilson	67	71	69	72	279	24,074
Matthew Baldwin	69	69	72	70	280	16,296
Michael Campbell	67	71	73	69	280	16,296
Anders Hansen	70	69	70	71	280	16,296
Dustin Johnson	72	71	67	70	280	16,296
Richard S. Johnson	71	69	70	70	280	16,296
James Kingston	68	69	70	73	280	16,296
Peter Lawrie	70	72	68	70	280	16,296
Joost Luiten	68	72	71	69	280	16,296
Graham DeLaet	71	69	69	72	281	11,481
Richard Finch	69	72	69	71	281	11,481
Tommy Fleetwood	66	73	72	70	281	11,481
Colin Montgomerie	71	70	69	71	281	11,481
Phillip Price	71	67	69	74	281	11,481
Jaco Van Zyl	72	69	70	70	281	11,481
Robert Rock	71	72	66	73	282	9,815
Tjaart van der Walt	72	70	69	71	282	9,815
Simon Khan	68	69	70	76	283	8,889
Soren Kjeldsen	69	73	69	72	283	8,889
Pablo Martin	67	70	74	72	283	8,889
Pat Perez	72	70	69	73	284	7,963
Charl Schwartzel	75	70	66	73	284	7,963
Rikard Karlberg	67	73	70	75	285	7,407
Fabrizio Zanotti	68	66	76	77	287	7,037

Turkish Airways World Golf Final

Antalya Golf Club, PGA Sultan Course, Belek, Antalya, Turkey
Par 35-36–71; 7,010 yards

October 9-12
purse, $5,200,000

FIRST ROUND

Matt Kuchar defeated Rory McIlroy, 70-76.
Charl Schwartzel defeated Tiger Woods, 69-70.
Justin Rose defeated Hunter Mahan, 71-75.
Lee Westwood defeated Webb Simpson, 72-73.

SECOND ROUND

Rose defeated Westwood, 66-69.
Simpson defeated Mahan, 65-67.
Schwartzel defeated McIlroy, 70-71.
Woods defeated Kuchar, 67-72.

THIRD ROUND

Rose defeated Simpson, 62-67.
Westwood defeated Mahan, 64-69.
Schwartzel defeated Kuchar, 63-65.
Woods defeated McIlroy, 64-70.

(Kuchar and Simpson received $450,000 each; McIlroy and Mahan received $300,000 each.)

SEMI-FINALS

Westwood defeated Schwartzel, 61-67.
Rose defeated Woods, 69-70.

(Schwartzel and Woods received $600,000 each.)

FINAL

Rose defeated Westwood, 66-67.

(Rose received $1,500,000; Westwood received $1,000,000.)

Portugal Masters

Oceanico Victoria Golf Course, Algarve, Portugal
Par 35-36–71; 7,157 yards

October 11-14
purse, €2,241,625

	SCORES			TOTAL	MONEY
Shane Lowry	67	70	67	66	270	€375,000
Ross Fisher	65	67	69	70	271	250,000
Michael Campbell	68	69	67	68	272	140,850
Bernd Wiesberger	70	65	65	73	273	112,500
Richard Finch	70	68	66	70	274	95,400
George Coetzee	69	73	67	67	276	56,550
Jamie Donaldson	67	71	72	66	276	56,550
Stephen Gallacher	65	70	72	69	276	56,550
Raphael Jacquelin	72	70	71	63	276	56,550
Henrik Stenson	70	70	68	68	276	56,550
Danny Willett	70	69	74	63	276	56,550
Gonzalo Fernandez-Castano	68	71	67	71	277	35,606
Lorenzo Gagli	72	69	67	69	277	35,606
Scott Jamieson	71	70	68	68	277	35,606
Matteo Manassero	71	71	70	65	277	35,606
Robert-Jan Derksen	70	72	70	66	278	26,591
Andrew Dodt	72	70	64	72	278	26,591
Mark Foster	71	67	67	73	278	26,591
Padraig Harrington	69	67	71	71	278	26,591
Keith Horne	69	72	67	70	278	26,591
Simon Khan	72	70	68	68	278	26,591
Francesco Molinari	71	71	66	70	278	26,591
Thorbjorn Olesen	69	70	73	66	278	26,591
Ricardo Santos	72	69	72	65	278	26,591
Lee Slattery	69	70	74	65	278	26,591
Anthony Wall	68	71	68	71	278	26,591
Thomas Aiken	68	71	69	71	279	19,375
Fredrik Andersson Hed	67	69	70	73	279	19,375
Johan Edfors	73	65	75	66	279	19,375
*Pedro Figueiredo	70	70	70	69	279	
Oscar Floren	73	68	67	71	279	19,375
Anders Hansen	71	70	69	69	279	19,375
Mikko Ilonen	73	69	68	69	279	19,375
Miguel Angel Jimenez	69	68	68	74	279	19,375

	SCORES				TOTAL	MONEY
George Murray	66	76	65	72	279	19,375
Peter Whiteford	70	71	67	71	279	19,375
Felipe Aguilar	72	70	69	69	280	13,950
Matthew Baldwin	73	69	69	69	280	13,950
Thomas Bjorn	70	70	73	67	280	13,950
Richard Bland	70	71	71	68	280	13,950
Richard Green	70	68	69	73	280	13,950
Peter Hedblom	72	70	68	70	280	13,950
David Howell	72	68	74	66	280	13,950
Damien McGrane	70	69	72	69	280	13,950
Christian Nilsson	67	70	69	74	280	13,950
Hennie Otto	70	71	69	70	280	13,950
Andy Sullivan	72	69	68	71	280	13,950
Steve Webster	71	68	74	67	280	13,950
Soren Kjeldsen	69	71	72	69	281	10,575
Peter Lawrie	73	67	72	69	281	10,575
Tom Lewis	69	73	70	69	281	10,575
Markus Brier	69	71	67	75	282	9,225
Bradley Dredge	72	69	71	70	282	9,225
Michael Hoey	70	72	70	70	282	9,225
Rich Beem	70	72	71	70	283	7,470
Gregory Bourdy	69	71	74	69	283	7,470
Rafa Cabrera-Bello	68	71	73	71	283	7,470
Jean-Baptiste Gonnet	72	68	73	70	283	7,470
Thomas Levet	69	72	69	73	283	7,470
Carlos Del Moral	69	72	74	69	284	6,412
Simon Dyson	72	68	70	74	284	6,412
*Ricardo Melo Gouveia	70	72	67	75	284	
Ricardo Gonzalez	69	72	68	76	285	5,738
Jbe' Kruger	67	71	77	70	285	5,738
Pablo Larrazabal	71	71	71	72	285	5,738
Matthew Zions	70	72	70	73	285	5,738
Shaun Micheel	74	68	69	75	286	5,175
Alejandro Canizares	70	72	72	74	288	4,838
Marcel Siem	72	68	68	80	288	4,838
Jamie Elson	71	69	75	74	289	4,500

ISPS Handa Perth International

See Australasian Tour chapter.

BMW Masters

Lake Malaren Golf Club, Shanghai, China
Par 36-36–72; 7,607 yards

October 25-28
purse, €5,331,668

	SCORES				TOTAL	MONEY
Peter Hanson	66	64	70	67	267	€888,561
Rory McIlroy	67	65	69	67	268	593,338
Luke Donald	70	67	68	66	271	333,762
Ian Poulter	70	69	68	65	272	268,792
Shane Lowry	72	64	69	68	273	226,367
Paul Casey	70	68	68	68	274	141,899
George Coetzee	69	68	66	71	274	141,899
Alexander Noren	68	68	69	69	274	141,899
Louis Oosthuizen	68	69	69	68	274	141,899
Justin Rose	68	68	69	69	274	141,899
Michael Hoey	67	70	68	70	275	92,416
Martin Kaymer	68	69	69	69	275	92,416

	SCORES			TOTAL	MONEY
Graeme McDowell	69	71	66	69	275	92,416
Nicolas Colsaerts	69	68	69	70	276	78,833
Lee Westwood	70	69	71	66	276	78,833
Jamie Donaldson	62	74	72	69	277	70,930
Oliver Fisher	74	67	70	66	277	70,930
Thongchai Jaidee	70	72	65	70	277	70,930
Charl Schwartzel	69	68	68	72	277	70,930
Ross Fisher	69	69	68	72	278	62,076
Robert Karlsson	71	64	75	68	278	62,076
Soren Kjeldsen	72	66	70	70	278	62,076
Liang Wen-chong	69	69	72	68	278	62,076
David Lynn	69	68	72	69	278	62,076
Wu Ashun	71	70	69	69	279	56,363
Richard Green	70	71	71	68	280	51,831
Joost Luiten	73	73	67	67	280	51,831
Edoardo Molinari	68	71	69	72	280	51,831
Henrik Stenson	72	69	70	69	280	51,831
Michael Campbell	71	71	70	69	281	45,776
Miguel Angel Jimenez	70	71	70	70	281	45,776
Danny Willett	72	70	69	70	281	45,776
John Daly	70	74	69	69	282	41,892
David Horsey	68	71	70	73	282	41,892
Thomas Aiken	71	68	72	72	283	37,169
Rafa Cabrera-Bello	70	75	69	69	283	37,169
Paul Lawrie	69	69	72	73	283	37,169
Francesco Molinari	66	74	73	70	283	37,169
Jose Maria Olazabal	67	72	73	71	283	37,169
Park Sang-hyun	72	72	71	69	284	32,295
Robert Rock	74	72	70	68	284	32,295
Bernd Wiesberger	69	74	72	69	284	32,295
Branden Grace	70	72	74	69	285	28,791
Anders Hansen	72	70	67	76	285	28,791
Richard S. Johnson	70	70	71	74	285	28,791
Gonzalo Fernandez-Castano	70	71	72	73	286	24,526
Tom Lewis	71	72	73	70	286	24,526
Matteo Manassero	70	73	72	71	286	24,526
Jeev Milkha Singh	72	69	74	71	286	24,526
Y.E. Yang	74	70	70	72	286	24,526
Sang-Moon Bae	70	73	69	75	287	19,727
Simon Dyson	71	70	71	75	287	19,727
Hu Mu	72	74	72	69	287	19,727
Marcel Siem	75	70	68	74	287	19,727
Simon Khan	71	71	73	73	288	16,642
Alvaro Quiros	70	69	75	74	288	16,642
S.S.P. Chowrasia	73	72	69	75	289	15,157
Pablo Larrazabal	77	69	72	72	290	13,672
Thorbjorn Olesen	71	76	75	68	290	13,672
Zhang Xin-jun	70	73	77	71	291	12,187
Rich Beem	74	70	75	73	292	10,892
Todd Hamilton	73	74	75	70	292	10,892
Darren Clarke	73	76	71	73	293	9,470
Huang Wen-yi	72	70	73	78	293	9,470
Richie Ramsay	75	74	71	73	293	9,470
Jin Daxing	73	75	74	72	294	8,378
Shaun Micheel	76	72	75	71	294	8,378
Li Hao-tong	71	73	78	73	295	7,769
Zhang Lian-wei	76	68	74	77	295	7,769
Paul McGinley	74	75	74	75	298	7,007
Su Dong	70	71	79	78	298	7,007
Tsai Chi-huang	75	76	72	75	298	7,007
Thomas Levet	75	77	79	68	299	6,398
Mike Weir	73	75	75	77	300	6,093
Huang Yongle	78	77	76	74	305	5,865

	SCORES				TOTAL	MONEY
Yuan Hao	76	76	78	75	305	5,865
Andres Romero	73	80	82	72	307	5,636
Wu Wei-huang	75	73	80	80	308	5,560

Barclays Singapore Open

See Asia/Japan Tours chapter.

UBS Hong Kong Open

See Asia/Japan Tours chapter.

South African Open Championship

See African Tours chapter.

DP World Tour Championship

Jumeirah Golf Estates, Earth Course, November 22-25
Dubai, United Arab Emirates purse, €6,174,996
Par 36-36–72; 7,675 yards

	SCORES				TOTAL	MONEY
Rory McIlroy	66	67	66	66	265	€1,041,429
Justin Rose	68	68	69	62	267	694,312
Luke Donald	65	68	66	71	270	359,302
Charl Schwartzel	68	67	67	68	270	359,302
Louis Oosthuizen	67	67	68	69	271	249,949
Branden Grace	69	65	70	68	272	203,240
Thongchai Jaidee	68	69	68	68	273	174,964
Henrik Stenson	68	68	69	68	273	174,964
Fredrik Andersson Hed	67	69	72	66	274	134,973
Jamie Donaldson	68	68	69	69	274	134,973
Gonzalo Fernandez-Castano	66	72	68	68	274	134,973
Sergio Garcia	73	64	73	64	274	134,973
Padraig Harrington	67	71	68	68	274	134,973
Scott Jamieson	68	69	72	66	275	109,353
Peter Lawrie	68	72	67	68	275	109,353
Stephen Gallacher	68	70	72	66	276	87,482
Peter Hanson	69	67	70	70	276	87,482
Raphael Jacquelin	69	67	71	69	276	87,482
Miguel Angel Jimenez	71	71	69	65	276	87,482
Joost Luiten	69	68	67	72	276	87,482
Anders Hansen	69	70	69	69	277	68,736
Thorbjorn Olesen	68	72	68	69	277	68,736
Robert Rock	72	70	69	66	277	68,736
Jeev Milkha Singh	71	74	64	68	277	68,736
Romain Wattel	70	68	67	72	277	68,736
George Coetzee	71	67	67	73	278	56,551
Martin Kaymer	67	70	72	69	278	56,551
Soren Kjeldsen	72	69	68	69	278	56,551
Ian Poulter	72	70	67	69	278	56,551
Richie Ramsay	67	68	73	70	278	56,551
Marc Warren	66	67	72	73	278	56,551
Danny Willett	71	65	70	72	278	56,551
Chris Wood	71	69	69	69	278	56,551
Nicolas Colsaerts	68	68	74	69	279	47,490
Francesco Molinari	72	71	71	65	279	47,490
Alejandro Canizares	74	68	71	67	280	44,366

	SCORES				TOTAL	MONEY
Victor Dubuisson	71	69	71	69	280	44,366
Pablo Larrazabal	70	72	72	66	280	44,366
Alexander Noren	70	73	71	67	281	41,866
Rafa Cabrera-Bello	70	70	70	72	282	39,992
Marcus Fraser	69	67	75	71	282	39,992
Thomas Aiken	70	66	71	76	283	34,993
Simon Dyson	69	69	73	72	283	34,993
Jbe' Kruger	72	70	70	71	283	34,993
Matteo Manassero	73	68	73	69	283	34,993
Marcel Siem	73	65	75	70	283	34,993
Bernd Wiesberger	72	70	68	73	283	34,993
David Drysdale	71	74	70	69	284	29,369
Paul Lawrie	71	72	70	71	284	29,369
Lee Westwood	67	74	71	72	284	29,369
Richard Sterne	74	74	67	71	286	26,870
Michael Hoey	70	71	71	75	287	24,995
Graeme McDowell	72	73	73	69	287	24,995
David Lynn	73	77	70	69	289	22,495
Lee Slattery	74	72	75	68	289	22,495
Richard Finch	76	74	74	71	295	20,621

Nelson Mandela Championship

See African Tours chapter.

Alfred Dunhill Championship

See African Tours chapter.

Challenge Tour

Gujarat Kensville Challenge

Kensville Golf & Country Club, Ahmedabad, India
Par 36-36–72; 7,224 yards

January 26-29
purse, €200,000

	SCORES				TOTAL	MONEY
Maximilian Kieffer	70	71	70	70	281	€32,000
Rahil Gangjee	68	69	73	71	281	22,000
(Kieffer defeated Gangjee on first playoff hole.)						
Paul Dwyer	71	72	72	68	283	12,000
Andreas Harto	73	70	69	71	283	12,000
Callum Macaulay	74	70	69	70	283	12,000
Chris Doak	74	70	72	69	285	7,200
Raymond Russell	73	69	74	69	285	7,200
Chris Lloyd	72	70	74	70	286	5,600
Seve Benson	70	68	76	73	287	4,600
Shiv Kapur	69	68	78	72	287	4,600

	SCORES				TOTAL	MONEY
Phillip Archer	73	71	68	76	288	4,000
Jens Dantorp	70	68	74	77	289	3,600
Dodge Kemmer	69	72	70	78	289	3,600
Peter Uihlein	76	72	71	70	289	3,600
Christophe Brazillier	72	70	74	74	290	2,900
Jordan Gibb	72	72	72	74	290	2,900
Luke Goddard	71	71	70	78	290	2,900
Oskar Henningsson	73	72	68	77	290	2,900
Bjorn Akesson	70	73	72	76	291	2,233
Gary Lockerbie	69	69	80	73	291	2,233
Steven Tiley	75	71	74	71	291	2,233
Matthew Cryer	73	73	74	72	292	1,900
Matt Ford	72	71	76	73	292	1,900
Chris Paisley	72	70	75	75	292	1,900
Anthony Snobeck	71	71	75	75	292	1,900

Pacific Rubiales Colombia Classic

Barranquilla Country Club, Barranquilla, Colombia
Par 36-36–72; 6,827

March 8-11
purse, €190,705

	SCORES				TOTAL	MONEY
Phillip Archer	71	71	68	70	280	€29,947
Chris Lloyd	73	73	68	67	281	16,845
Morten Orum Madsen	76	69	66	70	281	16,845
Nick Dougherty	71	70	68	73	282	9,358
Matt Haines	69	75	67	71	282	9,358
Chris Hanson	72	69	70	71	282	9,358
Michael Lorenzo-Vera	72	71	70	71	284	5,989
Tyrrell Hatton	73	70	67	75	285	4,866
Jamie McLeary	72	69	73	71	285	4,866
Andreas Harto	75	70	70	71	286	4,118
Benn Barham	74	68	70	75	287	3,556
Federico Damus	75	70	70	72	287	3,556
Paulo Pinto	70	75	70	72	287	3,556
Magnus A. Carlsson	74	71	72	71	288	2,714
Sebastian Fernandez	74	71	71	72	288	2,714
Espen Kofstad	70	71	75	72	288	2,714
Callum Macaulay	75	70	69	74	288	2,714
Racioppi Francisco Ojeda	73	72	67	76	288	2,714
Sebastian Saavedra	69	72	75	72	288	2,714
Graeme Clark	73	74	71	71	289	1,786
Matthew Cryer	74	69	75	71	289	1,786
Floris De Vries	75	72	71	71	289	1,786
Luke Goddard	72	72	74	71	289	1,786
Scott Henry	76	70	70	73	289	1,786
Jeppe Huldahl	73	73	69	74	289	1,786
Niklas Lemke	79	70	70	70	289	1,786
Jose-Filipe Lima	70	72	73	74	289	1,786
*Celia Ricardo	72	75	74	68	289	
Manuel Villegas	68	74	75	72	289	1,786

Barclays Kenya Open

Muthaiga Golf Club, Nairobi, Kenya
Par 36-35–71; 7,236 yards

March 29-April 1
purse, €193,135

		SCORES			TOTAL	MONEY
Seve Benson	66	71	71	66	274	€30,400
Lasse Jensen	69	71	65	69	274	20,900
(Benson defeated Jensen on first playoff hole.)						
Phillip Archer	71	71	69	65	276	12,350
Tyrone Ferreira	73	66	71	66	276	12,350
Gary Lockerbie	69	69	67	72	277	8,550
Justin Walters	68	70	72	67	277	8,550
Jason Barnes	69	74	69	66	278	6,080
Cesar Monasterio	70	73	68	68	279	4,940
Florian Praegant	68	75	66	70	279	4,940
Floris De Vries	69	73	69	69	280	3,752
Jordan Gibb	71	70	67	72	280	3,752
Carl Suneson	73	68	69	70	280	3,752
Jurrian van der Vaart	67	76	71	66	280	3,752
Oliver Bekker	70	74	68	69	281	2,577
Merrick Bremner	72	69	70	70	281	2,577
Matthew Cryer	69	71	74	67	281	2,577
Rafa Echenique	70	69	72	70	281	2,577
Trent Leon	71	69	73	68	281	2,577
Chris Lloyd	71	71	69	70	281	2,577
Jamie McLeary	67	73	70	71	281	2,577
Mark Tullo	68	74	68	71	281	2,577
Robert Dinwiddie	71	73	68	70	282	1,805
Joachim B. Hansen	71	73	68	70	282	1,805
Dismas Indiza	67	70	75	70	282	1,805
Brian Njoroge	68	70	71	73	282	1,805

Madeira Islands Open

See European Tour section.

Allianz Open Cotes d'Armor - Bretagne

Golf Blue Green, Pleneuf Val Andre, France
Par 35-35–70; 6,447 yards

May 10-13
purse, €160,480

		SCORES			TOTAL	MONEY
Eddie Pepperell	67	71	71	68	277	€25,600
Jeppe Huldahl	72	68	67	70	277	17,600
(Pepperell defeated Huldahl on first playoff hole.)						
Peter Baker	73	64	72	70	279	11,200
Carlos Aguilar	69	66	70	75	280	8,000
Ignacio Elvira	69	69	70	72	280	8,000
Mikko Korhonen	68	69	73	70	280	8,000
Gregory Molteni	68	70	71	72	281	5,120
Rasmus Hjelm	71	67	71	73	282	4,480
Kristoffer Broberg	70	72	69	72	283	3,680
Dominique Nouailhac	69	70	74	70	283	3,680
Jens Dantorp	74	63	74	73	284	3,120
Gary Stal	69	70	73	72	284	3,120
Floris De Vries	68	74	72	71	285	2,720
Matt Evans	71	71	74	69	285	2,720
Gary Lockerbie	72	70	71	72	285	2,720

	SCORES				TOTAL	MONEY
Jamie Abbott	71	68	77	70	286	2,240
Oliver Farr	73	68	77	68	286	2,240
Niklas Lemke	70	71	74	71	286	2,240
Jamie Howarth	76	65	72	74	287	1,661
Alexander Levy	74	66	79	68	287	1,661
Damien Perrier	69	69	74	75	287	1,661
Manuel Quiros	73	68	76	70	287	1,661
Will Roebuck	71	70	76	70	287	1,661
Darren Wright	71	71	72	73	287	1,661
Brendan McCarroll	70	73	72	73	288	1,472

Telenet Trophy

Ravenstein Royal Golf Club of Belgium, Tervuren, Belgium
Par 35-36–71; 6,612 yards

May 24-27
purse, €163,744

	SCORES				TOTAL	MONEY
Marco Crespi	68	65	70	67	270	€25,600
Carlos Aguilar	67	71	68	67	273	17,600
Jose-Filipe Lima	69	69	69	67	274	11,200
Bjorn Akesson	69	71	68	67	275	8,800
Alexandre Kaleka	69	66	69	71	275	8,800
Pedro Oriol	67	70	70	69	276	5,333
Eddie Pepperell	71	71	65	69	276	5,333
Olly Whiteley	69	66	70	71	276	5,333
Alessandro Tadini	71	72	69	65	277	3,840
Scott Henry	69	68	71	70	278	3,160
Jurgen Maurer	71	67	68	72	278	3,160
Andrea Perrino	69	68	69	72	278	3,160
Simon Wakefield	68	69	72	69	278	3,160
Jordi Garcia Pinto	71	71	70	67	279	2,480
Garry Houston	70	72	68	69	279	2,480
Mikko Korhonen	71	69	69	70	279	2,480
Andy Sullivan	64	76	68	71	279	2,480
Steven O'Hara	72	70	70	68	280	2,000
Steven Tiley	73	69	70	68	280	2,000
An Byeong-hun	67	74	73	67	281	1,546
H.P. Bacher	73	65	70	73	281	1,546
Eduardo De La Riva	75	67	75	64	281	1,546
Chris Doak	68	70	69	74	281	1,546
Matt Ford	72	68	73	68	281	1,546
Hugues Joannes	69	71	70	71	281	1,546
Adrian Otaegui	73	66	70	72	281	1,546
Scott Strange	72	70	68	71	281	1,546

Fred Olsen Challenge de Espana

Tecina Golf, La Gomera, Canary Islands, Spain
Par 36-35–71; 6,937 yards

May 31-June 3
purse, €163,744

	SCORES				TOTAL	MONEY
Eduardo De La Riva	68	63	69	65	265	€25,600
Simon Wakefield	69	68	63	66	266	17,600
Luis Claverie	66	65	71	66	268	9,600
Scott Henry	66	70	68	64	268	9,600
Alexander Levy	66	68	68	66	268	9,600
Charlie Ford	69	68	71	61	269	5,333

	SCORES				TOTAL	MONEY
Domenico Geminiani	65	68	67	69	269	5,333
Daniel Vancsik	65	64	68	72	269	5,333
Sebastian Garcia Rodriguez	65	65	74	66	270	3,680
Martin Rominger	63	69	66	72	270	3,680
Jamie Abbott	67	67	67	70	271	3,120
Niall Kearney	71	65	69	66	271	3,120
Daniel Brooks	69	67	68	68	272	2,320
Gavin Dear	67	71	67	67	272	2,320
Ignacio Elvira	73	67	70	62	272	2,320
Ben Evans	71	69	67	65	272	2,320
Sebi Garcia	67	64	68	73	272	2,320
Steven Jeppesen	69	66	71	66	272	2,320
Michael Lorenzo-Vera	66	66	71	69	272	2,320
Andrea Maestroni	71	68	64	69	272	2,320
Matt Ford	70	68	69	66	273	1,552
Jordi Garcia Pinto	67	70	68	68	273	1,552
Joachim B. Hansen	66	67	72	68	273	1,552
Antonio Hortal	70	66	68	69	273	1,552
Mark Tullo	68	69	69	67	273	1,552

Karnten Golf Open

Golfclub Klagenfurt-Seltenheim, Klagenfurt, Austria
Par 36-36–72; 7,053 yards

June 7-10
purse, €160,480

	SCORES				TOTAL	MONEY
Gary Stal	65	67	68	68	268	€25,600
Daniel Brooks	70	65	65	69	269	17,600
Justin Walters	67	72	69	63	271	11,200
Tyrrell Hatton	66	73	67	66	272	8,000
Gary Lockerbie	67	66	69	70	272	8,000
Michael Lorenzo-Vera	66	73	69	64	272	8,000
Max Glauert	66	69	72	67	274	5,120
Jordi Garcia Pinto	66	69	69	71	275	4,480
Callum Macaulay	70	70	68	68	276	3,840
Floris De Vries	68	70	72	67	277	3,360
Andreas Harto	67	72	70	68	277	3,360
James Busby	67	70	70	71	278	2,880
Robert Dinwiddie	68	72	70	68	278	2,880
Scott Henry	70	68	70	70	278	2,880
Jamie Abbott	70	70	69	70	279	2,240
Alexandre Kaleka	71	68	73	67	279	2,240
Mikko Korhonen	68	69	71	71	279	2,240
Peter Uihlein	74	67	66	72	279	2,240
Johan Wahlqvist	69	71	67	72	279	2,240
Gavin Dear	66	76	66	72	280	1,610
Matteo Delpodio	75	66	70	69	280	1,610
Jamie McLeary	68	68	71	73	280	1,610
Nicolas Meitinger	68	73	69	70	280	1,610
Roland Steiner	70	69	71	70	280	1,610
Leo Astl	69	73	71	68	281	1,376
Peter Erofejeff	72	69	71	69	281	1,376
Jeppe Huldahl	64	71	70	76	281	1,376
Lasse Jensen	68	70	72	71	281	1,376
Eddie Pepperell	70	69	69	73	281	1,376
Andrea Perrino	69	72	72	68	281	1,376
Mark Tullo	70	70	75	66	281	1,376

Saint-Omer Open

See European Tour section.

Scottish Hydro Challenge

Macdonald Spey Valley Golf Club, Aviemore, Scotland
Par 35-36–71; 7,100 yards
(Fourth round cancelled—rain.)

June 21-24
purse, €221,298

	SCORES			TOTAL	MONEY
Sam Walker	64	67	70	201	€35,200
Simon Wakefield	69	66	66	201	24,200
(Walker defeated Wakefield on third playoff hole.)					
Magnus A. Carlsson	67	69	66	202	15,400
Daniel Brooks	64	72	67	203	11,000
Chris Doak	70	67	66	203	11,000
John Parry	69	67	67	203	11,000
Chris Lloyd	73	62	69	204	6,600
Morten Orum Madsen	69	70	65	204	6,600
Nick Dougherty	69	69	67	205	4,840
Simon Lilly	71	68	66	205	4,840
Chris Paisley	71	69	65	205	4,840
Mark Tullo	67	68	71	206	4,180
Peter Baker	69	69	69	207	3,630
Sihwan Kim	69	71	67	207	3,630
Jose-Filipe Lima	69	68	70	207	3,630
Gary Lockerbie	68	70	69	207	3,630
Andre Bossert	67	70	71	208	2,326
Liam Burns	70	66	72	208	2,326
Laurie Canter	69	70	69	208	2,326
Neil Fenwick	69	69	70	208	2,326
Luke Goddard	71	68	69	208	2,326
Garry Houston	69	66	73	208	2,326
Maximilian Kieffer	67	71	70	208	2,326
Espen Kofstad	71	67	70	208	2,326
Michael Lorenzo-Vera	71	68	69	208	2,326
Nicolas Meitinger	71	68	69	208	2,326
Eddie Pepperell	68	72	68	208	2,326

Challenge Provincia di Varese

Golf Club Varese, Luvinate, Italy
Par 34-36–70; 6,433 yards

June 27-30
purse, €165,520

	SCORES				TOTAL	MONEY
Raymond Russell	63	67	66	67	263	€25,600
Daniel Vancsik	65	65	70	64	264	17,600
Marco Crespi	64	66	69	69	268	10,400
Alessandro Tadini	66	66	68	68	268	10,400
Gary Lockerbie	66	72	67	65	270	7,200
Andrew McArthur	64	68	68	70	270	7,200
Wil Besseling	68	69	68	66	271	4,032
Luke Goddard	69	65	70	67	271	4,032
Rikard Karlberg	69	66	70	66	271	4,032
Andrew Parr	69	71	65	66	271	4,032
Victor Riu	69	67	66	69	271	4,032
Espen Kofstad	72	68	65	67	272	2,800
Scott Strange	72	65	71	64	272	2,800

	SCORES				TOTAL	MONEY
Peter Uihlein	68	67	65	72	272	2,800
Justin Walters	64	70	68	70	272	2,800
Bjorn Akesson	69	69	67	68	273	2,013
Robert Dinwiddie	69	69	69	66	273	2,013
Matt Ford	70	68	67	68	273	2,013
Sihwan Kim	66	68	69	70	273	2,013
Mikko Korhonen	68	67	67	71	273	2,013
Andrea Maestroni	67	67	68	71	273	2,013
Phillip Archer	70	67	67	70	274	1,536
Jordi Garcia Pinto	67	68	68	71	274	1,536
Niklas Lemke	64	70	69	71	274	1,536
Raphael De Sousa	64	67	72	72	275	1,360
Joachim B. Hansen	68	71	68	68	275	1,360
Alexander Levy	69	63	70	73	275	1,360
Morten Orum Madsen	70	69	67	69	275	1,360
Andrea Perrino	71	68	67	69	275	1,360
Florian Praegant	71	66	66	72	275	1,360
Bernd Ritthammer	65	73	73	64	275	1,360
Mark Tullo	67	70	70	68	275	1,360

Credit Suisse Challenge

Golf Sempachersee, Lucerne, Switzerland
Par 36-35–71; 7,147 yards

July 12-15
purse, €160,000

	SCORES				TOTAL	MONEY
Gary Stal	69	67	67	70	273	€25,600
Alexandre Kaleka	70	65	70	68	273	17,600
(Stal defeated Kaleka on first playoff hole.)						
Andrea Perrino	69	66	68	72	275	11,200
Andreas Harto	69	70	69	68	276	8,800
Janne Mommo	69	65	69	73	276	8,800
Luke Goddard	71	64	70	72	277	6,400
Agustin Domingo	68	68	70	72	278	5,120
Nino Bertasio	71	70	69	69	279	3,493
Daniel Brooks	69	69	70	71	279	3,493
Baptiste Chapellan	70	69	70	70	279	3,493
Ben Parker	70	68	70	71	279	3,493
Roland Steiner	68	71	72	68	279	3,493
Daniel Vancsik	68	70	72	69	279	3,493
James Busby	69	67	72	72	280	2,400
Chris Doak	70	70	73	67	280	2,400
Daniel Gaunt	69	69	71	71	280	2,400
Garry Houston	69	65	72	74	280	2,400
Steven Tiley	67	72	69	72	280	2,400
Joachim B. Hansen	62	74	72	73	281	1,732
Roope Kakko	74	63	72	72	281	1,732
Colm Moriarty	67	70	73	71	281	1,732
Victor Riu	70	70	73	68	281	1,732
Lasse Jensen	66	71	74	71	282	1,488
Alexander Levy	67	73	71	71	282	1,488
Damian Ulrich	68	71	70	73	282	1,488
Oliver Wilson	66	74	70	72	282	1,488

Double Tree by Hilton Acaya Open

Acaya Golf Resort, Lecce, Puglia, Italy
Par 35-35–70; 6,855 yards

July 18-21
purse, €163,744

	SCORES				TOTAL	MONEY
Espen Kofstad	72	69	65	65	271	€25,600
Joachim B. Hansen	66	74	67	65	272	17,600
Roope Kakko	71	65	70	68	274	11,200
Matthew Southgate	68	73	69	65	275	9,600
Lloyd Kennedy	70	73	69	64	276	8,000
Christophe Brazillier	69	72	69	67	277	4,960
Eduardo De La Riva	71	68	70	68	277	4,960
Chris Paisley	71	70	71	65	277	4,960
Anthony Snobeck	72	69	68	68	277	4,960
Alexandre Kaleka	70	73	65	70	278	3,253
Peter Uihlein	70	66	72	70	278	3,253
Oliver Wilson	72	70	66	70	278	3,253
Klas Eriksson	69	73	67	70	279	2,720
Mikko Korhonen	73	68	70	68	279	2,720
Victor Riu	71	70	69	69	279	2,720
Benn Barham	72	69	70	69	280	2,160
Marco Crespi	80	64	68	68	280	2,160
Maximilian Kieffer	70	73	71	66	280	2,160
Raymond Russell	65	71	73	71	280	2,160
An Byeong-hun	73	71	69	68	281	1,527
Adrien Bernadet	72	68	70	71	281	1,527
Wil Besseling	70	71	71	69	281	1,527
Matthew Cryer	72	69	70	70	281	1,527
Sihwan Kim	69	71	70	71	281	1,527
Brooks Koepka	73	70	69	69	281	1,527
Chris Lloyd	68	74	70	69	281	1,527
Scott Strange	71	72	69	69	281	1,527
Daniel Vancsik	70	72	69	70	281	1,527

English Challenge

Stoke-by-Nayland Hotel, Golf & Spa, Stoke-by-Nayland, England
Par 36-36–72; 7,134 yards

July 26-29
purse, €160,480

	SCORES				TOTAL	MONEY
Chris Paisley	68	68	65	71	272	€25,600
Francis McGuirk	66	71	67	70	274	17,600
Espen Kofstad	70	68	67	71	276	11,200
Nick Dougherty	70	69	69	69	277	9,600
James Busby	69	68	67	74	278	7,200
Matthew Nixon	69	68	70	71	278	7,200
Robert Dinwiddie	65	65	77	73	280	3,726
Julien Grillon	67	70	74	69	280	3,726
Matt Haines	68	69	69	74	280	3,726
Brooks Koepka	72	66	67	75	280	3,726
Mikko Korhonen	70	69	72	69	280	3,726
Peter Uihlein	73	68	70	69	280	3,726
Justin Walters	73	71	70	66	280	3,726
Bjorn Akesson	71	71	71	68	281	2,480
Chris Lloyd	74	68	74	65	281	2,480
Stuart Manley	65	68	70	78	281	2,480
Simon Wakefield	70	72	72	67	281	2,480
Daniel Gaunt	72	65	72	73	282	1,860
Jeppe Huldahl	74	67	69	72	282	1,860

	SCORES				TOTAL	MONEY
Gary Lockerbie	73	67	69	73	282	1,860
Steven Tiley	72	70	71	69	282	1,860
Steven Brown	73	69	69	72	283	1,488
Jordi Garcia Pinto	71	68	71	73	283	1,488
Tyrrell Hatton	72	70	75	66	283	1,488
Garry Houston	74	69	68	72	283	1,488
Jose-Filipe Lima	70	72	70	71	283	1,488
*Ben Stow	74	69	67	73	283	
Dale Whitnell	69	69	71	74	283	1,488

Finnish Challenge

Kytaga Golf, Hyvinkaa, Finland
Par 35-36–71; 6,963 yards

August 2-5
purse, €170,510

	SCORES				TOTAL	MONEY
Kristoffer Broberg	69	66	66	68	269	€27,200
Wil Besseling	69	67	69	70	275	18,700
Bjorn Akesson	67	75	66	68	276	11,900
Peter Uihlein	72	65	68	72	277	10,200
Nick Dougherty	69	72	66	71	278	6,375
Brooks Koepka	67	73	72	66	278	6,375
Espen Kofstad	69	67	73	69	278	6,375
Andrew Tampion	71	67	68	72	278	6,375
Rafa Echenique	71	69	69	70	279	3,612
Chris Gane	68	69	70	72	279	3,612
Adrian Otaegui	73	70	67	69	279	3,612
Daniel Vancsik	74	67	68	70	279	3,612
Chris Doak	72	70	67	71	280	2,465
Daniel Gaunt	70	73	68	69	280	2,465
Scott Henry	73	66	67	74	280	2,465
Mikko Korhonen	71	70	73	66	280	2,465
Andrew McArthur	72	71	66	71	280	2,465
Victor Riu	72	67	72	69	280	2,465
Reinier Saxton	69	67	74	70	280	2,465
Mark Tullo	71	65	70	74	280	2,465
Jens Dantorp	74	68	68	71	281	1,694
Pelle Edberg	71	70	70	70	281	1,694
Matt Haines	67	71	74	69	281	1,694
Jason Barnes	71	68	73	70	282	1,462
Seve Benson	75	66	72	69	282	1,462
Luke Goddard	71	69	71	71	282	1,462
Maximilian Kieffer	70	70	70	72	282	1,462
Colm Moriarty	71	71	71	69	282	1,462
Raymond Russell	71	67	69	75	282	1,462
Kalle Samooja	70	70	74	68	282	1,462
Roland Steiner	67	69	73	73	282	1,462
Justin Walters	71	71	67	73	282	1,462

Norwegian Challenge

Byneset Golf Klubb, Trondheim, Norway
Par 36-36–72; 6,854 yards

August 9-12
purse, €176,522

	SCORES				TOTAL	MONEY
Kristoffer Broberg	67	64	65	70	266	€28,000
Alvaro Velasco	65	65	67	69	266	19,250
(Broberg defeated Velasco on second playoff hole.)						
Rafa Echenique	69	65	67	66	267	12,250
Steven O'Hara	67	67	69	65	268	9,625
Oliver Wilson	68	62	70	68	268	9,625
Jens Dantorp	70	65	67	67	269	5,833
Florian Praegant	69	67	69	64	269	5,833
Mark Tullo	67	68	69	65	269	5,833
An Byeong-hun	68	67	68	67	270	3,605
Agustin Domingo	72	67	64	67	270	3,605
Alexandre Kaleka	68	68	68	66	270	3,605
Alessandro Tadini	67	71	68	64	270	3,605
Justin Walters	70	68	67	65	270	3,605
Adrien Bernadet	69	64	68	70	271	2,800
Steven Brown	69	66	69	67	271	2,800
Chris Doak	69	66	68	68	271	2,800
*Anders Engell	69	68	65	69	271	
Knut Borsheim	70	68	66	68	272	2,275
Matthew Southgate	74	65	63	70	272	2,275
Gary Stal	68	66	69	69	272	2,275
Niall Kearney	70	67	70	66	273	1,789
Brooks Koepka	68	70	68	67	273	1,789
Chris Lloyd	68	68	68	69	273	1,789
Victor Riu	67	69	68	69	273	1,789
Tyrone Ferreira	71	67	70	66	274	1,610
Sihwan Kim	70	66	69	69	274	1,610
Jack Senior	67	68	69	70	274	1,610

ECCO Tour Championship

Stensballegaard Golf, Horsens, Denmark
Par 36-36–72; 7,577 yards

August 15-18
purse, €164,080

	SCORES				TOTAL	MONEY
Alessandro Tadini	69	71	67	69	276	€25,600
James Busby	68	71	67	70	276	17,600
(Tadini defeated Busby on third playoff hole.)						
Kristoffer Broberg	70	69	67	71	277	10,400
Klas Eriksson	70	62	73	72	277	10,400
Graeme A. Clark	71	66	69	72	278	4,498
Birgir Hafthorsson	69	70	69	70	278	4,498
Anders Schmidt Hansen	72	72	68	66	278	4,498
Sihwan Kim	70	73	69	66	278	4,498
Craig Lee	71	71	70	66	278	4,498
Nicolas Meitinger	69	69	70	70	278	4,498
Steven O'Hara	71	69	71	67	278	4,498
Chris Paisley	73	71	63	71	278	4,498
Mark Tullo	69	74	67	68	278	4,498
Joachim B. Hansen	67	75	64	73	279	2,640
Morten Orum Madsen	74	71	67	67	279	2,640
Jamie Abbott	71	74	70	65	280	2,160
Robert Dinwiddie	71	73	64	72	280	2,160
Mikko Korhonen	69	75	68	68	280	2,160

	SCORES				TOTAL	MONEY
John Parry	72	72	70	66	280	2,160
Daniel Brooks	69	71	71	70	281	1,587
Jordi Garcia Pinto	71	65	74	71	281	1,587
Luke Goddard	74	68	71	68	281	1,587
Alexandre Kaleka	71	73	68	69	281	1,587
Niklas Lemke	70	72	69	70	281	1,587
Lloyd Saltman	71	71	71	68	281	1,587

Rolex Trophy

Golf Club de Geneve, Geneva, Switzerland
Par 36-36–72; 6,727 yards

August 22-25
purse, €188,903

	SCORES				TOTAL	MONEY
Kristoffer Broberg	63	66	64	68	261	€24,400
Sihwan Kim	66	64	66	66	262	18,100
Daniel Vancsik	62	71	64	66	263	12,000
Joachim B. Hansen	65	65	66	68	264	10,000
Chris Lloyd	68	70	62	67	267	8,600
Peter Uihlein	64	68	66	70	268	7,200
Carlos Aguilar	67	67	67	69	270	6,300
Daniel Brooks	71	70	66	63	270	6,300
Eduardo De La Riva	67	66	68	70	271	5,250
Gary Lockerbie	65	67	67	72	271	5,250
Magnus A. Carlsson	65	71	67	69	272	4,160
Marco Crespi	71	68	68	65	272	4,160
Alexandre Kaleka	64	69	70	69	272	4,160
John Parry	68	65	71	68	272	4,160
Simon Wakefield	67	66	73	66	272	4,160
Andreas Harto	64	68	72	69	273	3,450
Jeppe Huldahl	67	66	69	71	273	3,450
Seve Benson	69	67	71	67	274	2,860
Lasse Jensen	73	71	66	64	274	2,860
Raymond Russell	69	65	68	72	274	2,860
Mark Tullo	67	70	66	71	274	2,860
Justin Walters	72	68	66	68	274	2,860
Wil Besseling	65	71	70	70	276	2,507
Eddie Pepperell	74	71	68	63	276	2,507
Alessandro Tadini	72	68	67	69	276	2,507

M2M Russian Challenge Cup

Tseleevo Golf & Polo Club, Moscow, Russia
Par 36-36–72; 7,491 yards

September 6-9
purse, €202,800

	SCORES				TOTAL	MONEY
Alexandre Kaleka	69	71	71	70	281	€32,000
Alessandro Tadini	67	69	73	73	282	18,000
Mark Tullo	68	70	75	69	282	18,000
Chris Doak	75	67	71	70	283	10,000
Joachim B. Hansen	69	70	76	68	283	10,000
Morten Orum Madsen	68	72	71	72	283	10,000
Agustin Domingo	68	74	71	71	284	6,400
Andreas Harto	73	73	69	70	285	5,200
Peter Uihlein	69	71	73	72	285	5,200
Espen Kofstad	67	75	74	70	286	4,067
Mikko Korhonen	70	71	73	72	286	4,067

	SCORES				TOTAL	MONEY
Florian Praegant	69	70	72	75	286	4,067
Magnus A. Carlsson	68	72	78	70	288	3,300
Jerome Lando Casanova	71	73	71	73	288	3,300
Chris Lloyd	70	68	73	77	288	3,300
Ben Parker	70	69	73	76	288	3,300
Matteo Delpodio	69	69	79	72	289	2,700
Daniel Vancsik	71	75	75	68	289	2,700
Carlos Aguilar	75	69	73	73	290	2,233
H.P. Bacher	70	74	76	70	290	2,233
Eduardo De La Riva	69	73	73	75	290	2,233
Phillip Archer	71	73	76	71	291	1,820
Adrien Bernadet	70	69	76	76	291	1,820
Maximilian Kieffer	71	72	72	76	291	1,820
Gary Lockerbie	70	76	72	73	291	1,820
Cesar Monasterio	74	73	74	70	291	1,820
Andrea Perrino	75	73	72	71	291	1,820
Lloyd Saltman	75	67	74	75	291	1,820
Gary Stal	75	72	76	68	291	1,820

Kazakhstan Open

Zhailjau Golf Resort, Almaty, Kazakhstan
Par 36-36–72; 7,197 yards

September 13-16
purse, €412,480

	SCORES				TOTAL	MONEY
Scott Henry	66	67	67	69	269	€64,000
H.P. Bacher	67	67	71	64	269	44,000
(Henry defeated Bacher on second playoff hole.)						
Alexander Levy	66	67	65	72	270	28,000
Lasse Jensen	65	72	67	67	271	20,000
Andrew McArthur	70	66	69	66	271	20,000
Jack Senior	70	69	65	67	271	20,000
Roope Kakko	69	69	67	67	272	11,200
Gary Lockerbie	67	68	68	69	272	11,200
Scott Pinckney	66	73	65	68	272	11,200
Magnus A. Carlsson	70	69	69	65	273	7,680
Andreas Harto	68	70	64	71	273	7,680
Alexandre Kaleka	68	68	69	68	273	7,680
Morten Orum Madsen	70	69	66	68	273	7,680
Chris Paisley	68	69	68	68	273	7,680
Chris Doak	69	69	67	69	274	6,000
Mark Haastrup	67	69	67	71	274	6,000
Jamie McLeary	71	66	66	71	274	6,000
Joachim B. Hansen	70	67	70	68	275	4,650
Michael Lorenzo-Vera	69	71	67	68	275	4,650
Pedro Oriol	68	69	68	70	275	4,650
Peter Uihlein	63	70	69	73	275	4,650
Robert Dinwiddie	71	65	70	70	276	3,720
Pelle Edberg	68	68	71	69	276	3,720
Jose-Filipe Lima	67	71	70	68	276	3,720
John Parry	68	70	70	68	276	3,720
Anthony Snobeck	68	71	66	71	276	3,720
Alessandro Tadini	69	68	68	71	276	3,720

Allianz Golf Open Toulouse Metropole

Golf de Toulouse-Seilh, Seilh, France
Par 35-36–71; 6,924 yards

September 20-23
purse, €161,392

	SCORES				TOTAL	MONEY
*Julien Brun	67	67	67	70	271	
Matteo Delpodio	65	67	70	70	272	€25,600
Eddie Pepperell	71	67	67	68	273	17,600
Michael Lorenzo-Vera	69	71	65	69	274	11,200
Anthony Snobeck	68	70	67	70	275	8,800
Peter Uihlein	68	72	68	67	275	8,800
Phillip Archer	69	72	65	70	276	4,960
Sebastian Garcia Rodriguez	68	71	67	70	276	4,960
Maximilian Kieffer	70	71	64	71	276	4,960
Mark Tullo	71	70	65	70	276	4,960
Richard Bland	66	72	68	71	277	3,360
Steven Jeppesen	68	70	70	69	277	3,360
Seve Benson	71	69	69	69	278	2,800
Jeppe Huldahl	70	70	70	68	278	2,800
Morten Orum Madsen	69	72	68	69	278	2,800
Tim Sluiter	67	69	75	67	278	2,800
*Edouard Espana	69	69	69	72	279	
Chris Hanson	66	71	70	72	279	1,950
Johann Lopez Lazaro	71	71	65	72	279	1,950
Cesar Monasterio	69	71	70	69	279	1,950
Matthew Nixon	66	72	72	69	279	1,950
Lloyd Saltman	67	72	68	72	279	1,950
Simon Wakefield	65	68	71	75	279	1,950
Justin Walters	65	75	69	70	279	1,950
Adrien Bernadet	70	68	70	72	280	1,456
James Busby	69	73	69	69	280	1,456
Lloyd Kennedy	69	67	69	75	280	1,456
Raymond Russell	67	72	71	70	280	1,456
Roland Steiner	70	70	66	74	280	1,456
Daniel Vancsik	65	78	66	71	280	1,456

Challenge de Catalunya

Golf La Graiera, Calafell, Tarragona, Spain
Par 36-36–72; 7,201 yards
(Event shortened to 54 holes—rain.)

September 27-30
purse, €163,024

	SCORES			TOTAL	MONEY
Brooks Koepka	68	67	65	200	€25,600
Alessandro Tadini	66	69	68	203	17,600
Robert Dinwiddie	68	68	68	204	11,200
Luke Goddard	66	69	70	205	8,000
Andrea Perrino	71	65	69	205	8,000
Steven Tiley	70	70	65	205	8,000
Stuart Davis	66	72	68	206	4,240
Roope Kakko	68	71	67	206	4,240
Espen Kofstad	66	70	70	206	4,240
Alexander Levy	71	70	65	206	4,240
Pelle Edberg	67	69	71	207	2,960
Jeppe Huldahl	64	70	73	207	2,960
Rikard Karlberg	69	70	68	207	2,960
Nicolas Meitinger	69	66	72	207	2,960
Chris Doak	65	74	69	208	2,160
Sebastian Garcia Rodriguez	69	70	69	208	2,160

	SCORES			TOTAL	MONEY
Anders Schmidt Hansen	68	69	71	208	2,160
Gary Lockerbie	70	68	70	208	2,160
John Parry	69	70	69	208	2,160
Raul Quiros	71	69	68	208	2,160
Carlos Aguilar	74	66	69	209	1,572
Luis Claverie	70	70	69	209	1,572
Jordan Gibb	68	73	68	209	1,572
Mikko Korhonen	69	71	69	209	1,572
Klas Eriksson	74	67	69	210	1,376
Thomas Feyrsinger	67	73	70	210	1,376
Chris Gane	67	70	73	210	1,376
Jordi Garcia Pinto	66	71	73	210	1,376
Mikael Lundberg	71	70	69	210	1,376
Andrew McArthur	68	71	71	210	1,376
Raymond Russell	68	73	69	210	1,376

Allianz Open de Lyon

Golf du Gouverneur, Monthieux, France
Par 36-35–71; 7,061 yards

October 4-7
purse, €160,944

	SCORES				TOTAL	MONEY
Chris Doak	70	67	68	66	271	€25,600
Tim Sluiter	69	67	72	63	271	17,600
(Doak defeated Sluiter on third playoff hole.)						
Jordi Garcia Pinto	69	69	69	65	272	9,600
Joachim B. Hansen	71	70	68	63	272	9,600
Lloyd Saltman	67	68	68	69	272	9,600
Sam Hutsby	69	63	72	70	274	5,760
Justin Walters	72	68	68	66	274	5,760
An Byeong-hun	71	65	68	71	275	3,947
Adrian Otaegui	68	70	69	68	275	3,947
Eddie Pepperell	66	72	71	66	275	3,947
Bjorn Akesson	66	71	71	68	276	2,960
Phillip Archer	67	67	72	70	276	2,960
Edouard Dubois	68	69	72	67	276	2,960
Andrew Johnston	70	65	72	69	276	2,960
Baptiste Chapellan	66	68	71	72	277	2,240
Roope Kakko	75	65	70	67	277	2,240
Bernd Ritthammer	68	67	76	66	277	2,240
Alessandro Tadini	70	68	73	66	277	2,240
Steven Tiley	68	69	71	69	277	2,240
Wil Besseling	70	65	73	70	278	1,527
Paul Dwyer	71	66	72	69	278	1,527
Steven Jeppesen	67	67	72	72	278	1,527
Chris Lloyd	70	66	73	69	278	1,527
Steven O'Hara	69	68	73	68	278	1,527
Chris Paisley	70	69	72	67	278	1,527
Raymond Russell	68	69	69	72	278	1,527
Gary Stal	69	67	73	69	278	1,527
Simon Wakefield	68	70	70	70	278	1,527

D+D Real Czech Challenge Open

Kuneticka Hora Golf Club, Drítec, Czech Republic
Par 36-36–72; 7,302 yards

October 11-14
purse, €160,480

	SCORES				TOTAL	MONEY
Andreas Harto	65	67	67	65	264	€25,600
Joachim B. Hansen	67	69	67	64	267	17,600
Garry Houston	69	68	66	67	270	11,200
Maximilian Kieffer	71	63	70	67	271	8,000
Mikko Korhonen	66	70	69	66	271	8,000
Steven Tiley	66	67	67	71	271	8,000
Alessandro Tadini	67	71	66	68	272	5,120
Agustin Domingo	69	69	66	69	273	4,160
Rasmus Hjelm	67	69	67	70	273	4,160
Marco Crespi	70	70	69	65	274	3,360
Charles-Edouard Russo	71	66	68	69	274	3,360
Daniel Gaunt	71	67	69	68	275	2,880
Callum Macaulay	69	70	67	69	275	2,880
Adrian Otaegui	69	71	65	70	275	2,880
H.P. Bacher	69	73	69	65	276	2,320
Julien Guerrier	71	67	66	72	276	2,320
Morten Orum Madsen	68	70	70	68	276	2,320
Daniel Vancsik	71	65	69	71	276	2,320
Carlos Aguilar	69	70	69	69	277	1,634
Bjorn Akesson	70	68	70	69	277	1,634
Chris Doak	69	66	71	71	277	1,634
Lloyd Kennedy	71	71	67	68	277	1,634
Francis McGuirk	70	70	72	65	277	1,634
Matthew Nixon	71	69	68	69	277	1,634
Bernd Ritthammer	68	73	69	67	277	1,634

Crowne Plaza Copenhagen Challenge

Royal Golf Club, Copenhagen, Denmark
Par 35-36–71; 7,045 yards

October 18-21
purse, €141,218

	SCORES				TOTAL	MONEY
Kristoffer Broberg	67	70	66	67	270	€22,400
Simon Wakefield	69	66	70	68	273	15,400
Daniel Brooks	68	69	68	74	279	9,100
Mikko Korhonen	75	70	67	67	279	9,100
Steven Jeppesen	73	71	69	67	280	5,693
Roope Kakko	68	70	72	70	280	5,693
Espen Kofstad	71	69	67	73	280	5,693
Jose-Filipe Lima	70	72	72	67	281	3,920
Sebastian Buhl	70	70	72	70	282	2,884
Matt Ford	69	70	74	69	282	2,884
Jordi Garcia	69	71	71	71	282	2,884
Matthew Nixon	70	74	67	71	282	2,884
Bernd Ritthammer	72	70	67	73	282	2,884
Phillip Archer	73	70	70	70	283	2,310
Jens Dantorp	71	68	72	72	283	2,310
Adrien Bernadet	71	69	76	68	284	1,890
Agustin Domingo	71	74	73	66	284	1,890
Joachim B. Hansen	67	74	69	74	284	1,890
Jeppe Huldahl	70	69	73	72	284	1,890
Chris Doak	72	68	71	74	285	1,336
Maximilian Kieffer	73	73	69	70	285	1,336
Alexander Levy	75	64	71	75	285	1,336

	SCORES				TOTAL	MONEY
Morten Orum Madsen	70	74	67	74	285	1,336
Adrian Otaegui	72	70	69	74	285	1,336
Chris Paisley	73	69	69	74	285	1,336
Raymond Russell	76	69	69	71	285	1,336
Daniel Vancsik	68	69	78	70	285	1,336
Johan Wahlqvist	76	68	71	70	285	1,336

Apulia San Domenico Grand Final

San Domenico Golf Club, Savelletri, Italy
Par 34-37–71; 7,031 yards

October 24-27
purse, €330,000

	SCORES				TOTAL	MONEY
Espen Kofstad	65	66	67	67	265	€56,650
James Busby	66	67	67	66	266	29,425
Joachim B. Hansen	67	62	67	70	266	29,425
Eduardo De La Riva	66	66	67	68	267	17,050
Seve Benson	68	69	65	68	270	13,805
Justin Walters	71	67	65	67	270	13,805
Kristoffer Broberg	69	67	67	68	271	10,428
Chris Doak	69	66	67	69	271	10,428
Andreas Harto	72	70	66	63	271	10,428
Maximilian Kieffer	68	66	69	68	271	10,428
Eddie Pepperell	70	67	69	65	271	10,428
Mikko Korhonen	66	71	67	68	272	7,645
Peter Uihlein	69	67	66	70	272	7,645
Wil Besseling	65	68	69	71	273	5,940
Gary Lockerbie	66	68	68	71	273	5,940
Raymond Russell	66	68	70	69	273	5,940
Magnus A. Carlsson	71	65	69	69	274	4,565
Marco Crespi	64	68	67	75	274	4,565
Nick Dougherty	70	66	69	70	275	3,878
Roope Kakko	69	67	67	72	275	3,878
John Parry	68	69	69	69	275	3,878
Alessandro Tadini	69	66	71	69	275	3,878
H.P. Bacher	66	68	70	72	276	3,520
Alexander Levy	69	66	70	72	277	3,355
Sam Walker	72	68	68	69	277	3,355

Asian Tour

Zaykabar Myanmar Open

Royal Mingalardon Golf & Country Club, Yangon, Myanmar
Par 36-36–72; 7,218 yards

February 2-5
purse, US$300,000

	SCORES				TOTAL	MONEY
Kieran Pratt	70	69	66	68	273	US$47,550
Adam Blyth	71	68	69	65	273	25,425
Kiradech Aphibarnrat	66	66	69	72	273	25,425
(Pratt defeated Kiradech on first and Blyth on second playoff hole.)						
Arnond Vongvanij	67	69	71	67	274	13,545
Scott Hend	64	67	69	74	274	13,545
Prayad Marksaeng	68	73	71	63	275	7,788
Anthony Kang	72	69	68	66	275	7,788
Chapchai Nirat	72	67	66	70	275	7,788
Ben Fox	64	69	69	73	275	7,788
Marcus Both	68	66	68	73	275	7,788
Thaworn Wiratchant	67	72	72	65	276	4,927.50
Makoto Inoue	72	66	69	69	276	4,927.50
Park Hyun-bin	69	71	66	70	276	4,927.50
Kodai Ichihara	67	67	70	72	276	4,927.50
Javi Colomo	71	70	70	66	277	3,966
Jesper Kennegard	71	63	74	69	277	3,966
Baek Seuk-hyun	67	71	70	69	277	3,966
Martin Rominger	67	70	70	70	277	3,966
Jonathan Moore	70	67	67	73	277	3,966
Park Jung-ho	68	73	69	68	278	3,330
Niall Turner	69	68	72	69	278	3,330
Chawalit Plaphol	68	67	72	71	278	3,330
Wade Ormsby	64	70	72	72	278	3,330
Tetsuji Hiratsuka	69	66	67	76	278	3,330
Chawinroj Rungsrichai	72	68	72	67	279	2,745
Sushi Ishigaki	69	72	70	68	279	2,745
Joon Lee	67	67	76	69	279	2,745
Nils Floren	72	67	71	69	279	2,745
Peter Karmis	70	67	72	70	279	2,745
Lee Sung	70	70	68	71	279	2,745
Kim Gi-whan	65	72	70	72	279	2,745
Adam Groom	71	67	68	73	279	2,745

ICTSI Philippine Open

Wack Wack Golf & Country Club, Manila, Philippines
Par 36-36–72; 7,222 yards

February 9-12
purse, US$300,000

	SCORES				TOTAL	MONEY
Mardan Mamat	69	70	70	71	280	US$47,550
Mo Joong-kyung	72	71	68	74	285	32,550
Antonio Lascuna	71	71	76	69	287	16,545
Azuma Yano	69	75	73	70	287	16,545
Ben Fox	69	73	74	72	288	12,300
Adam Blyth	73	70	75	71	289	9,450
Paul Donahoo	71	72	74	72	289	9,450
Arnond Vongvanij	73	72	74	71	290	6,680

	SCORES				TOTAL	MONEY
Kim Gi-whan	71	75	72	72	290	6,680
Hwang Inn-choon	77	72	67	74	290	6,680
Chawalit Plaphol	74	75	71	71	291	4,695
Angelo Que	73	76	71	71	291	4,695
Anthony Kang	69	75	75	72	291	4,695
Joonas Granberg	72	74	73	72	291	4,695
Marcus Both	72	72	74	73	291	4,695
Miguel Tabuena	71	72	67	81	291	4,695
Daisuke Kataoka	73	77	70	72	292	3,870
Danny Chia	75	69	74	74	292	3,870
Thitiphun Chuayprakong	72	78	74	69	293	3,472.50
Lu Wei-chih	72	77	74	70	293	3,472.50
Nils Floren	77	73	72	71	293	3,472.50
Wade Ormsby	70	76	73	74	293	3,472.50
Namchok Tantipokhakul	74	74	75	71	294	3,015
Chan Shih-chang	72	78	72	72	294	3,015
Ferdinand Aunzo	72	70	79	73	294	3,015
Jason Knutzon	72	77	72	73	294	3,015
Mars Pucay	70	74	74	76	294	3,015
Berry Henson	73	73	72	76	294	3,015

Avantha Masters

DLF Golf & Country Club, Gurgaon, India
Par 36-36–72; 7,156 yards

February 16-19
purse, US$1,800,000

	SCORES				TOTAL	MONEY
Jbe' Kruger	70	69	66	69	274	US$394,589.91
Jorge Campillo	72	71	66	67	276	205,633.95
Marcel Siem	69	69	68	70	276	205,633.95
Marcus Fraser	69	69	69	70	277	109,380.32
Jose Manuel Lara	74	69	64	70	277	109,380.32
Thorbjorn Olesen	71	67	70	70	278	66,527.86
Estanislao Goya	74	70	64	70	278	66,527.86
Prom Meesawat	72	64	71	71	278	66,527.86
Jean-Baptiste Gonnet	68	69	69	72	278	66,527.86
Kiradech Aphibarnrat	68	69	74	68	279	42,438.14
Ricardo Santos	73	69	69	68	279	42,438.14
Alejandro Canizares	66	73	69	71	279	42,438.14
Rhys Davies	70	69	69	71	279	42,438.14
Gregory Havret	68	70	71	71	280	34,802.83
Paul McGinley	70	69	68	73	280	34,802.83
Andrea Pavan	69	71	67	73	280	34,802.83
Siddikur	71	73	69	68	281	29,546.89
Chawalit Plaphol	75	69	68	69	281	29,546.89
Julien Quesne	72	71	68	70	281	29,546.89
Felipe Aguilar	73	68	69	71	281	29,546.89
Joost Luiten	70	69	70	72	281	29,546.89
Shamim Khan	70	68	74	71	283	26,753.20
Romain Wattel	71	73	73	67	284	24,267.28
Richard Sterne	71	71	71	72	284	24,267.28
Zaw Moe	73	71	68	72	284	24,267.28
Anirban Lahiri	69	69	72	74	284	24,267.28
Marcus Both	70	70	70	74	284	24,267.28
Chapchai Nirat	70	67	71	76	284	24,267.28
Robert Derksen	73	71	70	71	285	20,005.71
Vijay Kumar	72	69	71	73	285	20,005.71
Gareth Maybin	72	69	71	73	285	20,005.71
Mithun Perera	70	72	69	74	285	20,005.71
Soren Hansen	70	68	71	76	285	20,005.71

	SCORES			TOTAL	MONEY
Marc Warren	72	67	68	78	285	20,005.71
Andrew Dodt	72	67	76	71	286	16,572.78
Scott Barr	70	69	75	72	286	16,572.78
Berry Henson	70	70	74	72	286	16,572.78
Jamie Moul	71	68	73	74	286	16,572.78
Shiv Kapur	71	70	71	74	286	16,572.78
Liang Wen-chong	72	72	66	76	286	16,572.78
Gaurav Pratap Singh	72	72	74	69	287	13,494.97
Richard McEvoy	71	72	73	71	287	13,494.97
Oscar Floren	69	75	71	72	287	13,494.97
Scott Hend	74	69	71	73	287	13,494.97
Prayad Marksaeng	72	69	72	74	287	13,494.97
Thongchai Jaidee	68	70	73	76	287	13,494.97
Bernd Wiesberger	71	70	70	76	287	13,494.97
S.S.P. Chowrasia	71	72	75	70	288	11,127.44
Jeev Milkha Singh	69	72	75	72	288	11,127.44
Lorenzo Gagli	72	68	72	76	288	11,127.44
Rikard Karlberg	75	69	72	73	289	9,943.67
Jamie Donaldson	68	70	73	78	289	9,943.67
Joel Sjoholm	73	70	74	73	290	9,233.40
Himmat Rai	68	72	79	72	291	8,286.39
David Horsey	71	72	76	72	291	8,286.39
Manav Jaini	73	70	75	73	291	8,286.39
Mardan Mamat	70	74	74	74	292	7,102.62
Mars Pucay	74	70	73	75	292	7,102.62
Peter Uihlein	69	73	73	77	292	7,102.62
Scott Jamieson	69	72	77	75	293	6,510.73
George Murray	70	74	73	76	293	6,510.73
Sanjay Kumar	73	70	78	73	294	5,918.85
Mukesh Kumar	71	72	75	76	294	5,918.85
Kieran Pratt	71	66	75	82	294	5,918.85
Ross Bain	74	70	76	76	296	5,326.96
Vivek Bhandari	69	72	75	80	296	5,326.96

SAIL-SBI Open

Delhi Golf Club, New Delhi, India
Par 36-36–72; 6,963 yards

February 22-25
purse, US$300,000

	SCORES			TOTAL	MONEY
Anirban Lahiri	65	69	67	73	274	US$47,550
Prom Meesawat	72	64	68	70	274	32,550
(Lahiri defeated Prom on first playoff hole.)						
Scott Barr	71	68	65	71	275	18,300
Ben Fox	70	70	72	66	278	14,790
Siddikur	74	67	70	69	280	12,300
Shankar Das	74	69	70	68	281	8,810
Ashok Kumar	74	68	69	70	281	8,810
Gaganjeet Bhullar	68	69	70	74	281	8,810
Vinod Kumar	70	68	74	70	282	5,975
Stephen Lewton	72	73	66	71	282	5,975
Shamim Khan	71	68	71	72	282	5,975
Martin Rominger	72	69	73	69	283	4,765
Thaworn Wiratchant	69	71	69	74	283	4,765
P. Ghulfam	73	68	66	76	283	4,765
Rikard Karlberg	67	70	74	73	284	4,230
Ron Harvey, Jr.	66	75	69	74	284	4,230
Randhir Ghotra	70	71	73	71	285	3,870
Chapchai Nirat	70	70	69	76	285	3,870
Elmer Salvador	71	73	70	72	286	3,472.50

	SCORES				TOTAL	MONEY
Wade Ormsby	70	74	70	72	286	3,472.50
Sanjay Kumar	71	71	71	73	286	3,472.50
Abhinav Lohan	70	71	71	74	286	3,472.50
Harmeet Kahlon	70	71	75	71	287	3,060
Mithun Perera	71	69	73	74	287	3,060
Kunal Bhasin	74	69	70	74	287	3,060
Kim Gi-whan	74	70	68	75	287	3,060
Rahil Gangjee	73	67	71	76	287	3,060

Handa Faldo Cambodian Classic

Angkor Golf Resort, Siem Reap, Cambodia
Par 36-36–72; 7,279 yards

March 14-17
purse, US$300,000

	SCORES				TOTAL	MONEY
David Lipsky	73	68	67	65	273	US$47,550
Elmer Salvador	68	69	68	68	273	32,550
(Lipsky defeated Salvador on first playoff hole.)						
Niall Turner	67	67	68	72	274	18,300
Kalle Samooja	72	69	69	65	275	12,420
Chinnarat Phadungsil	69	64	76	66	275	12,420
Baek Seuk-hyun	66	71	69	69	275	12,420
Kim Gi-whan	69	71	70	66	276	7,620
Thanyakon Khrongpha	71	66	68	71	276	7,620
Kim Hyung-sung	68	65	68	75	276	7,620
Thaworn Wiratchant	71	70	71	66	278	5,280
Scott Barr	71	71	69	67	278	5,280
Berry Henson	68	72	70	68	278	5,280
Chawalit Plaphol	68	70	71	69	278	5,280
Sushi Ishigaki	73	69	68	69	279	4,230
Hirotaro Naito	72	70	67	70	279	4,230
Pablo Herreria	71	68	69	71	279	4,230
Sam Cyr	70	70	68	71	279	4,230
Anton Haig	72	71	67	70	280	3,585
Hu Mu	72	71	66	71	280	3,585
Sukree Othman	72	69	68	71	280	3,585
Ajeetesh Sandhu	69	68	69	74	280	3,585
Prom Meesawat	70	70	71	70	281	3,150
Danny Chia	71	72	70	68	281	3,150
Kwanchai Tannin	72	68	70	71	281	3,150
Shaaban Hussin	69	69	71	72	281	3,150
Dodge Kemmer	70	69	68	74	281	3,150

Panasonic Open India

Delhi Golf Club, New Delhi, India
Par 36-36–72; 6,963 yards

March 29-April 1
purse, US$300,000

	SCORES				TOTAL	MONEY
Digvijay Singh	70	73	68	66	277	US$47,550
Siddikur	71	67	73	68	279	25,425
Gaganjeet Bhullar	72	67	70	70	279	25,425
Boonchu Ruangkit	71	74	69	67	281	14,790
Sanjay Kumar	70	72	75	65	282	10,400
Ben Fox	73	71	69	69	282	10,400
Shankar Das	70	69	71	72	282	10,400
Anirban Lahiri	69	75	74	65	283	7,065

	SCORES			TOTAL	MONEY
Ashok Kumar	70	69	69	75	283	7,065
Harmeet Kahlon	72	71	75	66	284	5,124
Prom Meesawat	70	69	76	69	284	5,124
Kunal Bhasin	71	73	68	72	284	5,124
Manav Jaini	72	67	72	73	284	5,124
Wade Ormsby	73	67	71	73	284	5,124
Mithun Perera	75	70	73	68	286	4,320
Atthaphon Prathummanee	74	69	73	71	287	3,960
Raju Ali	74	73	69	71	287	3,960
Niall Turner	73	69	71	74	287	3,960
Mukesh Kumar	75	69	74	70	288	3,426
Jyoti Randhawa	71	77	69	71	288	3,426
Kwanchai Tannin	74	73	69	72	288	3,426
Rattanon Wannasrichan	73	70	72	73	288	3,426
Peter Karmis	75	67	72	74	288	3,426
James Byrne	70	75	74	70	289	3,060
Thaworn Wiratchant	74	72	72	71	289	3,060
Shamim Khan	72	72	73	72	289	3,060

ISPS Handa Singapore Classic

Orchid Country Club, Singapore
Par 36-34–70; 6,843 yards

April 5-8
purse, US$400,000

	SCORES			TOTAL	MONEY
Scott Hend	67	68	64	199	US$63,400
Mithun Perera	67	68	65	200	25,980
Lu Wei-chih	65	69	66	200	25,980
Javi Colomo	67	66	67	200	25,980
David Lipsky	63	69	68	200	25,980
Gaganjeet Bhullar	68	69	64	201	11,010
Hwang Inn-choon	69	67	65	201	11,010
Yuta Ikeda	69	66	66	201	11,010
Thaworn Wiratchant	61	71	69	201	11,010
Adam Groom	69	68	65	202	7,282.67
Kieran Pratt	67	66	69	202	7,282.67
Ben Fox	67	66	69	202	7,282.67
Rory Hie	69	68	66	203	6,024
Zaw Moe	69	69	65	203	6,024
Shaaban Hussin	66	65	72	203	6,024
Chawalit Plaphol	68	67	69	204	5,072
Hu Mu	68	66	70	204	5,072
Anton Haig	68	66	70	204	5,072
Jonathan Moore	65	68	71	204	5,072
Daisuke Kataoka	65	67	72	204	5,072
Joonas Granberg	66	71	68	205	4,260
Mo Joong-kyung	70	67	68	205	4,260
Jesper Kennegard	72	66	67	205	4,260
Unho Park	67	68	70	205	4,260
Rikard Karlberg	67	71	67	205	4,260
Peter Karmis	69	69	67	205	4,260

Maybank Malaysian Open

Kuala Lumpur Golf & Country Club, Kuala Lumpur, Malaysia   April 12-15
Par 36-36–72; 7,000 yards   purse, US$2,500,000

	SCORES				TOTAL	MONEY
Louis Oosthuizen	66	68	69	68	271	US$416,660
Stephen Gallacher	67	68	69	70	274	277,770
Rafa Cabrera-Bello	67	72	66	71	276	129,166.67
Danny Willett	69	69	67	71	276	129,166.67
David Lipsky	70	67	69	70	276	129,166.67
Charl Schwartzel	64	75	70	68	277	87,500
Matteo Manassero	70	72	68	69	279	60,875
Martin Kaymer	70	67	71	71	279	60,875
Romain Wattel	68	68	72	71	279	60,875
Hennie Otto	71	64	72	72	279	60,875
Scott Hend	70	71	73	66	280	40,850
Victor Dubuisson	72	68	69	71	280	40,850
Jeev Milkha Singh	65	73	70	72	280	40,850
Jyoti Randhawa	66	72	68	74	280	40,850
Jbe' Kruger	70	65	77	68	280	40,850
Soren Kjeldsen	68	72	71	70	281	33,062.50
Rikard Karlberg	73	69	71	68	281	33,062.50
Ben Fox	70	68	70	73	281	33,062.50
Mo Joong-kyung	71	71	70	69	281	33,062.50
Joost Luiten	72	69	73	68	282	28,687.50
Chapchai Nirat	71	73	69	69	282	28,687.50
Antonio Lascuna	67	74	72	69	282	28,687.50
Julien Quesne	69	72	73	68	282	28,687.50
Prom Meesawat	68	75	70	70	283	25,250
Ricardo Gonzalez	68	71	66	78	283	25,250
Simon Dyson	69	70	70	74	283	25,250
Rhys Davies	70	68	72	73	283	25,250
Pablo Larrazabal	69	73	67	74	283	25,250
Alvaro Quiros	72	68	73	71	284	21,875
Nicolas Colsaerts	72	68	73	71	284	21,875
Liang Wen-chong	72	68	70	74	284	21,875
Marcel Siem	69	73	70	72	284	21,875
Berry Henson	72	72	70	71	285	18,285.71
Mardan Mamat	73	71	70	71	285	18,285.71
Steve Webster	73	70	69	73	285	18,285.71
Scott Barr	73	70	70	72	285	18,285.71
Richard Green	69	74	71	71	285	18,285.71
David Howell	71	71	75	68	285	18,285.71
Gary Boyd	75	67	68	75	285	18,285.71
Joonas Granberg	68	73	71	74	286	14,750
David Drysdale	72	69	74	71	286	14,750
Daisuke Kataoka	70	71	72	73	286	14,750
Branden Grace	69	72	72	73	286	14,750
Panuphol Pittayarat	69	74	73	70	286	14,750
Tom Lewis	70	70	72	74	286	14,750
Gaurav Ghei	68	74	73	71	286	14,750
Jason Knutzon	66	75	71	75	287	11,750
Gregory Bourdy	75	69	74	69	287	11,750
Marcus Both	72	72	73	70	287	11,750
Robert-Jan Derksen	71	73	74	69	287	11,750
Lorenzo Gagli	69	71	74	73	287	11,750
Siddikur	72	71	73	72	288	9,500
Fabrizio Zanotti	72	71	75	70	288	9,500
Simon Khan	72	71	73	72	288	9,500
Shiv Kapur	69	72	72	75	288	9,500
Peter Karmis	72	70	74	73	289	8,250
Bernd Wiesberger	73	71	75	71	290	7,250

	SCORES				TOTAL	MONEY
Stephen Lewton	70	71	77	72	290	7,250
Anthony Kang	69	75	76	70	290	7,250
Prayad Marksaeng	73	70	69	78	290	7,250
Shaaban Hussin	70	72	75	73	290	7,250
Thanyakon Khrongpha	73	68	72	78	291	6,500
Michael Campbell	72	71	71	78	292	6,000
Zaw Moe	72	71	74	75	292	6,000
Alastair Forsyth	71	72	70	79	292	6,000
Lee Sung	69	75	75	74	293	5,250
Zhang Lian-wei	70	74	72	77	293	5,250
Richard McEvoy	72	71	75	75	293	5,250
Pariya Junhasavasdikul	76	68	72	78	294	4,750
Jean-Baptiste Gonnet	71	69	80	75	295	4,570
Keith Horne	72	72	78	74	296	3,749.54
Ignacio Garrido	71	70	81	89	311	3,745.57

CIMB Niaga Indonesian Masters

Royale Jakarta Golf Club, Jakarta, Indonesia
Par 36-36–72; 7,322 yards

April 19-22
purse, US$750,000

	SCORES				TOTAL	MONEY
Lee Westwood	65	68	65	74	272	US$118,875
Thaworn Wiratchant	72	69	66	67	274	81,375
Gaganjeet Bhullar	72	70	65	69	276	41,362.50
Shiv Kapur	68	71	70	67	276	41,362.50
Anirban Lahiri	74	68	66	69	277	30,750
Baek Seuk-hyun	72	70	68	68	278	25,425
Angelo Que	69	73	68	69	279	19,050
Lee Sung	68	71	67	73	279	19,050
Bernd Wiesberger	70	68	72	69	279	19,050
Berry Henson	69	73	69	70	281	13,199.75
Wade Ormsby	71	73	66	71	281	13,199.75
Masanori Kobayashi	69	68	74	70	281	13,199.75
Zaw Moe	68	67	75	71	281	13,199.75
Scott Barr	74	69	69	70	282	10,137.50
Ben Fox	73	70	68	71	282	10,137.50
Siddikur	71	73	67	71	282	10,137.50
Jonathan Moore	73	72	68	69	282	10,137.50
Adam Groom	72	69	70	71	282	10,137.50
Kieran Pratt	73	65	69	75	282	10,137.50
Jyoti Randhawa	68	75	68	72	283	8,550
Darren Beck	73	71	69	70	283	8,550
Antonio Lascuna	70	72	70	71	283	8,550
Mithun Perera	70	73	72	69	284	7,762.50
Adilson Da Silva	73	70	72	69	284	7,762.50
Boonchu Ruangkit	68	72	71	73	284	7,762.50
Daisuke Kataoka	72	68	71	73	284	7,762.50

Ballantine's Championship

Blackstone Resort, Seoul, South Korea
Par 36-36–72; 7,275 yards

April 26-29
purse, €2,200,000

	SCORES				TOTAL	MONEY
Bernd Wiesberger	72	65	65	68	270	US$480,289.43
Richie Ramsay	70	72	68	65	275	320,192.95

	SCORES				TOTAL	MONEY
Victor Dubuisson	68	75	68	66	277	162,241.77
Marcus Fraser	71	67	69	70	277	162,241.77
Anthony Wall	73	67	71	67	278	111,523.20
Miguel Angel Jimenez	72	68	69	69	278	111,523.20
George Coetzee	71	71	71	66	279	66,741.02
Ross Fisher	71	72	70	66	279	66,741.02
Alexander Noren	75	66	69	69	279	66,741.02
Paul McGinley	71	73	65	70	279	66,741.02
Felipe Aguilar	71	69	68	71	279	66,741.02
Adam Scott	71	76	68	65	280	46,684.13
Romain Wattel	72	73	67	68	280	46,684.13
David Howell	73	69	68	70	280	46,684.13
Jamie Donaldson	70	72	73	66	281	38,961.08
Ian Poulter	75	67	69	70	281	38,961.08
David Oh	73	70	68	70	281	38,961.08
Y.E. Yang	74	71	66	70	281	38,961.08
Kiradech Aphibarnrat	76	69	65	71	281	38,961.08
Thaworn Wiratchant	73	70	70	69	282	32,621.26
Brett Rumford	73	70	70	69	282	32,621.26
Sang-Moon Bae	75	68	69	70	282	32,621.26
Soren Kjeldsen	74	69	69	70	282	32,621.26
Prom Meesawat	72	72	68	70	282	32,621.26
Jeev Milkha Singh	72	74	68	69	283	27,376.50
Graeme Storm	72	69	72	70	283	27,376.50
Matthew Zions	74	71	70	68	283	27,376.50
Paul Casey	70	72	70	71	283	27,376.50
Siddikur	75	69	68	71	283	27,376.50
Thongchai Jaidee	71	71	69	72	283	27,376.50
Oliver Fisher	71	70	67	75	283	27,376.50
Shane Lowry	74	70	70	70	284	22,693.68
Mikko Ilonen	75	69	70	70	284	22,693.68
Andrea Pavan	72	74	70	68	284	22,693.68
Gregory Havret	76	69	66	73	284	22,693.68
Oscar Floren	72	67	75	71	285	20,748.50
Lee Tae-kyu	71	73	75	66	285	20,748.50
Gareth Maybin	72	76	67	71	286	18,154.94
Danny Willett	75	67	73	71	286	18,154.94
Richard Johnson	73	73	68	72	286	18,154.94
Berry Henson	74	72	68	72	286	18,154.94
Peter Karmis	77	69	69	71	286	18,154.94
Mark Foster	70	75	71	70	286	18,154.94
Choi Jin-ho	75	73	71	67	286	18,154.94
Choi Ho-sung	73	70	72	72	287	14,985.03
Estanislao Goya	76	70	71	70	287	14,985.03
Chris Wood	74	71	72	70	287	14,985.03
Kang Kyung-nam	76	72	71	68	287	14,985.03
Anirban Lahiri	71	73	71	73	288	12,391.47
Andrew Dodt	75	71	69	73	288	12,391.47
Richard McEvoy	78	70	69	71	288	12,391.47
Keith Horne	75	72	70	71	288	12,391.47
Scott Jamieson	76	68	73	71	288	12,391.47
Jung Ji-ho	70	71	74	74	289	9,365.64
Christian Nilsson	74	71	71	73	289	9,365.64
K.T. Kim	73	75	70	71	289	9,365.64
Ryu Hyun-woo	74	73	71	71	289	9,365.64
An Byeong-hun	73	75	73	68	289	9,365.64
Peter Whiteford	71	74	76	68	289	9,365.64
Marc Warren	76	72	69	73	290	8,068.86
Michael Jonzon	76	71	69	75	291	7,348.43
James Morrison	74	69	73	75	291	7,348.43
Damien McGrane	73	71	73	74	291	7,348.43
Kim Do-hoon	72	76	73	70	291	7,348.43
Tjaart van der Walt	75	73	70	74	292	6,195.73

	SCORES				TOTAL	MONEY
Lee Sung	75	71	73	73	292	6,195.73
Andrew Tschudin	74	73	73	72	292	6,195.73
Ricardo Gonzalez	75	70	75	72	292	6,195.73
Park Sung-kug	76	71	75	71	293	5,475.30
Joo Heung-chol	74	73	70	77	294	4,786.56
Digvijay Singh	73	70	78	73	294	4,786.56
Pablo Martin	80	68	72	75	295	4,318.03
Kao Shang-hung	72	74	75	80	301	4,314.11

Queen's Cup

Santiburi Samui Country Club, Koh Samui, Thailand
Par 35-36–71; 6,832 yards

June 14-17
purse, US$300,000

	SCORES				TOTAL	MONEY
Thaworn Wiratchant	70	67	72	68	277	US$47,550
Juvic Pagunsan	75	65	72	68	280	25,425
Siddikur	70	68	71	71	280	25,425
Himmat Rai	70	72	72	67	281	13,545
Guido van der Valk	70	72	69	70	281	13,545
Prayad Marksaeng	69	75	69	69	282	8,810
Anirban Lahiri	71	68	72	71	282	8,810
Varut Chomchalam	72	71	66	73	282	8,810
Boonchu Ruangkit	67	74	73	70	284	6,600
Chinnarat Phadungsil	76	70	75	64	285	5,662.50
Miguel Tabuena	67	70	72	76	285	5,662.50
Namchok Tantipokhakul	71	73	71	71	286	4,653.75
Kiradech Aphibarnrat	68	72	74	72	286	4,653.75
Baek Seuk-hyun	68	73	70	75	286	4,653.75
Jonathan Moore	72	72	67	75	286	4,653.75
Adilson Da Silva	73	69	71	74	287	4,140
Chiragh Kumar	76	72	71	69	288	3,605
Zaw Moe	72	72	73	71	288	3,605
Javi Colomo	70	73	73	72	288	3,605
Antonio Lascuna	71	73	72	72	288	3,605
Thanyakon Khrongpha	75	71	67	75	288	3,605
Panuwat Muenlek	71	73	67	77	288	3,605
Rick Kulacz	71	78	68	72	289	3,195
Hsu Chia-jen	74	72	70	73	289	3,195
Ben Leong	74	70	76	70	290	2,970
Wade Ormsby	74	72	69	75	290	2,970
Mars Pucay	70	76	68	76	290	2,970

Volvik Hildesheim Open J Golf Series

Hildesheim Country Club, Jecheon, South Korea
Par 72

June 21-24
purse, US$300,000

	SCORES				TOTAL	MONEY
Lee In-woo	71	68	69	68	276	US$60,000
Lee Sang-hee	66	73	71	67	277	24,000
Thaworn Wiratchant	69	71	68	69	277	24,000
Pariya Junhasavasdikul	68	70	71	69	278	14,400
Byun Jin-jae	69	71	69	70	279	11,220
Javi Colomo	69	70	69	71	279	11,220
Prom Meesawat	71	71	71	67	280	7,800
Makoto Inoue	70	71	70	69	280	7,800

	SCORES				TOTAL	MONEY
Park Boo-won	69	69	70	72	280	7,800
Park Jun-won	69	71	68	72	280	7,800
Kang Kyung-nam	71	71	70	69	281	5,520
Song Young-hoon	70	70	71	70	281	5,520
Stephen Lewton	69	73	69	70	281	5,520
Thanyakon Khrongpha	70	71	68	72	281	5,520
Lee Dong-min	73	71	69	69	282	4,080
Kim Gi-whan	72	71	69	70	282	4,080
Bae Sung-chul	70	72	68	72	282	4,080
Kim Dae-hyun	67	70	72	73	282	4,080
Ma Soo-kil	66	75	68	73	282	4,080
Siddikur	71	71	70	71	283	3,300
Wade Ormsby	72	71	67	73	283	3,300
Daisuke Kataoka	69	75	70	70	284	3,000
Kim Hui-soo	71	72	69	72	284	3,000
Adilson Da Silva	69	72	67	76	284	3,000
Park Hyun-bin	70	72	72	71	285	2,520
Choi Ho-sung	67	77	70	71	285	2,520
Lee Min-chang	68	75	72	70	285	2,520
Wang Jeung-hun	71	73	72	69	285	2,520
Berry Henson	73	69	74	69	285	2,520

Worldwide Holdings Selangor Masters

Kota Permai Golf & Country Club, Shah Alam, Malaysia   September 5-8
Par 36-36–72; 6,977 yards   purse, US$395,000

	SCORES				TOTAL	MONEY
Thaworn Wiratchant	66	69	68	69	272	US$60,900.25
Gaganjeet Bhullar	68	71	70	66	275	41,688.81
Siddikur	73	71	66	66	276	19,377.93
Javi Colomo	68	69	72	67	276	19,377.93
Michael Tran	67	68	73	68	276	19,377.93
Jason Knutzon	72	68	70	68	278	12,103.20
Jesper Kennegard	70	69	67	72	278	12,103.20
Mars Pucay	73	71	68	67	279	9,048.59
Marcus Both	67	69	73	70	279	9,048.59
Thanyakon Khrongpha	72	70	71	67	280	6,743.22
Kieran Pratt	67	71	71	71	280	6,743.22
Lam Chih Bing	70	70	69	71	280	6,743.22
Jonathan Moore	67	71	70	72	280	6,743.22
Lin Wen-tang	73	69	71	68	281	5,763.43
Gavin Flint	70	69	73	70	282	5,187.09
Panuwat Muenlek	70	71	71	70	282	5,187.09
Lindsay Renolds	68	70	73	71	282	5,187.09
Himmat Rai	70	70	71	71	282	5,187.09
Miguel Tabuena	73	71	70	69	283	4,508.29
Namchok Tantipokhakul	70	72	70	71	283	4,508.29
Niall Turner	71	70	70	72	283	4,508.29
Philip Matsson	74	70	69	71	284	3,919.13
Jaakko Makitalo	70	74	69	71	284	3,919.13
Thitiphun Chuayprakong	73	70	70	71	284	3,919.13
Berry Henson	73	69	71	71	284	3,919.13
Darren Beck	75	67	70	72	284	3,919.13
Thammanoon Sriroj	70	71	70	73	284	3,919.13
Antonio Lascuna	72	69	70	73	284	3,919.13

Yeangder Tournament Players Championship

Linkou International Golf & Country Club, Taipei, Taiwan
Par 36-36–72; 7,125 yards
(Event shortened to 54 holes and completed on Monday — typhoon.)

September 13-17
purse, US$500,000

	SCORES			TOTAL	MONEY
Gaganjeet Bhullar	66	69	69	204	US$79,250
Jason Knutzon	66	71	71	208	42,375
Thaworn Wiratchant	70	66	72	208	42,375
Lin Wen-tang	67	75	67	209	19,162.50
Hung Chien-yao	72	69	68	209	19,162.50
David Lipsky	72	67	70	209	19,162.50
Berry Henson	69	68	72	209	19,162.50
Yeh Wei-tze	68	72	71	211	12,550
Miguel Tabuena	71	71	70	212	9,220
Baek Seuk-hyun	71	71	70	212	9,220
Namchok Tantipokhakul	69	72	71	212	9,220
Mars Pucay	72	69	71	212	9,220
Himmat Rai	71	70	71	212	9,220
Panuphol Pittayarat	69	75	69	213	6,628.57
Yeh Chang-ting	73	69	71	213	6,628.57
Darren Beck	71	71	71	213	6,628.57
Kim Gi-whan	70	71	72	213	6,628.57
Gunn Charoenkul	74	67	72	213	6,628.57
Sung Mao-chang	74	67	72	213	6,628.57
Angelo Que	65	75	73	213	6,628.57
Huang Tao	72	72	70	214	5,325
Anirban Lahiri	68	74	72	214	5,325
Antonio Lascuna	70	72	72	214	5,325
Wang Ter-chang	72	74	68	214	5,325
Gavin Flint	70	70	74	214	5,325
Adam Groom	76	68	70	214	5,325

Asia-Pacific Panasonic Open

See Japan Tour section.

Mercuries Taiwan Masters

Taiwan Golf & Country Club, Taipei, Taiwan
Par 36-36–72; 6,923 yards

September 27-30
purse, US$600,000

	SCORES				TOTAL	MONEY
Tsai Chi-huang	74	69	65	76	284	US$120,000
Antonio Lascuna	70	73	72	73	288	72,000
David Lipsky	72	74	76	67	289	36,000
Chan Yih-shin	74	74	70	71	289	36,000
Danny Chia	72	72	72	74	290	24,000
Sung Mao-chang	72	75	75	69	291	19,500
Angelo Que	70	75	75	71	291	19,500
Baek Seuk-hyun	70	73	71	78	292	15,000
Thaworn Wiratchant	73	77	73	70	293	10,320
Adilson Da Silva	73	72	77	71	293	10,320
Lu Chien-soon	77	70	75	71	293	10,320
Sam Cyr	73	76	72	72	293	10,320
Gaganjeet Bhullar	75	74	68	76	293	10,320
Thitiphun Chuayprakong	72	78	75	69	294	7,725
Prom Meesawat	73	76	74	71	294	7,725

	SCORES				TOTAL	MONEY
Wang Ter-chang	73	76	72	73	294	7,725
Wang Shih-jui	70	73	77	74	294	7,725
Boonchu Ruangkit	73	72	77	73	295	6,600
Lin Wen-tang	71	73	77	74	295	6,600
Siddikur	72	72	73	78	295	6,600
Hsu Mong-nan	75	74	75	72	296	5,970
Jonathan Moore	77	73	72	74	296	5,970
Namchok Tantipokhakul	73	76	72	75	296	5,970
Hung Chien-yao	75	73	72	76	296	5,970
Mardan Mamat	77	71	77	72	297	5,460
Lin Keng-chi	73	74	76	74	297	5,460
Anirban Lahiri	71	75	75	76	297	5,460
Kalle Samooja	71	73	74	79	297	5,460
Lam Chih Bing	72	75	75	76	298	4,980
Elmer Salvador	75	74	73	76	298	4,980
Adam Groom	72	78	72	76	298	4,980
Guido van der Valk	73	72	73	80	298	4,980

CJ Invitational

Haesley Nine Bridges Golf Club, Yeoju, South Korea October 4-7
Par 71; 7,152 yards purse, US$750,000

	SCORES				TOTAL	MONEY
K.J. Choi	69	65	68	67	269	US$118,875
Jang Dong-kyu	68	71	65	67	271	63,562.50
Bae Sang-moon	69	68	66	68	271	63,562.50
Kim Dae-hyun	71	65	66	71	273	36,975
Scott Hend	69	69	66	70	274	28,087.50
Charlie Wi	67	70	67	70	274	28,087.50
Chinnarat Phadungsil	68	64	71	72	275	21,825
Arnond Vongvanij	70	70	68	68	276	18,825
Kim Meen-whee	69	67	69	72	277	15,637.50
Ryan Yip	64	71	70	72	277	15,637.50
Park Hyun-bin	67	74	67	70	278	12,318.75
Lee Dong-hwan	66	72	65	75	278	12,318.75
Prom Meesawat	68	69	70	71	278	12,318.75
Kim Woo-chan	73	72	67	66	278	12,318.75
Darren Beck	70	69	70	70	279	10,125
Lee Sang-hee	74	71	66	68	279	10,125
Lee Kyoung-hoon	69	68	71	71	279	10,125
Lee Sung	67	68	72	72	279	10,125
Angelo Que	68	73	75	64	280	8,565
Choi Hyuk-jae	70	70	69	71	280	8,565
Chapchai Nirat	67	71	74	68	280	8,565
Kang Kyung-nam	67	71	71	71	280	8,565
Adilson Da Silva	71	65	73	71	280	8,565
Park Sang-hyun	72	71	66	72	281	7,762.50
Han Min-kyu	73	72	68	68	281	7,762.50

Venetian Macau Open

Macau Golf & Country Club, Macau
Par 35-36–71; 6,624 yards

October 11-14
purse, US$750,000

	SCORES				TOTAL	MONEY
Gaganjeet Bhullar	63	68	69	68	268	US$118,875
Jonathan Moore	67	68	70	65	270	81,375
Siddikur	66	68	72	66	272	41,362.50
Thitiphun Chuayprakong	67	66	69	70	272	41,362.50
Shiv Kapur	70	67	70	67	274	30,750
Angelo Que	68	66	70	71	275	23,625
Scott Hend	65	70	69	71	275	23,625
Chinnarat Phadungsil	71	72	67	66	276	14,687.50
Thongchai Jaidee	66	68	73	69	276	14,687.50
Unho Park	69	68	70	69	276	14,687.50
Prom Meesawat	65	68	72	71	276	14,687.50
Adilson Da Silva	68	66	71	71	276	14,687.50
Berry Henson	67	69	68	72	276	14,687.50
Wade Ormsby	73	66	71	67	277	10,800
Jason Knutzon	67	68	73	69	277	10,800
Kieran Pratt	66	68	71	72	277	10,800
David Gleeson	72	71	71	64	278	9,300
Pariya Junhasavasdikul	71	69	72	66	278	9,300
Guy Woodman	72	69	71	66	278	9,300
Marcus Fraser	70	70	69	69	278	9,300
Shaaban Hussin	70	73	69	67	279	8,212.50
Niall Turner	66	73	71	69	279	8,212.50
Javi Colomo	72	70	67	70	279	8,212.50
Rikard Karlberg	69	68	70	72	279	8,212.50
Dodge Kemmer	71	72	71	66	280	7,087.50
Rattanon Wannasrichan	71	66	76	67	280	7,087.50
Varan Israbhakdi	68	73	72	67	280	7,087.50
Kwanchai Tannin	68	71	72	69	280	7,087.50
Lin Wen-hong	71	70	70	69	280	7,087.50
Hsu Mong-nan	75	66	67	72	280	7,087.50

Hero Indian Open

Karnataka Golf Association, Bengaluru, India
Par 35-36–71; 7,068 yards

October 18-21
purse, US$1,250,000

	SCORES				TOTAL	MONEY
Thaworn Wiratchant	69	68	67	66	270	US$198,125
Richie Ramsay	66	66	70	68	270	135,625
(Thaworn defeated Ramsay on first playoff hole.)						
Panuphol Pittayarat	67	68	69	67	271	76,250
Shiv Kapur	67	71	68	66	272	61,625
Anirban Lahiri	70	71	66	67	274	43,333.33
Arnond Vongvanij	71	67	67	69	274	43,333.33
Jaakko Makitalo	67	68	68	71	274	43,333.33
Peter Hanson	70	71	68	66	275	29,437.50
Chiragh Kumar	69	71	67	68	275	29,437.50
Angelo Que	68	68	69	71	276	23,562.50
James Morrison	66	71	67	72	276	23,562.50
Nils Floren	74	71	67	65	277	18,520.83
Namchok Tantipokhakul	69	71	71	66	277	18,520.83
Scott Barr	70	68	72	67	277	18,520.83
Kalle Samooja	67	72	69	69	277	18,520.83
Scott Hend	71	69	67	70	277	18,520.83

	SCORES				TOTAL	MONEY
Jyoti Randhawa	72	68	67	70	277	18,520.83
Pariya Junhasavasdikul	72	70	69	67	278	15,750
Mardan Mamat	69	70	72	68	279	14,666.67
Prom Meesawat	72	68	71	68	279	14,666.67
Chinnarat Phadungsil	75	65	70	69	279	14,666.67
Panuwat Muenlek	70	70	72	68	280	13,312.50
Adilson Da Silva	70	68	72	70	280	13,312.50
Gaganjeet Bhullar	68	69	70	73	280	13,312.50
Chapchai Nirat	67	68	70	75	280	13,312.50

CIMB Classic

Mines Resort & Golf Club, Kuala Lumpur, Malaysia
Par 35-36–71; 6,917 yards

October 25-28
purse, US$6,100,000

	SCORES				TOTAL	MONEY
Nick Watney	71	65	65	61	262	$1,300,000
Robert Garrigus	64	64	69	66	263	485,000
Bo Van Pelt	70	65	62	66	263	485,000
Brendon de Jonge	68	65	66	66	265	265,000
Chris Kirk	69	66	63	67	265	265,000
Tiger Woods	66	67	69	63	265	265,000
Carl Pettersson	69	67	68	62	266	200,000
Jbe' Kruger	66	64	69	68	267	175,000
Pat Perez	67	68	68	65	268	150,000
Gaganjeet Bhullar	65	72	65	67	269	102,500
Brian Harman	64	70	66	69	269	102,500
Kevin Na	67	66	69	67	269	102,500
Scott Piercy	75	68	64	62	269	102,500
Ben Crane	68	66	68	68	270	87,000
Seung-Yul Noh	71	66	67	66	270	87,000
Greg Chalmers	66	66	69	70	271	79,000
Jason Dufner	68	72	64	67	271	79,000
Bill Haas	70	65	68	68	271	79,000
Jeff Overton	64	70	68	69	271	79,000
John Senden	72	66	66	67	271	79,000
Thaworn Wiratchant	72	65	68	66	271	79,000
Ricky Barnes	66	71	66	69	272	71,000
J.B. Holmes	66	70	68	68	272	71,000
Marcus Fraser	70	70	65	68	273	67,000
Charlie Wi	69	66	71	67	273	67,000
Tom Gillis	65	70	66	73	274	60,600
John Huh	70	68	68	68	274	60,600
Masanori Kobayashi	69	71	66	68	274	60,600
Anirban Lahiri	71	66	68	69	274	60,600
Martin Laird	68	67	69	70	274	60,600
Trevor Immelman	72	63	68	72	275	56,500
Kevin Stadler	67	68	76	64	275	56,500
Bob Estes	69	68	70	69	276	53,500
Troy Matteson	63	69	73	71	276	53,500
Cameron Tringale	71	69	70	66	276	53,500
Johnson Wagner	70	69	67	70	276	53,500
Prom Meesawat	70	69	68	70	277	50,000
Sean O'Hair	69	72	65	71	277	50,000
Ryan Palmer	69	68	70	70	277	50,000
Marc Leishman	75	67	66	70	278	48,000
Kyle Stanley	69	70	74	66	279	46,500
Jimmy Walker	69	68	71	71	279	46,500
Danny Chia	66	75	73	67	281	45,000
David Lipsky	68	73	71	70	282	43,500

	SCORES				TOTAL	MONEY
William McGirt	70	70	73	69	282	43,500
Siddikur	73	74	69	68	284	42,000
Shaaban Hussin	74	73	70	68	285	41,000
Scott Hend	70	77	70	70	287	40,000

WGC - HSBC Champions

Mission Hills Golf Club, Olazabal Course, Guangdong, China
Par 36-36–72; 7,251 yards

November 1-4
purse, US$7,000,000

	SCORES				TOTAL	MONEY
Ian Poulter	69	68	65	65	267	$1,200,000
Jason Dufner	68	66	71	64	269	417,500
Scott Piercy	68	68	68	65	269	417,500
Ernie Els	70	63	69	67	269	417,500
Phil Mickelson	66	69	66	68	269	417,500
Louis Oosthuizen	65	63	70	72	270	190,000
Lee Westwood	70	67	61	72	270	190,000
Adam Scott	65	68	71	67	271	155,000
Martin Kaymer	68	69	67	68	272	140,000
Bill Haas	69	67	66	71	273	125,000
Hiroyuki Fujita	73	67	67	67	274	98,000
Marcel Siem	71	70	66	67	274	98,000
Thorbjorn Olesen	71	65	70	68	274	98,000
Prom Meesawat	67	70	69	68	274	98,000
Brandt Snedeker	72	71	60	71	274	98,000
Nick Watney	72	72	69	62	275	80,500
Carl Pettersson	70	68	66	71	275	80,500
Marc Leishman	73	68	65	70	276	75,000
Luke Donald	68	68	69	71	276	75,000
Gaganjeet Bhullar	73	68	63	72	276	75,000
Thomas Bjorn	72	70	68	67	277	70,000
Thongchai Jaidee	70	68	69	70	277	70,000
Keegan Bradley	71	68	68	71	278	67,000
Liang Wen-chong	72	73	66	68	279	62,250
Scott Hend	70	74	67	68	279	62,250
Peter Hanson	66	71	73	69	279	62,250
Justin Rose	72	70	67	70	279	62,250
John Senden	72	70	70	68	280	57,500
Bernd Wiesberger	72	72	68	68	280	57,500
Thomas Aiken	68	73	69	70	280	57,500
Gonzalo Fernandez-Castano	71	67	69	73	280	57,500
Shane Lowry	66	68	72	75	281	55,000
Bubba Watson	66	72	69	75	282	54,000
Tadahiro Takayama	73	69	70	71	283	52,500
I.J. Jang	68	71	72	72	283	52,500
Paul Lawrie	69	71	72	72	284	50,000
Joost Luiten	72	72	68	72	284	50,000
Wu Ashun	68	70	71	75	284	50,000
Thaworn Wiratchant	72	70	70	73	285	47,000
Francesco Molinari	74	69	74	68	285	47,000
Dustin Johnson	67	68	84	66	285	47,000
Julien Quesne	71	71	71	73	286	43,500
Graeme McDowell	71	75	68	72	286	43,500
Marcus Fraser	73	72	70	71	286	43,500
Jamie Donaldson	71	74	71	70	286	43,500
Brendan Jones	74	69	70	74	287	40,000
Mark Wilson	73	74	69	71	287	40,000
Jeev Milkha Singh	72	71	73	71	287	40,000
Greg Chalmers	71	71	68	77	287	40,000

	SCORES				TOTAL	MONEY
Rafa Cabrera-Bello	75	69	76	67	287	40,000
Robert Garrigus	76	68	69	75	288	38,000
Brad Kennedy	73	77	67	71	288	38,000
Geoff Ogilvy	75	74	72	67	288	38,000
Nicolas Colsaerts	73	73	71	72	289	36,750
Han Lee	73	70	75	71	289	36,750
George Coetzee	73	76	68	73	290	34,750
Robert Allenby	76	72	69	73	290	34,750
Garth Mulroy	70	74	73	73	290	34,750
Kim Hyung-sung	78	70	70	72	290	34,750
Jaco Van Zyl	74	75	70	71	290	34,750
Zhang Xin-jun	75	69	76	70	290	34,750
Danny Willett	74	73	71	73	291	32,500
Hennie Otto	76	73	71	71	291	32,500
Branden Grace	75	76	70	70	291	32,500
Alvaro Quiros	72	76	68	76	292	31,000
Richie Ramsay	78	71	72	71	292	31,000
Kyle Stanley	79	70	74	69	292	31,000
Jbe' Kruger	83	72	71	67	293	30,000
David Lynn	76	69	73	77	295	29,000
Toshinori Muto	74	71	76	74	295	29,000
Kenichi Kuboya	77	83	66	69	295	29,000
David Lipsky	78	74	69	76	297	27,500
Yuta Ikeda	70	70	82	75	297	27,500
Robert Rock	78	70	76	73	297	27,500
Johnson Wagner	75	74	73	76	298	26,500
Siddikur	77	76	76	72	301	26,000
Hu Mu	79	74	79	75	307	25,500
Masanori Kobayashi					WD	25,000

Barclays Singapore Open

Sentosa Golf Club, Singapore
Par 36-35–71; 7,372 yards

November 8-11
purse, US$6,000,000

	SCORES				TOTAL	MONEY
Matteo Manassero	70	68	64	69	271	$1,000,000
Louis Oosthuizen	70	69	65	67	271	666,660
(Manassero defeated Oosthuizen on third playoff hole.)						
Rory McIlroy	70	70	69	65	274	375,600
Thomas Bjorn	66	67	74	68	275	300,000
Adam Scott	71	66	69	70	276	232,200
Francesco Molinari	69	67	72	68	276	232,200
Chapchai Nirat	65	73	70	69	277	154,800
Anders Hansen	69	69	71	68	277	154,800
Chris Wood	70	65	70	72	277	154,800
Y.E. Yang	68	73	68	69	278	107,550
Paul Casey	68	73	67	70	278	107,550
Adilson Da Silva	72	70	66	70	278	107,550
Jaco Van Zyl	68	71	70	69	278	107,550
Richard Green	69	72	69	69	279	88,200
Phil Mickelson	73	70	69	67	279	88,200
George Coetzee	72	63	74	70	279	88,200
Prom Meesawat	70	70	69	71	280	74,880
Liang Wen-chong	74	66	69	71	280	74,880
Felipe Aguilar	70	72	70	68	280	74,880
S.S.P. Chowrasia	70	69	71	70	280	74,880
Rikard Karlberg	69	69	71	71	280	74,880
Gaganjeet Bhullar	71	69	69	72	281	66,900
Shiv Kapur	70	68	71	72	281	66,900

	SCORES				TOTAL	MONEY
Andrew Dodt	70	72	73	67	282	60,600
Gunn Charoenkul	69	70	74	69	282	60,600
Bernd Wiesberger	72	66	74	70	282	60,600
Thaworn Wiratchant	73	70	69	70	282	60,600
Simon Dyson	69	68	74	71	282	60,600
Thorbjorn Olesen	72	69	69	73	283	52,500
Lee Slattery	72	69	72	70	283	52,500
Darren Fichardt	72	68	77	66	283	52,500
Joost Luiten	71	68	68	76	283	52,500
Miguel Angel Jimenez	74	66	71	73	284	45,750
Marcus Fraser	70	70	73	71	284	45,750
Chan Yih-shin	71	69	68	76	284	45,750
Antonio Lascuna	71	71	74	68	284	45,750
Soren Kjeldsen	71	71	72	71	285	40,800
Mo Joong-kyung	72	70	71	72	285	40,800
Wisut Artjanawat	73	66	73	73	285	40,800
Anirban Lahiri	71	68	68	78	285	40,800
David Howell	69	71	72	74	286	33,000
Gregory Bourdy	70	70	72	74	286	33,000
Johan Edfors	71	71	71	73	286	33,000
Emiliano Grillo	71	71	72	72	286	33,000
Raphael Jacquelin	72	67	75	72	286	33,000
Scott Barr	72	70	73	71	286	33,000
Mardan Mamat	73	69	73	71	286	33,000
Chinnarat Phadungsil	67	71	74	74	286	33,000
Kiradech Aphibarnrat	73	70	71	72	286	33,000
Richard Sterne	70	71	71	75	287	24,000
Edoardo Molinari	70	72	73	72	287	24,000
Pablo Larrazabal	71	69	75	72	287	24,000
Rafa Cabrera-Bello	72	70	74	71	287	24,000
Baek Seuk-hyun	71	72	71	73	287	24,000
Jason Knutzon	72	71	73	71	287	24,000
Garth Mulroy	69	72	75	72	288	19,200
Choo Tze-huang	75	67	71	75	288	19,200
Simon Khan	67	74	75	73	289	17,400
Pablo Martin	67	72	75	75	289	17,400
Colin Montgomerie	72	71	71	75	289	17,400
Bio Kim	73	70	74	74	291	15,900
Quincy Quek	72	71	75	73	291	15,900
*Jonathan Woo	70	71	74	77	292	
Jyoti Randhawa	69	72	70	81	292	14,400
Gregory Havret	70	70	72	80	292	14,400
Michael Hoey	72	66	78	76	292	14,400
Danny Chia	73	69	76	75	293	12,900
Lee Sung	73	70	79	71	293	12,900
Berry Henson	71	71	81	72	295	12,000
Juvic Pagunsan	72	69	77	78	296	11,170
James Morrison	73	69	79	75	296	11,170
Kwanchai Tannin	68	74	78	80	300	8,999.95

UBS Hong Kong Open

Hong Kong Golf Club, Fanling, Hong Kong
Par 34-36–70; 6,734 yards

November 15-18
purse, US$2,000,000

	SCORES				TOTAL	MONEY
Miguel Angel Jimenez	65	67	68	65	265	US$333,330
Fredrik Andersson Hed	66	66	70	64	266	222,220
Marcus Fraser	67	69	68	64	268	125,200
Stephen Gallacher	68	68	68	65	269	84,933.33

	SCORES				TOTAL	MONEY
Peter Lawrie	68	68	67	66	269	84,933.33
Matteo Manassero	67	70	64	68	269	84,933.33
Matt Kuchar	69	69	66	67	271	60,000
Pablo Larrazabal	69	70	65	68	272	47,400
Michael Campbell	67	64	69	72	272	47,400
Chris Wood	72	70	68	63	273	34,800
Mark Foster	69	68	68	68	273	34,800
Paul Lawrie	69	69	67	68	273	34,800
Thongchai Jaidee	72	66	67	68	273	34,800
Anders Hansen	69	64	70	70	273	34,800
Ricardo Santos	71	65	73	65	274	27,600
David Horsey	67	70	71	66	274	27,600
Jose Maria Olazabal	66	71	69	68	274	27,600
Zhang Lian-wei	66	66	69	73	274	27,600
Simon Dyson	68	70	72	65	275	24,000
Paul Casey	70	71	67	67	275	24,000
James Morrison	70	67	70	68	275	24,000
Gregory Bourdy	67	73	70	66	276	20,500
Julien Quesne	68	72	69	67	276	20,500
Alejandro Canizares	74	68	67	67	276	20,500
Kim Gi-whan	70	69	69	68	276	20,500
Liang Wen-chong	71	70	67	68	276	20,500
Thaworn Wiratchant	70	68	69	69	276	20,500
Jyoti Randhawa	68	70	67	71	276	20,500
Raphael Jacquelin	72	68	64	72	276	20,500
Kiradech Aphibarnrat	70	72	68	67	277	16,085.71
Arnond Vongvanij	71	65	73	68	277	16,085.71
Chan Yih-shin	69	69	71	68	277	16,085.71
Prom Meesawat	70	71	67	69	277	16,085.71
Mardan Mamat	67	70	70	70	277	16,085.71
Kwanchai Tannin	68	69	69	71	277	16,085.71
Lorenzo Gagli	66	72	67	72	277	16,085.71
Gary Boyd	68	71	70	69	278	13,800
Kristoffer Broberg	71	70	67	70	278	13,800
Andrew Dodt	65	73	68	72	278	13,800
Juvic Pagunsan	72	68	72	67	279	11,800
Wade Ormsby	75	66	69	69	279	11,800
Joonas Granberg	70	70	69	70	279	11,800
Andrew Marshall	71	69	69	70	279	11,800
Berry Henson	71	70	68	70	279	11,800
Brett Rumford	73	68	68	70	279	11,800
Daisuke Kataoka	68	67	72	72	279	11,800
Alex Cejka	72	69	70	69	280	9,800
Pariya Junhasavasdikul	71	71	69	69	280	9,800
Javi Colomo	64	71	72	73	280	9,800
Soren Kjeldsen	72	69	74	66	281	8,400
Antonio Lascuna	71	71	70	69	281	8,400
Peter Hedblom	75	66	70	70	281	8,400
Rhys Davies	71	71	69	70	281	8,400
Steve Webster	71	71	73	67	282	6,371.43
Adam Blyth	71	70	72	69	282	6,371.43
Scott Strange	73	69	70	70	282	6,371.43
Chinnarat Phadungsil	70	69	72	71	282	6,371.43
Joel Sjoholm	67	72	72	71	282	6,371.43
Simon Khan	67	73	70	72	282	6,371.43
Mo Joong-kyung	69	71	68	74	282	6,371.43
Gregory Havret	74	68	71	70	283	5,000
Johan Edfors	70	71	71	71	283	5,000
Jordan Gibb	72	67	72	72	283	5,000
Lee Slattery	69	72	69	73	283	5,000
Lin Wen-tang	72	68	68	75	283	5,000
Kalle Samooja	69	73	72	70	284	4,200
Zaw Moe	72	68	71	73	284	4,200

	SCORES				TOTAL	MONEY
Jean-Baptiste Gonnet	72	69	69	74	284	4,200
David Howell	68	70	75	72	285	3,725
Richard Bland	70	72	71	72	285	3,725
Adilson Da Silva	69	72	72	75	288	3,000.30
Scott Hend	68	74	78	71	291	2,994.54
Timothy Tang	74	67	75	75	291	2,994.54

King's Cup

Singha Park Khon Kaen Golf Club, Khon Kaen, Thailand
Par 36-36–72; 7,546 yards

November 29-December 2
purse, US$500,000

	SCORES				TOTAL	MONEY
Arnond Vongvanij	65	70	67	64	266	US$79,250
Thaworn Wiratchant	69	66	65	68	268	42,375
Mardan Mamat	63	70	66	69	268	42,375
Thammanoon Sriroj	70	66	68	65	269	22,575
Udorn Duangdecha	65	68	69	67	269	22,575
Boonchu Ruangkit	67	67	71	67	272	12,980
Thongchai Jaidee	67	69	69	67	272	12,980
Prom Meesawat	65	69	70	68	272	12,980
Kiradech Aphibarnrat	67	68	68	69	272	12,980
Piya Swangarunporn	70	65	67	70	272	12,980
Quincy Quek	69	66	71	68	274	7,825
Simon Griffiths	69	70	67	68	274	7,825
Chris Rodgers	64	69	72	69	274	7,825
Chiang Chen-chih	70	64	71	69	274	7,825
Pawin Ingkhapradit	71	68	66	69	274	7,825
Javi Colomo	65	72	65	72	274	7,825
Baek Seuk-hyun	70	70	71	64	275	6,100
Antonio Lascuna	69	71	67	68	275	6,100
Prayad Marksaeng	70	69	67	69	275	6,100
Elmer Salvador	68	66	70	71	275	6,100
Pariya Junhasavasdikul	66	69	66	74	275	6,100
Jonathan Moore	70	69	70	67	276	5,325
Panuphol Pittayarat	69	70	68	69	276	5,325
Lin Wen-tang	66	68	69	73	276	5,325
Wade Ormsby	71	63	69	73	276	5,325

Thailand Golf Championship

Amata Spring Country Club, Bangkok, Thailand
Par 36-36–72; 7,453 yards

December 6-9
purse, US$1,000,000

	SCORES				TOTAL	MONEY
Charl Schwartzel	65	65	68	65	263	US$158,500
Bubba Watson	68	70	71	65	274	84,750
Thitiphun Chuayprakong	66	67	71	70	274	84,750
Sergio Garcia	69	69	68	70	276	49,300
Park Hyun-bin	68	74	67	68	277	41,000
Kiradech Aphibarnrat	68	71	72	67	278	25,960
Prom Meesawat	69	72	70	67	278	25,960
Simon Dyson	72	71	67	68	278	25,960
Scott Hend	70	68	69	71	278	25,960
Daniel Chopra	67	67	69	75	278	25,960
Jonathan Moore	73	72	67	67	279	16,425
Chapchai Nirat	70	73	67	69	279	16,425

	SCORES				TOTAL	MONEY
Ryo Ishikawa	70	66	73	70	279	16,425
Lee Westwood	70	69	70	70	279	16,425
Anirban Lahiri	70	69	70	71	280	14,100
Nicolas Colsaerts	72	67	70	71	280	14,100
Kalle Samooja	71	72	72	66	281	12,400
Yoshinobu Tsukada	70	72	72	67	281	12,400
Thongchai Jaidee	69	71	72	69	281	12,400
Darren Beck	69	70	72	70	281	12,400
Shiv Kapur	73	71	72	66	282	11,400
Gunn Charoenkul	73	70	72	68	283	10,350
Wade Ormsby	69	72	73	69	283	10,350
Javi Colomo	67	73	73	70	283	10,350
Darren Clarke	70	72	69	72	283	10,350
Hunter Mahan	71	69	70	73	283	10,350
Masanori Kobayashi	68	67	73	75	283	10,350

Iskandar Johor Open

Horizon Hills Golf & Country Club, Johor Bahru, Malaysia
Par 35-36–71; 6,783 yards
(Event shortened to 54 holes—rain.)

December 13-16
purse, US$2,000,000

	SCORES			TOTAL	MONEY
Sergio Garcia	68	69	61	198	US$317,000
Jonathan Moore	69	71	61	201	217,000
Thongchai Jaidee	66	71	65	202	122,000
Daniel Chopra	68	66	69	203	98,600
Thaworn Wiratchant	71	69	65	205	60,440
Masanori Kobayashi	71	67	67	205	60,440
Angelo Que	67	70	68	205	60,440
Antonio Lascuna	68	68	69	205	60,440
Chapchai Nirat	68	67	70	205	60,440
Shiv Kapur	67	70	69	206	37,750
S.S.P. Chowrasia	67	69	70	206	37,750
Gunn Charoenkul	72	68	67	207	31,766.67
Berry Henson	70	69	68	207	31,766.67
Mardan Mamat	70	69	68	207	31,766.67
Baek Seuk-hyun	66	72	70	208	27,600
Scott Barr	72	65	71	208	27,600
John Daly	74	69	65	208	27,600
Javi Colomo	72	67	70	209	24,700
Arnond Vongvanij	70	69	70	209	24,700
*Gavin Kyle Green	70	68	71	209	
Chawalit Plaphol	73	68	69	210	20,400
Gaganjeet Bhullar	71	70	69	210	20,400
Daisuke Maruyama	71	70	69	210	20,400
Himmat Rai	76	66	68	210	20,400
Kalle Samooja	67	73	70	210	20,400
Anirban Lahiri	70	69	71	210	20,400
Rick Kulacz	68	71	71	210	20,400
Marcus Fraser	70	68	72	210	20,400
Siddikur	72	71	67	210	20,400
Wade Ormsby	71	72	67	210	20,400
Unho Park	65	71	74	210	20,400

OneAsia Tour

Enjoy Jakarta Indonesia Open

Emeralda Golf Club, Jakarta, Indonesia
Par 36-36–72; 7,184 yards

March 22-25
purse, US$1,000,000

	SCORES				TOTAL	MONEY
Nick Cullen	72	66	67	74	279	US$172,000
David Smail	68	69	74	69	280	100,500
Michael Long	75	73	68	65	281	51,066.66
Yoshikazu Haku	70	69	74	68	281	51,066.66
David Oh	72	67	71	71	281	51,066.66
Satoshi Tomiyama	71	70	74	67	282	32,333.33
Hu Mu	73	68	71	70	282	32,333.33
Stephen Leaney	72	70	67	73	282	32,333.33
Rory Hie	73	70	72	68	283	24,666.66
Liang Wen-chong	69	73	72	69	283	24,666.66
Park Eun-shin	74	69	69	71	283	24,666.66
Prayad Marksaeng	74	68	74	68	284	19,000
Kim Meen-whee	70	70	74	70	284	19,000
Naoto Nakanishi	72	71	73	69	285	15,800
Jay Choi	71	72	71	71	285	15,800
Ashley Hall	70	74	67	74	285	15,800
Andik Mauludin	71	74	72	69	286	11,490
Masaya Tomida	72	70	76	68	286	11,490
Thaworn Wiratchant	75	71	69	71	286	11,490
Terry Pilkadaris	73	71	70	72	286	11,490
Hiroyuki Fujita	70	71	72	73	286	11,490
Scott Laycock	76	71	71	69	287	9,700
Mark Brown	76	72	71	68	287	9,700
Matthew Griffin	73	74	69	71	287	9,700
Mamo Osanai	71	72	69	75	287	9,700

Volvo China Open

Binhai Lake Golf Club, Tianjin, China
Par 36-36–72; 7,667 yards

April 19-22
purse, RMB20,000,000

	SCORES				TOTAL	MONEY
Branden Grace	67	67	64	69	267	US$526,675.62
Nicolas Colsaerts	68	67	66	69	270	351,117.08
Richard Finch	67	73	65	66	271	197,819.56
Victor Dubuisson	69	68	68	67	272	145,994.62
George Coetzee	72	67	64	69	272	145,994.62
Ricardo Gonzalez	68	73	65	67	273	83,678.30
Francesco Molinari	72	65	67	69	273	83,678.30
Marcus Fraser	67	69	67	70	273	83,678.30
Alexander Noren	68	72	63	70	273	83,678.30
Fabrizio Zanotti	70	68	64	71	273	83,678.30
Richard Green	69	70	69	66	274	54,458.31
Julien Quesne	70	68	69	67	274	54,458.31
Ignacio Garrido	67	69	67	71	274	54,458.31
Peter Hanson	71	69	70	65	275	45,504.82

	SCORES				TOTAL	MONEY
Matthew Baldwin	65	73	70	67	275	45,504.82
Paul Lawrie	72	67	68	68	275	45,504.82
Jean-Baptiste Gonnet	66	67	70	72	275	45,504.82
Peter Whiteford	70	68	72	66	276	38,047.08
Jbe' Kruger	66	72	69	69	276	38,047.08
Pablo Larrazabal	68	70	69	69	276	38,047.08
Robert-Jan Derksen	68	69	69	70	276	38,047.08
Joost Luiten	66	71	68	71	276	38,047.08
Scott Jamieson	74	67	69	67	277	32,390.58
Damien McGrane	67	71	71	68	277	32,390.58
Ricardo Santos	70	68	69	70	277	32,390.58
Edoardo Molinari	70	69	68	70	277	32,390.58
Choi Jin-ho	69	67	70	71	277	32,390.58
Fredrik Andersson Hed	66	74	64	73	277	32,390.58
Ian Poulter	71	71	70	66	278	26,273.61
Brett Rumford	73	69	69	67	278	26,273.61
David Drysdale	70	72	68	68	278	26,273.61
Soren Kjeldsen	68	72	69	69	278	26,273.61
Rafa Cabrera-Bello	70	70	68	70	278	26,273.61
Scott Strange	66	71	69	72	278	26,273.61
Gary Boyd	66	67	71	74	278	26,273.61
Anthony Wall	68	72	71	68	279	22,436.40
Simon Dyson	71	70	68	70	279	22,436.40
Andrea Pavan	72	67	68	72	279	22,436.40
Rhys Davies	72	69	71	68	280	19,908.36
James Morrison	71	69	70	70	280	19,908.36
Gareth Paddison	68	68	71	73	280	19,908.36
Danny Willett	69	68	69	74	280	19,908.36
Johan Edfors	71	69	66	74	280	19,908.36
Lorenzo Gagli	70	71	73	67	281	16,748.30
Bradley Dredge	70	72	72	67	281	16,748.30
Markus Brier	68	74	72	67	281	16,748.30
Keith Horne	72	68	72	69	281	16,748.30
Jamie Donaldson	71	71	70	69	281	16,748.30
An Byeong-hun	69	73	72	68	282	14,009.58
Soren Hansen	72	70	70	70	282	14,009.58
Shane Lowry	71	69	68	74	282	14,009.58
Richie Ramsay	67	75	72	69	283	10,862.69
Graeme Storm	67	75	72	69	283	10,862.69
Huang Wenyi	72	68	73	70	283	10,862.69
Oscar Floren	72	69	72	70	283	10,862.69
Estanislao Goya	73	69	71	70	283	10,862.69
Oliver Wilson	70	67	73	73	283	10,862.69
Thorbjorn Olesen	68	73	69	73	283	10,862.69
Ashley Hall	71	71	66	75	283	10,862.69
Jeev Milkha Singh	75	66	73	70	284	8,532.15
Michael Hoey	74	68	71	71	284	8,532.15
Colin Montgomerie	68	72	72	72	284	8,532.15
Peter Lawrie	69	71	74	71	285	7,900.14
Alejandro Canizares	69	73	75	69	286	6,952.12
Mikko Ilonen	72	70	74	70	286	6,952.12
Zhang Lian-wei	69	71	75	71	286	6,952.12
Niclas Fasth	71	71	71	73	286	6,952.12
Gareth Maybin	71	70	71	74	286	6,952.12
Felipe Aguilar	71	71	73	73	288	6,004.11
Carlos Del Moral	72	70	78	71	291	5,759.20

GS Caltex Maekyung Open

Nam Seoul Golf & Country Club, Seoul, South Korea
Par 36-36—72; 6,964 yards

May 10-13
purse, KRW1,000,000,000

	SCORES				TOTAL	MONEY
Bio Kim	69	69	67	68	273	US$171,146.42
Ryu Hyun-woo	73	71	68	66	278	102,687.85
Kang Kyung-nam	68	70	73	68	279	58,189.78
Park Sang-hyun	68	69	70	74	281	46,209.53
Lee Sang-hee	70	72	69	71	282	32,089.95
Choi Ho-sung	70	70	68	74	282	32,089.95
Kim Seung-hyuk	70	73	71	69	283	24,388.36
Lee Tae-hee	75	69	70	69	283	24,388.36
Lee Jung-hwan	69	74	73	68	284	17,884.80
Hur In-hoi	68	76	72	68	284	17,884.80
Park Jun-won	70	74	68	72	284	17,884.80
Jamie Arnold	69	74	73	69	285	11,695.00
Lee Seong-ho	70	69	73	73	285	11,695.00
Hwang Inn-choon	69	71	68	77	285	11,695.00
Yoon Jung-ho	71	70	75	70	286	8,999.45
Garrett Sapp	68	71	75	72	286	8,999.45
Stephen Leaney	71	71	72	72	286	8,999.45
*Kim Si-woo	73	73	68	72	286	
Jason Kang	70	72	70	74	286	8,999.45
Lucas Lee	71	70	70	75	286	8,999.45
K.T. Kim	70	72	70	74	286	8,999.45
Scott Laycock	71	72	72	72	287	7,482.52
David Oh	74	72	69	72	287	7,482.52
Lee Ki-sang	74	72	73	68	287	7,482.52
Thaworn Wiratchant	74	68	71	74	287	7,482.52
Koichi Kitamura	68	71	74	74	287	7,482.52

SK Telecom Open

Pinx Golf Club, Jeju Island, South Korea
Par 36-36—72; 7,366 yards

May 17-20
purse, KRW900,000,000

	SCORES				TOTAL	MONEY
Bio Kim	68	68	67	67	270	US$170,488.45
Park Sang-hyun	71	65	70	67	273	85,244.22
*Kim Si-woo	69	70	66	70	275	
Joo Heung-chol	72	68	65	70	275	51,146.53
Hur In-hoi	71	71	63	71	276	37,507.46
Kim Gi-whan	72	72	67	68	279	26,851.93
Mark Brown	72	66	72	69	279	26,851.93
Rory Hie	70	66	72	72	280	20,458.61
Simon Yates	71	70	70	70	281	17,475.07
Park Jun-won	70	70	70	72	282	15,770.18
Lee Tae-hee	73	69	70	71	283	13,639.07
Lee Sang-hee	72	71	67	73	283	13,639.07
Anthony Brown	73	68	72	71	284	11,579.00
Aaron Townsend	71	74	68	71	284	11,579.00
K.J. Choi	73	71	69	71	284	11,579.00
Kang Wook-soon	73	72	71	69	285	8,346.18
Ted Oh	75	69	72	69	285	8,346.18
Jung Ji-ho	75	68	72	70	285	8,346.18
Kim Seong-yong	70	75	71	69	285	8,346.18
Choi Ho-sung	72	70	72	71	285	8,346.18
Jamie Arnold	71	74	70	70	285	8,346.18

	SCORES				TOTAL	MONEY
Nam Young-woo	70	70	73	72	285	8,346.18
Chung Joon	73	68	77	67	285	8,346.18
Terry Pilkadaris	75	67	71	72	285	8,346.18
Mo Joong-kyung	72	67	72	74	285	8,346.18
Ashley Hall	71	70	70	74	285	8,346.18

Thailand Open

Suwan Golf & Country Club, Nalornpathom, Thailand
Par 36-36–72; 7,077 yards

August 9-12
purse, US$1,000,000

	SCORES				TOTAL	MONEY
Chris Wood	67	64	67	67	265	US$180,686
Jang Dong-kyu	68	69	67	63	267	105,575
Arnond Vongvanij	67	67	69	65	268	53,645.33
Wisut Artjanawat	66	64	71	67	268	53,645.33
Lee Dong-hwan	67	67	67	67	268	53,645.33
Mark Brown	70	65	70	65	270	37,818
Yasunori Yoshida	64	72	70	65	271	30,814.33
Kim Meen-whee	69	68	66	68	271	30,814.33
Chan Shih-chang	65	66	68	72	271	30,814.33
Scott Arnold	70	68	67	67	272	22,323
Choi Ho-sung	66	69	69	68	272	22,323
Udorn Duangdecha	70	65	68	69	272	22,323
David McKenzie	65	66	70	71	272	22,323
Pawin Ingkhapradit	70	66	72	65	273	13,767.87
Kenichi Kuboya	71	66	70	66	273	13,767.87
Michael Wright	70	69	67	67	273	13,767.87
Chapchai Nirat	70	70	66	67	273	13,767.87
Kiradech Aphibarnrat	66	70	69	68	273	13,767.87
Peter O'Malley	70	70	65	68	273	13,767.87
Thaworn Wiratchant	68	64	72	69	273	13,767.87
Prom Meesawat	66	63	72	72	273	13,767.87
Kim Hyung-tae	64	73	69	68	274	9,937.60
David Horsey	70	69	67	68	274	9,937.60
Terry Pilkadaris	68	71	66	69	274	9,937.60
Choi Jin-ho	66	66	72	70	274	9,937.60
Gareth Paddison	70	67	67	70	274	9,937.60

Charity High1 Resort Open

High1 Country Club, Gohan, South Korea
Par 36-36–72; 7,148 yards

September 6-9
purse, KRW1,000,000,000

	SCORES				TOTAL	MONEY
Matthew Griffin	67	70	69	72	278	US$177,777.78
Kang Kyung-nam	74	70	67	68	279	71,111.11
Park Sang-hyun	69	71	68	71	279	71,111.11
Choi Ho-sung	71	68	71	70	280	39,111.11
Bio Kim	72	70	67	71	280	39,111.11
Garrett Sapp	74	72	70	65	281	27,377.77
Park Jae-kyung	72	71	71	67	281	27,377.77
Aaron Townsend	70	69	70	72	281	27,377.77
Gareth Paddison	75	70	70	68	283	21,333.33
Lucas Lee	72	72	70	70	284	17,777.77
Son Joon-eob	72	72	70	70	284	17,777.77
David McKenzie	70	73	70	71	284	17,777.77

	SCORES				TOTAL	MONEY
Lee Jun-seok	70	67	73	74	284	17,777.77
Lee Jung-hwan	70	72	72	71	285	13,155.55
Choi Hyuk-jae	74	70	70	71	285	13,155.55
Mo Joong-kyung	70	72	70	73	285	13,155.55
Park Ju-hyuk	69	72	71	73	285	13,155.55
Jang Jun-hung	71	74	72	69	286	10,666.67
Lee Tae-hee	72	67	75	72	286	10,666.67
Rory Hie	73	70	70	73	286	10,666.67
Han Min-kyu	68	71	76	72	287	9,066.66
Hong Soon-sang	70	72	73	72	287	9,066.66
Park Hyun-bin	69	74	71	73	287	9,066.66
Jason Kang	66	74	73	74	287	9,066.66
Jamie Arnold	75	68	74	71	288	7,644.44
Kim Ki-soo	72	72	75	69	288	7,644.44
Kim Meen-whee	74	69	72	73	288	7,644.44
Song Young-hoon	74	65	73	76	288	7,644.44

Nanshan China Masters

Nanshan International Golf Club, Nanshan, China
Par 36-35–71; 7,151 yards

October 11-14
purse, US$1,000,000

	SCORES				TOTAL	MONEY
Liang Wen-chong	68	67	68	73	276	US$180,686
Y.E. Yang	71	68	68	69	276	105,575
(Liang defeated Yang on fifth playoff hole.)						
Aaron Townsend	69	67	69	72	277	69,333
Louis Oosthuizen	71	72	69	67	279	43,140.33
Wang Jeung-hun	69	71	70	69	279	43,140.33
Garrett Sapp	73	70	67	69	279	43,140.33
Michael Hendry	72	73	67	68	280	33,616
Steven Jones	68	74	72	67	281	28,363
Rory Hie	74	69	69	69	281	28,363
Scott Laycock	70	71	70	70	281	28,363
Mark Brown	73	68	75	66	282	22,060.50
Michael Wright	73	71	69	69	282	22,060.50
Simon Yates	71	70	74	68	283	17,858.33
Chris Campbell	70	72	72	69	283	17,858.33
David McKendrick	70	70	70	73	283	17,858.33
Douglas Holloway	73	70	73	68	284	13,796.33
Clint Rice	71	75	68	70	284	13,796.33
Gareth Paddison	70	69	73	72	284	13,796.33
Song Young-han	69	74	74	68	285	11,362.66
Andre Stolz	71	71	71	72	285	11,362.66
Terry Pilkadaris	71	71	69	74	285	11,362.66
Daniel Fox	70	74	71	71	286	10,435
Jamie Arnold	69	70	72	75	286	10,435
Mitchell Brown	73	71	67	75	286	10,435
Kim Hyung-tae	71	72	70	74	287	9,454

Kolon Korea Open

Woo Jeong Hills Country Club, Cheonan, South Korea
Par 36-35–71; 7,213 yards

October 18-21
purse, KRW1,000,000,000

	SCORES				TOTAL	MONEY
Kim Dae-sub	72	68	70	69	279	US$267,236.77
Kim Dae-hyun	71	73	66	71	281	87,297.35
Y.E. Yang	73	70	72	67	282	44,539.46
Kang Kyung-nam	68	69	77	68	282	44,539.46
Ryu Hyun-woo	75	69	73	66	283	30,286.83
Seung-Yul Noh	73	74	68	69	284	26,723.68
David Oh	73	72	72	68	285	22,566.66
Ryo Ishikawa	75	72	69	69	285	22,566.66
Choi Ho-sung	71	71	72	71	285	22,566.66
Chae Bum-geun	72	74	71	70	287	17,815.78
Sang-Moon Bae	79	72	72	65	288	14,341.70
Choi Jin-ho	74	72	71	71	288	14,341.70
Lee Sang-hee	77	68	69	74	288	14,341.70
Chung Joon	76	75	67	71	289	10,689.47
Park Eun-shin	79	73	71	67	290	8,961.34
Maeng Dong-seop	73	74	72	71	290	8,961.34
Mo Joong-kyung	78	70	71	71	290	8,961.34
Lee Seong-ho	74	70	73	73	290	8,961.34
Kang Wook-soon	73	71	69	77	290	8,961.34
Kim Seung-hyuk	74	73	74	70	291	7,928.02
Park Jun-won	74	76	70	71	291	7,928.02
Park Hyun-bin	73	72	69	77	291	7,928.02
Hwang In-choon	74	70	75	73	292	7,438.09
Byun Jin-jae	77	71	76	68	292	7,438.09
Park Sang-hyun	76	71	76	70	293	6,888.77
Rory Hie	73	72	78	70	293	6,888.77
Lucas Lee	72	71	76	74	293	6,888.77
*Lee Chang-woo	74	76	68	75	293	

Emirates Australian Open

See Australasian Tour.

Australian PGA Championship

See Australasian Tour.

Japan Tour

Token Homemate Cup

Token Tado Country Club, Kuwana, Mie
Par 35-36–71; 7,081 yards

April 12-15
purse, ¥130,000,000

	SCORES				TOTAL	MONEY
Brendan Jones	68	69	70	62	269	¥26,000,000
Ryuichi Oda	65	74	67	65	271	13,000,000
Mamo Osanai	66	71	68	67	272	8,840,000
Hideto Tanihara	69	70	69	65	273	5,373,333
Satoshi Tomiyama	68	67	71	67	273	5,373,333
Shingo Katayama	69	70	65	69	273	5,373,333
Yoshinori Fujimoto	72	68	70	64	274	4,290,000
Tomohiro Kondo	73	68	70	64	275	3,965,000
Masamichi Uehira	67	71	71	67	276	3,666,000
Hidemasa Hoshino	70	72	69	66	277	3,016,000
Yuta Ikeda	70	72	69	66	277	3,016,000
Hiroyuki Fujita	70	70	70	67	277	3,016,000
Ryo Ishikawa	69	69	68	71	277	3,016,000
Kim Do-hoon	67	71	72	68	278	2,301,000
Kenichi Kuboya	69	67	72	70	278	2,301,000
Kunihiro Kamii	69	71	74	65	279	1,976,000
Yui Ueda	66	69	75	69	279	1,976,000
Taichiro Kiyota	71	70	67	71	279	1,976,000
Toru Taniguchi	69	70	73	68	280	1,437,428
Kim Hyung-tae	70	71	71	68	280	1,437,428
Masatsugu Morofuji	71	71	69	69	280	1,437,428
Yasuharu Imano	67	76	71	66	280	1,437,428
Steven Conran	69	68	72	71	280	1,437,428
S.K. Ho	70	69	70	71	280	1,437,428
Kiyoshi Murota	68	71	70	71	280	1,437,428

Tsuruya Open

Yamanohara Golf Club, Kawanishi, Hyogo
Par 35-36–71; 6,767 yards

April 19-22
purse, ¥110,000,000

	SCORES				TOTAL	MONEY
Hiroyuki Fujita	68	66	68	67	269	¥22,000,000
Lee Kyoung-hoon	73	64	66	70	273	11,000,000
Masahiro Kawamura	67	70	70	67	274	5,720,000
Sushi Ishigaki	70	68	68	68	274	5,720,000
Ryuichi Oda	66	67	70	71	274	5,720,000
Masatsugu Morofuji	70	65	72	68	275	3,648,333
Cho Min-gyu	73	66	67	69	275	3,648,333
Kodai Ichihara	71	65	67	72	275	3,648,333
Azuma Yano	71	69	69	67	276	2,772,000
Hideto Tanihara	68	71	69	68	276	2,772,000
Kunihiro Kamii	69	69	66	72	276	2,772,000
K.T. Kim	69	66	68	73	276	2,772,000
Park Sung-joon	71	68	71	67	277	1,974,500
Brendan Jones	71	69	69	68	277	1,974,500

	SCORES				TOTAL	MONEY
S.K. Ho	68	68	67	74	277	1,974,500
Han Lee	67	69	63	78	277	1,974,500
Naomichi Ozaki	70	70	71	67	278	1,569,333
Yuta Ikeda	71	69	66	72	278	1,569,333
Shingo Katayama	62	73	69	74	278	1,569,333
Tomohiro Kondo	70	70	69	70	279	1,173,333
Ryo Ishikawa	73	68	67	71	279	1,173,333
Kiyoshi Miyazato	72	66	70	71	279	1,173,333
I.J. Jang	70	69	68	72	279	1,173,333
David Smail	69	70	68	72	279	1,173,333
Kim Hyung-sung	67	71	68	73	279	1,173,333

The Crowns

Nagoya Golf Club, Wago Course, Togo, Aichi
Par 35-35–70; 6,545 yards

April 26-29
purse, ¥120,000,000

	SCORES				TOTAL	MONEY
I.J. Jang	71	69	66	66	272	¥24,000,000
Steven Conran	66	65	73	70	274	10,080,000
Yoshikazu Haku	66	71	67	70	274	10,080,000
Hideto Tanihara	69	69	69	69	276	5,280,000
Prayad Marksaeng	69	71	67	69	276	5,280,000
Lee Kyoung-hoon	72	68	71	66	277	3,693,600
S.K. Ho	70	71	69	67	277	3,693,600
Kenichi Kuboya	65	70	73	69	277	3,693,600
Shigeru Nonaka	72	71	63	71	277	3,693,600
J.B. Park	68	70	68	71	277	3,693,600
Masamichi Uehira	72	70	69	67	278	2,214,000
Shinichi Yokota	71	70	70	67	278	2,214,000
Yui Ueda	74	68	69	67	278	2,214,000
Tomohiro Kondo	72	71	68	67	278	2,214,000
Tetsuya Haraguchi	70	68	71	69	278	2,214,000
Ryo Ishikawa	69	71	68	70	278	2,214,000
Kim Sung-yoon	68	71	68	71	278	2,214,000
Tadahiro Takayama	69	69	67	73	278	2,214,000
Sushi Ishigaki	73	68	71	67	279	1,416,000
Chinnarat Phadungsil	72	73	67	67	279	1,416,000
Azuma Yano	74	67	70	68	279	1,416,000
Masahiro Kawamura	74	69	66	70	279	1,416,000
Masanori Kobayashi	71	70	66	72	279	1,416,000
Daisuke Maruyama	73	70	69	68	280	1,080,000
Ryuichi Oda	71	72	67	70	280	1,080,000
Takashi Kanemoto	69	74	66	71	280	1,080,000

Japan PGA Championship

Karasuyamajo Country Club, Tochigi
Par 36-35–71; 7,193 yards

May 10-13
purse, ¥150,000,000

	SCORES				TOTAL	MONEY
Toru Taniguchi	65	70	76	73	284	¥30,000,000
Keiichiro Fukabori	72	66	76	71	285	15,000,000
Shunsuke Sonoda	69	72	74	73	288	10,200,000
Kim Do-hoon	75	69	75	70	289	6,600,000
Hideto Tanihara	67	73	74	75	289	6,600,000
Yuta Ikeda	76	69	75	70	290	4,452,500

	SCORES				TOTAL	MONEY
Lee Kyoung-hon	70	72	76	72	290	4,452,500
Lee Dong-hwan	72	71	75	72	290	4,452,500
Brendan Jones	70	71	76	73	290	4,452,500
Tomohiro Kondo	70	70	75	75	290	4,452,500
Yoshinobu Tsukada	73	72	71	74	290	4,452,500
Kaname Yokoo	71	72	76	72	291	2,730,000
Tetsuya Haraguchi	71	72	75	73	291	2,730,000
S.K. Ho	74	70	73	74	291	2,730,000
Masanori Kobayashi	72	70	74	75	291	2,730,000
Shingo Katayama	70	72	74	75	291	2,730,000
Yui Ueda	70	70	75	76	291	2,730,000
Kouki Idoki	70	74	77	71	292	1,770,000
Yoshikazu Haku	71	68	80	73	292	1,770,000
Toshinori Muto	73	71	78	70	292	1,770,000
Han Lee	73	71	74	74	292	1,770,000
Park Sung-joon	69	72	75	76	292	1,770,000
Koumei Oda	73	70	70	79	292	1,770,000
I.J. Jang	71	71	71	79	292	1,770,000
Hiroo Kawai	73	71	76	73	293	1,170,000
Tatsunori Nukaga	71	70	77	75	293	1,170,000
Norio Shinozaki	74	69	80	70	293	1,170,000
Akinori Tani	70	69	78	76	293	1,170,000
Kiyoshi Murota	73	72	72	76	293	1,170,000
Kunihiro Kamii	71	72	73	77	293	1,170,000
Akio Sadakata	73	71	72	77	293	1,170,000

Totoumi Hamamatsu Open

Grandee Hamanako Golf Club, Hamamatsu, Shizuoka — May 17-20
Par 36-36–72; 7,054 yards — purse, ¥100,000,000

	SCORES				TOTAL	MONEY
Jay Choi	68	71	68	65	272	¥20,000,000
Yoshinori Fujimoto	64	70	68	71	273	10,000,000
Hideto Tanihara	68	70	66	70	274	6,800,000
Kurt Barnes	68	74	68	65	275	4,800,000
S.K. Ho	67	73	67	69	276	4,000,000
Toshinori Muto	69	69	72	68	278	3,192,500
Ryu Hyun-wu	70	72	68	68	278	3,192,500
Tomohiro Kondo	68	70	71	69	278	3,192,500
Brendan Jones	65	71	72	70	278	3,192,500
David Oh	69	75	72	63	279	2,062,857
Koumei Oda	70	73	72	64	279	2,062,857
Hiroyuki Fujita	75	69	68	67	279	2,062,857
Yuta Ikeda	70	72	69	68	279	2,062,857
Hiroshi Iwata	66	70	73	70	279	2,062,857
Toru Taniguchi	70	73	66	70	279	2,062,857
Daisuke Kataoka	66	71	71	71	279	2,062,857
Prayad Marksaeng	68	73	71	68	280	1,303,333
J.B. Park	67	75	70	68	280	1,303,333
Wu Ashun	69	73	69	69	280	1,303,333
Steven Conran	68	75	68	69	280	1,303,333
Keiichiro Fukabori	70	73	68	69	280	1,303,333
Mamo Osanai	67	74	68	71	280	1,303,333
*Kenta Konishi	65	79	69	68	281	
Sushi Ishigaki	65	77	69	70	281	886,666
Koichi Sugimoto	69	73	69	70	281	886,666
Masahiro Kawamura	69	74	67	71	281	886,666
Kaname Yokoo	70	74	66	71	281	886,666
Satoshi Kodaira	72	68	69	72	281	886,666
Lee Dong-hwan	69	72	68	72	281	886,666

Diamond Cup

The Country Club Japan, Noda, Chiba
Par 36-36–72; 7,199 yards

May 24-27
purse, ¥120,000,000

	SCORES				TOTAL	MONEY
Hiroyuki Fujita	66	65	70	73	274	¥24,000,000
Kiradech Aphibarnrat	68	67	70	72	277	12,000,000
Yasuharu Imano	72	68	69	69	278	6,240,000
Hidezumi Shirakata	70	69	70	69	278	6,240,000
Jay Choi	64	70	72	72	278	6,240,000
Yoshinori Fujimoto	71	71	65	72	279	4,140,000
Takashi Kanemoto	67	70	67	75	279	4,140,000
Toshinori Muto	72	69	67	72	280	3,660,000
Park Eun-shin	68	73	72	68	281	3,144,000
Norio Shinozaki	68	70	72	71	281	3,144,000
Kim Sung-yoon	69	72	69	71	281	3,144,000
Kurt Barnes	68	70	75	69	282	2,664,000
K.T. Kim	66	72	74	71	283	2,154,000
Cho Min-gyu	72	69	74	68	283	2,154,000
Masahiro Kawamura	70	70	71	72	283	2,154,000
Toru Taniguchi	72	70	68	73	283	2,154,000
Sushi Ishigaki	71	68	74	71	284	1,314,000
David Oh	73	70	71	70	284	1,314,000
Kim Do-hoon	69	68	75	72	284	1,314,000
Shingo Katayama	69	69	74	72	284	1,314,000
Yuta Ikeda	72	68	72	72	284	1,314,000
Hideto Tanihara	73	67	72	72	284	1,314,000
Nobumitsu Yuhara	72	69	71	72	284	1,314,000
Chapchai Nirat	70	70	77	67	284	1,314,000
Tetsuji Hiratsuka	70	71	70	73	284	1,314,000
Hirofumi Miyase	69	67	74	74	284	1,314,000
Steven Conran	70	70	70	74	284	1,314,000
Hwang Jung-gon	75	67	67	75	284	1,314,000

Japan Tour Championship

Shishido Hills Country Club, West Course, Kasama, Ibaraki
Par 36-35–71; 7,313 yards

May 31-June 3
purse, ¥150,000,000

	SCORES				TOTAL	MONEY
Yoshinori Fujimoto	68	68	67	68	271	¥30,000,000
Masamichi Uehira	69	67	68	69	273	15,000,000
Yuta Ikeda	72	65	68	69	274	10,200,000
Juvic Pagunsan	70	74	66	65	275	7,200,000
Tetsuji Hiratsuka	74	65	70	67	276	5,450,000
K.T. Kim	70	64	73	69	276	5,450,000
Masahiro Kawamura	66	70	68	72	276	5,450,000
Prayad Marksaeng	67	74	68	69	278	4,402,500
Lee Dong-hwan	68	73	65	72	278	4,402,500
Kaname Yokoo	69	69	72	69	279	3,780,000
Brendan Jones	66	71	71	71	279	3,780,000
Azuma Yano	71	73	69	67	280	2,917,500
Hiroyuki Fujita	70	65	76	69	280	2,917,500
Koumei Oda	73	69	66	72	280	2,917,500
Kazuhiro Yamashita	71	72	65	72	280	2,917,500
Kim Hyung-tae	73	70	68	70	281	2,430,000
Chinnarat Phadungsil	72	70	73	67	282	2,140,000
Katsunori Kuwabara	73	66	71	72	282	2,140,000
Tomohiro Kondo	68	72	70	72	282	2,140,000

	SCORES				TOTAL	MONEY
Kenichi Kuboya	71	71	73	68	283	1,650,000
Park Eun-shin	70	75	69	69	283	1,650,000
Lee Kyoung-hoon	70	69	72	72	283	1,650,000
Shingo Katayama	67	72	72	72	283	1,650,000
Satoru Hirota	72	69	70	72	283	1,650,000
Hisashi Sawada	68	75	71	70	284	1,260,000
Kunihiro Kamii	71	70	71	72	284	1,260,000
Ryu Hyun-wu	69	73	68	74	284	1,260,000
Kim Do-hoon	67	67	75	75	284	1,260,000

Gateway to the Open Mizuno Open

JFE Setonaikai Golf Club, Kasaoka, Okayama
Par 36-36–72; 7,356 yards

June 21-24
purse, ¥110,000,000

	SCORES				TOTAL	MONEY
Brad Kennedy	72	68	65	66	271	¥22,000,000
Toshinori Muto	72	71	68	63	274	9,240,000
Toru Taniguchi	73	68	66	67	274	9,240,000
Koumei Oda	69	73	67	66	275	5,280,000
Hiroyuki Fujita	73	68	70	66	277	3,065,700
Kunihiro Kamii	75	68	67	67	277	3,065,700
Tomohiro Kondo	68	71	70	68	277	3,065,700
Mitsuhiro Tateyama	69	72	68	68	277	3,065,700
Ryuichi Oda	68	70	70	69	277	3,065,700
Taichi Teshima	68	69	71	69	277	3,065,700
Lee Kyoung-hoon	67	73	68	69	277	3,065,700
Lee Seong-ho	68	69	70	70	277	3,065,700
Kazuhiro Yamashita	71	71	65	70	277	3,065,700
Yui Ueda	67	68	70	72	277	3,065,700
Nick Cullen	69	71	71	67	278	1,782,000
Liang Wen-chong	70	69	70	69	278	1,782,000
Kim Hyung-sung	70	68	68	72	278	1,782,000
Tetsuji Hiratsuka	71	70	70	68	279	1,430,000
Ryutaro Nagano	71	68	71	69	279	1,430,000
Cho Min-gyu	70	69	70	70	279	1,430,000
Jay Choi	71	72	65	71	279	1,430,000
Wu Ashun	69	71	73	67	280	1,089,000
Chapchai Nirat	74	69	69	68	280	1,089,000
Brendan Jones	70	71	67	72	280	1,089,000
Lee Dong-hwan	72	71	65	72	280	1,089,000

Nagashima Shigeo Invitational

North Country Golf Club, Chitose, Hokkaido
Par 36-36–72; 7,127 yards

July 5-8
purse, ¥150,000,000

	SCORES				TOTAL	MONEY
Lee Kyoung-hoon	65	69	70	65	269	¥30,000,000
Kim Hyung-sung	69	67	68	67	271	15,000,000
Ryo Ishikawa	74	67	66	66	273	7,200,000
Lee Dong-hwan	69	70	68	66	273	7,200,000
Taichi Teshima	68	69	69	67	273	7,200,000
Katsumasa Miyamoto	71	67	67	68	273	7,200,000
Wu Ashun	69	67	71	68	275	4,585,000
Cho Min-gyu	66	72	69	68	275	4,585,000
Yasuharu Imano	69	65	72	69	275	4,585,000

	SCORES				TOTAL	MONEY
Prayad Marksaeng	71	69	73	63	276	3,630,000
Liang Wen-chong	69	68	68	71	276	3,630,000
Toru Suzuki	69	67	69	71	276	3,630,000
Toru Taniguchi	68	71	70	68	277	2,780,000
Koumei Oda	68	69	68	72	277	2,780,000
Ryu Hyun-woo	68	69	68	72	277	2,780,000
Ryuichi Oda	70	70	71	67	278	2,355,000
Toshinori Muto	74	65	69	70	278	2,355,000
Yoshinori Fujimoto	72	68	72	67	279	1,950,000
Kim Do-hoon	73	69	70	67	279	1,950,000
Daisuke Maruyama	70	71	68	70	279	1,950,000
Yasuki Hiramoto	74	66	68	71	279	1,950,000
Hwang Jung-gon	73	67	73	67	280	1,485,000
Keiichiro Fukabori	73	68	73	66	280	1,485,000
Yuji Igarashi	74	67	70	69	280	1,485,000
Jang Dong-kyu	70	70	69	71	280	1,485,000

Sun Chlorella Classic

Otaru Country Club, Otaru, Hokkaido
Par 36-36–72; 7,471 yards

July 26-29
purse, ¥150,000,000

	SCORES				TOTAL	MONEY
Brendan Jones	69	66	68	70	273	¥30,000,000
Lee Seong-ho	69	70	66	70	275	12,600,000
*Hideki Matsuyama	71	66	69	69	275	
Yoshinobu Tsukada	67	68	67	73	275	12,600,000
Kiradech Aphibarnrat	68	70	65	74	277	7,200,000
Shingo Katayama	75	67	66	70	278	6,000,000
Masatsugu Morofuji	69	70	70	70	279	5,400,000
Masahiro Kawamura	72	70	70	68	280	4,585,000
Keiichiro Fukabori	71	71	68	70	280	4,585,000
Park Eun-shin	69	71	68	72	280	4,585,000
Kim Sung-yoon	69	70	73	69	281	3,330,000
Shigeru Nonaka	69	71	72	69	281	3,330,000
Ryutaro Nagano	71	72	72	66	281	3,330,000
Norio Shinozaki	70	72	69	70	281	3,330,000
David Smail	71	70	68	72	281	3,330,000
Tatsunori Nukaga	73	66	73	70	282	2,220,000
Takashi Kanemoto	70	72	70	70	282	2,220,000
I.J. Jang	71	71	69	71	282	2,220,000
Wu Ashun	67	71	71	73	282	2,220,000
Daisuke Maruyama	72	70	67	73	282	2,220,000
Yoshinori Fujimoto	72	70	67	73	282	2,220,000
Masamichi Uehira	71	71	72	69	283	1,461,428
Hideto Tanihara	69	69	75	70	283	1,461,428
Prayad Marksaeng	72	70	71	70	283	1,461,428
Mamo Osanai	74	68	70	71	283	1,461,428
Kurt Barnes	73	68	71	71	283	1,461,428
Hiroo Kawai	70	71	70	72	283	1,461,428
Lee Kyoung-hoon	70	65	73	75	283	1,461,428

Kansai Open

Izumigaoka Country Club, Sakai, Osaka
Par 36-35–71; 6,929 yards

August 16-19
purse, ¥60,000,000

	SCORES				TOTAL	MONEY
Toshinori Muto	64	65	68	69	266	¥12,000,000
Kim Hyung-sung	68	64	68	67	267	6,000,000
Norio Shinozaki	65	68	66	70	269	4,080,000
Yuta Ikeda	70	67	62	71	270	2,880,000
K.T. Kim	67	72	67	66	272	2,400,000
Jang Dong-kyu	72	67	65	69	273	1,846,800
Kazuhiro Yamashita	72	64	68	69	273	1,846,800
Hwang Jung-gon	68	70	64	71	273	1,846,800
Han Lee	70	67	66	70	273	1,846,800
Shunsuke Sonoda	65	66	69	73	273	1,846,800
Hiroyuki Fujita	72	66	68	68	274	1,392,000
Ryu Hyun-woo	69	65	68	72	274	1,392,000
Cho Min-gyu	68	69	71	67	275	954,000
*Chun Jae-han	70	68	69	68	275	
Kim Do-hoon	68	71	68	68	275	954,000
Azuma Yano	66	71	69	69	275	954,000
Kiradech Aphibarnrat	69	68	69	69	275	954,000
Masafumi Kawase	71	66	69	69	275	954,000
Yosuke Tsukada	70	70	66	69	275	954,000
Hideto Tanihara	69	69	68	69	275	954,000
Yoshikazu Haku	70	68	66	71	275	954,000
Tetsuya Haraguchi	71	69	68	68	276	600,000
Mamo Osanai	71	67	69	69	276	600,000
Kunihiro Kamii	71	69	67	69	276	600,000
Tetsuji Hiratsuka	70	68	69	69	276	600,000
Lee Kyoung-hoon	66	69	69	72	276	600,000
Richard Lee	70	66	69	71	276	600,000

Vana H Cup KBC Augusta

Keya Golf Club, Shima, Fukuoka
Par 36-36–72; 7,146 yards

August 23-26
purse, ¥110,000,000

	SCORES				TOTAL	MONEY
Kim Hyung-sung	69	64	68	69	270	¥22,000,000
Akio Sadakata	66	66	70	69	271	11,000,000
Kazuhiko Hosokawa	68	71	66	68	273	7,480,000
Ryutaro Nagano	71	69	66	68	274	4,840,000
Kurt Barnes	67	64	73	70	274	4,840,000
I.J. Jang	68	68	71	68	275	3,960,000
Kaname Yokoo	72	68	69	67	276	3,126,200
David Smail	69	71	68	68	276	3,126,200
Jay Choi	69	66	72	69	276	3,126,200
Kim Do-hoon	70	70	66	70	276	3,126,200
Hiroyuki Fujita	69	66	70	71	276	3,126,200
Yusaku Miyazato	67	71	71	68	277	1,939,142
Kim Sung-yoon	69	69	72	67	277	1,939,142
Han Lee	72	68	67	70	277	1,939,142
Hidezumi Shirakata	65	73	69	70	277	1,939,142
Kiyoshi Miyazato	67	70	70	70	277	1,939,142
Daisuke Maruyama	69	67	70	71	277	1,939,142
Kazuhiro Yamashita	67	71	66	73	277	1,939,142
Toshinori Muto	68	72	70	68	278	1,386,000
Michio Matsumura	66	68	73	71	278	1,386,000

	SCORES				TOTAL	MONEY
Kunihiro Kamii	71	69	67	71	278	1,386,000
Masahiro Kawamura	69	68	72	70	279	960,666
Shigeru Nonaka	65	71	73	70	279	960,666
Lee Seong-ho	72	67	70	70	279	960,666
Yosuke Asaji	69	69	72	69	279	960,666
Takashi Kanemoto	71	67	71	70	279	960,666
Azuma Yano	70	68	71	70	279	960,666
Taichiro Kiyota	71	69	70	69	279	960,666
Lee Kyoung-hoon	70	67	71	71	279	960,666
Yoshinori Fujimoto	63	70	72	74	279	960,666

Fujisankei Classic

Fujizakura Country Club, Fujikawaguchiko, Yamanashi
Par 35-36–71; 7,437 yards

August 30-September 2
purse, ¥110,000,000

	SCORES				TOTAL	MONEY
K.T. Kim	70	70	68	68	276	¥22,000,000
Yuta Ikeda	73	70	67	67	277	11,000,000
Hiroyuki Fujita	69	72	67	70	278	6,380,000
Prayad Marksaeng	68	69	68	73	278	6,380,000
Takashi Kanemoto	73	68	68	70	279	4,400,000
Wu Ashun	72	70	70	68	280	3,648,333
Tomohiro Kondo	71	70	69	70	280	3,648,333
Kim Hyung-sung	71	66	70	73	280	3,648,333
Lee Kyoung-hoon	72	68	71	70	281	3,102,000
Satoru Hirota	73	70	70	69	282	2,552,000
Kazuhiro Yamashita	67	76	70	69	282	2,552,000
Yusaku Miyazato	73	70	69	70	282	2,552,000
Hiroshi Iwata	68	70	69	75	282	2,552,000
Kim Do-hoon	71	71	70	71	283	1,947,000
Taichi Teshima	72	68	70	73	283	1,947,000
Lee Seong-ho	68	74	73	70	285	1,529,000
Yasuharu Imano	70	72	71	72	285	1,529,000
Hidezumi Shirakata	68	74	74	69	285	1,529,000
I.J. Jang	72	70	71	72	285	1,529,000
Hwang Jung-gon	71	70	71	73	285	1,529,000
Chawalit Plaphol	68	75	69	73	285	1,529,000
Michio Matsumura	70	71	74	71	286	1,034,000
Yoshinori Fujimoto	73	71	72	70	286	1,034,000
Hideto Tanihara	71	69	72	74	286	1,034,000
Kurt Barnes	71	70	71	74	286	1,034,000
Koichiro Kawano	69	70	72	75	286	1,034,000
Kazuhiko Hosokawa	70	70	71	75	286	1,034,000

Toshin Golf Tournament

Ryosen Golf Club, Inabe, Mie
Par 36-36–72; 7,169 yards
(Event shortened to 54 holes—rain.)

September 6-9
purse, ¥80,000,000

	SCORES			TOTAL	MONEY
Wu Ashun	65	66	67	198	¥12,000,000
Yuta Ikeda	65	66	67	198	6,000,000
(Wu defeated Ikeda on fourth playoff hole.)					
Hiroo Kawai	66	68	65	199	3,480,000
Masamichi Uehira	66	63	70	199	3,480,000

	SCORES			TOTAL	MONEY
Kodai Ichihara	69	66	65	200	2,400,000
Ryutaro Nagano	66	69	66	201	1,915,500
Park Eun-shin	67	68	66	201	1,915,500
Koumei Oda	65	67	69	201	1,915,500
Ryu Hyun-woo	64	67	70	201	1,915,500
Liang Wen-chong	69	68	65	202	1,237,714
James McLean	67	70	65	202	1,237,714
Hwang Jung-gon	67	69	66	202	1,237,714
Yoshinori Fujimoto	68	68	66	202	1,237,714
Shingo Katayama	67	68	67	202	1,237,714
Kim Hyung-sung	68	67	67	202	1,237,714
Satoshi Kodaira	66	68	68	202	1,237,714
Chawalit Plaphol	64	71	68	203	831,000
Kiyoshi Miyazato	67	67	69	203	831,000
Han Lee	68	66	69	203	831,000
Yui Ueda	66	67	70	203	831,000
Yasunori Yoshida	69	69	66	204	616,800
Lee Seong-ho	69	70	65	204	616,800
Hiroyuki Fujita	70	69	65	204	616,800
Lee Kyoung-hoon	67	67	70	204	616,800
Masahiro Kawamura	70	69	65	204	616,800

ANA Open

Sapporo Golf Club, Wattsu Course, Kitahiroshima, Hokkaido
Par 36-36–72; 7,063 yards

September 13-16
purse, ¥110,000,000

	SCORES				TOTAL	MONEY
Hiroyuki Fujita	71	68	65	68	272	¥22,000,000
Liang Wen-chong	66	75	68	64	273	7,040,000
Kurt Barnes	70	67	69	67	273	7,040,000
Yuta Ikeda	68	71	67	67	273	7,040,000
Kim Hyung-sung	67	70	65	71	273	7,040,000
Kiyoshi Murota	69	69	68	68	274	3,795,000
Lee Dong-hwan	72	67	67	68	274	3,795,000
Hideto Tanihara	68	67	73	67	275	3,228,500
Tomohiro Kondo	68	68	70	69	275	3,228,500
Lee Kyoung-hoon	67	71	71	67	276	2,662,000
Michio Matsumura	69	67	70	70	276	2,662,000
Yusaku Miyazato	69	70	67	70	276	2,662,000
Toshinori Muto	70	68	70	69	277	1,914,000
Ryo Ishikawa	71	69	67	70	277	1,914,000
Kim Do-hoon	70	64	72	71	277	1,914,000
Masamichi Uehira	69	69	68	71	277	1,914,000
Kunihiro Kamii	67	70	69	71	277	1,914,000
Yosuke Asaji	72	71	65	70	278	1,562,000
Yui Ueda	69	71	72	67	279	1,298,000
Koumei Oda	69	71	71	68	279	1,298,000
Massy Kuramoto	70	70	70	69	279	1,298,000
I.J. Jang	69	72	69	69	279	1,298,000
Shingo Katayama	68	70	69	72	279	1,298,000
Kodai Ichihara	71	68	74	67	280	968,000
Tetsuji Hiratsuka	65	72	72	71	280	968,000
Kiyoshi Miyazato	69	70	69	72	280	968,000
Kim Sung-yoon	69	70	69	72	280	968,000

Asia-Pacific Panasonic Open

Higashi Hirono Golf Club, Miki, Hyogo
Par 35-36–71; 7,020 yards

September 20-23
purse, ¥150,000,000

	SCORES				TOTAL	MONEY
Masanori Kobayashi	74	64	67	62	267	¥30,000,000
Koumei Oda	64	69	68	67	268	16,500,000
Masamichi Uehira	66	68	65	71	270	11,550,000
Shiv Kapur	67	68	69	67	271	6,350,000
Tomohiro Kondo	66	69	66	70	271	6,350,000
Juvic Pagunsan	67	66	67	71	271	6,350,000
Hwang Jung-gon	67	70	67	68	272	3,637,500
Hideto Tanihara	67	67	69	69	272	3,637,500
Wu Ashun	67	69	67	69	272	3,637,500
Masahiro Kawamura	70	65	66	71	272	3,637,500
Liang Wen-chong	69	71	68	65	273	2,497,500
Darren Beck	68	65	70	70	273	2,497,500
Marcus Fraser	70	70	67	67	274	1,841,250
Kunihiro Kamii	69	72	64	69	274	1,841,250
Yoshinobu Tsukada	68	69	68	69	274	1,841,250
Hiroyuki Fujita	64	68	70	72	274	1,841,250
*Cameron Smith	67	71	66	71	275	
Lee Seong-ho	67	69	73	67	276	1,355,625
Brendan Jones	69	71	68	68	276	1,355,625
I.J. Jang	68	69	69	70	276	1,355,625
Kim Do-hoon	65	73	68	70	276	1,355,625
Toru Taniguchi	67	69	69	71	276	1,355,625
S.K. Ho	68	70	67	71	276	1,355,625
Gunn Charoenkul	70	68	66	72	276	1,355,625
Yusaku Miyazato	64	70	68	74	276	1,355,625

Coca-Cola Tokai Classic

Miyoshi Country Club, West Course, Miyoshi, Aichi
Par 36-36–72; 7,315 yards

September 27-30
purse, ¥120,000,000

	SCORES				TOTAL	MONEY
Ryu Hyun-woo	71	73	67	71	282	¥24,000,000
Shingo Katayama	71	72	73	66	282	12,000,000
(Ryu defeated Katayama on first playoff hole.)						
K.T. Kim	70	72	70	71	283	8,160,000
Kim Hyung-sung	69	72	71	72	284	5,760,000
Masamichi Uehira	70	74	71	70	285	4,800,000
Akio Sadakata	69	77	72	68	286	3,980,000
Ryo Ishikawa	73	74	71	68	286	3,980,000
David Smail	70	73	71	72	286	3,980,000
Kazuhiro Yamashita	73	75	71	68	287	3,384,000
Tadahiro Takayama	68	79	72	69	288	3,144,000
Koumei Oda	71	72	77	69	289	2,364,000
Daisuke Maruyama	75	71	74	69	289	2,364,000
Yosuke Asaji	74	74	71	70	289	2,364,000
Tatsunori Nukaga	71	71	75	72	289	2,364,000
Hwang Jung-gon	76	70	70	73	289	2,364,000
Masahiro Kawamura	70	70	72	77	289	2,364,000
Takashi Kanemoto	78	72	69	71	290	1,515,428
Kunihiro Kamii	72	73	73	72	290	1,515,428
Jeev Milkha Singh	75	72	71	72	290	1,515,428
Ryuichi Oda	72	72	71	75	290	1,515,428
Katsumasa Miyamoto	70	72	73	75	290	1,515,428

	SCORES				TOTAL	MONEY
Park Eun-shin	72	68	74	76	290	1,515,428
Park Sung-joon	70	72	72	76	290	1,515,428
Shunsuke Sonoda	76	74	72	69	291	1,080,000
Hiroyuki Fujita	73	71	78	69	291	1,080,000
Liang Wen-chong	73	73	72	73	291	1,080,000
Yusaku Miyazato	76	73	73	70	292	960,000
Tomohiro Kondo	73	70	73	76	292	960,000
Yuta Ikeda	73	73	74	73	293	819,000
Toru Taniguchi	70	74	76	73	293	819,000
Yuji Igarashi	72	76	70	75	293	819,000
Hiroshi Iwata	74	73	77	69	293	819,000

Canon Open

Totsuka Country Club, Yokohama, Kanagawa
Par 36-36–72; 7,191 yards

October 4-7
purse, ¥150,000,000

	SCORES				TOTAL	MONEY
Yuta Ikeda	66	68	68	69	271	¥30,000,000
Hwang Jung-gon	68	69	67	70	274	12,600,000
Taichi Teshima	67	72	65	70	274	12,600,000
Masamichi Uehira	69	68	70	70	277	6,600,000
Ryo Ishikawa	68	70	66	73	277	6,600,000
Toru Taniguchi	71	69	69	69	278	5,400,000
Kim Do-hoon	70	73	67	69	279	4,421,250
I.J. Jang	73	69	68	69	279	4,421,250
Brad Kennedy	68	69	71	71	279	4,421,250
Hiroyuki Fujita	72	66	70	71	279	4,421,250
Yasuharu Imano	71	68	70	71	280	3,480,000
Toshinori Muto	71	68	67	74	280	3,480,000
K.T. Kim	71	70	73	67	281	2,692,500
Yusaku Miyazato	71	71	70	69	281	2,692,500
Kazuhiro Yamashita	70	72	69	70	281	2,692,500
Makoto Inoue	72	69	69	71	281	2,692,500
Ryu Hyun-woo	71	70	72	69	282	2,016,000
Kim Hyung-sung	70	72	71	69	282	2,016,000
Masafumi Kawase	72	67	73	70	282	2,016,000
Tadahiro Takayama	71	73	68	70	282	2,016,000
Michio Matsumura	70	70	69	73	282	2,016,000
Kiyoshi Miyazato	71	70	72	70	283	1,410,000
Jeev Milkha Singh	68	70	74	71	283	1,410,000
Daisuke Maruyama	70	72	70	71	283	1,410,000
Brendan Jones	71	67	72	73	283	1,410,000
Jay Choi	69	71	70	73	283	1,410,000
*Masamichi Ito	73	71	72	67	283	
Shigeki Maruyama	68	69	69	77	283	1,410,000

Japan Open

Naha Golf Club, Naha, Okinawa
Par 36-35–71; 7,176 yards

October 11-14
purse, ¥200,000,000

	SCORES				TOTAL	MONEY
Kenichi Kuboya	74	73	75	70	292	¥40,000,000
Juvic Pagunsan	76	72	70	75	293	22,000,000
Tetsuji Hiratsuka	73	70	73	78	294	15,400,000
Wu Ashun	75	73	78	70	296	8,466,666

	SCORES				TOTAL	MONEY
Kim Do-hoon	78	73	72	73	296	8,466,666
Yusaku Miyazato	78	69	72	77	296	8,466,666
*Hideki Matsuyama	78	75	74	70	297	
Kiyoshi Miyazato	78	72	75	72	297	5,600,000
I.J. Jang	74	75	75	73	297	5,600,000
Hideto Tanihara	80	71	74	73	298	3,900,000
Yuta Ikeda	78	72	71	77	298	3,900,000
Koumei Oda	73	73	72	80	298	3,900,000
Yoshinori Fujimoto	74	77	78	70	299	2,695,000
Kazuhiro Yamashita	77	74	75	73	299	2,695,000
Hwang Jung-gon	72	77	75	75	299	2,695,000
Masanori Kobayashi	76	75	73	75	299	2,695,000
Kim Hyung-sung	77	75	75	73	300	2,150,000
Yosuke Tsukada	82	71	71	76	300	2,150,000
Tadahiro Takayama	78	75	75	73	301	1,824,000
Tsuneyuki Nakajima	73	74	79	75	301	1,824,000
Chun Jae-han	76	76	74	75	301	1,824,000
Han Lee	76	73	76	76	301	1,824,000
Kunihiro Kamii	82	71	72	76	301	1,824,000
Nobuhito Sato	72	75	78	77	302	1,580,000
Yoshinobu Tsukada	77	72	76	77	302	1,580,000
Ryu Hyun-woo	74	76	74	78	302	1,580,000
Hiroyuki Fujita	74	73	76	79	302	1,580,000

Bridgestone Open

Sodegaura Country Club, Chiba
Par 35-36–71; 7,119 yards

October 18-21
purse, ¥150,000,000

	SCORES				TOTAL	MONEY
Toru Taniguchi	66	71	69	66	272	¥30,000,000
Hiroyuki Fujita	64	72	69	68	273	15,000,000
Kunihiro Kamii	71	69	69	65	274	7,800,000
Ryuichi Oda	68	73	65	68	274	7,800,000
Lee Dong-hwan	69	69	67	69	274	7,800,000
Yusaku Miyazato	70	66	71	68	275	5,175,000
Sushi Ishigaki	68	68	70	69	275	5,175,000
Masamichi Uehira	69	72	68	67	276	4,402,500
Kiyoshi Miyazato	68	71	68	69	276	4,402,500
Hwang Jung-gon	69	71	68	69	277	3,930,000
Hideto Tanihara	68	72	71	67	278	3,480,000
Azuma Yano	70	70	69	69	278	3,480,000
Shingo Katayama	70	70	72	67	279	2,610,000
Prayad Marksaeng	70	68	73	68	279	2,610,000
Lee Kyoung-hoon	68	69	73	69	279	2,610,000
Masahiro Kawamura	67	74	68	70	279	2,610,000
Kazuhiro Yamashita	67	70	71	71	279	2,610,000
S.K. Ho	68	71	72	69	280	2,010,000
Daisuke Maruyama	68	72	71	69	280	2,010,000
Toshinori Muto	68	73	68	71	280	2,010,000
I.J. Jang	70	71	71	69	281	1,425,000
Brad Kennedy	70	71	70	70	281	1,425,000
David Smail	69	71	70	71	281	1,425,000
Kim Hyung-tae	71	70	69	71	281	1,425,000
Kenichi Kuboya	69	71	70	71	281	1,425,000
Han Lee	73	71	73	64	281	1,425,000
Keiichiro Fukabori	71	70	68	72	281	1,425,000
Takashi Kanemoto	72	71	66	72	281	1,425,000

Mynavi ABC Championship

ABC Golf Club, Kato, Hyogo
Par 36-36–72; 7,201 yards

October 25-28
purse, ¥150,000,000

	SCORES				TOTAL	MONEY
Han Lee	67	71	70	63	271	¥30,000,000
Katsumasa Miyamoto	67	68	69	68	272	15,000,000
K.T. Kim	67	65	71	70	273	8,700,000
Kaname Yokoo	67	70	68	68	273	8,700,000
I.J. Jang	71	65	69	70	275	6,000,000
Takashi Kanemoto	68	73	68	68	277	4,975,000
Kiradech Aphibarnrat	70	70	67	70	277	4,975,000
Ryo Ishikawa	70	66	71	70	277	4,975,000
Yusaku Miyazato	69	70	70	69	278	3,630,000
Kiyoshi Miyazato	68	75	66	69	278	3,630,000
Kazuhiro Yamashita	65	72	71	70	278	3,630,000
Shunsuke Sonoda	70	69	69	70	278	3,630,000
Toru Taniguchi	68	71	69	70	278	3,630,000
Hideto Tanihara	71	73	68	67	279	2,430,000
Taichi Teshima	69	73	69	68	279	2,430,000
Lee Kyoung-hoon	72	67	71	69	279	2,430,000
Koumei Oda	70	71	69	69	279	2,430,000
Yoshinori Fujimoto	70	72	64	73	279	2,430,000
Shigeki Maruyama	71	74	68	67	280	1,710,000
Kim Hyung-sung	70	71	71	68	280	1,710,000
Kurt Barnes	69	72	71	68	280	1,710,000
Satoshi Kodaira	69	71	69	71	280	1,710,000
Toshinori Muto	71	65	72	72	280	1,710,000
Daisuke Maruyama	69	68	69	74	280	1,710,000
Yosuke Asaji	67	75	69	70	281	1,290,000
Akinori Tani	70	72	69	70	281	1,290,000
Tomohiro Kondo	71	70	69	71	281	1,290,000

Mitsui Sumitomo Visa Taiheiyo Masters

Taiheiyo Club, Gotemba Course, Gotemba, Shizuoka
Par 36-36–72; 7,246 yards

November 8-11
purse, ¥150,000,000

	SCORES				TOTAL	MONEY
Ryo Ishikawa	67	69	69	68	273	¥30,000,000
Michio Matsumura	65	71	70	68	274	15,000,000
Yoshinori Fujimoto	67	70	70	69	276	10,200,000
*Hideki Matsuyama	72	70	66	69	277	
Han Lee	69	65	72	71	277	7,200,000
Hiroshi Iwata	67	70	74	67	278	6,000,000
Hwang Jung-gon	75	66	68	70	279	5,175,000
Kim Do-hoon	70	68	68	73	279	5,175,000
Ryu Hyun-woo	70	72	71	67	280	3,939,000
Brad Kennedy	75	68	69	68	280	3,939,000
Hideto Tanihara	73	68	70	69	280	3,939,000
Akinori Tani	75	67	69	69	280	3,939,000
I.J. Jang	71	68	68	73	280	3,939,000
Brendan Jones	67	72	71	71	281	3,030,000
S.K. Ho	71	74	69	68	282	2,163,333
Kazuhiro Yamashita	72	66	74	70	282	2,163,333
Yusaku Miyazato	69	69	74	70	282	2,163,333
Sushi Ishigaki	71	74	66	71	282	2,163,333
Steven Conran	73	72	66	71	282	2,163,333
Yasuharu Imano	71	71	69	71	282	2,163,333

	SCORES				TOTAL	MONEY
David Smail	68	68	74	72	282	2,163,333
Nobuhiro Masuda	69	68	73	72	282	2,163,333
Kurt Barnes	71	69	70	72	282	2,163,333
Lee Kyoung-hoon	70	70	74	69	283	1,395,000
Koumei Oda	71	70	73	69	283	1,395,000
Shingo Katayama	75	67	69	72	283	1,395,000
Kiyoshi Murota	68	70	72	73	283	1,395,000

Dunlop Phoenix

Phoenix Country Club, Miyazaki
Par 36-35–71; 7,027 yards

November 15-18
purse, ¥200,000,000

	SCORES				TOTAL	MONEY
Luke Donald	65	64	71	68	268	¥40,000,000
*Hideki Matsuyama	70	67	69	67	273	
Koumei Oda	73	70	67	64	274	20,000,000
Hiroyuki Fujita	69	66	70	70	275	11,600,000
Brendan Jones	65	72	67	71	275	11,600,000
Toshinori Muto	70	69	72	65	276	7,266,666
Alvaro Quiros	70	69	69	68	276	7,266,666
Hideto Tanihara	65	74	70	67	276	7,266,666
Koichiro Kawano	67	69	70	71	277	6,100,000
Gonzalo Fernandez-Castano	70	71	70	67	278	4,840,000
Jonas Blixt	70	70	70	68	278	4,840,000
Shingo Katayama	69	69	68	72	278	4,840,000
Hirohito Koizumi	68	69	68	73	278	4,840,000
Shunsuke Sonoda	67	66	71	74	278	4,840,000
Kim Hyung-sung	70	74	68	68	280	3,640,000
Lee Kyoung-hoon	71	69	72	69	281	3,140,000
Toru Taniguchi	71	70	71	69	281	3,140,000
David Smail	74	68	69	70	281	3,140,000
Kazuhiro Yamashita	72	69	70	70	281	3,140,000
Ryuichi Oda	72	71	69	70	282	2,600,000
Nobuhiro Masuda	69	68	71	74	282	2,600,000
Ryo Ishikawa	73	67	73	70	283	1,853,333
Yui Ueda	74	68	71	70	283	1,853,333
Nicolas Colsaerts	69	71	72	71	283	1,853,333
Sushi Ishigaki	74	72	68	69	283	1,853,333
Cho Min-gyu	70	72	70	71	283	1,853,333
Shigeru Nonaka	69	69	72	73	283	1,853,333
Park Sung-joon	69	70	71	73	283	1,853,333
Kurt Barnes	71	68	70	74	283	1,853,333
Daisuke Maruyama	71	70	66	76	283	1,853,333

Casio World Open

Kochi Kuroshio Country Club, Geisei, Kochi
Par 36-36–72; 7,300 yards

November 22-25
purse, ¥200,000,000

	SCORES				TOTAL	MONEY
Hwang Jung-gon	65	70	68	66	269	¥40,000,000
Kunihiro Kamii	67	69	68	68	272	20,000,000
Yoshinori Fujimoto	69	70	68	67	274	10,400,000
Kenichi Kuboya	67	71	67	69	274	10,400,000
K.T. Kim	69	67	68	70	274	10,400,000
Ryo Ishikawa	69	69	70	68	276	6,633,333

	SCORES			TOTAL	MONEY
S.K. Ho	65	72	71	68	276	6,633,333
Yui Ueda	68	71	67	70	276	6,633,333
Yosuke Asaji	70	73	67	67	277	4,315,000
Satoru Hirota	71	71	68	67	277	4,315,000
Yusaku Miyazato	68	67	74	68	277	4,315,000
Hiroyuki Fujita	68	69	71	69	277	4,315,000
Brad Kennedy	68	70	70	69	277	4,315,000
Kazuhiro Yamashita	70	70	68	69	277	4,315,000
Daisuke Kataoka	71	68	68	70	277	4,315,000
Hideto Tanihara	68	69	69	71	277	4,315,000
Shingo Katayama	69	70	72	67	278	2,770,000
Koumei Oda	71	72	69	66	278	2,770,000
Kim Do-hoon	69	69	71	69	278	2,770,000
Norio Shinozaki	68	72	68	70	278	2,770,000
Hiroshi Iwata	70	72	69	68	279	1,948,571
Cho Min-gyu	72	72	66	69	279	1,948,571
Hirofumi Miyase	71	70	69	69	279	1,948,571
Takashi Kanemoto	71	70	68	70	279	1,948,571
Hirohito Koizumi	71	71	67	70	279	1,948,571
Prayad Marksaeng	71	70	67	71	279	1,948,571
Yasuki Hiramoto	71	66	69	73	279	1,948,571

Golf Nippon Series JT Cup

Tokyo Yomiuri Country Club, Tokyo
Par 35-35–70; 7,023 yards

November 29-December 2
purse, ¥130,000,000

	SCORES			TOTAL	MONEY
Hiroyuki Fujita	61	66	68	67	262	¥40,000,000
Toshinori Muto	64	69	70	64	267	12,500,000
Han Lee	70	62	69	66	267	12,500,000
K.T. Kim	67	66	68	67	268	6,378,478
Toru Taniguchi	69	66	66	68	269	5,338,478
Kazuhiro Yamashita	70	66	70	65	271	4,623,478
Ryo Ishikawa	67	66	68	70	271	4,623,478
Shingo Katayama	69	69	71	63	272	4,103,478
Masanori Kobayashi	66	68	71	68	273	3,804,478
Tomohiro Kondo	71	71	67	65	274	3,414,478
Ryu Hyun-woo	69	66	70	69	274	3,414,478
Kenichi Kuboya	65	71	72	67	275	2,894,478
Wu Ashun	66	69	68	72	275	2,894,478
Yoshinori Fujimoto	69	69	70	68	276	2,439,478
Brad Kennedy	67	68	70	71	276	2,439,478
Hideto Tanihara	66	69	70	72	277	2,244,478
Jeev Milkha Singh	71	71	69	67	278	2,114,478
Koumei Oda	68	69	72	70	279	1,984,478
Kim Do-hoon	70	68	68	74	280	1,880,478
Masamichi Uehira	69	67	71	74	281	1,776,478
Kunihiro Kamii	75	68	72	67	282	1,620,479
Brendan Jones	70	76	68	68	282	1,620,479
Hwang Jung-gon	73	69	71	70	283	1,464,479
Jay Choi	77	69	69	70	285	1,360,479
Yuta Ikeda	73	70	73	73	289	1,308,479
Ryuichi Oda	74	76	69	72	291	1,256,479

Australasian Tour

Victorian Open

Spring Valley Golf Club, Melbourne, Victoria
Par 71; 6,738 yards

January 5-8
purse, A$125,000

	SCORES				TOTAL	MONEY
Scott Arnold	71	66	67	68	272	A$18,750
Kurt Barnes	71	68	68	66	273	11,875
Michael Hendry	65	66	73	73	277	8,750
Nick Cullen	73	69	71	66	279	4,921.87
Leigh McKechnie	69	71	73	66	279	4,921.87
Peter Lonard	70	74	68	67	279	4,921.87
Matthew Ballard	72	67	68	72	279	4,921.87
Daniel Popovic	69	73	70	68	280	3,500
Quinton Howe	72	73	67	69	281	2,906.25
Craig Parry	66	75	69	71	281	2,906.25
Aaron Townsend	75	66	71	70	282	2,000
Aaron Pike	71	70	71	70	282	2,000
Paul Donahoo	72	71	69	70	282	2,000
*Daniel Bringolf	72	73	69	68	282	
Peter Wilson	72	72	71	67	282	2,000
Rika Batibasaga	68	73	70	71	282	2,000
Matthew Griffin	72	71	73	66	282	2,000
Doug Holloway	75	69	69	70	283	1,500
Michael Long	73	72	69	69	283	1,500
Chris Gaunt	75	71	71	67	284	1,387.50
Heath Reed	73	71	68	72	284	1,387.50
Steve Jeffress	72	69	70	73	284	1,387.50
Craig Scott	71	72	75	67	285	1,250
Andrew Tschudin	71	73	68	73	285	1,250
Brad Andrews	71	71	73	70	285	1,250
Alistair Presnell	72	69	70	74	285	1,250
Terry Pilkadaris	74	68	73	70	285	1,250
Anthony Summers	73	70	68	74	285	1,250
Grant Scott	72	71	73	69	285	1,250

Adroit Insurance Group Victorian PGA Championship

Forest Resort, Creswick, Victoria
Par 36-36-72

February 16-19
purse, A$120,000

	SCORES				TOTAL	MONEY
Gareth Paddison	67	69	67	74	277	A$18,000
Leighton Lyle	67	69	73	69	278	11,400
Peter O'Malley	70	74	69	66	279	5,880
David McKenzie	70	73	70	66	279	5,880
Marcus Cain	70	71	69	69	279	5,880
Andre Stolz	68	69	71	71	279	5,880
Ashley Hall	72	71	68	69	280	3,360
Jin Jeong	71	70	68	71	280	3,360
James McLean	69	65	72	74	280	3,360
Jason Norris	67	75	70	69	281	2,640
Anthony Brown	71	74	68	69	282	2,280
Michael Long	72	70	67	73	282	2,280

	SCORES			TOTAL	MONEY
David McKendrick	73	65	72	73	283	1,740
Leigh McKechnie	71	69	70	73	283	1,740
Doug Holloway	74	68	68	73	283	1,740
Kurt Carlson	74	69	65	75	283	1,740
Aaron Townsend	75	70	69	70	284	1,327.50
Jason Scrivener	71	71	72	70	284	1,327.50
Matt Jager	71	73	70	70	284	1,327.50
Stephen Dartnall	66	74	73	71	284	1,327.50
Scott Laycock	67	73	73	71	284	1,327.50
Stephen Leaney	72	70	71	71	284	1,327.50
Matthew Griffin	69	71	72	72	284	1,327.50
John Wade	70	72	68	74	284	1,327.50
Andrew Kelly	68	73	74	70	285	1,188
Peter Cooke	68	71	76	70	285	1,188

Coca-Cola Queensland PGA Championship

City Golf Club, Toowoomba, Queensland
Par 35-35-70; 6,348 yards
(Event shortened to 54 holes—rain.)

February 23-26
purse, A$115,000

	SCORES			TOTAL	MONEY
Andrew Tschudin	67	68	64	199	A$17,250
Brody Ninyette	67	66	67	200	9,487.50
Andrew Martin	65	67	68	200	9,487.50
Paul Hayden	69	67	66	202	4,266.50
Hamish Robertson	69	66	67	202	4,266.50
Terry Pilkadaris	68	67	67	202	4,266.50
*Cameron Smith	68	66	68	202	
Ryan Haller	65	68	69	202	4,266.50
Rohan Blizard	71	68	63	202	4,266.50
Ashley Hall	66	67	70	203	2,817.50
Gavin Fairfax	70	68	66	204	2,185
Michael Hendry	68	68	68	204	2,185
Tim Hart	70	65	69	204	2,185
Ryan Fox	68	71	65	204	2,185
Nick Cullen	66	71	68	205	1,453.92
Matthew Griffin	69	67	69	205	1,453.92
Steve Jones	67	71	67	205	1,453.92
Andrew Evans	68	68	69	205	1,453.92
Scott Laycock	67	68	70	205	1,453.92
Leigh Deagan	69	65	71	205	1,453.92
David McKendrick	69	70	66	205	1,453.92
Brad Andrews	69	68	69	206	1,196
Christopher Wood	68	70	68	206	1,196
Samuel Eaves	69	69	68	206	1,196
Michael Wright	69	66	71	206	1,196
Marcus Cain	69	70	67	206	1,196

New Zealand PGA Pro-Am Championship

The Hills Golf Course, Queenstown, New Zealand
Par 36-36–72

March 29-April 1
purse, NZ$450,000

	SCORES				TOTAL	MONEY
Michael Hendry	69	68	67	68	272	A$61,917.12
Mark Brown	66	71	69	68	274	29,152.64

	SCORES				TOTAL	MONEY
Andrew Martin	67	64	71	72	274	29,152.64
Ryan Fox	74	69	64	68	275	16,511.23
Jin Jeong	76	62	69	69	276	13,759.36
Adam Crawford	67	73	71	66	277	11,122.15
Brendan Jones	72	67	72	66	277	11,122.15
Nick Cullen	73	69	67	68	277	11,122.15
Paul Sheehan	68	69	73	68	278	8,484.94
Josh Younger	70	70	68	70	278	8,484.94
Brody Ninyette	69	67	67	75	278	8,484.94
Terry Pilkadaris	70	71	69	69	279	6,535.69
Kristopher Mueck	71	68	69	71	279	6,535.69
Ashley Hall	71	68	71	70	280	5,434.94
Peter Cooke	68	71	71	70	280	5,434.94
Clint Rice	68	68	72	72	280	5,434.94
Stephen Leaney	68	72	71	70	281	3,815.76
David Frost	70	73	67	71	281	3,815.76
Chris Campbell	70	71	70	70	281	3,815.76
Mark Purser	70	66	74	71	281	3,815.76
Michael Moore	70	72	68	71	281	3,815.76
Daniel Fox	70	73	70	68	281	3,815.76
Matthew Griffin	71	69	70	71	281	3,815.76
Paul Spargo	68	71	72	71	282	3,302.25
Zhang Xin-jun	68	74	74	67	283	2,738.11
Craig Scott	70	68	72	73	283	2,738.11
Andrew Tschudin	72	70	70	71	283	2,738.11
Mahal Pearce	72	71	71	69	283	2,738.11
Leigh Deagan	69	74	71	69	283	2,738.11

South Pacific Golf Open Championship

Tina Golf Club, Noumea, New Caledonia
Par 71

September 26-29
purse, A$120,000

	SCORES				TOTAL	MONEY
Brad Shilton	67	68	65	71	271	A$18,000
Matthew Griffin	70	64	71	67	272	11,400
Adam Bland	71	70	68	64	273	7,200
Henry Epstein	63	74	66	70	273	7,200
Steve Jeffress	70	69	70	65	274	4,560
Aaron Townsend	70	67	69	68	274	4,560
Jason Norris	74	67	69	65	275	3,180
Anthony Brown	72	69	67	67	275	3,180
Gavin Flint	71	66	69	69	275	3,180
Kurt Carlson	70	68	67	70	275	3,180
Jean-Louis Guepy	65	69	72	70	276	2,400
Matthew Guyatt	67	67	73	70	277	2,160
Alex Hawley	70	69	75	64	278	1,860
Ryan Fox	66	68	70	74	278	1,860
Michael Wright	73	69	70	67	279	1,445.14
Tim Wood	71	67	73	68	279	1,445.14
Corey Hale	70	69	72	68	279	1,445.14
Paul Hayden	71	71	69	68	279	1,445.14
Anthony Summers	67	68	74	70	279	1,445.14
Samuel Eaves	70	67	71	71	279	1,445.14
Clint Rice	66	68	71	74	279	1,445.14
Ian Esson	74	66	71	69	280	1,236
Kim Felton	66	73	71	70	280	1,236
Craig Hasthorpe	72	68	70	70	280	1,236
Daniel Fox	67	73	69	71	280	1,236

Western Australia Goldfields PGA Championship

Kalgoorlie Golf Course, Kalgoorlie, Western Australia
Par 36-36–72

October 11-14
purse, A$110,000

	SCORES				TOTAL	MONEY
Peter Wilson	74	70	70	69	283	A$16,500
Glenn Joyner	68	77	68	72	285	10,450
Andrew Kelly	70	72	74	71	287	7,700
Brendan Smith	72	77	71	68	288	4,620
Kurt Carlson	69	74	73	72	288	4,620
Nick Cullen	77	71	68	72	288	4,620
Matthew Ballard	75	73	72	69	289	3,465
Kristopher Mueck	77	77	71	65	290	2,887.50
Jason Scrivener	73	76	70	71	290	2,887.50
Jordan Sherratt	79	72	67	73	291	2,420
Ryan Lynch	76	78	70	69	293	1,826
Michael Moore	76	72	75	70	293	1,826
Tarquin MacManus	78	71	74	70	293	1,826
Mark Varela	74	78	71	70	293	1,826
Scott Arnold	71	74	75	73	293	1,826
Jason Norris	76	75	74	69	294	1,331
Kim Felton	78	71	75	70	294	1,331
Matthew Guyatt	74	76	72	72	294	1,331
Josh Carmichael	73	72	72	77	294	1,331
Brad Shilton	77	74	69	75	295	1,221
Alex Benjamin	76	76	73	71	296	1,155
Brett Rankin	74	73	76	73	296	1,155
Ryan McCarthy	76	74	73	73	296	1,155
Peter Welden	75	74	72	75	296	1,155
Aaron Pike	71	79	75	72	297	1,078
Stephen Leaney	77	75	73	72	297	1,078
Ian Esson	69	77	79	72	297	1,078

ISPS Handa Perth International

Lake Karrinyup Country Club, Perth, Western Australia
Par 36-36–72; 7,014 yards

October 18-21
purse, US$2,000,000

	SCORES				TOTAL	MONEY
Bo Van Pelt	70	67	67	68	272	A$304,601.77
Jason Dufner	71	67	67	69	274	203,068.49
Alejandro Canizares	65	73	71	68	277	114,409.39
Michael Hendry	65	73	72	69	279	91,381.30
Paul Casey	67	75	71	67	280	56,583.30
Scott Jamieson	72	71	69	68	280	56,583.30
Rhys Davies	68	72	71	69	280	56,583.30
David Howell	71	68	70	71	280	56,583.30
Emiliano Grillo	66	67	73	74	280	56,583.30
Greg Chalmers	68	73	69	71	281	36,552.52
Knut Borsheim	70	71	72	69	282	32,531.74
Steve Jones	71	71	68	72	282	32,531.74
Steve Webster	72	73	72	66	283	28,693.73
Scott Laycock	71	72	71	69	283	28,693.73
Robert Coles	71	68	73	72	284	26,317.81
Mark Brown	71	69	72	72	284	26,317.81
Richard Bland	70	69	76	70	285	24,124.66
Ashley Hall	68	72	73	72	285	24,124.66
Matthew Baldwin	74	71	74	67	286	21,017.69
James McLean	75	70	74	67	286	21,017.69

	SCORES				TOTAL	MONEY
Aaron Townsend	71	71	73	71	286	21,017.69
Sam Little	72	71	72	71	286	21,017.69
Jason Scrivener	68	69	76	73	286	21,017.69
David McKendrick	72	71	70	73	286	21,017.69
Matthew Millar	71	70	75	71	287	18,459.02
Rika Batibasaga	73	71	72	71	287	18,459.02
Jason Norris	70	73	71	73	287	18,459.02
Tommy Fleetwood	75	70	74	69	288	15,466.28
Ryan McCarthy	73	73	72	70	288	15,466.28
Craig Lee	70	70	77	71	288	15,466.28
Matthew Zions	74	68	73	73	288	15,466.28
Edoardo Molinari	71	72	72	73	288	15,466.28
Andrew Dodt	68	73	73	74	288	15,466.28
Peter Cooke	73	66	74	75	288	15,466.28
Andre Stolz	70	73	68	77	288	15,466.28
Brett Rumford	74	70	75	70	289	12,976.14
Scott Strange	71	71	75	72	289	12,976.14
Ignacio Garrido	74	71	67	77	289	12,976.14
Terry Pilkadaris	71	74	73	72	290	11,331.28
Wade Ormsby	74	72	72	72	290	11,331.28
Daniel Fox	70	75	71	74	290	11,331.28
Thomas Petersson	70	72	73	75	290	11,331.28
Paul Spargo	78	68	69	75	290	11,331.28
Stephen Dartnall	72	67	74	77	290	11,331.28
Jin Jeong	70	72	78	71	291	9,320.89
David McKenzie	72	71	76	72	291	9,320.89
Matthew Stieger	75	71	71	74	291	9,320.89
Josh Younger	73	71	72	75	291	9,320.89
Kieran Pratt	74	69	72	76	291	9,320.89
Andrew Johnston	67	73	80	72	292	7,858.79
Anthony Summers	71	75	73	73	292	7,858.79
Ryan Haller	75	68	75	74	292	7,858.79
Rohan Blizard	73	73	75	72	293	6,762.21
Rick Kulacz	71	74	72	76	293	6,762.21
Matthew Guyatt	70	75	71	77	293	6,762.21
Hamish Robertson	76	69	76	73	294	5,519.43
*Oliver Goss	74	72	75	73	294	
Thomas Norret	72	74	74	74	294	5,519.43
Kristopher Mueck	74	70	74	76	294	5,519.43
Oliver Wilson	73	73	70	78	294	5,519.43
Edouard Dubois	71	71	70	82	294	5,519.43
Alastair Forsyth	70	70	79	76	295	4,843.21
Max McCardle	68	70	80	77	295	4,843.21
Anthony Brown	72	74	77	73	296	4,386.30
Peter Wilson	71	74	76	75	296	4,386.30
Jamie Moul	70	75	72	79	296	4,386.30
Mikael Lundberg	75	71	74	77	297	3,929.39
Tim Wood	74	70	75	78	297	3,929.39
Peter O'Malley	73	73	80	73	299	3,563.87
Federico Colombo	71	74	74	80	299	3,563.87
Ben Wharton	73	73	80	74	300	3,335.90
Matthew Giles	74	71	76	81	302	3,197.38

John Hughes Geely/Nexus Risk Services WA Open

Royal Perth Golf Course, Perth, Western Australia
Par 36-36–72

October 25-28
purse, A$110,000

	SCORES				TOTAL	MONEY
*Oliver Goss	72	66	68	66	272	
*Brady Watt	70	68	66	68	272	
(Goss defeated Watt on fifth playoff hole.)						
Brett Rumford	68	67	74	65	274	A$16,500
Rohan Blizard	70	70	68	67	275	9,075
Ashley Hall	72	67	67	69	275	9,075
Daniel Nisbet	69	73	69	65	276	4,620
Nick Cullen	70	68	71	67	276	4,620
Scott Strange	68	69	69	70	276	4,620
Anthony Brown	69	72	68	68	277	3,080
Andrew Kelly	71	69	68	69	277	3,080
Peter Wilson	69	72	66	70	277	3,080
Adam Crawford	67	70	73	68	278	2,420
*Daniel Hoeve	73	70	69	67	279	
Matthew Griffin	71	68	71	69	279	2,090
Scott Laycock	70	72	68	69	279	2,090
Terry Pilkadaris	68	73	73	66	280	1,503.33
Kim Felton	70	68	74	68	280	1,503.33
*Nathan Holman	73	72	66	69	280	
James McLean	69	72	70	69	280	1,503.33
Josh Younger	69	73	69	69	280	1,503.33
Michael Long	70	71	69	70	280	1,503.33
Pieter Zwart	73	69	67	71	280	1,503.33
Rick Kulacz	71	71	69	71	282	1,254
Jason Scrivener	74	69	69	71	283	1,204.50
Daniel Fox	72	70	69	72	283	1,204.50
*Michael Dennis	70	69	69	75	283	

Talisker Masters

Kingston Heath, Melbourne, Victoria
Par 72

November 15-18
purse, A$1,000,000

	SCORES				TOTAL	MONEY
Adam Scott	67	70	67	67	271	A$180,000
Ian Poulter	67	72	64	72	275	102,000
Gareth Paddison	71	71	69	68	279	57,750
Mark Brown	72	71	67	69	279	57,750
Adam Crawford	72	76	69	65	282	40,000
Peter Senior	74	74	68	68	284	34,000
Michael Hendry	67	69	79	69	284	34,000
Graeme McDowell	71	77	67	71	286	28,000
David Bransdon	71	69	74	72	286	28,000
Matthew Millar	73	67	76	71	287	22,333.33
Richard Green	71	72	72	72	287	22,333.33
*Jake Higginbottom	68	75	70	74	287	
Matthew Guyatt	65	69	75	78	287	22,333.33
Kalem Richardson	68	75	76	69	288	15,066.66
James McLean	73	73	72	70	288	15,066.66
Scott Laycock	75	71	71	71	288	15,066.66
Ryan Fox	73	73	71	71	288	15,066.66
Jason Norris	71	74	69	74	288	15,066.66
Craig Hancock	68	71	72	77	288	15,066.66
*Oliver Goss	71	72	74	72	289	

	SCORES				TOTAL	MONEY
Stuart Appleby	71	73	73	72	289	10,816.66
Paul Gow	68	73	73	75	289	10,816.66
Christopher Campbell	70	72	69	78	289	10,816.66
Peter Nolan	73	73	73	71	290	9,700
Peter Wilson	72	76	68	74	290	9,700
Brody Ninyette	69	76	70	75	290	9,700
Peter O'Malley	68	78	69	75	290	9,700

BMW New Zealand Open

Clearwater Resort, Christchurch, New Zealand
Par 36-36–72; 7,122 yards

November 22-25
purse, A$400,000

	SCORES				TOTAL	MONEY
*Jake Higginbottom	72	70	72	67	281	
Jason Norris	77	73	66	66	282	A$56,400
Peter Wilson	72	71	71	68	282	56,400
Mark Brown	72	73	66	73	284	27,000
Richard Lee	76	70	70	69	285	19,200
Brody Ninyette	80	69	69	68	286	14,400
Clint Rice	74	74	69	69	286	14,400
Peter O'Malley	74	73	68	71	286	14,400
Nick Cullen	71	77	69	70	287	11,600
Michael Moore	77	70	72	69	288	8,600
Mahal Pearce	72	72	74	70	288	8,600
Aaron Townsend	73	71	73	71	288	8,600
Aaron Pike	73	77	67	71	288	8,600
Craig Hancock	68	75	72	73	288	8,600
Michael Hendry	74	71	70	73	288	8,600
Andrew Tschudin	73	74	72	70	289	5,163.33
Ryan McCarthy	75	73	71	70	289	5,163.33
Daniel Pearce	76	72	71	70	289	5,163.33
Ryan Fox	70	73	75	71	289	5,163.33
Gareth Paddison	71	72	75	71	289	5,163.33
Marcus Cain	73	74	70	72	289	5,163.33
Steven Jones	75	73	72	70	290	3,846.66
Clarke Osborne	79	72	69	70	290	3,846.66
Ryan Haller	71	71	77	71	290	3,846.66
Pieter Zwart	72	76	71	71	290	3,846.66
David Bransdon	74	74	70	72	290	3,846.66
Martin Dive	79	71	67	73	290	3,846.66

NSW PGA Championship

Mt. Broughton Golf & Country Club,
Southern Highlands, New South Wales
Par 36-36–72; 6,619 yards

November 29-December 2
purse, A$100,000

	SCORES				TOTAL	MONEY
Matthew Stieger	67	67	71	68	273	A$15,000
Daniel Nisbet	70	69	68	69	276	9,500
Nick Cullen	69	71	70	67	277	7,000
Kyle Grant	70	68	72	68	278	4,550
Ryan Fox	67	70	71	70	278	4,550
Daniel Popovic	69	71	71	68	279	3,325
Thomas Petersson	67	68	73	71	279	3,325
*Callan O'Reilly	71	67	66	75	279	

	SCORES				TOTAL	MONEY
Chris Gaunt	75	71	69	65	280	2,483.33
Craig Hancock	71	68	72	69	280	2,483.33
Anthony Summers	68	69	73	70	280	2,483.33
Matthew Griffin	70	70	73	68	281	1,800
Marcus Cain	71	68	70	72	281	1,800
Adam Stephens	66	71	71	73	281	1,800
Jordan Sherratt	75	68	71	68	282	1,450
*Dimi Papadatos	73	70	71	68	282	
Deyen Lawson	68	70	72	72	282	1,450
Alex Katholos	71	75	68	69	283	1,190
Gavin Fairfax	68	76	70	69	283	1,190
Nick Gillespie	74	69	69	71	283	1,190
Timothy Wood	69	72	70	72	283	1,190
Jake Higginbottom	65	73	72	73	283	1,190
Taylor Cooper	75	68	69	72	284	1,060
Anthony Brown	68	70	73	73	284	1,060
Pieter Zwart	70	67	72	75	284	1,060

Emirates Australian Open

The Lakes Golf Club, Sydney, New South Wales
Par 35-37–72; 6,841 yards

December 6-9
purse, A$1,250,000

	SCORES				TOTAL	MONEY
Peter Senior	75	68	69	72	284	A$225,000
Brendan Jones	68	71	75	71	285	127,500
Cameron Percy	72	69	72	73	286	84,375
Kim Felton	68	75	72	72	287	51,666.66
Kieran Pratt	71	71	70	75	287	51,666.66
Justin Rose	68	73	70	76	287	51,666.66
Michael Hendry	72	71	74	71	288	36,666.66
Scott Gardiner	76	71	68	73	288	36,666.66
Stuart Appleby	70	73	70	75	288	36,666.66
Brett Rumford	73	69	75	72	289	26,562.50
Nick O'Hern	71	73	73	72	289	26,562.50
Rod Pampling	74	69	73	73	289	26,562.50
Matthew Jones	71	72	69	77	289	26,562.50
*Cameron Smith	72	74	69	75	290	
Steven Jones	73	68	73	76	290	19,750
Mathew Goggin	71	70	73	76	290	19,750
Adam Scott	72	71	71	76	290	19,750
Nick Flanagan	69	76	74	72	291	14,362.50
Jamie Arnold	72	72	72	75	291	14,362.50
Matthew Stieger	73	71	71	76	291	14,362.50
Nick Cullen	70	70	74	77	291	14,362.50
John Senden	66	73	70	82	291	14,362.50
Alistair Presnell	75	72	71	74	292	11,825
Matthew Griffin	75	69	71	77	292	11,825
Geoff Ogilvy	74	71	70	77	292	11,825
Greg Chalmers	71	75	69	77	292	11,825
Matthew Millar	74	71	69	78	292	11,825

Australian PGA Championship

Palmer Coolum Resort, Coolum, Queensland
Par 36-36-72

December 13-16
purse, A$1,250,000

	SCORES				TOTAL	MONEY
Daniel Popovic	64	70	69	69	272	A$225,000
Rod Pampling	71	67	69	69	276	105,937.50
Anthony Brown	73	68	64	71	276	105,937.50
Geoff Ogilvy	67	69	72	69	277	55,000
Brad Kennedy	69	68	70	70	277	55,000
Richard Green	71	68	70	69	278	42,500
Nathan Green	72	71	66	69	278	42,500
Marc Leishman	69	70	73	67	279	26,166.66
Steven Bowditch	70	67	74	68	279	26,166.66
Darren Clarke	70	69	72	68	279	26,166.66
John Senden	73	69	69	68	279	26,166.66
James Nitties	70	72	68	69	279	26,166.66
Michael Wright	70	73	66	70	279	26,166.66
Stephen Dartnall	68	72	68	71	279	26,166.66
Mathew Goggin	71	66	70	72	279	26,166.66
Matthew Griffin	69	67	70	73	279	26,166.66
Adam Crawford	70	71	70	69	280	14,703.12
Jason Kang	70	69	71	70	280	14,703.12
Matthew Millar	73	66	70	71	280	14,703.12
Brendan Jones	73	67	67	73	280	14,703.12
Peter O'Malley	73	68	71	69	281	12,875
Greg Chalmers	72	69	68	72	281	12,875
Kim Do-hoon	73	71	68	70	282	11,593.75
Terry Pilkadaris	70	74	69	69	282	11,593.75
Jason Scrivener	68	75	69	70	282	11,593.75
Kurt Barnes	74	65	71	72	282	11,593.75

African Tours

Africa Open

East London Golf Club, East London, Eastern Cape, South Africa
Par 37-36–73; 6,691 yards

January 6-9
purse, €1,000,000

	SCORES				TOTAL	MONEY
Louis Oosthuizen	69	62	67	67	265	R1,664,250
Tjaart van der Walt	69	64	65	69	267	1,207,500
Retief Goosen	65	68	66	69	268	726,600
Jaco Van Zyl	71	65	67	66	269	515,550
Alastair Forsyth	69	66	68	67	270	433,650
Richard Sterne	69	69	64	70	272	371,700
Danny Willett	67	68	65	73	273	309,750
Lyle Rowe	73	68	65	68	274	242,550
Craig Lee	68	67	68	71	274	242,550
Emiliano Grillo	73	66	71	65	275	183,487.50
Peter Karmis	68	70	69	68	275	183,487.50
Matthew Baldwin	72	64	70	69	275	183,487.50
Magnus A. Carlsson	69	66	70	70	275	183,487.50
Branden Grace	77	63	69	67	276	146,475
Jaco Ahlers	65	68	73	70	276	146,475
Shaun Norris	67	70	69	70	276	146,475
Thomas Aiken	64	69	72	71	276	146,475
David Drysdale	72	69	69	67	277	114,068.18
Reinier Saxton	71	70	69	67	277	114,068.18
Jacques Blaauw	70	69	70	68	277	114,068.18
Dawie Van der Walt	70	70	69	68	277	114,068.18
Tommy Fleetwood	69	66	72	70	277	114,068.18
Benn Barham	70	66	70	71	277	114,068.18
Tim Sluiter	68	69	69	71	277	114,068.18
Joshua Cunliffe	69	68	69	71	277	114,068.18
Adilson Da Silva	69	69	68	71	277	114,068.18
Darren Fichardt	71	70	65	71	277	114,068.18
Richard Bland	67	69	69	72	277	114,068.18
David Howell	68	69	72	69	278	89,460
George Coetzee	71	68	69	70	278	89,460
Doug McGuigan	70	69	68	71	278	89,460
Danie van Tonder	70	70	67	71	278	89,460
Tyrone Ferreira	68	68	69	73	278	89,460
Phillip Archer	73	67	72	67	279	76,650
Taco Remkes	68	70	71	70	279	76,650
Jorge Campillo	71	66	71	71	279	76,650
Maarten Lafeber	67	73	68	71	279	76,650
Garth Mulroy	68	72	68	71	279	76,650
Edouard Dubois	69	71	68	71	279	76,650
Grant Muller	69	69	68	73	279	76,650
Warren Abery	71	70	70	69	280	63,000
J.J. Senekal	67	71	71	71	280	63,000
Chris Wood	69	71	69	71	280	63,000
James Kingston	70	71	68	71	280	63,000
Allan Versfeld	69	70	68	73	280	63,000
Agustin Domingo	68	71	68	73	280	63,000
Matthew Nixon	70	71	74	66	281	49,350
Merrick Bremner	69	70	74	68	281	49,350
Desvonde Botes	69	71	71	70	281	49,350
Ariel Canete	71	68	71	71	281	49,350
Steven O'Hara	70	70	70	71	281	49,350

	SCORES				TOTAL	MONEY
Sam Walker	69	68	72	72	281	49,350
Andrew Marshall	74	65	69	73	281	49,350
Jamie Elson	70	71	71	70	282	36,960
Sam Hutsby	73	65	72	72	282	36,960
Alessandro Tadini	70	70	70	72	282	36,960
Alan McLean	70	71	68	73	282	36,960
Julien Quesne	69	71	68	74	282	36,960
Wil Besseling	69	70	73	71	283	31,500
Andrew Georgiou	75	66	71	71	283	31,500
Ruan de Smidt	69	70	67	77	283	31,500
Jamie Moul	70	71	72	71	284	26,250
Jordi Garcia	68	73	71	72	284	26,250
Hendrik Buhrmann	72	69	71	72	284	26,250
Bryce Easton	69	70	72	73	284	26,250
Albert Pistorius	71	69	71	73	284	26,250
Charles-Edouard Russo	67	72	71	74	284	26,250
Keith Horne	67	73	75	69	284	26,250
Scott Pinckney	69	72	67	77	285	22,050
Dean O'Riley	66	75	74	72	287	17,489.50
Vaughn Groenewald	73	68	73	73	287	17,489.50
Justin Walters	73	68	71	75	287	17,489.50
Knut Borsheim	70	68	76	74	288	15,671.25
Jean-Baptiste Gonnet	71	67	72	78	288	15,671.25
Titch Moore	74	66	75	74	289	15,624
Neil Cheetham	71	68	76	75	290	15,561
J.G. Claassen	68	72	75	75	290	15,561
Adam Gee	69	69	74	78	290	15,561
Ockie Strydom	70	69	81	73	293	15,482.25
Oliver Wilson	70	69	78	76	293	15,482.25

Joburg Open

Royal Johannesburg & Kensington Golf Club,   January 12-15
Johannesburg, South Africa   purse, €1,300,000
Par 37-35–72; 7,650 yards

	SCORES				TOTAL	MONEY
Branden Grace	67	66	65	72	270	R2,142,920
Jamie Elson	63	75	70	63	271	1,554,800
David Drysdale	65	72	69	67	273	561,305.33
Marc Warren	66	69	70	68	273	561,305.33
Jaco Van Zyl	67	69	69	68	273	561,305.33
Trevor Fisher, Jr.	68	68	69	68	273	561,305.33
Dawie Van der Walt	70	66	67	70	273	561,305.33
Michiel Bothma	68	66	68	71	273	561,305.33
George Murray	65	69	73	67	274	256,204
Bernd Wiesberger	70	66	69	69	274	256,204
Robert Rock	65	67	72	70	274	256,204
Jbe' Kruger	67	66	69	72	274	256,204
Andrew Parr	70	69	64	72	275	212,264
Danny Willett	69	67	68	72	276	195,364
George Coetzee	65	67	69	75	276	195,364
Retief Goosen	66	67	71	73	277	185,224
Lee Slattery	72	67	69	70	278	160,694.85
Craig Lee	64	74	70	70	278	160,694.85
Andrew Marshall	70	69	71	68	278	160,694.85
Chris Swanepoel	68	69	73	68	278	160,694.85
Magnus A. Carlsson	70	66	70	72	278	160,694.85
Reinier Saxton	64	73	69	72	278	160,694.85
Joakim Lagergren	70	67	68	73	278	160,694.85

	SCORES			TOTAL	MONEY
Lyle Rowe	66	69	74	70	279	127,933
Ulrich van den Berg	68	68	71	72	279	127,933
Julien Quesne	65	72	70	72	279	127,933
Thomas Aiken	68	68	70	73	279	127,933
Warren Abery	66	72	68	73	279	127,933
Shaun Norris	65	69	71	74	279	127,933
Scott Jamieson	68	67	70	74	279	127,933
Richard Finch	66	66	69	78	279	127,933
Adam Gee	69	70	69	72	280	106,808
Daniel Gaunt	69	67	73	71	280	106,808
Jean Hugo	68	67	72	73	280	106,808
Adilson Da Silva	71	68	72	69	280	106,808
Hendrik Buhrmann	72	66	73	69	280	106,808
Doug McGuigan	69	70	69	73	281	87,880
Sam Little	68	71	70	72	281	87,880
Tommy Fleetwood	66	73	70	72	281	87,880
Jordi Garcia	66	72	70	73	281	87,880
Divan van den Heever	67	70	73	71	281	87,880
Anthony Wall	73	65	73	70	281	87,880
Joel Sjoholm	65	74	73	69	281	87,880
Roope Kakko	71	68	73	69	281	87,880
Justin Walters	69	70	73	69	281	87,880
Jake Roos	69	68	72	73	282	68,952
Darren Fichardt	68	71	68	75	282	68,952
Damien McGrane	63	71	76	72	282	68,952
*Brandon Stone	72	65	73	72	282	
Brandon Pieters	66	71	73	72	282	68,952
Alastair Forsyth	74	65	72	71	282	68,952
Markus Brier	71	68	70	74	283	58,136
Phillip Archer	71	67	71	74	283	58,136
Peter Karmis	64	73	75	71	283	58,136
Theunis Spangenberg	69	68	72	75	284	50,024
Ryan Tipping	68	69	72	75	284	50,024
Matthew Nixon	70	67	70	77	284	50,024
Anthony Snobeck	72	67	74	72	285	43,940
Scott Pinckney	64	72	77	72	285	43,940
Benjamin Hebert	67	72	73	74	286	41,236
Keith Horne	72	67	74	73	286	41,236
Sam Hutsby	68	71	75	73	287	39,208
Carlos Del Moral	65	72	77	74	288	37,180
Steven Ferreira	74	65	78	71	288	37,180
Thomas Norret	66	71	77	75	289	35,152
Desvonde Botes	65	69	78	78	290	33,800
Bennie van der Merwe	67	72	81	73	293	32,448

Volvo Golf Champions

The Links at Fancourt, George, South Africa
Par 36-37–73; 7,388 yards

January 19-22
purse, €2,000,00

	SCORES			TOTAL	MONEY
Branden Grace	68	66	75	71	280	€350,000
Ernie Els	71	71	71	67	280	177,500
Retief Goosen	72	68	70	70	280	177,500
(Grace defeated Els and Goosen on first playoff hole.)						
Nicolas Colsaerts	64	76	69	72	281	110,000
Charl Schwartzel	75	67	68	72	282	93,000
Jose Maria Olazabal	71	68	72	73	284	80,000
Raphael Jacquelin	71	69	77	69	286	65,000
Louis Oosthuizen	69	71	72	74	286	65,000

	SCORES				TOTAL	MONEY
Thomas Aiken	68	70	77	72	287	53,000
Padraig Harrington	69	73	70	76	288	47,050
Paul Lawrie	72	68	74	74	288	47,050
Oliver Fisher	77	72	69	71	289	40,075
Robert Karlsson	74	70	72	73	289	40,075
Robert Rock	73	70	79	67	289	40,075
Lee Slattery	73	65	77	74	289	40,075
Thomas Bjorn	71	70	75	74	290	34,650
David Horsey	69	72	76	73	290	34,650
Alexander Noren	72	68	74	76	290	34,650
Hennie Otto	71	69	76	74	290	34,650
Darren Clarke	74	68	73	76	291	32,150
Simon Dyson	75	70	73	73	291	32,150
Tom Lewis	68	74	77	73	292	31,100
Matteo Manassero	76	73	76	68	293	30,400
S.S.P. Chowrasia	75	71	72	76	294	29,350
Miguel Angel Jimenez	71	72	79	72	294	29,350
Gonzalo Fernandez-Castano	74	72	78	71	295	27,600
Joost Luiten	69	72	77	77	295	27,600
Matthew Zions	70	75	77	73	295	27,600
Garth Mulroy	71	73	76	76	296	26,200
Kenneth Ferrie	71	76	80	70	297	25,500
Colin Montgomerie	70	75	80	75	300	24,800
Pablo Larrazabal	74	74	78	76	302	24,100
Michael Hoey	78	72	76	82	308	23,400
Thomas Levet	81	73	82	76	312	22,350
Pablo Martin	76	73	90	73	312	22,350

Dimension Data Pro-Am

Fancourt, George, South Africa
Par 36-36–72; 7,342 yards

February 16-19
purse, R3,200,000

	SCORES				TOTAL	MONEY
Oliver Bekker	65	70	71	70	276	R475,500
Tyrone Ferreira	69	70	70	69	278	276,300
Thomas Aiken	68	71	70	69	278	276,300
Shaun Norris	75	68	69	68	280	135,600
Merrick Bremner	72	72	63	73	280	135,600
Derik Ferreira	71	73	72	65	281	97,350
Jean Hugo	70	68	70	73	281	97,350
Charl Coetzee	74	69	70	70	283	58,050
Michael Hollick	71	71	72	69	283	58,050
Dawie Van der Walt	72	77	67	67	283	58,050
Divan van den Heever	67	67	75	74	283	58,050
James Kingston	68	72	68	75	283	58,050
Simon Wakefield	71	71	66	75	283	58,050
Kyle Scott	71	72	72	69	284	41,850
Desvonde Botes	69	74	69	72	284	41,850
Tjaart van der Walt	70	70	73	71	284	41,850
Anthony Michael	72	74	64	74	284	41,850
P.H. McIntyre	73	68	72	72	285	35,520
Doug McGuigan	72	72	71	70	285	35,520
Bruce McDonald	70	74	71	70	285	35,520
Jacques Blaauw	72	71	75	67	285	35,520
Hennie Otto	67	73	69	76	285	35,520
J.J. Senekal	79	70	68	69	286	31,950
Mark Murless	72	69	70	75	286	31,950
Michiel Bothma	69	71	76	71	287	29,700
Daniel Greene	72	72	68	75	287	29,700
Warren Abery	65	72	73	77	287	29,700

Telkom PGA Championship

The Country Club, Johannesburg, South Africa
Par 36-36—72; 7,546 yards

February 23-26
purse, R3,500,000

	SCORES				TOTAL	MONEY
Keith Horne	70	63	67	69	269	R554,750
Jaco Ahlers	69	68	69	66	272	272,183.33
Alex Haindl	69	65	68	70	272	272,183.33
Darren Fichardt	64	71	67	70	272	272,183.33
Ulrich van den Berg	69	69	68	67	273	123,900
James Kamte	67	67	69	70	273	123,900
Trevor Fisher, Jr.	65	69	69	70	273	123,900
Tyrone Ferreira	73	65	70	66	274	76,766.66
Jaco Van Zyl	69	68	70	67	274	76,766.66
Bryce Easton	69	66	70	69	274	76,766.66
Richard Sterne	71	68	68	68	275	60,550
Albert Pistorius	70	70	65	70	275	60,550
Allan Versfeld	71	70	71	64	276	47,337.50
Mark Murless	74	67	69	66	276	47,337.50
Jake Roos	69	71	68	68	276	47,337.50
Louis Moolman	70	66	71	69	276	47,337.50
Keenan Davidse	71	66	69	70	276	47,337.50
Andrew Curlewis	67	69	69	71	276	47,337.50
Joshua Cunliffe	71	66	66	73	276	47,337.50
Dean Burmester	66	66	70	74	276	47,337.50
Jbe' Kruger	70	68	70	69	277	39,375
Morne Buys	73	65	65	74	277	39,375
Merrick Bremner	72	69	66	71	278	37,800
Drikus van der Walt	69	71	72	67	279	36,225
Jean Hugo	70	70	69	70	279	36,225

Platinum Classic

Mooinooi Golf Club, Rustenburg, South Africa
Par 36-36—72; 6,835 yards

March 22-24
purse, R500,000

	SCORES			TOTAL	MONEY
Jake Roos	66	66	70	202	R79,250
Anthony Michael	72	67	63	202	48,750
Chris Swanepoel	66	71	65	202	48,750
(Roos won on fifth playoff hole.)					
Ulrich van den Berg	68	66	69	203	27,500
Dean Burmester	68	66	69	203	27,500
James Kamte	68	69	67	204	16,166.66
Warren Abery	67	67	70	204	16,166.66
Divan van den Heever	64	66	74	204	16,166.66
Graham van der Merwe	70	70	65	205	11,333.33
Doug McGuigan	71	67	67	205	11,333.33
Allan Versfeld	70	67	68	205	11,333.33
Albert Pistorius	69	68	69	206	9,750
Danie van Tonder	67	69	70	206	9,750
Louis de Jager	68	71	68	207	8,566.66
Mark Williams	68	70	69	207	8,566.66
Charl Coetzee	68	66	73	207	8,566.66
Oliver Bekker	72	68	68	208	7,650
Neil Cheetham	65	74	69	208	7,650
Shaun Norris	70	72	67	209	6,700
Bryce Easton	70	71	68	209	6,700
Grant Muller	70	71	68	209	6,700

	SCORES			TOTAL	MONEY
Vaughn Groenewald	71	69	69	209	6,700
Andrew Georgiou	69	70	70	209	6,700
Des Terblanche	68	72	70	210	5,850
Divan Gerber	68	71	71	210	5,850

Golden Pilsener Zimbabwe Open

Royal Harare Golf Club, Harare, Zimbabwe — April 19-22
Par 36-36–72; 7,149 yards — purse, R1,500,000

	SCORES				TOTAL	MONEY
Chris Swanepoel	71	69	69	64	273	R237,750
Trevor Fisher, Jr.	70	65	69	69	273	172,500
(Swanepoel defeated Fisher on second playoff hole.)						
Ruan de Smidt	70	65	69	71	275	103,800
Colin Nel	70	69	73	67	279	73,650
Jean Hugo	71	71	69	69	280	53,100
Titch Moore	71	74	65	70	280	53,100
Justin Walters	72	66	69	73	280	53,100
Desvonde Botes	71	69	72	69	281	36,900
Anthony Michael	73	71	72	67	283	27,450
Tyrone Ryan	71	75	70	67	283	27,450
Teboho Sefatsa	72	71	71	69	283	27,450
Danie van Tonder	72	71	68	72	283	27,450
Ulrich van den Berg	69	69	71	74	283	27,450
J.J. Senekal	71	73	71	69	284	20,925
Ben Mannix	72	71	68	73	284	20,925
Dean Burmester	75	68	67	74	284	20,925
Andrew Curlewis	68	70	71	75	284	20,925
Toto Thimba, Jr.	69	76	71	69	285	18,350
Jacques van Tonder	74	72	70	69	285	18,350
Des Terblanche	73	69	71	72	285	18,350
Jake Roos	71	70	77	68	286	16,425
T.C. Charamba	72	72	72	70	286	16,425
Jaco Ahlers	73	72	70	71	286	16,425
Justin Harding	76	70	68	72	286	16,425
Andrew Georgiou	72	71	75	69	287	14,625
Ryan Cairns	70	72	75	70	287	14,625
Matthew Carvell	67	72	75	73	287	14,625
Daniel Greene	71	71	70	75	287	14,625

Investec Royal Swazi Sun Open

Royal Swazi Golf Club, Mbabane, Swaziland — May 2-5
Par 36-36–72; 6,715 yards — purse, R1,000,000

	POINTS				TOTAL	MONEY
Christiaan Basson	10	17	11	12	50	R158,500
Desvonde Botes	11	18	10	10	49	93,200
Danie van Tonder	4	13	21	11	49	93,200
Dean Burmester	11	14	10	10	45	50,500
Oliver Bekker	4	16	15	9	44	42,400
Louis de Jager	11	7	8	17	43	30,533.33
Ruan de Smidt	8	11	6	18	43	30,533.33
Toto Thimba, Jr.	12	10	10	11	43	30,533.33
Daniel Greene	11	11	9	10	41	22,000
Merrick Bremner	8	14	8	10	40	19,900

	POINTS				TOTAL	MONEY
Andrew Curlewis	7	10	9	13	39	16,881
Tyrone Ferreira	14	5	9	11	39	16,881
Brandon Pieters	14	5	12	8	39	16,881
Albert Pistorius	14	6	14	5	39	16,881
Allan Versfeld	5	9	15	9	38	14,306
Wallie Coetsee	10	12	11	5	38	14,306
Jake Roos	11	16	5	6	38	14,306
Colin Nel	9	7	7	14	37	12,906
Neil Schietekat	11	10	9	7	37	12,906
Des Terblanche	20	2	8	7	37	12,906
Trevor Fisher, Jr.	15	1	13	7	36	11,956
Charl Coetzee	15	7	8	6	36	11,956
Theunis Spangenberg	10	13	4	8	35	11,356
Jacques Blaauw	12	4	8	11	35	11,356
Matthew Carvell	7	8	4	15	34	10,906

Vodacom Origins of Golf - Simola

Simola Golf & Country Estate, Eastern Cape, South Africa   May 9-11
Par 36-36–72; 7,003 yards   purse, R600,000

	SCORES			TOTAL	MONEY
Ryan Cairns	71	68	62	201	R95,100
Vaughn Groenewald	67	68	66	201	69,000
(Cairns defeated Groenewald on first playoff hole.)					
Louis de Jager	70	67	67	204	42,900
Jake Redman	69	64	71	204	42,900
James Kamte	70	68	67	205	25,500
Titch Moore	68	68	69	205	25,500
Trevor Fisher, Jr.	71	67	68	206	18,900
Christiaan Basson	70	71	66	207	14,900
Ulrich van den Berg	71	68	68	207	14,900
Albert Pistorius	66	72	69	207	14,900
Bryce Easton	66	72	70	208	12,000
Anthony Michael	70	66	72	208	12,000
Justin Harding	69	67	72	208	12,000
Branden Grace	70	71	69	210	10,280
Andrew Georgiou	69	72	69	210	10,280
Neil Schietekat	68	70	72	210	10,280
Jacques Blaauw	70	72	69	211	9,000
Peter Karmis	69	71	71	211	9,000
Ruan de Smidt	68	72	71	211	9,000
Chris Swanepoel	72	71	69	212	7,890
Jaco Ahlers	73	69	70	212	7,890
Mark Williams	72	70	70	212	7,890
Louis Calitz	71	70	71	212	7,890
Desvonde Botes	73	71	69	213	6,322.50
Alan McLean	76	68	69	213	6,322.50
Dean Burmester	74	69	70	213	6,322.50
Charl Coetzee	72	71	70	213	6,322.50
David Ryan	66	76	71	213	6,322.50
Keenan Davidse	69	72	72	213	6,322.50
Steven Ferreira	72	69	72	213	6,322.50
Merrick Bremner	69	71	73	213	6,322.50

Sun City Challenge

Lost City Golf Club, Sun City, South Africa
Par 36-36–72; 7,626 yards

May 24-26
purse, R550,000

	SCORES			TOTAL	MONEY
Bryce Easton	66	69	72	207	R87,175
Allan Versfeld	66	72	69	207	47,300
Brandon Pieters	65	71	71	207	47,300
Andrew Georgiou	66	70	71	207	47,300
(Easton won on first playoff hole.)					
Theunis Spangenberg	69	72	67	208	21,358.33
Justin Walters	70	67	71	208	21,358.33
James Kamte	69	65	74	208	21,358.33
Jake Roos	73	70	66	209	12,705
Des Terblanche	71	68	70	209	12,705
Neil Cheetham	68	70	71	209	12,705
Grant Muller	70	67	72	209	12,705
Johan du Buisson	66	71	72	209	12,705
Jacques Blaauw	71	70	70	211	9,460
Merrick Bremner	70	70	71	211	9,460
Doug McGuigan	68	71	72	211	9,460
Oliver Bekker	69	68	74	211	9,460
Callie Swart	67	69	75	211	9,460
Ryan Tipping	73	69	70	212	8,085
Ulrich van den Berg	72	68	72	212	8,085
Lindani Ndwandwe	70	71	72	213	7,507.50
Jake Redman	69	70	74	213	7,507.50
Toto Thimba	67	73	74	214	6,820
Daniel Hammond	66	74	74	214	6,820
Louis de Jager	71	69	74	214	6,820
Christiaan Basson	72	71	72	215	6,105
Ryan Cairns	70	73	72	215	6,105
Danie van Tonder	69	73	73	215	6,105

Lombard Insurance Classic

Royal Swazi Country Club, Mbabane, Swaziland
Par 36-36–72; 6,715 yards

June 1-3
purse, R900,000

	SCORES			TOTAL	MONEY
Jake Roos	66	70	63	199	R142,650
Justin Harding	68	64	67	199	103,500
(Roos defeated Harding on first playoff hole.)					
Andrew Georgiou	65	67	70	202	64,260
Mark Murless	66	70	68	204	41,805
Jacques Blaauw	67	67	70	204	41,805
Adilson Da Silva	71	66	68	205	27,480
Albert Pistorius	66	70	69	205	27,480
Jean Hugo	65	68	72	205	27,480
Jaco Ahlers	69	71	66	206	18,855
Louis de Jager	69	67	70	206	18,855
Justin Walters	69	70	68	207	16,160
David Hewan	68	70	69	207	16,160
Matthew Carvell	71	68	69	208	14,225
Ryan Tipping	67	70	71	208	14,225
Brandon Pieters	70	70	69	209	11,543
Tyrone Ryan	68	72	69	209	11,543
Danie van Tonder	68	71	70	209	11,543
Oliver Bekker	69	70	70	209	11,543

	SCORES			TOTAL	MONEY
Ulrich van den Berg	74	67	68	209	11,543
Desvonde Botes	72	70	67	209	11,543
Michiel Bothma	70	66	73	209	11,543
Charl Coetzee	69	73	67	209	11,543
Neil Cheetham	71	73	65	209	11,543
Christiaan Basson	68	67	74	209	11,543
Doug McGuigan	70	69	71	210	8,708
Des Terblanche	69	71	70	210	8,708
Dean O'Riley	71	69	70	210	8,708
Johan du Buisson	69	69	72	210	8,708
Merrick Bremner	68	69	73	210	8,708
Andrew Curlewis	71	71	68	210	8,708
Lindani Ndwandwe	71	71	68	210	8,708
Attie Schwartzel	69	68	73	210	8,708
Divan van den Heever	68	68	74	210	8,708
Ockie Strydom	74	69	67	210	8,708

Vodacom Origins of Golf - Zebula

Zebula Country Club, Limpopo, South Africa
Par 36-36–72; 7,469 yards

June 6-8
purse, R600,000

	SCORES			TOTAL	MONEY
Bryce Easton	68	64	68	200	R95,100
Doug McGuigan	66	66	71	203	69,000
Dean Burmester	67	69	68	204	48,000
Colin Nel	71	65	69	205	37,800
Andrew Georgiou	66	69	71	206	28,200
Neil Schietekat	69	71	69	209	20,850
Prinavin Nelson	64	76	69	209	20,850
Oliver Bekker	72	70	68	210	14,900
Ulrich van den Berg	71	70	69	210	14,900
Danie van Tonder	70	66	74	210	14,900
Jaco Ahlers	74	70	68	212	10,426.66
Trevor Fisher, Jr.	69	73	70	212	10,426.66
Michiel Bothma	70	72	70	212	10,426.66
P.H. McIntyre	73	69	70	212	10,426.66
Jake Redman	71	71	70	212	10,426.66
Shaun Norris	70	70	72	212	10,426.66
Albert Pistorius	67	73	72	212	10,426.66
Titch Moore	71	68	73	212	10,426.66
Louis de Jager	64	73	75	212	10,426.66
Andrew Curlewis	73	68	72	213	8,040
Vaughn Groenewald	72	68	73	213	8,040
Bradford Vaughan	70	69	74	213	8,040
Lean Boezaart	73	70	71	214	7,160
Matthew Carvell	72	70	72	214	7,160
Jean Hugo	73	68	73	214	7,160

Indo Zambia Bank Zambia Open

Lusaka Golf Club, Lusaka, Zambia
Par 35-38–73; 7,226 yards

June 14-17
purse, R1,200,000

	SCORES				TOTAL	MONEY
Justin Harding	71	72	69	68	280	R190,200
Divan van den Heever	75	70	68	69	282	138,000

	SCORES				TOTAL	MONEY
Des Terblanche	70	73	73	67	283	70,980
J.G. Claassen	69	73	73	68	283	70,980
Dean Burmester	73	73	71	69	286	42,480
Oliver Bekker	70	76	69	71	286	42,480
Chris Erasmus	68	70	76	72	286	42,480
Prinavin Nelson	74	72	76	65	287	27,720
Daniel Greene	72	71	73	71	287	27,720
Colin Nel	71	75	71	71	288	22,500
P.H. McIntyre	75	67	74	72	288	22,500
Titch Moore	74	72	74	69	289	17,297.14
Albert Pistorius	73	72	72	72	289	17,297.14
Jake Roos	73	73	71	72	289	17,297.14
Anthony Michael	68	72	76	73	289	17,297.14
Brandon Pieters	77	71	68	73	289	17,297.14
Charl Coetzee	69	75	71	74	289	17,297.14
Jake Redman	72	73	70	74	289	17,297.14
Thabo Maseko	75	74	73	68	290	14,160
Andrew Georgiou	72	67	79	72	290	14,160
Omar Sandys	74	72	69	75	290	14,160
Attie Schwartzel	76	72	74	69	291	12,420
Matthew Carvell	71	74	74	72	291	12,420
Riekus Nortje	73	75	71	72	291	12,420
Louis de Jager	77	72	70	72	291	12,420
Ulrich van den Berg	71	75	72	73	291	12,420
Doug McGuigan	69	76	72	74	291	12,420

Vodacom Origins of Golf - De Zalze

De Zalze Golf Club, Stellenbosch, South Africa
Par 36-36–72; 6,964 yards

July 25-27
purse, R600,000

	SCORES			TOTAL	MONEY
Allan Versfeld	65	66	67	198	R95,100
Ockie Strydom	64	64	73	201	69,000
Keith Horne	67	70	68	205	48,000
Shaun Norris	69	71	66	206	24,840
Mark Williams	71	67	68	206	24,840
Johan du Buisson	71	67	68	206	24,840
Louis de Jager	69	68	69	206	24,840
Jbe' Kruger	68	67	71	206	24,840
Jaco Van Zyl	72	68	67	207	13,600
Jaco Ahlers	67	69	71	207	13,600
Dean Burmester	68	67	72	207	13,600
Bryce Easton	67	71	70	208	11,700
Jean Hugo	66	68	74	208	11,700
Colin Nel	71	70	68	209	10,050
Matthew Carvell	71	69	69	209	10,050
Charl Coetzee	72	70	67	209	10,050
Darren Fichardt	66	70	73	209	10,050
Francois Haughton	67	73	70	210	8,505
Attie Schwartzel	72	68	70	210	8,505
Keenan Davidse	71	69	70	210	8,505
David Hewan	73	71	66	210	8,505
Chris Erasmus	68	73	70	211	7,440
Jacques Blaauw	72	67	72	211	7,440
J.G. Claassen	75	69	67	211	7,440
Riekus Nortje	71	71	70	212	6,540
Bradford Vaughan	71	71	70	212	6,540
Justin Harding	73	66	73	212	6,540
Des Terblanche	70	72	70	212	6,540

Vodacom Origins of Golf - Selborne

Selborne Hotel, Spa & Golf Estate, KwaZulu-Natal, South Africa
Par 36-36–72; 6,509 yards

August 22-24
purse, R600,000

	SCORES			TOTAL	MONEY
Adilson Da Silva	69	66	69	204	R95,100
Danie van Tonder	71	67	67	205	58,500
Doug McGuigan	68	66	71	205	58,500
Desvonde Botes	71	69	67	207	37,800
Allan Versfeld	70	69	69	208	21,600
Vaughn Groenewald	68	69	71	208	21,600
Charl Coetzee	69	66	73	208	21,600
Jared Harvey	67	68	73	208	21,600
Jaco Ahlers	73	68	68	209	13,200
Lindani Ndwandwe	75	65	69	209	13,200
Andrew Curlewis	70	68	71	209	13,200
Joshua Cunliffe	69	69	71	209	13,200
Matthew Carvell	71	70	69	210	11,100
Michiel Bothma	70	70	70	210	11,100
Theunis Spangenberg	71	71	69	211	9,600
Trevor Fisher, Jr.	68	72	71	211	9,600
Jacques Blaauw	69	69	73	211	9,600
Ulrich van den Berg	71	66	74	211	9,600
Riekus Nortje	76	66	70	212	8,340
Jake Redman	67	74	71	212	8,340
Martin du Toit	68	68	76	212	8,340
Des Terblanche	73	70	70	213	7,440
Andre Cruse	72	71	70	213	7,440
Ryan Tipping	75	67	71	213	7,440
Anthony Michael	72	72	70	214	5,910
Grant Muller	73	69	72	214	5,910
Dean Burmester	70	72	72	214	5,910
Bryce Easton	75	67	72	214	5,910
Neil Schietekat	74	68	72	214	5,910
Graham van der Merwe	69	73	72	214	5,910
Stuart Clark	72	68	74	214	5,910
Divan van den Heever	69	71	74	214	5,910
P.G. Van Zyl	69	70	75	214	5,910
Mark Williams	72	64	78	214	5,910

Wild Waves Golf Challenge

Wild Coast Country Club, KwaZulu-Natal, South Africa
Par 35-35–70; 6,149 yards

August 29-31
purse, R600,000

	SCORES			TOTAL	MONEY
Trevor Fisher, Jr.	64	67	66	197	R95,100
Ross Wellington	67	64	68	199	69,000
Oliver Bekker	69	65	66	200	48,000
Danie van Tonder	64	70	67	201	37,800
Ulrich van den Berg	67	68	67	202	28,200
Warren Abery	68	68	67	203	22,800
Charl Coetzee	68	69	67	204	18,900
Christiaan Basson	71	67	67	205	13,071.42
Matthew Carvell	68	70	67	205	13,071.42
Doug McGuigan	68	69	68	205	13,071.42
P.G. Van Zyl	70	67	68	205	13,071.42
Andrew Georgiou	68	68	69	205	13,071.42
Steven Ferreira	68	68	69	205	13,071.42

	SCORES			TOTAL	MONEY
Derik Ferreira	70	64	71	205	13,071.42
Neil Schietekat	64	73	69	206	9,408
Tyrone Ferreira	67	70	69	206	9,408
Adilson Da Silva	70	67	69	206	9,408
Justin Harding	68	67	71	206	9,408
Tyrone Ryan	67	66	73	206	9,408
Michiel Bothma	70	65	72	207	8,340
Louis Calitz	70	68	70	208	7,590
Brandon Pieters	67	71	70	208	7,590
Daniel Greene	66	71	71	208	7,590
Ruan de Smidt	72	65	71	208	7,590
P.H. McIntyre	69	71	69	209	6,540
Grant Muller	72	66	71	209	6,540
Mark Fensham	68	70	71	209	6,540
Grant Veenstra	72	66	71	209	6,540

Vodacom Origins of Golf - Sishen

Sishen Golf Club, Kathu, South Africa
Par 36-36–72; 7,054 yards

September 5-7
purse, R600,000

	SCORES			TOTAL	MONEY
Trevor Fisher, Jr.	67	69	66	202	R95,100
Christiaan Basson	66	71	65	202	69,000
(Fisher defeated Basson on first playoff hole.)					
Doug McGuigan	69	69	66	204	48,000
Danie van Tonder	66	72	68	206	37,800
Colin Nel	74	69	65	208	25,500
Justin Harding	69	70	69	208	25,500
Ulrich van den Berg	67	70	72	209	18,900
Michiel Bothma	67	75	68	210	16,500
Jake Roos	70	72	69	211	14,700
Divan van den Heever	74	73	65	212	12,700
Hendrik Buhrmann	69	71	72	212	12,700
Grant Muller	72	68	72	212	12,700
Brandon Pieters	70	73	70	213	11,100
Ryan Cairns	70	72	71	213	11,100
Jaco Ahlers	75	71	68	214	9,600
Bradford Vaughan	69	74	71	214	9,600
Ruan de Smidt	73	69	72	214	9,600
Jean Hugo	65	76	73	214	9,600
Andrew Curlewis	73	73	69	215	8,490
Mark Williams	72	70	73	215	8,490
Keenan Davidse	74	73	69	216	7,065
Jacques Blaauw	72	74	70	216	7,065
Thabo Maseko	75	71	70	216	7,065
Desvonde Botes	72	74	70	216	7,065
Dean O'Riley	70	75	71	216	7,065
Theunis Spangenberg	73	72	71	216	7,065
Chris Swanepoel	73	72	71	216	7,065
Matthew Carvell	71	71	74	216	7,065

Vodacom Origins of Golf Final

The Links, Fancourt, George, South Africa
Par 36-37–73; 7,579 yards

September 26-28
purse, R600,000

	SCORES			TOTAL	MONEY
Branden Grace	69	72	68	209	R95,100
Allan Versfeld	71	66	75	212	69,000
Divan van den Heever	69	71	77	217	48,000
Vaughn Groenewald	71	71	77	219	37,800
Andrew Georgiou	75	70	75	220	23,300
Grant Muller	73	70	77	220	23,300
Alex Haindl	72	67	81	220	23,300
Ulrich van den Berg	70	77	74	221	14,325
Oliver Bekker	73	73	75	221	14,325
Warren Abery	71	74	76	221	14,325
Neil Schietekat	70	72	79	221	14,325
Bradford Vaughan	77	74	71	222	9,953.33
Ryan Tipping	71	79	72	222	9,953.33
George Coetzee	75	73	74	222	9,953.33
Darryn Lloyd	73	73	76	222	9,953.33
Jean Hugo	75	71	76	222	9,953.33
James Kamte	73	73	76	222	9,953.33
Francois Haughton	72	74	76	222	9,953.33
Desvonde Botes	71	72	79	222	9,953.33
Ruan de Smidt	71	71	80	222	9,953.33
Danie van Tonder	73	76	75	224	7,065
Jake Roos	73	74	77	224	7,065
Michiel Bothma	71	75	78	224	7,065
Louis de Jager	72	74	78	224	7,065
Brandon Pieters	72	74	78	224	7,065
Andrew Curlewis	73	73	78	224	7,065
Alan Michell	73	72	79	224	7,065
Ross Wellington	72	73	79	224	7,065

BMG Classic

Glendower Golf Club, Johannesburg, South Africa
Par 36-36–72; 7,564 yards

October 19-21
purse, R600,000

	SCORES			TOTAL	MONEY
Teboho Sefatsa	70	68	68	206	R95,100
Merrick Bremner	73	65	69	207	69,000
Desvonde Botes	67	72	69	208	42,900
Matthew Carvell	68	69	71	208	42,900
Jake Redman	65	74	70	209	28,200
Neil Schietekat	73	71	66	210	22,800
Doug McGuigan	72	69	70	211	18,900
Trevor Fisher, Jr.	72	69	71	212	15,600
Tyrone Mordt	70	69	73	212	15,600
Pieter Moolman	70	72	71	213	12,700
Ben Mannix	69	71	73	213	12,700
Jean Hugo	71	73	69	213	12,700
Chris Swanepoel	74	68	72	214	9,697.50
Wallie Coetsee	74	69	71	214	9,697.50
Dean Burmester	71	70	73	214	9,697.50
Andre Cruse	67	73	74	214	9,697.50
Ockie Strydom	70	70	74	214	9,697.50
Ulrich van den Berg	78	66	70	214	9,697.50
Graham van der Merwe	68	71	75	214	9,697.50

	SCORES			TOTAL	MONEY
Divan Gerber	70	69	75	214	9,697.50
Alex Haindl	69	74	72	215	7,590
Warren Abery	75	69	71	215	7,590
Jacques Blaauw	69	71	75	215	7,590
Darryn Lloyd	70	74	71	215	7,590
Allan Versfeld	72	70	74	216	6,540
Andrew Curlewis	70	73	73	216	6,540
Jaco Ahlers	66	74	76	216	6,540
Dean O'Riley	74	70	72	216	6,540

Suncoast Classic

Durban Country Club, Durban, South Africa
Par 36-36–72; 6,732 yards

October 25-27
purse, R600,000

	SCORES			TOTAL	MONEY
Ruan de Smidt	69	68	71	208	R95,100
Vaughn Groenewald	74	70	68	212	69,000
Jacques Blaauw	72	70	71	213	48,000
Jake Roos	77	69	68	214	29,600
Titch Moore	73	71	70	214	29,600
Doug McGuigan	76	67	71	214	29,600
Teboho Sefatsa	73	69	73	215	17,700
Wallie Coetsee	71	69	75	215	17,700
Andre Cruse	75	71	70	216	14,100
James Kingston	74	72	70	216	14,100
Christiaan Basson	76	70	71	217	12,000
Grant Muller	69	79	69	217	12,000
Ryan Cairns	78	66	73	217	12,000
Louis de Jager	78	68	72	218	10,280
Jaco Ahlers	73	75	70	218	10,280
Alex Haindl	73	69	76	218	10,280
Trevor Fisher, Jr.	74	73	72	219	8,676
Ross Wellington	73	74	72	219	8,676
Daniel Hammond	74	72	73	219	8,676
Lyle Rowe	76	69	74	219	8,676
Andrew Curlewis	79	70	70	219	8,676
Bryce Easton	77	70	73	220	7,740
Daniel Greene	76	70	75	221	6,790
Omar Sandys	76	71	74	221	6,790
Danie van Tonder	73	72	76	221	6,790
Drikus van der Walt	77	71	73	221	6,790
Ryan Tipping	78	70	73	221	6,790
Hendrik Buhrmann	76	73	72	221	6,790

ISPS Handa Matchplay Championship

Zwartkop Country Club, Pretoria, South Africa
Par 36-36–72; 7,045 yards

October 30-November 5
purse, R2,000,000

QUARTER-FINALS

Jaco Ahlers defeated Wallie Coetsee, 3 and 1.
P.H. McIntyre defeated Steven Ferreira, 19th hole.
Doug McGuigan defeated Darren Fichardt, 2 and 1.
Merrick Bremner defeated Theunis Spangenberg, 3 and 2.

(Each losing player received R64,000.)

SEMI-FINALS

Ahlers defeated McIntyre, 5 and 3.

McGuigan defeated Bremner, 5 and 3.

PLAYOFF FOR THIRD-FOURTH PLACE

Bremner defeated McIntyre, 6 and 5.

(Bremner received R150,000; McIntyre received R100,000.)

FINAL

McGuigan defeated Ahlers, 1 up.

(McGuigan received R300,000; Ahlers received R200,000.)

Nedbank Affinity Cup

Lost City Golf Club, Sun City, South Africa
Par 36-36—72; 7,310 yards

November 6-8
purse, R650,000

	SCORES			TOTAL	MONEY
Trevor Fisher, Jr.	69	67	71	207	R103,025
Desvonde Botes	71	70	67	208	63,375
Bradford Vaughan	68	72	68	208	63,375
Grant Muller	69	72	68	209	32,066.66
Matthew Carvell	73	66	70	209	32,066.66
Grant Veenstra	68	69	72	209	32,066.66
Tyrone Ferreira	72	70	68	210	19,175
Allan Versfeld	69	68	73	210	19,175
Warren Abery	73	71	68	212	14,300
Jacques Blaauw	69	74	69	212	14,300
Justin Walters	69	71	72	212	14,300
Louis Calitz	68	69	75	212	14,300
Chris Swanepoel	71	73	69	213	10,715.71
James Kamte	71	73	69	213	10,715.71
Brandon Pieters	67	76	70	213	10,715.71
Lyle Rowe	71	71	71	213	10,715.71
Andrew Curlewis	71	70	72	213	10,715.71
Ulrich van den Berg	72	68	73	213	10,715.71
Dean Burmester	66	70	77	213	10,715.71
David Hewan	74	69	71	214	8,872.50
Neil Cheetham	73	68	73	214	8,872.50
Michael du Toit	74	71	70	215	7,774
Andre Cruse	72	71	72	215	7,774
Louis de Jager	70	73	72	215	7,774
Andrew Georgiou	69	73	73	215	7,774
Jared Harvey	68	69	78	215	7,774

South African Open Championship

Serengeti Golf & Wildlife Estate, Ekurhuleni, South Africa
Par 36-36—72; 7,761 yards

November 15-18
purse, €1,000,000

	SCORES				TOTAL	MONEY
Henrik Stenson	66	65	69	71	271	R1,754,595
George Coetzee	70	70	63	71	274	1,273,050
Thomas Aiken	73	66	69	67	275	654,790.50
Martin Kaymer	70	70	68	67	275	654,790.50

	SCORES				TOTAL	MONEY
Charl Schwartzel	68	68	74	67	277	457,191
Tommy Fleetwood	70	69	71	69	279	330,255
Darren Fichardt	68	70	68	73	279	330,255
Magnus A. Carlsson	68	67	68	76	279	330,255
Hennie Otto	71	72	75	62	280	228,042
Michael Jonzon	68	69	71	72	280	228,042
Oliver Bekker	68	69	74	70	281	191,511
Shaun Norris	72	70	67	72	281	191,511
Adrien Bernadet	68	71	74	69	282	161,345.25
Lloyd Saltman	70	66	75	71	282	161,345.25
Jake Roos	68	71	71	72	282	161,345.25
Trevor Fisher, Jr.	69	70	71	72	282	161,345.25
Marc Warren	70	69	71	73	283	140,589
Michiel Bothma	69	69	71	74	283	140,589
Allan Versfeld	69	69	70	75	283	140,589
Desvonde Botes	71	71	74	68	284	118,033.87
Richard Sterne	69	70	75	70	284	118,033.87
Michael Hollick	72	71	70	71	284	118,033.87
Markus Brier	71	71	70	72	284	118,033.87
James Kingston	71	68	72	73	284	118,033.87
Knut Borsheim	73	69	69	73	284	118,033.87
Martin Wiegele	72	69	70	73	284	118,033.87
Matthew Carvell	66	72	70	76	284	118,033.87
Peter Whiteford	69	69	72	75	285	102,951
Anthony Snobeck	69	73	73	71	286	95,478.75
Chris Swanepoel	73	69	71	73	286	95,478.75
James Kamte	69	74	68	75	286	95,478.75
Ryan Cairns	69	71	71	75	286	95,478.75
Jaco Ahlers	69	70	79	69	287	80,811
Tyrone Ferreira	72	69	77	69	287	80,811
Justin Harding	73	70	72	72	287	80,811
Estanislao Goya	69	72	74	72	287	80,811
Craig Lee	67	70	77	73	287	80,811
Peter Gustafsson	71	70	72	74	287	80,811
Andrew Johnston	71	70	71	75	287	80,811
Jaco Van Zyl	70	72	68	77	287	80,811
Merrick Bremner	64	70	73	80	287	80,811
Alastair Forsyth	71	72	73	72	288	65,313
H.P. Bacher	70	70	76	72	288	65,313
Neil Schietekat	73	69	73	73	288	65,313
Jorge Campillo	70	71	72	75	288	65,313
Espen Kofstad	69	70	73	76	288	65,313
Andy Sullivan	71	70	79	69	289	56,457
Bradford Vaughan	70	70	75	74	289	56,457
Titch Moore	71	69	74	75	289	56,457
Ross Wellington	72	71	74	73	290	47,601
Lasse Jensen	72	70	74	74	290	47,601
Aron Zemmer	73	69	73	75	290	47,601
Garth Mulroy	75	67	71	77	290	47,601
Matthew Southgate	70	71	72	77	290	47,601
Gareth Maybin	73	70	73	75	291	36,531
David Drysdale	69	72	74	76	291	36,531
Maarten Lafeber	71	71	72	77	291	36,531
Roope Kakko	70	72	72	77	291	36,531
Niclas Fasth	70	69	75	77	291	36,531
Ruan de Smidt	72	69	73	77	291	36,531
Sam Walker	71	72	78	72	293	30,996
Theunis Spangenberg	73	70	77	73	293	30,996
David Hewan	71	70	72	80	293	30,996
Oscar Floren	70	70	81	73	294	28,782
Branden Grace	72	69	78	77	296	27,675
Steven Tiley	69	71	81	79	300	26,568

Lion of Africa Cape Town Open

Royal Cape Golf Club, Western Cape, South Africa
Par 36-36–72; 6,818 yards

November 22-25
purse, R2,000,000

	SCORES				TOTAL	MONEY
Jake Roos	71	67	73	68	279	R317,000
Jaco Van Zyl	67	72	74	66	279	155,533.33
Tyrone van Aswegen	72	72	68	67	279	155,533.33
Mark Williams	66	67	75	71	279	155,533.33
(Roos defeated Van Zyl on first and van Aswegen and Williams on second playoff hole.)						
Keenan Davidse	73	68	70	70	281	76,700
Colin Nel	69	72	68	72	281	76,700
Darren Fichardt	69	74	73	67	283	45,280
Hennie Otto	75	66	74	68	283	45,280
Keith Horne	71	68	73	71	283	45,280
Darryn Lloyd	70	71	71	71	283	45,280
Christiaan Basson	70	70	70	73	283	45,280
Matthew Carvell	72	71	74	67	284	31,400
Attie Schwartzel	73	66	77	68	284	31,400
Bradford Vaughan	73	68	71	72	284	31,400
Riekus Nortje	76	71	72	66	285	28,400
Ruan de Smidt	70	72	76	68	286	26,400
Steve Surry	70	71	72	73	286	26,400
Dean Burmester	71	67	74	74	286	26,400
Ulrich van den Berg	72	74	74	67	287	23,600
Ross Wellington	70	71	73	73	287	23,600
James Kamte	71	71	72	73	287	23,600
Peter Karmis	78	66	74	70	288	21,000
Andrew Georgiou	70	73	74	71	288	21,000
Wallie Coetsee	71	73	73	71	288	21,000
Jared Harvey	72	68	75	73	288	21,000
Ryan Cairns	72	68	74	74	288	21,000

Nedbank Golf Challenge

Gary Player Country Club, Sun City, South Africa
Par 36-36–72; 7,831 yards

November 29-December 2
purse, US$5,000,000

	SCORES				TOTAL	MONEY
Martin Kaymer	72	69	70	69	280	$1,250,000
Charl Schwartzel	72	71	70	69	282	660,000
Bill Haas	70	73	71	71	285	450,000
Louis Oosthuizen	71	72	69	74	286	350,000
Lee Westwood	71	73	70	73	287	330,000
Paul Lawrie	71	69	75	74	289	310,000
Francesco Molinari	72	71	78	69	290	295,000
Carl Pettersson	72	75	74	69	290	295,000
Peter Hanson	72	73	73	73	291	280,000
Nicolas Colsaerts	70	78	74	71	293	270,000
Justin Rose	73	79	69	74	295	260,000
Garth Mulroy	75	73	75	74	297	250,000

Nelson Mandela Championship

Royal Durban Golf Club, Durban, South Africa
Par 34-31–65; 5,594 yards
(Event shortened to 36 holes—rain.)

December 6-9
purse, €1,000,000

	SCORES		TOTAL	MONEY
Scott Jamieson	66	57	123	R1,367,062.50
Steve Webster	63	60	123	794,362.50
Eduardo De La Riva	62	61	123	794,362.50
(Jamieson defeated De La Riva on first and Webster on second playoff hole.)				
Maximilian Kieffer	62	62	124	334,865.62
Matthew Nixon	63	61	124	334,865.62
Morten Orum Madsen	60	64	124	334,865.62
Tim Clark	60	64	124	334,865.62
Jaco Van Zyl	68	57	125	166,893.75
Julien Quesne	62	63	125	166,893.75
Sam Little	62	63	125	166,893.75
Colin Nel	62	63	125	166,893.75
Bjorn Akesson	63	62	125	166,893.75
Matthew Southgate	62	63	125	166,893.75
David Horsey	62	64	126	113,973.21
Robert Coles	63	63	126	113,973.21
Ruan de Smidt	66	60	126	113,973.21
Estanislao Goya	64	62	126	113,973.21
Carlos Del Moral	63	63	126	113,973.21
Jaco Ahlers	63	63	126	113,973.21
Justin Walters	65	61	126	113,973.21
Tyrone Mordt	65	62	127	85,465.90
Shaun Norris	62	65	127	85,465.90
Marc Warren	63	64	127	85,465.90
Trevor Fisher, Jr.	65	62	127	85,465.90
Mikael Lundberg	63	64	127	85,465.90
Seve Benson	64	63	127	85,465.90
Allan Versfeld	63	64	127	85,465.90
Joakim Lagergren	68	59	127	85,465.90
James Kingston	63	64	127	85,465.90
Christiaan Basson	62	65	127	85,465.90
Garth Mulroy	65	62	127	85,465.90
Alexandre Kaleka	69	59	128	66,412.50
Rhys Davies	64	64	128	66,412.50
Desvonde Botes	62	66	128	66,412.50
Andrew Marshall	63	65	128	66,412.50
Adilson Da Silva	64	64	128	66,412.50
Michiel Bothma	64	64	128	66,412.50
Moritz Lampert	65	63	128	66,412.50
Darren Fichardt	65	64	129	48,300
Peter Lawrie	66	63	129	48,300
Chris Paisley	66	63	129	48,300
Chris Lloyd	61	68	129	48,300
Steve Surry	66	63	129	48,300
Richard Bland	63	66	129	48,300
Peter Whiteford	66	63	129	48,300
*Dominic Foos	64	65	129	
Justin Harding	67	62	129	48,300
Branden Grace	66	63	129	48,300
Pablo Larrazabal	63	66	129	48,300
George Coetzee	66	63	129	48,300
Tyrone van Aswegen	64	65	129	48,300
Scott Arnold	69	60	129	48,300
Ignacio Garrido	65	64	129	48,300
James Morrison	65	65	130	25,982.81
David Hewan	64	66	130	25,982.81

	SCORES		TOTAL	MONEY
Simon Wakefield	67	63	130	25,982.81
Matthew Carvell	68	62	130	25,982.81
Oscar Floren	63	67	130	25,982.81
Martin Wiegele	66	64	130	25,982.81
Doug McGuigan	64	66	130	25,982.81
Kristoffer Broberg	67	63	130	25,982.81
Espen Kofstad	64	66	130	25,982.81
Warren Abery	65	65	130	25,982.81
Bryce Easton	65	65	130	25,982.81
David Howell	66	64	130	25,982.81
Lorenzo Gagli	65	65	130	25,982.81
Damien McGrane	66	64	130	25,982.81
Dean Burmester	66	64	130	25,982.81
Andrew Georgiou	66	64	130	25,982.81

Alfred Dunhill Championship

Leopard Creek Golf Club, Mpumalanga, South Africa
Par 35-37–72; 7,287 yards

December 13-16
purse, €1,500,000

	SCORES				TOTAL	MONEY
Charl Schwartzel	67	64	64	69	264	R2,658,045
Kristoffer Broberg	70	69	67	70	276	1,928,550
Scott Jamieson	70	68	71	68	277	817,537.50
Garth Mulroy	71	68	70	68	277	817,537.50
Andy Sullivan	73	71	64	69	277	817,537.50
Gregory Bourdy	66	65	74	72	277	817,537.50
Richard Sterne	70	68	70	70	278	423,163
Keith Horne	70	69	68	71	278	423,163
Steve Webster	67	69	70	72	278	423,163
George Coetzee	71	70	73	65	279	314,437.50
Richard Bland	67	73	71	68	279	314,437.50
David Howell	70	73	70	67	280	263,289
Tyrone van Aswegen	70	68	71	71	280	263,289
Branden Grace	68	71	67	74	280	263,289
Richard McEvoy	69	70	74	68	281	229,749
Peter Lawrie	70	71	69	71	281	229,749
Danie van Tonder	72	70	67	72	281	229,749
Magnus A. Carlsson	71	69	72	70	282	208,786.50
Danny Willett	70	73	67	72	282	208,786.50
Alessandro Tadini	72	70	71	70	283	186,482.40
Justin Walters	73	71	68	71	283	186,482.40
Tjaart van der Walt	72	68	71	72	283	186,482.40
Lorenzo Gagli	71	71	68	73	283	186,482.40
Darren Fichardt	67	68	73	75	283	186,482.40
Desvonde Botes	75	69	69	71	284	160,992
Gary Lockerbie	73	70	69	72	284	160,992
Bjorn Akesson	71	70	70	73	284	160,992
Oscar Floren	69	70	70	75	284	160,992
David Drysdale	69	72	68	75	284	160,992
Marc Warren	73	71	75	66	285	135,837
Eddie Pepperell	74	70	73	68	285	135,837
Espen Kofstad	69	71	74	71	285	135,837
Michael Jonzon	74	67	71	73	285	135,837
Doug McGuigan	71	71	68	75	285	135,837
Louis de Jager	67	69	73	76	285	135,837
John Parry	72	70	67	76	285	135,837
Richard Finch	70	68	78	70	286	112,359
Mikael Lundberg	71	72	73	70	286	112,359
Robert Rock	69	68	77	72	286	112,359

	SCORES				TOTAL	MONEY
Emiliano Grillo	73	71	69	73	286	112,359
Vaughn Groenewald	72	70	69	75	286	112,359
Maximilian Kieffer	68	69	72	77	286	112,359
Matteo Delpodio	72	68	69	77	286	112,359
Simon Wakefield	74	67	75	71	287	95,589
Divan van den Heever	73	71	69	74	287	95,589
J.B. Hansen	70	70	72	75	287	95,589
Peter Whiteford	75	68	75	70	288	85,527
Oliver Bekker	67	77	72	72	288	85,527
Jaco Van Zyl	69	71	69	79	288	85,527
Allan Versfeld	71	72	76	70	289	72,111
Sam Little	72	69	76	72	289	72,111
Tommy Fleetwood	69	69	74	77	289	72,111
Anton Haig	73	66	72	78	289	72,111
Alejandro Canizares	70	72	69	78	289	72,111
Eduardo De La Riva	72	69	77	72	290	54,382.71
Graeme Storm	68	74	76	72	290	54,382.71
Hennie Otto	71	71	75	73	290	54,382.71
Jean Hugo	71	71	74	74	290	54,382.71
Peter Uihlein	70	73	72	75	290	54,382.71
Estanislao Goya	70	74	71	75	290	54,382.71
Thomas Aiken	70	73	67	80	290	54,382.71
Tyrone Mordt	71	67	80	73	291	44,440.50
Christiaan Basson	70	72	75	74	291	44,440.50
Matthew Southgate	70	74	73	74	291	44,440.50
Ockie Strydom	69	69	76	77	291	44,440.50
Matthew Nixon	75	69	75	73	292	39,409.50
George Murray	73	69	73	77	292	39,409.50
Neil Cheetham	73	71	75	74	293	36,894
Matthew Baldwin	69	72	79	75	295	35,217
James Kamte	70	72	74	84	300	33,540
Louis Oosthuizen	73	67	72		WD	25,155

Women's Tours

ISPS Handa Women's Australian Open

See Australian Ladies Tour section.

Honda LPGA Thailand

Siam Country Club, Pattaya Old Course, Chonburi, Thailand
Par 36-36–72; 6,469 yards

February 16-19
purse, $1,500,000

	SCORES				TOTAL	MONEY
Yani Tseng	73	65	65	66	269	$225,000
Ai Miyazato	67	70	65	68	270	140,688
Jiyai Shin	70	66	68	67	271	102,059
Amy Yang	68	69	68	69	274	78,951
Jimin Kang	70	72	69	67	278	49,297
Shanshan Feng	70	70	70	68	278	49,297
Amanda Blumenherst	71	67	71	69	278	49,297
Stacy Lewis	70	69	69	70	278	49,297
Jenny Shin	71	70	67	71	279	32,736
Karrie Webb	68	65	71	75	279	32,736
Hee Young Park	72	71	69	68	280	28,884
Caroline Hedwall	72	65	74	70	281	26,958
*Ariya Jutanugarn	73	69	65	74	281	
Lexi Thompson	73	73	70	66	282	23,107
Cristie Kerr	74	68	71	69	282	23,107
Mina Harigae	74	68	68	72	282	23,107
Pornanong Phatlum	71	67	71	73	282	23,107
Sophie Gustafson	74	70	69	70	283	19,154
Anna Nordqvist	68	74	71	70	283	19,154
Angela Stanford	76	69	68	70	283	19,154
Mika Miyazato	72	72	71	69	284	16,792
Meena Lee	72	70	72	70	284	16,792
Brittany Lincicome	70	70	72	72	284	16,792
Suzann Pettersen	70	67	69	78	284	16,792
Catriona Matthew	74	71	72	68	285	14,173
Kristy McPherson	71	72	72	70	285	14,173
Azahara Munoz	75	69	69	72	285	14,173
Se Ri Pak	68	74	71	72	285	14,173
Na Yeon Choi	68	68	73	76	285	14,173
Vicky Hurst	76	73	68	69	286	12,555

HSBC Women's Champions

Tanah Merah Country Club, Singapore
Par 36-36–72; 6,547 yards

February 23-26
purse, $1,400,000

	SCORES				TOTAL	MONEY
Angela Stanford	66	70	71	71	278	$210,000
Na Yeon Choi	68	71	71	68	278	102,564
Shanshan Feng	69	71	69	69	278	102,564
Jenny Shin	69	67	71	71	278	102,564
(Stanford defeated Feng on first, Choi on second and Shin on third playoff hole.)						
Yani Tseng	71	72	67	69	279	60,780

	SCORES				TOTAL	MONEY
Ai Miyazato	69	70	73	69	281	45,677
I.K. Kim	68	72	71	70	281	45,677
Vicky Hurst	69	73	71	69	282	33,030
Hee Young Park	71	68	73	70	282	33,030
Jiyai Shin	70	70	70	72	282	33,030
So Yeon Ryu	68	73	71	71	283	26,705
Katie Futcher	69	67	71	76	283	26,705
Momoko Ueda	68	75	72	69	284	23,427
Sun Young Yoo	70	70	73	71	284	23,427
Karen Stupples	72	72	72	69	285	20,235
Sandra Gal	72	71	71	71	285	20,235
Ji-Hee Lee	71	69	73	72	285	20,235
Julieta Granada	70	73	74	69	286	16,376
Chella Choi	72	70	74	70	286	16,376
Catriona Matthew	74	70	72	70	286	16,376
Se Ri Pak	72	72	72	70	286	16,376
Amy Yang	68	75	73	70	286	16,376
Stacy Lewis	71	75	68	72	286	16,376
Azahara Munoz	70	70	74	72	286	16,376
Suzann Pettersen	73	69	78	67	287	13,040
Morgan Pressel	74	72	71	70	287	13,040
Karrie Webb	72	72	73	70	287	13,040
Maria Hjorth	73	74	69	71	287	13,040
Inbee Park	70	72	72	73	287	13,040
Kristy McPherson	69	75	73	71	288	11,567

RR Donnelley LPGA Founders Cup

Wildfire Golf Club, Phoenix, Arizona
Par 36-36–72; 6,568 yards

March 15-18
purse, $1,500,000

	SCORES				TOTAL	MONEY
Yani Tseng	65	70	67	68	270	$225,000
Na Yeon Choi	67	69	67	68	271	118,654
Ai Miyazato	68	68	66	69	271	118,654
So Yeon Ryu	68	71	68	68	275	77,182
Hee Young Park	65	72	73	67	277	62,123
Caroline Hedwall	70	71	67	70	278	41,039
Jennifer Song	69	70	69	70	278	41,039
Cristie Kerr	68	73	66	71	278	41,039
Hee Kyung Seo	67	71	69	71	278	41,039
Chella Choi	71	70	71	67	279	27,446
Mindy Kim	68	71	70	70	279	27,446
Stacy Lewis	68	70	70	71	279	27,446
Karin Sjodin	69	68	71	71	279	27,446
Haeji Kang	70	71	70	69	280	21,310
Se Ri Pak	70	69	69	72	280	21,310
Hee-Won Han	69	70	68	73	280	21,310
Karrie Webb	68	69	70	73	280	21,310
Jiyai Shin	66	71	75	69	281	17,658
Jodi Ewart	70	71	69	71	281	17,658
Paula Creamer	69	68	70	74	281	17,658
I.K. Kim	70	66	69	76	281	17,658
Anna Nordqvist	72	68	73	69	282	15,230
Katie Futcher	68	71	72	71	282	15,230
Julieta Granada	70	68	73	71	282	15,230
Lizette Salas	74	69	68	71	282	15,230
Jee Young Lee	74	70	70	69	283	12,575
Na On Min	70	70	72	71	283	12,575
Mika Miyazato	69	67	75	72	283	12,575

	SCORES				TOTAL	MONEY
Kristy McPherson	73	65	72	73	283	12,575
Suzann Pettersen	69	71	67	76	283	12,575
Inbee Park	68	69	69	77	283	12,575

Kia Classic

La Costa Resort, Legends Course, Carlsbad, California
Par 36-36–72; 6,500 yards

March 22-25
purse, $1,700,000

	SCORES				TOTAL	MONEY
Yani Tseng	67	68	69	70	274	$255,000
Sun Young Yoo	69	73	67	71	280	156,242
Shanshan Feng	72	71	71	67	281	100,511
Jiyai Shin	68	71	68	74	281	100,511
Ai Miyazato	72	70	71	70	283	64,156
Caroline Hedwall	67	72	70	74	283	64,156
Jodi Ewart	70	69	73	72	284	45,337
Se Ri Pak	71	66	73	74	284	45,337
Brittany Lincicome	68	73	73	71	285	38,066
Catriona Matthew	79	70	68	69	286	33,361
Chella Choi	71	71	70	74	286	33,361
Azahara Munoz	71	73	71	72	287	27,287
Suzann Pettersen	68	75	71	73	287	27,287
Inbee Park	72	70	70	75	287	27,287
Alison Walshe	73	66	73	75	287	27,287
Eun-Hee Ji	76	70	71	71	288	22,840
Mina Harigae	71	73	71	73	288	22,840
Vicky Hurst	73	74	69	73	289	20,787
Na Yeon Choi	73	73	69	74	289	20,787
Morgan Pressel	72	75	73	70	290	18,306
Lindsey Wright	72	74	73	71	290	18,306
Ha-Neul Kim	74	75	69	72	290	18,306
Brittany Lang	73	76	69	72	290	18,306
Meena Lee	73	70	70	77	290	18,306
Paula Creamer	72	75	76	68	291	15,141
Stacy Lewis	72	73	74	72	291	15,141
Amy Yang	69	73	75	74	291	15,141
Jennifer Johnson	68	73	73	77	291	15,141
Karrie Webb	73	70	71	77	291	15,141
Stephanie Sherlock	69	77	74	72	292	11,927
Haeji Kang	71	77	70	74	292	11,927
Jenny Shin	73	74	71	74	292	11,927
Nicole Castrale	73	71	73	75	292	11,927
Kris Tamulis	71	73	73	75	292	11,927
Hannah Yun	74	72	71	75	292	11,927
Sydnee Michaels	72	74	70	76	292	11,927

Kraft Nabisco Championship

Mission Hills Country Club, Dinah Shore Course,
Rancho Mirage, California
Par 36-36–72; 6,738 yards

March 29-April 1
purse, $2,000,000

	SCORES				TOTAL	MONEY
Sun Young Yoo	69	69	72	69	279	$300,000
I.K. Kim	70	70	70	69	279	182,538

(Yoo defeated Kim on first playoff hole.)

	SCORES				TOTAL	MONEY
Yani Tseng	68	68	71	73	280	132,418
Karin Sjodin	72	67	68	74	281	77,202
Amy Yang	66	74	72	69	281	77,202
Stacy Lewis	74	71	70	66	281	77,202
Hee Kyung Seo	69	72	69	71	281	77,202
Natalie Gulbis	76	71	70	65	282	44,806
Se Ri Pak	70	69	72	71	282	44,806
Na Yeon Choi	72	67	71	72	282	44,806
Ha-Neul Kim	71	71	70	71	283	34,003
Angela Stanford	72	71	70	70	283	34,003
Eun-Hee Ji	71	69	70	73	283	34,003
Vicky Hurst	70	70	71	72	283	34,003
Catriona Matthew	74	70	70	70	284	26,184
Suzann Pettersen	72	74	66	72	284	26,184
Karrie Webb	71	72	71	70	284	26,184
Haeji Kang	69	68	72	75	284	26,184
Azahara Munoz	73	72	67	72	284	26,184
Paula Creamer	69	73	71	72	285	22,586
Katherine Hull	69	73	69	74	285	22,586
Cristie Kerr	71	70	72	73	286	20,587
Shanshan Feng	72	70	73	71	286	20,587
Ariya Jutanugarn	71	73	71	71	286	20,587
Lexi Thompson	72	72	68	74	286	20,587
Brittany Lang	74	74	69	70	287	16,401
Inbee Park	71	74	68	74	287	16,401
Hee Young Park	72	71	70	74	287	16,401
Anna Nordqvist	74	74	67	72	287	16,401
Jiyai Shin	72	71	70	74	287	16,401
Beatriz Recari	72	76	70	69	287	16,401
Cindy LaCrosse	73	71	70	73	287	16,401
Jodi Ewart	69	73	73	72	287	16,401
Jennifer Johnson	72	71	73	71	287	16,401
Karine Icher	73	73	67	75	288	12,792
Julieta Granada	70	75	73	70	288	12,792
Mi Jung Hur	73	70	75	70	288	12,792
Kris Tamulis	72	75	68	74	289	11,068
Maria Hjorth	73	68	75	73	289	11,068
Sandra Gal	71	72	72	74	289	11,068
Mina Harigae	73	71	72	73	289	11,068
Charley Hull	71	77	68	73	289	11,068
Heather Bowie Young	74	70	73	73	290	9,594
Pat Hurst	75	73	71	71	290	9,594
Lindsey Wright	67	71	76	76	290	9,594
Morgan Pressel	73	74	73	71	291	8,495
Lizette Salas	76	70	71	74	291	8,495
Ji-Hee Lee	74	73	69	75	291	8,495
Hee-Won Han	70	74	73	75	292	7,195
Candie Kung	70	75	72	75	292	7,195
Becky Morgan	76	72	72	72	292	7,195
Seon Hwa Lee	76	72	68	76	292	7,195
Chella Choi	72	74	75	71	292	7,195
Caroline Masson	79	69	70	74	292	7,195
Austin Ernst	77	70	68	77	292	7,195
Wendy Ward	71	76	71	75	293	5,608
Ai Miyazato	71	72	74	76	293	5,608
Pornanong Phatlum	71	72	73	77	293	5,608
Jennifer Song	72	71	71	79	293	5,608
Diana Luna	76	68	75	74	293	5,608
Melissa Reid	77	70	71	75	293	5,608
Caroline Hedwall	74	72	71	76	293	5,608
So Yeon Ryu	74	74	73	72	293	5,608
Christel Boeljon	74	73	75	71	293	5,608
Jaye Marie Green	71	77	70	75	293	5,608

	SCORES			TOTAL	MONEY
Katie Futcher	72	72	73	77	294	4,647
Sarah Kemp	71	75	71	77	294	4,647
Momoko Ueda	71	69	80	74	294	4,647
Dewi Claire Schreefel	75	72	70	77	294	4,647
Reilley Rankin	73	73	70	79	295	4,197
Mo Martin	74	72	73	76	295	4,197
Amanda Blumenhorst	75	73	72	75	295	4,197
Cydney Clanton	70	76	75	74	295	4,197
Yukari Baba	75	73	72	75	295	4,197
Alena Sharp	75	73	73	75	296	3,897
Christina Kim	74	69	77	76	296	3,897
Karen Stupples	73	72	75	76	296	3,897
Leta Lindley	76	70	77	75	298	3,797
Nicole Castrale	69	73	81	76	299	3,728
Lorie Kane	74	73	72	80	299	3,728
Kyeong Bae	74	74	78	75	301	3,657
Ji Young Oh	74	72	81	76	303	3,611

LPGA LOTTE Championship

Ko Olina Golf Club, Kapolei, Oahu, Hawaii
Par 36-36–72; 6,421 yards

April 18-21
purse, $1,700,000

	SCORES			TOTAL	MONEY
Ai Miyazato	71	65	70	70	276	$255,000
Meena Lee	74	65	71	70	280	135,444
Azahara Munoz	72	64	73	71	280	135,444
Cristie Kerr	70	68	71	72	281	79,508
So Yeon Ryu	71	70	69	71	281	79,508
Suzann Pettersen	70	69	74	69	282	58,020
Brittany Lang	69	70	74	70	283	43,121
Jiyai Shin	69	71	70	73	283	43,121
Mariajo Uribe	77	65	73	68	283	43,121
Karen Stupples	72	70	73	69	284	33,522
Yani Tseng	69	72	69	74	284	33,522
Angela Stanford	69	71	70	75	285	26,645
Karrie Webb	71	71	71	72	285	26,645
Inbee Park	70	70	72	73	285	26,645
Momoko Ueda	74	69	70	72	285	26,645
Pernilla Lindberg	76	66	75	68	285	26,645
*Hyo Joo Kim	71	71	73	70	285	
Paula Creamer	73	67	74	72	286	19,868
Sophie Gustafson	71	71	74	70	286	19,868
Hee-Won Han	76	71	70	69	286	19,868
Candie Kung	71	74	71	70	286	19,868
Julieta Granada	74	70	71	71	286	19,868
Sun Young Yoo	70	73	71	72	286	19,868
Caroline Hedwall	73	70	71	72	286	19,868
Alena Sharp	73	70	74	70	287	16,718
Haeji Kang	74	67	71	75	287	16,718
Brittany Lincicome	70	71	73	74	288	14,354
Natalie Gulbis	75	72	70	71	288	14,354
Becky Morgan	75	70	71	72	288	14,354
Lindsey Wright	78	69	74	67	288	14,354
Karin Sjodin	74	72	72	70	288	14,354
Jessica Shepley	75	68	75	70	288	14,354

Mobile Bay LPGA Classic

Robert Trent Jones Golf Trail, Magnolia Grove-Crossings Course,
Mobile, Alabama
Par 36-36–72; 6,521 yards

April 26-29
purse, $1,250,000

	SCORES				TOTAL	MONEY
Stacy Lewis	68	67	67	69	271	$187,500
Lexi Thompson	70	71	66	65	272	114,347
Karine Icher	72	65	68	68	273	82,951
Brittany Lincicome	70	67	67	72	276	44,887
Karrie Webb	73	70	64	69	276	44,887
Sun Young Yoo	68	69	69	70	276	44,887
Azahara Munoz	69	69	70	68	276	44,887
So Yeon Ryu	69	67	72	68	276	44,887
Natalie Gulbis	69	70	68	70	277	25,563
Lindsey Wright	67	69	70	71	277	25,563
Hee Young Park	70	70	71	66	277	25,563
Nicole Castrale	71	70	69	68	278	19,407
Suzann Pettersen	73	68	69	68	278	19,407
Haeji Kang	68	70	69	71	278	19,407
Pornanong Phatlum	72	69	66	71	278	19,407
Caroline Hedwall	67	73	70	68	278	19,407
Meena Lee	69	69	71	70	279	15,568
Jennifer Rosales	67	72	69	71	279	15,568
Brittany Lang	72	69	70	68	279	15,568
Moira Dunn	71	67	72	70	280	13,157
Becky Morgan	74	65	70	71	280	13,157
Karin Sjodin	72	64	74	70	280	13,157
Eun-Hee Ji	74	68	67	71	280	13,157
Na Yeon Choi	70	70	75	65	280	13,157
Mariajo Uribe	68	69	71	72	280	13,157
Hee-Won Han	71	69	70	71	281	10,655
Cristie Kerr	70	71	70	70	281	10,655
Meaghan Francella	75	69	69	68	281	10,655
Hee Kyung Seo	71	71	69	70	281	10,655
Numa Gulyanamitta	69	70	70	72	281	10,655

HSBC LPGA Brasil Cup

Itanhanga Golf Club, Rio de Janeiro, Brazil
Par 73; 6,285 yards

May 5-6
purse, $720,000

	SCORES		TOTAL	MONEY
Pornanong Phatlum	66	67	133	$108,000
Amy Hung	72	65	137	83,990
Paula Creamer	69	69	138	54,031
Chella Choi	71	67	138	54,031
Amanda Blumenherst	72	67	139	27,637
Brittany Lang	68	71	139	27,637
Candie Kung	68	71	139	27,637
Katie Futcher	67	72	139	27,637
Karine Icher	66	73	139	27,637
Anna Nordqvist	73	68	141	16,761
Christina Kim	69	72	141	16,761
Beatriz Recari	71	70	141	16,761
Suzann Pettersen	68	73	141	16,761
Ryann O'Toole	73	69	142	14,163
Jeong Jang	74	69	143	12,967
Gerina Piller	71	72	143	12,967

	SCORES		TOTAL	MONEY
Victoria Tanco	71	73	144	11,680
Kyeong Bae	71	73	144	11,680
Julieta Granada	74	71	145	10,944
Cindy LaCrosse	73	73	146	10,576
Mindy Kim	75	72	147	9,841
Paige Mackenzie	75	72	147	9,841
Veronica Felibert	72	75	147	9,841
Mariajo Uribe	73	75	148	9,105
Paz Echeverria	74	77	151	8,783
Karen Stupples	75	77	152	8,300
Tiffany Joh	75	77	152	8,300
Angela Park	76	77	153	7,817
Victoria Alimonda	75	81	156	7,495
Luciana Bemvenuti	81	81	162	7,220

Sybase Match Play Championship

Hamilton Farm Golf Club, Gladstone, New Jersey
Par 36-36–72; 6,553 yards

May 17-20
purse, $1,500,000

FIRST ROUND

Anna Nordqvist defeated Beatriz Recari, 2 and 1.
Jiyai Shin defeated Jennifer Song, 6 and 5.
Natalie Gulbis defeated Mika Miyazato, 1 up.
Amy Yang defeated Amy Hung, 3 and 2.
Inbee Park defeated Hee-Won Han, 3 and 2.
Morgan Pressel defeated Mindy Kim, 5 and 4.
Jenny Shin defeated Jimin Kang, 4 and 2.
Na Yeon Choi defeated Grace Park, 2 up.
Jessica Korda defeated Hee Kyung Seo, 1 up.
Sun Young Yoo defeated Amanda Blumenherst, 4 and 2.
Sandra Gal defeated Pornanong Phatlum, 2 up.
Stacy Lewis defeated Pat Hurst, 4 and 3.
Azahara Munoz defeated Lindsey Wright, 4 and 3.
Karrie Webb defeated Tiffany Joh, 4 and 3.
Sophie Gustafson defeated Karen Stupples, 4 and 3.
Jodi Ewart defeated Suzann Pettersen, 3 and 1.
Haeji Kang defeated Caroline Hedwall, 3 and 2.
Candie Kung defeated Catriona Matthew, 3 and 1.
Katie Futcher defeated Chella Choi, 4 and 3.
Yani Tseng defeated Jeong Jang, 1 up.
Eun-Hee Ji defeated Maria Hjorth, 1 up.
Angela Stanford defeated Wendy Ward, 2 and 1.
Vicky Hurst defeated Meena Lee, 2 and 1.
Cristie Kerr defeated Belen Mozo, 2 and 1.
Karine Icher defeated Hee Young Park, 4 and 2.
Jennifer Johnson defeated Paula Creamer, 2 and 1.
Julieta Granada defeated Brittany Lang, 2 and 1.
Ryann O'Toole defeated Brittany Lincicome, 2 and 1.
Mina Harigae defeated Michelle Wie, 3 and 2.
So Yeon Ryu defeated Karin Sjodin, 2 and 1.
Katherine Hull defeated Song-Hee Kim, 3 and 2.
Mariajo Uribe defeated Ai Miyazato, 2 up.

(Each losing player received $3,865.)

SECOND ROUND

Ewart defeated Gustafson, 3 and 1.
Munoz defeated Webb, 2 and 1.

Lewis defeated Gal, 4 and 3.
Yoo defeated Korda, 2 up.
Tseng defeated Futcher, 3 and 1.
Kung defeated Haeji Kang, 1 up.
Icher defeated Johnson, 2 and 1.
Granada defeated O'Toole, 6 and 5.
Hull defeated Uribe, 1 up.
Ryu defeated Harigae, 3 and 2.
Hurst defeated Kerr, 19 holes.
Stanford defeated Ji, 4 and 3.
Choi defeated Jenny Shin, 3 and 2.
Pressel defeated Inbee Park, 3 and 2.
Nordqvist defeated Jiyai Shin, 2 and 1.
Yang defeated Gulbis, 5 and 4.

(Each losing player received $7,740.)

THIRD ROUND

Pressel defeated Choi, 19 holes.
Nordqvist defeated Yang, 3 and 1.
Ryu defeated Hull, 5 and 4.
Hurst defeated Stanford, 2 and 1.
Kung defeated Tseng, 3 and 2.
Granada defeated Icher, 1 up.
Munoz defeated Ewart, 2 and 1.
Lewis defeated Yoo, 1 up.

(Each losing player received $18,750.)

QUARTER-FINALS

Pressel defeated Nordqvist, 5 and 4.
Hurst defeated Ryu, 1 up.
Kung defeated Granada, 2 and 1.
Munoz defeated Lewis, 5 and 4.

(Each losing player received $37,500.)

SEMI-FINALS

Kung defeated Hurst, 2 and 1.
Munoz defeated Pressel, 2 and 1.

PLAYOFF FOR THIRD-FOURTH PLACE

Pressel defeated Hurst, 2 and 1.
(Pressel received $150,000; Hurst received $112,500)

FINAL

Munoz defeated Kung, 2 and 1.
(Munoz received $375,000; Kung received $225,000)

ShopRite LPGA Classic

Stockton Seaview Hotel & Golf Club, Galloway, New Jersey
Par 37-34–71; 6,155 yards

June 1-3
purse, $1,500,000

	SCORES			TOTAL	MONEY
Stacy Lewis	65	65	71	201	$225,000
Katherine Hull	71	66	68	205	134,854
Mika Miyazato	65	73	68	206	86,752
Azahara Munoz	69	68	69	206	86,752
Lexi Thompson	69	71	67	207	50,821
Hee-Won Han	71	67	69	207	50,821
Anna Nordqvist	69	67	71	207	50,821
Alison Walshe	73	66	69	208	34,701
Paula Creamer	67	70	71	208	34,701
Eun-Hee Ji	71	70	68	209	28,794
Ai Miyazato	70	69	70	209	28,794
Jenny Shin	73	68	69	210	22,272
Sophie Gustafson	71	69	70	210	22,272
Na Yeon Choi	70	69	71	210	22,272
Karine Icher	71	68	71	210	22,272
Amy Yang	74	65	71	210	22,272
Yani Tseng	71	67	72	210	22,272
Laura Davies	75	68	68	211	17,011
Inbee Park	73	69	69	211	17,011
Suzann Pettersen	74	67	70	211	17,011
Jennifer Johnson	77	63	71	211	17,011
Mariajo Uribe	67	71	73	211	17,011
Gerina Piller	74	68	70	212	14,914
Karrie Webb	72	70	70	212	14,914
I.K. Kim	72	74	67	213	13,327
Brittany Lang	78	68	67	213	13,327
Kris Tamulis	73	70	70	213	13,327
So Yeon Ryu	70	67	76	213	13,327
Haeji Kang	76	70	68	214	9,920
Seon Hwa Lee	70	75	69	214	9,920
Mindy Kim	70	74	70	214	9,920
Jeong Jang	74	69	71	214	9,920
Maude-Aimee Leblanc	68	75	71	214	9,920
Sarah Jane Smith	71	72	71	214	9,920
Lorie Kane	73	69	72	214	9,920
Ilhee Lee	73	69	72	214	9,920
Brittany Lincicome	72	70	72	214	9,920
Mo Martin	69	73	72	214	9,920
Shanshan Feng	70	70	74	214	9,920

Wegmans LPGA Championship

Locust Hill Country Club, Pittsford, New York
Par 35-37–72; 6,534 yards

June 7-10
purse, $2,500,000

	SCORES				TOTAL	MONEY
Shanshan Feng	72	73	70	67	282	$375,000
Mika Miyazato	70	72	73	69	284	158,443
Stacy Lewis	72	72	70	70	284	158,443
Suzann Pettersen	71	72	71	70	284	158,443
Eun-Hee Ji	75	68	69	72	284	158,443
Ai Miyazato	70	74	73	68	285	73,285
Gerina Piller	74	71	72	68	285	73,285
Karrie Webb	74	71	68	72	285	73,285

	SCORES				TOTAL	MONEY
Paula Creamer	70	72	73	71	286	51,742
Inbee Park	72	70	72	72	286	51,742
Giulia Sergas	69	76	69	72	286	51,742
Sandra Gal	71	71	75	70	287	42,956
Cristie Kerr	70	76	70	71	287	42,956
Hee Young Park	77	70	73	68	288	39,028
Mina Harigae	74	72	74	69	289	33,960
Karin Sjodin	75	69	73	72	289	33,960
Jeong Jang	70	74	71	74	289	33,960
Sun Young Yoo	72	72	71	74	289	33,960
Nicole Castrale	76	74	70	70	290	28,638
Se Ri Pak	70	71	76	73	290	28,638
Jenny Shin	71	75	71	73	290	28,638
Jennifer Johnson	73	71	71	75	290	28,638
Christel Boeljon	74	74	73	70	291	25,597
Marcy Hart	72	75	73	71	291	25,597
Brittany Lincicome	76	73	73	70	292	22,872
I.K. Kim	73	73	73	73	292	22,872
So Yeon Ryu	73	70	74	75	292	22,872
Lizette Salas	74	70	73	75	292	22,872
Candie Kung	71	77	75	70	293	20,655
Mo Martin	71	77	77	69	294	18,015
Mariajo Uribe	74	76	71	73	294	18,015
Mi Jung Hur	74	69	77	74	294	18,015
Lexi Thompson	74	72	74	74	294	18,015
Sophie Gustafson	73	72	74	75	294	18,015
Sydnee Michaels	72	71	72	79	294	18,015
Sarah Jane Smith	75	72	77	71	295	13,263
Alison Walshe	73	77	73	72	295	13,263
Chella Choi	75	74	74	72	295	13,263
Catriona Matthew	75	72	76	72	295	13,263
Haru Nomura	74	77	70	74	295	13,263
Pornanong Phatlum	75	74	72	74	295	13,263
Maude-Aimee Leblanc	72	73	75	75	295	13,263
Ryann O'Toole	69	76	75	75	295	13,263
Jodi Ewart	75	72	72	76	295	13,263
Karine Icher	75	75	74	72	296	9,820
Leta Lindley	78	73	72	73	296	9,820
Ji Young Oh	77	72	74	73	296	9,820
Beatriz Recari	69	78	75	74	296	9,820
Hee-Won Han	74	74	73	75	296	9,820
Morgan Pressel	74	75	69	78	296	9,820
Becky Morgan	75	73	77	72	297	8,363
Katherine Hull	75	76	73	73	297	8,363
Haeji Kang	77	73	73	74	297	8,363
Karen Stupples	76	75	74	73	298	7,858
Katie Futcher	74	77	76	72	299	7,349
Jessica Korda	74	74	79	72	299	7,349
Amelia Lewis	73	75	77	74	299	7,349
Anna Nordqvist	74	77	72	77	300	6,842
Yani Tseng	76	75	74	76	301	6,379
Belen Mozo	74	76	75	76	301	6,379
Amy Hung	76	75	73	77	301	6,379
Dewi Claire Schreefel	76	74	81	71	302	5,829
Kris Tamulis	74	74	80	74	302	5,829
Alena Sharp	77	71	78	76	302	5,829
Pat Hurst	74	76	75	77	302	5,829
Brittany Lang	72	75	76	79	302	5,829
Jennifer Rosales	73	77	78	75	303	5,322
Ilhee Lee	76	75	73	79	303	5,322
Meaghan Francella	76	74	73	80	303	5,322
Taylor Coutu	73	74	77	80	304	5,100
Stephanie Louden	73	78	80	74	305	4,974
Grace Park	75	75	76	79	305	4,974

Manulife Financial LPGA Classic

Grey Silo Golf Course, Waterloo, Ontario, Canada

Par 36-35–71; 6,354 yards

June 21-24

purse, $1,300,000

	SCORES				TOTAL	MONEY
Brittany Lang	69	65	67	67	268	$195,000
Chella Choi	69	66	70	63	268	90,231
Hee Kyung Seo	66	68	67	67	268	90,231
Inbee Park	69	64	66	69	268	90,231
(Lang defeated Choi on first, Park on second, and Seo on third playoff hole.)						
Stacy Lewis	72	64	69	64	269	48,610
So Yeon Ryu	70	65	70	64	269	48,610
Shanshan Feng	66	68	70	66	270	34,351
Anna Nordqvist	64	72	67	67	270	34,351
Mi Jung Hur	69	68	68	66	271	28,842
Karin Sjodin	67	68	69	68	272	25,277
Sandra Changkija	63	72	69	68	272	25,277
I.K. Kim	70	69	70	65	274	21,971
Karine Icher	72	68	66	68	274	21,971
Jacqui Concolino	69	70	69	67	275	18,342
Paula Creamer	69	68	71	67	275	18,342
Jodi Ewart	68	68	72	67	275	18,342
Lexi Thompson	66	69	70	70	275	18,342
Mindy Kim	68	73	71	64	276	14,933
Sandra Gal	72	68	69	67	276	14,933
Jeong Jang	70	68	69	69	276	14,933
Sun Young Yoo	68	67	72	69	276	14,933
Jennifer Song	71	67	68	70	276	14,933
Pornanong Phatlum	71	70	71	65	277	11,715
Anna Grzebien	70	71	69	67	277	11,715
Suzann Pettersen	67	70	72	68	277	11,715
Christel Boeljon	71	68	69	69	277	11,715
Jin Young Pak	69	70	69	69	277	11,715
Kris Tamulis	70	67	71	69	277	11,715
Amy Yang	68	70	68	71	277	11,715
Nicole Hage	72	65	67	73	277	11,715

Walmart NW Arkansas Championship

Pinnacle Country Club, Rogers, Arkansas

Par 36-35–71; 6,356 yards

June 29-July 1

purse, $2,000,000

	SCORES			TOTAL	MONEY
Ai Miyazato	68	68	65	201	$300,000
Mika Miyazato	70	65	67	202	159,739
Azahara Munoz	69	68	65	202	159,739
Inbee Park	67	68	68	203	93,770
Veronica Felibert	65	66	72	203	93,770
Hee Kyung Seo	73	65	66	204	68,427
Amy Yang	72	68	65	205	57,276
Brittany Lang	73	63	70	206	47,646
Anna Nordqvist	68	70	68	206	47,646
Catriona Matthew	69	68	70	207	36,950
Sarah Jane Smith	71	68	68	207	36,950
Jenny Shin	69	71	67	207	36,950
So Yeon Ryu	70	67	70	207	36,950
Giulia Sergas	73	68	67	208	27,979
Sun Young Yoo	70	71	67	208	27,979
Suzann Pettersen	70	69	69	208	27,979

	SCORES			TOTAL	MONEY
Mo Martin	70	70	68	208	27,979
Jennifer Rosales	70	69	69	208	27,979
Kyeong Bae	70	69	70	209	22,910
Katie Futcher	69	67	73	209	22,910
Shanshan Feng	66	70	73	209	22,910
Stacy Lewis	70	69	70	209	22,910
Angela Stanford	71	69	70	210	19,383
Karine Icher	67	72	71	210	19,383
Sandra Gal	70	70	70	210	19,383
Na Yeon Choi	70	69	71	210	19,383
Danielle Kang	72	68	70	210	19,383
Beth Bader	69	71	71	211	15,028
Katherine Hull	70	70	71	211	15,028
Paula Creamer	71	71	69	211	15,028
Julieta Granada	71	69	71	211	15,028
Beatriz Recari	72	69	70	211	15,028
Cindy LaCrosse	72	71	68	211	15,028
Jodi Ewart	73	70	68	211	15,028
Lizette Salas	73	67	71	211	15,028

U.S. Women's Open

Blackwolf Run, Kohler, Wisconsin
Par 36-36–72; 6,984 yards

July 5-8
purse, $3,250,000

	SCORES				TOTAL	MONEY
Na Yeon Choi	71	72	65	73	281	$585,000
Amy Yang	73	72	69	71	285	350,000
Sandra Gal	71	70	74	74	289	218,840
Giulia Sergas	74	71	73	72	290	128,487
Ilhee Lee	72	71	77	70	290	128,487
Shanshan Feng	74	74	71	71	290	128,487
Paula Creamer	73	73	71	74	291	94,736
Mika Miyazato	71	71	73	76	291	94,736
Cristie Kerr	69	71	77	75	292	72,596
Nicole Castrale	73	70	74	75	292	72,596
Inbee Park	71	70	76	75	292	72,596
Se Ri Pak	72	73	76	71	292	72,596
Suzann Pettersen	71	68	78	75	292	72,596
Cindy LaCrosse	73	74	74	72	293	55,161
Danielle Kang	78	70	71	74	293	55,161
So Yeon Ryu	74	71	74	74	293	55,161
Lexi Thompson	70	73	72	78	293	55,161
Brittany Lincicome	69	80	74	71	294	45,263
Vicky Hurst	71	70	75	78	294	45,263
Hee Kyung Seo	72	73	80	69	294	45,263
Jimin Kang	72	72	78	73	295	33,799
Brittany Lang	73	74	77	71	295	33,799
Azahara Munoz	73	73	73	76	295	33,799
Jennie Lee	70	74	79	72	295	33,799
Diana Luna	76	72	76	71	295	33,799
Numa Gulyanamitta	73	76	73	73	295	33,799
Yeon-Ju Jung	74	72	80	69	295	33,799
Ai Miyazato	70	74	75	77	296	23,604
Anna Nordqvist	72	74	79	71	296	23,604
Pornanong Phatlum	76	69	76	75	296	23,604
Mina Harigae	77	71	75	73	296	23,604
Sun Young Yoo	76	72	81	68	297	20,880
Jin Young Pak	73	72	80	72	297	20,880
Lizette Salas	69	73	75	80	297	20,880

	SCORES				TOTAL	MONEY
Michelle Wie	74	66	78	80	298	18,653
Beatriz Recari	70	75	76	77	298	18,653
Jenny Shin	76	71	76	75	298	18,653
Jennifer Johnson	76	70	76	76	298	18,653
Jeong Jang	73	72	75	80	300	15,491
Heather Bowie Young	75	73	77	75	300	15,491
Katie Futcher	73	75	74	78	300	15,491
Jessica Korda	74	71	75	80	300	15,491
Sakura Yokomine	75	70	75	80	300	15,491
*Lydia Ko	74	72	79	75	300	
Carlota Ciganda	76	72	77	75	300	15,491
Alison Walshe	74	71	75	81	301	12,651
Stacy Lewis	77	69	80	75	301	12,651
Jennifer Song	72	74	81	74	301	12,651
*Emma Talley	73	75	81	72	301	
Karrie Webb	75	72	81	74	302	10,532
Yani Tseng	74	72	78	78	302	10,532
Gerina Piller	73	71	81	77	302	10,532
Melissa Reid	79	69	75	79	302	10,532
Angela Stanford	75	71	81	76	303	9,484
Meena Lee	71	78	76	78	303	9,484
Sophie Gustafson	77	72	84	71	304	9,132
Katherine Hull	75	73	81	76	305	8,709
Angela Oh	75	74	80	76	305	8,709
Dewi Claire Schreefel	73	76	82	74	305	8,709
Kristy McPherson	75	71	81	79	306	8,267
*Alison Lee	75	74	79	78	306	
Ji-Hee Lee	79	70	83	74	306	8,267
Lorie Kane	76	73	82	76	307	8,055
Paige Mackenzie	75	74	83	77	309	7,922
Sue Kim	75	72	85	81	313	7,789

Evian Masters

See Ladies European Tour section.

Jamie Farr Toledo Classic

Highland Meadows Golf Club, Sylvania, Ohio
Par 34-37–71; 6,428 yards

August 9-12
purse, $1,300,000

	SCORES				TOTAL	MONEY
So Yeon Ryu	67	68	67	62	264	$195,000
Angela Stanford	66	70	69	66	271	119,765
Inbee Park	69	65	69	69	272	77,045
Chella Choi	66	67	70	69	272	77,045
I.K. Kim	69	67	66	71	273	49,178
Jennie Lee	69	70	67	67	273	49,178
Mika Miyazato	66	68	69	71	274	34,753
Jiyai Shin	69	67	66	72	274	34,753
Beatriz Recari	70	66	70	69	275	27,868
Hee Kyung Seo	68	66	68	73	275	27,868
Karine Icher	66	69	71	70	276	22,310
Jacqui Concolino	68	68	69	71	276	22,310
Hee-Won Han	68	67	70	71	276	22,310
Stacy Lewis	68	69	73	66	276	22,310
Jeong Jang	68	70	69	70	277	18,010
Lindsey Wright	69	68	73	67	277	18,010
Sandra Gal	69	71	68	69	277	18,010

	SCORES				TOTAL	MONEY
Karin Sjodin	73	68	68	69	278	15,650
Natalie Gulbis	69	71	69	69	278	15,650
Pernilla Lindberg	64	71	70	73	278	15,650
Na Yeon Choi	70	71	70	68	279	13,770
Amy Yang	67	73	69	70	279	13,770
Mo Martin	69	72	67	71	279	13,770
Sydnee Michaels	69	68	72	70	279	13,770
Janice Moodie	68	72	72	68	280	11,387
Brittany Lang	70	71	70	69	280	11,387
Kristy McPherson	72	69	71	68	280	11,387
Taylor Coutu	71	71	70	68	280	11,387
Mi Jung Hur	71	66	74	69	280	11,387
Numa Gulyanamitta	66	72	72	70	280	11,387

Safeway Classic

Pumpkin Ridge Golf Club, Ghost Creek Course,
North Plains, Oregon
Par 37-35–72; 6,611 yards

August 17-19
purse, $1,500,000

	SCORES			TOTAL	MONEY
Mika Miyazato	65	68	70	203	$225,000
Brittany Lincicome	67	71	67	205	118,654
Inbee Park	66	70	69	205	118,654
Cristie Kerr	66	70	70	206	63,377
Haeji Kang	71	69	66	206	63,377
So Yeon Ryu	67	68	71	206	63,377
Sydnee Michaels	65	72	70	207	42,545
Michelle Wie	69	70	69	208	37,274
Karine Icher	71	70	68	209	32,003
I.K. Kim	71	69	69	209	32,003
Yani Tseng	70	67	73	210	28,237
Brittany Lang	71	69	71	211	24,020
Jee Young Lee	67	73	71	211	24,020
Amy Yang	68	70	73	211	24,020
Lizette Salas	71	70	70	211	24,020
Ai Miyazato	70	75	67	212	19,628
Na Yeon Choi	69	71	72	212	19,628
Alison Walshe	67	72	73	212	19,628
Angela Stanford	75	68	70	213	16,125
Paula Creamer	68	69	76	213	16,125
Giulia Sergas	71	70	72	213	16,125
Shanshan Feng	72	71	70	213	16,125
Momoko Ueda	69	70	74	213	16,125
Dori Carter	69	71	73	213	16,125
Jennifer Johnson	72	68	73	213	16,125
Karrie Webb	72	73	69	214	11,220
Catriona Matthew	72	72	70	214	11,220
Paige Mackenzie	74	72	68	214	11,220
Sandra Gal	68	72	74	214	11,220
Suzann Pettersen	71	71	72	214	11,220
Hee-Won Han	68	70	76	214	11,220
Stacy Prammanasudh	74	73	67	214	11,220
Mindy Kim	72	68	74	214	11,220
Jiyai Shin	71	72	71	214	11,220
Cindy LaCrosse	73	72	69	214	11,220
Mariajo Uribe	71	74	69	214	11,220
Belen Mozo	69	71	74	214	11,220
Amelia Lewis	69	74	72	215	7,693

CN Canadian Women's Open

Vancouver Golf Club, Coquitlam, British Columbia, Canada
Par 35-37—72; 6,681 yards

August 23-26
purse, $2,000,000

	SCORES				TOTAL	MONEY
*Lydia Ko	68	68	72	67	275	
Inbee Park	68	71	70	69	278	$300,000
Na Yeon Choi	67	72	73	68	280	140,103
Chella Choi	72	64	73	71	280	140,103
Jiyai Shin	70	70	69	71	280	140,103
Stacy Lewis	72	71	66	72	281	75,478
Anna Nordqvist	74	70	68	69	281	75,478
Haeji Kang	72	71	72	67	282	56,860
Vicky Hurst	70	70	72	71	283	47,300
Jane Rah	71	71	72	69	283	47,300
Moira Dunn	69	70	72	73	284	36,682
Catriona Matthew	74	72	67	71	284	36,682
Gerina Piller	73	74	70	67	284	36,682
Azahara Munoz	73	71	71	69	284	36,682
Suzann Pettersen	71	69	73	72	285	26,568
Taylor Coutu	71	70	71	73	285	26,568
Mika Miyazato	71	71	73	70	285	26,568
Dewi Claire Schreefel	72	71	72	70	285	26,568
Mina Harigae	73	70	69	73	285	26,568
Sydnee Michaels	70	72	69	74	285	26,568
Jessica Korda	72	71	71	71	285	26,568
Ilhee Lee	73	73	72	68	286	21,134
Paige Mackenzie	70	76	71	69	286	21,134
Stacy Prammanasudh	72	73	72	69	286	21,134
Mo Martin	74	71	73	68	286	21,134
Katherine Hull	73	71	72	71	287	17,477
Angela Stanford	69	70	74	74	287	17,477
Meena Lee	72	74	72	69	287	17,477
Karrie Webb	71	73	71	72	287	17,477
Hee-Won Han	73	73	69	72	287	17,477
Amy Yang	70	76	70	71	287	17,477

Kingsmill Championship

Kingsmill Resort, River Course, Williamsburg, Virginia
Par 36-35—71; 6,384 yards
(Event concluded on Monday—darkness.)

September 6-10
purse, $1,300,000

	SCORES				TOTAL	MONEY
Jiyai Shin	62	68	69	69	268	$195,000
Paula Creamer	65	67	65	71	268	120,655
(Shin defeated Creamer on ninth playoff hole.)						
Karine Icher	70	68	67	65	270	77,618
Danielle Kang	67	64	70	69	270	77,618
Angela Stanford	69	67	71	64	271	49,544
Catriona Matthew	67	70	66	68	271	49,544
Mika Miyazato	66	70	70	66	272	35,011
Ai Miyazato	67	68	67	70	272	35,011
Maria Hjorth	65	69	71	68	273	26,010
Gerina Piller	67	69	68	69	273	26,010
Stacy Lewis	69	65	68	71	273	26,010
Azahara Munoz	65	68	69	71	273	26,010
Dewi Claire Schreefel	66	66	69	73	274	21,666
Pernilla Lindberg	71	68	72	65	276	17,092

	SCORES				TOTAL	MONEY
Anna Nordqvist	70	70	67	69	276	17,092
Karin Sjodin	67	70	69	70	276	17,092
Sandra Gal	69	67	69	71	276	17,092
Candie Kung	68	67	70	71	276	17,092
Lexi Thompson	67	66	72	71	276	17,092
Chella Choi	67	68	69	72	276	17,092
Hee Young Park	68	68	67	73	276	17,092
Mi Jung Hur	70	66	72	69	277	13,608
Julieta Granada	67	69	70	71	277	13,608
Taylor Coutu	72	67	66	72	277	13,608
Jane Park	68	72	71	67	278	11,258
Beatriz Recari	65	74	72	67	278	11,258
Jennifer Johnson	66	69	75	68	278	11,258
Mindy Kim	72	69	68	69	278	11,258
Karen Stupples	70	71	67	70	278	11,258
Pornanong Phatlum	69	69	68	72	278	11,258
Jennifer Song	66	69	69	74	278	11,258

Ricoh Women's British Open

See Ladies European Tour section.

Navistar LPGA Classic

Robert Trent Jones Golf Trail, Capitol Hill Course,   September 20-23
Prattville, Alabama   purse, $1,300,000
Par 36-36–72; 6,607 yards

	SCORES				TOTAL	MONEY
Stacy Lewis	66	70	65	69	270	$195,000
Lexi Thompson	63	69	74	66	272	120,962
Angela Stanford	67	68	68	70	273	70,089
Mi Jung Hur	68	65	72	68	273	70,089
Haeji Kang	70	68	67	68	273	70,089
Sarah Jane Smith	69	69	68	68	274	41,060
Beatriz Recari	70	71	66	67	274	41,060
Meena Lee	70	67	71	67	275	29,692
Hee Young Park	65	69	72	69	275	29,692
So Yeon Ryu	69	69	69	68	275	29,692
Azahara Munoz	72	66	73	65	276	23,245
Pernilla Lindberg	70	68	71	67	276	23,245
Jennifer Johnson	71	65	71	69	276	23,245
Nicole Castrale	69	68	70	70	277	19,801
Dori Carter	67	67	73	70	277	19,801
Sandra Gal	68	71	72	67	278	16,557
Dewi Claire Schreefel	71	69	72	66	278	16,557
Mina Harigae	69	72	67	70	278	16,557
Sydnee Michaels	67	68	72	71	278	16,557
Lizette Salas	65	69	70	74	278	16,557
Brittany Lincicome	72	70	68	69	279	13,170
Wendy Ward	66	73	72	68	279	13,170
Karin Sjodin	70	67	72	70	279	13,170
Suzann Pettersen	71	71	71	66	279	13,170
Amy Yang	69	71	69	70	279	13,170
Gerina Piller	68	67	74	70	279	13,170
Belen Mozo	70	68	73	68	279	13,170
Mindy Kim	68	65	76	71	280	9,632
Amy Hung	73	70	70	67	280	9,632
Kris Tamulis	72	70	69	69	280	9,632

	SCORES				TOTAL	MONEY
Karine Icher	72	71	70	67	280	9,632
Sun Young Yoo	73	69	68	70	280	9,632
Natalie Gulbis	68	68	72	72	280	9,632
Hee-Won Han	71	69	72	68	280	9,632
Vicky Hurst	68	69	70	73	280	9,632
Pornanong Phatlum	71	70	67	72	280	9,632

Sime Darby LPGA Malaysia

Kuala Lumpur Golf & Country Club, Kuala Lumpur, Malaysia
Par 35-36–71; 6,246 yards

October 11-14
purse, $1,900,000

	SCORES				TOTAL	MONEY
Inbee Park	69	68	65	67	269	$285,000
Na Yeon Choi	65	67	68	71	271	179,747
Karrie Webb	65	71	68	68	272	130,394
Catriona Matthew	68	68	70	67	273	100,870
So Yeon Ryu	68	73	67	66	274	81,189
Paula Creamer	69	67	70	69	275	61,014
Lindsey Wright	70	66	72	67	275	61,014
Jessica Korda	68	71	73	64	276	48,714
Ai Miyazato	68	69	68	72	277	38,749
Candie Kung	70	71	71	65	277	38,749
Mika Miyazato	66	69	71	71	277	38,749
Lizette Salas	68	67	76	66	277	38,749
*Ariya Jutanugarn	69	72	67	69	277	
Azahara Munoz	71	71	67	69	278	31,294
Sun Young Yoo	66	70	72	70	278	31,294
Karine Icher	70	69	71	69	279	27,030
Ilhee Lee	69	71	70	69	279	27,030
Eun-Hee Ji	70	67	72	70	279	27,030
Brittany Lang	69	68	70	73	280	21,875
I.K. Kim	70	67	72	71	280	21,875
Shanshan Feng	70	72	71	67	280	21,875
Suzann Pettersen	71	64	70	75	280	21,875
Stacy Lewis	70	69	73	68	280	21,875
Beatriz Recari	72	66	73	69	280	21,875
Sydnee Michaels	69	65	75	71	280	21,875
Cristie Kerr	68	77	69	67	281	18,108
Hee Young Park	67	72	70	72	281	18,108
Amy Yang	70	69	71	71	281	18,108
Momoko Ueda	68	67	74	73	282	16,729
Sandra Gal	72	71	70	70	283	14,860
Chella Choi	71	74	65	73	283	14,860
Gerina Piller	70	74	71	68	283	14,860
Lexi Thompson	69	71	76	67	283	14,860
Mina Harigae	70	71	74	68	283	14,860

LPGA KEB-HanaBank Championship

Sky 72 Golf Club, Ocean Course, Incheon, South Korea
Par 36-36–72; 6,364 yards

October 19-21
purse, $1,800,000

	SCORES			TOTAL	MONEY
Suzann Pettersen	63	68	74	205	$270,000
Catriona Matthew	68	70	67	205	168,366

(Pettersen defeated Matthew on third playoff hole.)

	SCORES			TOTAL	MONEY
Yani Tseng	67	70	69	206	122,138
Se Ri Pak	70	67	70	207	94,483
Sandra Gal	69	68	71	208	69,135
Lexi Thompson	68	70	70	208	69,135
Azahara Munoz	66	72	71	209	40,482
Ha-Neul Kim	66	72	71	209	40,482
Brittany Lincicome	72	70	67	209	40,482
Hee Young Park	69	73	67	209	40,482
Mina Harigae	68	72	69	209	40,482
So Yeon Ryu	66	70	73	209	40,482
Cristie Kerr	70	72	68	210	29,313
Karin Sjodin	64	75	71	210	29,313
Inbee Park	70	70	71	211	25,318
Haeji Kang	70	70	71	211	25,318
Jiyai Shin	71	71	69	211	25,318
Beatriz Recari	69	71	72	212	22,400
Danielle Kang	71	70	71	212	22,400
Ai Miyazato	66	75	72	213	20,833
Jodi Ewart	74	69	70	213	20,833
Julieta Granada	69	74	71	214	18,989
Brittany Lang	73	69	72	214	18,989
Jung-Min Lee	69	71	74	214	18,989
Gerina Piller	69	72	74	215	16,316
Yoon-Kyung Heo	69	74	72	215	16,316
Hyun-Hee Moon	66	75	74	215	16,316
Amy Yang	70	72	73	215	16,316
Hyo Joo Kim	68	73	74	215	16,316
Karine Icher	68	73	75	216	13,919
I.K. Kim	73	73	70	216	13,919
Michelle Wie	73	73	70	216	13,919

Sunrise LPGA Taiwan Championship

Sunrise Golf & Country Club, Yang Mei, Taoyuan, Taiwan
Par 36-36–72; 6,390 yards

October 25-28
purse, $2,000,000

	SCORES				TOTAL	MONEY
Suzann Pettersen	69	65	66	69	269	$300,000
Inbee Park	65	69	64	74	272	185,159
Yani Tseng	67	69	66	71	273	134,320
Catriona Matthew	70	66	68	70	274	103,907
So Yeon Ryu	71	70	69	68	278	83,633
Anna Nordqvist	71	69	68	71	279	62,852
Cristie Kerr	70	69	67	73	279	62,852
Azahara Munoz	71	68	69	72	280	45,449
Julieta Granada	70	69	68	73	280	45,449
Na Yeon Choi	74	67	66	73	280	45,449
Ai Miyazato	71	69	68	73	281	36,747
Belen Mozo	73	68	66	74	281	36,747
Paula Creamer	69	73	67	73	282	33,250
Chella Choi	69	71	68	75	283	29,465
Ilhee Lee	72	69	68	74	283	29,465
Lexi Thompson	72	69	69	73	283	29,465
Beatriz Recari	71	72	70	71	284	26,357
Momoko Ueda	73	70	71	71	285	24,634
Hyo Joo Kim	71	71	71	72	285	24,634
Giulia Sergas	75	74	69	68	286	22,505
Haeji Kang	72	70	68	76	286	22,505
Mariajo Uribe	73	73	68	72	286	22,505
Pornanong Phatlum	68	73	69	77	287	18,667

	SCORES				TOTAL	MONEY
Nicole Castrale	68	75	70	74	287	18,667
Mo Martin	74	72	69	72	287	18,667
Michelle Wie	71	72	68	76	287	18,667
Mina Harigae	72	73	71	71	287	18,667
Jennifer Johnson	73	69	69	76	287	18,667
Alison Walshe	71	67	75	74	287	18,667
Paige Mackenzie	72	71	70	75	288	15,611
Pernilla Lindberg	73	68	72	75	288	15,611

Mizuno Classic

See Japan LPGA Tour section.

Lorena Ochoa Invitational

Guadalajara Country Club, Guadalajara, Mexico
Par 36-36–72; 6,626 yards

November 8-11
purse, $1,000,000

	SCORES				TOTAL	MONEY
Cristie Kerr	67	69	67	69	272	$200,000
Angela Stanford	66	67	72	68	273	88,415
Inbee Park	67	68	66	72	273	88,415
Candie Kung	66	71	71	68	276	51,901
Stacy Lewis	67	70	71	68	276	51,901
Haeji Kang	74	68	68	67	277	34,788
So Yeon Ryu	67	70	67	73	277	34,788
Hee Kyung Seo	70	69	69	70	278	26,372
Katherine Hull	68	71	70	69	278	26,372
Anna Nordqvist	69	71	70	69	279	22,724
Karine Icher	67	71	69	73	280	21,041
I.K. Kim	68	70	71	72	281	19,021
Suzann Pettersen	70	74	68	69	281	19,021
Ai Miyazato	73	68	72	69	282	16,309
Brittany Lincicome	71	73	66	72	282	16,309
Michelle Wie	66	75	67	74	282	16,309
Beatriz Recari	69	73	71	70	283	14,589
Azahara Munoz	71	73	68	72	284	13,158
Vicky Hurst	71	70	73	70	284	13,158
Lorena Ochoa	71	72	70	71	284	13,158
Brittany Lang	73	71	69	71	284	13,158
Paula Creamer	71	76	67	71	285	11,559
Catriona Matthew	71	72	68	74	285	11,559
Jessica Korda	75	69	68	73	285	11,559
Julieta Granada	77	70	71	70	288	10,717
Sandra Gal	73	69	73	74	289	9,735
Lexi Thompson	71	77	70	71	289	9,735
Kristy McPherson	71	74	74	70	289	9,735
Yani Tseng	70	71	76	72	289	9,735
Chella Choi	76	74	72	68	290	8,809

CME Group Titleholders

TwinEagles Club, Naples, Florida
Par 36-36–72; 7,300 yards

November 15-18
purse, $1,500,000

	SCORES				TOTAL	MONEY
Na Yeon Choi	67	68	69	70	274	$500,000
So Yeon Ryu	66	72	68	70	276	106,379
Brittany Lincicome	68	69	70	70	277	77,171
Karrie Webb	69	69	71	69	278	59,698
Ai Miyazato	70	64	71	74	279	48,050
Karine Icher	67	70	70	73	280	39,313
Azahara Munoz	72	72	67	70	281	27,811
Anna Nordqvist	69	70	69	73	281	27,811
Cristie Kerr	67	74	71	69	281	27,811
Shanshan Feng	70	69	69	73	281	27,811
Inbee Park	70	70	72	70	282	20,442
Lizette Salas	68	71	73	70	282	20,442
Caroline Hedwall	70	69	73	70	282	20,442
Sandra Gal	70	68	72	73	283	16,482
Beatriz Recari	72	69	68	74	283	16,482
Cindy LaCrosse	69	72	72	70	283	16,482
Danielle Kang	69	75	70	69	283	16,482
Julieta Granada	68	72	70	74	284	13,658
Brittany Lang	71	69	69	75	284	13,658
Suzann Pettersen	66	71	72	75	284	13,658
I.K. Kim	72	70	69	73	284	13,658
Amy Yang	70	70	73	72	285	12,231
Jiyai Shin	68	73	71	73	285	12,231
Giulia Sergas	71	72	72	71	286	11,328
Sun Young Yoo	66	71	74	75	286	11,328
Lindsey Wright	67	74	74	72	287	10,309
Yani Tseng	75	73	69	70	287	10,309
Mina Harigae	72	71	75	69	287	10,309
Hee Kyung Seo	71	73	73	71	288	8,453
Stacy Lewis	70	72	72	74	288	8,453
Katherine Hull	70	72	74	72	288	8,453
Angela Stanford	70	74	72	72	288	8,453
Ilhee Lee	72	72	73	71	288	8,453
Catriona Matthew	72	77	70	69	288	8,453
Sydnee Michaels	74	75	71	68	288	8,453

Ladies European Tour

Gold Coast RACV Ladies Masters
See Australian Ladies Tour section.

ISPS Handa Women's Australian Open
See Australian Ladies Tour section.

ISPS Handa New Zealand Women's Open
See Australian Ladies Tour section.

World Ladies Championship

Mission Hills Vintage Course, Haikou, Hainan, China
Par 38-34–72; 7,363 yards

March 2-4
purse, US$600,000

	SCORES			TOTAL	MONEY
Shanshan Feng	66	69	71	206	€56,275.95
Pornanong Phatlum	68	69	70	207	38,080.06
Pernilla Lindberg	69	70	69	208	26,262.11
Diana Luna	66	71	72	209	18,083.34
Li-Ying Ye	68	67	74	209	18,083.34
Nontaya Srisawang	70	71	69	210	13,131.06
Giulia Sergas	71	73	68	212	9,154.22
Melissa Reid	70	74	68	212	9,154.22
Linda Wessberg	69	72	71	212	9,154.22
Beth Allen	67	71	74	212	9,154.22
Felicity Johnson	71	71	71	213	6,490.49
Lee-Anne Pace	71	70	72	213	6,490.49
Caroline Masson	70	70	73	213	6,490.49
Florentyna Parker	69	68	76	213	6,490.49
Candie Kung	67	77	70	214	5,815.18
Jennifer Rosales	70	73	72	215	5,304.95
Virginie Lagoutte-Clement	74	69	72	215	5,304.95
Carin Koch	68	75	72	215	5,304.95
Gwladys Nocera	73	70	72	215	5,304.95
Line Vedel	71	70	74	215	5,304.95

Lalla Meryem Cup

Golf de l'Ocean, Agadir, Morocco
Par 35-36–71

March 22-25
purse, €325,000

	SCORES				TOTAL	MONEY
Karen Lunn	72	66	68	66	272	€48,750
Tandi Cuningham	71	70	67	67	275	27,868.75
Marianne Skarpnord	70	65	71	69	275	27,868.75
Holly Aitchison	70	68	72	67	277	15,665
Jade Schaeffer	67	69	69	72	277	15,665
Sophie Giquel-Bettan	69	69	72	68	278	10,562.50

	SCORES			TOTAL	MONEY
Valentine Derrey	72	67	69	70	278	10,562.50
Carin Koch	69	68	74	68	279	8,125
Carlota Ciganda	70	68	73	69	280	6,586.67
Line Vedel	72	68	71	69	280	6,586.67
Bree Arthur	72	68	70	70	280	6,586.67
Stacy Lee Bregman	72	69	70	70	281	5,411.25
Malene Jorgensen	71	70	70	70	281	5,411.25
Rebecca Flood	72	71	73	66	282	4,631.25
Rebecca Hudson	71	71	72	68	282	4,631.25
Cassandra Kirkland	72	70	68	72	282	4,631.25
Linda Wessberg	68	70	71	73	282	4,631.25
Esther Choe	72	69	67	74	282	4,631.25
Stefania Croce	70	74	63	75	282	4,631.25
Stacey Keating	70	71	71	71	283	4,143.75
Marion Ricordeau	71	69	71	72	283	4,143.75

Aberdeen Asset Management Ladies Scottish Open

Archerfield Links, East Lothian, Scotland
Par 36-36–72; 7,000 yards

May 3-5
purse, €218,040

	SCORES			TOTAL	MONEY
Carly Booth	70	71	71	212	€32,706
Frances Bondad	71	75	67	213	18,696.93
Florentyna Parker	72	69	72	213	18,696.93
Trish Johnson	71	75	68	214	9,550.15
Stacey Keating	73	72	69	214	9,550.15
Melissa Reid	70	74	70	214	9,550.15
Sophie Giquel-Bettan	73	72	70	215	6,541.20
Gwladys Nocera	72	75	69	216	5,167.55
Becky Morgan	74	70	72	216	5,167.55
Cassandra Kirkland	71	76	70	217	3,898.56
Kylie Walker	74	74	69	217	3,898.56
Virginie Lagoutte-Clement	74	74	69	217	3,898.56
Lee-Anne Pace	70	74	73	217	3,898.56
Diana Luna	70	73	74	217	3,898.56
Caroline Masson	74	73	71	218	3,187.74
Kiran Matharu	73	75	70	218	3,187.74
Karen Lunn	74	71	73	218	3,187.74
Sarah Kemp	69	76	73	218	3,187.74
Anne-Lise Caudal	67	76	75	218	3,187.74
Catriona Matthew	74	72	73	219	2,725.50
Margherita Rigon	75	71	73	219	2,725.50
Pernilla Lindberg	74	74	71	219	2,725.50
Stacy Lee Bregman	71	70	78	219	2,725.50

Turkish Airlines Ladies Open

National Golf Club, Belek, Antalya, Turkey
Par 36-37–73; 6,211 yards

May 10-13
purse, €250,000

	SCORES			TOTAL	MONEY
Christel Boeljon	70	73	69	73	285	€37,500
Ursula Wikstrom	73	70	71	74	288	25,375
Carin Koch	72	77	68	73	290	15,500
Carlota Ciganda	73	76	66	75	290	15,500
*Charley Hull	73	72	73	73	291	

		SCORES			TOTAL	MONEY
Pernilla Lindberg	70	75	74	73	292	8,950
Holly Aitchison	74	74	70	74	292	8,950
Minea Blomqvist	72	72	70	78	292	8,950
Hannah Jun	74	75	71	73	293	5,925
Sophie Giquel-Bettan	73	73	74	73	293	5,925
Diana Luna	70	75	72	77	294	5,000
Danielle Montgomery	72	77	72	74	295	4,600
Esther Choe	75	72	77	72	296	4,058.33
Louise Larsson	75	70	73	78	296	4,058.33
Line Vedel	76	73	68	79	296	4,058.33
Miriam Nagl	74	78	74	71	297	3,608.33
Bree Arthur	73	75	72	77	297	3,608.33
Rebecca Hudson	72	75	71	79	297	3,608.33
Laura Davies	73	73	78	74	298	3,268.75
Caroline Masson	71	76	76	75	298	3,268.75
Anne-Lise Caudal	72	74	75	77	298	3,268.75
Sarah Kemp	73	80	68	77	298	3,268.75

UniCredit Ladies German Open

Golfpark Gut Hausern, Munich, Germany
Par 36-36–72; 6,204 yards

May 24-27
purse, €350,000

		SCORES			TOTAL	MONEY
Anne-Lise Caudal	74	67	67	67	275	€52,500
Laura Davies	69	71	68	67	275	35,525
(Caudal defeated Davies on second playoff hole.)						
Rebecca Hudson	71	68	67	71	277	24,500
Felicity Johnson	70	73	72	64	279	15,330
Trish Johnson	71	69	71	68	279	15,330
Bree Arthur	69	72	65	73	279	15,330
Caroline Afonso	70	71	71	68	280	7,558.33
Sophie Gustafson	69	72	71	68	280	7,558.33
Carlota Ciganda	69	74	69	68	280	7,558.33
Giulia Sergas	72	70	69	69	280	7,558.33
Sandra Gal	70	68	70	72	280	7,558.33
Pernilla Lindberg	68	69	69	74	280	7,558.33
Stefanie Michl	67	71	73	70	281	5,512.50
Carin Koch	67	74	69	71	281	5,512.50
Diana Luna	69	71	72	70	282	5,127.50
Caroline Masson	70	72	70	70	282	5,127.50
Nikki Garrett	72	72	72	67	283	4,641
Rebecca Artis	71	72	70	70	283	4,641
Becky Morgan	70	75	68	70	283	4,641
Minea Blomqvist	74	70	68	71	283	4,641
Joanna Klatten	69	69	73	72	283	4,641

Deloitte Ladies Open

Golfclub Broekpolder, Rotterdam, Netherlands
Par 36-35–71; 6,386 yards

June 1-3
purse, €250,000

		SCORES		TOTAL	MONEY
Carlota Ciganda	71	67	69	207	€37,500
Ursula Wikstrom	71	68	70	209	25,375
Lee-Anne Pace	71	70	71	212	17,500
Carin Koch	71	70	72	213	12,050

	SCORES			TOTAL	MONEY
Dewi Claire Schreefel	71	70	72	213	12,050
Mikaela Parmlid	72	71	71	214	7,025
Caroline Masson	71	72	71	214	7,025
Veronica Zorzi	73	69	72	214	7,025
Caroline Afonso	71	70	73	214	7,025
Florentyna Parker	68	72	75	215	5,000
Diana Luna	69	76	71	216	3,752.50
Hannah Burke	69	75	72	216	3,752.50
Christel Boeljon	70	73	73	216	3,752.50
Gwladys Nocera	76	70	70	216	3,752.50
Marion Ricordeau	72	74	70	216	3,752.50
Louise Larsson	72	71	73	216	3,752.50
Sophie Walker	72	74	70	216	3,752.50
Alison Whitaker	70	72	74	216	3,752.50
Stacy Lee Bregman	73	69	74	216	3,752.50
Elena Giraud	68	73	75	216	3,752.50

Allianz Ladies Slovak Open

Golf Resort Tale, Brezno, Tale, Slovakia
Par 35-37–72

June 8-10
purse, €225,000

	SCORES			TOTAL	MONEY
Line Vedel	71	69	69	209	€33,750
Caroline Masson	75	67	69	211	22,837.50
Nontaya Srisawang	70	73	70	213	13,950
Veronica Zorzi	70	72	71	213	13,950
Frances Bondad	72	71	71	214	8,707.50
Jessica Yadloczky	71	70	73	214	8,707.50
Caroline Rominger	73	72	70	215	5,211
Carin Koch	70	73	72	215	5,211
Carly Booth	70	72	73	215	5,211
Trish Johnson	73	68	74	215	5,211
Rachel Bailey	71	70	74	215	5,211
Esther Choe	72	73	71	216	3,746.25
Julie Greciet	73	72	71	216	3,746.25
Sophie Giquel-Bettan	74	72	71	217	3,206.25
Rebecca Artis	73	72	72	217	3,206.25
Tandi Cuningham	73	76	68	217	3,206.25
Lee-Anne Pace	74	70	73	217	3,206.25
Gwladys Nocera	71	72	74	217	3,206.25
Lucie Andre	69	73	75	217	3,206.25
Mikaela Parmlid	74	72	72	218	2,700
Barbara Genuini	71	75	72	218	2,700
Elisabeth Esterl	73	73	72	218	2,700
Stefania Croce	76	71	71	218	2,700
Anne-Lise Caudal	74	71	73	218	2,700
Nikki Garrett	71	73	74	218	2,700
Klara Spilkova	70	73	75	218	2,700

Deutsche Bank Ladies Swiss Open

Golf Gerre Losone, Ticino, Switzerland
Par 35-37–72; 6,266 yards

June 14-17
purse, €525,000

	SCORES				TOTAL	MONEY
Carly Booth	70	71	67	68	276	€78,750
Anja Monke	71	72	67	66	276	45,018.75
Caroline Masson	70	69	69	68	276	45,018.75
(Booth defeated Masson and Monke on fourth playoff hole.)						
Mikaela Parmlid	74	68	70	65	277	25,305
Marjet van der Graaff	69	71	67	70	277	25,305
Stacy Lee Bregman	71	67	70	70	278	17,062.50
Ashleigh Simon	68	72	66	72	278	17,062.50
Anne-Lise Caudal	69	72	70	68	279	12,442.50
Rebecca Artis	64	71	70	74	279	12,442.50
Lisa Holm Sorensen	72	72	73	63	280	8,925
Carlota Ciganda	69	70	72	69	280	8,925
Lee-Anne Pace	68	71	71	70	280	8,925
Karen Lunn	69	71	69	71	280	8,925
Diana Luna	67	70	71	72	280	8,925
Jessica Yadloczky	69	71	65	75	280	8,925
Rebecca Hudson	71	70	73	67	281	7,061.25
Stefania Croce	68	74	70	69	281	7,061.25
Barbara Genuini	67	71	73	70	281	7,061.25
Florentyna Parker	66	71	72	72	281	7,061.25
Linda Wessberg	69	70	70	72	281	7,061.25
Connie Chen	73	69	67	72	281	7,061.25

Raiffeisenbank Prague Golf Masters

Albatross Golf Resort, Prague, Czech Republic
Par 36-36–72; 6,354 yards

June 22-24
purse, €250,000

	SCORES			TOTAL	MONEY
Melissa Reid	68	67	72	207	€37,500
Diana Luna	70	69	69	208	25,375
Rachel Bailey	70	73	66	209	15,500
Rebecca Hudson	70	68	71	209	15,500
Joanna Klatten	71	72	67	210	9,675
Stacey Keating	69	69	72	210	9,675
Marjet van der Graaff	70	73	68	211	6,087.50
Nikki Garrett	69	71	71	211	6,087.50
Veronica Zorzi	66	72	73	211	6,087.50
Elisabeth Esterl	66	71	74	211	6,087.50
Connie Chen	68	76	68	212	4,100
Carlota Ciganda	73	70	69	212	4,100
Rebecca Codd	75	68	69	212	4,100
Ashleigh Simon	71	70	71	212	4,100
Lee-Anne Pace	68	71	73	212	4,100
Linda Wessberg	73	73	67	213	3,450
Gwladys Nocera	72	70	71	213	3,450
Karen Lunn	72	69	72	213	3,450
Stefania Croce	70	66	77	213	3,450
Anja Monke	74	72	68	214	2,887.50
Tandi Cuningham	76	69	69	214	2,887.50
Miriam Nagl	73	71	70	214	2,887.50
Laura Cabanillas	73	71	70	214	2,887.50
Mikaela Parmlid	72	72	70	214	2,887.50
Kiran Matharu	71	71	72	214	2,887.50

	SCORES			TOTAL	MONEY
Laura Davies	69	73	72	214	2,887.50
Marianne Skarpnord	71	71	72	214	2,887.50
Caroline Afonso	72	69	73	214	2,887.50
Sophie Giquel-Bettan	72	67	75	214	2,887.50

South African Women's Open

Selborne Park Golf Club, KwaZulu-Natal, South Africa
Par 36-36–72; 6,206 yards

July 13-15
purse, €260,000

	SCORES			TOTAL	MONEY
Caroline Masson	69	75	71	215	€39,000
Lee-Anne Pace	75	71	70	216	22,295
Danielle Montgomery	74	70	72	216	22,295
Tandi Cuningham	75	72	70	217	12,532
Joanna Klatten	71	73	73	217	12,532
Lindsey Wright	74	73	71	218	7,800
Julie Greciet	71	74	73	218	7,800
Ashleigh Simon	72	72	74	218	7,800
Melissa Eaton-Jackson	78	73	68	219	5,269.33
Felicity Johnson	72	76	71	219	5,269.33
Bree Arthur	77	69	73	219	5,269.33
Morgana Robbertze	73	74	73	220	4,329
Stacy Lee Bregman	71	75	74	220	4,329
Anne-Lise Caudal	74	73	74	221	3,939
Anais Maggetti	71	76	74	221	3,939
Sophie Walker	77	74	71	222	3,692
Gwladys Nocera	74	77	71	222	3,692
Nontaya Srisawang	73	77	73	223	3,484
Marion Ricordeau	77	72	74	223	3,484
Rebecca Codd	78	71	75	224	3,354

Evian Masters

Evian Masters Golf Club, Evians-les-Bains, France
Par 36-36–72; 6,457 yards

July 26-29
purse, €2,496,170

	SCORES				TOTAL	MONEY
Inbee Park	71	64	70	66	271	€397,068.75
Karrie Webb	70	69	67	67	273	210,392.29
Stacy Lewis	63	69	73	68	273	210,392.29
Shanshan Feng	68	72	68	66	274	123,504.43
*Hyo-Joo Kim	69	68	69	68	274	
Natalie Gulbis	69	69	68	68	274	123,504.43
Anna Nordqvist	72	67	69	68	276	90,125.10
Se Ri Pak	70	69	69	69	277	75,438.15
Beatriz Recari	71	66	75	66	278	59,861.39
Ilhee Lee	66	67	76	69	278	59,861.39
Paula Creamer	68	67	73	70	278	59,861.39
Giulia Sergas	71	72	69	67	279	45,428.73
Momoko Ueda	69	72	69	69	279	45,428.73
Karine Icher	70	72	68	69	279	45,428.73
Cristie Kerr	71	69	67	72	279	45,428.73
Meena Lee	69	69	72	70	280	34,981.75
Azahara Munoz	70	68	72	70	280	34,981.75
Mika Miyazato	67	69	73	71	280	34,981.75
Lindsey Wright	71	70	68	71	280	34,981.75

	SCORES				TOTAL	MONEY
Lee-Anne Pace	69	71	68	72	280	34,981.75
Ai Miyazato	71	70	70	70	281	29,641.03
Julieta Granada	74	65	71	71	281	29,641.03
Hee Young Park	65	72	71	73	281	29,641.03
Brittany Lang	71	69	74	68	282	24,586.67
Amy Yang	72	68	73	69	282	24,586.67
I.K. Kim	69	73	71	69	282	24,586.67
Hee Kyung Seo	71	69	71	71	282	24,586.67
Mirim Lee	73	68	70	71	282	24,586.67
Carlota Ciganda	73	69	66	74	282	24,586.67
Suzann Pettersen	69	71	68	74	282	24,586.67
Chella Choi	73	68	72	70	283	20,161.06
So Yeon Ryu	73	65	72	73	283	20,161.06
Jiyai Shin	69	69	71	74	283	20,161.06
Ha-Neul Kim	70	71	73	70	284	18,157.69
Hee-Won Han	72	69	69	74	284	18,157.69
Mariajo Uribe	67	74	74	70	285	16,089.31
Brittany Lincicome	73	67	73	72	285	16,089.31
Katherine Hull	71	70	72	72	285	16,089.31
Haeji Kang	72	70	68	75	285	16,089.31
Alison Walshe	76	69	72	69	286	13,084.70
Juli Inkster	71	75	70	70	286	13,084.70
Catriona Matthew	74	72	69	71	286	13,084.70
Na Yeon Choi	75	70	70	71	286	13,084.70
Pornanong Phatlum	72	70	72	72	286	13,084.70
Becky Morgan	70	71	69	76	286	13,084.70
Maria Hjorth	72	69	75	71	287	10,747.88
Jessica Korda	77	67	72	71	287	10,747.88
Sun Young Yoo	73	68	71	75	287	10,747.88
Jenny Shin	73	69	69	76	287	10,747.88
Pernilla Lindberg	74	72	70	72	288	9,545.86
Cheyenne Woods	71	69	70	78	288	9,545.86
Christina Kim	73	67	73	76	289	8,946.17
Ji-Na Yim	72	69	71	77	289	8,946.17
Miki Saiki	76	69	76	69	290	8,010.83
Jennifer Song	73	72	73	72	290	8,010.83
Ran Hong	74	68	75	73	290	8,010.83
Hye-Youn Kim	73	72	72	73	290	8,010.83
Danielle Kang	75	70	71	74	290	8,010.83
Carly Booth	72	73	74	72	291	7,076.80
Shin-Ae Ahn	74	72	72	73	291	7,076.80
Min-Young Lee	74	72	74	72	292	6,676.13
Amanda Blumenherst	73	73	77	70	293	6,475.79
Cindy LaCrosse	76	69	73	75	293	6,475.79
Laura Davies	73	72	79	70	294	6,008.52
Jennifer Johnson	73	70	78	73	294	6,008.52
Sandra Gal	69	76	76	73	294	6,008.52
Michelle Wie	73	72	76	73	294	6,008.52
Jodi Ewart	70	76	73	75	294	6,008.52
Mina Harigae	75	71	71	78	295	5,606.78
Kaori Ohe	74	71	68	83	296	5,474.11
Caroline Afonso	73	73	78	73	297	5,308.27
Anais Maggetti	76	69	76	76	297	5,308.27
Linda Wessberg	75	69	77	77	298	5,206.11
Gwladys Nocera	71	75	75	79	300	5,139.77
Felicity Johnson	73	73	79	76	301	5,073.43

Ladies Irish Open

Killeen Castle, Co. Meath, Ireland
Par 36-36–72; 6,477 yards

August 3-5
purse, €350,000

	SCORES			TOTAL	MONEY
Catriona Matthew	67	71	71	209	€52,500
Suzann Pettersen	72	69	69	210	35,525
Laura Davies	74	71	68	213	24,500
Nikki Garrett	73	72	70	215	15,330
Joanna Klatten	72	73	70	215	15,330
Pernilla Lindberg	68	72	75	215	15,330
Felicity Johnson	69	75	72	216	9,625
Carly Booth	71	69	76	216	9,625
Carlota Ciganda	74	75	68	217	6,587
Dewi Claire Schreefel	73	73	71	217	6,587
Jodi Ewart	73	72	72	217	6,587
Alison Walshe	73	71	73	217	6,587
Elizabeth Bennett	70	73	74	217	6,587
Becky Morgan	77	70	71	218	5,390
Holly Aitchison	76	73	70	219	5,051.67
Amelia Lewis	75	71	73	219	5,051.67
Sophie Gustafson	70	75	74	219	5,051.67
Diana Luna	75	76	69	220	4,308.89
Anais Maggetti	75	75	70	220	4,308.89
Stacey Keating	75	74	71	220	4,308.89
Caroline Afonso	74	75	71	220	4,308.89
Celine Palomar	76	71	73	220	4,308.89
Sophie Giquel-Bettan	73	74	73	220	4,308.89
*Charley Hull	71	76	73	220	
Giulia Sergas	72	74	74	220	4,308.89
Miriam Nagl	74	72	74	220	4,308.89
Gwladys Nocera	73	73	74	220	4,308.89

ISPS Handa Ladies British Masters

Buckinghamshire Golf Club, Denham,
Buckinghamshire, England
Par 36-36–72; 6,364 yards

August 16-18
purse, €357,226

	SCORES			TOTAL	MONEY
Lydia Hall	66	71	72	209	€57,395.10
Beth Allen	68	69	73	210	38,837.35
Trish Johnson	69	72	70	211	16,351.23
Stacy Lee Bregman	67	74	70	211	16,351.23
Rebecca Artis	71	70	70	211	16,351.23
Henrietta Zuel	66	75	70	211	16,351.23
Mikaela Parmlid	71	68	72	211	16,351.23
Ashleigh Simon	69	66	76	211	16,351.23
Caroline Martens	72	73	67	212	8,111.84
Lisa Holm Sorensen	71	71	70	212	8,111.84
Anais Maggetti	75	71	67	213	6,594.06
Lee-Anne Pace	68	73	72	213	6,594.06
Julie Greciet	70	69	74	213	6,594.06
Stefanie Michl	72	71	71	214	5,615.15
Diana Luna	70	73	71	214	5,615.15
Esther Choe	72	68	74	214	5,615.15
Nontaya Srisawang	70	70	74	214	5,615.15
Carlota Ciganda	70	76	69	215	4,884.96
Melissa Reid	69	76	70	215	4,884.96

	SCORES			TOTAL	MONEY
*Charley Hull	70	74	71	215	
Tandi Cuningham	69	75	71	215	4,884.96
Frances Bondad	72	72	71	215	4,884.96
Stacey Keating	67	74	74	215	4,884.96
Gwladys Nocera	69	70	76	215	4,884.96

UNIQA Ladies Golf Open

Golfclub Fohrenwald, Wiener Neustadt, Austria
Par 37-35–72; 6,179 yards

September 2-4
purse, €200,000

	SCORES			TOTAL	MONEY
Caroline Hedwall	67	66	70	203	€30,000
Mikaela Parmlid	68	71	68	207	17,150
Laura Davies	70	69	68	207	17,150
Linda Wessberg	70	69	69	208	8,760
Anne-Lise Caudal	69	70	69	208	8,760
Alison Whitaker	67	68	73	208	8,760
Henrietta Zuel	71	71	67	209	5,500
Veronica Zorzi	74	66	69	209	5,500
Margherita Rigon	73	69	68	210	3,950
Trish Johnson	69	71	70	210	3,950
Stacy Lee Bregman	69	70	71	210	3,950
Nontaya Srisawang	70	68	72	210	3,950
Lisa Holm Sorensen	70	71	70	211	3,116
Elizabeth Bennett	72	69	70	211	3,116
Julie Greciet	72	68	71	211	3,116
Laura Cabanillas	70	70	71	211	3,116
Melissa Reid	71	67	73	211	3,116
Caroline Afonso	73	70	69	212	2,740
Line Vedel	73	68	71	212	2,740
Carly Booth	71	69	72	212	2,740

Ricoh Women's British Open

Royal Liverpool Golf Club, Hoylake, England
Par 35-37–72; 6,660 yards

September 13-16
purse, €1,920,130

	SCORES				TOTAL	MONEY
Jiyai Shin	71	64	71	73	279	€331,936.21
Inbee Park	72	68	72	76	288	208,079.53
Paula Creamer	73	72	72	72	289	145,655.42
Mika Miyazato	71	70	72	77	290	113,948.85
So Yeon Ryu	70	74	71	76	291	87,195.57
Karrie Webb	71	70	68	82	291	87,195.57
Julieta Granada	74	71	74	74	293	73,323.48
Stacy Lewis	74	70	76	74	294	63,415.02
Katie Futcher	71	71	73	79	294	63,415.02
I.K. Kim	75	72	73	75	295	49,873.01
Chella Choi	72	73	72	78	295	49,873.01
Catriona Matthew	76	73	71	75	295	49,873.01
Na Yeon Choi	73	73	75	75	296	36,785.52
Cindy LaCrosse	73	75	72	76	296	36,785.52
Michelle Wie	75	70	72	79	296	36,785.52
Cristie Kerr	72	73	74	77	296	36,785.52
Carlota Ciganda	76	71	77	73	297	28,338.36
Lindsey Wright	76	72	75	74	297	28,338.36

	SCORES				TOTAL	MONEY
Lexi Thompson	74	75	76	72	297	28,338.36
Jenny Shin	75	68	71	83	297	28,338.36
*Lydia Ko	72	71	76	78	297	
Vicky Hurst	71	72	79	75	297	28,338.36
Lydia Hall	71	75	75	77	298	23,780.55
Juli Inkster	79	69	72	78	298	23,780.55
Angela Stanford	72	72	74	80	298	23,780.55
Hee Kyung Seo	72	73	75	79	299	19,941.02
Amy Yang	73	72	75	79	299	19,941.02
Beatriz Recari	72	77	73	77	299	19,941.02
*Holly Clyburn	72	73	74	80	299	
Yani Tseng	72	72	76	79	299	19,941.02
Yuki Ichinose	72	72	72	83	299	19,941.02
Ai Miyazato	71	72	73	83	299	19,941.02
*Bronte Law	75	71	77	77	300	
Karine Icher	75	72	76	77	300	16,596.94
Hee Young Park	78	71	76	75	300	16,596.94
Line Vedel	80	69	74	77	300	16,596.94
Katherine Hull	72	72	77	79	300	16,596.94
Candie Kung	73	76	75	77	301	15,358.14
Jane Park	74	72	78	78	302	14,119.66
Hee-Won Han	72	75	74	81	302	14,119.66
Erina Hara	75	73	77	77	302	14,119.66
Lee-Anne Pace	76	73	77	76	302	14,119.66
Amy Hung	72	74	79	78	303	12,137.85
Morgan Pressel	72	73	77	81	303	12,137.85
Carin Koch	72	71	78	82	303	12,137.85
Sarah-Jane Smith	74	75	77	77	303	12,137.85
Dewi Claire Schreefel	73	74	79	78	304	9,908.58
Becky Morgan	72	75	79	78	304	9,908.58
Sun Young Yoo	74	75	75	80	304	9,908.58
Stephanie Na	76	73	78	77	304	9,908.58
Haeji Kang	70	79	77	78	304	9,908.58
*Jing Yan	80	69	77	78	304	
Sydnee Michaels	75	71	82	77	305	8,174.84
Eun-Hee Ji	75	74	75	81	305	8,174.84
Florentyna Parker	77	72	76	81	306	7,430.88
Trish Johnson	72	77	83	77	309	6,935.73
Mo Martin	77	72	79	84	312	6,440.59

Tenerife Open de Espana Femenino

Las Americas Golf Course, Tenerife, Spain
Par 36-36–72; 6,403 yards

September 20-23
purse, €350,000

	SCORES				TOTAL	MONEY
Stacey Keating	70	69	70	70	279	€52,500
Caroline Masson	69	69	70	71	279	35,525
(Keating defeated Masson on first playoff hole.)						
Trish Johnson	67	74	72	67	280	24,500
Nikki Garrett	64	73	74	70	281	18,900
Carlota Ciganda	71	70	74	67	282	11,585
Tania Elosegui	69	74	71	68	282	11,585
Esther Choe	70	69	73	70	282	11,585
Lee-Anne Pace	68	72	72	70	282	11,585
Henrietta Zuel	73	72	71	67	283	6,587
Ashleigh Simon	70	73	72	68	283	6,587
Sophie Sandolo	69	70	75	69	283	6,587
Gwladys Nocera	70	73	71	69	283	6,587
Diana Luna	72	72	70	69	283	6,587

	SCORES				TOTAL	MONEY
Florentyna Parker	69	69	77	69	284	5,302.50
Nontaya Srisawang	71	69	72	72	284	5,302.50
Rebecca Artis	69	76	72	69	286	4,970
Hannah Burke	70	70	73	73	286	4,970
Connie Chen	72	72	75	68	287	4,631.67
Laura Davies	69	70	77	71	287	4,631.67
Rebecca Hudson	71	73	72	71	287	4,631.67

Lacoste Ladies Open de France

Chantaco Golf Club, Saint-Jean-de-Luz, Aquitaine, France
Par 35-35–70; 6,057 yards

October 4-7
purse, €250,000

	SCORES				TOTAL	MONEY
Stacey Keating	62	71	69	64	266	€37,500
Diana Luna	67	64	68	68	267	25,375
Hannah Jun	68	68	67	66	269	15,500
Azahara Munoz	66	71	66	66	269	15,500
Trish Johnson	69	69	69	63	270	8,950
Carlota Ciganda	68	67	67	68	270	8,950
Anne-Lise Caudal	70	65	67	68	270	8,950
Nontaya Srisawang	71	66	69	65	271	6,250
Titiya Plucksataporn	69	68	66	69	272	5,600
Julie Greciet	73	68	66	67	274	5,050
Jade Schaeffer	68	74	71	62	275	4,325
Lee-Anne Pace	71	66	70	68	275	4,325
Anja Monke	72	63	72	68	275	4,325
Rebecca Hudson	69	68	68	70	275	4,325
Maria Hjorth	70	74	67	65	276	3,812.50
Florentyna Parker	67	71	70	68	276	3,812.50
Sarah Kemp	71	66	73	67	277	3,600
Maria Hernandez	71	71	67	68	277	3,600
Sophie Giquel-Bettan	66	71	72	69	278	3,291.67
Anais Maggetti	67	73	69	69	278	3,291.67
Valentine Derrey	70	66	72	70	278	3,291.67

China Suzhou Taihu Open

Suzhou Taihu International Golf Club, Suzhou, China
Par 36-36–72; 6,320 yards

October 26-28
purse, €350,000

	SCORES			TOTAL	MONEY
Carlota Ciganda	65	70	64	199	€52,500
Caroline Masson	68	69	69	206	35,525
Julie Greciet	71	70	69	210	21,700
Florentyna Parker	67	74	69	210	21,700
Patcharajutar Kongkraphan	72	71	68	211	11,585
Lee-Anne Pace	68	73	70	211	11,585
Xi Yu Lin	71	70	70	211	11,585
Samantha Richdale	72	68	71	211	11,585
In Ji Bae	72	72	68	212	7,093.33
Veronica Zorzi	70	72	70	212	7,093.33
Felicity Johnson	71	67	74	212	7,093.33
Laura Davies	70	73	70	213	5,827.50
*Xin Ying Wang	71	71	71	213	
Tao Li Yang	71	69	73	213	5,827.50
Carly Booth	72	74	68	214	5,061

	SCORES			TOTAL	MONEY
Caroline Afonso	72	72	70	214	5,061
Ashleigh Simon	71	72	71	214	5,061
Yan Hua Shen	74	72	68	214	5,061
Tania Elosegui	66	74	74	214	5,061
Tiffany Tavee	74	71	70	215	4,515
Laurette Maritz	72	73	70	215	4,515
Rebecca Hudson	72	71	72	215	4,515

Sanya Ladies Open

Yalong Bay Golf Club, Sanya, China
Par 36-36–72; 6,433 yards

November 2-4
purse, €250,000

	SCORES			TOTAL	MONEY
Cassandra Kirkland	73	67	70	210	€37,500
Jade Schaeffer	71	72	69	212	21,437.50
Holly Aitchison	72	69	71	212	21,437.50
Becky Brewerton	71	73	69	213	7,344.44
Xi Yu Lin	72	72	69	213	7,344.44
Pernilla Lindberg	73	71	69	213	7,344.44
Patcharajutar Kongkrapan	73	70	70	213	7,344.44
Yue Xia Lu	72	70	71	213	7,344.44
Beth Allen	74	68	71	213	7,344.44
Carlota Ciganda	72	70	71	213	7,344.44
Sarah Kemp	71	70	72	213	7,344.44
Numa Gulyanamitta	70	69	74	213	7,344.44
Florentyna Parker	74	71	69	214	3,866.67
Caroline Masson	71	73	70	214	3,866.67
Elizabeth Bennett	72	70	72	214	3,866.67
Laura Davies	77	69	69	215	3,550
Jia Yun Li	73	70	72	215	3,550
Gwladys Nocera	75	71	70	216	3,268.75
J. Palakawong Na Ayutthaya	73	70	73	216	3,268.75
Joanna Klatten	69	73	74	216	3,268.75
Belen Mozo	74	68	74	216	3,268.75

Hero Women's Indian Open

DLF Golf & Country Club, New Delhi, India
Par 36-36–72; 6,202 yards

November 30-December 2
purse, €230,415

	SCORES			TOTAL	MONEY
Pornanong Phatlum	72	65	66	203	€34,704.60
Caroline Hedwall	76	62	69	207	23,483.45
Nontaya Srisawang	71	70	68	209	16,195.48
Carlota Ciganda	75	68	70	213	10,133.74
Trish Johnson	72	72	69	213	10,133.74
Stefania Croce	69	73	71	213	10,133.74
Laura Davies	71	69	74	214	6,940.92
Caroline Afonso	72	75	68	215	5,483.33
Elizabeth Bennett	72	69	74	215	5,483.33
*Aditi Ashok	69	74	72	215	
Joanna Klatten	76	70	70	216	4,442.19
Veronica Zorzi	74	70	72	216	4,442.19
Margherita Rigon	73	72	72	217	3,609.28
Thidapa Suwannapura	72	72	73	217	3,609.28
Gwladys Nocera	72	72	73	217	3,609.28

	SCORES			TOTAL	MONEY
Jaruporn Palakawong Na Ayutthaya	70	75	72	217	3,609.28
Bree Arthur	70	67	80	217	3,609.28
Beth Allen	75	71	72	218	3,106.06
Nikki Garrett	73	73	72	218	3,106.06
Celine Palomar	71	74	73	218	3,106.06
Stacey Keating	70	75	73	218	3,106.06

Omega Dubai Ladies Masters

Emirates Golf Club, Dubai, United Arab Emirates
Par 35-37–72; 6,425 yards

December 5-8
purse, €500,000

	SCORES				TOTAL	MONEY
Shanshan Feng	66	65	67	69	267	€75,000
Dewi Claire Schreefel	69	71	63	69	272	50,750
Becky Brewerton	70	73	68	65	276	31,000
Caroline Masson	68	68	69	71	276	31,000
Lorie Kane	68	70	68	71	277	17,900
Gwladys Nocera	68	68	68	73	277	17,900
Cindy LaCrosse	67	69	69	72	277	17,900
Line Vedel	69	72	68	69	278	11,850
Felicity Johnson	68	67	72	71	278	11,850
Veronica Zorzi	71	73	67	68	279	8,500
Holly Aitchison	70	72	66	71	279	8,500
Carlota Ciganda	70	68	73	68	279	8,500
Caroline Hedwall	69	71	67	72	279	8,500
Lexi Thompson	69	68	72	70	279	8,500
Nontaya Srisawang	68	73	68	70	279	8,500
Laura Davies	71	71	66	72	280	7,100
Julieta Granada	70	70	69	71	280	7,100
Pernilla Lindberg	74	70	70	67	281	6,800
Michelle Wie	70	73	70	69	282	6,300
Trish Johnson	70	71	71	70	282	6,300
Sarah Kemp	69	72	72	69	282	6,300
Stacy Lee Bregman	69	72	71	70	282	6,300
Florentyna Parker	66	74	69	73	282	6,300

Japan LPGA Tour

Daikin Orchid Ladies

Ryukyu Golf Club, Nanjo, Okinawa
Par 36-36–72; 6,439 yards

March 2-4
purse, ¥80,000,000

	SCORES			TOTAL	MONEY
Airi Saitoh	70	64	72	206	¥14,400,000
Yuko Mitsuka	73	67	66	206	6,320,000
Ji-Hee Lee	71	68	67	206	6,320,000
(Saitoh defeated Lee on first and Mitsuka on second playoff hole.)					
Erika Kikuchi	70	67	70	207	4,800,000
Mi-Jeong Jeon	70	73	65	208	3,100,000
Sakura Yokomine	71	69	68	208	3,100,000
Rui Kitada	69	69	70	208	3,100,000
Akane Iijima	73	65	70	208	3,100,000
Mayu Hattori	71	71	67	209	1,701,333
Bo-Mee Lee	70	71	68	209	1,701,333
Rikako Morita	74	67	68	209	1,701,333
Soo-Yun Kang	71	73	66	210	1,304,000
Megumi Kido	70	70	70	210	1,304,000
Miki Saiki	72	68	70	210	1,304,000
Yukari Baba	68	69	73	210	1,304,000
Teresa Lu	72	70	69	211	914,666
Da-Ye Na	71	70	70	211	914,666
Shinobu Moromizato	68	71	72	211	914,666
*Mamiko Higa	72	67	72	211	
Inbee Park	69	67	75	211	914,666

Yokohama Tire PRGR Ladies Cup

Tosa Country Club, Kanan, Kochi
Par 36-36–72; 6,232 yards

March 9-11
purse, ¥80,000,000

	SCORES			TOTAL	MONEY
Bo-Mee Lee	73	71	69	213	¥14,400,000
Sun-Ju Ahn	73	73	67	213	7,040,000
(Lee defeated Ahn on second playoff hole.)					
Ayako Uehara	73	70	71	214	5,600,000
Akane Iijima	73	74	69	216	4,000,000
Soo-Yun Kang	72	73	71	216	4,000,000
Mi-Jeong Jeon	69	74	73	216	4,000,000
Ritsuko Ryu	75	73	69	217	2,400,000
Mina Nakayama	76	72	69	217	2,400,000
Na-Ri Kim	74	73	70	217	2,400,000
Yuri Fudoh	68	75	75	218	1,600,000
Teresa Lu	77	68	74	219	1,448,000
Sakura Yokomine	72	77	71	220	1,168,000
Kumiko Kaneda	75	74	71	220	1,168,000
Na-Ri Lee	75	74	71	220	1,168,000
Saiki Fujita	73	73	74	220	1,168,000
Da-Ye Na	77	73	71	221	784,000
Mayu Hattori	74	77	70	221	784,000
Li-Ying Ye	73	78	70	221	784,000

T-Point Ladies

Takamaki Country Club, Kamo, Kagoshima
Par 36-36–72; 6,350 yards

March 16-18
purse, ¥70,000,000

	SCORES			TOTAL	MONEY
Ji-Hee Lee	71	69	69	209	¥12,600,000
Soo-Yun Kang	72	67	71	210	6,160,000
Ritsuko Ryu	70	69	72	211	4,550,000
Eun-Bi Jang	72	66	73	211	4,550,000
Na-Ri Lee	71	73	68	212	2,916,666
Hiromi Mogi	70	73	69	212	2,916,666
Mi-Jeong Jeon	70	71	71	212	2,916,666
Kaori Ohe	68	72	73	213	2,100,000
Ayako Uehara	68	75	71	214	1,270,000
Young Kim	73	70	71	214	1,270,000
Mayu Hattori	68	74	72	214	1,270,000
Sakura Yokomine	70	72	72	214	1,270,000
Yuri Fudoh	73	69	72	214	1,270,000
Teresa Lu	69	72	73	214	1,270,000
Harukyo Nomura	71	70	73	214	1,270,000
Maiko Wakabayashi	71	73	71	215	903,000
Akane Iijima	73	70	72	215	903,000
Junko Omote	70	74	72	216	728,000
Nachiyo Ohtani	69	74	73	216	728,000
Asako Fujimoto	71	71	74	216	728,000

Yamaha Ladies Open

Katsuragi Golf Club, Fukuroi, Shizuoka
Par 36-36–72; 6,587 yards
(Second round cancelled—rain.)

March 30-April 1
purse, ¥100,000,000

	SCORES		TOTAL	MONEY
Ritsuko Ryu	73	68	141	¥13,500,000
Li-Ying Ye	76	67	143	5,062,500
Yuki Ichinose	75	68	143	5,062,500
Mayu Hattori	69	74	143	5,062,500
Hiromi Mogi	72	71	143	5,062,500
Mi-Jeong Jeon	74	70	144	2,812,500
Young Kim	75	69	144	2,812,500
So-Hee Kim	73	72	145	2,062,500
Nikki Campbell	72	73	145	2,062,500
Mihoko Iseri	72	74	146	1,281,428
Ayako Uehara	72	74	146	1,281,428
Miki Saiki	73	73	146	1,281,428
Harukyo Nomura	76	70	146	1,281,428
Erina Hara	74	72	146	1,281,428
Hiroko Fukushima	75	71	146	1,281,428
Yuko Fukuda	73	73	146	1,281,428

Studio Alice Ladies Open

Hanayashiki Golf Club, Yokawa Course, Miki, Hyogo
Par 36-36–72; 6,483 yards

April 6-8
purse, ¥60,000,000

	SCORES			TOTAL	MONEY
Miki Saiki	71	69	69	209	¥10,800,000
Jiyai Shin	70	68	72	210	5,280,000
*Mamiko Higa	69	72	72	213	
Sun-Ju Ahn	69	73	72	214	4,200,000
Chie Arimura	74	72	70	216	3,000,000
Shinobu Moromizato	74	71	71	216	3,000,000
Mi-Jeong Jeon	73	69	74	216	3,000,000
Sakura Yokomine	75	73	69	217	2,100,000
Mayu Hattori	78	72	68	218	1,800,000
Hyun-Ju Shin	71	76	72	219	990,000
Rikako Morita	73	75	71	219	990,000
Yumiko Yoshida	77	72	70	219	990,000
Erina Hara	74	73	72	219	990,000
Ritsuko Ryu	70	76	73	219	990,000
Nozomi Inoue	74	72	73	219	990,000
Akane Iijima	74	72	73	219	990,000
Shiho Toyonaga	74	71	74	219	990,000
Na-Ri Lee	73	71	75	219	990,000
Inbee Park	74	70	75	219	990,000
Shanshan Feng	72	75	73	220	539,333
Natsuka Hori	73	74	73	220	539,333
Kotono Kozuma	73	74	73	220	539,333
Hiromi Mogi	73	74	73	220	539,333
Bo-Mee Lee	77	70	73	220	539,333
Teresa Lu	70	76	74	220	539,333
Satsuki Oshiro	71	74	75	220	539,333
Kaori Aoyama	73	72	75	220	539,333
Eun-Bi Jang	76	69	75	220	539,333

Nishijin Ladies Classic

Kumamoto Airport Country Club, Kikuyo, Kumamoto
Par 36-36–72; 6,482 yards

April 13-15
purse, ¥70,000,000

	SCORES			TOTAL	MONEY
Maiko Wakabayashi	70	70	69	209	¥12,600,000
Hiromi Mogi	71	72	68	211	6,160,000
Mihoko Iseri	71	72	69	212	4,550,000
Kumiko Kaneda	76	66	70	212	4,550,000
Miki Sakai	73	70	70	213	3,150,000
Bo-Mee Lee	70	72	71	213	3,150,000
Esther Lee	69	71	74	214	2,450,000
Ritsuko Ryu	76	73	66	215	1,627,500
Nobuko Kizawa	72	71	72	215	1,627,500
Miki Saiki	75	68	72	215	1,627,500
Chie Arimura	71	71	73	215	1,627,500
Teresa Lu	75	72	69	216	945,000
Ming-Yen Chen	72	74	70	216	945,000
Asuka Tsujimura	77	69	70	216	945,000
Akane Iijima	72	75	69	216	945,000
Soo-Yun Kang	72	72	72	216	945,000
Da-Ye Na	73	71	72	216	945,000
Inbee Park	72	71	73	216	945,000
Kaori Ohe	71	70	75	216	945,000

	SCORES			TOTAL	MONEY
Na-Ri Kim	73	74	70	217	602,000
Yumiko Yoshida	72	73	72	217	602,000
Sakura Yokomine	74	71	72	217	602,000
Na-Ri Lee	74	70	73	217	602,000
Mayu Hattori	76	68	73	217	602,000

Fujisankei Ladies Classic

Kawana Hotel Golf Club, Fuji Course, Ito, Shizuoka
Par 36-36–72; 6,407 yards

April 20-22
purse, ¥80,000,000

	SCORES			TOTAL	MONEY
Kaori Ohe	72	65	70	207	¥14,400,000
Mi-Jeong Jeon	70	68	70	208	7,040,000
Mayu Hattori	72	71	66	209	4,800,000
Sakura Yokomine	70	71	68	209	4,800,000
Yuko Fukuda	72	69	68	209	4,800,000
Teresa Lu	71	71	69	211	2,116,571
Bo-Bae Song	71	70	70	211	2,116,571
Miki Sakai	71	69	71	211	2,116,571
Hiromi Mogi	72	68	71	211	2,116,571
Erina Hara	69	70	72	211	2,116,571
Yukari Baba	69	69	73	211	2,116,571
Akane Iijima	68	67	76	211	2,116,571
Da-Ye Na	73	71	68	212	1,208,000
Rikako Morita	75	68	69	212	1,208,000
Saiki Fujita	70	69	73	212	1,208,000
Hiromi Takesue	70	70	73	213	1,008,000
Miki Saiki	68	70	75	213	1,008,000
Kaori Yamamoto	73	70	71	214	888,000
Miki Uehara	71	73	71	215	724,800
Maiko Wakabayashi	73	71	71	215	724,800
Esther Lee	73	70	72	215	724,800
Hiroko Fukushima	70	72	73	215	724,800
Ya-Huei Lu	73	69	73	215	724,800

Cyber Agent Ladies

Tsurumai Country Club, Ichihara, Chiba
Par 36-36–72; 6,400 yards

April 27-29
purse, ¥70,000,000

	SCORES			TOTAL	MONEY
Chie Arimura	68	68	65	201	¥12,600,000
Sakura Yokomine	69	71	66	206	6,160,000
Rikako Morita	72	70	65	207	4,550,000
Jiyai Shin	72	66	69	207	4,550,000
Sun-Ju Ahn	71	69	68	208	3,150,000
Inbee Park	68	70	70	208	3,150,000
Esther Lee	71	71	67	209	2,275,000
Nobuko Kizawa	70	69	70	209	2,275,000
Maiko Wakabayashi	73	71	66	210	1,431,500
Hiromi Mogi	72	69	69	210	1,431,500
Yuki Sakurai	71	68	71	210	1,431,500
Ji-Woo Lee	70	66	74	210	1,431,500
So-Hee Kim	75	68	68	211	1,008,000
Mayu Hattori	71	72	68	211	1,008,000
Mi-Jeong Jeon	68	74	69	211	1,008,000

	SCORES			TOTAL	MONEY
Akane Iijima	72	69	70	211	1,008,000
Ya-Huei Lu	69	71	71	211	1,008,000
Shinobu Moromizato	71	69	71	211	1,008,000
Mihoko Iseri	73	71	68	212	700,000
Toshimi Kimura	72	70	70	212	700,000
Miki Saiki	72	69	71	212	700,000
Yuri Fudoh	70	70	72	212	700,000

World Ladies Championship Salonpas Cup

Ibaraki Golf Club, West Course, Tsukubamirai, Ibaraki   May 3-6
Par 36-36–72; 6,649 yards   purse, ¥90,000,000
(First round cancelled—rain.)

	SCORES			TOTAL	MONEY
Sun-Ju Ahn	67	69	72	208	¥18,000,000
Inbee Park	67	73	68	208	7,875,000
Morgan Pressel	65	68	75	208	7,875,000
(Ahn defeated Park and Pressel on first playoff hole.)					
Shanshan Feng	68	69	72	209	5,400,000
Mi-Jeong Jeon	66	70	74	210	4,050,000
Jiyai Shin	65	70	75	210	4,050,000
Mika Miyazato	71	71	69	211	2,880,000
Ayako Uehara	70	70	72	212	2,115,000
Bo-Mee Lee	67	72	73	212	2,115,000
Hiromi Takesue	70	73	70	213	1,494,000
Yuri Fudoh	71	71	71	213	1,494,000
Hiromi Mogi	71	69	73	213	1,494,000
Ai Miyazato	67	73	73	213	1,494,000
Ji-Hee Lee	67	72	74	213	1,494,000
Kumiko Kaneda	69	74	71	214	939,857
Miki Sakai	71	72	71	214	939,857
Yuki Ichinose	70	71	73	214	939,857
Na-Ri Lee	69	76	69	214	939,857
Maiko Wakabayashi	71	70	73	214	939,857
Rikako Morita	72	74	68	214	939,857
Shinobu Moromizato	71	69	74	214	939,857

Fundokin Ladies

Fukuoka Century Golf Club, Wajiro Course, Asakura, Fukuoka   May 11-13
Par 36-36–72; 6,384 yards   purse, ¥80,000,000

	SCORES			TOTAL	MONEY
Inbee Park	70	69	68	207	¥14,400,000
Shanshan Feng	67	72	70	209	7,040,000
Mi-Jeong Jeon	71	75	65	211	5,200,000
Mihoko Iseri	71	74	66	211	5,200,000
Sun-Ju Ahn	71	71	70	212	4,000,000
Bo-Mee Lee	74	68	72	214	3,000,000
Erina Hara	72	69	73	214	3,000,000
Ji-Hee Lee	75	73	68	216	1,872,000
Satsuki Oshiro	73	74	69	216	1,872,000
Nachiyo Ohtani	77	68	71	216	1,872,000
Maiko Wakabayashi	73	71	72	216	1,872,000
Ayako Uehara	75	71	71	217	1,368,000
Mayu Hattori	74	71	72	217	1,368,000

	SCORES			TOTAL	MONEY
Teresa Lu	78	72	68	218	1,128,000
Megumi Shimokawa	73	73	72	218	1,128,000
Chie Arimura	74	72	72	218	1,128,000
Na-Ri Kim	72	71	75	218	1,128,000
Harukyo Nomura	72	76	71	219	888,000
Megumi Kido	77	70	72	219	888,000
Miki Sakai	72	77	71	220	728,000
Hiroko Fukushima	72	75	73	220	728,000
Kotono Kozuma	74	76	70	220	728,000
Lala Anai	77	70	73	220	728,000
*Haruka Morita	72	74	74	220	
Sakura Yokomine	72	73	75	220	728,000
Nozomi Inoue	72	71	77	220	728,000

Chukyo TV Bridgestone Ladies Open

Chukyo Golf Club, Ishino Course, Toyota, Aichi
Par 36-36–72; 6,462 yards

May 18-20
purse, ¥70,000,000

	SCORES			TOTAL	MONEY
Ji-Hee Lee	68	65	67	200	¥12,600,000
Rikako Morita	69	68	66	203	6,160,000
Mi-Jeong Jeon	68	68	68	204	4,900,000
Yumiko Yoshida	72	69	66	207	3,850,000
Ritsuko Ryu	72	66	69	207	3,850,000
Harukyo Nomura	72	72	64	208	2,450,000
Sun-Ju Ahn	74	65	69	208	2,450,000
Miki Saiki	70	68	70	208	2,450,000
*Mamiko Higa	71	71	67	209	
Chie Arimura	71	71	67	209	1,386,000
Megumi Kido	70	70	69	209	1,386,000
Lala Anai	73	66	70	209	1,386,000
Erina Hara	72	66	71	209	1,386,000
Mayu Hattori	72	65	72	209	1,386,000
Yui Kawahara	71	72	67	210	1,015,000
Eun-A Lim	71	70	69	210	1,015,000
Maiko Wakabayashi	71	68	71	210	1,015,000
Hiromi Mogi	69	69	72	210	1,015,000
Asako Fujimoto	70	73	69	212	840,000
Momoko Ueda	73	70	70	213	697,200
Rui Kitada	74	69	70	213	697,200
Na-Ri Lee	71	71	71	213	697,200
Mikiko Nishi	71	71	71	213	697,200
Mihoko Iseri	71	70	72	213	697,200

Yonex Ladies

Yonex Country Club, Nagaoka, Niigata
Par 36-36–72; 6,370 yards

May 25-27
purse, ¥60,000,000

	SCORES			TOTAL	MONEY
Shanshan Feng	70	69	69	208	¥10,800,000
Yukari Baba	69	67	72	208	5,280,000
(Feng defeated Baba on second playoff hole.)					
Bo-Mee Lee	72	70	67	209	3,900,000
Ritsuko Ryu	70	68	71	209	3,900,000
Teresa Lu	70	69	71	210	2,700,000

	SCORES			TOTAL	MONEY
Serena Aoki	69	68	73	210	2,700,000
Nikki Campbell	70	70	71	211	2,100,000
Nozomi Inoue	74	69	69	212	1,650,000
Sakura Yokomine	71	69	72	212	1,650,000
Mihoko Iseri	72	71	70	213	1,164,000
Maiko Wakabayashi	70	70	73	213	1,164,000
Satsuki Oshiro	73	71	70	214	978,000
Hiromi Mogi	70	73	71	214	978,000
Yeo-Jin Kang	72	71	71	214	978,000
Hiromi Takesue	71	71	72	214	978,000
Chie Arimura	73	71	71	215	738,000
Rui Kitada	71	71	73	215	738,000
So-Hee Kim	72	69	74	215	738,000
Yuri Fudoh	74	67	74	215	738,000
Hitomi Kai	73	71	73	217	558,000
Asako Fujimoto	75	69	73	217	558,000
Ya-Huei Lu	72	73	72	217	558,000
Yui Kawahara	70	72	75	217	558,000
Erika Kikuchi	73	73	71	217	558,000
Mi-Sun Cho	78	68	71	217	558,000

Resort Trust Ladies

Grandee Karuizawa, Miyota, Nagano
Par 36-36–72; 6,506 yards

June 1-3
purse, ¥70,000,000

	SCORES			TOTAL	MONEY
Mi-Jeong Jeon	65	68	69	202	¥12,600,000
Ji-Hee Lee	65	69	71	205	6,300,000
Mihoko Iseri	67	68	71	206	4,900,000
Soo-Yun Kang	69	69	69	207	3,920,000
Ritsuko Ryu	68	67	72	207	3,920,000
Shinobu Moromizato	71	72	67	210	2,310,000
Yukari Baba	68	73	69	210	2,310,000
Miki Saiki	71	67	72	210	2,310,000
Kaori Nakamura	69	69	72	210	2,310,000
Rui Kitada	71	67	73	211	1,400,000
Sun-Ju Ahn	69	73	70	212	1,246,000
Shiho Toyonaga	71	72	69	212	1,246,000
Yeo-Jin Kang	70	70	72	212	1,246,000
Natsu Nagai	72	68	72	212	1,246,000
Hye-Soo Lee	71	70	72	213	931,000
Hiromi Mogi	70	73	70	213	931,000
Natsuka Hori	67	73	73	213	931,000
Eun-Bi Jang	70	70	73	213	931,000
So-Hee Kim	69	70	74	213	931,000
Maiko Wakabayashi	70	72	72	214	686,000
Kotono Kozuma	70	72	72	214	686,000
*Haruka Morita	69	72	73	214	
Mika Takushima	70	71	73	214	686,000
Ah-Reum Hwang	68	73	73	214	686,000
Young Kim	69	69	76	214	686,000
Bo-Bae Song	68	66	80	214	686,000

Suntory Ladies Open

Rokko Kokusai Golf Club, Kobe, Hyogo
Par 36-36–72; 6,511 yards

June 7-10
purse, ¥100,000,000

	SCORES				TOTAL	MONEY
*Hyo-Joo Kim	71	71	68	61	271	
Miki Saiki	66	73	71	65	275	¥18,000,000
Yuki Ichinose	73	68	69	67	277	7,266,666
Mi-Jeong Jeon	71	69	68	69	277	7,266,666
Mayu Hattori	67	67	69	74	277	7,266,666
Bo-Bae Song	68	72	69	69	278	5,000,000
Sun-Ju Ahn	68	72	71	68	279	3,500,000
Sakura Yokomine	71	69	71	68	279	3,500,000
Soo-Yun Kang	69	71	70	69	279	3,500,000
Ji-Hee Lee	67	71	70	72	280	2,500,000
Yukari Baba	70	73	72	67	282	2,000,000
Da-Ye Na	73	73	70	67	283	1,670,000
Ritsuko Ryu	68	75	70	70	283	1,670,000
Ya-Huei Lu	69	72	71	71	283	1,670,000
Rikako Morita	68	73	68	74	283	1,670,000
Shinobu Moromizato	71	74	72	67	284	1,220,000
Miki Sakai	70	74	72	68	284	1,220,000
Bo-Mee Lee	70	72	73	69	284	1,220,000
Teresa Lu	73	71	70	70	284	1,220,000
Kaori Aoyama	72	67	71	74	284	1,220,000

Nichirei Ladies

Sodegaura Country Club, Shinsode Course, Chiba
Par 36-36–72; 6,548 yards

June 15-17
purse, ¥80,000,000

	SCORES			TOTAL	MONEY
Hyun-Ju Shin	67	71	67	205	¥14,400,000
Ritsuko Ryu	67	71	68	206	5,813,333
Chie Arimura	72	66	68	206	5,813,333
Soo-Yun Kang	68	67	71	206	5,813,333
Bo-Mee Lee	71	70	66	207	2,880,000
Yuri Fudoh	66	73	68	207	2,880,000
Na-Ri Lee	67	72	68	207	2,880,000
Esther Lee	68	71	68	207	2,880,000
Kaori Ohe	69	67	71	207	2,880,000
Young Kim	69	69	70	208	1,600,000
Yun-Jye Wei	69	71	69	209	1,480,000
Rikako Morita	68	73	70	211	1,360,000
Yumiko Yoshida	71	69	71	211	1,360,000
Erina Hara	68	74	70	212	1,120,000
Natsu Nagai	70	70	72	212	1,120,000
Miki Saiki	73	72	67	212	1,120,000
Mi-Jeong Jeon	70	66	76	212	1,120,000
Megumi Kido	75	69	69	213	784,000
Keiko Sasaki	68	75	70	213	784,000
Hiroko Fukushima	73	73	67	213	784,000
Kumiko Kaneda	72	71	70	213	784,000
Kaori Aoyama	70	72	71	213	784,000
Mihoko Iseri	72	70	71	213	784,000

Earth Mondahmin Cup

Camellia Hills Country Club, Sodegaura, Chiba
Par 36-36–72; 6,475 yards

June 22-24
purse, ¥100,000,000

	SCORES			TOTAL	MONEY
Mayu Hattori	67	66	68	201	¥18,000,000
Chie Arimura	68	66	68	202	7,900,000
Sakura Yokomine	67	66	69	202	7,900,000
Sun-Ju Ahn	64	69	70	203	6,000,000
Hsuan-Yu Yao	73	64	68	205	5,000,000
Ritsuko Ryu	69	69	68	206	3,000,000
Rikako Morita	70	68	68	206	3,000,000
Yuri Fudoh	70	68	68	206	3,000,000
Rui Kitada	69	68	69	206	3,000,000
Megumi Kido	68	67	71	206	3,000,000
Young Kim	70	67	70	207	1,810,000
Na-Ri Kim	70	71	67	208	1,560,000
Junko Omote	68	71	69	208	1,560,000
Bo-Mee Lee	73	66	69	208	1,560,000
Shiho Toyonaga	67	67	74	208	1,560,000
Hyun-Ju Shin	70	71	68	209	1,160,000
Ayako Uehara	70	70	69	209	1,160,000
Mihoko Iseri	72	68	69	209	1,160,000
Ji-Hee Lee	67	71	71	209	1,160,000
Yuko Saitoh	73	70	67	210	870,000
Natsu Nagai	70	71	69	210	870,000
Nachiyo Ohtani	73	68	69	210	870,000
Na-Ri Lee	71	68	71	210	870,000
Maiko Wakabayashi	71	68	71	210	870,000

Nichi-Iko Ladies Open

Yatsuo Country Club, Toyama
Par 36-36–72; 6,502 yards

June 29-July 1
purse, ¥60,000,000

	SCORES			TOTAL	MONEY
Mi-Jeong Jeon	66	71	71	208	¥10,800,000
Erina Hara	70	70	69	209	5,280,000
Mayu Hattori	68	72	71	211	4,200,000
Yeo-Jin Kang	69	69	75	213	3,300,000
Miki Saiki	70	67	76	213	3,300,000
Rikako Morita	72	71	71	214	2,250,000
Yumiko Yoshida	70	70	74	214	2,250,000
Yun-Jye Wei	72	71	72	215	1,650,000
Misuzu Narita	71	70	74	215	1,650,000
Megumi Kido	72	74	70	216	1,078,500
Da-Ye Na	70	71	75	216	1,078,500
Nachiyo Ohtani	70	71	75	216	1,078,500
Bo-Mee Lee	70	68	78	216	1,078,500
Chie Arimura	73	70	74	217	918,000
Teresa Lu	73	72	73	218	738,000
Ritsuko Ryu	73	72	73	218	738,000
Hyun-Ju Shin	73	71	74	218	738,000
Sun-Ju Ahn	76	67	75	218	738,000
Mihoko Iseri	70	75	73	218	738,000
Erika Kikuchi	71	73	75	219	522,000
Sayuri Takashima	71	73	75	219	522,000
Lala Anai	73	71	75	219	522,000
Yuko Fukuda	70	73	76	219	522,000

	SCORES			TOTAL	MONEY
Ikue Asama	72	71	76	219	522,000
Akane Iijima	73	70	76	219	522,000
Hiromi Mogi	73	68	78	219	522,000

Stanley Ladies

Tomei Country Club, Susono, Shizuoka
Par 36-36–72; 6,520 yards
(Event shortened to 27 holes—fog.)

July 13-15
purse, ¥90,000,000

	SCORES		TOTAL	MONEY
Chie Arimura	67	36	103	¥12,150,000
Bo-Bae Song	71	33	104	4,950,000
Tao-Li Yang	68	36	104	4,950,000
Rikako Morita	66	38	104	4,950,000
Esther Lee	72	33	105	2,615,625
Mi-Jeong Jeon	71	34	105	2,615,625
Yeo-Jin Kang	70	35	105	2,615,625
Miki Saiki	68	37	105	2,615,625
Yuko Fukuda	72	34	106	1,340,550
Erika Kikuchi	72	34	106	1,340,550
Akane Iijima	71	35	106	1,340,550
Hiromi Mogi	71	35	106	1,340,550
Inbee Park	69	37	106	1,340,550
Ayako Okazaki	74	33	107	815,400
Shinobu Moromizato	71	36	107	815,400
Hiromi Takesue	71	36	107	815,400
Keiko Sasaki	71	36	107	815,400
Harukyo Nomura	71	36	107	815,400
Saiki Fujita	70	37	107	815,400
Ayako Uehara	70	37	107	815,400
Junko Omote	69	38	107	815,400
Shiho Oyama	69	38	107	815,400
Erina Yamato	67	40	107	815,400

Samantha Thavasa Girls Collection Ladies

Eagle Point Golf Club, Ibaraki
Par 36-36–72; 6,535 yards

July 20-22
purse, ¥60,000,000

	SCORES			TOTAL	MONEY
Megumi Kido	66	66	70	202	¥10,800,000
Mi-Jeong Jeon	70	66	68	204	5,280,000
So-Hee Kim	69	70	66	205	3,900,000
Jiyai Shin	69	68	68	205	3,900,000
Yuri Fudoh	71	66	69	206	3,000,000
Eun-Bi Jang	66	75	66	207	2,250,000
Natsu Nagai	69	68	70	207	2,250,000
Rikako Morita	71	69	68	208	1,650,000
Asako Fujimoto	67	70	71	208	1,650,000
Eun-A Lim	70	71	68	209	1,083,000
Hsuan-Yu Yao	71	69	69	209	1,083,000
Miki Saiki	71	69	69	209	1,083,000
Ritsuko Ryu	68	69	72	209	1,083,000
Sakura Yokomine	68	73	69	210	834,000
Na-Ri Lee	72	69	69	210	834,000
Erika Kikuchi	69	71	70	210	834,000

	SCORES			TOTAL	MONEY
Esther Lee	71	66	73	210	834,000
Teresa Lu	73	69	69	211	582,000
Na Yeon Choi	68	73	70	211	582,000
Yumiko Yoshida	69	72	70	211	582,000
Nobuko Kizawa	72	69	70	211	582,000
Hyun-Ju Shin	70	70	71	211	582,000
Mihoko Iseri	71	69	71	211	582,000

Meiji Cup

Sapporo International Country Club, Kitahiroshima, Hokkaido   August 3-5
Par 36-36–72; 6,490 yards   purse, ¥90,000,000

	SCORES			TOTAL	MONEY
Shanshan Feng	72	70	67	209	¥16,200,000
Shinobu Moromizato	71	69	69	209	7,110,000
Sun-Ju Ahn	71	67	71	209	7,110,000
(Feng defeated Moromizato on first and Ahn on fourth playoff hole.)					
Yuri Fudoh	70	73	67	210	4,950,000
Yuki Sakurai	68	73	69	210	4,950,000
Young Kim	69	71	71	211	3,600,000
Bo-Mee Lee	70	71	71	212	3,150,000
Chie Arimura	67	73	73	213	2,700,000
Na-Ri Kim	71	74	69	214	1,719,000
Yui Kawahara	68	75	71	214	1,719,000
Maiko Wakabayashi	72	71	71	214	1,719,000
Yumiko Yoshida	73	70	71	214	1,719,000
Mayu Hattori	71	71	72	214	1,719,000
Esther Lee	72	69	73	214	1,719,000
Mayumi Shimomura	70	76	69	215	1,206,000
Rui Kitada	70	74	71	215	1,206,000
Mihoko Iseri	70	73	72	215	1,206,000
Yeo-Jin Kang	72	71	72	215	1,206,000
Yuki Ichinose	72	75	69	216	915,000
Li-Ying Ye	72	74	70	216	915,000
Kumiko Kaneda	69	74	73	216	915,000

NEC Karuizawa 72

Karuizawa 72 Golf Club, Karuizawa, Nagano   August 10-12
Par 36-36–72; 6,525 yards   purse, ¥70,000,000

	SCORES			TOTAL	MONEY
Yumiko Yoshida	71	67	67	205	¥12,600,000
Eun-Bi Jang	68	69	68	205	6,160,000
(Yoshida defeated Jang on sixth playoff hole.)					
Yuri Fudoh	69	68	70	207	4,900,000
Junko Omote	68	72	68	208	3,237,500
Sakura Yokomine	71	69	68	208	3,237,500
Sun-Ju Ahn	70	69	69	208	3,237,500
Harukyo Nomura	71	68	69	208	3,237,500
Rikako Morita	73	70	66	209	1,386,875
Na-Ri Lee	72	68	69	209	1,386,875
Esther Lee	71	68	70	209	1,386,875
Mi-Jeong Jeon	72	67	70	209	1,386,875
Kaori Ohe	69	69	71	209	1,386,875
Teresa Lu	70	68	71	209	1,386,875

	SCORES			TOTAL	MONEY
Miki Sakai	72	66	71	209	1,386,875
Tomoko Kusakabe	68	68	73	209	1,386,875
Kumiko Kaneda	69	73	68	210	819,000
Ritsuko Ryu	69	74	67	210	819,000
Na-Ri Kim	71	69	70	210	819,000
Miki Saiki	71	69	70	210	819,000
Bo-Mee Lee	72	68	70	210	819,000

CAT Ladies

Daihakone Country Club, Hakone, Kanagawa
Par 36-37–73; 6,687 yards

August 17-19
purse, ¥60,000,000

	SCORES			TOTAL	MONEY
Mi-Jeong Jeon	71	70	65	206	¥10,800,000
Rikako Morita	69	70	71	210	4,360,000
Bo-Mee Lee	71	68	71	210	4,360,000
Mayu Hattori	72	67	71	210	4,360,000
Miki Sakai	74	68	69	211	3,000,000
Yumiko Yoshida	71	68	73	212	2,400,000
Esther Lee	72	72	69	213	1,468,000
Hsuan-Yu Yao	74	68	71	213	1,468,000
Junko Omote	71	70	72	213	1,468,000
Airi Saitoh	69	71	73	213	1,468,000
Hiroko Fukushima	71	69	73	213	1,468,000
Onnarin Sattayabanphot	73	66	74	213	1,468,000
Shiho Toyonaga	73	69	72	214	1,014,000
Sae Yamamura	70	72	73	215	894,000
Kaori Ohe	71	71	73	215	894,000
Misuzu Narita	72	70	73	215	894,000
Tao-Li Yang	73	70	73	216	774,000
Chie Arimura	76	71	70	217	622,800
Mami Fukuda	72	73	72	217	622,800
Yukari Baba	73	72	72	217	622,800
Akane Iijima	72	71	74	217	622,800
Erika Kikuchi	71	70	76	217	622,800

Nitori Ladies

Katsura Golf Club, Tomakomai, Hokkaido
Par 36-36–72; 6,477 yards

August 24-26
purse, ¥100,000,000

	SCORES			TOTAL	MONEY
Sun-Ju Ahn	71	63	68	202	¥18,000,000
Mi-Jeong Jeon	69	68	67	204	8,800,000
Rikako Morita	72	70	65	207	6,500,000
Soo-Yun Kang	70	67	70	207	6,500,000
Lala Anai	66	70	72	208	5,000,000
Yeo-Jin Kang	70	69	70	209	4,000,000
So-Hee Kim	69	71	70	210	3,500,000
Kumiko Kaneda	71	68	72	211	2,750,000
Young Kim	70	68	73	211	2,750,000
Hiromi Mogi	71	72	69	212	1,775,000
Kaori Ohe	71	72	69	212	1,775,000
Yumiko Yoshida	69	71	72	212	1,775,000
Nachiyo Ohtani	68	70	74	212	1,775,000
Sakura Yokomine	70	75	68	213	1,450,000

	SCORES			TOTAL	MONEY
Miki Saiki	71	67	75	213	1,450,000
Ji-Hee Lee	71	73	70	214	1,063,333
Hsuan-Yu Yao	72	71	71	214	1,063,333
Onnarin Sattayabanphot	73	72	69	214	1,063,333
Ya-Huei Lu	69	72	73	214	1,063,333
Akane Iijima	72	68	74	214	1,063,333
Esther Lee	72	75	67	214	1,063,333

Golf 5 Ladies

Mizunami Country Club, Mizunami, Gifu
Par 36-36–72; 6,537 yards

August 31-September 2
purse, ¥60,000,000

	SCORES			TOTAL	MONEY
Sun-Ju Ahn	67	68	66	201	¥10,800,000
Ji-Hee Lee	67	69	66	202	5,280,000
Rikako Morita	69	69	65	203	3,900,000
Chie Arimura	67	67	69	203	3,900,000
Yukari Baba	68	69	67	204	2,700,000
Yun-Jye Wei	72	65	67	204	2,700,000
Esther Lee	68	68	69	205	1,950,000
Mayu Hattori	68	68	69	205	1,950,000
Yeo-Jin Kang	70	69	67	206	1,206,000
Yuko Fukuda	66	72	68	206	1,206,000
Ah-Reum Hwang	67	68	71	206	1,206,000
Megumi Kido	70	65	71	206	1,206,000
Miki Sakai	72	69	66	207	882,000
Yui Kawahara	73	66	68	207	882,000
Junko Omote	73	65	69	207	882,000
Misuzu Narita	70	66	71	207	882,000
Na-Ri Kim	69	70	69	208	642,000
Na-Ri Lee	67	71	70	208	642,000
Natsu Nagai	67	71	70	208	642,000
Yoshimi Koda	69	68	71	208	642,000

Japan LPGA Championship

Tarao Country Club, West Course, Koka, Shiga
Par 36-36–72; 6,670 yards

September 6-9
purse, ¥140,000,000

	SCORES				TOTAL	MONEY
Chie Arimura	69	65	69	72	275	¥25,200,000
Inbee Park	72	68	71	65	276	12,320,000
Yumiko Yoshida	64	71	71	71	277	9,800,000
Kumiko Kaneda	74	73	65	68	280	7,700,000
Ritsuko Ryu	71	70	70	69	280	7,700,000
Saiki Fujita	69	71	72	69	281	5,600,000
Bo-Mee Lee	69	72	71	70	282	4,550,000
Na-Ri Kim	68	71	71	72	282	4,550,000
Esther Lee	74	67	74	68	283	3,150,000
Junko Omote	69	72	74	68	283	3,150,000
So-Hee Kim	72	71	72	69	284	2,212,000
Sun-Ju Ahn	70	74	70	70	284	2,212,000
Megumi Kido	70	74	69	71	284	2,212,000
Rui Kitada	70	71	71	72	284	2,212,000
Mayumi Shimomura	70	72	68	74	284	2,212,000
Nikki Campbell	70	75	72	68	285	1,792,000

	SCORES			TOTAL	MONEY
Yuri Fudoh	71	73	71 71	286	1,582,000
Kaori Yamamoto	71	73	69 73	286	1,582,000
Yuki Ichinose	72	70	74 71	287	1,246,000
Na-Ri Lee	72	71	72 72	287	1,246,000
Mihoko Iseri	71	74	69 73	287	1,246,000
Kaori Ohe	68	70	72 77	287	1,246,000

Munsingwear Ladies Tokai Classic

Shin Minami Aichi Country Club, Mihama, Aichi   September 14-16
Par 36-36–72; 6,402 yards   purse, ¥80,000,000

	SCORES			TOTAL	MONEY
Natsu Nagai	67	71	66	204	¥14,400,000
Bo-Mee Lee	69	67	70	206	6,320,000
Miki Saiki	69	67	70	206	6,320,000
Mi-Jeong Jeon	64	69	74	207	4,800,000
Chie Arimura	69	68	71	208	4,000,000
Na-Ri Lee	70	72	67	209	2,800,000
Saiki Fujita	71	69	69	209	2,800,000
Esther Lee	72	66	71	209	2,800,000
Na-Ri Kim	69	70	71	210	1,706,666
Misuzu Narita	74	65	71	210	1,706,666
Da-Ye Na	71	65	74	210	1,706,666
Ya-Huei Lu	70	72	69	211	1,280,000
Rikako Morita	69	72	70	211	1,280,000
Hsuan-Yu Yao	70	71	70	211	1,280,000
Eun-Bi Jang	71	70	70	211	1,280,000
Rui Kitada	69	69	73	211	1,280,000
Mayu Hattori	69	72	71	212	920,000
Ji-Woo Lee	69	71	72	212	920,000
Hiroko Yamaguchi	71	69	72	212	920,000
Sakura Yokomine	73	67	72	212	920,000

Miyagi TV Cup Dunlop Ladies Open

Rifu Golf Club, Rifu, Miyagi   September 21-23
Par 36-36–72; 6,498 yards   purse, ¥70,000,000

	SCORES			TOTAL	MONEY
Rikako Morita	71	64	67	202	¥12,600,000
Hiromi Mogi	68	66	70	204	6,160,000
Esther Lee	71	64	70	205	4,900,000
Chie Arimura	70	69	67	206	4,200,000
Mihoko Iseri	72	65	70	207	3,500,000
Shanshan Feng	68	71	69	208	2,800,000
Junko Omote	70	68	71	209	2,450,000
Kumiko Kaneda	72	71	67	210	1,545,600
Ji-Hee Lee	73	70	67	210	1,545,600
Mi-Jeong Jeon	72	70	68	210	1,545,600
Akane Iijima	69	71	70	210	1,545,600
Mayu Hattori	69	70	71	210	1,545,600
Ayako Uehara	73	70	68	211	1,099,000
Asako Fujimoto	71	69	71	211	1,099,000
Airi Saitoh	75	68	69	212	770,000
Misuzu Narita	74	70	68	212	770,000
Megumi Shimokawa	72	69	71	212	770,000

	SCORES			TOTAL	MONEY
Miki Sakai	69	71	72	212	770,000
Hiroko Azuma	72	68	72	212	770,000
Sakura Yokomine	70	69	73	212	770,000
Yuri Fudoh	67	71	74	212	770,000
Soo-Yun Kang	69	68	75	212	770,000

Japan Women's Open

Yokohama Country Club, West Course, Yokohama, Kanagawa
Par 35-35–70; 6,545 yards

September 27-30
purse, ¥140,000,000

	SCORES				TOTAL	MONEY
Shanshan Feng	68	75	74	71	288	¥28,000,000
Inbee Park	73	76	70	70	289	15,400,000
Ji-Hee Lee	73	77	71	69	290	10,780,000
Mika Miyazato	72	75	73	71	291	7,000,000
Ah-Reum Hwang	76	77	68	71	292	5,390,000
Rui Kitada	77	73	70	72	292	5,390,000
Ayako Uehara	72	74	72	75	293	4,200,000
Akane Iijima	75	77	71	71	294	3,126,666
Hiromi Takesue	78	74	70	72	294	3,126,666
Jeong Jang	74	73	74	73	294	3,126,666
Natsu Nagai	76	76	72	71	295	1,999,200
Chie Arimura	76	75	71	73	295	1,999,200
Teresa Lu	72	74	75	74	295	1,999,200
Hiromi Mogi	75	75	71	74	295	1,999,200
Ai Miyazato	72	77	70	76	295	1,999,200
Maiko Wakabayashi	75	72	78	71	296	1,317,750
Esther Lee	75	77	72	72	296	1,317,750
Na-Ri Lee	74	75	74	73	296	1,317,750
Na Yeon Choi	77	76	70	73	296	1,317,750
Onnarin Sattayabanphot	74	76	72	74	296	1,317,750
Miki Sakai	73	77	72	74	296	1,317,750
Mi-Jeong Jeon	74	77	71	74	296	1,317,750
Soo-Yun Kang	71	80	71	74	296	1,317,750

Fujitsu Ladies

Tokyu Seven Hundred Club, Chiba
Par 36-36–72; 6,635 yards

October 12-14
purse, ¥80,000,000

	SCORES			TOTAL	MONEY
Misuzu Narita	71	69	67	207	¥14,400,000
Lala Anai	65	70	74	209	7,040,000
Shiho Oyama	70	70	70	210	4,800,000
Mamiko Higa	73	67	70	210	4,800,000
Ji-Hee Lee	68	71	71	210	4,800,000
Yuko Fukuda	68	71	72	211	3,200,000
Hiromi Mogi	70	72	70	212	2,200,000
Sun-Ju Ahn	73	69	70	212	2,200,000
Sae Yamamura	66	73	73	212	2,200,000
Mihoko Iseri	73	66	73	212	2,200,000
Na-Ri Kim	72	70	71	213	1,480,000
Yuki Ichinose	73	69	71	213	1,480,000
Yui Kawahara	71	71	72	214	1,280,000
Na-Ri Lee	72	69	73	214	1,280,000
Esther Lee	68	71	75	214	1,280,000

	SCORES			TOTAL	MONEY
Tao-Li Yang	71	74	70	215	1,040,000
*Mayu Hosaka	69	75	71	215	
Rikako Morita	71	73	71	215	1,040,000
Eun-A Lim	70	73	72	215	1,040,000
Yuko Shinsakaue	71	74	71	216	777,142
Soo-Yun Kang	75	70	71	216	777,142
Erika Kikuchi	69	75	72	216	777,142
Eun-Bi Jang	70	72	74	216	777,142
Miki Sakai	71	71	74	216	777,142
Erina Hara	74	68	74	216	777,142
Megumi Kido	70	68	78	216	777,142

Masters Golf Club Ladies

Masters Golf Club, Miki, Hyogo
Par 36-36–72; 6,458 yards

October 19-21
purse, ¥123,000,000

	SCORES			TOTAL	MONEY
So-Hee Kim	67	68	70	205	¥22,140,000
Yumiko Yoshida	72	66	67	205	9,717,000
Sakura Yokomine	65	67	73	205	9,717,000
(Kim defeated Yoshida on first and Yokomine on second playoff hole.)					
Yukari Baba	70	68	68	206	7,380,000
Rikako Morita	68	69	70	207	6,150,000
Paula Creamer	70	71	67	208	4,305,000
Misuzu Narita	72	69	67	208	4,305,000
Sun-Ju Ahn	69	71	68	208	4,305,000
Soo-Yun Kang	71	70	68	209	2,619,900
Bo-Mee Lee	72	69	68	209	2,619,900
Mi-Jeong Jeon	72	69	68	209	2,619,900
Shiho Oyama	72	71	67	210	2,140,200
Asako Fujimoto	74	68	68	210	2,140,200
Young Kim	73	69	69	211	1,771,200
Yuki Ichinose	68	72	71	211	1,771,200
Erina Hara	70	70	71	211	1,771,200
Kumiko Kaneda	72	64	75	211	1,771,200
Harukyo Nomura	72	71	69	212	1,276,740
Miki Saiki	71	72	69	212	1,276,740
Natsuka Hori	74	68	70	212	1,276,740
Teresa Lu	70	71	71	212	1,276,740
Chie Arimura	70	71	71	212	1,276,740

Hisako Higuchi Morinaga Weider Ladies

Morinaga Takataki Country Club, Ichihara, Chiba
Par 36-36–72; 6,652 yards

October 26-28
purse, ¥70,000,000

	SCORES			TOTAL	MONEY
Mi-Jeong Jeon	67	69	68	204	¥12,600,000
Young Kim	69	71	67	207	6,160,000
Asako Fujimoto	68	70	70	208	4,900,000
Junko Omote	69	74	68	211	2,600,000
Shanshan Feng	69	73	69	211	2,600,000
Ah-Reum Hwang	73	69	69	211	2,600,000
Na-Ri Kim	68	72	71	211	2,600,000
Mayu Hattori	70	70	71	211	2,600,000
Rui Kitada	69	70	72	211	2,600,000

	SCORES			TOTAL	MONEY
Sakura Yokomine	69	70	72	211	2,600,000
Kumiko Kaneda	71	73	69	213	1,141,000
Shiho Toyonaga	72	72	69	213	1,141,000
Chie Arimura	72	72	69	213	1,141,000
Sun-Ju Ahn	70	73	70	213	1,141,000
Hiromi Takesue	67	72	74	213	1,141,000
Harukyo Nomura	69	75	70	214	826,000
Onnarin Sattayabanphot	73	72	69	214	826,000
Natsu Nagai	72	72	70	214	826,000
Kaori Yamamoto	71	72	71	214	826,000
Esther Lee	72	72	71	215	623,000
Lala Anai	72	74	69	215	623,000
So-Hee Kim	71	75	69	215	623,000
Mihoko Iseri	71	71	73	215	623,000
Miki Sakai	71	71	73	215	623,000

Mizuno Classic

Kintetsu Kashikojima Country Club, Shima, Mie
Par 36-36–72; 6,506 yards

November 2-4
purse, ¥95,376,000

	SCORES			TOTAL	MONEY
Stacy Lewis	71	70	64	205	¥14,306,400
Bo-Mee Lee	70	64	72	206	8,704,888
Ayako Uehara	68	72	67	207	6,314,765
Yani Tseng	71	70	68	209	4,884,920
Anna Nordqvist	72	71	67	210	3,050,124
Hee Kyung Seo	73	69	68	210	3,050,124
Na Yeon Choi	69	71	70	210	3,050,124
Jenny Shin	71	69	70	210	3,050,124
Beatriz Recari	69	74	68	211	1,813,892
Chella Choi	74	69	68	211	1,813,892
So-Hee Kim	72	70	69	211	1,813,892
Karine Icher	71	69	71	211	1,813,892
Rikako Morita	70	68	73	211	1,813,892
Amy Yang	71	72	69	212	1,385,256
Sakura Yokomine	70	72	70	212	1,385,256
Jiyai Shin	68	73	71	212	1,385,256
Mika Miyazato	71	74	68	213	1,044,208
Akane Iijima	71	74	68	213	1,044,208
Inbee Park	70	73	70	213	1,044,208
Mariajo Uribe	72	71	70	213	1,044,208
Lizette Salas	73	69	71	213	1,044,208
Miki Sakai	72	70	71	213	1,044,208
Eun-Hee Ji	71	70	72	213	1,044,208
Junko Omote	73	68	72	213	1,044,208
Ilhee Lee	73	68	72	213	1,044,208
Angela Stanford	69	71	73	213	1,044,208
Giulia Sergas	73	71	70	214	794,720
Shanshan Feng	69	73	72	214	794,720
Pornanong Phatlum	71	71	72	214	794,720
Momoko Ueda	69	72	73	214	794,720

Itoen Ladies

Great Island Club, Chonan, Chiba
Par 36-36–72; 6,639 yards

November 11-13
purse, ¥90,000,000

	SCORES			TOTAL	MONEY
Bo-Mee Lee	69	67	68	204	¥16,200,000
Chie Arimura	64	70	70	204	7,920,000
(Lee defeated Arimura on first playoff hole.)					
Hiromi Mogi	66	68	71	205	6,300,000
Na-Ri Lee	71	69	66	206	5,400,000
Miki Saiki	69	69	69	207	4,500,000
Hyun-Ju Shin	71	69	68	208	2,529,000
Junko Omote	68	71	69	208	2,529,000
Akane Iijima	69	70	69	208	2,529,000
Soo-Yun Kang	67	71	70	208	2,529,000
Ji-Woo Lee	67	71	70	208	2,529,000
Momoko Ueda	68	70	70	208	2,529,000
Sakura Yokomine	68	75	66	209	1,494,000
Yukari Baba	70	71	68	209	1,494,000
Mayu Hattori	67	69	73	209	1,494,000
Megumi Shimokawa	74	69	67	210	1,179,000
Maiko Wakabayashi	69	71	70	210	1,179,000
Shinobu Moromizato	71	68	71	210	1,179,000
Erika Kikuchi	67	71	72	210	1,179,000
Li-Ying Ye	72	71	68	211	909,000
Yuki Ichinose	71	73	67	211	909,000

Daio Paper Elleair Ladies Open

Itsuura Teien Country Club, Fukushima
Par 36-36–72; 6,427 yards

November 16-18
purse, ¥90,000,000

	SCORES			TOTAL	MONEY
Miki Saiki	67	70	68	205	¥16,200,000
Mi-Jeong Jeon	66	70	72	208	7,920,000
Nobuko Kizawa	70	72	71	213	5,850,000
Yuri Fudoh	69	72	72	213	5,850,000
Yukari Baba	72	73	70	215	2,815,714
Ritsuko Ryu	70	74	71	215	2,815,714
Junko Omote	72	71	72	215	2,815,714
Shiho Toyonaga	69	73	73	215	2,815,714
Mayu Hattori	70	72	73	215	2,815,714
Na-Ri Kim	71	70	74	215	2,815,714
Mihoko Iseri	70	69	76	215	2,815,714
Kotono Kozuma	72	71	73	216	1,575,000
Rui Kitada	71	70	75	216	1,575,000
Na-Ri Lee	74	72	71	217	1,395,000
Erina Yamato	70	76	71	217	1,395,000
Rikako Morita	73	73	72	218	999,000
Ji-Hee Lee	71	75	72	218	999,000
Shinobu Moromizato	70	76	72	218	999,000
*Fumika Kawagishi	71	73	74	218	
Sakura Yokomine	71	73	74	218	999,000
Yuko Fukuda	72	72	74	218	999,000
Mina Nakayama	70	73	75	218	999,000
Esther Lee	70	77	71	218	999,000
Megumi Kido	69	72	77	218	999,000

Japan LPGA Tour Championship Ricoh Cup

Miyazaki Country Club, Miyazaki
Par 36-36–72; 6,467 yards

November 22-25
purse, ¥100,000,000

	SCORES				TOTAL	MONEY
Bo-Mee Lee	67	70	69	69	275	¥25,000,000
Inbee Park	70	68	70	69	277	14,500,000
Miki Saiki	70	72	74	65	281	10,000,000
Shanshan Feng	73	69	72	69	283	7,205,000
Yuri Fudoh	71	73	69	70	283	7,205,000
Sakura Yokomine	67	69	76	72	284	5,600,000
Ji-Hee Lee	68	70	77	70	285	3,125,000
Esther Lee	70	71	74	70	285	3,125,000
Kaori Ohe	74	68	73	70	285	3,125,000
Hiromi Mogi	70	68	76	71	285	3,125,000
Jiyai Shin	73	69	75	69	286	1,320,000
Rikako Morita	74	71	69	72	286	1,320,000
Hyun-Ju Shin	70	69	73	74	286	1,320,000
Mihoko Iseri	74	72	71	70	287	875,000
Ritsuko Ryu	71	69	73	74	287	875,000
Megumi Kido	72	70	76	70	288	553,333
Hyo-Joo Kim	73	71	74	70	288	553,333
Junko Omote	72	69	75	72	288	553,333
Misuzu Narita	71	70	75	72	288	553,333
Mayu Hattori	73	74	69	72	288	553,333
Mi-Jeong Jeon	70	72	72	74	288	553,333

Australian Ladies Tour

Women's Victorian Open

Spring Valley Golf Club, Melbourne, Victoria
Par 73; 6,099 yards

January 6-8
purse, A$125,000

	SCORES			TOTAL	MONEY
Joanna Klatten	74	70	68	212	A$19,500
Haeji Kang	72	72	68	212	13,000
(Klatten defeated Kang on second playoff hole.)					
Rebecca Flood	72	67	76	215	9,125
Rachel Bailey	75	75	66	216	6,125
Frances Bondad	73	73	70	216	6,125
Jessica Speechley	72	73	72	217	4,656.25
Karen Lunn	74	68	75	217	4,656.25
*Su-Hyun Oh	72	74	71	217	
Nikki Garrett	73	75	70	218	3,937.50
Bree Arthur	76	75	69	220	3,625
Kate Little	75	77	70	222	3,375

	SCORES			TOTAL	MONEY
*Minjee Lee	74	73	75	222	
Kristie Smith	81	76	66	223	3,000
Sarah Oh	79	73	71	223	3,000
Lindsey Wright	74	77	73	224	2,458.33
Sarah Kemp	75	74	75	224	2,458.33
Sarah-Jane Smith	81	69	74	224	2,458.33
Tamie Durdin	77	75	73	225	2,062.50
Julia Boland	75	77	74	226	1,837.50
Lisa Jean	74	79	73	226	1,837.50

Moss Vale Golf Club ALPG Pro-Am

Moss Vale Golf Club, Wollongong, New South Wales
Par 73; 5,300 yards

January 13-14
purse, A$25,000

	SCORES		TOTAL	MONEY
Cathryn Bristow	68	65	133	A$3,750
Joanna Klatten	71	66	137	2,166.67
Sarah Kemp	71	66	137	2,166.67
Nikki Campbell	69	68	137	2,166.67
Jessica Speechley	69	69	138	1,187.50
Rebecca Codd	69	69	138	1,187.50
Stacey Keating	71	68	139	937.50
Julia Boland	72	67	139	937.50
Frances Bondad	68	72	140	750
Joanne Mills	72	70	142	675
Katelyn Must	72	70	142	675
Sarah-Jane Smith	71	72	143	575
Sarah Oh	70	73	143	575
Jody Fleming	73	71	144	475
Courtney Massey	73	71	144	475
Bree Arthur	78	67	145	400
Shani Waugh	70	76	146	362.50
Jacinta Toberty	73	73	146	362.50
Kym Larratt	73	74	147	325
Katherine MacDouall	77	71	148	275
Corinne Furnell	75	73	148	275
Samantha Whittle	75	73	148	275

ActewAGL Royal Canberra Ladies Classic

Royal Canberra Golf Club, Yarralumla, ACT
Par 73; 6,442 yards

January 20-22
purse, A$130,000

	SCORES			TOTAL	MONEY
Karen Lunn	71	66	70	207	A$19,500
Vicky Thomas	72	71	68	211	13,000
Stacey Keating	73	70	69	212	7,930
Kym Larratt	70	70	72	212	7,930
Nikki Campbell	71	70	72	213	5,330
Lindsey Wright	72	71	71	214	4,940
Haeji Kang	73	70	72	215	4,355
Jessica Shepley	73	70	74	217	3,835
Lorie Kane	78	69	71	218	3,380
Jessica Korda	72	71	75	218	3,380
Felicity Johnson	76	74	69	219	2,405
Rebecca Codd	74	72	73	219	2,405

	SCORES			TOTAL	MONEY
Cathryn Bristow	74	71	74	219	2,405
Danielle Montgomery	72	73	74	219	2,405
Tamie Durdin	71	80	69	220	1,950
Julia Boland	77	71	73	221	1,690
Rachel Bailey	72	74	76	222	1,540.50
Sarah Oh	75	77	70	222	1,540.50
Jody Fleming	76	76	71	223	1,404
Kristie Smith	76	75	72	223	1,404
Mo Martin	75	73	75	223	1,404
Lynnette Brooky	73	74	76	223	1,404

Bing Lee Samsung NSW Open

Oatlands Golf Club, Sydney, New South Wales
Par 36-36–72; 6,008 yards

January 27-29
purse, A$125,000

	SCORES			TOTAL	MONEY
*Lydia Ko	69	64	69	202	
Becky Morgan	70	70	66	206	A$18,750
Kristie Smith	72	67	68	207	10,500
Lindsey Wright	71	66	70	207	10,500
Katherine Hull	73	69	66	208	6,500
Gwladys Nocera	70	68	71	209	4,812.50
Hae-Rym Kim	69	70	70	209	4,812.50
Sarah Kemp	71	70	69	210	3,750
Sophie Giquel-Bettan	71	70	69	210	3,750
Rachel Bailey	68	72	70	210	3,750
Julia Boland	72	72	68	212	2,906.25
Nikki Garrett	69	71	72	212	2,906.25
Sarah Oh	70	71	72	213	2,337.50
Stephanie Na	69	71	73	213	2,337.50
Tamara Johns	70	75	69	214	1,875
Marianne Skarpnord	69	71	74	214	1,875
Vicky Thomas	73	70	71	214	1,875
Mo Martin	76	67	72	215	1,432.50
*Charlotte Thomas	72	71	72	215	
Wendy Doolan	71	68	76	215	1,432.50
Melissa Reid	70	70	75	215	1,432.50
Stacey Keating	69	74	72	215	1,432.50
Karen Lunn	68	77	70	215	1,432.50

Gold Coast RACV Australian Ladies Masters

RACV Royal Pines Resort, Ashmore, Queensland
Par 36-36–72; 6,511 yards

February 2-5
purse, A$500,000

	SCORES				TOTAL	MONEY
Christel Boeljon	66	65	68	68	267	A$75,000
Ha-Neul Kim	72	65	64	67	268	36,500
Diana Luna	71	64	66	67	268	36,500
So Yeon Ryu	66	61	69	72	268	36,500
Gwladys Nocera	69	68	69	64	270	20,000
Felicity Johnson	67	68	70	68	273	15,875
Bo-Mee Lee	65	69	70	69	273	15,875
Lindsey Wright	70	71	66	68	275	10,666.67
Danielle Kang	70	71	66	68	275	10,666.67
Nikki Campbell	67	67	70	71	275	10,666.67

	SCORES				TOTAL	MONEY
Karine Icher	73	70	69	64	276	7,312.50
Caroline Hedwall	72	71	69	64	276	7,312.50
Giulia Sergas	70	68	68	70	276	7,312.50
Sophie Gustafson	69	70	70	67	276	7,312.50
Frances Bondad	68	72	63	74	277	6,025
Kylie Walker	71	71	66	69	277	6,025
Haeji Kang	73	66	71	67	277	6,025
Lexi Thompson	67	70	72	68	277	6,025
Stacy Lewis	70	73	67	68	278	5,516.67
Bree Arthur	70	66	71	71	278	5,516.67
Pernilla Lindberg	69	68	73	68	278	5,516.67

ISPS Handa Women's Australian Open

Royal Melbourne Golf Club, Melbourne, Victoria
Par 36-37–73; 6,505 yards

February 9-12
purse, US$1,100,000

	SCORES				TOTAL	MONEY
Jessica Korda	72	70	73	74	289	US$165,000
Stacy Lewis	69	73	77	70	289	63,784
Julieta Granada	70	72	76	71	289	63,784
Brittany Lincicome	70	75	73	71	289	63,784
So Yeon Ryu	71	69	76	73	289	63,784
Hee Kyung Seo	75	66	75	73	289	63,784
(Korda won on second playoff hole.)						
Jenny Shin	72	74	74	70	290	31,743
Katie Futcher	74	72	71	74	291	26,406
Yani Tseng	70	76	71	74	291	26,406
Anna Nordqvist	76	77	71	68	292	21,911
Beatriz Recari	76	72	72	72	292	21,911
Caroline Hedwall	73	77	74	69	293	16,948
Eun-Hee Ji	72	79	71	71	293	16,948
Sarah Kemp	69	79	73	72	293	16,948
Sophie Giquel-Bettan	72	74	74	73	293	16,948
Melissa Reid	71	71	77	74	293	16,948
Nikki Campbell	72	74	70	77	293	16,948
Jiyai Shin	72	74	74	74	294	13,933
*Lydia Ko	74	76	72	73	295	
Cydney Clanton	74	72	75	74	295	13,372
Mina Harigae	78	72	74	72	296	12,922
Suzann Pettersen	80	71	74	72	297	12,248
Lorie Kane	72	73	72	80	297	12,248
Kristy McPherson	76	75	76	71	298	10,346
Jennifer Song	74	79	73	72	298	10,346
Ha-Neul Kim	77	71	77	73	298	10,346
Kyeong Bae	77	75	72	74	298	10,346
Meaghan Francella	73	76	75	74	298	10,346
Mo Martin	76	73	74	75	298	10,346
Lexi Thompson	74	74	75	75	298	10,346

ISPS Handa New Zealand Women's Open

Pegasus Golf Course, Christchurch, New Zealand
Par 36-36–72; 6,343 yards

February 17-19
purse, €200,000

	SCORES			TOTAL	MONEY
Lindsey Wright	70	68	68	206	A$30,000
Jessica Speechley	69	73	65	207	16,800
Alison Walshe	68	70	69	207	16,800
Lorie Kane	72	67	69	208	9,200
Stephanie Na	70	69	69	208	9,200
Beth Allen	70	71	68	209	7,200
Danielle Kang	68	72	69	209	7,200
Rachel Jennings	72	70	68	210	5,000
Kris Tamulis	70	71	69	210	5,000
Haeji Kang	69	69	72	210	5,000
Gerina Piller	68	71	71	210	5,000
Cara Freeman	70	70	71	211	3,140
Sarah Oh	69	72	70	211	3,140
Pernilla Lindberg	70	72	69	211	3,140
*Cecilia Cho	70	72	69	211	
Carlota Ciganda	69	69	73	211	3,140
Marianne Skarpnord	73	73	66	212	2,520
Linda Wessberg	70	73	69	212	2,520
Mariajo Uribe	70	68	74	212	2,520
*Lydia Ko	69	69	74	212	

Senior Tours

Mitsubishi Electric Championship

Hualalai Golf Course, Ka'upulehu-Kona, Hawaii

Par 36-36–72; 7,053 yards

January 20-22

purse, $1,800,000

	SCORES			TOTAL	MONEY
Dan Forsman	67	65	69	201	$307,000
Jay Don Blake	69	67	67	203	185,500
Michael Allen	67	68	69	204	121,000
John Cook	69	67	68	204	121,000
Gary Hallberg	68	71	66	205	86,000
Jeff Sluman	68	66	71	205	86,000
Brad Bryant	70	64	72	206	60,000
Mark Calcavecchia	71	69	66	206	60,000
Jay Haas	66	69	71	206	60,000
Tom Watson	69	65	72	206	60,000
Fred Couples	72	66	69	207	45,000
Olin Browne	72	66	70	208	38,333.34
Tom Lehman	65	72	71	208	38,333.33
Bruce Vaughan	65	71	72	208	38,333.33
Russ Cochran	68	69	72	209	32,000
Bernhard Langer	68	72	69	209	32,000
Mark McNulty	68	70	71	209	32,000
David Eger	69	69	72	210	25,250
Brad Faxon	66	72	72	210	25,250
Larry Mize	69	70	71	210	25,250
Corey Pavin	66	72	72	210	25,250
John Huston	68	71	72	211	21,500
Loren Roberts	66	70	75	211	21,500
Larry Nelson	73	68	71	212	19,000
Nick Price	73	69	70	212	19,000
Rod Spittle	72	68	72	212	19,000
Tom Kite	69	72	72	213	15,875
Mark O'Meara	71	70	72	213	15,875
Ted Schulz	72	70	71	213	15,875
Mark Wiebe	72	69	72	213	15,875

Allianz Championship

Old Course at Broken Sound, Boca Raton, Florida

Par 36-36–72; 6,807 yards

February 10-12

purse, $1,800,000

	SCORES			TOTAL	MONEY
Corey Pavin	64	70	71	205	$270,000
Peter Senior	66	68	71	205	158,400
(Pavin defeated Senior on first playoff hole.)					
Michael Allen	70	67	69	206	118,350
Bernhard Langer	66	69	71	206	118,350
John Cook	71	67	69	207	78,750
Jay Haas	68	70	69	207	78,750
Mark Calcavecchia	67	68	73	208	57,600
Gary Hallberg	69	69	70	208	57,600
Nick Price	70	73	65	208	57,600
Olin Browne	70	70	69	209	39,960

	SCORES			TOTAL	MONEY
Brad Bryant	70	70	69	209	39,960
Russ Cochran	71	71	67	209	39,960
Fred Funk	66	72	71	209	39,960
John Huston	67	72	70	209	39,960
Brad Faxon	68	71	71	210	28,800
David Frost	68	71	71	210	28,800
Bill Glasson	68	71	71	210	28,800
J.L. Lewis	70	67	73	210	28,800
Joey Sindelar	68	69	73	210	28,800
Jay Don Blake	69	71	71	211	21,600
Mike Goodes	68	70	73	211	21,600
Jim Rutledge	70	73	68	211	21,600
Jeff Sluman	69	72	70	211	21,600
Loren Roberts	69	72	71	212	18,900
Tom Byrum	71	73	69	213	16,050
Joel Edwards	73	69	71	213	16,050
David Eger	71	72	70	213	16,050
Steve Lowery	70	75	68	213	16,050
Larry Mize	69	74	70	213	16,050
Mark Wiebe	72	74	67	213	16,050

ACE Group Classic

TwinEagles Golf Club, Talon Course, Naples, Florida
Par 36-36–72; 7,300 yards

February 17-19
purse, $1,600,000

	SCORES			TOTAL	MONEY
Kenny Perry	64	62	70	196	$240,000
Bernhard Langer	66	65	70	201	140,800
Bill Glasson	68	66	68	202	95,466.67
Mike Goodes	65	68	69	202	95,466.67
Tom Lehman	64	66	72	202	95,466.66
Jay Haas	66	68	69	203	64,000
Larry Mize	62	67	75	204	57,600
David Frost	68	66	71	205	51,200
Russ Cochran	64	70	72	206	41,600
Jeff Sluman	69	67	70	206	41,600
Rod Spittle	71	66	69	206	41,600
Mark Calcavecchia	69	67	71	207	31,600
Joe Daley	71	68	68	207	31,600
Nick Price	68	73	66	207	31,600
Loren Roberts	71	69	67	207	31,600
Michael Allen	66	72	70	208	24,032
Jay Don Blake	68	67	73	208	24,032
Jim Carter	68	68	72	208	24,032
J.L. Lewis	71	67	70	208	24,032
Joey Sindelar	68	66	74	208	24,032
Olin Browne	70	72	67	209	18,160
John Cook	69	67	73	209	18,160
Gary Koch	68	71	70	209	18,160
Jim Rutledge	70	68	71	209	18,160
Jim Gallagher, Jr.	69	68	73	210	15,253.34
Dan Forsman	69	66	75	210	15,253.33
P.H. Horgan	68	68	74	210	15,253.33
Chip Beck	70	68	73	211	12,960
Jeff Hart	75	67	69	211	12,960
Gil Morgan	72	66	73	211	12,960
Peter Senior	70	70	71	211	12,960

Toshiba Classic

Newport Beach Country Club, Newport Beach, California
Par 35-36–71; 6,591 yards

March 16-18
purse, $1,750,000

	SCORES			TOTAL	MONEY
Loren Roberts	66	70	69	205	$262,500
Tom Kite	66	72	69	207	128,041.67
Bernhard Langer	65	72	70	207	128,041.67
Mark Calcavecchia	67	67	73	207	128,041.66
Mark McNulty	67	70	71	208	72,041.67
Joey Sindelar	67	71	70	208	72,041.67
David Eger	66	71	71	208	72,041.66
Bobby Clampett	65	74	70	209	48,125
Fred Couples	67	69	73	209	48,125
John Huston	69	71	69	209	48,125
Steve Pate	66	73	70	209	48,125
Brad Bryant	72	72	66	210	31,750
John Cook	71	67	72	210	31,750
Jay Haas	69	69	72	210	31,750
Larry Mize	67	72	71	210	31,750
Mark O'Meara	68	71	71	210	31,750
Jeff Sluman	72	70	68	210	31,750
Stan Utley	72	69	69	210	31,750
Fred Funk	68	72	71	211	22,983.34
Tommy Armour	71	69	71	211	22,983.33
Nick Price	70	68	73	211	22,983.33
Michael Allen	67	73	72	212	17,600
Mike Goodes	67	72	73	212	17,600
Tom Jenkins	69	73	70	212	17,600
Tom Lehman	69	70	73	212	17,600
Chien Soon Lu	69	70	73	212	17,600
Jim Thorpe	70	75	67	212	17,600
Mark Wiebe	69	70	73	212	17,600
Ben Bates	71	72	70	213	12,403.13
Greg Bruckner	68	74	71	213	12,403.13
Wayne Levi	67	74	72	213	12,403.13
Corey Pavin	72	71	70	213	12,403.13
Olin Browne	65	76	72	213	12,403.12
Russ Cochran	68	72	73	213	12,403.12
Bob Gilder	74	70	69	213	12,403.12
Rod Spittle	70	68	75	213	12,403.12

Mississippi Gulf Resort Classic

Fallen Oak Golf Club, Biloxi, Mississippi
Par 36-36–72; 7,054 yards

March 23-25
purse, $1,600,000

	SCORES			TOTAL	MONEY
Fred Couples	63	70	69	202	$240,000
Michael Allen	68	69	66	203	140,800
Tom Pernice, Jr.	64	73	69	206	105,200
Jeff Sluman	69	64	73	206	105,200
Bobby Clampett	67	69	71	207	65,866.67
Bill Glasson	68	70	69	207	65,866.67
Jim Thorpe	70	65	72	207	65,866.66
Brad Bryant	68	72	68	208	48,000
Chien Soon Lu	67	69	72	208	48,000
Peter Senior	67	70	73	210	41,600
Gary Hallberg	70	75	66	211	38,400

	SCORES			TOTAL	MONEY
John Cook	68	74	70	212	32,533.34
Chip Beck	69	70	73	212	32,533.33
Fred Funk	69	70	73	212	32,533.33
Tom Purtzer	71	72	70	213	28,000
Joey Sindelar	70	69	74	213	28,000
David Frost	73	71	70	214	20,177.78
Jim Gallagher, Jr.	72	73	69	214	20,177.78
Mike Goodes	70	72	72	214	20,177.78
Jay Haas	73	69	72	214	20,177.78
P.H. Horgan	72	71	71	214	20,177.78
Bernhard Langer	72	71	71	214	20,177.78
Robert Thompson	72	73	69	214	20,177.78
John Huston	67	69	78	214	20,177.77
Jerry Pate	71	71	72	214	20,177.77
Mark Calcavecchia	71	73	71	215	13,600
Jeff Hart	72	72	71	215	13,600
Tom Lehman	70	73	72	215	13,600
Steve Lowery	78	68	69	215	13,600
Dick Mast	68	72	75	215	13,600
Mark Wiebe	70	71	74	215	13,600

Encompass Insurance Pro-Am

TPC Tampa Bay, Lutz, Florida
Par 35-36–71; 6,783 yards

April 13-15
purse, $1,600,000

	SCORES			TOTAL	MONEY
Michael Allen	66	67	68	201	$240,000
Kenny Perry	72	67	65	204	140,800
Peter Senior	67	72	67	206	115,200
Corey Pavin	67	71	70	208	95,200
Bernhard Langer	67	71	71	209	76,000
Olin Browne	72	66	72	210	60,800
Russ Cochran	67	72	71	210	60,800
Brad Bryant	67	73	71	211	42,240
David Eger	73	66	72	211	42,240
Bill Glasson	71	71	69	211	42,240
Jay Haas	69	71	71	211	42,240
Kirk Triplett	68	71	72	211	42,240
Jeff Hart	73	70	69	212	30,400
Sandy Lyle	69	69	74	212	30,400
Jim Thorpe	72	69	71	212	30,400
Jay Don Blake	69	72	72	213	24,800
Gary Hallberg	69	73	71	213	24,800
P.H. Horgan	72	74	67	213	24,800
Andy North	68	72	73	213	24,800
Dan Forsman	71	71	72	214	18,266.67
Larry Mize	73	72	69	214	18,266.67
Jeff Sluman	71	75	68	214	18,266.67
D.A. Weibring	72	74	68	214	18,266.67
Tom Jenkins	68	71	75	214	18,266.66
Jerry Pate	69	72	73	214	18,266.66
Dana Quigley	72	70	73	215	15,200
Bob Gilder	74	72	70	216	13,280
Morris Hatalsky	72	71	73	216	13,280
Gary Koch	76	73	67	216	13,280
Larry Nelson	70	71	75	216	13,280
Steve Pate	70	71	75	216	13,280

Liberty Mutual Insurance Legends of Golf

Savannah Harbor Golf Resort, Savannah, Georgia
Par 36-36–72; 7,087 yards

April 20-22
purse, $2,700,000

	SCORES			TOTAL	MONEY (Each)
Michael Allen/David Frost	62	63	62	187	$230,000
John Cook/Joey Sindelar	63	64	61	188	135,000
Chien Soon Lu/Andy Bean	63	64	62	189	91,333.33
Jeff Sluman/Brad Faxon	62	64	63	189	91,333.33
Brad Bryant/Tom Purtzer	60	65	64	189	91,333.33
Fred Couples/Jay Haas	63	63	64	190	58,000
Gary Hallberg/Corey Pavin	65	62	63	190	58,000
Bobby Clampett/Andy North	64	62	65	191	47,000
Ian Baker-Finch/Hale Irwin	66	63	64	193	37,312.50
Olin Browne/Steve Pate	64	64	65	193	37,312.50
Bruce Fleisher/Tom Jenkins	62	66	65	193	37,312.50
Bernhard Langer/Tom Lehman	64	63	66	193	37,312.50
Russ Cochran/Kenny Perry	62	65	67	194	27,150
David Eger/Mark McNulty	66	64	64	194	27,150
Tom Kite/Gil Morgan	65	61	68	194	27,150
Tom Pernice, Jr./Bob Tway	65	62	67	194	27,150
Loren Roberts/Scott Simpson	64	67	63	194	27,150
Morris Hatalsky/Larry Nelson	67	64	64	195	22,500
Peter Jacobsen/D.A. Weibring	65	65	66	196	20,250
Larry Mize/Hal Sutton	64	66	66	196	20,250
Mark Calcavecchia/Rod Spittle	66	66	65	197	17,000
Jim Gallagher, Jr./John Huston	66	63	68	197	17,000
Bob Gilder/Eduardo Romero	66	67	64	197	17,000
Sandy Lyle/Peter Senior	65	66	66	197	17,000
Jay Don Blake/Fred Funk	66	66	66	198	14,000
Keith Fergus/Wayne Levi	66	65	67	198	14,000
Mike Goodes/Craig Stadler	65	65	68	198	14,000
Mark Brooks/Bill Glasson	65	66	68	199	13,000
Chip Beck/Mark Wiebe	67	67	67	201	12,500
Allen Doyle/Bruce Vaughan	69	67	67	203	11,750
John Jacobs/Fuzzy Zoeller	67	70	66	203	11,750

Insperity Championship

The Woodlands Country Club, The Woodlands, Texas
Par 36-36–72; 7,018 yards

May 4-6
purse, $1,700,000

	SCORES			TOTAL	MONEY
Fred Funk	66	69	67	202	$255,000
Tom Lehman	65	70	68	203	149,600
Mike Goodes	69	67	70	206	122,400
Michael Allen	69	68	71	208	73,100
Brad Bryant	68	68	72	208	73,100
Bobby Clampett	70	67	71	208	73,100
Dan Forsman	71	69	68	208	73,100
Bernhard Langer	68	71	69	208	73,100
Tom Byrum	69	69	72	210	42,500
Gene Jones	69	71	70	210	42,500
Corey Pavin	71	70	69	210	42,500
Rod Spittle	68	73	69	210	42,500
Olin Browne	68	74	69	211	29,750
James Mason	72	71	68	211	29,750
Jim Rutledge	72	72	67	211	29,750
Peter Senior	73	70	68	211	29,750

	SCORES			TOTAL	MONEY
Jeff Sluman	72	71	68	211	29,750
Bobby Wadkins	72	68	71	211	29,750
Mark Calcavecchia	69	73	70	212	21,675
Kenny Perry	72	71	69	212	21,675
Loren Roberts	68	74	70	212	21,675
Jim Thorpe	70	73	69	212	21,675
Jim Carter	72	71	70	213	17,425
P.H. Horgan	70	69	74	213	17,425
Eduardo Romero	72	72	69	213	17,425
D.A. Weibring	72	73	68	213	17,425
David Frost	69	74	71	214	14,450
John Huston	68	75	71	214	14,450
Peter Jacobsen	70	73	71	214	14,450
Willie Wood	73	73	68	214	14,450

Senior PGA Championship

Golf Club at Harbor Shores, Benton Harbor, Michigan
Par 36-35–71; 6,822 yards

May 24-27
purse, $2,000,000

	SCORES				TOTAL	MONEY
Roger Chapman	68	67	64	72	271	$378,000
John Cook	69	66	69	69	273	227,000
Hale Irwin	71	66	69	68	274	43,000
Peter Senior	74	67	71	63	275	74,400
Sandy Lyle	74	71	66	64	275	74,400
Joe Daley	73	72	66	64	275	74,400
Bernhard Langer	73	68	69	65	275	74,400
David Frost	70	70	68	67	275	74,400
Kenny Perry	75	70	69	62	276	55,000
Steve Pate	70	69	67	71	277	51,000
Michael Allen	77	64	68	69	278	47,000
Mark Calcavecchia	73	68	74	64	279	34,428.57
Fred Couples	76	67	70	66	279	34,428.57
Boonchu Ruangkit	72	69	71	67	279	34,428.57
Jim Carter	70	71	70	68	279	34,428.57
Willie Wood	72	72	67	68	279	34,428.57
Loren Roberts	72	67	71	69	279	34,428.57
Joel Edwards	73	67	67	72	279	34,428.57
Gene Jones	71	71	70	68	280	24,000
Kirk Triplett	73	70	68	69	280	24,000
Barry Lane	74	73	68	66	281	19,500
Paul Wesselingh	71	72	72	66	281	19,500
Bill Glasson	74	72	67	68	281	19,500
Bob Tway	72	69	69	71	281	19,500
Lonnie Nielsen	71	70	72	69	282	15,625
Christopher Williams	74	71	68	69	282	15,625
Jeff Hart	72	73	68	69	282	15,625
Steve Jones	74	70	68	70	282	15,625
Jeff Freeman	74	73	72	64	283	12,550
Russ Cochran	73	74	71	65	283	12,550
Kiyoshi Murota	73	70	73	67	283	12,550
Tom Lehman	76	69	70	68	283	12,550
Jay Haas	70	74	70	69	283	12,550
Jay Don Blake	71	72	67	73	283	12,550
Tim Thelen	75	69	73	67	284	10,400
Gary Wolstenholme	79	67	69	69	284	10,400
Bill Britton	73	71	69	71	284	10,400
Wayne Levi	73	70	73	69	285	8,600
Tom Pernice, Jr.	76	70	70	69	285	8,600

	SCORES			TOTAL	MONEY
Larry Mize	74	69	72	70	285	8,600
Mark Brooks	78	67	70	70	285	8,600
Mark McNulty	71	72	71	71	285	8,600
Scott Simpson	75	67	70	73	285	8,600
Sonny Skinner	77	70	69	70	286	6,750
Mark Mouland	72	73	71	70	286	6,750
Jeff Sluman	70	75	73	68	286	6,750
John Huston	73	70	72	71	286	6,750
Dick Mast	73	71	74	69	287	5,850
Bobby Clampett	71	71	71	74	287	5,850
Jim Gallagher, Jr.	75	72	70	71	288	5,400
Bobby Wadkins	76	71	73	69	289	5,050
Kim Jong-duck	75	72	72	70	289	5,050
Anders Forsbrand	71	74	74	70	289	5,050
J.L. Lewis	70	73	71	75	289	5,050
Andrew Oldcorn	74	70	71	75	290	4,800
Jeff Coston	76	71	77	67	291	4,562.50
P.H. Horgan	72	74	77	68	291	4,562.50
Mark James	73	70	76	72	291	4,562.50
Rod Spittle	75	72	70	74	291	4,562.50
Andrew Magee	73	74	76	69	292	4,400
Bruce Vaughan	76	69	78	70	293	4,275
Tom Purtzer	77	70	74	72	293	4,275
Stan Utley	73	74	74	72	293	4,275
Tom Jenkins	75	70	72	76	293	4,275
Blaine McCallister	74	72	75	73	294	4,125
David J. Russell	76	69	74	75	294	4,125
Peter Fowler	75	71	78	71	295	4,075
Ted Schulz	73	73	75	76	297	4,037.50
Tom Atchison	76	71	72	78	297	4,037.50
Mike Hulbert	77	70	76	75	298	4,000
Tom Wargo	74	73	76	77	300	3,975

Principal Charity Classic

Glen Oaks Country Club, West Des Moines, Iowa
Par 35-36–71; 6,877 yards

June 1-3
purse, $1,750,000

	SCORES			TOTAL	MONEY
Jay Haas	66	65	66	197	$262,500
Larry Mize	66	68	68	202	140,000
Kirk Triplett	67	73	62	202	140,000
Fred Funk	70	67	66	203	93,625
Tom Lehman	68	67	68	203	93,625
Andrew Magee	68	68	68	204	70,000
David Eger	69	71	65	205	56,000
Jeff Freeman	68	70	67	205	56,000
Kenny Perry	68	69	68	205	56,000
Mark Calcavecchia	68	72	66	206	40,250
Bernhard Langer	70	69	67	206	40,250
Lonnie Nielsen	69	69	68	206	40,250
Mark Wiebe	71	70	65	206	40,250
Mark Brooks	67	71	69	207	30,625
Bob Gilder	70	69	68	207	30,625
Mike Goodes	64	74	69	207	30,625
Tom Pernice, Jr.	66	72	69	207	30,625
Jeff Sluman	67	73	68	208	24,558.34
Russ Cochran	67	71	70	208	24,558.33
Loren Roberts	73	68	67	208	24,558.33
Fulton Allem	71	69	69	209	18,929.17

	SCORES			TOTAL	MONEY
Brad Faxon	70	71	68	209	18,929.17
Jeff Hart	70	71	68	209	18,929.17
Willie Wood	71	69	69	209	18,929.17
Dan Forsman	67	70	72	209	18,929.16
Rod Spittle	68	70	71	209	18,929.16
Joel Edwards	69	71	70	210	15,575
Eduardo Romero	67	73	70	210	15,575
John Cook	71	67	73	211	13,230
Gary Hallberg	71	72	68	211	13,230
Morris Hatalsky	69	74	68	211	13,230
Dick Mast	68	70	73	211	13,230
Jim Rutledge	69	74	68	211	13,230

Regions Tradition

Shoal Creek, Shoal Creek, Alabama
Par 36-36–72; 7,197 yards

June 7-10
purse, $2,200,000

	SCORES				TOTAL	MONEY
Tom Lehman	69	69	68	68	274	$335,000
Bernhard Langer	68	71	71	66	276	177,460
Chien Soon Lu	72	69	69	66	276	177,460
Fred Couples	73	72	68	65	278	132,000
Russ Cochran	69	68	72	70	279	96,800
Bill Glasson	66	69	74	70	279	96,800
Brad Bryant	69	69	71	71	280	74,800
Jeff Sluman	70	68	70	72	280	74,800
Michael Allen	73	72	69	67	281	59,400
Fred Funk	67	71	71	72	281	59,400
Dan Forsman	66	73	71	72	282	50,600
Peter Senior	71	71	66	74	282	50,600
Jay Haas	73	72	68	70	283	39,600
Morris Hatalsky	70	73	70	70	283	39,600
Wayne Levi	70	71	73	69	283	39,600
Steve Pate	73	70	69	71	283	39,600
Kenny Perry	74	67	71	71	283	39,600
Mark Calcavecchia	73	69	73	69	284	32,010
David Frost	74	71	69	70	284	32,010
Mike Goodes	70	70	75	70	285	29,040
Jay Don Blake	74	74	69	69	286	26,400
Rod Spittle	73	70	70	73	286	26,400
Bob Tway	74	67	74	72	287	24,200
Peter Jacobsen	74	71	72	71	288	23,100
Tom Jenkins	71	73	73	72	289	20,064
Steve Jones	77	71	71	70	289	20,064
Larry Mize	70	70	73	76	289	20,064
Loren Roberts	72	75	73	69	289	20,064
Hal Sutton	73	72	73	71	289	20,064
Corey Pavin	72	73	74	71	290	16,573.34
David Eger	75	77	70	68	290	16,573.33
Scott Simpson	73	75	70	72	290	16,573.33
Bruce Fleisher	69	72	75	75	291	13,860
Sandy Lyle	75	73	73	70	291	13,860
David Peoples	78	69	74	70	291	13,860
Tom Pernice, Jr.	77	70	72	72	291	13,860
Kirk Triplett	70	73	74	74	291	13,860
Fulton Allem	72	71	76	73	292	10,726.72
Gary Hallberg	70	75	74	73	292	10,726.72
Larry Nelson	73	76	72	71	292	10,726.72
Mark Brooks	73	74	74	71	292	10,726.71

	SCORES				TOTAL	MONEY
John Cook	74	73	75	70	292	10,726.71
Eduardo Romero	72	75	75	70	292	10,726.71
Bruce Vaughan	74	73	74	71	292	10,726.71
Jerry Pate	76	70	74	73	293	8,580
Mark Wiebe	75	74	73	71	293	8,580
Tom Kite	80	71	71	72	294	6,820
Steve Lowery	76	74	72	72	294	6,820
Andrew Magee	72	74	74	74	294	6,820
Gil Morgan	75	72	77	70	294	6,820
Jim Thorpe	73	75	73	73	294	6,820
D.A. Weibring	76	73	72	73	294	6,820
Olin Browne	71	81	72	71	295	5,170
Hale Irwin	72	71	77	75	295	5,170
Roger Chapman	74	73	76	73	296	4,510
Brad Faxon	73	70	79	74	296	4,510
Jim Gallagher, Jr.	73	74	71	78	296	4,510
Craig Stadler	76	71	76	73	296	4,510
Bob Gilder	75	71	79	72	297	3,740
Mark McNulty	73	77	72	75	297	3,740
Dana Quigley	78	71	75	73	297	3,740
Denis Watson	74	74	74	76	298	3,300
Chip Beck	76	72	75	76	299	3,080
Andy Bean	74	78	73	75	300	2,640
Tom Purtzer	79	77	72	72	300	2,640
Mike Reid	71	78	79	72	300	2,640
Bobby Clampett	74	76	75	76	301	2,189
Allen Doyle	79	77	68	77	301	2,189
Vicente Fernandez	77	77	75	73	302	2,046
Ted Schulz	75	74	78	77	304	1,848
Fuzzy Zoeller	73	78	80	73	304	1,848
Keith Fergus	72	79	78	78	307	1,650
Bobby Wadkins	82	76	77	74	309	1,518
Mike McCullough	81	81	89	81	332	1,430
Joey Sindelar	70	75	74		WD	
J.L. Lewis	77	72	75		WD	

Montreal Championship

Vallee du Richelieu Vercheres, Sainte-Julie, Quebec, Canada
Par 36-36–72; 6,950 yards

June 22-24
purse, $1,800,000

	SCORES			TOTAL	MONEY
Mark Calcavecchia	69	67	64	200	$270,000
Brad Bryant	71	68	65	204	158,400
Russ Cochran	66	71	68	205	118,350
Bob Tway	70	65	70	205	118,350
Michael Allen	68	69	69	206	78,750
Jay Don Blake	70	67	69	206	78,750
Craig Stadler	71	68	69	208	64,800
Olin Browne	69	73	68	210	51,600
David Frost	71	73	66	210	51,600
Gary Hallberg	70	68	72	210	51,600
David Eger	69	72	70	211	38,250
Dick Mast	72	68	71	211	38,250
Jerry Pate	68	70	73	211	38,250
Peter Senior	69	72	70	211	38,250
John Cook	71	72	69	212	28,800
Fred Funk	71	72	69	212	28,800
John Huston	74	69	69	212	28,800
Hale Irwin	69	68	75	212	28,800

	SCORES			TOTAL	MONEY
Willie Wood	71	70	71	212	28,800
Bill Glasson	73	72	68	213	19,597.50
Mike Goodes	70	73	70	213	19,597.50
Larry Mize	68	74	71	213	19,597.50
Mark Mouland	71	68	74	213	19,597.50
David Peoples	69	75	69	213	19,597.50
Jim Rutledge	76	68	69	213	19,597.50
Jeff Sluman	69	74	70	213	19,597.50
Kirk Triplett	69	74	70	213	19,597.50
Fulton Allem	70	72	72	214	13,950
R.W. Eaks	73	70	71	214	13,950
Dan Forsman	69	72	73	214	13,950
Steve Lowery	72	70	72	214	13,950
Lonnie Nielsen	71	71	72	214	13,950
Tom Purtzer	71	72	71	214	13,950

Constellation Senior Players Championship

Fox Chapel Golf Club, Pittsburgh, Pennsylvania
Par 35-35–70; 6,710 yards

June 28-July 1
purse, $2,700,000

	SCORES				TOTAL	MONEY
Joe Daley	66	64	68	68	266	$405,000
Tom Lehman	66	67	66	69	268	237,600
Olin Browne	73	62	69	65	269	194,400
Mark Calcavecchia	69	65	64	72	270	144,450
Fred Couples	66	63	70	71	270	144,450
Bill Glasson	67	67	68	69	271	102,600
Kirk Triplett	71	69	65	66	271	102,600
Kenny Perry	68	69	67	68	272	86,400
Michael Allen	66	68	70	69	273	72,900
Fred Funk	65	72	64	72	273	72,900
Jeff Freeman	70	65	65	74	274	64,800
Chien Soon Lu	74	67	67	67	275	56,700
Willie Wood	70	66	70	69	275	56,700
Roger Chapman	70	68	66	72	276	44,550
Mike Goodes	74	67	68	67	276	44,550
Steve Lowery	73	69	67	67	276	44,550
Jim Rutledge	74	69	67	66	276	44,550
Bruce Vaughan	64	74	67	71	276	44,550
Mark Wiebe	71	73	64	68	276	44,550
Jay Don Blake	69	65	73	70	277	29,396.25
Brad Bryant	69	76	64	68	277	29,396.25
John Cook	74	67	68	68	277	29,396.25
Jay Haas	71	69	66	71	277	29,396.25
Morris Hatalsky	71	67	69	70	277	29,396.25
Steve Pate	68	69	68	72	277	29,396.25
Corey Pavin	70	70	70	67	277	29,396.25
Tom Watson	70	67	69	71	277	29,396.25
Mark Brooks	73	71	70	64	278	22,950
David Frost	71	69	68	70	278	22,950
Russ Cochran	71	71	69	68	279	18,258.75
Joel Edwards	73	66	70	70	279	18,258.75
David Eger	70	68	70	71	279	18,258.75
Hale Irwin	72	68	72	67	279	18,258.75
Tom Jenkins	73	71	65	70	279	18,258.75
Sandy Lyle	73	69	67	70	279	18,258.75
Larry Mize	70	65	70	74	279	18,258.75
Gil Morgan	70	71	71	67	279	18,258.75
Brad Faxon	69	73	70	68	280	13,770

	SCORES				TOTAL	MONEY
P.H. Horgan	72	68	69	71	280	13,770
Loren Roberts	70	73	66	71	280	13,770
Peter Senior	69	73	66	72	280	13,770
Rod Spittle	68	74	68	70	280	13,770
Bobby Clampett	68	72	69	72	281	11,340
Gary Hallberg	71	74	66	70	281	11,340
Steve Jones	72	66	70	73	281	11,340
Jeff Sluman	73	68	68	72	281	11,340
Jeff Hart	70	73	67	72	282	9,990
Jim Carter	74	66	67	76	283	8,640
Gene Jones	76	70	65	72	283	8,640
Larry Nelson	72	72	68	71	283	8,640
Tom Purtzer	69	73	71	70	283	8,640
Tom Kite	71	68	74	71	284	7,290
Phil Blackmar	72	73	68	72	285	6,210
Dick Mast	79	70	70	66	285	6,210
Greg Norman	67	74	73	71	285	6,210
Jim Thorpe	67	70	77	71	285	6,210
Bob Tway	72	72	70	71	285	6,210
Ted Schulz	69	72	73	72	286	5,265
Hal Sutton	74	68	76	68	286	5,265
Bob Gilder	73	73	74	67	287	4,725
Bobby Wadkins	75	71	68	73	287	4,725
Chip Beck	71	71	71	75	288	4,050
Peter Jacobsen	71	73	69	75	288	4,050
David Peoples	70	71	75	72	288	4,050
Bruce Fleisher	73	77	69	70	289	3,375
Lonnie Nielsen	71	75	66	77	289	3,375
Craig Stadler	70	70	72	78	290	2,970
Tommy Armour	74	67	74	77	292	2,538
Jim Gallagher, Jr.	73	69	72	78	292	2,538
Jerry Pate	75	74	74	69	292	2,538
Dan Forsman	75	73	69	76	293	2,052
John Huston	74	67	71	81	293	2,052
Eduardo Romero	73	70	71	79	293	2,052
Andy Bean	74	71	73	77	295	1,728
Scott Simpson	72	76	78	69	295	1,728
Andrew Magee	71	75	76	74	296	1,566
Mark McNulty	76	75	73	74	298	1,458
Ben Crenshaw	74	78	71	76	299	1,350
Wayne Levi	80	75	74	76	305	1,242
Tony Jacklin	81	80	78	81	320	1,161
D.A. Weibring	73	69			WD	

Nature Valley First Tee Open

Pebble Beach Golf Links: Par 36-36–72; 6,822 yards
Del Monte Golf Course: Par 36-36–72; 6,357 yards
Monterey, California

July 6-8
purse, $1,700,000

	SCORES			TOTAL	MONEY
Kirk Triplett	70	70	66	206	$255,000
Mark McNulty	68	71	69	208	149,600
Jay Haas	72	69	69	210	101,433.34
Brad Bryant	69	67	74	210	101,433.33
Bill Glasson	69	72	69	210	101,433.33
Mark Brooks	71	70	70	211	61,200
Gary Hallberg	69	71	71	211	61,200
Hale Irwin	74	68	69	211	61,200
Tom Kite	67	69	76	212	42,500

	SCORES				TOTAL	MONEY
Corey Pavin	69	71	72		212	42,500
Peter Senior	69	70	73		212	42,500
Jeff Sluman	71	74	67		212	42,500
Russ Cochran	72	69	72		213	31,450
Jeff Hart	71	71	71		213	31,450
Steve Jones	74	70	69		213	31,450
Chien Soon Lu	74	70	69		213	31,450
Joel Edwards	74	73	67		214	22,585.72
P.H. Horgan	73	71	70		214	22,585.72
Craig Stadler	71	75	68		214	22,585.72
Mike Goodes	71	72	71		214	22,585.71
John Huston	71	72	71		214	22,585.71
Tom Pernice, Jr.	68	74	72		214	22,585.71
Hal Sutton	73	69	72		214	22,585.71
Michael Allen	70	74	71		215	15,193.75
Tommy Armour	74	70	71		215	15,193.75
Mark Calcavecchia	69	73	73		215	15,193.75
Roger Chapman	76	69	70		215	15,193.75
Jeff Freeman	76	66	73		215	15,193.75
Andrew Magee	76	71	68		215	15,193.75
Steve Pate	73	71	71		215	15,193.75
Mark Wiebe	75	71	69		215	15,193.75

U.S. Senior Open Championship

Indianwood Golf & Country Club, Lake Orion, Michigan
Par 35-35–70; 6,828 yards

July 12-15
purse, $2,600,000

	SCORES				TOTAL	MONEY
Roger Chapman	68	68	68	66	270	$500,000
Fred Funk	67	71	67	67	272	177,739
Bernhard Langer	66	70	64	72	272	177,739
Tom Lehman	70	66	68	68	272	177,739
Corey Pavin	67	69	68	68	272	177,739
John Cook	69	72	67	66	274	87,348
John Huston	69	67	68	70	274	87,348
Mark Wiebe	69	68	70	68	275	76,614
Jay Haas	69	68	68	72	277	65,046
Peter Senior	71	72	66	68	277	65,046
Lance Ten Broeck	66	68	72	71	277	65,046
Mark Calcavecchia	68	70	69	71	278	53,463
Fred Couples	72	68	65	73	278	53,463
Tom Kite	65	70	74	69	278	53,463
Dick Mast	68	68	69	74	279	46,213
Tom Pernice, Jr.	67	71	66	75	279	46,213
Peter Fowler	70	74	66	70	280	38,142
Damon Green	68	72	72	68	280	38,142
Peter Jacobsen	70	70	68	72	280	38,142
Kim Jong-duck	73	71	70	66	280	38,142
Steve Lowery	70	68	69	73	280	38,142
Jay Don Blake	73	65	75	68	281	27,497
Joel Edwards	72	71	70	68	281	27,497
Gary Hallberg	70	74	68	69	281	27,497
Kiyoshi Murota	71	70	71	69	281	27,497
Kirk Triplett	69	69	72	71	281	27,497
Tom Watson	70	72	70	69	281	27,497
Brad Bryant	70	68	74	70	282	19,491
Chien Soon Lu	69	68	73	72	282	19,491
Jeff Sluman	67	71	73	71	282	19,491
Rod Spittle	70	69	71	72	282	19,491

	SCORES				TOTAL	MONEY
Robert Thompson	70	72	71	69	282	19,491
Michael Allen	74	70	68	71	283	17,017
Barry Lane	70	74	73	66	283	17,017
Jim Rutledge	72	72	73	66	283	17,017
Tommy Armour	69	69	75	71	284	14,084
Olin Browne	69	74	70	71	284	14,084
Tom Byrum	70	74	72	68	284	14,084
David Eger	69	70	74	71	284	14,084
Dan Forsman	69	71	72	72	284	14,084
Mike Goodes	71	73	66	74	284	14,084
Loren Roberts	71	69	74	70	284	14,084
Joey Sindelar	70	72	68	74	284	14,084
Brad Faxon	69	71	71	74	285	11,165
Steve Jones	69	72	71	73	285	11,165
Rick Lewallen	70	68	72	75	285	11,165
Mikael Hogberg	67	75	73	71	286	9,308
Andrew Magee	74	70	67	75	286	9,308
Andy Oldcorn	70	69	75	72	286	9,308
Jerry Pate	69	75	68	74	286	9,308
Ted Schulz	70	73	72	73	288	8,180
Bob Tway	72	71	72	73	288	8,180
Fulton Allem	68	75	70	76	289	7,774
Andy Bean	70	73	73	73	289	7,774
*Douglas Hanzel	71	72	71	75	289	
T.C. Chen	71	72	71	76	290	7,490
Jim Chancey	73	69	78	71	291	7,163
Gary Wolstenholme	70	70	73	78	291	7,163
Fuzzy Zoeller	70	74	69	78	291	7,163
Mark Brooks	72	71	74	75	292	6,827
Mike Reid	71	72	72	77	292	6,827
*Sean Knapp	70	72	76	74	292	
Larry Mize	71	72	75	75	293	6,659
Bob Gilder	72	72	74	77	295	6,547
Dave Eichelberger	70	74	78	78	300	6,436

The Senior Open Championship presented by Rolex

See European Senior Tour section.

3M Championship

TPC Twin Cities, Blaine, Minnesota
Par 36-36–72; 7,100 yards

August 3-5
purse, $1,750,000

	SCORES			TOTAL	MONEY
Bernhard Langer	67	69	62	198	$262,500
David Peoples	68	62	70	200	154,000
Olin Browne	68	67	66	201	115,062.50
Kenny Perry	69	68	64	201	115,062.50
Joel Edwards	66	69	67	202	83,125
Jeff Sluman	69	69	65	203	70,000
Tom Kite	69	67	68	204	56,000
Peter Senior	65	71	68	204	56,000
Craig Stadler	69	69	66	204	56,000
Mark Calcavecchia	71	68	66	205	37,625
Gil Morgan	65	73	67	205	37,625
Mark O'Meara	68	71	66	205	37,625
Steve Pate	65	71	69	205	37,625
Eduardo Romero	68	65	72	205	37,625

	SCORES			TOTAL	MONEY
Joey Sindelar	68	71	66	205	37,625
Fred Funk	69	71	66	206	28,000
Lance Ten Broeck	71	65	70	206	28,000
D.A. Weibring	67	72	67	206	28,000
David Frost	67	70	70	207	23,712.50
Gary Hallberg	70	68	69	207	23,712.50
Loren Roberts	71	66	71	208	20,912.50
Bob Tway	77	65	66	208	20,912.50
David Eger	72	70	67	209	16,775
Dan Forsman	69	73	67	209	16,775
Bill Glasson	70	71	68	209	16,775
Tom Lehman	68	70	71	209	16,775
Steve Lowery	70	69	70	209	16,775
Chien Soon Lu	65	71	73	209	16,775
Mark Wiebe	69	69	71	209	16,775
Jay Don Blake	74	71	65	210	11,588.89
Jeff Hart	67	71	72	210	11,588.89
John Huston	71	70	69	210	11,588.89
Wayne Levi	71	67	72	210	11,588.89
Blaine McCallister	70	71	69	210	11,588.89
Mark McNulty	66	70	74	210	11,588.89
Larry Nelson	72	67	71	210	11,588.89
Willie Wood	67	72	71	210	11,588.89
Joe Daley	67	67	76	210	11,588.88

Dick's Sporting Goods Open

En-Joie Golf Course, Endicott, New York
Par 37-35–72; 6,974 yards

August 17-19
purse, $1,800,000

	SCORES			TOTAL	MONEY
Willie Wood	67	68	68	203	$270,000
Michael Allen	66	71	66	203	158,400
(Wood defeated Allen on first playoff hole.)					
Brad Faxon	67	66	71	204	98,550
Tom Lehman	69	68	67	204	98,550
Kenny Perry	65	72	67	204	98,550
Joey Sindelar	67	71	66	204	98,550
Mark Calcavecchia	70	68	67	205	52,560
John Cook	66	72	67	205	52,560
Bernhard Langer	65	73	67	205	52,560
Mark O'Meara	68	69	68	205	52,560
Peter Senior	68	67	70	205	52,560
Dick Mast	69	67	70	206	37,800
Mark McNulty	67	70	69	206	37,800
Fred Funk	67	69	71	207	31,500
Bob Gilder	71	71	65	207	31,500
Andrew Magee	70	70	67	207	31,500
Loren Roberts	69	70	68	207	31,500
Tommy Armour	68	71	69	208	25,260
Jay Haas	70	70	68	208	25,260
Chien Soon Lu	69	71	68	208	25,260
John Huston	65	67	77	209	21,510
Mark Wiebe	68	72	69	209	21,510
Brad Bryant	72	67	71	210	18,900
Jeff Hart	75	66	69	210	18,900
Jeff Sluman	68	72	70	210	18,900
Jay Don Blake	69	70	72	211	15,660
Bill Glasson	68	69	74	211	15,660
Tom Jenkins	71	68	72	211	15,660

	SCORES			TOTAL	MONEY
Corey Pavin	70	71	70	211	15,660
Mike Reid	74	67	70	211	15,660

Boeing Classic

TPC Snoqualmie Ridge, Snoqualmie, Washington
Par 36-36–72; 7,264 yards

August 24-26
purse, $2,000,000

	SCORES			TOTAL	MONEY
Jay Don Blake	68	70	68	206	$300,000
Mark O'Meara	74	64	68	206	176,000
(Blake defeated O'Meara on second playoff hole.)					
Willie Wood	69	68	70	207	144,000
Michael Allen	73	68	67	208	107,000
Mark Calcavecchia	65	73	70	208	107,000
Tom Byrum	71	70	68	209	76,000
David Frost	72	70	67	209	76,000
Duffy Waldorf	75	68	67	210	57,333.34
Tom Kite	69	71	70	210	57,333.33
Jeff Sluman	68	73	69	210	57,333.33
John Cook	70	69	72	211	40,000
Joel Edwards	69	70	72	211	40,000
Mike Goodes	70	73	68	211	40,000
Bernhard Langer	73	69	69	211	40,000
Steve Pate	68	73	70	211	40,000
Mike Reid	70	68	73	211	40,000
David Eger	70	68	74	212	29,050
Gary Hallberg	72	73	67	212	29,050
John Huston	71	68	73	212	29,050
Corey Pavin	71	71	70	212	29,050
Bill Glasson	72	71	70	213	21,142.86
Steve Lowery	72	70	71	213	21,142.86
Kenny Perry	70	72	71	213	21,142.86
Loren Roberts	71	72	70	213	21,142.86
Gene Sauers	71	71	71	213	21,142.86
Jim Gallagher, Jr.	69	71	73	213	21,142.85
Tom Jenkins	70	65	78	213	21,142.85
R.W. Eaks	73	71	70	214	15,840
Jeff Hart	71	72	71	214	15,840
Gil Morgan	72	73	69	214	15,840
Jim Rutledge	72	73	69	214	15,840
Rod Spittle	69	70	75	214	15,840

Pacific Links Hawai'i Championship

Kapolei Golf Course, Kapolei, Hawaii
Par 36-36–72; 7,001 yards

September 14-16
purse, $1,800,000

	SCORES			TOTAL	MONEY
Willie Wood	68	68	66	202	$270,000
Bill Glasson	66	65	72	203	158,400
Peter Senior	65	70	69	204	129,600
David Frost	69	67	69	205	96,300
Tom Lehman	68	70	67	205	96,300
Dick Mast	69	68	69	206	68,400
Larry Mize	71	70	65	206	68,400
Andrew Magee	72	66	69	207	45,600

	SCORES			TOTAL	MONEY
Mark O'Meara	70	67	70	207	45,600
Corey Pavin	69	67	71	207	45,600
Eduardo Romero	67	72	68	207	45,600
Gene Sauers	70	69	68	207	45,600
Duffy Waldorf	68	71	68	207	45,600
Kirk Triplett	78	65	65	208	34,200
Mark McNulty	67	68	74	209	32,400
Jay Don Blake	66	72	73	211	26,220
Bobby Clampett	71	70	70	211	26,220
John Cook	71	71	69	211	26,220
Jeff Hart	71	71	69	211	26,220
Morris Hatalsky	70	69	72	211	26,220
Bruce Vaughan	70	72	69	211	26,220
Tommy Armour	72	72	68	212	16,230
Chip Beck	72	72	68	212	16,230
Mark Brooks	71	72	69	212	16,230
Tom Byrum	72	71	69	212	16,230
Joe Daley	72	69	71	212	16,230
Fred Funk	74	68	70	212	16,230
Steve Jones	74	70	68	212	16,230
Tom Kite	69	73	70	212	16,230
Gil Morgan	71	70	71	212	16,230
Tom Pernice Jr.	72	69	71	212	16,230
Jim Rutledge	72	70	70	212	16,230
Bob Tway	70	69	73	212	16,230

SAS Championship

Prestonwood Country Club, Cary, North Carolina
Par 35-37–72; 7,137 yards

October 5-7
purse, $2,100,000

	SCORES			TOTAL	MONEY
Bernhard Langer	68	72	63	203	$315,000
Jay Don Blake	67	70	68	205	184,800
Mark Wiebe	69	69	68	206	151,200
Tommy Armour	71	70	66	207	112,350
Fred Funk	67	69	71	207	112,350
Andrew Magee	67	70	71	208	71,400
Larry Nelson	72	66	70	208	71,400
Steve Pate	67	69	72	208	71,400
Kenny Perry	68	71	69	208	71,400
John Cook	72	71	66	209	45,150
John Huston	71	68	70	209	45,150
Tom Jenkins	69	73	67	209	45,150
Mark McNulty	70	68	71	209	45,150
Mark O'Meara	69	69	71	209	45,150
Gene Sauers	68	74	67	209	45,150
Russ Cochran	66	73	71	210	35,700
David Eger	73	70	68	211	32,550
Steve Jones	73	67	71	211	32,550
Michael Allen	71	70	71	212	25,375
Joel Edwards	73	71	68	212	25,375
Mike Reid	69	70	73	212	25,375
Craig Stadler	70	70	72	212	25,375
Duffy Waldorf	71	72	69	212	25,375
Willie Wood	69	74	69	212	25,375
Allen Doyle	68	75	70	213	17,523.34
Mike Goodes	73	70	70	213	17,523.34
David Peoples	70	73	70	213	17,523.34
Bill Glasson	70	69	74	213	17,523.33
Neal Lancaster	72	69	72	213	17,523.33

	SCORES			TOTAL	MONEY
Steve Lowery	75	69	69	213	17,523.33
Larry Mize	70	75	68	213	17,523.33
Peter Senior	72	71	70	213	17,523.33
Jeff Sluman	69	73	71	213	17,523.33

Greater Hickory Classic

Rock Barn Golf & Spa, Conover, North Carolina
Par 35-37–72; 7,046 yards

October 12-14
purse, $1,600,000

	SCORES			TOTAL	MONEY
Fred Funk	66	66	69	201	$240,000
Duffy Waldorf	69	67	66	202	140,800
Mark Wiebe	67	69	70	206	115,200
Chip Beck	69	67	71	207	68,800
Jay Don Blake	67	72	68	207	68,800
John Cook	68	71	68	207	68,800
Dan Forsman	65	72	70	207	68,800
Peter Senior	68	69	70	207	68,800
David Frost	66	71	71	208	41,600
Bernhard Langer	70	69	69	208	41,600
Loren Roberts	70	70	68	208	41,600
Larry Mize	66	67	76	209	31,600
Mark O'Meara	70	69	70	209	31,600
Gene Sauers	69	68	72	209	31,600
Jeff Sluman	69	71	69	209	31,600
Michael Allen	69	75	66	210	26,400
Hale Irwin	71	72	67	210	26,400
Bobby Clampett	69	71	71	211	23,200
Steve Pate	70	70	71	211	23,200
Roger Chapman	74	69	69	212	19,200
Tom Jenkins	69	74	69	212	19,200
Dick Mast	72	68	72	212	19,200
Mark McNulty	71	73	68	212	19,200
Russ Cochran	70	72	71	213	14,300
Tom Kite	68	77	68	213	14,300
Tom Lehman	68	74	71	213	14,300
Andrew Magee	73	71	69	213	14,300
Kenny Perry	74	70	69	213	14,300
Scott Simpson	68	72	73	213	14,300
Rod Spittle	71	71	71	213	14,300
Bruce Vaughan	68	73	72	213	14,300

AT&T Championship

TPC San Antonio, Canyons Course, San Antonio, Texas
Par 36-36–72; 6,932 yards

October 26-28
purse, $1,850,000

	SCORES			TOTAL	MONEY
David Frost	71	71	66	208	$277,500
Bernhard Langer	74	68	66	208	162,800
(Frost defeated Langer on second playoff hole.)					
Mark Calcavecchia	67	69	74	210	133,200
Tommy Armour	73	71	67	211	110,075
Kirk Triplett	74	69	69	212	80,937.50
Willie Wood	70	72	70	212	80,937.50
Tom Lehman	75	68	70	213	62,900
Mark Mouland	72	74	67	213	62,900

	SCORES			TOTAL	MONEY
Jay Don Blake	74	70	70	214	46,250
Jay Haas	72	73	69	214	46,250
Chien Soon Lu	74	71	69	214	46,250
Kenny Perry	70	70	74	214	46,250
Tom Kite	70	74	71	215	34,225
Sandy Lyle	75	73	67	215	34,225
Gil Morgan	72	73	70	215	34,225
Mark Wiebe	72	70	73	215	34,225
Joel Edwards	74	70	72	216	27,750
Fred Funk	73	69	74	216	27,750
Mike Goodes	76	71	69	216	27,750
Bill Glasson	73	72	72	217	21,645
Jeff Hart	76	70	71	217	21,645
Mike Reid	74	73	70	217	21,645
Ted Schulz	75	70	72	217	21,645
Esteban Toledo	74	67	76	217	21,645
Larry Mize	77	75	66	218	16,121.43
Larry Nelson	77	71	70	218	16,121.43
Corey Pavin	75	72	71	218	16,121.43
Loren Roberts	76	73	69	218	16,121.43
Peter Senior	73	73	72	218	16,121.43
Jim Thorpe	75	69	74	218	16,121.43
Chip Beck	71	71	76	218	16,121.42

Charles Schwab Cup Championship

Desert Mountain Club, Cochise Course, Scottsdale, Arizona
Par 35-35–70; 6,929 yards

November 1-4
purse, $2,500,000

	SCORES				TOTAL	MONEY
Tom Lehman	68	63	62	65	258	$440,000
Jay Haas	66	60	69	69	264	254,000
Jay Don Blake	64	71	65	66	266	213,000
Fred Couples	66	66	62	73	267	158,000
Fred Funk	71	65	66	65	267	158,000
Bernhard Langer	69	65	70	65	269	117,000
Russ Cochran	67	70	64	69	270	105,000
Olin Browne	66	67	69	70	272	87,500
Corey Pavin	67	68	69	68	272	87,500
Michael Allen	69	66	69	69	273	70,000
John Cook	71	64	70	68	273	70,000
David Frost	70	64	68	71	273	70,000
Brad Bryant	68	67	70	69	274	57,000
Mark Calcavecchia	68	66	68	72	274	57,000
Bill Glasson	66	70	69	70	275	50,500
Larry Mize	73	66	67	69	275	50,500
Joe Daley	70	71	67	70	278	40,700
Kenny Perry	69	68	69	72	278	40,700
Loren Roberts	71	70	67	70	278	40,700
Kirk Triplett	67	68	74	69	278	40,700
Willie Wood	71	70	68	69	278	40,700
Gary Hallberg	65	72	70	72	279	34,000
Chien Soon Lu	70	73	67	70	280	32,000
Peter Senior	72	66	72	71	281	30,000
Mark Wiebe	73	70	70	69	282	29,000
Mark McNulty	69	69	73	72	283	27,000
Jeff Sluman	67	72	72	74	285	26,000
Mike Goodes	77	68	70	71	286	25,000
Roger Chapman	69	70	74	78	291	24,500
Dan Forsman	75	70	75	72	292	24,000

European Senior Tour

Mallorca Senior Open

Pula Golf Club, Son Servera, Mallorca, Spain
Par 36-35–71; 6,745 yards

May 11-13
purse, €199,800

	SCORES			TOTAL	MONEY
Gary Wolstenholme	70	66	69	205	€30,000
Mike Harwood	70	67	70	207	15,000
Paul Wesselingh	68	68	71	207	15,000
Chris Williams	73	67	67	207	15,000
Juan Quiros	69	68	71	208	9,040
Barry Lane	71	69	69	209	8,000
Andrew Sherborne	72	67	72	211	7,200
Graham Banister	74	71	67	212	4,886
Gordon Brand, Jr.	74	67	71	212	4,886
Ross Drummond	73	68	71	212	4,886
Angel Franco	69	68	75	212	4,886
Dick Mast	68	72	72	212	4,886
Andrew Oldcorn	70	71	71	212	4,886
Tim Thelen	70	74	68	212	4,886
Bob Cameron	71	72	70	213	3,600
Roger Chapman	71	73	70	214	2,923
Anders Forsbrand	74	70	70	214	2,923
Peter Fowler	69	71	74	214	2,923
Gordon Manson	73	70	71	214	2,923
David J. Russell	68	72	74	214	2,923
Steve Van Vuuren	74	68	72	214	2,923

Benahavis Senior Masters

La Quinta Golf & Country Club, Benahavis, Spain
Par 35-36–71; 6,449 yards

June 1-3
purse, €199,800

	SCORES			TOTAL	MONEY
Gary Wolstenholme	67	67	66	200	€30,000
Mark James	67	67	67	201	17,000
Mark Mouland	64	69	68	201	17,000
Mike Harwood	70	64	68	202	10,020
Barry Lane	69	67	66	202	10,020
Kevin Spurgeon	67	68	68	203	8,000
Des Smyth	68	71	65	204	6,400
Archie Takamatsu	68	71	65	204	6,400
Paul Wesselingh	73	67	64	204	6,400
Anders Forsbrand	66	69	70	205	5,000
Steve Van Vuuren	68	69	68	205	5,000
Carl Mason	70	64	72	206	4,067
Juan Quiros	70	70	66	206	4,067
Chris Williams	65	75	66	206	4,067
Delroy Cambridge	66	71	70	207	3,204
Tim Elliott	68	68	71	207	3,204
Marc Farry	76	63	68	207	3,204
Tony Johnstone	67	74	66	207	3,204

	SCORES			TOTAL	MONEY
Andrew Sherborne	70	71	66	207	3,204
Bob Cameron	69	71	68	208	2,480
Roger Chapman	71	67	70	208	2,480
Jean Pierre Sallat	69	70	69	208	2,480

ISPS Handa PGA Seniors Championship

De Vere Slaley Hall, Hexham, England
Par 36-36–72; 7,036 yards
(Event shortened to 54 holes—rain.)

June 7-10
purse, €312,970

	SCORES			TOTAL	MONEY
Paul Wesselingh	72	71	67	210	€50,075
Anders Forsbrand	70	71	70	211	29,263
Andrew Oldcorn	72	69	70	211	29,263
Mark James	67	72	74	213	19,091
Steve Cipa	74	70	71	215	12,327
Peter Fowler	72	70	73	215	12,327
Peter A. Smith	70	73	72	215	12,327
Carl Mason	72	75	69	216	7,597
Peter Mitchell	71	73	72	216	7,597
Mark Mouland	72	73	71	216	7,597
Barry Lane	72	74	71	217	5,965
Gary Wolstenholme	72	74	71	217	5,965
Delroy Cambridge	73	71	74	218	5,061
Ross Drummond	73	73	72	218	5,061
Marc Farry	72	75	71	218	5,061
Stephen McNally	75	71	72	218	5,061
John Gould	72	76	71	219	3,696
John Harrison	76	70	73	219	3,696
David Merriman	71	75	73	219	3,696
Andrew Murray	72	71	76	219	3,696
Andrew Sherborne	76	71	72	219	3,696

Van Lanschot Senior Open

Royal Haagsche Golf & Country Club, The Hague, Netherlands
Par 36-36–72; 6,752 yards

June 22-24
purse, €249,750

	SCORES			TOTAL	MONEY
Massy Kuramoto	75	72	69	216	€37,500
Andrew Oldcorn	74	74	70	218	25,000
John Harrison	74	73	73	220	15,625
Juan Quiros	77	70	73	220	15,625
Jeff Hall	73	78	70	221	10,650
Chris Williams	75	73	73	221	10,650
Ross Drummond	74	75	73	222	8,500
Mike Harwood	74	73	75	222	8,500
Gordon Brand, Jr.	71	75	77	223	6,750
Glenn Ralph	78	73	72	223	6,750
Des Smyth	74	73	77	224	6,000
Mike Cunning	74	76	75	225	4,938
Peter Fowler	78	71	76	225	4,938
Domingo Hospital	73	77	75	225	4,938
Kevin Spurgeon	76	75	74	225	4,938
John Gould	73	74	79	226	3,881
Bill Longmuir	75	77	74	226	3,881

	SCORES			TOTAL	MONEY
Miguel Angel Martin	74	75	77	226	3,881
Boonchu Ruangkit	80	74	72	226	3,881
Angel Franco	80	73	74	227	3,100
Tony Johnstone	75	72	80	227	3,100
Andrew Sherborne	74	74	79	227	3,100

Berenberg Bank Masters

Worthsee Golf Club, Munich, Germany
Par 36-36—72; 6,902 yards

June 29-July 1
purse, €400,000

	SCORES			TOTAL	MONEY
Tim Thelen	66	68	67	201	€60,000
Peter Fowler	65	70	69	204	30,000
Barry Lane	65	70	69	204	30,000
Mark Mouland	66	67	71	204	30,000
Bernhard Langer	69	67	69	205	18,080
Rick Gibson	71	70	66	207	15,200
Andrew Oldcorn	73	66	68	207	15,200
Graham Banister	71	68	69	208	11,467
Ross Drummond	70	68	70	208	11,467
Paul Wesselingh	69	68	71	208	11,467
Anders Forsbrand	69	73	67	209	9,600
Andrew Sherborne	71	67	72	210	8,800
Mike Cunning	69	71	71	211	7,600
Mark James	72	71	68	211	7,600
Juan Quiros	67	70	74	211	7,600
John Gould	71	71	70	212	6,210
John Harrison	67	75	70	212	6,210
Tony Johnstone	73	69	70	212	6,210
Boonchu Ruangkit	69	71	72	212	6,210
Bob Cameron	70	71	72	213	4,267
Rodger Davis	71	71	71	213	4,267
Angel Franco	73	68	72	213	4,267
Mike Harwood	71	69	73	213	4,267
Carl Mason	71	70	72	213	4,267
Peter Mitchell	71	72	70	213	4,267
Gerry Norquist	68	74	71	213	4,267
David J. Russell	70	71	72	213	4,267
Ian Woosnam	74	68	71	213	4,267

Bad Ragaz PGA Seniors Open

Golf Club Bad Ragaz, Bad Ragaz, Switzerland
Par 35-35—70; 6,183 yards

July 6-8
purse, €280,000

	SCORES			TOTAL	MONEY
Tim Thelen	66	65	67	198	€42,000
Mark James	65	70	65	200	28,000
Ian Woosnam	68	66	67	201	19,600
Anders Forsbrand	69	67	66	202	12,334
Peter Fowler	66	69	67	202	12,334
Stephen McAllister	68	69	65	202	12,334
Des Smyth	66	70	66	202	12,334
Bill Longmuir	69	67	67	203	8,400
Paul Wesselingh	70	68	65	203	8,400
Gary Wolstenholme	69	67	68	204	7,280

	SCORES			TOTAL	MONEY
Rick Gibson	68	69	68	205	5,768
Mike Harwood	71	66	68	205	5,768
Andrew Sherborne	69	70	66	205	5,768
Sam Torrance	69	71	65	205	5,768
Chris Williams	68	66	71	205	5,768
Graham Banister	72	65	69	206	4,347
Mike Cunning	68	66	72	206	4,347
Marc Farry	69	68	69	206	4,347
Gordon Manson	67	72	67	206	4,347
Bob Cameron	70	70	67	207	3,472
Angel Franco	72	69	66	207	3,472
Denis O'Sullivan	70	70	67	207	3,472

The Senior Open Championship presented by Rolex

Turnberry, Ayrshire, Scotland
Par 35-35–70; 7,105 yards

July 26-29
purse, €1,629,543

	SCORES				TOTAL	MONEY
Fred Couples	72	68	64	67	271	€256,059
Gary Hallberg	71	63	73	66	273	170,787
Barry Lane	67	74	66	69	276	79,360
Carl Mason	69	74	67	66	276	79,360
Dick Mast	66	73	70	67	276	79,360
John Cook	69	72	66	71	278	43,167
Peter Fowler	68	72	65	73	278	43,167
Bernhard Langer	64	73	66	75	278	43,167
Mark Wiebe	70	71	70	67	278	43,167
Jay Don Blake	66	73	69	71	279	26,696
Mark Calcavecchia	72	72	69	66	279	26,696
Tom Lehman	66	71	73	69	279	26,696
Tom Watson	69	75	66	69	279	26,696
Ian Woosnam	71	70	68	70	279	26,696
David Frost	66	73	70	73	282	21,582
Corey Pavin	70	72	70	70	282	21,582
Kirk Triplett	69	74	72	67	282	21,582
Michael Allen	66	74	75	68	283	19,213
Olin Browne	69	73	71	70	283	19,213
Mark McNulty	65	75	75	68	283	19,213
Peter Senior	68	71	72	73	284	17,849
Gary Wolstenholme	70	73	70	71	284	17,849
Bob Gilder	72	74	72	67	285	17,071
Mike Goodes	69	73	71	73	286	16,032
Tom Kite	74	73	71	68	286	16,032
Chris Williams	71	73	72	70	286	16,032
Bobby Clampett	70	71	71	75	287	14,247
Mark Mouland	71	72	71	73	287	14,247
Loren Roberts	68	75	72	72	287	14,247
Boonchu Ruangkit	69	73	72	73	287	14,247
Ross Drummond	70	74	70	74	288	12,466
Jeff Hart	69	76	70	73	288	12,466
John Huston	70	72	70	76	288	12,466
Chien Soon Lu	66	77	73	72	288	12,466
David Eger	74	70	74	71	289	11,042
Marc Farry	71	74	71	73	289	11,042
Philip Golding	70	75	74	70	289	11,042
*Chip Lutz	70	76	67	76	289	
Des Smyth	75	70	72	72	289	11,042
Joel Edwards	69	77	70	74	290	9,412
Anders Forsbrand	71	72	71	76	290	9,412

	SCORES				TOTAL	MONEY
Angel Franco	73	73	67	77	290	9,412
Jay Haas	73	74	69	74	290	9,412
Eduardo Romero	68	74	77	71	290	9,412
David J. Russell	69	73	71	77	290	9,412
Jeff Sluman	70	76	72	72	290	9,412
Mark Brooks	70	71	69	81	291	7,513
Jeff Freeman	71	74	74	72	291	7,513
David Merriman	70	77	74	70	291	7,513
Larry Mize	71	74	74	72	291	7,513
Rod Spittle	72	74	72	73	291	7,513
Paul Wesselingh	69	76	75	71	291	7,513
Mark James	74	74	73	71	292	6,345
Bill Longmuir	71	77	71	73	292	6,345
Philip Jonas	73	71	74	75	293	5,769
Steve Pate	71	75	73	74	293	5,769
Fred Funk	69	74	75	76	294	5,233
Anthony Gilligan	69	73	78	74	294	5,233
Rossouw Loubser	74	71	78	72	295	4,362
Andrew Murray	69	78	76	72	295	4,362
Juan Quiros	71	76	73	75	295	4,362
Lee Rinker	67	78	77	73	295	4,362
Mike San Filippo	72	76	76	71	295	4,362
Kevin Spurgeon	72	73	74	76	295	4,362
Phil Hinton	70	75	76	75	296	3,575
Kouki Idoki	69	76	70	81	296	3,575
Tim Thelen	73	72	74	77	296	3,575
Tim Elliott	71	76	74	76	297	3,278
*Randy Haag	74	74	78	72	298	
Mike Cunning	73	75	76	75	299	3,059
John Harrison	73	74	78	74	299	3,059
Mitch Adcock	73	74	75	78	300	2,840
Denis O'Sullivan	76	72	81	72	301	2,621
Noel Ratcliffe	72	76	74	79	301	2,621
Seiki Okuda	73	74	72	83	302	2,402
John Ross	75	71	84	79	309	2,256

SSE Scottish Senior Open

Fairmont St. Andrews, Fife, Scotland
Par 35-37–72; 6,762 yards

August 17-19
purse, €316,380

	SCORES			TOTAL	MONEY
Anders Forsbrand	66	66	67	199	€47,457
Philip Golding	72	64	64	200	31,638
David J. Russell	69	66	67	202	22,147
Gordon Manson	69	68	70	207	13,937
George Ryall	72	66	69	207	13,937
Chris Williams	73	66	68	207	13,937
Ian Woosnam	69	71	67	207	13,937
Mike Harwood	68	73	67	208	9,491
Barry Lane	74	65	69	208	9,491
Mike Cunning	71	69	69	209	7,277
Miguel Angel Martin	73	70	66	209	7,277
Glenn Ralph	71	68	70	209	7,277
Des Smyth	68	74	67	209	7,277
Mark Mouland	72	71	67	210	5,537
Gerry Norquist	70	75	65	210	5,537
Tim Thelen	69	74	67	210	5,537
Sam Torrance	72	69	69	210	5,537
Jerry Bruner	72	67	72	211	4,076

	SCORES			TOTAL	MONEY
Steve Cipa	70	69	72	211	4,076
Mark James	68	74	69	211	4,076
Andrew Oldcorn	67	73	71	211	4,076
Ken Tarling	71	67	73	211	4,076
Gary Wolstenholme	72	70	69	211	4,076

Speedy Services Wales Senior Open

Conwy Golf Club, Caernarvonshire, Conwy, Wales
Par 35-37–72; 6,903 yards

August 24-26
purse, €317,275

	SCORES			TOTAL	MONEY
Barry Lane	72	67	70	209	€47,591
Philip Golding	64	74	72	210	31,728
Anders Forsbrand	67	76	69	212	19,830
Peter Fowler	71	69	72	212	19,830
Mark Mouland	66	74	73	213	13,516
Paul Wesselingh	71	73	69	213	13,516
Angel Fernandez	72	72	71	215	9,264
Tony Johnstone	69	76	70	215	9,264
Des Smyth	71	71	73	215	9,264
Katsuyoshi Tomori	71	71	73	215	9,264
Gary Wolstenholme	72	73	70	215	9,264
Rick Gibson	68	75	73	216	6,663
Mike Harwood	70	74	72	216	6,663
Roger Chapman	73	72	72	217	5,394
Andrew Oldcorn	70	74	73	217	5,394
David J. Russell	70	75	72	217	5,394
Roger Sabarros	73	75	69	217	5,394
Kevin Spurgeon	76	70	71	217	5,394
Ross Drummond	80	67	71	218	3,953
Miguel Angel Martin	69	74	75	218	3,953
David Merriman	72	75	71	218	3,953
Jim Rhodes	74	72	72	218	3,953
George Ryall	70	73	75	218	3,953

Travis Perkins plc Senior Masters

Woburn Golf Club, Duke's Course, Woburn, England
Par 35-37–72; 6,896 yards

August 31-September 2
purse, €379,770

	SCORES			TOTAL	MONEY
Des Smyth	72	66	68	206	€57,082
Peter Fowler	70	70	67	207	38,055
Mark James	76	65	67	208	26,638
Andrew Sherborne	70	71	69	210	20,930
Roger Chapman	74	68	69	211	14,575
Ross Drummond	70	71	70	211	14,575
Miguel Angel Martin	75	69	67	211	14,575
Juan Quiros	70	68	73	211	14,575
Mike Harwood	72	71	69	212	10,655
Katsuyoshi Tomori	71	72	70	213	9,133
Sam Torrance	75	68	70	213	9,133
Chris Williams	73	69	71	213	9,133
Bob Cameron	73	72	69	214	7,040
Mike Cunning	70	71	73	214	7,040
Tony Johnstone	70	72	72	214	7,040

	SCORES			TOTAL	MONEY
Tim Thelen	71	69	74	214	7,040
Philip Golding	74	72	69	215	5,899
Mark Mouland	77	69	69	215	5,899
Gordon Manson	72	70	74	216	5,036
Paul Wesselingh	73	69	74	216	5,036
Gary Wolstenholme	72	73	71	216	5,036

Pon Senior Open

Winston Open Course, Vorbeck, Germany
Par 36-36–72; 6,844 yards

September 7-9
purse, €400,000

	SCORES			TOTAL	MONEY
Terry Price	67	66	67	200	€60,000
Marc Farry	71	66	69	206	34,000
Barry Lane	73	67	66	206	34,000
Bill Longmuir	70	66	71	207	22,000
Glenn Ralph	70	66	72	208	16,160
Andrew Sherborne	71	68	69	208	16,160
Gary Wolstenholme	74	66	68	208	16,160
Bernhard Langer	68	73	68	209	12,000
Steve Van Vuuren	70	70	69	209	12,000
Mike Harwood	69	69	72	210	9,600
Carl Mason	71	72	67	210	9,600
Des Smyth	71	68	71	210	9,600
Paul Curry	70	70	71	211	6,431
Ross Drummond	67	72	72	211	6,431
Denis Durnian	72	71	68	211	6,431
Philip Golding	70	69	72	211	6,431
Miguel Angel Martin	71	71	69	211	6,431
David Merriman	72	68	71	211	6,431
Gerry Norquist	71	67	73	211	6,431
Kevin Spurgeon	70	69	72	211	6,431
Chris Williams	74	72	65	211	6,431

French Riviera Masters

Terre Blanche Resort & Golf Club, Tourrettes, Provence, France
Par 36-36–72; 6,955 yards

September 21-23
purse, €399,180

	SCORES			TOTAL	MONEY
David J. Russell	69	74	65	208	€60,000
Tim Thelen	76	66	66	208	40,000
(Russell defeated Thelen on third playoff hole.)					
Roger Chapman	71	67	71	209	25,000
Paul Wesselingh	71	69	69	209	25,000
Peter Fowler	71	69	71	211	16,160
Des Smyth	72	70	69	211	16,160
Ian Woosnam	71	71	69	211	16,160
Mike Cunning	73	71	68	212	12,000
Jean Pierre Sallat	68	74	70	212	12,000
Bob Cameron	70	70	73	213	10,000
Chris Williams	69	70	74	213	10,000
Anders Forsbrand	69	72	73	214	7,900
Mike Harwood	72	71	71	214	7,900
Gordon Manson	73	71	70	214	7,900
Gary Wolstenholme	74	68	72	214	7,900

	SCORES			TOTAL	MONEY
Miguel Angel Martin	75	72	68	215	6,800
Philip Golding	73	72	71	216	5,487
John Gould	73	72	71	216	5,487
Mark James	76	72	68	216	5,487
Barry Lane	77	70	69	216	5,487
Mark Mouland	73	71	72	216	5,487
Steve Van Vuuren	70	72	74	216	5,487

Fubon Senior Open

Miramar Golf & Country Club, Taipei, Taiwan
Par 36-36–72; 6,706 yards

November 9-11
purse, US$450,000

	SCORES			TOTAL	MONEY
Tim Thelen	66	67	69	202	€62,388
Frankie Minoza	72	64	71	207	29,374
Chris Williams	69	68	70	207	29,374
Boonchu Ruangkit	70	67	71	208	16,637
Paul Wesselingh	71	69	69	209	13,864
Andrew Murray	67	71	72	210	11,207
Gerry Norquist	71	69	70	210	11,207
Terry Price	73	69	68	210	11,207
Kim Jong-duck	67	63	81	211	9,358
Lin Chi-hsiang	70	67	75	212	8,665
Angel Franco	72	66	75	213	6,932
Chien Soon Lu	72	69	72	213	6,932
Katsuyoshi Tomori	72	69	72	213	6,932
Massy Kuramoto	70	73	71	214	5,476
David Merriman	70	69	75	214	5,476
George Ryall	72	68	74	214	5,476
Mark Belsham	73	71	71	215	4,333
Glenn Ralph	72	67	76	215	4,333
Rick Gibson	72	71	73	216	3,650
Mitch Kierstenson	73	69	74	216	3,650
Bill Longmuir	68	73	75	216	3,650
Zeke Martinez	70	73	73	216	3,650
Wang Ter-chang	68	71	77	216	3,650

Nedbank Champions Challenge

Gary Player Country Club, Sun City, South Africa
Par 36-36–72; 7,831 yards

November 29-December 1
purse, US$880,000

	SCORES			TOTAL	MONEY
Bernhard Langer	68	67	74	209	US$250,000
Jay Haas	71	68	72	211	130,000
Ian Woosnam	73	69	72	214	100,000
Jeff Sluman	74	70	73	217	90,000
Sandy Lyle	74	72	77	223	85,000
Tom Watson	74	75	75	224	80,000
Mark Calcavecchia	71	69	85	225	75,000
Fred Funk	76	77	74	227	70,000

ISPS Handa Australian Senior Open

Royal Perth Golf Club, Perth, Australia
Par 72

November 30-December 2
purse, A$100,000

	SCORES			TOTAL	MONEY
Peter Fowler	67	70	70	207	A$18,000
Mike Harwood	72	70	71	213	8,570
David Merriman	70	71	72	213	8,570
Michael Clayton	72	75	67	214	4,440
Tim Elliott	69	71	74	214	4,440
Peter Senior	71	73	71	215	3,700
Wayne Smith	75	71	71	217	3,120
Lyndsay Stephen	75	68	74	217	3,120
Anthony Gilligan	71	74	73	218	2,560
Terry Price	67	74	77	218	2,560
*Lester Peterson	72	76	72	220	
Ken Tarling	69	77	74	220	2,260
Mike Zilko	74	76	72	222	1,860
Gregory Engall	78	71	73	222	1,860
Wayne Grady	75	74	73	222	1,860
David Hill	79	74	70	223	1,560
Russell Swanson	77	74	74	225	1,373.33
Krishna Singh	77	71	77	225	1,373.33
Kenneth Oung	72	74	79	225	1,373.33
Terry Gale	75	77	74	226	1,140
Graham Banister	74	76	76	226	1,140
Allan Cooper	77	72	77	226	1,140

MCB Tour Championship

Constance Belle Mare Plage, Poste de Flacq, Mauritius
Par 36-36–72; 6,614 yards

December 7-9
purse, €400,000

	SCORES			TOTAL	MONEY
David Frost	64	67	74	205	€62,814
Peter Fowler	69	69	68	206	35,595
Barry Lane	70	66	70	206	35,595
Chris Williams	71	68	69	208	23,032
Jerry Bruner	69	68	72	209	18,928
Marc Farry	71	70	69	210	15,075
Kevin Spurgeon	71	69	70	210	15,075
Paul Wesselingh	73	65	72	210	15,075
Bob Cameron	72	68	71	211	10,888
Angel Franco	70	70	71	211	10,888
Tim Thelen	68	67	76	211	10,888
Tom Lehman	71	69	72	212	8,515
George Ryall	69	72	71	212	8,515
Des Smyth	71	70	71	212	8,515
Roger Chapman	70	69	74	213	7,328
Andrew Murray	71	70	72	213	7,328
John Gould	69	71	74	214	6,295
Juan Quiros	71	71	72	214	6,295
Steen Tinning	72	72	70	214	6,295
Gary Wolstenholme	73	71	71	215	5,528
Ross Drummond	70	75	71	216	4,763

Japan PGA Senior Tour

Starts Senior

Hirakawa Country Club, Chiba
Par 36-36–72; 6,997 yards

June 8-10
purse, ¥56,500,000

	SCORES			TOTAL	MONEY
Naomichi Ozaki	67	68	73	208	¥14,000,000
Seiki Okuda	68	71	70	209	6,800,000
Gregory Meyer	69	71	70	210	4,180,000
Kouki Idoki	68	75	70	213	2,390,000
Kiyoshi Murota	71	74	69	214	1,792,000
Kiyoshi Maita	70	71	73	214	1,792,000
Nobuo Serizawa	74	72	70	216	1,400,500
Massy Kuramoto	73	72	71	216	1,400,500
Katsunari Takahashi	73	74	70	217	1,198,000
Ikuo Shirahama	70	76	72	218	1,045,000
Kimpachi Yoshimura	71	75	72	218	1,045,000
Masami Ito	72	73	73	218	1,045,000
Satoshi Higasi	73	76	70	219	901,000
Nobumitsu Yuhara	76	70	73	219	901,000
Katsuyoshi Tomori	74	75	71	220	820,000
Tsukasa Watanabe	74	76	71	221	697,000
Tsuneyuki Nakajima	74	74	73	221	697,000
David Ishii	76	71	74	221	697,000
Yutaka Hagawa	67	79	75	221	697,000
Yoshinori Mizumaki	72	80	70	222	603,000

ISPS Handa Cup Shakunetsu-no Senior Masters

Kyusyu Golf Club, Yahata Course, Fukuoka
Par 36-36–72; 6,935 yards

August 2-3
purse, ¥20,000,000

	SCORES		TOTAL	MONEY
Takashi Miyoshi	71	71	142	¥3,600,000
Kiyoshi Murota	72	71	143	1,210,000
Takaaki Fukuzawa	72	71	143	1,210,000
Hideki Kase	70	73	143	1,210,000
Yasuo Sone	70	73	143	1,210,000
Gohei Sato	74	70	144	645,000
Yoshitaka Yamamoto	72	72	144	645,000
Satoshi Higashi	73	72	145	480,000
Tateo Ozaki	70	75	145	480,000
Tsukasa Watanabe	76	70	146	332,000
Takenori Hiraishi	73	73	146	332,000
Katsunari Takahashi	72	74	146	332,000
Hikaru Emoto	72	74	146	332,000
Tomoo Ozaki	71	75	146	332,000
Toshihiko Otsuka	76	71	147	240,000
Masanori Ushiyama	75	72	147	240,000
Masami Ito	74	73	147	240,000
Kouki Idoki	74	73	147	240,000
Gregory Mayer	73	74	147	240,000

	SCORES		TOTAL	MONEY
Nobuo Serizawa	75	73	148	198,142
Massy Kuramoto	75	73	148	198,142
Tadashige Kusano	75	73	148	198,142
Nobumitsu Yuhara	74	74	148	198,142
Yoichi Sugawara	74	74	148	198,142
Ikuo Shirahama	73	75	148	198,142
David Ishii	73	75	148	198,142

Fancl Classic

Susono Country Club, Susono, Shizuoka
Par 36-36–72; 6,865 yards

August 17-19
purse, ¥62,000,000

	SCORES			TOTAL	MONEY
Kazuhiro Takami	66	69	72	207	¥15,000,000
Frankie Minoza	73	67	67	207	5,400,000
Tsuneyuki Nakajima	68	69	70	207	5,400,000
(Takami defeated Nakajima on first and Minoza on second playoff hole.)					
Masami Ito	68	73	67	208	1,764,750
Satoshi Oide	69	71	68	208	1,764,750
Hideki Kase	75	64	69	208	1,764,750
Yoshinori Mizumaki	73	65	70	208	1,764,750
Naomichi Ozaki	70	67	71	208	1,764,750
Nobumitsu Yuhara	70	67	71	208	1,764,750
Takashi Miyoshi	71	66	71	208	1,764,750
David Ishii	66	68	74	208	1,764,750
Ikuo Shirahama	67	71	71	209	1,020,000
Hiroshi Tominaga	72	72	66	210	840,500
Satoshi Higashi	72	70	68	210	840,500
Koki Idoki	70	72	68	210	840,500
Takenori Hiraishi	69	72	69	210	840,500
Kiyoshi Murota	70	69	71	210	840,500
Gohei Sato	70	65	75	210	840,500
Tsukasa Watanabe	75	67	69	211	705,000
Nobuo Serizawa	69	71	71	211	705,000

Komatsu Open

Komatsu Country Club, Komatsu, Ishikawa
Par 36-36–72; 6,932 yards

September 6-8
purse, ¥60,000,000

	SCORES			TOTAL	MONEY
Naomichi Ozaki	68	69	66	203	¥12,000,000
Hiroshi Ueda	68	68	67	203	5,700,000
(Ozaki defeated Ueda on third playoff hole.)					
Kazuhiro Takami	69	68	67	204	4,020,000
Takashi Miyoshi	68	74	64	206	2,730,000
Gregory Meyer	69	72	67	208	1,805,400
Hideki Kase	71	69	68	208	1,805,400
Masami Ito	66	71	71	208	1,805,400
Tuneyuki Nakajima	67	71	70	208	1,805,400
Massy Kuramoto	66	70	72	208	1,805,400
Nobuo Serizawa	72	70	67	209	1,263,000
Nobumitsu Yuhara	73	68	68	209	1,263,000
Tatsushi Takamatsu	69	70	70	209	1,263,000
Hajime Meshiai	67	74	69	210	1,026,000
Ikuo Shirahama	69	71	70	210	1,026,000

	SCORES			TOTAL	MONEY
Katsunari Takahashi	70	69	71	210	1,026,000
David Ishii	71	72	68	211	789,600
Hisao Inoue	70	72	69	211	789,600
Kouki Idoki	67	74	70	211	789,600
Naonori Nakamura	72	68	71	211	789,600
Satoshi Oide	73	67	71	211	789,600

ISPS Handa Cup Akibare-no Senior Masters

Noboribetsu Country Club, Hokkaido　　　　September 28-29
Par 36-36–72; 6,914 yards　　　　purse, ¥20,000,000

	SCORES		TOTAL	MONEY
Gohei Sato	68	68	136	¥3,600,000
Satoshi Higasi	70	66	136	1,800,000
(Sato defeated Higasi on eighth playoff hole.)				
Yutaka Hagawa	71	66	137	1,200,000
Hiroshi Ueda	71	68	139	920,000
David Ishii	68	71	139	920,000
Hirokazu Hagiwara	72	68	140	603,333
Kouki Idoki	72	68	140	603,333
Tadashige Kusano	70	70	140	603,333
Junji Kawase	71	70	141	420,000
Katsunari Takahashi	70	71	141	420,000
Katsuyoshi Tomori	74	68	142	326,666
Kiyoshi Maita	71	71	142	326,666
Kazuhiro Takami	71	71	142	326,666
Ikuo Shirahama	75	68	143	229,600
Hajime Meshiai	74	69	143	229,600
Nobumasa Nakanishi	74	69	143	229,600
Shinji Ikeuchi	73	70	143	229,600
Hideki Kase	73	70	143	229,600
Joji Furuki	72	71	143	229,600
Takaaki Fukuzawa	72	71	143	229,600
Kazushige Oya	71	72	143	229,600
Tomohiro Maruyama	70	73	143	229,600
Masanori Ushiyama	71	72	143	229,600

Japan PGA Senior Championship

Tojonomori Country Club, Tojo Course, Hyogo　　　　October 4-7
Par 36-36–72; 7,237 yards　　　　purse, ¥50,000,000

	SCORES				TOTAL	MONEY
Kiyoshi Murota	70	67	69	71	277	¥10,000,000
Hajime Meshiai	71	68	68	72	279	5,000,000
Nobumitsu Yuhara	70	70	71	70	281	3,000,000
Marc Farry	69	73	68	71	281	3,000,000
Ikuo Shirahama	69	71	71	71	282	1,750,000
Kouki Idoki	72	68	71	71	282	1,750,000
Boonchu Ruangkit	72	72	72	67	283	1,300,000
Yutaka Hagawa	72	70	67	74	283	1,300,000
Frankie Minoza	74	71	73	66	284	1,100,000
Tateo Ozaki	72	68	75	69	284	1,100,000
Kazuhiro Takami	69	71	72	73	285	1,000,000
Barry Lane	72	70	74	70	286	800,000
Katsunari Takahashi	71	71	74	70	286	800,000

	SCORES				TOTAL	MONEY
Joji Furuki	69	73	74	70	286	800,000
Kim Jong-duck	70	71	73	72	286	800,000
Naomichi Ozaki	74	69	71	72	286	800,000
Tsukasa Watanabe	71	71	72	72	286	800,000
Peter Fowler	70	70	73	73	286	800,000
Massy Kuramoto	73	72	71	71	287	605,000
Yukio Noguchi	71	71	71	74	287	605,000

Japan Senior Open Championship

Higashi Nagoya Golf Club, Aichi
Par 36-36–72; 7,010 yards

October 25-28
purse, ¥80,000,000

	SCORES				TOTAL	MONEY
Frankie Minoza	69	72	72	71	284	¥16,000,000
Kiyoshi Murota	70	72	71	72	285	6,320,000
Tsuneyuki Nakajima	70	75	68	72	285	6,320,000
Kouki Idoki	70	70	72	73	285	6,320,000
Boonchu Ruangkit	72	74	69	73	288	3,360,000
Barry Lane	70	70	73	78	291	2,800,000
Satoshi Higasi	72	73	71	76	292	2,400,000
Peter Fowler	74	77	71	72	294	2,080,000
Shinji Ikeuchi	76	72	76	71	295	1,486,000
Seiki Okuda	71	75	75	74	295	1,486,000
Tsukasa Watanabe	75	72	72	76	295	1,486,000
Kiyoshi Maita	70	74	73	78	295	1,486,000
Masami Ito	75	73	74	74	296	1,052,000
Massy Kuramoto	75	73	72	76	296	1,052,000
Yoshinori Mizumaki	73	73	75	76	297	912,000
Hideki Kase	72	75	73	77	297	912,000
Tomoyuki Nagai	74	75	76	73	298	800,000
Marc Farry	77	72	75	74	298	800,000
Yoshitaka Yamamoto	73	77	71	77	298	800,000
Takashi Miyoshi	74	79	75	71	299	708,000
Kimpachi Yoshimura	72	71	77	79	299	708,000

Fuji Film Senior Championship

The Country Club of Japan, Chiba
Par 36-36–72; 6,953 yards

November 1-3
purse, ¥70,000,000

	SCORES			TOTAL	MONEY
Kouki Idoki	66	70	68	204	¥14,000,000
Naomichi Ozaki	70	69	69	208	5,775,000
Seiki Okuda	69	69	70	208	5,775,000
Kiyoshi Murota	70	68	71	209	3,500,000
Kazunari Matsunaga	73	69	68	210	2,012,500
Boonchu Ruangkit	68	71	71	210	2,012,500
Tsuneyuki Nakajima	70	68	72	210	2,012,500
Kim Jong-duck	68	69	73	210	2,012,500
Hiroyuki Iwabuchi	73	66	73	212	1,470,000
Barry Lane	70	70	73	213	1,365,000
Minoru Hatsumi	71	73	70	214	1,211,000
Massy Kuramoto	73	70	71	214	1,211,000
Katsuyoshi Tomori	70	70	74	214	1,211,000
Satoshi Higashi	68	71	75	214	1,211,000
Nobumitsu Yuhara	70	75	70	215	959,000

	SCORES			TOTAL	MONEY
Yoshinori Mizumaki	70	74	71	215	959,000
Peter Fowler	70	75	70	215	959,000
Anthony Gilligan	72	69	74	215	959,000
Hideki Kase	70	70	75	215	959,000
David J. Russell	71	73	72	216	703,500
Takashi Miyoshi	70	73	73	216	703,500
Tateo Ozaki	73	69	74	216	703,500
Yuji Takagi	75	67	74	216	703,500
Hiroshi Ueda	69	72	75	216	703,500
Atsushi Takamatsu	69	72	75	216	703,500